PRAISE FOR *MOUNTAINEERING: THE FREEDOM OF THE HILLS*

"It is fair to say that *Freedom* is the definitive guide to mountains and climbing." —CONRAD ANKER

"If the mountains are my church, then *Freedom* is my bible. . . . As a very young climber I read it cover to cover, then dug through it again and again for nuggets of wisdom. I still do." —WILL GADD

"Not long after I learned to read, I would grip the flashlight in my teeth and stay awake late into the night scouring my parents' copy of the 3rd edition of *Freedom of the Hills*. . . . What this book captured, what it meant, what it hinted at that was so crucial to my fascination with mountaineering was this: Freedom, itself, was the most important thing. Freedom to explore who I am. Freedom afforded by learned skills to explore any mountain wilderness. Freedom to move, to climb. It's what still drives me today." —STEVE HOUSE

"Growing up in Southern California in the 1960s, I couldn't find anyone who shared my passion to learn how to climb. So I bought an ice axe, crampons, and *Freedom of the Hills* and still remember being on a snow slope with axe in one hand, book in the other, trying to teach myself how to self-arrest. It worked: I'm still around and still climbing." —RICK RIDGEWAY

"For many generations of climbers, *The Freedom of the Hills* is more than just a book. It's a passport to a rare and wild place." —ANDREW BISHARAT

"I have never felt more alive than when adventuring in remote mountains, dependent on a rope, a rack, and the partner that's got my back. . . . *Freedom of the Hills*, risk's best friend, is that partner." —TIMMY O'NEILL

"A 'must-have' for any aspiring mountaineer's library." —ED VIESTURS

"In my early years of heading into the mountains I used *Freedom of the Hills* to learn how to calculate fuel needs for the backcountry, to study crevasse rescue, and in general to just muse about the alpine craft. Everyone should have a copy of this standard tome." —KIT DESLAURIERS

"There is no substitute for learning to climb from a skilled and tested mentor. . . . But sometimes it's nice to learn key skills at your own pace from the comfort of your own kitchen table. . . . For those times, there is no better book than The Mountaineers' *Freedom of the Hills*." —BREE LOEWEN

"The lessons I learned in The Mountaineers climbing course in 1945 stood me on the summit of Mount Everest in 1963. To see that knowledge put into a book was wonderful. That it has evolved into the best book on climbing, updated by active climbers, is remarkable. I have told many people, including my sons, 'If you want to climb mountains, read *Mountaineering: The Freedom of the Hills*. Then read it again so you know, for sure, how to get down.'" —JIM WHITTAKER

"This truly remarkable resource has no equal in any language." —MARK TWIGHT

"A notorious reference for climbers and outdoor enthusiasts!" —LYNN HILL

"*Freedom* does a remarkable job of staying not just current, but on the cutting edge. Turning on new climbers to this resource is one of the best things I can do to prepare them for life in the big hills." —DAVE HAHN

"*Mountaineering: The Freedom of the Hills* provided invaluable advice and inspiration during my early climbing days. Incorporating the expertise of talented climbers and guides, this essential guide continues to empower new generations of mountaineers." —GRAHAM ZIMMERMAN

"Since 1960, *Freedom of the Hills* has been part of the living heritage of mountaineering, preserving past traditions while evolving to reflect present and future needs. Its tenth edition provides a significant guide for our precarious age, when the climate crisis, species extinction, and overdevelopment compel us to a deeper and more attentive stewardship of wild places—it also reminds us of the importance of supporting the diverse, creative, and inclusive communities that can best protect them." —KATIE IVES

MOUNTAINEERING
THE FREEDOM OF THE HILLS

10TH EDITION

MOUNTAINEERING

THE FREEDOM OF THE HILLS

10TH EDITION

Edited by Eric Linxweiler

MOUNTAINEERS
BOOKS

MOUNTAINEERS BOOKS is dedicated to the exploration, preservation, and enjoyment of outdoor and wilderness areas.

1001 SW Klickitat Way, Suite 201, Seattle, WA 98134
800-553-4453, mountaineersbooks.org

Printed in Canada
Distributed in the United Kingdom by Cordee, www.cordee.co.uk

First edition, 1960. Second edition, 1967. Third edition, 1974. Fourth edition, 1982. Fifth edition, 1992. Sixth edition, 1997. Seventh edition, 2003. Eighth edition, 2010. Ninth edition, 2017. Tenth edition, 2024.

Project editor: Laura Shauger
Development editor: Kris Fulsaas
Copyeditor: Erin Moore
Design and layout: Kate Basart, unionpageworks.com
Illustrator: John McMullen
Cover photographs: front, Dawa Yangzum Sherpa climbing in Rocky Mountain National Park *(photo by Mark Fisher)*; spine, lead climbing in Geyikbayiri, Turkey *(photo by AscentXmedia, iStock)*; back, climbing Mont Blanc *(photo by ChrisPelle, iStock)*
Interior photographs: pp. 2–3, on Mont Blanc *(photo by VichoT, iStock)*; p. 8, climbing in Denali National Park *(photo by mtnpirate, iStock)*; p. 10, the first edition of *Freedom of the Hills*; p. 11, traversing a ridgeline in the Alps *(photo by janiecbros, iStock)*; pp. 152–53, early morning in the mountains *(photo by Mystockimages, iStock)*; pp. 344–45, ice climbing *(photo by frontpoint, iStock)*; pp. 488–89, traversing a rocky landscape *(photo by simonkr, iStock)*; pp. 552–53, trekking down a snowfield *(photo by Mystockimages, iStock)*
All versions of the Leave No Trace Seven Principles and their supporting text are copyrighted by the Leave No Trace Center for Outdoor Ethics.

Library of Congress Cataloging-in-Publication Data is available at https://lccn.loc.gov/2023050172.
LC ebook record is available at https://lccn.loc.gov/2023050173.

Mountaineers Books titles may be purchased for corporate, educational, or other promotional sales, and our authors are available for a wide range of events. For information on special discounts or booking an author, contact our customer service at 800-553-4453 or mbooks@mountaineersbooks.org.

♻ Printed on 100% recycled and FSC-certified materials

MIX
Paper | Supporting responsible forestry
FSC® C016245
FSC www.fsc.org

ISBN (hardcover): 978-1-68051-606-7
ISBN (paperback): 978-1-68051-607-4
ISBN (ebook): 978-1-68051-608-1

An independent nonprofit publisher since 1960

CONTENTS

PREFACE

"The quest of the mountaineer, in simplest terms, is for the freedom of the hills."

—THE FIRST LINE OF THE FIRST EDITION

Honing the skills and techniques contained within the pages of *Mountaineering: The Freedom of the Hills* is your key to unlocking the experience of joy of the outdoors. Whether you want to learn to camp and cook outdoors, hike in your local forest, climb hills, cross glaciers, scale rock walls, or summit the world's highest peaks, this how-to guide is for you. Welcome to the community of hikers, climbers, mountaineers, and other outdoor enthusiasts who count on *Freedom of the Hills*, affectionately called *Freedom*, as a critical part of their outdoor education. Whether this is your first copy or you own every edition, *Freedom of the Hills* will build and refresh your knowledge of most topics everyone needs to be familiar with, from beginners to more experienced mountaineers. Use this book to learn skills, participate in outdoor adventures with more confidence and competence, and discover new places to explore and recreate.

Origins of This Guide

A synopsis of this how-to guide's evolution encompasses a capsule history of The Mountaineers itself. From its beginnings, *Freedom of the Hills* has been the product of the concerted effort of a team of volunteer leaders. For each edition, contributors have sprung forth from across the organization's membership, representing the best it has to offer, along with climbers and educators from the broader climbing and mountaineering community. It has always been an honor to work on this project.

When The Mountaineers was founded in 1906, one of its major purposes was to explore and study the mountains, forests, and waterways of the Pacific Northwest. The direction and emphasis of *Freedom of the Hills* originated from the nature of climbing in this region, with its wild and complex mountains and abundance of snow and glaciers. Access was inherently difficult—there were few roads, crossing often rugged terrain, and initial explorations of them were essentially expeditions, often requiring the assistance of Indigenous guides. As interest in mountaineering grew in the region, so did a tradition of, and commitment to, education. Increasingly, experienced climbers took novices under their wings to pass on their knowledge and skills. The Mountaineers formalized that exchange, starting in 1935, by developing a series of climbing courses.

For the first several decades, The Mountaineers climbing courses used a number of European textbooks, particularly Geoffrey Winthrop Young's classic *Mountain Craft*. These books, however, did not cover the various subjects unique and important to mountaineering in the Pacific Northwest. To fill the gaps, course lecturers prepared and distributed outlines to students. First compiled as the *Notebook*, these outlines were subsequently published as the *Mountaineers Handbook*. By 1955, the tools and techniques had changed so drastically, and the climbing courses had become so much more complex, that a new, comprehensive textbook was needed.

Over the next five years, an eight-person editorial committee coordinated the efforts of more than seventy-five contributors in the publication of the first edition of *Freedom of the Hills* in 1960. Chief editor and committee chair Harvey Manning was the primary individual responsible for establishing the scope of the book. It was his idea to add the distinctive subtitle. Manning was joined on the committee by John R. Hazle, Carl Henrikson, Nancy Bickford Miller, Thomas Miller, Franz Mohling, Rowland Tabor, and Lesley Stark Tabor. A substantial portion of the then relatively small Puget Sound climbing community—including such mountaineering icons as Dee Molenaar, Jim Whittaker, Lou Whittaker, and Wolf Bauer—researched and wrote the chapters, while at least one hundred additional volunteers acted as reviewers, planners, illustrators, typists, proofreaders, financiers, promoters, retailers, warehouse workers, and shipping clerks. Most Mountaineers climbers at the time were involved somehow with this guide. Members who donated their time and effort were rewarded by how well that first edition was received, and members who donated money were repaid by the book's success, which has contributed for more than six decades to the success and stature of The Mountaineers. *Freedom of the Hills* was the first title released by award-winning nonprofit publisher Mountaineers Books.

Legacy and Scope

This guidebook embodies the collective wisdom and experience of thousands of climbers and mountaineers. The previous editions of *Freedom of the Hills* represent a tradition of compiling and integrating the knowledge, techniques, opinions, and advice of many practicing climbers. Both in training sessions and on climbs, students have always been a pivotal sounding board and testing ground for advancements in techniques, equipment, and methods. Each new edition has been carefully

built on the foundation of the preceding editions. An outgrowth of more than a century of hands-on mountaineering knowledge and instruction, the first edition included 430 pages, 134 illustrations, and 16 black-and-white plates organized into 22 chapters. In comparison, this tenth edition features 624 pages, with more than 400 technical illustrations, organized into 28 chapters.

Between 1960's first edition and the tenth edition you now hold in your hands, subsequent editions—each revised and updated, reviewed and enhanced—appeared in roughly seven-year increments, with the eighth edition published in 2010 marking the guide's fiftieth anniversary. Like all nine previous editions, this tenth edition covers current concepts, techniques, and challenges encountered in the pursuit of mountaineering, to help climbers grasp a fundamental understanding of what they can do to manage their risk and enjoy their outdoor experiences. In addition to informing novices, this guide can help more experienced climbers review and improve their skills. Coverage of some topics, such as rock climbing, ice climbing, and aid climbing, is detailed enough to be useful. To fully delve into the range and complexities of *all* the topics introduced, however, climbers will also want to reference more advanced how-to guides (such as the Mountaineers Outdoor Expert Series) and connect with mentors or take classes from more experienced climbers.

You cannot learn mountaineering simply by studying a book, and *Freedom of the Hills* is not meant to be exhaustive. Rather, it is an important source of fundamental information intended to complement thorough instruction featuring proven techniques. A textbook for students and instructors participating in organized climbing courses, *Freedom of the Hills* has always had its greatest impact in learning environments, and a climbing course taught by competent instructors is essential for all beginning climbers.

Climbing requires continual situational and environmental awareness: conditions, routes, and individual abilities and skills vary. Both the individual climber and the climbing team must apply their knowledge, skills, and experience to the circumstances they face and decide how they will proceed. To reflect this process, *Freedom of the Hills* presents a variety of widely used techniques and practices, and then outlines both their advantages and limitations. Material is presented, not as dogma nor the definitive word, but rather as the basis for making sound decisions. To explore while managing their risk, climbers must realize that mountaineering is about problem solving, not merely applying techniques.

The type of climbing described in this guide is frequently—and best—experienced in the wilderness. It is important that mountaineers take responsibility for helping steward our public lands for present and future generations, and recognize that preserving wilderness is crucial to protecting the health of our ecosystems.

Contributors to the 10th Edition

Throughout its history spanning more than a century, The Mountaineers has consistently celebrated its volunteer ethos, emphasizing the complementary goals of inspiring outdoor exploration and offering comprehensive mountaineering education. Thanks to the organization's initiatives over its lifetime, countless individuals have been introduced to the wonders of the outdoors. Many of these individuals, in turn, become volunteers, finding ways to contribute to the evolution of our shared community. The contributors to this tenth edition, called out below, form a special cohort of dedicated leaders, who generously invested their time, intellect, and expertise to bring this new edition into being. What you now hold in your hands transcends the efforts of a few individuals—it embodies the collective knowledge of an organization devoted to cherishing and sharing the wisdom and gifts of the mountains for more than a century.

In assembling the contributors for this tenth edition, we focused on securing world-class instructors and mountaineers. We sought out the expertise of exceptional teachers and guides, drawing from the ranks of secondary and college educators, professionals specializing in outdoor stewardship, fitness, climbing, and meteorology—even a two-time Piolet d'Or award winner. The collective efforts of these remarkable individuals ensure that this edition remains true to the book's original intent. It stands as a worthy steward, incorporating the knowledge base accumulated through decades of combined outdoor innovation, experience, exploration, and education.

Several other professionals played noteworthy roles in the development, editing, and production processes, particularly staff and contractors affiliated with Mountaineers Books. Senior editor Laura Shauger laid the groundwork

Chair, 10th Edition: Eric Linxweiler

Part I—Outdoor Fundamentals: Peter Hendrickson (chair)

Chapter 1—First Steps: Peter Hendrickson

Chapter 2—Clothing and Equipment: Otto Greule

Chapter 3—Camping, Food, and Water: Dan Greenfield

Chapter 4— Conditioning: Mercedes Pollmeier and Mire Kashikura

Chapter 5—Navigation and Communication: Peter Hendrickson, Travis Prescott, and John Godino

Chapter 6—Wilderness Travel: Mire Kashikura and Danielle Graham

Chapter 7—Protecting the Outdoors: Reed Waite and Betsy Robblee

Part II—Climbing Fundamentals: Nicholas Hunt (chair)

Chapter 8—Essential Climbing Equipment: Dan Greenfield and Nicholas Hunt

Chapter 9—Basics of Climbing: Nicholas Hunt

Chapter 10—Belaying: Allison Taylor and Nicholas Hunt

Chapter 11—Rappelling: Peter Tran and Nicholas Hunt

Part III—Rock Climbing: Ian Nicholson (chair)

Chapter 12—Sport Climbing and Technique: Ian Nicholson and Eric Linxweiler

Chapter 13—Rock Protection: Ian Nicholson

Chapter 14—Traditional Rock Protection: Allison Taylor

Chapter 15—Aid and Big Wall Climbing: Lance Colley

Part IV—Snow, Ice, and Alpine Climbing: Steve Swenson (chair)

Chapter 16—Basic Snow and Ice Climbing: Steve Swenson

Chapter 17—Technical Snow and Ice Climbing: Steve Swenson

Chapter 18—Waterfall Ice and Mixed Climbing: Steve Swenson and Ian Nicholson

Chapter 19—Glacier Travel and Crevasse Rescue: Steve Swenson and Nicholas Hunt

Chapter 20—Avalanche Safety: Joe Thompson

Chapter 21—Expedition Climbing: Steve Swenson

Part V—Leadership, Safety, and Rescue: Jerry Logan (chair)

Chapter 22—Leadership: Marko Pavela

Chapter 23—Risk Management: Bill Ashby

Chapter 24—First Aid: Keith Gates

Chapter 25—Self-Rescue: Jerry Logan

Part VI—The Mountain Environment: Eric Linxweiler (chair)

Chapter 26—Mountain Geology: Rick Morrison and Eric Linxweiler

Chapter 27—The Cycle of Snow: Eric Linxweiler

Chapter 28—Mountain Weather: Jeff Renner

for the revisions and provided immeasurable leadership throughout the project. Kris Fulsaas deftly performed a developmental edit, and Erin Moore skillfully copyedited the materials. Creative director Jen Grable designed the covers and managed the book design and illustration process. Kate Basart refined the design and meticulously laid out the text and illustrations. John McMullen expertly tackled brand-new illustrations and revisions to most existing illustrations, along with the monumental task of vectorizing and updating the figures for the big wall and aid climbing chapter; his deep knowledge of climbing techniques informed his work.

Dale Remsberg reviewed the technical climbing-related material and offered invaluable edits and suggestions to ensure that this edition aligns with modern best practices in the broader climbing community. Immense thanks to the following individuals for their review of and help with select chapters: Rachel Aldridge, Bob Boyd, Richard Brodsky, Michael Cecot-Scherer, Karen Conger, Anthony Cree, Nathan Foster, Katie Goodwin, Bob Keranen, Ryan Kitchen, Takeo Kuraishi, Lauren Linxweiler, Michael Loso, John Lynch, Maya Magarati, Steve McClure, Loren McWethy, Aaron Mike, Lisa Messerli, Erik Murdock, Liana Robertson, John Porter, Vikram Sahney, Doug Sanders, J D Tanner, Laura Tobias, Peter Tran, Ty Tyler, Holly Webb, Sawyer Wolters, and Siana Wong.

This foundational manual is designed to acquaint you with the skills and knowledge essential for a lifetime of outdoor adventures. Absorb these instructions and insightful tips, delve into the technical illustrations, and be inspired by the advice and the legacy. Then venture outside and begin to put all that you learn into practice. In doing so, you will experience firsthand the possibilities, personal growth, and lifelong friendships that await you in the outdoors—and ultimately, discover your own freedom of the hills.

PART I
OUTDOOR FUNDAMENTALS

CHAPTER 1

FIRST STEPS

Mountaineering offers us the chance to experience many rewarding opportunities: physical and mental challenge, problem-solving, camaraderie, endurance, expansive vistas, and wild lands. Mountains harbor adventure and mystery. By venturing beyond the confines of the modern world, we learn about ourselves and forge lifelong bonds with climbing partners.

Despite the risks and hardships climbers sometimes face—or maybe in part because of them—mountaineering can offer a sense of tranquility and spiritual communion. In the words of British mountaineer George Mallory, "What we get from this adventure is just sheer joy." But before we find joy or freedom in the hills, we must prepare by learning technical, physical, mental, and emotional skills. Becoming skilled at being in the mountains is a process, and everyone has to begin somewhere. This guide to acquiring those skills is your passport to the freedom of the hills.

Technical Knowledge and Skills

To travel safely and enjoyably in the mountains, we need skills. We need to know what clothing, basic equipment, and food to bring into the backcountry and how to spend the night outside safely. We need to know how to cover long distances while relying on what we carry in our pack, often navigating without trails or signs. We need technical climbing proficiency, including belaying (the technique of securing a rope partner in case of a fall) and rappelling (using the rope to descend), to competently scale and descend a mountain. And we must possess skills specific to the terrain—whether rock, snow, ice, or glacier. Mountaineers strive to manage and minimize risk, but mountain travel is not entirely predictable. Every mountaineer needs to be trained in risk management, navigation, wilderness first aid, and rescue techniques with the goal of becoming self-reliant.

Physical Preparation

Mountaineering is a physically demanding activity. Nearly every type of climbing has become increasingly athletic,

especially at higher levels of difficulty. Climbers today accomplish feats once considered impossible. New standards are being set regularly in rock, ice, and high-altitude climbing. Climbers are pushing limits not only on the way up peaks but also on the way down. Some climbers now ski or snowboard down steep routes once considered difficult or impossible to ascend. Among the changes to the landscape of climbing are the advances in and increasing popularity of steep ice climbing, canyoneering, and mixed climbing—the practice of ascending a combination of rock and ice. Although most people appreciate such extreme achievements from the sidelines, higher standards at these utmost levels of performance often result in increased standards across all levels.

Climbers come in different shapes, sizes, ages, and genders and from different cultures. Whatever a climber's skill level and aspirations, solid physical conditioning is indispensable. The stronger we are, the better prepared we are to face the challenges of climbing mountains and the more likely we are to enjoy trips rather than simply endure them. More important, the safety of a climbing or hiking party depends on the strength and competency of each member.

KEY TOPICS

TECHNICAL KNOWLEDGE AND SKILLS
PHYSICAL PREPARATION
MENTAL PREPARATION
JUDGMENT AND EXPERIENCE
CARING FOR CLIMBING PARTNERS
CARING FOR AND PRESERVING WILDERNESS
A CLIMBING CODE
GAINING THE FREEDOM OF THE HILLS

Mental Preparation

Just as important as physical conditioning in mountaineering is mental attitude. The ability to keep your mind clear and calm helps with everything from deciding whether to stay home because of a poor weather forecast to pushing through a difficult climbing move to rescuing a climbing partner who has fallen. Mountaineers need to be positive and realistic. A can-do attitude may turn into dangerous overconfidence if it is not tempered with a judicious appraisal of the circumstances and environment.

Many a veteran mountaineer will likely say the greatest challenges are mental. Perhaps one of mountaineering's biggest appeals is that while seeking the freedom of the hills, we come face-to-face with ourselves.

Judgment and Experience

The ability to solve problems and make wise decisions is essential to mountaineering. Sound judgment, perhaps a mountaineer's most prized skill, develops from integrating knowledge with hard-won experience. This book outlines equipment and techniques ranging from basic to advanced, but mountaineers must determine how best to use that education to answer the sometimes unpredictable challenges they face in the mountains. Mountaineers need to develop both coping and problem-solving skills—the ability to deal with external factors, such as adverse weather, long hikes, and accidents, as well as internal factors, including fear, exhaustion, and desire. As climbers experience challenging situations, they gain judgment and experience that informs their decision-making in the future.

Mountaineering, moreover, tends to involve novel situations that require careful judgment rather than automatic responses. Although climbers may rely on their experience to inform their choices in the mountains, each situation is unique, especially in light of changing factors like weather and time of year. While sometimes unsettling, this uncertainty is part of the allure of mountaineering.

Many situations in the mountains involve risk, challenge, and accomplishment. As Helen Keller observed in *The Open Door*, "Security is mostly a superstition. It does not exist in nature, nor do the children of men as a whole experience it. Avoiding danger is no safer in the long run than outright exposure. Life is either a daring adventure, or nothing."

FACING THE CLIMATE CRISIS

Glaciers are melting or collapsing at an increasing rate around the world. Wildfires are burning ever hotter and faster; in the western US, for example, tinder-dry forests contain abundant amounts of woody fuel, built up after decades of fire suppression. Lethal floods are destroying access to and obliterating routes. Crop failure, famine, and civil unrest threaten lives and livelihoods in places where we recreate.

Some long-used routes around the world are no longer accessible due to changed conditions, while others have shorter seasons with a wider variety of conditions. Extreme weather events—everything from heat waves to historic rainfall to massive snowstorms—are affecting local conditions. We mountaineers are not above it all. Failure to advocate for the environment and act to mitigate the climate crisis is equivalent to abandoning our future adventures in the high places. While it may seem logical to focus on personal actions—for instance, carpooling to trailheads or choosing local destinations as opposed to global ones—collective action and systemic change to transform our energy infrastructure will make a much greater difference in the long run.

Caring for Climbing Partners

One of the core values of The Mountaineers is community, a principle that focuses on expanding and diversifying the climbing community by offering outdoor opportunities for everyone who wants to participate. People who have savored adventure in the mountains should be among the first to invite and mentor newcomers, especially people who may somehow think they do not belong in the hills. We need to look beyond our personal moments of rapture and fear and understand that self-care includes caring for everyone in our climbing party as well as the broader climbing community.

Mountaineering offers the chance to undergo life-changing experiences and form bonds with friends through adventure. A diverse, inclusive outdoors community inspires respect and passion for the places we love, as well as a powerful voice for protecting those places.

Caring for and Preserving Wilderness

The mountaineering skills described in this book are tools that allow us to visit and enjoy remote areas of the world. But remember that the beauty of wilderness often becomes its undoing by attracting visitors—leaving the landscape touched by human hands and eventually less than wild.

People are using, managing, and irreparably changing wilderness at an alarming rate. For this reason, The Mountaineers and many other outdoor enthusiasts have adopted a set of principles and ethics referred to as the Leave No Trace seven principles (see Chapter 7, Protecting the Outdoors).

Mountains owe climbers nothing and ask nothing of them. A noted Sherpa on the first ascent of Annapurna, Ang Tharkay described arriving at Camp II in his memoir *Sherpa*: "Night had fallen, and the view was glorious and deeply moving. Annapurna's summit looked like a crown of flames that was gradually fading." The minimum charge for the privilege of traveling through the wilderness is to leave the hills as you found them.

Beyond leaving no trace, mountaineers have a responsibility to help preserve the wild environments that climbers love. These days, mountaineering involves environmental restoration projects, permit systems to limit overuse, legislative alerts, clashes among competing interest groups, and closures of roads, trails, and entire climbing areas, sometimes due to civil unrest (as in access points to the Himalaya through Pakistan). In addition to treading softly in the mountains, mountaineers must speak out in support of wilderness preservation, access and entry, and sensitive use of public wildlands. Climbers can no longer assume that they will have access to explore a given area, nor that a beloved region will remain unchanged in the face of accelerating climate change. Mountaineers, climbers, and adventurers need to become active wilderness advocates if they want to continue to enjoy the grand expanses that have often been taken for granted.

A Climbing Code

The Mountaineers has devised a set of guidelines to help people maximize their chances of safety in the mountains. Based on careful observation of the habits of skilled climbers and a thoughtful analysis of accidents, these guidelines (see the "Climbing Code" sidebar) have served well not only for climbers but, with slight adaptation, for all wilderness travelers. Beginners will especially benefit from becoming familiar with this code. Careful planning and preparation go a long way in minimizing risk.

This Climbing Code is not a step-by-step formula for avoiding danger while reaching summits but, rather, a set of guidelines for managing the risks in mountaineering. People new to mountaineering have not yet developed the judgment that comes from years of experience. Common sense is hard won, rarely claimed without that experience.

CLIMBING CODE

- Leave your trip itinerary with a responsible person.
- Carry the necessary clothing, food, and equipment—the Ten Essentials (see The Mountaineers' Ten Essentials in Chapter 2).
- Wear a helmet to minimize your risk of traumatic brain injury from rockfall or other hazards.
- Rope up in exposed areas and for glacier travel. Anchor all belays. Always double-check a rappel setup before you trust it with your life.
- Keep the party together, and obey the leader or the majority.
- Challenge yourself, but do not climb beyond your ability and knowledge without a trusted mentor and/or guide.
- Do not let desire overrule your judgment when choosing a route or deciding whether to turn back.
- Follow sound mountaineering principles as set forth in books of recognized merit.
- Behave in a manner that reflects favorably upon mountaineering—for example, by exercising caution while climbing, paying attention to other parties, and adhering to the Leave No Trace seven principles.
- Carry effective communication devices that meet the needs of the trip (see Chapter 5 for details).
- Be prepared to care for an injured climber.
- Consider purchasing global rescue insurance. Not all jurisdictions provide free evacuation and/or rescue services.

Seasoned mountaineers often modify these guidelines in practice, making judgments based on an understanding of the risks as well as the party's skill level.

Climbers sometimes question the need for such standards in a sport notable for a lack of formal rules. However, serious accidents can often be avoided or minimized when climbing parties follow these simple principles. This code is built on the premise that mountaineers want a high probability of safety and success, even in risk-filled or uncertain situations, and they want an adequate margin of safety in case they misjudge their circumstances or those circumstances change.

Gaining the Freedom of the Hills

The "freedom of the hills" is a concept that combines the simple joy of being in the mountains with the skill, equipment, and strength to travel without harming yourself, others, or the environment. The hills offer this freedom in exchange for your training, preparation, and desire.

These days, avoiding civilization with all its technology and conveniences requires individuals to make a conscious choice. In the modern digital world, many people are accessible online every minute of every day. Although we do not have to leave our devices and connectivity behind to go to the mountains, for those who want to step out of—if only briefly—our mechanized, digitized world, the mountains beckon. They offer a place of richness and communion with the natural world—the exception now rather than the rule.

The mountains and wilderness are indifferent to human needs. Not everyone has the desire to or is willing to pay the price for mountaineering's intense physical and spiritual rewards, but people who aspire to climb mountains can use this book to pursue that dream. And if you learn to climb safely and skillfully, you too can enjoy wilderness while respecting it, experiencing life-changing adventures, forming bonds with friends forged through time spent exploring nature, and tasting the freedom of the hills.

CHAPTER 2

CLOTHING AND EQUIPMENT

Packing everything you may need to stay safe, dry, and comfortable on a wilderness trip can paradoxically lead to danger, chill, and misery. The challenge is limiting your load so you can travel fast and light while carrying enough to succeed and survive. All those ounces add up to limit how far and efficiently you can climb and how quickly you can retreat.

To strike a balance, monitor what you take on a trip, and then afterward, determine what you used and genuinely needed to achieve a reasonable margin of safety. When buying equipment, opt for lightweight, low-bulk alternatives that offer performance and durability. If you are new to mountaineering, rent, borrow, or improvise for early outings to gain hands-on experience before you invest, particularly for expensive items such as boots or backpacks. Ask seasoned climbers for advice, browse outdoor stores, and consult gear reviews to compare prices and features. The latest, greatest products or most expensive items are not always the best. Many local outdoor retailers offer a wide selection of used garments and gear, as well as end-of-season sales.

This chapter covers essential wilderness gear, including guidelines for gauging whether equipment is reliable. Though it does not recommend specific brands, it will help you select high-quality items that work together flexibly. Gear specific to eating and sleeping is covered in Chapter 3, Camping, Food, and Water.

Fabrics

To construct outdoor clothing and gear, companies use a wide range of natural and synthetic fibers and fill materials. Each material has particular advantages and drawbacks.

MICROFIBERS AND LEAVE NO TRACE ETHICS

The durability of garments and equipment is a paramount consideration for mountaineers, and synthetic fabrics, often durable, are commonly used for outdoor gear. But items made of what are essentially plastic yarns have environmental costs. Over time they break down into microplastics, pieces smaller than 3/16 inch (5 millimeters).

Synthetic yarns release microfibers every time they are washed and dried; these fragments end up in the air, on land, and in waterways, and from there into the digestive systems of marine organisms and seabirds. Microplastics are undigestible and typically leach toxins, leading wildlife to starve or cause their immune systems to fail. Mountaineers and other advocates of the Leave No Trace ethic are confronted with a sobering projection by World Economic Forum experts: by 2050, there will be more plastic in the ocean by weight than fish.

Using recycled plastics to make the polyesters in many fabrics reduces dependency on petroleum as a source for raw materials, but it is only part of the solution. As a mountaineer, prioritize durability by making informed decisions when shopping. Buy fewer garments overall and fewer made of virgin fibers, and extend the life of your garments by repairing, reusing, and recycling them. Wash clothing and gear less frequently. A front-loading washing machine causes less friction than a top-loading machine, which reduces the amount of microfibers shed per load of laundry. Consider using a microfiber-filter bag when machine-washing garments.

KEY TOPICS

FABRICS
CLOTHING
CARING FOR OUTDOOR CLOTHING
FOOTWEAR
PACKS
ESSENTIAL EQUIPMENT
PREPARING FOR THE FREEDOM OF THE HILLS

TABLE 2-1. KEY FEATURES OF GARMENTS MADE OF SYNTHETIC FABRICS				
GARMENT TYPE: FABRIC(S)	**WIND RESISTANCE**	**BREATHABILITY**	**WATERPROOFNESS**	**STRETCHINESS**
Midlayer shirt and/or hoodie: polyester fleece	Poor	Excellent	Poor	Excellent
Double-weave softshell: polyester, nylon, and fleece	Fair	Excellent	Poor	Excellent
Laminated softshell: polyester, nylon, and fleece	Good	Good	Fair	Good
Waterproof, breathable laminated softshell: polyester fleece, membrane, and nylon	Excellent	Fair	Good to excellent	Fair
Waterproof, breathable hardshell: waterproof, breathable interior fabric, inner membrane, and nylon	Excellent	Fair	Excellent	Poor

SYNTHETIC FABRICS

While synthetic fibers have mostly held favor in mountaineering fabrics over the past few decades, natural fibers such as merino wool are regaining popularity. Synthetic fibers (polyester, nylon, spandex, and acrylic) are synthesized from petrochemicals and commonly supplemented with chemicals known to be detrimental to both human health and the environment. The ill-health effects of long-term exposure to these chemicals remain vastly understudied.

Synthetic fibers are hydrophobic and tend to repel moisture. Garments made of synthetic fabrics absorb water only between the fibers and/or filaments making up each thread. Bacteria thrive in these spaces, turning your sweat into stink (for solutions, see Caring for Outdoor Clothing, below). Synthetic fabrics are also slicker than natural fibers, a disadvantage if you fall on steep snow or ice while wearing them. Table 2-1 compares key features of outdoor clothing made from synthetic fabrics.

Polyester. Many garments from base layers to outer layers are made from high-quality polyester threads, each of which can contain more than 100 filaments, giving the final fabric a soft, cotton-like feel. Polyester fabrics are often chemically treated or shaped to help wick away moisture. In outdoor garments, polyester has largely replaced polypropylene, offering a softer feel against the skin and less odor retention. Some polyester thread is made from recycled plastic.

Synthetic fleece. Also known as polar fleece, fleece, or pile, this warm, lightweight polyester fabric began replacing wool in many climbing garments in the 1980s. Synthetic fleece absorbs little moisture and retains loft and reasonable insulating properties when wet. Fleece has a good warmth-to-weight ratio but does little to block the wind, and it can be bulky.

Spandex. This stretchy fiber, also known as elastane or the brand name Lycra, is often added to fabrics for a snug fit that allows a full range of motion. Base layers close to the skin help the body's heat move moisture to the next layer (although some nonspandex knit fabrics work this way too). When it comes to mid- and outer layers, wearing items that fit snugly minimizes the bellows effect that blows away some of your hard-earned warm air layer as you move. Spandex adds significantly to a garment's weight and drying time. Look for blends containing no more than 10 percent to optimize fit, stretch, and warmth while minimizing extra weight and drying time.

Nylon. Fabrics made of nylon, technically known as polyamide, are very strong, resulting in better abrasion resistance than polyester. These characteristics lead to nylon's use in ropes and outerwear, including the surface layer of waterproof, breathable laminated fabric. Nylon fabrics also feel softer to the touch and on the skin than polyesters, leading to their use in many garments. Nylon retains twice as much water as polyester but only one-fourth as much as cotton or wool; water-repellent finishes further reduce nylon's water retention. Ripstop nylon incorporates a sewing pattern that resists tearing.

Waterproof, nonbreathable fabrics. The simplest way to create a waterproof fabric is to coat or impregnate nylon with waterproof, nonbreathable polyurethane or silicone (silnylon). Such coatings are lightweight and relatively inexpensive but are often subject to abrasion or mildew.

Although they keep rain out, they also seal in sweat and water vapor. If sweat cannot evaporate through your clothes, you will get wet.

Waterproof, breathable fabrics. Incorporating billions of microscopic pores per square inch, waterproof, breathable fabrics contain several laminated layers to repel rain and snow while allowing perspiration to escape. Since the individual water molecules we perspire are much smaller than droplets of rain, the holes are designed to be large enough to let vapor escape but too small for raindrops to get in (fig. 2-1). Most have a factory-applied durable water-repellent (DWR) finish so that rainwater beads up rather than coats the micropores. A wetted-out, waterproof, breathable shell fabric can become cold, increasing condensation inside the garment.

Many DWR finishes contain the chemicals perfluorooctane sulfonate (PFOS) and perfluorooctanoic acid (PFOA). These chemicals can harm the environment and human health through their toxicity and tendency to last a long time and bioaccumulate. Products labeled "PFOA- and PFOS-free" may use different but similar chemicals. (See the "Caring for Waterproof, Breathable Fabrics" sidebar below.)

Coated fabrics are less expensive and less durable than laminated fabrics. Waterproof, breathable laminated fabric is, however, more expensive to make. It consists of three layers or laminations: an innermost liner or membrane-protective coating to spread out any condensed perspiration, a waterproof, breathable interior membrane, and a breathable outer nylon shell that protects the membrane. These laminated fabrics tend to last longer since the primary membrane is protected.

Ultra-high-molecular-weight polyethylene. These strong, lightweight fibers (with strength-to-weight ratios eight times those of high-strength steels) are commonly used in climbing runners and utility cord. They are better known by their brand names, Dyneema and Spectra. Dyneema is usually woven to create featherweight, abrasion-resistant fabrics for backpacks; it is also often sandwiched into ultralightweight, waterproof, nonbreathable Dyneema Composite Fabric for tents and raingear.

Softshell Materials

Typically a dense, flexible cloth woven out of two interconnected layers, softshell fabrics have a fleecy interior for warmth and a smooth nylon or polyester exterior with DWR treatment that deflects and sheds some snow and wind. Newer softshell fabrics are laminated with an abrasion-resistant, stretchable nylon face. Some types include a waterproof, breathable membrane for additional wind and weather resistance. Softshell materials generally fall into one of the following three categories.

Double-weave softshell. The original ski pant material, this softshell fabric is ideal for intense activity and cool conditions. Usually made with woven nylon or polyester, it stretches to allow freedom of movement. A relatively hard finish resists wind, snow, and abrasion.

Laminated softshell. Better suited to colder conditions, but also a little heavier, this softshell significantly blocks wind, sheds snow, and adds some protection from rain. It consists of a stretchy woven fabric, such as polyester, nylon, or spandex, added or laminated to an interior layer typically made of fleece.

Waterproof, breathable laminated softshell. This material sandwiches a waterproof, breathable membrane between polyester fleece on the inside and woven nylon on the outside. The result is a soft-to-the-touch, slightly stretchy fabric with weather resistance comparable to that of a breathable waterproof fabric.

Hardshell Materials

Hardshells—rain parkas and rain pants—are generally made of nylon or nylon blends. Since nylon is not waterproof, hardshells derive their waterproofing either from fabric treatments (nonbreathable), fabrication methods

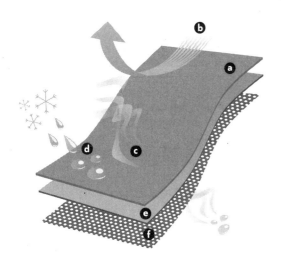

Fig. 2-1. *Waterproof, breathable fabric system:* **a,** *outer nylon fabric;* **b,** *outer layer repels wind;* **c,** *sweat as water vapor transpires through the outer layer;* **d,** *snow and water bead up on DWR finish;* **e,** *interior waterproof, breathable film;* **f,** *inner liner (optional).*

(breathable), or a combination of both. A person who is working hard will create more moisture than a waterproof, breathable garment can manage, causing sweat to condense inside the shell. When sweat can no longer escape, the wearer is once again dealing with the original problem of becoming wet over time.

Construction techniques and features such as zippered vents improve ventilation, but they add weight, introduce another possible point of failure, and are often more expensive. A base layer helps by absorbing liquid sweat, spreading it out, and allowing it to vaporize from body heat and then escape directly through the fabric or a vent. Mountaineers can minimize perspiration by wearing as few layers as possible on top of their base layer—start out a little cold and assume you'll warm up as you move.

NATURAL FIBERS

In the early days of mountaineering, natural-fiber clothes were the only option. Cotton, with the possible exception of a T-shirt on a hot day or in base camp, now has no place in a climber's pack. The rise of synthetic fleece allowed climbers to dismiss ragg wool as coarse and itchy. Base layers, knit shirts, and socks made from merino wool and blends have since resurged in popularity.

Cotton. Comfortable to wear when dry, cotton loses its insulating qualities when wet, absorbs many times its weight in water, generally takes a long time to dry, and gets cold quickly. Do not rely on it to keep you warm. Cotton plays a common role in many hypothermia tragedies, leading to the adage "cotton kills." Wet cotton also chafes, particularly annoying in underwear and socks or under pack straps. Yet in hot, dry weather, cotton offers reasonable sun protection and ventilates well—plus sweat evaporating from a wet cotton T-shirt on a hot day may cool you off.

Rayon, modal, and viscose. These fibers, a hybrid of sorts between synthetic and natural fibers, are chemically extruded from wood pulp and made to mimic natural fabrics like silk, wool, linen, or cotton. They exhibit all the downsides of cotton. Avoid them in the outdoors.

Merino wool. Under such brands as Darn Tough Vermont, Smartwool, Ibex, and Icebreaker, modern wool fabrics use small-diameter silky fleece, primarily made from the coats of merino sheep. Chemical descaling removes most of the itchiness and tendency to shrink. Making wool fabric is also easier on the environment, but such garments often cost more and lightweight options are delicate and prone to holes. Wool weighs more when wet and dries more slowly than synthetics (see the "Warm When Wet?" sidebar). Nevertheless, merino wool gets high marks for

---

WARM WHEN WET?

Wool used to carry the banner of "warm when wet," a badge now heralded by synthetic fabrics and fills. And though wet wool will usually keep you warmer than wet cotton, there is no getting past physics—converting the liquid in damp clothes into vapor requires a lot of energy. If you want to stay warm, *stay dry*.

---

comfort and warmth. Wool has amazing natural antistink qualities unrivaled by synthetics and appreciated by tentmates on longer trips.

INSULATING FILLS

Insulation for outdoor clothing and gear, such as sleeping bags, is made of either down or synthetics.

Down. High-quality goose or duck down is the warmest, lightest, most compressible fill available. Down compresses well yet regains its loft—and therefore its warmth—quickly when unpacked. High-quality goose down has 650 to 900-plus fill power, which means that each ounce, uncompressed, expands to fill 650 to 900-plus cubic inches (376 to 520-plus cubic centimeters per gram). Down's low weight-to-warmth ratio makes it popular for cold-weather jackets and especially for sleeping bags. Down is a byproduct of the poultry industry, however, so look for the Responsible Down Standard (RDS) certification label, which ensures the humane treatment of animals within a traceable supply chain.

Down is expensive yet lasts longer than other insulating fills. Unfortunately, it loses all its insulating value when wet and is almost impossible to dry in damp conditions. Although DWR treatment may shorten an item's drying time, it only briefly delays the time that a garment becomes soaked in damp or wet conditions, which may offer a false sense of security.

Synthetic fill. Unlike down, synthetic fills keep their loft when wet, providing more reliable insulation in damp climates. Heavier and less compressible than down, they are also less expensive and easier to clean. Compared with down, most synthetic fills may not withstand as many compression cycles (stuffing and unstuffing), which means they lose their loft and insulation properties more quickly. This may be changing with the advent of active insulation, which responds to your output level and retains warmth but allows heat and moisture to escape. Originally invented for the US military, it is now firmly rooted in the broader outdoor-garment market. A few examples are Polartec Alpha, PrimaLoft, and Patagonia's Nano-Air.

Clothing

Clothing helps you stay comfortable by creating an insulating cushion of air next to the skin. The right clothes preserve that insulating layer from precipitation, wind, heat, and cold. Inclement weather often leads to conditions far below most people's definition of comfort. Still, the key to being comfortable is to stay dry—or, after getting wet, to stay warm and dry out quickly. When venturing into remote territory, climbers need a layering system that helps them endure difficult conditions for however long those conditions last (see the "Choosing a Starter Ensemble" sidebar).

Even in moderately cool temperatures, prolonged periods of dampness can cause your body's core temperature to fall, possibly triggering hypothermia, a frequent cause of death in the mountains. Wind exposes you to windchill and can contribute to hypothermia, frostnip, or frostbite (see Cold-Related Conditions in Chapter 24, First Aid). Layer your clothes to ensure that you can survive sustained exposure to cold, wet, and windy conditions (see the "Managing Moisture" sidebar).

Outdoor clothing must also protect climbers from overheating (and sun exposure) on hot days and reduce excessive sweating, which can dampen layers and lead to severe dehydration. Ventilation, breathability, and sun protection are other key considerations.

Assembling a layering system for the first time can be daunting. Ask questions and read tags. Evaluate garments for functionality, durability, fit, and versatility: Will it

---

CHOOSING A STARTER ENSEMBLE

Start by purchasing high-quality, well-fitting pieces to serve as the core of your layering system:

- Light- or medium-weight base layer, including two tops and one bottom
- One or two synthetic or wool (knit) tops of varying weights, including one with a zip collar or full-length zip and another with a lightweight hood
- Synthetic pants and shorts
- Insulated ("puffy") coat
- Hardshell jacket and pants
- Warm hat and gloves
- Sunglasses
- Boots and socks

MANAGING MOISTURE

Managing moisture, particularly from sweat, is key to staying warm. Follow these tips to protect midlayers from precipitation and perspiration and keep your clothing system functioning at its best:

- Start up the trail feeling a little cool. Readjust your layers shortly after you start, and then whenever practical during the day.
- Avoid waterproof, breathable fabrics until necessary— then wear minimal clothes underneath.
- Use zippers and vents to shed excess heat.
- Dry damp clothes when possible.
- Just say no to cotton.

---

work when wet? Will it keep you comfortable in a wide range of conditions, especially wet and/or cold ones? Be skeptical; clothing companies often make strong marketing claims supported by weak data. Clothes designed for other sports may also be suitable for climbing.

Climbers may select markedly different layers as a result of their body structure, metabolism, or preference. Personalizing core garments lets you adapt to the season, weather conditions, and activity. Thoughtful additions expand your clothing quiver to meet the challenge of upcoming adventures. Eventually, you will pare down the layers you bring on any given trip. But if you are new to wilderness travel, start out carrying more than enough to stay warm and dry. Leave items at home only when you are certain that you can survive and thrive without them. Before heading out, check the weather forecast, consider the temperature and weather extremes you may encounter, and then pack accordingly.

FOCUS ON LAYERING

The goal of dressing for changeable mountain conditions is to minimize clothing weight and bulk while efficiently maintaining a comfortable body temperature and avoiding sweat. Experienced mountaineers develop a basic layering strategy consisting of a few functional, versatile garments that they use in combination. They may swap in a new base layer, carry more or fewer midlayers or a different outer garment, or try something new—but this system has withstood the test of time and the elements. It consists of four types of layers, starting with the one closest to your skin and working outward:

1. **Base layer.** The base layer, next to your skin, allows perspiration to evaporate, keeping you warm and dry.
2. **Midlayers.** Midlayers trap warm air close to your body. The thicker the layer of trapped air, the warmer you will be. Several loose-fitting light layers can trap a lot of insulating air, and such an arrangement is more adjustable than a monolithic block of "dead" air (as in a down parka, for example).
3. **Shell layer.** Shells protect midlayers from wind and precipitation. The shell layer could consist of a waterproof, breathable hardshell, softshell, or wind shell, depending on conditions.
4. **Belay jacket.** If you put it on as soon as you stop moving, an insulated jacket sized to fit over all your other layers can preserve hard-won warmth.

Think of layers as a system intended to maintain comfort in a wide variety of weather conditions, which can also be worn all together to survive an unplanned bivouac. Try them in combination before a climb to make sure the shell layer fits comfortably over all the midlayers without compressing insulation or restricting movement. Similarly, make sure your belay jacket fits over your first three layers in case an unplanned bivy becomes a reality.

Armed with knowledge of outdoor fabrics and the strategy of layering, you can assemble an effective mountaineering layering ensemble. Figure 2-2 shows how to mix and match various articles of clothing and accessories to function throughout a spectrum of weather conditions and levels of physical exertion. Exact garments will vary from climber to climber, but the goal is to create a flexible, productive system.

Cool conditions with rain or wet snow are the most difficult to prepare for. Waterproof, breathable garments are the best options but condensation is still a concern. Dress minimally underneath to avoid overheating, vent as much as possible, and assume the clothes you are wearing are going to get wet. Wearing gaiters under rain pants (when you are not wearing crampons) helps keep boots, socks, and feet dry and free of debris, while allowing you to unzip the lower legs of the rain pants. A rain kilt or poncho is an option for the approach hike. Colder conditions and snow are simpler to dress for than rain. Cold snow often sluffs off garments before it has a chance to melt. Waterproof, breathable garments do not breathe as well as other outer layers; a more breathable, laminated softshell may be sufficient in snow.

Monitor your personal temperature closely. To avoid overheating, ventilate as much as possible and adjust your layers. Start off feeling a little cool; as you work harder, you will warm up. Remove waterproof garments as soon as possible. To get warm when resting, belaying, or hanging out in camp, don more midlayers under your shell and your belay jacket over your shell.

BASE LAYER

Protecting yourself from the cold begins with a base layer, also known as long johns or thermal long underwear. Wicking fabrics made of merino wool or polyester are popular. A dependable base layer sops up liquid sweat, disperses it, and allows your body heat to vaporize it. Dark colors dry more quickly in sunlight than light-colored layers do, but light colors reflect sun and are better on hot days, when a base layer worn alone protects from sunburn or insects.

For rock climbing, a base layer of spandex-blended polyester tights allows a full range of motion. Versatile lightweight nylon or double-weave softshell pants can be worn alone against the skin.

T-shirts and shorts, or other light layers. In hot weather, a cotton T-shirt or tank top may seem to be a comfortable base layer. But even on a moderately cool day, cotton will soak up sweat during a steep ascent, chilling you when you take a break. Noncotton fabrics are the better choice, and long sleeves or a long-sleeved hoodie provide more sun and insect protection. Warm-weather shirts should be light colored for coolness and loose enough to allow for ventilation. For shorts or skorts, seek out ventilation and a durable design and fabric. Loose-fitting nylon shorts with an integral mesh brief can work well. A popular combination for mild conditions is a lightweight base layer under synthetic shorts (fig. 2-2a and g). Lightweight nylon pants with zip-off legs that convert to shorts are particularly versatile.

Underwear and sports bra. As the layer below your base layer, underwear and sports bras add warmth and insulation and need to perform well. Cotton chafes when damp and is a poor choice for tight-fitting garments.

MIDLAYERS

The workhorse of any layering system, midlayers allow perspiration to evaporate while protecting your core from the elements. Climbers carry and wear a variety of midlayers, mixing and matching fleece vests and jackets, down or synthetic-fill jackets or sweaters (puffies), and double-weave softshells, depending on the challenge (see Table 2-2).

a

- helmet
- lightweight wind shell
- lightweight gloves
- midlayer
- synthetic or wool medium-weight base layers
- pants (zip-off legs optional)
- high gaiters

b

- helmet with headlamp
- warm hat
- buff
- insulated jacket
- medium- or heavy-weight base layer
- liner and outer gloves
- double-weave softshell pants
- built-in gaiters

c

- knit hat
- cap with brim
- midlayers
- puffy coat
- medium-weight gloves or mittens
- medium-weight or double-weave softshell pants
- high gaiters

d

- warm hat or balaclava
- goggles
- buff
- belay puffy over midlayers
- mitten harness security cord
- liner gloves with mittens
- puffy pants
- expedition gaiters
- insulated boots

e

- wide-brimmed rain hat
- waterproof, breathable hardshell jacket
- rain pants
- gaiters
- crampons

f

- helmet
- waterproof, breathable softshell
- gloves with liners and cuffs
- softshell pants with integrated gaiters

g

- sun hoody over ball cap
- sunglasses
- lightweight sun-protective top
- sun gloves
- shorts or pants
- low gaiters

Fig. 2-2. *Layering for a variety of conditions: **a,** high exertion, dry and cool; **b,** high exertion, dry and cold; **c,** low exertion, dry and cool; **d,** low exertion, dry and cold; **e,** high exertion, rain and wet snow; **f,** high exertion, dry snow; **g,** high or low exertion, hot.*

Synthetic shirt and pants. Simple nylon or polyester shirts and pants are lightweight pieces that provide sun and insect protection while being adaptable to cold weather. Shirts (and fleece tops) should be long enough to be tucked in or pulled below your hips to prevent gaps and drafts.

Merino wool knit shirt. This luxurious fabric's allure comes from its warm-to-the-touch feel and renewable source—

a welcome contrast to a pack full of yardage derived from petroleum.

Synthetic fleece. Core elements of the midlayer are synthetic fleeces and noncotton hoodies. Full-length zippers offer versatility over half-zips. Climbers usually combine a thin to medium-weight fleece shirt with other options. Having one fleece layer with a hood and one or two with

TABLE 2-2. OPTIONS FOR MIDLAYERS

TYPE OF MIDLAYER	WARMTH-TO-WEIGHT RATIO	BREATHABILITY
Synthetic shirt and pants	Good	Good
Wool knit shirt	Fair	Good
Synthetic fleece	Good	Excellent
Synthetic-fill puffy	Good	Fair
Down puffy	Excellent	Fair
Active insulation puffy	Good	Excellent
Double-weave softshell	Good	Excellent

zip-up collars adds warmth and sun protection. Snow tends to stick to fleece pants; double-weave softshell pants are a better choice.

Insulated jacket. Compressible, lightweight jackets, often called puffies, have largely replaced bulkier fleece jackets. Down is ideal for cool, dry conditions or cool, wet settings if worn under a hardshell. An indispensable pillar of most layering systems, synthetic and down puffy vests and jackets are light enough to wear when active, yet trim enough to work well with other layers. This go-to garment is especially useful when resting, belaying, or camping.

Insulated pants or skirt. Insulated ("puffy") pants (typically filled with synthetic insulation) help your legs retain heat in colder conditions. Look for full-length side zippers that allow you to put them on over boots, crampons, or snowshoes. A puffy skirt helps climbers avoid deeply chilled thighs. Puffy pants or a puffy skirt can extend the range of your sleeping bag, allowing you to carry a lighter bag.

Double-weave softshell. This type of midlayer garment provides reasonable wind and weather resistance for most conditions. The fabric's spandex content makes for trim-fitting garments and a warm and flexible fabric for skiing or climbing in cool or snowy conditions. (Softshell laminates offer even more waterproofing and are used for outer shells.)

SHELL LAYER

The ideal shell would be fully waterproof, windproof, and breathable. Though no single garment achieves all these objectives, various strategies come close. Many mountaineers carry two shells: a lighter, breathable, wind-resistant jacket and a somewhat heavier (breathable waterproof) hardshell jacket and pants. Climbers wear the more breathable wind-resistant gear in cool, windy, and even lightly drizzling conditions and for periods of heavy exertion, and reserve the hardshell for harder workouts or heavier rain. (See the "Choosing a Shell Jacket" sidebar.)

Wind shells. Compressible to the size of an apple but light as 2 ounces (60 grams), a wind shell conserves the heat captured by the midlayers. It packs more warmth per gram than any other garment. Wind shells are often highly breathable, and if they have a DWR coating, they can shed light precipitation.

Softshells. Laminated softshells are stretchy and more breathable than a hardshell while still offering some resistance to wind and dry snow. Breathable waterproof laminated softshells are another step up in waterproofness, albeit with reduced breathability comparable to that of a hardshell. Yet when there is a risk of extended exposure to precipitation, skip softshells entirely and pair your midlayers with a hardshell.

Hardshells. Stormy weather requires serious protection. Made of waterproof, breathable fabric with two or three layers, hardshells sacrifice breathability for improved weatherproofing. A high-quality hardshell jacket may be the most expensive garment in your arsenal. For ventilation, hardshells have full-length front zippers plus a variety of breathability tricks, including adjustable openings at the front, waist, underarms (pit zips), sides, and cuffs.

Hardshell pants (rain pants) should have full-length zippers so you can don or remove them over boots, crampons, or snowshoes, or vent them from top to bottom. Because rain pants tend to be worn less often than parkas—and because they can be ruined by bushwhacking or glissading—choosing a nonbreathable pair can save money.

In cold conditions, some climbers use waterproof, breathable bib pants held up by suspenders as a lower-body shell layer. Insulated bibs are considerably warmer than rain pants because they cover much of the torso and keep snow from entering around your waistline. They are a good option for backcountry skiing, waterfall ice climbing, and mixed climbing. Some mountaineers use one-piece, 8,000-meter suits, the warmest but least versatile option.

BELAY JACKET

In cold weather, a thickly insulated jacket, commonly referred to as a belay parka or belay puffy, helps keep you warm and attentive when stationary, such as for long stints of belaying. Keep it handy for rest stops and camp—

CHOOSING A SHELL JACKET

Evaluate the fabric and features when comparing shell jackets.

Fabric makes a difference:

- Uninsulated shells are lighter and versatile.
- Two-layer breathable waterproof shells work well in moderate weather (and they cost and weigh less than ones made of three layers).
- Three-layer waterproof, breathable shells perform better in severe weather.
- Jackets made of laminated or waterproof, breathable softshell fabric are alternatives for cold, dry conditions where climbers are most likely to encounter dry snow.

These features are important:

- Large enough to fit over all midlayers and a climbing harness
- A hood with a brim that fits over a helmet
- Neck construction that covers the chin comfortably and allows the head to move freely
- Sufficient ventilation
- Waterproof zippers
- Pockets that are easily accessible even while wearing gloves and carrying a pack
- Lengths sufficient to seal the waistline and cover the wrists

it also makes a great pillow. Desired features include an integral hood, thick but compressible insulation, and water-resistant, lightweight shell material. If it is large enough to fit either member of a rope team (on top of all their other layers), one belay jacket can suffice. But bringing a jacket for each climber could save lives in adverse weather or in the event of an accident.

HEADWEAR

There's truth to the adage "If your feet are cold, put on a hat." When you are cold, your body reduces blood flow to your arms and legs to warm other more vital areas. Putting on a hat, balaclava, or neck gaiter reduces heat loss from your head, allowing more to go to your feet. (See the "Choosing a Cold-Weather Strategy" sidebar.) Climbers often carry several types of hats to adapt to changing temperatures. To

prevent a brimmed hat from blowing off and sailing over a cliff, choose one with a strap or leash. Thin hats can be worn beneath most climbing helmets. Skiers wear helmets for both protection and warmth.

Insulating caps come in wool, acrylic, or polyester fleece. Balaclavas cover the face and neck or can be rolled up to allow ventilation around your neck. Stretchy knitted cylinders called neck gaiters or buffs help seal the neck opening of a jacket (see Figure 2-2b and d); they cover the head and ears and are thin enough to wear under a helmet. On a very cold day, pulling a buff up from around your neck to cover your mouth can help protect you from such hazards as yak-dung dust that contributes to the so-called Khumbu cough on the trek to Everest Base Camp.

A waterproof, breathable brimmed hat allows for ventilation while protecting your head and neck from the rain (see Figure 2-2e). A long-sleeved hoodie offers excellent sun protection, especially on snow or sand or near water (see Figure 2-2g). Some people wear a long-billed cap with a neck flap, or a large bandanna or hoodie under a baseball cap. A hat brim shades your eyes and keeps rain and snow off glasses, but it can also impede visibility in certain situations. Consider a hat with a narrower brim for ascending a steep slope or a stiffened brim for windy conditions. Remember to check that your hat is compatible with your helmet.

HANDWEAR

When the body sacrifices blood flow to the extremities to warm the core, you may experience cold hands and stiff fingers. Simple things like pulling zippers, adjusting buckles, and tying knots become a chore that can slow a climbing party's progress. Selecting mittens and gloves usually entails a compromise between dexterity and warmth. The more technical a climb, the more significant the compromise. As with other insulating garments, mittens and gloves must be made of fabrics that stay warm when wet but dry quickly. Outdoor handwear comes in synthetics, wool-synthetic blends, wool, and leather. Bulkier materials add warmth but decrease dexterity. Double-weave softshell fabric is common in alpine gloves.

The layering concept for clothing also applies to hands. The first layer may be a thin pair of gloves; other layers are usually thicker, more durable gloves or mittens. Mittens are warmer because they allow fingers to share warmth.

Climbers need to protect their hands from rock features, ropes, and cold. Some handwear features removable inner gloves or mitts, making them versatile and quicker to dry. A nonslip coating on the palms improves grip. To combat cold, handwear cuffs should overlap the parka sleeve about

4 to 6 inches (10 to 15 centimeters), with Velcro closures that cinch around the forearm (see Figure 2-2f). Security cords tether mittens so that climbers can easily remove them to climb rock or apply sunscreen (see Figure 2-2d). Heated gloves aid ice climbers or climbers with conditions such as Raynaud's disease. Touchscreen compatibility on fingertips helps navigators in cold or inclement weather.

In camp, layering mittens with glove liners or fingerless gloves allows for greater dexterity for delicate chores while exposing a minimum of bare skin (see Figure 2-2g). Though synthetics can melt in high heat (from a backpacking stove, for instance), they are also less likely to stick to frozen metal. Fingerless gloves are often best for rock climbing in cold weather. Handling a wet rope or scrambling over wet rocks can saturate handwear, even in dry weather. Some climbers carry several pairs, rotating them when they become wet and cold so that they start each pitch with dry gloves and warm hands.

Often worn for rope handling such as rappelling or belaying, leather gloves feature a better grip and prevent rope burns. While most leather gloves dry slowly and insulate poorly when wet, some climbing versions have waterproof, breathable liners and water-resistant leather. Mechanics' work gloves with leather palms are an inexpensive alternative for scrambling, belaying, and rappelling.

SLEEPWEAR

Many climbers carry a set of base layers and socks for camp and sleeping. Changing into these dry clothes in camp will help you retain body heat as you cool down after strenuous activity and nighttime settles in. Alternately, a climber may have to dry damp clothes by setting them in their sleeping bag or wearing them to bed.

Caring for Outdoor Clothing

There are several steps to caring for outdoor clothing. The first is keeping waterproof, breathable garments clean of dirt, oils, sunscreen, and insect repellent, which clog fabric pores and reduce breathability. The second is laundering outdoor garments based on their fabrics and construction. The third step is reviving the DWR finish (see the "Caring for Waterproof, Breathable Fabrics" sidebar).

CLEANING OUTDOOR CLOTHING

The key to laundering most outdoor fabrics is simply to follow the manufacturer's instructions, though washing less frequently reduces microfiber shedding. Close all zippers and fasteners; wash in cold or warm water with

CHOOSING A COLD-WEATHER STRATEGY

In addition to layering, these tactics can also help with your cold-weather defense:

- Manage moisture carefully.
- Add midlayers that can function with the system.
- Add a belay jacket and puffy pants.
- Eat more, starting with a big breakfast. Fat and calories correlate directly with body heat. Keep high-calorie snacks in a pocket where they can be eaten gradually. (See "Fat" in Composition of Foods in Chapter 3, Camping, Food, and Water.)
- Drink more water, even when urinating may be inconvenient. Dehydration results in low blood volume that will make you even colder.
- Manage cold feet and hands. Evaluate whether your gloves, hats, and socks are doing their job. Rotate wet gloves or mittens and socks with dry ones. Do not go to sleep wearing wet socks. Try chemical hand and foot warmers, but avoid direct contact with your skin, especially while asleep, to prevent burns.
- Monitor for frostbite: check for ears, toes, or a nose that is turning red or losing color or fingers that become tingly or are losing feeling. Before your trip, identify the nearest treatment facility in case you need to evacuate. (See Frostbite in Chapter 24, First Aid.)
- Even on a day trip, bring hot water in an insulated container and a stove to warm up food and water.
- For extreme cold at high elevations, consider wearing a one-piece climbing suit for vastly superior warmth.
- Accept that at times you will likely be somewhat cold, but be vigilant about distinguishing between discomfort and injury.

a liquid sports wash or mild laundry soap; then line or tumble dry on low. Avoid using fabric softeners (they ruin water repellency), scented detergents (they attract bears and bugs), chlorine bleach (it ruins colors, except for polyester), and hot irons (they melt synthetics), as well as dry cleaning down garments (which strips feathers of their essential oils).

Launder double-weave softshell fabric like most garments, but pay attention to their DWR treatment (see DWR on Hardshells and Softshells, below). Launder both

CARING FOR WATERPROOF, BREATHABLE FABRICS

Durable water-repellent (DWR) finishes fail slowly over time. Following these steps will help keep this finish functional:

- **Keep it clean.** Wash the garment as needed with a liquid sports wash, and do not use fabric softener.
- **Rinse it well.** After washing, put the garment through a second rinse.
- **Dry it.** Drip-dry or use a dryer set on medium (140 degrees Fahrenheit, 60 degrees Celsius).
- **Revive it.** Once the garment is completely dry, tumble dry for an additional 20 minutes on medium heat to revive the DWR.
- **Conduct a spray test.** Water should bead up on the surface.
- **Reapply DWR.** If the garment fails the test, reapply the coating.

laminated and waterproof, breathable laminated softshells the same as waterproof, breathable hardshells: clean gently, rinse thoroughly, dry carefully, and touch up or reapply the DWR coatings to help your gear last.

Funk. Bacteria thrive in synthetic thread and even survive the gentle laundering recommended above. On each outing, this microbiome generates its factory of funk, making sweaty clothes stink. Fabric labels to the contrary, most polyester fabrics (but not nylon or other synthetics) can be laundered with chlorine bleach. For other smelly garments, try presoaking in a nonchlorine bleach followed by normal cleaning.

Waterproof, breathable garments. The functionality of these shells depends on relatively delicate components, which need to be kept clean. It's best to use a sports wash detergent. Do not use fabric softener. Because detergent is hydrophilic (attracts or has a tendency to mix with water), rinsing the garment a second time is critical. Line dry or tumble dry on medium (140 degrees Fahrenheit, 60 degrees Celsius), then test the finish as explained below.

DWR ON HARDSHELLS AND SOFTSHELLS

DWR may be durable, but it will not last the lifetime of a garment. Maintaining that finish is important. Eventually, rainwater wets out the outer shell, making the fabric

appear dark; water vapor is blocked and can no longer pass through. The fabric becomes heavy and cold, compounding the problem by causing vaporized sweat to condense on the inside.

During manufacturing, DWR is applied to many other garments besides shells, including fleece jackets, wind shells, pants, hats, and gloves. These treatments also can be revitalized as described below.

Test the DWR. At home, test the garment with a spray bottle. When water no longer beads up on the surface, use heat to revive it.

Revive the finish with heat. After your shell is clean and completely dry, tumble dry for an additional 20 minutes on medium heat. If you are unable to tumble dry, you can try ironing the dry garment on a gentle setting (warm, no steam), placing a towel or cloth between the garment and the iron.

Apply a home treatment. When heat no longer revives the fabric, try applying a spray-on or wash-in DWR. These procedures may work to revive an expensive hardshell or softshell. Home-applied products fall into two main categories: nonfluorinated and fluorinated. Nonfluorinated DWRs repel water but are more susceptible to contamination from oils—sunscreens, insect repellents, and body oils. Fluorinated DWRs are more environmentally harmful but also more resistant to oil and water.

Always treat clean garments, following the manufacturer's instructions. Spray-applying these do-it-yourself remedies to clean wet garments allows the DWR to penetrate the surface of the fabric slightly better, displacing the water as it evaporates. For a more uniform application, use a wash-in DWR product. Read the instructions carefully: there are some incompatibilities when using wash-ins on coated (nonlaminated) waterproof, breathable fabrics. Wash-in DWRs are particularly helpful for softshells. Hand-washing can ensure that more of the product ends up on the garment. After applying the DWR, dry the garment according to the reviving directions noted above.

When you start to see signs of wetting out on the garment's surface, reapply the DWR coating, or simply touch up high-abrasion areas after every trip or two.

Footwear

Your feet are the means for reaching an objective. Mountaineers need suitable, well-fitting footwear, including boots, socks, gaiters, and sometimes specialized gear (see the "Choosing Specialized Footwear" sidebar).

Depending on the trip, a climber may wear one kind of boot for the approach hike, another type in camp, and yet another when climbing. If you are willing to carry the extra weight, consider these options:

- **Lightweight sticky rubber approach shoes:** less likely to cause blisters; less fatiguing than full-fledged boots on easy approaches; may not provide enough support to carry a heavy pack, especially on rough ground or descents
- **Lightweight athletic shoes, sandals, or neoprene socks or booties:** comfortable in camp; give boots a chance to dry; can be used for stream crossings
- **Insulated booties or fleece socks:** warmer for lounging and sleeping
- **Rock shoes:** lightweight and compact for climbing technical rock

BOOTS

A reliable alpine climbing boot is a compromise between performance and suitability for the likely range of conditions. No single boot type or design will do everything well. The rigidity of the sole, the stiffness and support provided by the upper, and how the sole and upper interact when you wear the boot are key features. Proper fit will keep your feet happy. A full mountaineering boot (fig. 2-3) must strike a balance between being tough enough to withstand rock abrasion, rigid enough for kicking steps in hard snow and wearing crampons, and yet comfortable enough for an approach hike. In a single day of mountaineering, climbers may cross trails, mud, streams, gravel, brush, scree, steep rock, hard snow, and ice.

While respected for its versatility, the classic all-leather-upper boot has been supplanted by new designs: boots with plastic-composite shells, pieces of leather, fabric panels, synthetic leather, waterproof linings, integrated gaiters, and overall lighter construction. Most mountaineering boots feature a seam-sealed waterproof outer bootie. Boots with these materials are usually more expensive, and they are no panacea: they may make feet uncomfortably damp or warm in hot weather, and the membrane can degrade from exposure to dirt and sweat. Boot designs are evolving, but the many conditions that climbers subject them to are not.

Lightweight Mountaineering or Scrambling Boots

Some boots that incorporate synthetic fabric panels—used to reduce weight and increase breathability—are suitable for climbing. These lightweight mountaineering or scrambling boots (fig. 2-4) are basically a rigid hiking boot with several advantages: reduced weight, improved comfort for long approaches, a shorter break-in time, a more flexible sole for better friction climbing, a faster drying time, and lower cost.

However, lightweight boots have significant drawbacks compared with full mountaineering boots, including less stability when edging and toe holding, and insufficient weight or stiffness for step kicking in firm snow or for wearing crampons. They are usually less waterproof and less durable.

When considering scrambling boots for climbing, check that the uppers are rigid and tall enough to protect your ankles, that a stiff rand wraps around the heel and toe,

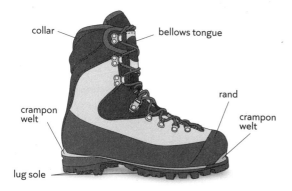

Fig. 2-3. *Full mountaineering boot.*

Fig. 2-4. *Lightweight mountaineering or scrambling boot.*

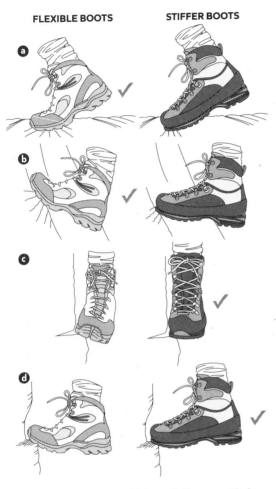

FLEXIBLE BOOTS   **STIFFER BOOTS**

*Fig. 2-5. Performance of flexible boots (left) versus stiffer boots (right) in various situations: **a,** approach hiking; **b,** friction climbing or smearing; **c,** edging; **d,** toe holding.*

and that areas subject to heavy abrasion are reinforced. If a boot is too flexible, your body wastes energy as your feet flex with each step on difficult ground. A flexible boot may also not edge well or be suitable for some models of crampons. A rigid boot acts as a tiny platform wherever you step so that bigger muscle groups perform simpler movements, saving energy.

Full Mountaineering Boots

Full mountaineering boots include fabrics and features that make them more robust, durable, and expensive than lightweight climbing boots. Typically lined with neoprene-like

padding, they are also warmer and more likely to remain waterproof. The best choice depends on how the boots will be used and is generally a compromise between comfort and technical capability.

For trails and easy snow or rock routes, boots with moderately stiff soles and uppers provide enough support while being comfortable and flexible (fig. 2-5a and b). For technical alpine rock climbing, a rigid boot is desirable for edging. Flexible boots, while sometimes used on technical rock, are usually a poor substitute for rock shoes (for more about rock shoes, see Footwear in Chapter 12, Sport Climbing). Stiffer boots can make walking less comfortable (as in Figure 2-5a), but they greatly reduce leg fatigue when a climber is standing on small rock nubbins. Look for boots stiff enough to permit edging on narrow ledges with either the side of the boot (fig. 2-5c) or the toe (fig. 2-5d).

For traveling on hard snow, a highly flexible boot is a disadvantage. Kicking useful steps or plunge-stepping with confidence requires a stiff boot. Snowshoes and (especially) crampons may not stay on if boots are too flexible for the bindings. Ice climbing demands an even higher level of support, as well as very stiff soles and uppers. Extremely stiff leather boots or plastic-composite boots (plastic and stiff leather) are generally best (see Chapter 17, Technical Snow and Ice Climbing).

Plastic Mountaineering Boots

Plastic mountaineering boots consist of hard synthetic outer shells with inner insulating boots (see Figure 2-2d). The synthetic shells are usually quite stiff, which makes them suitable for use with crampons or snowshoes. Straps and bindings can be cinched tightly on such shells without impairing circulation in the feet, and they provide solid support when edging and kicking steps.

Plastic mountaineering boots are waterproof, making them great in wet snow, especially on multiday treks. The inner insulating boot keeps feet warm. In camp, the inner boot can be removed and warmed, which helps dry out perspiration. Unfortunately, the factors that make plastic boots ideal for snow and ice, such as rigidity, waterproofness, and warmth, make them a poor choice for general trail use.

BOOT CARE

With proper care, well-made boots can last many years. Keep them clean and dry when not in use. Avoid exposing boots to high temperatures, which can damage leather, linings, and adhesives. During an outing, water can seep into boots through the uppers and seams. Apply waterproofing agents regularly to help limit that tendency. Worn tread can lead to slips, trips, and falls—check its condition after trips. For boots that fit well and are reliable, consider having them repaired at a local shop when they need a new sole, a patch, and so on. Before waterproofing according to product instructions, clean boots with a mild or special-purpose soap and a stiff brush.

A waterproof bootie functions like DWR on a hardshell. Similar to caring for DWRs, an approved waterproofing solution should be applied a year after the boots are purchased and then once or twice a year after that. Apply the waterproofing to clean, damp boots.

With plastic-composite boots, remove the inner boots after use and allow them to dry. Shake or wipe out any debris in the shells to reduce abrasion and wear.

PROPER FOOTWEAR FIT

The key to happy feet is proper fit, and the key to proper fit is to consider boots, socks, and insoles as components of a footwear system. Purchase insoles and socks at the same time as your boots; try on not only different boot types and sizes but a variety of insoles and socks.

Boots

Proper fit is pivotal when it comes to boots. Try on several makes and styles before choosing a pair. A boot's shape is defined by the unique last, or form, on which it is built, and its complex dimensions are not fully captured by length and width. Some brands are available in multiple widths; others offer both men's and women's models. Some people's feet fit better in one model than in another.

After lacing the boots firmly, test stability by standing on a narrow edge or pitching your feet from side to side. Walk in the boots, carrying a loaded pack if possible, to approximate conditions you may encounter. Note whether you can feel uncomfortable seams or creases or whether the boots pinch anywhere. In boots that fit properly, the back two-thirds of your foot will feel firmly anchored in place while your toes have plenty of room to wiggle. Stand facing downhill on an incline to evaluate how much space your toes have. Kick something solid to check that your toes do not jam against the toe box.

Tight boots, including those that place pressure on the bridge of the foot, will constrict circulation, leading to cold feet and increasing the chance of frostbite. Overly tight or excessively loose boots can also cause blisters. Be especially careful that boots intended for use in extreme cold and/or at high altitudes do not constrict your feet or impede circulation. Because fit is critical for comfort and performance, climbers with difficult-to-fit feet may need custom-made boots or perhaps custom insoles. Buying from a store with a liberal return policy may spare you from having to endure a less than acceptable boot.

Socks

Socks cushion and insulate the feet and reduce friction between the boot and foot. Socks made of nylon or merino wool reduce friction; those made of cotton do not. Cotton socks become abrasive when wet, leading to blisters. Socks need to fit snugly; socks that are too big lead to wrinkles and folds that irritate the skin. Threadbare, worn sections can cause blisters. Because boots do not breathe, sweat generated by feet accumulates inside them. In dry conditions, some climbers change their socks once or twice each day, putting on a dry pair while drying out the other one. Synthetic socks dry faster than wool ones.

Some climbers wear two pairs of socks. Thin liner socks worn next to the skin help resist blisters by moving perspiration away from the foot while staying somewhat dry. Liner socks also allow a climber to fine-tune fit. The thicker outer sock absorbs the moisture passing through the inner sock and cushions against the boot lining. Other climbers prefer a single medium- or heavyweight blended sock. Climbers do not often wear socks with rock shoes, which they generally want as snug as possible. Hikers wearing trail shoes on a warm day may wear a single pair of socks; climbers on very cold winter days may wear three pairs of socks inside oversize boots. Whatever the strategy, keep your toes free enough to wiggle; another pair of socks will not improve warmth if they constrict circulation.

Before putting on socks, consider protecting your feet at places prone to blisters, especially the back of the heel, with specialized tape, gel bandages, sticky padding like Moleskin, or blister bandages (see Blisters in Chapter 24, First Aid). Lubricants such as Vaseline may reduce friction, but if overall traction is reduced too much, especially on your sole, your foot may shift around and possibly compound the problem. Use any lubricants sparingly on a targeted area.

When worn over a pair of standard socks, waterproof, breathable socks can improve comfort in wet conditions, functioning much like boot liners while providing a higher, snugger cuff. In extremely cold weather, a vapor-barrier sock worn between the two main sock layers can reduce the danger of frostbite. Because vapor-barrier socks do not breathe, your feet get damp but retain more heat and stay warmer. Having damp feet for too long, however, increases your risk of developing immersion foot, a serious condition that may require medical treatment (see Chapter 24).

If you use vapor-barrier socks, dry your feet thoroughly at least once each day.

Insoles

Most climbers discard the cheap stock insoles that come with boots or trail runners. Aftermarket insoles come in an array of arch sizes and thicknesses ("high volume" means very thick). They provide additional comfort, insulation, and support—and affect fit considerably. If you prefer or need custom insoles, consult your local boot fitter or podiatrist.

GAITERS

Gaiters seal the boundary between bare legs or pants and boots, keeping out water, snow, and debris. Climbers often carry gaiters year-round and put them on to keep rain, dew, mud, or snow from saturating their pants, socks, and boots. Wet socks and boots are uncomfortable and can lead to serious foot problems.

Short trail gaiters (fig. 2-6a) that extend above the tops of the boots are adequate for summer treks. Deep snow, however, usually calls for alpine gaiters (fig. 2-6b) that extend up to the knee. Expedition gaiters (fig. 2-6c) are made from beefier materials and sized to accommodate large plastic boots; insulation built into some pairs covers

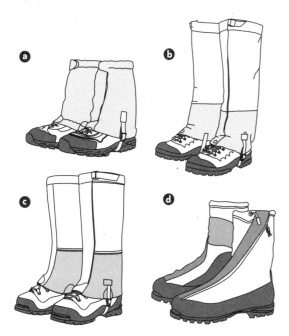

Fig. 2-6. Gaiters: **a,** trail; **b,** alpine; **c,** expedition; **d,** integrated.

the boots for added warmth. Boots with nonremovable (integrated) gaiters (fig. 2-6d) are a growing trend in winter mountaineering.

Gaiters are usually held closed with snaps, zippers, or hook-and-loop fasteners like Velcro, which are easiest to use in cold weather. If you select gaiters with zippers, be sure the teeth are heavy-duty. A flap over the zipper protects it from damage and keeps the gaiter closed and functional even if the zipper fails. Elastic or a strap at the top of the gaiter keeps it from sliding down. A snug fit around the calf helps prevent crampon points from catching on the gaiters, leading to a fall. When you are wearing crampons, layering gaiters on top of rain pants helps prevent tripping.

A close fit around your boot prevents snow from entering under the gaiter, especially useful when you are plunge-stepping during descents. A cord, lace, strap, or shock cord runs under the foot to help the gaiter hug the boot. The parts underfoot will wear out during the life of the gaiter, so look for designs that allow you to replace them easily. Neoprene straps work well in snow but wear out quickly on rock, whereas cord survives rock better but snow can ball up on it. Women's-specific gaiters are typically shorter and a little wider at the top (see Figure 2-2c).

Packs

Climbers usually own at least two packs: a small pack designed for day trips and a much larger backpack for multiday trips. A pack's capacity, its interior volume, is measured in liters. All packs should allow climbers to carry the weight close to their body and centered over their hips and legs (see Tips on Packing, below).

BUYING A BACKPACK

First, determine the pack capacity suitable for the demands of the climb; see Table 2-3. Then find a pack that fits your body, specifically one adjustable to be compatible with the length of your torso. Some backpacks adjust to a wide range of body sizes; others do not. Try on various packs and see which one you prefer (see the "Choosing a Pack" sidebar). Figure 2-7a and b shows a typical 50-liter climbing pack with a streamlined design.

Take your time when fitting a backpack. Load it up as you would on an actual climb—bring your personal gear to the store, or rely on their weighted stuff sacks. Without a typical load, you cannot tell if the pack fits you comfortably. To test the fit, follow the steps in the next section, Fitting and Adjusting a Backpack. Look in a mirror to see if the frame follows the curve of your back. Determine whether the stays or frame can be bent to improve the fit. The point where the shoulder straps attach to the backpack should be positioned between your shoulder blades; there should be at most a very small gap between the straps and your back.

Once the backpack is adjusted, check your head clearance while wearing a hat or helmet. Can you look up without hitting the back of your head on the pack? Next, check for adequate padding wherever the pack touches your body. Pay particular attention to the comfort of the shoulder straps and hip belt; evaluate the padding's quality, but note that thicker and softer does not necessarily mean more comfortable. The hip belt should be substantial; its padding should cover your hip bones with adequate margins to account for how it shifts as you move. To be sure the pack's load transfers properly to your hips, check that the belt wraps directly across the top, not the sides, of your hips and not around your waist.

Women's backpacks. Many people prefer a women's-specific design, which usually involves a shorter torso length, a narrower shoulder width, a belt that flares wider at the hips, and shorter, narrower, and higher shoulder straps. Although hips that flare more widely from a person's waist can be accommodated somewhat by adjusting the angle of the belt's webbing, a women's-specific hip belt is often best. Women's hip belts also feature more, but narrower padding than men's to avoid putting pressure on the lower rib cage. However, some women find that men's or unisex packs fit better.

FITTING AND ADJUSTING A BACKPACK

First, loosen all the straps. Then shoulder a full pack and follow these steps, as shown in Figure 2-8.

Step 1. Position the middle of the hip belt over the top of the iliac crest (hip bones). Raise your shoulders and

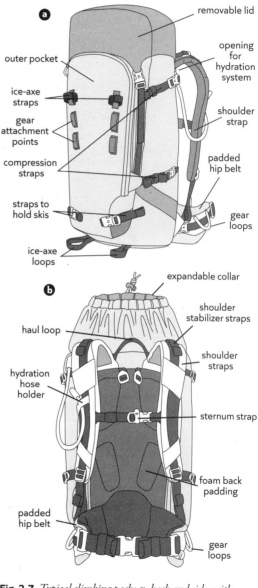

Fig. 2-7. *Typical climbing pack: **a,** back and side, with removable lid in low-volume position; **b,** back pad and straps, with lid removed.*

TABLE 2-3. TYPES OF BACKPACKS

TYPE	CAPACITY	NOTES
Day pack	30–50 liters; 20–30 lb. (9–14 kg)	Best for single-day climbs or hikes. Efficient packers facing good weather can overnight with a pack this size.
Overnight pack	50–80 liters; 30–55 lb. (14–25 kg)	Most popular size for overnight trips, winter day trips, or backcountry skiing. Compression straps minimize size for day trips. Packing carefully may accommodate longer trips.
Expedition or winter pack	70-plus liters; 55+ lb. (25+ kg)	Larger for extended trips of five days or more or winter treks, to accommodate extra food and clothes, warmer sleeping bag, and four-season tent.

CHOOSING A PACK

First, decide on capacity: day, overnight, or expedition. Consider the weight and volume of what you plan to carry, then factor in trip length. Your torso length matters more than your height. Beyond those factors, consider key features and details:

- Does the pack have a smooth profile? Or will it get tangled up in heavy brush or snagged when hauled up a steep rock face?

- How sturdy and durable are the zippers, suspension system, and stitching?

- How convenient is storing, arranging, and accessing gear? Does it have features compatible with a hydration system if you use one?

- Can it carry special items such as crampons, skis, snowshoes, snow shovel, trekking poles, phone, or satellite communication device?

- Does it have a haul loop, ice-axe loops, ski straps, and compression straps (to reduce volume and prevent the load from shifting)?

- Can the capacity be increased for extended trips? For example, does it have an expandable collar, gear loops, and side-pocket accessories?

tighten the hip belt *firmly*. Nearly all the pack's weight should now be on your hips, with the shoulder straps slack.

Step 2. Tighten the shoulder straps—snugly but not too tight—so they form a smooth arc over the top of your shoulders. The shoulder stabilizer straps should still be slack. The bulk of the pack weight should be on the hip belt, with minimal load carried by the shoulders.

Step 3. Gently tension the shoulder stabilizer straps (optional on day packs) to bring the pack close to the body. Ideally, these stabilizer straps should end up at around a 45-degree angle. Excess tension interferes with the smooth arc of the shoulder pad over the shoulder.

Last, tension any hip belt stabilizers and sternum straps. Each time you put on your backpack, adjust the straps in the same sequence, from bottom to top: position the hip belt and tighten it firmly, then tighten the shoulder straps, and finally tension all stabilizer straps. Readjust the backpack periodically while wearing it to help reduce soreness and fatigue; straps can loosen as the pack shifts over time.

BUYING A DAY PACK
Day packs for climbing usually have volumes of between 30 and 50 liters, enough to carry 20 to 30 pounds (9 to 14

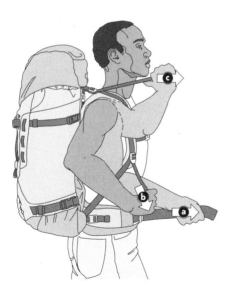

Fig. 2-8. *Fitting and adjusting a backpack:* **a,** *adjust hip belt;* **b,** *tighten shoulder straps;* **c,** *tension shoulder stabilizer straps.*

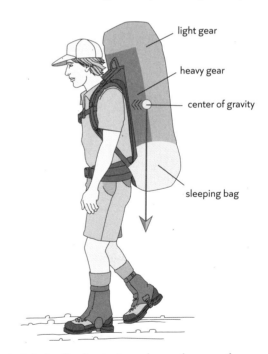

light gear

heavy gear

center of gravity

sleeping bag

Fig. 2-9. *Loading heavier items closer to the center of your back improves your balance and endurance.*

kilograms). The large selection on the market covers a wide spectrum of sturdiness. Some are designed without rigid frames or padded hip belts and may be too flimsy to carry heavy climbing gear—rope, rack, crampons, ice axe. Seek a pack with a sturdy internal frame and a hip belt at least 2 inches (5 centimeters) wide at the buckle and 4 inches (10 centimeters) wide where it covers the hips. Try on and compare day packs as you would a full-size backpack.

A LIGHTWEIGHT PERSPECTIVE

Yosemite climber Ray Jardine popularized an ultralight approach to backpacking, while Reinhold Messner and many contemporary alpinists have pushed the techniques of alpine-style climbing in small teams to the limit. More than just choices about gear, these lightweight approaches embody a philosophy rooted in environmental responsibility. A lightweight perspective harmonizes seamlessly with the Leave No Trace principles, as discussed in Chapter 7, and stands in sharp contrast to mid-twentieth century Himalayan expeditions that often relied on the labor of hundreds of porters, often Sherpa people, to transport tons of equipment.

A lightweight approach revolves around two fundamental principles:

1. **Minimalism:** Ultralight backpackers and climbers select gear that performs essential functions while shedding excess weight. This approach emphasizes efficiency, with its advocates often using multipurpose items to reduce their load and environmental impact and weighing each item to assess the trade-offs.

2. **Self-reliance:** These concepts promote self-reliance, encouraging individuals to be self-sufficient and responsible for their needs and risk-taking in the wilderness. This ethic encourages climbers to develop the skills and knowledge that allow them to return home and minimize their impact on fragile ecosystems.

By embracing ultralight principles, climbers reduce their ecological footprint while experiencing the mountains, ultimately leaving no trace to ensure the preservation of wild places for future generations. This way of interacting with the natural world is rooted in the rich history of outdoor adventure and environmentally conscious exploration.

Most features you would consider when choosing a full-size pack apply to day packs. Insist on ice-axe loops, a haul loop, and compression straps. Other useful features include an integrated whistle in the sternum strap, a snug-fitting deep pockets for water bottles, and an expanding front pocket on the hip belt for items you want to stow and retrieve quickly.

TIPS ON PACKING

Strategically loading items in a pack can dramatically improve your speed, endurance, and enjoyment. Generally, climbers will feel best if they can concentrate the load on their hips. Pack heavy items as close to your back as possible to bring in and lower your center of gravity, which allows a more upright, efficient walking stance. Centering heavy items in the pack vertically helps you stay balanced (fig. 2-9). Heavy items such as ropes placed high in the pack may make it top-heavy and affect your balance and stability.

Along with arranging items for optimum weight distribution, organize them for convenient access. Carry the gear that you will need most often close at hand. Stash gloves, hats, sunglasses, and insect repellent in side and top pockets or jacket pockets. A waist pack or SAR (search and rescue) chest pack worn in combination with the main pack allows you to retrieve snacks, water, maps, and time-critical first-aid items in a few seconds. In cool weather, keep a puffy coat at the ready.

Determine a strategy to keep pack contents dry in rainy weather. Even packs constructed from waterproof materials are rarely waterproof. Water can leak through seams, zippers, pockets, the top opening, and wherever the waterproofing is worn. Individual plastic bags or waterproof stuff sacks and a waterproof pack cover can keep gear dry. Some climbers prefer to line their entire pack with a 2- or 3-millileter-thick trash compactor bag.

Essential Equipment

Certain equipment deserves space in every pack (see The Mountaineers' Ten Essentials, below). A climber will not need every item on every trip, but essential equipment can save your life in an emergency. Exactly how much equipment "insurance" should be carried is a matter of healthy debate (see the "Ultralight Travel" sidebar). Some respected minimalists argue that a heavier pack slows people down, increasing your chances of getting caught by a storm or nightfall. "Carry bivy gear, and you will bivy. Instead, go fast and light," they argue. The other side of this debate is that, even without extra weight, climbers still may be forced

THE MOUNTAINEERS' TEN ESSENTIALS

The Ten Essentials list is a fundamental guide that adventurers follow and tailor to their trip.

To prevent an emergency and respond should one occur:

1. Navigation
2. Headlamp
3. Sun protection
4. First aid
5. Knife

To spend at least one night outside:

6. Fire
7. Shelter
8. Extra food
9. Extra water
10. Extra clothes

to bivouac. Each party must determine what they believe will keep them safe.

Most climbers carefully select what they carry to survive the unexpected. Whatever your approach to equipment, a checklist (see Table 2-4) will help you remember what to bring as you prepare. Adapt this list to suit your needs and get in the habit of checking it before each trip. First developed by The Mountaineers in the 1930s, The Mountaineers' Ten Essentials forms the foundation for such checklists.

THE MOUNTAINEERS' TEN ESSENTIALS

The point of The Mountaineers' Ten Essentials is to ensure that you can confidently answer two basic questions: (1) Can you prevent and respond to an emergency? (2) Can you spend at least one night outside?

Tailor your choices to your trip and factor in the weather forecast, remoteness from help, terrain expected, and trip complexity. The first seven essentials are compact and vary little from climb to climb; group them together to pack efficiently. Add extra food, water, and clothes, and you are ready to go.

The brief list in the sidebar above is intended to be easy to remember as a mental checklist, but the following limerick written by Steve McClure (with essentials indicated by bold) may be more fun: To **navigate**, **head** for the **sun** / With **first aid** and **knife** on the run. / Bring **fire** and **shelter**. / **Extra food** is a helper, / But **water** and **clothes** weigh a ton.

1. Navigation

Mountaineers carry five essential tools while navigating the backcountry: map, altimeter, compass, Global Positioning System (GPS) device or phone with GPS app, and a means to contact emergency first responders (a personal locator beacon, satellite communication device, or satellite phone). Wilderness navigators need to carry these tools and know how to use them. If you or a member of your party becomes injured or lost, you need to be able to alert emergency responders. Using multiple navigation tools increases confidence in location and route, provides backup when a tool fails, and increases situational awareness (see "The Importance of Situational Awareness" sidebar in Chapter 5, Navigation and Communication). For in-depth information on navigation tools and techniques, see Chapter 5.

Map. Maps synthesize a vast amount of information about a region that cannot be replicated by written descriptions or memory. The key to getting the most out of a map is keeping it handy so you can refer to it often. If it is buried in a backpack, you will not use it. Stow your map so that it is as readily accessible as an altimeter or GPS watch worn on your wrist. Modern resources enable mountaineers to create customized maps. If your primary map is a battery-powered electronic device, carry at least one redundant device and backup power. Each climber needs to carry at least a copy of a physical topographic map, ideally printed on Rite in the Rain paper and protected in a case or resealable plastic bag. A printed map does not require electricity or battery power and serves as a backup while also displaying the big picture about a region, which cannot be replicated by a tiny

CHOOSING A GPS DEVICE

Mountaineers have several options when it comes to GPS technology:

■ **A phone combined with a good app** has become the most popular way for climbers to navigate by GPS. These apps have extensive libraries of free digital worldwide maps that, if downloaded before your trip, allow freedom to travel hills near and far.

■ **Dedicated GPS units** are more difficult to use and have fewer maps, but they are more rugged and weatherproof, and easier to read in bright daylight.

■ **Digital wristwatches** can provide GPS coordinates and altitude, to be used in conjunction with a printed topographic map. Some of these devices even show tiny maps and pair with phones.

screen. Carrying an extra copy allows you to share it with any wayward hikers you may encounter.

Altimeter. Mountaineers have long understood the importance of knowing elevation for navigation. If you refer to a topographic map and know your elevation, you can solve half of the navigation equation, day or night, in clear skies or fog. With just one more scrap of data—a trail, stream, ridge, or bearing to a known peak—climbers can often determine where they are. Altimeters these days are made of a sliver of silicon that determines altitude by measuring air pressure or using GPS satellite signals—or a combination of the two. Practiced mountaineers tend to use an altimeter far more frequently than a compass.

Compass. Robust and easy to use, a compass allows wilderness travelers to orient the map and themselves to the landscape. A compass with a baseplate is essential for measuring and following field bearings and matching them up with the map. Virtually all smartphones, GPS devices, and navigational wristwatches contain an electronic compass.

GPS device. GPS has greatly increased how quickly and accurately you can determine your location (point position) in the wilderness, though the location data derived from a GPS unit has value only when understood within the context of a digital or paper topographic map. You must first understand a map's iconography to interpret and assimilate that data into a cohesive routefinding strategy. GPS augments but does not replace a map.

Phones with a reliable GPS (satellite) app rival the best dedicated GPS units for accuracy and are easier to use (see Chapter 5, Navigation and Communication). Phones are becoming ever more useful for communicating with search and rescue authorities, even beyond cell service range. Apps often have extensive free map libraries; download the ones you need while at home before you are out of data range. Together with downloaded digital maps, GPS-capable phones can guide climbers even if they are far from any cell towers. The caveats? Phones are fragile. An application can quickly drain a phone battery, discouraging climbers from comparing the map to the topography, an important way that far less experienced navigators learn how to orient themselves and interpret maps. Plus, a touchscreen interface can be problematic in cold or bright conditions. Climbers should take steps to armor these delicate devices, keep them dry, and extend their battery life. Bringing a fully charged power bank is an important precaution. Dedicated GPS devices are often more rugged and weatherproof than phones, making them a better choice on long trips, on expeditions, or in extreme environments (see the "Choosing a GPS Device" sidebar).

PLBs and satellite communicators. Historically, mountaineers have needed to be completely self-reliant, and climbers should still have that mindset when entering the wilderness. But when an emergency unfolds despite reliable tools, preparation, and training, most climbers welcome help. Personal locator beacons (PLBs) and satellite

CHOOSING A HEADLAMP

Headlamps are essential for outdoor ventures. Consider and compare their features carefully.

- **Beam type, output, and distance.** Choose a headlamp with both wide and spot beams. Each headlamp has an output rated in lumens, a beam distance measured in meters, and a run time measured in hours. For general-purpose mountaineering, look for a lamp rated at least 50 lumens that casts a beam at least 160 feet (50 meters) and has a run time of at least 24 hours. Keep in mind that the amount of daylight varies significantly depending on time of year and latitude. Brighter illumination consumes more battery power; if you anticipate significant nighttime operations (for example, search and rescue), choose a headlamp with a brighter beam, a top strap, and a larger battery pack (positioned on the back of the head).

- **Weight.** The typical headlamp weighs 3–4 ounces (85–115 grams). High-powered models are bulkier and heavier (up to 11 ounces or 300 grams). Ultralight models can weigh less than an ounce (28 grams). Choose according to how you plan to use it.

- **Brightness modes.** Most headlamps offer a range of brightness settings. Use the low beam or red mode to conserve battery life and avoid annoying your partners. A high beam is useful for moving through terrain at night.

- **Battery type.** Choose a headlamp powered by AA or AAA batteries, which are often used for other electronics, such as a dedicated GPS device or SPOT messenger (see Batteries later in this chapter). Consider a model with a rechargeable battery.

- **Additional features.** Some headlamps include a blinking mode for a beacon, a red mode to preserve nighttime vision, and regulated output to keep the beam brightness constant until the batteries are exhausted. Other models are rechargeable in the field.

communicators determine your position using GPS and then send a message to emergency responders using government or commercial satellite networks. These devices have saved many lives; carrying one in the backcountry can offer peace of mind, especially for solo travelers. Satellite phones are reliable in the wilderness, whereas smartphones—which rely primarily on proximity to cell towers for calling, texting, and to run apps—are not. Do not assume that the call function of your phone will work in the backcountry. With a weak signal, texts may go through even when calls cannot.

2. Headlamp

The flashlight of choice for climbers, headlamps free the hands for everything from cooking to climbing. Even if a climbing party plans to return before dark, each climber must carry a headlamp and spare batteries. A headlamp is a critical piece of gear. Consider carrying a charged backup headlamp if there is a possibility the party could become benighted. In the dark, switching to a backup is easier than finding and replacing batteries, especially in cold conditions—plus another party member may need to borrow one. To economize, consider a simpler backup model that uses the same batteries as your primary one (see the "Choosing a Headlamp" sidebar). Headlamps with rechargeable batteries are gaining favor, but the downside is that if the battery runs down, you need a power bank to replenish it.

Many headlamps carried by outdoor shops are weatherproof, and a few models can survive being submerged in water, at least for a short time. The lamps on most models can be tilted down to focus the beam for up-close work, such as cooking, and pointed up to look off into the distance. Some headlamps feature a low-power red beam.

3. Sun Protection

Carry and wear sunglasses, sun-protective clothes, and broad-spectrum sunscreen rated at least SPF 30. Sun damage can lead to sunburn or snow blindness; long-term unpleasantness includes cataracts or pterygiums (surfer's eye) and, more seriously, skin cancer. See the "Choosing a Sun Protection Strategy" sidebar.

Sunglasses. In alpine country, high-quality sunglasses are critical. Eyes are particularly vulnerable to solar radiation, and corneas can easily burn before you feel any discomfort, resulting in an excruciatingly painful condition known as snow blindness. Ultraviolet rays penetrate cloud layers—do not let cloudy conditions fool you into leaving your eyes unprotected. It is advisable to wear sunglasses whenever you are outside and it is bright. This protection becomes critical on snow, ice, and water and at high altitudes.

CHOOSING A SUN PROTECTION STRATEGY

Consider these options when planning how to protect yourself.

- Wear appropriate sunglasses. Check your local daily UV forecast at the EPA's website.
- Wear sun-protective clothes: long-sleeved hoodie, wide-brimmed hat, long pants.
- Liberally apply a broad-spectrum sunscreen, minimum SPF 30, on all exposed skin.
- Protect lips with sunscreen or an SPF-rated lip balm.
- Reapply sunscreen frequently; seek shade where appropriate.
- When using both sunscreen and insect repellent, first apply sunscreen and allow it to dry. After it has bonded to your skin, apply repellent.

When trying on sunglasses, look in a mirror: if it is easy to see your eyes, the lenses are too light. The tint should allow only a fraction of the visible light through the lens to the eyes. Sunglasses should filter at least 99 percent of ultraviolet (UV) light, including both UVA and UVB. Sunglasses, when rated, are usually scored by visible light transmission (VLT) or, occasionally, by percentage of light blocked. For glacier glasses, a lens should have a VLT rating of 5 to 10 percent. For conditions that do not involve snow or water, sports sunglasses with a VLT rating of 5 to 20 percent are sufficient. Many sunglasses do not have a VLT rating, making them cornea-scorching fashion accessories. Look in a mirror when trying on sunglasses—if your eyes can easily be seen through the lenses, they are too light. Gray or brown lens tints provide the truest color; yellow provides better contrast in overcast or foggy conditions. While polarized lenses can decrease glare, they black out camera and smartphone LCD screens in certain orientations. Photochromic lenses automatically adjust to changing light intensity, but most lack a sufficient VLT rating for snow and adjust slowly in cold conditions.

Sunglass lenses should be made of polycarbonate or Trivex (a form of polyurethane). While glass is more scratch-resistant, it is heavy and can shatter. High-quality sunglasses can have a variety of helpful lens coatings, including ones that repel water or minimize scratches or fogging. Rather than scratching up expensive sunglasses while bushwhacking, consider wearing an inexpensive pair of personal protective equipment (PPE) safety glasses, available in clear and tinted versions—clear is preferable in lower-light conditions such as beneath a forest canopy on a cloudy day. Sunglass frames should be a wraparound style or have side shields to reduce the light reaching your eyes, while allowing adequate ventilation to prevent fogging. Skiers and some climbers use VLT-rated ski goggles. Applying an antifog product to your lenses can reduce fogging.

Groups should carry at least one spare pair of sunglasses in case a party member loses or forgets a pair. To improvise eye protection, cut a strip of Mylar from an emergency blanket or make slits in a piece of cardboard or cloth.

Sun-protective clothes. Clothes easily offer more sun protection than sunscreen. Long underwear or wind garments are frequently worn on sunny glacier climbs. The discomfort of long underwear, even under blazing conditions, may be a minor nuisance compared with the hassle of smearing on sunscreen (or suffering through a sunburn later). Some garments have a UPF (ultraviolet protection factor) rating, a system calibrated the same as the SPF rating described below. A UPF 50–rated garment allows $\frac{1}{50}$ of the UV radiation that falls on it to pass through. Most clothes block UV rays sufficiently, but don't expect a thin T-shirt to protect you on a long glacier climb. For the most part, UPF ratings are not critical except to those with sensitive skin. Whenever possible, wear a hat, preferably one with a wide enough brim to protect your face and neck. A baseball-style cap combined with a sun-protective hoody offers great protection, keeps your hat on in the wind, and works under a helmet (see fig. 2-2g).

Sunscreen. Sunscreen is vital to protecting skin not covered by clothing, and most people sensitive to sun use both clothing and sunscreen. People vary widely in natural pigmentation, the amount of sun protection their skin requires, and their propensity for or history of skin cancer. The penalty for underestimating the protection you need is severe. Some diseases, such as lupus, and some medications, such as antibiotics and antihistamines, can cause extra sensitivity to the sun's rays.

While climbing, use a broad-spectrum sunscreen that blocks both UVA and UVB rays. UVA rays are the primary preventable cause of skin cancer; UVB rays primarily cause sunburn. To protect skin from UVB rays, use a sunscreen with a sun protection factor (SPF) of at least 30; if you are near snow or water, use at least SPF 50 on thin-skinned areas such as the hands, nose, and ears. When your sunscreen is past the expiration date or more than three years old, replace it.

The Environmental Protection Agency highly recommends using sunscreens labeled "broad spectrum." While there is no standard rating for UVA protection, broad spectrum means "the product provides UVA protection that is proportional to its UVB protection." Most sunscreen ingredients absorb UV light through a chemical reaction—although titanium dioxide and zinc oxide physically block UV and cause the fewest skin reactions. Of all the chemicals used in sunscreen, these four are most likely to cause adverse skin reactions: aminobenzoic acid (PABA), dioxybenzone, oxybenzone, and sulisobenzone. There are two types of sunscreens—chemical-based and mineral-based. Chemical sunscreens can contain an active ingredient (octocrylene) and a contaminant (benzene) that pose a health risk to humans. Using mineral sunscreens, like those based on zinc oxide, avoids this exposure.

Sunscreen can wash off into the environment. The chemicals it can contain, including benzophenone-1, benzophenone-8, 4-methylbenzylidene camphor, 3-benzylidene camphor, octinoxate, and octocrylene, are known to be harmful to marine life (for more information, see Resources).

The effectiveness of all sunscreens is diminished by sweat, so reapply frequently. If reapplying is impractical on a climb, apply a heavy layer of sunscreen in the morning, wear sun-protective clothes, and reapply when you can. When you sweat, sunscreen can end up in your eyes and sting relentlessly. Some climbers prefer "no-tear" sunscreen intended for children, which is pH balanced to help prevent this problem.

Generously apply sunscreen to all exposed skin, including the undersides of your chin and nose, the insides of your nostrils, and your ears. Even if you are wearing a hat, apply sunscreen to all exposed areas on your face and neck to protect against reflection from snow, sand, or water. Apply chemical-based sunscreen at least 20 minutes before exposure to the sun, because it usually takes time to start working. Mineral sunscreens start working immediately. Lips burn, too, and require protection to prevent peeling and blisters. Reapply lip protection frequently.

4. First Aid

Carry and know how to use a first-aid kit, and understand its strengths and limitations. Make sure your kit is clearly identifiable and readily accessible. Some items such as Emergency Bandages (e.g., Israeli Bandages) may need to be administered within seconds, not minutes. Chapter 24, First Aid, covers much more about first aid for climbers.

Training in wilderness first aid or wilderness first responder skills is worthwhile and goes beyond most first-aid training aimed at urban or industrial settings. In the mountains, trained response may be hours—even days—

TABLE 2-4. SAMPLE EQUIPMENT LIST

On any given trip, you do not put all your gear in your pack. Depending on the adventure, you will wear some gear and leave some in the car or at home. Some items are optional, depending on personal preference and the nature of the trip. See various other chapters for details about some of this gear. Items in brackets [ ] can be shared by a group.

ITEMS LEFT IN OR NEAR THE TRAILHEAD VEHICLE

- Copy of trip itinerary, listing people in the party
- List of equipment carried, including PLBs, etc.
- Map and directions to trailhead; weather forecast
- Extra water
- Refreshing drinks (optional)
- Spare key hidden outside of or near the car (optional)
- Pack scale for checking pack weight at start of trip (optional)
- Clean, comfortable clothes for the drive home (optional)

ITEMS WORN OR CARRIED

An underlying assumption of this list is that you are starting cool, most likely in the morning, dressed as in Figure 2-2a.

- Pack: day pack or backpack for overnight or longer trips
- Boots; gaiters (optional)
- Socks (synthetic or wool); liners (optional)
- Brimmed hat
- Base-layer top
- Long-sleeved shirt
- Base-layer bottoms (optional)
- Underwear (optional)
- Shorts (optional)
- Lightweight nylon pants (zip-off legs optional)
- Wristwatch altimeter
- Trekking poles
- Keys to trailhead vehicle

GEAR PACKED FOR ALL TRIPS

The Mountaineers' Ten Essentials

Because they are typically small and change little from trip to trip, keep Essentials 1–7 grouped together and ready to go.

1. **Navigation:** map, altimeter, compass, [GPS: smartphone with GPS app or dedicated GPS device], [PLB, satellite communicator, or satellite phone], [extra batteries], [power bank]
2. **Headlamp:** plus extra batteries [extra headlamp (optional)]
3. **Sun protection:** sunglasses, sun-protective clothes, sunscreen
4. **First aid:** including foot-care supplies, insect repellent (optional)
5. **Knife:** plus repair kit
6. **Fire:** matches, lighter and tinder, or stove (as appropriate)
7. **Shelter:** tent, bivy, or emergency shelter (as appropriate and carried at all times)
8. **Extra food:** beyond minimum expectation
9. **Extra water:** beyond minimum expectation, or means to purify
10. **Extra clothes:** beyond minimum expectation (detailed below)

CLOTHING

This section includes garments worn while actively climbing as well as extra clothes to survive the inactive long hours of an unplanned bivouac. Choices depend on probable worst-case weather, thus none are marked as optional.

Base Layer
- Top(s) and bottom(s) to wear while active
- Extra dry set for camp and to wear while sleeping

Midlayers
- Synthetic shirt(s) and pants
- Synthetic fleece (vests, shirts, or jackets)
- Wool knit shirt(s)
- Double-weave softshell jacket and pants
- Puffy jacket (synthetic, down, or active insulation)

Shell Layers and Belay Jacket
- Wind-shell jacket and wind pants
- Laminated softshell jacket
- Waterproof, breathable laminated softshell jacket
- Hardshell jacket and pants (rain pants)
- Belay jacket

Headwear, Handwear, and Footwear
- Warm hat
- Warm under-helmet hat
- Waterproof wide-brimmed hat
- Balaclava
- Buff or neck tube(s)
- Gloves or mittens (extras), plus glove or mitten liners
- Socks (extras)
- Waterproof, breathable socks
- Stream-crossing footwear
- Gaiters (short, alpine, or expedition)

TABLE 2-4. SAMPLE EQUIPMENT LIST

ESSENTIAL CLIMBING GEAR FOR ALL CLIMBS

- Helmet
- Climbing harness
- Personal anchor with locking carabiner
- Carabiners, including at least one large pear-shaped locking carabiner (pearabiner)
- Runners
- Belay and/or rappel device
- Leather gloves for belaying and rappelling (optional)
- Prusik slings
- [Climbing rope]
- Approach shoes (optional)

OTHER (NONCLIMBING) GEAR

- [Dedicated GPS device suitable for extreme environments]
- Lunch and/or snacks sufficient for the climb
- Water (minimum 2 quarts or liters)
- Toilet kit: toilet paper, blue bags, hand sanitizer or wipes, [trowel]
- N95 masks (optional, helpful for wildfire smoke)
- Insect repellent (optional)
- Local communication device (optional): whistle, walkie-talkie
- Spare eyeglasses (optional)
- Cup (optional)
- Nylon cord (optional)
- Camera (optional)
- Extra batteries and/or power bank for electronic gear
- Binoculars (optional)
- Bandanna (optional)
- Protective phone cover (optional)

OTHER ITEMS FOR AN OVERNIGHT TRIP

- Sleeping bag, stuff sack, sleeping pad
- [Tent], [tarp], or bivy sack (optional)
- [Ground cloth] (optional)
- [Food]
- [Water container(s)]
- [Group first-aid kit]
- [Group repair kit]
- [Stove, accessories, fuel]
- [Pot(s), cleaning pad]
- Spoon, fork (optional), bowl (optional)
- Toiletries (optional)
- Alarm clock or alarm watch (optional)
- Clothes to wear in camp and while sleeping (optional)
- Camp footwear (optional)
- Pack cover (optional)
- Hand and foot warmers (optional)
- Thermos bottle (optional)

OTHER GEAR FOR ROCK CLIMBS

- [Rack: climbing protection, nuts, cams, etc.]
- [Nut tool]
- Rock climbing shoes (optional)
- Chalk (optional); athletic tape (optional)

OTHER GEAR FOR SNOW, GLACIER, OR WINTER CLIMBS

- Ice axe
- Chest sling or harness
- Waist and foot prusik slings
- Rescue pulley
- [Snow shovel]
- Snowshoes (optional) or skis (optional)
- Avalanche transceiver (optional)
- Avalanche probes (optional)
- [Wands] (optional)
- [Snow saw] (optional)
- [Pickets, ice screws]
- Crampons adjusted to boots
- Spike traction devices (optional)
- Powder baskets for trekking poles (optional)

OTHER WARM CLOTHES TO CONSIDER

- **Base layer:** heavier-weight top and bottom
- **Midlayers:** additional and heavier-weight layers for insulation
- **Shell layer:** sturdier or additional shell layers
- **Belay jacket:** one for each climber (rather than shared)—increasingly important as temperature drops
- **Head, hands, and feet layers:** more items that can work as a system, plus backups
- **Boots:** more-robust mountaineering boots

OTHER GEAR

- [Spare sunglasses]

away. The best course of action is to take steps to avoid injury or illness in the first place.

A first-aid kit should be compact and sturdy, with the contents wrapped in waterproof packaging. Most commercial first-aid kits are inadequate. A basic first-aid kit (see the "Basic First-Aid Kit" sidebar in Chapter 24) includes bandages, skin closures, gauze pads, dressings, roller bandage or wrap, and tape; antiseptic; blister prevention and treatment supplies; nitrile gloves; tweezers; a sewing needle; nonprescription painkillers; anti-inflammatory, antidiarrheal, and antihistamine tablets; a topical antibiotic; and important personal prescriptions, including an EpiPen for people with severe allergies. Consider your trip parameters (e.g., high-altitude climbing) when deciding what to add to these basics.

5. Knife

Knives are so useful in first aid, food preparation, repairs, and climbing that every party member needs to carry one: a leash helps prevent loss. Many climbers carry a small multitool and a short piece of cordage as part of a small repair kit. More-remote trips may require even more tools, and climbers carry a variety of supplies depending on previous experience: pliers, a screwdriver, an awl, and scissors can be part of a knife or pocket tool or carried separately. Other useful repair items include safety pins, a sewing needle and thread, wire, duct tape, nylon fabric repair tape, cable ties, plastic buckles, webbing, and replacement parts for equipment such as a water filter, tent poles, a stove, crampons, snowshoes, and skis. If your sleeping pad is inflatable, it is a good idea to carry a repair kit for it.

6. Fire

Bring the means to start and sustain an emergency fire. Most climbers carry a disposable butane lighter (or two) instead of matches. Firestarters, including chemical heat tabs, cotton balls soaked in petroleum jelly, and commercially prepared wood soaked in wax or chemicals, are indispensable for igniting wet wood to make a campfire in an emergency. Alternatively, on a high-altitude snow or glacier climb where there is no firewood, carry a stove as an emergency source of heat and water (see Stoves in Chapter 3, Camping, Food, and Water).

7. Shelter

For every trip, carry some sort of emergency shelter (in addition to a rain shell), such as a plastic tube tent or a jumbo plastic trash compactor bag. Single-use bivy sacks made of heat-reflective polyethylene are an excellent option at less than 4 ounces (115 grams). Emergency or space blankets, while cheap and lightweight, are inadequate for keeping out wind, rain, or snow while retaining body heat. A tent serves as an essential extra shelter only if a climbing party carries it with them even on day trips. Pack an insulated sleeping pad so you can sit or lie down, if necessary, on snow or wet terrain.

Some climbers carry a bivy sack as part of their everyday survival gear. A bivy sack, at about 1 pound (0.5 kilogram), protects you and your clothing from the weather, minimizes the effects of wind, and traps much of the heat that escapes from your body. See Shelter in Chapter 3 for details on tents, insulated pads, and bivy sacks.

8. Extra Food

For shorter trips, a one-day supply of extra food is a reasonable emergency stockpile for delays caused by foul weather, faulty navigation, or injury. A long trek may require more food, and on a cold trip, remember that food equals warmth. Extra food should not require cooking and should be easy to digest and store well for long periods. A combination of jerky, nuts, candy, granola, and dried fruit works well. Carrying a stove allows you to have a hot beverage or soup, and a few servings of instant coffee can help a dedicated coffee drinker keep a clear head. See more on food in Chapter 3.

9. Extra Water

Carry sufficient water and have the skills and tools required to obtain and purify more. Always carry at least one reusable water bottle or hydration bladder. Widemouthed containers are easier to refill. While hydration bladders are designed to be stored in a pack and feature a plastic hose and valve that allow you to drink while in motion, they are prone to leaking and freezing and can be difficult to keep clean.

Before you start out on the trail, fill water containers from a reliable source. Personal daily water consumption varies. For most people, 1.5 to 3 quarts (approximately the same in liters) of water per day is enough; in hot weather or at high altitudes, 6 quarts may be too little. Plan for enough water to accommodate heat, cold, altitude, exertion, or emergency.

In most environments, you will need to treat water—by filtering, using purification chemicals, or boiling—obtained from rivers, streams, lakes, and other natural sources. In cold environments, you will need a stove, fuel, lighter, and pot for melting snow. See Water in Chapter 3.

10. Extra Clothes

In the context of the Ten Essentials, "extra clothes" refers to what you would need for an unplanned bivouac. Ask yourself: What extra clothes would I need to survive the night in my emergency shelter in the worst conditions I could realistically encounter on this trip?

An extra layer of long underwear, a hat, or a balaclava can add warmth and weighs little. For your feet, bring an extra pair of thick socks; for your hands, an extra pair of mittens. For winter and expedition climbing in severe conditions, bring more insulation for your torso as well as your legs. See the "Choosing a Cold-Weather Strategy" sidebar earlier in this chapter.

OTHER IMPORTANT ITEMS

Many items in addition to the Ten Essentials are, of course, useful for climbing. Think ahead. Take time periodically to envision scenarios of possible accidents and unexpected circumstances, including what you would need to do should you be separated from your party, lost and alone. What equipment would you need to survive? How much risk are you willing to accept?

Ice Axe

Indispensable for preventing or arresting falls on steep snow and glaciers, an ice axe is also useful on snow-covered alpine trails; for traveling in steep heather, scree, or brush; for crossing streams; and for digging sanitation holes. For uses of ice axes, see Chapter 6, Wilderness Travel, and Chapter 16, Basic Snow and Ice Climbing.

Crampons and Spikes

While an ice axe is indispensable, especially for arresting a fall on steep snow or ice, crampons help prevent a fall from occurring. On icy alpine trails, spike traction devices—essentially tire chains for your boots—can prevent an unintended triple axel into a tree. See Spike Traction Devices and Crampons in Chapter 16.

Trekking Poles

Trekking poles help propel climbers uphill and brake on the way down. They offer stability for crossing streams and traveling on snow or scree. Plus, they redistribute effort across arms and legs, minimizing the peak loads on leg muscles to increase overall endurance. See the "Choosing Trekking Poles" sidebar.

Some climbers shorten adjustable trekking poles when traveling uphill (fig. 2-10a) and lengthen them when traveling downhill (fig. 2-10b). To adjust the length briefly—for example, when traversing a short section of uneven terrain—simply slide your uphill hand down the shaft (fig. 2-10c).

Using the wrist strap is a bit counterintuitive. First, put your hand up through the strap from below, then grab both the strap and pole grip so the strap comfortably supports your wrist. To scramble a short, steep section, let the poles dangle by the straps so you can shift your grip along them as needed. For a longer stretch, collapse the poles and stow

Fig. 2-10. *Using trekking poles while traveling:* **a,** *shorten poles to go uphill;* **b,** *lengthen poles to go downhill;* **c,** *slide hand down the uphill pole for quick changes as needed when scrambling on uneven terrain.*

them in your pack. Some ultralight tents use trekking poles in lieu of tent poles to save weight (see Shelter in Chapter 3, Camping, Food, and Water).

Toilet Kit for Managing Human Waste

The best way to manage waste in the backcountry is to use an existing pit toilet or privy. Alpine areas, however, typically lack such facilities. The next best way is to pack it out using either a "poop tube" or a waste alleviation and gelling (WAG) bag. "Poop tubes" are available commercially or are easy to construct using 4-inch-diameter (10-centimeter) PVC pipe, but note that untreated poop should not be thrown away in garbage containers whose contents end up in landfills; check local regulations for proper disposal. A pee bottle will spare you from having to leave your shelter on a cold night. If you find it useful, consider bringing a female urination device (see Figure 7-1).

When you factor in the aggregate number of visitors to a popular site, digging a "cat hole" and burying human waste may be detrimental to the land. Alpine areas often have little or no soil to decompose feces or toilet paper that, if left behind, fouls an area for decades. Lower-elevation sites may have sufficient soil or forest duff for feces, but not TP, to decompose. If you plan to dig a cat hole in a suitable environment, include a lightweight trowel in your toilet kit and extra bags for used TP. Consider including sanitizer or wipes, extra hygiene products, and latex or nitrile gloves. Pack out used TP and wipes.

Location and regulations may dictate actions, but each climber must act responsibly to prevent human waste from fouling the wild spaces we all love. Wipes, for example, are typically made of polyester. Be skeptical of manufacturers' claims of biodegradability, as that process depends on environmental conditions. See Managing Human Waste in the Mountains in Chapter 7, Protecting the Outdoors.

Insect Repellent

Some insects—mosquitoes, ticks, chiggers, biting flies, and no-see-um gnats—feast on the human body. According to the Centers for Disease Control and Prevention (CDC), the United States has seen a substantial increase since 2004 in reported cases of mosquito-borne and tick-borne (vector-borne) diseases. For winter trips or for snow climbs any time of year, insect repellent may be unnecessary; a low-elevation approach trail in summer is another story.

When traveling in areas in the US with disease-carrying mosquitoes or disease-carrying ticks, take extra precautions to avoid being bitten (see the "Bug Defense Strategy" sidebar). Mosquitoes can carry Zika virus, malaria, and West Nile virus, while ticks can carry at least sixteen diseases, including Lyme disease and Rocky Mountain spotted fever. Internationally, the situation is more complicated and the risk of malaria, Zika, and dengue fever looms large. In tropical areas, you may need to take antimalarial medications and use bed netting. Before you travel abroad, consult resources from the CDC for recommendations.

Be extra vigilant about protecting yourself around dawn and dusk, when bugs bite most. Mosquitoes have trouble tracking targets in windy conditions, so camp and take breaks accordingly. To minimize your attractiveness to insects (and bears!), avoid wearing fragrances. In tick country, especially on days when you have been thrashing through brush, check your clothes, body, and hair thoroughly at night.

The first line of defense against voracious insects is to cover up with tightly woven clothing, including gloves and head nets. In hot weather, long shirts and pants made of netting may prove worthwhile. Keep in mind that mosquitos favor red, orange, black, and cyan.

The next defensive measure is to wear factory- or home-applied permethrin-treated clothes as a chemical barrier and apply a spritz of non-permethrin repellent (for example, picaridin) to the outer layer of your clothing as needed in the field. A solid application to a hat and scarf helps protect the face, and to socks, the ankles. If necessary, apply an appropriate insect repellent to exposed skin, being especially careful around your face. When using both sunscreen and insect repellent, first apply sunscreen and allow it to dry, then apply the repellent.

Read the warning label of repellents, as they may be harmful to pets and toxic to aquatic organisms. In the US, insect repellents must be registered with the Environmental Protection Agency (EPA) and have solid evidence for all claims of safety and effectiveness. There are only five active ingredients with EPA registrations that claim to repel mosquitoes and ticks for more than two hours: DEET, picaridin, permethrin, IR3535, and oil of lemon eucalyptus. Botanical oils (citronella, soybean, lemongrass, cedar, et cetera) are only minimally effective. Insect repellents come in various forms (spray, liquid, cream, stick, and wipe on) and concentrations; sprays are the easiest to apply to clothes. Treated wristbands, vitamin supplements, garlic, and ultrasonic repellents are all equally ineffective.

Sometimes, retreating to a tent with a full bug screen may be the only way to preserve your sanity.

LOCAL COMMUNICATION DEVICES

A climbing party may need tools to communicate locally. Whistles, avalanche transceivers, and handheld two-way radios can be useful when climbers end up spread out along a route or need to locate a lost or incapacitated member. Three signals, repeated several times in sequence, is universal for "SOS."

Whistle. A whistle's shrill, penetrating blast greatly exceeds the range over which a person's voice can be heard by others and can serve as a crude means of communication when shouts for help cannot be heard—such as when a climber is trapped in a crevasse or a party becomes separated in fog, darkness, or thick forest. Whistles prove much more useful if a climbing party designates specific signals for "Where are you?," "I'm here and OK," and "Help!" before a trip.

Avalanche transceiver. Conditions may call for mountaineers to carry avalanche transceivers, or beacons, used to locate victims of a snowslide. See Avalanche Rescue Transceivers in Chapter 20, Avalanche Safety.

Handheld two-way radio. The noise of wind or water and physical obstacles between people at the two ends of a climbing rope often make communication difficult. Handheld two-way radios can greatly ease communication between climbing partners or between a climbing party and base camp (see Communication Devices in Chapter 5, Navigation and Communication). Bring sufficient batteries or a power bank (see the next section). To summon help in remote mountain areas, carry a satellite communicator (see Chapter 5); two-way radios are not reliable for that purpose.

Route markers. In the field, route markers can aid the return trip where the party lacks redundant GPS capability, and glacier wands can mark dangers such as crevasses. Remove route markers after using them to follow Leave No Trace practices.

Satellite communicators. Party members may be able to text each other using satellite communicators.

Batteries

An expanding list of backcountry electronics—including GPS devices, satellite communicators, headlamps, walkie-

---

TIPS FOR USING ELECTRONIC DEVICES IN COLD WEATHER

- Use lithium batteries for single-use battery devices; bring extras.
- Use your pockets, body, and sleeping bag to keep electronics as warm as possible, but avoid intense heat.
- Cycle batteries and their backups through warm pockets.

TABLE 2-5. BATTERY PERFORMANCE IN COLD TEMPERATURES				
	SINGLE-USE ALKALINE	LITHIUM	RECHARGEABLE NIMH	LI-ION
Minimum recommended operating temperature	-4°F (-20°C)	-40°F (-40°C)	32°F (0°C)	-40°F (-40°C)
Performance at 32°F (0°C)	70%	100%	75%	90%
Performance at -4°F (-20°C)	25%	80%	25%	80%
Performance at -40°F (-40°C)	0%	50%	0%	50%
Overall performance	Poor	Excellent	Poor	Excellent

talkies, and avalanche beacons—run on batteries, so battery type and size are part of the equipment checklist. The standard batteries for most devices are 1.5 volt AA and AAA. AA cells have roughly twice the capacity of smaller AAA batteries. Batteries operate through chemical processes adversely affected by cold temperatures; see the "Tips for Using Electronic Devices in Cold Weather" sidebar and Table 2-5's comparison of overall battery performance in low temperatures. Regardless of what you choose, make sure you start each trip with batteries compatible with your headlamp and navigation tools, all fully charged to handle any reasonable emergency.

Alkaline batteries. Alkaline batteries are single use and the most commonly available general-purpose batteries. Their major problem is that voltage (hence, brightness) drops significantly as they discharge. Cold temperatures drastically accelerate this voltage drop, resulting in much shorter battery life.

Lithium batteries. Much longer lasting and lighter than alkaline, lithium batteries also cost more. They are single use and not rechargeable. Do not dump them in garbage or recycling bins; take them to a location that accepts hazardous waste. Voltage remains almost constant over their charge, and they are nearly as efficient at 0 degrees Fahrenheit (minus 18 degrees Celsius) as at room temperature. The more powerful the electronic device, the bigger the advantage lithium batteries have over alkalines. Ability to operate at cold temperatures compounds this advantage. For cold-weather trips, lithium batteries are the clear choice for high-powered headlamps, GPS units, and satellite communicators.

Rechargeable batteries. One popular strategy is to use rechargeables for main batteries and single-use batteries as spares. Rechargeable nickel–metal hydride (NiMH) batteries have replaced once-common nickel-cadmium (NiCd) in standard AA and AAA sizes, while lithium-ion (Li-ion) batteries are usually found in higher-voltage consumer electronics such as smartphones. *Caution:* NiMH batteries tend to discharge rapidly in storage, losing approximately 30 percent per month. Always start an outing with a full charge.

Lithium-ion rechargeable batteries. Li-ion batteries (not to be confused with single-use lithium batteries) are found in phones, digital cameras, and most portable power banks (see below). Li-ion batteries are not available in standard 1.5-volt AA and AAA sizes, due to the possible dangers associated with inserting them into a noncompatible charger. Li-ion batteries perform well in cold temperatures. It is best to recharge them often to avoid a full discharge. Dispose of them as you would single-use lithium batteries.

Portable power banks. Also called battery packs, power banks using rechargeable Li-ion technology are a handy way to store power to recharge Li-ion-powered devices such as phones and cameras. A battery pack's capacity is rated in milliamp hours (mAh), with about 4,000–5,000 mAh needed to recharge a smartphone.

Portable solar panels. Solar panels can be an effective way to recharge power banks to keep electronics running on longer climbs and expeditions. See Batteries in Chapter 5 for information about charging with solar panels.

Preparing for the Freedom of the Hills

When you go into the wilderness, it is important to carry essential gear and leave the rest at home. Achieving that balance requires knowledge and solid judgment, both of which are gained with experience. Understanding the basics of clothing and equipment will help you decide which essentials you need to minimize your risk and stay dry and comfortable in the mountains. This is only the beginning of your discovery of the freedom of the hills. The next chapter on camping, food, and water will expand your horizons.

CHAPTER 3

CAMPING, FOOD, AND WATER

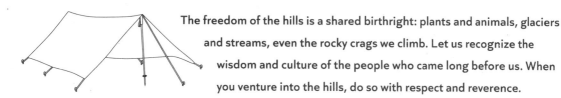

The freedom of the hills is a shared birthright: plants and animals, glaciers and streams, even the rocky crags we climb. Let us recognize the wisdom and culture of the people who came long before us. When you venture into the hills, do so with respect and reverence.

Choose wisely long before you arrive at the trailhead. While technology may provide us exceptional equipment for safety and comfort, always consider the broader impact of the gear you acquire. Long-lasting, responsibly produced camping gear helps us experience the solitude of the mountains, the star-filled skies, and the beauty of nature. As much as possible, step lightly and leave no trace of your passing.

The Sleep System

The sleep system gets you through the night in safety and comfort. It is your "shelter from the storm." Choose sleep system components—clothes, a sleeping bag, ground insulation, and shelter—to endure the worst conditions you are likely to encounter while also traveling fast and light.

CLOTHES AND ACCESSORIES

When they arrive at camp, experienced climbers change out of their damp clothes and don a dry base layer, hat, gloves, and socks. Cozy, dry clothes, a puffy coat, camp shoes, and a hot drink boost the revitalization process. This ritual also keeps your sleeping bag dry and clean. While wearing camp clothes, climbers may attempt to dry out their climbing clothes by hanging them up if conditions allow. A few accessories can help climbers get a good night's sleep. For example, side sleepers in particular may appreciate a small inflatable pillow, and a conveniently placed (well-marked!) pee bottle will help minimize the chill of middle-of-the-night bathroom breaks.

SLEEPING BAG

Ideally, a sleeping bag is light and compressible and fits you well. For cold conditions, nothing beats an efficient mummy bag (fig. 3-1). The fill material traps an insulating layer of air around the climber's warm body. A bag's thermal efficiency depends on your physiology, how well the bag fits you, and the type, amount, and loft (thickness) of the insulation.

Physiological Factors

A sleeping bag only slows your body's inevitable loss of heat (see the "Key Factors That Affect How You Sleep" sidebar). Depending on muscle mass, age, and gender, individuals vary considerably in their ability to generate heat and tolerate cold. People with more muscle mass tend to generate more heat because their bodies burn more calories to fuel that mass. Experienced mountaineers and people who work outside may feel more comfortable in cold environments than people who work in offices.

Sizing and Fit

Choose a design that fits you well. If a sleeping bag is too long or wide, it will be harder for your body to heat the excess interior volume. Plus, an overly large bag adds weight to your pack. Too tight a fit and your body compresses the insulation, making the bag colder. Yet for winter camping or expedition use, a bag sized a little larger allows extra room that, together with your body heat, helps dry small items such as wet gloves, socks, and boot liners. Use caution, however, when using your sleeping bag as a dryer: excess moisture can collect in the insulation, particularly on longer trips or in humid conditions.

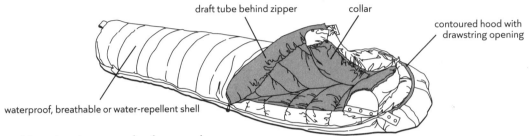

Fig. 3-1. *Mountaineering mummy bag features and components.*

Insulation, Fabric, and Environmental Factors

Insulation for mountaineering sleeping bags is either natural down (goose or duck), synthetic fill, or a blend. Goose-down bags have the highest warmth-to-weight ratio and are well suited to alpine environments, but they lose their warmth when wet. (See Chapter 2, Clothing and Equipment, for more about quality of down.) Synthetic bags may be preferred for trips where moisture cannot be avoided. Sleeping bags with either type of insulation can

now be treated with waterproof, breathable water-repellent (DWR) chemicals to increase their hydrophobic properties (see Insulating Fills in Chapter 2).

The nylon or polyester fabrics used in mountaineering sleeping bags are tightly woven to keep the insulation in place. Waterproof, breathable fabrics are expensive but advantageous in damp environments, such as a snow cave or wet tent; they are especially desirable for a down bag. Shell materials are treated with DWR, giving the same advantages and limitations as when used in clothing (see "Waterproof, breathable fabrics" under Synthetic Fabrics in Chapter 2).

Any attempts to waterproof a sleeping bag, including using waterproof, breathable materials, will decrease the bag's ability to transfer body moisture to the atmosphere. The trade-off is between the risk of water getting inside the bag from external sources—rain, snow, dew, and condensation inside a tent—and the risk of perspiration and damp clothing being trapped inside the bag. In wet environments, most climbers will want to use a bag with synthetic insulation or waterproof, breathable fabrics.

Dew is particularly insidious. As evening air cools, it releases moisture, condensing as dew, especially on cold objects. In humid environments, as the temperature falls in camp and the night air cools, keep tents zipped, sleeping bags in their stuff sacks, and clothes stowed until bedtime to minimize the surface area exposed to dampness.

Bag Rating Systems

Historically, a sleeping bag rating gave only rough guidance of the coldest temperature at which an average person would stay warm through the night, assuming use of long underwear, a hat, and an insulated pad. Now, many sleeping bags—though not all, including some high-quality bags—are independently rated by the International Organization for Standardization's ISO 23537 or EN13537. (These standards do not apply to use by children or military personnel

---

KEY FACTORS THAT AFFECT HOW YOU SLEEP

As the night gets progressively colder, the insulation of your sleeping bag and pad retains the heat you generate.

- **Warm air (convection).** The body continually warms the air around it. Clothes and sleeping bags trap this warm air, slowing its escape to the atmosphere.

- **Breathing and sweat (respiration and evaporation).** People lose about a quart (liter) of water every night. In colder environments, the warm, moist air you breathe out can result in a significant amount of heat loss.

- **Cold ground (conduction).** Direct contact with cold ground sucks away heat. Rock and snow are the most conductive surfaces outside; grass, dry dirt, and forest duff, the least. Camping mattresses and pads insulate you from cold ground and protect underlying grass and vegetation. Look for pads with higher R-values for sleeping on colder surfaces.

- **Radiant heat (infrared radiation).** Our bodies radiate heat, representing up to 10 percent of our heat loss. Sleeping pads and clothes made with reflective materials instead of insulation capture and reflect back some of this heat.

TABLE 3-1. SEASONAL GUIDELINES FOR SLEEPING BAGS

SEASON	TEMPERATURE RANGE
Summer	Above 40°F (above 4°C)
Three-season (spring, fall, summer at high altitudes)	15°F to 40°F (-9°C to 4°C)
Winter	-10°F to 15°F (-23°C to -9°C)
Polar and extreme alpine	Below -10°F (below -23°C)

or in extremely cold conditions.) Each bag is assigned four temperature ratings:

1. **Upper limit:** The highest temperature for a "standard man" to sleep without sweating.
2. **Comfort:** The lowest temperature for a "standard woman" to have a comfortable night's sleep.
3. **Lower limit:** The lowest temperature for a standard man to have a comfortable night's sleep.
4. **Extreme:** The survival rating for a standard woman.

Women and men should use the comfort and lower limit ratings, respectively, when choosing a sleeping bag. Table 3-1 offers rough seasonal guidelines. For an example applicable to three-season camping, Table 3-1 gives a low temperature of 15 degrees Fahrenheit (minus 9 degrees Celsius). The average woman would want a bag with a comfort rating of 15 degrees Fahrenheit, and the average man would want a bag with a lower limit rating of 15 degrees Fahrenheit. Climbers must consider their metabolism, body makeup, and any insulation they may wear in the sleeping bag. Other factors that affect warmth are level of hydration or fatigue and quality of shelter and ground insulation (see the "Tips for Staying Warm in a Sleeping Bag" sidebar).

Features and Components

A sleeping bag's features and components affect efficiency and ventilation (see Figure 3-1). A close-fitting hood surrounds your head, retaining precious heat while leaving your face uncovered for breathing. Collars that seal around the neck and draft tubes along the length of the zipper help hold heat inside. Long zippers make it easy to get in and out and help ventilate excess heat. Some designs offer complementary left- and right-hand zippers so that two bags can be zipped together. Using a half- or three-quarter-length zipper saves weight and bulk but sacrifices ventilation flexibility.

Accessories

Washable sleeping bag liners add a few degrees of warmth and keep body oils from soiling the bag's interior and insulation. The same objective can be accomplished by wearing a dry set of base layers and an extra insulating layer on your torso if needed.

Vapor-barrier liners (VBLs) are either a sleeping bag liner or a full multipiece suit constructed of a waterproof, nonbreathable material. In frigid conditions and especially on longer trips, VBLs can be used to protect clothing and sleeping bag insulation from perspiration condensing *inside* the insulation. You sleep inside the VBL (typically wearing a base layer), nested inside the sleeping bag. These liners reduce evaporative heat loss and the amount of moisture (or, in arctic environments, ice) buildup within the sleeping bag's insulation. Clothing insulation, especially that of gloves and socks, can be similarly protected. Test out a VBL before using it; many climbers find them awkward and clammy.

Most sleeping bags come with a semi-waterproof stuff sack for storage during trips and a larger breathable sack for storage between trips. In wet conditions, use a waterproof stuff sack, dry bag, or plastic bag. A large plastic bag can serve double duty as extra rain protection while traveling and as a roomy storage option in camp or to collect snow to melt for water. Compression stuff sacks save pack space. A fleece-lined stuff sack can double as a pillow.

Specialty Bags

Some climbers prefer to go as light as possible, sacrificing comfort in order to carry less weight. Used in conjunction with an insulating jacket, half- or three-quarter-length bags can be adequate to just below freezing. Even more minimal is an ultralight, zipperless, hoodless quilt with down or polyester insulation. These weight-saving alternatives may also be less expensive and more comfortable for some tent partners, for example, during warm desert trips.

Care and Cleaning

With a little care, a sleeping bag will last for many years.

Storage. Always store a bag fully lofted. Keep it in a compression stuff sack for only short periods of time.

Cleaning down and synthetic bags. Spot-clean soiled areas with soap specified by the manufacturer; wash the whole bag only when necessary. Never dry-clean a down sleeping bag. Professional cleaning by a down specialist is recommended, but you can also clean your bag carefully at home. Before washing, secure all zippers and snaps and remove detachable pieces, and turn the bag inside out so that the waterproof, breathable shell is on the inside. Wash the bag with mild nondetergent (preferably down-specific) soap on the gentle cycle in a large front-loading washing machine. Run the bag through the rinse cycle several times to remove all soap. Treat the DWR finish as required (see Caring for Outdoor Clothing in Chapter 2, Clothing and Equipment) while the bag is still wet, and dry the bag in a large clothes dryer on medium. Toss a few tennis balls into the dryer to break up clumps of down, and squeeze the insulation periodically to check for moisture. It takes several hours to dry a bag.

GROUND INSULATION

The foundation of a comfortable night in the outdoors is reliable insulation under the sleeping bag. A sleeping pad reduces the amount of heat you lose to the cold ground or snow beneath you. If you are forced to sleep without a pad, use extra clothing, your pack, the climbing rope, or boots for padding and insulation.

Type

There are four common types of sleeping pads.

Closed-cell foam. Bulkier than pneumatic options, a thin pad of closed-cell foam is inexpensive and provides reliable lightweight insulation that cannot fail from a puncture. Foam pads can also be used for a splint in an emergency. Consider bringing foam pads on trips, particularly when sleeping on snow. Textured designs lend a softer sleeping surface, lower weight, and increased ability to trap air, resulting in greater thermal efficiency. Molded patterns that are Z-folded rather than rolled are compact.

Self-inflating pad. The bulky, water-absorbing open-cell foam pad of long ago has evolved into the self-inflating pad, with Therm-a-Rest being the most well-known brand. The open-cell foam is enclosed in an airtight, waterproof chamber that compresses well.

Non-insulating air mattress. A basic inflatable mattress is typically compact and provides plenty of cushion to cover bumps, rocks, and roots, but the air in the mattress convects heat away from the body by internal air circulation. Pairing a non-insulating air mattress with a closed-cell foam pad is an effective and inexpensive solution for colder weather.

Insulating air mattress. Modern versions of the air mattress employ complex internal chambers and insulation to minimize air convection currents, and they use radiant-heat-reflective materials to reflect infrared radiation back to the sleeper. Once inflated, these comfortable, lightweight, extremely small sleeping pads have high warmth ratings—very useful on snow and ice. However, these

TABLE 3-2. OPTIONS FOR GROUND INSULATION

TYPE OF GROUND INSULATION	TYPICAL R-VALUE(S)	TYPICAL USES
Closed-cell foam: 0.38 in., 0.63 in., 0.75 in. (1 cm, 1.5 cm, 2 cm)	R1.5, R2.7, R3.5	Least expensive; puncture-proof. Multipurpose pad for sitting, dressing, cooking. Frequently combined with self-inflating pad or insulating air mattress.
Self-inflating pad: 1.5–2 in. (3.8–5 cm)	R2–R5	General purpose.
Non-insulating air mattress	R1	Not appropriate for mountaineering except in mild weather.
Insulating air mattress	R2–R7.8	General purpose.

mattresses can puncture and offer no insulation when deflated. Always bring a repair kit when using an inflatable pad. A lake or pond may be handy for assessing a leak.

Warmth

Pads are rated for warmth by R-value, a measure of thermal resistance. For example, pads with a rating of R2.5 protect well down to about freezing; R4, to about 15 degrees Fahrenheit (minus 9 degrees Celsius); and R5-plus, in colder temperatures. Higher R-values are needed for sleeping on wet ground, rock, and snow. Table 3-2 shows typical R-values and uses of different types of ground insulation.

Size

Self-inflating pads and insulating air mattresses come in various lengths, but a shorter length (4 feet, 120 centimeters) is usually adequate for general mountaineering. You can use a smaller closed-cell foam sit pad to pad and insulate feet and legs. For greater insulation when camping on snow or in winter or arctic environments, use a short inflatable pad on top of a full-length or three-quarter-length closed-cell foam pad.

SHELTER

The seventh of the Ten Essentials, shelter is key to surviving a night in the wilderness and usually means a tent, tarp, or bivy sack. Even on a day trip, or if you will be away from your primary shelter on a summit attempt, it is recommended that you carry an emergency shelter sufficient for the entire party (see Bivy Sacks later in this section, as well as "7. Shelter" in The Mountaineers' Ten Essentials in Chapter 2, Clothing and Equipment).

Tents, the most common and versatile mountain shelter, are relatively easy to set up and provide rainproof privacy and refuge from wind, sun, and insects. They are usable in almost any terrain and are often roomy enough for people and their gear. Tents usually are the first choice above timberline, on glaciers, in winter, and in bear, mosquito, and/or biting fly country.

A lightweight alternative to tents, tarps can be used together with bivy sacks to provide effective shelter from rain and sun. Bivy sacks also make great lightweight emergency shelters.

When selecting a tent or tarp, climbers must counterbalance protection (sturdiness and cover from the elements), weight, and interior space. There are trade-offs. Consider how and where you will use the shelter as well as your personal preferences (see the "Choosing a Tent" sidebar).

CHOOSING A TENT

Before purchasing a tent, try it out at the store to check its space, protection, and weight. Consider how easy—or challenging—it is to set up.

- **Space:** Tents are rated for the number of sleepers, usually assuming cozy conditions and storing minimal gear inside. Is there sufficient head- and foot room? How much do the walls slope, which helps determine usable interior space? Does each side have a door? Are the doors easy to maneuver through? Does the tent have pockets or vestibules? Will your sleeping pads fit?

- **Protection:** Consider how much conditions and terrain can vary, for example, from summer in the Sierra to autumn in the Alps, winter in the Cascades, or spring in the Andes. Will the shelter need to withstand above-timberline wind? Heavy snowfall? A four-season tent provides more protection than an ultralight one at the expense of added weight.

- **Weight:** What does it really weigh? Break out the scale, since manufacturers are notoriously optimistic. With a two-person, four-season tent weighing anywhere from 3.3 to almost 10 pounds (1.5 to 4.5 kilograms), a tent can be your heaviest piece of gear. Tents often list a minimum or packed weight (excluding stakes, stuff sacks, et cetera) and a packaged weight (which includes everything). Use minimum weight for comparisons.

Moisture Strategies

Shelters, from tents to tarps to bivy sacks, serve two competing functions in managing moisture: keeping out as much as possible while venting as much as possible. A person exhales and perspires a substantial amount of water overnight. If a tent were waterproof, this water vapor would dampen sleeping bags and clothing. A tent must "breathe."

Double-wall tents. Double-wall construction consists of an inner, breathable wall separated from an outer, detachable, waterproof rain fly. Body moisture escapes from the vented space between these two layers. The fly of a mountaineering tent should come fairly close to the ground, covering the tent and entryway and shedding wind-driven rain (fig. 3-2a). Tent floors are typically coated nylon with a sill that extends up the sides (fig. 3-2b). A higher sill offers more protection from rain blown in under the fly but can reduce the amount of breathable fabric and gather condensation.

To avoid unnecessary seams, the floor and sill are typically one continuous piece of fabric, known as a bathtub floor. All seams in the rain fly and floor should be factory-taped to keep water out.

Single-wall waterproof, breathable tents. Lightweight, rugged, and expensive, these tents use just one layer of waterproof, breathable fabric (fig. 3-2c). The inside is a fuzzy, blotter-like facing that holds and distributes excess moisture to disperse it outside. The great advantage of a single-wall tent is its light weight. A solo tent can weigh less than 1 pound (about 450 grams). Lighter two-person versions can weigh less than 2 pounds (0.9 kilogram). They are also quieter in high winds because there is no outer fly to flap against the tent walls. Their major disadvantages are their price tags and tendency to collect moisture during warm, wet weather.

Ultralight single-wall waterproof, nonbreathable tents. These tents trade efficient breathability for reduced weight (fig. 3-2d). Moisture is managed through vents.

Tarps. Tarps easily vent moisture and are usually paired with ground sheets (fig. 3-2e). Campers using tarps in marginal weather will often use an all-weather "splash bivy" for additional protection (see Bivy Sacks later in this chapter).

More options. Some manufacturers offer floorless lightweight nylon tents and usually at least one pole. Similarly, the rain fly of some double-wall tents can be set up without the tent, and with or without the tent's footprint, to serve as a freestanding lightweight shelter (fig. 3-2f). Bivy sacks are a solo option (fig. 3-2g and h). Evaluate a bivy's breathability and comfort carefully.

Three- and Four-Season Tents

Tents for mountaineering are either three-season (for non-winter use) or four-season (for all situations, including snow camping). All-season climbers often own both types and perhaps a tarp and bivy sack as well.

Fig. 3-2. *Shelters come in many shapes and sizes:* **a,** *classic four-season dome tent (shown with rain fly and tunnel-style vestibule);* **b,** *classic three-season tent (shown with rain fly rolled back);* **c,** *four-season single-wall (waterproof, breathable fabric) tent;* **d,** *ultralight single-wall waterproof, nonbreathable tent using trekking poles for support;* **e,** *tarp with trekking poles for support;* **f,** *rain fly and ground sheet only, without inner tent;* **g,** *lightweight bivy sack;* **h,** *hoop-style bivy sack.*

Three-season tents. The side or top panels of many three-season tents are made with transparent netting, providing ventilation, bug protection, stargazing opportunities, and lower weight (see Figure 3-2b) but are also open to snow and dew. Adequate for mountaineering in a wide variety of conditions from late spring to early fall, these tents can be ideal for longer trips where weight is more of a concern.

Four-season tents. Usually heavier, more expensive, and built to withstand winter conditions of high winds and snow loading, four-season tents have higher-strength aluminum or carbon fiber poles and more-durable reinforcing. The doors, windows, and vents have solid panels that zip, and the fly extends close to the ground (see Figure 3-2a). Four-season tents often have more than two poles and a greater emphasis on guylines. Usually, the tent shape is some variation on a dome.

Ultralight tents. Often associated with long-distance hikers and moderate weather, ultralight tents can be used by climbers in moderate conditions (some models weigh less than a pound!). They are made of Dyneema Composite Fabric or silnylon or silpoly and may use trekking poles as tent poles to save weight (see Figure 3-2d). These designs are not freestanding (see Tent Design and Features, below) and so are less suited to windy, wet alpine environments.

Tent Design and Features

Designers shape tents to maximize interior space, load-bearing strength, and ability to withstand wind while minimizing weight. A great tent must be easy to pitch and disassemble but tenacious when storms attempt to take it down. Mountaineering tents use a variety of clever criss-crossing pole architectures to form various dome or tunnel shapes. Some shapes are freestanding and do not require stakes. Such tents are easy to pick up and move but must be secured with stakes and perhaps guylines to prevent them from being blown away, especially when unoccupied—a real danger in a storm.

The two-person tent is the most popular tent size for mountaineering, offering the greatest flexibility in choice of campsite. For a group, it is generally more versatile to bring two two-person tents rather than one larger tent. Many two-person tents can handle three people in a pinch, yet are light enough to be used by one person. A tent is generally warmer, however, with more than one occupant.

Some three- and four-person tents are light enough to be carried by two people who crave luxurious living (or two large people who crave adequate space). Larger tents, especially those tall enough to stand in, are big morale boosters

during an expedition or long storm but are burdens to carry. Before you set out, distribute the tent parts (tent, fly, poles, and stakes) among the party to share the weight.

A well-designed mountaineering tent keeps out most of the rain and snow as climbers get in and out. Manufacturers offer many different features, such as extra doors, interior pockets, gear loops, tunnels, vestibules, and hoods. Of course, most extra features add both weight and cost. Go out a few times with a few different tents, either rented or borrowed, and decide what you like best.

Vestibules. Some tents include a protruding floorless protected area known as a vestibule. Expedition rain flies often come with their own poles for extending the vestibule area (see Figure 3-2a). Vestibules shelter the entrance and provide more room for storing gear, dressing, and cooking. In foul weather, cooking in the tent vestibule is an art to be appreciated—carefully (see Stove Safety later in this chapter). Some four-season tents provide two vestibules, allowing for specialization (for example, cooking in one, storing boots in the other).

Vents. Vents near the ceiling allow rising warm, moist air to escape. Mosquito netting allows air to flow freely when the doors are unzipped yet bars rodents, reptiles, and insects (see Figure 3-2b and d).

Color. Warm tent colors such as yellow, orange, and red are cheerier, helpful if you are stuck inside, and they make it easier to spot your camp from afar. On the other hand, subdued hues blend into the landscape.

Setting Up, Caring for, and Cleaning a Tent

When setting up (or taking down) a tent, push the poles through the tent sleeves rather than pulling them. Pulling can separate the pole sections and risks breaking the joints. If party members are familiar with the design, they will be able to set up a tent quickly. Modern fast-clip tents speed up the process. For anchoring, see the next section.

Consider bringing a tarp or ground cloth to protect the exterior floor from abrasion. Footprints—ground cloths shaped for a specific tent—can be purchased from manufacturers or made from durable lightweight material, such as Tyvek. Be careful to tuck the edges under the tent to keep rainwater from collecting under it. Bring fabric repair tape in your repair kit.

To protect the tent floor from water, dirt, and abrasion, discourage people from wearing boots inside. Do not touch tent fabric immediately after applying DEET-based insect repellents; they can ruin fabric coatings. Before packing up, lift the tent, doors open and upside down, to shake out debris and remove condensation or rain.

Tents last longer when carefully cleaned and air-dried after each trip. Hose it off or hand-wash it with mild soap and water. Scrub stains with a sponge. Spot-clean any tree sap. Hang to dry.

High heat and prolonged sun exposure damage tent material, so do not leave a tent set up outside for unnecessary periods of time. Exposure to ultraviolet light can ruin a rain fly in a single season.

Anchoring a Tent

Bring stakes designed to handle the terrain. In forest duff, short plastic or heavy-gauge wire stakes, such as those that come with most tents, are just fine. For rocky alpine terrain, use metal skewer-type stakes (fig. 3-3a) or sturdier triangular stakes (fig. 3-3b). In sand or snow, a broader surface area on the stake will help (fig. 3-3c).

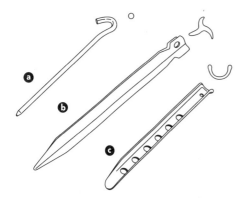

Fig. 3-3. *Tent stakes (note profile cross sections at upper right): **a,** skewer; **b,** triangular with notches; **c,** snow or sand stake.*

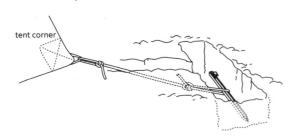

Fig. 3-4. *T-slot anchor: Dig a T-shaped trench about 12 inches (30 centimeters) deep, fasten the tent's guylines around the anchor, and place the anchor in the trench's crossbar. Pull the line taut to tension the tent. Backfill the trench and stomp on the snow to compact it over the anchor.*

Stakes driven into snow in the normal fashion will pull out in heavy wind and melt out during the day. Ice axes, skis, and trekking poles can make solid anchors but cannot be used for anything else in the meantime. For extra security, tie the tent to a rock or tree. In snow, the best anchors are T-slot anchors (fig. 3-4), made from stakes, stuff sacks packed with snow, metal plates called flukes made specifically for this purpose, or even rocks or sticks. If you arrange the knots for the cords attached to rocks or sticks above the snow, you will be able to untie them rather than dig them up. Don't skimp on anchors when camping on an exposed, windy area on a glacier.

First, dig a T-shaped trench at least 12 inches (30 centimeters) deep, with the long leg of the T facing the tent. Tie the T-slot anchor to the tent guyline or form a loop in the line and slip the anchor material into it. Put the T-slot in the trench, then backfill and stomp on the snow to compact it over the anchor.

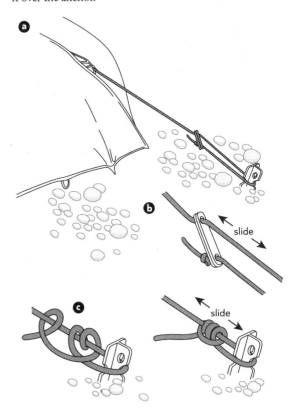

Fig. 3-5. *Tensioning guylines: **a,** guyline with a tensioner device; **b,** close-up view of a tensioner; **c,** tying and adjusting a taut-line hitch.*

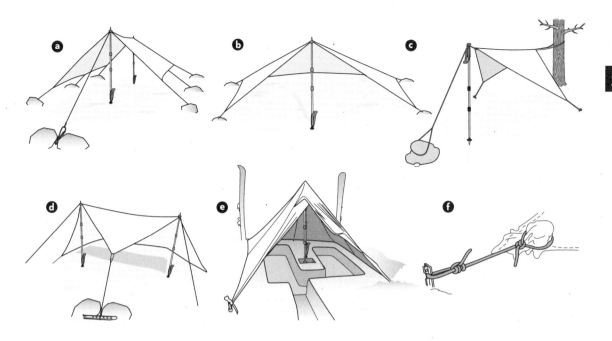

Fig. 3-6. *Improvised tarp shelters:* **a,** *A-frame using two trekking poles, one secured by a wedged rock;* **b,** *arrowhead using a trekking pole;* **c,** *dining fly with tree and trekking pole anchored with a rock;* **d,** *dining fly using two trekking poles and a snow stake wedged between rocks;* **e,** *dining fly for kitchen in snow using skis, a trekking pole, and a stake;* **f,** *tying off corners of a tarp that has no grommets or tie-off loops.*

Guylines can be kept taut with adjustable small plastic or metal tensioners (fig. 3-5a and b) or with a simple taut-line hitch (fig. 3-5c), also easy to adjust.

Tarps

Lightweight and inexpensive, a tarp may offer adequate shelter—from all but extreme weather—in lowland forests and among subalpine trees. Compared with a tent, a tarp offers less protection from heat loss and wind and none at all from insects or rodents (see Figure 3-2e). A tarp also requires ingenuity and use of landscape features to set up; it's a poor choice as a main shelter above timberline unless you bring ice axes or trekking poles (fig. 3-6a, b, and d). A tarp makes a helpful shelter for a cooking and eating area in camp during inclement weather (fig. 3-6c and e). Avoid wrapping yourself in a tarp as if it were a blanket because perspiration will condense inside the waterproof material.

Plastic tarps are unsuitable for mountaineering. Coated nylon, silnylon, and Dyneema Composite Fabric tarps are stronger and lightweight. Many tarps come with reinforced grommets or tie-off loops for easy rigging. Alternatively,

create corner tie-in points by wrapping a small piece of the tarp's fabric around a pine cone or small rock from camp (fig. 3-6f). Bring lightweight cord and a few light stakes, and use taut-line hitches (see Figure 3-5c) to string the tarp up.

BIVY SACKS

A lightweight alternative to a tent, a bivouac sack (often called a bivy sack) is a large fabric bag with a long side zipper and, typically, zippered mosquito netting at the head. Bivy sacks provide insulative value and the moisture-management functions of a tent, keeping out external water while venting internal water vapor. The bottom is usually waterproof-coated nylon; the upper is either a waterproof, breathable or weather-resistant material. Bivies come in three main types:

1. **All-weather bivies** are able to fully function as a shelter, weighing from about 1 to 2.5 pounds (about 0.5 to 1.1 kilograms).
2. **Splash bivies** are weather-resistant on top, allowing them to be extremely lightweight (as light as 6 ounces, 170 grams) and breathable. Intended for

mild weather, they protect from splashing rain and drifting snow when used with tarps.

3. **Emergency bivies** weigh so little, about 4–9 ounces (113–255 grams), that each member of the climbing party can always carry one as an emergency shelter.

Styles vary from spartan sacks (see Figure 3-2g) to mini-tents that may be staked out and have a hoop to keep the fabric off the sleeper's face (see Figure 3-2h). Bivies are typically designed for one person or two in an emergency. Test that the length and circumference can accommodate the sleeper in a fully lofted sleeping bag and with ground insulation inside, not outside, the bivy.

A bivy can be used as a primary shelter or carried only as an emergency shelter. In mild conditions, a bivy sack with a tarp set up over it offers protection equal to most tents. In wet conditions, a bivy sack inside a tent keeps a sleeping bag dry. Smaller and more versatile than a tent, a bivy bag can be used to hunker down in a snow trench or on a narrow shelf on an exposed ridge.

Selecting a Campsite

The ideal campsite has great views, a nearby water source, protection from the elements, and flat space for tents and cooking. But selecting a campsite usually involves trade-offs. Climbers may walk past an idyllic forest spot in favor of a cramped mountain ledge closer to a summit.

Wind. Prevailing winds are an important consideration in choosing a campsite. A ridgetop camp is exposed, and a notch or low point on a ridge is windiest of all. Alpine breezes can be capricious. An afternoon breeze blowing upslope may reverse at night as heavy, chilled air rolls downslope from snowfields. Chilly air flows downward during settled weather, following valleys and creek beds, and collects in depressions and basins. Air is often several degrees cooler near a river or lake at night than on the knolls above. Alternatively, a campsite on a ridge with a gentle breeze may provide relief from mosquitoes on a warm summer night.

Consider wind direction when pitching a tent. Pitching camp on the lee side of a clump of trees or rocks is often best. Facing the door into the wind in fair weather minimizes flapping. In stormy conditions, pitch the tent door away from wind-driven rain and snow.

Location. Consider how changing conditions may affect the campsite. For example, avoid camping in washes or gullies, which are susceptible to flash floods during a

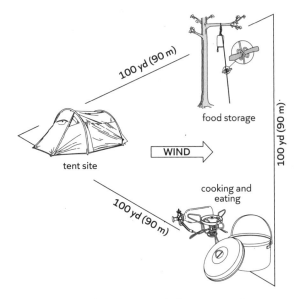

Fig. 3-7. *Optimal campsite triangle for camping in bear habitat: camp kitchen with clear visibility in all directions; separate storage area for food, cooking gear, and aromatic items; tent site upwind.*

thunderstorm. Consider that a river or stream may rise if conditions change. The braided rivers in the interior of Alaska, for example, often rise considerably from glacial runoff as the temperature warms up throughout the day. In winter or in the high country, make sure the tent is clear of possible avalanche paths or rockfall. If you camp under trees, look up to assess their health. Avoid camping near potential blowdowns or falling branches.

Leave No Trace. The more human traffic and the more fragile the setting, the more careful climbers need to be in selecting a campsite (see the "Three Cardinal Rules for Leave No Trace Camping" sidebar). The detailed campsite discussion related to the seven principles of Leave No Trace in Chapter 7, Protecting the Outdoors, can be summarized as follows:

- **Best choices:** Well-used, established sites; snow; rock slab
- **Adequate choices:** Sandy, gravelly, or dirt flat; duff in deep forest
- **Poor choices:** Grass-covered meadow; plant-covered meadow above timberline
- **Worst choice:** Waterfront along lakes and streams

Bear country. Many wild areas are also home to bears, and camping in bear country means thinking about how

3

THREE CARDINAL RULES FOR LEAVE NO TRACE CAMPING

1. **Camp gently.** Use established campsites or durable surfaces whenever possible. Research special issues for the areas where you intend to climb. Use a camp stove, not a campfire. Wash bodies and dishes well away from campsites and water sources.

2. **Do not disturb.** Leave flowers, rocks, and wildlife undisturbed by "taking only pictures and leaving only footprints." Keep human food from wildlife to minimize the chance of unwanted human-animal encounters.

3. **Dispose of waste properly.** To dispose of human waste properly, go stealthily at least 80 steps (200 feet, 60 meters) away from water sources, trails, and campsites. In forests, dig a cat hole at least 6 inches deep to bury your poop. In the alpine, pack out human waste in a container or bag (see Chapter 7). Pack out all scraps of food and garbage, including toilet paper and hygiene products.

to avoid potential conflict. Access to human food threatens bears as well as people: bears attracted to human food sometimes become threatening and have to be killed by land managers. As you choose a campsite and set up camp, consider that bears have powerful noses and can smell you from up to a mile away.

In treeless bear country, set up camp in a triangle configuration (fig. 3-7) that is at least 100 yards (90 meters) on each side, or at least as far apart as is feasible. Establish the cooking and eating area at the point of the triangle with the best all-around visibility. Next, store food, kitchen gear (stove, pots, scrubber), and anything else with an aroma (toothpaste, lotions, and blue-bagged human waste) at another point of the triangle. Finally, station the tent site at the point of the triangle upwind of the other two points. See Cooking and Eating in Bear Country, below.

Large animals such as bears and cougars are not known to attack parties of four or more—if everyone stays together—so that can be a useful minimum group size for extended trips in wilder areas. In bear country, it is generally safer to sleep in a tent rather than out in the open. Keep in mind that bear and cougar attacks are extremely rare.

PROTECTING FOOD FROM ANIMALS

Do not leave food inside a tent. Bears, rodents, skunks, raccoons, birds, mice, and other animals can smell food and will tear into plastic bags, stuff sacks, and even packs. Ravens, crows, and jays can peck through mesh tent windows; weasels can skillfully fiddle with zippers; other animals simply gnaw through the fabric, taking food, making a mess, and ruining your shelter.

Hiding a food cache in the wilderness is generally a poor practice and prohibited in some areas. Where land managers allow you to cache with a bear-resistant container (see below), you can choose that approach. When animals discover an improperly protected cache, they get in the habit of seeking out people for food. If a bear or cougar becomes habituated to campsites as a food source, the animal may become a "problem animal" that must be relocated or killed. Remember the adage "a fed bear is a dead bear."

Bear-resistant containers are also great for protecting food from smaller critters. Best yet are permanent fixtures such as metal storage cabinets, poles, or steel wire highlines, provided more and more frequently by land managers, especially in US and Canadian national parks. Check before you go.

A less desirable, but sometimes necessary method of securing food, especially in remote locations, is to hang a stuff sack from a tree. In thickly forested areas, hanging can be a viable choice provided the food is at least 15–20 feet (4.5–6 meters) from the ground and at least 4 feet (1.2 meters) from the tree trunk. The most reliable method is the two-tree method: Sling rope or cordage as high as you can over the first tree using a weighted stuff sack or anything that won't get caught in the branches. Allow for plenty of slack and secure the middle of it with weight or by clipping it to yourself. Then toss the other end over a second tree that is at least 20 feet (6 meters) from the first tree. Clip the middle of the rope to the food bag using a girth hitch or slipknot, tie off the line from one tree, and hoist from the second until the food is high between the two trees. The line can be tied off to the trunk, a branch, or any secure anchor.

Trees may be in short supply in the alpine. If a single tree is the only option, try the Pacific Crest Trail (PCT) method and find a branch high enough and long enough to thwart climbing animals (fig. 3-8). Plan to bring a canister or Ursack for destinations without trees.

Bear-resistant canisters and bags. Managers of numerous wilderness areas in the western United States find that special bear-resistant, unbreakable plastic food canisters (fig.

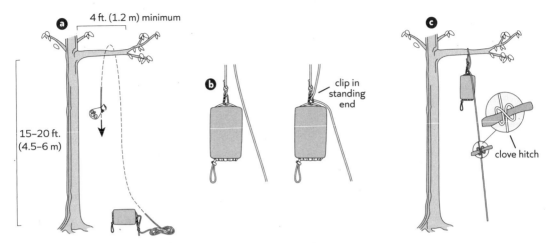

Fig. 3-8. *PCT method for hanging food: **a,** fill small stuff sack with rocks, attach it to a line, and toss sack over sturdy tree limb 15–20 feet (4.5–6 meters) from the ground, positioning it at least 4 feet (1.2 meters) from the trunk and lowering it until you can grab the line; **b,** remove stuff sack and attach food bag to line, clipping standing end through carabiner; **c,** hoist bag up to limb, then, reaching as high as you can, tie a stick into lower line with a clove hitch (see Knots, Bends, and Hitches in Chapter 8) and lower bag until stick jams against carabiner.*

3-9a) are more effective than the traditional hanging food bag. In places with significant bear populations, land managers often loan or rent these containers. Some areas require them, and hikers who don't use them may be charged significant fines. Although bulky and heavier than sacks, canisters are the most effective choice and can also double as a camp stool. In many areas, collapsible lightweight bear bags

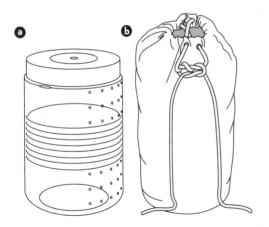

Fig. 3-9. *Bear-resistant containers: **a,** bear canister; **b,** Ursack. For the latter, cinch the bag tight, leaving no gaps, and secure cord with square knot with one or more extra wraps (shown loose for clarity).*

such as the Ursack (fig. 3-9b) are allowed as an alternative to rigid bear canisters. These bags are made of extremely strong and durable fabrics, like Spectra, advertised as impervious to bears; optional aluminum inserts help keep the food from being mashed. These sacks are often not permissible in national parks, such as Yosemite in California. Check the regulations for your destination before you leave home.

COOKING AND EATING IN BEAR COUNTRY

When you prepare a meal, remove only the items you need for that meal from your food storage area and bring them to the cooking and eating site. Maintain a lookout when cooking and eating. If a bear starts ambling toward the group, quickly clean up and pack the food in the food storage area, as long as that doesn't involve getting any closer to the bear.

At the end of the meal, wash up well with unscented soap to remove food odors from people, clothes, and cooking gear. Dispose of wash water downwind from the campsite and well away from lakes and streams (see Leave No Trace in Chapter 7, Protecting the Outdoors). Return all the cooking equipment and leftover food to the food storage site. Do not keep any food in the tent, and avoid bringing in clothes with food stains or cooking odors. When storing food to protect it from animals, include such odorous objects as toothbrushes, toothpaste, deodorants, used feminine-hygiene products, the garbage bag, and even Esbit fuel (see Types of Stove Fuel later in this chapter).

Snow and Winter Camping

To stay comfortable while camping in winter, a reliable shelter, proper insulation, and the skills to stay dry are essential. Tents are the preferred choice when weather conditions are changing, with temperatures near the freezing point, as well as in terrain with little snow, on short trips, or when you must set up camp quickly. If the sun is out at midday, the inside of a tent can be up to 40 degrees Fahrenheit (20 degrees Celsius) warmer than the air outside it, allowing climbers to dry clothes or sleeping bags. Simple snow shelters like trenches are relatively easy to create. Making more complex snow shelters such as snow caves and igloos requires more time, effort, and skill, but they may be stronger, more spacious, and even warmer in very cold weather.

TOOLS

A mountaineering snow shovel is essential for preparing tent platforms, building wind-blocking walls, digging emergency shelters, excavating climbers from avalanche debris, and sometimes even clearing climbing routes. In winter, each party member should carry a shovel. For summer snow camping, bring one shovel per tent or rope team, with a minimum of two shovels per party.

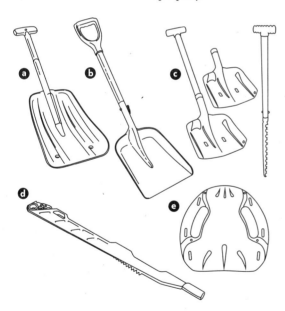

Fig. 3-10. *Snow tools:* **a,** *scoop-style shovel with T-shaped handle;* **b,** *straight-blade shovel with D-shaped handle;* **c,** *combination shovel and saw;* **d,** *saw that attaches to a ski pole;* **e,** *flat disk-shaped shovel with two side handles.*

Look for a lightweight shovel with a compact sectional or telescoping handle and a sturdy aluminum blade for chopping into icy snow. The blade may be scoop-shaped (fig. 3-10a), easier for moving large volumes of snow, or relatively straight-bladed (fig. 3-10b), easier for cutting snow blocks. A D-shaped handle (as in Figure 3-10b) or T-shaped handle (as in Figure 3-10a) can provide leverage and a firm grip.

Some snow shovel handles contain a snow saw (fig. 3-10c), the best tool for cutting blocks to make a wind-blocking snow wall around your tent (see Figure 3-11, below), a snow trench, or an igloo. A standalone snow saw that attaches to a ski pole is another option (fig. 3-10d). Snow saws are also handy for avalanche assessment. A flexible disk-shaped shovel with two side handles (fig. 3-10e) can be used in its flat form or folded into a scoop; it can also function as a snow anchor, sled, or emergency splint.

TENTS IN WINTER

Camping on snow is gentle on the landscape, and snow can provide an exceptionally level and comfortable campsite. In snow-covered terrain, camp away from hazards such as crevasses, avalanche paths, and cornices. Observe the local wind patterns: A rock-hard or sculpted snow surface indicates frequent wind, whereas an area with loose, powdery snow indicates a lee slope where wind-transported snow is deposited. An area deep in powdery snow may be protected from wind, but the tent may have to be cleared of snow frequently (see Chapters 19, Glacier Travel and Crevasse Rescue; 20, Avalanche Safety; and 27, The Cycle of Snow).

If possible, start with a flat spot. The great advantage of snow is how easy it is to create a level campsite. Establish a platform by compacting an area large enough to hold the tent and allow you to move around it. A straight-bladed shovel (as in Figure 3-10b) works well to flatten the site, tromping around in snowshoes compacts it, and a ski does a great job of grading it. Flatten and smooth the platform to keep occupants from sliding downslope and to avoid uncomfortable bumps that will ice up in the night. If the site is not level, sleep with your head toward the high side. Stake the tent at snow level: a tent in a pit will be buried faster by falling snow. For securing a tent in snow, see Anchoring a Tent, above.

After pitching the tent, dig a doorway pit about 1 foot (30 centimeters) deep (fig. 3-11), where climbers can sit comfortably to put on boots and gaiters. In bad weather, the vestibule-protected pit is a convenient, wind-protected location for the stove.

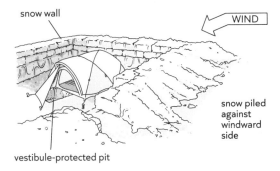

snow wall

WIND

snow piled against windward side

vestibule-protected pit

Fig. 3-11. *Typical winter camp: tent placed with its door downwind, with vestibule-protected pit as a kitchen area and bermed snow walls built upwind.*

Stormy weather may require a snow wall around most mountaineering tents to protect them from the wind and prevent a tent from collapsing (see Figure 3-11). If possible, avoid fully surrounding the tent or tents, which tends to trap new snow. Build the wall in an arc on the windward side with walls 3 to 6 feet (1 to 2 meters) high. Piled snow walls are most common, but blocks cut with a snow saw or straight-bladed snow shovel make the easiest, quickest walls and cut the wind more effectively than a rounded pile. Keep snow walls at least as far from the tent as they are high: for example, a 3-foot-high (1-meter-high) wall should be at least 3 feet away from the tent, because wind will quickly deposit snow on the wall's leeward side. Piling snow against the wall's windward side strengthens the blocks and helps minimize drifting on the leeward sides.

During most storms, snowdrifts deepen on the leeward side of tents and snow walls. Even a partially buried tent poses a risk of asphyxiation, especially if climbers use stoves inside. Snow can load the tent enough to break poles and collapse the tent. Party members will periodically have to clear snow away from the tent's top and sides. Shake the walls regularly and shovel out around the tent, taking care to remove snow from below the lower edge of the fly to maintain airflow. Be careful not to cut the tent or lines with the shovel, especially when digging out stakes; nylon slices easily when tensioned. In a severe or prolonged storm, a tent may begin to disappear between neighboring snowdrifts, making it necessary to reestablish the tent on top of the drifted snow.

Useful items for winter camping. Bring a small whisk broom to sweep snow off tents and gear. Keep a sponge handy for cleaning up spills and removing condensation from the inside of tent walls. An LED lantern can add cheer during long winter nights; for a larger community tent, a gas or solar lantern can offer tremendous brightness and warmth.

House rules for tent-bound hours. To make time spent tent-bound more pleasant, agree on a few house rules. It often helps to have one person enter the tent first to lay out sleeping pads and organize gear. If the tent is small, packs may have to be stored outside. If the tent has vestibules, brush snow from packs there or outside before bringing them inside. House rules may also dictate that climbers take their boots off outside, brush them free of snow, and place them in a waterproof boot bag to bring them inside the tent. Mountaineering or ski-touring boots with removable liners are a real advantage; you can leave the shells outside and bring the liners inside. Use stuff sacks to reduce clutter and protect personal gear. Put dry clothing inside your sleeping bag or a waterproof sack so it does not get wet or frosty from condensation.

Drying and warming gear. Sleeping bags offer an opportunity to dry out gear. Add boot liners, gloves, and socks to your bag before you go to sleep, to help dry them for the morning. Do not wear large, damp garments to bed; they will just make you and the bag wet and cold. In extreme cold, put boots inside an oversize stuff sack next to the sleeping bag to keep them from freezing. To prevent a water bottle from freezing or a compressed-gas fuel canister from getting chilled (and performing poorly at breakfast), place them inside the sleeping bag overnight.

IMPROVISE USING NATURAL FEATURES

The best shelter in snow is a four-season tent, and setting one up is quicker and easier than building a snow shelter. Knowing how to construct a snow shelter could, however, prevent an unplanned bivouac from becoming fatal. With a little improvisation, natural features can be converted into snow hideaways. Such shelters occur under logs, along riverbanks, and in the pits or wells formed when the limbs of large conifer trees deflect snow from the tree trunks.

For a tree-well shelter, enlarge the natural hole around the trunk and make a roof from any available covering, such as snow blocks, tree limbs, an emergency space blanket, or a tarp. Blocking the wind is often essential for survival, and boughs and bark can insulate and support, but only cut live trees in an emergency. Make sure your chosen location is not in the path of a potential avalanche (see Chapter 20, Avalanche Safety).

SNOW SHELTERS

In general, experienced mountaineers will not rely on snow shelters for regular camping because they are time-consuming to construct, can be dangerous, and can have a deleterious effect on the environment. That said, knowing how to build a quick snow trench in an emergency can be a lifesaver. Also see the "Improvise Using Natural Features" sidebar.

A basic emergency snow-trench shelter can be built by digging a trench some 4 to 6 feet (1.2 to 2 meters) deep, wide and long enough for the party to sleep in. Dig a narrow entryway a little deeper than the sleeping platform. Stretch a tarp over the top and weigh the edges down with snow (fig. 3-12). On a flat site, provide some slope to the tarp by building up the snow on one side of the trench. This quick shelter works moderately well in wind or rain, but a heavy snowfall can collapse the roof. Extended snow probes or ski poles can be used as a

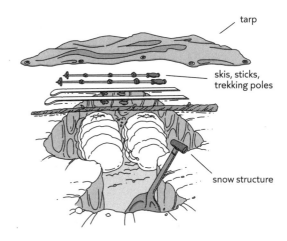

Fig. 3-12. Basic snow trench roofed with a tarp: dig a narrow entryway a little deeper than the sleeping platform.

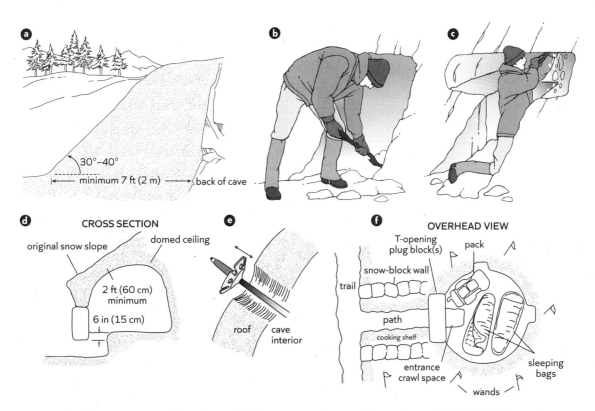

*Fig. 3-13. Building a snow cave: **a,** choose location; **b,** dig entrance; **c,** dig inward, expanding up, left, and right; **d,** expand to desired size, with platform above entryway; **e,** create ventilation holes; **f,** smooth ceiling, dig meltwater path, erect wind blocks and cooking shelf, and mark cave perimeter.*

supporting roof lattice for the tarp. As with all snow shelters, the smaller the trench, the easier it is to keep warm. Mark all snow shelters (including tents) with wands for visibility.

Snow caves should be reserved for special situations and not relied on in most snow-camping situations. The snow must be deep enough to leave about 2 feet (60 centimeters) of ceiling thickness. A strong and stable cave also requires somewhat consolidated snow. Several people can shelter in one snow cave, and a well-built cave dug in firm snow is a secure structure. However, if the outside temperature is warming toward freezing, a tent or tree-well shelter may be a better choice, since the collapse of a snow cave roof can cause serious injury.

Find a short snowdrift—7 feet (2 meters) deep at minimum—on a short 30- to 40-degree slope (fig. 3-13a) clear of any potential avalanche hazard (see Chapter 20, Avalanche Safety). The snow must be deep enough that you will not hit ground before the entire cave is excavated. Dig an entry about 3 feet (1 meter) into the slope, making it about 1.5 feet (0.5 meter) wide and 5 feet (1.5 meters) high (fig. 3-13b). Then create a temporary construction-debris exit slot by digging a waist-high platform centered on the entryway, forming a T that is 4 feet (1.2 meters) wide by 1.5 feet (0.5 meter) high (fig. 3-13c). Develop this platform so that it forms a horizontal slot extending into the slope, allowing for easy snow removal. Shovel snow out through the horizontal slot; a second person, working outside, can clear the snow away.

When digging a snow cave, it is important to keep the sleeping area above the entrance so that the occupants' body heat can warm the space (fig. 3-13d). Doming and smoothing the ceiling prevents dripping. Make sure to allow for ventilation (fig. 3-13e). The snow cave can be finished with snow-block walls and a cooking shelf shielded from the wind, plus wands to mark where the structure is to avoid people walking on it and collapsing it (fig. 3-13f). Do not cook inside the cave.

Snow kitchens are common for both small and large groups for melting water out of the wind (fig. 3-14). A snow kitchen allows campers to socialize and enjoy each other's company.

If conditions are right, igloos are undeniably fun to build and use, but their complex and time-intensive construction makes them impractical on most mountaineering trips or in an emergency. A possible exception might be for a long-term base camp in a remote flat area.

Fig. 3-14. *A snow kitchen is a sociable, useful open-air feature for any snow shelter setup.*

Stoves

Fire is the sixth Ten Essential, and for fire, mountaineers rely on camp stoves. Stoves are faster, cleaner, and more convenient than campfires for backcountry travel, and safer for forests around the world that are at increasing risk of wildfire. They will operate under almost any conditions with minimal environmental impact. Whatever stove and fuel you choose, practice using your stove at home first. When choosing the right stove (see Types of Stoves, below), consider four key factors:

Fuel preference. Canister fuel dominates the outdoor industry in most places these days, but in some countries liquid or alternative fuels (see Types of Fuel, below) are sometimes easier to find or more suitable for cold weather, high altitudes, or ultralightweight travel.

Boil or simmer. Some stoves are tiny infernos optimized to boil water and melt snow, while others are appropriate for more complex cooking. Consider your cooking preferences when choosing your stove.

Windy weather. A wind of merely 5 miles (8 kilometers) per hour can double to triple the fuel consumption of an unprotected stove-on-top canister stove. To conserve fuel if you anticipate windy conditions, a windproof canister system stove or a remote-fuel stove is highly recommended. Remote-fuel stoves allow a full windscreen to protect the burner from the heat-stealing wind while keeping the fuel reservoir safely away from the inferno. If you are using a stove-on-top canister stove or personal canister system stove, shield the windward side with rocks or gear, but *do* *not* encircle the stove with a windscreen or the trapped heat will have you serving a Molotov cocktail.

Cooking for a crowd. For one or two climbers sharing a pot up to about 1.5 quarts (liters), stove-on-top and canister system stoves are best. Groups of four or more, or those with substantial snow to melt, need a 2- to 5-liter pot paired with a remote-fuel stove, which is low profile and therefore sufficiently stable for larger pots. Canister system stoves currently can accommodate their specially designed pots of up to 2.5 quarts (liters).

TYPES OF FUEL

Because the type of fuel drives a stove's design and functionality, it is helpful to learn about fuels. Table 3-3 compares advantages and disadvantages of different types of fuel. Whatever the fuel, avoid spills and flare-ups to spare your gear and the increasingly fire-prone landscape.

Canister fuel. A convenient fuel type, canisters of liquefied petroleum gas (LPG) are blends of isobutane, propane, and butane. As the self-sealing valve opens, the pressure in the canister forces fuel out, eliminating both priming and pumping. The stoves they power are popular and easy to light, with good flame control, immediate maximum heat output, and no chance of fuel spills. But because the gases are liquefied (pressurized), cold and high altitude often hinder stove performance. Also, not all canisters are interchangeable. Butane canisters, which are usually the cheapest, work best in warm weather. For reasonable performance at high altitude and cold temperatures, purchase blends of isobutane and propane.

Liquid fuels. White gas and kerosene used to be the most popular mountaineering stove fuels in North America and Europe, respectively. These fuels pack about the same heat output per ounce or gram as LPG and so are still favored for expeditions due to their low cost, wide availability, sustainability (fuel bottles can be refilled), and performance in cold high-altitude locations. Some stoves run only a single type of liquid fuel. Multifuel stoves, with their ability to burn white gas, kerosene, diesel, and others, are a reliable choice for international trips where fuel may be difficult to find; unleaded automobile gas can be used, but fuel additives are prone to clogging stoves.

TYPES OF STOVES

Once you have chosen your preferred fuel, you can then choose the type of stove for your trip.

Canister stoves. Simple canister stoves come in two types and run on canisters of compressed gas. Stove-on-top canister stoves (fig. 3-15a) simply screw onto the canister, which forms the base. The Snow Peak GigaPower stove and MSR PocketRocket are both lightweight and compact, but susceptible to wind and prone to tipping over. Do not use a full windscreen since that can superheat a canister and possibly cause it to explode. Remote-fuel canister stoves are low-profile stoves that attach the canister to the burner via a flexible hose (fig. 3-15b). They accommodate larger pots and are compatible with full windscreens. Some remote-fuel canister stoves permit the canister to be inverted to supply liquid fuel to the burner, improving performance in cold weather.

TABLE 3-3. COMPARISON OF POPULAR STOVE FUELS			
FUEL TYPE	**ADVANTAGES**	**DISADVANTAGES**	**BEST USED FOR**
CANISTER: Blends of isobutane, propane, and butane	No priming or pumping required. Almost no maintenance. Immediate maximum heat output. Some stoves able to simmer. Readily available in North America, Patagonia, the Himalaya, Pakistan, Europe, South Africa, and Mexico.	Spent canisters must be carried out. Not available everywhere. Tricky to judge fuel level (see "Calculating the Contents of a Fuel Canister" sidebar). Less efficient in cold temperatures.	Short, light trips under any conditions. Good at high altitudes if temperatures are above freezing or somewhat colder (with pressure-regulated stove).
LIQUID: White gas or naphtha (for example, Coleman fuel, MSR fuel), kerosene, diesel, jet fuel, aviation gas, unleaded automobile gas	Widely available and inexpensive. Stable stove designs. Simple to judge fuel level and pack exact amounts. No spent canisters.	Heavier stove that requires priming. Requires separate fuel bottle. Fuel spills possible and may increase forest fire risk. Stoves require periodic maintenance and tinkering (for example, matching jets to fuel).	Winter (very cold) or high-elevation areas. International expeditions where fuel availability is unknown. Large groups.

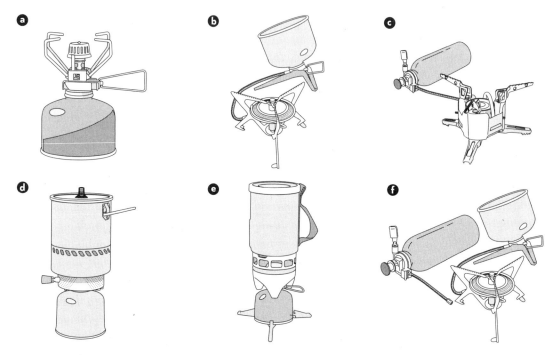

Fig. 3-15. *Types of mountaineering stoves:* **a,** *stove-on-top canister stove;* **b,** *remote-fuel canister stove;* **c,** *liquid fuel stove;* **d,** *windproof canister system stove;* **e,** *personal canister system stove;* **f,** *dual-fuel stove.*

Liquid fuel stoves. Most liquid fuel stoves connect to refillable fuel bottles and run on white gas (fig. 3-15c). If you travel to remote places, consider a stove that can burn other liquid fuels (see below). The liquid fuel bottle must be pumped up to operating pressure by hand each time the stove is lit and periodically during use for full heat output. This hand pumping of a liquid fuel stove to full operating pressure allows the user to compensate for cold and elevation.

Since liquid fuel bottles are refillable, their use generates no empty canisters that you must pack out for recycling. Some models run only on white gas (naphtha). Multifuel models, however, like the MSR XGK EX, burn a wide variety of "petrol" found around the world, including white gas, kerosene, diesel, and even, in a pinch, unleaded automobile gas—although diesel fuels generally work well only on specifically engineered stoves fitted with the proper jets.

Canister system stoves. These stoves also use compressed-gas canisters, but they up the ante with specially integrated pots with built-in heat exchangers to capture as much heat as possible. These stoves are medium-weight and compact, with the stove and fuel stowable within the pot. Canister- system stoves come in two types. Windproof systems (fig. 3-15d) like the MSR Reactor hide the flame and are

the most efficient stoves available, remaining almost as efficient in windy conditions. They do not need a windscreen. Personal canister system stoves (fig. 3-15e) are designed to allow you to cook and eat from a single container but are susceptible to wind and incompatible with windscreens. If you can see the flame, the stove is not windproof.

Dual-fuel stoves. Hybrid-fuel stoves (fig. 3-15f) like the MSR WhisperLite Universal run off either liquid fuel or compressed-gas canisters, delivering the convenience of canister fuels but easily switching over to liquid fuels for longer trips, cold weather, or use in international locales.

Accessories

A few stove accessories, such as windscreens and hanging kits, can be quite helpful.

Windscreens. A full wraparound aluminum windscreen (fig. 3-16a) is necessary for many stoves to be efficient. Never wrap a windscreen around any canister stove, however, unless you can exclude the canister itself from the windscreen, such as with a remote-fuel canister stove. Using a windscreen incorrectly may cause the canister to explode.

Hanging kits. Stove-on-top canister stoves and canister system stoves are prone to tipping. Hanging kits allow the

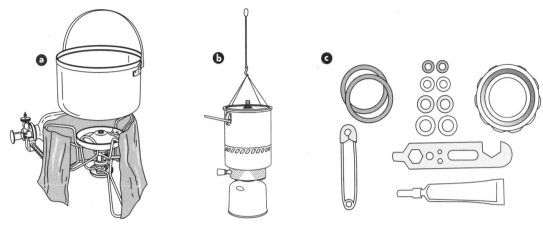

Fig. 3-16. *Stove accessories: **a,** windscreen; **b,** hanging kit; **c,** liquid-fuel stove maintenance kit.*

stove and pot to hang as an integral unit from a chain or wire (fig. 3-16b). They are primarily used for big wall climbing and at high camp on expeditions.

Maintenance kit. Liquid fuel stoves can require replacement seals and pump cups. A maintenance kit should also include a tightening tool and other components (fig. 3-16c).

ALTERNATIVE FUELS AND STOVES

Biofuel stoves efficiently burn fuel including small pieces of dead wood and are an option in some forests. Freedom from buying or carrying fuel gives these stoves a unique appeal. For ultralightweight cooking, solid fuel stoves (using Esbit or hexamine fuel tablets) and alcohol stoves (running off 95 percent grain alcohol, marine stove fuel, and/or other alcohols) barely register on the weight scale. These featherweights are sufficient for heating water for drinks and freeze-dried meals but not for melting snow and ice. MSR PocketRocket stoves are the standard for long-distance thru-hikers, for example on the Pacific Crest and Appalachian Trails.

Alternative stoves are often frowned on in the backcountry because of the risk of spilling and wildfire ignition. Burning alcohol or wood is prohibited in many backcountry areas in the US. With climate change and the increased risks of wildfire, these concerns are growing.

HOW STOVES OPERATE

A stove ignites when a spark or flame is applied to vaporized fuel at the burner. While some stoves have integrated piezo igniters (which create a small electric charge), they are notoriously unreliable. With most stoves, you must use matches or a lighter. In stormy conditions, you may need

TIPS FOR IMPROVING PERFORMANCE OF CANISTER STOVES

There are some very simple ways to improve the performance of canister stoves. Consider these tips to get the most out of your stove and fuel canisters:

- Use a windproof canister system stove.
- Alternatively, use a remote-fuel canister stove that allows a liquid feed (upside-down cartridge) mode. Wrap a windscreen around the pot, allowing about a ½-inch (1- to 2-centimeter) gap.
- Use a pressure-regulated stove, which makes sure the stove receives fuel at a steady pace and precise (low) pressure. Look for this feature on your stove specs.
- Use isobutane fuel mixes and, prior to use, keep them warm in a sleeping bag or inside your puffy coat.
- Insulate canisters from the cold ground. A circle of cardboard wrapped in foil is inexpensive.
- Keep a lid on the cook pot and do not boil contents unless necessary.
- While a stove is in use, the evaporating liquid chills the canister exterior; it may even cause frost to form on the canister. To minimize a loss of pressure and performance, swap out cold canisters for warm ones or sit the canister in a bowl of tepid (even warm) water during use.
- Run the stove slightly below maximum for increased efficiency.

waterproof or stormproof matches or several disposable lighters. Keep matches and lighters dry.

With canister stoves running in upright mode, the fuel is already vaporized. Starting the stove is simply a matter of turning the regulating valve and lighting the released fuel. See the "Tips for Improving Performance of Canister Stoves" sidebar for once the stove is in operation.

In contrast, a liquid fuel stove must be primed by preheating the generator tube. Using the stove's valve, release a small amount of fuel (or alcohol carried for the purpose) into the priming cup and light it, with the stove off, thus preheating the generator tube. When the flame from the priming process wanes, open the fuel regulator valve. The liquid fuel vaporizes as it passes through the now-hot generator tube toward the jet, igniting from the residual priming cup flame. Be aware of pitfalls: Using too much priming fuel prolongs the process and wastes fuel. Opening the regulator valve too soon may cause a dangerous flare-up; wait for the flame to subside but not go out. Opening the regulator valve after the priming fuel has extinguished requires quick, careful action with a match or lighter.

Stoves can stop working, often at inconvenient times. In windy, dusty conditions, debris can clog the jet and cause a stove to fail. With more than two climbers, bring a backup stove: modern stoves are compact and lightweight, making the added burden a reasonable trade-off—one integral to having the eighth and ninth Ten Essentials, "extra food" and "extra water."

Liquid fuel stoves are finicky. Clean them regularly and rebuild them periodically, replacing seals and pump cups as necessary. Read the manufacturer's instructions to learn what tools are needed and practice repairing the stove at home.

STOVE SAFETY PRECAUTIONS

Careless stove operation has resulted in tents being blown up, equipment burned, fires started, and injuries. Before lighting a stove, check fuel lines, valves, and connections for leaks.

Let a stove cool completely before changing canisters or adding liquid fuel. Change pressurized fuel canisters and fill and start liquid fuel stoves, outside tents and away from other open flames. Avoid spill fuel; in subfreezing temperatures, liquid petroleum fuel or alcohol can quickly freeze skin.

Never use a full wraparound windscreen with any canister stove unless you can exclude the canister from the windscreen, such as with a remote-fuel stove. An incorrectly used windscreen can superheat the canister and cause it to explode.

TABLE 3-4. COMPARING BASELINE PERFORMANCE OF STOVES

STOVE TYPE	TIME REQUIRED TO BOIL 1 QUART OF WATER	EFFICIENCY FACTOR
Canister		
Stove-on-top	3–4 minutes	1.8
Remote-fuel	3–4 minutes	1.8
Liquid Fuel		
Single-fuel or multifuel	3–4 minutes	1.6
Canister System		
Windproof	3–4 minutes	2.5
Personal	3–4 minutes	2.5
Alternative Fuel		
Esbit (solid fuel)	10 minutes or longer	1.0
Alcohol	10 minutes or longer	0.7

Notes: *Efficiency factor is quarts boiled per ounce of fuel. For canisters, 1 oz. (28 g) is by fuel weight; for liquid fuels, 1 oz. is a fluid ounce, which weighs 0.66–0.8 oz. (19-23 g), depending on fuel's specific gravity. Baseline performance calculated at 70°F (21°C) with no wind.*

HOW MUCH FUEL?

Taking sufficient fuel is key to the success of any wilderness trip. Fuel, like water, is heavy, and you may be tempted to carry less to keep your pack light. Yet when an open fire is not an option, running out of fuel means eating cold food, and running out when snow is the only source of drinking water puts climbers and the journey at risk.

To calculate how much fuel is needed for a wilderness trip, consider your party's needs, the stove type, and the fuel type. Longer trips require careful computation tempered by experience, plus a cushion for the unexpected. For amounts of water needed per person, a good estimate is between 0.75 and 1 quart (liter) of hot water per meal and 3 quarts (liters) of drinking water per day per climber. Dividing the quarts that need to be boiled by your type of stove's efficiency factor (see Table 3-4) gives the baseline number of ounces of fuel required. For example, on a simple overnight glacier climbing trip under baseline conditions, a single 8-ounce (227-gram) canister used with a stove-on-top system will provide 6 quarts (liters) of drinking water and 4 quarts (liters) of boiled water with 3.6 ounces (102 grams) of fuel to spare.

Remember that when snow and ice are the only sources of water, you will need considerably more fuel to melt drinking water. If possible, it is best to save fuel by melting snow (see the "Tips for Melting Snow" sidebar), not boiling it, and then purifying the melted snow as you would for water from any other natural source (see Water Treatment later in this chapter).

Tips for melting snow. Melting snow or ice from its frozen state at 32 degrees Fahrenheit (0 degrees Celsius) to liquid water requires a surprising amount of fuel. In fact, it takes almost the same amount of energy to first melt ice as it does to increase the water's temperature to boiling. Always start with some water in the pot with the snow or ice to prevent overheating and improve heat transfer. Yes, it is possible to burn a pot filled with snow!

To save fuel, melt snow on the stove and purify it by means other than boiling. Consider a large, aluminum pot for big groups and working an "assembly" line to feed snow, melt it, and purify the water. On a sunny summit day, a black plastic bag filled with snow may fill a large pot ready for thirsty climbers returning to camp.

Adverse factors. When preparing for a trip, it is critical to calculate how much fuel you will need, adding any adverse environmental factors into the equation. Baseline calculations assume that you are starting with room-temperature

---

CALCULATING THE CONTENTS OF A FUEL CANISTER

To calculate the fuel remaining in a canister, do one of the following:

- At home, weigh the used canister on a kitchen scale. Using the canister's original weight, determine how many ounces of fuel are left. Write that value on the side of the canister.

- Float canister in water (first "burping" the bottom concavity) and compare the float line against a full canister's (some have an index).

- Shake and guess. Experience will improve accuracy.

After a trip, record approximately how much fuel is left with a permanent marker on the side of the container.

---

water (70 degrees Fahrenheit, 21 degrees Celsius) and heating that water to boiling in still air. Yet real-world climbing conditions typically require heating cold water, or perhaps even snow, at high elevations and often in windy weather. These adverse factors can increase fuel consumption significantly. For details, see Table 3-5.

The impact of wind on fuel consumption is highly stove dependent. Breezy conditions can double or triple the fuel consumption of an unprotected stove-on-top canister stove

---

TABLE 3-5. SAMPLE FUEL CALCULATIONS FOR ONE PERSON PER DAY

FUEL NEEDED TO MELT SNOW FOR WATER	CANISTER STOVE-ON-TOP	LIQUID FUEL	WINDPROOF[a] CANISTER SYSTEM
Melt snow or ice to 33°F (1°C) to yield 5 liters water: 5 liters water ÷ stove's efficiency factor = fuel required	5 liters water ÷ 1.8 = 2.8 ounces fuel	5 liters water ÷ 1.6 = 3.1 fluid ounces fuel	5 liters water ÷ 2.5 = 2 ounces fuel
Warm 5 liters 33°F (1°C) water up to 70°F (21°C) for drinking or boiling: 5 liters water ÷ by stove's efficiency factor × 25% = fuel required	5 liters ÷ 1.8 × 25% = 0.7 ounce	5 liters ÷ 1.6 × 25% = 0.8 fluid ounce	5 liters ÷ 2.5 × 25% = 0.5 ounces
Boil 2 liters water from 70°F (21°C): 2 liters divided by stove's efficiency factor	2 liters ÷ 1.8 = 1.1 ounces	2 liters ÷ 1.6 = 1.3 fluid ounces	2 liters ÷ 2.5 = 0.8 ounce
Subtotal	4.6 ounces	5.2 fluid ounces	3.3 ounces
Additional fuel required in windy conditions	add 100%	add 20%	add 10%
Subtotal × % (windy conditions) for each stove type	4.6 ounces	1.0 fluid ounce	0.3 ounce
Total	9.2 ounces	6.2 fluid ounces	3.6 ounces

Notes: *Liquid fuel column assumes use of white gas and a windscreen. Fuel needed depends on stove's efficiency factor: 1.8 for canister stove-on-top; 1.6 for liquid fuel, white gas plus windscreen; 2.5 for windproof canister system. Totals exclude weight of canisters and fuel bottles. One liter equals approximately one quart. To convert ounces to grams, multiply by 28.35. To convert fluid ounces to milliliters, multiply by 29.6. To convert milliliters to grams, multiply by 66% to 80%, depending on specific gravity of fuel type (fuel is lighter than water); this example uses specific gravity of white gas (70%).*

DANGERS OF COOKING INSIDE A TENT

Do not cook inside a tent unless it is so windy that the stove will not operate outside or so cold that the cook risks developing hypothermia. The risks of cooking inside a tent range from relatively minor (spilling hot water or food onto sleeping bags or clothes) to deadly (catching your tent on fire or exposing your climbing team to carbon monoxide poisoning). If it is absolutely necessary to cook inside a tent, follow these safety rules:

- Light a liquid fuel stove outside or near a tent door so you can toss it away if it flares. Wait until it is running smoothly before bringing it inside and putting a pot on top.

- Cook near the tent door or in a vestibule for better ventilation. In an emergency, you can also throw the stove outside quickly.

- Run stoves on a high setting to make sure as much fuel combusts as possible. Colorless and odorless, carbon monoxide is absorbed into the blood faster at high altitudes. Be sure you allow for plenty of ventilation.

or a personal canister system, and stronger wind can prevent boiling altogether. Stoves that allow a windscreen do much better, and windproof stoves are almost unaffected. Temperatures substantially below freezing require additional fuel to first heat the snow or ice up to freezing before it can be melted further.

Sample fuel calculation. Table 3-5 details a step-by-step example calculation for fuel needs for one climber per day when conditions are just below freezing. The baseline calculation assumes 2 quarts (or liters) of "room-temperature" water is heated to boiling in windless conditions for cooking meals (two meals, each requiring 0.75 to 1 quart or liter). "Cooking" for this example requires simply bringing water to a boil without simmering. Then the adverse conditions are factored in: First the climber must melt snow or ice to cold water (33 degrees Fahrenheit, 1 degree Celsius), which requires twice as much fuel as the baseline. The climber will also melt snow or ice and warm it to "room temperature" for an additional 3 quarts (3 liters) of drinking water; this requires an additional 25 percent fuel beyond the baseline. (These water requirements may be insufficient, depending on conditions.)

After subtotaling these calculations, the sample calculation factors in windy conditions: the stoves are exposed to an 8-mile-per-hour (13-kilometer-per-hour) wind. The effect of wind can be dramatic but varies greatly depending

on the stove design. The calculations in Table 3-5 demonstrate that this climber will require anywhere from 3.4 to 8.6 ounces (96 to 244 grams) of fuel per day—without factoring in a cushion for the unexpected.

STORING LIQUID FUEL

Carry extra white gas or kerosene in a metal bottle designed to store fuel, with a screw top and intact rubber or synthetic gasket (some synthetics are safer than rubber). Clearly label the fuel container to distinguish it from other containers, such as water bottles, and stow it in a place where any leaks will not contaminate food.

Leave about 1 inch (2.5 centimeters) of air space in the stove's fuel reservoir, rather than filling it to the brim, to prevent excessive pressure buildup. At the end of the season, empty stoves of any fuel. Date any leftover fuel to be sure to use it by the end of the next season. Aging fuel becomes gummy and prone to clogging.

RECYCLING CANISTERS

Because they are made of steel, fuel canisters are recyclable in many places when empty. Make sure the canister is empty before you puncture it with an ice axe or screwdriver. Then you can flatten the container walls. (See the "Calculating the Contents of a Fuel Canister" sidebar.)

Water

With the sustained exertion of mountaineering, skin, mucous membranes, and lungs release large amounts of moisture into high-altitude mountain air. Do not ignore your thirst—the body's fine-tuned notification system—and also monitor your urine: a darker-than-normal color means you are dehydrated. At high elevations, dehydration can contribute to nausea that reduces your desire to take in fluids. It can also cause fatigue, disorientation, and headaches. Dehydration becomes debilitating more quickly than you might expect: it is a factor in several mountain maladies, including acute mountain sickness (see Dehydration in Chapter 24, First Aid). High-altitude climbing results in increased urination in response to the body's acid-base balance and aids in the acclimatization process. Your body needs a lot more water when climbing at altitude.

"Extra water" is on the list of Ten Essentials. Plan ahead so that you will have sufficient water on mountaineering adventures. To combat dehydration, drink more water than usual, perhaps up to 2 extra quarts, during the 24-hour period before a climb. (*Note:* Since a quart is nearly the same quantity as a liter, metric conversions for quarts are not given in this section.) It is wise to drink a cup or two of water immediately before beginning a climb.

During the climb, keep water handy and hydrate regularly, even if you do not feel thirsty. Keep a bottle within easy reach. Some climbers use a hydration bladder in their pack, with a tube clipped to the shoulder strap for convenient sipping. Under winter conditions, protect the bladder, hose, and mouthpiece from freezing, for example, by running the hose through an insulated backpack sleeve. Some climbers blow into the hose to keep it from freezing, but bottles are a less risky alternative. Climbers may add flavors or electrolytes to make drinking water more appealing.

Hydration is essential and, except for critical emergencies, drinking clean water is imperative (see the "Essential Water Tips" sidebar). Use only purified water (or tap water from home, as long as it lasts) for dishwashing and brushing teeth. On longer trips, climbers must replenish water on the go. Getting water from natural sources and making it potable (drinkable) requires tools and knowledge.

Everyone needs to drink plenty of water to stay hydrated and avoid fatigue. Climbing parties should allow climbers the time and opportunity to urinate on a regular basis to avoid dehydration, embarrassment, and dangerous situations (see Leave No Trace in Chapter 7, Protecting the Outdoors). Finding a safe and private place to pee is more difficult for women. Some are comfortable undoing the quick-release rear riser straps on their climbing harness for their leg loops and pulling down their pants. Alternatively, female urination devices (commercially developed pee funnels) allow women to urinate through their pants fly while standing. Never remove your climbing harness or untie from the rope unless you are in a safe situation.

SOURCES OF WATER

Some climbs have abundant streams and snowfields to replenish water supplies, but often the high peaks are bone-dry or frozen solid, and climbers must either carry water or melt snow or ice. For most people, 1.5 to 3 quarts of water per day is enough. Take more than you think you will need. During a tough three-day climb, each person might drink 6 quarts while hiking and climbing, plus another 5 quarts in camp. It is preferable to replenish supplies from lakes, streams, and snow than to try to carry that much water, which weighs about 2 pounds per US quart (1 kilogram per liter).

When the only water source along the trail is snow, fill up a water bottle with snow and hang it on the outside of your pack. Adding some water to the snow in the bottle hastens melting time. Try catching the drips from overhanging eaves of melting snow. Or find a tongue of snow that is slowly melting into a trickle, dredge a depression below, let the silt settle, and channel the resulting puddle into a container.

Melt enough snow in the evening to fill all water bottles and cooking pots. A full pot of water buried in snow overnight will usually not freeze. If you have sufficient sun and time, set out pots of snow to melt in the sun while you summit. A black plastic garbage bag filled with snow can provide a surprising volume of water. Otherwise, use the stove. Either way, get the snow from a drinking snow pit, well away from the designated toilet and cleaning areas. The snow need not be boiled if it will be otherwise purified, and with care it can be filtered directly from the pot as it melts. A pot can burn if it contains only dry snow—add a little water to it. If you are cooking in the tent vestibule, collect snow in a stuff sack before bringing it inside.

PATHOGENS IN WATER

There are few joys as supreme as naively drinking refreshing alpine water right from the source. We still lack data on water quality in remote areas, and although most of it may be free of pathogens, purifying it is the best practice. Animal and human waste can contaminate water and older snow, and microscopic organisms can survive freezing temperatures. As tainted snow melts, it trickles and percolates its way to contaminate other snow a long distance away. Purify melted snow just as if it were any other water source. Treat water to guard against the three types of waterborne pathogens: parasites, bacteria, and viruses.

ESSENTIAL WATER TIPS

- **Always carry some method to treat water for drinking.** Chlorine dioxide is reliable, lightweight, cheap, and compact.

- **Clean your hands after using the bathroom** to avoid the common "fecal-oral" route to illness.

- **Check for risk of virus contamination in wilderness waters in the location you will visit.** The greatest risk for water-associated viral infections is other humans. Hand hygiene and cleaning cooking and other shared equipment are the most important interventions to prevent disease transmission. While animal viruses may be found in wilderness water sources, human viruses are uncommon in those same sources in North America.

TABLE 3-6. PURIFYING WATERBORNE PATHOGENS				
	PATHOGENS TREATED			
PURIFICATION METHOD	Parasites and Protozoa	Bacteria	Viruses	Treats All Pathogens
Boiling	Yes	Yes	Yes	Yes
Gravity-fed purifier-filter	Yes	Yes	Yes	Yes
Microfilter	Yes	Yes	No	No
Chlorine dioxide drops or tablets	Yes	Yes	Yes	Yes
Chlorine or iodine	Unreliable	Yes	Yes	No
UV light purifier plus microfilter	Yes	Yes	Yes	Yes

Note: Pathogens in column subheads are listed in order from largest (parasites and protozoa) to smallest (viruses).

Parasites. Larger parasites include amoebas, tapeworms, and flatworms. Smaller parasites include single-cell protozoa such as *Giardia lamblia* ("giardia") and *Cryptosporidium parvum* ("crypto"), which are between 1 and 20 microns in size (for context, the period at the end of this sentence is roughly 500 microns). Exposure to giardia and crypto are major health concerns for alpine travelers. Both are found in backcountry waters worldwide, including all of North America, but there are insufficient data to accurately assess frequency and risk. The illnesses giardiasis and cryptosporidiosis take two to twenty days to manifest, with symptoms including intense nausea, diarrhea, stomach cramps, fever, headaches, flatulence, and belches that reek like rotten eggs. Some parasites have tough cell walls that are resistant to chemical treatment. But because of their larger size, they are easily filtered, and boiling kills them.

Another protozoan, *Cyclospora*, which commonly contaminates water in Nepal during spring and summer, is increasingly found in other areas, including North America. About the same size as crypto and susceptible to the same chemicals, it can be treated in the same way.

Bacteria. Mountain waters contain a wide range of bacteria, tiny living organisms between 0.1 and 10 microns in size. Common harmful waterborne bacteria include *Salmonella* species (incubation period 12–36 hours), *Campylobacter jejuni* (incubation three to five days), and *Escherichia coli*, or *E. coli* (incubation 24–72 hours). In some parts of the world, water may contain bacteria that cause severe illnesses such as cholera, dysentery, and typhoid. Like viruses, most bacteria can be effectively killed with chemicals. Bacteria are larger than viruses, so they can be removed more easily with the proper filters. Boiling kills all bacteria.

Viruses. Viruses such as *Hepatovirus* (causes hepatitis A), *Rotavirus* (causes diarrhea), *Enterovirus* (causes respiratory ailments, among others), and *Norovirus* (causes vomiting and diarrhea) are exceptionally tiny pathogens causing diseases that can be contracted by drinking water contaminated with feces. (SARS-CoV-2, the virus that causes COVID-19, which emerged as a global pandemic in 2019 and persists, is airborne, not waterborne.) Viruses are often species-specific, and therefore viruses that infect humans via water sources are usually spread through contamination by human waste. Each climbing location has its own risk level for different viruses, so it is wise to consult a reputable public health source as part of trip planning.

Although wilderness waters in North America are usually free of pathogenic human viruses, the risk comes from human visitors and how they handle waste, so it never hurts to treat against viruses. Every year people get sick from viruses in heavily used lakes. Viruses are easily killed with chemical treatment but are too tiny to be removed by most filters. Boiling kills viruses.

Table 3-6 summarizes the major water purification methods to eliminate human pathogens from water sources in the wilderness.

WATER TREATMENT

Water treatment is a combination of filtering and purification. The principal methods of backcountry water treatment are boiling, filtering, and chemical treatment (see Table 3-7). No single method is best for every situation—boiling is not always practical due to fuel-carrying limitations, and cold water and turbidity affect some purification methods. See More Considerations for Water Treatment, below.

Boiling

Boiling, the surefire method of water purification, kills all waterborne pathogens and does not affect how water tastes.

TABLE 3-7. COMPARISON OF WATER TREATMENT METHODS

METHOD	PURIFIES	ADVANTAGES	DISADVANTAGES
Boiling	Yes	Simple. Water's flavor not altered. Very effective against parasites, protozoa, bacteria, and viruses.	Slow. Inconvenient. Requires additional fuel, which adds weight to pack.
Gravity-fed purifier-filter	Yes	Quick. Comprehensive treatment. Great for groups. Water's flavor and clarity improved. Very effective against parasites, protozoa, bacteria, and viruses.	Some are bulky or heavy. May clog or break. Must be protected from freezing. Possible cross-contamination from hoses.
Microfilter	No	Quick. Pump-style microfilter allows filtering from a pot while melting snow. Water's flavor and clarity improved. Very effective against parasites, protozoa, and bacteria. Prevents some bottle-thread and stirring contamination.	Some are bulky or heavy. May clog or break. Squeeze and straw-style filters must be protected from freezing. Ineffective against viruses, but may be combined with chemical treatment or UV light to protect against viruses. Possible cross-contamination from hoses.
Chlorine dioxide tablets or drops	Yes	Water's flavor not altered significantly. Lightweight and compact. Inexpensive.	Waiting times can be long. Tablets may be difficult to dissolve in cold water.
Chlorine or iodine	No	Lightweight and compact. Inexpensive.	Iodine alters how water tastes. Ineffective against protozoa and parasites like cryptosporidium. Waiting times vary.
UV light purifier plus microfilter	Yes	Water's flavor not altered.	Requires clear water from a microfilter. Fragile UV lamp requires batteries.

Note: "Yes" in "Purifies" column means the method is effective against all pathogens: parasites (including protozoa), bacteria, and viruses.

The US Centers for Disease Control and Prevention recommends bringing water to a rolling boil and maintaining the boil for one minute, or three minutes above 6,500 feet (2,000 meters); see Table 3-8. Other reliable sources, including the World Health Organization, state that simply bringing water to a boil is sufficient, even at elevations as high as Everest Base Camp in Nepal. This method does require additional fuel as well as the time to set up and light a stove.

Filtering

Water filters are relatively quick and easy to use and result in clear, palatable water. Look for a compact, lightweight model that is easy to use, clean, and maintain in the field. Filters come in many gravity-fed (fig. 3-17a), pump (fig. 3-17b and c), squeeze (fig. 3-17d), and straw-style (fig. 3-17e) formats. Water passes through a hollow-fiber membrane or porous ceramic filter to separate parasites, bacteria, and sometimes viruses, depending on the type of filter. This microscopic strainer collects the pathogens, still alive, on its surface. There is a risk of cross-contamination from the two hoses in a pump filter; be careful handling them. Follow the manufacturer's instructions to periodically clean the filter by backflushing (pump filters), scrubbing, boiling, and using chemical disinfecting.

Purifier-filters. Purifier-filters are effective against viruses, the smallest of pathogens. Purifier-filters work either by physical filtration or by the process of adsorption. Physical filtration occurs through a method using medical-grade

TABLE 3-8. BOILING POINT OF WATER

ELEVATION IN FEET (METERS)	TEMPERATURE AT WHICH WATER BOILS (IN °F AND °C)
Sea level (0)	212° (100°)
5,000 (1,525)	202° (94°)
10,000 (3,050)	193° (89°)
15,000 (4,575)	184° (84°)
20,000 (6,100)	176° (80°)
25,000 (7,620)	168° (75°)
29,029 (8,848)	162° (72°)

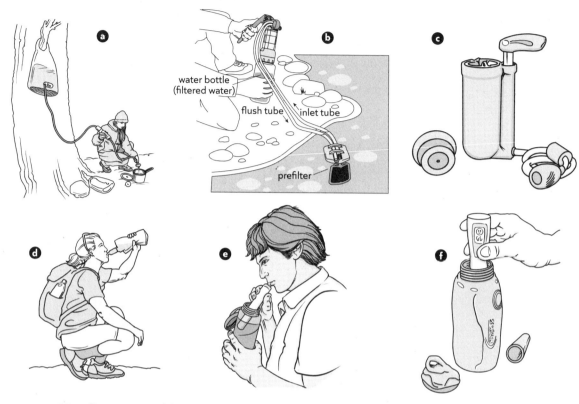

Fig. 3-17. *Water filters:* **a,** *gravity-fed purifier-filter hanging from a tree limb—speed up filtration by keeping the unfiltered-water bag as high as possible and the filtered-water end as low as possible;* **b,** *pump-style microfilter attached directly to a water bottle, with a prefilter at the hose intake end (this model offers two-hose continuous self-cleaning);* **c,** *another pump microfilter;* **d,** *squeeze microfilter;* **e,** *straw-style microfilter;* **f,** *UV light purifier.*

hollow-fiber membrane technology, currently used by relatively few filters on the market. These filters need to be replaced when it becomes difficult to pump, a sign that the filter is clogged. Adsorption-based purifier-filters force viruses to cleave to a special material. However, they are difficult to monitor for ongoing effectiveness. Depending on how much water passes through these purifier-filters and how dirty that water is, the useful life of this material is often very short, silently ending when the cleaving sites are full, with no indication to the user.

Microfilters. The effectiveness of microfilters to remove parasites, protozoan cysts, and bacteria depends on the filter's pore size. Manufacturers describe filter pore size in various ways, so look for an absolute pore size that is 0.2 micron or less. However, even at the smallest pore size, *microfilters do not remove viruses.* To guard against viruses,

use a purifier-filter instead, or post-treat the water with UV light or any of the chemical disinfectants listed below. Tannins (dissolved tea-colored solids) clog filters and can be impossible to remove, so backflush often. Squeeze and straw-style microfilters use hollow-fiber membrane filters that when wet are damaged by freezing temperatures. Keeping these small filters next to your body while hiking may help protect them from freezing.

Chemical Disinfecting

Treating water chemically may be the lightest, most inexpensive, and most effective way to purify water. After adding chemical disinfectants to water, loosen the water-bottle lid and slosh a little of the treated water onto the threads around the bottle's top and cap to eliminate any pathogens lurking there.

Chlorine dioxide. Water treatment using chlorine dioxide (not to be confused with chlorine) is the most effective of the chemical treatments and does not significantly alter how the water tastes. Chlorine dioxide is available in tablet or two-part liquid forms. You simply add the tablets, a lightweight, inexpensive method, to untreated water, though they do not dissolve well in cold water. Liquid chlorine dioxide is mixed with phosphoric acid before being added to untreated water; the treatment is ready to use when it turns from clear to bright yellow, about five minutes. For either tablet or liquid form, the treated water is ready after 15–30 minutes—or up to four hours to kill crypto.

Chlorine and iodine. The two chemicals chlorine and iodine are equally effective against all bacteria and all viruses but unreliable against parasites and protozoa (see Table 3-6 above). They are somewhat effective against giardia but not effective against crypto. Both chemicals are halogens; another halogen, bromine, is used on US Navy ships but is impractical for backcountry travel. Chlorine (not to be confused with the fundamentally different chlorine dioxide described above) is available as household bleach, sodium dichloroisocyanurate, or troclosene sodium tablets. Iodine is available as tablets, drops, or crystals. After the disinfectant is added to untreated water, wait until the process is complete (times vary) before adding vitamin C, electrolytes, or drink powders to help eliminate any bad flavor, or use a microfilter with a carbon element after waiting the full disinfectant time.

UV Light

Municipal water systems widely use ultraviolet light to purify water, but backcountry versions, such as the Steripen, are fragile, battery-operated UV lamps (fig. 3-17f). Even clear-looking water can contain enough particles (turbidity—see the next section) to shield pathogens from UV light, and since users cannot reliably assess turbidity, prefiltering with a 0.2-micron microfilter is recommended. (A microfilter combined with a chemical treatment costs less.) UV light purifiers are lightweight, convenient, and effective when used properly. Consider using a rechargeable purifier to reduce environmental impact.

More Considerations for Water Treatment

Factors such as water temperature, turbidity, cleanliness of hands, and agricultural runoff can affect your method for treating water.

Cold water, freezing temperatures, snow, and ice. Cold water slows the processes of chemical treatment, so longer contact time is needed; other methods are not affected. Freezing temperatures can destroy water filters, especially hollow-fiber membranes, in a manner difficult to detect; pump the filter dry and place in a sleeping bag at night to protect it. Freshly fallen snow can be considered pure, but deciding whether to purify melted snow or ice requires judgment, since giardia, crypto, and many bacteria can survive freezing. Avoid drinking pinkish watermelon snow (from algae) found in older snowbanks: it can be a laxative.

Turbidity. Organic turbidity (suspended organic solids such as sediment or debris) creates a "demand," which depletes chemical disinfectants faster than clear water; use additional disinfectant to offset. Organic turbidity can clog filters. Inorganic turbidity (for example, glacial silt) creates hiding places for pathogens from UV light. It can also clog filters. If not removed by filtering, glacial silt acts as a laxative. Before using any water treatment method, reduce turbidity significantly by prefiltering with a cloth, a paper coffee filter, or a paper towel; by using a chemical (flocculant) to help sediments settle; or by waiting for the solids to settle. Using a water filter, chemical disinfectant, and even UV light is more efficient if turbid water is prefiltered.

Dirty water and hands. Water storage bottles, bags, and hydration devices can become contaminated easily by dirty water or dirty hands. Disinfect water storage containers with any of the chemical water treatment methods described above, or with diluted bleach or very hot water. Thoroughly wash hands before handling food. If hand-washing is impractical, scrub hand grime with river or lake sand, then clean with hand sanitizer gel or wipes. Backcountry health issues attributed to drinking wilderness water often are actually caused by fecal-oral contamination from poor hand sanitation.

Chemicals and toxins. None of the treatment methods described above are effective against chemicals or toxins, including agricultural runoff (pesticides and herbicides) and industrial runoff (mine tailings and heavy metals). Filters with an activated carbon element offer limited protection. If you are suspicious about a water source, find another.

Food

As with hydration, proper nutrition begins long before the trip. Climbers need to consume a variety of foods to tackle a strenuous, demanding activity like mountaineering. With planning, it is possible to choose foods that last a long time, are lightweight, and meet all your nutritional needs. Mountain trips are a great place to indulge in the kind of high-calorie foods that you may normally limit at home. The longer the trip, the more variable and complex the menu should be. Food that tastes appealing will help you meet the goal of fueling your body well and quickly.

Adequate caloric intake is essential for climbers. Most climbing expeditions plan on roughly 4,000 to 5,000 calories per day for each climber. Energy expenditure on a climb can reach as high as 6,000 calories per day, possibly even higher for some people. In comparison, most people require only about 1,500 to 2,500 calories per day to fuel a sedentary lifestyle. Your food plan depends on the demands of the trip and your body's needs. Never restrict calories during a mountaineering trip. Adequate sustenance and energy are essential for performance and well-being.

COMPOSITION OF FOODS

For your body to function well, eat from all three basic food components—carbohydrates (sugars and starch), protein, and fats. In addition to these macronutrients, climbers also need particular vitamins and minerals, such as sodium, potassium, magnesium, and calcium. On longer trips, replenishing these micronutrients becomes even more important.

Carbohydrates. The easiest food for the body to convert into energy, carbohydrates should constitute most of your calories—50 to 65 percent—per day. Think of them as the main fuel to keep your body functioning most efficiently. Excellent sources of complex carbohydrates include oats, brown rice, quinoa, pasta, whole wheat tortillas, potatoes, cereals, breads, crackers, pretzels, beans or lentils, fruit or dried fruits, and a wide variety of prepackaged energy or granola bars. Simple sugars, also a great source of quick energy while climbing, include honey, jam, sugar, hot cocoa, energy gels, candy, chocolate, and drink mixes. Most athletes need 0.01 to 0.16 ounce of carbohydrates per pound (6 to 19 grams per kilogram) of body weight per day, depending on gender and individual physical fitness level.

Protein. Protein helps your body repair and rebuild muscle tissue after exercise. It also helps to replenish depleted energy stores and support the immune system. Our bodies cannot store protein, so once we have met our daily requirement, the body converts the excess to energy or stores it as fat. Protein should make up about 15 to 20 percent of caloric intake per day. Most athletes need 0.04 to 0.06 ounce per pound (2 to 4 grams per kilogram) of body weight per day. High-protein foods include cheese, nuts, nut butters, dried jerky, canned or vacuum-packed meats and fish, beans or lentils, tofu, powdered milk and eggs, dehydrated meals containing meat or cheese, and a variety of prepackaged protein bars.

Fats. Because fats pack more than twice as many calories per gram as protein or carbohydrates, they are an important source of energy even in small portions, which is helpful in packing light. Our bodies digest fats more slowly than carbohydrates or protein, so they help keep you satisfied longer and help you stay warm on cold nights. Fats should make up about 20 to 30 percent of your daily calorie intake. High-fat foods include butter, margarine, avocados, nuts and nut butters, hard sausage or salami, eggs, seeds, cheese, and jerky made from beef, fish, or turkey. Oils and canned sardines are other great sources of fat but can be messier on the go—and sardines are used to bait bears.

Hydration. It is difficult to know the exact amount of water or fluids each climber should drink because it depends on individual conditioning, weather conditions, altitude, et cetera. Dehydration can lead to headaches, fatigue, impaired mental and physical performance, dry mouth, chills, and clamminess. Monitoring urine color and volume is one way to monitor your hydration status. Urine should be pale to light yellow. Urine that is darker or comes out in lower volumes indicates you need to drink more.

Electrolytes. A well-balanced diet replaces most electrolytes that are lost during heavy sweating, but you may need replacement fluids in addition to water. Some climbers like to use high-performance sports drinks (often diluted) to replace water, carbohydrates, and electrolytes simultaneously, but powders or tablets are lighter and more practical than bottled drinks on a climb. Try some options at home before relying on them in the mountains.

TIMING OF MEALS

The better your physical condition, the more efficiently food and water will provide energy during strenuous exercise. It can be especially hard to eat large meals while exerting yourself because the body diverts blood away from muscles to the stomach during digestion. Eating smaller, more frequent meals and snacks can be more sustainable and comfortable. Most athletes need around 1 to 2 ounces (30 to 60 grams) of carbohydrates per hour to prevent low blood sugar and to support energy levels. Start off with a hearty breakfast and consume carbohydrates and water steadily, beginning one to two hours into a climb.

PLANNING AND PACKAGING FOOD

As a rough guideline, provide 1.5 to 2.5 pounds (0.7 to 1.1 kilograms) or 2,500 to 4,500 calories of food per person per day. The precise amount will vary based on conditions, exertion, and metabolism. Keep in mind that extra food is the eighth of the Ten Essentials, but do not weigh yourself down with excess provisions.

Try to minimize waste by buying foods with less packaging. Bulk dates and nuts in reusable plastic bags are every bit as tasty and nutritious and more budget-friendly than expensive energy bars.

On very short trips, climbers can pack standard on-the-go foods such as sandwiches, fresh fruit and vegetables, cheese sticks, et cetera. Water-heavy fruit such as apples and oranges that would be prohibitive on overnight trips are fine on day trips; you can consider them part of your water rations for the day. Taking only ready-to-eat food saves the weight of a stove, fuel, and cook pots—a good idea for lightweight bivouacs. In nasty weather, this approach allows you to retreat directly to the tent without the hassle of cooking. Use firm bread, rolls, or bagels for a sandwich that will stand up to packing. Leave out ingredients that spoil easily if you will be out for more than one day.

For longer trips, food planning becomes more complicated and food weight more critical. Freeze-dried food is compact, lightweight, and easy to prepare but is relatively expensive. Outdoor stores carry a large selection, including main courses, vegetables, soups, breakfasts, and desserts, most of which require little or no cooking. Simply add hot water, let it soak for a while, and eat the meal straight out of the package. Others require cooking in a pot.

By shopping at local stores and using a food dehydrator, climbers can enjoy a more varied menu at substantial savings. Simple and nutritious mountaineering foods can be made from scratch using fruit, dairy, vegetables, and meat. Dehydrated produce can be eaten as is or added as an ingredient to a cooked dish. Fruit leather, easy to prepare with a dehydrator, is a delicious snack. Dehydrate sauces—for example, pesto—to serve with thin, lightweight angel-hair pasta (which cooks quickly). Dehydrated foods require simple rehydration rather than cooking, which means food will be ready to eat faster. Vacuum-sealing, or removing all air from the package, thereby reducing spoilage, extends the longevity of dehydrated food. Dehydrate the food first, then vacuum-seal it.

Having a small kitchen scale at home is useful for precise planning and packaging of food. Weigh the portions and transfer the food from bulky packaging into resealable plastic bags or other lightweight containers. Enclose identifying labels and cooking instructions, or write this information on the outside of the bag with a permanent marker. Place ingredient or meal packages inside larger bags labeled with broad categories, such as "breakfast," "dinner," or "drinks."

Meal Planning with Groups

On group climbs meals can become social events, and often groups collaborate to plan their food. An appealing menu can boost morale, and with planning and coordination, sharing food planning and prep can reduce the pack weight each person carries. Due to daily schedules or other variables, some groups may decide to share only one meal per day, commonly dinner.

Group meals can be planned collectively or by a chosen individual. Canvass members for food preferences and cultural norms, needs, and allergies; one person may be a vegetarian, another may refuse to eat freeze-dried entrées. Discussing the menu in advance can go a long way toward maintaining group harmony around cooking and eating.

The ideal number of people in a cooking group is two to three per stove, four maximum. Above that, the complexities of large pots, small stoves, and increased cooking and waiting times outweigh the efficiency of cooking in a group.

High-Altitude Cooking

Cooking raw food becomes impractical above about 10,000 feet (3,050 meters). The boiling point of water decreases with altitude (as shown in Table 3-8 above), which increases the time to cook raw food by two to four times at 10,000 feet (3,048 meters) and by four to seven times at 15,000 feet (4,575 meters). The practical solution is to bring foods that require only warming, such as meat or fish or sauces in a foil pouch; dehydrated or instant meals, such as instant rice or quick oats; and freeze-dried meals. Dedicated high-altitude chefs may consider a lightweight pressure cooker.

The rigors of ascending rapidly to higher altitudes also require special attention to the choice of food. Altitude can affect appetites and tolerance of certain foods. Under these conditions, food also becomes more difficult to digest. Climbers must continue to eat and drink; staying hydrated is particularly essential. To cope with aversion to food, eat light and often, emphasizing carbohydrates, which are easiest to digest. Trial and error will determine what foods your body can tolerate.

MENU SUGGESTIONS

Try out various food combinations before taking them on an extended trip in the mountains. See Table 3-9 for a sample one-person, one-day menu for about 4,500 calories.

TABLE 3-9. SAMPLE MENU TO SUPPLY 4,500 CALORIES FOR ONE PERSON IN ONE DAY				
	CALORIES	CARBS	PROTEIN	FATS
Breakfast				
Instant oatmeal (3 packets)	480	99 g	12 g	6 g
Cashews (¼ cup)	197	11 g	5 g	16 g
Dried fruit (¼ cup)	110	25 g	1 g	0
Hot cocoa (1 packet)	150	30 g	2 g	0
Black coffee	0	0	0	0
Total	937	165 g	20 g	22 g
Midmorning Snack				
Trail mix (½ cup)	350	34 g	10 g	22 g
Dehydrated apple slices (1 cup)	200	55 g	0	0
Total	550	89 g	10 g	22 g
Late Morning Snack				
Candy bar	280	35 g	4 g	14 g
Total	280	35 g	4 g	14 g
Lunch				
Whole wheat tortillas (2)	184	40 g	6 g	2 g
Tuna (2 packets)	200	18 g	26 g	2 g
Mayonnaise (2 packets)	180	0	0	20 g
Cashews (¼ cup)	197	11 g	5 g	16 g
Raisins or dried fruit (¼ cup)	110	25 g	1 g	0
Total	871	94 g	38 g	40 g
Midafternoon Snack				
Beef jerky (1 oz.)	120	3 g	9 g	7 g
Fig bars (4)	180	44 g	2 g	0
Total	300	47 g	11 g	7 g
Late Afternoon Snack				
Dried mango (2 oz.)	200	45 g	3 g	0
Crunchy granola bar (Nature Valley)	190	28 g	5 g	7 g
Total	390	73 g	8 g	7 g
Dinner				
Dehydrated meal (Mountain House fettucine alfredo with chicken)	810	64 g	34 g	46 g
Total	810	64 g	34 g	46 g
After Dinner Snack				
Granola (½ cup)	300	32 g	9 g	15 g
Total	300	32 g	9 g	15 g
Daily Total	4,438	599 g (21.1 oz.)	134 g (4.7 oz.)	173 g (6.1 oz.)

Note: *To convert grams to ounces, divide by 28.35. Source for data is www.calorieking.com.*

Breakfasts

So that you can start quickly, package each standard meal separately before your trip. A single bag can contain oatmeal, cold cereal, or granola with dried or dehydrated fruit; powdered milk; and sweet spices such as nutmeg or cinnamon. Stir in water, whether cold or hot, and breakfast is ready. Other quick options include bakery items, dried fruit and meat, nuts, energy bars, dehydrated applesauce, and freeze-dried breakfasts that combine eggs, meat, and potatoes. Common hot drink choices are instant cocoa, instant cider, coffee, powdered milk, tea, and instant breakfast drinks. For some, caffeine is a pleasant way to start the day, and many studies show it brings a measurable increase in endurance and delays exhaustion.

Lunches and Snacks

During a climb, lunch begins shortly after breakfast and continues throughout the day. Eat small amounts, and eat often, every one to two hours. At least half of a climber's daily food allotment should be for lunch and snacks. A reliable munching staple is gorp (originally, "good old raisins and peanuts"), a mixture that can contain nuts, small candies such as chocolate chips, and dried fruit or ginger. One handful makes a snack; several make a meal. Granola is another option, with its mixture of grains, honey or sugar, and bits of fruit and nuts. Other popular snack items are fruit leather, candy bars, energy bars, and dried fruit. A basic lunch can include any of the following:

Protein. Sources include vacuum-sealed meats and fish, jerky, salami, powdered hummus, powdered peanut butter, hard cheese, nuts, and seeds.

Starch. Carbohydrates include whole-grain breads, bagels, pita bread, granola, firm crackers, tortillas, rice cakes, chips, pretzels, and energy bars.

Sweets. Some treats are cookies, candy bars, hard candy, muffins, pastries, jam, and chocolate.

Fruit. Sources include fresh fruit; fruit leather; dried fruit such as raisins, figs, and apples; and freeze-dried strawberries, blueberries, or mango.

Vegetables. Some vegetables that travel well are fresh carrots and celery sticks, sliced sweet peppers, and dehydrated vegetables.

To encourage rehydration, mix up a flavored beverage such as lemonade or fruit punch at lunch. In cold weather, fill a lightweight thermos with hot water at breakfast, then enjoy a cup of instant soup or hot tea at lunch.

Dinners

The evening meal should be nourishing and delicious, yet easy and quick to prepare, since you will likely be tired. To supplement liquid intake, include some items that take a lot of water, such as soup, hot cider, herbal tea, fruit drinks, or cocoa. A cup of soup makes for a quick and satisfying first course. A heartier soup can also serve as the main course. Some choices include miso, minestrone, bean, beef barley, lentil, chili, or chicken noodle. Add instant potatoes, dehydrated vegetables, rice, crackers, tortilla shells, cheese, or bread, and the meal is complete.

One-pot meals with a carbohydrate base of pasta, rice, beans, potatoes, or grains are easy and nutritious. To ensure that you get adequate protein, fat, and flavor, add other ingredients such as chicken, beef, or fish that has been dried or packaged in a foil pouch; sausage; freeze-dried vegetables or fruit; margarine; or a dehydrated soup or sauce mix. Outdoor retail and online stores carry a variety of freeze-dried entrées that are nutritionally balanced and easy to prepare, though expensive. Prepackaged dishes from the grocery store—such as noodle dishes and rice mixes—are also good, easy, and less expensive. Freeze-dried or dehydrated vegetables add variety. Prepare them as side dishes or add to soups or stews. Freeze-dried cooked beans or processed soy products in powdered or textured forms are excellent low-cost options for adding protein. Natural food stores often have a wide selection of these ingredients. Climbers can also prepare and dehydrate sauces and many other ingredients at home.

Margarine, which keeps better than butter, and oils, such as olive oil, improve flavor and add significant calories with minimum weight. For seasonings, try salt, pepper, herbs, garlic, chili powder, bacon bits, curry powder, dehydrated onions, grated Parmesan cheese, hot sauce, brewer's yeast, or soy sauce (just not all together). Desserts could be dates, cookies, candy, chocolate, no-bake cheesecake, applesauce, cooked dried fruit, instant pudding, or freeze-dried ice cream. Dessert time, accompanied by a cup of hot herbal tea, can provide a pleasant backdrop while the group talks about the next day's itinerary and decides who will provide the morning wake-up call.

Boiled-water cooking. Cooking dinner for many alpine chefs simply means boiling water. Most freeze-dried entrées are designed to be reconstituted in their packaging. Food that does not require any cooking is simple, fast, and easy to clean up. Dinner can also be prepared directly in a bowl or

Fig. 3-18. *Cookware and utensils:* **a,** *alpine pot with small fry pan and lids;* **b,** *pot lifter;* **c,** *two designs of sporks;* **d,** *nested bowls;* **e,** *cup with lid and measuring marks;* **f,** *containers with screw-top lids.*

cup. Start with some instant soup. The main course could be a starchy food (instant mashed potatoes, instant rice, or couscous) with added protein, vegetables, and condiments. Follow with a dessert of instant applesauce or instant pudding, and end with a rehydrating hot drink of noncaffeinated tea or cider. The only items to wash up are the spoon, cup, and maybe a bowl.

COOKWARE AND UTENSILS

On an ultralightweight trip with just cold food, fingers are the only utensils needed. (Wash hands before preparing food or eating, or at least use a hand-sanitizing gel.) Making dinner with the boiled-water cooking methods described above requires only one cup and one spoon or spork (combination spoon and fork) per person, plus one cook pot with a bail or handle for each group of three or four; bowls are convenient but optional.

The popular canister system stoves have a built-in cook pot or a small set of integrated pots optimized for boiled-water cooking. For less spartan menus, other stoves accept a variety of cooking pots. Bring one pot for boiling water, another for cooking, and unbreakable lightweight bowls for eating. Alpine cook sets (fig. 3-18a) come in aluminum,

stainless steel, and titanium. Aluminum, which is light and inexpensive, is the most common. Stainless steel is strong and easy to clean but heavy. Titanium is light and strong but expensive. For big groups, consider a large pot part of the group gear. A large water pot is useful for melting snow. A wide pot is more stable than a tall, narrow one and more efficient because it catches more of the stove's flame. Be sure all pots have bails or handles, or bring a small metal pot lifter (fig. 3-18b). Tight-fitting pot lids conserve heat. (See "Cooking for a Crowd" under Stoves earlier in this chapter.) Some cooking pans have a nonstick coating for easy cleaning but require plastic or silicone utensils to avoid scratches.

Sporks, bowls, and cups (fig. 3-18c, d, and e) come in the same materials as cook sets or in strong, lightweight polycarbonate plastic. Screw-top containers (fig. 3-18f) are handy and prevent spills. A coffee press is an accessory for some canister system stoves. A small silicone spatula is useful for cooking and efficiently getting food out of the pan, whether for eating or cleaning up. Bring a plastic scrub pad and a synthetic-fabric pack towel for cleaning. Many specialized pieces of camp kitchenware, such as bake ovens, Dutch ovens, pressure cookers, and espresso makers, are impractical on mountaineering trips.

"It's Just Camping"

Pioneer American alpinist Paul Petzoldt once said, in an interview about climbing in the Himalaya and Karakoram, "It's just camping." His point was that technical climbing skills are less important than the ability to survive—and even less so than the resourcefulness necessary to be at home and comfortable in the mountains.

Camping skills are the basis upon which all the more-technical mountaineering skills rely. Once climbers develop and hone the skills to stay in the mountains, they will have the confidence to venture farther and begin to understand what it means to experience the freedom of the hills.

CHAPTER 4

CONDITIONING

Mountaineering requires a unique combination of endurance and key strengths. An effective and rewarding climbing conditioning program blends aerobic and anaerobic cardiovascular training, strength training, flexibility training, skill development, cross training, mental conditioning, proper fueling, and adequate rest and recovery based on fundamental training concepts.

Many mountaineers dedicate an hour or two several days a week to sport-specific conditioning, reserving weekends for longer outings in the mountains. The best way to train is to do the desired activity. When that is not possible, other training options can help climbers prepare for their sport. This chapter provides guidelines for developing a systematic conditioning program to optimize your training time.

With any new endeavor comes a learning curve, and while learning and experimenting, you may encounter aches and pains—or sometimes, an injury. Injuries often result from increasing volume and intensity too rapidly, not the new activity itself. When starting a new training program, pace the intensity and amount of exercise, and focus on moving in ways in which you feel in control.

Setting Goals

Each climber must first understand what being fit means for them. Fitness is defined in this context as the full-body conditioning needed to move easily and confidently in the mountains, while maintaining a reserve of strength and stamina to handle unforeseen challenges. Before designing a suitable training program, each climber needs to assess and establish their current conditioning, set realistic goals, and outline the steps needed to reach those goals. Physical conditioning has many benefits, including faster speed heading uphill and reduced stress on joints going downhill.

SMART goals. First, set goals that are Specific, Measurable, Action-oriented, Realistic, and Time-stamped: SMART. For example, you may choose to set a goal to "climb Mount X by Y route in three days by the end of the coming summer, through a workout program that includes five weekly workouts and a 6- to 8-mile (10- to 13-kilometer) hike gaining 3,000 feet (915 meters) of elevation every other week, gradually increasing pack weight

by 3 to 5 pounds (1.4 to 2.3 kilograms) per outing." Such a specific, clearly delineated target with all the elements of a SMART goal is more motivating than a vague goal like "get fit for mountaineering." And the more motivated you are, the more likely you are to stick with your training program.

Components of Fitness

The level of fitness required for a beginning-level one-day rock climb differs from that needed for an advanced two-day ice climb. The fitness programs for those two objectives will look different from that of someone training for a three-week trek. With an end goal in mind, each climber can individualize their training.

CARDIOVASCULAR TRAINING

Cardiovascular endurance is your ability to perform a continuous activity for an extended time. When working cardiovascularly, the body uses large muscle groups simultaneously, either aerobically or anaerobically. A strong cardiovascular base is mandatory for all aspects of mountaineering.

Aerobic Exercise

Any cardiovascular activity that elevates heart rate in order to supply a significant amount of oxygen to muscles for

> ### KEY TOPICS
>
> SETTING GOALS
> COMPONENTS OF FITNESS
> FUNDAMENTAL TRAINING CONCEPTS
> BUILDING AN ANNUAL TRAINING PROGRAM
> MENTAL CONDITIONING
> BEYOND TRAINING: RECOVERY

sustained effort is aerobic exercise. It can be categorized as being of short (two to eight minutes), medium (eight to thirty minutes), or long (more than thirty minutes) duration. Aerobic workouts performed for longer durations and at a lower intensity build the aerobic base and ultimately the cardiovascular endurance required for a long day in the mountains. Lower intensity is defined as being able to maintain nasal breathing or speak complete sentences without difficulty, and not needing to stop and rest frequently.

If you have little experience with endurance training, it is best to start slow and progress gradually. Start with a combination of slow jogging and walking for a few miles or kilometers. Longer distances at the beginning will quickly lead to burnout and injury. Gauge how you feel after your first few endurance sessions. If those sessions go well, increase your distance. A useful starting schedule is two to four sessions a week separated by rest days. For athletes who are 55 and older, training consistently at lower intensity is more important because building an aerobic base takes longer and requires more effort than it does at a younger age.

A solid first goal to work toward as a beginner mountaineer is to complete a 5-mile (8-kilometer) roundtrip hike with roughly a 13-pound (6-kilogram) pack, ascending and descending 2,000 feet (610 meters) in less than two and a half hours. After establishing this baseline, climbers can then build to four or more cardiovascular workouts per week, depending on their objective, as they approach their targeted goal. Consider increasing aerobic sessions by five minutes each week or increasing your mileage by 10 percent each week.

While some of these workouts should be in the mountains or at least emphasize uphill travel, most can be done close to home. Cardiovascular training options for mountaineering should include activities that load the spine in an upright position. Suitable examples are using an inclined treadmill, elliptical cross-training machine, stair machine, vertical climber, or revolving stair climber; hiking, hill walking, snowshoeing, or cross-country skiing; participating in aerobic classes; and trail running. Some lower impact aerobic activities like biking, paddling, and swimming don't train the body for mountain sports, but they make great off-season activities, rehabilitative alternatives to allow you to continue training, or supplemental cross-training alternatives (see Cross-Training later in this chapter).

Anaerobic Exercise

Near-maximal cardiovascular training that takes climbers to the upper levels of their aerobic training zone and beyond is anaerobic exercise. Such training involves working at a heart rate higher than what you can sustain during aerobic sessions. Anaerobic exercise prepares climbers for when they need a sudden burst of energy to respond to emergencies in the mountains or to link powerful moves on a climbing wall. Anaerobic training helps climbers increase their speed across varied terrain (known as leg turnover rate). It boosts climbers' entire aerobic zone so that activities that once made them breathless feel more comfortable. Examples include pack-loaded stair climbing, walking quickly uphill while wearing a pack, or sprinting uphill without a pack.

Tracking Cardiovascular Fitness

Keeping track of workouts and how you felt during and after is an important element of maintaining an effective training plan, because fitness improves as the body recovers from the stress it endured during the workouts. Putting the body under too much stress without adequate time to recover can lead to plateaus in fitness gain, fatigue, and injuries.

Quantifying the stress of a workout is helpful. Heart rate is easy to measure and can provide useful insight. Using a heart-rate monitor with one of many available training apps (Garmin, Polar, Strava, TrainingPeaks, SportTracks, Intervals.icu, et cetera) can simplify this task, but even keeping an old-school training log noting how you felt while exercising can suffice. A GPS-based sports watch with a heart-rate monitor can record activities and feed data directly to an app, allowing you to track your fitness and analyze various elements to gauge your performance. For example, you may note: "I did the hike as fast as last time, but my heart rate was 10 beats lower per minute." Because you performed the same activity with less energy output, you can easily measure and see the results of your progress.

Another way to periodically assess your cardiovascular fitness is to choose a hike nearby that is mostly snow-free year-round and use it as a test piece every few weeks. Each time you hike it, challenge yourself: add weight to your pack—no more than 10 percent per week, or 3 to 5 pounds (1.4 to 2.3 kilograms) per outing. Hike as fast as or faster than you did on a previous hike. Meeting these challenges indicates that your cardiovascular fitness has increased.

An easy way to add weight is to fill several 2-quart (2-liter) bottles with water and put them in your pack. Early in your training program, dump the water before descending if you need to in order to save wear and tear on your joints. As you near your training goal, however, carry down the weight that you carry up. If you struggle with breathlessness while carrying a light pack, concentrate on developing endurance during training sessions. If your legs feel heavy when you increase pack weight, focus on building strength.

STRENGTH TRAINING

Crucial to success in mountaineering, strength training gives climbers the power and force to withstand challenges, whether predictable or unforeseen, in the mountains. Strength training can prevent injuries by helping the body adapt to overload, providing muscle balance, improving performance, boosting metabolism, and increasing lean muscle mass. Preteen climbers might not need as structured a strength-training program, while loss of elasticity in connective tissues for climbers 55 and older means that strength training is more important than when they were younger, to prevent injury.

Climbers should strive to be stronger than they think they will need to be. The endurance demands on a climber's body during an ascent result in a loss of strength. Incorporating extra strength training into your program will offset that loss. Mountaineers benefit from full-body strength training year-round to maintain baseline strength, then building as needed at appropriate times.

Strength training can be done in phases that match your season. For early- and midseason strength, opt for general strength training; for late-season strength, opt for more specific strength training, aiming for muscular endurance, doing between 10 and 15 repetitions for two or three sets. If you are new to strength training, start with muscular endurance for a few weeks to become familiar with the exercises and balance out any weaknesses.

Unilateral Free-Weight Exercises

During the preseason training program, use single-limb (unilateral) free-weight exercises to correct any weaknesses in your legs and hips, particularly in the full range of motion encountered on alpine outings. Exercises such as static lunges, step-ups, step-downs (see Figure 4-1), and one-legged dead lifts (see Figure 4-2) ensure that your legs and hips share the workload. Many of these exercises can be performed at home, using body weight initially, then with a loaded pack as your balance and strength improve. Since your calves take the brunt of the load on steep terrain, include straight-leg variations of calf exercises (see Resources).

Step-down. This is one of the most effective and specific unilateral mountaineering exercises to strengthen the quadriceps for downhill travel. Ideally, use a 6- to 12-inch (15- to 30-centimeter) box or step whose height allows you to do the exercise under control without any lateral (side-to-side) knee movement. If this height is too much, start with a shorter step and gradually increase the height. Start on top of the step, with toes pointing forward. Start with just

body weight at first, then add a 2-pound (0.9-kilogram) dumbbell in each hand. Gradually increase the weight each week up to 30–50 percent of your body weight, or use your planned pack weight as a guide (fig. 4-1a).

Slowly step off the front of the step as if walking downstairs, controlling the downward movement as though you are stepping onto eggshells. Focus on the leg on the step, your working leg. When your foot reaches the floor (fig. 4-1b), reverse the movement, pushing from your toes and using the leg on the step to lift yourself back up. Keep your working knee tracking over your middle toe rather than collapsing toward your body's midline. Control both the lifting and lowering portions of this exercise. Complete two or three sets of 4 to 6 repetitions for a strength-training phase and 10 to 15 repetitions per leg for muscular endurance, then repeat with the other leg.

One-legged dead lift. This excellent sport-specific unilateral mountaineering exercise contributes to stability by strengthening the ankles, knees, hips, and lower back. Stand balancing on one foot while holding a dumbbell in

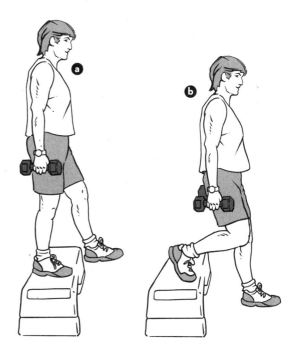

Fig. 4-1. Step-down: a, step off the step slowly as if walking downstairs; b, slowly reverse the movement, starting by raising yourself onto the toes of your downward foot and using the leg still on the step to lift yourself back up. Keep your knee tracking directly over your middle toe.

one or both hands (fig. 4-2a). Keep the other foot lifted but near the floor in case you need to touch it down for balance. Hinge forward at the hips with as much or as little knee bend as desired and reach the dumbbell(s) to the floor (fig. 4-2b). Exhale and return to a fully upright position with each repetition. Complete two or three sets of 4 to 6 repetitions for a strength-training phase and 10 to 15 repetitions per leg for muscular endurance, then repeat with the other leg. Start with a lighter weight and increase weight as you get stronger.

Snow shoveler. This mountaineering-specific movement integrates the upper and lower body with torso rotation, preparing climbers to lift heavy packs onto their backs, dig snow pits or latrines, or carve snow blocks for windbreaks and snow shelters. In both hands, hold a dumbbell that you can comfortably press overhead with both hands; practice the movement first, then increase weight gradually to make it more challenging. Stand with your feet wider than shoulder-width apart. With a neutral spine, keeping your lower spine from bending, squat toward the floor (fig. 4-3a). Keep the dumbbell directly below your chin.

As you rise to a standing position, pivot to one side as though you are completing a golf swing, keeping the dumbbell's weight close to your shoulder (fig. 4-3b). Follow the dumbbell with your eyes as you move it to the top of the arc, ending near your shoulder, not overhead. Squat again, then lift to the other side, alternating sides with each repetition. Keep your abdominals tight to avoid overextending your back. Complete two to three sets of 4 to 6 repetitions for a strength-training phase and 10 to 15 repetitions for muscular endurance.

Full-Body, Range-of-Motion Exercises

During the middle of the training program, once you have developed reliable muscle balance and core strength, incorporate full-body, full-range-of-motion exercises, including variations on the squat, dead lift, bench press, pull-up, and row, among others. The core involves all of the muscles that make up the front, sides, and back of the torso. It includes the pelvic floor and muscles that stabilize the hips and aid in balanced movement. Because of the dynamic and unpredictable nature of performing self-arrests with an ice axe, climbers need full range of motion in their shoulders as well as strength and joint integrity throughout their chest, shoulders, and torso. Pull-ups, push-ups, and core exercises enable climbers to get into position rapidly and hold the ice axe in place more securely on icy slopes while stopping themselves.

Options that help increase strength and stamina throughout the whole body include lifting weights, dragging a sled, carrying a weighted pack, training with body-weight exercises (using your own body for resistance, as in push-ups or pull-ups), and using resistance bands. Bouldering and hang boards are useful options for climbers to develop strength in specific areas, especially fingers and forearms.

Consider which muscles your upcoming activities will involve and match your training exercises to the movements they require. For example, if you plan to snowshoe on an approach for a winter mountaineering outing, develop strength endurance in your hip flexors for repeated high-steps. Add ankle weights or ski boots to short anaerobic uphill or strength workouts. Do not, however, add ankle weights to long endurance workouts, as they can alter your natural stride, not to mention cause an overuse injury. If you are weak on overhanging movements, develop your core and grip by training your abdominals, obliques (side abdominal muscles involved in rotating the torso), forearms, and fingers, in addition to the larger muscle groups in your upper body.

Use the hiking test piece (see Tracking Cardiovascular Fitness, above) as a guideline for refining your strength-training program. If your ankles fatigue on uneven terrain, add unilateral balance exercises or incorporate short weekly training sessions on gravel or sand or traversing slopes to

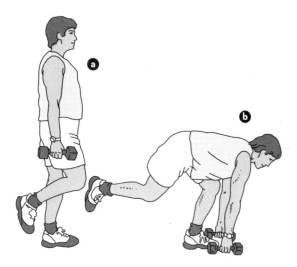

Fig. 4-2. *One-legged dead lift:* **a,** *stand balanced on one leg, holding dumbbell(s);* **b,** *breathing in, hinge forward at the hips, reaching dumbbell(s) to the floor, then exhale and return to upright position.*

Fig. 4-3. *Snow shoveler: **a,** holding dumbbell in both hands, squat with a neutral spine; **b,** stand up, pivoting to one side and swinging dumbbell up to shoulder, following it with your eyes and keeping abdominals tight. Repeat, pivoting to the other side.*

help them adapt. If your quadriceps muscles are sore following steep hikes, strengthen them by increasing the number of sets of step-downs, front squats, or lunges you do. If your shoulders and neck get tired as you increase pack weight, add exercises such as upright rows or shrugs. By tracking such challenges on training hikes, climbers can determine what body areas to focus on.

Building Strength Intensity

In building strength and conditioning, you can use the rate of perceived exertion (RPE) to rate the intensity of an exercise as you are doing it: to improve strength, you need to work at a high enough intensity. For effective, injury-free progression in strength training, use a weight that gets you to an RPE of 7 or 8 on a scale of 1 to 10, with 1 being easiest and 10 almost impossible. Using this scale allows you to self-regulate. Some days you will feel strong and may use a heavier weight, while other days you may feel off and will want to use a lighter weight. As long as you target an RPE of 7 or 8, you are making progress.

Rest Times

To build strength, allow your muscles to rest between sets. When doing four to six repetitions, rest 90 to 120 seconds or until you feel recovered from the last set of repetitions. Without this rest, you will not be able to lift as heavy a weight—which results in building muscle endurance, not strength. When you are just starting out in a strength-training program or are aiming for muscle endurance, rest around 30 seconds between exercises and sets. Rest enough to move with control. Stop for a moment if you start to lose control, then continue when you are ready.

Delayed Onset Muscle Soreness

A methodical strength-training program will most of the time not leave you sore and tired. Delayed onset muscle soreness (DOMS)—which can include mild pain, stiffness, and joint aches—occurs most often after a change in physical activity, after a too-strenuous workout, or after taking time off. DOMS also occurs from the eccentric or lowering phase of an exercise, such as extended downward travel with a heavy pack, downhill trail running, or bouldering that requires dropping from a height onto your feet.

Although it may be tempting to rest to avoid pains caused by DOMS, muscles need oxygen and nutrients to recover, and the most efficient way to deliver them to your muscles is to engage in light physical activity like a brisk walk after your workout or strenuous activity, to increase blood flow without subjecting muscles to more stress. When you return to strength training following time off, ease back into the routine by lowering the intensity, weight, duration, and volume (fewer sets and repetitions) of the exercises, to prevent DOMS.

FLEXIBILITY TRAINING

You can move only as far as your joints allow, so increasing your range of motion allows you more freedom of movement. The active and passive range of motion of muscles around a particular joint determines your flexibility.

Strength training can improve your range of motion if you always move through the full range. However, when you add more weight, use caution because it takes time to develop strength and capacity at the end ranges of motion. Done right, strength training can allow you to leverage your body's ability to move freely. When in doubt, tailor your movements to your sport-specific needs.

Stretching is another way of increasing range of motion in a joint. Stretching muscles can help relax your nervous system after a strenuous workout, which helps you recover. When starting a new training routine, it is normal to experience minor stiffness—stretching may offer ease of movement.

You can stretch as part of your warm-up; pairing the stretch with active movements opens up ranges of motion you will need in your targeted activity. The best way to improve your flexibility is to add dedicated flexibility sessions to your training program or to integrate stretches into your strength workouts, perhaps during your rest times between sets (see Rest Times, above). Either way, work consistently on flexibility for the best results.

Sample Stretches

Some stretches that can increase flexibility include the frog stretch, deep squat, and seated gluteal stretch.

Frog stretch. This lower-body stretch increases flexibility in the hips, groin, and inner thighs. Starting on all fours, support your torso with your hands or forearms on the floor, pointing straight ahead and in line with your shoulders. Engage the core. Slide your knees out as far as is comfortable, keeping them in line with your hips (fig. 4-4). Keep your knees bent at right angles (90 degrees) and feet turned out. Hold for two to five minutes, and do this exercise a few times each week.

Deep squat. This lower-body stretch is great for opening your hips for rock climbing. Stand with your feet apart, slightly wider than shoulder width, and sink into a full squat, keeping your heels flat on the floor and allowing your torso to lean forward slightly but not collapse over your knees (fig. 4-5). Press your elbows against the insides of your knees to increase the stretch in your hips and inner thighs. Hold for at least 30 to 60 seconds. For best results, hold this squat for two to five minutes several times a week.

Seated gluteal stretch. This stretch targets the glutes and lower back. Sit on a bench, armless chair, or car bumper with your knees at a right angle (shins perpendicular and

Fig. 4-5. *Deep squat: keeping heels on the floor and leaning torso slightly forward, squat down as low as is comfortable and press elbows against knees to open up hips.*

Fig. 4-6. *Seated gluteal stretch: sitting with shins perpendicular to ground and thighs parallel to ground and to each other, cross right ankle over left knee, press chest forward with a straight spine, and hold. Repeat with left ankle over right knee.*

thighs parallel to the ground). To stretch the right hip, cross the right ankle over the left knee (fig. 4-6). Press your chest forward with a straight spine (avoid collapsing your chest toward your knee) until you feel a deep stretch in the outer right hip. Hold for 30 to 60 seconds, then repeat with the left ankle over the right knee. Repeat the stretch two to three times. Note which hip is tighter (if either), and in future stretching sessions start by stretching that hip first.

Fig. 4-4. *Frog stretch: Slide knees out in line with hips as far as is comfortable. Engage your core, keeping your knees bent at a 90-degree angle and feet splayed out.*

SKILL DEVELOPMENT

Skill refers to technique and mastery of coordination. Skilled mountaineers move more precisely and use less energy than novices. A beginner climbing four days a week may risk overtraining, whereas a highly conditioned climber can perform the movements with less exertion and strain and may be able to climb at a higher frequency without overdoing it. Experienced mountaineers have a sense of when to back off of the intensity or volume (length of time) of their training sessions and work on less taxing but equally important skills. Develop skill by putting all the techniques discussed in this book into practice and seeking out appropriate training when you need it.

CROSS TRAINING

The final component in preparing for mountaineering adventures is cross training: doing supplemental physical activities not directly related to your targeted sport. At higher skill levels, cross training recruits muscle groups in different patterns and provides psychological and physiological breaks from excessive repetition. Cross training provides body and muscle balance for sports that require repetitive motion from small muscle groups.

While cross training may not relate directly to performance in your chosen sport, keeping your joints healthy and preventing overtraining *does* relate to performance long term. Cross training for the climber may involve horizontal pulling movements or rowing training to balance out the vertical component that dominates the sport. Many mountaineering programs rely on cycling for cross training; this seated activity does not load the spine as mountaineering does, but it is gentler on the legs and has far less impact than running.

Fundamental Training Concepts

Once climbers understand the training components of mountaineering conditioning, they can manipulate them to create a customized training program.

FITT PARAMETERS

The four FITT parameters constitute the training load, or stress. They are Frequency (how often you exercise), Intensity (how hard you exercise), Time (how long you exercise, also called volume), and Type (what exercise modes you do). A person who trains for a one-day beginner rock climb has a low workload: low frequency, low intensity, low time (duration). An advanced high-altitude mountaineer getting ready for an expedition has a high workload: high frequency, low to high intensity, high time (duration). The greater the

workload, the more carefully designed the training program needs to be, with sufficient rest and recovery days to prevent physical and psychological burnout.

Frequency

How often climbers train depends on their current fitness level, end goal, and desired level of achievement. According to the American College of Sports Medicine and the American Heart Association, a suitable fitness program for average healthy adults includes three to five aerobic workouts per week of 20 or more minutes each *and* activities that maintain or increase muscular strength and endurance, a minimum of two nonconsecutive days a week. Mountaineering is a strenuous activity that requires far more training than an average healthy adult needs on a daily basis. As climbers progress to more demanding alpine goals, they will need to increase the frequency of their cardiovascular, sport-specific, and strength-training workouts, and their workouts will vary in intensity and time (duration).

Intensity

How hard a workout is determines its intensity. For information regarding heart rate and optimal cardiovascular intensity for fitness improvement, see Resources. Early in a training program most aerobic workouts should be at a low intensity. Gradually build cardiovascular endurance before adding high-intensity anaerobic workouts late in a training program.

Strength training should also start with low-intensity workouts. Work with lighter weights for a moderate number of repetitions (for example, two or three sets of eight to ten repetitions), especially if you are relatively new to strength training. Next, progress to a phase emphasizing gaining strength by performing more sets with heavier weight and fewer reps. As you peak in reaching your training goal, focus on increasing muscular endurance by using lighter weights but completing more repetitions. Table 4-1 indicates how strength sets and repetitions vary according to the training phase.

Time

Cardiovascular and strength workouts range in length, also known as duration or volume, according to your end goals, training cycle, and exercise type. Climbers should perform aerobic exercise in their training zone for at least 15 to 20 minutes per session in order to see improvements. A strength workout as short as 8 to 10 minutes can provide some benefits, although a typical strength workout ranges from 20 to 60 minutes, depending on the frequency of the strength training.

Type

Workout types vary according to the specific cardiovascular exercises and strength exercises they encompass. Exercise selection depends on individual preference, location (climate and terrain), season, and sport discipline. Choices will vary from one athlete to the next: a rock or ice climber may spend more time at indoor climbing gyms and focus on upper-body and core training in the off-season, while a high-altitude alpine climber may opt for backpacking trips year-round and focus on core and lower-body conditioning exercises in the off-season. Supplemental cross training outside of your chosen sport offers your body the chance to rest and recover, while also providing additional training stimulus for the cardiovascular and musculoskeletal systems.

TRAINING GUIDELINES

In addition to properly balancing the four FITT parameters, climbers should also adhere to a few key training guidelines.

Train Specifically

Do your best to match the cardiovascular modes and intensities of a training program to the primary movements of your intended sport. Sometimes it is difficult to practice a sport: ice climbing is challenging in a warm winter, rock climbing is difficult in the middle of a city, high-altitude trekking may be impossible for those who live at sea level. And sometimes it is beneficial to include cross training for rehabilitation or injury prevention.

To the extent possible, choose comparable activities that work the muscle groups in the same ways the intended sport works them. In a well-rounded program for mountaineering, spinal-loading choices such as hill climbing, stair climbing, and using an inclined cardiovascular machine (for example, an elliptical trainer, treadmill, stair climber, or stepmill)—all with or without a pack—as well as trail running without a pack should be the dominant cardiovascular choices. Non-spinal-loading cardiovascular activities such as biking, rowing, and swimming may be included for cross-training purposes.

Increase Gradually

Increase training volume by no more than 5 to 15 percent at any given time. If a training program starts with 20-minute workouts, add 2 minutes to subsequent cardiovascular sessions. This suggested progression is based on the amount of musculature used, impact on joints, and relative support provided for the body. Activities that rely heavily on smaller upper-body musculature or rigorous full-body movements (for example, cross-country skiing or technical climbing) should be increased by no more than 5 percent at a time. High-impact activities that rely more on large muscles (such as trail running or telemark skiing) should be increased by no more than 10 percent at a time. And finally, low-impact activities (for instance, hiking or scrambling) or seated, supported activities (such as biking) should be increased by less than 15 percent at a time.

For strength training, increase in no more than 2- to 5-pound (1- to 2-kilogram) increments each week for upper-body exercise and in no more than 5- to 10-pound (2- to 5-kilogram) increments for lower-body exercise (remember to self-regulate workouts to hit an intensity of 7 to 8 RPE each workout).

Include Adequate Recovery Time

High-intensity workouts require more recovery time. Endurance days may be done at low intensities, but if you add pack weight or hilly terrain, follow these days with a recovery day. Low-intensity recovery cross-training exercises include walking, swimming, dancing, easy flat-terrain

TABLE 4-1. SAMPLE YEAR-ROUND STRENGTH-TRAINING PROGRAM						
	EARLY TRAINING	MIDDLE TRAINING	LATE TRAINING	ACTIVITY SEASON	POST-ACTIVITY	OFF-SEASON
FOCUS	Establishing baseline; keep volume low.	Strengthening	Strengthening, building endurance	Maintenance	Addressing imbalanced areas developed from sport-specific activities	Training weak points
SETS	Fewer: 2–3	Moderate: 3–5	Fewer: 2–3	Fewer: 2–3	Fewer: 2–3	Moderate: 3–5
REPETITIONS	Moderate: 8–10	Fewer: 4–6	More: 10–15	Few: 3–5	Moderate: 8–10	Few: 3–5

Note: *Number of sets and repetitions are examples and can vary with type of strength-building exercise.*

biking, yoga, and yard work. Such light days help prevent overtraining by allowing tired muscles to rest before they perform again. As climbers grow older, they may need more recovery and training time to reach their training goals.

Adapt to Sex and Hormonal Differences in Training

For people who experience a menstrual or hormonal cycle every month, if it involves physical pain and emotional discomfort, it can be detrimental to consistency in training. However, if you know enough about your body during your cycle, you can plan ahead with training and event days to get an edge on your performance. The first place to start is to track your cycle days and note how you feel in your workouts. Several available apps allow you to track this data, since this area is finally attracting interest among athletes, coaches, and researchers. Your cycle can affect your performance in many ways. For instance, during the follicular phase, you may find that you can exercise harder, go farther, and carry heavier weight in your activities, but during the luteal phase, you may find it harder to perform your endurance workouts. Fluctuating hydration levels and eating certain foods may help or hinder your performance. Do not ever feel less capable because of your biology. With a little preparation and adjustment, you can leverage the timing of your hormones each month and perform at the level you want.

Menopause, another factor that affects performance, also requires some adaptations. With age, people undergo hormonal changes—biological females experience a steep drop in hormones; biological males, a more gradual decline—that require better planning for training and more time for recovery. Rest days play a more significant role, as well as doing other enjoyable activities for cross training. And as you age, your strength and power levels decline; it is important to continue both strength and power training on a regular basis.

NUTRITION HABITS

Comprehensive nutrition guidelines are beyond the scope of this chapter, but the fuel and nutrients you consume directly affect your physical fitness. Six basic habits for sound nutrition focus on healthy choices—without any calorie counting, measuring food, or giving up favorites (for other food and water considerations, see Chapter 3, Camping, Food, and Water). These habits are as applicable to the weekend sport climber as they are to the die-hard mountaineer who wants to climb the Seven Summits. All that you need to adopt these six habits are your own hands.

Habit 1. Eat *slowly*, and try to stop eating when you feel 80 percent full (that is, still slightly hungry), to teach yourself what comfortably full feels like for you. After eating slowly for 20 minutes (the approximate amount of time it takes for satiety signals to reach the brain), if you are still hungry, eat some more.

Habit 2. Include vegetables with each meal. A cup of leafy greens or a half cup of other vegetables qualifies as one serving. Try to include between one and four servings with every meal, depending on your biological sex, age, body size, and nutritional needs. Eat from every color of the rainbow to maximize your phytonutrient benefits.

Habit 3. Include protein with each meal. Think palm-sized based on your own hand—anywhere from one to two palms' worth, depending on your biological sex, age, body size, and nutritional needs. Good sources of protein include whole eggs; lean beef, pork, or lamb; poultry; or seafood. For plant-based eaters, focus on legumes (such as lentils, beans, and tofu), nutritional yeast, and high-protein grains (including spelt, quinoa, and seitan).

Habit 4. Make sure to get healthy fats with each meal—fats that are rich in omega-3 fatty acids and low in omega-6 fatty acids. Nuts, nut butters, seeds, extra-virgin olive oil, avocados, and fish oils are excellent choices. Try to include between one to two thumb-sized portions with each meal, depending on your biological sex, age, body size, and nutritional needs.

Habit 5. Focus on starchy carbohydrates and include between one and two fist-sized portions (size after cooking), depending on your biological sex, age, body size, and nutritional needs. Choose from such foods as rice, sprouted grains, other whole grains, potatoes, squash, and pasta. Ideally, athletes should focus on eating whole unprocessed foods whenever possible. Eat any sweet snacks in moderation slowly so you can fully enjoy them. They are made with not just sugar but also fats, which drives up their energy density.

Habit 6. Drink plenty of water, and consider adding in an electrolyte (sodium, potassium, magnesium) if you sweat a lot. The amount of water you need is based on how active you are, how much you sweat, and the size of your body. Start with 2 quarts (liters) a day at minimum, and consume more on days when you are training longer than an hour—enough to keep your urine output relatively clear.

FITNESS PROGRAM TRAINING BLOCKS

To develop a suitable training program, start by noting the date you want to attain your end goal. In many cases, registering for a climb or making a deposit on a trip provides a deadline that is hard to change. There may also be a short window of opportunity for a given climb—for example, for ice climbs in most parts of the world. Once you have a firm date, break the time between that end goal and the training program's starting point into six distinct training blocks, each with a different objective based on the target activity in your end goal. Table 4-2 illustrates how an entire year may be divided into training blocks.

1. Early training. In the early phase of your training program, the goal is to establish a solid foundation, or baseline, on which to build the rest of the training. Frequency, intensity, and time for both cardiovascular training and strength training will probably be fairly low, and the type of activity is more general.

2. Middle training. In the middle phase, the training focus shifts to increasing cardiovascular endurance, so increase frequency and time of cardiovascular exercise gradually while keeping intensity low. Focus on building strength specific to the chosen activity with increased intensity (more weight, fewer repetitions, more sets) for strength exercises.

3. Late training In the late stages of training, as the end-goal date or start of activity season approaches, the focus shifts to increasing stamina and enhancing mental toughness (see Mental Conditioning later in this chapter). This could mean adding intensity in the form of one or two weekly anaerobic sessions, adding pack weight and distance to long weekend conditioning trips, and training for more strength endurance (lighter weight, higher repetitions). The late phase is devoted to peaking (performing at our best) and tapering (engaging in less overall volume) for a climb or for the start of the intended sport's season. The training program leading up to the activity season can last from one to six months.

4. Activity season. A sport's activity season might consist of getting out into the mountains several times or more a month. The end goal might encompass a series of climbs or trips or a single targeted climb, generally from late spring through summer and early autumn, depending on location; ice climbing and some climbs would take place in winter. The training goal in this period is to maintain peak performance level during the intended activity; however, this window can be quite short. Peak performance often comes a few weeks after the training program's late phase and a good week of tapering (less overall volume of activity). The activity season might last from one to six months. Therefore, FITT parameters (Frequency, Intensity, Time, Type) of the training program for a climber planning to ascend Mount Everest will look quite different from the training program for a climber whose goal is to climb technical but low-altitude mountains every week throughout summer or year in some climates.

5. Post-activity. After the active season, training ideally focuses on addressing any imbalances that arose from those activities. Common to climbing is the need to balance a season of horizontal and vertical pulling by adding horizontal and vertical pressing movements, thus improving shoulder stability. This period lasts two to four weeks.

6. Off-season. The off-season is when the sport or activity cannot be engaged in, due to weather and/or terrain conditions. During this period, training prioritizes any weak points that have emerged, such as quadriceps that tired on steep downhills, hips that got tight on longer trips, or lower-back muscles that fatigued with heavier pack weight. The off-season is the time between post-activity and the next training program—generally several months, unless a climber participates in multiple sports.

A sample year. If a novice climber is training for a very easy first mountaineering outing, the early phase of the training program may last only one to two weeks, with two or three weeks for each of the other five training blocks. A more experienced mountaineer or climber working toward complex goals that require more than half a year of training might spend a month in each training block, cycling through the middle phase of the training program several times, alternating between strength building and

TABLE 4-2. SAMPLE TRAINING BLOCKS AND GOALS FOR ONE YEAR					
EARLY TRAINING	**MIDDLE TRAINING**	**LATE TRAINING**	**ACTIVITY SEASON**	**POST-ACTIVITY**	**OFF-SEASON**
Establish baseline.	Increase cardiovascular endurance and build strength.	Enhance mental toughness and stamina; peak and taper.	Maintain performance level.	Focus on imbalances developed from sport-specific activities.	Prioritize training of weak points.

endurance building and separating each ramp-up with a week of active recovery (tapering). Each block in a training program has a different focus, which the daily workouts should reflect.

Building an Annual Training Program

This section provides details on how to set up an annual training program, with a sample calendar based on a northern-hemisphere mountaineer who typically climbs most during late spring through early autumn. This calendar varies depending on where and when climbers do most of their mountaineering.

Post-activity. After an intense season of mountaineering, the body needs a break. This period includes shorter aerobic workouts, reduced pack weights, and cross-training workouts unrelated to the sport's activity. The goal in this training block is to rest, both physically and mentally (see Mental Conditioning later in this chapter). For the example northern-hemisphere climber, post-activity would generally encompass October; after several weeks of reduced intensity, the climber might shift to training for winter activities, to get ready for snow sports such as snowshoeing, cross-country skiing, downhill skiing, and/or winter ice climbing.

Off-season. This is the ideal time to evaluate what worked well in the training program from the previous activity season. Strength-training sessions address any muscle imbalances that may have developed or been identified during the sport's activity season. This is a great time to add focused flexibility training to improve range of motion and tissue health. Training intensity and time remain low, but frequency may increase once the climber is fully recovered from the activity season. For the example northern-hemisphere climber, off-season would be November and December. But if that climber is participating in winter ice climbing during the off-season, adding a focus on calf, core, and forearm training would be appropriate to support swinging ice axes overhead for longer periods of time.

Training program. In the early phase of the program, include unilateral strength exercises for balance and agility to address any problems detected in the off-season. Introduce pack carrying and other sport-specific training at somewhat reduced intensities from those of the previous post-activity period, gradually building back up to weight-carrying and distance-traveling goals for the intended activity. As you work through the middle to late training phases, increase intensity and decrease volume in strength training. Cardiovascular training time (volume) can increase by 15 percent or less per week. For the example northern-hemisphere climber, a program would run from January through April.

Activity season. In this period, the training focus shifts to maintenance, with full-body strength training twice a week and weekly anaerobic training when appropriate. Climbers might participate in as many trips, climbs, or events as desired and schedule suitable recovery time following each outing. For the example northern-hemisphere climber, the activity season would be from May through September. If a climber is aiming for a specific objective on a specific date, such as climbing Mount Rainier on June 15, instead of participating in trips or climbs randomly, they should thoughtfully choose trips as secondary goals that build toward the primary goal, allowing for an adequate tapering period leading up to the date of the primary objective.

Training for two activity seasons. A mountaineer who climbs in two seasons—for example, both summer rock and winter ice—can take one to two weeks of off-season for evaluation and flexibility training between the end of one activity's season (summer rock climbing or winter climbing) and the beginning of the next. Such climbers will have two seasons to prepare for and shorter training periods for each sport. The advantage is that participating in two sports helps a climber maintain a baseline of climbing strength and flexibility, so the training program does not have to be as extensive.

Training for year-round climbing readiness. The climber who is outdoors year-round—for example, climbing rock in spring and fall and alpine ice in summer, then traveling over glaciers in austral summer—may need a program with four seasonal cycles leading up to specific high-priority climbing objectives. *Off-season* might refer to any season that is lower priority, and training frequency, intensity, time, and type would vary according to the highest-priority goal.

SAMPLE TRAINING PROGRAM

When climbers assemble their goals and exercise preferences, evaluate their skill level, and combine all the fitness components and training parameters, they have a personalized training program that will work uniquely for them. Each climber's program will look different, based on individual body type and size, goals, age, and social environment. A single program *cannot possibly* work for every mountaineer.

The template shown in Table 4-3 illustrates just one example of how all the training variables might fit together in a six-week training program suitable for a goal such as a 7-mile (11.3-kilometer) outing with a 20-pound (9-kilogram) pack covering an elevation gain and loss of 3,200 feet (975 meters). The weekend progression begins with baseline hiking of 5 miles (8 kilometers) roundtrip with 2,300 feet (700 meters) of elevation gain while carrying a 13-pound (6-kilogram) pack and gradually transitions to steeper terrain—by increasing elevation gain by 300 to 500 feet (90 to 150 meters) per outing—and a heavier pack weight, up to 23 pounds (10.4 kilograms).

At each step along the way, climbers choose types of cardiovascular exercise and specific strength movements to fit personal preferences, lifestyle factors, and individual body needs. Modern endurance training regimes recommend dedicating 70 to 80 percent of the training to building and maintaining aerobic capacity, supplemented with anaerobic and strength training.

Mental Conditioning

Most accomplished climbers agree that mountaineering involves both physical and mental demands. Skilled mountaineers are more comfortable and confident in situations that may cause novice climbers to panic, make mistakes, exercise poor judgment, or experience accidents that could lead to injury. Aspiring mountaineers would be wise to dedicate as much, if not more, time to mental conditioning as they do to physical conditioning. There are many elements to mental conditioning, but the following are key starting points.

UNDERSTANDING AND MANAGING FEARS

Fear is a series of chemical reactions in the brain triggered by psychological or physical stress stimuli. When we are faced with an imminent threat, fear is the mechanism through which our brain sounds the alarm by releasing adrenaline. Adrenaline (also called epinephrine) activates the sympathetic nervous system, which causes physiological

TABLE 4-3. SAMPLE SIX-WEEK TRAINING PLAN TO PREPARE FOR STRENUOUS DAY HIKES						
WEEK	DAY 1	DAY 2	DAY 3	DAY 4	DAY 5	WEEKEND (1 DAY)
BUILD STRENGTH						
1	40 minutes aerobic; 30 minutes strength	60 minutes aerobic, 15-pound pack	Off	60 minutes aerobic, no pack	30 minutes full-body, sport-specific strength	2,300 feet gain, 5–6 miles roundtrip, 13-pound pack
2	40 minutes aerobic; 30 minutes strength	60 minutes aerobic, 17-pound pack	Off	60 minutes aerobic, no pack	45 minutes full-body, sport-specific strength	2,600 feet gain, 5–6 miles roundtrip, 16-pound pack
3	45 minutes aerobic; 40 minutes strength	30 minutes uphill or stair intervals, 20-pound pack	Off	70 minutes aerobic, no pack	45 minutes full-body, sport-specific strength	2,600 feet gain, 5–6 miles roundtrip, 19-pound pack
BUILD STAMINA						
4	45 minutes aerobic; 45 minutes strength	35 minutes uphill or stair intervals, 22-pound pack	Off	60 minutes aerobic, no pack	45 minutes full-body, sport-specific strength	2,900 feet gain, 6–8 miles roundtrip, 19-pound pack
5	45 minutes aerobic; 45 minutes strength	40 minutes uphill or stair intervals, 25-pound pack	Off	65 minutes aerobic, no pack	45 minutes full-body, sport-specific strength	2,900 feet gain, 6–8 miles roundtrip, 23-pound pack
6	60 minutes recovery (easy cardio)	30 minutes cardio; 45 minutes strength	Off	45 minutes aerobic, no pack	Off	3,200 feet gain, 7 miles roundtrip, 20-pound pack

Note: *To convert feet to meters, multiply by 0.3048. To convert miles to kilometers, multiply by 1.6. To convert pounds to kilograms, multiply by 0.4536. Source is* The Outdoor Athlete *by Courtenay W. Schurman and Doug G. Schurman (see Resources).*

responses: the heart beats faster, your breathing becomes shallower, palms start to sweat, and muscles tense to prepare the body for "fight or flight" from the threat or danger. Mountaineering elements that could trigger climbers' anxiety or fear often coincide with situations of higher perceived risk and consequences, such as being high up on a multipitch route on a rock wall or down-climbing a steep, icy couloir. Climbers need to learn to recognize what triggers their fear and have an approach for managing those triggers so their physiological responses do not become debilitating.

Mental-conditioning tools include desensitizing yourself by incrementally increasing exposure to fear factors, visualizing yourself safely moving through key sections of a planned route, and using fear to bring your focus back to the task at hand. These are all proven ways to break the brain's chemical feedback loop. Deep breathing (longer exhalations engaging the diaphragm that squeeze out every last pocket of air) also activates the parasympathetic nervous system, which controls the brain's "rest and digest" function and allows you to relax. To explore other methods of addressing fear in more depth, see the Resources for this chapter and chapter 23, Risk Management. These techniques require you to be self-aware and practice them regularly.

DEVELOPING SELF-AWARENESS

Some key internal factors that could influence the outcome of a mountaineering trip are a climber's motivations, tendencies, emotions (including fears), and honest assessment of current limitations. Not recognizing when decisions are being guided by "summit fever" or being unaware of a tendency to overestimate your skills when planning a climbing trip can lead to catastrophic results. Developing self-awareness requires conscious, regular practice. Establish a habit of evaluating your decision-making process through the lens of someone you trust (for example, "What would my climbing mentor do if faced with the same decision?") so that you can recognize and catalog personal tendencies.

Another way to develop self-awareness is by journaling, or writing down your thoughts when you experience a specific emotion, such as fear. What physical cues emerge during stressful situations? By documenting these instances, you can start to understand how and why you react to certain situations. You can then use this information to manage your emotions, such as fear, and replace your initial reactions with better strategies.

BUILDING SKILLS THROUGH PRACTICE

The only way for mountaineers to build confidence is by knowing that they have the skills to address varying situations in the mountains, and those skills develop over time from experience. A dependable way for beginner climbers to gain skills and experience is by setting incremental, attainable goals and practicing the skill successfully several times before moving on to a new objective. The act of setting goals and systematically achieving them provides mental comfort when you tackle a new skill. Successfully climbing a challenging route once may be the result of luck, but being able to do so every time is a source of confidence climbers can fall back on when trying a new route of equal or slightly higher difficulty.

Beyond Training: Recovery

All the hard training in the world will mean nothing if you do not allow your body the time it needs to repair damage, replenish muscle glycogen stores, and prepare to work hard again. High-intensity cardiovascular and strength workouts require more recovery time than endurance or recovery workouts do. While endurance days (for example, aerobic workouts lasting more than an hour) are done at lower intensities, as soon as you add pack weight or hilly terrain, insert a rest day, unless your specific program calls for back-to-back training to prepare for a multiday trip. Recovery days at lower intensity may include cross-training exercise such as easy walking or biking, dancing, or relaxed yard work. Such easy days help avoid strain by allowing tired muscles to rest before they perform again. You also have the option of resting completely. Mountaineers 55 and older may need to plan on even more recovery time and training time to reach their fitness goals.

Pay close attention to your body. If you feel tired or sore from a workout or climb, reduce the intensity of your current workout or work out for a shorter period of time than scheduled. If your finger or elbow tendons are tender to the touch following a hard climb or workout, try cross training to allow them to recover adequately. Plan strength-training sessions or highly demanding rock or ice climbs at least 48 hours apart so that the targeted muscles, tendons, and ligaments can recover before they are stressed again. If you expect to climb multiple days in a row, try to alternate days of higher-intensity workloads (or carries, in the case of expeditions) with those of lower-intensity workloads (or "climb high, sleep low," in the case of high-altitude expeditions). Tendons and ligaments take longer than muscles to adjust to increased workloads. They also take a frustrating amount of time to heal once they are injured.

Other factors that help you recover include getting adequate sleep (seven to nine hours per night), managing daily stress, eating well, staying hydrated, meditating, and reflecting on your experiences. Limited research supports that massage or vibration therapy (massage guns) enhance recovery. You may want to try one out to see if it helps you recover. The more you train, the more you need to recover.

Although most mountaineers find it difficult to take time off from a favorite activity, it is better to let your body heal completely before resuming a sport. Otherwise, an acute irritation may turn into a chronic injury that requires a much longer time away. Knowing that you have done the physical training necessary to succeed will empower you to face challenges or worst-case scenarios not only in your chosen activity but also in daily life. To achieve mountaineering goals, you must first acquire the knowledge to get there, and then dedicate yourself to the physical and mental conditioning you need to reach the high hills and enjoy the freedom they offer.

CHAPTER 5

NAVIGATION AND COMMUNICATION

 Hiking on a manicured, well-signed trail rarely requires much in the way of navigation skills, but alpine climbers, mostly far away from this luxury, must possess competent wilderness navigation skills and feel confident applying them in the field.

5

odern tools like digital mapping software, high-quality GPS phone apps, and two-way satellite communication devices have made trip planning and navigation easier. But climbers still need to hone the foundational skills of planning their route, evaluating terrain, reading topographic maps, and using a compass and altimeter. This chapter details the skills you need to achieve greater success when you step off the beaten path.

Mountaineers have access to a broad set of tools to accomplish the two key objectives of a climb. First, they need to know where they are and how to get to their objective and back again safely. Second, they need to be able to communicate with emergency responders in the event of an accident or other unfortunate event. Modern-day navigation tools allow the mountaineer to accomplish both objectives with far more confidence than in the past. Using multiple tools increases mountaineers' confidence in their location and route, provides backup when tools fail or are lost, and increases situational awareness. Mountaineers rely on five primary tools to navigate and communicate in the backcountry: paper and digital maps, a GPS (Global Positioning System) device or phone with GPS app, an altimeter, a compass, and satellite-based communication device(s) to contact emergency first responders.

This book assumes that mountaineers travel through relatively remote backcountry where timely outside support is unlikely. Returning safely depends on climbers' experience, preparation, skill, and judgment. Mountaineers need to decide where to walk, scramble, or climb, and they do this by knowing where they are, where they are going and by what route, how long it will take, and what they expect to encounter along the way. Orientation is the process of determining your position relative to your surroundings. Navigation is the process of using skills and tools to reach a destination. Routefinding is selecting the most efficient and least risky path to that destination. Routefinding, which is covered in Chapter 6, Wilderness Travel, requires a solid foundation in the tools and skills described in this chapter.

Map

Every mountaineer needs to carry at least one map. Traditionally, paper maps were printed by government agencies or commercial companies, but these maps have waned in popularity with the availability of digital maps. Many traditional printed maps have been converted to digital map layers that depict the same details but can be printed at a variety of scales and on different paper sizes. Digital maps contain the same details but are more likely to be up to date, especially those based on publicly maintained sources such as OpenStreetMap (OSM).

Digital map layers abound, including all the USGS maps (historical and US Topo); US National Park Service and Forest Service maps; Mexico Topo and other Latin American national layers; European national and other layers; CanMaps (Canada); OSM; National Geographic; Green Trails Maps; road, nautical, and cycling maps; satellite imagery; and overlays for shaded relief, slope, and contours.

A GPS device manufacturer, such as Garmin, sells proprietary map packages that customers install on their devices, and some devices come with topographic maps installed. Phone apps such as Gaia GPS, CalTopo, and Avenza Maps allow a user to download select digital map layers and custom sources. When displayed on phone apps or GPS devices (see GPS Devices later in this chapter), digital maps indicate your location, rendering orientation trivial. Climbers can download multiple map layers targeting a single trip and smaller area, or a much larger seamless map area to address unexpected changes in plans.

For trip planning, one of the benefits of digital maps is that you can combine their layers to create hybrid map views. Some digital map layers contain useful geocoded information such as weather, snow depth, or slope angles for overlay onto navigational map layers, amplifying the information (these geocoded layers are sometimes called overlays). A relief shading overlay illustrates terrain slope and type in hues of green, gray, and brown. Digital maps can be customized with waypoints, routes, and notes, and climbers can upload these customized maps to phones or GPS devices for field use.

Though digital maps are valuable, they become inaccessible when the phone or device is lost or damaged or its battery is drained. Sharing digital maps with your climbing partners and carrying physical maps ensures that you will always have a usable map. Maps at a suitable scale can be printed from software like CalTopo (see Printing and Protecting Physical Maps, below).

TYPES OF MAPS

Several types of maps are useful to climbers. Topographic maps (topos), essential for off-trail travel, are usually the best choice for mountaineers. Other maps include commercial recreation maps, guidebook maps, and maps created by land management agencies. Additional visual tools include climbers' sketch maps and satellite imagery.

Topographic maps. These maps depict the shape of Earth's surface, its topography, by showing contour lines that represent constant elevations above sea level (see Figures 5-1 and 5-2). Elevations may be in units of either feet or meters; be sure to check the map key.

For many decades, the only topographic maps available in the US were those produced by the US Geological Survey (USGS). The entire continental US is mapped at a scale of 1:24,000 (see Reading a Topographic Map, below) in USGS 7.5-minute series maps. Each map sheet covers 7.5 minutes of latitude and 7.5 minutes of longitude (more about coordinates below), or about 6 miles (10 kilometers) by 9 miles (14.5 kilometers). Based on aerial photos, these USGS maps portray the terrain with carefully drawn contour lines and show areas of vegetation, water, rock, and glaciers as of their publication date.

Historical 7.5-minute maps have shortcomings for backcountry use and are no longer the best option for mountaineers. They are difficult to locate and purchase. Roads and trails are often out of date, trails can be difficult to see, a UTM grid (see Coordinate Systems, below) and relief shading are often lacking, and section lines irrelevant to wilderness travelers add clutter. Finally, these maps are printed at a fixed scale and on a fixed paper size rather than centered on a climber's specific trip.

Commercial companies and mapping software often use these USGS topographic maps as a base layer but improve them by adding current trails, points of interest, shaded relief, land ownership, and other features useful to climbers. These commercially printed maps, such as Green Trails Maps and National Geographic Maps, or mapping software such as CalTopo, are usually a better choice than 7.5-minute USGS maps.

Land management and recreation maps. Because recreation maps are updated frequently, they are useful for current details on roads, trails, ranger stations, and other human constructions. They usually show only a flat view of natural features, without contour lines that indicate the shape of the land. These recreation maps, published by the US Forest Service and other government agencies, are suitable for trip planning.

Guidebook maps. Some guidebook maps are sketches; others are detailed interpretations of topographic maps. Though they vary greatly in quality, most contain useful details on roads, trails, and climbing routes.

Climbers' sketch maps. Often called climbing route topos, sketch maps made by climbers are two-dimensional sketches whose route detail may make up for what they lack in draftsmanship. They represent climbing features on vertical terrain rather than the bird's-eye perspective of traditional maps. Such drawings can effectively supplement map and guidebook information.

Satellite images. Although they are not maps, satellite images can be of significant help in researching wilderness routes. For example, websites such as Gaia GPS and CalTopo provide frequently updated, high-resolution imagery of snowpack. Satellite imagery can be downloaded like any other map layer on some phones and GPS devices.

PRINTING AND PROTECTING PHYSICAL MAPS

Sometimes more than one map is needed to cover the area of a trip. With mapping software like CalTopo, you can print pages that cover your entire route; using larger sizes of paper (like 11" × 17" or A3) can be helpful. Commercial copy centers may be your best choice for color printing. (See the "Printing Digital Maps" sidebar below.) If using commercial maps, either fold adjoining maps at the edges and tape them together or create a customized map by cutting and splicing. Include plenty of territory to generate an overview of the trip area and the surrounding terrain.

Physical maps—precious objects that they are—deserve tender care in the wild. Some custom maps can be obtained or printed on waterproof paper or plastic that will withstand wet conditions. Storing a physical map in a protective case or resealable plastic bag also helps protect it. On the climb, carry the map in an easily accessible place where you can reach it without taking off your pack. Clever climbers also access (and enlarge) paper maps by taking backup photos with their phone.

READING A TOPOGRAPHIC MAP

Topographic maps are essential to wilderness travel, and mountaineers need to be able to glean as much information from them as possible (fig. 5-1). Understanding features on topographic maps such as coordinate systems, datums, scale, and contour lines is a crucial navigation skill.

Most all topographic maps have a legend of symbols and colors used for the map's features. For example, in a historical USGS map (see "Topographic Maps" under Types of Maps, above), contour lines are brown except on permanent snowfields or glaciers, where they are blue. Blue is also used for water features such as lakes, rivers, and oceans. Multiple methods and colors are used to show roads, trails, vegetation, and other features.

Coordinate Systems

Two common geographic coordinate systems used to define a location on Earth are latitude-longitude and Universal Transverse Mercator (UTM).

Latitude and longitude coordinates divide Earth into the 360 degrees of a circle. A measurement east or west around the globe is called longitude; a measurement north or south is called latitude. Longitude is measured 180 degrees east and 180 degrees west, starting at the north-south line (meridian) that goes through the Royal Observatory at Greenwich, England. Latitude is measured 0 to 90 degrees north and 0 to 90 degrees south, starting at the equator. This system allows each place on the planet to be identified by a unique set of coordinates. For example, Kathmandu, Nepal, is situated near 27 degrees north latitude and 85 degrees east longitude.

Each degree of latitude or longitude is divided into 60 minutes, and each minute is further subdivided into 60 seconds—just as for units of time. On a map, a latitude of 27 degrees, 42 minutes, 2 seconds north is written as 27°42'2"N. Search and rescue organizations, as well as phone and mapping applications, tend to use decimal degrees converted from minutes and seconds; the latitude in the previous example would be written in decimal degrees as 27.7005°, with the positive number indicating north (a negative number indicates south). Longitudes east of Greenwich, to 180 degrees east, are written as positive numbers, while those west of Greenwich, to 180 degrees west and throughout the western hemisphere, are written as negative numbers.

The UTM coordinate system is another method for identifying a point on a map. Because the UTM system is metric-based, it allows easy computation of distances between points and can be easier to use with a printed map. (To learn more about UTM, see Orienting Using GPS later in this chapter.)

Datums

The two coordinate systems in the preceding section describe locations on Earth's surface. A datum is a frame of reference for representing the position of locations on Earth, and worldwide there are many different ones. When you plot a point on a map using a phone app or GPS device, the datums of device and map need to match—otherwise, you may find yourself hundreds of feet off. Whatever map you are using, it is important to set the datum on the device to match the datum on the printed map. Fortunately, simplifying things, nearly all modern paper and digital maps are based on a datum called WGS84.

The North American Datum of 1927 (NAD27), used on the USGS's historical topos, was based on points on Earth's surface similar to surveyors' benchmarks. The World Geodetic System of 1984 (WGS84), used on the USGS's digital US Topo maps, is based on the center of the Earth. In 1987, WGS84 became the default standard datum for coordinates stored in GPS apps and devices; it is international in scope rather than local or national.

The datums NAD27 and WGS84 will appear to produce the same location on Earth. But because they are based on two different systems, the actual locations they produce differ. That difference is called the datum shift and it varies depending on location. Near Seattle, Washington, for example, the shift between these two datums on a UTM grid is about 720 feet (220 meters) at a bearing of about 335 degrees; the latitude-longitude shift is about 300 feet (90 meters) at a bearing of about 256 degrees.

Scale

The scale of a map is the ratio between measurements on the map and in the real world. There are three ways to indicate scale; a map may have one, two, or all three: (1) a bar

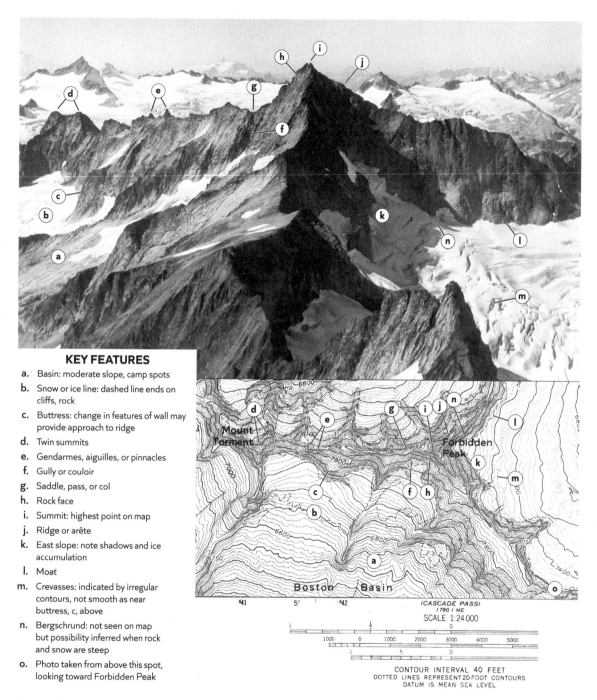

KEY FEATURES

a. Basin: moderate slope, camp spots

b. Snow or ice line: dashed line ends on cliffs, rock

c. Buttress: change in features of wall may provide approach to ridge

d. Twin summits

e. Gendarmes, aiguilles, or pinnacles

f. Gully or couloir

g. Saddle, pass, or col

h. Rock face

i. Summit: highest point on map

j. Ridge or arête

k. East slope: note shadows and ice accumulation

l. Moat

m. Crevasses: indicated by irregular contours, not smooth as near buttress, c, above

n. Bergschrund: not seen on map but possibility inferred when rock and snow are steep

o. Photo taken from above this spot, looking toward Forbidden Peak

Fig. 5-1. *Key features of a mountainous area are indicated on this topographic map and the corresponding photograph. The glaciers on Forbidden Peak in Washington's North Cascades have receded significantly since this photo by Tom Olson was first published in the late 1960s.*

scale, a graphic representation often printed at the bottom of a map; (2) a ratio scale, such as 1:24,000 (which means "1 inch on the map equals 24,000 inches in the real world"); and (3) a verbal scale, such as "1 inch equals 1 mile." (See the bottom right of Figure 5-1 for examples of bar scale and ratio scale.) Typically, a bar scale is the most helpful because it allows climbers to put a twig, finger, or string (such as a compass lanyard) on the bar scale and quickly measure real-world distance on the map.

Ratio scale is less useful with nonmetric maps: "1 inch equals 24,000 inches" is difficult for most people to visualize: 24,000 must first be divided by 12 to arrive at feet. A ratio scale is more helpful on metric maps, because the distance conversion of centimeters to meters is straightforward. For example, on a metric map with a ratio scale of 1:50,000, 1 centimeter on the map equals 500 meters (or 0.5 kilometer) in the field. Metric maps are used in nearly every country outside of the US.

With mapping software, you can usually print a map at whatever scale ratio you want (see the "Printing Digital Maps" sidebar). A scale of around 1:24,000 or 1:25,000 can be a good choice to show greater terrain detail—useful for off-trail or cross-country travel—while a scale of 1:50,000 might be good for a backpacking trip when you are staying on existing trails.

Contour Lines

The heart of a topographic map is its overlay of contour lines. Each contour line indicates a constant elevation in the actual landscape. A map's contour interval is the difference in elevation between adjacent contour lines. In mountainous areas, this interval is often 40 feet (12 meters). To make contour lines easier to use, every fifth contour line, or index contour line, is printed darker than the other lines and is labeled periodically with the elevation. Metric maps usually use a contour interval of 5, 10, or 20 meters (16, 33, or 66 feet). Mapping software may offer choices of contour intervals (see the "Printing Digital Maps" sidebar).

A topographic map shows whether a route travels uphill or downhill. If the route crosses contour lines of increasingly higher elevation, it goes uphill; if it crosses contour lines of increasingly lower elevation, it goes downhill. Flat or sidehill travel is indicated by a route that crosses few or no contour lines. The direction perpendicular to contour lines is the fall line—that is, the direction of the slope.

Contour lines also indicate cliffs, summits, passes, and other terrain features (fig. 5-2). Climbers can improve their interpretation of these lines by periodically comparing the terrain with a map (see Figure 5-1). Climbers increase their

---

PRINTING DIGITAL MAPS

Regardless of the printing capabilities of different software packages, these key tips will guide you when printing a digital map for backcountry use:

- **Base topo.** Use a relatively clean and high-contrast topographic layer for the base map.

- **Grid.** Choose a coordinate system (UTM or latitude-longitude) for the map, in order to produce a grid overlay.

- **Datum.** Set the datum to WGS84, the default for most phone apps and GPS devices.

- **Scale.** For maximum compatibility with physical navigation tools (compass, Romer interpolation scales, et cetera), use a fixed scale that matches your tools (1:24,000 and 1:25,000 are common). For larger overview maps, if you opt for a custom scale (1:50,000 is common), some scales may render a map incompatible with some navigation tools; thus, climbers may have to print two or more maps at different scales.

- **Terrain shading.** This feature can make the map easier to interpret by visualizing slopes and gullies independently from contour lines. However, on many home printers, terrain shading can result in muddy areas that are difficult to read; if this occurs, choose map layers that do not have terrain shading.

- **Print settings.** If your printer has a "fit to page" setting, turn it off, especially when the map has a fixed scale. Print the map at 100 percent or "actual" size for a true-scale map.

- **Cropping.** Do not simply center the map on your route. Include significant landmarks and features such as surrounding peaks that can aid in navigation. Or print two maps, one with greater detail.

- **Water protection.** Laser-jet printouts are less likely to smear when they get wet than inkjet printouts. To further improve water resistance, consider printing on waterproof paper such as Rite in the Rain.

---

situational awareness when they can refer to a topographic map and form a clear mental image of the lay of the land. Following are the main features depicted by contour lines:

Flat areas have no contour lines at all or contour lines very far apart (fig. 5-2a).

Gentle slopes have widely spaced contour lines (fig. 5-2b; see also Figure 5-1a).

Steep slopes have closely spaced contour lines (fig. 5-2c; see also Figure 5-1k).

Cliffs have contour lines extremely close together or touching (fig. 5-2d; see also Figure 5-1h).

Valleys, ravines, gullies, or couloirs have contour lines in a U or V pattern pointing uphill, the direction of higher elevation. An uphill-pointing U pattern shows a gentle, rounded valley or gully; an uphill-pointing V pattern shows a sharp valley or gully (fig. 5-2e; see also Figure 5-1f).

Ridges or spurs have contour lines in a U or V pattern pointing downhill, the direction of lower elevation. A downhill-pointing U pattern shows a gentle, rounded ridge; a downhill-pointing V shows a sharp ridge (fig. 5-2f; see also Figure 5-1j). Confused about whether a contour shows a valley or a ridge? Valleys and ravines often display streams in the V.

Peaks or summits have concentric patterns of contour lines, with the summit the innermost and highest ring (fig. 5-2g; see also Figure 5-1d and i). A peak may also be indicated by an "X," an elevation number, a benchmark (BM), and/or a triangle symbol.

Cirques or bowls have patterns of contour lines forming a semicircle, rising from a low spot in the center of the partial circle, showing a natural amphitheater at the head of a valley or along a bluff (fig. 5-2h).

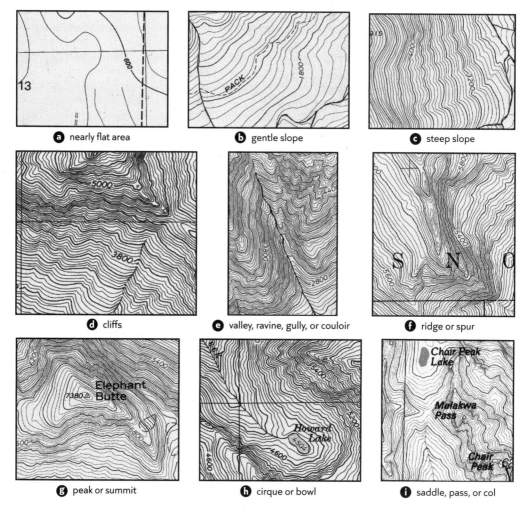

Fig. 5-2. *Contour lines showing basic topographic features:* **a,** *flat area;* **b,** *gentle slope;* **c,** *steep slope;* **d,** *cliffs;* **e,** *valley with stream;* **f,** *ridge;* **g,** *peak;* **h,** *bowl;* **i,** *pass.*

Saddles, passes, or cols have an hourglass shape, with higher contour lines on each side, indicating a low point on a ridge (fig. 5-2i; see also Figure 5-1g). The closer the contour lines, the steeper the terrain.

Other Information

Map margins can have important information, such as date of publication and revision, contour interval, and scale. The margin also may give the area's magnetic declination (discussed later in this chapter), which is the difference between true north and magnetic north.

Topographic maps have certain limitations. Only so much information can be drawn on a map without it becoming unreadable. Features shorter than the contour interval may not be shown; for instance, if climbers navigate with a map that has a 40-foot (12-meter) contour interval, the map may not indicate a 30-foot (9-meter) cliff.

Most commercial maps have their publication dates printed on them. Check the map's date before relying on it because information on forests, magnetic declination, roads, trails, streams and rivers, and other changeable features could be out of date. For example, a forest may have been logged, a road may have been extended or abandoned, or a river may have shifted course since the map was last revised. Most default layers for popular mapping apps rely heavily on OpenStreetMap and are more likely to be up to date.

Although topographic maps are essential to wilderness travel, climbers may need to supplement them with information from visitors to the area, trip reports, blog posts, Forest Service or Park Service rangers, guidebooks, and other maps. Annotate changes on your maps as you learn about or encounter them, or print a fresh version of your map from updated digital or paper map sources.

GPS

The US Department of Defense and similar agencies in other countries have satellites or space-based navigation systems. The current primary systems are: US Global Positioning System (GPS); Russia's Global Navigation Satellite System (GLONASS); the European Galileo System; and China's BeiDou (BDS). This chapter refers to these systems collectively as GPS.

Satellite-based systems have revolutionized navigation. From orbits of about 12,000 miles (20,000 kilometers) above Earth's surface, GPS satellite signals are available nearly anywhere on the planet. Because phone apps can be used for GPS navigation, this section includes other signal types, such as cellular phone signals, with a range of a few

miles, and local Wi-Fi networks, with a range of several hundred feet. Unlike satellite-based systems, neither cellular phone signals nor Wi-Fi is dependably available in the wilderness at the time of publication.

For GPS navigation and increasingly for SOS texts (though not yet for calls), smartphones work effectively even out of range of cell phone towers—a condition encountered frequently in the wilderness.

GPS DEVICES

From here on, this chapter uses "GPS device" to refer to any device that can receive a GPS signal, including dedicated GPS units, phones and tablets with a GPS app, trackers, and GPS watches. These devices can receive and simultaneously use the signals from satellites to give the user's position and elevation to within about 10 feet (3 meters) under an open sky. GPS devices have various features that allow users to display specific positions (waypoints), determine the compass bearing and distance to distant waypoints, plot routes comprising a series of waypoints from one position to another, and record tracks (approximations of the actual route taken along a path) as the party travels. Mountaineering parties should bring a GPS device for every climb. It can cost as little as $20 per year to turn a smartphone into a GPS device with an app or up to hundreds of dollars for a more durable dedicated GPS unit. Some reliable GPS apps are even free.

GPS devices can break or get lost, their software can malfunction, and their batteries can die, so a climbing party needs to bring multiple devices (see Mountaineering with a GPS Device later in this section). Ideally, every team member has a GPS phone app. When trees or mountains block the view of the sky, adequate satellite signals may not reach you, resulting in poor GPS accuracy or sometimes even the inability to obtain a position at all. For this reason, also always carry a detailed printed topographic map (or maps) of the travel area, an altimeter, and a baseplate compass.

Phones with GPS App

Phones can receive GPS signals from satellite systems from various countries and agencies, even far from cell tower coverage. To navigate by phone, you must first install a GPS app and download the required digital maps while the device is still connected to the internet. Phone GPS apps offer a large high-resolution screen, usually a broad range of map base layers, and a familiar interface (fig. 5-3a).

The phone's effectiveness as a GPS navigation device—inside or outside of cellular phone signal range—enables its use for backcountry navigation on all climbs where navigation may take the climber off well-known paths. In more

Fig. 5-3. *Devices commonly used to glean or employ GPS data:* **a,** *smart phone displaying a topographic map app;* **b,** *smart watch;* **c** *and* **d,** *sport and GPS watches;* **e,** *dedicated satellite messenger unit.*

extreme conditions or colder climates, the ruggedness of dedicated GPS units may be more appropriate. For other cautions regarding using GPS-enabled phones, see Limitations in the Backcountry later in this chapter.

GPS Watches

GPS watches include both standalone GPS-enabled watches (fig. 5-3b) and sport watches (fig. 5-3c–d), which combine navigation tools such as GPS and altimeter with fitness-tracking features like step counting and heart-rate monitoring. Unlike phones, most GPS watches come preloaded with the necessary software, though they often pair and sync with a companion phone app. Some premium watches have full-color screens and digital maps, though many more provide GPS coordinates only on demand or as a bread-crumb feature when recording a track. When using this type of watch, it is crucial to have a physical map to make use of the GPS coordinates. Compared with phones, more-expensive GPS watches tend to be more rugged. For additional concerns, see Limitations in the Backcountry later in this chapter.

Dedicated GPS Units

Handheld GPS units also receive GPS signals from various satellite systems. Topographic maps can be added to most such devices, for some by purchasing Secure Digital (SD) or microSD cards containing maps of specific areas (such as a large state or several smaller states), or by downloading the maps from the internet. Some of the more-expensive dedicated GPS units come with topographic maps already installed.

Dedicated GPS units, which are usually more rugged and weatherproof and are operable in a wider range of temperatures than phones, are a better choice in extreme environments. One downside compared with phone GPS apps is that the maps on a dedicated GPS device usually need to

---

THE IMPORTANCE OF SITUATIONAL AWARENESS

Experienced navigators both respect and are wary of using a GPS device to navigate. Too often climbers hike with "heads down," following their tiny screen while remaining unaware of their surroundings. When a navigator ignores cues from the passing terrain, situational awareness erodes. Lower situational awareness limits a mountaineer's ability to assess, anticipate, and manage risk. A climber using GPS must fight this tendency by applying key routefinding strategies (see the "Five Routefinding Tips to Remember" sidebar later in this chapter).

Maintaining situational awareness is crucial to risk management in general. Ask yourself these types of questions:

- How is the weather? And how is it changing or predicted to change?
- What is the party's condition?
- How many hours of daylight remain?

Maintaining a high level of situational awareness can help keep climbers on course and reduce risk, thus enabling everyone to more fully enjoy the experience.

be updated manually, whereas phone app maps are usually updated automatically and seamlessly. For additional concerns, see Limitations in the Backcountry later in this chapter.

Basics of Using GPS

To get the most benefit from a GPS device, read the instruction manual carefully. Review the device's settings and select which units to use: miles or kilometers, feet or meters, magnetic or true bearings, et cetera. Next—very important—select the datum that agrees with the datum of the topographic map you will be using. GPS devices and mapping software use WGS84 as the default datum (for details, see Datums earlier in this chapter).

Practice using the GPS device to master its features. Try it out at home, in local parks, and on hikes on clearly marked trails before taking it on a climb. Talk with friends familiar with GPS use, take a class to obtain helpful hints for using GPS, or consult trustworthy videos and websites that explain GPS in greater detail (see Resources).

MOUNTAINEERING WITH A GPS DEVICE

GPS devices are marvelous tools for the mountaineer. Using them can significantly aid in navigation. Keep in mind, however, that they are not foolproof and that topography, forest cover, battery life, electronic failure, extremely high or low temperatures, and inadequate user knowledge can hamper their effectiveness. The first rule of using a GPS device is to avoid becoming dangerously dependent on it (see "The Importance of Situational Awareness" sidebar).

Having multiple GPS devices in the party can help mitigate the consequences if a single device fails. In addition, for complex routefinding, carry route-marking materials such as flagging and wands, regardless of whether a GPS device is carried.

Download Maps Before You Go

Most phones when combined with a reliable app have the same GPS capability as a dedicated GPS unit. Popular apps feature several types of map layers, overlays, and satellite images, and they can display your position on a map (fig. 5-4). However, the digital maps themselves are still not downloadable through a GPS signal. A party must download maps for the area they will travel through ahead of time from the internet while in range of Wi-Fi or a cellular network.

While most GPS apps can automatically download map tiles via cellular data or Wi-Fi, this is unreliable: the GPS app caches the new tiles while erasing the oldest tiles without warning, potentially leaving you without a map. The best practice is to proactively download the map layers you need before you leave town. Be sure to do this in an area

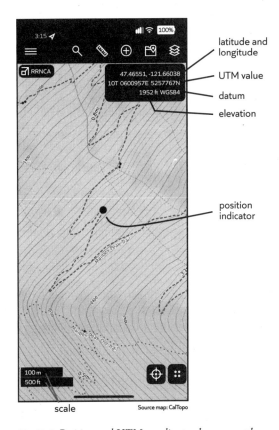

latitude and longitude

UTM value

datum

elevation

position indicator

scale

Source map: CalTopo

Fig. 5-4. *Position and UTM coordinates shown on a phone within cellular range or using a previously downloaded topo map.*

with a strong internet signal, since attempting to download these big files while driving to remote trailheads can be slow and frustrating, if possible at all.

If the party has not downloaded a map of the area, the GPS device may show the party's location as a dot on a blank grid or low-resolution map (fig. 5-5). The app will nevertheless allow them to find their location by displaying their coordinates in latitude and longitude or UTM. The party can then find their position on the physical map. Alternatively, they can take and save waypoints along the route or record a track and then follow this bread-crumb trail back to the starting point. The same techniques apply for GPS watches that lack mapping capability.

Batteries

Unlike a paper map and compass, GPS devices require battery power. Being familiar with your device's features, how quickly the battery drains in various modes and weather conditions, and how you can recharge it in the field is critical to using these devices effectively in the field. A GPS device with a dead battery is of no use at all.

Phone with GPS app. Phones run off an internal battery that is rechargeable with a suitable cable or charging stand and power source. Fully charge the phone before the trip, and carry a rechargeable power bank (see the "Power Banks: An Electronics Essential" sidebar) or power bank with a solar charger for multiday climbs, though both options add to overall pack weight. Phone firmware may defeat attempts to charge directly from a solar source. In this case, you can use the solar source to charge a power bank and then in turn charge the phone.

GPS watches. Though GPS watches are generally compatible with the same external power banks as phones, they can be more difficult to charge in the field due to their smaller size and proprietary cables. Some newer GPS watches have built-in solar charging capability to increase their battery performance.

Dedicated GPS units. Start each trip with a fresh set of batteries and carry spares. Fully charge rechargeable batteries for a dedicated GPS unit, along with spares, prior to a trip. For even better battery performance, use disposable lithium cells: they cost more but last longer, perform better at cold temperatures, and weigh considerably less than alkaline or NiMH cells (see Batteries in Chapter 2).

Common Uses in the Mountains

The wide variety of features that GPS devices have can be applied in many different ways in the mountains. How a GPS device is used on a climb depends on user knowledge, navigational preference, terrain, weather, intended destination, type and length of climb, and more. This section provides some examples of how using a GPS device can help in mountaineering situations. These examples cover the most common uses and do not represent an all-inclusive list.

Identify your position. The primary feature of a GPS device is to provide its user's position. An example is provided in Orientation later in this chapter.

Create and follow waypoints. A basic feature of a GPS device is the ability to create and use waypoints for point-to-point navigation. Waypoints can be locations such as trailheads, trail intersections, summits, campsites, gear stashes, and other places you want to pinpoint or remember. The coordinates for waypoints can be obtained from maps, guidebooks, websites, mapping software, and other sources; waypoints can also be entered into the GPS device before or during a trip. It is a best practice to create (or "drop") a waypoint at any place to which the party wants to return, such as a car, camp, or any crucial point along the route. At any later time, it is then possible to tell the GPS device to "go to" that waypoint, and the device will display the straight-line distance and direction or bearing to it. Climbers can then travel to that destination either by observing the GPS screen or by setting and then following the bearing on a baseplate compass. Turn off the GPS device to save battery power. An example of this is provided in Navigation by Instrument later in this chapter.

Create and follow a track. Another useful feature of GPS devices is the ability to create a track. If the GPS device is left on during an entire climb or a critical portion of a trip, another party can follow those tracks, or the original party can follow their own track back to the trailhead. For example, in Figure 5-6, a track was made from the trailhead to the

5

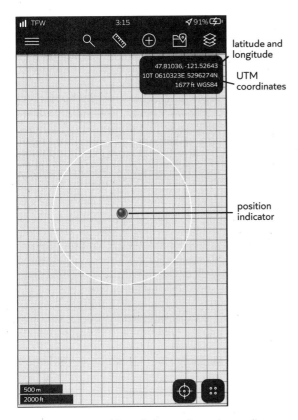

Fig. 5-5. *Position and latitude-longitude coordinates shown on a phone that is out of cellular range and does not have a downloaded topo map.*

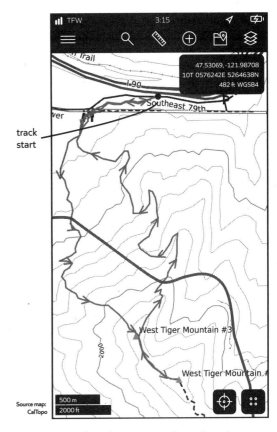

Fig. 5-6. *GPS tracks and routes: a saved sample track, or route that can be reused and shared. A route can also be created at home.*

summit of West Tiger Mountain #2 in western Washington and was saved; later, another user can follow the same track. (See Use GPS Data in Mapping Software, below, for how other users can access the information in these tracks.)

Provide trip data. Most GPS devices have a "trip computer" feature that displays data such as current location, speed of travel, distance traveled, and elevation climbed while recording a track. This information can be useful for the return trip or for future climbers, but if the device loses satellite reception for part of the trip (which can happen in thick forests, in narrow canyons, or when it is turned off to conserve battery power), some of these trip data may not be accurate.

Use GPS data in mapping software. Waypoints and tracks can be uploaded into mapping software such as Cal-Topo, Gaia GPS, or proprietary software that comes with a particular GPS device, such as Garmin's BaseCamp or the Suunto app. This feature allows climbers to see the entire route on a computer screen and modify or save it for future

reference. With mapping software, data can usually be exported in the universal GPX or GeoJSON file formats, providing the ability to transfer the data into another GPS unit so that other climbers can use these routes, tracks, and waypoints. Additionally, others can view and print a map of the area overlaid with selected routes, tracks, and waypoints—useful both for planning a trip and on the actual climb.

Limitations in the Backcountry

A GPS device is tremendously useful for navigation, but it should be used along with the other three essential tools: map, altimeter, and compass (as well as a means of contacting emergency first responders—see Communication Devices later in this chapter). Below are some important limitations of GPS devices and strategies for mitigating these limitations.

They can be damaged. Protect a GPS device from impact during a climb by using a sturdy case and perhaps a lanyard. Most dedicated units and some phones are waterproof; protect them against water and sweat as necessary. Have the party carry two or more devices in case a single unit fails.

They are not a substitute for a physical map. GPS devices can plot a route straight from one point to another, but neither digital nor paper maps can automatically find a route around rivers, lakes, or cliffs. It is often impractical to use certain features of a traditional baseplate compass with a GPS device, such as plotting a bearing. Such tasks are best accomplished using a physical map.

They may not work in extreme temperatures. Some GPS devices will not work at temperatures much below freezing. Lithium batteries are helpful in extending cold-weather battery life for dedicated GPS units. Phones are more temperature sensitive than dedicated GPS units: a cold phone may not respond to a cold finger, or it may just immediately shut down, and it may not function at temperatures near or above about 95 degrees Fahrenheit (35 degrees Celsius)—when it is too hot, you may get a warning screen.

They are unreliable if they cannot pick up enough signals. A GPS device must be able to pick up signals from at least four satellites to provide an accurate horizontal and vertical position. Because GPS devices receive signals from different constellations of satellites (US, Russia, Europe, China, India, Japan), this is usually not a problem. Under some conditions, such as in deep canyons or under dense forest cover, a GPS device may be unable to receive signals from enough satellites to accurately determine its position. When this occurs, the device sacrifices elevation information in favor of horizontal position.

They depend on batteries. The display is usually the largest power consumer on any device; be strategic and sparing in screen time. The best way to conserve power for any GPS device is, of course, to turn it off completely when it is not needed. When navigation is straightforward, such as on easy trails or roads or at rest stops or camps, turn the device on only at key locations, obtain an accurate position that makes sense, save the waypoint, and turn it off again. You can also use the device to take a needed travel bearing, and then shut it off and follow the bearing using a baseplate compass. Use the GPS device as little as necessary to conserve battery.

External chargeable power banks can charge your phone multiple times, and it is good practice to carry one (see the "Power Banks: An Electronics Essential" sidebar above), along with a charging cable, if you plan to rely on devices with batteries. The GPS function significantly drains a phone battery, especially when used continually, as when recording tracks. Thrifty use of phone battery power is advisable on trips that last a full day or longer. To extend battery life while using the GPS function, put the phone into airplane mode, which still allows a climber to use the GPS app and the camera functionality. When the phone is not in airplane mode, it is wise to completely shut down any unnecessary apps, since some apps refresh in the background, consuming power.

Like phones, many GPS watches use proprietary rechargeable batteries that are difficult to replace. Battery life can be significantly shorter when using GPS than when not. Conserve the battery by configuring the watch for navigation rather than fitness (for example, by turning off the heart-rate monitor) and turning it off at night. It is also possible to modify some settings, either on the watch itself or through its companion app, such as reducing the display backlight or changing the track-point resolution.

Battery life for dedicated GPS devices is ordinarily limited to a day or two, depending on the model and how it is used. These devices can be recharged in the field. Reducing the track-point resolution or disabling the device's compass or barometer helps extend battery life. Other useful tricks include decreasing the amount of time for the autolock feature that puts the device into sleep mode and turning down the display brightness. Even a slight dimming of the display correlates to increased battery life. That said, on a bright day above tree line or on snow, while wearing sunglasses, climbers will find a dimmed display harder to read. Viewing the screen in the shade, such as in a shadow, may help.

Altimeter

Mountaineers have long understood the importance of knowing elevation. An altimeter provides a simple elevation-point estimate. With a topographic map and one identifiable landscape feature—a trail, a stream, a ridge, or a compass bearing to a known peak—it is usually possible to determine your location. By monitoring elevation and checking it against a topographic map, mountaineers can track their progress, pinpoint their location, and find their way to critical route junctions. Every climber should carry some type of altimeter. Table 5-1 summarizes the features of altimeters used for mountaineering.

Barometric altimeters. Sometimes called pressure altimeters, barometric altimeters are basically modified barometers. Both barometers and altimeters measure air pressure (the weight of air), but a barometer is calibrated in inches of mercury, hectopascals, or millibars, whereas an altimeter is calibrated in feet or meters above sea level based on the predictable decrease in air pressure with increasing altitude. Barometric altimeters, available in digital wristwatches and on many GPS devices, are affected by changes in weather and so must be calibrated at known elevations.

Digital altimeters. A digital altimeter might have one or two sensors: a sliver of silicon that can measure air pressure (barometrically) and/or one that receives GPS satellite signals. Though inexpensive standalone models exist, the most popular digital altimeters are on cell phones, but the most readily accessible is worn on the wrist, often as a feature of popular GPS sport watches (see Figure 5-3). A wearable altimeter combines multiple functions in a single piece of equipment and is more convenient to use. Some digital altimeters display additional information, such as air temperature and rate of elevation gain or loss.

Though a digital altimeter requires a battery, the batteries in some standalone models are good for years, while others are rechargeable. The battery of a GPS sport watch that is actively tracking location, or of a phone that is running a GPS app with an altimeter function, will last a highly variable time unless other functions are turned off. Some brands offer watches that can be charged via solar power. Climbing parties typically carry more than one altimeter, so if one malfunctions or its battery dies, the party can use another climber's altimeter.

Another drawback to digital altimeters is that their liquid crystal display (LCD) screens may go blank at temperatures near freezing or lower, though this is usually not a problem if they are worn on the wrist and under sleeves. To keep a watch from being damaged on rock or ice on a technical pitch of climbing, attach it to your pack or put it in a pocket or pack. Inexpensive wristwatch altimeters are adequate for mountaineering use.

It is convenient to refer to a wristwatch altimeter to check your elevation, but climbers often turn off dedicated GPS devices (see earlier in this chapter) to conserve battery power. Plus, those devices require at least a minute to acquire satellite signals and display a position and elevation.

Altimeter as a function of GPS devices. GPS devices determine position in three dimensions—horizontal position from east to west and from north to south, as well as elevation above sea level—and can therefore display a climber's elevation as determined by the information its sensor receives from GPS satellites, rather than by barometric pressure. Some newer phones, as well as dedicated GPS units, have an internal altimeter that uses a barometric pressure sensor. They can display elevation either derived from multiple sources, based on the two types of sensors, or one elevation calculated using both sensors. Many GPS apps for phones (see GPS earlier in this chapter) include elevation readouts as well as horizontal position; other apps display elevation only.

HOW ALTIMETERS AID MOUNTAINEERS

Altimeters can help mountaineers in several key ways: calculating the party's rate of ascent, determining position (orientation) and navigating, and predicting the weather.

Calculating Rate of Ascent

By letting mountaineers calculate their rate of ascent, the altimeter helps them decide whether to continue a climb

TABLE 5-1. COMPARISON OF ALTIMETERS			
TYPE OF ALTIMETER	**COST**	**ADVANTAGES**	**DISADVANTAGES**
Digital wristwatch or smartwatch	Up to $1000+	Convenient to carry. Elevation displayed at a glance. Inexpensive unit is adequate. Long battery life; some offer solar charging. Can sync with phone app.	Some must be recalibrated to account for changes in weather. LCD screen can go blank at subfreezing temperatures. Battery occasionally needs to be replaced once it no longer holds a charge (battery life of one year or more).
Phone with altimeter or GPS app	Free or low-cost app	Same advantages as smartwatch	Same disadvantages as smartwatch. Must remove from pocket to read. Device is fragile; requires a protective case to make it rugged enough for mountaineering.
Dedicated GPS unit	Internal barometer adds to device cost	GPS (satellite-derived) elevation reading unaffected by weather. Elevation and position displayed together. May display elevation from GPS or from internal barometric altimeter.	Needs time to access satellites before displaying elevation. LCD screen can go blank at subfreezing temperatures.

or turn back. For example, a party that takes altimeter readings to check time and elevation hourly during a climb sees that they have gained only 500 feet (150 meters) in the past hour. The summit is at an elevation of 8,400 feet (2,560 meters), and an altimeter reading shows the party is now at 6,400 feet (1,950 meters), so they still have 2,000 feet (610 meters) to gain. The climbers can predict that if they maintain their present ascent rate, it will take roughly four more hours to reach the summit. That data, courtesy of the altimeter, combined with a look at the weather, the time of day, and the condition of the party members, gives the group the information they need to make a decision to proceed with the climb or turn back. Some GPS apps display rate of ascent.

Determining Position and Navigating

While a GPS phone app is a faster, more accurate tool, an altimeter can help a party determine where they are (orientation). If they are climbing a ridge or hiking up a trail shown on the map but they do not know their exact position along the ridge or trail, they can check the altimeter for elevation. The likely location is where the ridge or trail reaches the contour line closest to that elevation on the map.

Another way to use an altimeter to determine a climbing party's location is to start with a compass bearing to a summit or some other known feature (see Compass, below). Find that peak on the map, and plot the bearing line from the mountain back toward the climbing party. The group now knows it must be somewhere along that line—but where? Take an altimeter reading and find out the elevation. The party is most likely where the compass bearing line crosses a contour line at that elevation on the map.

An altimeter also makes route finding easier. If climbers find a convenient couloir that gains the summit ridge, they can note the elevation of the top of the couloir, and on the way back, they can descend the ridge to that same elevation to easily find the couloir again. Some guidebook descriptions direct climbers to change course at particular elevations; doing so is much easier when using an altimeter.

An altimeter may reveal whether the party is on the true summit, not a false one—for example, when the visibility is too poor to allow climbers to tell by looking around. (Again, a GPS unit or app also serves this function.) And the prospect of a long slog back to the trailhead can be lightened by measuring altitude yet to lose.

Predicting Weather

Some digital wristwatch altimeters can be adjusted to read barometric pressure instead of, or in addition to, altitude.

But remember that changes in barometric pressure are caused by changes in both weather and elevation—even wind speed—during a climb. Such changes may lead to erroneous conclusions regarding barometric pressure. Weather reports on phones or satcom devices provide superior weather forecasting.

GPS devices whose altitude display is derived from GPS satellites only (devices that do not use an internal barometric sensor) are not useful by themselves for weather forecasting. To differentiate between changes in air pressure readings caused by changes in elevation and those caused by changing weather conditions, first calibrate the barometric altimeter to the GPS elevation and then see if they diverge significantly over the next few hours. If the barometric altimeter diverges from the GPS altitude, weather conditions are likely changing. (For more on interpreting barometric changes, see Chapter 28, Mountain Weather.)

CAUTIONS REGARDING ALTIMETER USE

A change in weather is generally accompanied by changes in air pressure and temperature; both affect the reading of a barometric altimeter. During periods of unstable weather, the elevation reading for a given location may change by as much as 500 feet (150 meters) in one day. Even when conditions seem stable, an apparent change in elevation of 100 feet (30 meters) per day is not uncommon.

Because barometric altimeters are strongly affected by weather, do not be misled into trusting them to an accuracy greater than is possible. Though a typical high-quality barometric altimeter may have a resolution of 3 feet (1 meter), this does not mean that the altimeter will be that accurate. Changes in weather could easily throw the reading off by hundreds of feet or meters. *Do not trust the instrument until it has been set at a location with an elevation you know.* While traveling, check the reading when you reach points of known elevation (or every so often using GPS) and reset the altimeter if necessary. A combined GPS–barometric altimeter can usually produce better results. Modern GPS receivers store a lookup database of altitudes at known locations to further improve accuracy.

Get to know your own altimeter, use it often, check it at every opportunity, and note differences in information between it and the map or GPS device. Recalibrate barometric altimeters at known elevations (for instance, saddles, streams, or summits). Compare readings with other party members. You will soon know what level of accuracy to expect, and your altimeter will then be a dependable aid.

Compass

A compass is essentially a balanced, rotating magnetized needle or hub (depending on the model) that aligns itself with Earth's magnetic field and is marked on one end (usually red) to indicate north. Options include the traditional baseplate compass, compass apps for smartphones, and features in dedicated GPS units and watches. Compasses are either adjustable or nonadjustable for declination. A declination-adjustable compass is much easier to use and therefore strongly recommended.

The baseplate compass is an essential tool for navigation, not only to determine direction but also to measure and plot bearings on a map. The baseplate compass does not require batteries or daily calibration, and it operates fine in subzero temperatures.

Below are its essential features (fig. 5-7a):

- **Magnetic needle:** rotating magnetized needle or hub marked (usually red) on one end to indicate north.
- **Rotating housing (bezel):** usually filled with fluid to dampen (reduce) magnetic needle's vibrations.
- **Dial around circumference of housing:** usually graduated clockwise in degrees from 0 to 360.
- **Parallel orienting lines:** used to align rotating housing (bezel) with north on a map.
- **Orienting arrow:** adjustable, easy-to-use tool for correcting for magnetic declination. Gear-driven adjustability using a tiny screwdriver is easier and more dependable than tool-free adjustability.
- **Orienting arrow:** provides the "shed" to align the magnetic needle.
- **Transparent baseplate:** includes a **direction-of-travel line.**
- **Rulers:** used to measure distances on a map.
- **Index line:** where bearings are read and set; index line may be one end of direction-of-travel line.

Optional features (fig. 5-7b) include the following:

- **Sighting mirror:** improves accuracy and permits emergency signaling; often has a sighting notch at top of housing. Direction-of-travel line may extend from notch across center of mirror. Some compasses have a sighting window at mirror's base.
- **Clinometer:** used to measure angle of a slope and upward or downward angle to another object (see Clinometer later in this chapter).
- **Romer scale:** an interpolation scale used to measure UTM position.
- **Lanyard:** a cord used to attach the compass to a belt, jacket, shirt, or pack. Putting it around your neck is unsafe, particularly for any technical climbing. It can

be used to measure distance along irregular paths on a map.

- **Magnifying glass:** helps you read closely spaced contour lines or small labels.

When covering how to use the orienting arrow, navigation classes teach the mnemonic phrase "put red in the shed," reminding you to align the red (north) end of the magnetic needle with the roof-shaped end of the orienting arrow.

Some compasses omit the mirror for a good cost compromise. A compass that is corrected for compass dip (see later in this section) anywhere in the world may have "global" in its name or a notation on the package; these

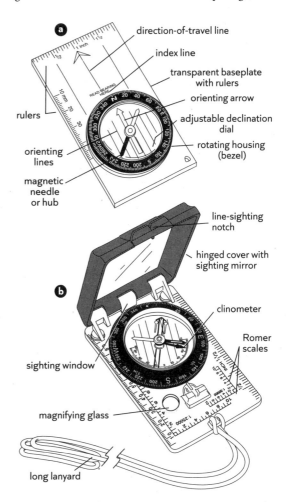

Fig. 5-7. *Features of mountaineering compasses:* **a,** *essential features;* **b,** *useful optional features.*

5

TABLE 5-2. COMPARISON OF COMPASSES			
TYPE	**COST**	**ADVANTAGES**	**DISADVANTAGES**
Simple baseplate, lacks adjustable declination	Up to $40	Price, weight.	Field adjustments for declination correction prone to error.
Full-featured with gear-driven adjustable declination	Up to $50; up to $100 with sighting mirror	No need to correct for magnetic declination mentally or by modifying compass.	Higher cost. Slightly less accurate without mirror.
Electronic compass on GPS device or your phone	Often included in cost of digital unit	Convenience of one instrument for several functions.	Cannot use to measure or plot bearings on map. May require recalibrations. Battery-dependent. May not display at subfreezing temperatures.

compasses are generally more expensive. Table 5-2 summarizes characteristics of compasses designed for mountaineering use.

BEARINGS

A bearing is the direction from one place to another, measured in degrees of angle from true north. The round dial of a compass is divided into 360 degrees (fig. 5-8). The cardinal directions are north at 0 degrees (the same as 360 degrees), east at 90 degrees, south at 180 degrees, and west at 270 degrees. The intercardinal directions are halfway between the cardinal directions: northeast is at 45 degrees; southeast, 135 degrees; southwest, 225 degrees; northwest, 315 degrees.

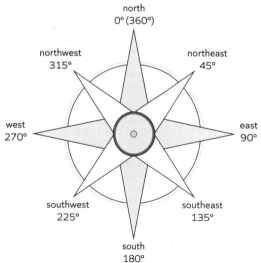

Fig. 5-8. *Cardinal and intercardinal directions and corresponding compass bearings in degrees.*

There are five primary uses for a compass: one starts with a digital bearing obtained from a GPS app; two of them use a compass alone (see Bearings in the Field, below); and two of them use a map and compass together (see Bearings on a Map and the "Map and Compass Checklist" sidebar, both below).

1. **Following a digital bearing:** Retrieve a bearing from a digital waypoint. Set and then follow that compass bearing.
2. **Measuring a bearing in the field:** Measure a bearing to a landscape feature and then follow that bearing to the feature.
3. **Following a bearing in the field:** Turn the compass dial to a specific direction or bearing, such as east 90 degrees, and then follow that bearing in the desired direction.
4. **Measuring a bearing on a map:** Measure a bearing from your position to another location on a map, then follow that bearing to the location.
5. **Plotting a bearing on a map:** Measure a bearing to a landscape feature, then plot that bearing on a map.

Bearings in the Field

All bearings in the field are based on where the magnetic needle points. The first two examples below, for the sake of simplicity, ignore the effects of magnetic declination (covered in the next section).

Measuring a bearing in the field. Square up your feet and shoulders to face your target and hold the compass level in front of you at waist level (near your navel, fig. 5-9), with elbows at your sides. First, point the direction-of-travel line at the object whose bearing you want to determine (fig. 5-10). Now, rotate the compass housing (bezel) until the pointed end of the orienting arrow is aligned with the north-seeking (red) end of the magnetic needle. Finally, if you have a mirrored compass, raise it to eye level, elbows slightly bent, and make slight adjustments as necessary.

If your compass has a sighting mirror, fold the mirror back at about a 45-degree angle and hold the compass at eye level, with the sighting notch at the top of the mirror pointing at the object (fig. 5-11). Observe the magnetic needle and the orienting arrow in the mirror while rotating the housing to align the needle and the arrow.

Whether or not a compass has a mirror, hold it level and read the bearing on the dial where it intersects the index line; for example, in Figure 5-10 the bearing is 270 degrees. Keep the compass away from ferrous metal objects, which can easily deflect the magnetic needle (see Cautions for Using a Compass, below).

Following a bearing in the field. Simply reverse the process used to measure a bearing in the field in order to follow a bearing in the field. Start by rotating the compass housing (bezel) until the desired bearing—say, 270 degrees (due west)—is set at the index line (see Figure 5-10). Hold the compass level in front of you, then turn your entire body (including your feet) until the north-seeking red end of the magnetic needle is aligned with the pointed end of the orienting arrow ("red in the shed"). The direction-of-travel line is now pointing due west—now follow that bearing. (For a back bearing, keep the same bearing set at the index line, but turn your body to align the south-seeking end of the magnetic needle with the pointed end of the orienting arrow.) The combination of

a bearing and a back bearing tends to reduce compass error. This procedure can be very slow and tedious.

Bearings on a Map

The compass can be used as a protractor to both measure and plot bearings on a map. Magnetic north and magnetic declination have nothing to do with these operations. Therefore, you can ignore the magnetic needle and orienting arrow (which is adjusted for declination) when measuring or plotting bearings on a map. The only time the magnetic needle is used on the map is whenever you align the map with true north in the field (see Orientation later

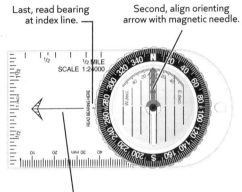

Last, read bearing at index line.

Second, align orienting arrow with magnetic needle.

First, point direction-of-travel line at object.

Fig. 5-10. *Measuring a compass bearing in the field in an area with zero declination: point direction-of-travel line at object; align orienting arrow with magnetic needle; read bearing at index line.*

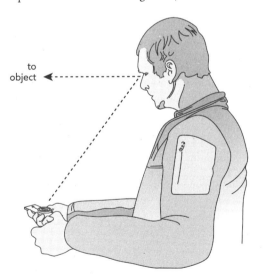

Fig. 5-9. *Square up body to target and hold compass (with or without a sighting mirror) at waist level to point it at the object whose bearing you want to measure.*

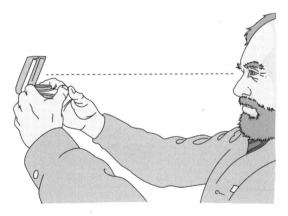

Fig. 5-11. *Using a sighting mirror to measure a bearing in the field.*

in this chapter), but there is no need to align the map to measure or plot bearings.

Measuring a bearing on a map. Place the compass on the map, with one long edge of the baseplate running directly between two points of interest (fig. 5-12). While measuring the bearing from point A to point B, make sure that the compass's direction-of-travel line always points in the direction from point A to point B, as shown—do not reverse the compass 180 degrees so the direction-of-travel line points from B to A.

Then turn the rotating housing (bezel) until its orienting lines are parallel to the north-south grid lines on the map. If the map does not have north-south lines, draw some in, parallel to the edge of the map and at intervals of 1 to 2 inches (2.5 to 5 centimeters). Be sure that "N" (360 degrees) on the bezel and the orienting lines point to the top of the map—to north. If the "N" on the bezel points toward the bottom of the map, to south, the reading will be

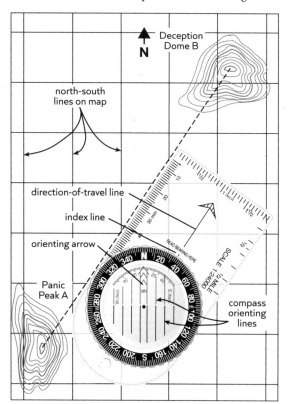

north-south lines on map

direction-of-travel line

index line

orienting arrow

Panic Peak A

compass orienting lines

Fig. 5-12. *Measuring a bearing on a map with the compass as a protractor (magnetic needle omitted for clarity).*

180 degrees off. (In Figure 5-12, the magnetic needle has been omitted to provide a better view of the orienting lines and the "N" mark on the bezel.)

Now read the number on the dial that intersects with the index line. This is the bearing from point A to point B. In the example shown in Figure 5-12, the bearing from point A, Panic Peak, to point B, Deception Dome, is 34 degrees.

Plotting a bearing on a map. There are really only two instances when you need to plot a bearing onto a map: (1) if you are lost and attempting to determine your approximate position, or (2) if you want to identify a landmark such as a distant peak. In scenario one, you can plot a bearing to a known point that is on your map—a task that you do not need to do if you have access to your location via GPS. Scenario two usually arises out of curiosity, not necessity.

In a hypothetical example, while you are enjoying a break on a mountaintop, you see another peak several miles away and wonder what mountain it is. Measure a bearing from your known location to the nearby peak (as described above in Measuring a Bearing in the Field), then place the compass on the map, with the long edge of the baseplate on the feature from which you wish to plot a bearing. Turn the entire compass to align its orienting lines with the map's north-south lines. The edge of the baseplate is the bearing line, which should pass through the mountain on your map, showing you the name of the peak. Phone apps can perform the same function.

MAGNETIC DECLINATION

A compass needle or hub is attracted to magnetic north, whereas most maps are aligned with a different point on Earth: the geographic North Pole, called true north. This difference between the direction to true north and the direction to magnetic north is called magnetic declination (sailors or aviators call it magnetic variation). It is usually expressed in degrees east or west of true north. A simple compass adjustment or modification is necessary to correct for magnetic declination.

The three lines connecting all points where true north aligns with magnetic north are called agonic lines (or literally, "lacking an angle"), that is, lines of zero declination. One runs through the middle of the United States and west of most of South America; one runs through Europe, Africa, India, and central Asia; and one runs from eastern Russia south through the western Pacific to Australia. The agonic line in North America now runs from Hudson Bay to Minnesota to Louisiana (fig. 5-13). In areas west of this agonic line, the magnetic needle points somewhere to the

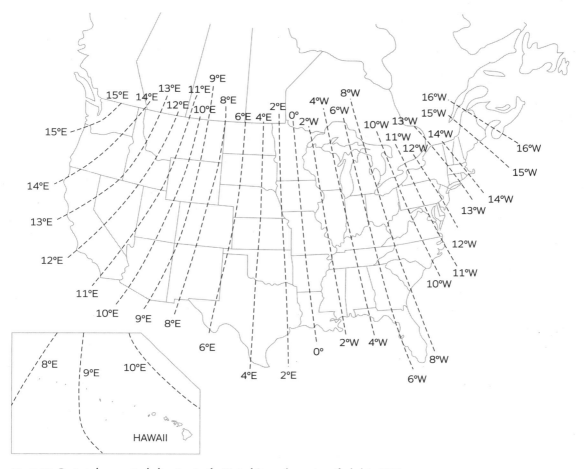

Fig. 5-13. *Projected magnetic declination in the United States (excepting Alaska) in 2025.*

east of true north, so these areas are said to have east declination. It works just the opposite east of this agonic line, where the magnetic needle points somewhere to the west of true north: these areas have west declination.

Changes in Magnetic Declination

Declination changes with time (hence, figures show projected declination) because the molten magnetic material in Earth's core is continually moving. Declination printed on older maps may be out of date. High-quality mapping apps and software display correct magnetic declination.

The map in Figure 5-13 shows the projected declination for the year 2025 for the contiguous US and Hawaii, and it may be accurate to within about half a degree for most such locations from 2024 to about 2029. The map in Figure 5-14 shows the declination for the year 2025 for the state of Alaska, and it may be accurate to within about 1 degree through 2026. Check magnetic-declination.com to determine the correct declination for any location.

As an example of declination change, a USGS map of the Snoqualmie Pass area of Washington State dated 1989 stated a declination of 19.5 degrees. Another map of the same area in 2023 gave a declination of 15.4 degrees. Declination change varies widely throughout the world (fig. 5-15). In Washington, DC, declination is barely changing as of 2024. The degree of change can vary dramatically in different parts of the world, so printed declination on maps more than a few years old should generally not be trusted. It is important to find the latest declination information to prevent errors in navigation by compass.

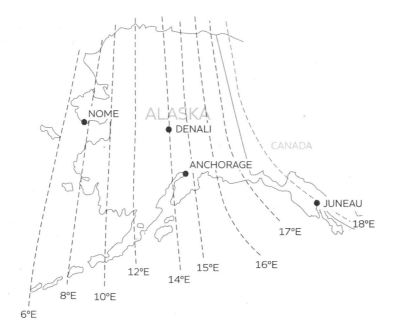

Fig. 5-14. *Projected magnetic declination in Alaska in 2025.*

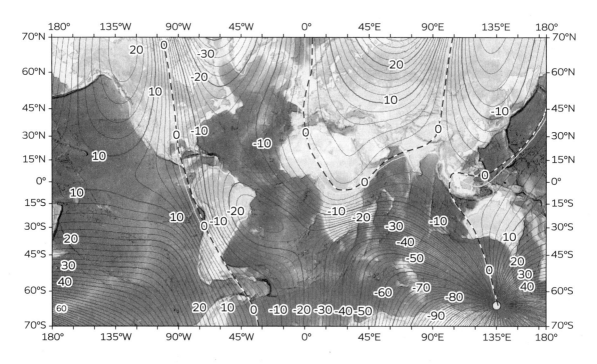

Fig. 5-15. *Projected world magnetic declination map for the year 2025: faint lines of constant declination are at 2-degree intervals. Positive numbers indicate east declinations, and negative numbers indicate west declinations.*

MAP AND COMPASS CHECKLIST

Do you understand how to use a map and compass? To practice, run through the whole procedure, check off each step as you do it, and remember the following:

- Never use the magnetic needle or the orienting arrow when measuring or plotting bearings on the map.

- When measuring or following a bearing in the field, always align the pointed end of the orienting arrow with the north-seeking (usually red) end of the magnetic needle ("put red in the shed").

Measuring a Bearing in the Field

Follow these steps to measure a bearing in the field:

1. Square up your feet and shoulders to face the target. With your elbows at your sides, hold the compass level at your waist (near your navel) with the direction-of-travel line pointed at the target.

2. Rotate the housing (bezel) to align the orienting arrow with the magnetic needle; if using a mirrored compass, adjust at your waist, then raise it to eye level to check. In either case, make adjustments as needed.

3. Read the bearing at the index line.

Following a Bearing in the Field

Follow these steps to follow a bearing in the field:

1. Many navigators first set a GPS waypoint at the target to generate a bearing.

2. Rotate the compass housing (bezel) to set the desired bearing at the index line.

3. Rotate your body to align the magnetic needle with the orienting arrow ("put red in the shed"). Hold the compass level in front of you, elbows bent at your sides, at waist level, keeping the direction-of-travel line pointed at the target.

4. Travel in the direction shown by the direction-of-travel line.

Measuring a Bearing on a Map

Follow these steps to measure a bearing on a map:

1. Place the compass on the map, with the long edge of the baseplate joining the two points of interest. Be sure the direction-of-travel arrow is pointing toward the object you want to travel to.

2. Rotate the housing (bezel) to align the compass's orienting lines with the north-south lines on the map. The north end of the baseplate must face toward the north end of the map.

3. Read the bearing at the compass's index line.

Plotting a Bearing on a Map

Follow these steps to plot a bearing on a map:

1. Rotate the compass housing (bezel) to set the desired bearing at the index line (as described above in Measuring a Bearing in the Field).

2. Place the compass on the map, with the long edge of the baseplate on the feature from which you wish to plot a bearing.

3. Turn the entire compass to align its orienting lines with the map's north-south lines. The edge of the baseplate is the bearing line.

Adjusting Bearings for Magnetic Declination

Pretend that you are in northern Idaho with a simple baseplate compass that is not adjusted for declination, which is 14 degrees east (fig. 5-16a). You want to walk to the geographic North Pole. If you set your compass dial to 0 degrees and box the needle, you will be facing 14 degrees to the right (east) of true north. To face true north, you must subtract 14 by turning the dial to 346 degrees and boxing the needle once more.

West of the agonic line that runs through North America, compasses point east of north. Travelers in western Washington State make a correction of about 15 degrees.

East of this agonic line, the declination can be added to the magnetic bearing to get the true bearing. In central Maine, for example, the magnetic bearing is 15 degrees greater than the true bearing (fig. 5-16b). Adding the declination of 15 degrees gives a climber in Maine the true bearing.

Adjustable declination. Adjusting for magnetic declination is simple in theory but can be confusing in practice, and in the wilderness, errors in mental arithmetic can have potentially serious consequences. A recommended way to handle declination is to always use a compass with adjustable declination rather than one with a fixed arrow. The declination arrow can quickly be adjusted for any declination

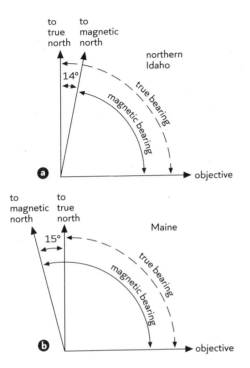

Fig. 5-16. *Magnetic and true bearings:* **a,** *in northern Idaho, east declination;* **b,** *in Maine, west declination.*

by following the instructions supplied with the compass. Then the bearing at the index line will automatically be the true bearing, and there will be no need for concern about a declination error. If climbers travel to a location with a different declination, they can make a simple adjustment to set the compass for the new declination value.

Measuring or following bearings in the field. To measure or to follow a bearing (that has been adjusted for magnetic declination) in the field, follow the same procedure used in the earlier examples (see Bearings in the Field, above), where the declination is near zero. The only difference is that you will now align the magnetic needle with the orienting arrow. *Note:* For all bearings in the field, align the needle with the orienting arrow; unless otherwise stated, all bearings referred to in this chapter are true bearings, not magnetic.

COMPASS DIP

A compass's magnetic needle is affected not only by the horizontal direction of Earth's magnetic field but also by its vertical pull. The closer a compass user gets to the magnetic North Pole, the more the north-seeking end of the

needle tends to point downward, toward the ground. Near the equator, the needle is level; at the magnetic South Pole, the north-seeking end of the needle tries to point upward. This phenomenon is referred to as compass dip.

To compensate for this effect, most compass manufacturers purposely introduce a slight imbalance to the magnetic needles of their compasses, so that their dip is negligible for the geographic area where they will be used. However, if a climber buys a compass in the northern hemisphere—say, in North America or Europe—and then tries to use it in the southern hemisphere—say, in New Zealand or Chile—the difference in dip may be enough to introduce errors in compass readings or even make it impossible to use. For this reason, if a climbing party brings compasses to a far-away place, as soon as they get to the country they are visiting, they must first try out the compass in an urban area to make sure it works properly before heading out into the wilderness, and if it does not work, they must purchase one balanced for dip in that area.

Some compass manufacturers produce compasses that are not affected by dip. Some such compasses may have the term "global" in their names or a notation on the package that the compass is corrected for dip anywhere in the world, though these are generally more expensive. Some brands magnetize the needle hub and the plastic needle floats free. Climbers planning worldwide climbing expeditions might consider a global compass.

PRACTICING WITH A COMPASS

Before counting on your compass skills in the wilderness, test them near where you live (see the "Map and Compass Checklist" sidebar, above). The best place to practice is someplace where you already know all the answers, such as an intersection where the roads run exactly north-south and east-west.

Take a bearing in a direction you know to be east. When the direction-of-travel line or arrow is pointed at something that you know is due east of you—such as the edge of the sidewalk or a road or a curb—and the orienting arrow is lined up with the magnetic needle, the number on the dial that intersects with the index line should be within a few degrees of 90. Repeat for the other cardinal directions: south, west, and north.

Then do the reverse: Pretend you do not know which way is west. Set 270 degrees (west) at the index line and hold the compass in front of you as you turn your entire body until the magnetic needle is again aligned with the orienting arrow. The direction-of-travel line should now point west. Does it? Repeat for the other cardinal directions. This set of exercises will help develop skill and self-confidence at compass reading and also will check the compass's accuracy.

Look for chances to practice in the mountains, especially a known location—such as a summit or a lakeshore—from which identifiable landmarks can be seen. Take bearings as time permits, plot them on the map, and see how close the result is to the actual location.

CAUTIONS FOR USING A COMPASS

It pays to understand some common errors made while using a compass and other factors that may affect its functioning.

Map and compass versus fieldwork. When measuring and plotting bearings on a map, ignore the compass needle and orienting arrow. The compass is simply being used as a protractor, so just align the orienting lines on the compass housing with the north-south lines on the map. To measure and follow bearings in the field, however, do use the magnetic needle and orienting arrow.

Interference from metal. The presence of nearby metal can interfere with a compass reading. Ferrous objects—iron, steel, and other materials with magnetic properties—will deflect the magnetic needle and produce false readings. Keep the compass away from watches, phones, avalanche beacons, belt buckles, ice axes, and other metal objects such as a vehicle. Iron in nearby rocks (for example, if the compass is resting on the ground) can make the bearing information nearly useless. If a compass reading does not seem to make sense, move 10 to 100 feet (3 to 30 meters) and check to see if it changes. If so, it is likely being affected by nearby metal. Avoid using a baseplate compass inside a car.

Errors of 180 degrees. Keep your wits about you when pointing the orienting arrow and the direction-of-travel line. If either is pointed backward—an easy thing to do— the reading will be 180 degrees off: if the bearing is north, the compass will say it is south. (Noting where the sun is in the sky can often help jog your directional presence of mind.) Remember that the north-seeking (red) end of the magnetic needle must be aligned with the pointed end of the orienting arrow ("red in the shed") and that the direction-of-travel line must point from you to the objective, not the reverse (unless you are taking a back bearing).

There is yet another way to introduce a 180-degree error in a compass reading: by aligning the compass orienting lines with the north-south lines on a map but pointing the rotating housing backward. The way to avoid this is to check that "N" on the compass dial is pointing to north (usually the top) on the map.

Trust the compass. If you are in doubt, trust the compass. The compass, when used correctly, is almost always right, whereas a climber's judgment may be clouded by fatigue, confusion, or haste. If you get a nonsensical reading, check to see that you are not making one of those 180-degree errors. Have your partner try making the same measurement, then compare results. Double-check using other navigation tools: altimeter and GPS. If other navigation devices provide the same answer, trust the tools over hunches and intuition.

CLINOMETER

Useful for measuring the angle of a slope in profile or the upward or downward angle to another object, clinometers are essential for assessing snow slopes for avalanche risk (see Chapter 20, Avalanche Safety). Some compasses include a clinometer feature, and these are used to measure slope angle in profile. Clinometers are also available as small devices that attach to ski or trekking poles and as phone apps: both are generally faster and easier to use than a compass clinometer.

The compass clinometer (see Figure 5-7b) consists of a small nonmagnetic needle that points, due to gravity, downward toward the degree scale on the compass's rotating housing (bezel). To use the compass clinometer, first rotate the housing to set either 90 or 270 degrees at the index line. Then hold the compass on edge and with the direction-of-travel line level, so that the clinometer needle swings freely and points downward toward the numbered scale. The needle should point to 0 degrees. Tilting the compass up or down to match a slope's angle then causes the clinometer needle to point to a degree of inclination.

You can align the baseplate edge of a compass with a distant slope in profile to measure it and up slope and up slope. inclination (fig. 5-17a), or use the sighting notch to evaluate a slope (fig. 5-17b). There are several options available for ski or trekking poles, ranging from inexpensive decals that wrap around the pole to small electronic devices that attach to the pole with Velcro and measure slope angle when a button is pushed. Phone clinometer apps measure slope angle by using the edge of the phone or, for distant points, eyeing through the camera.

Orientation

The goal of orientation is to determine the approximate point where you are standing on Earth. Finding your position is faster and more accurate using GPS, but it is still worthwhile to know how to find your position using a map

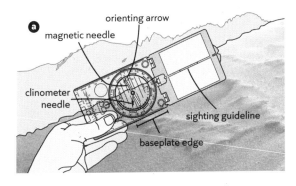

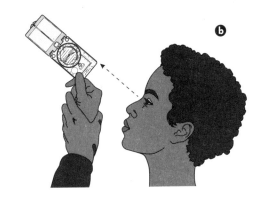

Fig. 5-17. *Using a baseplate compass clinometer: **a**, aligning the baseplate edge with a distant slope in profile; **b**, to measure a distant slope and upslope.*

and compass. That position can then be represented by a mere dot on a map, known as the point position. There are two less-specific levels of orientation. One is called line position: the party knows it is along a certain line on a map—such as a river, a trail, or a bearing or elevation line—but does not know where it is along the line. The least specific is area position: the party knows the general area it is in, but that is about it.

POINT, LINE, AND AREA POSITION

The primary objective of orientation is to determine an exact (or approximate) point position. First, simply look around and compare what you see around you with what the map depicts. Sometimes there is little nearby to identify on the map. The usual solution then is to use the compass to measure bearings on landscape features or use an instrument to determine your orientation. (Orientation using

GPS, which is different, is described later in this chapter.) When climbers know their point position, they can proceed to identify on the map any major feature visible on the landscape. They can also identify on the landscape any visible feature shown on the map.

Finding Point Position from a Known Line Position

With line position known, the goal is to determine point position. When climbers know they are on a trail, a ridge, or some other identifiable line, they need only one more trustworthy piece of information. For example, a climbing party knows it is on Unsavory Ridge—but exactly where? Off in the distance to the southwest is Mount Majestic. A bearing on Majestic reads 220 degrees. Plot 220 degrees from Mount Majestic on the map. Run this line back toward Unsavory Ridge, and where it intersects the ridge is the point position where the climbers are (fig. 5-18).

Finding Point Position from a Known Area Position

Suppose a climbing party knows only its area position: the general area of Fantastic Crags (fig. 5-19). To move from knowing area position to knowing point position, two

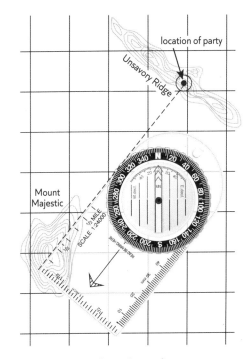

Fig. 5-18. *Orientation from a known line position to determine point position (magnetic needle omitted for clarity).*

trustworthy pieces of information are needed. The climbers will first determine line position and then, from that, point position.

Climbers may be able to use bearings on two visible features. Suppose they measure a bearing on Fantastic Peak and get a reading of 39 degrees. They plot a line on the map, through Fantastic Peak, at 39 degrees. They know they must be somewhere on that bearing line, so they now have their line position. They can also see Unsavory Spire. A bearing on the spire shows 129 degrees. They plot a second line on the map, through Unsavory Spire, at 129 degrees. Creating two bearing lines that intersect shows their approximate point position. The closer an angle of intersection is to 90 degrees, the more accurate the point position will be.

Climbers should use every scrap of information at their disposal, but they must be sure their conclusions agree with reasoning honed through experience (how you acquire "common sense"). If they take bearings on Fantastic Peak and Unsavory Spire and find that the two lines on the map intersect in a river, but they are on a high point of land, something is wrong. They should take a bearing on another landmark and plot it. If the lines intersect at a map location with no similarity to the terrain surrounding you, something is wrong. Perhaps you made an error in measuring or

plotting bearings, there might be some magnetic anomaly in the rocks, or the map may be inaccurate. In this example, who knows? Maybe those peaks are not really Fantastic and Unsavory in the first place.

Finding Line Position from a Known Area Position

When the area position is known and there is just one visible feature to take a bearing on, the compass cannot provide anything more than line position. That can be a big help, though. If the climbers in the preceding example are in the general vicinity of Fantastic River, they can plot a bearing line from the one visible feature to the river and then know they are near where the bearing line intersects the river. Perhaps from a study of the map, the climbers can then figure out their point position. They can also read the altimeter and find the spot on the map where the bearing line intersects the contour line for that elevation, which may provide an unambiguous position.

ORIENTING A MAP

To interpret a map, it helps to hold it so that north on the map is pointed in the direction of true north. This is known as orienting a map, and it is a great way to understand the relationship between the map and the terrain.

It is a simple process. Set 0 or 360 degrees at the index line on the compass and place the compass on the map near its lower left corner (fig. 5-20). Put the edge of the compass's baseplate along the left edge of the map or one of its north-south grid lines, with the direction-of-travel line or the mirror's notch pointing toward north on the map. Then turn the map and compass together until the north-seeking (red) end of the magnetic needle is aligned with the pointed end of the compass's orienting arrow. The map is now oriented to the scene before you. (Map orientation can give a general feel for the area but is less accurate than the more precise methods of orientation by map and compass described above.)

ORIENTING USING GPS

Suppose a climbing party wants to identify its point position on a topographic map. If you have a GPS device with a decent base map, this process is easy. Look at your GPS, know your position, and then transfer that position onto your printed map.

If you have only GPS coordinates and no base map, turn on the GPS device and let it acquire an accurate position. The device will probably read latitude-longitude, the usual default coordinate system. For mountaineering, the UTM system (which uses metric measurements) is easier and more accurate to use for manual plotting because the UTM

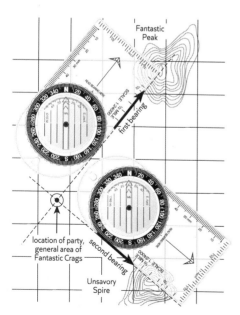

Fig. 5-19. *Orientation from a known area position to determine point position (magnetic needle omitted for clarity).*

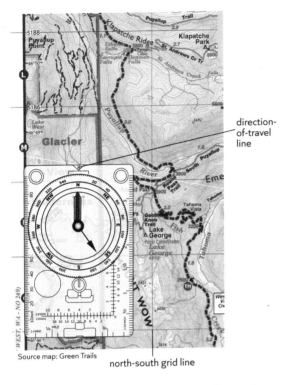

direction-
of-travel
line

north-south grid line

Source map: Green Trails

Fig. 5-20. *Using a compass to orient a topographic map in an area with 14 degrees east declination. This particular map uses WGS84 datum and UTM.*

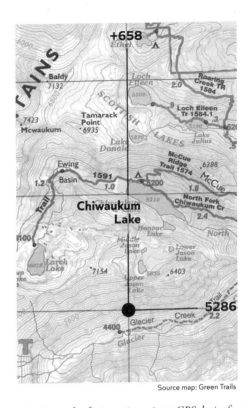

Source map: Green Trails

Fig. 5-21. *Example of orientation using a GPS device for coordinates and a topo map: point position is on Chiwaukum Lake, Alpine Lakes Wilderness in Washington State. A lot of detail and small type call for an enlarged smartphone photo.*

reference lines on many maps are much closer together (typically 1,000 meters, 0.62 mile apart) than the reference lines for latitude-longitude, which are usually about every 2.5 minutes (approximately 2 to 3 miles, 3 to 4 kilometers).

Using the GPS device's setup screen, the climbers should be able to change the coordinate system from latitude-longitude to UTM. They can then correlate the UTM numbers on the device's screen with the UTM grid on the map. Without using a scale or a ruler, climbers usually can visually estimate their position to within about 100 meters (about 300 feet), which is often close enough to get to within sight of an objective. If greater accuracy is desired, use the meters scale at the bottom of the map, the Romer (interpolation) scale on some compasses, or a separate plastic Romer scale.

For example, suppose a party is approaching McCue Ridge and clouds obscure all visibility. They reach an alpine lake, but which one on their route? They turn on a GPS device and let it acquire a position. The UTM numbers on the screen of the device are as follows: 10 U658000E, 5286 000N (fig. 5-21).

The "10" is the UTM zone number, which can be found in the lower left corner of the Green Trails topographic map. The "U" is a latitude band, used by most, but not all, GPS devices; each letter indicates a certain range of latitudes. The first long number, 658000E, called the easting, indicates that the climbers' position is 658,000 meters east of the reference line for their area. Along the top edge of the map, they can find the number 658. This is the partial easting, which omits the "000E." Their 1:63,360 map has 2,000 meter grid squares and their location in on a grid intersection.

The second long UTM number, 5286000N, is the northing, which indicates the climbers are 5,286,000 meters north of the equator. (In the northern hemisphere, the northing is the number of meters north of the equator; in the southern hemisphere, where it is sometimes designated with a minus sign, it is the number of meters north of the South Pole. Along the right edge of the map in Figure

5-21 is the number 5286, a partial northing that omits "000N." This partial northing is also at a grid intersection. Finding this point in Figure 5-21 shows that climbers are just off-trail near Chiwaukum Lake.

Navigation by Instrument

Getting from point A to point B is usually a matter of keeping an eye on the landscape and watching where you are going, helped by an occasional glance at the map. However, if your objective is out of sight, you can navigate by instrument: take compass in hand, measure a bearing, and follow the direction-of-travel line to your goal.

Navigation by instrument is sometimes the only practical method for finding the way. It also supplements other methods and verifies that the party is on the right track. Again, use reasoning and experience to question a compass bearing that seems wrong. For example, is the orienting arrow pointing the wrong way, sending the party 180 degrees off course?

USING MAP AND COMPASS

The most common situation requiring instrument navigation comes when the route is unclear because the topography is featureless or because landmarks are obscured by forest or fog, snow or smoke. In this case, if the climbers know exactly where they are and where they want to go, they can identify on the map both their current position and their destination. They must measure the bearing to the objective on the map and then follow that bearing.

Suppose you measure a bearing of 344 degrees on the map (fig. 5-22a). Read this bearing at the compass's index line and leave it set there. Then hold the compass in front of you as you rotate your body until the north-seeking end of the magnetic needle is aligned with the pointed end of the orienting arrow. The direction-of-travel line on the compass now points to the objective in the terrain (fig. 5-22b). Start walking in that direction.

USING COMPASS ALONE

Navigators often travel by instrument alone in the air and on the ocean—climbers can too. For example, if a party is approaching a pass and clouds begin to obscure it, they can measure a quick compass bearing to the pass. Then they follow the bearing, compass in hand if desired. It is not even necessary to note the numerical bearing; just align the magnetic needle with the orienting arrow and keep it aligned, then follow the direction-of-travel line.

Likewise, if climbers are heading from a ridge into a valley where fog or forest will hide the mountain that is the

goal, they can measure a bearing on the peak while it is still visible, before dropping from the ridgetop into the valley (fig. 5-23). Then they can follow the bearing—navigate by compass—through the valley. This method becomes more reliable if two or more people travel together with compass in hand, checking one another's work.

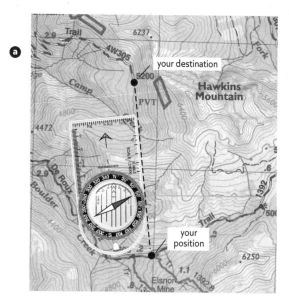

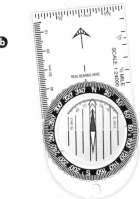

Fig. 5-22. *Navigation using map and compass (magnetic needle omitted to help with readability):* **a,** *measure a bearing on map from your position to your destination and, maintaining the bearing at compass's index line, pick up compass;* **b,** *turn yourself to align compass's magnetic needle with orienting arrow's pointed end ("red in the shed") and follow compass's direction-of-travel line for that bearing.*

USING INTERMEDIATE OBJECTIVES

The technique of using intermediate objectives is handy for those frustrating times when climbers try to follow a compass bearing exactly but keep getting diverted by obstructions such as cliffs, dense brush, or crevasses. They can sight past the obstruction to a tree, a rock, or another object that is exactly on the bearing line between their position and the principal objective (fig. 5-24). This is the intermediate objective. Then they scramble over to the tree or rock by whatever route is easiest. When they get to the intermediate objective, they can be confident that they are still on the correct route. Then they repeat the process toward the next intermediate objective. This technique is useful even when there is no obstruction. Moving from one intermediate objective to another means it is possible to put the compass away for those stretches, rather than having to check it every few steps.

Often there are no natural intermediate objectives on snow or glaciers or in fog, simply an undifferentiated white landscape. Similarly, in a forest, all the trees may look the same. In most situations, another party member can serve as the intermediate objective, the preferred method for search and rescue. That person travels out to near the limit of visibility or past the obstruction. The rest of the group waves that party member left or right until the person is directly on the bearing line. That person can then improve the accuracy of the route by measuring a back bearing on the rest of the party. Headlamps improve accuracy too, even during the day.

USING GPS

Suppose a climbing party can identify its desired destination on the map but cannot actually see it in the field. With a GPS device, simply add a waypoint on your objective,

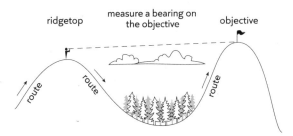

Fig. 5-23. *Following a compass bearing when the view of the objective is obscured: measure the bearing from the ridgetop from which you can see the objective before descending into the valley where the view of the objective is obscured.*

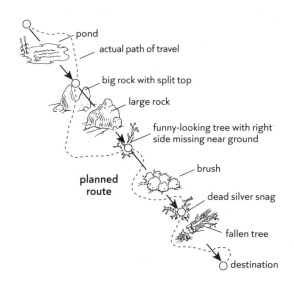

Fig. 5-24. *Using intermediate objectives: in a forest, where obstructions might include a pond, a large rock, brush, and a fallen tree, intermediate objectives can be a prominent rock or a distinctive tree. Note that party members should not stand beside each other during roped glacier travel.*

then use the "go to" function to get a distance and compass bearing. This will get you headed in the right direction.

With a GPS device that provides only coordinates (such as a GPS watch), read the UTM position of the destination off the map and enter it into the GPS device as a waypoint. For example, in the Chiwaukum Lake topo shown in Figure 5-21, suppose you want to find a route to the summit of McCue Ridge (elevation 6,288 feet, 1,917 meters). This point is about two-thirds of the way between the eastings of 658000 and 660000, according to easting labels on map border, so the easting is roughly 10 U659340E (the zone number is 10 in this example). They can also see that the summit is about one-quarter of the way between the northings of 5288000 and 5290000, so you can estimate the full northing to be 5288250N. Then you can enter these coordinates into the GPS device by activating its "create waypoint" function and entering the UTM coordinates of 10 U659340E and 5288250N, name the waypoint (for example, "MCCUEPK"), and save it.

When using a phone or dedicated GPS unit that displays topographic maps, a climber can simply tap or click on the desired location on the screen to mark and save a waypoint, an easier and more accurate process than interpolating the UTM position from the map.

Once the climbers have entered their destination into the GPS device, they can ask it to "go to" the name of the new waypoint ("MCCUEPK" in this example); the device will display the distance and compass bearing from wherever they are to the summit of McCue Ridge. They can set this bearing on their baseplate compasses, turn off the GPS device and put it away, and follow the compass bearing until they arrive at the summit of McCue Ridge. Alternatively, some devices have a built-in compass that can be used, but it may need to be calibrated prior to use and may not be as accurate as a baseplate compass.

What if a party gets off route due to a landslide or other obstruction? After passing the obstruction, turn on the GPS device and again ask it to "go to" the destination waypoint. The device will then display the new distance and compass bearing to the destination. Set the new bearing on the compass and follow it to the destination.

Navigation Workflow

Modern navigation tools offer more certainty, but coordinating the information gleaned from a map, altimeter, compass, and GPS device requires careful work. It is helpful to think of this effort as a workflow that begins at home, continues at the trailhead and en route, and then wraps up after the trip.

Before the Trip

Given the prevalence of electronic devices, the navigation workflow usually begins at home while connected to the internet. Although trip planning can be done solely using paper maps, digital mapping software brings an unprecedented level of power and efficiency to the navigational process.

Research the trip. Start by researching routes from guidebooks, blogs, trip reports, climbing sites, and other sources. What is the approach to the trailhead? Are fire, flood, or other weather events an issue? What is the roundtrip distance? What is the general steepness? Are you mostly on trail, off trail, or a mix? Will you be in tree cover, on rocks, or on snow or a glacier? If it will be an overnight trip, where are your intended campsites? Is it an out-and-back trip or a loop? Do you know the way down as well as the way up? Obtain GPS data such as routes, tracks, and waypoints from trustworthy sources that were ideally recorded recently.

Anticipate routefinding problems. Before the trip, anticipate specific routefinding problems. For example, if the route traverses a glacier or any large, featureless area such as a snowfield, consider carrying route-marking wands (see Chapter 16, Basic Snow and Ice Climbing). Identify any escape or bailout routes that can be used in case of sudden bad weather, loss of visibility, or other setbacks.

Prepare a route plan. Prepare a well-thought-out route plan for how the party will navigate to its objective and back. Import collected GPS data into your mapping software and study the terrain by examining several map layers, since each layer provides a unique perspective of the terrain you plan to travel through. Customize the map with your planned route and waypoints. A few minutes with your map, the intended route, and three-dimensional tools like Google Earth or FATMAP can give you a solid mental image of your real-world outing.

Prepare GPS devices. Load your custom GPS data into your GPS device. This is often a very different process from downloading map layers. For phone apps, data can sometimes be imported directly, but it is usually easiest to upload the data to the app's companion website and let the two synchronize. Then download useful map layers and overlays to the GPS device at the appropriate level of detail (in most phone apps, this feature requires a paid subscription). Include an area that surrounds the intended travel area in case plans change; the larger map can be at a lower level of detail if storage space is an issue.

Identify handrails and baselines. Look at the map for any linear feature that parallels the direction of travel—a handrail—which helps a party stay on route. The handrail needs to be something you can easily see (or hear, like running water) along the route. Roads, trails, powerlines, borders of meadows, valleys, streams, cliff bands, ridges, and lakeshores could all be useful handrails. When planning the trip, also pick out a baseline (also called a catch line or backstop), an unmistakable line that can help the party find its way home if they get off track. A baseline can be a road, the shore of a large lake, a river, a trail, a powerline, or any other feature that is at least as long as the area the party will travel in. For example, if the party knows the shore of a large lake always lies west of the trip area, heading west will get the party to this identifiable landmark and may save the group from becoming truly lost.

Adjust compass declination. Always confirm that your compass is set for the amount and direction of magnetic declination at the trip location. An easy way to find this is the website magnetic-declination.com. If the trip is to a location far from home, remember to reset declination. Mapping software should provide correct declination.

Obtain a physical map. Ensure you have a hard copy of your map, either by printing one from your mapping software or purchasing one commercially and tracing your intended route onto it.

A Day or Two Before the Trip

While trips can be planned weeks, months, or even years in advance, a few key things can be done only in the few days leading up to the trip.

Review time-critical conditions. Research weather trends, road and trail conditions, civil unrest, disease restrictions, wildfire closures, streamflow, rockfall, and avalanche conditions (see Chapters 6, Wilderness Travel, and 20, Avalanche Safety). Evaluate these conditions against your route plan to ensure that your plan is still achievable and reasonable from a risk management perspective. Revise your turnaround time if desired.

Confirm all electronics are ready. While still connected to the internet, ensure your data is downloaded, batteries are charged, that you have all the necessary charging cables, satcom devices are registered, and any preset ("canned" or user-definable) messages have been updated (see Communication Devices later in this chapter). Try out any device that is new to you.

Notify someone. Before leaving on the trip, give the trip itinerary to a responsible person. Include your estimated departure time, all group members' contact details, relevant medical conditions, make and model of vehicle, license plate, expected route, turnaround time and/or point, and procedure for reporting to authorities should such actions become necessary. Remember to tell that same person when you have returned (see Organizing and Leading a Climb in Chapter 22, Leadership, for more details).

At the Trailhead

Get off on the right foot by making sure that everyone in the party understands the route and the general travel plan.

Review the route. Discuss the route and make contingency plans in case the party gets separated. It may be helpful to gather the party around the physical map and correlate the map to the surroundings, and set a turnaround time.

Confirm with GPS. Ensure the GPS device's datum matches that of the physical map. Create a GPS waypoint at the trailhead and note your start time.

Check altimeters and compasses. Have the party calibrate all barometric-based altimeters to the trailhead elevation using a map or GPS device. Note magnetic declination, and adjust compasses as needed.

Inform contact. If plans change, let your contact person know.

Record track. If desired, begin recording a GPS track.

Conserve batteries. Put your phone in airplane mode, and take other steps with your devices to conserve power.

During the Trip

Everyone on a trip should be familiar with the intended route, have their own map, know the route plan, know how to get back, and not aimlessly "follow the leader." Your mind is your most valuable navigational tool.

Think about the route. As the party heads upward, ask questions: How will we recognize this important spot on our return? Would we be able to find our way out in a whiteout or if snow covered our tracks? What will we do if the leader is injured? Should I mark and save a waypoint here? Ask questions as you go, and act on the answers.

Monitor the rate of travel. Part of navigation is having a sense of the party's speed, by estimating the rate of travel along with elapsed time. Given all the variables, will it take the party one hour to travel 2 miles (3.2 kilometers), or will it take two hours to travel 1 mile (1.6 kilometers)? The answer is rather important if it is 3:00 PM and base camp is still 5 miles (8 kilometers) away. After enough trips into the wilds, climbers are good at estimating their speed (see the "Typical Speeds for Average Fit Party" sidebar). There will be much variation; for example, in heavy brush the rate of travel can drop to a third or even a quarter of what it would be on a good trail. At high altitudes, the rate of travel will also greatly decrease, perhaps down to as little as 100 feet (30 meters) of elevation gain per hour.

TYPICAL SPEEDS FOR AVERAGE FIT PARTY

- Hiking on a gentle trail with a light day pack: 2–3 miles (3–5 kilometers) per hour

- Hiking up a steep trail with a heavy full-size pack: 1–2 miles (2–3 kilometers) per hour

- Traveling cross-country up a moderate slope with a light day pack: 1,000 feet (about 300 meters) of elevation gain per hour

- Traveling cross-country up a moderate slope with a heavy full-size pack: 500 feet (150 meters) of elevation gain per hour

Monitor progress. Record times at various locations in a notebook or on a map or create waypoints in a GPS device, since waypoints are time-stamped; many GPS devices have a trip computer that will calculate average pace and average moving pace while recording a track. Note the times when the party reaches important identifiable features along the route, such as streams, ridges, trail junctions, and cols or passes; this helps on the return trip. Make estimates—and reestimates—of what time the party will reach the summit or other destination, as well as what time the party will get back to base camp or the trailhead. Experienced climbers regularly assess their party's progress and compare it with trip plans, including turnaround time. If it begins to look as though the party could become trapped in tricky terrain after dark, the group may decide to change plans and bivouac in a safer place or call it a day and return home.

Periodically recalibrate barometric altimeters. Occasionally, at known locations on the map or GPS device, recalibrate barometric-based altimeters. If the party has a barometric-based altimeter, check changes in barometric pressure that might be weather related. Do not get caught unawares by precipitation, lightning, or high winds.

Relate surroundings to the map. Along the way, keep relating the terrain to the map using multiple navigation tools (see the "Five Routefinding Tips to Remember" sidebar). Whenever a new landmark appears, connect it with the map. At every chance—at a pass, a clearing, or when the clouds break—update your fix on the group's exact position so you can plan each successive leg of the trip and help to prevent climbers from getting lost. It also may turn them into expert map readers, because they will know what a specific valley or ridge looks like compared to its representation on the map.

Look ahead to the return trip. Familiarize the party with the appearance of the return trip. The route always looks amazingly different on the way back. Avoid surprises and confusion by glancing back over your shoulder from time to time on the way in to see what the route should look like on the return. Maybe take a photo and annotate it with a line or two to show the correct return route. If you cannot keep track of it all, jot down times, elevations, landmarks, and so on in a notebook or on your phone. A few cryptic words—"7,600, intersect ridge"—can be a very helpful reminder on the descent. If using a GPS device, mark waypoints at crucial locations along the way; some GPS apps permit photographs to be linked to waypoints. Also consider recording a track, especially if the party may need to renegotiate complex terrain on the way back.

FIVE ROUTEFINDING TIPS TO REMEMBER

1. **Where am I?** Place your finger on that spot on the map.
2. **Where am I going?** Place your finger at the objective on the map.
3. **What route do I want to take?** Trace the route with your finger on the map.
4. **How long will it take to get there?** Figure your time using your typical speed for this distance and elevation gain.
5. **What should I expect to see along the way?** Note and mention aloud the names of landmarks and landforms you expect to see.

Mark the route if necessary. At times, it may be useful to mark the route going in so it can be found again heading out. Marking the route can be helpful when traveling over snowfields or glaciers during changeable weather, through heavy forest, or in fog or approaching nightfall. On snow, climbers sometimes use wands to mark the path. In forest, plastic surveyors' tape is sometimes tied to branches to show the route, but can be a blight and lasts a long time. A short length of unbleached toilet paper is the best marker from an ecological standpoint, because it will usually disintegrate during the next rainfall should you overlook any pieces. If you are certain of dry weather, use toilet paper; if not, use thin rolls of white crepe paper—it will survive an approaching storm but will disintegrate over the winter. If you mark a route, always remove the markers afterward; if there is any chance the party will not come back the same way and will be unable to remove the markers, use biodegradable paper markers. Waypoints recorded in a GPS device serve the same purpose as markers and leave no trace.

Piles of rocks used as markers—cairns—sometimes dot an entire route and at other times signal the point where a route changes direction. These heaps of rock are another imposition on the landscape, and they can confuse people—do not build new ones. If you must build a cairn, tear it down on the way out. But leave existing cairns as they are on the assumption that someone, perhaps even land managers, may depend on them.

On Technical Portions of a Climb

When the going gets tough, it is easy to forget about navigation and start worrying about the next foothold—but keep the map and other route information handy for use during occasional rests. On rock or ice climbs, do not let the mechanics of technical climbing overwhelm the need to stay on route or stick to the agreed-on turnaround time.

On a Summit

Remind one another that once the party has reached the summit, the climb is only half complete, so avoid letting your guard down regarding safety and care in navigation. Review your descent route plans at the summit or turn-around point, remembering that many more routefinding errors happen on the way down than on the way up. Repeat the trailhead get-together by discussing the route plan and emergency strategies. Stress the importance of keeping the party together on the descent, when some climbers will want to race ahead while others may lag behind.

The summit also provides a golden opportunity to rest, relax, and enjoy—and to learn more about the area and about map reading by comparing the actual view to the way it looks on the map. "Augmented reality" phone apps like PeakFinder can aid in identifying distant summits. If you can see a portion of your return route, taking photos from the summit can be a great help with routefinding.

Give yourselves enough time to reach the camp or trail-head in daylight on the way down. A rule of thumb for estimating the amount of time after sunset that usually has enough light to navigate by (at the latitude of the Pacific Northwest) is 30 minutes; conversely, the first usable light in the morning is about 30 minutes before sunrise. These times vary with latitude, so consult online sources for civil twilight and civil dawn for your location.

While Descending

The descent is a time for extra caution, as mountaineers fight fatigue and inattention. As on the ascent, maintain a good sense of the route and how it relates to the map. Stay together, do not rush, and be even more careful if the party is taking a descent route that is different from the ascent route.

Intentional offset. If a party fears it might get into nav-igational trouble—for instance, if they forgot to record a GPS waypoint at the trailhead—they can use the concept of intentional offset, or aiming off. Imagine that the climb-ing team is almost back to the car after a tough 12-hour climb. The car is parked along an access road. The party fol-lows a compass bearing directly back to the road, but get-ting there they cannot see the car because they have gotten off route by a few degrees. At the road the party will have

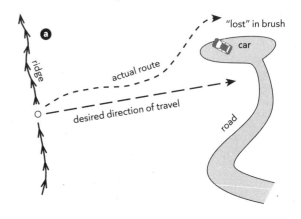

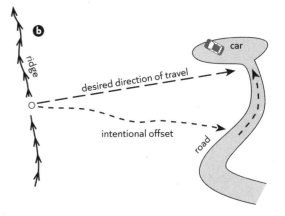

Fig. 5-25. *Navigating to a specific point on a line:* **a,** *inevitable minor errors can sometimes have disastrous consequences;* **b,** *to avoid such problems, follow a course with an intentional offset.*

to guess which way to go. It will be a frustrating ending to a good day if the car is to the right and the party goes left. It will be even worse if the car is parked at the end of the road and a routefinding error takes them beyond the road-end and on through the forest (fig. 5-25a).

To avoid this situation, the party can travel in a direc-tion that is intentionally offset some relatively large amount (say, 20 to 30 degrees) to the right or the left of where they want to be (fig. 5-25b). When the group inter-sects the road (or river, ridge, or whatever linear feature), they will be more confident about which way to turn. The correct location can sometimes be confirmed using an altimeter.

Back at the Trailhead

When the party reaches the trailhead, stop recording any GPS tracks and ensure all party members are accounted for.

After the Trip

Back home, while the details are still fresh in your mind, write a description of the route and any problems, mistakes, or unusual features. Imagine what you would like to know if you were about to take this trip for the first time. If you found a great campsite, note the GPS coordinates. If a guidebook or map was confusing or wrong, write to the publisher. You can post your trip reports or GPS data on one of the numerous websites available (such as peakbagger.com) to aid future climbers. Since you likely used such information to plan your climb, it is a valuable practice to give back to the community this way.

Communication Devices

Historically, mountaineers have needed to be self-reliant, and people entering the wilderness today should absorb that ethic (see the "Ethic of Self-Reliance" sidebar). But when you find yourself in a life-threatening situation despite your planning and preparation, help from emergency responders will be welcome. A climbing party in need of outside assistance has several means of requesting help. Whatever emergency communication device you carry, always carry a backup battery or a means of recharging the device.

Satellite communication systems. In 1982, an international satellite-based search and rescue (SAR) system was launched for aviation and maritime uses, the latter using devices known as EPIRBs (Emergency Position-Indicating Radio Beacons). Personal locator beacons (PLBs) were introduced in 2003, using the same government-based system as EPIRBs but intended for land-based emergency services.

PLBs. Personal locator beacons determine a party's coordinates using GPS and transmit them through international government satellites to the appropriate emergency responders. Registration is required, and some charge subscription fees to use the government-based system. Remember that using this beacon will initiate a full-scale rescue and you may be held liable for some or all of the rescue costs in certain situations and locations. These rescues may cost thousands of dollars! PLBs are only to be used in dire emergencies. Many climbers elect to carry emergency evacuation and medical treatment insurance.

ETHIC OF SELF-RELIANCE

Understanding the limits of satellite communication (satcom) devices and other communication tools is as important as understanding their usefulness: Batteries deplete; electronics fail; cellular phone signals are limited in most mountain locations; a rescue may not be possible due to weather conditions or availability of rescuers.

A satcom device or phone is not a substitute for self-reliance. No party should set out ill prepared or inadequately equipped, nor should they attempt a route beyond their ability and assume that emergency help can be summoned. The climbers who wrote the early editions of this book had no easy options for rescue in the mountains. They knew that the freedom of the hills could come at great cost and that a safe return depends on the party's experience, preparation, skill, and judgment.

Satellite communicators or messengers. Over the past fifteen years or so, various companies have introduced multifunctional PLBs (and even a wristwatch PLB), as well as devices that function similar to PLBs. Collectively these are known as satellite communicators or messengers. As popular satellite communicator brands, models, and features change frequently, consult with more experienced colleagues and trusted reviewers such as Outdoor Gear Lab.

All these devices determine the party's position using GPS, then send a message using commercial satellite networks. Some units allow for short, preset nonemergency text messages to be sent (for example, "camping here tonight"); some allow free-form text messages to be sent; some allow for two-way texting. Satellite communicators require subscriptions for using their services, and each device manufacturer offers plans of varying costs, based on factors such as the number of messages transmitted, tracking, or other services used.

Some users find the distinction between PLBs and other satellite devices important, but both are commonly referred to using either term. Both are powerful, but satellite communicators have additional functionality; see Table 5-3 for a comparison.

PLBs and other satellite devices have saved many lives, and *parties are strongly advised to carry at least one to reduce their risk.*

Satellite phones. In use since 1962, satellite phones have come down in price and weight, so they have become a reasonable option, especially for larger and longer expeditions, although they are expensive per minute of call time. They allow for communication detail and nuance that PLBs and satellite communicators cannot provide, as well as reliable connection in remote backcountry where cellular signals will not work.

OTHER COMMUNICATION DEVICES

Mobile phones and two-way radios are land-based communication devices for climbers. A phone with a GPS app can also be used for navigation.

Phones. As a communication device, phones are the obvious first choice for requesting outside help—when the climbing party is within range of a cellular signal (or perhaps satellites), which is the only time these phones work for this purpose. In such cases, phones can dramatically shorten the time it takes to summon rescuers. Phones are also useful for telling people back home that the party will be late but is not in trouble, which can forestall unnecessary rescue efforts. Some phones employ the accelerometer to signal a crash, but they can trigger a false alarm.

However, unless the climbing party is certain they are in range of a cellular data signal or can reliably acquire a satellite using their service plan, they *must assume that their phone will not function for making calls from the backcountry.* The signals for land-based phones rely on terrestrial towers, and reception is unreliable in the backcountry. A text (SMS, or short message service) may get through when calling is nonfunctional.

Handheld two-way radios. Modern handheld amateur radios, also called ham radios, are inexpensive, lightweight, and compact but cannot be consistently relied on for emergency communications from the backcountry. These battery-powered amateur radios can communicate either directly from radio to radio or, in many locations worldwide, via repeaters (electronic devices stationed at high locations that receive the ham radio signal and retransmit it at a higher power level so that communication can occur over longer distances). In some locations, ham radio repeater coverage is equal to or better than cellular phone signal coverage but, like cellular phone coverage, cannot be consistently relied on in the backcountry. Amateur radios are regulated by the federal government, and their operation requires a license.

Family radio service (FRS) two-way radios (walkie-talkies) are useful as local, short-range communication devices (up to a few miles or kilometers) between climbing partners or between a climbing party and base camp. FRS two-way radios, citizens band (CB) radios, and general mobile radio service (GMRS) radios have limitations both in range and strength of signal propagation.

If you plan to use handheld two-way radios, make sure they conform with local radio-frequency regulations. To be useful, all radios in the party must be set to operate at the same frequency. Wait a second or two to start talking after you press the "talk" button so that your first couple of words are not lost.

TABLE 5-3. COMPARISON OF SATELLITE COMMUNICATION DEVICES			
DEVICE	**SATELLITE SYSTEM**	**FUNCTIONALITY**	**ADVANTAGES AND DISADVANTAGES**
Personal locator beacons (PLBs)	Dedicated government search and rescue system	Sends location to emergency responders via government-based satellites.	Transmission signal is somewhat stronger than that of commercial systems. Requires registration.
Smartphones	Commercial systems	One- or two-way texting in backcountry.	Emergency SOS available on some newer phones. Costs unknown. Requires clear skies.
Satellite communicators or messengers (satcoms)	Commercial systems	Sends location to emergency responders via private companies. Some models have one- or two-way messaging options. Can send location to friends and family. Some models also provide GPS navigation functions.	Some models also function as a full GPS device. Requires monthly subscription fee (cost varies depending on services).
Satellite phones	Commercial systems	Two-way backcountry telephone communications. Some allow SMS messaging.	Some are GPS enabled. Expensive call time.

Lost! What Now?

Why do people get lost? Some travel without a map because the route seems obvious. Some people trust their instincts over the compass; others do not bother with the map homework that can give them a mental picture of the area. Some do not pay enough attention to the route on the way in, and some rely on the skill of their climbing partners. Some do not take the time to think about where they are going, so they miss trail junctions or wander off on game paths or casual trails. Some become lost due to an overreliance on technology, and some people get separated from their party.

Have everyone be aware of the route and travel plan. Take steps to keep group members together (especially on the descent), and assign a sweep (or rear guard) to keep track of stragglers. Having learned humility through years of experience, skilled navigators always carry the Ten Essentials, including enough food, extra clothing, and bivouac gear, and they are familiar with the agency managing the area they are exploring.

WHAT IF YOUR PARTY GETS LOST?

If your party becomes lost, the first rule is to stop. Try to determine where the party is. If you cannot, figure out the last time the party knew its exact location. If that spot is fairly close, within an hour or so, retrace your steps to that point. If that spot is hours away, the party may instead decide to head toward the baseline they established when they started out (see Navigation Workflow, above). If darkness falls or your party tires before it has found its way out, safely bivouac for the night. Traveling at night when you are lost will usually compound the problem. In the morning, the party members may be able to gain a fresh perspective on their location.

WHAT IF YOU BECOME LOST WHILE ALONE?

The prime directive if you are lost and alone is, again, to stop. Look for other members of the party, shout or blow a whistle, and listen for a response. If the only answer is silence, sit down, regain your calm, and combat panic with reason.

Once you have calmed down, look at the map to determine your location and plan a route to the car or trailhead in case you do not connect with the other climbers. Mark your location with a cairn or other objects, and then scout in all directions, perhaps 100 paces out, each time returning to the marked position. Find a nearby open area where you can be seen from the air and spread out everything brightly colored that you have with you—clothing, a tarp, a rain fly,

> ### HOW TO SEEK HELP VIA PHONE WHEN YOU ARE LOST
>
> If you still have service, call 911 and cell towers may help determine your location. Tell search and rescue your status. If your service is marginal, text 911 (in certain locations) or your primary contact. Some phone services may use satellites to text emergency services.
>
> Conserve battery and power bank charge. A rescue operation will likely take much longer than you anticipate.
>
> Other cellular forensics may help locate the lost party. Alternatively, airborne drones or planes may be able to use your phone as a beacon to pinpoint your location. If you are able to text or call someone, the first and most important information you should share is your precise latitude and longitude if you know it, in decimal degree format, for example 45.1234 degrees, -121,1234 degrees.

or whatever is available—to give searchers something to see. Staying busy will raise your spirits; try singing—it will give you something to do and searchers something to hear. Well before dark, prepare for the night by finding shelter (most important) and water.

After a night alone, if you are not reunited with your party, you may decide to hike out to a baseline feature picked out before the trip. If the terrain is too difficult for you to travel alone, or if you are injured or sick, you may need to concentrate on letting rescuers find you. Staying in one place in the open and shouting and whistling periodically may improve your chances of being found by a rescue party.

Finding the Freedom of the Hills

The mountains await those who have learned the skills of orientation, navigation, and routefinding. In large part, navigation is the subject of this entire book because it is essential to all off-trail adventure. In medieval times, the greatest honors a visitor could receive were the rights of a citizen and the freedom of the city, sometimes even today symbolized by presenting a guest with the "keys to the city." For the modern alpine traveler, navigation is the key to wandering at will through valleys and meadows, up cliffs and over glaciers, thereby earning the rights of a citizen in an exhilarating land—a mountaineer with the freedom of the hills.

CHAPTER 6

WILDERNESS TRAVEL

Climbing a mountain is one thing; getting from the trailhead to its slopes is another. Wilderness travel is the art of getting there—along trails, around brush, across rock, over snow, and across streams. By learning the skills of wilderness travel, climbers open the gateway to the summits.

Working out an efficient route from trailhead to summit within the abilities of the climbing party is the art of routefinding in the wilderness. Intuition and luck play a role, but it takes skill and experience to surmount the hazards and hurdles between the trailhead and the top.

Routefinding in the Wilderness

The orientation and navigation skills described in Chapter 5, Navigation and Communication, form the foundation for wilderness travel. Complementary to these tools, climbers hone their abilities to interpret trail, rock, snow, and weather conditions to skillfully travel over different types of terrain and to comprehend the clues that the wilderness offers.

GATHER ROUTE INFORMATION

The more information you gather ahead of time, the better your ability to make sound decisions during the trip. Take time to research the terrain and climate of the party's selected area, in addition to your specific objective. Each mountain range has its own peculiarities that affect routefinding and travel. For example, mountaineers accustomed to the broad valleys and open forests of the Canadian Rockies must embrace new rules to contend with the narrow and heavily vegetated canyons of British Columbia's Coast Range. The Pacific Northwest mountaineer familiar with deep snow in June at 4,000 feet (1,200 meters) may discover drastically different June conditions in the California Sierra.

Guidebooks offer detailed climb descriptions, including information on the climbing route, the estimated time necessary to complete it, elevation gain, and distance. But guidebooks can become outdated—one bad winter can completely alter an approach; make sure to consult the latest editions of two or three different guidebooks, if available. Publications that cover other aspects of the area—its skiing, hiking, geology, or history—may also have something to offer as the party plans its trip.

Check online resources for weather forecasts, flooding, snow or fire conditions, and the land manager's information. Check also for information from other climbers, for example on trip report websites such as Mountain Project or from people you know. Climbers who have made the same trip can describe landmarks, hazards, and routefinding difficulties, and quite often their trip reports contain helpful photographs. As always, exercise judgment when using online sources.

Useful details are packed into maps of all sorts: Forest Service maps, road maps, aerial maps, climbers' sketch maps, and topographic maps. More and more maps and topographic materials are available online and are downloadable or printable to take with you; see details in Chapter 5, Navigation and Communication.

Prepare in depth for trips into areas new to you. This might include scouting, making observations from vantage points, or studying oblique (taken at an angle) aerial photos. Forest Service or Park Service rangers can usually provide information on road and trail conditions. Popular climbing areas sometimes have designated climbing rangers who are regularly in the mountains and give informed current reports. Satellite imagery, such as that provided by Google Earth, provides invaluable three-dimensional views of maps from any chosen vantage point.

Some of the best route details come out of conversations with locals. Area outfitters or gear shops are excellent places to ask about current conditions, including snow levels, fire danger, trail closures, and the best places to ford streams.

Always consider the season and the amount of snowfall in a given year when preparing for a climb. Early in the season, avalanche danger may be high on steep slopes, especially if there is a heavy accumulation of snow from winter. Late in the season, or following a warm winter with low snowfall, a slope that is usually covered in snow may be exposed as talus (see Negotiating Difficult Terrain near the end of this chapter).

Finally, do not let outdated information ruin a trip. Check beforehand with the appropriate agencies about roads and trails, especially closures, and about climbing routes and regulations, permits, limitations on party size, and camping requirements.

LEARN FROM EXPERIENCE

There is no substitute for firsthand experience. When climbers are learning, travel with seasoned mountaineers, watch their techniques, and ask questions. The more familiar climbers are with the wilderness, the greater their freedom to find their own way.

BE OBSERVANT ON THE APPROACH

Climb with your eyes. Study the mountain for climbing routes. A distant view can reveal patterns of ridges, cliffs, snowfields, and glaciers, as well as the degree of incline. At closer range, details of fault lines, bands of cliffs, and crevasse fields appear. Look for clues indicating routes: ridges with an incline less steep than the faces they divide; cracks, ledges, and chimneys leading up or across faces; snowfields or glaciers offering easy or predictable pitches. Look for climbable sections and link them together visually. With experience comes a critical eye for what you know you can climb.

If the approach skirts a mountain's base, take the opportunity to view the peak from various perspectives. Even moderate slopes can appear steep when viewed head-on. A system of ledges indistinguishable from background cliffs may stand out when viewed from another angle or as shadows cross the mountain.

The presence of snow sometimes promises a modest angle and easy climbing because it does not last long on

6

slopes steeper than 50 degrees. Snow and shrubs on distant rock faces often turn out to be "sidewalks" with smaller ledges between. However, snow can be deceptive. What appears to be snowfields high on the mountain may be ice. Deep, high-angle couloirs often retain snow or ice year-round or stay icy late in the day, especially when shaded.

WATCH FOR HAZARDS

Stay alert to climbing hazards by continuously assessing not just what is ahead but also what is above and below the party. Is there a group of climbers above who could trigger rockfall? How likely is that in the given environment, and what would the consequence be if it were to happen? Study snowfields and icefalls for avalanche danger and cliffs for signs of possible rockfall. Snowfields reveal recent rockfall by the appearance of dirty snow or rock-filled craters. If the route goes through avalanche and rockfall territory, travel in the cold hours of night or very early morning, before the sun melts the ice that bonds precariously perched boulders and ice towers. Move through such places quickly. For more on this topic, see Chapter 20, Avalanche Safety.

Before entering danger zones, evaluate the party's exposure. Ask these questions when making a risk-adjusted decision: "How long will I be exposed to this hazard?" "How quickly can I get to resources if things go wrong?" When you enter danger zones, try not to get caught behind slower parties. If possible, avoid these risky areas in heavy rain. Also watch for changing weather conditions (see Chapter 28, Mountain Weather). Keep evaluating hazards and looking for the most appropriate route, given the conditions. If the route that the group initially planned on climbing begins to look questionable, search for alternatives and make decisions as early as possible.

THINK ABOUT THE RETURN

Consider the descent while on the approach. Terrain that you may find easy while going up may be much more challenging going down, or perhaps even difficult to find. Look back frequently, take notes and photos, mark GPS waypoints, take altimeter readings, and, if necessary, mark the route and/or record a GPS track. Some climbers even photograph key turns while facing the return route. (For additional information, see Chapters 5, Navigation and Communication; 7, Protecting the Outdoors; and 16, Basic Snow and Ice Climbing.)

The approach is also a time to look ahead to the end of the day. Consider where the party has to be by dark and whether the area will be safe to travel through by headlamp, if necessary. Keep an eye out for emergency campsites, water supplies, and anything else that may make the return trip easier and less risky. Notice how long it takes the party to travel in so you can estimate how long it might take to return. If the group has not already done so while planning the trip, establish a turnaround time—the time when the party will need to begin the return journey whether or not you have achieved your objective. Make sure that others on the trip have this information so that they can also plan and understand the expectations for the outing.

Hiking

Reaching the summit often involves more hiking than climbing. Walking is as important as any other skill climbers learn. Before hitting the trail, stretch your legs, hips, back, and shoulders. Drink some water. Consider taping or using blister bandages such as Moleskin or New-Skin on areas prone to blisters. Take time to adjust your pack and boots to avoid later aches and pains.

Use the pack's outside pockets and pouches for items you plan to access repeatedly throughout the day, such as snacks, water, jacket, hat, gloves, gaiters, sunglasses, and headlamp, positioning them so that you and other members of your party can easily reach these items without stopping or slowing the pace. Strap your ice axe and trekking poles to the outside so they are readily available for rough terrain. An ice axe is often useful even before you reach the snow line.

TRAVELING WITH A GROUP

Traveling with others involves certain considerations that make a trip more efficient and enjoyable:

- **Set a steady pace that does not burn out slower climbers.** Adjust the party's pace so that slower climbers do not fall far behind. Do not allow anyone to travel alone, either last or first. At rest stops, give the last person time to catch up with the party—and time for that person to rest once they get there.
- **Try putting the slowest person in front to set the pace.** This approach helps keep the group together and may motivate a slower hiker to set a faster pace.
- **Redistribute group gear to energetic people.** This approach may help slow a fast hiker to keep the group together.
- **Stay four to 12 steps behind the person ahead.** Give the climber in front of you some space. You don't want to end up running into them or, worse, their ice axe or trekking poles.
- **Stay close to the group.** Do not lose contact with other party members or make them continually wait for you or wonder how far ahead you are.
- **Step off the trail when you stop.** Do not block the trail for others.
- **Ask permission to pass.** And pick a good spot to do so.
- **Mind the person behind you when you move branches.** Before releasing branches, look back and call out "Branch."
- **Be courteous when meeting an oncoming party.** When meeting horseback riders or pack animals, move aside to the downhill side of the trail. When hiking downhill, yield to an ascending party by stepping aside on the uphill side of the trail, allowing them to continue upward without breaking pace.
- **Best practice is to keep climbing groups together.** However where routefinding is not a concern, some leaders may decide to designate gathering points for the party during long approaches and descents.
- **Be positive and helpful.** Act like someone you would want to climb or adventure with.

PACE

Setting the right pace from the start ensures a stronger, more comfortable day of climbing. The most common mistake is moving too fast to begin with, perhaps out of concern about the long miles ahead or from a desire to perform well with companions. But why get worn out on the first mile of a 10-mile (16-kilometer) approach if the whole day is available? You are going too fast if you cannot sustain your pace hour after hour or if you cannot converse without losing your breath. Take your time and enjoy yourself (see the "Traveling with a Group" sidebar).

The other mistake is moving too slowly, which prolongs the hike and leaves less time to negotiate the more technical portions. If you are moving slowly due to fatigue, remember that the body has considerable reserves. Muscles may ache but still have many miles left in them. A degree of discomfort is inevitable; moving too fast or too slow only creates additional fatigue.

At the start, move slowly to allow your body to warm up. Before you start to sweat, take a break and remove some clothing. Then increase the pace and accept the pain as your body works harder to experience its second wind. Physiologically, your heartbeat and circulation increase and muscles loosen. As endorphins kick in and the feelings of physical stress subside, you feel strong and happy.

Vary the pace depending on the trail. Plod slowly and methodically up steep hills. As the grade lessens, pick up the tempo—"stretch your legs." Eventually you will find a natural pace that adapts to pack weight, terrain, weather, and other conditions. The pace will inevitably slow late in the day as fatigue sets in. Adrenaline may fuel short bursts of exertion, but there is no "third wind."

Whether you are hiking, snowshoeing, snowboarding, or skiing, if your party meets another group on the trail, traditionally the party heading downhill steps aside to let the ascending party continue upward without breaking pace. However, if the terrain is steep or if the descending party is larger, the ascending climbers may step aside and take a few breaths. Generally, stand on the uphill side of the trail to let others past. However, when a party meets horseback riders or pack animals, it is often expected that those on foot will move aside and stand on the downhill side of the trail, speak quietly, and make no sudden movements. Cyclists should always yield to those on foot.

THE REST STEP

Slow and steady is a pace that gains the summit. On steep slopes, in snow, and at high altitudes, the rest step controls your pace and reduces fatigue. Use this technique instead of

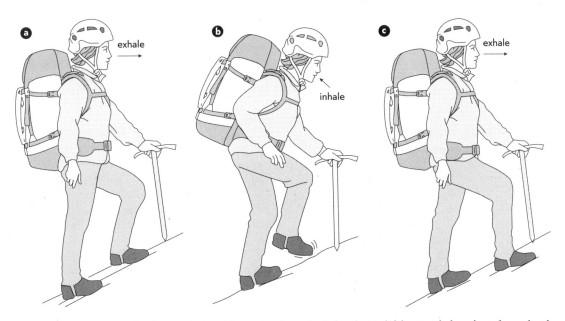

Fig. 6-1. *The rest step:* **a,** *stand with entire body weight on right leg and exhale, relaxing left leg;* **b,** *inhale and step forward with right leg, shifting weight to left leg;* **c,** *place entire body weight on left leg and exhale, relaxing right leg.*

frequent rest stops whenever legs or lungs need to recuperate. The rest step is simple but subtle; practice it.

The essence of the technique is to end every step with a momentary but complete stop, giving your leg muscles a rest. Swing one foot forward for the next step. Stand upright and exhale while letting your rear leg support your entire body weight (fig. 6-1a). Straighten your rear leg so that you are supported by bone, not muscle. Feel the weight sink into your bones and foot. Now relax and soften the muscles of your forward leg, especially the thigh. This momentary rest, no matter how brief, refreshes the muscles. The momentary rest also tends to make your foot placement more secure. Then take a breath and swing your rear foot forward for the next step (fig. 6-1b), and repeat the rest step for your other leg (fig. 6-1c).

Synchronize your breathing with your leg movements. Inhale and take a step up; exhale while pausing and letting your front leg rest as your rear leg supports your weight. Keep repeating the sequence. Many experienced climbers find a tune they replay in their head to help them keep a comfortable rhythm. The number of breaths per step depends on the difficulty of the route or slope and your level of fatigue. At high altitudes, climbers sometimes take three or four deep breaths, concentrating on breathing deeper and exhaling more forcefully, before each step.

The rest step requires patience. For some, its monotony can undermine morale, especially when following another climber up a snowfield when there is no routefinding or step kicking to occupy your thoughts. But focus on the rhythm or hum a tune in your head (settle on an upbeat tune if that helps). Trust the technique to chew up the miles, even though the summit may seem far away.

RESTS

Rests allow your body to recover from strenuous activity and maintain an efficient pace. Take rests only when necessary; otherwise, keep moving. Stopping frequently can easily turn a 10-hour day into a 15-hour day, affecting group morale or even the team's chance of reaching a summit.

During the first half hour, stop to allow the group to readjust bootlaces and pack straps, add or take off layers of clothing, stretch warmed-up muscles, et cetera. Take short breathers—every one to one and a half hours—during the early part of the day, while bodies are fresh. Rest in a standing or semireclining position, leaning against a tree or hillside to remove pack weight from your shoulders. If there is nothing to rest against, point your toes up the fall line and lock your knees, then rest. Take deep breaths and have a bite to eat and something to drink. Stay hydrated—drink at every stop.

Remember to declare regular party separations (toilet stops), especially out of courtesy to the person who may be too shy to express the need. However, to minimize impact on the mountains, make the first toilet stop at the last available restroom facility found at or before the trailhead.

Later in the day, feelings of fatigue may demand more thorough relaxation, and the party can take a full rest every two hours or so. Look for a place with advantages, such as water or a convenient slope for removing packs and enjoying a view. Stretch muscles and put on additional clothing to avoid stiffness and chilling. Remove extra clothing before starting out again, to prevent another stop a few minutes down the trail.

Be efficient about your breaks, minimizing how much of your gear you unpack. Clearly establish how long the break will last. When the group stops, it is a good time to sit down, have a snack, drink some water, reapply sunblock, or empty your bladder. Even if you were not quite ready to do so, it saves the group from having to make another stop too soon. When the leader prepares to leave, that's your signal to get ready too.

UPHILL

As the party climbs uphill, in addition to watching for specific hazards, monitor the steepness and general nature of what you are climbing into. Consider whether continuing will lead into territory so steep and technical that the group will have difficulty downclimbing or otherwise retreating. If you notice that retreating may be difficult, especially if there is any chance the party is not on the trail it intended to follow, confirm that the group is on route and that there are no other options. Otherwise, retreating while the party still feels comfortable with the terrain is likely the best option.

DOWNHILL

Traveling downhill is a mixed blessing. The pace quickens without increasing fatigue; however, climbers may feel pain long after the day is over. When walking downhill, your body and pack weight drop abruptly on your legs, knees, and feet. Toes jam forward. The impact of your feet landing on the ground jolts up your spine and jars your entire body. Use a few of the following tricks to avoid a host of injuries, including blisters, damage to knee cartilage, sore toes, blackened toenails, headaches, and back pain:

- **Trim your toenails** short before starting out.
- **Tighten your laces and buckles**, especially on the upper part of boots, to reduce foot movement inside boots and avoid jamming toes against the front.

- **Bend your knees** with each step to cushion the shock and engage your core. As dancers like to say, "Remember your plié."
- **Place each foot lightly,** as if it were already sore.
- **Use ski or trekking poles** to reduce the load on your knees and to provide additional stability.
- **Maintain a measured pace** that is slower than the one urged by gravity.
- **Use an ice axe** for balance or for braking when necessary. The ice axe is not just for snow. It is also helpful in steep meadow, forest, and heather. (To learn ice-axe techniques, see Chapter 16, Basic Snow and Ice Climbing.)
- **Find a place to sit briefly** every 45 to 60 minutes, if necessary, to reduce knee fatigue.

SIDEHILL

The ups and downs of climbing are far preferable to the torments of cross-country sidehilling (traversing). Traveling across the side of a slope twists your ankles, contorts your hips, and undermines balance. If possible, abandon the sidehill, hike straight up, and drop down into a brush-free valley, or go up onto a rounded ridge. If you must traverse, look for rocks, animal trails, and the ground just above clumps of grass or heather for flat spots that may offer relief. Switchback regularly to avoid hip or ankle strain in one leg.

Trail Finding

For a wilderness traveler, a "trail" is any visible route—no matter how ragged—that efficiently gets the party where they want to go. The goal is to find the easiest route using the resources at hand: awareness of the terrain, navigational skills, weather conditions, and tips from guidebooks and experts.

Even in popular areas with heavy foot traffic and signage, keep alert to find and stay on the trail. Missing a turnoff is easy if a sign is gone or if logging, erosion, an avalanche, treefall, or rockfall obliterates the trail. On an established forest trail in deep snow or through a lot of woody debris, saw-cut log ends peeking through may be the only indication of the trail's location.

Old blazes cut in tree trunks or surveyors' ribbon tied to branches often mark the trail through a forest; rock cairns (piles of rocks placed along the route as markers where the path is not obvious) may show the way above timberline. These pointers may be unreliable. A tiny cairn or a wisp of ribbon may indicate nothing more than a lost climber, a route to an alternate destination, or an old route now obstructed by rockfall. Navigation tools like the map, GPS, altimeter, and compass stand you in good stead too (see Chapter 5, Navigation and Communication).

The trick, however, is to stay on the trail until the inevitable moment it disappears or until it becomes necessary to head off trail in order to head in the right direction. Choose a course that a trail would follow if there were a trail. Trail builders look for the easiest way to go. Do as they do.

Sharing the Wilderness

6

Alpine wildlife is fascinating and often charming, but enjoy the birds and animals from a distance and do not disturb them. When you encounter wildlife on the route, move slowly and allow them plenty of time to drift away. Try to pass on their downhill side—typically they head uphill to escape. Give them plenty of room. An animal rushing from a close encounter with a human is in danger of stress or injury. If it has too many of these encounters, it may feel forced to abandon its home grounds for poorer terrain.

BEARS, COUGARS, AND WOLVES

In bear country, try not to surprise bears. Whenever possible, go around brushy ravines with poor visibility rather than through them, even if it makes the route longer. Make plenty of noise in lower-visibility areas to warn animals of your approach. Pepper spray is a last resort. Store food properly and well away from your tent to avoid bear encounters at camp. (For more about handling animal encounters, see Resources. For more about proper food storage, see Chapters 2 and 7.)

If you surprise a bear or cougar, do not turn around and run. Running may elicit a chase response in large predators, and bears and cougars can run very fast. Instead, stand your ground, face the animal, talk, and slowly edge away while still facing it. Do not crouch or squat down.

Do not ever approach wolves, to avoid habituating them to humans. If a wolf approaches you, try scare tactics before it is within 100 yards (90 meters). Raise and wave your arms, make noise, and toss sticks, rocks, and sand to scare wolves away. If the wolf is aggressive, stand your ground as you would with a bear.

LOCAL LAND USERS

Some approaches travel through working farms or logging areas (legal or otherwise). Respect local conventions or postings to avoid conflict: close all gates after using them, find another route if there are No Trespassing signs, et cetera. Be alert to guard dogs that may announce or discourage your approach. If dogs are aggressive, stand your ground as you would with the wild animals described above.

Negotiating Difficult Terrain

The biggest barriers on the way to a mountaintop often appear below the snow line.

BRUSH

Brush thrives in younger forests or in low-altitude, wet, subalpine areas that have few trees. A river that changes course prevents large-tree growth and permits brush to thrive. In gullies swept by winter avalanches, the shrubs simply bend undamaged under the snow and flourish in spring and summer. Downward-slanting vine maple and slide alder are slippery.

Bushwhacking through brush makes travel difficult, dangerous, and slow. Brush obscures the peril of cliffs, boulders, and ravines. It also snares ropes and ice-axe picks. The best policy is to avoid brush, but if that is not possible, try the following techniques (also see the "Tips to Minimize Brush Hassles" sidebar):

- **Use trails as much as possible.** Five miles (8 kilometers) of trail may be less work and take less time than 1 mile (1.6 kilometers) of brush.
- **Travel when snow covers brush.** Some valleys make for easy going in the spring when it is possible to walk on snow, but they are almost impossible in summer when it is necessary to burrow through the brush.
- **Avoid avalanche tracks.** When ascending a valley wall, stay in the trees between avalanche tracks to avoid the brush.
- **Aim for big trees, where brush is thinner.** Mature forests block sunlight and stifle brush growth.
- **Travel on scree, talus, or snow remnants.** Avoid thickets adjacent to rock or snow.
- **Look for game trails.** Animals generally follow the path of least resistance, but game trails can be steep and rugged. Use these trails, but take care not to startle large animals in heavy brush.
- **Travel on ridges and ridge spurs.** Creek bottoms and valley floors are often choked with vegetation, but ridges and spurs may be dry and brushless.
- **Scout both sides of a stream.** Evaluate which bank involves the least amount of bushwhacking.
- **Consider going into the stream channel.** If the route parallels a stream, wading through its bed can be easier than bushwhacking through the brush. Dry streambeds are often ideal. Take care in deep canyons where waterfalls and fallen trees interrupt a stream. Beware of flash floods in canyons and washes.
- **Take a high route.** Climb directly to timberline or a ridgetop.
- **Go up to the base of side bluffs.** There is often an open, flattened corridor next to the rock.

SCREE, TALUS, AND BOULDERS

Mountain peaks crumble regularly, dropping rock fragments that pile up below as scree, talus, and boulders. Most of the rubble pours from gullies and spreads out in alluvial fans that often merge into one another, forming a broad band of broken rock between valley greenery and the peaks. These fans can alternate in vertical strips with forest. Scree is the smallest—from the size of coarse sand up to a couple inches (5 centimeters) across—and some pieces may flow around your feet when you step on it. Talus consists of larger fragments, usually big enough to step on individually. When even larger rocks fall off cliff faces, they form boulder fields. Slopes of scree, talus, and boulders can either help or hinder a climber. Most offer handy, brush-free pathways to the mountains, but some are loose and dangerous, and the footing is unpredictable, with sharp-edged rock that can cause injury.

Scree. Loose scree can make going uphill a slow-motion torment, with part of each step lost as your foot settles in. Stepping on or just above a larger rock in scree can pry or wedge it out. However, descents can be fun. It may be possible to move down the scree in a sliding stride—something like cross-country skiing or plunge-stepping down snow. Ice axes are helpful; the technique on scree is similar to that on snow (see Chapter 16, Basic Snow and Ice Climbing). Nonetheless, be aware that scree can sometimes consist of only a thin cover of ball bearing–sized fragments over large rocks. If

---

TIPS TO MINIMIZE BRUSH HASSLES

Some skirmishes with brush are inevitable, especially in off-trail or cross-country travel where bushwhacking is simply part of the process. Here are some bushwhacking tips:

- **Choose the shortest route** across the brushy area.
- **Look for animal trails** through the brush.
- **Use fallen trees** with long, straight trunks as elevated walkways.
- **Push and pull bushes apart**, sometimes by stepping on lower limbs and lifting and clinging to higher ones, to make a passageway.
- **Use hardy shrubs** as hand- and footholds on steep terrain.

there is vegetation on the slope, avoid setting off scree slides that can damage the plants. Although riding a scree slope can be fun, bits of rock can work their way into your boots. Consider wearing lightweight gaiters if scree is expected.

Talus. Gradually, over the ages, talus slopes build up; on the oldest slopes, soil fills the spaces between the rocks, locking them together to create smooth pathways. But talus can be loose on volcanoes and younger mountains, where vegetation has not filled in the spaces. Even large rocks can roll or teeter. Whether ascending or descending, try for a route where the rock is lichen covered, which indicates that the rock has remained in place for a long time. Move

nimbly on talus, ready to leap away if a rock shifts underfoot. Use your eyes and plan four or five steps ahead. Try to set your foot smoothly and flex your foot to accommodate the angle of the surface you are stepping on. That may help the piece remain stable. Take care on wet talus.

Boulders. Normally, boulders form a steep slope beneath the cliff they detached from—the steepest slope that such boulders can pile up on is called the angle of repose. The boulders landing on even steeper slopes tend to fall off unless stabilized by vegetation. Boulder fields can be pleasant alternatives to torturous scree slopes, but they have their own dangers. The most commonly traveled routes

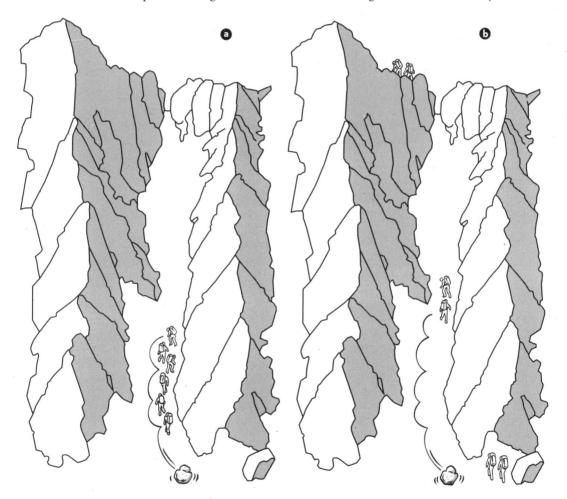

Fig. 6-2. *Traveling on loose rock:* **a,** *climbers stay close together so a dislodged rock does not gain dangerous momentum before reaching the climbers below;* **b,** *climbers ascend in pairs (or small groups) out of one another's fall line, so a dislodged rock passes the climbers below.*

over boulder fields are usually quite stable, since foot traffic has gradually shifted the riskiest boulders to more stable places. Beware the unfrequented boulder field—where there are no boot marks on the boulder moss, for instance.

Rockfall

Sometimes a route ascends a steep gully filled with a mix of boulders embedded in talus and scree—this is a classic scenario for party-induced rockfall. Disturbing one key stone on a glacial moraine or a talus slope can set off a rock avalanche. Travel outside the fall line of climbers above and below you if possible, to avoid rockfall. If you are in a narrow gully where this is not possible, tread gently and be ready to loudly shout "Rock! *Rock!* **Rock!**" if a stone dislodges. Keep the party close together so a rock set off by one climber cannot gain dangerous momentum before reaching others (fig. 6-2a). Consider allowing just one climber or two (or small groups keeping closely together) to move at a time while the rest of the party remains in protected spots (fig. 6-2b).

Party-induced rockfall is by no means the only hazard in loose gullies. Even rainfall can set off rockfall. Other times, rockfall may be set off by another climbing party out of your party's sight. Overall, rockfall is one of the most common causes of mountain accidents, so beware! Consider wearing a helmet any time you are traveling over terrain where a climber may be exposed to rockfall from above or could have a serious fall.

Descending

Facing exposure while descending scree, talus, or boulders can be intimidating. Move in short, smooth, quick steps, and know where the next step is, so you are ready to quickly get off a moving rock and avoid injury. Hesitating or moving too slowly can be dangerous. Trekking poles or an ice axe are helpful for balance; keep your pole or axe in front of you to avoid it becoming caught between rocks or disturbing rocks above you. Pole baskets that may help in snow are apt to snag on rock.

SNOW

Snow can be very helpful for wilderness travel. Many peaks are best climbed early in the season when consolidated snow covers talus, brush, and logging slash and when snow bridges provide easy access over streams. However, in a different season or with less-than-ideal snow conditions, snow can be a curse. Trails are lost under snow or are washed out by avalanches or heavy thaw. Thin snow is unstable and may obscure dangerous conditions. Watch for terrain traps if spring avalanches are a possibility (see Chapter

16, Basic Snow and Ice Climbing). A party may encounter different snow conditions on the approach, the climb, and the descent, given the time of day, the pace, or changing weather conditions. Be sure to study weather and snow conditions before the climb. (See Chapter 20, Avalanche Safety, for an overview of evaluating snow conditions.)

When you are traveling on snow, watch for visible terrain features that may indicate thin or melting snow. Snow next to logs and boulders often covers holes and soft spots called moats, where the snow partially melts away from the wood and the rock. A moat called a tree well is common around trees where lower limbs keep the snow from filling in next to the trunk. Probe with an ice axe to avoid likely trouble spots, step wide off logs and rocks, and stay away from treetops poking above the snow. If snow is thin on a talus slope, watch out for large voids under the snow that are easy to punch through. Especially if the day is warm and the snow is thin, go slow on talus on the return trip.

Streams will melt the underside of a snow bridge until it can no longer support a climber's weight. To guard against a dunking (or worse), watch for depressions in the snow and variations in color or texture, and listen for sounds of running water. Water emerging at the foot of a snowfield indicates the existence, and perhaps the size, of a cavity beneath the snow. Probe for thin spots with an ice axe.

With experience, climbers recognize both the advantages and dangers of snow and learn to use the medium to make wilderness travel easier and more enjoyable. For more information, see Chapters 16, Basic Snow and Ice Climbing, and 27, The Cycle of Snow.

RIVERS AND STREAMS

When the party's objective lies on the far side of a sizable river or stream, crossing it is a major factor in route selection. Crossings can consume huge amounts of time and energy, and they can be the most dangerous part of the trip.

Finding a Place to Cross

Try to get a distant, overall view of the river and scope out crossing possibilities. This can be more useful than a hundred close looks from the riverbank. When a distant view is impossible or unhelpful, the party may have to choose between either thrashing through river-bottom brush to find a way across or traversing slopes high above the river in hopes of a sure crossing.

The surrounding landscape indicates the options. In a deep forest, there is a good chance of finding easy passage on a large log or logjam, even over wide rivers. Higher in the mountains, foot logs are harder to come by, especially if the river frequently changes course and prevents the growth of large trees near its channel.

If it is necessary to wade across, find the widest part of the river. The narrows may be the shortest way, but they are also the deepest, swiftest, and most dangerous. If snowmelt feeds a river, its flow will be at a minimum in the early morning before turning into a dangerous, raging torrent in the afternoon. Sometimes a party may camp overnight to take advantage of this morning low water.

Crossing a Stream

Unfasten your pack's hip belt and sternum straps before trying any stream crossing that may require swimming if you fall. Make sure you will be able to remove your pack in a hurry.

Logs. A foot log is a great way across. If the log is thin, slippery, or steeply inclined, use a trekking pole (or poles), an ice axe, a sturdy stick, crampons or boot spikes, or a tightly stretched hand line (see below) to help with balance, traction, and support. Sit down and scoot across if that allows you to keep your balance.

Boulder hopping. Another way across is stepping on boulders. Before crossing, mentally rehearse the path you will follow. Try to make smooth and steady progress over stones that may be too slippery and unsteady to stop on for more than a few seconds. Use an ice axe or trekking pole(s) for additional balance. Avoid mossy or algae-covered stones if possible.

Wading. If you will be wading, try to keep your gear, including boots, dry. If the water is placid and the stones rounded, put your boots and socks in your pack and wade across barefoot or in sandals, water shoes, or lightweight tennis shoes brought for that purpose. In tougher conditions, wear your boots but put your socks and insoles in the pack; on the far side, drain your boots and replace the dry insoles and socks. In deeper crossings, consider removing your pants or other clothing: loose clothing increases the water's drag; however, it also reduces chilling and may permit a longer crossing.

If you are trying to cross where the water is deep but not swift, cross with the least force against your body by angling downstream at about the same speed as the current. However, the best way to cross is to face upstream, lean into the current, and firmly plant an ice axe, trekking pole, or stout stick upstream for a third point of support. First, probe with your leading foot for solid placement on the shifting river bottom; next, advance your following foot; then thrust the axe or pole into a new position.

It is easy to underestimate swift water. With one false step, you can be pushed under and dashed against rocks and logs or sent bouncing along in whitewater. A swift stream flowing only shin-deep can boil up against your knees—water is dangerous above knee level. Knee-deep water may boil above your waist, leading to a disconcerting sensation of buoyancy. Frothy water, containing a great deal of air, is wet enough to drown you but may not be dense enough for the human body to float. A stream fed by glaciers has an additional difficulty: milky water from glacier-milled rock flour hides the streambed and any rocks that may lurk there.

Team crossing. Two or more travelers can cross together, each moving in turn to a solid new stance while remaining secured to the other(s) by linked arms or hands. Team crossing with a pole is another method: Team members enter the water, each grasping the pole and holding it horizontal and parallel to the stream's flow; for more than two people, use a pole between each pair. The upstream member breaks the current's force. Anyone who slips can hold onto the pole while the other(s) keeps the pole steady.

Hand lines. For small stream crossings, a hand line can be helpful. Angle the line downstream so that if any climbers lose their footing, they will be swept to shore. If a nylon climbing rope is the only available option, consider the rope stretch (see Chapter 8, Essential Climbing Equipment). Always use appropriate anchors (see Chapter 10, Belaying).

Using ropes for stream crossings in deep, swift water can be hazardous. If someone is belayed across the river, it is possible that the crossing person can be held by the belay but trapped underwater. Consider adding a belay line to the pack, however. That way, if a climber falls and sheds the pack, it will not get swept away.

Falling In

If falling off a log into the water seems imminent, try to fall on the downstream side to avoid getting swept under the log. If you are swept downstream by a swift current, the safest position is facing downstream and on your back with your feet pointed up; use a backstroke to steer. This position vastly improves your chances for survival with minimal injuries. Be alert. If you approach a "strainer" (a small dam of wood, branches, or debris), switch quickly to normal headfirst swimming and swim furiously toward shore but away from the debris. If the pile is unavoidable, do all you can to stay high in the water and on top of it, not strained under it.

If a party member falls in, those on shore can try to reach out with a pole, ice axe, or branch. It may be possible to throw out a floating object, such as an inflated water bag or a whitewater rope-throw bag. Make a realistic evaluation of the danger to yourself before you decide to go into the stream to attempt a hands-on rescue.

Ready for the Wilderness

Traveling in the wilderness is like wandering in a foreign country: The unfamiliarity of a place is part of the attraction, yet that same quality can also limit the journey.

Preparation is essential, and nothing rivals the knowledge gained from personal experience.

Immerse yourself in the wilderness again and again; study it as if it were a new language. Use all five senses to master the "vocabulary" of the terrain. Some of the best moments come when you discover your ability to respond well to what the wilderness asks of you. With fluency comes the freedom to roam, and with that freedom comes the exhilaration of discovery.

CHAPTER 7

PROTECTING THE OUTDOORS

When climbers traverse mountain landscapes, they move through Indigenous land, fragile ecosystems, wildlife habitat, and some of the most beautiful places on earth. Climbing, therefore, comes with enormous responsibility as well as rewards. By approaching these areas with respect, reciprocity, and reverence, and by leaving no trace and providing active stewardship, we can continue to enjoy the freedom of the hills.

7

Mountaineers seek the uncharted way, the trail less traveled, and a well-earned view from the summit. Climbing requires physical effort, honed skills, and dexterity, and mountaineers embrace low-impact recreation skills as an integral part of their technical pursuits. They leave no trace of their time outdoors because they have both enthusiasm for the natural environment and a deep desire to protect it for the next trip, as well as for the next generations. As more people turn to the mountains and these landscapes become increasingly challenged by a changing climate, stewardship and responsible recreation are paramount for protecting these wild places.

Leave No Trace

All mountaineers have witnessed evidence of overuse, carelessness, and thoughtlessness in the backcountry. Climbers on Mount Rainier, Denali, and Everest (Chomolungma), for instance, are required to pack out their excrement due to increased recreation on those mountains. On Denali, the first chunks of 75 tons (68 tonnes) of poop, thrown into Kahiltna Glacier between 1951 and 2012, will begin to melt out in the late 2020s. Pathogenic outflow will continue downstream for decades.

During the 1960s, visitation to national parks increased dramatically, companies started to make better backpacking equipment, and ecological consciousness began to rise. An ethical evolution in climbing emerged in the 1970s when the first chocks replaced rock-deforming pitons. Federal land agencies developed national campaigns in the 1980s, attempting to mitigate the effects of increasing visitation: "Minimum Impact Camping," "Tread Lightly," "No Trace Camping." In 1994, the Leave No Trace

Center for Outdoor Ethics was established as a nonprofit educational organization to promote a consistent set of minimum-impact guidelines, now referred to as Leave No Trace.

Leave No Trace principles and practices are based on recreation ecology studies and scientific social research. These principles (see the "Seven Leave No Trace Principles" sidebar) extend common courtesies to other outdoor visitors and to the natural world itself. Leave No Trace ethics and low-impact skills are transferable to other recreational pursuits and subalpine environments.

1. PLAN AHEAD AND PREPARE

Planning ahead achieves more than a summit; it is essential to practicing Leave No Trace skills.

Protect the Climbing Party, Protect the Place

A climbing group that stretches itself to the limit, and perhaps gets into trouble, may not be able to practice Leave No Trace. For example, they may grow fatigued and have to set up camp in a fragile alpine meadow. They may get cold and start a campfire in a fire-ban zone, putting warming forests at risk. If rescuers must be called, human safety is prioritized regardless of environmental damage. Realistic planning can often prevent these kinds of dire situations in the first place.

> **KEY TOPICS**
>
> **LEAVE NO TRACE**
> **MINIMIZING CLIMBING IMPACTS**
> **ACCESS AND STEWARDSHIP**
> **THE FUTURE OF MOUNTAINEERING**

SEVEN LEAVE NO TRACE PRINCIPLES

1. Plan ahead and prepare.
2. Travel and camp on durable surfaces.
3. Dispose of waste properly.
4. Leave what you find.
5. Minimize campfire impacts.
6. Respect wildlife.
7. Be considerate of others.

See Resources to learn more about sustainable practices related to the outdoors from the Leave No Trace Center for Outdoor Ethics, which partners with US land managers and other organizations worldwide to instill responsible recreation.

Before You Go

Success begins long before the first pitch. How a climbing party gets to the trailhead, packs for the route and weather, and sets adequate safety margins are but a few preclimb considerations (see Table 22-2 in Chapter 22, Leadership). Research required permits and other possible regulations ahead of time. For example, permits are not required to climb mountains in Europe, but places like the Matterhorn do restrict the number of people who can stay in huts.

In the US, land management norms vary across agencies and at popular locations. These norms include area closures to protect sensitive wildlife, habitat restoration projects, and other conservation efforts. Likewise, climbers need to understand required waste-disposal systems, forest fire danger ratings, and ecological sensitivities before arriving at the trailhead. Because regulations change from time to time, well-prepared climbers consult agency resources and officials before they head out, inquiring about sensitive lands and waters, unique flora and fauna, and archeological and cultural areas.

Meal Planning

As with many Leave No Trace skills, meal planning not only protects the environment but also makes for more efficient mountaineers. Mastering two techniques—repackaging food and preparing one-pot meals—speeds cooking, lightens loads, decreases garbage, and protects the environment (see Food in Chapter 3, Camping, Food, and Water).

The more packaging climbers carry, the greater the chance of leaving unintentional litter in the backcountry. Wrapped or twist-tied foods can readily be repackaged into resealable containers or bags. Place empty bags inside one another for packing out. Sealing up food and food waste (and other odiferous items—sunscreens, toiletries, soaps, perfumed items) protects climbers from hungry critters and protects those same animals.

One-pot meals, prepared quickly on a backpacking stove, require minimal cooking utensils and cleanup. Plan meals so that, except for emergency rations, the group takes only the amount of food necessary. If there are leftovers, do not bury, burn, or dump them; pack them out as waste.

Consider Conditions

Planning continues beyond the trailhead. Weather, along with objective and subjective hazards (termed mountain and human hazards in Chapter 23, Risk Management), can change in minutes. Be willing to modify your plans. Failing to prepare is preparing to fail.

2. TRAVEL AND CAMP ON DURABLE SURFACES

The depth of a climber's footprint or size of a camper's shelter may seem infinitesimal amid the canyons of the American Southwest, vistas of Europe's Alps, or heights of Asia's Himalaya. However, as climbing and mountaineering continue to grow in popularity, these areas and others host millions of visitors a year. Whenever possible, hike on established trails and camp in established sites. As climbers move off trail into pristine environments, practicing responsible recreation with Leave No Trace skills becomes even more critical.

Hiking

Think of trails as wilderness highways. Staying on established trails and following best hiking practices make it possible for wild places to stay wild. Trails that are properly designed can withstand high foot traffic, channel users through fragile areas, manage water flow, and prevent soil erosion. Always obey trailside signs.

On-Trail Travel

While mountaineers venture beyond the beaten path, nearly every outing involves some established trails. Observe these practices to help preserve trails and the areas they pass through:

- **Always use trails where they exist.**
- **Stay on the established trail.** Even if a trail is muddy or rutted, stay on it, hiking single file. These practices protect trailside vegetation and keep hikers from unintentionally widening trails. It takes mere hours to dry waterproof footwear and gaiters, but it may take decades to repair a braided trail in an alpine

landscape. Take care along stream banks to avoid erosion.

- **Never cut switchbacks.** Shortcutting between switchbacks accelerates erosion, kills plants, and increases chances of slipping and injury.
- **Travel on snow when possible.** Snow is a natural protective layer between boots and the ground. Take extra care when traveling through the fragile transition zone between dirt and a thin snow layer, where the soil is saturated with water and prone to rutting, especially during spring and late fall.
- **Select resilient areas, such as rocks, sand, or unvegetated areas, for rest breaks.** To remain unobtrusive to fellow hikers, move away from the trail and onto durable surfaces for rest breaks. If this is not possible due to fragile or dense vegetation, find a wide spot in the trail to rest or yield to other hikers.
- **Pick up scraps of litter.** Put litter somewhere secure in your bag or pockets. Check for microtrash—foil ends of bar wrappers, crumbs, scraps of paper, fabric, or plastic—after each break and meal or when packing up camp. Carry a garbage bag to haul out larger materials, especially on the way out.

Off-Trail Travel

Generally, a climbing objective lies well off any established trail. Mountaineers traveling off trail minimize damage by incorporating the following skills into how they climb:

- **Keep a thoughtful pace.** Travel slowly enough to be aware of the surroundings and to plan a low-impact route.
- **Spread out the group.** Have each member take a separate path, especially in fragile meadows. Avoid traveling in a straight line, which can create a new linear "trace."
- **Walk on durable surfaces.** Bare ground (patches between vegetation, wildlife trails) not covered by biological soil crust, rock (bedrock, large stones, talus, scree, stream gravel), and sedge grasses are durable surfaces. In many arid and semi-arid ecosystems, biological soil crust, or biocrust, is commonly found on the surface of the soil. Consisting of cyanobacteria, algae, mosses, lichen, and fungi, biocrust is one of the oldest known life-forms. Avoid tromping on woody or herbaceous vegetation, even if it appears to be hardy. Walking on durable surfaces is especially important at higher elevations where native vegetation experiences shorter growing seasons and harsher conditions and it is harder for plants to recover from harm.

- **Leave areas free of cairns and flagging.** Leave markers that are already there, but don't build new rock piles. Never carve tree bark. Use electronic GPS software to record the way. If your party needs to physically mark the route on the way up, remove the markers on the way back down (see During the Trip in Chapter 5, Navigation and Communication). Let the next party experience its own routefinding adventure.

Camping

Many of the world's most popular summit routes and back-country trails have a number of established campsites. Use those to avoid creating a new campsite and further disrupting the natural landscape. Look for previously used, established campsites. Resist the temptation to use a less disturbed site because it has a better view or is closer to a water source.

If a pristine location is all you have, stay only a night or two and then find another spot, which allows the area to recover. If there is a choice between a pristine campsite and a slightly impacted one, the better choice could be the pristine site, if Leave No Trace guidelines are carefully applied. Although this choice may be contrary to first instinct, it allows the slightly affected area to revive rather than receive more use.

In pristine sites, observe these recommendations:

- **Avoid grouping tents together.**
- **Disperse toilet sites and vary walkways.** Ensure that no single path gets so trampled that the vegetation cannot recover. Carry sandals or lightweight soft-soled shoes to wear around camp; heavy lug-soled boots are hard on soil and vegetation.
- **Never "landscape" a site.** Do not level a site, remove vegetation, or dig trenches, for example.
- **An ideal campsite is a found campsite, not an engineered one.** Find a tent spot with a slight natural slope so water will not pool beneath a tent, which might tempt campers to dig a trench.

When selecting a campsite, apply the 200-foot rule (about 80 big steps for an adult): camp at least 200 feet (60 meters) away from water and trails. Land managers may allow use of already hardened sites even though they are close to water; if so, use them, but do not create a new site in the same vicinity. In a pristine area, enhance the sense of solitude for yourself and others by choosing an out-of-the-way site or one with natural screening.

Use established mountaineering bivy sites or high camps. Avoid moving alpine rocks, which may kill fragile plants that are often tiny and nestled up against rocks and stones.

7

It takes years for alpine plants to grow. Moving rocks may also disturb the habitat of insects and other wildlife.

Keep track of gear and maintain a tidy camp so equipment and food are not misplaced or forgotten. Leave the site in better condition than you found it, with a micro-trash sweep before you go. Pristine sites require a little extra effort: covering used areas with native materials, brushing out footprints, and fluffing up matted grasses.

3. DISPOSE OF WASTE PROPERLY

For decades, climbers practiced a laissez-faire approach to human sanitation, blithely defecating in shallow snow holes or tossing poop in paper bags down while on big wall climbs. Watersheds worldwide have been contaminated by fecal waste, wastewater, and garbage.

Mountaineers are self-reliant. They pack in food, coordinate equipment like stoves and lighting, and assemble temporary shelter. They also pack out their trash and manage sanitation.

Managing Human Waste in the Mountains

Properly disposing of human waste is critical to both human well-being and environmental health. How does a climber deal with bladder and bowel functions away from carefully engineered sewage-treatment and garbage systems?

It is important to understand four objectives for backcountry waste disposal: (1) minimizing the chance of ground- and surface-water pollution, (2) minimizing the spread of disease, (3) minimizing the aesthetic impact on the outdoors so that others can enjoy natural beauty, and (4) maximizing the decomposition rate of human waste. If any one of these four objectives cannot be accomplished,

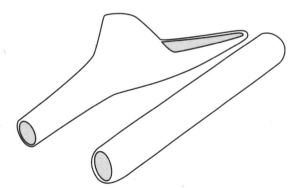

Fig. 7-1. *Female urination device (FUD): one of several reusable products. The Shewee shown is made of recyclable polypropylene. Disposable FUDs are also available.*

pack it out. Below are strategies for meeting these four objectives:

- **If there is an outhouse or similar toilet facility, use it.** Land managers place these amenities near trails, peaks, and camps where they can be easily used and serviced.
- **If an outhouse is unavailable and there is vegetated soil, use a cat hole.** Cat holes should be a minimum of 200 feet (60 meters)—about 80 big steps for an adult—from water, camp, trails, and drainages. Research ahead of time to know if this is an option or whether to pack out your waste. Digging cat holes and packing out poop are explained in more detail below.
- **If you use toilet paper, use unscented and pack it out.** Paper takes a very long time to decompose in dry alpine environments, it attracts animals, wind moves it easily, and burning it is a fire hazard. A small plastic bag will easily hold a day's worth of paper.
- **Instead of toilet paper, consider using natural materials.** Smooth stones, conifer cones, and broad leaves are some natural substitutes that can be buried (to avoid spreading pathogens) rather than packed out. Be careful to avoid vegetation that is fragile, prickly, or could cause a skin reaction, like poison oak or ivy.
- **Consider using a menstrual cup and bagging fluids to pack out.** Bulky menstrual products can add up on longer trips.
- **Pack out used personal hygiene products and pet waste.** Tampons, disposable diapers, bandages, and incontinence and menstrual pads must all be packed out after use.
- **Urinate on bare ground or rocks—not vegetation.** The salt in urine attracts animals that might dig soils and damage plants while trying to get to it.
- **On snow or ice, concentrate urine in designated downslope locations.** In camp or at rest stops, rather than creating a proliferation of pee holes, designate one location. Be sure it is well away from any water sources hidden by snow—use the 200-foot (60-meter) rule. Cover yellow snow.
- **On steep rock or ice faces, stream urine away from the climbing route.** You might have to wait until you reach a suitable place. On long routes or in tents, some climbers use a pee bottle to collect urine for later disposal. Women can use a female urination device (fig. 7-1)—without removing their climbing harnesses (see Water in Chapter 3, Camping, Food, and Water).

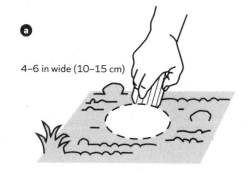

4–6 in wide (10–15 cm)

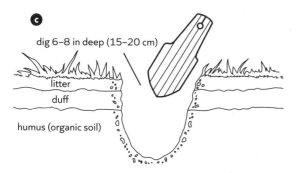

dig 6–8 in deep (15–20 cm)

litter
duff
humus (organic soil)

Fig. 7-2. *Creating a cat hole:* **a,** *cut a plug from top layer of vegetation and soil;* **b,** *remove plug and set it aside;* **c,** *dig the cat hole.*

- **On a slope, stay uphill of your pee.** Position yourself so any urine heads away from your feet.

Digging and Covering a Cat Hole

Using a cat hole to bury feces is most suited to lower elevations where there is a deep layer of organic soil; a cat hole is not suitable in snow unless organic soil can be found underneath it, possibly in a tree well (see the "Tips for Using Cat Holes" sidebar). Carry a waste-disposal bag or

---

TIPS FOR USING CAT HOLES

Keep these tips in mind when you need to dispose of solid human waste in the outdoors.

- **Have a waste-disposal kit ready.** Keep a trowel, toilet paper, bags for used hygiene products or diapers, wipes, latex or nitrile gloves, and hand sanitizer at the ready.

- **Plan ahead and prepare.** Begin to scout for a place when you first realize that you'll need to relieve yourself soon.

- **Go a minimum of 80 big steps away.** Find a location 200 feet (60 meters) away from trails, campsites, and water.

- **Cut a plug separately, then dig the hole.** Keep the plug intact to cover the top of the cat hole when you are done. Pile the dug material upslope to make it easier to backfill when you are done.

- **Face downhill during your deposit.** Facing downhill helps you balance, and you might have a view.

- **Keep the trowel sanitary.** Do not use it to pack down poop or soil; use sticks, stones, or your boot sole on the topmost layer of duff.

If you prefer, skip the cat hole completely and pack it out, using a pack-out container or bag (see the next section).

---

kit with trowel, toilet paper, bag for used toilet paper, and hand sanitizer.

Find a secluded area away from trails, campsites, gathering areas, or water sources—apply the 200-foot (60-meter) rule. Remember, if the spot is easy for you to reach, it will be easy for others too.

When you find a suitable location, use the trowel to remove the top layer of vegetation and soil as a plug about 4 to 6 inches (10 to 15 centimeters) in diameter (fig. 7-2a), and set it aside (fig. 7-2b). Dig down 6 to 8 inches (15 to 20 centimeters)—deeper than litter and duff, but not deeper than the humus, the dark organic soil containing microbes and insect life that breaks down fecal matter over time (fig. 7-2c). If there is a thin organic layer, such as in desert areas, make your hole wider and shallower—or, better yet, bag and pack out waste.

After making your deposit, fill the hole with soil, then replace the plug. Tamp the soil and distribute area vegetation to create a natural appearance. After bagging your toilet paper and checking the area, clean your hands with hand sanitizer, or wash them with soap and water.

Packing Out Poop

Mountaineers are already accustomed to packing out used toilet paper and personal hygiene products. Increasingly, climbers must be prepared to pack out feces as well. Packing out waste is the preferred practice on popular glacier routes, in alpine areas with thin mineral soils, in desert country, on steep rock and ice routes including big wall climbs, in canyons, on arctic tundra, and during winter travel. Climbers on Mount Rainier started using "blue bags" in the early 1980s, and mandatory carry-everything-out programs later spread to other popular peaks and environmentally sensitive areas. Today you will still encounter the term "blue bags" for human waste pack-out kits. Below are some steps for packing out poop and disposing of it once the party returns.

1. Double-bag it. Two resealable plastic bags work effectively and securely. With careful aim, make a direct deposit into the first resealable bag, or poop on the ground and, like a dog owner picking up after a pet, invert the bag over your hand like a glove, scoop up the solid waste, and turn the bag inside out to envelop the waste. With either method, seal the filled bag and place it inside the second bag, also sealing it well.

You can reduce odor in the first bag by adding some chlorinated lime, cat-box filler, or chemical gelling treatments like Poo Powder. Commercially available waste alleviation and gelling kits such as the GO Anywhere Toilet Kit (formerly WAG BAG), the Double Doodie, the RESTOP2, and the Biffy Bag use a double-bag system approved for deposit in landfills, with the inner bag containing powder that gels waste and neutralizes odors. In some wilderness areas, land managers hand out ready-made double-bag sets, gelling kits, or other supplies. Be aware of the available options and those promoted for the area the group is visiting.

2. Securely transport the bags. Most climbers will want more protection for the filled double bags. This could be as simple as an old stuff sack, a black plastic garbage bag, a watertight dry bag (such as those used on river trips), or a sturdy commercial product, all of which can be reused. Products designed for big wall climbers include the Metolius Waste Case, which is made out of haul-bag material and has sturdy straps to allow for secure hauling, and Clean Mountain Can, a hard-sided large-capacity cylinder developed on Denali that can be used as a toilet. Climbers can fashion their own transport system using durable, watertight lightweight plastic containers.

3. Dispose properly of packed-out poop. There are no easy answers to the question of how to properly dispose of packed-out waste. At popular climbing and mountaineering areas, land managers often provide specially marked collection bins for human waste once climbers are out of the backcountry. Usually, however, it is up to each group to properly dispose of waste after they have finished a trip.

Do not put human waste in a garbage can unless the waste is in an approved commercial gelling bag. Do not put paper or plastic bags into pit, flush, or composting toilets; empty waste from plastic bags into these toilets and wash the bag before throwing it into a garbage container. Be sure to thoroughly wash your hands with soap and water or use hand sanitizer after handling fecal waste.

Don't Bury Waste in Crevasses

It was once standard practice to drop waste into crevasses on glaciers in remote areas. However, these places are melting out faster all the time and climber waste is polluting communities downstream. Research the latest and best options for managing waste with the local land manager.

Handling Food and Garbage

Leave No Trace applies to everything people bring into nature. Developing efficient systems for handling food waste and garbage lightens the load for climbers and the environment. As discussed in Plan Ahead and Prepare earlier in this chapter, repackaging food results in less garbage to pack out and less weight to carry in.

Keep your backcountry kitchen away from water sources: apply the 200-foot (60-meter) rule—about 80 big steps for adults. When cooking and eating, be careful not to drop food scraps. Food not native to the environment's habitat can have unintended consequences, such as feeding wildlife that then become habituated. Food remnants that decompose—such as apple cores and banana peels—are not native to the mountain environment and can take years to decompose; pack them out. Pack out all leftover food.

After cooking in the backcountry, strain cookwater through a small piece of screen or cloth to collect food particles, and pack them out with other trash. Scrape pots and dishware with a plastic scrubber rather than sand or grass; use biodegradable soaps sparingly and 200 feet (60 meters) from water sources. Dispose of gray water—strained wash and rinse waters—at least 80 big steps away from water sources and camp. Either dig a sump—a small cat hole—downwind from the campsite and pour the gray water into the hole, where it will filter through the soil, or fling the gray water in an arc with a fast, sweeping motion, which disperses the water in fine droplets.

Washing

Never wash anything directly in a river eddy or other water source. Wash pots and dishware, your hands, and yourself at least 200 feet (60 meters) away from camp and water sources, using very small quantities of biodegradable soap (keeping it off plants), or use quick-drying liquid disinfectant. If you have applied sunscreen or insect repellent, wash it off at least 200 feet (60 meters) from camp and water sources before getting into a lake or stream; the chemicals and oils can harm aquatic plants and wildlife and leave an oily surface film.

4. LEAVE WHAT YOU FIND

Leave rocks, plants, archaeological artifacts, and other natural resources as you find them, allowing others to experience a similar sense of discovery and wonder. Do not touch or remove fossils you may discover. Leave untouched any area with evidence of archaeological artifacts, such as those left by prehistoric or Native populations. Where a fossil or artifact is found can yield important insights for members of scientific or cultural communities (see Access and Stewardship, below).

Report vandalism, theft, or any dangerous condition to local authorities so they can take care of the situation. Be specific: make note of time, extent, and location, and ideally take photos to document the incident and/or site.

If you post trip information and photos to social media, consider how this might adversely harm the area, its infrastructure, and the local population. Be sure your use of GPS coordinates and geotags sends people to places that can handle an increase in use.

When traversing fenced or private property, remember to leave gates as you found them. Avoid disturbing vegetation or rocks on a climbing route (see Environmental Impacts later in this chapter). Observe, draw, or photograph wilderness flora rather than picking or collecting. As the adage says, "Take only photos, leave only footprints."

5. MINIMIZE CAMPFIRE IMPACTS

For more than 400,000 years, humans have gathered around campfires for cooking, heat, and comfort. Yet on alpine climbs above tree line, there is little to no fuel to start a wood fire, so portable stoves and adequately insulated clothing are a must.

Lightweight backpacking stoves, igniting quickly and creating heat in seconds, make fast and light travel possible, unencumbered by hatchet or saw and the need to gather dry wood or build, start, maintain, and extinguish a campfire. Stoves do not consume wild materials, do not fill the mountain air with smoke, and are much less likely to be the source of forest fires, a growing concern in climate-changed landscapes.

Campfires are permitted in many frontcountry and wilderness areas, so if the group decides one is needed, research and plan ahead accordingly. Check for fire bans and restrictions. Use existing fire rings at established campsites. When gathering fuel, remember the four D's: collect branches that are Dead, Down (on the ground), Dinky (no thicker than your wrist), and Distant (far from the area around camp, to avoid denuding the site). Never strip standing trees and shrubs, even dead ones—this greatly diminishes wildlife habitat. Burn wood completely, and scatter the cold ashes well away from camp so there is no visual evidence—blackened rocks and charred wood are visual scars that last for decades.

6. RESPECT WILDLIFE

Animals are part of complex ecosystems, and our responsibility in the backcountry is to let these processes continue

LEAVE NO SCENT

When you visit wild places, remember that humans' sense of smell is much less acute than that of the wild creatures around us. Use unscented products, such as sunscreen, soap, toilet paper, and personal hygiene products, in the backcountry. In the words of Edward O. Wilson, in *The Social Conquest of Earth*, "Our greatest weakness, however, is our pitifully small sense of taste and smell. Over 99 percent of all living species, from microorganisms to animals, rely on chemical senses to find their way through the environment. . . . In contrast, human beings, along with monkeys, apes, and birds, are among the rare life forms that are primarily audiovisual, and correspondingly weak in taste and smell. We are idiots compared with rattlesnakes and bloodhounds." Out of respect for wildlife's highly sensitive sense of smell, plan to reduce your olfactory impact.

unfettered (see the "Leave No Scent" sidebar). As visitors to wildlife's home, climbers must act with great care and decorum:

- **Never approach or touch wildlife.** Keep safe distances, for both your safety and that of the animals. Binoculars, useful for scouting rock faces, offer a safely distanced way to observe animal behavior.
- **Never feed wildlife.** Giving human food to wild animals threatens their health and creates dangerous dependence. This is true for all animals, even birds and chipmunks. A fed animal is a dead animal.
- **Clean up microcrumbs.** Even the smallest specks of processed food at trail stops and campsites are not natural to the environment—pack them out.
- **Watch for nesting birds, especially raptors.** On rock routes, do not disturb nesting birds. Check with land managers for nesting seasons and closures. If you do encounter nesting birds, back off or take another route.
- **Do not allow pets and wildlife to mix.** The mere presence of a dog can cause wild animals to flee, using up energy and decreasing survival rates. Animal diseases cross both ways. Always collect, bag, and pack out pet feces. Consider leaving pets at home; if you bring them, do so only where permitted. In many areas, pets must be leashed at all times.

7. BE CONSIDERATE OF OTHERS

Most people go into the wilderness to experience untrammeled areas and a sense of solitude. Mountaineers can nurture the wilderness experience for other visitors by spatially distancing campsites and keeping camp colors and sounds discreet. Respect the privacy of others, traveling through their space only if necessary.

Enjoy the sounds of the wilderness. Soon enough, we all return to our daily routines and electronic sounds. You may want to listen to music on long expeditions, but for most backcountry trips, audio devices can be distracting to you and have a worse impact on others. Check trip companions' feelings about music and podcasts beforehand. If you are listening, wear earphones and keep the volume down. If you must make a summit call, distance yourself from others. Mute audible signals from phones and personal electronic devices. Drones may annoy others, and their use is restricted at many locations; check with land managers.

Think Small

Limit the size of the group. Outdoor trips are often social events, but keeping groups smaller enhances the sense of solitude for the party and other visitors. If local land managers have a party size limit, consider making your group even smaller. Ask yourself, "What is the minimum group size we need for safety?"

Minimizing Climbing Impacts

Mountaineers can do their part to protect and preserve wild regions they explore by applying the seven principles of Leave No Trace, using sound judgment, and educating others. There is no more positive way to help ensure continued outdoor access. While approaching, summiting, and descending, climbers are active stewards contributing to the lasting protection of natural resources for themselves and future generations. Being aware of their potential impacts helps climbers protect and enjoy natural landscapes. In addition to practicing low-impact recreation skills, climbers are responsible for educating themselves about Indigenous and local customs, land rules and regulations, and any access restrictions where they wish to climb.

ENVIRONMENTAL IMPACTS

Stewardship starts with the natural environments that attract mountaineers in the first place. Alpine ecosystems are typically fragile, with delicate and shallow-rooted vegetation. The alpine environment is easily affected by humans. If a single mountaineer fails to use Leave No Trace principles, the damage may alter the environment for months or years.

Cliff environments often have unique features—cliffs may create their own microclimates and provide conditions either drier or wetter than the surrounding area. The tops and bases of cliffs may feature plant and wildlife concentrations unique to an area, such as nesting raptors, bat colonies, and highly specialized (and sometimes very rare) plant communities. Climbers affect both the cliff faces themselves, through wildlife disturbance and passive or active devegetation like cleaning a route, and the cliff tops and bottoms, through erosion and damage to soils and plants from concentrated foot travel and group gatherings.

This damage can lead to access restrictions. Climbers trails, belay and/or rappel stations, and backcountry camping often conflict with regulations intended to protect

BEST PRACTICES TO MINIMIZE ENVIRONMENTAL IMPACTS FROM CLIMBING

Climbers have a special obligation beyond observing Leave No Trace principles. Simply put, implement best practices such as these:

- **Use as little chalk as possible.** Use rock-colored chalk and remove chalk-line tick marks that are an eyesore.

- **Use natural-colored webbing at rappel points and remove excess webbing if it is not needed.**

- **Never chip holds or alter the rock structure.** Rather than pushing loose rocks off during an alpine climb, try adjusting them to make them stable. At popular sport climbing crags, it may be better to move loose rocks away from a route or anchor point because of the danger they pose in crowded areas.

- **Limit your use of pitons, bolts, and new permanent fixed anchors or rappel points.** Modern climbing ethics dictate using these only when clean climbing gear cannot be used, where there are no other options for protection, and where they are needed to minimize risk. Consult the local climbing community and land managers before making a decision about placing permanent protection.

- **Break down snow shelters.** Before you leave, deconstruct snow shelters to reduce visual impact and inadvertent safety hazards.

places, including laws to protect habitat for threatened plants and animals. Most regulations accommodate some level of impact and vary depending on who manages the land. Impacts acceptable in a park managed for recreation may be unacceptable in an area managed for habitat preservation.

To minimize environmental harm, climbers practice Leave No Trace principles and follow land manager regulations and restrictions. Become familiar with the agency who manages your climbing destinations, and learn the usage rules of those areas. Strive to minimize your impacts everywhere, and go to even greater lengths in wilderness and environmentally sensitive areas. Climbers can also help reduce the environmental costs of their travel by carpooling to the trailhead, flying less, and purchasing carbon offsets.

CULTURAL CONSIDERATIONS

When we venture into the mountains or visit a local crag, we are often on Indigenous, and sometimes sacred, land. In many cases, Indigenous communities still hold a strong connection to these lands; and while sacred significance may vary across landscapes, natural formations can be foundations of Indigenous identity. From Chomolungma (Mount Everest) and Denali (formerly Mount McKinley) to Bear Lodge (Devils Tower) and Tsé Bit' a'í (Shiprock), natural formations that attract climbers have served as sacred places for Indigenous tribes since time immemorial. These formations appear in tribal creation stories, which inform their sacred practices.

Indigenous cultural values and climbers' recreational objectives are often in direct conflict. For example, the US has a chaotic history of poaching routes on sovereign Indigenous lands, ignoring ceremonial closures, and destroying Indigenous artifacts. And yet there are other examples of Native tribes working together with recreation groups to protect an important place for its cultural and recreational value.

To address these complexities and historical injustices, the climbing community must move forward with a greater understanding of the direct connection Indigenous communities have with the land. Developing this understanding will allow us to foster deeper relationships and define and work toward shared goals in stewarding, protecting, and strengthening our connections with the outdoors.

Before visiting an area, consider learning about the local Indigenous history, customs, and place names to inform your experience. Approach decision-making from a culturally sensitive perspective, and make sure your choices align with local land management practices and norms. For instance, stewardship means not disturbing or altering artifacts and rock art (petroglyphs and pictographs) or trampling traditional medicinal plants growing alongside trails. Approaching the land in this way improves climbers' experiences and brings them into reciprocity with the land in a manner like that of the land's original stewards, Indigenous tribes.

AESTHETIC IMPACTS

The use of fixed gear such as bolts, in situ pitons, and rappel slings are at the center of many access issues because of their aesthetic and environmental effect on natural places. When climbing has a visual impact on the outdoors, such as a high density of bolts on a cliff or rappel anchors that stand out from a distance, or even a preponderance of chalk marks showing closer up, it diminishes the outdoor experience of climbers and nonclimbers alike. Climbers can turn to the Access Fund, a nonprofit organization focused on climbing access and stewardship (see Resources), for more information on climbing-specific, low-impact recreation skills.

FEES AND PERMITS

Access fees that apply to all recreational users can also affect climbers. While such fees can create economic barriers for some mountaineers, climbing and mountaineering fees and permits help pay for management and stewardship of the land. Particularly in Asia, fees are used to reduce environmental impacts, pay for rescue services, and raise revenue for often impoverished countries. If an area is especially popular and overcrowded, a land manager may restrict access through permits. Be aware of the requirements in the area where you wish to climb, and apply for a permit before your trip.

Access and Stewardship

Climbers and mountaineers have a long history of protecting wild places. Their love for experiencing the outdoors sparks a desire to take care of these lands and preserve their beauty for future generations.

Access and stewardship are intertwined. Access to places to climb, hike, and explore is one of the foundations of a stewardship ethic. Stewardship is simply taking care of the areas we love to explore—through individual actions like perfecting Leave No Trace skills and through collective actions like maintaining trails, advocating for wilderness protection and preservation, and working with land

MINIMIZE IMPACT AND MAXIMIZE STEWARDSHIP

- **Recreate responsibly.** Follow Leave No Trace principles and respect Indigenous peoples and their lands.
- **Steward the natural environment.** Protect wild places through both small actions and organized stewardship activities.
- **Participate as a stakeholder.** Take part in land management and recreation planning decisions.
- **Build an inclusive outdoors.** Help to make the outdoors accessible and welcoming for all.

management agencies. People protect what they love: having meaningful outdoor experiences nurtures an inclination to work for these places as stewards and advocates.

Stewardship ensures that climbers can continue to access the outdoors. If mountaineers neglect or damage the cherished places where we climb, we risk losing entry to them. Practicing stewardship is also key to minimizing access conflicts. On public and private lands, recreation is often just one of many activities that occur. Land managers responsible for balancing multiple uses on public lands sometimes must place restrictions on the areas where mountaineers climb. Maintaining access to wild places depends deeply on minimizing the actual and potential conflicts between mountaineers, other users, and the interests of those who manage these areas.

ACCESS AND INCLUSION

Everyone deserves to have access to the outdoors and to experience wild places. Unfortunately, many barriers prevent people from enjoying these benefits, including lack of funds, gear, transportation, and knowledge, as well as systemic barriers reinforced by discrimination, racism, histories of oppression, and lack of representation. These factors can be as much of a barrier to access as a road or trail closure. Not everyone feels free to explore the hills.

Climbers can play an active part in making the outdoors safe and welcoming for all identities and abilities. Consider learning about the history of exclusion in the outdoors, listening to the experiences of others, choosing your language carefully, welcoming people who are newer to the outdoors, mentoring others, learning from your mistakes, and supporting organizations that introduce diverse communities to the outdoors. Cultivating a diverse and inclusive outdoors inspires respect and stewardship for natural landscapes and helps build a strong constituency dedicated to protecting wild places.

PROTECT THE PLACES YOU LOVE

As people who enjoy the outdoors, climbers have both a responsibility to protect outdoor places and a stake in preserving access to them. This section describes a few important ways mountaineers can act to protect outdoor experiences for everyone (see also the "Minimize Impact and Maximize Stewardship" sidebar).

Speak Up as a Stakeholder

If climbers want to have a say about how to protect and access the places where they love to climb, one place to start is with a country's land management agencies. These agencies—for example in the US, the National Park Service, Forest Service, and Bureau of Land Management—manage public lands, mountains, and forests on behalf of all residents. On public lands, every user is a stakeholder. Land management agencies in many countries employ public processes to gather input about management decisions and solicit feedback from stakeholders, including advocacy groups such as The Mountaineers, environmental organizations, local businesses, developers, and the wider public.

For instance, if climbers love visiting a local national forest, they can get involved in protecting their access to climbing there by participating in ongoing public processes or by contacting their local land managers. Since these agencies can be huge (sometimes with hundreds or thousands of employees that take care of millions of acres of land), it can sometimes be overwhelming to get involved. A local advocacy organization that works with these agencies can help climbers figure out the most effective ways to be sure our voices are heard.

Join a Membership Group
Membership organizations such as The Mountaineers, the Access Fund, the Alpine Club of Canada, the American Alpine Club, Outdoor Alliance, and local climbing organizations are active in access issues, stewardship projects, and advocating for wild places. These organizations work hard to protect climbing access and can also connect climbers to opportunities for sharing their voices with land managers. When climbers join one of these groups, they help give advocacy groups more political power to protect the places and the climbing access that matter to them. If you are in a financial position to do so, consider donating to these groups as an additional way to give back.

These kinds of organizations influence policy and often share with members multiple opportunities to contribute to those efforts, such as contacting legislators and land managers about important recreation and conservation issues. Such groups work with agencies that develop management plans for climbing and provide grants for land acquisition, trail building, trailhead maintenance, and other conservation projects. Some local and regional climbing organizations have been formed at specific climbing areas to address access issues close to home. These organizations also advocate for issues that weigh heavily on the future of mountaineering, including land and water conservation, climate action, equitable access to the outdoors, and respect for Indigenous rights.

Exert Influence as a Steward
Acts of stewardship matter greatly for protecting places and a climber's access to them. All mountaineers have the responsibility to minimize their impact on the natural environment, but climbers can also consider small acts of stewardship that restore the natural environment and improve the recreation experience. This can be as simple as picking up someone else's litter or abandoned gear or a bigger step such as participating in organized stewardship activities like trail building and revegetation projects. Strive to be a positive ambassador for climbing by interacting respectfully with other recreationists, wildlife, and the natural environment.

The Future of Mountaineering
Mountaineers pursue unconfined exploration. And yet the future of mountaineering relies on all climbers taking care to mitigate their impacts and thinking of themselves as stewards of wild places, for current and future generations. As more people recreate outdoors and our beloved wild places become more beleaguered by the accelerating effects of climate change, it is incumbent on all climbers to safeguard the mountains and steward shared lands and waters. By doing so, they and the generations of mountaineers who follow can continue to enjoy the experience of a new trail, a challenging climb, or a mountain summit—the freedom of the hills.

7

PART II
CLIMBING FUNDAMENTALS

CHAPTER 8

ESSENTIAL CLIMBING EQUIPMENT

Climbers rely on ropes to protect them when they fall, whether as they make a difficult move or due to a loose rock, a slip on snow, or some other unexpected occurrence.

Rope safety systems are used when climbing in situations where a fall would likely result in injury or death. Primary components of roped climbing include the knots, carabiners, and runners that firmly attach the climbing rope to the terrain. Using this system to manage risk requires more than just mechanics. Climbers must exercise judgment and decide when and where a rope will improve safety. Confidence, ability, conditions, and terrain are critical components of this essential system.

Avoid using any critical climbing equipment if you are unfamiliar with its history. Secondhand equipment, whether found or passed along without an account of its use, can have damage or wear that is hard to see, possibly introducing a weak link into the essential safety system that protects you and your climbing partners.

Ropes

Elastic, lightweight, and strong, dynamic climbing ropes can bear a load of more than two tons. They also have the remarkable quality of elasticity, critical for protecting a climber in a fall. Rather than bringing a falling climber to an abrupt, jolting stop, nylon ropes stretch to dynamically dissipate much of the energy generated by a fall and greatly reduce the associated forces.

Early nylon ropes were of "laid" or "twisted" construction, composed of many tiny nylon filaments bunched into three or four major strands twisted together. Gradually, twisted nylon ropes were replaced by kernmantle ropes designed specifically for climbing. Modern kernmantle ropes (fig. 8-1) are composed of a core of braided or parallel

nylon filaments encased in a smooth, woven nylon sheath. Kernmantle rope features the advantages of nylon but minimizes the problems associated with twisted rope construction: stiffness, friction, and excessive elasticity.

Kernmantle ropes are now the only climbing ropes approved by the International Climbing and Mountaineering Federation (Union Internationale des Associations d'Alpinisme; UIAA), the internationally recognized authority in setting standards for climbing equipment, and the European Committee for Standardization (Comité Européen de Normalisation; CEN, listed as "CE" on equipment labels), the European group responsible for creating and maintaining standards for all equipment, including climbing gear (fig. 8-2).

Fig. 8-2. *The logos of the two organizations that approve kernmantle ropes.*

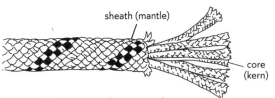

Fig. 8-1. *Construction of a kernmantle rope.*

> ### KEY TOPICS
> ROPES
> KNOTS, BENDS, AND HITCHES
> HELMETS
> HARNESSES
> RUNNERS
> CARABINERS
> KNIFE
> KEEPING THE SAFETY NET STRONG

TABLE 8-1. COMPARISON OF DIFFERENT TYPES OF ROPES					
DIAMETER	**TYPE**	**WEIGHT**	**SINGLE OR DOUBLE**	**COMMON USE**	**ADVANTAGES AND DISADVANTAGES**
10–11 mm	Dynamic	Heavy	Single	Rock and ice climbing	More durable than lighter ropes. *Less popular due to their heavier weight.*
9:4–9.9 mm	Dynamic	Moderate	Single	Rock and ice climbing	Versatile. Most common diameter for single ropes.
8.6–9.3 mm	Dynamic	Light	Single	Rock and ice climbing; glacier travel	Lightweight option when labeled for use as a single rope. *Generally less durable than thicker ropes.*
8–9 mm	Dynamic	Light	Single or double	Half-rope system for rock and ice climbing; single rope for simple glacier travel	Lightweight option when labeled for single-rope use. Allows for longer rappels in half-rope systems.
7–8 mm	Dynamic	Very light	Twin	Twin-rope system for rock and ice climbing	Allows for longer rappels than single-rope systems.
9–13 mm	Static	Variable	Single	Fixed lines for rescues, expedition-style climbing; haul lines; aid-route rappels	Low-stretch material for hauling and rappelling. *Not for lead climbing.*

8

VARIETIES OF CLIMBING ROPE

Climbing ropes are available in a great variety of diameters, lengths, and characteristics. Any rope used for climbing should have the manufacturer's label, a UIAA or CEN rating, and specifications such as length, diameter, elongation or impact force, and fall rating. Ropes are measured universally using the metric system; in this book, imperial units of measurement (inches, feet, and so on) are occasionally listed in parentheses as well.

Dynamic. Kernmantle ropes designed to catch a fall are known as dynamic ropes. These ropes achieve low impact forces by stretching under the force of a fall. One of the most important considerations when looking at rope specifications is the impact force, and lower is generally better. Using a rope with a lower impact force means that a climber's fall will be stopped less abruptly (a "softer catch") and less force will be imparted onto the fallen climber, belayer, and anchor system.

Dynamic ropes come in a variety of diameters acceptable for technical climbing. Table 8-1 illustrates some typical ropes and their common uses. Smaller-diameter dynamic ropes (down to about 7 millimeters) are typically used in pairs as part of either a twin- or half-rope system (see Chapter 14, Traditional Rock Climbing). These small-diameter rope systems rely on the elastic properties of both ropes to

protect the climber and must be used as a pair. The current trend in manufacturing dynamic ropes—and, therefore, in using them—is toward thinner and lighter ropes, but every rope is rated for certain intended uses indicated on the rope's label.

Dynamic ropes also come in a variety of lengths. Useful lengths range from 30 meters to 70 meters. Although 60 meters (200 feet) is the most common length for all-around recreational climbing, some climbers may want a shorter or longer rope, to minimize weight or better align with a particular route or rappel. Discrete sections of a technical route, or pitches, are generally 100 feet (30 meters) long, based on the maximum rappel distance of a standard 200 foot (60-meter) rope.

Static. In contrast to dynamic ropes, static ropes—as well as nylon slings and cord—stretch very little. A fall of even a few feet on these materials can generate impact forces severe enough to cause an anchor to fail or to severely injure a climber.

Although climbing stores often sell static ropes alongside dynamic ropes, static ropes should never be used for lead climbing. They are typically used as a haul line, jug line, or rappel line during aid climbing and for activities such as exploring caves, performing rescues, or setting fixed lines on expedition-style climbs.

Color

The color(s) used on a rope's sheath is largely an aesthetic choice. Many manufacturers use color patterns to make the middle of the rope stand out; often the sheath transitions from one pattern to another at the rope's midpoint. Alternatively, manufacturers may use a single color for the sheath but apply a special dye with a contrasting color to mark the middle. The UIAA warns against marking a rope with any substance that has not been specifically approved by the rope manufacturer. Do not mark the midpoint yourself, unless you are certain the substance you are using will not harm the rope.

Solid black and solid white are typically reserved for static ropes, though that is not an industry standard. Always check the manufacturer's label on the rope to confirm the intended use.

Water-Repellency

When a rope gets wet, it can become heavy and difficult to manage, possibly even freezing in cold enough temperatures. Studies show that wet ropes hold fewer falls and can have anywhere from 30 to 70 percent less dynamic strength than dry ropes. Manufacturers treat some ropes with either a silicone-based coating or a synthetic fluorine-containing resin coating (such as Teflon) to make them more water-repellent ("dry") and therefore stronger in wet conditions. These dry rope treatments improve the rope's abrasion resistance and also reduce friction as it runs through carabiners. Dry ropes usually cost slightly more than untreated ropes, and the treatment wears off over time.

PERFORMANCE TESTS

The UIAA and CEN test equipment to determine whether gear meets their standards. Because climbing is a sport in which equipment failure can be fatal, be sure to purchase equipment that has earned UIAA or CEN approval.

In its rope tests, the UIAA checks the strength of the single ropes used in most styles of climbing—usually between 8.9 and 11 millimeters in diameter—and also the thinner ropes used in half- or twin-rope climbing. To receive UIAA approval, a rope must hold a required minimum number of falls. The tests measure the impact force of the rope, which determines the stress of the fall on the climber's body and on the pieces of protection. The UIAA also applies static tension tests to determine how much ropes elongate under load; approved ropes do not stretch by more than a specified percentage. For more information on the UIAA certification process, see "The Standard Drop-Test Fall" sidebar in Chapter 10, Belaying.

ROPE CARE

A climbing rope protects your life. Treat it with care, both on route and in storage. A rope's life span depends entirely on the circumstances of its use and how well climbers care for it (see the "Expected Life Span of a Rope" sidebar).

Preventing Damage to the Rope

By stepping on a rope you risk grinding sharp soil particles into and through the sheath. Over time, sand and grit act like tiny knives slicing the nylon filaments in the rope's core. Climbers wearing crampons must be especially careful: a misstep in crampon points may damage the rope's core without leaving any visible gash on the sheath. Specialized tarps or bags made for packing up and moving ropes double as clean spots to place the rope at the base of a climb.

When transporting a rope, keep it away from substances that may damage it. For example, a parking lot or a vehicle trunk may harbor corrosive chemicals (especially acids), paints, and petroleum products, any of which could damage a rope. Manufacturers recommend that climbers destroy and discard a rope if it comes into contact with these substances.

EXPECTED LIFE SPAN OF A ROPE

It is impossible to predict how long climbing ropes are generally safe to use. For best guidance on a particular rope, check the manufacturer's website.

These general recommendations assume that the rope is properly cleaned and stored:

- **A rope used daily:** retire after a year.
- **A rope used on most weekends:** retire after about two years.
- **All ropes:** retire 10 years after manufacture, even if unused and stored properly. The nylon deteriorates over time, especially with use and exposure to UV light, metal climbing hardware, and other elements.

Unfortunately, these recommendations do not tell the whole story. Leader falls, abrasion from rocks, and damage by crampons can all significantly shorten the rope's life span, sometimes even requiring it to be retired immediately. Track the history of your rope, and consult the rope's manufacturer for instructions on how to inspect the rope.

Washing and Drying

Follow the manufacturer's recommendations for care. Most ropes can be washed when necessary with tepid water and mild soap, although some manufacturers recommend against using petroleum-based or other detergents on water-repellent ropes. Aftermarket products can renew a water-repellent finish. Wash a rope in a bathtub by hand—not a washing machine, unless the manufacturer recommends it. Rinse it several times in clean water and then hang it to dry out of direct sunlight.

Storing

Before storing any rope, remove all knots, coil the rope loosely (see Coiling the Rope, below), and make sure it is completely dry. Store it in a cool, dry area away from sunlight, heat, moisture, petroleum products, paints, and corrosive chemicals such as acids.

Retiring a Rope

When evaluating when to retire a rope, consider the rope's history and other factors affecting its condition. When inspecting a rope, refer to the rope manufacturer's detailed instructions as well as their guidelines to interpret your findings. Once you have decided to retire a rope, it is best to cut the rope into smaller sections to make sure no one uses it for climbing.

Examine a rope's sheath to evaluate overall condition. When flaking or coiling a rope, run your hands along it, feeling for soft or flat spots. Inspect ropes frequently, especially after a fall, to ensure the sheath is intact and does not have any abrasions. Seriously question the rope's integrity if the sheath looks tattered, whether from being stepped on by a crampon, excessively abraded, damaged by rockfall, or run across a sharp edge. If the core is visible, retire the rope.

If the sheath does not have any obvious soft spots or scars, it can be difficult to decide when to retire a rope. Its condition depends on many factors, including frequency of use, the care it has received, the number of falls it has endured (particularly long leader falls), and its age. After a severe fall, it may be wise to replace a rope, particularly if any segment feels mushy or flat.

COILING THE ROPE

Ropes are normally coiled, most commonly in the butterfly coil, when carried or stored. Fast to create and easy to undo, a single butterfly coil does not kink the rope. The rope can also be coiled starting from the middle, coiling two strands at a time to form a double coil. While a double coil is somewhat faster, it is much more likely to tangle the rope and

therefore is not recommended. Once the rope is coiled, tying it snugly to your body (if you are not wearing a pack) makes it easy to carry.

Butterfly coil. Create a single butterfly coil by using your arms as a measure and your neck and shoulders to support the coils. Start by holding one end of the rope with your left hand, leaving an ample tail—two "wingspans" (the length of both outstretched arms) is a good guideline—and slide your right hand out along the rope to lift the length of rope between your hands up and over your head, draping it on the back of your neck. Next, let go of the rope with your left hand and bring that hand over to your right hand (fig. 8-3a), then use your free left thumb to pull a bight of the free end of the rope up and over your head while keeping your right hand in place holding the end of the coil (fig. 8-3b). Continue to hold this coil in place while this time using your right hand to pull a new bight of rope to drape up and over your head. Continue alternating these moves, making and placing new coils, until you reach the end of the rope, leaving a tail equal in length to the first tail. To keep the coil neat, try to make the loops the same length; the last coil can be shorter if necessary to adjust the tail length. This technique results in a stack of multiple coils in the shape of a horseshoe (fig. 8-3c). Carefully grasp each side of the horseshoe with each hand, then lift the horseshoe up off your neck and over your head.

Holding the horseshoe of coils with one hand, wrap the two tail ends tightly and neatly around the middle of the horseshoe several times (fig. 8-3d), avoiding twists; this step creates a loop at the top of the horseshoe. Bring a bight of the tail ends through this loop (fig. 8-3e). Pull enough through to form a good-sized loop. Then bring the rest of the tail ends through this loop, and cinch the loop tight (fig. 8-3f).

To tie the butterfly coil to your body, place the coil against your back and draw one end over each shoulder and around your back, crossing them over the coil and bringing them around your waist to tie them in front (fig. 8-3g).

Flaking out the rope. It is important to uncoil the rope carefully, to minimize the chance of tangles causing problems while belaying. Do not simply drop the coils and start pulling on one end. Instead, untie the cinch knot in Figure 8-3f, unwrap the strands from around the horseshoe, open the horseshoe, and then uncoil the rope. Putting the tails where you can easily find them, uncoil the rope (in a process known as flaking out the rope) into a small, compact pile in a well-chosen spot, usually where you intend to belay. Be sure to flake the rope before every climb or pitch.

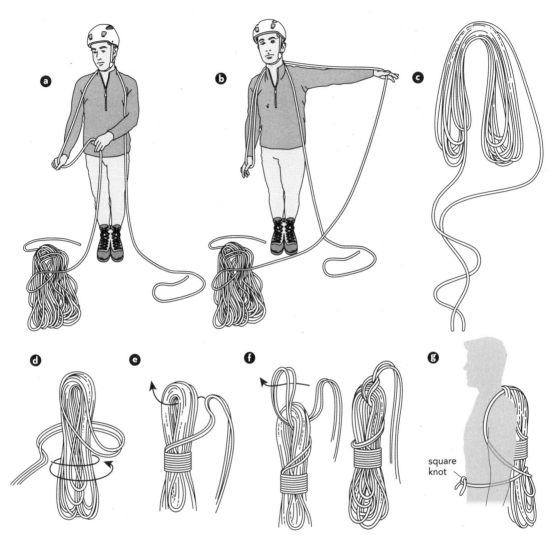

Fig. 8-3. *Butterfly coil for a rope carry:* **a** *and* **b,** *after draping one rope end (leaving ample tail) behind your neck, reach toward the strand of uncoiled rope to draw a bight overhead and behind your neck again, bringing the uncoiled strand to the opposite side;* **c,** *repeat this step, alternating hands, until most of the rope is coiled, leaving an equally long final tail and then lift the horseshoe of coils off your shoulders;* **d,** *wrap tails around middle of horseshoe several times;* **e,** *starting from last wrap, make a bight with both strands of loose rope and feed it through horseshoe's upper loop;* **f,** *bring both tail ends completely through this bight and cinch loop;* **g,** *for the carry, put a rope end over each shoulder, bring the ends around behind your back, cross the ends over the coiled rope and then bring them forward around your waist, and secure with a square knot.*

Knots, Bends, and Hitches

Climbers know their knots. Knots are used to tie in to the rope for climbing, to anchor to a mountain, to tie two ropes together for long rappels, to use slings to ascend the rope itself, and much more. Technically, there are knots, bends, and hitches. A knot is material tied on itself; a bend is a knot that joins two ropes or materials; and a hitch secures a rope or webbing around a solid object, such as a carabiner or tree. In this book, *knot* is often used to collectively refer to all of the above.

Climbers rely most heavily on a dozen or so basic knots, described below. Practice them until tying the knot becomes second nature. Being able to tie knots quickly and correctly under stress, in the dark, or during inclement weather is an essential skill for all mountaineers. Online sources such as the Animated Knots website and app (see Resources) are invaluable tools.

All knots weaken a rope, some more than others. When a rope breaks in drop or pull tests, it typically fails at the knot. Table 8-2 shows how much some knots typically reduce the strength of a single kernmantle rope compared with an unknotted rope. Some knots may be preferable for some purposes because of their holding power; others are easier to tie or are less likely to come undone in use.

Some terms and techniques are common to all knot tying. The end of the rope that is not being actively used is called the standing end; the other end is the loose end or working end. A 180-degree bend in the rope is a bight. A loop is formed when the rope is curled around in a complete circle, 360 degrees, so that both ends join or overlap. A double knot is tied in a pair of ropes or in a doubled portion of one rope.

Tie knots neatly, keeping the separate strands parallel and free of twists, a process known as dressing the knot. Tightly cinch every knot by pulling on each loose strand, and tie off loose ends with an overhand knot (see below). Tying knots consistently in perfect form will make it easier to recognize and check them. Develop the habit of inspecting your knots and those of your climbing partners, particularly before beginning a pitch or a rappel. As a general rule, keep knots away from points of great stress, friction, and abrasive sharp edges and corners.

BASIC KNOTS

Basic knots are used for tying harnesses to ropes, for tying ropes together for rappel, for tying slings, and for anchoring and rescue procedures.

Overhand Knot

An overhand knot is frequently used to secure loose rope ends after another knot has been tied. To tie it, pass the loose end of the rope through a bight of it (fig. 8-4a). An overhand knot can be used to secure both rope ends after tying a square knot (fig. 8-4b) or a rewoven figure eight (fig. 8-4c).

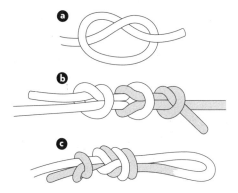

Fig. 8-4. *Overhand knot:* **a,** *tying it;* **b,** *backing up both sides of a square knot;* **c,** *backing up a rewoven figure eight.*

Flat Overhand Bend

A flat overhand bend (or offset overhand bend) is tied using the loose ends of two ropes (fig. 8-5a) to set up a double-rope rappel. Be sure to leave at least 12 to 18 inches (30 to 46 centimeters) of tail (fig. 8-5b) to prevent it from working loose. With a lower profile than the double fisherman's bend (see below), this knot is less likely to become caught on edges, stuck in cracks, or tangled on trees when climbers retrieve a rappel rope.

Overhand Loop

An overhand loop is often used for creating leg loops in accessory cord as part of a prusik system (described in Chapter 19, Glacier Travel and Crevasse Rescue) or to make a loop in a doubled rope or a length of webbing. It is tied using a bight in the rope (fig. 8-6a and b).

TABLE 8-2. HOW KNOTS AFFECT STRENGTH	
KNOT	**REDUCTION IN BREAKING STRENGTH**
Double fisherman's bend	20%–35%
Figure eight on a bight	23%–34%
Figure-eight bend	25%–30%
Clove hitch	25%–40%
Girth hitch	25%–40%
Bowline	26%–45%
Butterfly knot	28%–39%
Water knot (ring bend)	30%–40%
Overhand loop	32%–42%
Square knot	53%–57%

Note: *These values are for a single kernmantle rope.*

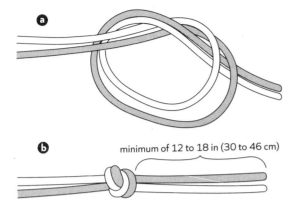

Fig. 8-5. *Flat overhand bend:* **a,** *tie an overhand knot in two strands of rope;* **b,** *pull all four strands tight, leaving a long tail.*

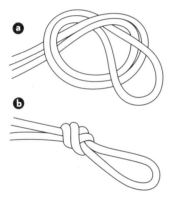

Fig. 8-6. *Overhand loop:* **a,** *tie an overhand knot in a bight of rope or cord;* **b,** *dress and pull all strands tight.*

Square Knot

A square knot can be used to join two ends of a rope—for example, to secure the ends of a butterfly coil when it is carried on a climber's back (see Figure 8-3g). Cross two loose ends over each other (fig. 8-7a); bring one end up around the other and through the loop (fig. 8-7b); dress all four strands (fig. 8-7c) and pull them tight (fig. 8-7d). Make sure both ends are parallel as they cross through the bights. While a useful utility knot, because square knots may work loose over time, do not use them in safety-critical applications.

Double Fisherman's Bend

A double fisherman's bend (or grapevine knot) is used to join two ropes or create a closed loop from a length of round accessory cord. To tie it, overlap a loose end of each

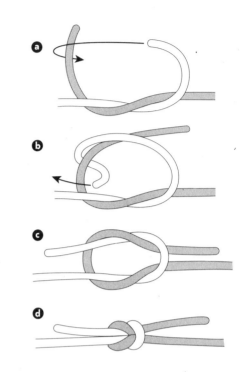

Fig. 8-7. *Square knot:* **a,** *cross two loose ends over each other and bring one up and around the other;* **b,** *bring end through loop;* **c,** *dress all four strands;* **d,** *pull all strands tight.*

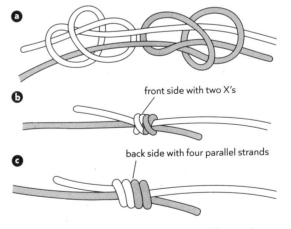

Fig. 8-8. *Double fisherman's bend:* **a,** *pass each loose end twice around the other rope's standing end, then tie an overhand knot;* **b,** *pull all four strands tight;* **c,** *back side.*

rope, pass each loose end around the other rope's standing end two times, then pull each end through both of its two loops (fig. 8-8a). Pull both knots tight (fig. 8-8b).

It is important that the two parts of this knot are symmetrical. Verify that the front has two X's (the knot itself, as shown in Figure 8-8b) neatly nested together and the back has four neat parallel strands (fig. 8-8c). A double fisherman's bend tied on a single strand, called a barrel knot, serves as a reliable backup knot during rappel (see Figure 11-12 in Chapter 11, Rappelling).

With low-friction material, such as Spectra cord, use a triple fisherman's bend for added security. Tie it like the double fisherman's described above, but with three wraps on each end instead of two.

Figure Eight on a Bight

A figure eight on a bight is easier to untie and stronger than an overhand on a bight. It can be tied quickly to create a fixed loop, and is commonly used to back up a clove hitch or as a secure attachment on an anchor. Bring a bight under and over standing ends to form an eight (fig. 8-9a and b), then bring the bight down through the bottom loop of the eight (fig. 8-9c) and pull it tight (fig. 8-9d).

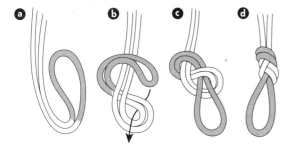

Fig. 8-9. *Figure eight on a bight:* **a,** *bring a bight back parallel to standing ends;* **b,** *bring the bight under and then over standing ends to form an eight;* **c,** *bring the bight down through the bottom loop of the eight and dress the strands;* **d,** *pull all four strands tight.*

Rewoven Figure Eight

A rewoven figure eight is the most common knot for tying in at the end of a rope. First, tie a single-strand figure eight near the end of the rope with a long tail (fig. 8-10a). Then pass the loose end through the tie-in points of the harness and reweave it around the original figure eight (fig. 8-10b) to create the final knot (fig. 8-10c). Follow the manufacturer's guidelines to identify the tie-in points of your particular harness. Dress the knot so that all strands lie flat.

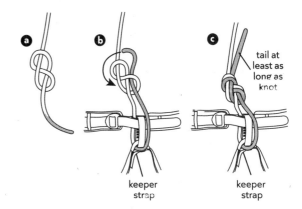

Fig. 8-10. *Rewoven figure eight:* **a,** *tie a figure eight;* **b,** *pass loose end through harness tie-in points and double back to retrace the eight, so loose end is parallel to standing end;* **c,** *pull the standing ends and the end loop tight.*

When finished, the tail of the knot should be about the same length as the knot itself to ensure the knot's security (see Figure 8-10c). The tail can optionally be tied around the standing end of the rope with an overhand or barrel knot to help keep it in place, for convenience only—this does not add to the security of the original knot.

Flemish Bend

A Flemish bend is used to join two ropes together for rappelling or to create a cordelette or equalette for building anchors (see Chapter 10, Belaying). After being weighted,

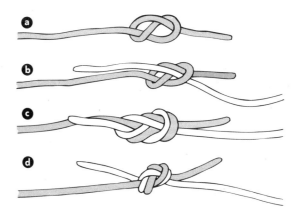

Fig. 8-11. *Flemish bend:* **a,** *tie a figure eight in loose end of one rope;* **b,** *retrace the eight using other rope's loose end;* **c,** *verify tails come out of opposite ends of knot;* **d,** *tighten all four strands.*

the Flemish bend is easier to untie than the double fisherman's bend. Tie a figure eight in the loose end of one rope (fig. 8-11a). Use the loose end of the other rope to retrace the figure eight, going toward the standing end of the first rope (fig. 8-11b). The two tails should come out of opposite ends of the dressed knot (fig. 8-11c and d).

Caution: Do not confuse the Flemish bend with an offset figure eight, which looks similar but ends with both tails coming out of the same side of the knot. The offset figure eight is known to roll and collapse under relatively small loads and *can be fatal if used for a rappel.*

Water Knot

A water knot (or ring bend) is frequently used to tie the two ends of a length of tubular webbing to create a runner (see Runners later in this chapter). Pull a loose end of webbing through a bight (fig. 8-12a). Bring the other loose end through the bight, around the first end, and under itself (fig. 8-12b). Draw the ends well through the knot to make the tails at least 2 to 3 inches (5 to 7.5 centimeters) long (fig. 8-12c). Pull each of the four strands tight (fig. 8-12d). A water knot can work loose over time, so check it often. "Dress" the knot so that the webbing lies flat throughout.

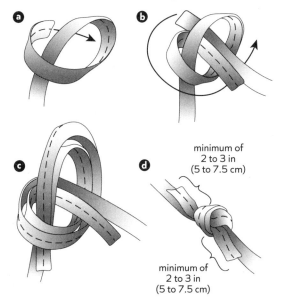

minimum of
2 to 3 in
(5 to 7.5 cm)

minimum of
2 to 3 in
(5 to 7.5 cm)

Fig. 8-12. *Water knot (ring bend):* **a,** *draw a loose end through a bight of webbing;* **b,** *bring other loose end through the bight, around the first end, and under itself;* **c,** *draw ends through knot, leaving 2- to 3-inch (5- to 7.5-cm) tails;* **d,** *pull all four strands tight.*

Single Bowline

A single bowline makes a loop at the end of the climbing rope that will not slip, and it can secure the rope around a tree or other anchor. This knot is easy to untie after it has been loaded, making it a viable alternative to the rewoven figure eight as a tie-in for top-roping. Start by forming a loop in the loose end of the rope (8-13a). Then pass the working end up through the loop, around the standing end, then down through the original loop; the tail should come out on the inside of the bowline's loop (fig. 8-13b). Tie off the loose end with an overhand knot (fig. 8-13c) and dress both knots (fig. 8-13d). The bowline knot tends to loosen when not under constant load; leave a long tail and inspect it frequently.

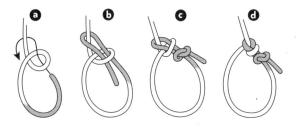

Fig. 8-13. *Single bowline:* **a,** *make a loop and pass loose end of rope under and through it, then around the back of standing end;* **b,** *bring loose end back down through the loop;* **c,** *pull ends tight and tie an overhand knot;* **d,** *dressed and backed-up knot.*

Single Bowline with a Yosemite Finish

Popularized by Yosemite climbers, a single bowline with a Yosemite finish is started the same as a single bowline (fig. 8-14a). For the finish, bring the loose end under and over

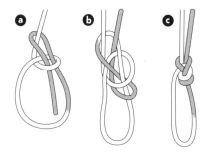

Fig. 8-14. *Single bowline with a Yosemite finish:* **a,** *tie a single bowline, keeping knot loose;* **b,** *bring loose end under and over the rope and under entire knot, then up through topmost loop;* **c,** *pull all strands tight.*

the rope, under the entire knot, and then up through the topmost loop until it is parallel with the standing end (fig. 8-14b); tighten the knot (fig. 8-14c). This finish avoids the need to tie off the single bowline with an overhand knot.

Butterfly Knot

A butterfly knot is commonly used to tie in to a rope for glacier climbing (see Chapter 19, Glacier Travel and Crevasse Rescue). It can also be used in a rescue to isolate a damaged section of rope. To form it in the middle of a rope, make two loops (fig. 8-15a), then pull the endmost loop over and through the other loop (fig. 8-15b). This knot can sustain a pull from either end of the rope or from the loop itself (fig. 8-15c). Many climbers use the hand method to tie the butterfly knot while on a route (fig. 8-16).

Clove Hitch

A clove hitch is a quick knot for clipping in to a locking carabiner attached to an anchor. This hitch is excellent for adjusting the length of the rope between the belayer and anchor without unclipping the rope. Make two loops side by side (fig. 8-17a), then stack the left-hand loop behind the other (fig. 8-17b). Clip a locking carabiner through both loops (fig. 8-17c). Dress it by tightening both strands firmly (fig. 8-17d). If the knot is tied correctly, it will stop the pull when loaded.

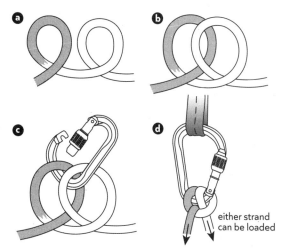

either strand can be loaded

Fig. 8-17. *Clove hitch:* **a,** *form two identical loops, side by side;* **b,** *bring left-hand loop behind the other;* **c,** *clip a locking carabiner through both loops;* **d,** *pull both ends tight.*

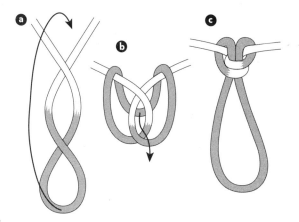

Fig. 8-15. *Butterfly knot:* **a,** *form a double loop;* **b,** *pull lower loop over and then back up through upper loop;* **c,** *pull loop and both strands tight.*

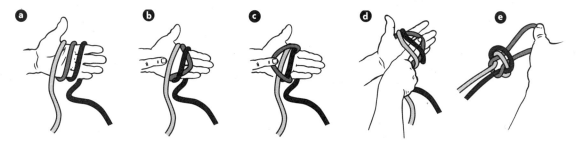

Fig. 8-16. *Hand method for tying butterfly knot:* **a,** *lift rope and loop it twice around one hand (from thumb to fingertips);* **b,** *reach under the outermost loop and pull the second strand under it;* **c,** *holding onto that same loop, pull it over the other two;* **d,** *then pull that loop up through the inside of the other loops;* **e,** *pull this bight through, removing hand and tightening final loop.*

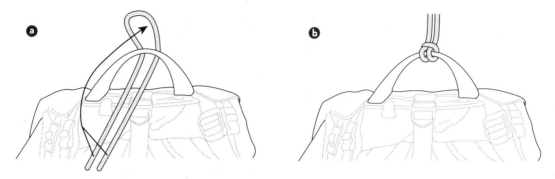

Fig. 8-18. *Girth hitch: **a,** reach a bight behind or around an object, such as a pack's haul loop; **b,** pull both loose ends through the bight and tighten.*

Girth Hitch

A girth hitch can serve many purposes, such as attaching webbing or cord to a natural anchor or to a pack's haul loop, or tying off a piton (see Figure 13-7 in Chapter 13, Rock Protection). To tie this simple knot, reach a bight behind or around an object (fig. 8-18a), then pull both loose ends through the bight and pull them tight (fig. 8-18b).

Overhand Slipknot

Another simple knot, the overhand slipknot may be used to attach a tie-off loop (see Runners, below) or a personal anchor (see Personal Anchors, below) to a carabiner. Make a loop (fig. 8-19a), then bring a bight up through the loop and draw it closed to tie off the bight (fig. 8-19b). The overhand slipknot has the added benefit of immobilizing a runner's knot or sewn bar tacks on the carabiner (fig. 8-19c).

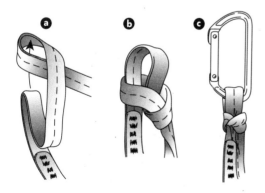

Fig. 8-19. *Overhand slipknot: **a,** make a loop, then bring a bight up through loop; **b,** draw loop closed to tie off bight; **c,** clip bight in to carabiner and pull both ends tight.*

Like the girth hitch, it can also be used to cinch a runner to a rock feature or to tie off a short-driven piton.

Mule Knot

A mule knot is a variant of the overhand slipknot that can be used by a belayer to temporarily free their hands from the rope. It can also be used in an emergency to free the belayer from the system altogether (see Escaping the Belay in Chapter 10, Belaying). When used with a belay device, this knot is called a device-mule.

While holding your brake hand back in the braking position, use your guide hand to pull a bight of rope through the locking carabiner on your harness (fig. 8-20a). Continue to hold the braking strand with your brake hand. Pull the bight behind the loaded strand of rope going to the fallen climber, then bring another bight over the loaded strand and through the first bight to tie an overhand slipknot (fig. 8-20b). Remove any slack and cinch the knot tight against the belay device (fig. 8-20c). Since the mule knot is releasable, prevent it from releasing accidentally by backing it up with an overhand knot tied around the loaded strand (fig. 8-20d), pulling on the braking strand if more rope is needed.

When used with a munter hitch (described below), the mule knot is called a munter-mule. Hold the fallen climber with your brake hand and use your guide hand to make a loop in the rope under the loaded strand, then bring a bight over the loaded strand and through the loop (fig. 8-21a). Finish the munter-mule the same as the device-mule: complete the overhand slipknot around the loaded strand and cinch it against the belay carabiner (fig. 8-21b), then finish with an overhand knot, pulling on the braking strand if more rope is needed (fig. 8-21c).

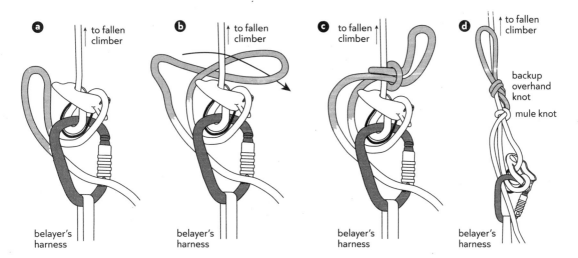

Fig. 8-20. *Mule knot with belay device (or device-mule):* **a,** *pull a bight of rope through the locking carabiner;* **b,** *pull the bight behind the loaded strand, then bring another bight over the loaded strand and through the first bight to tie an overhand slipknot;* **c,** *remove slack and cinch knot against the device;* **d,** *back up with an overhand knot.*

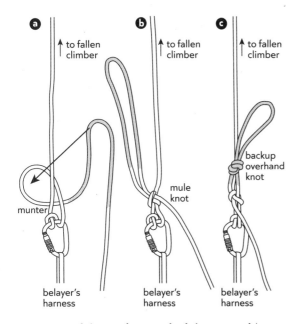

Fig. 8-21. *Mule knot with munter hitch (munter-mule):* **a,** *make a loop under loaded strand, then bring a bight over the loaded strand and through the loop to tie an overhand slipknot around the loaded strand with the braking strand;* **b,** *tighten knot by pulling on loop of overhand slipknot;* **c,** *back up with another overhand knot.*

FRICTION HITCHES

Friction hitches grip the climbing rope only when weighted. They are a quick and simple way to back up a rappel or to set up a system for ascending or descending a climbing rope without mechanical ascenders. The best-known friction hitch is the prusik, but others, such as the bachmann, klemheist, and autoblock, are also useful. Materials with relatively low melting points, such as Spectra or Dyneema, should not be used for friction hitches since they could melt from the heat generated by the hitch should it slip.

Prusik Hitch

By attaching two cords to a climbing rope with prusik hitches, climbers can ascend or descend the rope; Chapter 19, Glacier Travel and Crevasse Rescue, explains the prusik method of ascending the rope using prusik hitches. They are also used in the systems to raise and lower people and equipment during rescues and to pass safety knots in the rope (described in more detail in Chapters 19 and 25, Self-Rescue).

To tie a prusik hitch, attach an accessory cord loop to the climbing rope via a girth hitch (fig. 8-22a), followed by a few additional wraps around the climbing rope (fig. 8-22b and c). A tie-off loop of 5- to 7-millimeter accessory cord, for example, is usually wrapped twice (fig. 8-22d) or three times (fig. 8-22e) around the rope. Icy ropes, thinner-diameter ropes, or heavy loads require more wraps of the hitch to ensure sufficient friction to hold the load.

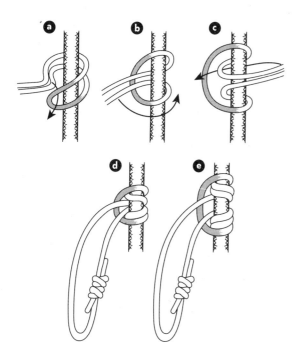

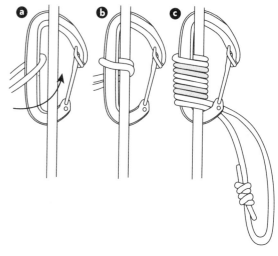

Fig. 8-23. *Bachmann hitch:* **a,** *with a carabiner under the rope, clip a loop of cord in to carabiner;* **b,** *wrap cord around rope and through carabiner;* **c,** *repeat three to five times.*

Fig. 8-22. *Prusik hitch:* **a,** *girth-hitch loop of cord around rope;* **b,** *bring loose ends around rope and through loop of cord;* **c,** *wrap loose ends around rope and through cord loop again;* **d,** *two-wrap prusik hitch;* **e,** *three-wrap prusik hitch.*

To create the friction necessary to hold when weighted, the cord must be smaller in diameter than the climbing rope; the greater the difference in diameter, the better the hitch grips. However, very small-diameter cords make the prusik hitch more difficult to manipulate than do cords of larger diameter. Experiment to see which diameter of cord works best. Webbing is not usually used for prusik hitches because it provides less friction than cord.

Bachmann Hitch

A bachmann hitch is used for the same purposes as a prusik hitch. Tie this hitch around a carabiner and the climbing rope, which makes the bachmann much easier to loosen and slide than a prusik. The bachmann hitch also has the virtue of sometimes being self-tending: it will feed rope in the non-load-bearing direction without requiring the belayer to actively manipulate it. To tie the bachmann hitch, position a carabiner under the rope and clip a loop of cord in to the carabiner (fig. 8-23a); wrap the cord around the rope and through the carabiner (fig. 8-23b), then repeat three to five times (fig. 8-23c).

Klemheist Hitch

A klemheist hitch is another alternative to the prusik. It can be made from either accessory cord or webbing, which may be important if a climber has an ample supply of webbing but little cord. Wind a tied loop of cord or webbing around the main rope in a spiral, then thread loose ends through the loop created by the top wrap of the cord or webbing (fig. 8-24a). Pull the cord or webbing down to create the basic klemheist (fig. 8-24b), which can be clipped to a carabiner (fig. 8-24c). Tying off the klemheist with a half hitch (fig. 8-24d) makes this klemheist less likely to jam and easier to loosen and slide than the basic klemheist. The klemheist can also be tied around a carabiner (fig. 8-24e), which provides a good handhold for sliding the knot along the rope.

Autoblock Hitch

An autoblock hitch is similar to the klemheist. In general, an autoblock is easier than a prusik to release once it has been loaded. It does not, however, provide as much friction; it simulates the grip of a hand rather than supporting full body weight. This hitch is commonly used as a backup during rappels by tying it around the braking strands of the rope, below the rappel device, and clipping it to the harness belay loop (or a leg loop if the rappel is a short one) with a locking carabiner (see Figure 11-18c in Chapter 11, Rappelling).

To tie an autoblock hitch, wrap a short loop of cord or webbing (either sewn or tied with a double fisherman's

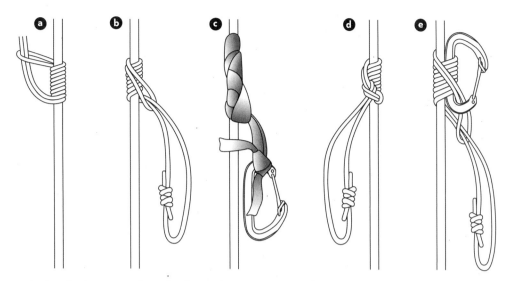

Fig. 8-24. *Klemheist hitch:* **a,** *wrap a loop of cord around the rope five times and draw loose ends through the end loop;* **b,** *pull ends down;* **c,** *klemheist hitch tied using webbing and clipped to a carabiner;* **d,** *to tie off the klemheist with a half hitch, bring loose ends up, then under and over the top loop, forming a new loop, and bring loose ends down through this loop, pulling ends tight;* **e,** *klemheist tied around a carabiner.*

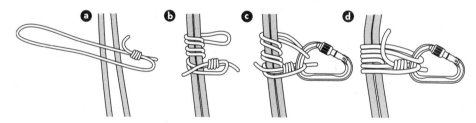

Fig. 8-25. *Autoblock hitch:* **a,** *lay a loop of cord, tied with a double fisherman's bend near one end, perpendicular to the climbing rope;* **b,** *wrap the cord around the rope three times, making sure there are no twists or overlapping strands;* **c,** *clip both ends of the cord to a locking carabiner;* **d,** *dress the hitch.*

bend) three or more times around the rope, making sure there are no twists or overlapping strands (fig. 8-25a and b), and clip both ends of the loop in to a locking carabiner (fig. 8-25c). Finally, make sure the knot is neither in the wrap nor squarely on the carabiner (fig. 8-25d).

Munter Hitch

A munter hitch (originally dubbed the *halbmastwurf sicherung,* meaning "half clove-hitch belay") is an excellent method of belaying a leader or lowering a climber, because it is reversible, meaning that the rope can be fed out of or pulled back in through the carabiner. The knot also provides sufficient friction for the belayer—by holding the

braking strand of the rope—to stop a falling climber or a climber who is lowering. A munter hitch can also be used for rappelling, though it twists the rope more than other rappel methods. Even if climbers prefer using a specialized belay device, this hitch is worth knowing as a backup if they lose or forget their belay device.

A munter hitch is very easy to set up and use, but it feeds rope effectively only on a pear-shaped locking carabiner, or pearabiner—a carabiner large enough at its wider end to accommodate multiple turns of the rope. Tie the munter as a simple hitch in the rope (fig. 8-26a) that is clipped in to a locking carabiner (fig. 8-26b) to create friction (fig. 8-26c).

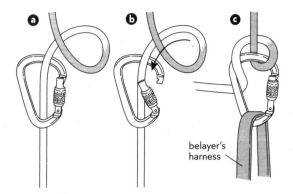

Fig. 8-26. *Munter hitch:* **a,** *draw rope up through carabiner and form a loop;* **b,** *clip carabiner through loop;* **c,** *pull rope ends in opposite directions and lock carabiner.*

The munter offers a variable amount of friction depending on the angle of the two strands. The braking position of the munter, when used as a belay, is when the two strands are parallel. This position offers the most friction.

Helmets

Climbing helmets help protect a climber's head from falling rocks or gear, and from hitting hard surfaces such as rock or ice. Climbers can take such blows in many ways: a fall to the ground or onto a ledge, a leader fall that swings the belayer into a wall, or a quick move upward against a sharp outcropping. A helmet only works when it is on your head. Choose one that is comfortable, and make sure it is easy to reach and wear in situations where you may need it.

Modern climbing helmets are lightweight, ventilated, and available in many designs, but know that no helmet can protect climbers from all possible impacts. Buy a helmet

with UIAA and/or CEN certification, which ensures minimum standards of impact resistance.

HELMET TYPES

Climbing helmets come in hardshell and lightweight foam construction. Both styles typically include headlamp clips.

Hardshell helmets, also called suspension or hybrid helmets, have a thick outer shell, usually ABS plastic, covering a thin layer of polystyrene foam combined with a suspension system (fig. 8-27a). The ABS shell is durable and ding-resistant. Hardshell helmets are suitable for all styles of climbing.

Typically lighter and more ventilated, lightweight foam helmets are constructed primarily of polystyrene covered in a thin polycarbonate shell (fig. 8-27b)—or, in rare cases, foam without a shell. These helmets dissipate impact forces via deformation. Because their outer shell is thin, lightweight foam helmets need to be handled more carefully and may need to be replaced more often. For these reasons, they are probably better suited for experienced climbers.

CHOOSING AND FITTING A HELMET

Before picking out a helmet, consider the type of climbing you plan to do. For example, helmets with large air vents add comfort on hot days but do not protect as well against smaller rocks or other projectiles.

Because normal skull shapes and sizes vary, fit is individual. Try on many different styles and brands. Choose

Fig. 8-28. *Wearing a helmet:* **a,** *properly adjusted;* **b,** *adjusted incorrectly, leaving forehead exposed to rockfall and icefall.*

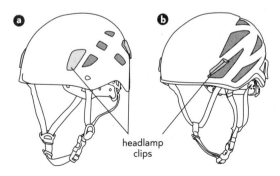

Fig. 8-27. *Climbing helmets:* **a,** *hardshell helmet;* **b,** *lightweight foam helmet.*

a helmet that fits well and can be adjusted to fit whether you are bareheaded or wearing a hat or balaclava. To protect your forehead and frontal lobe, wear the helmet as intended, securely fitted to your head (fig. 8-28a), not tipped back (fig. 8-28b).

CARING FOR HELMETS

To maximize the life of your helmet, protect it from banging against hard surfaces and chipping or cracking when it is not on your head, and store it out of direct sunlight. Follow all manufacturer's recommendations for storage. Follow these steps after each use:

- Test to see that the chin buckle and adjustment hardware are in good working order.
- Verify the suspension and other webbing are free of frays or gashes.
- Make sure any foam casing is secure and that all components are free of cracks and dents. Minor dings are OK; major dents are not.

When to replace a helmet. Climbing helmets have a limited life span. Even with ultraviolet radiation inhibitors, the plastics in helmets are vulnerable to sunlight and weaken with exposure; also, helmets can be damaged and not show obvious wear and tear. With even minimal use, helmets should be retired no later than 10 years after the date of manufacture (stamped on some brands); frequent climbers may want to cut this time in half. Retire a helmet when it is obviously dented, cracked, or damaged or the straps are worn or torn. Replace a helmet as soon as possible after a significant impact: any time you take a hard hit and think to yourself, "I would have been seriously hurt if not for my helmet," the helmet has done its job and it is time to get a new one.

Harnesses

In the early days of climbing, mountaineers looped the climbing rope around their waist several times and then tied the waist loop in to the rope with a bowline on a coil. Long falls onto waist loops, however, can severely injure a climber's back and ribs. Additionally, falls that leave the climber hanging, such as a fall into a crevasse or over the lip of an overhang, could cause the rope to ride up and constrict the climber's diaphragm, leading to suffocation. Improvising leg loops and attaching them to the whole coil can help prevent injury, but a bowline on a coil is best avoided. In case of emergencies, an improvised sling harness (see below) would be a better choice.

These days mountaineers connect to the rope using a harness designed to distribute the force of a fall over a larger percentage of the climber's body. A climber at the end of a climbing rope ties in to the harness with a knot such as a rewoven figure eight (see Figure 8-10) or a single bowline with a Yosemite finish (see Figure 8-14). A climber in the middle of a rope usually ties in to the harness by clipping a butterfly knot (see Figures 8-15 and 8-16) or a figure eight on a bight (see Figure 8-9) with a locking carabiner (see Carabiners, below).

Plan ahead about when to put on your harness in the alpine environment. It is often easier to put on a harness on low-angle terrain. And when you are descending, it may be better to leave your harness on until you are certain you no longer need it.

Harnesses deteriorate over time. Inspect them often and replace them with the same frequency as a climbing rope.

SEAT HARNESSES

With properly fitted leg loops, a seat harness rides snugly above a climber's hip bones yet transfers the force of a fall across the entire pelvis. It also provides a comfortable seat for hanging belays and rappelling. Throughout this book, when not otherwise specified, *harness* refers to a seat harness.

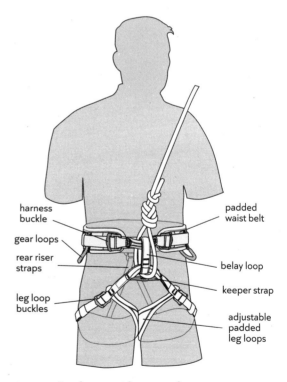

Fig. 8-29. *Seat harness with common features.*

Manufactured Seat Harness

Several features are particularly desirable in a mountaineering seat harness (fig. 8-29). Adjustable leg loops maintain a snug fit no matter how many layers of clothing are worn. Padding on the waist belt and leg loops can provide additional comfort, particularly if the climber will be hanging for any length of time, although padding adds to the harness's bulk and weight. Harnesses made especially for alpine climbing often do not include this padding, relying instead on the climber to wear layers under it.

Leg loops that can be unbuckled and/or that have rear riser straps that can be unclipped from the back of the waist belt allow the climber to put the harness on without stepping into and out of them, as well as to put on rain pants or answer toilet calls without removing the harness or untying from the rope. Some minimalist alpine harnesses lack a belay loop. A belay loop can make it easier to attach a belay device for belaying or rappelling, while having the harness buckle located toward one side helps avoid conflict with the rope tie-in or the locking carabiner that attaches to the harness for belaying and rappelling in the absence of a belay loop. Gear loops are desirable for carrying carabiners and other pieces of climbing gear.

Before buying a harness, try it on to be sure it fits properly over climbing clothes. With the profusion of harness styles on the market, consult each manufacturer's instructions to learn how to securely wear and tie in to that particular harness. Printed instructions accompany any new harness, and they also are usually sewn inside the waist belt. With some harnesses, the climber for security *must pass the waist strap back over and through the main buckle a second time* (on these models, climbers must usually do the same for the leg loop straps and buckles). Be sure at least 2 to 3 inches (about 5 centimeters) of strap extends beyond the buckle after the waist strap is rewoven.

Improvised Sling Harness

In an emergency, a sling harness may be improvised as a substitute for a commercial seat harness. The sling harness takes about 10 feet (3 meters) of webbing tied in a large loop. With the loop behind your back, pull each end around your sides to your stomach (fig. 8-30a). Bring one piece of the webbing loop down from behind your back and between your legs, then up to your stomach to meet the other two loop ends (fig. 8-30b). Clip all three loops together in front with two opposite and opposed carabiners (see Figure 8-37a) or a locking carabiner (fig. 8-30c).

Improvised sling harnesses are not a substitute for the effective reliability of a modern commercial seat harness,

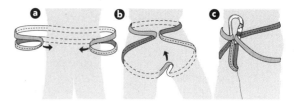

Fig. 8-30. *Improvised sling harness: **a,** bring large loop around waist from the back; **b,** bring lower loop on the backside between your thighs and up to meet the other two ends of the loop at the waist; **c,** clip all three loops together with a locking carabiner (shown here) or two opposite and opposed carabiners.*

but knowing how to build one could be useful in an emergency situation where a manufactured harness is damaged or otherwise unavailable.

CHEST HARNESS

A chest harness helps keep a climber upright after a fall or while ascending a rope using prusiks or mechanical ascenders. After a fall, simply clip the climbing rope through the carabiner of the chest harness to help you stay upright and stable. If you were to keep the chest harness clipped in while climbing, it would deliver some of the force of a fall to your chest, which is injured more easily than your pelvis (where the force is directed by a seat harness). Some snow or glacier climbers travel with the rope passing up through a carabiner on the chest harness, but if the climber needed to arrest and hold a fall while clipped in this way, the force would come high on the body and could spin the climber out of arrest position. It is therefore preferable to leave the

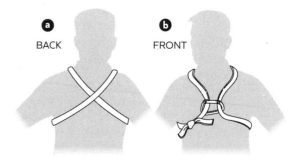

Fig. 8-31. *Carabiner chest harness: Using webbing tied into a loop with a water knot, twist the loop and put an arm through each of the resulting two loops; **a,** lift the runner over your head and let the crossed portion drop against your back; **b,** clip a carabiner through the two front sides.*

rope unclipped from a chest harness until it is needed after a fall into a crevasse. The chest harness is also useful when rappelling with a heavy backpack, to help the climber stay upright.

A chest harness may be purchased or readily improvised with a long runner. One popular design depends on a carabiner to bring the ends together at your chest. To make a carabiner chest harness, start with 9.5 feet (2.9 meters) of ⁹⁄₁₆- or 1-inch tubular webbing. Tie the webbing into a loop with a water knot (see Figure 8-12); adjust the size of the loop to fit comfortably. Give the loop a half twist to create two temporary loops and put one arm through each loop. Lift the runner over your head and let it drop against your back, with the crossed portion at your back (fig. 8-31a). Then pull the two sides together in front and clip a carabiner through them at your chest (fig. 8-31b). Keep the knot in front of you and out of the way of the carabiner. Another option is called the Parisienne *baudrier* (see Resources).

FULL-BODY HARNESS

Full-body harnesses, which incorporate both a seat and a chest harness, have a higher tie-in point (fig. 8-32), which reduces the chances of flipping backward during a fall. Because a body harness distributes the force of a fall throughout the trunk of the body, there may be less danger of lower-back injury.

Although body harnesses may be safer in some circumstances, they are not recommended for general climbing or glacier travel: if a climber must arrest to hold a fall, the force will be exerted high on the body and could spin the climber out of arrest position. Body harnesses are more expensive, restrict movement, and complicate clothing adjustments such as adding or removing layers. Most climbers use a seat harness and then improvise a chest harness when one is warranted, such as when climbing with a heavy pack, crossing glaciers, or aid climbing under large overhangs. Full-body harnesses are necessary, however, for children whose hips are not yet fully developed, because they could slide out of a seat harness when upside-down. Pregnant climbers may also want to use a full-body harness, but that is a decision climbers should make in consultation with a health care professional.

Runners

Loops of soft material, such as tubular webbing or round accessory cord, are called runners or slings. (Note that flat webbing is used for things like pack straps, while tubular webbing—so-called even though it lies flat—is designed for use in climbing-specific applications.) Among the simplest, most useful pieces of climbing equipment, runners are a critical link in climbing systems. Their lengths are often standardized to be a multiple of 2 feet (60 centimeters), and the names given to the different lengths reflect that: single-length runners are 2 feet (60 centimeters), double-length runners are 4 feet (120 centimeters), triples are 6 feet (180 centimeters), and quads are 8 feet (240 centimeters). A beginning climber needs many single runners and a few doubles. Triple- and quad-length slings are often used for anchor material (see Belay Anchors in Chapter 10, Belaying). To help identify the different lengths of runners at a glance, choose a consistent color of webbing for each length.

Runners should be retired regularly, using the same considerations as for retiring a rope (see Rope Care, above). For a tied webbing runner, writing your initials and the date the runner was made on one of the tails of the water knot helps you identify your runner and decide when to retire it.

It is very important to remember that webbing and accessory cord are not dynamic. If they are used without a dynamic rope, a fall of even a few feet can impart

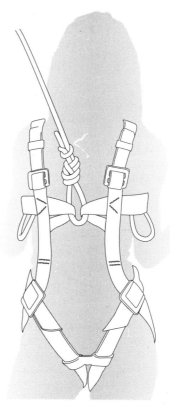

Fig. 8-32. *Full-body harness.*

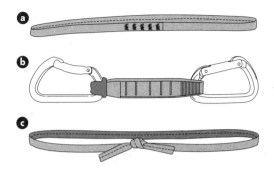

Fig. 8-33. *Runners made of webbing:* **a,** *sewn runner;* **b,** *sewn quickdraw;* **c,** *tied runner.*

catastrophic force onto the anchor system and climber (see How a Dynamic Rope Limits Impact Force in Chapter 10).

SEWN RUNNERS

High-strength presewn runners (fig. 8-33a) are manufactured by several companies in the standard lengths described above, as well as in nonstandard lengths. Sewn runners also come in a variety of widths, with ⁵⁄₁₆-, ⅜-, ⁹⁄₁₆-, ¹¹⁄₁₆-, and 1-inch (8-, 10-, 14-, 17-, and 25-millimeter) widths the most common. Sewn runners are generally stronger, lighter, and less bulky than tied runners. Using a sewn runner also eliminates the possibility of the knot coming untied.

Sewn runners are often made from Dyneema and Spectra, high-performance polyethylene fibers that are stronger, more durable, and less susceptible to ultraviolet deterioration than nylon. However, these materials have a lower melting temperature and provide less friction than nylon, which can affect their use in friction hitches. Additionally, these materials are less dynamic than nylon and should always be used in conjunction with another dynamic component (such as the climbing rope).

Quickdraws. Some runners are specially sewn into preformed quickdraws, which are typically 4 to 8 inches (10 to 20 centimeters) long and have carabiners attached at each end (fig. 8-33b).

TIED RUNNERS

Tied runners, while bulkier and heavier than commercially sewn runners, are inexpensive to make, can be untied and threaded around trees and natural chockstones (rocks firmly lodged in cracks), and can be untied and retied with another runner to create longer runners. To make a

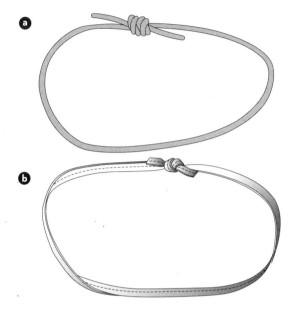

Fig. 8-34. *Tie-off loops:* **a,** *loop of cord tied with a double fisherman's bend;* **b,** *loop of webbing tied with a water knot.*

tied runner, tie ⁹⁄₁₆- to 1-inch tubular webbing or 7- to 9-millimeter Perlon accessory cord into a loop.

A webbing runner is usually tied with a water knot (see Figure 8-12) to make the loop (fig. 8-33c). Avoid putting twists in the webbing while tying it. A cord runner is typically tied with a double fisherman's bend (see Figure 8-8); slicker fibers such as Spectra or aramid fiber (Kevlar) cord require a triple fisherman's bend. Make the tails on tied runners 2 to 3 inches (5 to 7.5 centimeters) long. If the webbing or cord is cut to make the runner, melt the ends with a small flame to keep them from unraveling.

Tie-off loops. Also called hero loops or prusik loops, tie-off loops are short runners usually made of 5- to 8-millimeter cord tied into a loop (fig. 8-34a), although webbing can be used in a pinch (fig. 8-34b). (Presewn tie-off loops are commercially available as well.) The loop's length depends on its intended use, though 19 inches (48 centimeters) is common. Tie-off loops are often used for escaping belays (see Chapter 10, Belaying), for self-belay during a rappel (see Chapter 11, Rappelling), for aid climbing (see Chapter 15, Aid and Big Wall Climbing), and for attaching the anchor to the rope in crevasse rescue (see Reacting and Responding to a Crevasse Fall in Chapter 19, Glacier Travel and Crevasse Rescue).

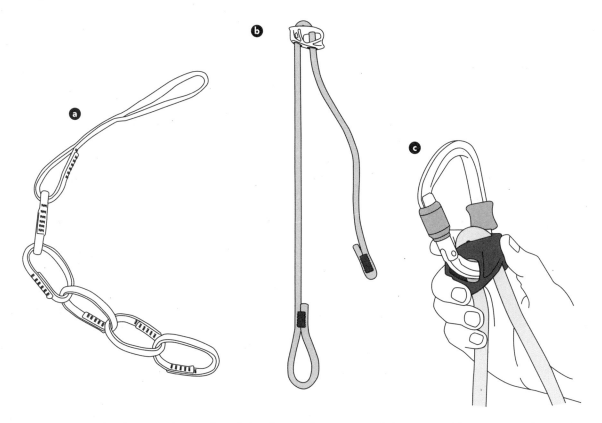

Fig. 8-35. *Personal anchors: **a,** with series of interlocking loops; **b,** dynamic PA, with short section of dynamic rope; **c,** close-up of clip-in point on dynamic PA.*

PERSONAL ANCHORS

On multipitch alpine rock climbs, most climbers use the climbing rope to tie in to the anchor (see Tying In to the Belay Anchor in Chapter 10, Belaying), which provides a dynamic tether without using any additional gear. Nevertheless, it is sometimes necessary—for instance, in setting up a rappel—to use a dedicated personal anchor or leash instead of the rope to attach yourself to belay and rappel anchors (see Figure 11-1 in Chapter 11, Rappelling).

A personal anchor can be made with a double-length runner (see Runners, above) girth-hitched to the tie-in points of a seat harness. Connect the other end of the runner to the anchor with a locking carabiner (see Figure 11-18 in Chapter 11). Use a more dynamic material, such as nylon webbing, or an anchor made from climbing rope rather than static or low-stretch materials, such as Dyneema, to make a runner for a personal anchor.

A variety of commercially made personal anchors are available as well. Almost all styles allow a climber to adjust length: some are made from a series of full-strength interlocking loops (fig. 8-35a), while others are constructed with a short section of dynamic rope and an adjustable clip-in point (fig. 8-35b and c). Commercially made personal anchors can be bulkier than a tether made from a runner but are usually much easier to adjust. When using commercially made anchors, make sure to follow all recommendations by the manufacturer on how to attach and use the device.

Daisy chains are unsuitable for use as general-purpose personal anchors. They are made specifically for aid climbing (see Chapter 15, Aid and Big Wall Climbing), and the stitches of the sewn links are rated for body weight only. If a climber cross-clips only a sewn link—that is, clips in to the anchor through two loops of the daisy chain—a fall can break the relatively weak bar tacks separating the loops and completely detach the climber from the anchor. The result can be catastrophic failure.

When you are not using your personal anchor, wrap it around your waist and clip it to the seat harness or otherwise neatly stow it on the harness gear loops.

Carabiners

Carabiners are another versatile and indispensable tool for belaying, rappelling, and many other tasks. All modern carabiners are marked with the "working load limit," the force at which the carabiner will fail. At a minimum, a CEN-certified carabiner should have a working load limit of 20 kilonewtons closed-gate strength and 7 kilonewtons open-gate and minor-axis strength. Those values mean that the carabiner should be able to withstand the force of up to a 20-kilonewton pull when its gate is closed, a substantial margin of safety beyond the forces generated by a falling climber (see Why Fall Factors Are Significant in Chapter 10, Belaying).

Carabiners come in many shapes, styles, materials, and sizes. Most climbers use aluminum carabiners because they are lighter, although steel may be preferred for heavy-use applications, such as permanent top-rope anchors. Some carabiners are made from metal bars with cross sections that are oval, T-shaped, cross-shaped, or wedge-shaped (as opposed to round) to save weight. Traditionally, the gate latches to the frame with a hook on the inside of the carabiner. Because this hook can interfere with unclipping, several models now use a keylock connection without a hook (fig. 8-36a).

NONLOCKING CARABINERS

Carabiners that do not lock are called "nonlocking" or "regular" carabiners. They vary in shape and feature different gates suited for specific climbing purposes.

Shapes. Ovals (fig. 8-36b) were once very popular for general mountaineering because their symmetry makes them good for many purposes. D carabiners (fig. 8-36c) are also good for general purposes, plus their shape makes them stronger than ovals. Offset Ds (fig. 8-36d) have the strength advantage of standard Ds, but the offset D's gate opens wider, making it easier to clip in awkward situations.

Gates. Bent-gate carabiners (fig. 8-36e) facilitate clipping, allowing climbers to quickly clip and unclip the carabiners by the feel of the gates alone. They are often used in

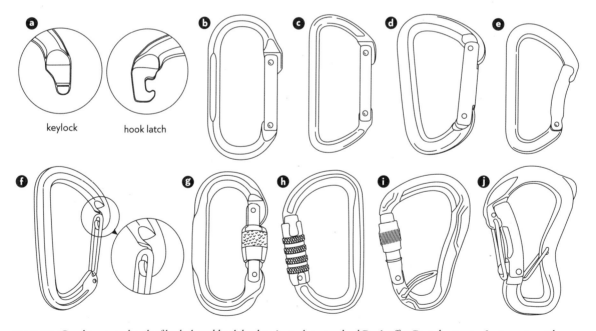

Fig. 8-36. *Carabiners:* **a,** *details of keylock and hook latches;* **b,** *oval;* **c,** *standard D;* **d,** *offset D;* **e,** *bent-gate;* **f,** *wire-gate, with detail of hook latch;* **g,** *standard locking;* **h,** *auto-locking pear-shaped (pearabiner);* **i,** *pearabiner with screw-lock gate and internal spring bar that prevents twisting;* **j,** *S-shaped carabiner with twin-gate lock and independent wire gate for belay loop.*

quickdraws for sport climbing (see Figure 8-33b). With a trend toward lighter and stronger gear, wire-gate carabiners have become very common (fig. 8-36f). They provide a lighter-weight, strong gate that is less prone to freezing shut or having its clipping action become sticky. Some studies also indicate that wire-gate carabiners are less prone to gate fluttering, which can occur when a rope passes quickly through a carabiner during a leader fall.

LOCKING CARABINERS

With a sleeve that covers one end of the gate to minimize accidental opening, locking carabiners provide greater risk management for rappelling, belaying, and clipping in to anchors. Locking carabiners also have different types of

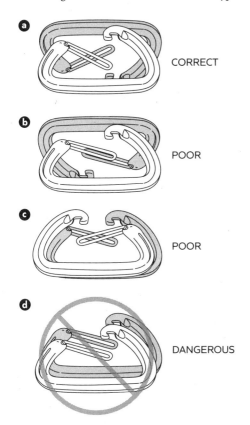

Fig. 8-37. *Substituting two nonlocking carabiners for a locking carabiner:* **a**, *gates on opposite sides and same ends, opposite and opposed (correct);* **b**, *gates on opposite sides and ends, opposite and parallel (poor);* **c**, *gates on same sides and opposite ends, parallel and opposed (poor);* **d**, *gates on same sides and ends, doubly parallel (dangerous).*

locking gates. Most have a sleeve that screws down over one end of the gate (fig. 8-36g and i). Commonly referred to as autolocking carabiners, others have a spring that rotates the sleeve into place whenever the gate is closed (fig. 8-36h), rather than the climber having to screw it down. There are advantages to each, and climbers often carry different types. Regardless of the carabiner's particular locking mechanism, always check to make sure that the carabiner is properly locked. Test it manually before relying on it.

Pear-shaped locking carabiners, also called pearabiners (fig. 8-36h and i), are much larger at the gate-opening end than at the hinge end; they are ideal for belaying with the munter hitch (see Figure 8-26). They are also a good choice for use with a seat harness. The extra cost and weight of pear-shaped locking carabiners are justified by the increased ease they provide in loading and managing all the ropes, knots, cords, and runners used at the harness's anchor point. Some locking carabiners have an independent wire gate for securing to the belay loop, which can be very handy to prevent accidentally cross-loading the carabiner while belaying (fig. 8-36i and j).

Using Two Nonlocking Carabiners Like a Locking Carabiner

Two nonlocking carabiners can be substituted for a locking carabiner if joined correctly. Align the carabiners with their gates on opposite sides, and position them so their gate-opening ends face the same direction. The two gates should open toward—or opposed to—each other (fig. 8-37a). This "opposite and opposed" configuration helps prevent the gates from unclipping, as they could if configured as in Figure 8-37b, c, or d. To check that the carabiners are in the proper configuration, open both gates at the same time; in profile, they should appear to cross, forming an X, as shown in Figure 8-37a.

USING AND CARING FOR CARABINERS

A few basic rules apply to the use and care of all carabiners. Always make sure the force falls along the long axis and closer to the spine side; be especially careful not to load the gate (see Figure 9-16 on clipping technique in Chapter 9, Basics of Climbing).

Check the gates occasionally. A gate should always close automatically and open easily, even when the carabiner is loaded, and the gate should have solid side-to-side rigidity when open.

To clean a dirty gate, apply a solvent or lubricant (lightweight oil, citrus solvent, or products such as WD-40) to the hinge, working it until it operates smoothly again. Then dip the carabiner in boiling water for about 20 seconds to remove the cleaning agent.

Avoid exposing carabiners to corrosive chemicals, especially acids. Do not store them in damp or acidic environments.

Knife

A knife is an essential tool that experienced mountaineers always keep within easy reach. It could prove invaluable if an item becomes caught in the rappel device, for example. Attach the knife to the harness with a carabiner and secure it with an arm's-length lanyard (fig. 8-38) to avoid dropping it when it is unclipped for use. Always use caution when wielding a knife to avoid nicking the rope, especially when the rope is weighted. Ropes under tension are particularly subject to slicing. Because the knife is used infrequently, some climbers will lightly tape the blade shut to avoid opening it accidentally.

Keeping the Safety Net Strong

Ropes, helmets, harnesses, runners, and carabiners, as well as belay devices (see Chapter 10, Belaying) and protection pieces (see Chapter 13, Rock Protection), are all vital links in the climber's chain of protection. Being familiar with key equipment and knowing how to use it are essential for managing risk when climbing. Climbing partners commonly check each other's equipment, knots, and setup before every climb, belay, or rappel. Developing and following a routine safety checklist (see Chapter 9, Basics of Climbing) helps ensure that you do not overlook anything. But the most important part of this essential system is you. Your safety net, and the experience, judgment, and awareness for using it properly, will reduce your risk in the climbing environment.

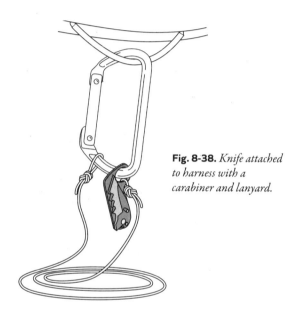

Fig. 8-38. *Knife attached to harness with a carabiner and lanyard.*

CHAPTER 9

BASICS OF CLIMBING

Climbing routes can range from short single-pitch routes at a local crag to long multiday climbs in remote alpine settings. In all cases, climbing efficiently with solid technique makes for a less risky and more enjoyable experience.

This chapter introduces the principles of efficient movement and basic techniques for climbing in technical terrain. When ascending technical terrain, climbers should always be on belay, as described in Chapter 10. However, to clearly show body positions in most of this chapter's illustrations, the essential system including ropes, harnesses, and protection is omitted.

Types of Climbing

Scrambling, or nontechnical climbing, generally occurs on less difficult, rocky terrain that a party typically does not rope up for. However, just because one person or party scrambles a section does not mean that everyone will feel comfortable crossing the same terrain without the increased security of a belay.

Technical climbing begins when the party's safety requires the use of anchored belays. Climbers rely on technical climbing on routes across or up rocks (described in Part III) or on snow, glaciers, ice, or mixed terrain (described in Part IV).

Traditional (or trad) climbing is a style of rock climbing in which the leader places removable protection as they ascend and another climber follows the leader's route and "cleans" (removes) this equipment. Ideally, nothing is left behind on the route. Placing gear correctly is a skill that requires a lot of learning and practice. Trad climbing and gear placement is covered in detail in Chapter 14.

Sport climbing generally involves rock routes with pre-placed or fixed protection (most commonly bolts) that allow climbers to focus on the physical and mental aspects of rock climbing, rather than evaluating and placing protection. When compared with trad routes, sport climbing routes are typically less remote and in relatively lower-risk environments. Chapter 12 covers sport climbing.

Free climbing involves ascending a route using natural handholds and footholds, with a rope and placing protection to catch a climber only if they fall, rather than actively using the rope and protection to make upward progress. Free climbing contrasts with aid climbing, in which the protection placed by the leader is itself pulled on or otherwise weighted by the climber to ascend the route. To learn more about aid technique, see Chapter 15, Aid and Big Wall Climbing.

Ice climbing refers to using any climbing style to ascend near-vertical or vertical ice with the aid of ice tools and crampons. Ice climbing routes are further classified as either water ice or alpine ice. Water-ice routes ascend a frozen water feature, such as a waterfall or water runoff (see Chapter 18, Waterfall Ice and Mixed Climbing), whereas on alpine ice routes, the climber ascends frozen headwalls or steep glaciers in an alpine environment (see Chapter 17, Technical Snow and Ice Climbing).

Solo climbing is, of course, climbing alone, but it is often used synonymously with free soloing, in which the climber ascends unroped and unprotected. Alternatively, a climber can rope-solo a route by using gear to provide a self-belay. Both of these forms of solo climbing are advanced techniques and should not be attempted by beginning climbers.

9

KEY TOPICS

TYPES OF CLIMBING
EQUIPMENT
CLIMBING EFFICIENTLY
ESSENTIAL CONCEPTS OF MOVEMENT
COMBINING MOVEMENTS
LEADING A CLIMB
STYLE AND ETHICS
CLIMBING WELL

RATING CLIMBS

The system used to describe a route's technical difficulty depends not only on the type of climbing involved (for example, rock or ice) but also on the geographic location of the route, since different countries have developed distinct forms of rating.

The Yosemite Decimal System (YDS) is used in North America to assign a numeric difficulty to rock and alpine routes. In this system, nontechnical climbs, or scrambles, are referred to as second-, third-, or even fourth-class terrain. Technical routes are referred to as fifth-class terrain, which is further subdivided by specifying a second number after a decimal point: the larger the number after the decimal, the more difficult the route. For instance, a route rated 5.4 would generally be considered easier than one rated 5.9, though both are considered fifth-class terrain and would typically be climbed with a rope and protection. For a comparison of the YDS to systems used outside of North America, see Appendix: Rating Systems.

Ice climbing routes use a system to describe difficulty that takes into account the nature of the ice being climbed—water or alpine. Water-ice routes use a prefix of WI, and alpine ice routes use the prefix AI. The difficulty is then indicated with a numeric value beginning at one, with higher difficulty indicated with increasing values. A climb rated WI1 would be considered an easier water-ice route, and a route rated AI5 would be a much more technical alpine-ice route.

A climb is rated by its most difficult pitch. Portions of a long route may be considerably easier than the overall rating. Climbers, depending on their skills and experience and the route condition, may choose to tackle some easier sections unroped, with the rope held in coils, or with a running belay (see Leading on Nontechnical Terrain later in this chapter). Mountaineers often make these compromises around security to climb a longer route faster or with less gear. Experts may classify climbs or sections of climbs as hard as mid-fifth class in this category, despite the possible fatal consequences should a climber fall.

Equipment

The rack refers to the collection of gear used for protection on a climb, and it can include nuts and cams for rock routes or ice screws and pickets for steep snow and ice. The rope connects two or more climbers and is clipped to the gear placed by the leader. Collectively, the "rack and rope" are the climbers' protection (see Chapter 13, Rock Protection).

To limit a fall, the leader periodically places individual pieces of protection, or pro, while climbing each section of a route. A second climber, the follower, belays from below. The follower ascends on the same gear, and the last follower removes the equipment and carries the pieces to the top of the pitch. Between each pitch, the team reorganizes the rack and the leader organizes the gear for the next pitch.

The terrain and the climbers' comfort levels determine what gear they should bring. If a climb is described in a guidebook or on a reliable online resource such as Mountain Project (see Resources), refer to that resource for general information such as the type and size range of gear the route requires.

RACKING GEAR

The next consideration is where the climber will carry the gear on route. The three most common options are on the leader's harness, on a dedicated gear sling, or on some combination of the two. Commercially available padded slings (fig. 9-1a) may be the most comfortable choice, but climbers can use a single-length runner instead. Some commercial gear slings feature partitions (fig. 9-1b), which may be helpful for organizing protection.

The ideal racking method allows the leader to place protection efficiently and often enough to protect the pitch but still climb smoothly while carrying gear. Climbers should aim to organize the rack in a way that also allows them to transfer gear easily between pitches (swinging leads) or blocks of pitches (see Multipitch Climbs in Chapter 14, Traditional Rock Climbing). Climbers often have a preferred racking method, but it is best to be familiar with racking on the harness as well as using a gear sling. Certain

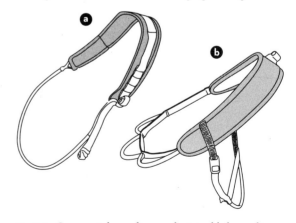

Fig. 9-1. *Commercial gear slings: **a,** basic padded gear sling; **b,** partitioned gear sling.*

routes, styles, or individual pitches are far better suited to one or the other of these two methods.

Rack the protection systematically so that it is easy to find a particular piece. Clip each piece of pro with an individual carabiner, or group similar kinds of pro on the same carabiner. Use the same orientation for each carabiner so that the leader can unclip each one in exactly the same way. Racking carabiners uniformly allows climbers to unclip by feel.

Agreeing on a racking method before a climb will help climbers be more efficient, especially when they are relatively inexperienced at transferring gear, to avoid devoting precious time to reracking later.

Climbers also rack runners, either on the harness or carried over a shoulder (for details, see Chapter 14, Traditional Rock Climbing). When climbing with a pack, put on the pack first, then add the rack, then drape runners over one or both shoulders. On the harness gear loops carry cordelette or other anchor-equalizing cord or webbing, a belay device, and at least one rappel ring where they are easily accessible. Clip other items of gear, such as a knife with a tie-off loop, to the harness so they are out of the way but accessible.

OTHER IMPORTANT ITEMS

It is a good idea to bring along a recent route description, a route topo, and routefinding notes, especially for unfamiliar multipitch routes.

Packs. It is common for at least one member of a climbing team to carry a pack containing food, water, and extra clothing on a multipitch route. On alpine routes, all team members usually carry their own pack. The number and size of packs varies, depending on the route and the party's speed.

Footwear. Individual climbers may choose various types of footwear for the approach and the climb. Very lightweight to heavyweight mountaineering boots or lightweight approach shoes are typically used for the approach—and sometimes on the climb itself. Climbers usually prefer to wear rock shoes (see Figure 12-1 in Chapter 12, Sport Climbing and Technique) on more difficult technical leads and on virtually all sport climbs. Climbers generally wear mountaineering boots for both the approach and climb on snow, glaciers, and ice.

Climbing Efficiently

Moving efficiently makes climbing more enjoyable, enabling climbers to ascend at a reasonable pace. Climbers must have enough strength for not only the approach to the climb and the climb itself but also the descent and hike

back out. Solid climbing technique involves a combination of balance, footwork, and hand movements while expending as little strength as possible. To climb efficiently, both the leader and follower(s) need to be proficient with the technical gear described in Chapter 8, Essential Climbing Equipment, and Parts III, Rock Climbing, and IV, Snow, Ice, and Alpine Climbing. It takes time and practice to develop and hone these skills.

Some types of climbing require significant arm strength. But while strength alone may allow climbers to bull their way up certain routes despite using poor technique, relying on arm strength alone leads to excess fatigue. Many natural features require proper technique, and when combined with physical training in strength, power, and endurance (see Chapter 4, Conditioning), climbers have the greatest advantage. The following general guidelines about technique apply to all types of climbing, whether on rock, ice, or glaciers.

FOCUS ON SPEED AND SAFETY

Although speed is often not an important consideration when climbing in a gym or at a sport crag, it can make a dramatic impact on the climbing team's security in the alpine environment or on longer multipitch routes, whether on rock, snow, or ice. Less time climbing means less time exposed to rockfall, icefall, and changing weather. Proficiency in climbing allows more time to solve routefinding problems, deal with injury in case of an accident, get off the mountain before dark, or handle any number of possible risks inherent in these environments. Do not, however, sacrifice reasonable caution for speed. Focus on moving efficiently and using proper technique whenever you climb. Practice on shorter, easier routes and move to longer, more difficult routes as your efficiency improves.

Aim to move smoothly over the terrain and set up belays, exchange gear, and manage the rope with a minimum of wasted time. Alpine climbing often necessitates carrying a pack, and choices regarding packs depend on the route and personal preference. Pack enough gear to do the climb and survive unexpected situations, but be spartan. Depending on the situation, for speed and safety all climbers in a team may choose to carry similar packs, or the follower(s) might carry either the only pack or a larger one.

Keep small snacks and water readily accessible for nibbling or sipping at belay stations. Many a climber has gotten dangerously tired and slow (bonked) from inadequate nutrition or hydration. Be aware of your own—as well as your partners'—food and water intake and energy levels.

The size of the climbing party and the number of rope teams affect overall trip speed. All else being equal, it will take longer for an entire party to finish if it has more rope teams.

CLIMB WITH YOUR EYES

Observe the terrain. On a rock climb, notice where the holds are—the edges, the cracks—before you even set foot on the rock. For multipitch routes, look for likely belay stations (see Chapter 10, Belaying). On a snow or glacier climb, look for hazards such as moats and crevasses. Climbers cannot memorize the specifics of an entire pitch beforehand, but it is possible to get a general idea. Look to both sides as well as up and down while climbing—and rappelling (see Chapter 11, Rappelling)—to continually evaluate the route and locate places for your hands and feet. Easy to moderate routes have many choices; do not let tunnel vision stop you from seeing them.

When options are limited on more difficult terrain, a calm attitude can help. Tune in to how your balance feels as you move deliberately, smoothly, and fluidly. A relaxed yet alert mind will help you make decisions and movements methodically.

USE PROPER FOOTWORK

Footwork and balance are the foundations of most climbing. Careful footwork offers a climber steady balance and requires less exertion than hand movements do. Larger and stronger than arm muscles, leg muscles provide the most efficient use of muscle power. That is why climbers are frequently told to climb with their feet.

Look for footholds and placements that are comfortably spaced. Shorter steps take less energy than longer, higher steps, and you will stay in balance more easily. However, steps too close together take up more time in relation to upward progress.

Stand erect over your feet—this position keeps your body weight centered over your feet, and the resulting downward pressure helps keep your feet on the placements, not sliding off (fig. 9-2a). Anxious climbers tend to hug or lean into the terrain, which pushes their feet away from the terrain because the pressure is out, not down (fig. 9-2b).

MAINTAIN THREE POINTS OF CONTACT

Whether on ice or rock, try to keep three body points—any combination of hands and feet—weighted on the terrain at all times. You can use two hands and one foot (fig. 9-3) or

Fig. 9-2. *Stance in relation to feet:* **a,** *keep weight over feet and push hips away from terrain (good);* **b,** *avoid leaning into the slope, which pushes feet away from the slope (poor).*

Fig. 9-3. *Three points of contact: Keep three body points weighted at all times; here, the climber's hands and right foot provide a secure stance while she moves her left foot higher.*

Fig. 9-4. *Loose features: **a,** look for loose rocks (circled); **b,** test loose features before using them.*

one hand and two feet. Keep your balance over your feet until you release a hold to move for the next one. This is an especially useful approach when testing a feature for looseness without weighting it, because it allows you to balance securely on three holds while testing the new one.

Staying directly above your feet is usually the most stable stance. Moving your center of gravity over a new foot- or handhold causes your weight to shift to that new hold.

On more difficult climbs, it is not always possible to keep three body points in contact with the terrain. If there are only one or two sound holds, use your body position to maintain a delicate balance over them. Regardless of the number of body points you have in contact, the same principle applies: keep your weight over your holds.

CHECK FOR LOOSE FEATURES

Loose rock, unstable snow or ice, and other movable terrain features are all too common in the mountains. Some foot- or handholds are obviously loose, but be alert for those that are not. Look for fracture lines in rock and ice (fig. 9-4a); hollow-sounding features are more likely to be detached or weak. Gently nudge any suspect feature, or give it a push with the heel of your hand (fig. 9-4b). Make sure your testing does not actually dislodge the feature! If loose features cannot be avoided, move with extra care and deliberation through that section. Sometimes you can still use a loose hand- or foothold if you carefully push downward and in on it while weighting it—but be careful.

Essential Concepts of Movement

This section covers concepts, rather than specific moves, that can be used in all kinds of climbing, including downward pressure, counterforce, flagging, how to position your body to reach farther, dynamic moves, and more.

DOWNWARD PRESSURE

Downward pressure, or down-pressure, refers to pressing down on a hold with any part of your hand (fig. 9-5). Pressing down with the thumb can be useful on very small holds. A common technique is to pull down on a hold from above, then press down on the hold after you move above it. Downward pressure may be used alone or in combination with other techniques, such as in counterforce with a lieback hold or as part of a stemming move (see Crack Climbing in Chapter 12, Sport Climbing and Technique).

Fig. 9-5. *Downward pressure: using left hand to press down on a hold.*

COUNTERFORCE

Counterforce, which plays a part in many climbing maneuvers described in Chapter 12, refers to applying pressure in opposing directions to stay in place. Specific counterforce techniques, such as chimneying, stemming, and hand and arm jams, are useful in rock climbing on faces or cracks.

FLAGGING

Flagging is the principle of distributing your body weight in a way that maintains your balance, by putting a hand or foot in a particular location, even without an obvious hold, to counterbalance the rest of your body (fig. 9-6). Your hips and shoulders also come into play as you move them. Flagging extends a climber's reach.

LONG REACHES

When the next available hold is far away or even out of reach, climbers use several techniques. Make the most of available holds by moving as high as possible on them, though remember that standing on your toes to reach higher contributes to muscle fatigue. On rock, some climbers may be able to reach farther by standing on the outside edge of a shoe, called backstepping, which tends to turn the body sideways to the terrain. Flagging a foot out to the side may also extend your reach. For most climbers, their longest possible reach is with the hand on the same side of the body as the foot they are standing on.

DYNAMIC MOVES

Another option for overcoming a long reach—particularly on rock routes—is to make intermediate moves, using marginal holds just long enough to move quickly to the next better hold. This technique leads to a dynamic move (or dyno): a lunge or quick move made before you lose your balance. For a dynamic move, you want to grab the next higher hold at the "dead point," the apex of the arc of movement when your body is weightless for a fraction of a second.

Make a dynamic move only after calculating and accepting the consequences of failure. If a dynamic move fails, you will likely fall. Ensure beforehand that the protection is secure and that a fall will not result in hitting a ledge or the ground.

EXCHANGING HANDS OR FEET

Sometimes a climber needs to move a foot onto the same small hold as their other foot, or a hand onto a hold their other hand is already gripping. Either move can be made several different ways.

To exchange a foot placement, make an intermediate move using a poorer, even marginal, hold to get the foot off the good hold long enough for the other foot to take it over. Or hop off the hold while replacing one foot with the other. Or try matching feet, moving one foot to the edge of the hold to make enough room for the other.

The crossover is another technique: cross one foot in front of the other (fig. 9-7a and b) to occupy a small spot on the hold while the first foot moves off that hold (fig. 9-7c) to another (fig. 9-7d).

To trade hands, similar to how you exchange your feet, consider making an intermediate move. Place both hands on the same hold, one on top of the other, or if space is limited, try picking up the fingers of one hand, one finger at a time, and replacing them with the fingers of the other hand. The crossover technique also is occasionally useful. When ice climbing, climbers can switch hands by temporarily grabbing (sharing) a single ice tool with both hands.

Fig. 9-6. *Two examples of flagging, for an extended reach: **a,** left foot flagged to the side; **b,** left foot flagged behind the right.*

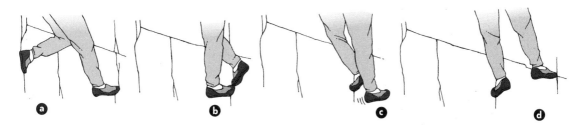

Fig. 9-7. *Using a crossover to exchange foot placements on a small hold: **a,** right foot is on a hold; **b,** cross left foot in front of the right and press down with it; **c,** press left foot on the hold while moving right foot away; **d,** right foot shifts to next hold.*

Combining Movements

Terrain features such as overhangs, roofs, horizontal or diagonal sequences, and ledges challenge climbers to employ a variety of movements, tactics, and body positions.

NEGOTIATING OVERHANGS AND ROOFS

To climb overhangs and roofs, remember the main points for any style of climbing: stay in balance and conserve strength. Identify handholds for moving up and over the bulge. Make the most of footholds with counterforce: keep feet high on the rock and hips low to press weight against the footholds (fig. 9-8). In some situations, press your hips into the terrain, with your back arched, to keep your weight over your feet while poised under an overhang.

To conserve strength, weight your feet as much as possible, even when negotiating a roof (fig. 9-9a). Keep your arms straight while raising your feet (fig. 9-9b). Avoid hanging on bent arms, which quickly exhausts arm strength. Push your body up with your legs rather than pulling with your arms (fig. 9-9c). Move quickly to minimize the time spent in these strenuous positions. Occasionally you may need to rise up on your feet while making a dynamic long reach to a handhold. Another trick is to throw one foot up onto a ledge, then push with the other foot and pull with your arms to swing up onto the top foot (fig. 9-9d).

Fig. 9-8. *Climbing an overhanging route: keep feet high and hips low.*

TRAVERSING

Going sideways across a section of rock or ice, or traversing, calls for a wide variety of climbing techniques. Staying in balance and being aware of your center of gravity are especially important during traverses.

Usually climbers face into the terrain when traversing. On rock, their feet often point away from each other (fig. 9-10a). Climbers often shuffle their hands and feet sideways, or they match or exchange hands or feet on a single hold. Rock climbers may occasionally cross one foot behind the other or one hand over the other to reach the next hold (fig. 9-10b and c). When ice climbing, it is often easier to find suitable placements for ice tools and crampons that do not require crossing your feet or hands.

When footholds are marginal or nonexistent, climbers may need to rely exclusively on friction between their shoes and the rock for placement (a technique called smearing). While gripping a series of holds or shuffling along an edge, climbers can use their feet to push against the rock (fig. 9-11a), as in a lieback or undercling (see Chapter 12, Sport Climbing and Technique). Keep your feet high and center of gravity low, to increase friction and keep your feet from slipping. Cross one hand over the other (fig. 9-11b). Again, keep your arms straight to conserve strength and let your legs do as much of the work as possible.

EXITING ONTO LEDGES

When approaching a ledge from below, continue to walk your feet up the surface, then press down with your hands near the ledge's edge if on rock (called a mantel; see Figure 9-12a and Chapter 12), or reach far back onto the ledge with your ice tool if on snow or ice. Avoid the temptation to simply lean forward and pull your torso onto the ledge; shifting your weight like that may throw you off balance and also make it impossible to keep an eye on footholds (fig. 9-12b).

DOWN-CLIMBING

Efficient down-climbing is useful on many alpine climbs. Down-climbing is sometimes faster, safer, or easier than rappelling, and it offers another retreat option. Holds are harder to see when climbing down, and the steeper the face, the harder they are to see. While down-climbing it is also difficult to test holds before you are committed to them.

When climbing down a low-angle slope, face outward for the greatest visibility (fig. 9-13a). Keep hands low and use down-pressure holds whenever possible. Keep your weight over your feet to maximize friction, especially when descending rock slabs. It may help to keep your center of

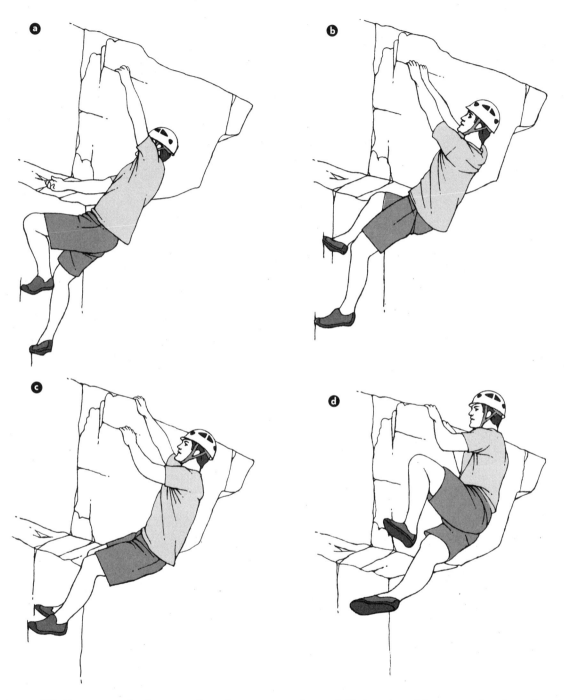

Fig. 9-9. *Climbing over a roof:* **a,** *lean out and stretch your arm up to locate a hold above the roof, keeping your hips close to the rock and feet weighted;* **b,** *move your other hand up above roof, keeping your arms straight;* **c,** *move your feet up and push them against the rock to move your body up;* **d,** *bring one foot up and begin to pull over the roof.*

Fig. 9-10. *Traversing a steep face:* **a,** *start with right foot on a hold in the direction of the traverse;* **b,** *twisting the body, reach through with left hand and shift weight over right foot;* **c,** *move right hand to new hold, while shifting both feet to right.*

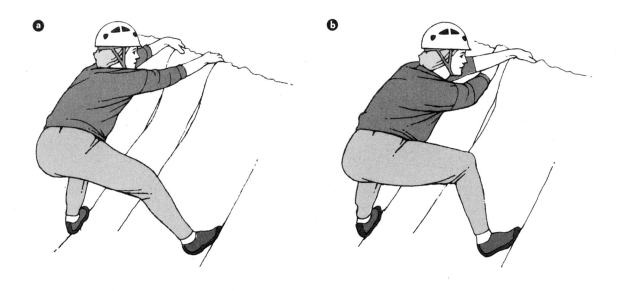

Fig. 9-11. *Hand traverse:* **a,** *push feet against rock, providing counterforce;* **b,** *cross one hand over the other.*

9

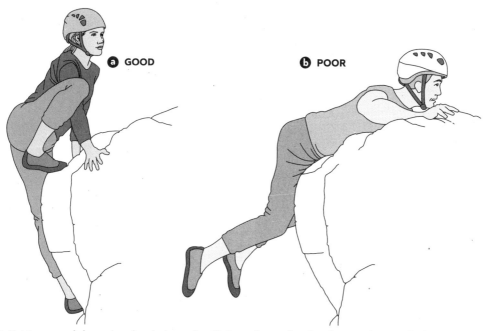

Fig. 9-12. *Exiting onto a ledge:* **a,** *keep hands close to lip of ledge and mantel up (good);* **b,** *reaching too far forward may cause your feet to slip off (poor).*

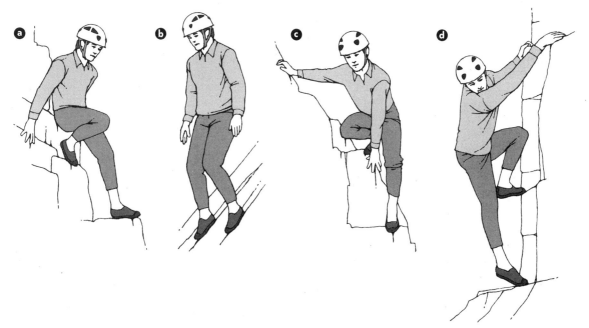

Fig. 9-13. *Down-climbing techniques:* **a,** *face out on a low-angle slope;* **b,** *keep weight over feet going down a friction slab;* **c,** *face sideways on steeper slopes;* **d,** *face in on even steeper terrain.*

gravity low, with knees well bent (fig. 9-13b). As the slope steepens, turn sideways, leaning away from the rock to improve your ability to see the route (fig. 9-13c). If the angle gets even steeper, face into the slope and look down and around behind you (fig. 9-13d).

Leading a Climb

Leading a climb requires the complementary skills of both the leader and the belayer. The lead climber reads the route, makes the moves, places protection, and then clips the rope in to the protection—all while risking a fall. The belayer watches the leader, feeds out rope, anticipates the leader's need for tension or slack, and on longer routes communicates about remaining rope length, the route description, and more (for details, see Chapter 10, Belaying). Although the leader incurs additional risk while on the "sharp end" of the rope, the belayer and leader both play critical roles in making each pitch secure and successful.

The quality and location of the protection that the lead climber places largely determine the consequences of a potential fall. If a climber falls while leading, the length of the fall will be about twice the distance between the climber and the last point of protection, plus rope stretch (fig. 9-14). If the last piece placed pulls out, the fall increases in length by double the distance to the next piece that holds the fall (see Understanding Impact Force in Chapter 10). Climbers need to be skilled in both selecting solid locations for protection and making the placement. (See Chapters 13, Rock Protection, and 16, Basic Snow and Ice Climbing, for details on placing protection.)

Fig. 9-14. *Leader fall with intermediate points of protection in place.*

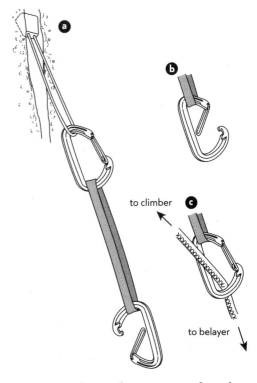

Fig. 9-15. *Correct down-and-out positioning of a carabiner:* **a,** *clip the carabiner into the protection's runner in a downward direction;* **b,** *then rotate it out and away from the climbing surface (gate opening is now down and facing out);* **c,** *clip the rope through the carabiner in direction of travel.*

CONNECTING THE ROPE TO PROTECTION

Carabiners and runners are the equipment climbers use to connect the climbing rope to protection. One carabiner is attached to the protection, the other is attached to the rope, and the two carabiners are connected with a runner (fig. 9-15a). The carabiner attached to the rope should almost always be used in the down-and-out position: the gate should point down and away from the climbing surface (fig. 9-15b). This position lessens the chance that the carabiner gate will accidentally open during a fall—potentially disastrous. The rope should be clipped in so that it runs freely through the carabiner in the direction of travel (fig. 9-15c): the rope should travel from the climbing surface upward through the carabiner and then out toward the climber. If the climbing route does not take the climber straight upward, the rope exits the carabiner on one side or the other—it should exit on the side opposite from the gate. This minimizes the chance that the rope will twist across the gate and open it during a fall (see Clipping Technique, below).

Runners or slings are used to lengthen the distance between the point of protection and the rope. This extra distance helps to isolate rope movement from the protection, keeping protection from wiggling or "walking" from its intended placement or dislodging completely. Using runners, slings, or cordelette also helps to minimize friction or rope drag on the climbing rope by allowing it to run closer to straight.

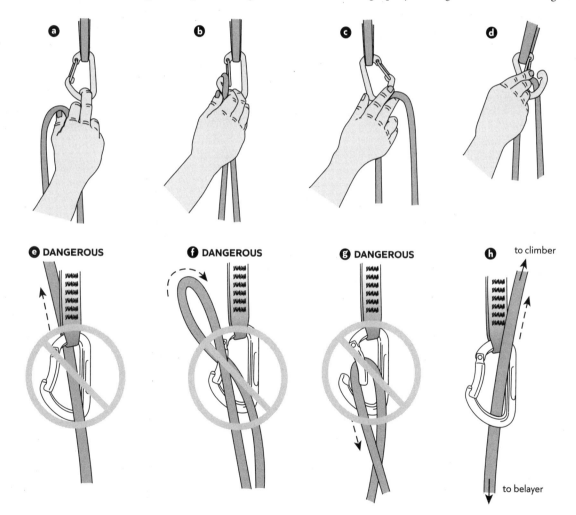

Fig. 9-16. *Clipping technique: **a** and **b**, gate facing left, right hand; **c** and **d**, gate facing right, right hand; **e**, rope is back-clipped (dangerous); **f** and **g**, back-clipped rope causes carabiner gate to open in a fall; **h**, correctly clipped carabiner.*

CLIPPING TECHNIQUE

Not only does being able to quickly and correctly clip the rope in to protection while leading decrease the climber's risk, as well as the belayer's, it also helps reduce the distance the climber may fall. Clipping well boosts confidence, which helps you climb better. It is a critical skill to gain.

Remember that the gate of the carabiner clipped in to the rope should always face away from the direction the rope is traveling. If the climb proceeds to the right after a protection point, the gate should face left (fig. 9-16a and b). If the climb proceeds to the left, the gate should face right (fig. 9-16c and d). If this principle is not followed, the rope could travel over the gate and open the carabiner when the leader falls, causing the rope to unclip. When the climb travels straight up from the last protection point, the gate can face either direction.

One common mistake among novice leaders is back-clipping: clipping the leader's end so that it travels *behind* the carabiner (fig. 9-16e) as the leader ascends above this piece of protection. Back-clipping can lead to the rope accidentally opening the carabiner gate (fig. 9-16f and g) during a leader fall.

In a correct clip, the leader's end of the rope travels out the front of the carabiner to which it is clipped and up to the lead climber (fig. 9-16h). On the ground and well before your first lead climb, practice clipping with each of your hands and with the gate facing both directions until the process is fluid and fast.

LEADING ON NONTECHNICAL TERRAIN

A climbing party may elect to travel unroped or unbelayed over second- and third-class terrain. A party should make this decision only after carefully evaluating their climbing abilities and confidence and weighing the risk and likelihood of a fall. If the risks of unroped climbing escalate beyond the party's comfort level, the leader has several options, short of full belayed climbing, for using a rope to help minimize danger.

Hand Line

A fixed hand line can be set up for members of an unroped party on less technical but exposed terrain to save the time it would take to belay multiple party members. The leader can either be belayed up or scramble up this section, bringing along the loose end of the rope and placing protection along the way, if warranted. At the top, the leader anchors the rope, taking care not to place the rope under tension over sharp edges.

The other climbers then move through this section, either holding the line or being prepared to grab it if needed. Alternatively, if they are wearing harnesses, they can clip in to the line with a carabiner attached to a runner from their harness (fig. 9-17), or they can clip a carabiner directly from their harness to a sling attached to the line with a prusik hitch. The rope may also be anchored at the start of this section to make it easier to prusik along the

Fig. 9-17. *A hand line offers limited protection for an unroped party.*

rope—that is, to push along the climber's prusik sling tied to the rope (see Friction Hitches in Chapter 8, Essential Climbing Equipment). The last climber removes the protection and breaks down the hand line while ascending, while on belay or prusiking up the hand line.

Running Belay

The running belay, also known as simul-climbing, is another useful option when a team is climbing over relatively easy terrain but is still roped together. This technique is generally used by two-person teams on rock or by rope teams of three to five people on glacier climbs.

To establish a running belay, the lead climber places protection at appropriate intervals and simply clips the rope in to the protection. The follower(s), rather than remaining behind and providing a belay, climbs at the same time as the leader (fig. 9-18), with the last climber removing the protection along the way. If one climber falls, the rope will remain linked to the protection—and the weight of the other climber(s) will naturally arrest the fall at some point.

If a party decides to use a running belay, the climbers must decide how much rope to leave between the leader and follower. Having more rope out has the advantage of absorbing more force should a climber fall, but on rock or alpine routes, it introduces rope drag, makes it more likely that the rope will snag on terrain, and can inhibit communication between the leader and follower. See Chapter 19, Glacier Travel and Crevasse Rescue, for recommendations on how to choose the rope interval in glaciated terrain. When the situation calls for it, coils (see below) can be used to shorten the rope to the appropriate length.

The running belay is less secure than belayed climbing but considerably safer than no protection at all. Given the advantages and disadvantages of this technique, the party must carefully decide whether to simul-climb, weighing the potential risks and benefits for the given party and the specific situation. Important factors to consider include the skill and comfort level of the climbing party, the degree of time pressure experienced during the climb, the degree of runout (distance between consecutive pieces of protection) and exposure (how hazardous the terrain is or how steep it is—the fall exposure), the likelihood of falling, and the consequences of falling in the given situation.

The lead climber needs to be sensitive to the skill level of the other climbers and should be ready to set up an anchored belay if anyone following needs that degree of security. Communication is imperative between the climbing team. An anchored belay would also need to be set up if the lead climber runs out of protection while simul-climbing, so that the follower(s) can either transfer gear back to the leader or switch leads and continue the running belay. For anchored belays, see Chapter 10.

Climbing in Coils

Sometimes, between sections of more technical terrain where running or fixed belays are used, climbers coil most of the rope between them, leaving themselves tied in and with about 10–16 feet (3–5 meters) of climbing rope separating them. This is called climbing in coils (see Shorten the Rope with Coils in Chapter 19). Climbers coil the extra rope over their shoulders and tie in short to a locking carabiner attached to their harness. This method can increase efficiency, saving time because climbers can forgo untying from the rope and packing it up in between more technical pitches. Also, by climbing closely together, climbers can minimize rope-induced rockfall and improve communication among the team members.

Style and Ethics

Climbers have debated endlessly over which styles are fair and which are less than sporting, as well as which practices hurt the environment and which protect it. Getting to the end of a pitch or the top of a peak is not the only goal. Many climbers care about getting there in a way that feels right, respects the terrain, and tests their skill and resolve. These are matters of style and ethics. Sometimes used interchangeably by climbers, *style* generally refers to each climber's personal mode of climbing, whereas *ethics* pertains to the overall application of the pursuit and covers issues concerning preservation of the crags and peaks.

DIVERSITY OF STYLES

Styles change and attitudes evolve, but the core of the debate is about how to maintain the challenge of climbing a particular route or summit in a way that aptly tests a climber. Climbers adhering to traditional style (trad) prefer to climb each route strictly from the ground up, or onsight, without help from such aids as top ropes or preplaced protection such as bolts. They explore and protect new routes only on lead. This type of climbing characterizes rock climbing in the alpine setting, but it is also found at many popular crags.

Climbers following the sport climbing style (see Chapter 12), which was influenced by European climbers, are more likely to find other techniques acceptable as well, including inspecting the route on rappel before trying to lead it from below. This approach can also mean cleaning the route on

9

rappel, removing placed pro, and perhaps placing protection on rappel before climbing. Climbers may climb routes with multiple falls, by resting on the rope while checking out the next moves (hangdogging) or by rehearsing moves with the help of a top rope. These techniques make it possible to climb harder and harder routes with the climber assuming less risk.

Often, due to the commitment and remoteness of alpine ascents, climbers will pull on gear or stand in a sling to climb through a hard section faster and with more security. Just as alpine climbers can improve their technique by cross training with sport climbing, they also can benefit from a knowledge of aid climbing (see Chapter 15, Aid and Big Wall Climbing).

A particular climbing area may lend itself more to one style than another because of the type of rock, the difficulty of the routes, or the prevailing custom among local climbers. In the climbing world, there is room for a diversity of styles, and most climbers experience a variety of them.

ETHICS AND THE TERRAIN

Ethics has to do with respecting the terrain and every person's chance to use it. Unlike climbing style, ethics involves personal decisions that affect other peoples' experience and enjoyment, including the sticky question of the manner in which bolts are placed on a route. Are bolts placed on rappel different from—that is, less "ethical" than—bolts placed on lead? Some climbers may argue that bolts placed on rappel rob others of the chance to try the route from the ground up, and such bolts are often placed at less convenient places than they would be if they were placed on a ground-up ascent. But other climbers may say that placing the bolts on rappel gives them a chance at an otherwise unclimbable route.

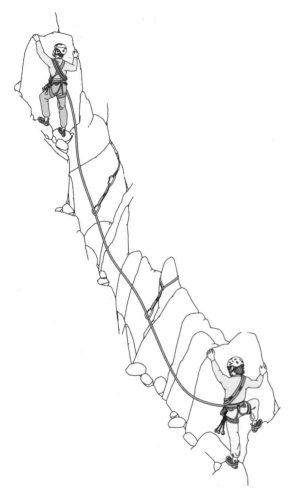

Fig. 9-18. *A running belay, shown here for a two-member rock climbing team, offers limited protection.*

THE SAFETY CHECK

Climbing partners commonly check each other's equipment setup at the start of a climb. Following a routine checklist before every climb or descent helps ensure that you do not overlook or forget anything. One example of a coherent system for safety checking involves starting with the rock, mountain, or glacier and working outward toward the climber (see Chapter 11, Rappelling).

Establish a preclimb safety checklist. The list varies by type of climb, but there are commonalities. For example: Is all equipment that will be needed for the route in the party's possession (see Chapter 8, Essential Climbing Equipment)? On technical routes, are all climbers properly tied in, their knots complete and correct, and their harnesses securely buckled? Are anchors for belaying or rappeling solidly constructed and redundant? Have climbers shared what they know (beta) about the pitches to come and have they established clear communication commands (see Communication in Chapter 10, Belaying)?

Safety checks are vital *before* the exhilarating part—the climbing—begins.

Each climbing area has its own tradition of what styles and ethics are acceptable. Visiting climbers should observe the local standards, which are usually described in local guidebooks, as well as any land management regulations, since some areas prohibit any bolting or placing of permanent anchors. Sometimes locals may disagree among themselves. This book does not try to resolve issues of style and ethics, but there is general agreement on a couple of principles.

Preservation of the rock is paramount. Chipping the rock to create new holds is unacceptable and destroys a natural feature. And who knows? It may be climbed someday as it is.

Bolting should not be indiscriminate. Although bolt-protected routes are common in many areas, it is particularly important in the mountains or other wilderness areas, away from concentrated centers of rock climbing, to preserve the environment for those who follow. If possible, stick to clean climbing, using only removable gear for protection (see Chapter 13, Rock Protection).

It is almost never justifiable to add a bolt to an existing route (retro-bolting). If you feel you cannot safely climb the route as it is, do not try it. Retro-bolting usually occurs when a consensus of local climbers agree—and the first ascensionists concur—that more bolts should be placed to promote security and enjoyment.

There should be no objection to replacement of an old bolt with a newer, stronger one at an established belay or rappel point, provided you have the necessary skills and experience to replace it.

COURTESY

Climbers should keep others in mind when they are out climbing. If a climbing party is moving up a multipitch route at a much slower pace than that of the people behind them, the first group should let the following party pass at a safe spot, such as a belay ledge. Passing can be awkward or dangerous on some longer, harder routes, so a party traveling more slowly than the norm for such a route may leave many frustrated climbers waiting for several hours or having to retreat.

Climbing Well

Moving efficiently on a route makes climbing more enjoyable and less risky. It also boosts confidence and permits climbers to tackle longer, harder, and more remote climbs. Practice moving efficiently whenever you climb. Pay attention to the techniques you find most difficult and seek out routes that allow you to practice those specific skills. Mastering the basic climbing techniques will allow you to unlock the freedom of the hills.

9

CHAPTER 10

BELAYING

A fundamental technique for reducing risk while climbing, belaying is a system of using a rope to stop a fall. This system controls the enormous energy that a falling climber generates, but belaying well takes practice and requires an understanding of the system's underlying principles.

In its simplest form, a belay consists of a rope that runs from a climber to another person—the belayer—who is ready to stop a fall. Three elements make the system work: a method of applying and amplifying a stopping force to the rope, an anchor strong enough to resist the pull of the fall, and a skilled belayer. There are different ways to apply this stopping force and many methods of setting up and tying in to a belay anchor, a secure point to which the rest of the system is attached. This chapter introduces the principal techniques and options related to belaying so climbers can choose the methods that work best for them and their route.

How Belays Are Used

On a climb, belay setups are usually established on the ground or on a reasonably comfortable ledge with solid anchors. A long climb is divided into sections, with one climber taking the lead and moving up the route to the next desirable stopping spot while being belayed from below. The lead climber then sets up a new belay station and, from above, belays the following climber. The distance between belays is known as a pitch. Rope length and terrain usually determine the length of each pitch. A short climb can be climbed in a single pitch; routes longer than a single pitch are called multipitch climbs. This section discusses how the mechanics work in three types of belay scenarios.

TOP-ROPE BELAY

In this scenario, the anchor is at the top of the route. The rope runs from the belayer up to the anchor, then back down to the ground (fig. 10-1). This scenario typically applies to single-pitch routes and is a common setup at a climbing gym or a cragging area.

In a top-rope belay, the belayer pulls the rope in, taking in slack as the climber moves upward. The direction of rope travel never changes. As long as the belayer keeps the slack out of the rope, the force of a climber fall is similar to the weight of the climber.

The belayer is not always connected to a ground anchor and instead often uses body weight as a counterforce. Certain factors may, however, require a ground anchor—for example, if there is a significant weight difference between the climber and belayer or if the climb or pitch begins from an exposed ledge.

LEAD BELAY

In a lead belay, the climber leads the route, placing protection while ascending. Lead climbing is the primary way to establish an anchor for top-roping if the top of the route is not accessible by other means. Both single-pitch and multipitch climbs can use a lead belay.

During a lead belay, the climbing rope normally moves up and away from the belayer, who pays out slack as the climber ascends. If the leader clips the rope to a piece of protection above waist height, a bit more rope must be paid out to enable the clip. The rope sags down before going up again as the leader resumes climbing. The belayer is responsible for managing the rope and keeping slack to a minimum, without pulling on the leader. In Figure 10-2, the leader has climbed above the last piece of protection he has placed.

In a lead belay, the force of a fall depends in large part on how far the climber is above the last piece of protection.

> **KEY TOPICS**
>
> HOW BELAYS ARE USED
> CHOOSING A BELAY SPOT
> HOLDING A FALL
> HOW TO APPLY BRAKING FORCE
> BELAY ANCHORS
> POSITION AND STANCE
> ROPE HANDLING
> COMMUNICATION
> ESCAPING THE BELAY
> SECURING THE FREEDOM OF THE HILLS

Fig. 10-1. *Top-rope belay.*

Fig. 10-2. *Lead belay.*

The force exerted by a falling climber can greatly exceed the force of that climber's body weight. It is much more common for the belayer to tie in to a ground anchor when belaying a leader to avoid being yanked off the ground, especially when a lead climber could take a long fall. This precaution is extremely important if the belay is on an exposed ledge or under a roof, to keep the belayer firmly on their perch.

BELAYING A FOLLOWER

After leading a pitch, a lead climber might belay a follower (or second; both terms are used interchangeably throughout this book) from the top of the pitch (fig. 10-3) for several reasons: they are climbing a multipitch route; the route is too long for top-roping; there are high amounts of rope drag (friction that impedes the rope's travel); or long traverses make this scenario less risky than top-roping.

In this scenario, the rope always moves up and toward the anchor. As long as the belayer keeps the slack to a minimum, the force of a fall should be similar to the follower's body weight. The belayer is usually tied in to the belay anchor, unless it is possible to belay directly off the anchor on a sizable ledge, making a fall unlikely. (See Belaying Off the Anchor, later in this chapter.)

10

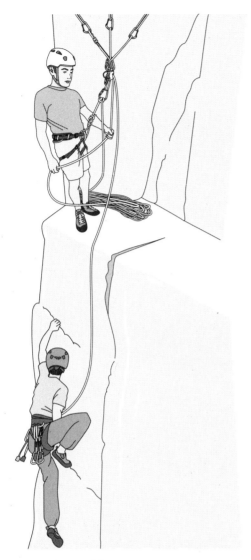

Fig. 10-3. *Belaying a follower.*

Choosing a Belay Spot

Belaying is an essential but often boring task that can take a long time and sometimes requires the belayer to sustain an awkward body position. It demands constant vigilance and is much easier from a comfortable, secure position.

Climbers need to consider many factors when choosing a belay spot. Longer leads are more efficient, so if an area has several suitable belay ledges, climbers generally pick the highest one. However, the leader may decide to stop and set up the next belay early to mitigate rope drag. The

protection, or pro, available on the leader's rack for building an anchor may also limit options for belay spots. Three attributes are key for choosing a belay location:

Solid placement for anchors. Critical to reducing risk for a belay, solid anchors are of paramount concern.

Secure position for the belayer. Being secured to an anchor severely limits a belayer's mobility. It may become difficult for them to move out of the way of falling rock or ice. Check for the possibility of rockfall or icefall and pick a stance with natural shelter from these hazards. If a location is exposed to imminent danger from above, it may be less risky to set up the belay somewhere that offers more shelter, even if there are less desirable placements for anchors.

Reasonable belayer comfort. A comfortable stance makes belaying significantly easier and more enjoyable. Finding a position where climbers have line-of-sight communication can also improve team well-being (see Communication later in this chapter). A leader may shorten a pitch because a comfortable stance at a partial rope length provides a greater advantage than pushing the lead as far as possible.

Holding a Fall

A belay serves two equally important purposes: to catch a fall so the climber does not hit the ground and to limit the impact force exerted on a falling climber.

BASIC CONCEPTS

Being familiar with some basic concepts of climbing physics will help you understand impact force.

Mass. In simple terms, mass is the amount of material an object has. The bigger and the denser an object is, the larger its mass.

Gravity. The downward force exerted by the earth is gravity, which gives weight to objects that have mass. The magnitude of gravity's pull is proportional to an object's mass. The direction of pull is always downward.

Acceleration. The rate at which an object's velocity changes is called acceleration. Velocity is the speed and direction in which an object travels. If the speed and direction of travel do not change, the acceleration is zero. Note that deceleration is also acceleration, but in the opposite direction of the velocity.

UNDERSTANDING IMPACT FORCE

With an understanding of these three concepts, we can explore how Newton's laws of motion apply in climbing.

Newton's first law of motion: An object at rest stays at rest. An object in motion travels at the same velocity unless acted on by a force or forces that do not cancel each other (an unbalanced force). This means an object's acceleration is zero unless there is an unbalanced force on it. Acceleration is not zero for a falling climber because of the force of gravity. And because any object on the earth that has mass is acted on by gravity, for an object to stay at rest there must be another force or forces to counter gravity's pull. When a climber hangs on a rope, the rope provides that counterforce by holding the climber in the air against gravity's pull.

In a somewhat simplified model that ignores rope stretch and slippage, when a climber is on a top rope, whether leading or following, and the belayer always holds the rope tight, the climber's velocity is zero before and after a fall—therefore the acceleration is also zero during the fall. The rope needs to provide only enough force to counter the climber's weight.

However, when a climber is on a lead belay, the scenario becomes rather complicated. The lead climber places intermediate pieces of protection and clips the rope in to these pieces, then climbs past them until placing another piece. If the climber falls from above the last piece of protection, they will experience a free-fall for double the distance from the last piece of protection (the climber falls to the last piece of protection, and then that much again beyond it before the rope catches the fall).

Newton's second law of motion: The net force on an object is equal to the object's mass multiplied by its acceleration. In intuitive terms, the more mass an object has, the more force it exerts; the more acceleration an object has, the more force it exerts.

Due to gravity (an unbalanced force), a falling climber's velocity will increase as the climber free-falls. This acceleration will remain constant because the earth's gravity does not change. The longer a climber free-falls, the faster they will fall. A belayer uses the rope to exert upward force, an impact force, to catch a climber, reducing the falling climber's velocity to zero.

How a Dynamic Rope Limits Impact Force

When a rope slips or stretches as the belayer catches a falling climber, the climber falls farther and for a longer time. But stopping the fall also takes longer. The magnitude of the deceleration is reduced, and thus less force overall is required to stop the fall. Stopping a fall quickly may prevent the falling climber from hitting something, such as a ledge; however, stopping a fall too suddenly subjects every component of the system, including the falling climber, to dangerously high impact forces. There is a trade-off between minimizing the length of the fall and minimizing

its impact force. Climbers say a catch is "soft," or a belay is "dynamic," when the rope slips or stretches to keep the impact force within a comfortable range.

Because modern belay devices limit rope slippage, the stretching of a dynamic climbing rope and often the belayer's movement contribute to a soft catch for a falling climber. In some situations, rope stretch is the only means of limiting impact force. Modern dynamic climbing ropes

---

THE STANDARD DROP-TEST FALL

In the standard UIAA-CEN drop-test fall for single dynamic ropes, an 80-kilogram (176-pound) mass affixed to a solid fixed anchor is dropped 5 meters (16 feet, 5 inches) on a 2.8-meter (9-foot, 2-inch) section of rope running over a 1-centimeter (⅜-inch) steel bar. To pass the test, the rope must withstand at least five standard drops and not exceed a 12 kilonewton (kN) impact force on the first drop.

This maximum 12 kN figure is derived from studies showing that the human body can briefly withstand 15 times its weight when dropped. Maximum impact forces for current single ropes usually range between 8.5 and 10.5 kN. Be aware that as a rope ages, it loses some capacity to absorb energy. A frequently used rope may generate considerably higher forces than these figures for new test ropes (see Rope Care in Chapter 8).

By design, the standard drop test produces a fall that would be considered severe in normal climbing situations. First, in most real-life situations any belay is, to a certain extent, a dynamic belay. Rope slippage, belayer movement, and rope friction against rock and through carabiners all dissipate impact force. The standard drop test is not a dynamic belay; the rope absorbs virtually all of the impact force of the fall.

Additionally, the standard drop-test fall is set up with a high fall factor, which is the length of the fall divided by the length of rope fallen on. In the UIAA-CEN standard drop test described above, the fall factor is calculated as 5 m ÷ 2.8 m = 1.78.

This test gauges the rope's properties to ensure that it will absorb the impact force generated by a severe fall without subjecting the system to excessively high loads. While the maximum fall factor of 2.0 could be encountered under normal climbing circumstances, such high-factor falls are uncommon enough that 1.78 is an acceptable and more realistic fall factor.

are designed to prevent dangerously high impact forces by elongating under load to absorb energy.

A rope that will be used for leading, an activity in which falls occur, must be an approved dynamic climbing rope. The International Climbing and Mountaineering Federation (UIAA) and European Committee for Standardization (CEN) test the designs of new climbing gear prior to production and help set safety ratings. All safe, tested climbing equipment depicts the UIAA safety label and/or the CEN mark (see Figure 8-2 in Chapter 8, Essential Climbing Equipment). For detailed information on how ropes are tested, see "The Standard Drop-Test Fall" sidebar above.

Static ropes, webbing, slings, and accessory cord, while fine for rappelling, constructing anchors, or other uses, do not stretch enough to safely catch a dynamic fall. Look at the manufacturer's specifications for climbing ropes: they are rated not by tensile strength but by impact force. This is because the rope does more than simply not break under the impact of a falling climber, it also stretches to absorb the energy of multiple falls. These two criteria align with the two purposes of the belay: to catch a fall and to limit the impact force.

Because dynamic ropes limit the impact force of a fall, less force is exerted throughout the system. As a result, the anchor is subjected to lower stresses, a climber receives a softer catch when falling, and the belayer can more easily hold a fall.

Why Fall Factors Are Significant

The impact force generated by a fall onto a dynamic rope is determined by both the length of the fall and how much dynamic rope is available to absorb the fall's energy. Together, these two lengths determine the fall factor: the length of the fall divided by the length of rope fallen on. The fall factor, not the length of the fall, determines the impact force: the longer the fall, the bigger the fall factor; the more rope to fall on, the smaller the fall factor. Therefore, lower fall factors always mean lower impact forces because there is more rope relative to the length of fall, hence more rope to stretch and absorb impact.

In any normal climbing situation, the biggest fall factor a climber could ever encounter is 2.0, which would mean falling exactly twice the length of rope the climber has run out. For example, if two climbers are on a smooth vertical face with no ledges or other hazards to hit in a fall and the leader falls from 10 feet (3 meters) above the belay without any protection, the climber would end up 10 feet below the belay stance (the only point of protection), having fallen 20

feet (6 meters) on 10 feet of rope. The fall factor would be 20 feet ÷ 10 feet = 2.0, or a fall factor of 2.0, also referred to as a factor 2 fall.

Such a fall would generate the maximum impact on anchors and climbers, creating a hazardous situation. If there is any slack in the rope, intermediate points of protection, rope slippage, or belayer movement, the fall factor will always be less than 2.0. When more rope is payed out, falls of a similar length will generate much lower impact forces, putting less stress on the system. That same 20-foot fall on a 100-foot section of rope would still involve exciting air time—but with a fall factor of 0.2 (20 feet ÷ 100 feet), the catch would be quite gentle by comparison.

Any length of fall of the same fall factor will generate the same impact force, although this is not immediately obvious. An intuitive explanation without involving math is that the length of the fall determines the maximum speed the falling climber reaches before being caught by the rope and starting to decelerate. Obviously, the longer the fall, the greater the speed. On the other hand, the length of rope catching the fall determines how fast the fall is stopped. The more rope, the more it stretches and the longer it takes to stop the fall. So although a longer fall involves higher speed, if the fall factor is constant, reducing that speed to zero also takes longer. The deceleration rate remains the same.

Take the 5-meter UIAA-CEN drop-test fall described in "The Standard Drop-Test Fall" sidebar above and multiply it by 5; now it is a 25-meter (82-foot) fall on 14 meters (46 feet) of rope, but the fall factor remains the same: 1.78. The fall is much longer (and clearly riskier for the falling climber), but because the amount of rope available to absorb shock is also greater, the amount of impact force that the belay system is subjected to remains the same.

PROTECTING THE LEADER

Understanding the fall factor and how it determines impact forces is fundamental to minimizing risk when leading. Because a leader fall would be at least twice the distance between the climber and the last piece of protection, the leader places intermediate points of protection while climbing to reduce fall length. As described in the preceding section, the impact forces are highest in a fall with a fall factor of 2.0. This would happen when the leader starts up a pitch and falls before any intermediate protection has been placed to limit the distance of that fall.

It is important to establish a solid first placement of protection as soon as possible after starting a new lead, not only to reduce the chance for a high-factor fall but also to establish the direction from which the force of a leader fall will come (see Anticipating Fall Forces in Chapter 14, Traditional Rock Climbing). Understanding the dynamics involved will help climbers make more sense of how belaying protects the leader and belayer.

How to Apply Braking Force

With the dynamic climbing rope acting as the shock absorber in the system, a belayer's job is to stop the rope from running as quickly as possible. Rope that runs through the system as a belayer catches the fall has two related effects: reducing the impact forces and lengthening the distance a climber falls. Occasionally a belayer may want to provide a more dynamic belay—for instance, if the climbers suspect that the protection they have placed is weak. But a longer fall increases the possibility that a lead climber may hit a ledge or other hazard.

It is important to consider the factors that affect the braking force applied by a belayer's grip. Grip strength varies considerably, with the average being somewhere around 50 pounds (about 0.2 kilonewton). Being substantially fatigued or awkwardly positioned reduces grip strength. Thinner ropes are more difficult to grip, and reduced friction, as occurs with wet, icy, or (possibly) dry-treated ropes, lowers braking force too. Conversely, as ropes age, their sheath becomes rougher, which offers more friction and makes them easier to grip.

The belayer's hand that holds the rope coming from the climber and pays the rope in and out is known as the guide hand. The other hand, the brake hand, must always grip the rope, ready to catch a fall at any time. Grip strength alone will not stop a fall, however. Belayers amplify their stopping power by relying on a component of the system that produces friction: a belay device, a munter hitch on a carabiner, or the belayer's hips.

For all belays, the rope from the climber goes around or through the part of the system that produces friction and then to the belayer's brake hand. The brake hand gripping the rope produces the initial force. The braking method is the essential means by which the belayer can control the large impact forces generated in a fall.

To stop a fall, a belayer assumes the braking position, grips the rope tightly with the brake hand, and then pulls back on the free end of the rope (for example, see Figure 10-10). Climbers must practice this action until it becomes automatic; the best way for belayers to stop a fall is to immediately assume the braking position as soon as they sense a fall.

Some belayers prefer to wear gloves to protect their hands from friction burns in case the rope slips. Glove

material should be rough enough to add friction to the system, essentially increasing grip strength. Make sure they fit snugly enough to avoid wrinkled or folded fabric. Some climbers dislike how gloves can interfere with dexterity and that hands are left damp and soft when they remove the gloves, which can make it harder to grip holds. Wearing fingerless gloves can allow climbers to maintain dexterity while protecting their palms.

The most important task for all belayers is to perfect whichever braking method they use. Having one method that you can count on is the first priority. After that, learning other methods for versatility is valuable.

BELAY DEVICES

When used correctly, belay devices multiply the rope friction and the belayer's grip strength by passing the rope through an aperture, wrapping it around a locking carabiner, and passing the rope back out through the aperture. This configuration creates a wrap, or bend, in the rope to assist in producing a stopping force. The belayer's brake hand is the initial, and critical, source of friction; if the brake hand is not on the rope, the climber is not on belay.

The total braking force exerted on the rope when arresting a fall depends on three things: (1) the degree of bend that the belay device produces in the rope, as well as the rope's inherent resistance to bending and deforming; (2) the friction generated as the rope runs over the surfaces of the belay device; and (3) the force exerted by the belayer's grip. Fortunately, despite the variations in grip strength among belayers, when modern belay devices are used properly, the belayer can generate adequate stopping force with even modest grip strength.

To stop a fall, the belayer pulls back on the free end of the rope with the brake hand to create an angle of at least 90 degrees between the rope from the climber entering the belay device and the rope leaving the device to the brake hand. This angle of separation between the two strands of the rope is critical to the strength of the belay. Figure 10-4 shows how pulling the rope farther back with the brake hand to increase the angle of separation from 90 degrees toward 180 degrees increases the braking force. The belayer must ensure that the brake hand is free to move to the braking position without being impeded by the terrain or requiring an unnatural body position or motion.

One of the simplest and most convenient belay methods is to clip the belay device in to a locking carabiner that is typically clipped through a sewn belay loop on the harness, as shown in Figure 10-10. It is important to follow manufacturer's instructions for clipping in properly; loading a

10

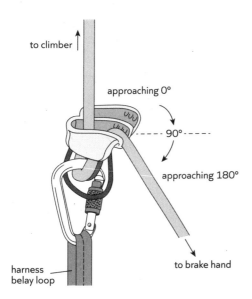

Fig. 10-4. *Angle of separation between the two rope strands, using a belay device and locking carabiner.*

harness in ways it was not designed for may lead to failure. Many harnesses have a sewn-in label showing the proper way to wear the harness and clip in to it.

Types of Belay Devices
Before mechanical belay devices were invented, climbers relied on the friction of a rope run around their hips to arrest a fall. Nowadays, with advanced dynamic-rope technologies and mechanical belay devices, climbers seldom need to rely on their body as a belay device, though the hip belay may be useful in some situations (see Hip Belay later in this chapter). Some of the most popular belay devices are described below. Always read and follow manufacturer's instructions, and check that the device is rigged properly each time you use it. Note that each belay device works with only a certain range of rope diameters.

Tubular belay devices. Figure 10-5 shows a variety of tubular, or tube-style devices, all of which work in a similar fashion: the belayer pushes a bight of rope through an opening in the device, then clips it to a locking carabiner on the harness belay loop, as shown in Figure 10-10. The devices shown are the Petzl Reverso (fig. 10-5a), Black Diamond ATC-Guide (fig. 10-5b), the Black Diamond ATC-XP (fig. 10-5c), and Edelrid Mega Jul (fig. 10-5d). This style of tubular device has replaced earlier plate-style devices, such as the Stitcht plate or figure-eight belay device, due to their improved rope handling and added capabilities.

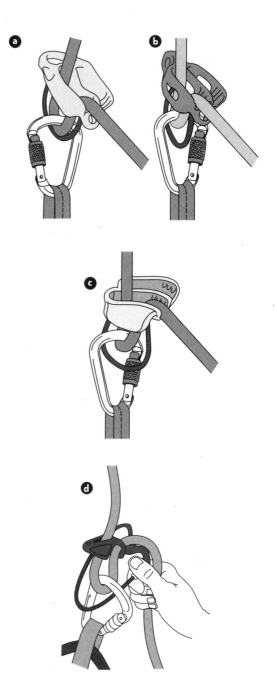

Fig. 10-5. *Tubular belay devices:* **a** *and* **b,** *tubular devices that can be used for belaying off a harness or anchor and offer an autolocking mode;* **c,** *tubular device with friction grooves;* **d,** *tubular device with thumb-loop release to manage slack.*

Tube-style devices must be kept from sliding up the rope and out of reach when in use, so they all include a wire loop that is clipped in to a locking carabiner on the belay loop, along with the climbing rope, as shown in Figures 10-4 and 10-5.

Many current tubular devices have two modes: regular-friction and high-friction. The latter is usually achieved by adding V-shaped slots and/or ridges to one side of the aperture. Figure 10-6a shows the regular-friction mode. In high-friction mode (fig. 10-6b), the device is rigged so that the rope going to the brake hand is pulled over the ridges (or into the narrower V slot, as in Figure 10-5a–c) to increase the braking force—useful when climbers want extra friction for belaying or rappelling. In practice, most climbers will almost always use the high-friction mode of these devices for both belaying and rappelling, only opting to utilize the regular-friction mode in circumstances where high-friction mode is too awkward or difficult to manage. Low-angle rappels on easier terrain might be one such scenario.

Auto-locking belay devices. These devices function in the same way as a standard tube device when belaying a leader, but they also have an alternative rigging mode that provides a secure means of belaying one or two followers directly off an anchor. Most of these devices work in a similar way; typical examples include the Petzl Reverso (fig. 10-5a), Black Diamond ATC-Guide (fig. 10-5b), and Edelrid Mega Jul

(fig. 10-5d), but many climbing-equipment companies manufacture their own versions of auto-locking belay devices. Follow the manufacturer's instructions to use these devices correctly. Note that auto-locking belay devices are not hands-free devices: they still require the belayer's brake hand to provide the initial braking force. The brake hand must never lose its grip on the rope.

Auto-locking belay devices look similar to other tube-style devices and may be used off the harness in the same way. But in auto-locking mode, these devices are connected directly to the anchor with a locking carabiner while the rope runs through both the device and a second locking carabiner (fig. 10-7). With the device rigged this way, the belayer can easily pull the rope in, but if the climber's strand

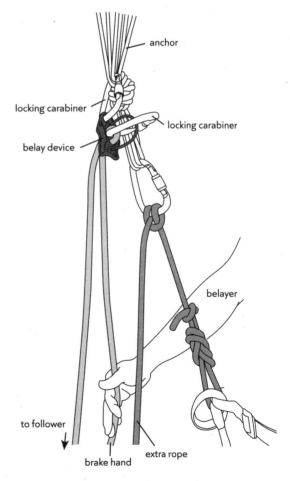

Fig. 10-7. *Auto-locking belay device rigged in auto-locking mode.*

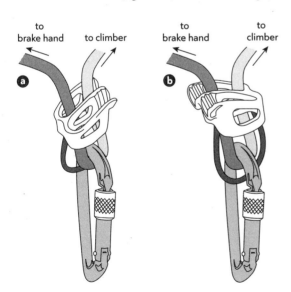

Fig. 10-6. *Tube-style belay device in two modes: **a,** regular-friction mode; **b,** high-friction mode.*

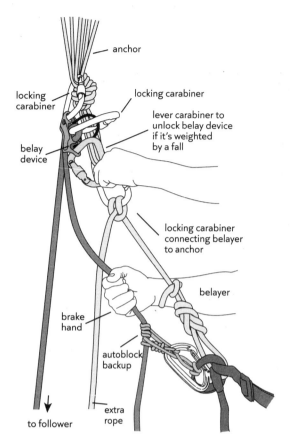

Fig. 10-8. *Using a lever carabiner to release a loaded auto-locking belay device weighted by a fall.*

is loaded, as in a fall, the rope locks down on itself: when the climber falls, their body weight loads their strand of the rope, and that loaded strand presses on the braking strand, preventing it from moving.

If a climber falls and is unable to unload the device, the belayer must have a way to lift the loaded climber's strand off the braking strand. Fingers are not strong enough to lift this load. The belayer can use a carabiner (or any rod that is strong enough) as a lever (fig. 10-8) or attach a cord and redirect their own body weight to pull against the load. Many newer auto-locking devices have a hole specifically designed for attaching a cord or carabiner for this purpose, as shown in Figure 10-8.

Note that releasing the auto-locking mechanism in this manner opens the device and allows the rope to run; the belayer must be prepared to carefully manage lowering the fallen climber before beginning to release. For short lowers, adding an autoblock backup on the braking strand (as shown in Figure 10-8) is sufficient. For longer lowers, it may be easier to redirect the braking strand through a carabiner higher on the anchor to ensure the rope remains in the braking position once the device has opened. Always consult the manufacturer's directions for a specific device for the recommended procedure, and practice releasing the device in a low-risk environment before putting it to use on a climb.

Assisted-braking belay devices. These specialized devices have an internal cam that locks down on the rope when the rope suddenly accelerates (fig. 10-9a). This locking action creates a braking force that does not depend on resistance from the belayer's grip. Models include the Petzl

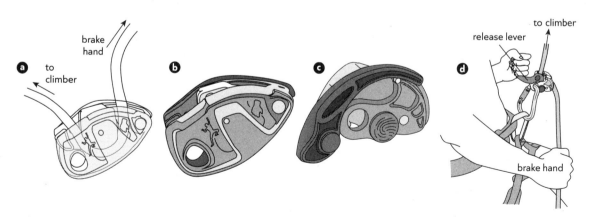

Fig. 10-9. *Assisted-braking belay devices:* **a,** *Petzl Grigri+ in belaying mode;* **b,** *Grigri+;* **c,** *Trango Vergo;* **d,** *Vergo in lowering mode.*

Grigri+ (fig. 10-9a and b), Trango Vergo (fig. 10-9c), and Edelrid Eddy. Popular for gym, sport, and aid climbing, assisted-braking belay devices have definite advantages when used properly. For example, they enable a smaller, lighter belayer to arrest and hold even heavy partners and stop long falls. All current models have a release lever that allows for controlled rappelling or lowering of a climber on a top rope (fig. 10-9d).

These devices tend to lock up when a lead climber moves up suddenly or a belayer feeds the rope too quickly. It is extremely important to follow the manufacturer's instructions and check the setup each time you rig a device. Disadvantages include their greater weight and bulk. Assisted-braking belay devices also catch the rope much more quickly, making it harder to give a soft, dynamic belay. With these devices, the belayer often must move forward a few steps or even jump slightly upward when the rope goes taut to soften the catch. This type of dynamic belay trades a slightly longer fall for a lower impact force on the climber. These devices also cannot be used to rappel on two strands, making them unsuitable for alpine climbing. Note that assisted-braking belay devices are not hands-free devices: they still require the belayer's brake hand to initiate the braking force.

Technique for Using a Belay Device

This section describes the technique of belaying a climber off the harness using a belay device. To assume the belay position, grab the rope with your brake hand, with your thumb pointing upward and your palm facing yourself or the ground. This natural position allows you to make use of your hand's full grip strength. Make sure the belay device, the rope, and the harness's belay loop are not twisted. Grip the rope with your guide hand at eye level, feeling the rope's slack but not pulling it (fig. 10-10a).

Taking in the rope. Known as PBUS (Pull, Brake, Under, Slide), this standard technique is taught at most climbing gyms and by most guides. With both hands on the rope, start in the belay position shown in Figure 10-10a. First, pull down on the climber's strand of the rope with the guide hand, and at the same time pull the brake hand away from your body, to pull the rope through the belay device (fig. 10-10b).

Then without losing your grip, drop the brake hand down to the braking position, and place the guide hand under the brake hand and grasp the rope (fig. 10-10c). Without removing the brake hand from the rope, slide it up until it is close to the belay device, and grasp the rope again (fig. 10-10d). Then move the guide hand back up to the climber's strand as shown in Figure 10-10a. Repeat

Fig. 10-10. *Taking in rope from a standing belay, with the brake hand never leaving the rope: **a,** start with both hands on the rope, with guide hand extended and brake hand close to the body; **b,** pull guide hand toward your body and brake hand away from your body; **c,** drop brake hand into braking position and move guide hand to grasp the rope under brake hand; **d,** slide brake hand back along rope toward your body while maintaining the braking position.*

this sequence as often as needed to take in the appropriate amount of rope. Remember that the brake hand must never leave the rope.

Letting out the rope. It is easy and intuitive to let out the rope. With the guide hand, pull the rope away from your body while using the brake hand to feed the rope toward the climber. Again, the brake hand must never leave the rope. If you are letting out a lot of rope quickly, slide the brake hand away from your body until your arm is fully extended, maximizing the amount of rope you can feed to the guide hand in one motion.

MUNTER HITCH

An effective alternative to using a belay device, the munter hitch uses only the rope, a locking carabiner, and the hitch to provide the friction necessary to stop a fall. Efficient belaying with a munter hitch requires a pear-shaped carabiner (pearabiner) with an opening large enough to allow the hitch to feed through smoothly (see Carabiners in Chapter 8). As a result of its configuration, the munter hitch multiplies the effect of the brake hand, with friction created by the rope being wrapped on itself and around the carabiner (see Munter Hitch and Figure 8-26 in Chapter 8).

The munter hitch is unique in that it provides sufficient friction regardless of the angle at which the belayer holds the braking strand of the rope. With regular aperture belay devices, the belayer generates maximum friction by holding the braking strand of the rope at an angle approaching 180 degrees from the climber's strand, as shown in Figure 10-4. These devices are useless when both strands are nearly parallel. In contrast, the munter hitch, because of the way it wraps around the pear-shaped carabiner, actually generates *more* friction when both strands of the rope are aligned; when the strands are at an angle of 180 degrees, the munter hitch still provides about 85 percent of the maximum friction. In other words, a belayer can hold the munter hitch at any position and still have sufficient friction.

Because it requires no special braking position, the munter hitch has an advantage over most belay devices in that if a climber fall takes a belayer by surprise, the hitch will function even if the belayer does no more than firmly grip the rope. Rope handling is quick and easy with the munter hitch, making it an ideal method when climbers are moving rapidly over easy ground. Because it requires no specialized equipment other than a locking carabiner, the munter hitch provides a ready backup belay method if a belay device is lost.

The munter hitch has some drawbacks. It can kink the rope more than other belay methods, though allowing the rope to feed freely unless you need to arrest a fall can minimize kinking. To unkink the rope, shake out the end that is hanging free. The munter hitch can also unscrew the lock on a carabiner gate as the rope runs across the gate—set it up so that the braking strand is on the spine side of the carabiner instead of the gate side, if possible. Pay attention to the carabiner gate when using a munter hitch.

HIP BELAY

Also called the body belay, the hip belay is a belay method in which the rope is wrapped around the belayer's body to generate enough friction to stop a climber's fall. Though device and munter belays have become more common in recent years, the hip belay is still useful in certain situations. The belayer clips in to a solid anchor and assumes a stable stance, facing the direction of an anticipated pull on the rope. The rope from the climber passes around the belayer's back and rides just below the top of the hips (fig. 10-11a). To arrest a fall, the belayer grips the rope tightly with the brake hand and pulls the straightened brake arm across the stomach into the braking position (fig. 10-11b). The braking position increases the amount of friction-producing wrap of the rope around the body, thereby increasing the stopping force.

Climbers need to practice this braking action so that it becomes automatic. The hip belay is most effective if a belayer assumes the braking position as soon as they sense a fall is about to occur. Because the hip belay requires more time for the belayer to attain braking position and generates less braking force than any other method, more rope slippage generally occurs and the climber usually falls farther. If a belayer cannot maintain their stance, the belayer is much more likely to lose control of the rope than with other methods. In summary, all elements of the hip belay must come together to make it work effectively during a long, hard fall; see Special Considerations for the Hip Belay, below.

Because the force of a fall is dissipated as friction against the belayer's body, a belayer stopping a severe fall can suffer serious rope burns. Climbers must wear clothing that protects themselves. Even fairly minor leader falls can melt and severely damage expensive synthetic garments. If a belayer is burned badly enough, they could drop a falling climber. Because the belayer's hands provide a greater proportion of friction in the hip belay than in other methods, gloves are essential to protect the hands from burns. A tighter grip causes less severe burns because stopping the rope faster and allowing less of it to slip through the hands or across the body generates less heat. Also, if the climbing rope runs over the anchor, it may burn the anchor attachment during a fall.

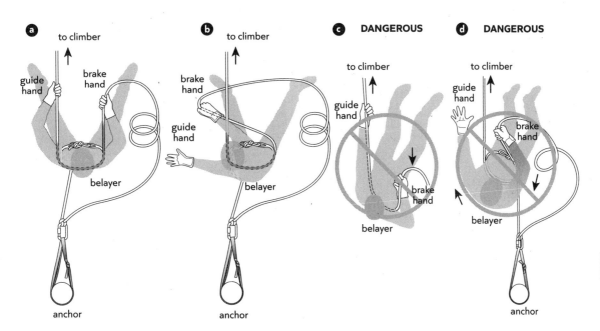

Fig. 10-11. *The hip or body belay:* **a,** *belayer anchored and ready to arrest a fall—the rope goes from the brake hand around the back at the top of the hips (to produce friction) and to the climber;* **b,** *the braking position—with braking arm extended across the stomach to create additional friction;* **c,** *if the belayer does not straighten their elbow before beginning to brake, their arm may be pulled into a helpless position (dangerous);* **d,** *having the anchor attachment on the same side as the brake hand can allow the hip belay to unwrap (dangerous).*

Despite these drawbacks as a general-purpose belay method, the hip belay does have advantages that make it worth learning. The belayer can take in rope much faster than with other methods and can set up the hip belay quickly with minimal equipment. It is probably most useful when belaying a fast-moving partner over moderate terrain. A common and efficient practice is to use a simple hip belay to bring a following climber up a relatively easy pitch, then switch to another method when the climbing becomes more technical. The hip belay can also be useful for belaying on snow, where a more dynamic belay may be desirable because anchors are absent or suspect (see Chapters 16, Basic Snow and Ice Climbing, and 17, Technical Snow and Ice Climbing). Also, if climbers lose or forget their belay device and do not have an appropriate carabiner for a munter hitch, the hip belay may be their only choice.

Special Considerations for the Hip Belay

Climbers must consider several factors when using the hip belay. To catch a fall, the belayer must first straighten the elbow of the braking arm before beginning to grip hard. Then the belayer must bring the braking arm across the front of their body to increase the amount of wrap for maximum friction. Most people's natural reaction is to grip the rope first, but doing so may pull the braking arm into a helpless position (fig. 10-11c), requiring the belayer to let go and slide their brake hand along the rope to grasp it elsewhere. Learning how to assume the optimal braking position requires practice, ideally by catching and holding actual weights.

When the belayer attaches to the anchor, rig the connection to the side opposite the brake hand. Note that this method is different from tying in for belaying with a mechanical device. If the brake hand and anchor rope are on the same side of your body, the force of a fall can partly unwrap the rope from around your body (fig. 10-11d), decreasing both friction and stability.

Another precaution is to clip a control carabiner through the two hard points of your harness (fig. 10-12). The carabiner goes in front, or on the same side as the rope coming from the climber, but well forward of your hip bone. Clipping the rope in to this carabiner keeps the rope where it is needed (at your hip), counteracts body rotation, and adds friction to the system.

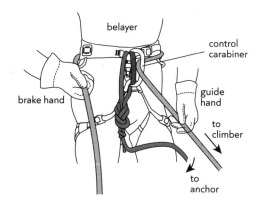

Fig. 10-12. *Control carabiner added to a hip belay.*

To keep from losing control of the belay, maintain a stable stance and take advantage of the anchor attachment to maintain your body position. Wrapping the rope around your back and above the anchor attachment will prevent the rope from being pulled below your seat. If you may be pulled from above but definitely not downward, wrap the rope around your back and below the anchor attachment to prevent the rope from being pulled over your head.

CHOOSING A BELAY METHOD

Choosing a belay method may seem like a simple matter of choosing whatever exerts the most stopping force. However, even if the maximum stopping force of two methods differs significantly, they may involve little practical difference. For most falls, a belayer can exert sufficient force regardless of the method.

However, in the case of a high-factor fall on steep terrain, where the belay is the primary source of friction, the belay method can mean the difference between the rope running or not. These types of falls have little margin for error.

If the rope starts to run while the belayer is holding a fall, the climber will fall farther—often less desirable and more dangerous. However, in any protected leader fall, it is important to consider that the force acts on the protection as well as the climber: the maximum force on the top piece of protection is one and a half to two times as much as the maximum force on the climber—in a high-factor fall on vertical rock, the maximum force on the climber can easily reach 7 kilonewtons (more than 1,500 pounds). If the protection fails under this force, the climber will fall farther. To reduce this force on the protection, some belayers choose a relatively weak method of belaying, one that will let the rope start to run at a lower force to lessen the likelihood of the protection failing.

Belay Anchors

Secure anchors are vital to a sufficient belay: climbers cannot always anticipate the moment when they will have to stop an extreme leader fall, and in that moment, the anchor must hold, or both climbers could suffer catastrophic consequences. The word *anchor* refers to a whole system. An anchor has many components and one or more anchor points. In addition to the climbing rope, it may include natural features, fixed protection pieces, removable protection pieces, runners, and carabiners.

SELECTING A BELAY ANCHOR

This section offers a few tips on selecting reliable anchors for belays, but to learn even more about using natural features and setting artificial anchors on rock, snow, and ice, study Chapters 13, Rock Protection; 14, Traditional Rock Climbing and Technique; 16, Basic Snow and Ice Climbing; and 17, Technical Snow and Ice Climbing (also see Resources for all these chapters).

When selecting a position for the belay anchor at the top of a pitch, consider every possible direction from which a

Fig. 10-13. *When the leader belays a follower, if the follower falls, the direction of pull on the belayer is from the last piece of protection.*

force may load the anchors. Ideally, the anchor should be directly above the last piece of protection or as close to it as possible. When the leader belays a follower, if the follower falls, the direction of the pull is from the last piece of protection (fig. 10-13). Once that piece is removed or fails, then the follower risks penduluming to and past the fall line (fig. 10-14). A belay anchor directly above the last piece, rather than to the side, will minimize such a pendulum.

In a lead belay, if the leader falls, the belayer is pulled toward the first piece of protection, which is usually upward. This is a good reminder to make sure the belay anchors will withstand a pull from any conceivable fall. See more about natural and fixed protection in Chapter 13.

Natural Anchors

A large natural feature, such as a well-rooted, reasonably sized live tree or a pillar of sound rock, can make an ideal anchor. Climbers can build and remove an anchor very quickly on such features. Trees and large bushes are obvious choices, but do not trust any features that appear weak, loose, or brittle; be aware that wood can become brittle in very cold weather. Carefully evaluate trees that may have shallow roots near or on cliff faces. Test trees by pushing against them. Attaching to a stout tree branch rather than low on the trunk helps limit the rope's contact with the ground, reducing abrasion and the risk of rockfall. However, connecting to a branch exerts more leverage on the tree, increasing the possibility that it could uproot. If you use a bush as an anchor, consider placing a piece or two in the rock for backup.

Many different rock features—horns, columns, rock tunnels formed by the contact point between two boulders, or flat-bottomed large boulders—are useful anchors. However, it is easy to overestimate the stability of large boulders. Consider the shape of the boulder's base and of the socket it sits in, the angle of the slope it rests on, and its height-to-width ratio. Imagine the hidden undersurface and the block's center of gravity: Could a big load pull it over the edge? Test it gently at first. Occasionally, climbers have to set up a belay at a jumble of large boulders. A boulder underneath other large boulders might be solid but can be difficult to assess.

Check any rock feature you plan to use as an anchor for fracture lines, which may be subtle, such as at the base of a rock horn or near the edge of a crack. When placing protection in a crack for an anchor, check to see whether one side may be a detachable block or movable flake; a crack that widens only a fraction of an inch under the force of a fall may allow the protection to pull out.

Fig. 10-14. *If the last piece of protection fails, then the follower will pendulum to and past the fall line.*

Always evaluate the probable strength and stability of a rock feature or chockstone before using it as an anchor. Place a sling on a rock feature well below its center of gravity to reduce the chance of it tipping or dislodging. If a natural anchor is questionable, test it before you attach gear or the rope.

Fixed Anchors

Artificial (manufactured) anchors include bolts and pitons that are usually left "fixed" permanently in place. On established routes, climbers may encounter bolts and pitons placed by earlier climbers; in unknown alpine terrain, some climbers carry pitons and a hammer to set anchors.

Bolts are permanent pieces of artificial protection driven into a hole that has been drilled into the rock. Bolt hangers, which may or may not be permanent, allow carabiners to be attached to bolts (see Figure 12-6 in Chapter 12, Sport Climbing). Pitons are metal spikes with a blade that is pounded into cracks; the eye is the point of attachment for a carabiner (see Figure 13-6 in Chapter 13). On rock climbing route topos, bolts and fixed pitons are often shown as "x" and "fp" (for "fixed piton"), respectively (see Figure 14-1 in Chapter 14).

Climbers may also encounter other hardware such as nuts, hexes, and so forth that became fixed when someone could not remove them. Evaluate any such fixed pieces thoroughly. Bolts and fixed pitons are often solid if they are of recent vintage, but older placements are notoriously difficult to assess. Old ¼-inch bolts should not be trusted.

Many popular routes feature fixed anchors at belay stations; commonly, these anchors consist of two or more bolts, sometimes connected with a short section or sections of chain.

Removable Anchors

Where natural features or fixed protection are unavailable, climbers build anchors and remove them as they complete a pitch (see Chapters 13 and 14 for rock anchors, 16 for snow anchors, and 17 for ice anchors).

EQUALIZING THE BELAY ANCHOR

Commonly, belays use two or three placements to create an anchor, so the system has redundancy and does not depend on any single placement. If one placement fails, the other anchor placements may still hold.

In building a multipoint anchor, the first factor to consider is how many anchor points it needs. There is no universal answer. It depends on a lot of factors: the maximum expected impact force, the quality of rock or natural protection, the quality of removable placements, et cetera. But the general rule of thumb is to build an anchor with two solid pieces or three good pieces. As your confidence in pieces lowers, add more pieces and do a better job of equalizing them.

The second factor to consider is the angle formed by all the legs at the power point—the main connection point of the anchor system. This angle is sometimes called the V-angle because the legs form the shape of a V. Figure 10-15 shows a two-point anchor in which the two legs are symmetric. According to the rules of physics, the bigger the angle, the greater the force that is delivered to each anchor point and the less effective the equalization. At a V-angle approaching 0 degrees, or when the two anchor points are

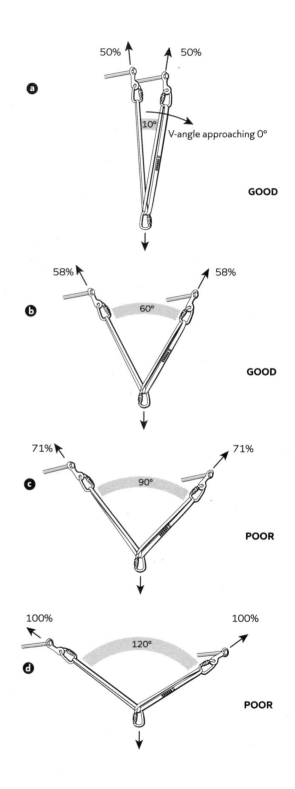

Fig. 10-15. *V-angle effect on percent of load or force on a two-point anchor system equalized with sewn runners: **a,** at a V-angle approaching 0 degrees, each anchor point receives half the load; **b,** strive to keep the V-angle less than 60 degrees; **c,** as the V-angle increases beyond 60 degrees, the load on each anchor point increases; **d,** at a V-angle of 120 degrees, the load is 100 percent on each anchor point.*

perfectly parallel, each anchor point receives half the load (fig. 10-15a). Strive to keep the V-angle of a belay anchor system less than 60 degrees (fig. 10-15b).

With a V-angle greater than 60 degrees, the load on each anchor point increases significantly (fig. 10-15c). When the V-angle is 120 degrees, the force on either anchor point is the same as the load itself (fig. 10-15d). In this case, the force is not reduced at all—the equalization serves no purpose other than providing redundancy (if one anchor point fails, the other takes over).

When the V-angle exceeds 120 degrees, the force is amplified, and it grows rapidly as the V-angle increases (fig. 10-16). An anchor system with more than two anchor points is a little harder to analyze, but the principles remain the same: keep the overall V-angle relatively small.

Distributing the load among the placements, a technique called equalization, increases the anchor's reliability. Most ways of equalizing the load on multiple anchor points use runners or loops of accessory cord (both of which are called legs) to connect the anchor points into a single power point (or master point). These equalization methods can be roughly divided into two types: static and dynamic equalization. Static equalization distributes the load in only one direction, while dynamic equalization distributes the load in a range of directions.

All equalization methods have advantages and disadvantages. It is important to understand the variables involved, to know how anchors function in different situations, and to make informed decisions about how best to construct anchors in various configurations. Ultimately, any multipart anchor is only as solid as its individual components, and skillful placement of individual pieces reduces the risk that the anchor will fail.

Static Equalization

With static equalization, the anchor is built to take the load from only one anticipated direction of pull; if the anchor is pulled in a different direction, the effect of equalization may be lost.

Two anchor points. To statically equalize two anchor points, a common method is to clip a double-length (48-inch, 120-centimeter) runner in to the two anchor points—one end of the runner to one anchor point, the other end of the runner to the other anchor point—and then gather the resulting four strands of the runner in a bight, tie them in an overhand or figure-eight knot, and clip a locking carabiner to the resulting loop (the power point) that is on the opposite side of the knot from the anchor points (fig. 10-17).

The main drawback of this method is that the knot is hard to untie after it has been heavily loaded. Also, if the runner is skinny, the knot is usually very small, and a small knot on a skinny runner significantly weakens the runner's

10

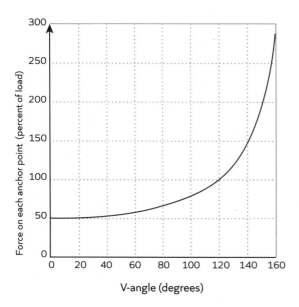

Fig. 10-16. *Force exerted on each anchor point for different V-angles, expressed as a percentage of the load on the anchor.*

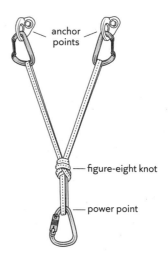

Fig. 10-17. *Statically equalizing two anchor points with a double-length runner.*

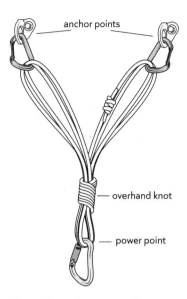

Fig. 10-18. *Statically equalizing two anchor points with a cordelette by doubling it and tying an overhand knot in the resulting eight strands to create a power point.*

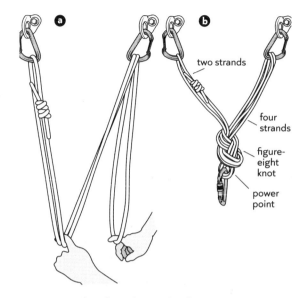

Fig. 10-19. *When the anchor needs to be longer, alternative method of statically equalizing two anchor points with cordelette: **a,** clip one bight of cordelette in to one anchor point and clip both strands of the cordelette to other anchor point; **b,** knot the resulting six strands together, here with a figure eight, to create a power point.*

strength. To mitigate this problem, climbers often use a cordelette, a loop made from about 20 feet (6 meters) of 7- to 8-millimeter nylon accessory cord or from small-diameter, high-strength cord made of a material such as Spectra or Dyneema. First, double the cordelette to half its length, then gather the resulting eight strands in a bight and tie them to create a power point with the loop (fig. 10-18), as you would for a double-length runner.

If the power point must be extended a little farther from the anchor points, start by clipping one bight of the cordelette in to one anchor point and both strands of the cordelette to the other anchor point (fig. 10-19a), then gather the resulting six strands in a bight and tie them to create the power point (fig. 10-19b).

Another increasingly popular technique for creating a statically equalized anchor uses a simple girth hitch. Aside from being quick to set up, this anchor is also easy to untie after it has been loaded and is easy to adjust to equalize force distribution. Clip the runner or cordelette to the two anchor points as described above for Figures 10-17 and 10-18, but rather than tying a knot with the gathered ends, pass the ends through, then around, a locking carabiner (fig. 10-20a) to create a girth hitch (fig. 10-20b). This locking carabiner itself becomes the power point; additional locking carabiners used for belaying and tethers are clipped directly to the power-point carabiner (fig. 10-20c).

Three or more anchor points. To equalize three or more anchor points, clip the cordelette in to each anchor point's carabiner and pull down the top segments between the anchor points (fig. 10-21a). Join the top segments with the bottom segment of the cordelette by gripping the resulting three loops (fig. 10-21b) and connecting a locking carabiner to all of them; shift the carabiner around while you gather the strands together to even out the tension in all strands as best you can. Then, while pulling in the anticipated direction of force, tie all segments together in an overhand or figure-eight knot (fig. 10-21c).

Either knot is acceptable; the overhand requires less cord than the figure eight, but it will be harder to untie if it is heavily loaded. Pull on the carabiner at the end loop (power point) to make sure all legs are weighted. To equalize the girth-hitch anchor described above with three or more anchor points, use all gathered strands to form the girth hitch.

The shelf. In either a two-point or three-point anchor, the end loop (the power point or master point) created by the overhand or figure-eight knot is the main attachment point to the belay anchor. More connection points, such as for a second climber to clip in to on arrival at the belay

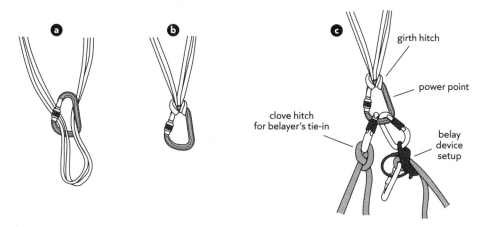

Fig. 10-20. *Girth-hitch anchor:* **a,** *gather individual legs of cordelette or runner and pass ends through locking carabiner;* **b,** *pass all strands around carabiner, forming a girth hitch around the power-point carabiner;* **c,** *clip additional locking carabiners directly to the power-point carabiner.*

10

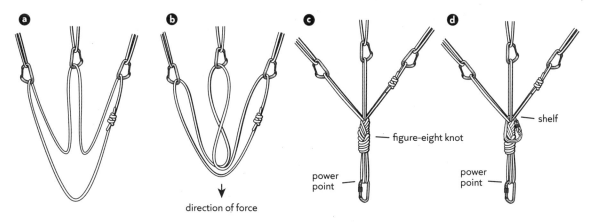

Fig. 10-21. *Static equalization of three anchor points with cordelette:* **a,** *clip in to each of three anchor-point carabiners and pull down top segments between anchor points;* **b,** *gather strands together at an even length;* **c,** *clip resulting three loops to a locking carabiner and tie all six strands in an overhand or figure-eight knot to create a power point;* **d,** *clip another locking carabiner in to the shelf.*

station, can be made by creating a "shelf" consisting of all anchor placements above the power point: clip a carabiner to one strand coming from each of the anchor points, as in Figure 10-20d. It is very important to clip only *one* strand from each anchor point.

A shelf does not exist in an anchor system unless each anchor point has two strands. This shelf can simplify clipping in to or unclipping from a loaded anchor and can avoid much clutter and confusion. When using this method, do not directly load the shelf without having at least one

carabiner also clipped to the anchor's power point, as shown in Figure 10-21d, to prevent the power point's knot from rolling and possibly releasing.

Uneven distribution of forces in static equalization. Load-testing of cordelettes shows that the even distribution of forces is not usually achieved using three anchor points: even under ideal circumstances—three anchor placements that are symmetrically arranged—the middle leg may be subjected to twice the load of the two side legs (fig. 10-22a). Asymmetrical configurations tend to primarily load the

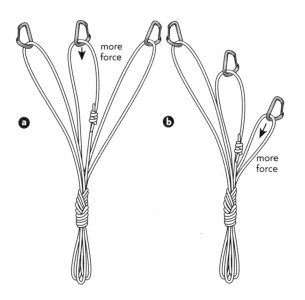

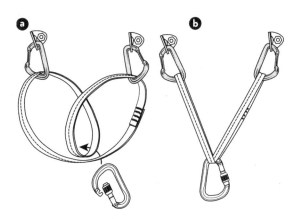

Fig. 10-22. *Uneven distribution of forces in static equalization: a, in a symmetrical anchor, pull appears equal on both side strands, but middle strand may be subjected to twice their load; b, in an asymmetrical anchor, the load is shifted to one side—now the lowest anchor point is subjected to higher loads than the two longer legs.*

Fig. 10-23. *Sliding X dynamically equalized anchor; a, grasp top segment of runner between two anchor points and put a half twist in it, making an X and forming a loop; b, clip the loop and the bottom segment of the runner together with a locking pearabiner, making that carabiner the power point.*

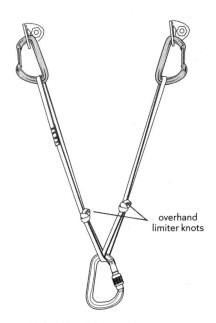

Fig. 10-24. *Sliding X with limiter knots.*

two legs closest to the direction of pull. As the different legs become more uneven in length (common when an anchor is rigged in a vertical crack), the lowest leg is subjected to much higher loads than the longer legs (fig. 10-22b) due to the greater elongation that occurs with longer sections. The effects of unevenly rigged configurations can be reduced by extending the individual placements with low-stretch runners to equalize the length of the elastic cordelette legs. Any slack in a leg of the cordelette means that it supports negligible weight and is not equalized.

Dynamic Equalization

Dynamic equalization is intended to allow the anchor to react to changing load direction and to redistribute any force among all the components. This section discusses a few methods of dynamic equalization.

Sliding X. Two-point equalizing is the simplest example of dynamic equalization. Clip a runner in to the two anchor carabiners. Grasp the top segment between the two anchor points and put a half twist in it, making an X and forming a loop (fig. 10-23a). Then clip the loop and the bottom segment together with a locking carabiner, which becomes the power point (fig. 10-23b). Without that essential loop in the runner, if one anchor point fails, the runner will simply slip through the carabiner, leaving the rope unanchored. With a longer runner, the sliding X can work well to equalize more than two anchor points.

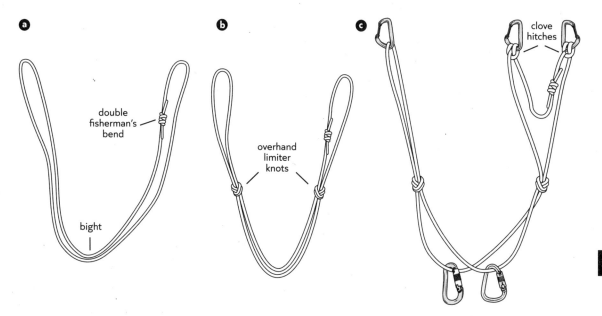

Fig. 10-25. *Dynamic equalization with an equalette:* **a,** *grab a bight of cord to form a two-stranded* ∪, *with the cord's fisherman's bend slightly offset from one end of the loop;* **b,** *tie overhand limiter knots on both sides, creating an isolated center section with two longer side loops;* **c,** *connect the side loops to one or more anchor components, and clip in to the central section with two carabiners, one per strand. Here, the right-hand loop is connected to two anchors and equalized with clove hitches.*

The sliding X method depends on the carabiner attachment sliding freely along the runner to self-equalize as the direction of pull changes. Take care in rigging this system to minimize friction between the sliding carabiner and the X. Newer, thinner sewn runners work better with this method than bulky ⁹⁄₁₆-inch or wider webbing. Larger-diameter carabiners like pearabiners reduce friction.

Dynamic equalization always conflicts with the "No Extension" principle described in the "SERENE Anchor Systems" sidebar below. To mitigate, either use shorter slings or tie limiter knots (usually overhand knots) in the runner (fig. 10-24). Limiter knots minimize the length the anchor can extend as well as limit the extent to which the anchor is equalized. But without such limiter knots, if one anchor point fails, the resulting anchor extension can magnify the impact force on the remaining anchor points, increasing the risk of catastrophic failure.

Equalettes. To overcome the disadvantages of friction and elongation associated with the sliding X and with the potentially poor static equalization of a cordelette, the equalette was developed to combine elements from both the sliding X and the cordelette. Equalettes are normally constructed from 20 feet (6 meters) of 7-millimeter nylon or smaller-diameter high-strength cord. Tie the cord into a loop with a double or triple fisherman's bend, as appropriate to the material.

Grab a bight to form a double-stranded ∪, with the fisherman's bend slightly offset from one end of the loop (fig. 10-25a), then tie overhand limiter knots on both sides of the ∪ to create a center section about 10 inches (25 centimeters) long (fig. 10-25b). As with the sliding X, the limiter knots would keep extension to a reasonable minimum if one side were to fail.

Now connect each end to one or more anchor components. To connect multiple components on one side, use clove hitches to equalize the strands (fig. 10-25c). Once the anchor is constructed, clip in to the bottom center section of the equalette, preferably using two locking carabiners, one for each of the two central strands, as shown in Figure 10-25c. If you use one carabiner, put a half twist in one of the strands, just as with the sliding X, in case one side of the equalette fails.

Though it may seem complicated at first, the equalette addresses the disadvantages of static and dynamic systems, and it does not add much complexity or time to anchor setups.

The quad. When an equalette is tied with a doubled-over cord, it is known as a quad. Start with a long cordelette that

SERENE ANCHOR SYSTEMS

When evaluating an anchor system, follow this simple yet highly effective set of principles. SERENE stands for Solid, Efficient, Redundant, Equalized, and No Extension. Strive to fulfill these requirements, but note that the principles of "Equalized" and "No Extension" conflict. Climbers must make compromises and understand the potential consequences.

- **Solid.** Each individual component in the system should be as strong as it can be, given the constraints of the anchor location and available equipment.

- **Efficient.** An anchor system should be built and dismantled in a timely manner and should not make use of excessive amounts of equipment.

- **Redundant.** Failure of any single component of the anchor should not result in catastrophic failure of the entire system.

- **Equalized.** Use a rigging method that tries to equally distribute the load among the various individual anchor points, which greatly increases the reliability of each part of the system.

- **No Extension.** Minimize the possibility that failure of one component in the system will shift and cause the anchor to suddenly extend, subjecting the remaining components to dangerously high impact forces.

has been tied into a loop with a double or triple fisherman's bend. Create a half twist at the loop's midpoint to make two equal loops (fig. 10-26a). With the fisherman's bend slightly offset from the end of the loops, tie overhand limiter knots on both sides of the U. Clip each double-stranded loop end to an anchor carabiner (fig. 10-26b).

Once the anchor is constructed, clip carabiners in to the center section of the quad between the limiter knots, capturing two or three of the four strands. Figure 10-26b and c shows a belayer's clove-hitch tie-in and a belay device setup. It is important not to clip a single strand or all four strands—neither of these techniques provides a redundant connection to the anchor.

Although quads are popular for anchors with two solid placements, such as at a bolted station on a sport climb, they can be extended to three or four placements by clipping the legs on each end (fig. 10-26c). When climbers tackle a route with bolted anchors, they often prebuild quads and carry them as part of the rack. Building the anchor at the next bolted station is then as simple as clipping the prebuilt quad to the hangers.

TYING IN TO THE BELAY ANCHOR

The best way for the belayer to connect to the anchor is to use the first few feet of rope coming from the tie-in at the belayer's harness to make a clove hitch and clip it in to the anchor's power point or shelf with a locking carabiner (see Figures 10-20c and 10-26 b and c). This approach ensures that there will be a dynamic link between the belayer and anchor.

Climbers may instead connect to the anchor using runners or commercially made personal anchors, though there are hazards associated with this practice. Runners and personal anchors usually do not stretch much nor react dynamically under load, so if a climber falls from above the anchor, they may experience a high-factor fall, and even short falls on relatively static materials can generate extremely high impact forces. Although runners and carabiners are quite strong, they have both failed under these circumstances. An even bigger risk in the case of a high-factor fall is the high impact force on the climber's body. If you choose to use a personal anchor for this purpose, keep the slack minimal, and do not climb above the anchor.

Position and Stance

When choosing a belay position, think through what could go wrong in case of a fall. Plan for worst-case scenarios and make sure that the anchor will catch a fall before a belayer's stance is affected, which would then entail the very real possibility that the belayer could lose control of the rope.

BELAYING A LEADER OR TOP-ROPE CLIMBER

When belaying a leader or a top-rope climber, belay directly off the harness so that you can use your hands and arms to manage the rope and brake the instant a climber falls. It is best to stand close to the rock, with a stable bent-knee athletic stance. No matter which direction you face, stay in line with the anchor and the anticipated direction of pull. Otherwise a fall will spin you into an awkward position. A poorly anchored belayer could be pulled upward into rocks, ledges, or other objects in the way.

If the belay is anchored, tie in to the anchor at most at an arm's length away, so that the belayer can still reach the anchor if their tie-in is pulled tight by a fall. At the same time, leave a little room for the brake hand, as well as a little slack in the rope should the belayer need to move their body to give the climber a soft catch.

When belaying a leader, there are many advantages to facing in toward the mountain. Facing in usually allows the belayer to watch their partner climb, anticipate the

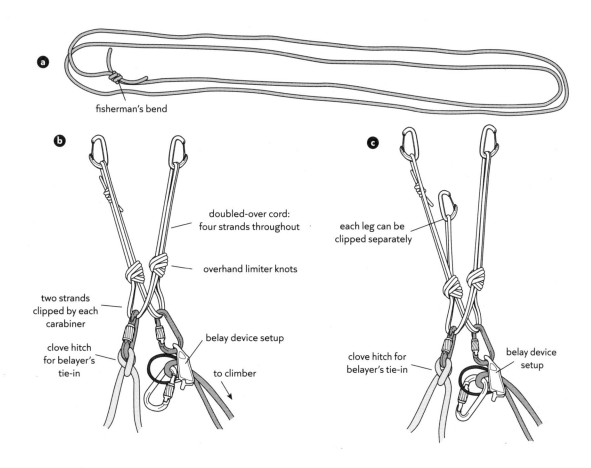

10

Fig. 10-26. *Quad anchor: **a,** doubled-over cordelette; **b,** two-piece quad anchor with belayer's and belay device carabiners each clipped to two strands; **c,** quads can also be built with three or four pieces of pro by clipping the individual strands on each leg of the quad.*

climber's movements, and pay out or take in rope more efficiently (see Rope Handling, below). Watching how their partner moves through difficult sections may also help the belayer negotiate any cruxes when it is time for them to climb. The belayer is also more likely to see rockfall early and take cover. And this is the best position from which to see when a leader starts to fall, so the belayer can brace quickly and go into the braking position. Being able to anticipate a leader's fall is a particular advantage when the first piece of protection is low and the force of the fall may pull the belayer into the rock.

Of course, these advantages evaporate when belaying in an alcove with a roof or bulge overhead. In this situation, it is probably much better to face out so a leader fall will not spin the belayer around.

When belaying a leader, the most likely direction of pull in the case of a leader fall is upward. But in the severe situation in which the leader falls past the anchor before placing the first piece of protection (a factor 2 fall), the force is downward. A belayer with a fairly long attachment to an anchor at about waist height or lower—very commonly seen—is not prepared to stop an unprotected leader fall. If the belayer is standing on a ledge and the partner falls past the belayer, the downward force builds quickly beyond the point that the belay stance can hold. The belayer would then be pulled violently off the ledge or driven sharply down onto it, with almost certain loss of control of the belay and probable injuries. To prevent this possibility, attach tightly to an anchor above waist level so that you cannot be pulled down more than a few inches.

Labels within figure:

a — fisherman's bend

b — doubled-over cord: four strands throughout; overhand limiter knots; two strands clipped by each carabiner; clove hitch for belayer's tie-in; belay device setup; to climber

c — each leg can be clipped separately; clove hitch for belayer's tie-in; belay device setup

BELAYING A FOLLOWER

A direct belay from the anchor is preferred in most cases when belaying a follower. Though belaying off the harness was once traditional, belaying off the anchor is now considered a standard practice. Harness belays and redirects can serve as alternatives in some situations.

Belaying Off the Anchor

The preferred method of belaying a follower is directly off the anchor, using a belay device or munter hitch, sometimes also called a direct belay. One big advantage of this method is that the belayer is out of the system and therefore not subject to the forces created by a fall and less likely to be injured or lose control of the belay. When something goes wrong, it is also easy for the belayer to "escape" (see Escaping the Belay, below). This method is also very useful if the follower is less experienced and needs to be coached from above.

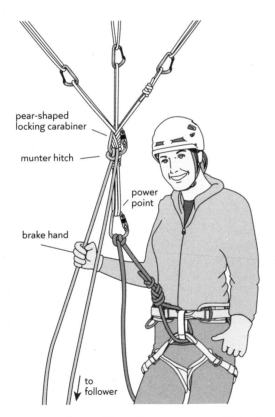

pear-shaped
locking carabiner

munter hitch

power
point

brake hand

to
follower

Fig. 10-27. *Belaying off the anchor using a munter hitch: clip the munter's locking carabiner to the anchor shelf.*

A common method for a direct belay is to use an assisted-braking belay device, or an auto-locking belay device in its auto-locking mode, clipped directly in to the anchor, as shown in Figure 10-7. Manufacturers use different terminologies for auto-locking mode (for instance, Black Diamond calls it "guide mode"); consult the manufacturer's instructions. An alternative method for a direct belay is to belay with a munter hitch on the anchor (fig. 10-27). This approach does not require any specialized equipment, but it may introduce twists in the rope.

Do not use a regular non-auto-locking belay device to belay directly off the anchor. To arrest a fall in such a setup, the belayer would have to awkwardly push the brake hand away from the body and behind the device to separate the rope strands by the minimum of 90 degrees, making for a comparatively weak brake-hand grip.

Regardless of the method used to belay off the anchor, position the tie-in so that the anchor's power point is at roughly shoulder level when weighted by the belayer. This way, the belayer has enough work space between the tie-in and anchor to make pulling and coiling the rope easier. If the power point is too low, consider using the anchor's shelf if there is one.

Belaying Off the Harness

The traditional way to belay a second has been off the harness—that is, the belay device is clipped directly to the belay loop on the harness (fig. 10-28). The advantage is that the belayer can use body movement to provide a soft belay, which is useful when the anchor is less than ideal. However, this method does not work very well if the terrain below is vertical, because the follower's weight will pull the belayer to the fall line. When that happens, the belayer could be pulled out of the belay stance and end up being suspended awkwardly, unable to get the brake hand back into the braking position. Most belay device manufacturers do not recommend belaying the second off the harness.

Belaying Off the Harness with a Redirect

An improvement over belaying off the harness is to redirect the rope through a carabiner above the belayer's harness (fig. 10-29). Consider using the strongest point in the anchor system for redirection, usually the power point or anchor shelf. Once the belay is redirected, the fall force would come from above instead of below, and the belayer would be in a more comfortable position when holding a fall.

When the belayer catches the fall, however, the force on the redirect carabiner will be twice the body weight of the follower (not considering friction) due to the pulley

Fig. 10-28. *Belaying a follower off the harness.*

Fig. 10-29. *Belaying a follower off the harness with a redirect: clip a carabiner to anchor power point.*

effect. Be aware of the multiplied force when choosing this method. However, the force multiplication is irrelevant in a hanging belay, wherein the weight of the belayer is already on the anchor.

Rope Handling

In addition to stopping a fall, a belayer needs to maintain and adjust tension on the rope. Belayers must prevent excess slack, anticipate the climber's movements and rope needs, let out rope as the climber moves up or clips in to protection, take rope in as needed, and manage the accumulating rope. The techniques below are described in the context of belaying the leader off the harness, but they can easily be modified for other belay methods. Practice until you learn to quickly take in or let out rope with the guide hand as needed while never removing the brake hand from the rope.

ADJUSTING SLACK

Keeping enough slack in the rope during a belay is a skill that requires practice. Too much slack results in a longer fall and increases the impact force and risk of the climber

getting injured (fig. 10-30a). Too much slack also makes it hard for the belayer to feel the rope movement and needs of the climber.

Too little slack, on the other hand, can impede the climber's movement and balance. A skilled belayer uses the guide hand to be aware of how much slack is in the rope. Ideally, when belaying a follower, there is almost no slack in the rope, but at the same time, the rope should not be taut, especially on a traverse when balance is crucial.

ANTICIPATING ROPE NEEDS

To minimize the distance they could fall, leaders preparing to make difficult moves often place protection well above their harness tie-in and clip in to that protection before moving up. In these cases, the leader needs more slack, and the direction of rope movement will reverse twice. After letting out rope so the leader can make the clip, the belayer needs to take in slack as the climber moves up to the protection. The belayer then pays out rope again once the climber moves past the protection and uses up most of the slack. These transitions call for

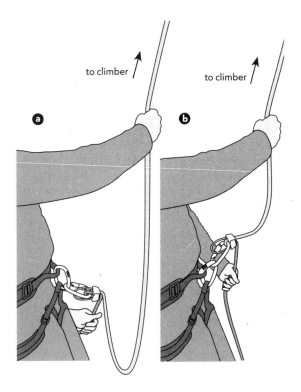

to climber

to climber

a

b

Fig. 10-30. *Rope slack: **a,** too much; **b,** just right.*

extra attention, especially because they tend to happen at the most difficult spots on a route. The belayer needs to remain alert, keeping in mind that a leader is momentarily subject to a longer fall when pulling up rope to clip in above waist level.

When belaying a leader, an alert belayer keeps just a little slack in the system (fig. 10-30b) and responds immediately to the leader's advance by paying out more rope. The belayer needs to be ready to transition between paying out rope and pulling in slack when the leader clips in to protection. Any friction applied by the belayer is multiplied; if a leader says that rope drag is a problem, keep about a foot or so (a third of a meter) of slack in the rope and do everything possible to eliminate any pull.

If there is a lot of friction in the system, the belayer may not even realize that a climber has fallen. If it is impossible to communicate with the climber, the belayer can find out by letting out a few inches of rope. If the same tension remains, then the belayer is probably holding the climber's weight.

MANAGING THE ROPE

Before belaying a leader, carefully flake out the rope (see Chapter 8, Essential Climbing Equipment), shaking out unwanted twists and stacking the rope on the ground with the climber's end on top. Ensure that the rope does not interfere with the leader at the start of the climb or get caught around their foot or ankle higher up on the route. A belayer needs to monitor and adjust slack while a climber is leading. Preparing the rope beforehand and managing it while climbing are essential.

When belaying a follower up to the belay station, either stack the rope on the ground or coil it. To create a butterfly coil, drape loops of rope across the belayer's anchor tie-in as the follower climbs up (fig. 10-31a). It helps to keep the tie-in under a little tension even if it is not a hanging belay. If the belayer stacks the rope on the ground, make sure the pile has a small footprint and is not tangled with rock flakes or tree branches (fig. 10-31b).

If the climbing team is swapping leads—that is, the follower will become the new leader on the next pitch—the belayer does not need to do anything with the rope before the new leader starts the next pitch. The leader's end is already on the top, and the rope should be nicely piled or coiled for the next pitch.

However, if the climbing team is leading in blocks—that is, the climber who led the last pitch will lead the next—the belayer must reverse the rope. If the rope is butterfly-coiled, grab the middle of the coil and flip it onto the follower's anchor tie-in. Reversing the rope is a little more difficult if the rope is stacked in a pile. The belayer can carefully flip the whole pile like a pancake, but if that fails, the whole rope must be reflaked, which is a time-consuming task.

Communication

Effective and efficient communication is key to efficient ascents with minimal risk. Relying on a set of standardized concise commands can tremendously reduce confusion and save time and hassle. Make sure everyone in the climbing party agrees on the commands before they start climbing, especially if any of the climbers are new to the sport or have not climbed together before. The commands in Table 10-1 below have been developed to produce a distinctive pattern, and they are used universally, even among non-English-speaking climbers.

As the climber and belayer get farther apart, they may begin to have difficulty hearing each other. It is often

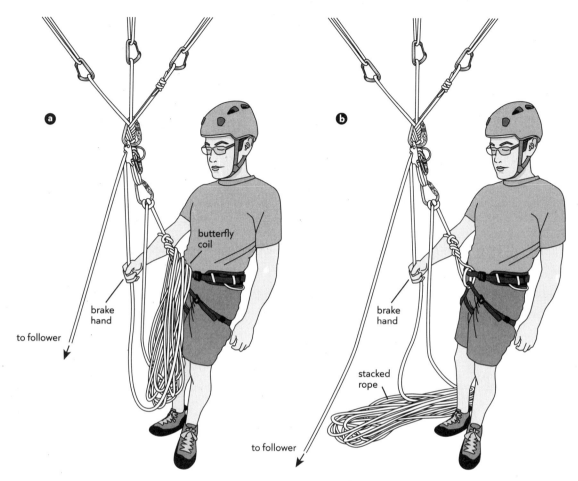

Fig. 10-31. *Managing rope at the belay:* **a,** *butterfly coils laid across belayer's anchor tie-in;* **b,** *stacking rope on the ground.*

impossible to communicate in full sentences, and sometimes the first syllable is not heard. Shout as loudly as possible and draw out the syllables, especially if there are echoes. In a crowded area, clearly preface commands with your partner's name to avoid confusion about who is being safely belayed or lowered, who is off belay, et cetera. Using climbers' names also has the advantage of making them pause on hearing their name, thus improving your chances of communicating. Sometimes climbers may rely on a third party to relay their commands.

Verbal communication often becomes impossible because of weather, obstructions, or distance. In such cases, some people have suggested tugging on the rope to communicate. However, there is no universal protocol for rope signals. If verbal communication is impeded, conditions and distance may interfere with rope tugs as well. Some climbers use handheld two-way radios for communication (see Chapter 5, Navigation and Communication). Be aware that battery life is shorter in cold conditions. If batteries run out, make sure you have alternative means of communication.

Always use positive commands instead of negative ones. For example, when there is too much slack in the rope, use "Up rope" instead of "Too muck slack," because the latter can be misheard or mistakenly interpreted as "Slack," the opposite of what you mean. Always try to stick to the standard commands listed in Table 10-1, because everyone can understand them. The rule of thumb is to keep it simple.

COMMON CLIMBING COMMANDS

Specific actions are associated with particular commands that the belayer and follower use.

Slack is especially useful to a climber who is leading or traversing.

Watch me is used when the climber is about to make some difficult moves.

Clipping warns the belayer that the leader is about to pull up rope to clip, meaning the belayer needs to feed rope out. If the protection is above the leader's waist, the rope will first travel away from the belayer, as they pay out enough slack for the leader to clip, then back toward the belayer, and then away again as the leader continues upward.

Half rope gives the leader a sense of the length of the route.

X feet (X meters) is used in a multipitch scenario to help the leader decide when and where to build an anchor. Outside of the United States, people usually use meters (a meter is roughly 3 feet).

TABLE 10-1. COMMANDS COMMONLY USED IN CLIMBING		
COMMAND	**SAID BY**	**MEANING**
"On belay?"	Climber	Do you have me on belay? Are you ready to catch my fall?
"Belay on."	Belayer	Yes, I have you on belay (can be a response to "On belay?").
"Climbing."	Climber	I'm about to climb.
"Climb on."	Belayer	Go ahead and climb (response to "Climbing").
"Off belay."	Climber	I'm safe, either on the ground or attached to an anchor. Please take the rope out of the belay device.
"Belay off."	Belayer	You are no longer on belay (response to "Off belay").
"Take."	Climber	Pull up all the slack in the rope and I'm going to put my weight on it.
"Got you."	Belayer	All slack has been pulled in. Go ahead and lean on the rope (response to "Take").
"Lower me" or "Lower."	Climber	I have finished climbing. Please lower me to the ground. Or I have finished cleaning this piece of protection. Continue lowering me.
"Lowering."	Belayer	I'm starting to lower you (response to "Lower me").
"Stop."	Climber	Pause the lower so I can clean protection.
"That's me."	Follower	You have taken in all the slack in the rope. The resistance to your pull is my body.
"Slack."	Climber	Give me some slack. The rope is too tight.
"Up rope."	Climber	Pull up some slack. The rope has too much slack.
"Watch me."	Climber	Give me an attentive belay. I may fall.
"Falling!"	Climber	I'm falling. Catch my fall.
"Rope!"	Anyone	I'm tossing a rope in preparation to rappel, or pulling a rope, and it is about to fall.
"Rock!" or "Ice!"	Anyone	Rock, ice, or other objects are falling. Take cover, everyone!
"Clipping."	Leader	I'm about to clip the rope in to a piece of protection.
"Half rope."	Belayer	You have led half the length of the rope.
"X feet" or "X meters."	Belayer	You have X feet (X meters) of rope left.
"On rappel!"	Anyone	I'm set up to rappel and about to start descending.

EXAMPLES OF HOW TO USE CLIMBING COMMANDS

Below, the recommended commands in Table 10-1 are configured for exchanges in two different climbing scenarios.

Single-Pitch Climb

In this scenario, the belayer is belaying a climber who is either leading or top-roping. This exchange takes place after both parties have done the safety check (see Chapter 9, Basics of Climbing).

CLIMBER: "On belay?"
BELAYER: "Belay on."
CLIMBER: "Climbing."
BELAYER: "Climb on."

The climber climbs to the top. If the climber is leading, they set up the top-rope anchor and clip the rope in to the anchor. Now the climber is ready to weight the rope and be lowered.

CLIMBER: "Take."
BELAYER: "Got you."
CLIMBER: "Lower me."
BELAYER: "Lowering."

The belayer lowers the climber to the ground.

CLIMBER: "Off belay."
BELAYER: "Belay off."

If the leader cleans the protection on the way down, they may also ask the belayer to pause at each protection point so they can remove them. The commands are "Stop" for pausing and "Lower" for resuming.

Multipitch Climb

In this scenario, the follower belays the leader. When the leader gets to the top of a pitch, they set up an anchor and belay the follower up (the follower and leader may or may not exchange roles for the next pitch). This exchange takes place at the start of the pitch.

LEADER: "On belay?"
FOLLOWER: "Belay on."
LEADER: "Climbing."
FOLLOWER: "Climb on."

The leader arrives at the top of the first pitch, sets up an anchor, and secures themself to the anchor.

LEADER: "Off belay."
FOLLOWER: "Belay off."

The leader pulls the rope, and the follower gets ready to follow the pitch. As the rope becomes taut, they communicate:

FOLLOWER: "That's me!"
LEADER: "Belay on."

The follower removes the previous anchor, then pauses to alert the leader before ascending.

FOLLOWER: "Climbing."
LEADER: "Climb on."

After climbing the pitch, cleaning protection on the way up, the follower arrives at the belay station and secures themself to the anchor.

FOLLOWER: "Off belay."
LEADER: "Belay off."

Escaping the Belay

Most climbers hope they will never have to tie off and escape the belay to help an injured partner (or themselves). If a climbing partner is seriously injured and other climbers are nearby, it is usually best to let them help while you continue to belay. By staying in place, you could also help in raising or lowering the victim. But if two climbers are alone, the belayer may need to tie off the climbing rope so that they can investigate, help the injured partner, or go for help. Escaping the belay is the first step of many rescue scenarios. The goal is to connect the load directly to the anchor so that the belayer can leave the system.

A device-mule knot with an overhand backup knot or a munter-mule-overhand (MMO) knot is used in transferring a live load. Such a knot is a load-releasing or releasable

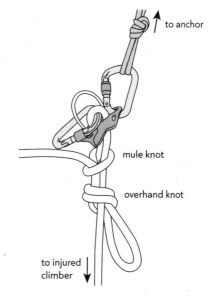

Fig. 10-32. *Escaping a belay off the anchor: tie off below autolocking belay device with mule knot and overhand knot.*

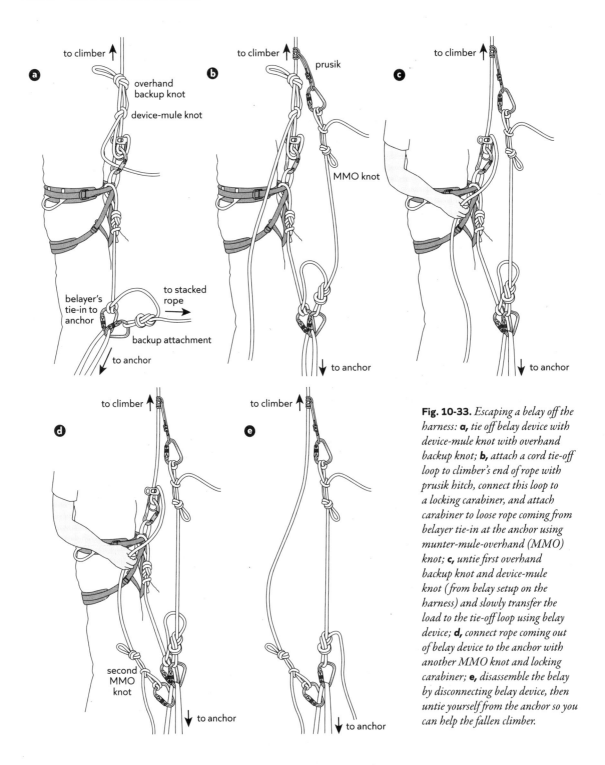

a, to climber
overhand
backup knot
device-mule knot
belayer's
tie-in to
anchor
to stacked
rope
backup attachment
to anchor

b, to climber
prusik
MMO knot
to anchor

c, to climber
to anchor

d, to climber
second
MMO
knot
to anchor

e, to climber
to anchor

Fig. 10-33. *Escaping a belay off the harness:* **a,** *tie off belay device with device-mule knot with overhand backup knot;* **b,** *attach a cord tie-off loop to climber's end of rope with prusik hitch, connect this loop to a locking carabiner, and attach carabiner to loose rope coming from belayer tie-in at the anchor using munter-mule-overhand (MMO) knot;* **c,** *untie first overhand backup knot and device-mule knot (from belay setup on the harness) and slowly transfer the load to the tie-off loop using belay device;* **d,** *connect rope coming out of belay device to the anchor with another MMO knot and locking carabiner;* **e,** *disassemble the belay by disconnecting belay device, then untie yourself from the anchor so you can help the fallen climber.*

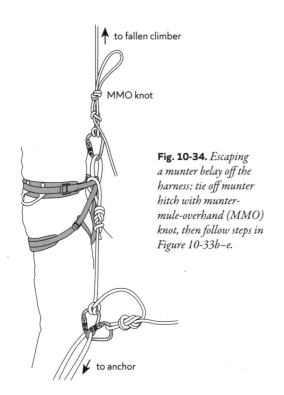

to fallen climber

MMO knot

to anchor

Fig. 10-34. *Escaping a munter belay off the harness: tie off munter hitch with munter-mule-overhand (MMO) knot, then follow steps in Figure 10-33b–e.*

is now in line with the load. Use your free hand to tie a device-mule knot (see Mule Knot in Chapter 8) with an overhand backup knot (fig. 10-33a). Both of the belayer's hands are now free.

The next steps involve transferring the climber's weight to the anchor so the belayer can get out of the system. First, attach a cord tie-off loop or hero loop to the climber's end of the rope with a prusik hitch and connect this loop to a locking carabiner. Then attach this locking carabiner to the loose rope coming from the belayer's tie-in at the anchor using a munter hitch with a mule knot, backing it up with an overhand knot—this entire knot is called a munter-mule-overhand, or MMO, knot (fig. 10-33b; see also Figure 8-21 in Chapter 8). Now reestablish a brake hand on the braking strand coming from the belay device and untie the first overhand backup knot and device-mule knot (from the belay setup on the harness), then slowly transfer the load to the tie-off loop by lowering the climber a few inches (fig. 10-33c).

The fallen climber's weight is now secured to the anchor, but on the potentially weak tie-off loop. Connect the rope from the fallen climber to the anchor with another MMO knot as a backup, leaving just enough slack to disassemble the belay (fig. 10-33d). To disassemble the belay, disconnect the belay device from the system, and untie from the anchor (fig. 10-33e).

FROM A MUNTER BELAY OFF THE HARNESS

The steps involved when belaying with a munter hitch attached to the harness are very similar to the preceding section, except for the first step. To free your hands, with the brake hand still holding the rope, tie a munter-mule with an overhand backup, or MMO, knot (fig. 10-34). The rest of the steps are exactly the same as for Figure 10-33.

knot. Releasable knots are extremely helpful in a rescue scenario because the belayer should always assume that the fallen climber is incapacitated and cannot release their load from the rope, even momentarily. This technique provides the flexibility needed later to either lower the fallen climber using the belay device or munter hitch, or rig a raising system.

FROM A BELAY OFF THE ANCHOR

When you are belaying off the anchor (a direct belay) with an assisted-braking belay device, an auto-locking belay device, or a munter hitch, the fallen climber's weight is already on the anchor. The only thing you need to do is free your brake hand. To do so, use your guide hand to tie a mule knot with the braking strand while still holding on to the braking strand with your brake hand, then back up the mule knot with an overhand knot (fig. 10-32).

FROM A DEVICE BELAY OFF THE HARNESS

When belaying from the harness with a belay device, the fallen climber's weight is directly on the belayer. Escaping the belay is more complicated. The first step is to free the belayer's hands. With the brake hand still holding the rope, stick a couple fingers of your guide hand through the belay carabiner and pull a bight of rope over so that now your guide hand becomes the brake hand. The braking strand

Securing the Freedom of the Hills

Belaying and belay anchor setup are the fundamental skills of technical climbing. Practice belaying often, alternating between using your right hand and left hand as the brake hand. Study and practice anchor techniques. There are many different ways of anchoring yourself. Always use the SERENE principles to evaluate your anchors.

Being proficient with belay technique and anchor setup helps climbers become solid team partners. These methods are also related to skills required for rappelling. Once climbers become proficient in belay skills, they will have more confidence when it comes to rappel. Overall, solid skills in belaying and anchor setup will help climbers secure the freedom of the hills.

CHAPTER 11

RAPPELLING

Indispensable to technical climbing, rappelling uses friction to control a climber's rate of descent on an anchored rope. Climbers sometimes overlook the inherent risks of rappelling, which can make it one of the most dangerous aspects of climbing. Proper technique is vital; without it, it can be a long fall to the ground.

In the words of climber Ed Viesturs, "Getting to the top is optional; getting down is mandatory." Rappelling requires a trustworthy anchor, rope, and proper technique. If any element of this system fails, the result will likely be catastrophic. Unlike the belay system—a setup that reacts to impact forces only *if* a fall occurs on ascents—the rappel system absorbs the forces exerted on it the entire time it is used. There is no room for error when setting up or using it. The annual publication *Accidents in North American Climbing* regularly notes that most rappelling accidents are preventable with simple checks, with common causes of rappel system failure being (1) uneven rope lengths, (2) an inadequate anchor system, and (3) an inadequate rappel backup.

The best way to avoid a rappelling accident may be to descend another way. For instance, in single-pitch climbs with bolted anchors, lowering from the permanent anchors has become a more popular way to clean and descend when finished with a route (see Chapter 12, Sport Climbing and Technique). On alpine climbs, a team may also be able to down-climb instead. Party size and experience, timing, weather, terrain, and available equipment are all factors in deciding whether to rappel.

Down-climbing, when possible, can be faster and pose a lower risk than rappelling. It is particularly attractive in terrain rated Class 4 and below, where slope angle and loose rocks increase the likelihood of getting a rope stuck or pulling rocks down while rappelling or retrieving the rope. When members of a climbing team have varying skill levels, it may be appropriate to set up a down-climbing hand line for less experienced climbers to hold or to connect to with a prusik (see Hand Line in Chapter 9, Basics of Climbing). If the team chooses to rappel, risk management and efficiency are imperative; this chapter describes best practices to ensure risk-averse, efficient rappels.

The Rappel System

A rappel system has five basic elements: an anchor, a rope, a rappel method for applying friction to the rope, the person rappelling, and their personal anchor attaching them to the rappel anchor (fig. 11-1). Each element is equally and vitally important. Especially when you are cold, tired, hungry, or racing to beat nightfall, double-check that each element is in place, functioning properly, and connected to form an integrated system.

It is common practice for climbing partners to check each other's equipment setup, anchors, rope tie-ins, et cetera at the start of a climb (see "The Safety Check " sidebar in Chapter 9, Basics of Climbing). Routine partner checks while descending are equally important. If the last person to rappel cannot set up before the second-to-last person leaves the anchor (see Finishing the Rappel later in this chapter), the last climber must take extra measures to check, recheck, and test their own setup. Another important measure to confirm correct setup is to weight the rappel while staying connected to the anchor with a personal anchor.

Following a routine checklist before every rappel can help ensure that you do not miss anything. One example

KEY TOPICS

THE RAPPEL SYSTEM
SETTING UP RAPPEL ANCHORS
SETTING UP THE ROPE
RAPPEL METHODS
RAPPEL TECHNIQUE
SAFETY BACKUPS
FINISHING THE RAPPEL
MULTIPLE RAPPELS
EXPERIENCING THE FREEDOM OF THE HILLS

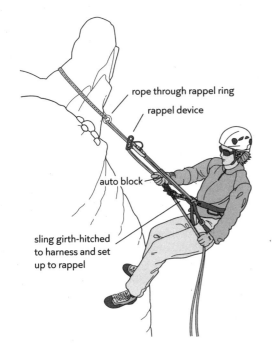

rope through rappel ring

rappel device

auto block

sling girth-hitched to harness and set up to rappel

Fig. 11-1. Components of mechanical rappel system: anchor (here, a rock horn), rope, rappel method for applying friction (here, a mechanical friction device), rappeller, and personal anchor. Each element is equally and vitally important. Here the climber is ready to rappel on extension.

of a coherent system involves starting with the rock or mountain and working outward toward the climber. Check that the anchor is attached to the rock and that the rope is attached to the anchor. Ensure that the rope is threaded properly through the rappel device (assuming a mechanical system is used—see Rappel Method, below). Then verify that the device is properly attached to the rappeller's harness and the harness is properly fastened to the rappeller. Each of these elements is briefly described below, followed by expanded sections in the rest of this chapter.

RAPPEL ANCHOR

The first element of the rappel system is the anchor: the point on the rock or mountain to which the system is attached. Carefully select the anchor for strength and reliability. Once you have begun to rappel, an error-free descent depends on the anchor's integrity; returning to the anchor to make adjustments can be problematic, if not impossible.

ROPE

The second element is the rope. Typically, the midpoint of the rope is looped through a metal ring (called a rappel ring) at the anchor, with the two ends of the rope hanging down the descent route. The rappeller descends both halves of the doubled rope and then retrieves it from below by pulling on one end.

Rappels shorter than half a rope length can be made with just one rope. Longer rappels need the extra length of two ropes tied together. Research a route beforehand to determine whether the rappels will require one or two ropes. If two ropes are required (often called a double-rope rappel), place the knot joining the ropes near the anchor, with the two equal-length ends hanging down the route. Using two ropes of different colors or patterns can help rappellers remember which rope to pull when retrieving the ropes.

RAPPEL METHOD

The third element is the method used to apply friction to the rope to control the rate of descent while the rappeller remains firmly attached to the rope. There are two types of systems for applying friction:

Mechanical system. The rope passes through a friction device attached to the harness.

Nonmechanical system. The rope is wrapped around the rappeller's body to provide the necessary friction.

In either case, the brake hand grasps the rope to control the amount of friction and the rate of descent. Be aware of atypical circumstances that could reduce the friction in the system, such as a heavier pack, a new, small-diameter rope, an icy rope, and so forth.

RAPPELLER

The most variable element in the rappel system is the rappeller, who must use proper technique both to attach into the rappel system and to descend with best practices. Transient circumstances, such as the rappeller's attitude and levels of fatigue, anxiety, attentiveness, skill, and training, as well as poor weather, impending darkness, and presence of rockfall or icefall, can affect the level of risk of a rappel.

RAPPELLER'S PERSONAL ANCHOR

The final element in the rappel system is the rappeller's personal anchor or leash, described in detail in Personal Anchors in Chapter 8, Essential Climbing Equipment.

11

Setting Up Rappel Anchors

A rappel anchor attaches the rappel system to the rock, snow, or ice that the climbers will descend. The rappel anchor must be strong enough to support the climbers' full weight as well as any additional forces that may occur, such as the dynamic force of bouncing or a sudden stop during the rappel.

Set up the anchor as close to the edge of the rappel route as possible, while ensuring it is solid, to afford the longest possible rappel and minimize the risk of the rope getting stuck or inducing rockfall when you retrieve it. Think about how the rope will run from the anchor to the ground or the next rappel anchor. Consider any sharp edges that might damage the rope when it is loaded. Choose a location that minimizes chances of the rope being pulled into a crack or otherwise hanging up on horns or other features when you retrieve it from below. And after the first rappeller is down, double-check the path the rope takes down the rappel route. In winter conditions, the rope can freeze in place if it cuts into snow or ice.

Rappel anchors can be fixed in place or use natural features or removable anchors built by the climbing party (see Selecting a Belay Anchor in Chapter 10, Belaying). For details on placing removable protection in rock, using natural features, and clipping bolted anchors, see Chapter 13, Rock Protection. For information on anchors in snow and ice, see the sections on anchors in Chapters 16, Basic Snow and Ice Climbing, and 17, Technical Snow and Ice Climbing.

A commonly found anchor consists of bolts with chains and rappel rings at the end of the chains (fig. 11-2). Use rappel rings *only* for rappelling—do *not* top-rope through them, which quickly wears out and weakens the rappel rings. The rappel rope can be run directly through the rappel rings. If the bolts at the anchor do not have chains and rappel rings, add webbing and rappel rings. For information on how to clean a bolted anchor with chains on single-pitch sport routes, see Chapter 12, Sport Climbing and Technique.

On popular alpine climbs, established rappel anchors will have slings, webbing, and/or cord, and perhaps rappel rings left behind by prior parties, with some parties adding a newer sling to back up the rappel station. Closely scrutinize these remnants for wear and damage (fig. 11-3):

- **Slings with significant wear, damage, nicks, et cetera.** Consider such slings risky, and remove them.
- **Slings that are bleached or washed-out in color or feel dry and stiff.** If slings exhibit such evidence of damage from ultraviolet light, do not use them. New slings have saturated color and are supple. Note that

UV exposure may weaken nylon and aramid fiber (Dyneema, Technora) as well, which are becoming more commonplace on anchors. Such damage may not cause any outwardly visible effects.

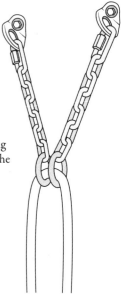

- **Slings routed around large boulders.** Do not trust existing slings unless you can inspect the entire length.
- **Slings not equipped with a rappel ring or carabiner.** Rappel ropes may have been pulled through such slings on previous rappels, which generates friction capable of weakening and eventually melting the slings.

Fig. 11-2. *Rappel anchor: rope threaded through rappel rings at ends of bolted chains.*

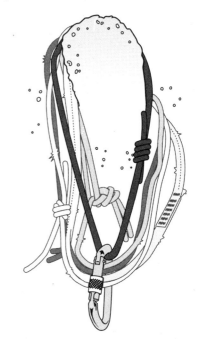

Fig. 11-3. *Anchor slings on a rock horn, with locking carabiner clipped to new sling as well as layers of old webbing and cord tied around the horn.*

Sometimes so many slings compose an anchor that total failure of every sling is unlikely. Still, a prudent rappeller might cut out a few of the oldest slings and add a new one before attaching the rope. If you are using more than one sling, make them equal in length to help distribute the load should one fail. If you are using any webbing or cord with knots, inspect them carefully before you weight them.

When two anchor points are used, it is common to run a separate sling from each point to the rappel ring. Adjust the slings so the force is comparable on each anchor point. Keep the V-angle between the two slings less than 60 degrees (fig. 11-4). For methods of equalizing anchor points, see Chapter 10, Belaying, and Figures 10-15 and 10-16 for an explanation of forces at work on anchors.

When climbing and belaying, climbers build strong and redundant anchors in case a climber falls. But when climbers rappel, their life depends on the loaded anchor from start to finish. It is essential to build rappel anchors that are SERENE: Solid, Efficient, Redundant, Equalized, and with No Extension (see the "SERENE Anchor Systems" sidebar in Chapter 10).

NATURAL ANCHORS

Often the best natural anchor is a healthy, live, large, well-rooted tree (see Natural Anchors in Chapter 10). The rope usually goes through a rappel ring attached to a runner (or sling) that is attached to the tree (fig. 11-5a). The rope could be looped directly around a tree without using a sling (fig. 11-5b), but this causes unnecessary damage to the tree and abrades the rope, soils it with tree resins, and makes it harder to retrieve.

Attaching a runner to an unquestionably stout tree branch rather than low on the trunk often makes it easier to retrieve the rope (the rope runs more directly to the person retrieving it) and reduces the risk of rockfall. However, connecting to a branch rather than the trunk puts more leverage on the tree; do not use this practice unless the trade-offs have been considered.

Another useful natural anchor is a rock horn slung with a runner. Never run the rope directly around a rock horn. Always inspect and test the horn carefully to be sure it is

11

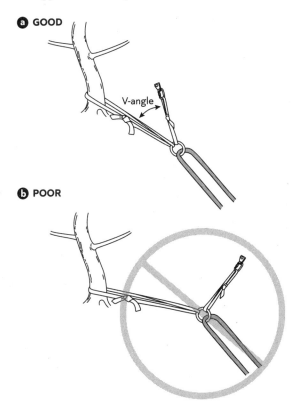

Fig. 11-4. *Two anchor points, with separate slings meeting at a rappel ring: **a**, a V-angle of less than 60 degrees between slings makes for an overall stronger anchor; **b**, an angle that is too wide significantly increases the load on each anchor point.*

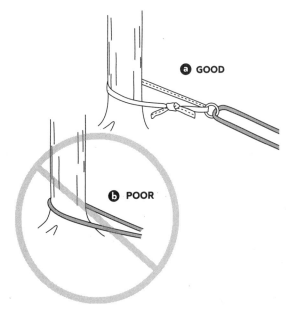

Fig. 11-5. *A tree as a natural rappel anchor: **a**, rappel rope through a rappel ring on a sling tied around tree (good); **b**, rappel rope looped directly around tree (poor).*

not in fact a loose rock masquerading as a solid feature. Place the runner as low as possible on the horn (fig. 11-6a) to guard against the dire possibility that a runner placed too high on the horn (fig. 11-6b) could slide up and come off the horn during a rappel (fig. 11-6c).

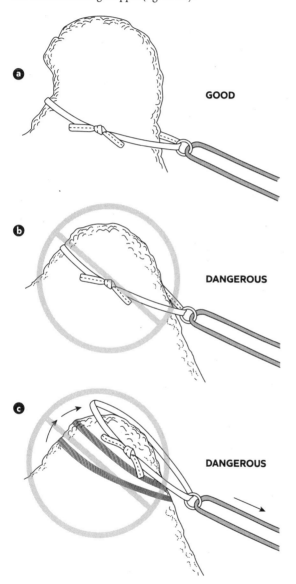

Fig. 11-6. *Using a rock horn as a natural rappel anchor:* ***a,*** *good runner placement—as low as possible on rock horn;* ***b,*** *dangerous runner placement—too high on horn;* ***c,*** *runner can ride up and slip off horn.*

A single anchor point might be used if it is an unquestionably solid, dependable natural anchor, but if there are any doubts, add another equalizing feature (or two) to the anchor (see Equalizing the Belay Anchor in Chapter 10). If there are no other natural features for creating a multipoint anchor, back up the anchor with cams or nuts, allowing the heaviest climbers to rappel first, then removing the backup for the last rappeller if the natural anchor performed well on the first rappels. Note that the natural anchor must carry all the weight under this test scenario. The backup protection must be extremely robust to handle the excess force should the natural anchor fail and the weight suddenly shift to the backup. Single natural anchors are not recommended if multiple people need to rappel simultaneously, such as in a rescue situation.

MANUFACTURED FIXED OR REMOVABLE ANCHORS

As a rule, when using manufactured fixed or removable protection for a rappel anchor, use two or more anchor points and equalize the load between them. The most common manufactured rappel anchors are bolts or pitons in the rock that have been left in place by previous climbers. These fixed anchors must be evaluated for damage, corrosion, and improper installation just as they would if they were being used for belaying or protection while climbing. *Never put the rope directly through the eye of a bolt hanger or piton*—friction may make it impossible to pull the rope back down from below, and the hanger's or piton's sharp edges can damage the rope.

Removable protection such as nuts, hexes, and cams are usually used only if no good alternative is available, because using these requires leaving gear behind. But it is better to leave equipment behind and minimize risk than to rely on a dubious natural anchor. Be suspicious of removable protection found already in place, perhaps left by climbers who were unable to remove the pieces. Also be wary of slings attached to such protection—they may be old, damaged, and unsafe. If fully set and immovable in the rock, an abandoned nut or hex may be used like a natural chockstone by looping a runner directly around it, ignoring the original sling.

Setting Up the Rope

Before setting up the rappel, run your hands along the entire length of the rope to check for cuts, fraying, or other damage that may have occurred during the climb or on a previous rappel.

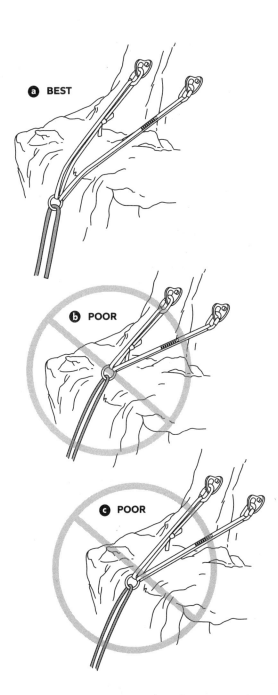

Fig. 11-7. *Location of point of connection between rappel rope and rappel sling (through attached ring);* **a,** *rope clear of edge and free to move (best);* **b,** *rope will not bind but will abrade (poor);* **c,** *rope placed at lip or edge will bind and abrade (poor).*

ATTACHING THE ROPE TO THE ANCHOR

To prepare the rope for rappelling, attach it to the anchor by suspending the rope's midpoint through rappel ring(s) attached to one or more runners or slings attached to the anchor (for example, see Figures 11-4a and 11-5a). Ropes are sometimes designed so that the color or pattern changes at the midpoint to make finding the middle easier. Some manufacturers sell ropes with the middle point marked with a special color. Keep the point of connection between the rappel anchor sling and the rope away from the rappel route's edge of rock, snow, or ice (fig. 11-7a) to help prevent rope abrasion (fig. 11-7b) or binding (fig. 11-7c).

Rappel Rings

The best practice is to use a rappel ring instead of looping the rope directly through the sling(s); if the rope rubs significantly on the sling(s), friction will create heat that may weaken or melt them. Rappel rings (also known as descending rings or rap rings) are simply continuous rings of aluminum, steel, or titanium about 1.5 inches (4 centimeters) in diameter, made for rappelling. Quick links—metal ovals with threaded sleeves for opening, closing, and locking the link (fig. 11-8)—may be used instead, but be sure to use links made specifically for climbing.

The rappel ring (fig. 11-9a) does add another possible point of failure, and some climbers insist on using two rings for redundancy (see Figure 11-2). An alternative is a single ring backed up by a non-weight-bearing sling from the anchor through the rope, ready to hold the rope if the ring fails (fig. 11-9b). Carabiners can be used in place of rappel rings, but as part of the anchor they also must then be left behind (see Figure 11-3).

Fig. 11-8. *Rappel quick link with threaded sleeve.*

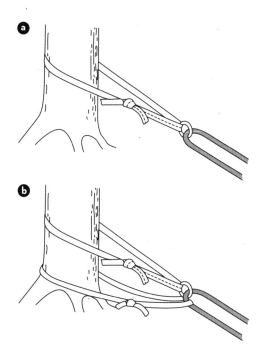

Fig. 11-9. *Rappel rope attached to anchor through a rappel ring:* ***a,*** *single ring;* ***b,*** *single ring with loose backup sling.*

One Rope

If the rappel is shorter than half a rope length, put one end of the rope through the rappel ring, pull it through to the rope's midpoint, and check the ends to ensure they are even. If you are using a rope with a middle mark, verify the mark's accuracy before the first rappel: check that the ends are even when the mark is at the anchor.

Two Ropes

For longer rappels, join two ropes together. If the rope lies with one strand against the rock and the other strand on top of the first, friction will impede retrieval, and it may be possible to pull only the strand closest to the rock. When using two ropes, place the knot joining them below the anchor, on the side of the strand to be pulled, which is also the lower of the two strands (fig. 11-10a)—otherwise, the rope may pinch between the rock and the end of the rope being pulled, and retrieval may not be possible (fig. 11-10b). As you rappel, keep the ropes side by side, not twisting or wrapping under one another. If the ropes are two different colors, designate the color to be pulled at the end of the rappel: for example, "Pull on red."

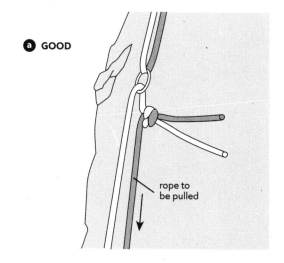

a GOOD

rope to
be pulled

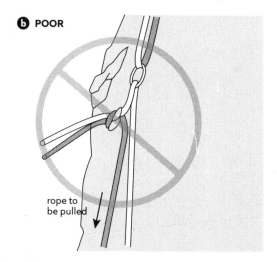

b POOR

rope to
be pulled

Fig. 11-10. *Knot placement with two-rope rappel:* ***a,*** *to retrieve the rope without it getting stuck, make sure the knot is on the lower of the two adjacent stands;* ***b,*** *having the knot on the side of the upper strand can lead to the lower strand getting pinched between the rock and loaded strand during retrieval.*

There are multiple ways to tie the rappel ropes together, each having benefits and drawbacks; Knots, Bends, and Hitches in Chapter 8, Essential Climbing Equipment, describes all of these knots. The sections below highlight knots for joining rappel ropes—knots that are easy to untie following tension.

Flat overhand bend. This knot, also called an offset overhand bend, is very safe when tied properly: hold one end of each rope together, with the tails 12 to 18 inches (30 to 46 centimeters) long, and tie an overhand knot, then dress the knot carefully, tightening it by pulling on each of the four strands (fig. 11-11a). It is important for the tails to be long enough, because the knot has been known to roll (or "capsize") under extreme loads. When the knot rolls, one side of the knot flips over the other side (toward the tail), shortening the tails. The rolled knot is identical to the original knot but has shorter tails. If rolled enough times, the knot will roll off the ends of the rope. If high forces are expected during the rappel (for example, multiple people rappelling simultaneously), the double fisherman's bend (described below) may be a better choice for joining the rope ends.

Because the flat overhand bend's knot lies offset from the axis of the direction of force, it is less likely than other knots to get stuck in cracks or on edges (fig. 11-11b).

Double fisherman's bend. This very secure knot is preferred if more than one person must rappel at the same time. It must be tied with long tails (see Figure 8-8 in Chapter 8). However, it is bulkier and more likely to become stuck in cracks than the flat overhand bend.

USING BACKUP KNOTS

Even very experienced rappellers have inadvertently rappelled off the ends of their ropes, with tragic results. When using a rappel device, put a large knot, also called a stopper knot—such as a double barrel (fig. 11-12a, b, and c) or triple barrel (fig. 11-12d), or a figure eight (see Figure 8-9)—as a backup in the ends of the rope to reduce this danger. If you add knots, do not rely blindly on them. Knots can come untied, and in any case, rappellers must keep an eye on the ends of the rope to plan where to stop. Knots also may jam in a crack or the rappel device. To prevent the knots from becoming lodged in a crack below the next rappel station, the ends of the rope can be secured to your harness while you descend.

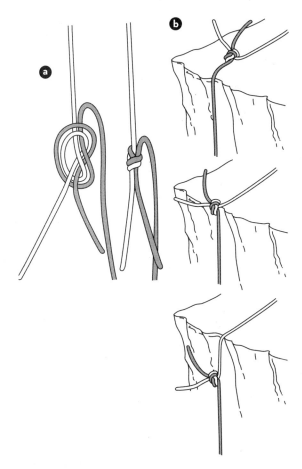

Fig. 11-11. *Joining rappel ropes with a flat overhand bend: **a,** tying and dressing the bend; **b,** since knot lies offset from the axis of the direction of force, it is less likely to catch on an edge or in a crack when you retrieve it.*

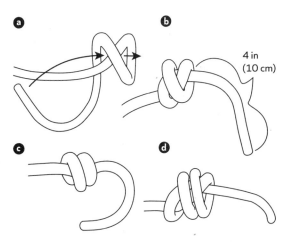

Fig. 11-12. *Barrel knot: **a,** for a double barrel knot, wrap end of rope around itself twice, pulling end through the loops; **b,** cinch down loose end and make sure tail is at least 4 inches (10 centimeters) long; **c,** back side of knot; **d,** add another wrap for a triple barrel knot.*

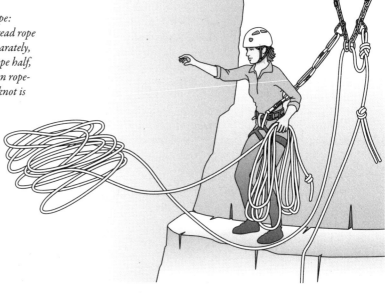

Fig. 11-13. *Throwing down the rope: With rope secured at midpoint, thread rope through rap rings and coil sides separately, two butterfly coils each. For each rope half, first toss coil nearest the anchor, then rope-end coil. Here, rope half on side of knot is already down.*

THROWING OR CARRYING THE ROPE DOWN

After threading the rappel rope through an anchor and equalizing the ends, prepare the rope for the rappel. The goal is to reduce rope snags and tangling, as well as to move the rope toward the bottom of the climb or pitch.

Throwing the Rope

Below is the standard method for throwing a rope (fig. 11-13). If the rope tangles or hangs up on the rappel route below, it is usually best to pull it back up, recoil it, and toss it again. Sometimes, however, it is possible to free the rope during the rappel. The following steps describe tossing both ends of a single rope; the process is the same for two ropes tied together.

1. **Attach yourself to an anchor.** Use a personal anchor to secure yourself, preferably with a locking carabiner (see Personal Anchors in Chapter 8, Essential Climbing Equipment). Make sure your waist is not above the anchor: a slip could significantly load the anchor because the personal anchor system is static.

2. **Attach the rope to the anchor.** Tie an overhand knot or figure eight on a bight of rope near its midpoint and clip it to the rappel anchor with a carabiner to prevent the disaster of losing the rope when tossing the coils.

3. **Tie backup knots at the ends of the rope.** See Using Backup Knots, above.

4. **Coil the rope.** Beginning from the rope's middle, coil each half of the rope separately into two butterfly coils—for a total of four butterfly coils, two on each side of the anchor.

5. **Evaluate wind and terrain before throwing the coils out.** Compensate for any significant wind. Avoid throwing the coils onto snags, pinch points, or sharp edges below.

6. **Alert others below by shouting "Rope!" before making the toss.** It is a good idea to shout the word two times and wait a few seconds after the warning before throwing the rope, to give anyone below time to respond.

7. **Toss the rope.** Start on one side of the anchor, tossing the coil nearest the anchor out and down the route, then the rope-end coil. Repeat for the other half of the rope (in Figure 11-13, one half of the rope has already been dropped below). In windy conditions, it may be prudent to throw the ropes toward the wind and down the route, or carry the rope down using one of the techniques described below.

8. **Detach the rope from the anchor.** After all coils have been tossed, remove the carabiner and bight added in step 2 above to leave the rope running free in the rappel ring(s).

Carrying the Rope Down

An alternative is to flake the rope into the rappeller's pack or a rope bag and feed it out while rappelling. In windy conditions, these approaches work better than tossing the rope.

Another option is to fashion the two strands of rope into two butterfly-coil saddlebags secured to the rappeller's harness: Girth-hitch two single-length runners to the harness wherever convenient, one runner on each side of the rappeller. Cradle the butterfly coils in these runners next to the harness, one coil on each side of the harness, and clip the other ends of the runners to the harness with two carabiners (fig. 11-14), orienting the butterfly coils so that they feed freely during the rappel.

A rappeller may need to actively tend the rope when feeding it out of a rope bag or using the saddlebag method to get it to feed out properly.

KEEPING ROPE LENGTHS EQUAL

As noted at the start of this chapter, rappelling with ropes of unequal length was found to be the top cause of accidents reported in *Accidents in North American Climbing*. Both strands of the rappel rope must either touch the next stance or hang equally. If not, one end may pull through the rappel device before the rappeller reaches a stance at the end of the rappel, leaving the rappeller out of control and in free fall. Also, be aware that ropes that are nominally equal in length, even from the same manufacturer, are often actually somewhat different lengths.

Watch for the potential problems discussed later in this chapter. Stopper knots at the ends of the rope are strongly recommended (see Using Backup Knots, above). They keep the climber from rappelling off the ends of the rope should the rope be too short.

When using two ropes of unequal diameters, take extra care to monitor the length of each strand during the rappel. The differing diameters and elastic characteristics of the ropes may cause one rope to advance through the rappel device more quickly than the other, thereby altering the relative lengths of the rope strands. Place the knot joining the two ropes on the side of the anchor with the rope that is most likely to slide—usually the smaller-diameter rope.

Rappel Methods

Once the rappel anchor and rope are set up, climbers need a way to connect to the rope and apply friction to control the rappel. Typically, a mechanical device provides a secure means of attachment, but climbers may also wrap the rope around their body.

MECHANICAL RAPPEL SYSTEMS

Most rappellers use a system consisting of their climbing harness and a belay-rappel device as their principal rappelling method. All these aperture devices operate in essentially the same manner: by applying varying degrees of friction to the rope. With some belay devices, the rope does not feed through the device smoothly on rappel. Others may easily heat up from rope friction. Before using any new device, closely read and follow the manufacturer's instructions. If climbers rely on a mechanical rappel device, it is imperative that they be skilled in a secondary mechanical rappel method such as the carabiner brake or the munter hitch in case they drop their rappel device midclimb (see below).

To set up the rappel device, make a bight in each strand of rope at the rappel anchor and insert them into the rappel device, then clip both bights with a locking carabiner to the climber's harness, in much the same way as for belaying. During the rappel, the bends in the rope that pass through the device and around the locking carabiner apply friction, magnifying the force exerted by the climber's brake hand (fig. 11-15). The position of the brake hand, which holds both strands of rope below the device (see Figure 11-14), provides a controlled descent. The rappel device and the brake hand together control the speed of descent and allow the rappeller to halt the descent at any time.

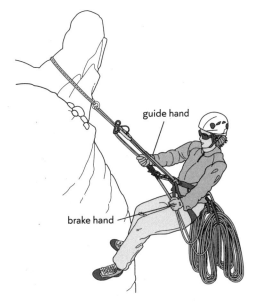

Fig. 11-14. *Setting up the rappel with two saddlebags of rope clipped to the harness, one coil on each side of the harness.*

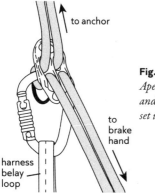

Fig. 11-15.
Aperture-style belay and/or rappel device set up for rappelling.

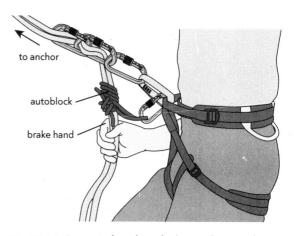

Fig. 11-16. *Improvised carabiner brake rappel system: three locking carabiners clipped to harness.*

The weight of the rope hanging below the device adds friction, making it easier to control the rate of descent near the top of a rappel than at the bottom. This is especially so on very steep or overhanging rappels where most of the rope hangs free. But no matter how little grip strength may be required to control the descent, never take your brake hand off the rope. You may slide your guide hand, or uphill hand (see Figure 11-4), along the rope to maintain your balance. With some setups, wrapping the rope partly around your back further increases friction. A leather glove is recommended to protect the brake hand, which is important when a rappel exceeds the desired speed and could burn a bare hand.

Rappelling with a mechanical system requires a harness (see Chapter 8, Essential Climbing Equipment). Never rappel with just a waist loop (a simple loop of webbing tied around your waist); it can constrict your diaphragm enough to cause you to lose consciousness. In an emergency, an improvised sling harness may be used for rappelling, even though it would not ordinarily be used for climbing (see Chapter 8).

Carabiner Brake Method

Though somewhat complex to set up, the carabiner brake method for rappelling does not require any special equipment. Employing three locking carabiners, this technique (fig. 11-16) is useful if a climber does not have an aperture-style rappel device.

This method generally provides less friction than other rappelling methods but does not twist the rope, a common problem with the munter hitch (see below). Because of the reduced friction, it is important to use an autoblock on the braking side of the ropes (see Figure 11-26). Here are the steps to set up the carabiner brake method:

1. Clip and lock one locking carabiner to the harness belay loop.
2. Clip and lock a second locking carabiner to the first.
3. Pull a bight of both ropes through the second carabiner.
4. Clip and lock a third locking carabiner to this bight and to the rope strands running to the anchor.
5. Ensure all carabiners are locked, and take care that the ropes do not run against the screw gates of any of the carabiners.
6. Add an autoblock backup (see Safety Backups later in this chapter).

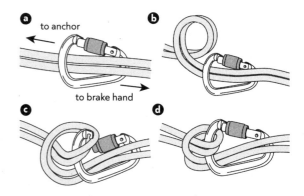

Fig. 11-17. *To rappel using a munter hitch: **a,** clip locking carabiner around both strands of rope; **b,** create loop using both strands above carabiner, with anchor strand behind braking strand; **c,** hook carabiner into loop; **d,** lock carabiner gate.*

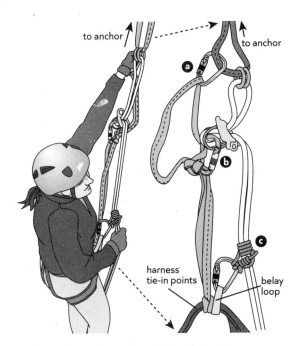

Fig. 11-18. *Rappel extension with double-length runner tied in the middle with a figure-eight knot: **a,** for personal anchor, clip runner's upper loop to rappel anchor with locking carabiner; **b,** clip locking carabiner in to both loops of runner (on either side of knot) and clip it through rappel device and both rope strands; **c,** wrap autoblock around both strands of rappel rope and clip ends to belay loop with locking carabiner.*

Munter Hitch

The same hitch used for belaying can work for rappelling (see Chapter 10, Belaying). It is worthwhile to learn this method as insurance because it requires only one locking carabiner and no other equipment. Though it is easy to set up and very secure, it puts significantly more twists in the rope than other rappel methods do. The rappeller must be very sure to keep the braking side of the ropes on the spine side of the carabiner (fig. 11-17), because if the rope runs over the gate, it may unlock the carabiner during the rappel. For additional security, a backup is recommended, such as an autoblock or a firefighter's belay (see Safety Backups later in this chapter).

EXTENDING THE RAPPEL DEVICE

Most climbers extend the rappel device connection to their harness with a personal anchor so that the rappel device rides higher on the rappel rope and in front of their chest (see Figures 11-18 and 11-19). Rappel extensions are recommended for the following reasons:

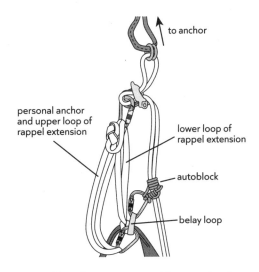

Fig. 11-19. *Rappel extension setup with personal anchor stowed on harness belay loop.*

- The rappeller can comfortably use either hand (or both hands) to brake the rappel and can add—and manage—a superior autoblock (see Safety Backups later in this chapter).
- Both ends of the autoblock can be clipped in to the harness's belay loop, which is more convenient than attaching it to a leg loop.
- The autoblock is less likely to jam against the rappel device and fail.
- The personal anchor is readily available for clipping to anchors.

The disadvantages of rappel extension are that this technique introduces one more piece into the rappel system—the runner used for the extension—and it brings the rappel device closer to long hair, which may get caught in the device; it is essential to have a knife handy to remedy this situation.

Here is how to create the extension with a double-length runner (although a manufactured personal anchor can be used as well). Tie a figure-eight or overhand knot in the middle of the runner to create two loops of equal length. Keeping the runner's stitching clear of the girth hitch, girth-hitch one loop of the runner to your harness tie-in points, not your belay loop. Clip a locking carabiner to the far end of the runner's upper loop and to the anchor (fig. 11-18a). Then clip another locking carabiner to both the upper and lower loops and set up the rappel device and rope (fig. 11-18b). Keep the runner's knot and stitching points clear of the carabiner clipping points.

Fig. 11-20. *The* dulfersitz, *a nonmechanical rappel method.*

Fig. 11-21. *The arm rappel, a nonmechanical rappel method.*

To add an autoblock, attach both of its ends directly to a locking carabiner on the harness belay loop instead of to the harness leg loop, and wrap the cord around both rope strands below the rappel device (fig. 11-18c). When the personal anchor and component is not in use, simply stow it by clipping and locking the upper loop's carabiner to the harness belay loop (fig. 11-19).

NONMECHANICAL RAPPEL METHODS

Two traditional rappel methods use no hardware whatsoever to create friction on the rope. Instead, the rope is simply wrapped around parts of the climber's body. Though uncomfortable and potentially painful, these methods can be especially helpful if climbers find themselves without a harness.

Dulfersitz

A simple, all-purpose method, the *dulfersitz* should be practiced by every climber in the event that a harness or carabiners are not available. To set up, face the anchor and straddle the rope. Bring the rope from behind you and around one hip, up across your chest, over the opposite shoulder, and then down your back to be held by the brake hand (the downhill hand) on the same side as your wrapped hip (fig.

11-20). Your other hand is the guide hand, which holds the rope above and keeps you upright. Add padding if possible between your body and the rope.

The *dulfersitz* has a number of drawbacks compared with mechanical rappel systems. Aside from being uncomfortable to the rappeller, it can unwrap from your leg, especially on high-angle rappels, though this risk can be mitigated by keeping your wrapped leg slightly lower than your other leg. As with all rappel methods, stay under careful control. If you are wearing a pack, the *dulfersitz* is even more awkward. The *dulfersitz* is rarely used in modern climbing, and only when there is no reasonable alternative.

Arm Rappel

The arm rappel is occasionally helpful for quick descent of a low-angle slope, such as a set of fixed lines on an alpine climb. Lay the rappel rope behind your back, bring it under your armpits, and wrap it once around each arm (fig. 11-21). Be sure the rope does not run over any exposed flesh, which can cause rope burns. Control the rate of descent with your brake (downhill) hand. For an arm rappel with a pack, be sure the rope goes around your pack rather than on top of or underneath it.

Fig. 11-22. *Starting to rappel from a high anchor (personal anchor omitted for clarity).*

Fig. 11-23. *Down-climbing to get below a low anchor before starting to rappel (personal anchor omitted for clarity).*

Rappel Technique

The first rappeller is typically one of a group's more experienced members. They usually fix any tangles or problems with the rope and clears the anchor area and route of debris that following rappellers may dislodge.

GETTING STARTED

First, double-check your knots and device setup. Before descending, shout "On rappel!" to warn others. Take up any slack between you and the anchor before leaning out or weighting the rope. To maintain stability during the rappel, keep your legs nearly perpendicular to the rock by leaning backward, out over the edge of the cliff (fig. 11-22), and commit to weighting the rope for rappel. If the terrain allows it, ease the transition by down-climbing several feet before leaning out and weighting the rope (fig. 11-23).

You may be able to sit or crouch on the edge (fig. 11-24a) and wiggle gently off of it (fig. 11-24b), simultaneously turning to face the slope and keeping your legs nearly perpendicular to the rock (fig. 11-24c). This technique, referred to as a "sit-and-spin," is particularly useful if the rappel starts above an overhang or if your harness is above the anchor when you stand at the start of the rappel.

MAKING THE RAPPEL

When they rappel, climbers must consider three things: position, speed, and movement.

Position

Seek to maintain a stable body position: feet shoulder-width apart, knees flexed, body at a comfortable angle to the slope and facing a little toward the brake hand for a view of the route (see Figure 11-24c). Common beginners' mistakes include keeping the feet too close together and not leaning back far enough, which can cause feet to slip off the rock. Some climbers go to the other extreme and lean too far back, increasing their chance of flipping over. If you should tip over or lose your footing, remember to maintain your hold on the rope with your brake hand.

Some climbers prefer to brake with both hands, using an alternating, hand-over-hand, shuffle-brake motion to feed the rope through the rappel device. Others feel more secure with a nonbraking hand high on the rope, to help keep them upright and to fend off any hazards (see Potential Problems While Rappelling, below). Either way, it is imperative that you keep one hand on the braking rope at all times.

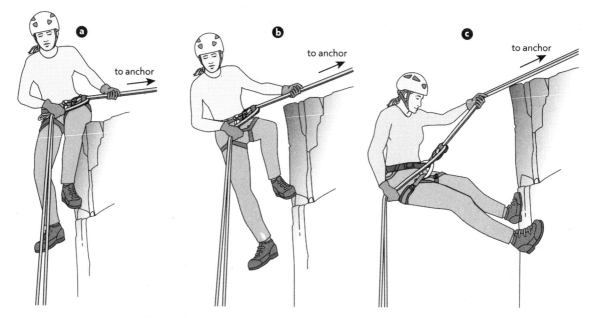

Fig. 11-24. *Starting to rappel from a steep ledge and a low anchor (personal anchor omitted for clarity):* **a,** *sit down on the ledge;* **b,** *squirm off it to get started, pressing one of your feet against the wall or on a hold if possible;* **c,** *turn inward to face the slope.*

Speed and Movement

As you rappel, move slowly and steadily, without bouncing or leaping. Feed the rope slowly and steadily into the rappel system, avoiding fast stops and jerks, which subject the anchor to greater force. Rappelling faster puts more heat and stress on the system; rappelling too fast can damage a rope or cause you to lose control of it.

STOPPING MIDRAPPEL

If you need to stop partway down a rappel, you can secure the rope by relying on an autoblock, by wrapping the rope around your leg, or by tying off with a mule knot. Some belay and/or rappel devices offer ways to stop the rope in the device; consult the manufacturer's instructions or obtain reliable instruction on using the device this way.

Autoblock

If you are using an autoblock as a rappel backup (see Safety Backups, below), simply allow the hitch to grab the rope and stop the rope from moving through the device. Before you remove your brake hand(s) from the rope, tie a large knot (such as an overhand on a bight) below the autoblock, using both strands of the rappel rope. This knot serves as a backup in case the autoblock slips.

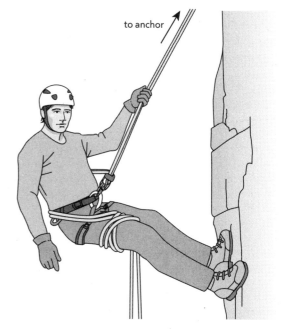

Fig. 11-25. *Leg wrap: stopping midrappel by wrapping the rope around one upper leg can free up the brake hand.*

To continue rappelling, reestablish your hand(s) on the braking side of the rappel rope, remove the backup knot, then release the autoblock hitch by sliding it away from the rappel device.

Leg Wrap

Another method for securing the rope midrappel is to wrap the rope two or three times around one upper leg. The friction of the wrap, increased by the weight of the rope hanging below the wrap, is usually enough to halt further descent. Keep the brake hand on the rope while passing the rope behind your back, and use the guide hand to assist with the wrapping; keep the brake hand in position until you have completed and tested the wraps (fig. 11-25). For even more friction, tuck a bight of the loose end of the rope under all the leg wraps.

To continue the descent, reestablish your brake hand before releasing the leg wraps. On steep rappels, while holding the rope with the brake hand, simply remove your foot and leg from contact with the rock and shake the wraps off.

Mule Knot

A mule knot can also be used to tie off the rappel, just like tying off a belay; see Mule Knot and Figures 8-20 and 8-21 in Chapter 8, Essential Climbing Equipment. The mule knot is a load-releasing knot; other knots may be difficult to remove once they are loaded.

POTENTIAL PROBLEMS WHILE RAPPELLING

It is important to be aware of the many problems you may encounter when rappelling, especially because climbers are often tired when setting up to rappel. These tips will help you troubleshoot.

Loose rock. Use extreme caution when rappelling a face with loose or rotten rock. You or the rope may displace rocks as you descend. Loose rocks can injure you or damage the rope. Another danger is that the next rappeller could knock rocks down on you. Position yourself in a safe area (out of the fall line or under a rock outcropping) before calling "Off rappel!" and stay there until the entire party has rappelled. Rocks are often knocked loose when the last rappeller pulls the rope. Keep an eye above you while pulling the rope, and make sure party members keep their helmets on until the rope has been safely retrieved after the final rappel.

Overhangs. It is easy to swing into the face below an overhang, smashing your hands and feet. It is also possible to stall the braking system on the lip of an overhang. A couple of methods can help you make the difficult transition from above the lip of an overhang to below it.

One method is to bend your knees deeply with your feet at the uppermost edge of the overhang, then release enough braking tension to slip down 3 or 4 feet (about 1 meter) at once, and then lock off the rappel by braking suddenly, which halts further acceleration once you are past the lip of the overhang. The abrupt halt and resulting bounce stress the rappel system, but this method helps reduce your chances both of swinging into the face below and of jamming the braking system on the lip.

Another method is to work your feet onto the lip of the overhang and, with knees bent, push your rear out (into space) until it is just lower than your feet. Then work your feet down the underside of the overhang until the rope above makes contact with the lip of the rock face above.

Below an overhang, you will dangle free on the rope. Assume a sitting position, use the guide hand on the rope above to remain upright, and continue steadily downward. Often you will slowly spin as twists in the rope unwind.

Pendulums. Reaching the next rappel stance may require you to move to the right or left of the fall line, walking down the face diagonally instead of moving straight down. If a slip occurs, you will pendulum back toward the fall line. After such a fall, it may be difficult to get reestablished on the proper rappel course without climbing back up the rope with prusik slings or mechanical devices.

To avoid this potentially dangerous situation, try to set up rappel routes so that you stick to the fall line as much as possible. A pendulum fall presents a risk of injury and may cause the climber to let go of the brake strand, making a backup method imperative when you must rappel diagonally (see Safety Backups, below).

Loose ends. Clothing, long hair, pack straps, helmet chin straps, and just about anything with a loose end all could get pulled into the braking system. Keep a knife handy to cut foreign material out of the system, but be extremely careful with a sharp knife around rope, especially a rope under tension, which is easy to cut.

Rope tangles. If the rope gets tangled or jammed, you must correct the problem before you can rappel past it. Stop at the last convenient ledge above the area, or stop with a leg wrap (see Stopping Midrappel, above). Pull the rope up, correct the problem, then throw the rope down again. Sometimes the solution is simple; for instance, when rappelling down blank slabs, shake tangles out as you encounter them. Keep an eye out for tangles or other possible problems below you.

Jammed rappel device. If the rappel braking system jams on something (such as a shirt) despite your precautions,

11

it can most likely be freed by unweighting it. First, free your hands by using a leg wrap or a backup mule knot (see Stopping Midrappel, above). Next, unweight the braking system by either standing on a ledge or tying a prusik hitch above your braking system and chaining slings together until they are long enough to stand in. In the worst case, you might even prusik some distance up the rappel ropes (see Prusik System in Chapter 19, Glacier Travel and Crevasse Rescue) or climb the wall. Then, if you still are unable to free the jammed material, cut it away from the braking system, taking care not to nick the rope. Always keep a prusik loop, three or four slings, and a knife on hand when rappelling.

Safety Backups

A few special methods and backup knots at the end of rappel ropes reduce your risk while rappelling. Safety backups can add security to particularly challenging or unnerving rappels and possibly save the life of a rappeller hit by rockfall. The backup methods described below also help beginner rappellers gain confidence.

SELF-BELAY WITH AN AUTOBLOCK

A friction hitch enables the rappeller to stop without gripping the ropes. The rappeller should tie the hitch onto both strands of the rope below the rappel device and clip it into their harness belay loop. A friction hitch such as an autoblock or prusik works best (see Friction Hitches in Chapter 8). These self-belay hitches grip the rope and halt the descent even if you do not actively tend them. If your brake hand releases the rope—for instance, as the result of rockfall—a self-belay friction hitch can prevent you from accelerating out of control.

For a self-belay friction hitch, use a sewn runner or accessory cord tied in a loop (see Runners in Chapter 8, Essential Climbing Equipment). The appropriate diameter and length of runner or cord varies with rope diameter—always test compatibility before using the hitch by making sure the hitch will grab the rope. The runner or loop must be short enough that the hitch cannot either jam the rappel device or be tended by the rappel device (which could result in the hitch failing to hold).

To set up the autoblock, attach the runner or loop to the harness belay loop with a carabiner (or use a girth hitch).

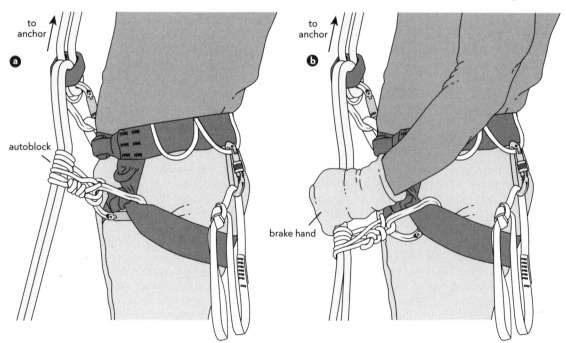

Fig. 11-26. *Self-belay autoblock on an unextended rappel:* **a,** *wrap autoblock and clip to harness leg loop;* **b,** *tend the friction hitch by sliding it down the rope with the brake hand. Personal anchor is stowed on harness in this example.*

Wrap the loop around both strands of the rappel rope(s) below the rappel device. Typically, three wraps provide enough (but not too much) friction. Then clip the end of the runner or loop to the belay loop with the same carabiner. The autoblock should be connected to the harness's belay loop in a rappel extension setup (see Extending the Rappel Device, above). But if the rappel system is not extended, use the leg loop to prevent the cord from being pulled into the rappel device (fig. 11-26a). Tend the autoblock by manually sliding it down the rope with the brake hand (fig. 11-26b). After engaging the hitch, reestablish the brake hand and slide the hitch away from the rappel device to continue descending.

These hitches require some testing and adjustment before each rappel in order to establish the runner or loop's proper length (so the hitch does not jam in the rappel device) and the proper amount of friction (adjusted by the number of wraps) to accommodate the climber's weight, rappel device, comfort, and any other individual considerations.

FIREFIGHTER'S BELAY

A person standing at the bottom of a rappel can easily control the rappeller's movement or stop it altogether—thus providing an effective backup—simply by pulling down on the rope, which puts friction on the braking system (fig. 11-27). To provide a backup for the rappeller with this method, the person at the bottom simply holds the rope strands loosely, ready to pull them tight the instant the rappeller has difficulty.

TOP BELAY

A rappeller can also be protected by a belay from above with a separate rope. If the belayer uses a separate anchor, the entire system, even the rappel anchor, has redundancy. A top belay is too time-consuming for routine use, but it may be used with beginners, climbers with minor injuries, or the first person descending on a suspect anchor.

Finishing the Rappel

Near the end of the rappel, it becomes much easier to feed rope through the rappel device because there is considerably less rope and therefore less friction below the rappeller. Given that the rope stretches when weighted while you are rappelling, when you clear it from your device and let go of it, it could contract and suddenly be up out of reach. It's better to end the rappel near the end of the rope rather than at the very end of it.

As you near the end of the rope, look for a suitable place to finish the rappel. Establish a solid stance and anchor yourself in before clearing the rope from the rappel device. Consider the possibility of rockfall and icefall, and do your best to be out of the way of the next rappeller.

Shout "Off rappel!" only after you are detached from the rope and safely away from the fall line, to avoid rock

Fig. 11-27. *Firefighter's belay: rappel can be halted by a climber below, who pulls down on the rope ends.*

or ice the next rappeller might dislodge. If you are the first person down a double-rope rappel, tug on the rope that has the knot to check that it is running smoothly. Recenter the knot before the second person descends as needed.

THE LAST RAPPELLER

With a double-rope rappel, it is critical to know which rope to pull on from below when you are done rappelling. Pulling the wrong one will cause the knot to jam in the rappel ring (see Figure 11-10).

The last rappeller should take a thorough final look at the rope(s) and the rappel sling to check that everything is in order and that the rope(s) will not catch on the sling or any rocks, snow, or ice. Before the last person starts to descend, have a person at the bottom perform a test pull on the proper strand to check that it moves freely. The last rappeller should confirm that the rope does not bind on itself when pulled and that the knot in a double-rope rappel can be pulled free of the edge (see Figures 11-10a and 11-11b).

On a double-rope rappel, the last person down may want to stop at the first convenient ledge and pull enough rope down so that the connecting knot is clear of the edge. However, this practice also shortens one rope end, so be sure there is still enough rope to reach the next rappel stance and that there are still stopper knots in the ends of both ropes.

PULLING THE ROPE(S) DOWN

Once everyone has finished the rappel, take out any visible twists in the rope(s) and remove any safety knots in the ends of the strands. Stand away from the rock, if possible, then pull the proper strand slowly and steadily. Before the pulled strand starts to travel freely, yell "Rope!" to warn of falling rope. Others should take shelter to stay out of the way of falling rope, rocks, or other debris. Until all climbers and ropes are on the ground, everyone should keep their helmets on.

Rope Jams

A jammed rappel rope may be a serious problem, perhaps even stranding a party on a descent that requires further rappels. If the rope gets stuck, either before or after the end clears the anchor, try flipping it with whipping and circular motions before attempting to pull it. Often a change in angle, back from the rock face or to the right or left, can free it. Sometimes pulling on the other end of the rope (if it is still in reach) or using a seesaw motion to pull on each end alternately can free the rope. Be alert and cautious when pulling a stuck rope; as it springs free, it may dislodge rocks, snow, or ice.

If the rope gets stuck, below are some options, in descending order of preference. Because climbing up to free a stuck rope may require building a new anchor to rappel from after the rope is freed, the climber must bring up enough gear to build a new solid anchor. If the stuck rope is not necessary to complete the descent, consider leaving it rather than undertaking risky maneuvers to free it.

1. **Climb with a secured prusik.** If both ends of the rope(s) are still in reach, it is possible to securely prusik up both strands (see Prusik System in Chapter 19, Glacier Travel and Crevasse Rescue, for one method of ascending a free-hanging rope), clear the jam, and rappel back down. Tie in to the rope at frequent intervals to back up the prusiks.

2. **Climb with a belay.** If you can reach only one rope end, you may need to climb up and free the rope(s). If there is enough rope available from the pulled strand, lead climb with a belay to reach the knot. There is a risk you may end up stuck, unable to be lowered or to rappel, if you cannot reach the spot where the rope is stuck, so do not attempt this method if you are unsure whether the available rope will reach.

3. **Climb self-belayed.** If there is not enough rope available from the pulled strand, lead climb with a self-belay by attaching to the available rope with a prusik. Anchor the end of the rope at the belay ledge, then secure it to the mountain with conventional protection as you climb. If the rope suddenly pulls free from above, hopefully the combination of the prusik attachment, periodic placement of protection, and the anchor will limit the length of the fall. If there is not enough rope available from the pulled strand, there are some alternative approaches appropriate for advanced climbers, but they are beyond the scope of this book.

4. **Climb with an unsecured prusik.** If it is not possible for someone to belay you, and if the party cannot proceed without the rope, a final resort is to attempt the desperate and very dangerous tactic of ascending the stuck rope with a prusik or mechanical ascenders. The extreme danger of climbing an unsecured rope must be weighed against the consequences of remaining stranded until another rope is available. If it is possible to place protection during the ascent, tie in to the loose end and attach the rope to protection with clove hitches; the consequences of the rope pulling free from above might be mitigated.

Multiple Rappels

A descent route often involves a series of rappels. These multiple rappels, especially in alpine terrain, present special problems and require maximum efficiency to keep the party moving. (See Multipitch Climbs in Chapter 14, Traditional Rock Climbing, for techniques specific to these types of routes.)

As a party moves through a series of rappels, the first person down each pitch usually carries gear for setting up the next rappel—setting it up only after finding a secure stance, establishing an anchor, and attaching to it out of the path of icefall and rockfall. More experienced climbers in a party can take turns being first and last. It is best for beginners to be in the middle of the rotation so that assistance is available at the start and end of each rappel.

UNKNOWN TERRAIN

The trickiest multiple rappel is one that goes down an unfamiliar route. Avoid this if possible. If an unfamiliar rappel is necessary, check out possible rappel lines as carefully as time and terrain permit. If there is a photo of the rappel route, bring it for reference. Keep in mind that the first few rappels down an unfamiliar route may, for better or worse, commit the party to that route.

If the bottom of an unfamiliar rappel pitch cannot be seen, the first person down must be prepared to climb back up in case the rappel hangs free at the end of the rope before there is a good stance or anchor. This rappeller should carry prusik slings or mechanical ascenders for ascending the rope if necessary.

Rappelling down unfamiliar terrain brings an increased risk of the rope getting hung up. Minimize the problem by down-climbing as much as possible instead of rappelling. Also, consider rappels using just one rope, even if two ropes are available. Although this increases the number of rappels and the time spent descending, one rope is less likely to hang up than two. If one rope does get stuck, the second rope is available to protect a climb back up to free the stuck rope. You may then carefully climb back down or establish an intermediate rappel where the problem occurred.

Although it is efficient to gain the maximum distance from each rappel, do not bypass a good rappel anchor spot—even well before the end of the rope—if there are doubts about finding a good place farther down.

Experiencing the Freedom of the Hills

Rappelling is central to climbing. Learn this skill thoroughly and employ it carefully to minimize your risk. Avoid becoming complacent about rappelling. This essential, specialized technique enables climbers to experience the freedom of the hills.

PART III
ROCK CLIMBING

CHAPTER 12

SPORT CLIMBING AND TECHNIQUE

Many rock climbers begin top-roping in a gym before transitioning to outdoor crags and sport routes. The progression from gym to crag allows the climber to learn and refine the technical skills to climb natural rock without having to focus on placing protection. As climbers gain skills and practice, they can begin to lead sport routes. Sport climbing generally features climbing using ropes with bolts or other fixed protection. Consider hiring a guide for your first lead climb or pairing up with an experienced mentor.

This chapter focuses on the basics of climbing single-pitch face and crack sport routes with fixed protection. It forms a foundation for transitioning to traditional climbing, including routes in more remote areas. Chapter 13 covers rock protection used in traditional climbing, and Chapter 14 focuses on traditionally protected routes where it is up to the lead climber to place appropriate gear to protect the route should the climber fall. Bouldering is another popular form of climbing performed relatively close to the ground without a rope; it is not covered in this book. Sport climbing allows climbers to focus on the physical and mental aspects of rock climbing in less remote, relatively lower-risk environments. Because sport climbing routes usually involve technical terrain, climbers should always be concerned about what would happen in a fall. In the sport of bouldering, climbers protect themselves from a fall with a foam crash pad. On sport climbs, climbers use a rope to protect themselves from getting seriously injured or dying if they fall.

Climbers can climb sport routes with either a top-rope belay or on lead. When leading a sport route, the climber brings the rope up and clips it in to fixed (permanent) protection as they ascend a predefined route. In this scenario, the lead climber is belayed by another climber from below. In traditional (trad) climbing, the leader does all this while also placing removable gear and identifying where the route moves up the rock.

There are several advantages to learning to climb sport routes before tackling trad routes. Because sport climbing does not involve placing removable protection, climbers can focus on moving on the rock, clipping protection, and managing the rope. Sport climbing also requires a lot less equipment than trad climbing. To get started, you will need a belay device, harness, climbing shoes, helmet, climbing rope, plus some quickdraws and locking carabiners.

Equipment

Whether you are sport climbing or trad climbing, moving efficiently on rock requires solid technique that takes time to develop. To bridge that gap, choose gear appropriate for the terrain that will help you manage the risks associated with being in such places. This section discusses a few items of rock climbing equipment beyond the basic climbing gear discussed in Chapter 8, Essential Climbing Equipment. Rock shoes, appropriate clothing, tape or gloves, chalk, and quickdraws all directly affect your experience on the rock and can help you move more efficiently.

FOOTWEAR

On easy rock climbs, including sport climbs, the boots or approach shoes mountaineers wear on the approach generally work well for climbing too. (For more information on mountaineering boots, see Chapter 2, Clothing and Equipment.) When the climbing is more difficult, specialized footwear—rock shoes—offers a significant advantage.

> ### KEY TOPICS
> EQUIPMENT
> TRANSITIONING FROM A GYM TO THE
>   OUTDOORS
> FACE CLIMBING
> CRACK CLIMBING
> BEING PREPARED

Most rock shoes have flexible uppers, plus smooth, flexible soles and rands of sticky rubber. These soles create excellent friction when weighted on rock, allowing purchase on features that can amaze a beginning climber.

On a carryover—a climb where climbers do not return to their starting point or base camp on the way down—using rock shoes on the route means climbing with the weight and bulk of boots in their packs. If the climbing includes patches of snow or ice between the rock sections, wearing boots for the entire route avoids time-consuming breaks for changing footwear. Some advanced climbers ascend through short sections of snow with rock shoes, or one climber will lead the rock pitches in rock shoes and the other climber will lead the mixed pitches of rock, snow, and ice in boots. For difficult rock climbing, especially narrow cracks, the superior grip and thinner profile afforded by rock shoes may enable faster, more secure movement.

The choice of footwear depends on personal preference and the type of route. Mountaineering boots are commonly worn on alpine rock routes without technically difficult rock sections. Rock shoes are used on more technical rock terrain, usually rated 5.6 or harder, that requires face or crack climbing.

Approach shoes (fig. 12-1a) are a compromise between mountaineering boots and rock shoes. Useful when the approach is snow free, they can also be worn on easy to moderate routes. To avoid the burden of carrying heavier boots on a sustained rock climb, some experienced climbers carry running shoes and crampons instead to negotiate short snow crossings, such as a small pocket glacier.

When choosing rock shoes, climbers may find the confusing array at outdoor stores daunting. Remember that climbing technique is far more important than your choice of shoes! Until you have mastered the techniques necessary to climb at the 5.10 or 5.11 level, the type of rock shoe you are wearing will likely not make a significant difference. That said, below are some useful guidelines for choosing rock shoes.

Stiff-soled, more cambered shoes are better at edging (fig. 12-1b), while flexible shoes are better at frictioning and smearing (see Using Footholds later in this chapter). Shoes with laces and higher tops that cover the anklebones (fig. 12-1c) offer protection when climbers jam their feet in cracks. The shoes shown in parts b and c have flat lasts, or soles, as opposed to parts d and e, which have a more aggressive downturned toe. Velcro-closure shoes (fig. 12-1d) and laceless slippers (fig. 12-1e) are easier to take off and are often great for highly technical moves. But ultimately the choice of Velcro or laces comes down to personal preference

Fig. 12-1. *Rock shoes: a, combined approach and climbing shoe; b, more specialized shoe, good for edging; c, all-around shoe (flat last, high ankles); d, Velcro-closure climbing shoe; e, slip-on moccasin.*

and fit. If you own only one pair of rock shoes, it's probably best to choose a pair with all-around characteristics.

Rock shoes should fit snugly to allow dexterity and a sense of the rock's features, yet not tight enough to cause pain. Sport climbers at local crags often have the luxury of taking their shoes off after each pitch, but alpine rock climbers should choose rock shoes comfortable enough to wear all day. Some makes of rock shoes are sized for wider or narrower feet. Try on different styles to find what fits. Thin liner socks add comfort and a little warmth—a bonus in chilly conditions. Some climbers prefer to have a pair of alpine rock shoes sized to fit over their mountain-boot socks. All rock shoes stretch somewhat, usually only a quarter to a half size in width and much less in length. Leather shoes stretch more than synthetic shoes. Lined shoes stretch the least.

Rock shoe rubber oxidizes and hardens over time. To expose a stickier new layer, try scrubbing the rubber briskly with a wire brush. When the rubber wears down, rock shoes can often be resoled, particularly if a hole has not yet worn all the way through. Resoling is significantly less expensive than buying a new pair.

12

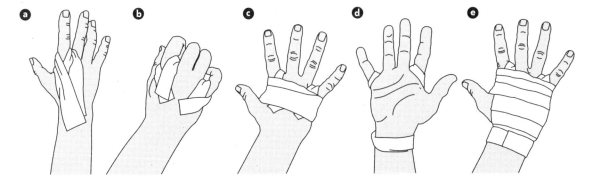

Fig. 12-2. *Hand taped for rock climbing:* **a,** *wrap tape around first finger or thumb, depending on coverage desired;* **b,** *wrap tape around pinky;* **c,** *cover back of hand with overlapping tape strips;* **d,** *leave palms mostly exposed;* **e,** *add wraps down to wrist to protect entire back of hand, continuing to leave palm open. Wrapping around fingers aids in securing the tape to the hands throughout a climb.*

CLOTHING

The clothing you wear while climbing needs to be comfortable and allow free range of movement. Long sleeves and pants will protect your skin from rock abrasion, particularly when crack climbing. In the alpine environment, dress in layers so you can easily adapt to changing weather conditions. For details on fabrics and general information on alpine clothing, see Chapter 2, Clothing and Equipment.

Remove rings, bracelets, and delicate watches before rock climbing. They will probably get scratched at the least; much worse, jewelry and watches can catch in a crack and damage your hands. A stuck ring can cause serious injury, even perhaps amputation of the finger.

HAND PROTECTION

Athletic tape protects hands from abrasive rock. Tape is advisable for climbers learning crack techniques and attempting more difficult cracks, especially on rock with sharp crystals. Wrapping tape around your fingers can support and protect your tendons.

Taping methods vary; Figure 12-2, for example, shows a method that leaves the palm untaped, to ensure sensitivity while face climbing. Flex your hands while taping them to ensure that the tape will not be too tight when you make a fist or hand jam later. After climbing, it often is possible to cut off your tape "gloves" and save them to use again.

Manufactured crack climbing gloves are an increasingly popular option (fig. 12-3). Typically minimal fingerless gloves with sticky rubber on the backs of the hands, they offer both protection for your hands and increased friction on the rock. They are also more durable than tape. The big

Fig. 12-3. *Manufactured crack climbing gloves: fingerless, with a Velcro wrist strap.*

advantage of manufactured gloves is that they're easy to take off; you can wear them only when you need them.

CHALK

Available as loose powder, a crushable block, or a liquid, chalk can improve a rock climber's grip by absorbing sweat, especially in hot weather. Climbers usually carry chalk in a designated bag attached to their harness or on a strap around their waist so that it is accessible but does not interfere with movement. Refillable mesh balls that allow smaller amounts of chalk to sift out into the chalk bag can minimize spillage.

Use chalk sparingly, especially in sensitive or heavily used areas. Chalk marks on a route identify the holds climbers have used in the past, detracting from the next climber's experience. Plus, excess chalk on holds can make them slippery, and such residue can affect other users. Some climbing areas require colors of chalk that match the rock.

QUICKDRAWS

Quickdraws are used to attach the rope to either bolts on a sport route or protection on a trad route. Using manufactured quickdraws rather than creating them out of slings is not only cleaner and faster for leading but also more secure and easier on all your gear in the long run. All sewn quickdraws have a rope-end fixed carabiner that does not spin, making it easier to clip the rope to this carabiner (fig. 12-4a), and a bolt-end side that, if made from aluminum, may develop burrs and nicks since aluminum is softer than the steel that nearly all bolt hangers are made of (see Bolts later in this chapter). These burrs can damage ropes or slings, and several accidents have been associated with them. Inspect your quickdraws regularly and replace damaged parts as necessary.

A tripled-up single-length (24-inch, 60-centimeter) sling works on occasion (fig. 12-4b), but sewn quickdraws are a better option for regular use. As always, inspect all climbing gear before using it to ensure it is in proper order, and retire or destroy any suspect gear.

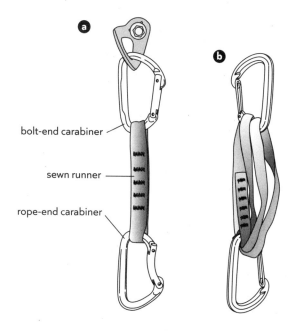

Fig. 12-4. *Quickdraws:* **a,** *sewn quickdraw with fixed carabiner at rope end for easier clipping;* **b,** *quickdraw created with tripled-up single-length sling clipped to two carabiners.*

bolt-end carabiner

sewn runner

rope-end carabiner

Transitioning from a Gym to the Outdoors

Transitioning from climbing inside a gym to sport climbing outside involves the familiarity of a top-rope belay, clipping fixed protection, and managing the rope. But learning to move on a variety of natural rock features, such as faces and cracks, presents new challenges (see Face Climbing and Crack Climbing later in this chapter). In sport climbing, always be careful to evaluate the soundness of fixed protection. The terrain sometimes dictates whether climbers lower off the route, rappel, or walk off.

Always discuss your descent plan before you leave the ground. For example, are you going to lower the leader, rappel, or walk off? You don't want to make that kind of important decision while the leader is on belay and you have to shout at each other.

SETTING UP A TOP ROPE

Unlike in a gym with preset top ropes, for a sport route the climbing team must bring their own rope up to establish a top rope. Nearly all sport climbing locales and cragging venues have fixed anchors at the top of each pitch. Most commonly these anchors are chains affixed to bolts (see Figure 11-2 in Chapter 11, Rappelling). On some sport routes, climbers can walk up to the top anchor to set up a top rope. Other routes require a lead climber to bring the rope up and run it through a fixed top anchor, or to perhaps even build the top anchor. Once the top rope is set up, both halves of the rope hang free from the top anchor and the belayer's tasks are the same as described in Chapter 10, Belaying. The first climber to top-rope the route unclips the rope from the fixed protection used for the lead climb, and then is either lowered off from or rappels at the top of the pitch.

It is best to avoid top-roping directly through a route's fixed rappel rings or chains because a weighted rope running through the anchor will wear it out quickly. A fixed anchor worn down this way long enough could become dangerously weak. Instead, top-rope through your own gear until it is time to lower off or rappel. Fixed mussy hooks are becomingly increasingly more common at anchors, and at some crags, the expectation is that climbers will use those for top-roping.

LEADING

The biggest difference between top-roping and leading a sport climbing pitch is that the leader accepts the possibility of a much greater fall. The fall will be slightly longer than twice the distance the leader was above the last point of protection because of rope stretch, slack in the system, and belayer reaction time. For instance, a leader who has

12

climbed 3 feet above the last clipped quickdraw would fall at least 6 feet plus rope stretch. Other factors that can affect a fall include a significant weight difference between the leader and belayer and whether or not the belayer gives a soft catch, an advanced technique whereby a belayer jumps to introduce slack into the system so the leader experiences less impact in a fall. The leader must decipher the challenges of the pitch while leading "on the sharp end" of the rope. Remember that a steep or close-to-vertical route is generally safer to lead than a blocky, easier-rated route with ledges, since a blocky route involves the risk of falling onto a ledge.

To maintain strength and power that you may need later on a pitch, balance your weight on your feet as much as possible. It may sound obvious, but make sure your climbing ability is consistent with the route you decide to lead. For example, you may be good at face climbing but struggle to climb cracks. In that case, if a route requires crack climbing, make sure that it is within your ability.

An aspiring leader who climbs well below their climbing ability can focus on learning the mechanics of leading without the distractions of climbing at the peak of their ability. Mock leading, climbing on top rope with a lead rope tied to your harness that you clip into quickdraws, is a great way for an aspiring leader to learn the mechanics with much less risk. To mentally prepare, start with routes well within your ability so you can focus on movement and the technical systems (anchors, protection points and gear, et cetera) instead of struggling to execute moves.

CLIMBING WITH FIXED PROTECTION

At sport climbing areas—and even at heavily traveled trad climbing areas—climbers will encounter many types of permanently placed (fixed) pieces of protection, or pro. Bolts are the most common type of fixed pro (see the next section) climbers will encounter. They are used at many rock climbing venues for lead, rappel, and belay anchors, and they are installed on sport climbing routes where naturally placed protection is limited and local ethics find bolts acceptable as permanent features.

In some areas, fixed protection might include pitons (hammered or drilled into place) or natural anchors like trees or boulders (see Belay Anchors in Chapter 10, Belaying). Fixed protection on a sport route can also include traditional gear that has been left behind—because the climbers who placed it were unable to remove it or left it intentionally for rappels or to best protect an otherwise tricky-to-protect section of rock.

Bolts

Bolts have been used for years as a method of attaching an anchor to rock. (For more on placing bolts, see Minimizing Climbing Impacts in Chapter 7 and Spirit of Aid Climbing in Chapter 15.) Unlike pitons, which are hammered into a crack, bolts can be installed in a variety of ways. A climbing bolt is fixed into a hole drilled into the rock. Newer bolts include self-anchoring expansion bolts and adhesives to make a stronger, more weather-resistant fixed anchor. They are usually stainless-steel concrete fasteners ranging from ⅜ inch to ½ inch in diameter and 2¼ inches to 4 inches in length, depending on the hardness of the rock and style in which they were placed.

Well-placed bolts will last for years, but age and weather can compromise their strength, with new bolts being significantly stronger and longer-lasting than models used more than three decades ago. Be especially wary of ¼-inch-diameter bolts, placed primarily in the 1960s and 1970s. Well-placed new bolts are stronger than most carabiners and capable of holding 5,000 to 7,000 pounds (about 2,300 to 3,200 kilograms), depending on their diameter and the quality and type of rock they are placed in. Most older

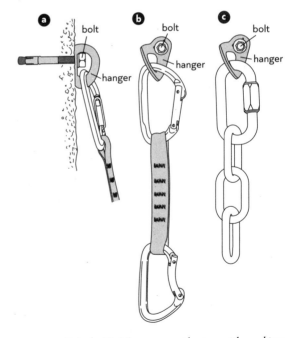

Fig. 12-5. *Bolts and bolt hangers: **a,** side view, with carabiner clipped to hanger; **b,** front view, with quickdraw clipped to hanger; **c,** front view, with quick link and chain attached to hanger.*

¼-inch bolts, which may have held 1,500 pounds (about 680 kilograms) when new, may be barely capable of holding body weight as a result of age and weathering.

In most cases, when a bolt has been placed, it includes a hanger, which allows a climber to attach a carabiner or quickdraw to it (fig. 12-5a and b). Chains, commonly used on bolted anchors (fig. 12-5c) intended for rappelling, are superior to webbing. They are not affected by UV rays, are more difficult to cut, and are unlikely to be damaged by wildlife. Chains are often attached to the bolt hangers by quick links. (See Figure 11-2 in Chapter 11 for a bolted rappel anchor setup.)

Be cautious of homemade-looking or sheet-metal-style hangers or any bolt hanger with heavy rust. Any bolt that can be moved in any direction, however slightly, is probably not trustworthy. Back up any suspect bolt with another point of protection nearby wherever possible, or better yet, use a different anchor altogether.

Clipping Fixed Protection

When you clip a quickdraw to a bolt hanger, make sure to orient the carabiner gate away from your direction of travel (fig. 12-6a and b). Otherwise, the carabiner attached to the hanger may rotate or slide in such a way that the gate makes direct contact with the bolt hanger (fig. 12-6c). If the leader

falls, the gate could strike the bolt hanger and possibly open or break. Not all carabiners and bolt hangers are alike, and a leader must evaluate each circumstance, trying to safeguard against situations that could lead to the carabiner gate unclipping from the hanger if force were suddenly applied.

The same principle applies when clipping in to pieces of fixed protection other than bolts. Avoid placing a carabiner in a position wherein the gate could open if it were to strike the rock or any other contact point.

A bigger concern is to make sure that you clip the gate of the carabiner so that the rope faces away from your direction of travel. For example, if the climb heads up to the right after a protection point, the gate clipped to the rope should face left (as in Figure 12-6a and b). If the climb heads up to the left, the gate should face right. Ignoring this principle

Fig. 12-7. *Lead climber preparing to clip in to a quickdraw while belayed from the ground.*

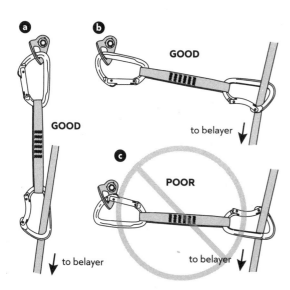

Fig. 12-6. *Clipping a carabiner in to a bolt hanger:* **a** *and* **b,** *gates face opposite the direction of the climb, which here goes up and right, and are not in danger of unclipping (good);* **c,** *gate faces direction of climb and is in danger of unclipping (poor).*

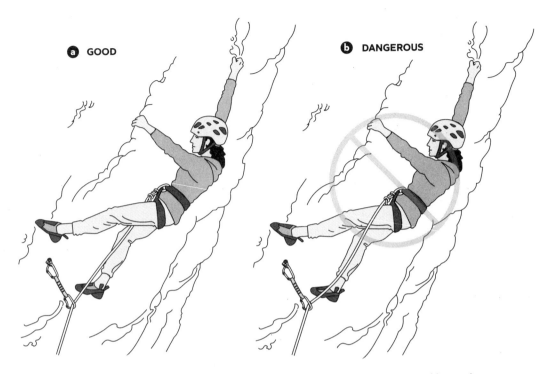

Fig. 12-8. *Rope management:* **a,** *when leading, aim to keep the rope between your legs (good);* **b,** *avoid letting the rope run over or behind one leg (dangerous).*

increases the risk that the rope will move over the gate if the leader falls, which could cause the gate to open and the rope to unclip. When a climber travels straight up from the last protection point, the gate direction does not matter. If there is a long runout above a protection point, consider using a locking carabiner to connect the rope to significantly reduce the chance of the rope becoming unclipped.

MANAGING THE ROPE ON LEAD

The lead climber progressing up the route trails the rope behind them, clipping in to protection, until they reach an anchor point and clip in to it—or possibly fall. If a lead climber falls, the rope is now above them, which means that during the frenzied moments of a fall, the leader and rope need to pass each other without becoming entangled. Generally the rope needs to be between a lead climber and the rock (fig. 12-8a). A leader must not climb with the rope running behind (over) their leg (fig. 12-8b): in a fall, the rope could flip them upside down violently, tangle them in the rope, cause rope burn, or otherwise increase their likelihood of injury from the very equipment meant to protect them.

A roped pitch along a simple diagonal illustrates this concept clearly (see Figure 12-8). However, on more intricate pitches with diagonal moves, bulges, short traverses, and protection on both sides of the climbing moves, keeping the rope aligned can quickly become complicated (see Chapter 14, Traditional Rock Climbing). Tracking how the rope and climber may interact in a fall is a lead climbing skill that requires coordinated problem-solving while placing protection.

CLEANING AND DESCENDING FROM A SINGLE-PITCH CLIMB

Nearly all sport climbing and most cragging venues feature fixed top anchors to facilitate lowering off. Most commonly these are chains affixed to bolts with double rappel (rap) rings (see Figure 11-2 in Chapter 11, Rappelling), but you may also find single rings in some climbing areas (see Figure 12-9). Generally speaking, it is OK to lower the final climber to the ground directly off the fixed anchor's chains. But in a handful of areas, climbers frown on lowering off through chains, which means the final climber will have to rappel down from them.

"Cleaning" refers to removing your gear from a climb—the quickdraws clipped in to the bolts and any quickdraws, carabiners, or runners attached to the fixed top anchor—and threading the rope directly through the anchor ring(s) or chains for lowering or rappelling. If it is possible to lower off from the top of the route, and the final climber leads the route, they will remove the quickdraws put in for protection as they descend; if the final climber top-ropes the route, they can remove the quickdraws on the way up or while lowering off (depending on the orientation of the bolts relative to the anchor). If you plan to rappel or hike off the route, the last climber to ascend will clean the route as they climb.

Whether you opt to lower off or rappel, make the decision on the ground before starting to climb and clearly communicate your plans to your belayer. *You do not want them to accidentally take you off belay when you expect them to lower you.* Also ask them about the type of anchor you will encounter at the top: Are there chains, or is the anchor equipped with fixed steel carabiners for lowering? Some routes feature the latter, making cleaning the anchor and lowering off particularly easy (see below).

Transitioning to Lowering Off

There are distinct safety advantages to lowering off rather than rappelling: among these, the climber never has to be off belay, they have no chance of dropping the rope, and it is not necessary to have a prerigged personal anchor system (see Personal Anchors in Chapter 8, Essential Climbing Equipment). The preferred method follows these steps. (Note that the anchor featured in Figure 12-9 is vertically oriented, with a chain connecting the rap ring to a second, higher bolt for redundancy; sport anchors vary somewhat, depending on local features and rock quality.)

1. **Clip in to either the anchor hangers or chains** with your personal anchor (fig. 12-9a), carabiners, slings, and/or quickdraws. Test your personal anchor setup by weighting it.
2. **Ask your belayer for slack, then pass a bight** of the climbing rope through the rappel ring(s) (fig. 12-9b) or chains.
3. **Tie a figure eight on this bight** and clip the knot in to your harness belay loop with a locking carabiner (fig. 12-9c). Test this new setup by weighting it.
4. **Untie your original tie-in knot**, and feed the end of the rope through the rap ring (fig. 12-9d).
5. **Clean any gear** used to top-rope from the anchor.
6. **Ask your belayer to take your weight** to confirm that you are still on belay. Examine the anchor carefully to make sure you threaded the rope correctly.
7. **Unclip your personal anchor** (fig. 12-9e). As your belayer lowers you, clean any quickdraws still on the route.

A climber on top-rope would begin with their rope clipped through their party's own gear—quickdraws or locking carabiners—attached to the anchor. They will need to remove those items after they have threaded the rope through the rap ring. Some modern sport climbs

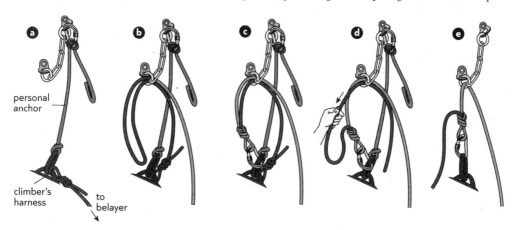

Fig. 12-9. *Cleaning a bolted anchor to transition from leading to being lowered: **a,** clip personal anchor (here, girth-hitched to belay loop) in to top anchor bolt; **b,** ask belayer for slack and pass bight of rope through rap ring; **c,** tie bight into a figure eight and clip it to harness belay loop with locking carabiner; **d,** untie original tie-in knot and feed end of rope through rap ring; **e,** have belayer pull in the slack, then remove your personal anchor—you are now ready to be lowered.*

feature permanent anchors with two stainless-steel carabiners or mussy hooks designed specifically for lowering. When you are finished with the route, simply clip your rope through both fixed carabiners and then clean your anchor quickdraws.

Transitioning to Rappelling

After cleaning the pitch on the way up and anchoring in, the last climber must untie from the rope. While threading the rope through the rappel anchor, the climber risks dropping it. Before you start climbing, make sure you and your partners agree about using this descent method.

To rappel, the last climber follows these steps:

1. **Clean the route as you ascend**, by unclipping the quickdraws from the bolts. Then remove the quickdraws from the rope in front of you and move them to your harness gear loops or a gear sling.

2. **When you reach the anchor, attach your personal anchor to it.** Make sure both bolts are engaged in the system. *Never rely on a single bolt.*

3. **Pull up some rope, tie an overhand on a bight, and secure the knot** to a harness gear loop using a locking carabiner.

4. **Untie the rope from your harness, then thread it through the rappel anchor chains.** Tie a stopper knot in the end of the rope.

5. **Pull the rope through the chains**, removing it from your harness gear loop when you get to that point. When you reach the halfway mark, have the climber who was belaying you confirm that both ends are clearly visible on the ground.

6. **Set up your autoblock and extended rappel** (see Figure 11-1 in Chapter 11).

7. **Rappel to the ground**, untie any stopper knots, and then pull the rope down.

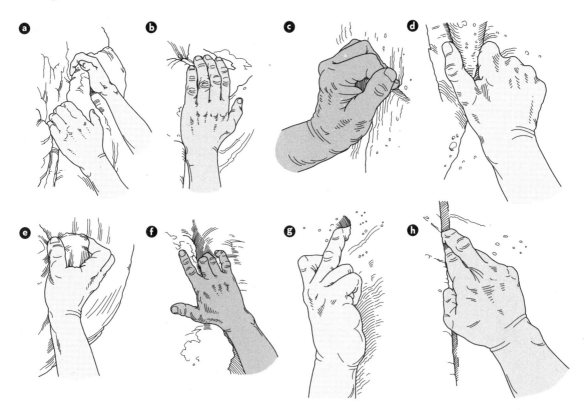

Fig. 12-10. *Handholds:* **a**, *hands on a jug with fingers close together;* **b**, *smaller open-grip hold;* **c**, *crimping on a smaller hold (more stressful on finger joints);* **d**, *finger pinch;* **e**, *thumb pinch;* **f**, *two-finger pocket;* **g**, *mono pocket;* **h**, *stacked fingers.*

Face Climbing

Face climbing refers to a style of climbing using the features on a rock wall or slab. A climber may use a particular hold or rock feature in a variety of ways with feet and hands while moving up the rock. Face climbing also includes ascending nearly featureless slabs, which requires techniques for smearing, friction, and balance. *Note:* To clearly show body positions in this section's illustrations, essential safety gear such as ropes, harnesses, and protection is omitted.

USING HANDHOLDS

Handholds can be used for balance, to help you raise yourself by pulling down on the hold, for providing counterforce or counterpressure, and to allow you to rest. Handholds head height or higher but not too far up are best, as long as they do not require you to overreach, which can be very tiring.

Handholds offer maximum security when you put all your fingers on them. Keeping your fingers close together strengthens your grip. A large hold, commonly known as a jug, allows the entire hand to be cupped over the hold (fig. 12-10a). A smaller, open-grip hold (fig. 12-10b) may allow room for only fingertips. If the hold is too small for all your fingers, crimp it, curling your fingers and placing your thumb over your index finger, which permits the fingers in use to get the most force from the muscle and tendon system (fig. 12-10c). Crimping requires caution, however: be careful not to overstress your fingers and injure yourself by using holds that are too small or difficult for your level of technique or conditioning.

Because climbers depend mainly on their legs to move upward, handholds are sometimes used only for balance. The finger pinch (fig. 12-10d) is a handhold that may allow climbers to maintain a balanced stance on good footholds long enough to shake out their free arm before reaching for a higher, more secure handhold or placing protection.

Smaller holds require different techniques. For example, with fingers holding on to a tiny ledge, climbers may use the thumb in opposition on a minor wrinkle for additional strength, as in a thumb pinch (fig. 12-10e); or in small holes, they may use more than one finger, as in a two-finger pocket (fig. 12-10f). On a narrow hold or a small pocket in the rock, climbers can use one or two fingers in a mono pocket (fig. 12-10g). On a very narrow hold or in a tight fissure, climbers can stack fingers on top of each other to increase down-pressure on the hold (fig. 12-10h).

Handholds at about head height are ideal for hanging straight-armed for a rest (fig. 12-11), which is less tiring

than hanging from bent arms. Lower your center of gravity by bending your knees or leaning out away from the rock. Letting an arm hang down and shaking it out can allow you to recover briefly before you continue climbing.

Some other types of handholds include slopers and side pulls. Slopers require an open hand and skin friction, and the holds, true to their name, slope downward. A side pull is a vertically oriented hold off to one side. You lean away from it as you pull on it.

Other techniques can also be useful on friction slabs. Face holds and cracks may be intermittently available for hands or feet. On small edges or irregularities, use down-pressure with your fingertips, thumb, or the heel of your hand. You may be able to use tiny edges to lieback with one hand. Look for an opportunity to stem, which could offer you a chance to rest your arms. For more about liebacking and stemming, see Using Counterforce in Crack Climbing later in this chapter.

12

Fig. 12-11. *Resting an outstretched arm while hanging on a straight arm.*

USING FOOTHOLDS

Climbers employ one of two techniques for most footholds: edging or smearing. On many holds, either technique will work; your choice will depend on personal preference and the stiffness of your footwear. A third technique, foot jamming, is covered in Crack Climbing later in this chapter.

When edging, the climber weights the edge of their sole over the hold (fig. 12-12a). Climbers usually prefer the inside edge for greater ease and security. The ideal point of contact may vary, but generally, it is between the ball of the foot and the end of the big toe. Keeping the heel higher than the toes offers greater precision but is more tiring. Using the toe of a boot or rock shoe on a hold (toeing in) is also very tiring. With practice, climbers can become proficient at using progressively smaller footholds.

In smearing, climbers point their foot uphill and "smear" the sole of the shoe over the hold (fig. 12-12b). Smearing works best with rock shoes, approach shoes, or flexible boots. On lower-angle rock, climbers may need to use only the smooth rock face, not a distinct hold, to create enough

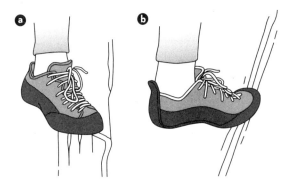

Fig. 12-12. *Footholds: **a,** edging; **b,** smearing.*

Fig. 12-13. *Bucket hold: **a,** use only as much of the hold as you need; **b,** putting your foot too far into a bucket can force your lower leg outward.*

friction. On steeper terrain, smearing the front of your foot over a hold allows even tiny irregularities in the rock to provide significant friction and security. Slab or friction climbing requires liberal use of smearing, or frictioning moves. Balance and footwork are the keys to success, and the primary technique is smearing with the feet.

When smearing, remember to flex the ankle (lowering the heel) and to keep your weight directly over the ball of your foot for maximum friction between rock and sole. Avoid leaning your body into the slope, which will cause your feet to slide down and out from under you. Instead, keep your weight over your feet, bending at the waist to touch the rock, and push your hips and buttocks away.

In using footholds, make the best use of the direction of force on the hold. Flexing the ankle may increase the surface area of contact between sole and rock, offering maximum holding power. Leaning away from the rock creates inward as well as downward pressure, further improving the hold.

When using large footholds, called buckets, place only as much of your foot as necessary on the hold (fig. 12-13a). Putting your foot in too far can sometimes force your lower leg outward, making for an out-of-balance stance (fig. 12-13b).

Avoid placing your knees on a hold: knees are susceptible to injury and offer little stability. Nevertheless, even experienced climbers may occasionally use a kneehold to avoid an especially high or awkward step. The main considerations are to avoid injury from pebbles and sharp crystals and to avoid becoming trapped on your knees, unable to rise beneath a bulge or roof.

Fatigue, often aggravated by anxiety, can lead to troublesome spastic contractions of the leg muscles, jocularly known among climbers as "sewing-machine" or "Elvis" leg. The best way to stop the spasms is to pause for a moment, take a few deep breaths, and change your leg position somehow—by moving on to the next hold, lowering your heel, or straightening your leg.

Take short steps to maintain balance, with your weight over your feet. Look for the small edges, rough spots, or changes in angle that make for the best foot placements. Sometimes climbers have to feel with their hands or feet to find irregularities that are hard to see.

Try to walk up the rock from foothold to foothold, as if you are going up a ladder—relying on your feet and using your hands merely for balance. When you raise a foot toward the next foothold, eye the hold and aim for it precisely. Once your foot is placed, hold firm, committing to it and the smear. Adjust your balance by shifting your hips over the new hold. Continue transferring your weight through your leg down to that foot. Complete the move: use your leg muscles to stand up.

MANTELING

A specific downward-pressure technique, the mantel lets climbers push down with their hands to lever their feet up onto the same hold when there are no higher handholds.

The classic mantel is easiest if the ledge is at about chest height (fig. 12-14a). As you grip the ledge, walk your feet up the rock (fig. 12-14b) until you can place both hands flat on the ledge, palms down, with the fingers of each hand curled over the edge, pointing down. Then raise up onto straight arms (fig. 12-14c). Continue to walk your feet up the rock or, if you can, spring up from a good foothold, lifting one foot up onto the ledge (fig. 12-14d). Stand up, reaching for the next handholds for balance (fig. 12-14e).

It is not always possible to execute a down mantel, however. A ledge is often higher, smaller, or steeper than you would prefer. To mantel on a narrow ledge, use the heels of your hands, with your fingers pointed down. If the ledge is over your head, pull down on it first, then use down-pressure as you move upward. If the ledge is too small for both hands, mantel up with just one arm and use your other hand on any other available hold (or perhaps just balance your hand against the rock). Remember to leave room for your foot.

Avoid using your knees on a mantel because it may be difficult to get your feet back under you, especially if the rock above is steep or overhanging. Sometimes it is possible halfway through manteling (see Figure 12-14c and d), when you are in a stable position, to reach up to a handhold to help you stand.

USING COUNTERFORCE IN FACE CLIMBING

Climbers can use counterforce to pull in on widely spaced holds—a pulling-together action (fig. 12-15a)—or to press in on both sides of a sharp ridge (fig. 12-15b) to create inward pressure. The hands can also be used in counterforce to the feet, as in an undercling (see below).

Stemming on a Face

A valuable counterforce technique, stemming allows climbers to push between two spots on the rock that may have few prominent features or holds. Where no holds are apparent, you may simply be able to press in opposing directions with your feet or with a hand and a foot.

Stemming may open an avenue of ascent on a steep face, where climbers can press one foot against a slight protrusion while the other foot or a hand gives opposing pressure against another rugosity or wrinkle in the rock (fig. 12-16).

Underclinging

On downward-facing ledges or flakes that are at about waist height, you can use a counterforce grip called underclinging.

Fig. 12-14. *Mantel:* **a** *and* **b,** *with ledge about chest high, walk feet up;* **c,** *place both hands flat on ledge, palms down and fingers of each hand pointing out and down;* **d,** *place one foot on the ledge;* **e,** *stand up and reach for next handholds.*

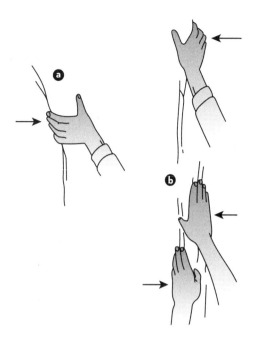

Your hands (palms up) pull outward beneath the flake or lip of rock while your body leans out and your feet push against the rock (fig. 12-17). Your arms pull while your feet push, creating a counterforce. Try to keep your arms extended. Both hands can undercling at the same time, or one hand can undercling while the other uses a different type of hold.

An undercling may have multiple uses. For example, from below a rock flake, climbers may hold the flake's bottom edge in a finger or thumb pinch and then convert to an undercling as they move up the flake.

Crack Climbing

Many climbing routes follow the natural lines of cracks in the rock. Cracks have the advantage of offering handholds and footholds virtually anywhere along their length, as well as protection opportunities (see Chapter 13, Rock Protection). Some climbers find crack climbing technique more difficult to develop than face climbing technique. Perhaps this is because even easy crack climbs demand a higher proportion of technique to strength than face climbs do. This type of climbing is also very individualized, depending on the size of each climber's hands, fingers, and feet. A crack

*Fig. 12-15. Counterforce: **a,** inward pressure, pulling together; **b,** inward pressure, pressing in on a sharp ridge.*

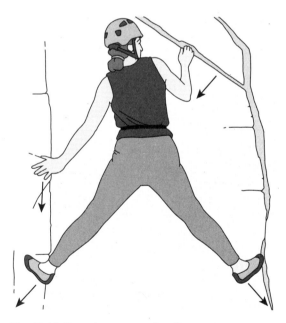

Fig. 12-16. Stemming on a steep face: feet press in opposite directions while left hand uses down-pressure and right hand pulls down on a crack.

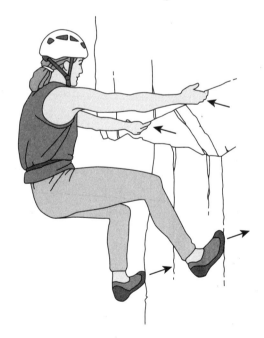

Fig. 12-17. Underclinging: arrows show direction of counterforce—hands pull out, feet push in.

climb of a certain width that is easy for one climber may be tricky for others with smaller hands, for example, or vice versa.

Experiment with what works for you. As with face climbing, balance and practice are the keys to success. That said, the following techniques—jamming and counterforce—are essential tools. *Note:* To clearly show body positions in this section's illustrations, essential safety equipment such as ropes, harnesses, and protection is omitted.

JAMMING

The basic technique of crack climbing is jamming. To jam, place a hand or foot into a crack, then rotate from your hip to turn your foot or flex your hand so that it is in snug contact with both sides of the crack. This foot or hand must be secure enough that it will hold when weighted. Look for constrictions in the crack, and place hand and foot jams just above them. When learning to crack climb, it is a good idea to weight-test jams—while remaining balanced on the other points of contact—before trying to move up on them.

Fig. 12-18. *Combining jamming (hands) with face climbing (feet).*

Cracks may be climbed with a pure jamming technique, with both feet and hands using jams, or in combination with other types of holds. While moving up on a jam, maintain the jammed position by using down-pressure. For many cracks, as you move along, one hand will be jammed thumb-up, the other, thumb down (fig. 12-18). Of course, there is nothing to stop you from using any nearby face holds for your feet or hands as well.

The following techniques are basic guidelines that you can adapt depending on the size and configuration of individual cracks. With practice, you will become more adept at selecting the appropriate technique to apply in a given situation.

Hand-Sized Cracks

The easiest crack to master is the hand-sized crack. As the name implies, climbers insert their entire hand into the crack. Relax your hand when you insert it, and then clench or expand your hand to wedge it in the crack. Different ways to increase hand width include flexing the thumb toward the palm so that the lower "meaty" part of the hand firmly contacts the walls of the crack, and cupping the hand for full contact (fig. 12-19a). To increase pressure against the walls, climbers sometimes tuck their thumb below their fingers and across the palm, especially in wider cracks (fig. 12-19b). To improve the hold, try bending your wrist so your hand points into the crack rather than straight up and down.

Hand jams are done with the thumb either up or down. The thumb-up technique is often the easiest and most comfortable for a vertical crack (as in Figure 12-19a and b; see also the bottom hand in Figure 12-19d) because it allows you to reach higher. The thumb-up configuration is most secure when your body leans to the same side as your jammed hand.

The thumb-down technique (fig. 12-19c; see also the top hand in Figure 12-19d) may allow for a more secure jam when the thumb-up technique may feel less secure to some climbers. However, you cannot reach as high with this jam in a vertical crack, which means having to use more hand jams and expend more energy. Because twisting the hand increases friction, climbers can lean in any direction off this jam. Climbers use a combination of thumbs up and thumbs down, especially in diagonal cracks, where it is often useful to jam the upper hand thumb down and the lower hand thumb up (fig. 12-19d).

With hand jams, climbers must keep alert to the effect of their elbow and body position on the security of the hold. As they move up and above the jam, they may have

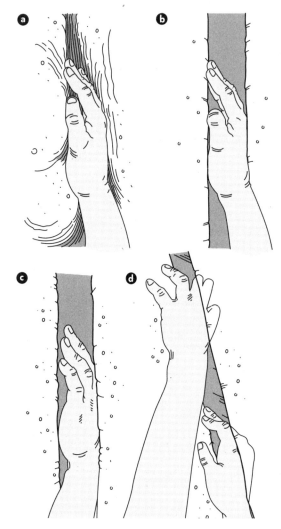

Fig. 12-19. *Hand jams: **a**, thumb-up jam; **b**, with thumb tucked across palm; **c**, thumb-down jam; **d**, combining thumb-down and thumb-up jams in a diagonal crack.*

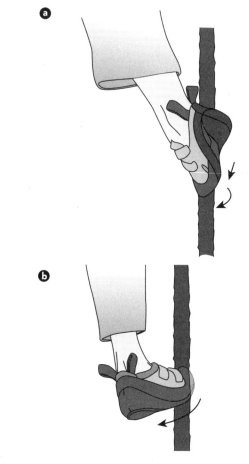

Fig. 12-20. *Foot jams: **a**, with foot facing sideways, stick toes in crack; **b**, then twist foot sole-down to jam.*

to rotate their shoulder or trunk to keep sufficient torque and downward pressure to maintain the hold. Direction of force should be pulling down, not out of the crack. In general, keep your forearm parallel to the crack while climbing.

In dealing with hand jams, climbers encounter variations at both ends of the size scale: from thinner cracks too big for finger jams but too small for the entire hand, up to wider cracks that are not quite large enough for a fist jam but require extra hand twisting to create enough expansion

for a secure hand jam. The size of a climber's hand is a major factor in determining the appropriate technique and degree of difficulty of any particular crack. Of course, crack size can change over the length of the crack. Generally some types of rock, like sandstone, yield cracks that are more consistent. They are beloved when they are a perfect fit and stay consistent for many vertical feet.

Hand-sized cracks are often suitable for foot jamming too, and it is generally possible to wedge a shoe in as far as the ball of the foot. Insert your foot sideways (fig. 12-20a), with your sole facing the side of the crack (big toe facing up), then rotate your hip inward to twist your foot sole-down to jam it (fig. 12-20b). The trick is to avoid twisting your foot so securely that it gets stuck.

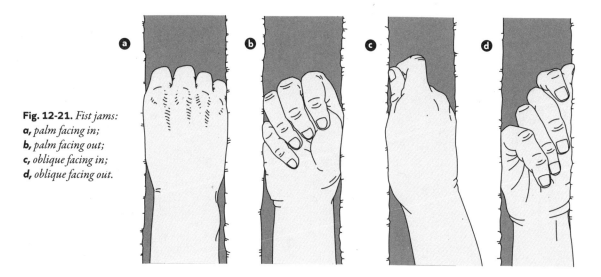

Fig. 12-21. *Fist jams:*
a, *palm facing in;*
b, *palm facing out;*
c, *oblique facing in;*
d, *oblique facing out.*

Fist-Sized Cracks

In a crack that is too wide for a hand jam, climbers can insert a fist. You can put your thumb inside or outside your fist, whichever provides the best fit. Your palm may face either the back of the crack (fig. 12-21a) or the front (fig. 12-21b). If the crack is not wide enough for a full fist jam, try turning your hand slightly to do an oblique fist jam (fig. 12-21c and d). If it is a bit too wide, try flexing your fist for a better fit. Fist jams, while often painful, can be very solid and useful. For the most secure hold, look for a constriction in the crack and jam your fist above it. If the crack is too wide for a hand but too small for your fist, you may be able to shove your entire forearm into the crack and flex it for purchase.

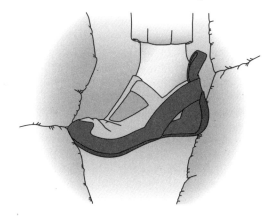

Fig. 12-22. *Heel-toe foot jam.*

Generally, most climbers can fit their entire foot in a fist-sized crack. As with hand-sized cracks, insert your foot sideways, sole facing the side of the crack, and rotate your foot to jam it securely in place. In even wider cracks, most often off-widths, it is possible to jam a foot diagonally or heel to toe (fig. 12-22).

Finger-Sized Cracks

Finger jams make it possible to climb some of the narrowest cracks, where a climber may be able to insert only one finger or perhaps just the fingertips. Finger jams are commonly done thumb down. Slip your fingers into the crack and twist your hand to lock your fingers in place (fig. 12-23a). Make your jam stronger by stacking your fingers or pressing your thumb against your index finger to form a ring jam (fig. 12-23b and c).

In slightly wider cracks, try a thumb lock, also called a thumb cam (fig. 12-23d). Place an upward-pointing thumb in the crack, the thumb pad against one side of the crack and a knuckle against the other. Slide the tip of your index finger tightly down over the first joint of your thumb to create the lock.

The pinkie jam is done with a thumb up (fig. 12-23e and f). Put your little finger in a crack and stack your other fingers on top—fingertips down, fingernails up. In slightly larger cracks, it may be possible to wedge the heel and smallest fingers of your hand into a crack that is not quite wide enough for a full hand jam. The heel of your hand bears the weight in this position.

12

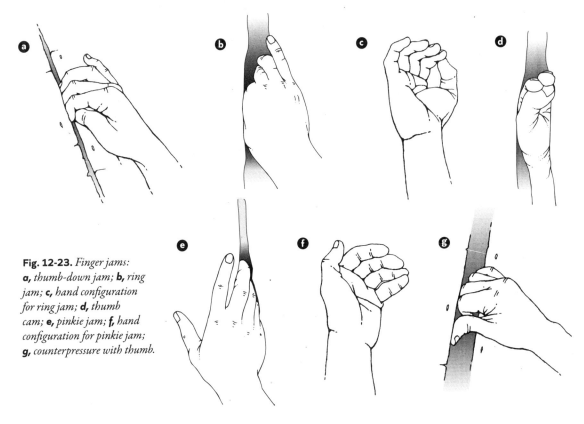

Fig. 12-23. *Finger jams:* **a,** *thumb-down jam;* **b,** *ring jam;* **c,** *hand configuration for ring jam;* **d,** *thumb cam;* **e,** *pinkie jam;* **f,** *hand configuration for pinkie jam;* **g,** *counterpressure with thumb.*

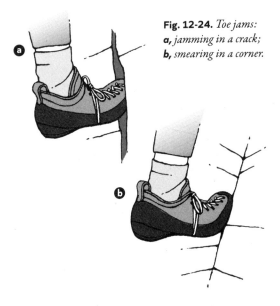

Fig. 12-24. *Toe jams:* **a,** *jamming in a crack;* **b,** *smearing in a corner.*

For another thumb-down variation, use the counterpressure of a thumb pushing against one side of the crack and the fingers pushing against the other (fig. 12-23g).

Finger-sized cracks are not big enough for a climber's foot, but there is often room for toes. Turn your foot sideways—usually with the inside of the ankle up—and insert your toes in the crack (see Figure 12-20a), then twist your foot to jam it (fig. 12-24a). Climbers also wedge their toes into a steep inside corner with a smearing technique, keeping their heel lower than their toes and putting pressure down and in to keep their toes in place (fig. 12-24b). Smearing and using your feet in a way that increases friction can also work well in a finger-sized crack. For thin cracks, a softer, narrower climbing shoe often performs well.

USING COUNTERFORCE IN CRACK CLIMBING

To use counterforce in a vertical crack, place both hands in the crack and pull in opposite directions on the sides of the crack—a pulling-apart action (fig. 12-25)—to create outward pressure. Two other types of counterforce are described below.

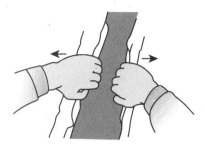

Fig. 12-25. *Using counterforce in a vertical crack to exert outward pressure.*

Classic Stemming

One classic way that climbers apply stemming is when climbing a rock chimney. It also comes into play in climbing a dihedral (also called an open book), where two walls meet in an inside corner. One foot and hand press against one wall of the chimney or dihedral, while the other foot and hand push against the other wall (fig. 12-26).

Liebacking

For the classic lieback technique, another form of counterforce, a climber uses their hands pulling and feet pushing in opposition to move upward in shuffling movements

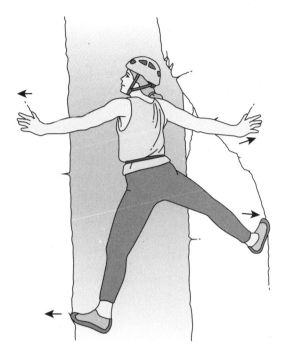

Fig. 12-26. *Stemming across a chimney: feet and hands on the left push to the left and on the right push to the right.*

Fig. 12-27. *Lieback:* **a,** *classic lieback;* **b,** *combining a lieback (right hand and foot) with face holds (left hand and foot). Arrows indicate direction of force.*

(fig. 12-27a). It is used to climb a crack in a corner, a crack with one edge offset beyond the other, or along the edge of a flake. Grasp one edge of the crack with both hands and lean back and to the side, away from the crack, on straight arms. At the same time, push your feet against the opposite wall of the crack. Keep your arms extended to minimize muscle stress. Keep your feet high enough to maintain friction on the rock, but not so high that the technique becomes arduous. As always, feel for your body's balance and adjust accordingly. This is a strenuous technique, and it is difficult to place protection when liebacking.

The lieback can be used along with other holds as the rock allows. Climbers can lieback on a single handhold in combination with other holds, or use one hand and foot in a lieback while using face holds for the opposite hand and foot (fig. 12-27b).

When using the lieback technique, a climber's body may have a tendency to swing sideways out of balance toward the crack, in what is known as a "barn-door," which usually results in a fall. To avoid barn-dooring outward, do not apply too much pressure with the leg closest to the rock (the left leg in Figure 12-27a).

CHIMNEYING

A chimney is any crack big enough to climb inside. They range in size from those that will barely admit a climber's body (called squeeze chimneys) to those that a climber's body can barely span. The basic principle is to span the breadth of the chimney with your body, using counterforce to keep from falling. Depending on the width of the crack, either face one side of the chimney or face directly into or out of it. The best body position and technique to use depends on the situation, your body size, and whether you are wearing a pack. If you are wearing a pack, you may want to consider options for hauling and/or dragging it, if it could get in your way and/or get damaged in the chimney. Which direction to face may depend on what holds are available outside the chimney and the best way to climb out of it.

In squeeze chimneys, wedge yourself in whatever way works best (fig. 12-28a) and twist and turn to work upward (fig. 12-28b). Look for handholds on the outside edge or inside the chimney. Arm bars and chicken wings (see Using Jams and Counterforce in Off-Width Cracks, below) may be useful. It is helpful, sometimes, to press a foot and knee of one leg (fig. 12-28c) or both legs (fig. 12-28d) against opposite sides of the chimney. Try stacking both feet in a

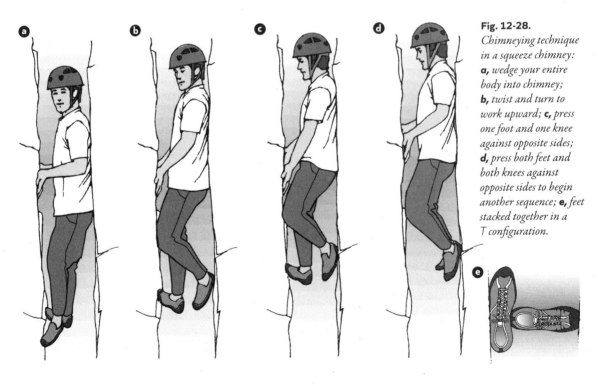

Fig. 12-28.
*Chimneying technique in a squeeze chimney: **a,** wedge your entire body into chimney; **b,** twist and turn to work upward; **c,** press one foot and one knee against opposite sides; **d,** press both feet and both knees against opposite sides to begin another sequence; **e,** feet stacked together in a T configuration.*

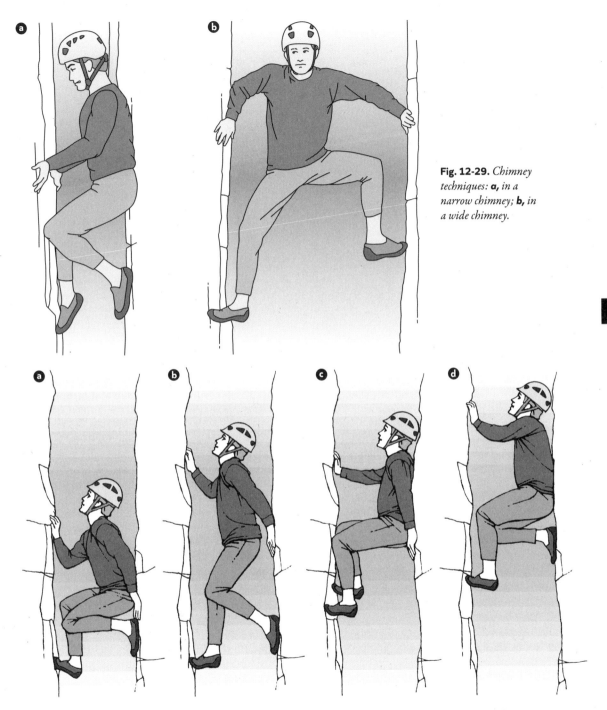

Fig. 12-29. *Chimney techniques:* **a,** *in a narrow chimney;* **b,** *in a wide chimney.*

Fig. 12-30. *Chimney techniques in a moderate-width chimney:* **a,** *using counterforce between hands and between feet;* **b,** *straightening legs to move up;* **c,** *using counterforce between buttocks and feet;* **d,** *beginning the sequence again.*

Fig. 12-31. *Chimneying technique in a dihedral.*

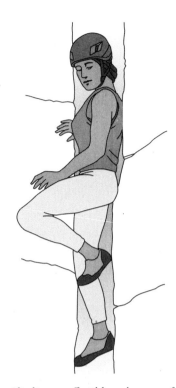

Fig. 12-32. *Climbing an off-width crack: counterforce between hip or knee and foot, plus heel-toe jams.*

T configuration, with one foot parallel to one side of the rock and the other perpendicular to it, jammed between the first foot and the opposite wall (fig. 12-28e). Climbing squeeze chimneys can be very taxing.

A crack somewhat wider than a squeeze chimney offers more room to maneuver. Press your back and feet against one side of the chimney as your knees and hands push against the other side (fig. 12-29a). Move upward by twisting and turning. Or try a sequence of wedging your upper body while raising your feet and knees, then wedging your feet and knees to raise your upper body.

A wide chimney calls for a stemming technique in which a climber faces directly into or out of the chimney and applies counterforce between the right hand and foot on one side of the chimney and the left hand and foot on the other side (fig. 12-29b). Press down as well as against the sides, especially if there are holds on the sides of the chimney. Ascend either by alternately moving arms and legs (cross-laterally) or by moving each leg and then each arm.

To climb a moderate-width chimney, perhaps 3 feet (1 meter) wide, face one wall of it with your back toward the other wall. Press one foot against each wall and one hand against each wall (fig. 12-30a). Move upward by straightening your legs and then reestablishing your hand positions

(fig. 12-30b). Immediately bring your back-wall leg across to the same side as the forward leg (fig. 12-30c), then swing your forward leg across to the back-wall position (fig. 12-30d). Now move upward again by straightening your legs. Alternatively, push your hands against one wall in counterforce to your back pressed against the other, or push your feet against one wall in counterforce to your buttocks against the other (see Figure 12-30c).

Though it may feel more secure psychologically, getting too far inside a chimney can make it difficult to move back out. You have a better chance of finding useful handholds and footholds near the outside of the chimney. Climbing deep inside can also make it harder to exit at the top. The transition from the top of the chimney to other types of climbing is often a challenge that requires extra thought, creativity, and skills.

Try using chimney technique in places other than classic chimneys, for example, in dihedrals (fig. 12-31) or along short, wide sections of otherwise narrower cracks. Knee pads can be very useful when climbing routes with extensive chimney sections.

USING JAMS AND COUNTERFORCE IN OFF-WIDTH CRACKS

Climbers have figured out ways to jam their arms, shoulders, hips, and knees into the difficult and awkward features known as off-width cracks, which are too wide for hand or fist jams but too narrow to admit the entire body for chimneying. The basic off-width technique calls for standing sideways to the crack and inserting one full side of your body into it (fig. 12-32). When confronted with an off-width crack, first decide which side of your body to put inside the crack, gauging the kinds of holds inside the crack versus on the face, the direction in which the crack leans, and whether the opening flares larger in some places than others.

After settling on which side to use, put your inside leg in the crack to form a counterforced knee bar, usually using either your foot and knee or foot and hip. This foot is often placed in a heel-toe jam (see Figure 12-22). The outside foot is also inside the crack in a heel-toe jam. Try to keep your toes below your heels (for better friction) and your heels turned into the crack (to allow the outside knee to turn out).

A primary body-jam technique is the arm bar. With your body sideways to the crack, insert one arm fully into the crack, with your elbow and the back of your upper arm on one side of the crack giving counterforce to the heel of the hand on the other side (fig. 12-33a). Get your shoulder in as far as possible, and have your arm bar extend diagonally down from the shoulder.

To perform a chicken wing, a variation of the arm bar, fold an arm in at the elbow, insert it in the crack, and press your palm against the opposite side in counterforce to your shoulder (fig. 12-33b). In either the arm bar or the chicken wing, use the outside arm to provide down-pressure to help hold you in the crack, or bring it across the front of your chest and push it against the opposite side of the crack, elbow out.

You are now wedged securely in the crack. To climb, move your outside leg upward to establish a higher heel-toe jam. When this jam is set, stand up on it. Then reestablish your inside leg bar and arm bar (or chicken wing), and reposition your outside arm to wedge your body in the crack again. You are now ready to move your outside leg upward to establish another higher heel-toe jam. Continue repeating this procedure.

Climbers may use their outside foot occasionally on face holds, but watch out for the tendency for these outside footholds to pull you out of the crack. For especially awkward crack sizes, climbers may have to stack hand jams—known as the "butterfly technique" (fig. 12-34a)—a hand jam and a fist jam (fig. 12-34b), or fist jams in the crack (fig. 12-34c), or jam with the knee.

Many alpine climbs have short sections of off-width cracks, but some climbs with long, strenuous off-widths have a cultlike following. For these, specialized rock protection (such as Big Bros; see Chapter 13, Rock Protection) and extra clothing and padding to protect your skin are all must-haves. Check resources online and guidebooks focused on this type of climbing for details (see Resources).

12

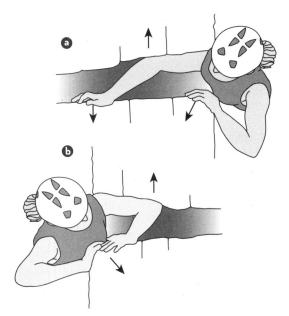

Fig. 12-33. *Off-width climbing techniques:* **a,** *arm bar;* **b,** *chicken wing.*

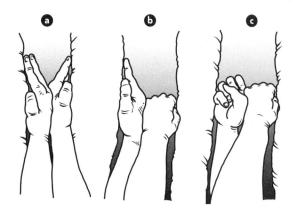

Fig. 12-34. *Hand jams using both hands:* **a,** *stacked hand jams (the "butterfly technique"); ***b,** *hand jam stacked with a fist jam;* **c,** *stacked fist jams.*

Fig. 12-35. *Liebacking with one hand combined with face holds.*

COMBINING CRACK AND FACE CLIMBING TECHNIQUES

Cracks may be climbed with a pure lieback technique (see Figure 12-27a. Or climbers can lieback with one hand and foot (see Figure 12-27b) or with one hand in combination with face holds for the other hand (fig. 12-35), which may result in a kind of stemming action.

Dihedrals may be climbed by using various combinations, such as hands jammed in a crack splitting the dihedral, combined with feet stemming on opposite sides of the feature (fig. 12-36).

Climbers may find useful edges or other holds hidden within cracks—on the sides, or even at the back of wide cracks. It is also possible to pull down on a horizontal crack like a regular hold or ledge.

Fig. 12-36. *Climbing a dihedral using stemming and hand jams.*

Being Prepared

Be wary of tackling climbs that are beyond your skill level. Try climbs at your limit on the crags rather than in the mountains, where inexperience can get a climbing party into trouble. You do not want to have to ask other climbers to help with a time-consuming and dangerous rescue. Come prepared to handle the possibilities inherent in the climb you have chosen, and aim to be self-reliant within your climbing party and capable of rescuing yourselves. This foundational competence adds to your confidence and enjoyment as you continue to climb higher, more challenging routes.

CHAPTER 13

ROCK PROTECTION

Rock protection, also called pro, refers to all types of protection: natural (existing natural features), fixed (bolts or hammered pitons), and traditional (removable protection). To limit a fall, the lead climber periodically places protection and clips their rope to it while ascending. Learning to place rock protection secures the way to new climbing adventures.

With time and experience, lead climbers become skilled at deciding where and how often to place protection. A leader chooses the right gear to make solid, secure placements. The quality and location of the protection that climbers place and the anchors that they build largely determine the consequences of any potential fall. An anchor can be natural, such as a live tree, composed of fixed pieces, or created from several pieces of removable protection.

Natural Protection

Trees and monolithic rock features like boulders, horns, and chockstones (rocks firmly lodged in cracks) provide excellent points of protection for rock climbing. These types of natural protection can even serve as single-point anchors should you and/or your climbing party deem their size and strength adequate. Using natural protection helps conserve gear, may offer a quicker alternative to placing traditional gear like cams or nuts, and may sometimes be the only option. Carefully evaluate all natural pro for its stability, integrity, and strength. "Test before you trust" is a good rule to follow.

Natural features used for anchors on popular routes often accumulate slings as each party rappels from a route and leaves yet another sling behind. Do not trust this mix of slings without inspecting and testing their strength. Sunlight, weather, and age degrade them; they can be cut by sharp edges or chewed on by animals. Inspect any existing webbing or cord for damage before trusting your life to it.

TREES

Trees used as anchors should be alive, well rooted (fully in soil with few visible roots), and larger than 8 inches (20 centimeters) in diameter—roughly the size of the average adult human thigh. Never trust dead trees: using them

could result not only in failed protection but in a tree crashing down on the climber, the belayer, and other parties on the route.

When using natural protection midpitch, loop a single- or double-length runner around the tree trunk's base, with the ends clipped together with a carabiner (fig. 13-1a). You can also untie a knotted sling and retie it around the trunk, using a water knot for webbing and a double fisherman's bend for cord (see Basic Knots in Chapter 8, Essential Climbing Equipment). A third method is to use a girth hitch (fig. 13-1b). To use the natural protection point as an anchor, loop a cordelette around the trunk's base and tie it with a figure eight, clipping the resulting power point (see Chapter 10, Belaying) of all figure-eights to a locking carabiner (fig. 13-1c). The cordelette should usually be as close to the tree roots as possible, although with a strong tree, the cordelette may be placed higher if necessary. Often a cordelette needs to be at least 20 feet long to fit all the way around the tree and allow you to tie a knot to form a power point.

ROCK FEATURES

Rock features, such as large boulders, horns (spike-shaped features), and chockstones, are common forms of natural protection. In evaluating a rock feature, consider how likely it is for a sling, rope, or cordelette to slip off. Always evaluate rock features for their relative hardness. Attempt to move the rock—being careful not to pull it loose—and

13

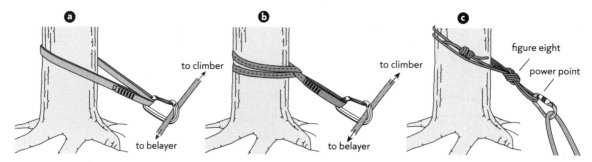

Fig. 13-1. *Using a tree trunk as a protection point:* **a,** *sewn sling wrapped around trunk;* **b,** *sewn sling girth-hitched around trunk;* **c,** *anchor setup with cordelette tied around trunk using a figure eight.*

whack it a few times with a hand or fist or give it a solid kick. Beware of hollow sounds, brittleness, or any sort of movement. Reliable boulders can also serve as belay or top-rope anchors (fig. 13-2). Use the feature's natural shape to determine a secure position for sling or cordage. Be careful to make sure your anchor to the boulder can't slide off or under the boulder.

Horns are another of the most common kinds of natural rock protection. Test them by pushing against them with your foot. To attach to a rock horn, loop a runner over the horn and clip it in to the rope (fig. 13-3a), but take care that the runner cannot be pulled off the horn by rope movement or as the leader climbs past. Use a clove hitch (fig. 13-3b) or slipknot (fig. 13-3c and d) to tighten the runner and prevent it from slipping off. A slipknot can easily be tied with one hand and requires less sling material than a

girth hitch or clove hitch (see Knots, Bends, and Hitches in Chapter 8).

To attach to a rock column, chockstone, or pinch, thread a sewn runner around the feature, then clip both ends of the loop with a carabiner. Alternatively, thread the runner around the rock feature, then secure it with a girth hitch (fig. 13-4), or untie a knotted runner and retie it after threading it through the point of protection.

Take extra care when using freestanding boulders. They should not tip or budge in any direction when tested. Consider both the size and shape, what it rests on, and how it might have been affected by changing conditions such as snow or ice. Avoid any boulder with a rounded bottom or a narrowed base, as well as boulders that rest on gravel, sand, or downsloping ledges. When you find a likely candidate,

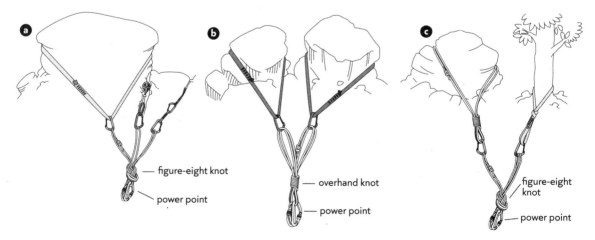

Fig. 13-2. *Large boulders as natural protection for belay anchors:* **a,** *wrapped sling follows natural rock feature;* **b,** *rope anchored around bulk of each of two boulders;* **c,** *boulder as one of two anchors for top rope.*

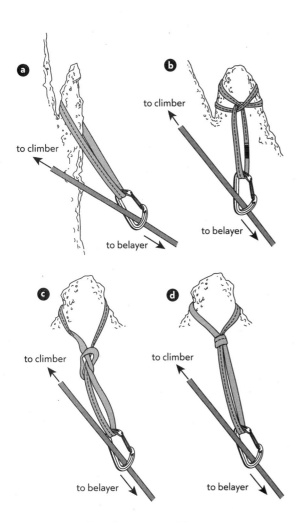

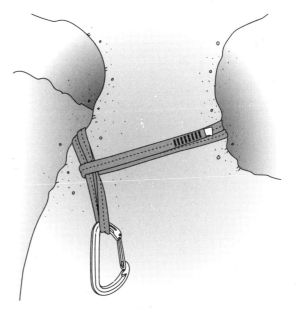

Fig. 13-4. *Attaching a sewn runner around a rock column using a girth hitch.*

Fig. 13-3. *Attaching the rope to a rock horn:* **a,** *using a runner and a carabiner to link the rope to a rock horn;* **b,** *securing a runner to a rock horn with a clove hitch;* **c,** *slinging a horn with a slipknot on a runner;* **d,** *the dressed slipknot.*

sling it around its base. Keep the pulling point low to minimize leverage on the boulder.

Fixed Protection

On established routes, climbers may encounter previously placed bolts and pitons. On rock climbing route topos (see Figure 14-1 in Chapter 14, Traditional Rock Climbing), bolts and fixed pitons are often shown as "x" (for bolt) and "fp" (for fixed piton).

BOLTS

Bolts, a defining feature of many crag and sport climbing routes, are described more closely in Chapter 12, Sport Climbing and Technique. At a fixed anchor with chains (see Chapter 12), what you clip in to depends on the type of anchor. For many modern bolted anchors, such as Fixe anchors, climbers should clip in to the rings. For a horizontal Fixe anchor, climbers should *not* clip the hangers. Be aware too that some carabiners may not fit through the chains' upper links.

Bolts without hangers can still offer reliable protection if a hanger is added. If you expect to encounter bolts without hangers, carry extra hangers and nuts. A last resort is to slide the nut of a wired nut down its wires (fig. 13-5a), slip the upper wire loop around the bolt stud and snug the nut up again against the bolt (fig. 13-5b), and then attach a runner to the lower end of the nut wire. In any case, a bolt without a hanger should be considered suspect, prompting serious concerns about why it is located where it is and why it does not have a hanger.

PITONS

Pitons were commonly used in rock climbing and mountaineering up until the 1970s, but today there are many protection alternatives, such as active cams (see Traditional

271

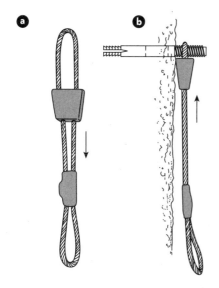

Fig. 13-5. *Placing a wired nut on a hangerless bolt: **a,** create a loop by sliding the nut down its wires; **b,** slide the nut up its wires to form a snug noose around the bolt.*

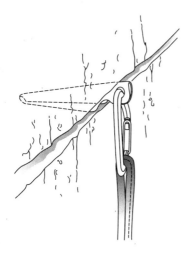

Fig. 13-6. *Piton driven into rock, with carabiner (with runner attached) clipped through piton's eye.*

Protection, below). Placing and cleaning pitons while leading is time-consuming, and repeatedly placing and removing them scars the rock. These days pitons are used primarily for rappel anchors in wilderness or alpine settings, where allowed by land managers. As glaciers continue to recede, mountaineers have begun to use pitons more often in alpine terrain for rappel anchors on newly exposed rock slabs;

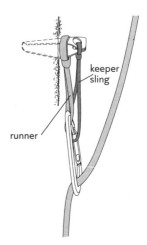

Fig. 13-7. *Partially driven piton, with a runner girth-hitched to it close to the rock to reduce leverage and a keeper sling added to catch the piton if it pulls out.*

pitons are more suitable for such compact rock than cams or nuts.

Climbers often encounter fixed pitons on alpine routes and popular rock climbs. But it is difficult to assess the integrity of an older piton. When you have a choice, it is generally better to rely on your own removable protection. Pitons, even more so than bolts, are vulnerable to weathering. Years of melt-freeze cycles expose and loosen them as time widens cracks in the rock. Examine pitons closely for signs of corrosion or weakness, and examine the cracks they are in for deterioration. Heavy use, failed attempts at removal, and falls on a piton can lead to cracks in the metal around the eye or other damage.

Ideally a piton will be driven in all the way to its eye, so that the eye is close to the rock and the length of the piton is perpendicular to the likely direction of pull. If the piton appears secure and in good condition, clip a carabiner (with runner attached) through its eye (fig. 13-6). Orient the carabiner so that it will not lever against the rock when under a load.

If a piton is driven in only partially but otherwise is secure—or if the eye is damaged and can't accept a carabiner—use a runner and tie the piton off next to the rock with a girth hitch (fig. 13-7) or clove hitch to reduce the leverage on the piton under the impact of a fall. If the eye of a partially driven piton is usable, you may want to girth-hitch a keeper sling to the eye and clip the carabiner in to it to catch the piton if it fails. Do not rely on this setup if there is better protection available.

OTHER FIXED PIECES

Removable protection may become "fixed" if a party is unable to remove it and abandons it. If you encounter one of these pieces, examine it carefully and consider that the party may have abandoned it because they were planning to retire it anyway. Also examine the quality of the rock where the piece is placed, and note whether the sling attached to the fixed gear appears to be worn or damaged. Because of fixed gear's questionable history and integrity, consider it primarily as backup protection. Do not trust removable gear that someone else placed.

Traditional Protection

Traditional protection (trad pro) generally refers to protection other than bolts and pitons and commonly consists of a removable metal device that can be secured into the rock, with a sling and carabiners used to link the protection to the rope. Place removable protection in high-quality rock to maximize strength.

There are two main types of traditional protection: passive (without moving parts) and active (with moving parts). Both types possess strengths and weaknesses, and climbers commonly use both in conjunction. In all cases, be sure you are knowledgeable about how to use any equipment per the manufacturer's instructions.

PASSIVE REMOVABLE PROTECTION

Passive traditional pro pieces—often collectively referred to as nuts, or perhaps chocks—are made from a single piece of metal connected to a sling or cable. Typically, nuts are set into a constriction in a crack. Nut shapes vary from a tapered wedge—also called a stopper (see Figure 13-8)—to a deformed hexagonal tube—often called a hex (see Figure 13-9a, b, c, and d)—to more unusually shaped, passive camming pieces such as the Tricam (see Figure 13-9e). Tricams can be active camming pieces when they are loaded.

Most nuts and some hexes are slung with metal wire cable, which is much stronger than fabric cord or webbing of the same size. The cable's stiffness sometimes aids in placing a nut—for example, all the way at the back of a constriction in a crack. Other nuts have sewn slings of cord, nylon webbing, or high-strength materials such as Spectra (see Synthetic Fabrics in Chapter 2, Clothing and Equipment). A few pieces are available without slings, which the climber must tie with sling material rated for climbing forces. Start with material twice as long as the desired sling length, plus about 12 inches (30 centimeters) for the knot and 1-inch-long (2.5-centimeter-long) tails—or 28 to 32 inches (70 to

80 centimeters) of material to make a loop 8 to 10 inches (20 to 25 centimeters) long. Due to the greater stiffness and slipperiness of Spectra and other high-strength materials, tie the sling with a high-friction knot, such as a triple fisherman's bend (see Figure 13-11b). Inspect cables and slings regularly for damage, and follow manufacturer's instructions for replacing or repairing them.

Passive Nuts

Nuts come in a wide variety of shapes and sizes, but most are generally wedge-shaped and can be placed in two different orientations—using either their narrower or wider diameter one. In addition, most nuts are narrower at the base than at the top (fig. 13-8a), which lets them slip down into a constriction. Variations of nuts include flat faces, curved faces (fig. 13-8b), more-curved faces (fig. 13-8c), faces with notches or grooves (fig. 13-8d), and sides that may be parallel or offset, with both horizontal and vertical tapers. Climbers might find that multiple nut shapes fit into multiple cracks, yet a nut is strongest when as much of its surface area as possible is in contact with the rock in which it is placed. Nuts have a primary placement direction but are frequently designed for multiple placement options to maximize adaptability. Manufacturers rate the breaking strength of gear; in general, bigger nuts have a higher breaking strength.

The smallest of the smallest nuts, referred to as micronuts (fig. 13-8e), are designed for very thin cracks and for aid climbing. Manufacturers usually construct micronuts with softer metals so that the rock bites into the micronut's head better than it does into standard aluminum nuts. This characteristic increases micronuts' holding power but also makes them less durable. The thinness of the micronut's cable makes it more prone to damage from normal use. Inspect micronuts and their cables often for nicks and other signs of wear, and retire them if the cable is damaged.

Passive Camming Protection

Some passive pieces can be positioned so they will cam when loaded. Hexes and other similar pieces take their name from their hexagonal shape (fig. 13-9a, b, c, and d). Opposing sides on a hex are different lengths, permitting three different placement options per piece. The off-center sling creates the camming action (fig. 13-10a), with the force on the sling or the wire rotating the device into the rock. Or the piece can be wedged in a constriction (used similar to a nut). More rounded versions of the hex work on the same principles.

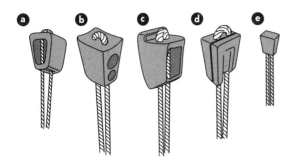

Fig. 13-8. *Nuts:* **a,** *stopper;* **b,** *curved nut;* **c,** *Wallnut;* **d,** *offset nut with grooves;* **e,** *micronut.*

Tricams have curved rails along one side, opposite a point, or "stinger," on the other side (fig. 13-9e). Their camming action is produced by running the sling between the curved side rails and setting the stinger in a small depression or irregularity in the crack (fig. 13-10b): the load on the sling rotates the device into the rock. Tricams also serve as simple nuts when set into a constriction in a crack (see Figure 13-18b), particularly those that narrow sharply.

A tube-shaped device such as the Big Bro has a spring-loaded inner sleeve that telescopes out to bridge a crack (fig. 13-11a) when a release button is pressed. The extended sleeve is then locked into place by spinning the collar down snugly against the outer tube. The sling is attached at one end, so a torquing action adds to the Big Bro's stability when loaded (fig. 13-11b).

ACTIVE REMOVABLE PROTECTION

Spring-loaded protection devices expand the limits of free climbing by providing protection that climbers can easily place with one hand and adapt to fit a variety of cracks.

Spring-Loaded Camming Devices (SLCDs)

The first spring-loaded cams, called Friends, were introduced in the mid-1970s and evolved for the world's first 5.13-rated route, a parallel-sided crack in Yosemite called the *Phoenix.* Now spring-loaded camming devices (SLCDs, or cams) are manufactured in a wide size range and with multiple designs (see Figure 13-13). The basic design has four lobes—called a four-cam unit—that rotate from one or two axles, connected to a trigger mechanism on a stem. The trigger pulls wires that retract the lobes (fig. 13-12a), narrowing the device's profile so that climbers can sneak it as far as possible into a crack or pocket. When the trigger is released, the lobes open up again, against the sides of the rock (fig. 13-12b).

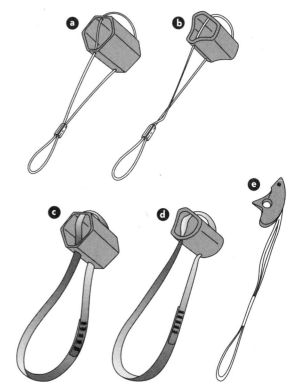

Fig. 13-9. *Passive camming protection:* **a,** *wired hex;* **b,** *wired curved hex;* **c,** *hex slung with high-strength webbing;* **d,** *curved hex slung with high-strength webbing;* **e,** *Tricam.*

Within their given range, the four (or three, for three-cam units) individual cams in the device adjust to the width and irregularities of the crack as the trigger is released. The cams move independently, permitting each to rotate to the point needed for maximum contact with the rock. This movement sets the device in place. If a climber falls, the stem is pulled downward or outward, increasing both the camming action and the outward pressure of the cams on the rock.

Variations of SLCDs abound, with each manufacturer providing differences for the climber to consider. They include double-axle cams called Camalots (fig. 13-13a); specialized SLCDs that fit into narrower placements (side to side) such as three-cam units (TCUs; fig. 13-13b), and Aliens (fig. 13-13c), and two-cam units; and cams with rigid stems or flexible stems or different trigger designs. Some specialized cams—called Fat Cams—are designed to hold better in sandstone. There are cams designed for flaring cracks, such as the Hybrid Alien; lightweight

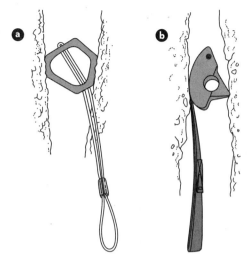

Fig. 13-10. *Passive camming protection in a vertical crack:* **a,** *hex-centric;* **b,** *Tricam.*

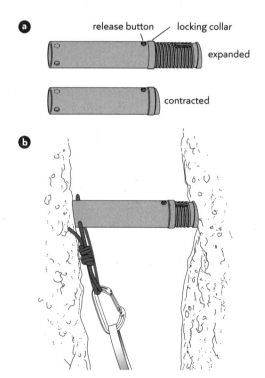

Fig. 13-11. *Spring-loaded tube (Big Bro):* **a,** *expanded and contracted;* **b,** *correctly placed in a vertical crack, where it acts as a cam.*

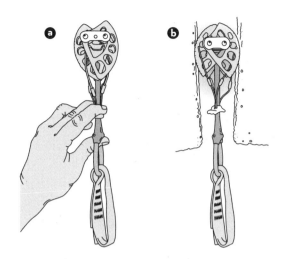

Fig. 13-12. *Spring-loaded camming device (cam):* **a,** *retracted;* **b,** *correctly placed in a vertically oriented crack.*

cams that cover a wide range of sizes (fig. 13-13d); cams for small cracks (fig. 13-13e); extended-range cams (fig. 13-13f) that maximize the range of a single piece of gear; and flexible-body cams (fig. 13-13g) with a wide expansion range. Some manufacturers, such as Metolius, offer a helpful feature that indicates the optimal camming range with colored dots on the sides of the camming units. In all cases, ensure you are following the manufacturer's instructions in the use of these devices (and all manufactured equipment).

Slider Nuts

Slider nuts (fig. 13-14a) use a small sliding piece to expand the nut's profile after it is placed in a crack. To place one, first pull back on the spring-loaded trigger to retract the smaller piece, thereby narrowing the nut's profile (fig. 13-14b). Then once it is in place, release the trigger, permitting the smaller piece to press up between the larger piece and the rock, filling in the gap and increasing the area of the nut that is in contact with the rock (fig. 13-14c).

Slider nuts work particularly well in small, parallel-sided cracks where other devices may be difficult or impossible to place. But like micronuts, slider nuts have less holding power than larger nuts without any moving parts because their smaller surface area is less adept at gripping the rock. Sliders are also less secure because the spring may allow them to move—or walk—within the crack after they are placed.

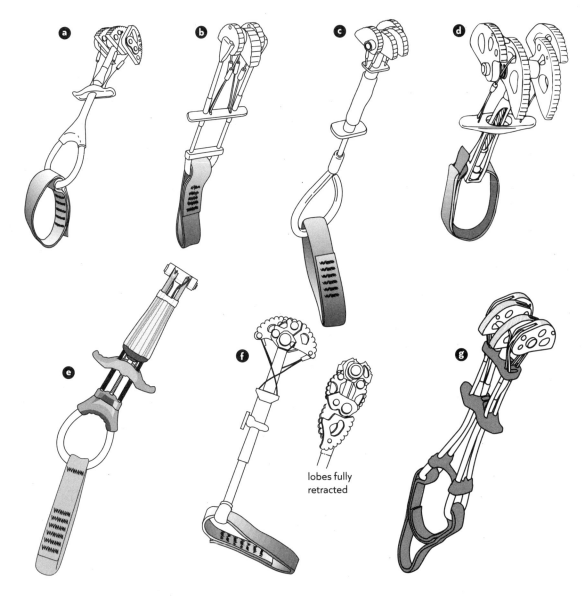

Fig. 13-13. *SLCDs:* **a,** *Black Diamond Camalot C4;* **b,** *Metolius three-cam unit (TCU);* **c,** *Fixe Hardware Alien;* **d,** *Wild Country Technical Friend;* **e,** *Black Diamond Camalot C3;* **f,** *Omega Pacific Link Cam;* **g,** *Totem Cam.*

PLACING REMOVABLE PROTECTION

Placing solid protection is both an art and a science. Developing an eye for suitable sites and securely and efficiently placing the right piece in the right place requires practice to perfect (see the "What to Consider When Placing Removable Protection" sidebar). Trustworthy placements start with reliable rock; in poor rock, even seemingly secure placements may not hold a fall.

When placing protection, look for constrictions in a crack, irregularities in crack surfaces, and prominences behind a flake. A useful site for placing pro has solid rock sides—free of vegetation, dirt, or deteriorating rock. Avoid

WHAT TO CONSIDER WHEN PLACING REMOVABLE PROTECTION

To climb confidently and securely, climbers must know how to place protection effectively and efficiently. Consider these guidelines when choosing where to place protection on difficult terrain:

- **Select high-quality rock.** Avoid rock that crumbles or flakes.

- **Estimate the size and shape** that will work best for a particular placement. Use your eyes and hands to gauge the size of the crack compared to your equipment. Check a guidebook or other source for a route so that you "know before you go."

- **Select the piece best suited to the type of crack.** Cams or hexes often work best in parallel cracks. Offset cams or Tricams work best in flaring cracks.

- **Use your fingers to place the piece** precisely where you want it. Avoid dragging it blindly through a crack and hoping it catches.

- **Reinforce placements that seem insecure** with a second piece or find a better placement.

- **Remember the follower** who will remove the protection. Make secure placements, but try to make them reasonably easy to remove and within your follower's reach.

- **Let the follower know (if possible) if you had to execute an intricate series of moves** to place the piece, so that they can more readily reverse the moves and collect the gear.

- **Avoid shallow placements** where protection can easily pull out of the crack. But avoid overly deep placements that may be hard for a follower to retrieve.

- **Check the piece after you have placed it.** Look to see that it is in close contact with the rock. Give the piece a strong tug in the direction of pull to set it and test its reliability.

- **Clip a runner between the protection and rope** to minimize the effect of rope movement on the piece. An adequate length of runner not only prevents a tug or pull on the piece but also reduces rope drag (see Chapter 14, Traditional Rock Climbing).

- **Use a camming device or two nuts in opposition for a first placement** to avoid the zipper effect caused by an outward or upward pull in a fall (see Using Opposition Placement later in this chapter).

13

crystals or irregularities that may be weakly bonded. Check for loose blocks or flakes by shaking or hitting the rock with your fist; if the rock moves or sounds hollow, look for a more solid placement.

Next, consider the type of protection. Wedge-shaped nuts work best when placed behind constrictions in a vertically oriented crack. Hexes or Tricams work well in horizontal cracks and behind small irregularities in cracks or flakes where it may be difficult or impossible to position wedges. Tricams often are the only pieces that will work in shallow, flaring pockets. Spring-loaded camming devices are easier to place, but they are more expensive than nuts and relatively heavy, and their placement integrity can be more difficult to evaluate. However, active cams often work well in parallel-sided or slightly flaring cracks where it is difficult or impossible to get anything else to hold.

More than one type of device may work in a given spot. Choose based on the gear you have available, the ease of placement, and the protection that the rest of the pitch may require. Ration the pieces that you will need higher up.

Placing Nuts

The basic procedure for placing nuts (or other passive wedging protection) is simple: find a crack with a constriction, place an appropriate piece of protection above the constriction (fig. 13-15a), slide the nut into place (fig. 13-15b), and pull down on the cable or sling to set the nut firmly in position (fig. 13-15c). Slot the nut completely into the crack, matching the crack's taper to the nut and maximizing the surface area of all sides of the nut that are in direct contact with the rock.

The best choice of nut for a given placement is whichever size and shape offers the best fit. As a general rule, greater contact between nut and rock means a stronger placement. Therefore, larger nuts generally are stronger than smaller ones, and wide-side placements (fig. 13-16a), which present more surface area, are generally stronger than narrow-side placements (13-16b). It is, however, the overall fit that is most important. Micronuts, given their tiny size and lower strength, must be placed especially carefully and be in excellent contact with the rock.

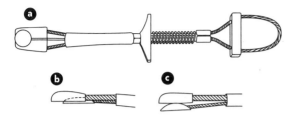

Fig. 13-14. *Slider nuts:* **a,** *C.A.M.P. USA ball nut;* **b,** *retracted;* **c,** *expanded.*

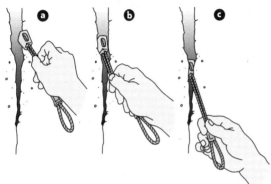

Fig. 13-15. *Placing a nut:* **a,** *position nut above a crack constriction;* **b,** *slide it into place;* **c,** *tug on nut wire to set the piece.*

Evaluate nut placements from multiple directions if possible. Even if the front looks secure, the back may not have much contact with the rock. If the placement looks doubtful from other angles, find a better placement or use a different piece.

Carefully evaluate the potential effects of rope drag and the direction of loading in the event of a fall. Nuts are more susceptible than cams to being pulled out by tension; add a long sling to minimize the outward pull the nut may receive. In vertical cracks, consider setting the nut with a strong downward pull to help keep it in place. While this practice will likely make it more difficult for the follower to clean the piece, the nut is more likely to stay in place in the event of a leader fall.

An advanced technique is to place two nuts side by side and equalize them to create a stronger, combined placement (see Equalizing Protection later in this chapter). In rarer cases, climbers can oppose two nuts for greater security (see Using Opposition Placement later in this chapter).

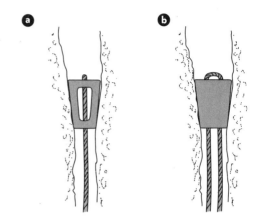

Fig. 13-16. *Nut placements:* **a,** *stronger placement with wide sides in contact with rock;* **b,** *weaker placement with narrow sides in contact with rock.*

Placing Hexes and Tricams

In addition to being used as nuts in a constriction, hexes and Tricams are also designed to cam under load. A secure placement is tight enough that the piece has sufficient contact with the rock and is unlikely to be displaced by the rope, yet is positioned to allow camming action under load. In vertical cracks, these pieces are more secure just above a constriction or irregularity and oriented so that the camming action pulls them tightly against any constriction or irregularity (figs. 13-17a and 13-18a and b). Placed as a passive wedging piece, a hex's camming surfaces face out (fig. 13-17b).

In horizontal cracks, place these pieces so that the downward or outward pull of a fall would maximize the camming action. Position hexes so that the sling exits the crack closer to the roof than to the floor (fig. 13-17c) to maximize the camming action. Place Tricams to optimize overall fit, with the sling and rails either down or up (Figure 13-18c shows rails and sling up).

Tube-shaped pieces, often called by their proprietary name Big Bros (see Figure 13-11), are specialized for wide parallel cracks known as off-widths. Place the tube horizontally in the crack, and press the release button to telescope it out to maximum size. Then spin the collar down to the desired size and lock it into place. The cord threaded on one end helps the entire tube cam into place when loaded.

Placing Cams (SLCDs)

An SLCD, better known as a cam, can be placed swiftly and is strong in a multitude of directions. As such, it is the piece of pro that the majority of climbers place the most.

Cams are the only choice for parallel-sided cracks that lack the constrictions or irregularities needed for wedging passive pro or for camming pieces of passive protection like Tricams or hexes. Spring-loaded camming devices can work for slightly flaring cracks, though the crack can be only *slightly* flaring. A crack that widens too abruptly provides too little contact for a cam to have sufficient holding power. Cams can also be used in cracks under roofs where passive protection may be slow or difficult to place. SLCDs work best in harder rock such as granite, rather than sandstone, and in cracks with relatively even sides.

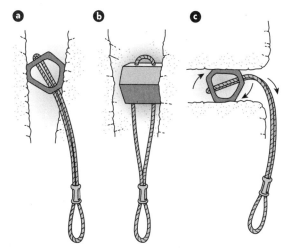

Fig. 13-17. *Hex placements:* **a,** *in a vertical crack as a passive cam;* **b,** *sideways in a vertical crack as passive wedging protection;* **c,** *facing out in a horizontal crack as a passive cam.*

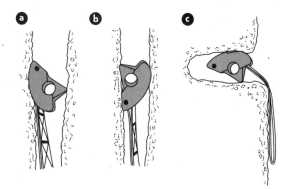

Fig. 13-18. *Tricam placements:* **a,** *in a vertical crack as a passive cam;* **b,** *passively wedged in a vertical crack;* **c,** *in a horizontal crack as a passive cam.*

For most cams on the market, to provide maximum strength and help keep the piece from being pulled out of position, the device's stem must be pointed in the likely direction of pull during a fall. Aim for all lobes to be in firm contact with the rock, with the internal angle formed by the cam's opposing lobes being less than 90 degrees on the trigger end, and with the lobes' tips being just past each other opposite the trigger end (fig. 13-19a). If a crack is too wide or too narrow for your SLCD sizes, it is better to err on the side of overretracting a larger cam setting it too tight (fig. 13-19b), rather than overexpanding a smaller cam and setting it too loose (fig. 13-19c). If a cam's lobes are overretracted, the hold of the piece is still quite strong—it just may be difficult to remove—whereas lobes that are overexpanded are likely to fail.

Larger cams offer a greater margin for error and are stronger than smaller cams. If a cam's lobe shifts due to a small rock crystal failing, that shift will affect the strength of a smaller cam more than it would a larger cam.

SLCDs have a flexible stem that will hang out over the edge of horizontal or near-horizontal cracks (fig. 13-20). After clipping a runner to the cam and the rope, wiggle the rope to make sure the SLCD's lobes will not "walk" back into the crack as the rope shifts around.

13

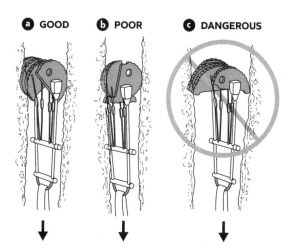

Fig. 13-19. *SLCD placements, with stem in likely direction of pull:* **a,** *cam expanded to midpoint—angle of lobes at stem end is less than 90 degrees (good);* **b,** *cams overretracted—no open angle of lobes at stem end means piece will be hard to remove (poor);* **c,** *cam overexpanded—angle of lobes at stem end of greater than 90 degrees means piece is likely to lose contact and fail (dangerous).*

When placed correctly (see the "Tips for Placing Cams" sidebar), SLCDs can protect against somewhat multidirectional loads, decreasing chances of the zipper effect (see Chapter 14, Traditional Rock Climbing).

Placing Slider Nuts

Climbers use spring-loaded nuts, more commonly referred to as slider nuts, almost anywhere a passive nut would be used. But slider nuts really come into their own in nearly parallel-sided, very thin cracks (fig. 13-21). A slider nut is small and its jamming (sliding) range narrow; take care to select just the right size of slider to fit a crack precisely. As with any piece of protection, place the device so it is strongest in the direction of the force of a potential fall. Because the movement of the rope can pull a slider nut out of place, always attach a runner to it.

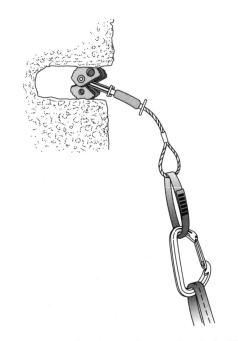

Fig. 13-20. *SLCD placement in a horizontal crack: flexible cable stem bends and adjusts to the direction of pull.*

TIPS FOR PLACING CAMS

The power of spring-loaded camming devices (SLCDs) comes from the high surface area of their camming lobes. Setting them requires a thoughtful and site-specific approach.

- Place SLCDs with their stems pointing in the direction of pull from a fall.

- Be certain the cam's lobes are in sufficient contact with the rock so the placement is stable (see Figures 13-12b and 13-19a).

- Aim to place the cam so that the internal angle formed by its lobes is less than 90 degrees on the trigger end and the tips of the lobes are just past touching one another opposite the trigger end (see Figures 13-12b and 13-19a).

- If a crack is between cam sizes, aim to place a larger cam too tight (overretracted) rather than a smaller cam too open (overexpanded).

- Include more cams on your rack and place them at closer, more regular intervals in softer sandstone and certain types of soft limestone. SLCDs placed in soft rock can be pulled out by a hard fall, even when placed properly.

- Make a careful placement and use a suitable runner. Rope movement can cause the entire piece to "walk," moving it either deeper into or out of the crack, jeopardizing the placement's stability.

- Be cautious of placing cams in flaring or uneven cracks.

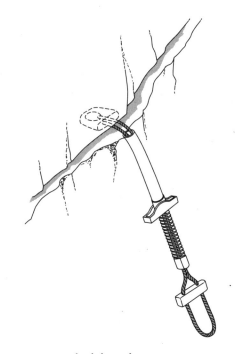

Fig. 13-21. *Spring-loaded nut placement.*

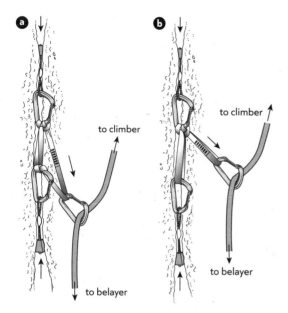

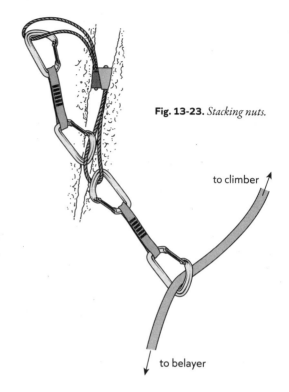

Fig. 13-23. *Stacking nuts.*

Fig. 13-22. *Opposing nuts in a vertical crack:* **a,** *connected by a runner secured with clove hitches to each nut's carabiner;* **b,** *connected by a runner clove-hitched to the upper nut's carabiner, which tensions the lower carabiner.*

USING OPPOSITION PLACEMENT

Sometimes a leader must place a second piece of passive protection to keep the initial piece from wandering—particularly important, for example, as the first placement on a pitch to avoid the zipper effect from a fall. Single placements can sometimes be dislodged by sideways or upward pulls on the rope as the leader advances, because of changes in the route's direction (see Figure 14-8 in Chapter 14).

To create an opposition placement, place two pieces so they will pull toward each other when linked. Use carabiners and sling(s) to link the pieces. Ideally, the pieces should be held together under a small amount of tension. Use clove hitches to tie a runner between the carabiners on the pieces' slings, then cinch up the runner; the climbing rope may then be clipped to the long loop of the runner (fig. 13-22a). Or just clove-hitch the runner to the upper carabiner, which tensions the lower carabiner, and clip the climbing rope to the runner (fig. 13-22b).

EQUALIZING PROTECTION

When faced with a hard move or questionable protection, a lead climber may decide to place two pieces of protection close together. That way, if one piece fails, the other remains as a backup. Another option is to equalize the load over two protection points, subjecting each to only a portion of the total force. (For equalizing protection to establish an anchor, see Equalizing the Belay Anchor in Chapter 10, Belaying.)

It is possible to equalize the forces between two points of protection using only one hand and a single runner. First, clip the runner in to both pieces. Next, put a half twist in the middle of one length of the runner, then pull the resulting loop down to meet the other side of the runner (see Figure 10-23, the sliding X, in Chapter 10). Clip an extra carabiner through both runner strands, with the rope attached to this carabiner. If one piece later pulls out, the twist in the runner will slide down and catch around the carabiner—though some extension will occur. Clipping in to the twist is essential to bind the pieces: without it, the entire setup will fail if one comes loose.

STACKING

If nothing on your rack will accommodate a spot in a crack where you need to place protection, an advanced technique called stacking can sometimes help. Place two passive wedges in opposition, with the larger one on top (fig.

13-23). Use only pieces that seat well against one another; otherwise, stacking is not effective. A downward pull on the larger piece will wedge it between the inside of the crack and the side of the other piece. Seat the larger piece with a firm tug before using it, and connect it to the rope in the usual way. Use a runner to clip the smaller piece in to the wire of the larger piece or another runner. This keeps the smaller one from becoming a flying missile when the follower removes it or if it comes loose in a fall.

REMOVING PROTECTION

Even traditional protection that went in easily can be difficult to remove, whether by a leader who wants to swap it out for a different piece or by the follower cleaning the pitch. A nut tool (also known as a cleaning tool) is a specialized piece of gear that assists in removing pro (see Figure 14-2 in Chapter 14, Traditional Rock Climbing). Nut tools are often racked separately on the harness, sometimes with a retractable cord to avoid losing them if dropped. Wield this tool to push underneath a stubborn piece to remove it up

and out, reversing how it was placed. For a piece lodged in a narrow crack, use the tool to grab the cable at the top and pull it out from above.

Building Skills

The way to become proficient at placing protection is very simple: practice. First, practice by placing protection while standing on the ground. When following as a second, observe closely how the leader places protection. Practice placing pieces while climbing on a top rope.

When you believe you are ready to try leading, choose an easy pitch that you have already climbed as a second or while on top rope. Place more pieces than you need, and do not be discouraged if the first time turns out to be challenging. Bringing along a knowledgeable, experienced climber as your second is a great way to get valuable feedback. Keep practicing, and soon you will be the one giving advice. Learning how to use protection properly will lead to a lifetime of climbing adventure.

CHAPTER 14

TRADITIONAL ROCK CLIMBING

Traditional rock climbing, or "trad" climbing, consists of routes where a lead climber protects pitches by placing gear and using natural features rather than relying on bolted or fixed protection. Trad climbing is more challenging than sport climbing because the protection the leader places along the way is what keeps them from hitting a ledge or the ground in the event of a fall.

Learning to lead traditional climbs merges climbing skill, technical savvy, a robust understanding of a wide range of protection options and limitations, routefinding abilities, and psychological readiness. How do climbers decide whether they are ready to transition to lead climbing on traditional routes? They have perhaps first learned to lead on single- and multipitch sport routes (see Chapter 12, Sport Climbing and Technique) before climbing as seconds on traditional routes. Every climbing pitch an aspiring leader follows is an opportunity to observe and learn. Climbers practice and gain confidence by placing rock protection and building anchors on the ground or other safe venues and asking for direct feedback from experienced trad leaders. Experience helps refine judgment.

When transitioning from sport to trad climbing, start with easier routes. Be conservative in estimating your climbing abilities and avoid jumping onto climbs that challenge you physically while you are also getting used to placing quality protection, or pro, on lead. The need to figure out the sequence of the route and place pro makes a trad climb more difficult than a bolted sport climb of the same rating. On top of all that, as a newer trad leader, you are learning to quickly and accurately select the correct piece that fits in a given feature and to assess the quality of each placement.

In single-pitch trad climbing, the end of a route is clearly indicated by an established anchor, and the pitch is often short enough (less than half a rope length) that a belayer can lower the leader back to the ground. In multipitch traditional climbing, each pitch is led and belayed. In either case, the lead climber always has farther to fall and accepts more risk than the second climber. Having to carry a pack and wear or carry mountaineering boots magnifies the difficulty of trad climbs. On a long alpine climb, even if the route is rated relatively easy, the consequences of a fall can be monumental. Evaluate routes in terms of potential risk and your ability to manage the consequences of a fall, and be conservative when choosing an alpine route and selective about the gear you need to climb it.

Equipment

From the basics like harnesses and a rope to route topos and a rack of protection, rock climbing requires a fair amount of gear and familiarity with using it to minimize your risk.

GUIDEBOOKS AND OTHER RESOURCES

Guidebooks and collaborative online resources provide climbers with diagrams, or "topos," depicting an entire route and its individual pitches (fig. 14-1). These sketches may map the widths of cracks, amount of fixed protection (labeled as "fp" for "fixed piton" and "x" for bolts) and natural protection along the route, length and direction of each pitch, difficulty of each section and of the overall climb, and perhaps even the precise sizes of pieces of traditional protection needed. More detailed information regarding specific recommended protection, descriptions of specific moves, and more—particularly for commonly climbed routes—can sometimes be found online in trip reports or on community blogs or websites.

14

KEY TOPICS

EQUIPMENT
LEADING ON ROCK
MULTIPITCH CLIMBS
TWO-ROPE SYSTEMS
PERSONAL RESPONSIBILITY

Route information for remote or less-traveled areas can be harder to come by. Generally, taking more than enough protection is slightly better than taking too little. An extra two to four cams can make a huge difference sometimes and are not burdensome in terms of weight or bulk. Research a climb by consulting guidebooks and online resources and seeking out other climbers who have climbed the route.

PROTECTION

Occasionally, guidebooks or websites recommend taking a "standard rack" of pro, which varies because each climbing venue is different. However, for those looking to begin trad climbing, a valuable start—and the closest, most universal

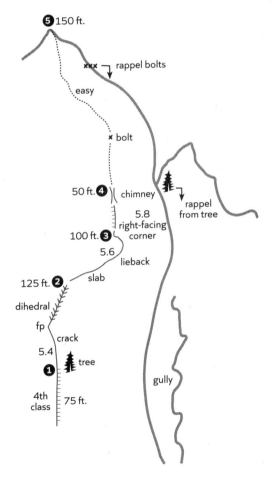

Fig. 14-1. *A typical climbing route topo for a five-pitch route featuring ratings, lengths of pitches, location of protection, and terrain features.*

size range for a basic gear rack—includes a selection of 8 to 12 cams, sized from less than ½ inch to 3 inches, as well as a set of 7 to 12 nuts and some runners and quickdraws.

More commonly, the pro climbers take varies slightly with each route. A long, thin crack might dictate a number of small wired nuts and cams, all narrower than 1 inch, whereas a wide crack climb may require only larger cams or even a tube (Big Bro) or two. A long, parallel hand crack often calls for multiple 2-inch cams. Many rock pitches are less clear-cut, requiring a full range of sizes. In addition, individual climbers often have their own preferences for gear that they never leave home without.

RUNNERS AND QUICKDRAWS

On some routes, a leader may be able to connect a cam or nut directly to the rope with a single carabiner. Much more commonly, a leader will extend many pieces of pro by clipping them to the rope with either a quickdraw or two nonlocking carabiners and a runner. Extension has two purposes; it minimizes the chance that a piece of protection will change position or orientation, which could compromise its strength or stability, and it reduces rope drag, the friction created as the rope runs through all the pro on a pitch. The sharper the angles made by the rope or each piece of pro, the more severe the rope drag.

Similar to there being no standard rack, there is no set number of slings or quickdraws to carry. Each route requires an approach tailored to its specific nature. But a combination of 8 to 12 quickdraws and slings in a variety of sizes will generally get climbers up the majority of trad routes.

Ideally, a runner used to extend a piece of pro is just long enough to keep the rope in as straight a line as possible over the course of the pitch. Keeping the rope running in a straight line minimizes the risk of the leader hitting the ground or a ledge or taking an unnecessarily long fall. A runner that is longer than necessary lengthens a fall; one that is shorter than needed causes rope drag. A too-short runner also compromises the quality of the overall protection placement by multiplying the forces if a fall occurs. Clipping directly to the piece of protection works fine for a fairly straight-up section of a climb. A zigzagging section that also turns a roof or a bulge, however, needs frequent quickdraws and longer runners, often stowed as alpine draws (see Figures 14-4 and 14-7b). It is important to balance the use of sufficiently long runners for reducing or preventing rope drag with the risk of hitting the ground or taking an unnecessarily long fall.

More runners may be needed for belay anchors, unanticipated protection placements, and rappel slings. Especially on alpine climbs and any routes that deviate from a direct vertical line, bring several longer slings—multiple singles and at least a few doubles—since quickdraws will be insufficient. Slings are inexpensive and light, and they can be shortened and used as quickdraws for straight pitches (see Racking Quickdraws and Runners, below).

OTHER GEAR

Each climber carries a nut tool (also called a cleaning tool), a thin metal device designed to help the second extract pieces of protection (fig. 14-2) as they follow a pitch. The nut tool helps the follower retrieve pieces of protection that do not come out easily. A nut tool is also useful when a leader needs to reset, move, or replace a piece of protection. The tool works for cams as well as nuts. Try hooking the trigger or the lobes with the hook of the tool when removing a stuck cam. See more about cleaning gear in Chapter 13, Rock Protection.

In addition to carrying pieces of pro, carabiners, runners, and a nut tool, a rock climber may carry chalk to keep their hands dry (see Chapter 12, Sport Climbing and Technique). Carefully consider and plan the equipment you bring, depending on the setting and the type and length of the rock climb.

RACKING GEAR

When organizing gear, aim for a less bulky rack with better weight distribution, which makes climbing easier and allows you to place gear more efficiently. Gear can be racked on an over-the-shoulder gear sling and on harness gear loops. Below are a couple of strategies for grouping pieces of protection on slings or loops.

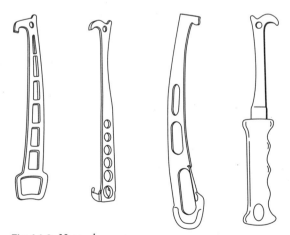

Fig. 14-2. *Nut tools.*

Group passive pieces or small cams on a single carabiner. Lead climbers often choose to group several pieces of passive protection, such as a partial or full set of nuts, on a single carabiner (see Figure 14-3a). Sometimes they use two carabiners when the rack contains a large number of nuts or doubles in certain sizes, splitting the whole into smaller and larger sizes. The same method works for small cams.

This strategy reduces the number of carabiners needed to carry these pieces. But because each piece of pro itself lacks a carabiner, climbers carry several quickdraws (see Quickdraws in Chapter 12) or alpine draws (two carabiners preattached to a runner; see Figure 14-4). When placing pro, the leader attaches one carabiner of the quickdraw or alpine draw to the piece and the other to the rope (see Figure 10-2 in Chapter 10).

To choose the best piece for a rock placement, unclip the racking carabiner holding the range of sizes you believe you need and hold the whole batch up to the placement to determine which piece will fit. Then place the protection in the rock, unclip the racking carabiner, and return it and the unused pieces to the gear sling. This method of racking increases the risk of dropping gear, since a climber handles more gear each time they place a piece, but it might help in selecting the best piece available.

Place other pieces on separate carabiners. Most climbers prefer to rack cams or other active pieces such as tubes on separate carabiners (see Figure 14-3). By design, active pieces of protection (like medium-size to large cams) cover a wider range of sizes than passive pieces (such as nuts or hexes). With experience, it becomes easier in a given situation to select the right cam for a placement than to identify the right nut. Arranging medium-sized to large cams on separate carabiners is less awkward than juggling multiple large pieces of protection on the same carabiner. After placing the appropriate cam, the leader can simply clip the cam's pre-attached carabiner to the rope or, if the route requires it, add a quickdraw or alpine draw and attach that to the rope.

Where to Rack Gear

When choosing where to rack your gear, remember that racking the hardware on the side of your body that will be away from the rock will make the gear easier to access. For instance, when climbing an inside corner with your left side in toward the rock, it is easier to use a sling to hang the rack from your left shoulder and under your right arm. No matter where they rack their gear, most climbers start with the smallest wired nuts at the front of the rack and larger pieces at the back.

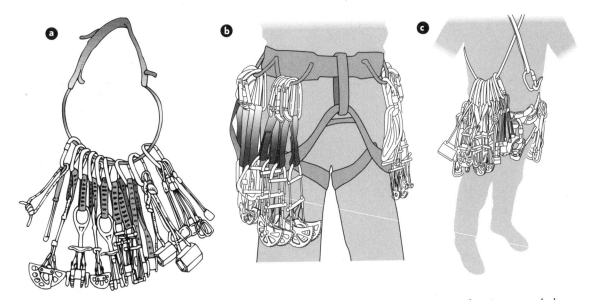

Fig. 14-3. *Examples of racking methods:* **a,** *individual pieces—as well as grouped pro—racked on a gear sling;* **b,** *pro attached to gear loops on the seat harness;* **c,** *hybrid method, with gear racked on both a gear sling and the harness, and a double-length runner looped over one shoulder.*

On a sling. To rack protection on a gear sling (fig. 14-3a), place the sling over one shoulder and under your opposite arm (see Figure 14-3c). This racking method has the advantage of smoother gear transfers because a belayer can pass the entire rack to a leader all at once at an anchor station. It also reduces the risk of dropping individual pieces. This method is also better for managing larger quantities of gear on longer routes or pitches that require a number of larger (heavier) cams that would be uncomfortable on a harness. Be very intentional and careful when transferring a rack of gear, however, to avoid dropping it. Racking on a sling also works better for climbing chimneys, because climbers can move the rack from one shoulder to the other to keep it out of the way as they ascend. The primary disadvantage is that climbers may feel top-heavy, and a sling full of gear can be cumbersome and obstruct the view of their feet, especially on slabs.

On harness gear loops. Using the gear loops on a climbing harness to rack gear (fig. 14-3b) distributes the rack's weight evenly on the waist. It allows climbers to separate the different types of protection—although the latter can also be done with a partitioned gear sling (see Figure 9-1b, in Chapter 9, Basics of Climbing; aid and big wall climbers use a similar big wall gear sling). This racking method can make for longer transition times at belay stations, since the climbers must transfer gear between multiple gear loops rather

than handing over a single gear sling. Yet for some climbers this time difference is worth the increase in comfort.

The primary disadvantage of racking on the harness is that it puts some gear out of reach when a climber is wedged into a larger crack or chimney. Climbers also need to be careful that the gear does not hang down so far that it interferes with their footwork. It is a good idea on many climbs to rack runners, carabiners, and quickdraws on both sides of the harness for easy access when clipping the rope in to protection.

On both harness and gear sling. Many climbers use a hybrid system (fig. 14-3c). For example, a climber could rack all the pieces of protection on a sling over their shoulder but carry runners and carabiners on the harness. Conversely, a climber could place the pro on their harness, the runners and carabiners on a sling, or some mixture of the two.

Racking Quickdraws and Runners

Quickdraws can be racked on the harness or on a sling. Single-length runners generally fit well over a shoulder (across the climber's torso). But if a climber is carrying several runners, it can be difficult to retrieve just one without tangling the lot. To carry a single-length runner quickdraw-style, attach two carabiners to it and thread one carabiner through the other (fig. 14-4a). Then clip the resulting loop with the first carabiner (fig. 14-4b) and

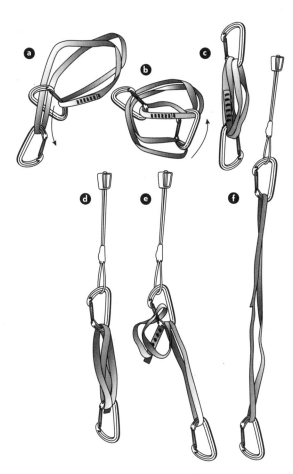

Fig. 14-4. *Racking and extending a single-length runner quickdraw-style (also known as an alpine draw): **a,** clip two carabiners to a single-length runner and pass one carabiner through the other; **b,** clip the first carabiner back in to the newly formed two-strand loop, tripling the runner; **c,** straighten the loops; **d,** clip one carabiner in to the protection; **e,** unclip the other carabiner from two of the three loops of the runner; **f,** straighten and extend the runner.*

then pull the carabiners away from each other to straighten the runner (fig. 14-4c). Also called an alpine draw or a tripled-up runner, this configuration allows a runner to be clipped in to protection (fig. 14-4d) just as you would clip in a quickdraw. To quickly extend an alpine draw, unclip one carabiner from all runner strands except one (fig. 14-4e), then pull this carabiner down to fully extend the runner (fig. 14-4f). Double stacking runners on an alpine draw can save space.

14

Climbers can carry double-length runners looped over a shoulder and connected with a carabiner, known as a daisy chain (see Figure 14-3c). Alternatively, climbers can chain the runner by tying a slipknot (fig. 14-5a) and pulling the runner through the loop formed by the slipknot (fig. 14-5b). Repeat these steps (fig. 14-5c), then clip a carabiner to the chained runner (fig. 14-5d) before attaching it to the harness. To use the runner, simply pull it or shake out the loops. Climbers can also fold a double- or triple-length runner several times and tie it in an overhand or figure-eight knot before clipping it to the harness.

Leading on Rock

Whether leading the next pitch or the next ascent, a climber must plan their route, evaluate the rope and rack requirements, and know what to expect on the descent. Leading is a complex business. Beginners usually learn by moving

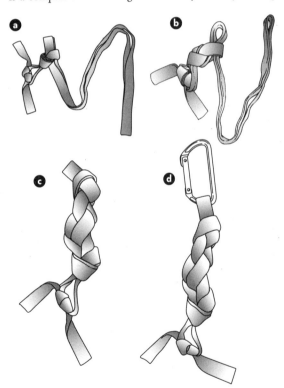

Fig. 14-5. *Chaining a long runner:* **a,** *tie a slipknot;* **b,** *pull runner through loop formed by slipknot;* **c,** *repeat process until runner is chained;* **d,** *attach final loop to a carabiner to carry chained runner and prevent it from unraveling.*

behind seasoned climbers before they can confidently "take the sharp end" of the rope (lead). Never take the lead if you do not feel ready, and do not pressure others into leading a pitch or climb if they are not feeling up to it (see the "Questions to Ask Before Leading a Pitch" sidebar above). Keep the art of leading exciting, challenging, satisfying, and as secure as it can reasonably be.

PROTECTING THE LEAD

Deciding how often to place protection requires practice and sound judgment to balance your party's risk. Placing pro every few feet requires a bigger rack than most climbers are willing to carry or that they may own. However, placing very little protection, known as running it out, increases a leader's risk of taking a long fall and being injured, a practice that eventually catches up to even the strongest climbers.

Protect moves you expect to be hard, but overall, focus on protecting the pitch as a whole, not just a particular sequence of moves. Space the protection you place to avoid excessively long or dangerous falls, such as hitting the ground or colliding with a midpitch stance or ledge. In deciding when to place another piece of protection, consider the quality of the placements made below. Avoid placing "mental pro": pieces you put in because you feel you

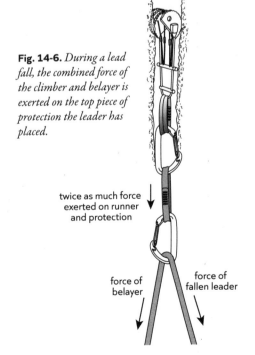

Fig. 14-6. *During a lead fall, the combined force of the climber and belayer is exerted on the top piece of protection the leader has placed.*

twice as much force exerted on runner and protection

force of belayer

force of fallen leader

should but that are not very strong. Only place gear you are willing to fall on; otherwise, keep going until you reach a better placement option. One exception is when a leader may place gear to keep the rope from becoming stuck in a constriction, but that is inadequate for enduring a lead fall.

ANTICIPATING FALL FORCES

The leader must anticipate the direction of forces on the protection in order to make placements, but this assessment must take the entire climbing system into account. A protection point may seem solid for a fall as you place it, but it could pop out later when the system causes pulls in directions you did not anticipate.

During a lead fall, the top piece of protection is loaded with high forces: the force of the falling climber, plus the force of the belayer holding the fallen climber. Other factors can increase this force, such as how far the climber falls, the amount of slack in the rope, the rope diameter,

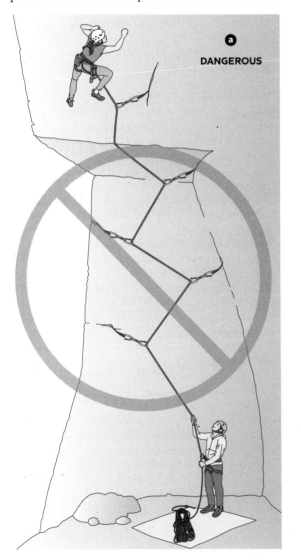
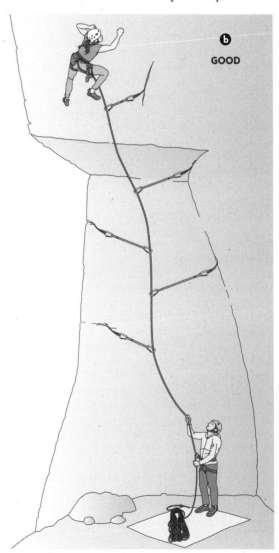

Fig. 14-7. *Avoid rope drag:* **a,** *zigzagging rope can result in severe rope drag on the leader;* **b,** *use runners to extend the connection to each piece of pro and make the line of the rope more direct, reducing drag and keeping the pieces from being loaded from the side.*

and how the belayer is anchored. Consider, too, the friction forces in the system between the fallen climber and belayer, which absorb some of the fall forces at the belay point. Typically a piece of protection sees around two times the forces exerted below it when arresting a fall (fig. 14-6). All protection placements should be solid, but consider backing up protection before hard moves if the options are less than ideal.

Minimize Rope Drag

Consider how to minimize strenuous rope drag, which is exacerbated by steep rope angles as it runs through the protection or drags around blunt terrain. Protection that allows the rope to follow a straight line minimizes rope drag. Extend protection where needed by using longer runners to connect it to the rope (see Figure 14-7b).

Rope drag not only makes climbing harder for the leader (increasing the weight of the rope on the climber on lead), it also decreases the rope's ability to absorb forces in the case of a fall—effectively increasing the fall factor (see Understanding Impact Force in Chapter 10, Belaying). When you must create a bend in the climbing line, make placements multidirectional by using natural protection, opposing nuts, or cams that can rotate with minimal walking (see Using Opposition Placement in Chapter 13, Rock Protection). Or consider placing the belay on the other side of the bend.

Keep the Rope Running Vertical

A zigzagging climbing rope causes severe directional forces as well as rope drag that can hinder or immobilize the leader (fig. 14-7a). Pieces of protection that were placed to hold only a downward pull may now be in danger of taking sharp pulls from different directions. In catching a fall, the rope loads and straightens from the belayer up to the highest protection point, then back down to the falling climber. When the rope runs in a zigzag between pieces of pro, the tightening rope can pull pieces sideways or upward. Pieces placed to protect only from a downward pull can be pulled out by falls higher up the pitch. To mitigate this hazard, use runners to extend pro so that the overall line of the rope running from belayer to leader is more vertical than zigzagging (fig. 14-7b).

Avoid the Zipper Effect

The zipper effect dramatically demonstrates the importance of anticipating force directions. The zipper effect occurs most readily when a belay station is established away from the base of the pitch (fig. 14-8a) or where the rope zigzags up the route (see Figure 14-7a). When a leader falls and loads the rope, it can exert a tremendous outward pull on the bottom piece of protection. If that first piece pulls out, the next piece becomes subject to the same outward pull. Each piece in turn could fail, causing the nuts and cams to be yanked out one by one, unzipping from the bottom up (as in Figure 14-8a). Overhangs and sharp traverses also have the potential to zipper.

Prevent the zipper effect by making the suspect placements multidirectional in two ways: by using multidirectional cams (fig. 14-8b) and by extending pieces with runners to eliminate the potential for outward pull. Having the belayer stand closer to the base of the route can also help reduce that outward pull (see Figure 14-8b).

SELECTING AND MAKING A PLACEMENT

The perfect pro placement comes just before the next hard move, can be placed from a comfortable stance, and slips readily into a crack in a textbook manner. While it is often not possible to find a placement possessing all these characteristics, one or two out of three is not too bad. When on the sharp end of the rope, place protection right before you make a hard move. If you anticipate encountering harder climbing above, doubling up on protection is an excellent strategy. Avoid making difficult moves far away from the last piece of protection. If a climb generally remains hard, continue to place gear. It is better to take a short fall on well-placed gear than to take an uncontrolled fall after you get tired on a more sustained, longer-than-anticipated crux.

Always double-check the rock's quality and the placement itself before trusting it with your life (see Chapter 13, Rock Protection, for details on protection and solid placements). Then, to place the piece, find a secure enough stance that allows you to release one hand. Climbers must be able to quickly place sound pro and clip in to it, using either hand, without falling (see Chapter 12, Sport Climbing and Technique, for clipping tips). Practice this skill on the ground until you can use either hand to clip the rope in to the carabiner with the gate facing either left or right.

If you face the unfortunate choice between questionable protection or none at all, by all means, place something, but plan to place more protection as soon as possible. Placing and equalizing two pieces can also help (see Chapter 13, Rock Protection). Do not let such a placement give you a sense of false security, however. If you have little faith that the piece will hold a fall, consider taking it with you, and put in a fall-worthy piece at the next available opportunity.

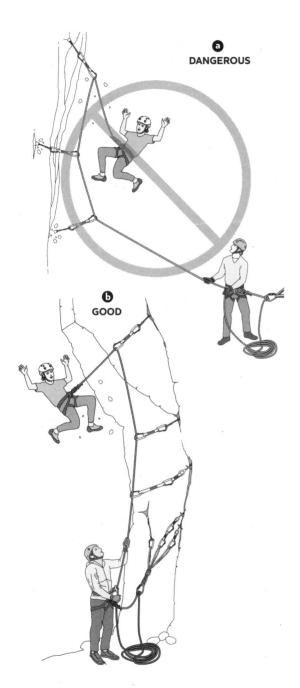

a
DANGEROUS

b
GOOD

Fig. 14-8. *The zipper effect:* **a,** *this dangerous effect in action;* **b,** *well-placed cams (or opposing nuts) at the bottom of a pitch—here, as part of the belay anchor and as the first piece— provide multidirectional protection against the zipper effect.*

PROTECTING SPECIAL SITUATIONS

Leading on overhangs or traverses requires special considerations to keep the following climber(s) safe.

Overhangs

Keep the rope running as free of an overhang as possible. Extend it with runners, as far as you need to, to reduce rope drag (fig. 14-9a), prevent dangerous fall forces such as the zipper effect, and keep the rope from being cut by the edge of the overhang (fig. 14-9b). On a small overhang, the most effective strategy may be leaning out and placing protection above it.

Traverses

When leading a traverse, place protection both before and after a hard move (fig. 14-10a) and along the entire pitch. This approach guards not only the leader but also the follower from the possibility of a long pendulum fall (fig. 14-10b). Pendulum falls seem like they should be less severe than leader falls, but climbers can take swinging falls into features with dire consequences. In addition to the danger of injury, that kind of fall could leave the second in a tough spot, off route and with no easy way to get back on.

When leading a diagonal or traversing section, keep in mind the effect each placement could have on the second climber. Put yourself in the second's shoes and ask, "Would I like some protection here?" If so, place it. Asking this question will help beginning leaders avoid a common, potentially dangerous mistake: inadequately protecting the follower on a traverse. If the party has enough equipment

14

CHOOSING PROTECTION

To choose among possible gear and placements, think through these questions:

- Which placement combines the best fit with stability in the direction(s) of pull?
- Which placement will be the strongest?
- What size nuts or cams should be conserved for use higher on the pitch or at the anchor?
- Which placement will be easier for the follower to remove?
- Will either of the possible placements interfere with a foothold or handhold? Sometimes, in crack climbing, you have no other option.
- Which placement minimizes rope drag?

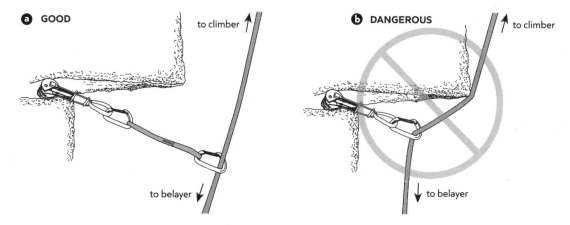

Fig. 14-9. *Placements under overhangs: **a,** rope running free of the overhang (good); **b,** bends cause rope drag, and rope could be cut by rock edge during a fall (dangerous).*

and it seems prudent, consider belaying the second with an extra rope, which may help protect against a long pendulum fall and provide better protection than using the leader's rope. If the party is using the half-rope technique (see Half- and Twin-Rope Techniques later in this chapter), the leader should clip only one rope in during the traverse, so that the leader can belay the follower from above on the unclipped rope.

ROCK PROTECTION ETIQUETTE

The issue of ethics in placing protection affects all climbers (see Chapter 9, Basics of Climbing). Specifically, many climbing areas expressly forbid placing, or even replacing, bolts. It is each climber's responsibility to understand the rules before installing a bolt. Some land managers request that climbers ask for permission before placing or replacing bolts. It is common practice for the first ascensionist of a sport climbing route to place the only bolts.

Popular routes with natural features, such as trees and horns, that serve as common rappel stations often collect slings from various parties over time. If you find damaged slings, cut them off and remove them from the route. Many climbing areas encourage climbers to use natural-colored bolts and slings when leaving gear on routes, to address aesthetic concerns of nonclimbing visitors.

Multipitch Climbs

Imagine two climbers high on a rock face. One is climbing up a crack and thin, airy face holds with the rope clipped through a half dozen well-spaced points of protection. The follower is anchored and attentively belaying, with their feet on a small stance and their body weight resting in their harness. The leader places a stopper in the crack, clips a runner to it, and then pulls down on it to test it. The leader grasps the rope extending from their tie-in, pulls it up, and clips it in to the freshly placed protection. The follower yells up to the leader "Half rope!" to indicate that they have reached the rope's midpoint.

The leader exhales deeply, switching hands, feet pasted to small features, and shakes out their arms before looking up to study the route ahead. The discontinuous, thin crack continues up steeply, with a few uneven pockets that may have some nice footholds to place gear from. The leader readies a cam from the rack that will likely work in the next placement.

PLANNING BEFORE THE TRIP

Multipitch routes generally require more research and preparation than single-pitch objectives, and planning for the route begins with background research at home. Look for climb descriptions in guidebooks and online, and talk to others who have climbed the route. For alpine climbs, obtain needed maps (paper or digital) for the approach, and check the weather forecast for the dates you are considering (see Chapters 5, Navigation and Communication, and 28, Mountain Weather). The skill the route requires depends on its location and the nature of the climb, as well as any potential difficulties on the approach and descent.

Routefinding can be as easy as following a guidebook picture with a route overlay or interpreting the symbols in a climbing topo (see Figure 14-1), but it can also be as difficult as tackling an off-trail multiday approach and then

ⓐ GOOD

ⓑ DANGEROUS

Fig. 14-10. *Protecting a traverse:* **a,** *placing protection both before and after a hard move on a traverse reduces the chances of a long pendulum fall (good);* **b,** *the follower faces a long pendulum in case of a fall because of inadequate protection (dangerous).*

an ambiguous technical climb with a vague route description. Routefinding on alpine climbs and some long crag routes can be complex, and longer routes are often less clearly defined. The guidebook description may be sketchy: "Ascend northeast buttress for several hundred feet of moderate climbing." The descent may be complicated and described only vaguely. Climbers rarely come back from a long route and say they "overplanned." As a general rule,

the bigger and more complex the route, the more planning and research it requires. Bring information in printed or digital form. Take photos of the guidebook pages, save route overlay photos, and consider bringing a printed version of the topo and description of the descent (as well as a digital backup).

For any multipitch climb, confirm the descent and—in case it is not obvious—perhaps check with others who have done the route. Decide whether the route will be a carryover, requiring your party to carry approach shoes or mountaineering boots up and over the route. Are there places where you can rappel? Where are they? How many are there? How long are the rappels? Answer all of these questions before your trip.

Multipitch Packs

For routes that require carrying some amount of clothing, shoes, or other equipment up (and potentially over) a route, consider bringing a small multipitch pack (fig. 14-11). This pack can be carried by itself from the trailhead, often overloaded, but on more substantial approaches, most climbers carry it inside another larger pack. Some modern packs have options for users to make them smaller and/or larger as they wish.

14

Fig. 14-11. *A useful multipitch pack rides close to the body, with features for carrying a rope on the outside.*

The pack you carry needs to be large enough to hold all the equipment needed for the climb, but not so large as to be cumbersome or limit efficient climbing movement up a route. Note that packs promoted as "multipitch" are designed to ride high, and many have handy features for strapping a rope on the outside or easily accessing a guidebook. Depending on the route, some parties opt to have only the follower wear a multipitch pack, allowing the leader to climb with as little extra weight as possible.

PLANNING ON THE WAY IN

Once the climbing party is on the way in, study the route on the approach if possible. Often the best view of a route is some distance from the start of the climb. Consider taking a photo with your phone that you can reference later. Look for major features that the line of ascent may follow, such as crack systems, dihedrals, chimneys, or areas of broken rock. Note clumps of small trees or bushes that may indicate belay ledges or rappel anchors. Identify landmarks that, when reached, will help determine the party's position on the route. Your eyes will reveal important details that a route topo or map cannot.

Watch out for deceptively tempting lines leading to poor-quality rock, broad roofs, blank walls, or false summits. If your party climbs these features in error, you may end up at a dead end after several pitches.

Develop a plan for the line of ascent, but keep likely alternatives in mind. Continue planning with regard to route-finding even as you begin to climb, looking for more local features and landmarks. Seek out natural lines to follow when leading the route. Form a tentative plan for each pitch, perhaps including a place for the first piece of protection and a spot for the next belay station. Do not hesitate to look around the corner for easier route alternatives that were invisible from below. When faced with a choice between pitches of varying difficulty, consider the rest of the climb. Two moderate pitches are better than an easy pitch followed by one beyond the party's ability.

On the way up, keep track of retreat possibilities in case the climb is aborted, and study—to the extent possible—the party's planned descent route. Rain, lightning, unexpected wind or cold, injury, or illness may make it prudent to retreat from the route. As the climb progresses, evaluate changing route conditions, the weather conditions and forecast, and the climbing party's stress levels and comfort with proceeding. Consider whether the party is equipped to deal with an unplanned bivy while on the climb. Be aware of any descent or escape routes in case you end up needing them. See Part V, Leadership, Risk Management,

and Rescue, for more about dealing with unexpected or emergency situations.

SWINGING LEADS VERSUS BLOCK LEADING

On a multipitch route, climbers have two strategies, each with distinctly different advantages, so the party must decide which option to apply.

The first strategy is known as swinging leads: for every pitch, the climbers trade leads (fig. 14-12a). This technique involves very little rope management, because the rope is stacked in the correct direction, with the next leader's end on top once they get to the belay. If the route is difficult, however, this technique is slower, more tiring, and a lot less efficient: each climber gets only a brief rest between following a demanding pitch and then attempting to lead the next one. It is a challenging approach if a climber is leading at their limit; they are unlikely to climb as well as they would if they were able to fully rest between the two rope lengths. Conversely, each climber gets ample rest while belaying their partner up to their anchor and then again as their partner leads the next pitch.

The second strategy is block leading (fig. 14-12b), in which the climbers lead in blocks, or groups of pitches, typically three or four at a time. This technique allows the designated leader of the block to rest while they belay their partner up to each anchor. The follower also gets to rest while belaying the leader up to the next pitch, rather than swinging through. Block leading offers generally faster gear transfers, because the climbers do not have to transfer the entire rack at the top of every pitch. Block leading does, however, require pancaking or restacking the rope so that the leader's end is on top (see Figures 14-13 and 14-15), but most climbers can restack rope faster than they can hand over an entire rack.

Many climbers go through a cycle regarding this choice. In the beginning, when they are climbing routes that are easier for them, it makes sense to swing leads, which simplifies rope management. However, as a climber's skills develop, and as they begin attempting more difficult routes, they may start block leading more often. They have honed their rope management skills, and they see and feel the physical advantages of leading while *fresh* rather than after having just followed a long pitch.

DETERMINING A PITCH'S LENGTH

On traditional crag climbs—and most alpine rock climbs—pitches vary in length and the end of a given pitch may be considerably more ambiguous. Pitches are often marked with bolted belay anchors, but climbers may need to use

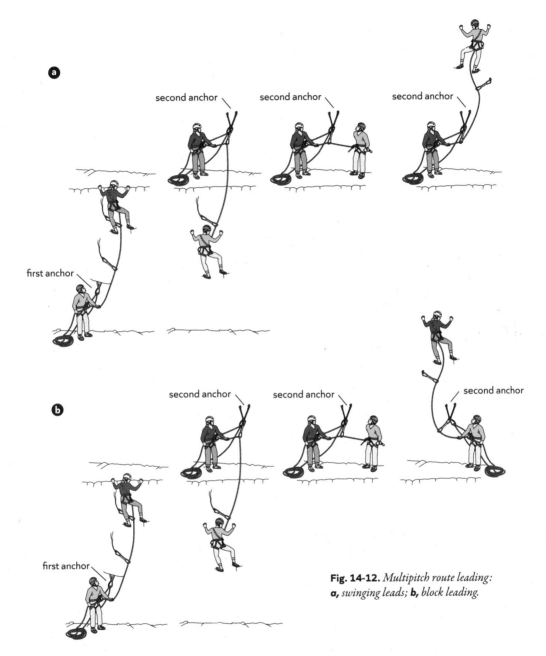

second anchor

second anchor

second anchor

first anchor

second anchor

second anchor

second anchor

first anchor

Fig. 14-12. *Multipitch route leading: a, swinging leads; b, block leading.*

natural anchors or construct gear anchors, which requires more routefinding and discretion.

The length of a given pitch is dictated by several factors. A pitch does not exceed the length of a typical dynamic rope, which ranges from 50 to 70 meters (164 to 230 feet)—with 60 meters (197 feet) being the most common rope length for most rock climbs. However, in most cases, the ideal pitch length is less—often considerably less—than a full rope length. A ledge or other secure site for the belay anchor often determines where the pitch naturally ends. The leader must be prepared to climb pitches of varying lengths, depending on the circumstances.

Avoid the temptation to make every pitch a full rope length, which can result in slower climbing, especially when the longer rope causes rope drag, arrives at an awkward belay station, or requires down-climbing to a more secure belay location that the leader earlier passed up as they ran the rope out to its end. New climbers often try to climb routes in fewer pitches because their transitions at anchors are slow. However, with shorter pitches and faster transitions, climbers can carry less gear, have the gear a pitch requires (rather than running it out on a needlessly longer pitch), communicate better, avoid rope drag, and just flow more quickly through most tasks.

When determining pitch length, use information from route descriptions and topos. On the route itself, seek out and use good belay spots. When in doubt about where a pitch ends, do not pass up a great location to set up a belay anchor with a comfortable stance while you still have enough rope to establish the belay. Try to maintain communication, particularly in windy conditions, when long pitches can significantly compromise communication with a climbing partner, and work to prevent or minimize rope drag. If rope drag becomes a problem, look for and establish a belay spot sooner rather than later.

LEADER ARRIVING AT THE BELAY

At the top of the pitch, the leader builds and clips in to a solid anchor before signaling "Off belay." (For more on building anchors and using climbing commands, see Chapter 10, Belaying.) A clove hitch, the most common tie-in, is easy to adjust and uses the strongest material you have with you: the rope.

Keep the belay system simple. Strive for straight, easy-to-trace lines from the anchor points to you. It is advantageous to belay directly off the anchor—not through a redirect or directly off your harness—using an auto-locking device that helps catch a fall. Climbers should still keep their brake hand on the rope. Think about your strategy before you start pulling rope up. Where is it best to belay from? Where will you stack the rope? Can you see the second from your stance, and where will the second secure themselves when they arrive?

When everything is set, pull up the rope. Once you think you may be pulling on the follower down below, immediately put them on belay. You may have to pull a little more rope through your device, but if you are pulling on the rope without the device and they unclip from the belay and fall, the result could be disastrous. Ideally, when you have pulled out the slack and the rope comes taut on the second

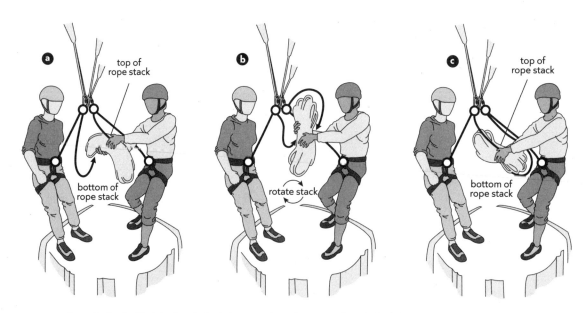

Fig. 14-13. *Pancake flip for block leads at belay ledge: **a,** pick up the rope stack with the follower's end on top; **b,** flip the "pancake"; **c,** block leader's rope end is now on top.*

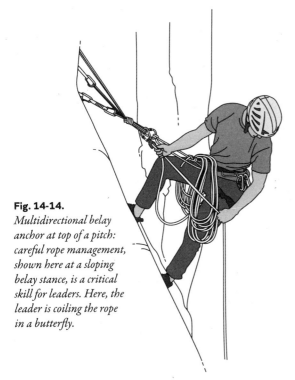

Fig. 14-14.
Multidirectional belay anchor at top of a pitch: careful rope management, shown here at a sloping belay stance, is a critical skill for leaders. Here, the leader is coiling the rope in a butterfly.

TIPS TO SAVE TIME AND ENERGY

After belaying the leader on a pitch, your job as the second climber has just begun.

- **Start preparing to climb as soon as the leader is off belay.** Put on your rock shoes, remove a layer of clothing, shoulder your backpack—do whatever can be done securely. Once the leader pulls up the rope and puts you on belay, begin breaking down the belay station.

- **Give the area a last look to make sure you leave nothing behind.** Then, once you are on belay, yell "Climbing!" and start up.

- **Remove protection by reversing the way each piece was placed.** If a stopper was slotted down and behind a constriction, remove it by pushing it back away from the constriction and up.

- **Be persistent but careful.** Use a nut tool to tap on a stubborn nut to loosen it, taking care to avoid hitting the piece's wires, then gently lift the nut out. Pieces of protection are a lot stronger than you are, and being "rough" with pro is rarely the answer. Approach placed pro with a thoughtful mindset, trying to reverse the moves the leader made to place it.

- **Use a nut tool to retract the triggers of a cam that has walked back into a crack.** If you cannot retract its trigger with your fingers, try using a nut tool, or use the wires of two stoppers to snare the trigger device so you can retract the cam.

- **Consider asking your belayer for tension** so you can put your weight on the rope, freeing both hands to work on removing a stuck piece that refuses to budge.

- **As a final option, abandon protection if necessary.** Climbers can waste a lot of time and effort on a piece of thoroughly stuck protection.

---

climber, they will yell "That's me." After placing the second on belay, yell "Belay on," cueing them to start breaking down the belay and begin climbing.

Never lay belay devices, gloves, carabiners, or other items on the ground or on a ledge. If you are not using an item, keep it attached to your harness, a sling, or an anchor. Have only one item, such as the rope, a nut, or a carabiner, in your hands at a time. The moment you no longer need an item for whatever you are doing, reattach it to your harness, a sling, or the anchor. It is too easy for unattached objects to be dropped or blown off the belay ledge. Take off your pack and rack and attach them to the anchor, but keep them within easy reach. That way, you will be more comfortable while belaying the second.

Managing the Rope at Belay Stations

With a party of two climbers, effective rope management techniques are pretty straightforward. The most common method if the terrain allows is for the belayer to flake or stack the rope neatly on a small ledge—the tighter the pile, the better. That way, if you are swinging leads, the rope is ready to go when the second arrives at the belay stance.

If your party is block leading, simply "pancake" the small stack (flip it over like you would a pancake) so that the belayer, now preparing to lead, has the rope paying out from the top of the stack, not the bottom (fig. 14-13). If the stack is not in a small, tight pile, reflake the rope rather than attempting to flip it.

If the belay station you have established does not have a ledge, butterfly coil the rope in neat, even loops over your clip-in point (fig. 14-14). It is tempting to make very large loops, but they often tangle and require more care to keep them from catching on nearby features in all but the slabbiest terrain. Start with large loops, and then make them progressively smaller to avoid tangles.

Rope management is critical to belaying, especially at a hanging or sloping belay stance (see Figure 14-14). However, it is less important than belaying well. If your follower is outpacing your ability to simultaneously belay and manage the rope, tell them to slow down, or give up on managing the rope until they reach the belay station.

CLEANING A PITCH

The follower tries to climb as quickly and efficiently as possible once they are on belay (see the "Tips to Save Time and Energy" sidebar above). While ascending, the second climber cleans the pitch. Cleaning involves removing the protection from the rock in an orderly way and organizing it on the harness or a sling. At the end of the pitch, unless the climbers are swinging leads, the second needs to efficiently transfer the cleaned gear to the leader.

In general, cleaning from rock to the rope is best. That way, the pieces are clipped to something at all times, and there is little possibility of dropping any gear. In any racking procedure, minimize the handling of unattached gear to also lessen the risk of dropping it. The cleaning procedure may depend on the method used to rack the hardware. If your party is swinging leads, the second climber can begin racking it the way they intend to lead with it. When climbers are block leading, a common technique is for the second climber to rack all the gear on a single runner. Then they can (carefully) hand off all the gear at once, and one climber can rerack while the other restacks the rope.

The following procedure is an efficient way to clean gear placed with runners that minimizes the risk of dropping gear:

1. Remove the cam or nut from the rock.
2. Holding the carabiner clipped to the nut, clip the carabiner-nut combination directly to the gear sling or harness gear loop.
3. Unclip the carabiner-nut combination from the runner that is clipped to the rope.
4. Loop the runner over your head, unclip the runner-carabiner combination from the rope, and rotate the runner-carabiner combination so that it is under one arm.
5. Continue climbing to the next piece of protection, then repeat.

If a placement uses a quickdraw instead of a runner, follow this procedure:

1. Remove the cam or nut from the rock.
2. Holding the carabiner that is clipped to the nut, clip this end of the quickdraw in to the gear sling or harness gear loop.
3. Unclip the other carabiner from the rope.

FOLLOWER ARRIVING AT THE BELAY

When the follower arrives at a belay station, the first thing they need to do—before being taken off belay—is clip in to the belay anchor, most commonly with a clove hitch and the rope end closest to them. The rope is the strongest piece of material in the system, is faster to connect, and potentially makes rope wrangling easier than if you clip in with a sling or other manufactured tether.

If the climbers are swinging leads, the belayer does not need to remove the rope from the belay device, but they can back it up with an overhand or figure eight on a bight and shift the device from the anchor to their harness. If they are block leading, they heed the saying "You stack, I rack," meaning one climber reracks while the other reflakes or pancakes the rope.

In either case, if the second is neat, organized, and efficient in cleaning the pitch, the climbers can transfer gear at the belay station quickly, whether the original leader transfers the rest of the rack to the second, who will now lead, or the second transfers the cleaned pieces back to the leader's rack. Follow this sequence, remembering that both climbers always stay anchored to the rock:

1. Reconstruct the rack. Clip the cleaned pieces to the rack, whether the original leader or the new leader has it. Be careful not to drop any gear.
2. Hand the removed runners and quickdraws over to whoever will lead.
3. If either climber is wearing a pack, remove it and clip it to the anchor.
4. If the original leader plans to lead the next pitch, pancake the rope stack, flip the butterflied coils, or reflake the rope so that the second's end of the rope is on the bottom and the leader's end is on top. The second then settles into the belay position.

The new leader shoulders the reconstructed rack and racks the runners according to the climbers' chosen system. The new leader rechecks and adjusts the rack to ensure that everything is ready for the next pitch. A look at the route description may be in order. At the very least, the leader examines the next pitch to gain a sense for the general line to be traveled. The follower places the leader on belay, and the leader unclips from the anchor and begins to climb again.

Two-Rope Systems

Throughout this guide, most of the climbing situations that are described use a single rope. However, climbers can opt for one of several methods that use two ropes: climbing in a party of three, rappelling with a static rope (often carried as a tag line), or using two smaller-diameter ropes in either half-rope or twin-rope technique. Several multipitch routes require two ropes to descend, and each of the several options climbers can choose from offers specific advantages and disadvantages. It goes without saying that a team of three climbers is already bringing two 60-meter ropes, so they do not need to consider the other options below.

CLIMBING WITH A PARTY OF THREE

Most rock climbing is commonly done in pairs, but a party of three climbers can be fun and, when efficiently executed, is not much slower than two climbers. If you are new to multipitch climbing, practice climbing in a two-person team to refine techniques and belay-station management first. Then a three-person team will not feel awkward, overwhelming, or significantly less efficient than a two-person team. A three-person team has the advantage of an extra person for hauling, rescue, et cetera, and is faster than two teams of two. Unless the pitches are extremely short, climbing as a party of three requires two ropes. As with a party of two, each of the three climbers must remain securely anchored when not climbing.

One of the most important decisions when climbing as a team of three is whether to climb in caterpillar or parallel technique. In caterpillar technique, the climbers ascend the pitch one at a time (fig. 14-15a), whereas in parallel technique, both followers climb the pitch at the same time while the belayer manages both ropes with an auto-locking

belay device clipped directly to the anchor (fig. 14-15b). Many rope manufacturers allow a following climber on a half-rated or twin-rated rope, particularly while rock climbing, but it involves more risk than single-rated ropes. The odds of cutting these thinner ropes are higher. Only climb in caterpillar or parallel with single-rated ropes.

The three-person team can switch back and forth between these two techniques over the entire route. Most experienced climbers climb the majority of multipitch routes in parallel except for the hardest pitches, where they might switch to caterpillar, because it is easier and more efficient for the leader to drag only one rope up the pitch; it is also cleaner for the seconding climbers to have to deal with only their rope.

Caterpillar Technique

In a team of three using two ropes sequentially, known as caterpillar technique (see Figure 14-15a), the leader climbs with one rope while the second belays and the third remains anchored at the belay station. At the top of the pitch, the leader sets up a belay and brings up the second, who is belayed on the first rope and has the second rope either clipped with a locking carabiner to the harness's back haul loop or tied in at the front of the harness. The third climber then uses the second rope.

If the pitch follows a straight line up, the second can clean it. Remember, being belayed from above is very safe—should the climber slip, they would fall only a very short distance. If the pitch includes some traversing, keep some or all of the protection in place for the third climber,

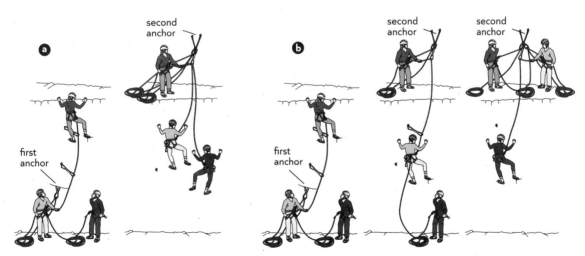

Fig. 14-15. *Caterpillar versus parallel rope techniques:* **a,** *climbing in parallel, both seconds climb at the same time;* **b,** *climbing in caterpillar, only one second climbs at a time.*

to help prevent them from enduring a pendulum fall. In this situation, the second climber unclips each piece of protection from the first rope and clips the protection to the second rope. Once the second climber is at the top of the pitch, the full length of the first rope is now at the top belay. One of the two climbers at the belay station puts the third climber on belay using the second rope, and that third climber then cleans the pitch. When the third climber reaches the top of the pitch, the climbers may decide to swing leads, with the third climber leading the next pitch using the second rope. For the second climber to lead, the ropes may need to be retied and perhaps restacked.

Parallel Technique

Another way for a party of three to climb is using two ropes simultaneously, also known as parallel technique (fig. 14-15b): the leader ties in to both ropes while the second and third climbers each tie in to one of the two ropes. Half ropes can be used for this method instead of two larger-diameter single ropes (see Half-Rope Technique, below). The leader then climbs the pitch, belayed on both ropes. Preferably, one person belays the leader with two ropes in one device (see Figure 14-16), or two belayers can each take one rope. At the top of the pitch, the leader sets up a belay station, then can either belay one follower at a time or bring both up together, one slightly ahead of the other,

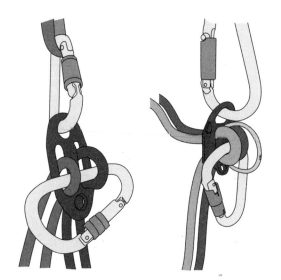

Fig. 14-16. *Two examples of auto-locking belay device setups for managing two ropes when belaying followers who are climbing in parallel.*

making sure to leave sufficient space between the climbers so that they will not collide if the higher climber falls.

With two climbers in parallel, the leader should use an auto-locking belay device to belay both climbers (fig. 14-16; see also "Auto-locking belay devices" under Types of Belay Devices in Chapter 10)—never belaying directly off the harness or through a redirect. This technique takes more rope management but allows three climbers to ascend nearly as fast as two. To manage the two ropes, the belayer uses split-finger technique, keeping strands separated between two fingers on the brake hand and taking in or yielding rope with the pulling hand as each climber climbs. When using parallel technique, it is simplest for the original leader to remain on lead throughout the climb (block leading). With the additional rope and climber involved in a three-person team, belay stations can become more confusing and messy.

While climbing in parallel, it is important for the second and third to ascend around 12 to 15 feet (4 to 4.5 meters) apart, to protect the lower climber should the upper climber fall. The upper (second) climber must unclip the sling on each piece of protection from their rope and reclip it to the lower (third) climber's rope. *Tip:* When belaying two climbers, use a round-stock carabiner and the skinniest single-rated ropes to reduce rope friction in the device.

SINGLE LEAD ROPE WITH A TAG LINE

This two-rope system involves using a typical single-rated lead rope, 50 to 70 meters long, coupled with a thinner, frequently static, smaller-diameter rope (see Ropes in Chapter 8, Essential Climbing Equipment). Some prefer to trail or hang the thinner rope from the back of their harness as they climb, while others tightly coil it and have the second climber carry it in their backpack. A single lead rope with a tag line is the most commonly used two-rope system.

HALF- AND TWIN-ROPE TECHNIQUES

In either the half-rope or twin-rope technique, two ropes are available for rappelling. But in areas with tricky or limited protection options, two ropes can also be used to help reduce rope drag. Half- and twin-rope techniques—less common on rock—are more popular on ice, where two-rope rappels are common and running across ice generally causes less wear and tear on ropes than running over rock does.

Half-Rope Technique

In this technique, two ropes serve as independent belay lines for a single climber. Each rope is referred to as a "half rope," is approved by the UIAA and/or CEN for such use,

Fig. 14-17. *Half-rope technique: **a**, two ropes should not cross but run reasonably straight to reduce rope drag (good); **b**, two ropes crossing and running in a zigzag increases both rope drag and sideways stress on the protection (dangerous).*

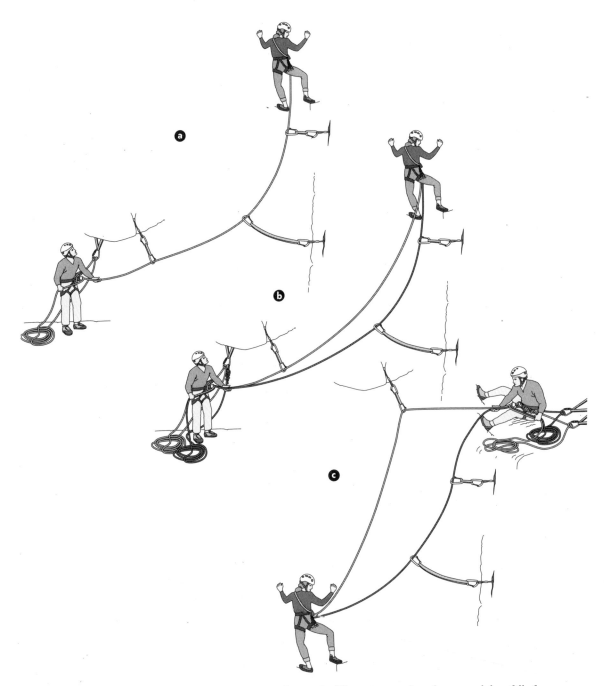

Fig. 14-18. *Advantages of half-rope technique:* **a,** *using a single rope, the follower is exposed to a longer pendulum fall after traversing beyond the first piece of protection;* **b,** *one rope through the first piece of protection can belay the follower on the traverse, while the second rope protects the leader on the direct ascent;* **c,** *off-line protection (placed off the route line) can be used to minimize or eliminate the risk of a pendulum fall.*

and is marked by a "½" on the end of the rope. Half ropes are usually 7 to 8.5 millimeters in diameter and are each by themselves rated strong enough to protect the leader. The ropes should be different colors to allow for clear communication about which rope needs slack or tension.

The leader clips each rope in to its own protection on the way up, and the belayer manages the ropes separately. Most belay devices with two slots can be used, but some are specially designed for use with double ropes. See the manufacturer's guidelines for more details on the approved use of different devices.

Although using two ropes is more complicated than using a single rope, half-rope technique has some advantages. It can greatly reduce rope friction, and climbers may fall shorter distances. Plus, two ropes are less likely than one to be severed by rockfall or sharp edges, and the climbers also have two ropes available for rappelling. This technique is widely used by European climbers and ice climbers—and an increasing number of climbers everywhere—to increase protection on highly technical routes.

The half-rope technique also offers great advantages when a route meanders. With a series of zigzag placements, a leader can clip one rope in to the pieces on the left and the other rope in to those on the right, allowing the ropes to remain relatively straight, in roughly parallel lines that do not cross (fig. 14-17a). Be careful to keep each rope on its designated side so that rope drag does not become a serious problem (fig. 14-17b). When both ropes are clipped to the same protection placement, they generally run through the same carabiner.

The half-rope technique also allows climbers to protect traverses better, especially when the route traverses at the start of a pitch and then heads straight up. The leader can use one rope for protection on the traverse and leave the other free to belay the second climber from above. If the climbers use only a single rope, the second climber could risk a long pendulum fall (fig. 14-18a). But with half ropes (fig. 14-18b), the belay on the free rope can minimize or prevent a long pendulum (fig. 14-18c).

Another major advantage of this technique is that it reduces worries for the leader straining to clip in to the next piece of protection. When climbers are using only one rope, the rope is slack as the leader pulls up a big length to clip in to the next placement. But with a half rope, the slack for clipping is provided on one rope, and the other rope is held snug by the belayer. Thus, when the leader is clipping in to a newly placed piece of protection, a potential fall is shorter.

One disadvantage of the half-rope technique is that the belayer's job is more complex, handling the movements of

two ropes at the same time—often letting out slack on one rope while taking it in on the other. Also, the two ropes weigh and cost more than a single rope or twin ropes. Another drawback is that the technique requires more practice for both leader and belayer than single-rope technique does. However, many climbers find that on long,

Fig. 14-19. *Twin-rope technique: two small-diameter ropes are used as one, with both attached to each piece of protection.*

challenging, complex rock pitches, the advantages of half ropes greatly outweigh the disadvantages.

Twin-Rope Technique

UIAA- and/or CEN-approved twin ropes are generally 7 to 8.5 millimeters in diameter, and they are not rated for use as single ropes. Twin ropes *must* be used in tandem. The rope ends are marked with a symbol of two overlapping circles.

The twin-rope technique shares some characteristics with single-rope technique and some with half-rope technique. Climbers use two ropes, but they clip each rope in to the same pieces of protection, as they would with a single larger-diameter rope (fig. 14-19). Twin ropes are commonly used for a route that requires a half-rope rappel. A team of two can climb the route without having to carry an extra rope to use for rappelling at the end.

Another advantage of twin ropes is that together they absorb more energy and can withstand more falls than a single rope. Though twin ropes are smaller-diameter, the likelihood of severing both at one time is less than that of severing one larger-diameter rope.

One significant disadvantage is that the thinner the rope, the more likely it is to tangle. Also, a pair of twin ropes weighs and costs more than a single rope, and the twin-rope technique lacks the specific advantages of the half-rope system on meandering routes, traverses, and shorter falls. As with half-rope technique, the belayer has to deal with two ropes, though the separate management of each rope is less challenging.

Personal Responsibility

Leading on rock is a thrilling but serious commitment. Climbers face decisions where choosing poorly could prove fatal. It is impossible to have and follow a rule for every situation climbers may encounter. Memorized dogma will not ensure security. Accurately evaluating the risks of climbing requires a fundamental understanding of the risks of the environment and the consequences of each climber's actions. Base your decisions and actions on the knowledge you gain through study and experience—and the freedom of the hills will open before you.

CHAPTER 15

AID AND BIG WALL CLIMBING

Aid climbing is the technique of using gear to support your weight while ascending. It can be as simple as pulling on a quickdraw, or as complex as climbing an entire multiday route on a big wall with your weight suspended from gear you have placed. Aid climbing tactics are typically used to climb terrain—single moves or entire routes—that cannot be free climbed.

Historically, nearly all rock climbs included piton placements and aid climbing, and many classic free climbs were first established as aid climbs. Pioneers such as Fred Beckey, Royal Robbins, Warren Harding, Allen Steck, and Layton Kor relied heavily on aid climbing to achieve historic first ascents. Today, climbers of all abilities free climb many routes originally climbed with aid.

As free-climbing skills continue to improve, climbers are freeing many more routes originally climbed with aid. But despite the rise in free-climbing standards and skill level, there will always be tempting routes that are more difficult still—and routes so devoid of climbable natural features—that a climber will need some of the aid climbing skills described in this chapter. And whereas today's elite climbers may be able to free an aid route, most climbers will likely still perform aid climbing to complete these routes.

Knowing how to aid climb can also help climbers overcome unexpected difficulties while free climbing. Climbers can use aid techniques to move up or down when bad weather or an accident jeopardizes a climbing party. Many routes have short sections of very difficult climbing or poor rock that may be better negotiated by aid climbing. Finally, aid climbing techniques give climbers access to the vertical world of big walls, such as El Capitan in Yosemite National Park, California, that inspire the dreams of so many mountaineers around the world.

There is nothing comparable to climbing thousands of feet off the ground on the world's biggest, steepest walls. Big wall routes demand extreme levels of commitment because retreat may be very difficult or even impossible. Some climbers pursue big wall climbing to find unclimbed wilderness, to follow in the footsteps of lifelong heroes, or to access an emotional and physical state that they cannot attain on flat ground. Regardless of why climbers begin their pursuit of big wall climbing, it will test their resolve, but the rewards can be glorious. This chapter is not a complete step-by-step guide to big wall climbing, but it provides aspiring wall climbers with basic tools and skills to inspire them and foster success. As a big wall climber, you must constantly think creatively and critically. Every pitch, climb, problem, and climbing partner is an opportunity to learn and expand your knowledge of gear and techniques.

Learning to climb big walls is daunting: only the most persistent climbers make headway. The new wall climber might break down big wall climbing into four activities: leading, following, hauling, and living on the wall. These four categories are not exclusive: to be proficient in each, it is important to be aware of the others. It is essential to practice these skills on flat ground with a climbing partner before having to rely on them in the vertical realm.

Note: The anchor setup and hauling diagrams in this chapter assume anchors that include one or more bolts properly installed in solid rock, which is the situation you are most likely to encounter on well-traveled aid routes. In the event that climbers must construct anchors, they should carefully evaluate the strength of each piece of protection, or pro, used and consider fixing the lead line or attaching the hauling device to the anchor's power point rather than directly to one point of protection.

15

KEY TOPICS

CLEAN AID CLIMBING
AID EQUIPMENT
AID PLACEMENTS
BASIC AID TECHNIQUES
FOLLOWING
CHANGING LEADS
MULTIDAY TECHNIQUES FOR BIG WALLS
SPIRIT OF AID CLIMBING

Clean Aid Climbing

Aid climbing involves a lot of gear, but it does not need to damage the rock. Traditionally, aid climbing involved hammering in pitons of various sizes, and in the early development of climbing, the entire gear rack consisted exclusively of pitons. But over time, placing and removing pitons permanently damages the rock, creating pin scars and ever-widening placements. On popular routes, tiny cracks sometimes evolve into finger- or hand-sized cracks from generations of climbers forcing them to accept pitons. With modern nuts, spring-loaded camming devices, hooks, and other gear, climbers have a better chance and a responsibility to climb aid routes "clean."

CLIMBING CLEAN

A clean aid placement is made without using a hammer. Gear placed cleanly can almost always be removed without defacing the rock, leaving no trace of the party's ascent. Climbing clean not only preserves the rock and route for future parties, but also means climbers can ascend faster, because nailing in gear with a hammer is more time-consuming for both leader and follower.

Because the first-ascent party may have left fixed protection (see Fixed Protection in Chapter 13, Rock Protection) such as bolts, pitons, or copperheads (similar to a nut but with a malleable head that is form-fitted in place), a clean ascent of an aid route often entails using fixed gear while also carrying some pitons, copperheads, and other nailing hardware in case previously fixed gear has been removed or is no longer usable. Thus, most clean ascents rely on some protection that earlier parties left in place.

Aid and big wall climbers almost always bring a big wall hammer, even if they intend to make only clean placements, because it is a critical tool with a wide range of functions. Its flat striking surface is useful for driving pitons and its blunt pick can be used to pry out protection (including gear necessary to continue the route) and to clean dirty cracks. Route conditions may require unexpected hammered placements. A hammer can also extend a climber's reach. However, some experienced aid climbers enjoy the added challenge of climbing without a hammer on established aid routes with known fixed gear, or even on new routes. Clean and hammerless styles of climbing both present elevated levels of commitment; climbers choosing these styles must accept the possibility of retreat.

USES OF AID CLIMBING

Aid climbing can be roughly categorized based on the extent of its use on a particular climb. (See Aid Climbing in Appendix: Rating Systems for information on the various grades of difficulty for aid climbs.) When ascending a route in the alpine environment, climbers usually try to climb without weighting any gear. However, climbers may use aid techniques and equipment to overcome sections of a route that are blank or extremely difficult.

This type of climbing often requires little to no specialized aid equipment; usually climbers simply use the free-climbing gear they have with them. Techniques could include pulling on gear, stepping in a sling, or even creating a makeshift aider or two from slings to get through a section. Sometimes climbers pull on gear to speed progress and minimize exposure to objective hazards or other risks in the mountains. Some routes have one pitch of aid climbing (or a relatively small number of aid pitches), allowing climbers to ascend an otherwise free line. Packs may be hauled on a difficult pitch, or climbers may perform a pendulum swing to reach the next section of free climbing.

Aid may also be used on alpine climbs for extended distances and with aid-specific equipment. Long one-day climbs may involve fixing the initial pitches (putting up ropes and leaving them in place on a preceding day) so that climbers can use mechanical ascenders (a technique called jugging) to reach the previous day's high point and then complete the route. For more on jugging, see Using Ascenders later in this chapter.

Aid Equipment

The range of equipment used in modern aid climbing (fig. 15-1) builds on all the gear and techniques described in Chapters 13, Rock Protection, and 14, Traditional Rock Climbing. Technical equipment used in free climbing is designed to protect climbers in the event of a fall. Unique to aid climbing is the use of gear intended to bear only the body weight of the climber. This equipment is designed only for upward progress on the climb; it is neither expected to catch a fall nor rated to hold a fall.

ESSENTIAL EQUIPMENT FOR AID CLIMBING

Aid climbing relies heavily on standard free-climbing equipment. The following gear used in free climbing is also used in aid climbing, with some differences at times in how it is used.

Camming Devices

The same spring-loaded camming devices (SLCDs, or cams) used in free climbing are used on aid climbs. Units with shorter clip-in points are preferred in aid placements

*Fig. 15-1. A collection of aid climbing equipment: **a,** hammer; **b,** standard hook; **c,** Black Diamond Pecker piton; **d,** mechanical ascender.*

to help gain the maximum elevation out of each placement. Most units feature a large clip-in point in addition to the sewn sling (see Figure 13-13 in Chapter 13, Rock Protection). This feature makes it possible to clip an aider (a webbing ladder used in aid climbing, also called an *etrier*; see below) directly to the piece of protection, which is a higher and more convenient clip-in point than the cam's sewn sling.

Specialty cams such as Totem Cams, hybrid and offset cams, microcams, and giant cams have vastly improved options for aid climbers in tricky placements. Totem Cams (see Figure 13-13g in Chapter 13) feature clip-in points that weight only some lobes, useful when it is not possible to place the cam with all lobes contacting the rock. This feature is unmatched for use in pin scars and unusual placements like pockets. Totem Cams also have a narrow head, softer metal, and longer lobes, all of which increase camming strength and "stickiness" (the tendency of gear to stick to the rock).

Offset cams or hybrid cams feature different-sized lobes on each side of the unit; these cams typically fit well in flaring pin scars. Microcams with a traditional design but an extremely small size and low load rating are also helpful to make upward progress on aid climbs. Giant cams protect wide pitches that were previously unprotectable. It can be helpful to mix cams of various brands when aid climbing because sometimes the perfect piece for a

particular crack will be in between the sizes made by one manufacturer.

Nuts, Offset Nuts, and Micronuts

The nuts from a free-climbing rack are also very useful for an aid climb. More-specialized offset nuts and micronuts, an important part of an aid climbing rack, work well in pin scars and can often be used instead of thin pitons. An offset nut has both horizontal and vertical tapers, making it more secure in flaring cracks and pin scars. Offset nuts come in all sizes, from 1 inch (2.5 centimeters) wide to micro sizes (less than ½ inch or 4 to 13 millimeters).

Micronuts can be offsets or the same shape as larger nuts but are much smaller (see Figure 13-8e in Chapter 13). The heads of these small nuts are usually made from softer metals, such as brass or copper-iron mixtures. Rock bites into these softer material so that these nuts tend to hold better in marginal placements. Most manufacturers' smallest micronuts are not rated to take falls; they are intended only to aid upward progress.

Small and offset nuts can be difficult or impossible to remove after they have been weighted. Due to their size and material, these smallest nuts are especially fragile and require very careful cleaning so they can be used on subsequent pitches. The cable blocks the area that a climber would normally hit while removing the piece with a nut tool (see Chapter 14, Traditional Rock Climbing). Sometimes the only way to remove micronuts once they have been weighted is with a hammer and a funkness device (see Universal Aid-Specific Equipment, below), but this method frequently results in a bent cable.

Carabiners

Aid climbing employs many different types of carabiners: to rack protection; sling protection (see Slings, below); build anchors; clip the haul bag to the haul line; clip critical gear to gear loops inside the haul bag; attach aiders, daisy chains, and ascenders (see the next section for details about all this equipment)—and for many other purposes. There are endless variations and designs of carabiners; climbers will eventually find that specific carabiner styles work especially well in certain situations and circumstances. The more organized and efficient climbers are, especially at building anchors and packing gear inside the haul bag, the fewer carabiners they will need.

Traditionally, aid climbers preferred oval carabiners for the entire rack to minimize "carabiner shift." Carabiner shift happens when a climber clips multiple carabiners, including asymmetrical carabiners like D carabiners, into a

15

sling, carabiner, or bolt, then a carabiner shifts when the climber weights them, making a sound similar to that of a piece of gear popping out of its placement. In the context of aid climbing, this can be a terrifying false alarm. However, modern aid techniques—like clipping directly in to the aid protection with the aider and using oval keylock carabiners (see Figure 8-36b in Chapter 8, Essential Climbing Equipment) on both aiders—eliminate carabiner shift most of the time. Most aid climbers now carry lighter, wire-gate carabiners (see Figure 8-36f in Chapter 8) as much as possible, such as for protection and slings, to reduce overall weight. Generally, conventional-gate carabiners should be used in big wall anchors and hauling systems.

Ropes

Big wall and aid climbing is tough on ropes. Leading, pendulums, jugging, rappelling, and hauling cause extreme wear. Big wall routes by nature are longer and more committing, frequently climbing through terrain where sharp edges are a concern.

Big wall climbers typically lead with a dynamic kernmantle rope 60 to 70 meters long and ranging from 10 to 11 millimeters thick, depending on the chosen objective. A thinner-diameter rope may be acceptable for shorter routes or when very little jumaring or hauling will be done. In rare circumstances, a separate rope may be needed if the route involves unusually long pendulums, multiple pendulums on a single pitch, or other uncommon problems. This rope could be another dynamic kernmantle rope or a static rope whose length and diameter depend on the expected use.

When there is too much for the second climber to carry comfortably and efficiently, a separate rope is used as a haul line. Climbers almost always need a haul line when they are spending multiple days on a route, but a haul line may also be useful on routes with consistently steep terrain, even if the party does not plan to stop and bivy. A 9- to 10-millimeter static rope is a suitable haul line for multiday big wall climbs; lighter-weight ropes, such as 8-millimeter tag lines, are sometimes used on short aid climbs with light loads and no overnight gear. The haul line could also be a second lead rope carried as a backup, but it is important to consider the stretch of a dynamic rope under heavy loads (hence why static ropes are preferred).

Examine your ropes often and consider retiring aid ropes earlier than you would a free-climbing rope. When they use ascenders on a fixed line, climbers are trusting the rope with their life.

Slings

Single-length slings are essential for extending placements to reduce rope drag, establishing anchors, and other normal rock climbing uses. Single-length slings are the most useful because they are easy to carry over the shoulder or like a quickdraw (referred to as an alpine draw or tripled-up runner; see Figure 14-4 in Chapter 14, Traditional Rock Climbing). In the latter configuration, they are easy to extend to full length after the first half is clipped to the placement. Cordelettes and other sling materials used to create anchors for free climbing are equally useful for anchors while aid climbing. (See Chapters 8, Essential Climbing Equipment, and 10, Belaying, for more information on slings and cordelettes.)

Belay Devices

Assisted-braking belay devices are essential on big walls and while aid climbing. While big wall routes can be climbed without these multipurpose tools, they are helpful in many tricky situations on an aid climb. The Petzl Grigri (see Figure 10-9a and b in Chapter 10, Belaying) is by far the best of such tools on a big wall. During long belays, for example, a Grigri helps climbers belay while accomplishing other tasks such as managing the haul line, eating, drinking, and even relieving themselves. These devices are also a backup when a climber is following; they can be used during hauling; they can substitute as a mechanical ascender if one is dropped; and they allow superior control during rappels on a single line. Many of these devices are designed for a specific range of rope diameters, so be sure to select a device that functions properly with the ropes you intend to climb with. An aperture belay device, such as the Black Diamond ATC, is also valuable on a big wall—for descending with heavy haul bags, for belaying a following climber, or in case a climber drops their primary belay device. A climbing team might decide to bring one to share.

Helmet

A helmet is indispensable for aid climbing (see Chapter 8). Tricky placements may pop out unexpectedly and send leaders flying. Steep terrain and large racks tend to lead to headfirst falls. Other hazards include rockfall, other climbers dropping gear, and roofs. When choosing a helmet, consider the extra rigors and length of aid and big wall climbs.

Gloves

Gloves are essential to protect your hands while leading, hauling, jugging, and removing protection, as well as from rope burn when rappelling and catching falls. Big wall climbing is hard on gloves; they will need to be replaced often. Some climbers use leather gardening gloves with the fingertips cut off; using tape to reinforce the cut edges can keep them from unraveling. Be sure the gloves can be clipped to your harness in case you need to execute any free-climbing moves.

Shoes

If a route involves only a small amount of aid, normal rock shoes perform best. If you anticipate a route will require sustained aid climbing, shoes or boots with greater sole rigidity provide a better working platform and more comfort. Sticky rubber approach shoes are very popular for aid climbing, including on big walls. They provide arch support and good torsional rigidity for aid climbing, yet have a flexible toe and a soft friction-rubber sole for reliable free-climbing capabilities.

Eye Protection

It is especially important for aid climbers to protect their eyes—from debris from cleaning out cracks, pieces of rock that may detach while hammering in pitons, and other hazards. Sunglasses typically provide adequate protection. A lanyard such as Croakies makes removing sunglasses and letting them hang more convenient. Photochromic or changeable lenses allow you to wear eye protection even when the weather is overcast or the route is in the shade.

Knife

A sharp knife is required on big wall routes. Climbers sometimes need to remove webbing or cord from a fixed piece to be able to clip it, to replace worn webbing, or simply to remove unnecessary or old fixed slings from the rock to keep the climb pristine for later climbers. A knife is also useful for repairing or making homemade gear.

UNIVERSAL AID-SPECIFIC EQUIPMENT

In addition to equipment normally used in free climbing, aid climbers need some specialized gear that can be hard to source. Plan ahead and ask around for the gear you need.

Big Wall Gear Sling or Chest Harness

A big wall gear sling features double or multiple gear loops on both sides of the climber's body (fig. 15-2), increasing the racking options for the large racks carried on aid-intensive pitches. It improves balance and comfort and reduces neck strain caused by the single load-bearing point of a traditional free-climbing gear sling. It can also serve as a chest harness, if designed for this use, and a chest harness can serve as a

Fig. 15-2. *Double gear sling with some racked cams and nuts.*

high-placed gear sling (also see Harnesses in Chapter 8). Racking methods vary widely, but given the weight and volume of gear carried on aid climbs, double gear slings are standard equipment that help distribute weight.

Aid-Specific Seat Harness

While they are not required, seat harnesses made specifically for aid climbing typically feature an extra-wide belt and larger leg loops with extra padding, which make it more comfortable for long belays and multiple days. Some harnesses have other aid climbing features such as a hammer holster, multiple belay loops, and reinforced gear loops.

Belay Seat or Bosun's Chair

During long hanging belays, a belay seat is a great comfort. Hanging in a harness for a long period can restrict bloodflow. Belay seats can be purchased, or climbers can make their own out of wood, a little padding, and some slings. A triangular cloth with straps at each corner is a simple but effective belay seat.

Warning: Never let the belay seat be your sole means of attaching to an anchor. Clip in from your harness to the anchor with the climbing rope as usual, and attach the belay seat to any secure point with its own carabiner.

Knee Pads

A climber's knees are frequently in contact with the rock during low-angle aid climbing and while hauling; wearing comfortable knee pads protects them. To avoid sweaty knees, choose knee pads with sufficient ventilation. Many climbers prefer skateboard-style kneepads with plastic caps and velcro straps.

Aiders (*Etriers*)

When ladders of webbing, called aiders or *etriers*, are clipped to a piece of protection, they allow the climber to step up from one placement to the next. In choosing aiders, consider their intended use. For alpine climbs, minimize weight by using a lightweight pair of aiders. For most aid climbing, offset-step (fig. 15-3a) or straight-style (fig. 15-3b) five- or six-step, ladder-type aiders sewn from 1-inch (2.5-centimeter) webbing are standard. They are used, usually in pairs, in leapfrog fashion as the climber ascends.

Aiders should be long enough to allow the climber to reach the bottom step of the higher ladder when testing aid placements from a comfortable stance on the lower ladder. More difficult aid routes usually require six-step ladders, because the distances between placement options may be longer, and because down-climbing to the lower piece is more common. Most big wall climbers prefer a straight-style aider with a spreader bar at the top (see Figure 15-3b), which prevents the rungs from collapsing when the climber stands in the aider and makes climbing the ladder easier and more comfortable. Spreader bars can, however, get in the way in corners, especially if there is a mix of free sections.

The basic aid sequence (see Basic Aid Techniques later in this chapter) uses two aiders. Climbing with only two aiders is lighter and more efficient; however, a third aider loose on the harness may make it easier to position your body in tricky sequences. Some aid climbers use four aiders, permanently set up in pairs. Using more than two aiders is common only on difficult aid and steep routes; ultimately, the number of aiders used depends on personal preference.

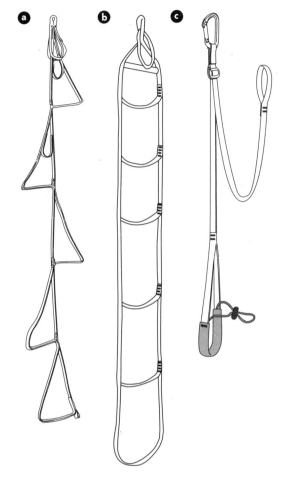

Fig. 15-3. *Types of aiders:* **a,** *offset-step style;* **b,** *straight style;* **c,** *adjustable.*

An adjustable aider with a foot loop (fig. 15-3c), most commonly used only for jugging, tends to be lighter and is well suited for quick adjustments. However, the ladder-type system remains the most commonly used.

Daisy Chains

Traditional daisy chains are sewn slings with multiple loops (fig. 15-4a)—formed by stitching—every 3 to 6 inches (7.5 to 15 centimeters). Daisy chains are used as tethers to keep new placements and aiders attached to the lead climber and are an integral part of the jugging setup. Daisy chains are made specifically for aid climbing. They are unsuitable for use as personal anchors in rock climbing; the stitches of the

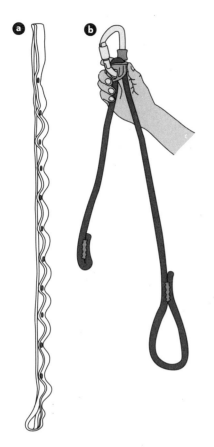

Fig. 15-4. *Lanyard and daisy chain:* **a,** *loop-style daisy chain;* **b,** *adjustable lanyard or personal anchor.*

sewn links are rated for body weight only (see Chapter 8) and, if not used correctly, will fail under a dynamic load or fall. A daisy chain attached to the harness should reach at least as far as the climber's raised hand. Typical daisy chains are 45 to 55 inches (115 to 140 centimeters) long. Longer daisy chains are helpful for difficult aid routes, because they permit the climber to down-climb longer distances below a piece of protection, which allows for adequate testing (see Leading the Basic Aid Sequence later in this chapter).

The sewn loops are used to shorten the daisy chain when it is used in the jugging mode. This shortening must be done in accordance with the manufacturer's guidelines.

Aid climbers usually carry two daisy chains, one for the left-side aider and one for the right-side aider. One end of each daisy chain is girth-hitched to the climbing harness through the tie-in points. The other end is attached to the appropriate aider with a carabiner, preferably an oval keylock carabiner. Connecting the aider to the daisy chain prevents a climber from losing an aider if it is dropped or a placement fails. The loops in the daisy chain provide a convenient method for weighting a placement by using a fifi hook (see below). Adjustable daisies, which are becoming a more popular alternative, have special features outside of their use as a tether (see Fifi Hooks below).

Positioning lanyards such as the Petzl Adjust (fig. 15-4b) are sometimes grouped by climbers into the adjustable daisy category. These lanyards have been tested to absorb falls and incorporate dynamic rope into their design, which decreases the forces created by a fall onto the lanyard. Most climbers find adjusting these positioning lanyards slightly easier and smoother to use than the adjustable daisies featuring flat webbing. With all daisies and positioning lanyards, it is important to understand the product's intended uses and limitations as well as how it is designed to be connected to the harness.

Fifi Hooks

The fifi hook is an integral part of aid climbing, used to quickly connect yourself to gear and so provide a third hand. How you attach a fifi hook to your harness depends on a number of factors, including the stance you desire. The classic fifi hook (fig. 15-5a) is girth-hitched to the harness with a sling that reaches 2 to 4 inches (5 to 10 centimeters) away from the harness after the girth hitch is tied. An adjustable fifi hook (fig. 15-5b) is rigged with slippery 6-millimeter accessory cord and is tied in to the harness with one end, typically with a rewoven figure-eight knot. The adjustable fifi hook can initially be placed higher, farther away from the harness, than the classic fifi hook; a climber can then pull on the cord to shorten it as needed.

A fifi hook can be a critical part of the basic aid sequence (see Basic Aid Techniques later in this chapter), especially on steep terrain. It is used to hook in to a placement and hold the climber's body weight while the climber looks for the next placement (fig. 15-5c). The fifi hook also provides supportive countertension when used to hook a piece at waist level, after which the climber stands up above it to top-step (see Figure 15-20) or to make difficult reaches above protection, such as on overhangs.

Two adjustable daisies can be used in place of a fifi hook. You can extend the adjustable daisy and clip in to a piece from a low position, shortening it as you climb up to the piece. Once you are at your preferred position, the

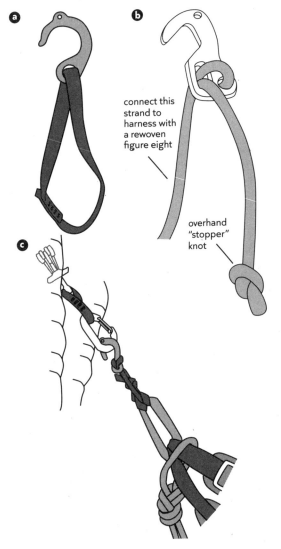

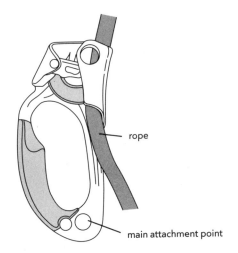

connect this
strand to
harness with
a rewoven
figure eight

overhand
"stopper"
knot

rope

main attachment point

Fig. 15-6. *Handled mechanical ascender for left hand (right-hand ascender is a mirror image): Carabiner holes at top and bottom are used for a number of purposes.*

are less tiring to use. Jumars are designed for use by a specific hand, either the left or the right, and when using two, climbers carry one for each hand (see Using Ascenders later in this chapter). The devices are also advantageous for hauling bags up big walls.

All ascenders employ a cam, allowing them to slide freely in one direction on a rope and to grip tightly when pulled in the opposite direction. Ascenders also have a trigger or locking mechanism to keep them from accidentally coming off the rope. Some triggers are difficult to release, making it harder to get the ascender off the rope when you want to remove it. In addition to the main opening at the bottom, the primary attachment point, carabiner holes at the top and bottom of the ascender come in handy for a number of purposes.

Big Wall Hammer

A basic tool for all aid climbing despite its name, the big wall hammer (see Figure 15-1a) has a flat striking surface for cleaning and driving pitons and a blunt pick for prying out protection, cleaning dirty cracks, and placing malleable pieces. A carabiner hole in the head's blunt pick is useful for cleaning pieces.

A sling attached to the handle (fig. 15-7) and to the climber with a carabiner or sling is essential to prevent the hammer from being lost if dropped. On difficult aid climbs, the hammer is essential for progress and descent—dropping it could have serious consequences. A dropped hammer can also be a serious hazard to climbers below. Hammer slings

Fig. 15-5. *Fifi hooks: **a,** classic, with sling; **b,** adjustable, attached to harness with cord; **c,** fified in to pro. Previous pieces, aiders, and lead rope omitted for clarity.*

adjustable daisy will be tight and can help you stand tall in strenuous positions.

Mechanical Ascenders

When aid climbing was pioneered, climbers ascended fixed ropes with prusik hitches. Mechanical ascenders (fig. 15-6)—often referred to as jugs or jumars—perform the same function, but they allow climbers to move faster and

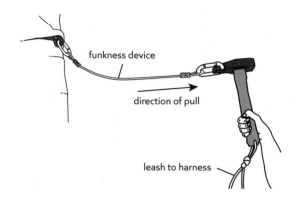

Fig. 15-7. *Big wall hammer with a leash made from a sling.*

can be clipped to the harness, worn across the body, or even clipped to an aider or piece of gear when the hammer is in use. Make the sling long enough so that you can fully extend your arm when using the hammer. Commercial holsters that attach to the harness for when the hammer is not being used are also available; holstered hammers must still be attached to the climber to prevent loss in an upside-down fall.

Funkness Device

A funkness device, also called simply a funkness, is a metal cable with loops on each end for clipping carabiners. The device is used as a static sling to assist in cleaning pieces; it is helpful for removing pins and nuts that have been weighted by the leader. A climber clips one of the carabiners to the piece and the other to the big wall hammer and then jerks upward and outward to remove the wedged piece (see Figure 15-7 and the "Tips for Cleaning Pins" sidebar later in this chapter). Removing pins may require multiple directions of pull. A climbing team shares one funkness, which they pass between climbers as they change leads, so the device must work with all the climbers' hammers. Use conventional (not wire-gate) carabiners that fit comfortably in all hammers used on the climb, so that you can easily clip in the funkness and have adequate range of movement. A Dyneema sling can also be used as a funkness.

Tie-Off Loops

Climbers sometimes carry a few loops of inexpensive thin 9/16-inch webbing tied with a water knot (see Figure 8-34b in Chapter 8) to leave behind on a route—for example, girth-hitched to fixed gear to lower off of a fixed piece when following a pitch. These body-weight tie-off loops are

also used to prevent the loss of stacked pieces (see Placing Pitons later in this chapter).

Ususally commercially sewn short slings, but also hand-tied webbing, both with a higher strength rating than tie-off loops used for lower-outs, full-strength tie-off loops are used on a placement expected to hold a fall. These loops may be threaded through the head of a fixed piton if the eye does not accommodate a carabiner, for tying off partially driven pins (see Figure 13-7 in Chapter 13, Rock Protection), or for improvising a quickdraw. Thinner full-strength tie-offs, such as 8 millimeters, are helpful to thread small holes in fixed gear.

Hooks

Sometimes called "standard" hooks (with the advent of camming hooks; see below), hooks for aid climbing come in many shapes. They are typically made of chromium molybdenum steel for strength and curved for stability. Commonly used to grip ledges or small holes, hooks are used to take body weight only and, by their nature, are almost never left behind as protection (see Placing and Using Hooks later in this chapter).

Many different sizes and types of hooks can be useful on a big wall. Some popular models no longer commercially available are still considered critical gear for certain types of ascents and popular routes. (This situation creates a sourcing challenge for aspiring aid climbers.) In general, for most routes, consider carrying at least one basic hook (fig. 15-8a), one bat hook (fig. 15-8b), and one large hook (fig. 15-8c). One model, the Talon, features three hooks with different shapes (fig. 15-8d). Because the Talon's two extra hooks can serve as "legs," this hook can be the best fit for some features. It is a good idea to carry two of each type of hook on longer aid routes, in

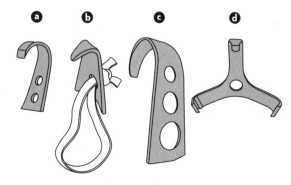

Fig. 15-8. *Standard hooks: **a,** basic hook; **b,** bat hook; **c,** large hook; **d,** Black Diamond Talon.*

case you need the same type of hook twice in a row or in case you drop a hook.

Hooks do not come with a sling; attach one, usually ½-inch tie-off webbing, by feeding a tie-off loop from the front of the hook through until the knot jams (see Figure 15-8b). The sling hangs from the rock side of the hook, with the knot on the other side. This orientation puts the line of force next to the rock, keeps the tip of the hook from rotating off the rock feature, and keeps the knot out of the way.

Filing a hook's tip to a point that can be set into small holes drilled at the back of tiny ledges can offer greater stability for some placements. Bat hooks are used almost exclusively in shallow, ¼-inch-diameter (6-millimeter-diameter) holes drilled for their use. The hooks shown in this guide are merely a sample of the shapes and sizes climbers can choose from.

Camming Hooks

Cam or camming hooks are simple, hard-steel levers used in any crack that is at least as wide as the metal is thick and no wider than the hook's tip. Secure them with a sling as you would for standard hooks. While they are all made from metal of about the same thickness, cam hooks have different tip widths and "arm" lengths (fig. 15-9a), which produce

different leverage (fig. 15-9b and c). Too much leverage may bite into the rock or expand a flake, whereas too little may make the placement insecure. Narrow cam hooks tend to have higher leverage than wider cam hooks. Often, a cam hook can be used to avoid placing a pin, especially in scars made by wedge pitons. Cam hooks can be used in leapfrog style to advance quickly on relatively easy terrain.

Rivet Hangers

Wire rivet hangers are loops of wire ⅛ inch or 3⁄32 inch (3 or 2 millimeters) in diameter with a slider to cinch the wire tight (fig. 15-10a and b). They are attached to bolt studs and rivets, shallowly driven ¼-inch bolts with a wide head. Small nuts with wire slings can be used in a similar manner, with the nut acting as the slider (see Figure 13-5 in Chapter 13, Rock Protection). However, because nuts have a longer wire loop and therefore hang lower, they offer less upward progress. Wire rivet hangers primarily assist with upward progress and may not catch a fall; be wary if relying on them as protection.

Regular and keyhole hangers are rivet hangers made from shaped pieces of metal (fig. 15-10c) that are useful when using a rivet or hanger-less bolt for protection expected to catch a fall, or in anchors. It is also wise to carry a few loose ¼-inch and ⅜-inch nuts to screw onto bolts and rivets without out hangers.

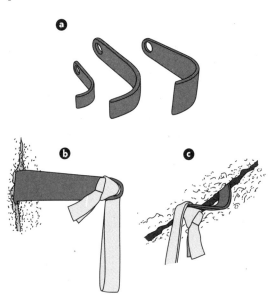

Fig. 15-9. *Cam hooks:* **a,** *typical cam hook sizes—small, medium, large;* **b,** *cam hook placement in vertical crack;* **c,** *cam hook placed upside down under a roof.*

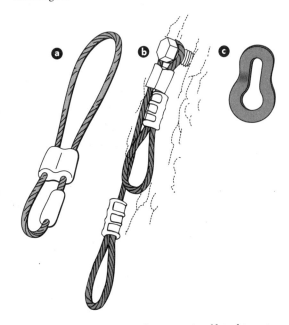

Fig. 15-10. *Rivet hangers:* **a,** *basic wire;* **b,** *self-cinching wire;* **c,** *keyhole.*

IRON HARDWARE AND BOLTS

To master the full range of aid climbing techniques, a climber must be familiar with pitons, malleable hardware, and bolts. With advancements in cams, the advent of cam hooks, and the presence of fixed gear, pitons are placed less often today, especially on well-traveled big wall climbs. Modern cams have largely replaced the need for pitons larger than a small angle or medium-sized Lost Arrows. Fixed pins are common on many routes, and climbers may carry pins for descent anchors in alpine environments.

Pitons

Modern pitons—also called pins—are made of hardened chromium molybdenum steel or other suitable metal such as titanium alloys. Rather than molding to cracks the way the older first-generation malleable pitons did, modern pitons are more unyielding and force the crack to their form. The key to effectively placing a piton is to choose the best size for the crack. To fit the diverse cracks climbers encounter on rock walls, pitons vary tremendously in size and shape.

Realized Ultimate Reality Piton. The RURP is the smallest piton—a postage-stamp-sized, hatchet-shaped pin (fig. 15-11a) used in incipient horizontal cracks. It will usually support only body weight.

Birdbeaks. Also called beaks, birdbeaks (fig. 15-11b) range from those close in size to RURPs to larger units that fit in placements similar to those in which knifeblades or even wedge pitons (see below) fit. Many modern climbers prefer beaks over other pitons. It is not uncommon to carry a dozen or more beaks of various sizes and only a handful of other pitons in other sizes. In an excellent beak placement, the beak's nose goes back into the crack away from the climber and also angles down into the crack, so that the follower not only must nail it up and down when removing it, as with a typical piton (see Following, below), but also pry outward.

When placing a beak, it is important to consider how it will be cleaned. If there is no room for a follower to get their hands or tool close to the piece—such as for a placement under a roof—the beak may be impossible to clean. It

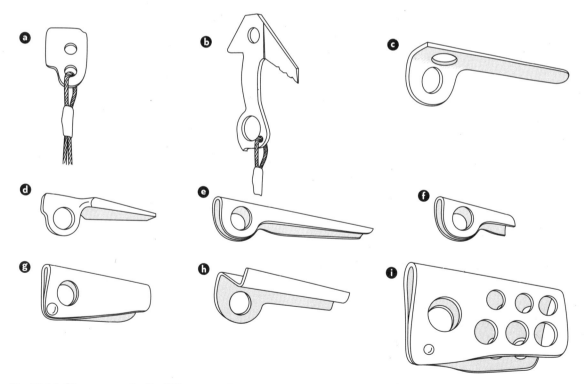

Fig. 15-11. *Piton types:* **a,** *Realized Ultimate Reality Piton (RURP);* **b,** *Pecker (birdbeak);* **c,** *knifeblade;* **d,** *Lost Arrow (wedge piton);* **e,** *angle;* **f,** *sawed-off angle;* **g,** *large sawed-off angle;* **h,** *Leeper Z;* **i,** *bong.*

is common to damage a beak's cable when cleaning, so take care and consider backing up the cable with webbing.

Knifeblades. Also called blades, knifeblades are long and thin and have two eyes: one at the end of the blade and a second in the offset portion of the pin (fig. 15-11c). They come in different lengths and in thicknesses ranging from ⅛ to 3/16 inch (3 to 5 millimeters) and are commonly used to fit cracks too thin for tiny nuts. Many routes have plenty of fixed blades in place, but because beaks tend to be more secure in cracks of the same size, fixed blades are used less often.

Wedge pitons. Known commonly by the brand name Lost Arrows, or just as arrows, wedge pitons are versatile. They have a single eye centered and set perpendicular to the end of the pin (fig. 15-11d), and they come in several lengths, in thicknesses ranging from 5/32 to 9/32 inch (4 to 7 millimeters). Among other uses, arrows work well in horizontal cracks, but they are easy to drop while cleaning. A funkness device (see above) is very useful for cleaning arrows.

Angles. Pitons formed into a V shape are called angles (fig. 15-11e, f, and g). The V varies in height from ½ to 1½ inches (13 to 38 millimeters). The strength of these pitons is derived from the metal's resistance to bending and spreading. Angles are commonly used in angle pin scars, since oftentimes nothing else will fit in a pin scar except a pin. Otherwise, a crack large enough to accept an angle will normally accept clean climbing equipment if the crack has never been used for pin placements.

Leeper Z pitons and bongs. The Leeper Z piton has a Z-shaped profile (fig. 15-11h), while bongs are large angle pitons, varying from 2 to 6 inches (5 to 15 centimeters) wide (fig. 15-11i). Big wall climbers may encounter fixed bongs occasionally on routes, but modern wall climbers no longer carry either type.

Sawed-off pitons. Angles (and Leeper Z pitons) with a few inches cut off the end (see Figure 15-11f and g) are useful for shallow placements on routes that have been heavily climbed using pitons, which leave shallow pin scars. Pins with the proportions of sawed-off angles are sometimes available commercially; otherwise, climbers saw their own pitons using a vise and a hacksaw. Angles of widths from ¾ to 1½ inches (19 to 38 millimeters) are the most common size to saw off.

Malleable Hardware

Generally called copperheads (even when not made of copper), or just heads, malleable hardware is designed to hold weight when the soft head of the piece melds to the irregularities of the rock, such as a small constriction or corner. The security of heads varies greatly, and it is difficult to gauge the strength of a copperhead when placed, making them last-resort equipment generally capable of holding only body weight. Most big wall routes have a few fixed heads; it is a good idea to carry a few heads of various sizes in case one fails and you need to replace it.

Placing heads is more of an art than any other aspect of big wall climbing, and time spent practicing on the ground can save climbers from desperate circumstances on big wall routes. Use the largest head the rock feature will best accommodate, and look for a placement option like a downward-tapered groove or crack with parallel sides, similar to a nut placement but shallower. Spend as much time as you need to make the placement as secure as possible, using the hammer to pound the head in.

Copperheads. Copperheads have a sleeve, called a ferrule, of copper or aluminum—this is the "head"—swaged to one end of a short cable that has a clip loop swaged at the other end (fig. 15-12a). They are placed by pounding the relatively soft metal head end into an irregularity in the rock. Copper conforms well and is more durable than aluminum. Aluminum copperheads (made of a softer aluminum than that used in carabiners) are weaker but more malleable and, therefore, easier to place correctly. Aluminum is the best choice for most placements; copper is generally used for only the smallest copperheads.

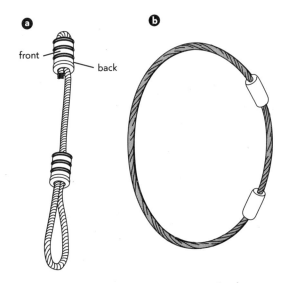

Fig. 15-12. *Malleable hardware types:* ***a,*** *copperhead;* ***b,*** *circlehead.*

Circleheads. Circleheads consist of a wire loop with one or more copper or aluminum ferrules swaged on the loop (fig. 15-12b), one of which is pounded into the rock in the same manner as a copperhead. They are used in horizontal cracks, overhead placements, and other applications wherein the symmetry of the wire loop's attachment point is preferable to a regular head because of the anticipated direction of pull.

Bolts

Chapter 13, Rock Protection, includes a section on the use of existing bolts found on climbing routes. Beyond the scope of this book, bolt placement is best left to the judgment and skill of very experienced climbers. (See also Rock Protection Etiquette in Chapter 14, Traditional Rock Climbing.)

BIG WALL EQUIPMENT

Climbers undertaking a big wall need to consider other specialized equipment needs. It is easy to drop gear on a big wall; safeguard important equipment by using tie-in loops or lanyards. Bring gear that will get the party through the worst possible weather, because retreating is often quite difficult. Be sure all equipment is durable, and consider reinforcing it, with duct tape, when applicable. Portaledges, haul bags, and other items can be protected from failure with some preventive maintenance.

Hauling Devices

Because hauling the gear required for multiple days on a big wall is grueling work, hauling devices, or haulers, are necessary to ease this chore. Devices that have a pulley with a self-locking cam to capture progress, such as the Petzl Pro Traxion and Micro Traxion, are commonly used (fig. 15-13a and b). A large pulley combined with a locking carabiner, two slings, and one ascender—all gear that is usually carried on an aid climb—can be assembled to form a basic hauling system (fig. 15-13c).

Haul Bags

To carry clothing, water, food, sleeping bags, and other climbing and nonclimbing paraphernalia, a well-designed haul bag (fig. 15-14a) offers more than adequate cargo capacity, a solid haul suspension, durable fabric, no snag points, and a removable backpacking harness system. To cover the knot connecting the haul bag to the haul line and reduce snags, an effective knot protector can be fashioned from the top of a 2-liter plastic bottle and some keeper cord (fig. 15-14b). (See also "Hauling" under Multiday Techniques for Big Walls later in this chapter.)

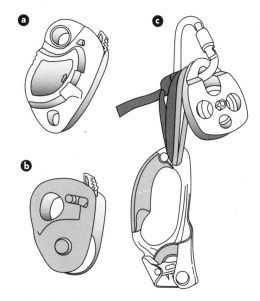

Fig. 15-13. *Hauling devices, or haulers:* **a,** *Petzl Pro Traxion;* **b,** *Petzl Micro Traxion;* **c,** *basic hauling system composed of an ascender attached with two slings to a pulley and locking carabiner.*

Swivel. Attaching a swivel to the top of the haul bag's suspension system improves the bag's movement over features and slabs. Swivels are especially important to reduce tangles in the rope on low-angle and traversing pitches. Without a swivel, the lower-out line (see below) can become tangled with the haul bag. The swivel links the locking carabiner attached to the bag's haul straps to the one clipped to the haul line (see Figure 15-14a).

Lower-out line. To safely lower out the haul bag after the leader completes a traversing pitch, a lower-out line is necessary. It can be a dedicated 50-foot (15-meter) piece of 8-millimeter cord tied to the haul bag. It could also be the docking cord (see below) or the tail end of the haul line (see Figure 15-14a). This latter setup requires the haul bag to be tied in short, usually with a butterfly knot, so there is extra rope available for the lower-out line; this method works on all but the most extreme traversing pitches, reducing the need for another rope. To use the end of the haul line, you will need a separate docking cord.

Docking cord. Before leaving the ground, equip the haul bag with a docking cord, typically 10 to 20 feet (3 to 6 meters) of 8-millimeter cord. This cord can be attached to the haul bag's primary locking carabiner (see Figure 15-14) or directly to the haul bag's primary haul strap with a rewoven figure eight.

15

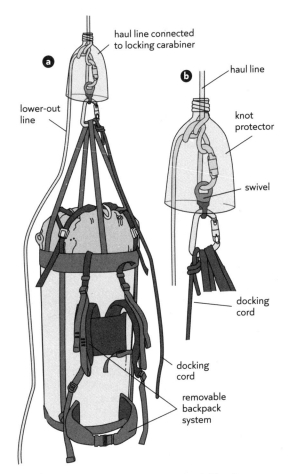

a haul line connected to locking carabiner

lower-out line

b haul line

knot protector

swivel

docking cord

docking cord

removable backpack system

Fig. 15-14. *Haul bag: **a,** features include solid haul suspension straps and removable and stowable backpacking shoulder straps and waist belt; **b,** detail of knot protector and swivel. Keeper cord omitted for clarity.*

Cheater Sticks

Cheater sticks allow climbers to clip the rope or an aider in to a piece of hardware beyond their reach. The most important reason to carry some kind of cheater stick on a big wall is for use in down-aiding (making placements and clipping the rope in to them while rappelling) in the event that you need to retreat through steep terrain. If a fixed placement is missing or broken, using a cheater stick to reach another placement might provide an alternative to placing new pitons, copperheads, or bolts.

A tent pole or hiking pole can be fashioned into a cheater stick in an emergency by taping a carabiner onto

one end. Cheater sticks as simple as a quickdraw reinforced and taped to be rigid may be mandatory for shorter climbers, especially when intermediate placements are not available.

Duct Tape

On big walls, most climbers bring some duct tape for a variety of uses. Duct tape is used to repair equipment and to fashion homemade aid-specific equipment. While climbing, it can be used to tape down hooks, to tape the edges of hangerless bolts to prevent rivet hangers from sliding off, to attach rivet hangers to the aider carabiner and extend the climber's reach to a rivet, or to tape the nut tool or hammer to aiders, hooks, or protection to reach an especially high placement. Duct tape can also be used to pad sharp edges on the rock and protect the rope. Small-diameter rolls can be slung with cord and carried on the harness.

Portaledges

A climber's sleeping platform, called a portaledge (fig. 15-15a), is like a lightweight cot that provides a place for climbers to sleep reasonably well on a big wall without having to reach a natural ledge. Portaledges can be folded up and hauled with the haul bag. When equipped with a rain fly, they provide protection in a storm (fig. 15-15b). Styles vary; some rain flies are more suitable for big storms than others. Inflatable portaledges (fig. 15-15c), a lighter option than traditional designs, are becoming more common. A hammock is significantly lighter but less comfortable. As with belay seats (see Universal Aid-Specific Equipment earlier in this chapter), when resting or sleeping, climbers must always be anchored directly to the rock, not to the portaledge or hammock.

Waste Containers

On big wall ascents, parties need to carry waste containers to haul and pack out human waste. Climbers typically attach these containers to the haul bag's underside. It is essential that the container's haul straps be reliable and attached securely, so that the container will not detach during the climb. Not only do such detachments leave the team without an appropriate waste container, they also leave human waste on the rock or at the base and can injure parties below. While homemade containers may survive the rigors of a big wall, commercial containers specifically designed for big wall climbing, such as the Metolius Waste Case, tend to be more reliable. Outer containers are usually used in combination with internal packaging (see Leave No Trace in Chapter 7, Protecting

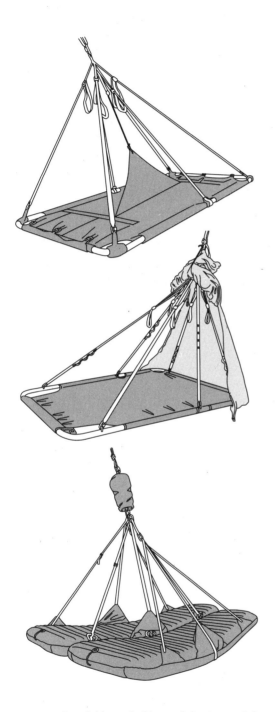

Fig. 15-15. *Portaledges:* **a,** *double portaledge;* **b,** *portaledge with rain fly pulled back;* **c,** *two inflatable portaledges, set up side by side.*

the Outdoors). It is never appropriate to toss waste off a cliff during a climb.

Aid Placements

The general rule for aid climbing is to place each aid piece as high as possible. For example, making most placements at 4-foot (1.2-meter) intervals rather than at 3-foot (1-meter) intervals over the course of a 160-foot (approximately 50-meter) pitch saves more than 10 placements and much time.

Most techniques for placing free-climbing protection apply to aid climbing; however, unlike in free climbing, some aid climbing placements are generally suitable to hold only body weight. Also more often used in aid climbing is the practice of back-cleaning: when a leader removes the previous piece to use it again higher on the climb. From the next higher placement, a leader will step or reach down to the lower piece to remove it (see the "Tips for Leading Aid Pitches" sidebar later in this chapter). As you back-clean, use informed basic protection skills and free-climbing concepts, and leave quality protection at adequate intervals.

Always keep in mind that if the follower will be jugging (using ascenders; see Following, below), the leader must leave protection close enough together for the follower to reach and clean it. When a climb changes direction or angle, removing too many pieces can create problems for the follower jugging a rope under tension.

Using a solid cam hook placement rather than a nut or piton can save considerable time for both leader (placement is much simpler) and follower (there is nothing to clean), but it offers no protection in a fall.

Placing nuts during an aid climb is similar to placing them on a free climb, but because aid nuts take the weight of the lead climber, and because they may be smaller than the nut tool, they can be difficult to remove. Consider using nuts only for protection and not weighting them if possible.

Evaluate fixed pins, bolts, and other fixed gear before using it (see Chapter 13, Rock Protection). Whenever possible, clip a carabiner directly to fixed gear rather than to old fixed slings attached to it. For example, cut old slings from piton eyes so that the eye can accept a carabiner. If for some reason a carabiner will not fit in the eye—because the pin is bent or is too close to an obstruction, or because fixed webbing cannot be removed—thread a full-strength sling through the eye, then either girth-hitch it or clip the two ends of the tie-off loop with a carabiner.

PLACING PITONS

A properly sized pin can be placed one-half to two-thirds of the way by hand and then hammered the rest of the way in. Select the correct pin to fit the crack. It is important before placing to consider the damage to the rock caused by pins. A pin that inserts smoothly, with sufficient contact with the rock, and that reasonably matches the shape of the crack will do less damage when hammered in than a pin that is too large or the wrong shape. Using an ill-fitting pin can mar the rock.

A soundly placed piton rings with a higher-pitched *ping* with each hammer strike. After the pin is driven, bounce-test the piece (see Leading the Basic Aid Sequence later in this chapter). Well-placed pins or fixed pins can flex when weighted, but they should not shift. Knowing just how much to hammer a piton is a matter of touch and experience. Excessive hammering wastes energy, makes it harder for the follower to remove the piton, and needlessly damages the rock. Underdriving a piton, however, increases the risk of it pulling out. Several underdriven pins in a row could result in a long fall as the series zippers out (see Avoid the Zipper Effect in Chapter 14, Traditional Rock Climbing).

Here are additional guidelines for placing pitons soundly:

■ **Place pitons by hand, without using the hammer,** if possible, to eliminate damage to the rock. Use an existing scar and do not hammer the pin. Hand-placed pitons may be less secure for upward progress and are less likely to catch a fall than hammered pitons, but with practice some placements can be accomplished this way.

■ **Try to determine what type of pin was previously placed** and how it was placed. Since most piton placements now occur in pin scars, climbers should try to use the scar in the same manner in which it was created.

■ **Place pins in wider portions of a crack,** in the way nuts are placed. If the crack is thinner above and below, the pin will be supported when it has to take your weight (fig. 15-16a).

■ **Add a full-strength tie-off loop** to the piton if its position causes the connecting carabiner to extend over an edge, to keep from cross-loading the carabiner (fig. 15-16b).

■ **Keep the three points of the V in contact with the rock** when placing angles (fig. 15-16c). The back (the point of the V) must always be in contact with one wall, while the edges (the two tips of the V) are in contact

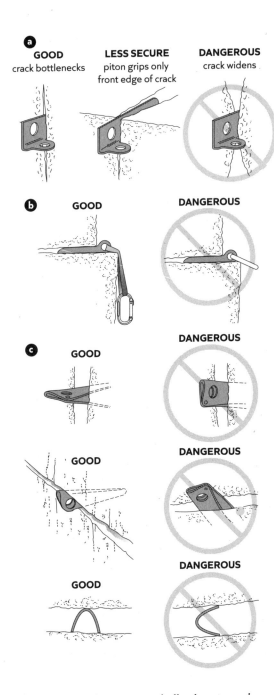

Fig. 15-16. *Piton placements:* **a,** *ideally, place pitons where crack constricts above and below it;* **b,** *extend a piton with a tie-off loop to avoid cross-loading the carabiner;* **c,** *place angle pitons so all three points of the V are in contact with the rock.*

with the opposing wall. In a horizontal crack, put the back of the angle up and the edges down.

- **Stop hammering when a pin bottoms out in a crack—** that is, cannot be driven in all the way. The piton must be tied off around the shaft at the point where it emerges from the rock. A tie-off loop connected with an overhand slipknot, girth-hitched or clove-hitched to the pin, supports the climber's weight and reduces levering action (see Figure 13-7 in Chapter 13, Rock Protection). Loop a longer sling (or a second carabiner) through the pin's eye, and clip this keeper sling in to the tie-off loop or its carabiner. The keeper sling does not bear weight but will catch the pin if it pops out.

STACKING

When no single pin, nut, or cam fits a crack, aid climbers get very creative. Whether you have run out of pieces or are facing a beat-out, pod-shaped pin scar, improvise by driving in two or more pins together. This technique, known as stacking, can be done many different ways, depending on the size of the crack and the pins available, as shown in Figure 15-17.

When pins are stacked, girth-hitch them together with a tie-off loop (fig. 15-17a and c), to ensure that if the stacked pins fail, any pins not clipped directly in to the rope will not be lost. It is typical to clip in directly to only one pin (fig. 15-17b); if the eyes of the stacked pins are blocked (as in Figure 15-17a), it may be necessary to clip directly to the tie-off loop.

PLACING AND USING HOOKS

Nearly every aid route has hook placements, and since hooks are relatively unfamiliar to most climbers, learning to place them on a top rope will increase your efficiency and confidence. To place a hook, set it on the ledge, flake, or hole where it will be used. When learning, try several hooks to see which one sits most securely in the feature. Move the hook around to find the most secure positioning by feel, and if you can see the hooked feature, visually inspect the quality of the placement as well. Hooks can sometimes be placed on top of a fixed copperhead missing its wire (called a "dead head").

After selecting the hook and placement position, clip an aider and daisy chain to the hook. Test all hooks before applying full body weight (or gently shift your body weight onto it if it is off to the side or otherwise cannot be tested). Climbers usually start very low in their aiders, with their weight and stance well below the hook, before they move up one step at a time. It is best to look down or away, so if the hook pops it will hit your helmet and not your face. Avoid standing with your face directly in front of it.

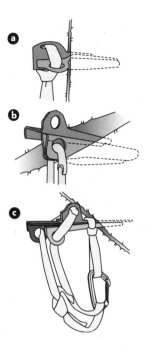

Fig. 15-17. *Examples of pitons and angles stacked and nested (some keeper slings omitted for clarity):* **a,** *arrow and knifeblade stacked back-to-back;* **b,** *Leeper Z and angle nested;* **c,** *two arrows and knifeblade stacked.*

Once your weight is on the hook in one aider (or one pair), it can be helpful to fifi in—to hook, in to the aider's carabiner and hang your body weight. Always keep constant downward pressure on the hook when standing in the aiders, especially when moving up in the aiders and shifting your weight from one foot to the other.

Place cam hooks in a crack or pocket so that the hook binds up and rotates: these placements rely on the force created by the hook's torque (camming action) into the rock (see Figure 15-9). With practice, climbers can place cam hooks in many seemingly unlikely positions and orientations. The tighter the cam hook fits into the crack (in other words, the closer the width of the metal is to that of the crack), the more secure the placement and the less potential damage to the rock. Hitting a cam hook once with a hammer when needed can increase the placement's security. Sometimes a hammer is needed to remove a cam hook, even when it has supported only body weight. Climbers generally agree that cam hooks should not be used in certain rock, such as sandstone, because their camming action may damage the rock.

15

Basic Aid Techniques

Before starting to lead any aid pitch, study the pitch and topo and make a plan. Decide what gear the leader needs and what the follower can carry. Generally, the leader carries an appropriate rack for the length and style of pitch, as well as gear for building an anchor and for hauling. The leader should also have a plan for ascending the rope in the event of a large fall. Figure out where to minimize rope drag and scope out any loose features on the pitch or features that may be dangerous in a fall. Identify any obstructions that might create hauling problems. Decide whether to save aid pieces of certain sizes for the end of the pitch.

RACKING

Efficiently racking and organizing the necessary gear for leading an aid climb is essential to increase efficiency and conserve energy. Racking styles vary significantly between climbers and even between pitches for the same climber. Spend some time thinking about the racking system and how to use the gear loops on the gear sling or chest harness (optional) and your climbing harness.

Generally, most climbers rack cams on a wire-gate carabiner of matching color. They put a set of cams on each side of their body in order from small to large and clip a third set to the gate side of the carabiner of one set already clipped to the harness. Offset cams and specialty aid gear such as hooks can go on the front of the harness if the leader anticipates frequent tricky placements or on the back if such tricky placements are less frequent. Gear for the anchor and hauling can go on the very back of the harness.

Consider racking half the SLCDs, nuts, pins, and slings of each size on each side of your body so that all sizes are available from both sides. It is not uncommon to drop or lose gear on big walls, so consider racking similar gear on different carabiners and different gear loops. For example, if all your nuts are racked on one carabiner and you drop it, the team will lose a significant amount of protection. Some climbers rack all their slings on their seat harness and all their protection on their gear sling (see Universal Aid-Specific Equipment earlier in chapter) or chest harness. Making sets of two or three slings—called "two-packs" or "three-packs"—reduces the amount of space the slings take up on the harness (fig. 15-18a). Or rack single slings over one shoulder.

It is helpful to rack pitons on an oval carabiner because it allows pieces to rotate on and off the carabiner smoothly in either direction (fig. 15-18b); specialized oval wire-gate carabiners weigh less. Do not overload a carabiner to the point that gear is difficult to access. Alternate the direction of angles and Lost Arrows to nest better on the carabiner, which allows more pins per carabiner. Consider racking nuts and hooks onto traditional latch-style (not keylock) carabiners (see Figure 8-36a in Chapter 8, Essential Climbing Equipment). The hook of latch-style carabiners makes it that much harder for nuts or hooks to accidentally come off. Free carabiners can be racked as "footballs" in groups of five or seven carabiners (fig. 15-18c) to make them easy to organize and to use less space on the rack.

It is often useful for the leader to have a nut tool to remove unsettled placements and clean grass, dirt, and other debris out of cracks. Finally, check that the hammer is accessible, with its sling secured but untangled.

LEADING THE BASIC AID SEQUENCE

The basic aid sequence is the same no matter where the leader starts: from the ground, from a comfortable free stance, or from the top step of the aiders. The following assumes that the climber is using two aiders:

1. Using your hands and eyes, **study the terrain above and select an aid piece** to place at the highest suitable spot within reach (fig. 15-19a).
2. **Place the piece and visually inspect it if possible.** Clip the free aider and daisy chain combination in to the new piece with its dedicated oval keylock carabiner (fig. 15-19b).
3. **If testing is warranted, test the new piece** (fig. 15-19c; see also Testing Placements below). Some climbers prefer to unhook the fifi before testing the new piece.
4. **Commit your weight to the new placement**, and unhook the fifi hook from the lower piece and **fifi in to the upper piece**, or **clip in the adjustable daisy strap** (fig. 15-19d). If you are not using an adjustable fifi hook or an adjustable daisy, climb up to the second or third steps in the aiders at this point in order to get closer to fifi in to the new piece. With a classic fifi hook, it is also possible to fifi in to one of the traditional daisy-chain loops.
5. While weighting the new piece, **reach back to the previous piece**. If you are clipping this piece for protection, add a carabiner, quickdraw, or sling and clip in the rope, then remove the aider and daisy chain combination and clip the oval keylock carabiner of that combination to your harness, preferably in the same place every time for ready access (fig. 15-19e). Or clip the free aider and daisy chain combination to the dedicated keylock

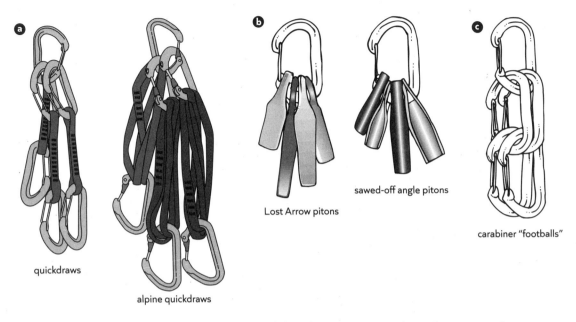

quickdraws

alpine quickdraws

Lost Arrow pitons

sawed-off angle pitons

carabiner "footballs"

Fig. 15-18. *Racking gear:* **a,** *"three-packs" of quickdraws and alpine draws;* **b,** *pitons nested on oval wire-gate carabiners;* **c,** *carabiners racked in "footballs."*

carabiner of the higher aider, and use the two aiders together on the new piece.

6. **Climb as high as possible in the aiders**, possibly to the second or top steps, moving or adjusting the fifi or adjustable daisy while advancing higher (fig. 15-19f). Resist the temptation to look for the next placement until you have climbed as high as you plan to in the aiders so that you do not get distracted.

Repeat the process starting with step 1 (see also the "Tips for Leading Aid Pitches" sidebar). The basic sequence described and pictured here assumes easier terrain and the use of two aiders. This approach can easily be modified for harder placements or steeper terrain by using two aiders per daisy chain, for a total of four aiders. For difficult or steep terrain, you can move the lower aider in step 5 to clip in to the oval keylock carabiner of the higher aider, instead of clipping into the seat harness. Then use two aiders to move up on the highest piece, and stand in two aiders to restart the sequence and make a new placement (fig. 15-19a).

Testing Placements

Testing placements takes time and can tediously extend lead time if every piece is extensively tested. To speed up leads, resist the urge to test obvious cam placements on

routes rated C1 (see Aid Climbing in Appendix: Rating Systems), especially any you would not normally test if you had placed them while free climbing. With practice, climbers can rely on experience and knowledge to set good placements and forgo testing. Of course, tricky and marginal placements still require such precautions.

If you feel that testing is necessary, bounce-test the new piece in this typical sequence: (1) Tug down firmly one or more times on the aider with a hand; (2) step one foot into the aider and give a few solid down-forcing "kicks" with that foot (keep all your weight supported on the previous piece during this first leg test); (3) transfer about half your weight to the new piece and give a few more vigorous hops (keep a hand on the aider of the previous piece and the other foot in that aider so that you can hold yourself upright and on the previous piece should the new piece fail; if possible, stay fifed in to the previous piece); and then (4) transfer all of your weight to the new piece and bounce more vigorously (see Figure 15-19c).

If the new piece is questionable, is not intended for more than body weight, or is behind an expanding feature, some climbers may decide to avoid aggressive bounce-testing. Instead, (1) hand-set the placement (if appropriate) with a firm tug, and then (2) shift your weight as gradually and smoothly onto the new placement as possible.

15

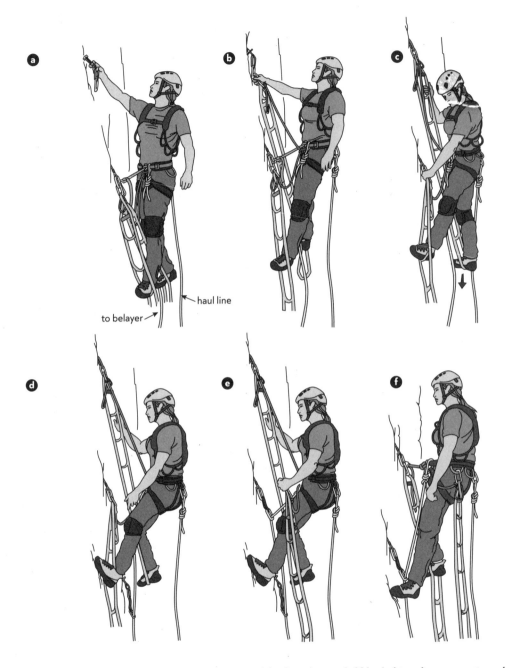

to belayer

haul line

Fig. 15-19. *The basic aid sequence (some equipment omitted for clarity):* **a,** *with fifi hooked in to lower protection, select and place piece of higher protection;* **b,** *clip aider-daisy to the new protection;* **c,** *inspect and if warranted, test the pro;* **d,** *shift weight to newly placed aider and pro, transferring adjustable fifi hook to new pro, then rest on fifi hook;* **e,** *clip rope to previous piece of protection if leaving and remove lower aider-daisy;* **f,** *clip lower aider-daisy to harness, and prepare to climb high in aiders, adjusting fifi as you go, then repeat the sequence.*

TIPS FOR LEADING AID PITCHES

Aid climbing is as much mental as physical. You need to focus, breathe deeply, and triple-check everything.

Minimize rope drag, as in free climbing. Consider each placement carefully, and extend slings to keep the rope running straight. If the follower is using ascenders, pay attention and set protection and slings so that the rope does not rub over sharp edges. If necessary, pad edges, usually with duct tape.

Think strategically while climbing about which pieces can be left and which should be removed (back-cleaned) to be used later on the pitch. Some pitches will require a large number of pieces of the same size, or the leader may have only one or two of certain critical pieces, so back-clean these pieces often. Avoid back-cleaning low on the start of a pitch, and leave protection at close enough intervals to prevent serious falls.

Consider when to clip the rope, which depends on personal preference and the quality of the lower and higher pieces of protection. Some climbers prefer to clip the rope in to the lower placement before completing the final bounce-testing or before committing their full weight to the new placement; if the new placement fails, the leader will not take a fall onto the lower piece, where they could be caught only by the daisy chain and not the rope. Other climbers rely on bounce-testing to ensure that the new higher piece will hold their weight long enough for them to reach down and clip the rope to the lower piece.

Generally, climbers do not want to pull up rope in order to clip it to the highest piece before moving past it, as this increases the length of a potential fall. However, the more suspect the new higher piece, the more likely the climber is to clip the current piece as protection *prior* to moving onto the higher piece, rather than after moving onto the higher piece, as in the basic sequence. On pitches rated A1 or C1, where all placements should be secure, generally follow the basic sequence.

TOP-STEPPING

Moving onto the top step of the aiders can be unnerving, but being able to do so greatly improves the efficiency of aid climbing. The process is simple on low-angle rock, where the top steps are used like any other foothold and the climber's hands provide balance (fig. 15-20). Sometimes

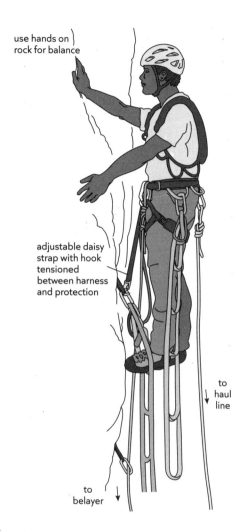

use hands on rock for balance

adjustable daisy strap with hook tensioned between harness and protection

to haul line

to belayer

Fig. 15-20. *Top-stepping on easy terrain: using handholds for balance and keeping heels together and toes spread apart against rock for stability. Some equipment omitted for clarity.*

it is faster and less fatiguing to make multiple placements from steps lower than the top step, such as on very steep terrain or when aiding deep inside awkward cracks and corners. On such terrain, climbers may find that they can move faster by always placing from the second step. However, top-stepping as much as possible is ideal.

Vertical and overhanging rock can make this technique difficult because your center of gravity moves away from the rock and above the point where the aiders are clipped to the aid placement. If the rock offers any features, use your

15

hands or an intermediate placement as a handhold to provide balance. If the rock is blank and the placement suitable, keep your weight on your feet, usually in two aiders on steep terrain, while standing up and applying tension to the fifi hook or adjustable daisy strap with daisy strap with hook strap between your harness and the aid placement. That tension provides the means of balancing yourself. When using a classic fifi, an alternative method is to clip a quickdraw in to the piece and pull upward on the quickdraw with one hand while making the next placement with the other hand.

Generally, standing with heels together and toes spread apart against the rock offers the most stability when top-stepping. This position can be very helpful when standing high in the aiders and stretching up to make a difficult placement.

CONSERVING ENERGY

Big walls by nature are long and arduous; it is important to conserve energy. Strategy, efficient systems, and teamwork allow climbers to move faster and have more fun. The best way to conserve strength is to rest by fully weighting a newly tested piece, freeing your feet completely before using the aiders to move up on the piece. Doing so allows you to switch feet between aiders as needed or reach sideways to attach aiders to a new piece or execute whatever the next move may be.

Aid pitches can be long and strenuous. Do not wear yourself out by carrying gear you do not need on a specific pitch; it is more efficient to leave it in the haul bag. If the leader is less than halfway up the rope and needs gear, the belayer can attach it to the haul line for the leader to bring up. Leading with a backpack is tempting but also very hot and tiring; instead, consider putting snacks in a pocket and a small water bottle on your harness.

The fifi is your friend. Rest on it when needed and be aware of inefficient or unnecessary efforts. Constantly ask if there is an easier way to accomplish a task using one of the many tools at your disposal. Applying brute force is a good way to wear yourself out, injure yourself, or break a vital piece of gear.

SWITCHING BETWEEN AID AND FREE CLIMBING

Stowing and deploying aiders and free climbing with aid gear, a large rack, and a haul line—these are just some of the difficulties climbers face when switching between aid and free climbing on a big wall climb. For free climbers, reorienting to a different style and repurposing free gear into aid gear is the main challenge. Weighting the first piece on aid

after free climbing can be scary when the last piece of protection is far away or untested. Communicate clearly with your partner on transitions between aid and free.

From Free to Aid

Switching from free climbing to aid climbing is the easier transition. If the route accepts rock protection, the climber simply calls for tension or clips the belay loop directly in to a piece.

If the climber has been free climbing because the rock did not accept protection, the last piece may be far below, making for a trickier transition. Whenever possible, start the transition at a piece of reliable protection and consider placing two pieces. Either way, test the first piece of aid protection carefully by looking at it and tugging on it before weighting it. If you are using aiders to aid climb the section, release them and the daisy chains (see Daisy Chains earlier in this chapter), and move into the basic aid sequence (see Leading the Basic Aid Sequence above).

If a climber does not expect to use aid and suddenly needs it, problems arise. When in this bind, prepare slings or quickdraws by interconnecting several slings, and then use these improvised aiders to move through the aid section. Be careful not to drop the improvised aiders.

From Aid to Free

A climber may wish to transition from aid to free climbing when encountering a section that cannot be aided (such as face climbing terrain where it is not possible to place protection) or when free climbing is faster and more efficient than aid climbing. Make sure your belayer knows you will be moving faster as you transition. Switching from aid to free can be very mentally challenging. Make sure the terrain is well suited for free climbing before you try it. Two methods are commonly used to switch to free climbing:

On easier or low-angle terrain, it is often possible to move out of the aiders and onto the rock with all your weight on your hands and feet and still reach back to unclip the aiders to bring them along. If the transition occurs at a ledge or stance, simply clip the aiders and daisy chains to the harness gear loops and start free climbing. Make sure that the aid equipment will not hinder your movement.

When the aid climbing is steep just before the transition to free climbing, you have multiple options, depending on the situation. If you will be free climbing the last section to the anchor, simply leave an aider clipped to the last piece. The follower can clean the aider with the piece of protection, or you could lower off the anchor to retrieve it.

Use a similar strategy if you know you will be able to clip a solid piece of pro or a bolt after the free-climbing section. Simply leave the aider clipped to the last piece, climb out of the ladder to the solid piece, and ask the belayer to lower you back to the aider. You can also leave pieces of the rack with the aider if you do not need them.

Another option is to clip a single- or double-length runner to the last piece of aid protection. Then stand in the runner, using it as an improvised aider. Remove the aiders and stow them on the harness. You can now make free-climbing moves without having to reach down to retrieve the aiders. If possible, clip the rope to the sling before stepping into it and free climbing away—otherwise, the piece will not help catch a fall. Also, if it is not connected to the rope, the piece and sling might be out of reach for the follower to clean.

If you are moving from a hook to free climbing, simply pull up on the aider(s) from the first free moves, and the hook and aider should release.

LEADING HORIZONTALLY

To move horizontally across unclimbable territory into climbable terrain, climbers use tension traverses and pendulum swings. First ascensionists use these techniques to avoid placing bolt ladders to reach the new system.

The main difference between a tension traverse and a pendulum is that a pendulum requires the climber to run across the face in order to reach the new system. For a tension traverse, the climber does not run but uses friction on small holds to work hands and feet sideways. Pendulums and tension traverses can be difficult, and they pose special problems for the second climber, who must both follow and clean protection.

For both techniques, the leader starts by placing a solid piece of protection at the top of the planned traverse or pendulum and clipping the rope in to this protection (or clipping in to fixed gear at this point). Usually the equipment used for the tension or pendulum point cannot be retrieved, unless it is possible to come back to it from above, so these points on most routes are equipped with fixed gear. Climbers might use a locking carabiner on a tension or pendulum point for extra security.

Tension Traverse

After clipping in the rope to protection at the top of the traverse, the leader takes tension from the belayer, lowers some amount, and starts to move toward the new crack system, using hands and feet to move across the rock (fig. 15-21a). Some tension traverses require climbers to achieve a sideways or even nearly upside-down position as they move.

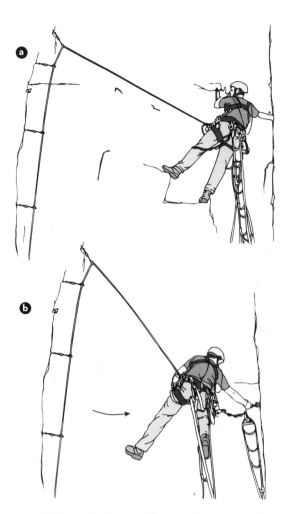

Fig. 15-21. *Leading horizontally:* **a,** *tension traverse, using hands and feet to move across the rock;* **b,** *pendulum swing, running back and forth across the rock to the new feature. Here, the climber has reached a point where they can place protection and continue climbing upward.*

Often during tension traverses, leaders call for more slack as they make progress. Maintain clear communication with the belayer, with standard "Lower me," "Stop," or "Hold" commands. Once you reach the final destination, you may need to call for slack so that you can continue climbing in the new crack.

Pendulum Swing

The leader clips in to the pendulum point with the rope and has the belayer take tension, as for a tension traverse. Then the leader calls for a lower. The belayer lowers the leader until there is enough rope out for the leader to run back and forth across the rock, gaining distance to swing into the new crack system (fig. 15-21b). When being lowered by the belayer, it is better to be lowered too little, because if you are too low, it may be very difficult to correct the error or reach your mark. Stop early and try the pendulum. If necessary, have the belayer lower you farther until you reach the best position. While running back and forth across the rock, start slow and increase your speed each time. Stay in control to avoid spinning and hitting the rock.

Tips for Moving Horizontally

Some pendulums and traverses are difficult due to length, angle of the face, or other factors. Climbers may want to attach a cam or hook to their aider so that they can jam it into the new crack very quickly (as in Figure 15-21b). If a climber has barely reached the new crack but has managed to dynamically bury the right piece into it, the piece and the daisy chain will catch the climber's weight before they swing back into the old plumb line. Once in the new crack system, climb as high as you can securely before clipping the rope in to aid pieces for protection. The higher a climber gets before placing protection, the easier it is for the belayer, who will second the pendulum (see Following Tension Traverses and Pendulum Swings later in this chapter).

A Grigri is helpful for belaying on tension traverses and pendulums. In a tension traverse, such a device enables the belayer to provide the perfect amount of tension for the leader. In a pendulum, it allows the belayer to hold the leader in the exact position required.

LEADING OVERHANGS AND ROOFS

Although they can appear intimidating, overhangs and roofs are often easier to "aid through" than they look, especially because fixed gear tends to be prevalent in roofs. Keep ascenders handy, because if a piece pulls out and you end up hanging, you may need them to climb back up to the last secure piece.

Under a steep overhanging wall or a roof, you may not be able to place your feet against the rock. In this situation, start by hanging as far below the piece as possible and in the low steps on the aiders. To move up and reach the next placement, use the fifi hook or adjustable daisy strap to hang from the harness rather than trying to stand with your full weight in the aiders. After making the new placement, test it and clip in an aider, then step into the lowest possible step and fifi in.

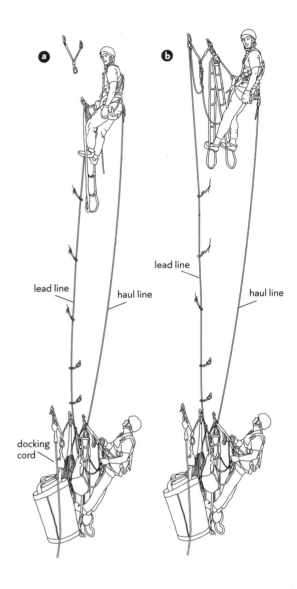

Fig. 15-22. *Establishing a belay: **a,** leader builds anchor and pulls up all the slack; **b,** leader fixes lead line; (continued on facing page)*

When climbing very steep overhangs, you will probably make placements close together. Be careful not to remove gear during these sections, because the follower will need more gear left in place in order to successfully clean the pitch. Or consider back-cleaning the entire section to allow

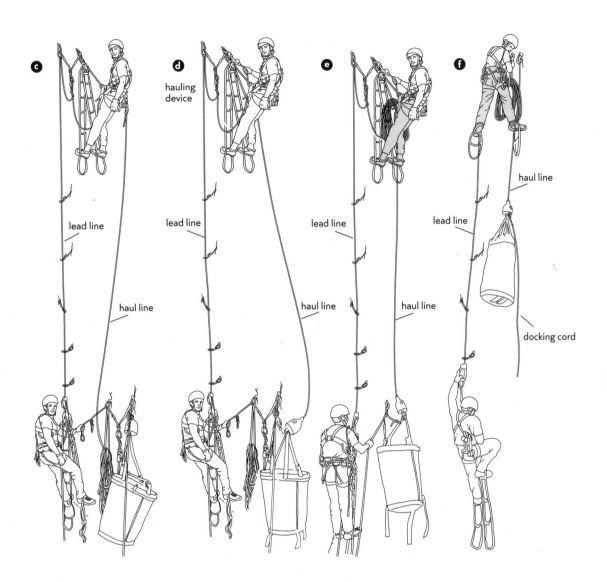

Fig. 15-22. *(continued from facing page)* **c,** *follower attaches to lead line and begins dismantling lower anchor;* **d,** *leader sets up the hauling system while second prepares to jug and clean;* **e,** *second releases haul bag;* **f,** *leader hauls while second jugs and cleans.*

the follower to simply ascend the fixed line. As an overhang becomes horizontal, it becomes easier to aid because you can stand fully erect in the aiders under the roof, possibly in the bottom steps, and aid sideways through the horizontal crack system.

Despite the difference in balance in aiding over a roof, climbers use the same basic sequence described earlier. Reach up and over the roof to find the next placement. You may need to use your hands to feel the placement rather than being able to see it. When you first move onto the aider clipped to the piece above the roof, it may be difficult to pull yourself up over the roof. Stepping into the lowest step and standing up can help you get started. Then, it should be possible to fifi in to the piece above the roof.

Rope drag is a common side effect of overhangs. Try not to give in to the temptation to put long slings on these placements, because it will make cleaning very difficult for the follower. Some climbers pull along a second belay rope and start climbing on it after clearing the lip of the overhang.

Finally, try to relax when working out moves over a big roof. Have confidence in your pieces. Clutching at them will only drain your strength.

ESTABLISHING BELAYS

On reaching the end of a pitch, the leader must establish an anchor. Many routes have bolts, but climbers may have to place their own gear. It is important to have a conversation about anchors with your teammate before climbing. Figure 15-22 shows a two-bolt anchor with one master point.

A big wall anchor is similar to the anchor you might build in multipitch climbing but has slightly different requirements. Typically, the follower is fixed (tied directly) to the anchor rather than belayed. The anchor also needs a point to haul from and a point to dock the bags to after the haul. Generally, try to keep the haul line in a straight line out of the route's path so that the follower does not have to push past the haul bag(s). It is helpful to build an anchor with extra-large locking carabiners and nylon slings or cordelette (fig. 15-22a), tying in with the climbing rope, depending on the team's strategy. At every anchor, assess the quality of all bolts and any pieces you have placed. Be extra careful placing gear behind flakes and in poor rock. Remember, a big wall anchor protects the lives of the team. It must withstand the extra forces involved with hauling—and could potentially be your campsite for the night.

The Lead Line

Usually the leader fixes the climbing rope to the anchor's master point with a clove hitch or similar knot that can be untied easily, then backs it up to another piece of the anchor (fig. 15-22b). The lead line could also be fixed to a solid piece of the anchor on either side of the master point, if the follower will be traversing to the anchor, and then fixed again ("backed up") to the master point. Make sure there is enough rope between where the follower is fixed to the anchor and the leader's position to allow the leader to haul the bags. As soon as the lead line is fixed and backed

up, the leader relays that information down to the follower, which also means that the leader is off belay (or the leader may shout "Off belay" separately).

The follower immediately attaches to the lead line with ascenders and a backup, removes most of the anchor from the belay station, and unties the backup knot in the haul line (fig. 15-22c). Until the haul starts, the follower leaves any pieces directly weighted by the haul-bag docking cord.

The Haul System

After fixing the lead line and while the second is preparing to jug and clean, the leader sets up the haul system (fig. 15-22d; see also "Hauling" under Multiday Techniques for Big Walls later in this chapter). The hauling system can be on any solid point of the anchor except for wherever you wish to dock the bag. Typically, hauling from a higher point on the anchor is more convenient.

Once the haul system is ready, the leader uses the command "Ready to haul." Then the follower releases the haul bag from the belay anchor (fig. 15-22e) so that the leader can haul, removes any pieces that the haul bag was directly weighting, and begins to ascend the fixed lead line (fig. 15-22f). When deciding where to dock the bag, consider where the bag will go on the next haul. If the pitch traverses, dock the bag where the follower can conveniently release it without the bag going over or under them. Constantly be aware that once a line is weighted, anything under it is trapped. To avoid this problem, a good plan generally is to dock the bag under everything else.

After hauling and docking the bag, the leader neatly stacks or restacks the haul line so it is ready to go for the next lead, with the end attached to the leader on top. The leader prepares for the follower to arrive and makes a plan for the next pitch. This is also a good time to eat, drink, and savor the view.

LEADING TYROLEAN TRAVERSES

To move between two rock features, such as a main wall and a detached pinnacle, climbers may use Tyrolean traverses. They are also useful for crossing rivers and other spans. Climbers string ropes between points on each side of the span and attach themselves to the rope to traverse through the air. As an example, the instructions that follow are for a Tyrolean traverse between a main wall and a detached pinnacle, such as Lost Arrow Spire in Yosemite National Park, California.

1. **Connect one end of a single-strand rappel line to a SERENE anchor** on the main wall—one that can take both a horizontal and a vertical pull. The rappel

line must be greater than two times the distance of the span between the main wall and the detached pinnacle, with the extra length more than two times what is needed for tying two knots.

2. **Rappel this rope to the saddle between the main wall and the detached pinnacle.**

3. **Climb the pinnacle** (using an additional climbing rope if needed) **and build an anchor** at the top for a horizontal pull (or, as in many cases, use the fixed anchors that are provided). Note that after the traverse, the equipment used for the pinnacle anchor cannot be recovered.

4. **The follower brings up the free end of the rappel line** if it was not used as the climbing rope (consider also tying in to this line to avoid dropping it). Both climbers are now atop the pinnacle and attached to the pinnacle anchor.

5. **Pull the rappel line tight against the anchor on the main wall** and fix this rope (which becomes the traverse line) to the pinnacle anchor. Feed the free end of the traverse line through the anchor just as you would to set up a rappel (if using two ropes, untying and retying is best). If you are using the free end of the rappel line to initiate the traverse (see step 7 below), consider fixing the second rope to the pinnacle anchor for redundancy and to avoid passing a knot on the rappel.

6. **Select the gear to attach to the traverse line and use for crossing.** If the traverse line is mostly horizontal or if the destination is higher than the starting point, many methods can be used to cross the span on the traverse line: (a) using a Petzl Micro Traxion clipped to the harness and one ascender, perhaps with an aider or foot sling attached to the ascender (fig. 15-23a); (b) using two ascenders, with one ascender clipped to the harness, and again with perhaps an aider or foot sling clipped to the other ascender (fig. 15-23b); or (c) using a combination of pulleys, carabiners, and prusik hitches. In addition to the two primary devices used for connecting to the traverse line, always rig a backup, such as a double-length runner girth-hitched to the harness tie-in points and clipped around the traverse line with a locked carabiner.

7. **The first climber connects to the tensioned traverse rope** and traverses from the pinnacle to a new location on the main wall, taking the free end of the traverse line with them (consider tying in to the end to ensure that it is not dropped) and building a new

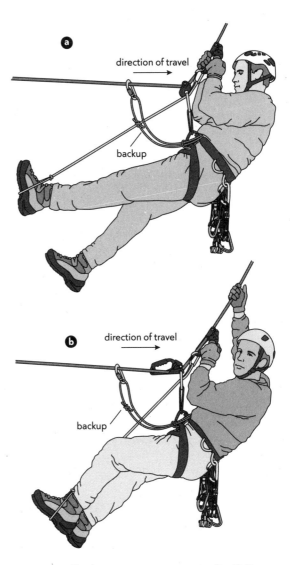

Fig. 15-23. *Tyrolean traverse setups: **a**, using Petzl Micro Traxion and one ascender; **b**, using two ascenders.*

anchor at the new main-wall location. Depending on the terrain, span distance, elevation difference, rope stretch, and traverse-line tension, a short lower-out, rappel, down-jugging, or down-prusiking may be necessary to start the traverse and prevent the climber from careening away from the detached pillar at an uncontrolled speed. Often, the first climber may rappel on the nontensioned free end of the traverse line to initiate the traverse. Do not attach a rappel device to the tensioned traverse rope, because this device will likely become tensioned and stuck near the traverse's midpoint.

In this example of the Lost Arrow Spire where the destination is higher than the starting point, only a short rappel or lower-out is required before ascending comes into play. However, if the destination is lower, all the climbers will likely have to rappel the entire traverse, and will need ascending equipment only for the final few feet. Plan ahead to ensure that you have adequate equipment and lines to perform the traverse.

8. **The follower unfixes the first rope from the pinnacle anchor**, ensuring that the rope is threaded through the anchor; if using two ropes, the follower takes note of the correct rope to pull when the traverse is complete, just as when preparing a two-rope rappel.

9. **The first climber tightens and fixes the free end of the traverse line to the new anchor** at the new main-wall location, which retensions the original line and tensions the free end for the first time so that now two tensioned lines cross the span.

10. **The follower sets up for the traverse using the system of choice** (see steps 6 and 7 above); if using two ropes, the follower selects the strand of traverse rope without a knot so that no knot pass is required on the traverse. Now both climbers are at the new main-wall location.

11. **Both climbers untie the ends of the traverse line** from the main wall anchor and pull the rope, taking care that the ends of the lines do not tangle.

If you are hauling a bag, find a way to send it across the traverse on the line. Hanging it off someone trying to cross is unpleasant at best.

Following

On short sections of aid, the second climber usually follows the same sequence as the leader, but is belayed from above. The second might use aiders to follow a short section, clipping them to the protection left by the leader, or just pull on the protection and use the rock for counterpressure or stances. The follower's technique depends on the steepness and difficulty of the section.

Long sections of aid and big walls call for a different strategy. The leader fixes the lead line to the anchor, and the second uses mechanical ascenders to ascend the fixed climbing rope and also cleans the protection (see the "Tips for Cleaning Pins" sidebar). If the team is hauling a bag, the

second must release the bag for hauling before leaving the lower anchor (see Figure 15-22e). If the bag hangs up along the way, the follower can help to free it.

USING ASCENDERS

When you are first learning to jug, you may find it easier to try an alternate method: using one ascender and one Grigri to hoist your body up. This description details the standard two-ascender method. Climbers commonly use a locking

Fig. 15-24. Using ascenders: **a,** *efficient jugging technique, with dominant left hand's ascender higher and right foot one step higher in its aider's ladder;* **b,** *proper method to shorten daisy chain for attaching to ascender.*

carabiner for each ascender (left and right). Smaller oval or D-shaped carabiners with a regular locking gate (not an auto-locking gate) are usually most convenient.

Setting Up

When preparing to follow a pitch, attach the ends of each daisy chain to the ascenders' locking carabiners. The ascender should always be clipped in to the end of the daisy chain rather than to one of its loops. Ensure that the attachment to the daisy chain is secure before weighting it, and lock any locking carabiners in the system. Ascending is easiest with your dominant hand's ascender higher on the rope, but it is important to be comfortable with either hand in the top position (fig. 15-24a).

For most ascending, shorten the overall length of the upper ascender's daisy chain so that it draws tight prior to or exactly at full arm extension. The amount that this daisy chain is shortened varies based on the steepness of the pitch and may change many times during an individual pitch. In general, the goal is to weight the ascender and not your arm. It is not necessary to shorten the daisy chain for the lower ascender.

To shorten the daisy chain, first place the ascender at approximately full arm extension. Pull up the daisy chain from the harness and find the loop that touches the locking carabiner attached to the ascender. Use a free carabiner (usually the dedicated carabiner belonging to the aider-and-daisy-chain combination) to attach this loop of the daisy chain directly to the aider's carabiner. This method of shortening the daisy chain ensures the daisy chain is shortened safely, in accordance with manufacturer's instructions (fig. 15-24b). Another option is to use an adjustable daisy strap. Experiment with jugging with the daisy chain shortened to different lengths to find what is most comfortable and efficient.

Moving Up

When jugging, offset your feet in the aider steps: If your left hand is dominant and that ascender is higher, and if the left foot is in the fifth step from the top, your right foot would typically be in the fourth step from the top (see Figure 15-24a). This way, your feet are at roughly the same height, an efficient stance for jugging.

When you begin to move the ascenders up, the upper one will move easily while you stand with your weight on the lower ascender and aider, but because initially there is no weight on the rope below your lower ascender, it will be more difficult to slide the ascender up the rope. Resist the temptation to hold or pull down on the rope below

---

TIPS FOR CLEANING PINS

Pitons by nature are more difficult to remove from placements than cams or nuts. Assessing the placement and using a funkness and hammer correctly is important.

First, tap the pin lightly to get an idea of how much it moves initially. Attaching a carabiner to one too early makes it harder to hit and slows the cleaning. For all pins except sawed-off angles, it should be possible to move the pin before the sling is attached. But be careful because if an unslung pin flies out, it will probably be lost.

Attach either a carabiner with a sling or the funkness device once the pin is loosened—or, for sawed-off angles, before hitting at all. Clip one end to the pin and one end to yourself, possibly to the aider or daisy chain or the climbing rope. Continue to hit the pin, side to side, loosening it back and forth until it comes out. Try not to hit and break the funkness carabiner. Use one hand to hold the carabiner to the side while you make blows. It might be a good idea to use the pick side of the hammer. For sawed-off angles, err on the side of putting the sling on early. They do not visibly move much, and it is hard to know when they might pop out.

Try clipping the free end of the funkness to the hammer (see Figure 15-7) if the pin does not come out with back-and-forth hits. Then "funk" on the pin by making a big jerk out and up with the hammer and then another separate "funk" with a jerk out and down. "Funk" the pin up and down multiple times, as needed, to loosen it. Sometimes jerking straight out away from the rock is helpful, especially with angles. Be careful not to hit your face when using the funkness.

15

---

the lower ascender to be able to move it up. It is an inefficient and inadequate technique for covering long distances. Instead, practice "thumbing"—using your thumb to slightly open the cam on the lower ascender so that it will move upward. Most ascenders can be thumbed open without risk of opening fully and detaching from the fixed line. Thumbing is very efficient, and you may need to do it every time you move the lower ascender up.

Ascending Steep Terrain

When ascending very steep terrain, rather than fully weighting the aiders during the entire process, drastically shorten the upper daisy chain, probably to about the third loop from your harness, and rest your body weight directly on the upper ascender after moving it up. In this sequence, move up the upper ascender and then rest with all your weight hanging in the harness from the ascender. Move the lower ascender up, stand up, push the upper ascender up a few feet, and hang again. There are variations of this technique, so experiment to find out what works best for you.

Backing Up Ascenders

While ascending the rope, the follower may need to remove the top ascender to pass pieces or to lower out, making it important to be backed up to decrease the possibility of a long fall. Remaining tied in to the end of the climbing rope serves as a backup but could still result in a huge fall to the end of the rope should both ascenders fail. To further decrease the likelihood of a long fall, periodically "tie in short," using the climbing rope as the backup. To do this, stop periodically and tie any knot, such as an overhand on a bight, just below the ascenders, and clip the loop in to your harness with a locking carabiner.

An alternative is to attach a Grigri directly below the ascenders. This device not only acts as a backup but it can also be employed in other simple and extremely efficient techniques for following pitches and cleaning gear (for example, the Grigri lower-out method, described later in this section). Following with a Grigri backup has many advantages, but it takes some practice to manage: you must tend the big loop of slack rope below you to avoid snags.

Some followers use a progress capture pulley, such as a Micro Traxion, as a backup because the rope feeds very nicely through it. But it is important to remember that the Micro Traxion adds another toothed device to the rope, and releasing rope through it is difficult.

Keep in mind that ascenders are most likely to come off on a traverse and less likely to come off when you are simply jugging up a straight line of ascent. Tying in short or providing a backup below the ascenders is an easy precaution that has saved lives. Conversely, mistakes in attaching and backing up ascenders have led to many deaths.

Other Precautions While Using Ascenders

While ascending, the follower should take other precautions. First, carry a spare prusik sling just in case an ascender fails or is dropped. A Grigri is a much more effective and efficient lower ascender than a prusik, so this is the first

backup to an ascender. As in all climbing, beware of sharp edges. Jugging places the rope under tension, and sharp edges can cut it. Ascend as smoothly as possible to minimize any sawing action on the rope running over an edge.

Be aware that high winds or "rope-eating" cracks may snag the rope; be sure to manage rope hanging below as you follow. Leaving the rope hanging for the entire pitch may be appropriate when the pitch is overhanging or there is little risk of the rope hanging up. As the follower ascends, the weight of the hanging rope will eventually make moving the lower ascender easier, eliminating the need to thumb the cam (see Moving Up, above).

FOLLOWING HORIZONTALLY

Seconding traverses when aid climbing can be both strenuous and technical. Some of the most common and useful methods are described below. These basic methods can often be applied to overhangs as well.

Re-aiding

When traversing horizontally, it may be more efficient to aid climb across the traverse, using aiders, as if leading (called re-aiding). Aiding in this fashion, the follower can self-belay by using a Grigri as an attachment point to the rope to keep the rope tight from above.

Following Short or Diagonal Traverses

The second can use normal jugging techniques to cross short traverses and sections of pitches that are more diagonal than horizontal. Two main techniques are used to second (and clean) a short diagonal traverse this way, rather than re-aiding as described above:

Grigri lower-out method. The first technique is very easy and requires a Grigri. Jug up to the piece you plan to pass, moving both ascenders as close to the piece as possible (fig. 15-25a). Then bring the Grigri up under the lower ascender and rest all your weight onto the Grigri (fig. 15-25b). Remove the top ascender and place it above the piece, and then repeat with the lower ascender (fig. 15-25c). Then open the handle of the Grigri and feed out rope, lowering yourself onto the ascenders and daisy chains (fig. 15-25d). Reestablish your weight in the aiders and reach back to clean the piece (fig. 15-25e).

Alternate method without a Grigri. Although this alternate method is a little trickier, it works if the follower does not have a Grigri. When approaching a piece of protection, leave the lower ascender about an arm's length or so below the piece, depending on the steepness of the terrain and the distance to and position of the next piece. Tie

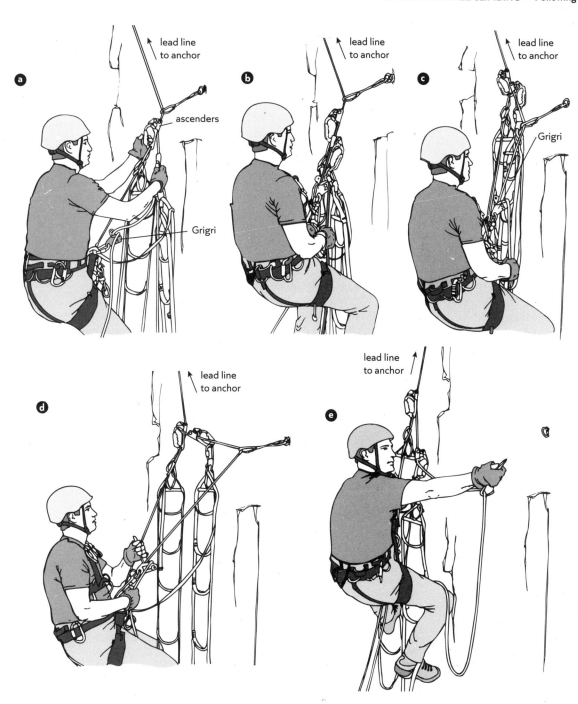

Fig. 15-25. *Grigri lower-out method:* **a,** *move ascenders to just below protection;* **b,** *bring Grigri below lower ascender and transfer weight to it;* **c,** *remove ascenders—upper first, then lower—and reinstall them above protection;* **d,** *lower with Grigri until weight is transferred to ascenders in new plumb line;* **e,** *clean the piece.*

yourself into the rope short as backup before you detach an ascender. With your weight on the lower ascender, remove the upper ascender and attach it as far as possible above the weighted piece. Then transfer your weight to the upper ascender, which will pull the lower ascender up toward the piece. If you have allowed enough space, the lower ascender will not jam into the piece's carabiner, and you will be able to remove the piece and move up the lower ascender.

Following Longer or Horizontal Traverses

The best way to follow longer traverses, tension traverses, and horizontal traverses is often to "lower-out," using the methods described below. If the leader has left some kind of piece suitable for lowering off of (as a "lower-out point") and then cleans all of the traversing pieces, the follower can lower from the beginning of the traverse to the next piece left by the leader. This method is often faster than others, but whether to use it is largely up to the leader, who has to decide whether a piece of gear can be left fixed for the lower-out and if they are willing to back-clean all the traverse pieces or not.

FOLLOWING TENSION TRAVERSES AND PENDULUM SWINGS

The best method for seconding a mostly horizontal long span between gear—including spans resulting from the leader performing a tension traverse or a pendulum swing—depends on the distance to be traveled and the ropes available. As described in Leading Horizontally earlier in this chapter, the lower-out point is usually fixed and is often a carabiner, a rappel ring, or a piece(s) of webbing. If the leader climbs a long distance without leaving gear, expecting the second to lower out to reach the new plumb line, the leader should ensure that there is adequate fixed gear left for the second to lower out from.

The term *lower-out* is used to describe a variety of methods for the follower to lower into a new plumb line, including the two techniques discussed below for following shorter and longer distances.

Short Pendulum Swings and Tension Traverses ("Stay Tied In" Method)

One clever and useful method of accomplishing a shorter lower-out is shown in Figure 15-26. The follower stays tied in to the climbing rope during the entire sequence, making it a secure and preferable method. This method requires the available rope to be four times as long as the distance to be traveled.

1. **Jug up to the fixed protection of the lower-out point.** If possible, fifi in to something without blocking the opening of the lower-out point (fig. 15-26a). Often, the leader will place protection near but separate from the lower-out point itself. Or, if using a Grigri as a backup, hold your weight on the Grigri.
2. **Clip a carabiner to the belay loop on your harness.** Then find the end of the rope that is tied in to the harness. Take this rope out to about arm's length from the harness tie-in knot and make a bend in it. Push this bight of rope through the lower-out point, then bring the bight back toward the harness (fig. 15-26b).
3. **Clip the bight in to the carabiner attached to the belay loop.** Pulling on the free end that comes out of the lower-out point, cinch yourself up and hold your weight on the climbing rope through the lower-out point (fig. 15-26c). Retrieve all the team gear before lowering out. Two additional optional steps are to clip any type of carabiner as a backup around the rope and through the top hole of either (or both) ascender(s), to ensure that the ascenders stay on the rope (fig. 15-27), and shorten the daisy chain on the upper ascender to reduce the overall lower-out distance.
4. **To lower out, let the rope feed through your hand** (fig. 15-26d). At first, there will be considerable friction, but be diligent as you lower yourself to avoid dropping the rope and lowering too fast. As your weight shifts onto the ascenders in the new plumb line, continue to feed rope through the lower-out system.
5. **Unclip the bight of rope from the carabiner on the harness belay loop** once you have all your weight on the ascenders in the new plumb line. Pull the ends of the rope so that the bight that was clipped to the harness is pulled through the lower-out point (fig. 15-26e). The rope has now been freed.

Sometimes climbers can second distances without lowering out, especially when the terrain is not steep. The follower moves up to the piece and finds a stance or a nearby crack or feature to hold on to so that they can take their weight off of the piece to be cleaned. Then the follower removes the piece and, prepared to swing, lets go without lowering out, swinging into the new plumb line while hanging from the ascenders and daisy chains. When used with sound judgment, this approach can be a fast, reliable way of following a short, low-angle pendulum swing.

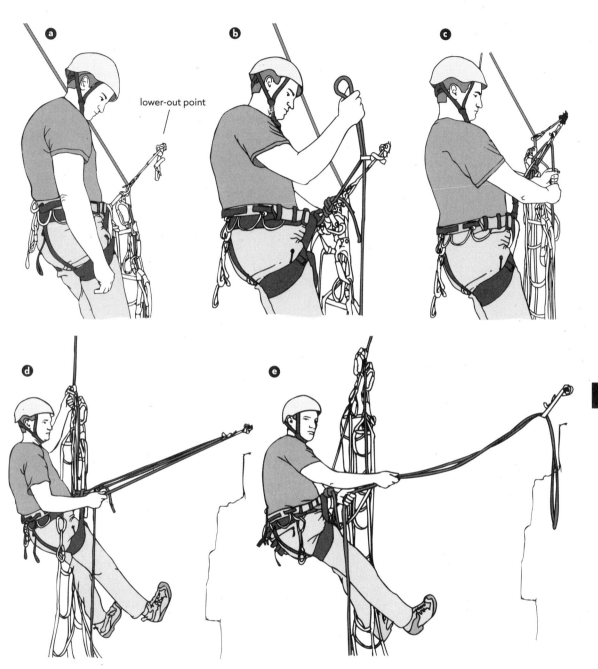

Fig. 15-26. *Lower-out method ("stay tied in" method) for following short pendulum or tension traverse:* **a,** *jug until ascenders are just below protection at lower-out point, then fifi in to protection (here, a quickdraw);* **b,** *clip a carabiner to harness belay loop, then pull a bight of rope from the tie-in knot through the lower-out point;* **c,** *clip bight to the carabiner on the harness belay loop and transfer weight to the bight through the lower-out point;* **d,** *remove fifi and quickdraw and feed the rope through the harness carabiner until ascenders are weighted;* **e,** *unclip the bight of rope from harness and pull it through the lower-out point.*

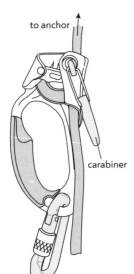

to anchor

carabiner

Fig. 15-27. *Carabiner clipped through ascender top hole and around the rope to prevent ascender from detaching from the rope.*

Long Pendulum Swings and Tension Traverses ("Untie" Method)

The lower-out method discussed above requires the available rope to be four times as long as the distance the follower must span, so it works well for seconding short pendulum swings and tension traverses. If the horizontal distance to the plumb line is less than 10 feet (3 meters), it is possible to use a 20-foot cordelette instead of the rope. It is thinner and easier to deal with.

For longer lower-outs, or when the follower does not have that much rope available, a different method that involves untying from the climbing rope must be used. Since it is preferable to stay tied in to the climbing rope, this technique is used only when the above technique suggested for shorter distances is not possible. For this alternative method, the available rope must be twice as long as the distance the follower needs to span.

1. **Ascend the rope to the fixed piece; your ascenders should be just below it.** Then attach a Grigri to the rope under the ascenders (if it is not already attached). Pull any slack through the Grigri to put all your weight fully on it. Tie in to the rope short with a backup knot below the Grigri. Then clip a ladder and daisy assembly to the lower-out piece (somewhere other than the lower-out ring). Remove the other ascender from the rope. Now untie from the end of the rope (fig. 15-28a).

2. **Thread the lead line through the lower-out point,** beginning with the tail you untied from your harness (fig. 15-28b). For large lower-outs on established routes, the lower-out point is likely to be a sturdy metal rappel ring.

3. **Put yourself on rappel on the tail side of the rope,** in the manner of a single-rope rappel. This can be accomplished with a belay device or a munter hitch. The climbing rope from above should be running through your Grigri, through the lower-out point, then through the second rappel hitch or device. The tail of the rope should be hanging below the follower without a knot tied in it. Stand in the ladder and pull the rappel device tight to the lower-out point; the goal is to take all your weight on the rappel device so that you can remove the quickdraw and the ladder and daisy from the lower-out piece. Before doing so, clip one or both ascenders to the lead line, above the Grigri (fig. 15-28c). It is possible to make the lower-out shorter by pushing the ascenders up the rope as high as possible. Consider clipping a carabiner through the hole of the ascender(s) and around the rope for added security (see Figure 15-27).

4. **Rappel the pendulum** until all your weight is on the ascenders in the new plumb line (fig. 15-28d).

5. **Remove the rope from the rappel device and pull the end of the rope through the lower-out point.** The rope has now been freed. Tie back in to the end of the rope before continuing to follow the pitch (fig. 15-28e).

Changing Leads

Unorganized belay stations can become a rat's nest of tangled ropes, twisted slings, and jumbled hardware. Basic organization keeps the belay station manageable and the team functioning efficiently. It is easy to judge a team's proficiency by looking at the time spent at changeovers: a dialed-in team can transition comfortably in minutes. The following methods improve organization at the belay station:

Keep the anchor simple. If you find yourself idle at the belay, look at your anchor and figure out how to simplify it and make it cleaner.

Use ropes of different colors when possible, so that they are easy to differentiate.

Always stack the haul line while hauling the bag, using rest intervals to stack the line in a rope bag or on a sling. After hauling, quickly restack the line, organize what remains of the rack, and put it all on one side of your body or on a sling on the anchor so that the follower can rerack

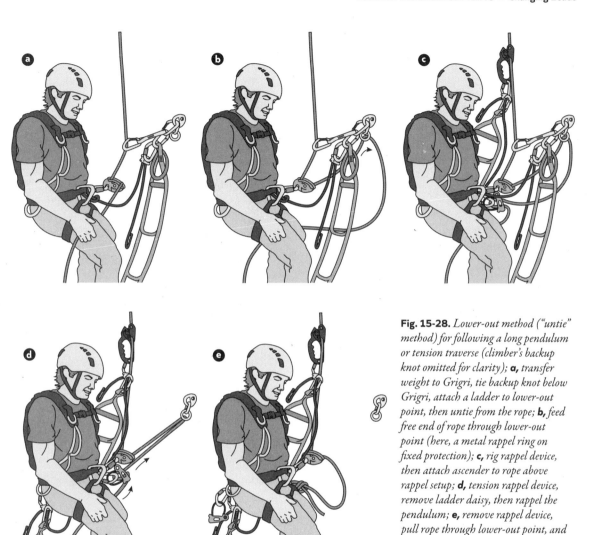

Fig. 15-28. *Lower-out method ("untie" method) for following a long pendulum or tension traverse (climber's backup knot omitted for clarity);* **a,** *transfer weight to Grigri, tie backup knot below Grigri, attach a ladder to lower-out point, then untie from the rope;* **b,** *feed free end of rope through lower-out point (here, a metal rappel ring on fixed protection);* **c,** *rig rappel device, then attach ascender to rope above rappel setup;* **d,** *tension rappel device, remove ladder daisy, then rappel the pendulum;* **e,** *remove rappel device, pull rope through lower-out point, and tie back into the rope.*

for the next pitch, freeing the leader for other chores after the second arrives.

Plan where the follower will come up, and have a locking carabiner ready to clip the second in to the anchor, or ask the second for one as soon as they arrive.

Focus on the needs of the new leader when the second arrives. Get the weight of the lead rope off the second as soon as possible. While the second reracks, pull up the lead line and restack it if necessary. Put the new leader on

belay immediately, even if that climber is not ready to lead. Transfer gear as necessary for the next pitch.

For a smooth belay transition, each team member should be doing some chore at all times to advance the team, until the leader starts out on the next pitch. If you are the next belayer, try not to eat, drink, adjust your clothing, or take care of yourself when the new leader is still at the belay. These needs can be taken care of after you finish hauling and before the follower arrives or while the new leader heads out on the next pitch. Watch the new leader attentively until they place protection on the new pitch. Then consider your needs while belaying the leader farther up the pitch.

Multiday Techniques for Big Walls

For some climbers, only the reward of a big Grade VI wall could entice them to pick up ascenders and aiders and undertake the process of aid climbing. Big wall climbing is sometimes referred to as vertical backpacking, because climbers haul heavy bags with water, food, and camping supplies and typically cover ground very slowly compared with free climbing. Climbing big walls is hard work, with endless chores of rope stacking, bag hauling, and ascending. Efficiency, organization, and proper conditioning are critical to success.

Big walls also call for a high degree of mental composure. Inexperienced wall climbers easily find themselves the victim of heightened fears brought on by prolonged, severe exposure. Climbers who are new to the game can perhaps soothe their fears by realizing that techniques for dealing with major walls are much the same as those needed for smaller climbs. Concentrate on the problem at hand, and work away at the objective one move at a time.

Guidebooks and other climbers are helpful sources of information in preparing for a big wall. Beware, however, of depending too heavily on climbing route topos and equipment lists. Routes change over time, especially if climbers use pins on them regularly.

Solid, efficient aid technique is a prerequisite for completing a major wall within the time constraints dictated by reasonable food and water supplies. To succeed, develop competence hoisting heavy haul bags up a route and living comfortably in the vertical world for days at a time. Amazing journeys to seldom-visited places amid a sweeping sea of granite await those who accept this adventure.

HAULING

The leader anchors in and fixes the climbing rope for the follower, then begins hauling, using one or more of the techniques described below. Regardless of which methods the team uses, the climbers should be connected to the anchor with the climbing rope. Hauling is the biggest chore on a big wall; spend time practicing and understanding your haul system. Consider practicing on a smaller wall at a local crag.

1. **Load the hauling device with the haul line.** Tie an overhand knot on a bight in the end of the haul line and attach it to the locking carabiner on the hauling device. Clip this hauling device to the haul anchor (fig. 15-29a). Clip a quickdraw or sling from an anchor point to the slack side of the hauling device; this quickdraw backs up the system in case the hauling device fails. If you are not using a hauling device, set up a haul system with a pulley and one ascender (see Figure 15-13c), using a sling (or two, for redundancy) to connect the ascender to the pulley's locking carabiner. Prepare a sling or rope bag to stack the haul line into. Pull up all the slack in the line, through the device, until it tightens. The follower should then call out "That's the bag."

2. **Connect one ascender to the belay loop on the harness and lock the carabiner.** Attach this ascender to the haul line on the slack side of the rope coming out of the hauling device. This could also be accomplished with a Grigri, which would probably already be on the leader's harness, allowing a climber to easily lower the bag if it snags. Haul a short distance, just a few inches at a time, as described in step 3 below, to unweight the bags off of the lower anchor, and stack the haul line (fig. 15-29b). Then the follower can free the haul bag from the anchor and call out "Bags are free. Haul away."

3. **Begin the regular hauling process.** Push back from the wall using your legs and palms to raise the haul bag (fig. 15-29c). An upward tug on the weighted haul line often helps start the hauling movement, as the pulley gets momentarily unweighted, changing from static to dynamic friction. As the bag comes up, the climber's body lowers until the rope between harness and anchor tightens. Then stop, stand up (maybe in the aiders), move the ascender back up the rope toward the hauling device, and reset. Repeat. When you stop hauling, the cam in the hauling device captures progress. You need slack—usually a few feet—in the climbing rope between yourself and the anchor to allow hauling movement.

You can also haul by allowing greater slack of 6 to 8 feet (2 to 2.5 meters) between the tie-in knot and attachment point to the anchor. Then walk down the wall 6 to 8 feet until the anchor rope tightens. Climb back to your original position by jugging, possibly with one aider and daisy chain on an ascender and with one Grigri. Repeat the process. This method works best with lighter bags.

Counterweight Hauling

If two people are needed to lift a very heavy bag, they can use a counterweight method. The leader can stay at the anchor station and haul the bag normally, while the follower can

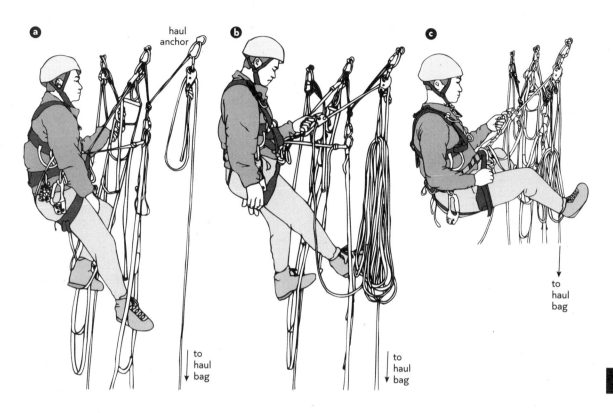

to haul bag

to haul bag

to haul bag

haul anchor

Fig. 15-29. *Hauling:* ***a,*** *install haul rope in hauling device, then pull up rope until it is taut;* ***b,*** *use one ascender or a Grigri (clipped to harness belay loop) to haul rope until haul bag is lifted from lower anchor;* ***c,*** *haul away after the second releases the haul bag from the lower anchor.*

attach their ascenders on the pulling side of the haul rope, about 6 to 8 feet (2 to 2.5 meters) below the leader. As the leader hauls, the follower hangs on the haul line to provide counterweight and walks down the wall. The follower must use a longer tie-in to the anchor, about 12 to 16 feet (4 to 5 meters). To prevent the follower's tie-in to the anchor from becoming tight, the follower must jug periodically.

Docking the Bag

Once the leader has completed the haul, the haul bag must be "docked" in order to attach it to the wall and free the haul line for the next pitch. First, always be sure to stop hauling before the knot in the line reaches the hauling device's pulley. This is a critical point—if the knot gets too close, it will be sucked into and jam the hauling device. Select a spot in the anchor to dock the bag, and attach a carabiner to this location. Pull the docking cord up from

the top of the haul bag and tie the cord to the carabiner as close to the haul bag as possible, using a load-releasing hitch such as a munter-mule (see Figure 8-21 in Chapter 8). Back up the hitch with an overhand knot in the docking cord (fig. 15-30a).

Then use the hauling system to raise the bag just an inch or so and allow the hauling device cam to disengage. Unlock the device, then carefully lower the bag, using your weight and the ascender clipped to the harness belay loop, so that the bag's weight rests on the docking cord (fig. 15-30b).

You may need to reengage the cam on the hauling device and repeat this mini-haul process one or more times before the bag's weight completely rests on the docking cord, allowing the leader to disengage and remove the hauling device. With the bag free from the hauling system, also tie the haul line from the bag in to the anchor with a figure eight on a bight as a backup (fig. 15-30c) in case the docking cord should fail.

Dock the bag as high as possible on the anchor, so that the bag is accessible while at the belay. The leader can then restack the haul line so the free end is on top.

Living in the Vertical World

Clip in all vital items when not in use or in the haul bag. Use "Got it" to confirm gear handoffs between partners. Consider bringing duplicates of key items such as another knife, a second communication device, an extra aider or two, et cetera. Know the location of every item in the haul bag and have it accessible when needed, especially storm gear, the first-aid kit, and the waste kit. Big wall climbers must carry all their water with them, generally a gallon per person per day, and pack out all garbage.

FIXING PITCHES

On long aid climbs, climbers often "fix" pitches: putting up ropes and leaving them in place so they can be climbed quickly with mechanical ascenders later to reach the previous high point. Climbers frequently fix one or two pitches above the ground or beyond the bivouac site, and at the high point they leave gear they do not need for the bivouac. The lower end of each fixed rope is attached to the anchor of the previous pitch.

When fixing pitches, take care to protect the rope from sharp edges or abrupt contours by using duct tape or other material to cover sharp features. Use intermediate anchor points, if available: they reduce rope stretch, contour the rope toward the direction of travel, and help avoid abrasion points. Leave enough slack in the rope when fixing it to the lower anchor to allow for reversal of rope stretch after rappelling, but not so much that loops of rope can blow around when unattended. Make a tidy coil of any rope left on the ground.

Never ascend someone else's fixed rope without knowledge of its rigging and permission from the rope's owner. Close calls have occurred when climbers ascended unknown "fixed ropes" that were not rigged for that purpose.

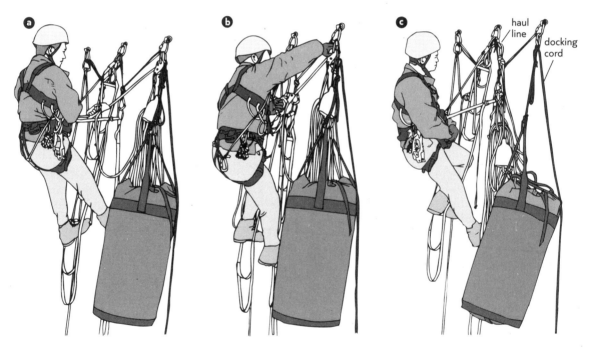

Fig. 15-30. *Docking the haul bag:* **a,** *attach the haul bag's docking cord to the anchor with a munter-mule and an overhand backup;* **b,** *haul enough to release the hauling device and lower the haul bag onto its docking cord;* **c,** *remove the haul rope from the hauling device and, to back up the docking cord, tie a figure eight on a bight in the haul rope and attach it to the anchor.*

Retreating

Before a major aid climb, plan retreat lines in case of bad weather, an accident, or another emergency. Locate other easy-to-reach routes that offer a speedier descent or fixed retreat lines.

If there is no retreat route, consider carrying a bolt kit for emergencies, so that you can place rappel anchors if necessary. Also, as you climb each pitch, consider how to descend it. On major walls, rescues, if possible, may be slow and difficult. It may be up to the climbing team to get back down in an emergency. Rappelling with haul bags can be difficult, so practice this skill.

Descending

After completing a major wall, climbers need to get their gear back down. Before packing the haul bag, consider whether the ropes need to be accessible for rappelling. If you are rappelling, set aside all the personal gear you will need for that before you pack the bags.

Before packing the haul bag, make sure that the backpack harness is attached. Pack the heaviest items on the bottom for the hike out. Attempt to fill all the small spaces in the bag from the bottom up so the bag is compact. Sleeping bags, bivy sacks, and clothing make pliable space fillers. Consider loading climbing gear into the haul bag loose—unclipping carabiners from protection and unclipping gear from slings—to pack the bag much more efficiently. A tightly packed haul bag can be carried off a difficult descent much more easily than a floppy, top-heavy one. If the team has to carry multiple bags, consider packing the smaller bag(s) with the heavier items and making any larger haul bags a little lighter to compensate for carrying a tall, bulky load.

As is true for all long climbs, the hike out can be a dangerous time, because climbers are exhausted from the effort expended on the climb. Take your time, watch your step, and double-check your systems when rappelling or performing other technical maneuvers.

Spirit of Aid Climbing

The pioneers of rock climbing developed aid climbing to open up the vertical world and its fabulous summits, including legendary walls such as El Capitan and Half Dome in Yosemite National Park, California. In following the path of aid climbing's pioneers, you will reach locations visited by relatively few climbers, imagining and experiencing the great vision and dedication required by the first ascensionists to establish these routes.

Aid routes require technical skill in placing gear and boldness to climb thin cracks and steep walls while relying on the proper use of equipment. Keep aid climbing adventurous by resisting the temptation to alter established routes by adding bolts, drilling holes, nailing pitons, or leaving behind excess fixed gear. Clean up routes by removing tired old fixed slings, and in general try to leave the route in better condition than you found it. Always practice Leave No Trace ethics on the wall, doing your part to safeguard the mountains. The rewards of all alpine trips are great, but most likely, your memories of long multiday wall routes will stand out in a lifetime of climbing as unique and special experiences.

15

PART IV
SNOW, ICE, AND ALPINE CLIMBING

CHAPTER 16

BASIC SNOW AND ICE CLIMBING

Climbing on snow and ice is fundamental to mountaineering. Becoming familiar with how snow and ice change over time and how to move through and over these surfaces is an essential challenge for alpine climbers.

Snow falls in a variety of forms ranging from big, wet flakes to tiny crystals or coarse pellets. The snowpack can initially consist of up to 90 percent air by volume. After snow has fallen and is on the ground, a cyclic process of melting and freezing begins. As the air in it is displaced, snow becomes increasingly dense, and ultimately some of it becomes ice or perhaps part of a glacier. Snow and ice display a broad spectrum of physical characteristics (see Chapter 27, The Cycle of Snow).

This chapter describes basic snow and ice climbing techniques on low-angle and gentle slopes no steeper than 30 degrees. Techniques for steeper, technical terrain are discussed in Chapters 17, Technical Snow and Ice Climbing, and 18, Waterfall Ice and Mixed Climbing. Climbers often use multiple movement techniques, depending on slope angle and conditions, and many skills for basic and technical snow and ice climbing overlap. New climbers begin by mastering basic skills for negotiating low-angle snow and ice (see Table 16-1) before attempting more difficult climbing. All climbers who travel on snow and ice must manage the risks described in Chapter 20, Avalanche Safety.

For many combinations of slope angle and snow conditions, climbers choose from several techniques (see Table 16-1). The best technique in a particular situation depends on your experience, skill, athleticism, and conditioning, as well as the consequences of a fall. A skilled climber might face out and scurry down a particular route, while another climber feels more comfortable facing in. Adopting a technique appropriate for the slope angle, the conditions, and your skill level is important, even if others decide to do it differently. A beginning climber using a slower technique that provides greater security may be motivated to improve their skill and comfort level with practice after observing more experienced climbers moving quickly and confidently over the same terrain using a different technique.

Traveling on snow and ice is trickier than hiking a trail or climbing a rock wall because the snowpack changes throughout the year, affected by terrain, shifts in weather, and time of day. Snow and ice can present widely different surfaces, depending on how consolidated it is—from seemingly bottomless powder, to wind slabs, to a firm, resilient surface, to bulletproof alpine ice. A snowfield may consist of thin snow over a brushy slope or only scattered snow patches; it could be a bowl full of powder ready to avalanche or a solid surface offering firm footing. Snow can change from firm in the morning to slush in the afternoon. Under certain conditions, snow that appears stable can suddenly release and flow (avalanche) and then quickly set up as hard as concrete. A snow bridge that is solid on a cool morning can easily collapse in the afternoon heat. Traveling and minimizing risk on snow and ice requires judgment based on experience (see Chapter 20, Avalanche Safety).

Snow and ice can make climbs easier by covering brush and loose rock, or serve as an alternative to stretches of technical rock climbing. Snow and ice conditions also affect routefinding and decisions about technique. Should a climbing party hike up the snow-covered valley slopes that are easier to traverse? Or follow the ridge crest to avoid the possibility of an avalanche? Should climbers step-kick up the sunny slope? Or try the more labor-intensive climb on firmer snow on the shaded hillside? Which option involves less risk: traveling roped or unroped? The changeable nature of snow and ice requires you to be flexible and ready to use different types of equipment such as snowshoes, skis, spike traction devices, or crampons.

KEY TOPICS

EQUIPMENT
BASIC TECHNIQUES
ROPED TECHNIQUES
ROUTEFINDING ON SNOW
PRACTICING FOR THE FREEDOM OF THE HILLS

TABLE 16-1. TECHNIQUES FOR BASIC SLOPE ANGLES UNDER DIFFERENT CONDITIONS

SLOPE ANGLE	CONDITIONS	ASCENDING: BOOTS	ASCENDING: ICE AXE OR ICE TOOL	DESCENDING: BOOTS	DESCENDING: ICE AXE OR ICE TOOL	COMMENTS
Low-angle: 0° to 20°	Soft snow	Flat-footed; possibly with spike traction devices or crampons	Ski pole(s) or ice axe or ice tool in cane or self-arrest position	Plunge-stepping or flat-footed facing out or glissade; possibly using spike traction devices or crampons	Ski pole(s) or ice axe or ice tool in self-arrest position	
Low-angle: 0° to 20°	Hard snow	Flat-footed or duck walk; likely with crampons or spike traction devices	Ski pole(s) or ice axe or ice tool in cane or self-arrest position	Flat-footed facing out likely with crampons or spike traction devices	Ski pole(s) or ice axe or ice tool in self-arrest position	If snow is too hard to safely descend flat-footed, spike traction devices or crampons are needed.
Low-angle: 0° to 20°	Hard ice	Flat-footed or duck walk; with sharp crampons	Ice axe or ice tool in cane or self-arrest position	Flat-footed facing out or descending diagonally with sharp crampons	Ice axe or ice tool in self-arrest or cane position	Nearly impossible to stop a fall with self-arrest. In the event of a slip, use the ice axe self-belay or a desperate swing of the axe to drive in the pick.
Gentle: 20° to 30°	Soft snow	Step-kick, with or without diagonal ascent; possibly alternating with hybrid technique; consider using crampons	Ice axe or ice tool in cane, self-arrest, or cross-body position	Plunge-stepping or possibly glissade; consider using crampons	Ice axe or ice tool in self-arrest position	While ascending, possible to use sturdy ski pole in cross-body position, but only on nontechnical terrain when consequences of an unchecked slide are not a concern.
Gentle: 20° to 30°	Hard snow	Duck walk or diagonal ascent; possibly alternating with hybrid technique; all with crampons	Ice axe or ice tool in cane, self-arrest, or cross-body position	Plunge-stepping or descending diagonally with crampons	Ice axe or ice tool in self-arrest position	Plunge-stepping may not be possible if snow is too hard. Self-arrest may be impossible if snow is too hard.
Gentle: 20° to 30°	Hard ice	Duck walk or diagonal ascent; possibly alternating with hybrid technique; all with sharp crampons	Ice axe or ice tool in cane or cross-body position	Descending diagonally or facing in and backing down with sharp crampons	Self-arrest position; cross-body position; or traction position if facing in (see *Traction Position* in Ch. 17)	While descending, it may be better to front-point while facing in (see Ch. 17). Self-arrest impossible.

16

A rock route is likely to be unchanged for years or decades. But snow and ice is changeable and ephemeral. What was a water-ice route in the morning may be nothing but a jumbled pile of ice blocks or a wet spot by afternoon. A single route often morphs throughout the year: in early season the climb is a straightforward jaunt up perfect smooth névé, but by August or September (in the Northern Hemisphere) it becomes a sheet of ice with exposed crevasses.

Equipment

Ice axes and crampons are essential equipment for basic snow and ice climbing. Snowshoes, skis, ski poles, and shovels are also important. On a warm, sunny day, it may be comfortable to walk or climb on low-angle and gentle snow and ice in lightweight clothing and gloves with an ice axe in hand. In windy or cold weather or in winter, the same slope requires more protection (see Chapter 2, Clothing and Equipment).

ICE AXE

Climbers use an ice axe to ascend and descend, self-arrest, self-belay, and anchor, as well as for many other tasks. There are three main types of this essential, versatile tool. General mountaineering ice axes are intended for low-angle and gentle snow and ice climbing described in this chapter. Technical mountaineering ice axes are meant for steeper alpine snow and ice climbing and are described in Chapter 17. Ice tools for waterfall ice and mixed climbing are covered in Chapter 18. Skilled use of ice axes allows climbers to venture onto all forms of snow and ice, enjoying a variety of mountain terrain year-round.

When selecting an ice axe, consider the features designed for these three specific uses. A long axe is suitable for cross-country travel and scrambling or for low-angle and gentle snow and ice, where it is used as a cane to provide security. On steeper slopes, a shorter, technical ice axe is better. Ice tools have even shorter shafts and specialized features. Be sure to select an axe designed for your intended use.

General mountaineering ice axes that meet the European Committee for Standardization (CEN) standards (see Chapter 8, Essential Climbing Equipment) are designated by a "B," generally stamped on the ice axe. Technical mountaineering ice axes and waterfall and mixed ice tools are designated by a "T" CEN standard. Ice axes designated with a "T" rating meet higher strength requirements than "B"-rated axes.

Parts of an Ice Axe

The main parts of a general mountaineering ice axe include the head, pick, adze, shaft, and spike (fig. 16-1a).

Head. An ice axe's head, generally composed of steel alloy, has a pick on one side and an adze on the other. Most climbers attach a leash to the carabiner hole in the axe head (see Wrist Leash or Umbilical, below).

Pick. The pick is curved or drooped, which provides better hooking action in snow or ice, enabling the axe to dig in when climbers seek purchase or try to stop themselves (self-arrest) after a fall. Ice axes designed for general mountaineering typically have aggressive teeth only at the end of the pick. The pick can also be used to chop footsteps in hard ice.

Adze. Climbers use the adze mainly to scoop or chop footsteps into soft or hard snow, or for digging to create a bivouac platform, snow shelter, or the like. Most general mountaineering ice axes have a relatively flat, straight-edged adze with sharp corners, which provides a firm, comfortable platform for a hand when a climber uses the cane position (see Basic Techniques later in this chapter).

Shaft. The shafts of most general axes are made of aluminum, while a few are made with a composite material such as carbon fiber. Shafts can be either straight (see Figure 16-1a) or slightly bent (fig. 16-1b). Some shafts are covered at least partly by a rubber material, which offers insulation from the metal, a more secure grip, and better control of the axe when swinging it.

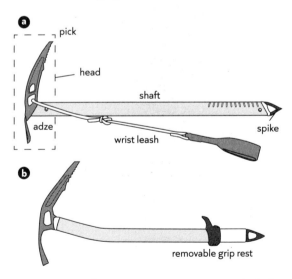

Fig. 16-1. *General mountaineering ice axes:* **a,** *straight shaft, with parts labeled;* **b,** *bent shaft.*

Spike. The spike, at the bottom end of an axe, should be sharp enough to penetrate snow and ice easily. Using an ice axe for balance on rocky trails and talus slopes dulls the spike (see Maintenance and Handling, below).

Length
General mountaineering ice axes, described only in metric units, range in length from 50 to 90 centimeters. The optimal length depends on both the intended use and the climber's height. Climbers who use the ice axe as a cane for cross-country travel or scrambling on easy terrain, such as lower-angle snow (or glaciers where it is useful to probe for crevasses), may want a longer axe where the spike barely reaches the ground when held by the head loosely at their side. Climbers on steeper snow may find a shorter axe easier to use—one with a spike that reaches their ankle when loosely held at their side.

Wrist Leash or Umbilical
For low-angle and gentle snow and ice climbing, tethering the ice axe to your wrist or harness with a wrist leash (see Figure 16-1a) or umbilical helps secure it, preventing this critical safety tool from being dropped. Using a wrist leash allows you to let the axe hang free should you need to scramble on rocks between sections of snow climbing. It also helps reduce arm fatigue for the occasional *piolet traction* move (see Chapter 17, Technical Snow and Ice Climbing) needed to climb a short, steep slope on an otherwise low-angle or gentle snow and ice climb. A leashed axe can, however, prove hazardous, bouncing around in the event of an uncontrolled fall.

Often, climbers choose not to use the wrist leash on their axe in situations such as switchbacking up a slope, where at every turn they need to switch hands. Some manufacturers offer a single-strand leash (also called an umbilical) that attaches to the harness and eliminates the need to move the wrist leash from hand to hand. Choosing when to use a wrist leash or umbilical is a personal judgment based on conditions, slope, comfort level, and risk of losing the axe.

Leashes and umbilicals are typically available from the ice-axe manufacturer. They can also be made with a piece of webbing attached to the carabiner hole in the head. For a wrist leash, adjust length so you can reach and grasp the end of the shaft near the spike when you place your hand through the wrist loop.

Maintenance and Handling
Ice axes require very little special care. Before each use, inspect the shaft for deep dents that might weaken it to the point of failure under load (but do not worry about minor nicks and scratches). After each climb, clean the axe of mud and dirt and store it dry. Check the pick, adze, and spike regularly for sharpness. To sharpen, use a hand file, not a power-driven grinding wheel. High-speed grinding can overheat the metal and change the temper, diminishing its strength. Guards are available to cover the sharp edges and points of the pick, adze, and spike for travel or storage.

SPIKE TRACTION DEVICES AND CRAMPONS
Spike traction devices consist of a stretchy rubber harness with light chains holding a dozen or more short 8-millimeter (5/16-inch) spikes. Fitted over a boot or trekking shoe, they provide traction on low-angle snow and ice or on hard, frozen dirt when crampons would be excessive (fig. 16-2a and b). Traction devices with wire coils or small cleats intended for preventing falls on icy sidewalks are not suitable for climbing snow or ice.

Crampons boast a set of long metal points integrated into frames that attach to the bottoms of boots. They penetrate hard snow and ice where boot soles alone cannot gain sufficient traction. Crampons are useful for both ascending and descending snow and ice.

Modern crampons are now categorized into four main types. This chapter describes very lightweight ski-touring and snow-approach crampons (see Figure 16-3), for occasional use on low-angle and gentle terrain, and general mountaineering crampons (see Figures 16-4 and 16-5), intended for glacier travel or low-angle and gentle snow and ice climbing. Technical mountaineering crampons are described in Chapter 17, and waterfall ice and dry-tooling crampons are described in Chapter 18. Be sure to select crampons designed for the intended use; crampon

16

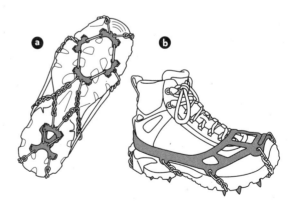

Fig. 16-2. *Spike traction device:* **a,** *bottom of shoe;* **b,** *side view.*

manufacturers specify the intended use for different models in their marketing materials.

In particular, the front points of different models vary in important ways. Ski-touring and snow-approach crampons, as well as general mountaineering crampons, each have a pair of horizontal front points consisting of a blade that is wide from side to side. These horizontally oriented front points are designed for snow conditions encountered in most general mountaineering situations. They provide a larger surface area and are more supportive in soft snow.

Choosing whether to wear crampons depends on a variety of factors, including slope angle, snow conditions, and the climber's confidence and experience (see Table 16-1). Climbers generally wear crampons in harder, icy conditions, especially where there is potential for a dangerous fall. Crampons can also provide security on steeper slopes of soft snow.

Sticky, soft snow can build up ("ball up") under crampons. If this stuck snow becomes thicker than the length of the crampon points, it can cause a climber to lose traction and possibly fall. To minimize this hazard, nearly all ski-touring and snow-approach crampons and general mountaineering crampons have antiballing plates—plastic, rubber, or vinyl pieces attached to the bottom of the crampon.

Ski-Touring and Snow-Approach Crampons

Ski-touring and snow-approach crampons that fit to boots (not ski crampons that attach to backcountry skis) usually have 10 points, including the front points (fig. 16-3). These crampons are intended for use on low-angle and gentle snow and are often made with aircraft-grade aluminum alloys, which are about 50 percent lighter than steel but also much softer. Aluminum crampons are mainly used for glacier travel, approaches to alpine rock climbs, or early-season climbs with snow but not hard ice. Some ski-touring and snow-approach aluminum crampons use a high-modulus polyethylene cord to link the front and back pieces to make them very lightweight.

General Mountaineering Crampons

Made from an extremely strong, lightweight steel alloy, general mountaineering crampons have either 10 or 12 points including front points (fig. 16-4). They are intended to be used all day on glaciers, low-angle and gentle snow and ice, and short sections of technical snow and ice climbing. Snow and ice routes often include short sections of rock that climbers navigate while wearing crampons, and most steel crampons can take the punishment, but extended travel on rock will dull the points.

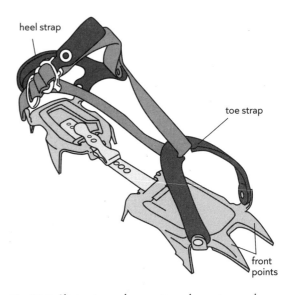

Fig. 16-3. *Ski-touring and snow-approach crampon made of aluminum, with horizontal front points and strap-on, or universal, attachment system.*

Crampon Attachment Systems

The three main attachment systems are strap-on, clip-on, and hybrid. In general, strap-on systems work best with flexible boots. Rigid boots without a front welt are compatible only with a strap-on or hybrid attachment system. The latter is a combination of a rear clip and a strap over the front of the boot. Rigid boots with a front welt that accommodates a crampon toe bail work with clip-on crampons. Ultimately, the choice of attachment system is largely dictated by the boot's rigidity and platform, as well as how a climber intends to use the crampons.

Strap-on. Modern strap-on, or universal, bindings (see Figure 16-3) make the crampons easy and fast to put on and provide a secure attachment with the widest selection of footwear.

Hybrid. Hybrid bindings feature toe straps combined with a heel clip (see Figure 16-4). These bindings are popular because they work well on boots that have a pronounced heel welt or groove but may lack a wide enough toe welt or groove. The heel clip should decisively snap into place, forcing the boot into the front posts attached to the toe strap. Hybrid bindings include a safety strap connecting the heel bail to the toe strap.

Clip-on. With clip-on bindings, the crampons attach to the boot with a wire toe bail and a heel clip or lever (fig. 16-5). These systems are also fast and easy to use. With

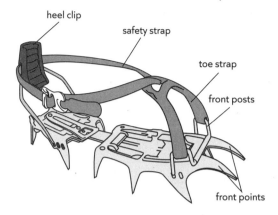

Fig. 16-4. *General mountaineering crampon, with 12 points and hybrid attachment system.*

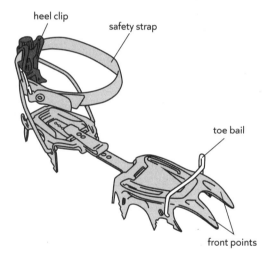

Fig. 16-5. *General mountaineering crampon, with 12 points and clip-on attachment.*

clip-on bindings, it is critical to have a rigid sole and a pronounced welt (lip or groove) at both the boot heel and toe. When the crampon is sized correctly for a boot that can accommodate this type of binding, the heel clip should be hard to lift and decisively snap into place on top of the boot heel welt, forcing the wire toe bail firmly into the boot toe welt. Clip-on bindings typically include a safety strap wrapped around the ankle to secure the crampon if it pops off the boot. If the boots are also used for alpine rock climbing, be sure that the toe welt has not been worn down so much that it will no longer securely hold the toe bail.

CRAMPON SAFETY RULES

Following a few rules helps maintain your crampons and protects you, your gear, and your companions from sharp crampon points:

- When carrying crampons inside your pack, use a crampon pouch.
- Always bring any tools you may need to adjust the crampons. On longer trips, bring spare parts.
- While climbing with crampons on, step deliberately to avoid snagging your pants or gaiters, gashing your leg, or stepping on the rope.
- Make sure gear hanging from your harness gear loops does not extend below your thighs to avoid snagging it with your crampons.

Crampon Fit, Maintenance, and Safety

It is critical that crampons fit boots securely. When purchasing crampons, bring your boots to the shop or follow the manufacturer's instructions carefully. If the crampons will be used on more than one pair of boots, check the fit on all pairs. Purchase crampons that match your intended usage. Most crampons also have a set of holes for attaching the toe bail or toe strap to adjust how the front part of the crampon is positioned on the boot. For low-angle and gentle snow and ice climbing, adjust the position of the front part of the crampons so that the front points don't protrude too far beyond the toe of the boot and that your foot can roll through its natural pattern on a hard surface like glacial ice without catching too much. For steeper technical snow and ice climbing, the front points should be adjusted so that they protrude farther (see Chapter 17, Technical Snow and Ice Climbing).

Practice putting on your crampons at home until you can do it easily. You will have plenty of opportunities to put them on in less-than-ideal conditions: by feel in dim light or with the limited illumination of a headlamp, fumbling with cold, numb fingers.

Regular maintenance keeps crampons safe and dependable (see the "Crampon Safety Rules" sidebar). After every climb, clean and dry the crampons and inspect them for wear. Repair or replace worn straps, nuts, bolts, wire bails, and screws. Tighten loose nuts and bolts. Maintaining sharp points is less important for most snow climbing but essential for icy conditions. If crampon points are overly dull, sharpen them with a file. Retire a pair of crampons when the points have been bent or filed down too far.

16

Crampons (especially toe bails) develop stress fractures after repeated use and normal wear and tear. Replace them when they look beat up or after about one hundred days of use. At a minimum, proactively replace the toe bails on clip-on crampons after using them for about fifty days. Having a crampon break or fall off during a climb can cause a serious accident.

SKI POLES

Climbers can use ski or trekking poles when traveling on a firm surface and ski poles with baskets when traveling on soft snow. When traveling over level or low-angle snow, slippery ground, or scree or when crossing a stream or boulder field, poles are better for balance than an ice axe. They

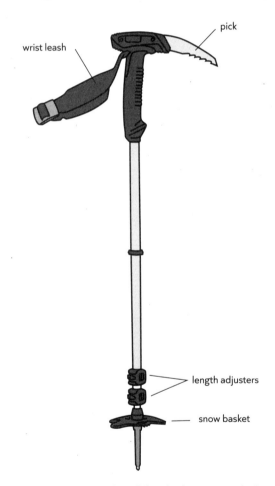

Fig. 16-6. *Whippet ski pole with length adjusters, snow basket, pick, and wrist leash.*

also take some weight and impact off the lower body, especially on descents. Use poles with baskets at the bottom to keep them from penetrating too deeply in soft snow.

Some ski and trekking poles have very useful features. Adjustable poles can be modified to suit the conditions or the terrain. Some adjustable poles can also be compressed for easy packing. After each trip, they need to be disassembled, cleaned, and dried. Whippet ski poles have handles with permanent or removable picks for self-arresting (fig. 16-6); however, on steep terrain a whippet ski pole is less effective than an ice axe at stopping a fall.

SNOWSHOES

For approaches in deep, soft snow, snowshoes offer flotation. (These conditions can also pose avalanche hazards; see Chapter 20, Avalanche Safety.) Most modern snowshoes have lightweight metal frames with durable decking materials (fig. 16-7). Modern bindings are easy to use with almost any footwear and include crampon-like toothed metal plates designed to improve traction on hard snow. Many models also include serrated heel and side plates that decrease side-to-side slippage.

Snowshoes enable efficient travel in soft snow that might otherwise involve sinking deeply with each step (postholing). Snowshoes can be used on low-angle slopes to kick steps uphill. Although travel on snowshoes may be slower than travel on skis, snowshoes can be used in brushy or rocky terrain where skis would be awkward. It takes less skill to use snowshoes than it does to use skis.

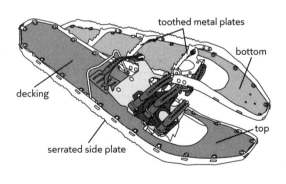

Fig. 16-7. *Snowshoes for winter mountaineering, with toothed metal plates, durable decking materials, and easy-to-use bindings.*

SKIS

For approaches in deep, soft snow, climbers can use mountaineering skis fitted with climbing skins. Ski mountaineering is a complex sport beyond the scope of this book (to learn more about special equipment and techniques, see Resources).

SHOVEL

A broad-bladed shovel is both a tool and a rescue device for the snow traveler, a necessity for uncovering an avalanche victim. Mountaineers use shovels to construct snow shelters and tent platforms, and even as tools to ascend particularly snowy routes.

A useful shovel has a blade large enough to move snow efficiently and a handle long enough for good leverage but short enough for use in a confined area: 2 to 3 feet (60 to 90 centimeters) long (see Figure 3-10 in Chapter 3, Camping, Food, and Water). Some shovels have extendable or detachable handles.

In dry, powdery snow, a plastic-bladed shovel provides a decent compromise of weight to strength. However, metal-bladed shovels are much stronger and therefore better for chopping through hard snow or avalanche debris and should be used when traveling in avalanche terrain. Shovels are also used in various snow stability tests (see Chapter 20, Avalanche Safety).

Basic Techniques

When traveling on snow, your top priority is to avoid slipping or falling. It is difficult to arrest a fall and easy to build up speed sliding down a slope. Failure to arrest could result in hitting trees or rocks and getting seriously injured. Climbers can learn techniques to stop and regain control should they slip, but snow conditions can make it very hard to stop once you pick up speed. On steep or exposed slopes where a fall would be difficult to control, prudent climbers carry an ice axe and wear crampons—and know how to use them.

To determine the route, terrain, and equipment choices for secure snow travel, ask the following questions: Are the snow conditions suitable for self-arrest, or is it too hard for a pick to penetrate? What does the runout look like? What technique should climbers use (see Table 16-1), and will crampons help or hinder? What are the climbers' levels of experience and skill? Is everyone comfortable with the situation? Are climbers wearing heavy overnight packs? It is critical to understand the limits of self-arrest (see Preventing and Stopping a Fall later in this chapter) and to always assess the runout.

ASSESSING RUNOUT

Because a falling climber's acceleration rate on a 30-degree snow slope can approach that of free-falling, it is important to evaluate a slope's runout. Are there rocks, crevasses, a moat, a bergschrund, or cliffs below the slope (fig. 16-8)? Being aware of the runout is the first thing to consider when deciding whether traveling on a particular snow slope is risky and what techniques and equipment to use.

If the runout is dangerous or unknown, carefully consider how to proceed. Does it require a belay with anchor and rope? If on the way up a party realizes they will face a perilous runout on the descent—one they would need to set up a belay to protect, but the party does not have the time, skill, or necessary equipment to do so—then turning around is always an option.

Fig. 16-8. *Assessing runout: rocks below a snow slope make for a dangerous runout.*

16

Fig. 16-9. *Carrying an ice axe when not in use:* **a,** *attached to pack's ice-axe loop;* **b,** *in hand while walking, with spike forward and pick down;* **c,** *between back and pack temporarily, so ice-axe head is easy to grasp.*

USING ICE AXE OR SKI POLES

An inherently simple tool to aid snow and ice travel, an ice axe can be used as a walking cane for balance and a tool to prevent or stop a fall. Ski poles are also useful for snow travel, but only in low-angle terrain where a fall would not have serious consequences. To decide when and how to use an ice axe or ski poles, consider these questions: Will using an ice axe or ski poles help? Will they make walking on snow easier and more efficient? If a slope has an exposed, dangerous, or unknown runout, it is crucial to carry an ice axe to stop a fall.

Carrying an Ice Axe

Always carry an ice axe carefully. Be aware of what its sharp points and edges can do to you and others. When you do not need the axe, carry it using the pack's attachment system (fig. 16-9a). To carry the axe in one hand, grasp the shaft with the spike forward and the pick down to avoid jabbing the person behind you (fig. 16-9b).

When snow alternates briefly with areas of rocks or steep brush, where climbers need both hands free, slide the spike and then the shaft under one of your shoulder straps and shift the axe so that it is hanging diagonally between your back and the pack (fig. 16-9c). Place the spike down and the pick between the pack's shoulder straps, so the axe head is clear of your neck. In this position, the axe can be stowed and retrieved quickly.

Climbing Techniques

The choice of different techniques for using an ice axe or ski poles depends on slope angle, snow conditions, and the climber's strength and skill (see Table 16-1). This section describes the techniques of walking with ski poles, using an ice axe in the cane position or self-arrest position, and using an ice axe or ski pole in cross-body position.

Walking with ski pole(s). On low-angle soft snow, using a ski pole, which is longer, is more helpful for maintaining balance than using an ice axe. Because standard ski poles do not have a pick that can be used to make a self-arrest and stop a fall, they are useful only when the consequences of an unchecked slide are not a concern. Ski poles equipped with whippet grips that have picks can be used to help stop a fall, but they are not as effective for this as an ice axe.

Ice axe in cane position (self-belay grasp). When ascending low-angle and gentle slopes or descending while facing in, climbers usually find it easier to stop a fall from becoming a slide by gripping the axe in the cane position (*piolet canne*). Holding the ice axe in the cane position enables you to lean over in the event of a small slip, push the pick forward into the snow, and push down on the ice axe head to catch yourself and regain balance (which is why some people call this the self-belay grasp); more on fall prevention and how to use the cane position is discussed later in this chapter. To climb in the cane position, rest your palm on top of the adze and wrap your thumb and index finger

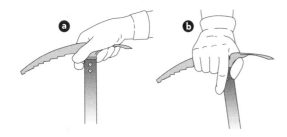

Fig. 16-10. *Grasping an ice axe: **a,** cane position; **b,** self-arrest position.*

under the pick (fig. 16-10a). While climbing, point the pick forward and set the spike firmly in the snow before each step.

Ice axe in self-arrest position. When descending low-angle and gentle slopes while facing out, climbers usually find it is easier to stop a fall from becoming a slide by gripping the axe in the self-arrest position. With the ice axe in this position, a climber who is descending while facing out can prevent a slip onto the buttocks from becoming an out-of-control fall by pushing the pick backwards into the snow and pushing down on the ice-axe head. To climb in the self-arrest position, place your thumb under the adze and your palm over the pick, wrapping your fingers around the pick (fig. 16-10b). While climbing, point the adze forward and set the spike firmly in the snow before each step.

Ice axe or ski pole in cross-body position. When making a diagonal ascent (see the next section), using the ice axe or a sturdy ski pole in the cross-body position (*piolet ramasse*) can make it easier to balance as the slope angle increases. Hold the ice axe with both hands, one in the cane or self-arrest position on the head and the other in the middle of the shaft or nearer the spike, depending on the steepness of the slope. Place or jab the spike into the snow next to you with the shaft diagonally in front of you (fig. 16-11). Push down gently with the hand on the shaft while the hand on the axe head holds the axe firmly in position.

Pros and cons of grips. The pros and cons of the cane grip and the self-arrest grip affect how you use an ice axe to stop a fall. (To learn more, refer to the "Pros and Cons of Ice-Axe Grips" sidebar, later in this chapter.)

USING CRAMPONS OR SPIKE TRACTION DEVICES

The choice of different techniques for using boots alone or with crampons or spike traction devices depends on slope angle, snow conditions, and the climber's strength and skill (see Table 16-1). The sections below describe how to

perform these different techniques on low-angle and gentle snow and ice (for technical snow and ice, see Chapter 17).

For low-angle snow and ice, spike traction devices are less bulky and easier to use than crampons and can be attached to a wide range of footwear, but use them only for slope angles and snow conditions shown in Table 16-1. For better purchase in steeper or icier conditions, or where the consequences of an out-of-control fall are a concern, crampons provide greater security. Crampons are necessary in icy conditions, but they can also be useful on snow, even soft snow.

Learn how and when to use crampons or spike traction devices. Ask these questions: Will footwear determine whether crampons or spike traction devices are needed, since rigid-soled boots can kick steps that are more stable and secure than steps made with softer, more flexible shoes or boots? Does using crampons or spike traction devices make walking on snow easier and more secure? Does the slope have a dangerous or unknown runout, and is traction without crampons or spike traction devices questionable? The answers to these questions will help you determine whether to use crampons or spike traction devices.

16

Fig. 16-11. *Holding an ice axe in cross-body position with hand in cane position.*

Learning to walk in crampons without tripping takes practice. In soft, sticky conditions, when snow is balling up under your crampons, it is easy to slip and fall, and travel might be easier without them. But in situations where the snow may be hard under a sticky surface layer or the slope is steep enough, crampons may be required even when the snow sticks to them. In this situation it may be necessary to knock the snow free by hitting the boot with the lower shaft of the ice axe or the spike, sometimes with every step.

For some techniques, French terms are given in parentheses. The French word *pied* (pronounced "pee-AY") means "foot"; the French word *piolet* (pronounced "pee-oh-LAY") means "ice axe." Terms including the word *pied* refer to footwork; terms including the word *piolet* refer to ice-axe positions (see Figures 17-14 and 17-15 in the next chapter).

Flat-Footed

On low-angle snow or ice slopes, it is possible to walk straight up flat-footed (*pied à plat*) like walking up an inclined sidewalk (fig. 16-12). If the snow is soft, crampons are probably not needed; on harder snow or ice, it may feel more secure to use spike traction devices or crampons. When walking flat-footed, flex the ankle and keep the entire bottom of the boot (with or without crampons or spike traction devices) in contact with the snow or ice for maximum grip. Climbers need flexible ankles to keep boot soles parallel to the surface, and boots that flex at the ankle facilitate walking flat-footed. With practice, walking flat-footed reduces strain on the calf muscles—by relying on the larger muscle groups to do most of the work—and offers a more stable platform.

Keep feet slightly farther apart than normal to avoid snagging a crampon point on clothing or the other boot. Use the ice axe in the cane or self-arrest position. (See the "Pros and Cons of Ice-Axe Grips" sidebar, later in this chapter.)

Step-Kick

As a slope with soft snow steepens, it is probably most efficient to kick steps straight up the slope. Facing into the slope and kicking steps creates a path of foot platforms going upward like a staircase in the snow (fig. 16-13). The leader at the front does the most work to kick fresh steps and look for the best route up. Climbers following behind move in single file up the steps, kicking down and into the existing foot platforms to further consolidate and strengthen them as they go.

The most efficient way to kick steps in soft snow is to lift and swing your leg, allowing the weight and momentum of your boot to generate most of the impact. If the platform collapses when weighted, kick again and create subsequent steps with a more vigorous foot swing to cut deeper into the slope. In firmer snow, climbers must kick harder to create steps, which requires more effort, and the steps may be smaller and less secure, which might necessitate wearing crampons.

Fig. 16-12. *Walking flat-footed (shown in hard, icy snow, with crampons) with ice axe in cane position.*

Fig. 16-13. *Step-kicking in soft snow, without crampons and with ice axe in cane position.*

In soft snow, kick the step deep enough and stomp it down so that it will not break when you step up on it. Steps in these conditions will be at least as deep as from your toes to your arch, and most likely the length of your entire foot. The leader will determine the size and depth of the steps to make based on the snow conditions and skill of the party. If the steps created with a single kick are too small or too weak for the party members to balance and step up on, the leader should kick into the slope multiple times to create a stable enough platform (or use crampons). When kicking steps, keep other climbers in the party in mind, particularly the shortest team member, and space your steps evenly.

Switch leads occasionally to share the heavy work. Like drafting with a group of cyclists, the leader can step aside and fall in at the end of the line.

Duck Walk

As a low-angle slope steepens, splay your feet outward to use the duck walk (*pied en canard*), keeping your knees bent and weight balanced over your feet (fig. 16-14). Continue to use the axe in the cane position. Splay your toes out so that your feet make a V in the snow and more of your weight is on the inside of the boot. With each step, rock your weight directly over your foot, then repeat the process with your other foot.

Fig. 16-14. *Duck walk, with ice axe in cane position.*

Diagonal Ascent

If the snow is too steep or firm to kick steps straight up the slope and too steep for the duck walk, a diagonal ascent, switchbacking up the slope, may work best. Depending on the snow conditions, foot placements in a diagonal ascent are a sideways version of either walking flat-footed or step-kicking.

When performing a diagonal ascent, face sideways to the slope with a downhill foot on the side of your body away from the slope, and an uphill foot on the side closest to the slope (fig. 16-15a). To climb the slope, cross your downhill foot in front of and above your uphill foot, then step up and forward by kicking a step or walking flat-footed (fig. 16-15b). Next, swing the now lower foot around from behind in a wide enough arc to avoid tripping (or, if wearing crampons, to avoid snagging your front points on a pant leg) and return it to the uphill position (fig. 16-15c). After completing this two-step crossover sequence, you will be back in the starting position but higher up. To ascend diagonally, simply repeat this sequence.

This normal crossover sequence for the diagonal ascent is an intermediate skill. Many beginner climbers have difficulty crossing their downhill foot up past the uphill one, executing a movement where accuracy is important because of a crampon passing by the opposite pant leg. Beginners may find it helpful to modify this sequence by eliminating the crossover and bringing the lower leg up next to and below the upper leg in an uphill shuffling motion. Once they have perfected this simpler shuffle, beginner climbers can progress to the normal crossover sequence.

To switchback up the slope using the diagonal ascent, follow these steps to change directions:

1. Start with your uphill foot in front of and above your downhill foot. Jab the ice-axe shaft straight down into the snow directly above you (fig. 16-16a).
2. Cross your downhill foot in front of and above the uphill foot (fig. 16-16b).
3. Grasp the ice-axe head with both hands, and move the now-downhill foot up into a duck-foot stance facing uphill, turning the insides of both feet toward the slope (fig. 16-16c).
4. Turn your body toward the new direction of travel, placing your new uphill foot in front of and above your new downhill foot (fig. 16-16d). Grasp the axe head with your new uphill hand in either the cane or self-arrest position (the latter is shown in Figure 16-16d).

16

Fig. 16-15. *Diagonal ascent combined with ice axe in cane position:* **a,** *start with uphill foot in front of and above downhill foot;* **b,** *cross downhill foot in front of and above the uphill foot;* **c,** *swing the now lower foot around from behind in a wide arc to the uphill position.*

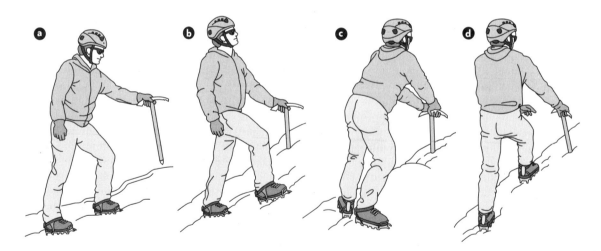

Fig. 16-16. *Changing directions on a diagonal ascent:* **a,** *start with uphill foot in front of and above downhill foot, combined with ice axe in cane position;* **b,** *cross downhill foot in front of and above the uphill foot;* **c,** *grasp ice axe with both hands and bring the now-downhill foot up into duck-foot stance, facing uphill with feet splayed;* **d,** *turn in new direction of travel, placing your new uphill foot in front of and above your new downhill foot, with the now-uphill hand shown in self-arrest position (remaining in cane position would also be fine).*

Hybrid Technique

On gentle snow or ice it may feel easier and more secure to go directly up the slope using a hybrid technique (*pied troisième*) that combines step-kick (or front-pointing when on ice, see Chapter 17) and duck walk (fig. 16-17). Face into the slope and kick the uphill foot straight into the snow or ice, then place the downhill foot even with it using a duck-walk stance. Make a direct ascent by repeating this sequence with one foot facing straight uphill and the other foot's instep facing uphill with the toes pointing away from your body at two or three o'clock (hence, the French term). It's common after several steps of using hybrid technique to get calf-muscle fatigue on the leg you're using to kick straight into the snow or ice. In that event, switch the straight-in foot to the duck-walk stance and the other foot to straight into the slope.

Climbing without Crampons

Sometimes climbers encounter short sections of low-angle or gentle hard snow or ice that might not merit taking the time to put on crampons, or perhaps crampons were left behind. If the section is short, climbers can make progress by cutting a few steps with their ice axe using the adze or the pick (fig. 16-18a). Advance up the steps in a diagonal ascent. The pick works better for cutting steps in hard ice (fig. 16-18b).

Cutting steps to climb even short sections of hard snow or ice without crampons or spike traction devices requires great caution because it would be difficult or impossible to self-arrest. When climbers do not have the proper equipment for the situation, it is usually best to turn around.

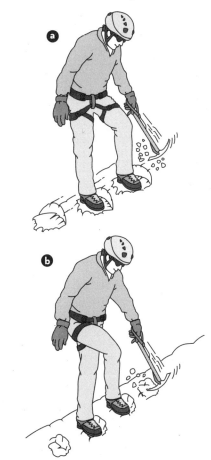

16

Fig. 16-17. *Hybrid technique: with downhill foot in duck-walk stance and uphill foot in step-kick stance, with ice axe in cane position.*

Fig. 16-18. *Cutting steps for short distances without crampons:* **a,** *use the adze to cut a step in hard snow;* **b,** *cut a step in ice using the pick.*

Climbing Low-Angle Rock with Crampons

Climbers commonly encounter short sections of low-angle rock next to low-angle or gentle snow and ice that they must cross while wearing crampons. Rather than taking the crampons off, time is saved by walking across the rock with them on. Place your feet parallel to the rock using all the crampon points and if possible avoid stepping onto smooth rock, where the points will skate. At first it may be difficult to keep your balance, but your confidence will increase with even a small amount of practice. Take care not to turn an ankle.

DESCENDING

The ability to go downhill efficiently and safely is a critical skill for a snow and ice climber. Descending is frequently more challenging than ascending the same slope, in part because it is easier to slip. Many otherwise competent climbers are intimidated at the prospect of going down a steep, exposed snow slope facing out. The best technique for descending low-angle and gentle snow and ice slopes depends on the slope angle, the snow conditions, and the climber's strength and skill. See Table 16-1 earlier in this chapter for when to use different descent techniques, including the plunge step, flat-footed facing out, diagonal descent, facing in (backing down), and glissading.

The Plunge Step

The plunge step is a confident, assertive downhill stride that creates a step in soft or not-too-hard snow. Face outward,

holding the ice axe in one hand and using your other arm for balance. Step away from the slope, shift your weight slightly forward, and land solidly on your heel with your straightened leg vertical, transferring your weight solidly to the new step (fig. 16-19). Avoid leaning back into the slope, which can result in a less effective plunge and perhaps an unplanned sitting glissade. Keep knees slightly bent, not locked, and lean forward to maintain balance. Take care (especially in deep, soft snow) not to plunge so deeply that your leg gets stuck and you fall forward, injuring your knee.

For most climbers, the plunge step without crampons feels secure when the snow is soft enough that the steps created are at least the size of the boot heel. But with crampons, most climbers feel secure plunge-stepping in firmer snow, even if the steps created are small. Highly skilled climbers are able to trust shallower steps in firmer snow without crampons. When plunge-stepping, maintain a steady rhythm, almost like marching, to help maintain balance. Typically, it is easier to plunge-step by picking your own line rather than following others' footsteps, because the undisturbed snow will compress in a more consistent and even way.

Flat-Footed Facing Out

On low-angle snow, face outward to simply walk down flat-footed, with the ice axe in the self-arrest position (fig. 16-20). Crampons may be needed on hard snow and necessary on hard ice.

Fig. 16-19. *Plunge step, with ice axe in self-arrest position.*

Fig. 16-20. *Flat-footed descent wearing crampons, with ice axe in self-arrest position.*

Diagonal Descent

While descending a gentle slope, it is often easier to walk sideways across and down the slope than it is to walk straight down the slope, especially if the snow is hard or icy. A diagonal descent is the same as a diagonal ascent, except it involves stepping down instead of up. Face sideways to the slope with the downhill foot on the side of your body away from the slope and the uphill foot on the side closest to the slope. To descend the slope, cross your uphill foot in front of and below your downhill foot, then step down by kicking a step or walking flat-footed. Next, swing the now-uphill foot around from behind in a wide enough arc to avoid tripping (or, if wearing crampons, to avoid snagging your front points on a pant leg), and kick a step or walk flat-footed to return it to the downhill position.

After completing this two-step sequence, you will be in the same position from which you started, but lower down. If you are wearing crampons, plant all points firmly into the snow or ice with each step. Hold the axe in the cane or self-arrest position. As the descent angle steepens, bend your knees more and keep your feet farther apart. Your thigh muscles should do the bulk of the work.

Switchbacking down the slope using a diagonal descent requires periodically changing the direction of descent, which is slightly different from how this is done in a diagonal ascent. Here are the steps to do this:

1. Start with your uphill foot in front of your downhill foot.
2. Turn your downhill foot in the new direction of travel. Jab the ice-axe shaft into the snow with the hand on the same side as your downhill foot turned toward the new direction.
3. Turn your body toward the new direction of travel by bringing your uphill foot in front of and below your downhill foot. Your downhill foot is now your uphill foot.

Like the diagonal ascent, the normal two-step cross-over sequence for the diagonal descent is an intermediate skill. Many beginner climbers have difficulty crossing their uphill foot in front of and below the downhill one, executing a movement where accuracy is important because of the crampon passing by the opposite pant leg. For beginners it may be helpful to modify this sequence by eliminating the crossover; simply step down with the lower leg and then bring the upper leg down next to it in a downhill shuffling motion. Beginner climbers can progress to the normal crossover sequence once this simpler shuffle is perfected.

Facing In (Backing Down)

Even on a gentle slope, if the snow is hard or icy and you do not feel confident facing out, it is more secure to face in and back down by kicking steps (fig. 16-21) or if it is icy, by front-pointing (see Front-Pointing in Chapter 17). Facing in restricts your view, so be aware of your surroundings. Try to plunge the axe shaft as low on the slope as is comfortable before stepping down. If the snow is too firm for a solid spike placement or the slope feels too steep, use the ice axe in the low- or middle-dagger position or use *piolet traction* (see Chapter 17 for these techniques). Try to keep your weight centered over your feet as much as possible; leaning into the slope can affect your balance.

direction of travel

Fig. 16-21. *Facing in (backing down), with ice axe in cane position.*

Glissading

A controlled slide down a snow slope is a fast and easy way to descend. But if it turns into an out-of-control fall down a slope into a moat, rocks, or trees below, it can result in injury. Done properly on low-angle soft snow slopes where climbers can control their speed, glissading is an efficient alternative to flat-footed or plunge-step descents.

16

Do not glissade in terrain where there are crevasses, moats, or similar hazards. Glissade only when there is a safe runout so that a climber will not become injured if they lose control. When glissading in an established track with others, take care to maintain enough space between climbers. Unless the party can see the entire descent route, the first person down must use extreme caution and stop frequently to look ahead. The biggest risk is losing control at such a high speed that it is impossible to self-arrest. Before performing a glissade, remove your crampons and stow them on or inside the pack where the points will not cause an injury. Wear gloves to protect hands from the abrasive snow, and wear a helmet too. If the party needs to be roped up, they should not glissade.

Always maintain control of the ice axe. If you wear an ice-axe leash, do not allow the axe to be knocked loose—a flailing axe risks injury. If you are not wearing a leash, do not lose your axe and the means to control the glissade or to self-arrest.

On certain types of soft snow slopes that don't pose a serious risk of initiating a large avalanche (see Chapter 20, Avalanche Safety), it is still possible for a glissader to set off a localized mass of surface snow, which slides down the slope ahead or with the glissader aboard. You can escape from this snow cushion while in a sitting glissade by rolling sideways and self-arresting, or when in a standing glissade by stepping out of the path of the moving snow.

Whether you use the sitting or standing glissade depends on the slope's steepness, the snow conditions, the runout, and your mastery of the techniques.

Sitting glissade. To perform a sitting glissade, sit upright in the snow, bend your knees, and plant the soles of your boots flat along the snow surface (fig. 16-22a). Hold the ice axe in self-arrest position with one hand and wrap the other hand around the shaft near the spike. To maintain control of your speed, push the spike into the snow on one side of you while holding the head firmly in position. The standard posture, with knees bent and feet flat, also reduces speed. Wear waterproof hardshell pants (see Chapter 2, Clothing and Equipment) to keep your backside dry and protect your pants.

To stop, use the spike to slow down, then gradually dig in your heels. If you dig in your heels too abruptly at high speed, you may end up somersaulting. To stop in an emergency, roll over and self-arrest.

It is almost impossible to turn in a sitting glissade. The best way to get around an obstruction is to stop, walk sideways to a point that is not directly above the obstacle, and then glissade again.

Standing glissade. The most maneuverable technique, the standing glissade also keeps your clothes from getting wet and abraded. The best conditions for a standing glissade are a firm base with soft snow on top. When the snow is crusty, pitted with icy ruts or small suncups (hollows melted by the sun), or dotted with rocks or shrubs, a standing glissade might still be possible and much easier on your body than bumping your way down these types of features in a sitting glissade. The softer the snow, the steeper the slope needs to be to maintain speed. A standing glissade is possible down slopes of firmer soft snow, but to maintain control in these conditions, it may be necessary to choose lower-angle slopes with a safe runout.

The standing glissade is like downhill skiing, except on "skis" the length of your boots. Crouch slightly, leaning forward over your feet, bend your knees, and spread your arms slightly for balance (fig. 16-22b). Either spread your feet out or place them together—whatever offers the most stability. Sometimes it helps to place one foot slightly forward. Hold the ice axe in one hand in self-arrest position.

To slow down or stop, stand up and dig in your heels, or turn your feet sideways and dig their edges into the slope. It is possible to turn as you would when skiing by rotating your lower body and knees in the direction you want to turn and to rock your feet onto your boot edges.

Responding to changes in the snow texture is tricky. If you hit softer, slower snow or harder, faster snow, you may need to move one boot forward for stability or lean

Fig. 16-22. *Glissade positions, with ice axe in self-arrest position:* **a,** *sitting;* **b,** *standing.*

forward or backward to maintain your balance. Switching to taking a few plunge steps can help you regain control before returning to a standing glissade.

PREVENTING AND STOPPING A FALL

When climbing snow and ice, falling is very dangerous. To avoid falling on snow and ice, climb in balance and practice the boot and ice-axe techniques mentioned previously until you feel secure and confident on the slopes you attempt. When encountering snow and ice slopes you are not adept at climbing, it is best to turn around, or at a minimum to use the appropriate roped techniques discussed later in this chapter for protection. Wear gloves on snow slopes where there is any chance of slipping; snow is quite abrasive and hand protection increases your ability to catch a slip or stop a fall. Climbers should first try to stop a slip from becoming a slide, and in turn stop a slide from becoming an uncontrolled fall; if climbers end up in an uncontrolled fall, they must know how to perform a self-arrest. There are pros and cons of using different ice axe grips when trying to stop a fall (see "Pros and Cons of Ice-Axe Grips" sidebar).

Catching a Slip and Catching a Slide

If a small slip does occur, prevent it from becoming a slide and then an out-of-control fall. When ascending, and also

push pick into snow

foot slips

Fig. 16-23. *Catching a slip before it becomes a slide while ascending.*

PROS AND CONS OF ICE-AXE GRIPS

When ascending and descending, climbers can use two methods to grip an ice axe: the cane or self-belay grip. (See fig. 16-10a for the cane grip; see fig. 16-10b for the self-arrest grip.) It is important to learn both methods. There are pros and cons of each grip when you are trying to keep a slip from becoming a slide, and failure to stop a slide could escalate into an uncontrolled fall.

Pros of cane grip: It's easy to push the pick into the snow to try and stop a slip. If a slip becomes a slide, it's still possible to use an ice axe self-belay (see fig. 16-29) to prevent it from becoming an uncontrolled fall.

Cons of cane grip: If a slip becomes a slide and escalates into an uncontrolled fall, it's harder to perform a self-arrest because you first have to switch to a self-arrest grip. With some slope angles and snow conditions, it is very difficult to stop a slip by pushing the pick into the snow using the cane grip. Using a self-arrest grip in these situations makes it easier to attempt a full self-arrest if a slide turns into an uncontrolled fall.

Pros of self-arrest grip: If a slip escalates into a slide that becomes an uncontrolled fall, it's easier to attempt to self-arrest because you are already using the self-arrest grip. If a slip becomes a slide, it's still possible to use an ice axe self-belay (see Fig. 16-29) to prevent it from becoming an uncontrolled fall.

Cons of self-arrest grip: It's difficult to try and stop a slip from becoming a slide. With some slope angles and snow conditions, the cane grip allows a climber to push the pick into the snow to try and stop a slip. Using a self-arrest grip in this situation would likely result in a slip becoming a slide at the very least.

It is vital that climbers practice the methods described in this chapter for stopping a fall using both grips. Practice on different slopes and in a variety of snow conditions to decide which way you want to grip your ice axe in different situations. You may find that you prefer using a self-arrest grip in certain situations when the cane grip is ineffective at stopping a slip and you must perform an extra step to self-arrest if a slip escalates into a slide that becomes an uncontrolled fall. In other situations, you may prefer the cane grip because it is easier to prevent a slip from becoming a slide in the first place. Whatever grip you choose, the real benefits come with understanding their pros and cons and knowing how and when to use each one.

16

when descending while facing in, this can be accomplished by holding the ice axe in the cane position, leaning over and pushing the pick forward into the snow, and then pushing down on the ice-axe head (fig. 16-23). This allows you to catch yourself and regain your balance.

When descending while facing out, hold the ice axe in the self-arrest position so that if a slip occurs onto the buttocks, it doesn't become a slide; push the pick backward into the snow, pushing down on the ice-axe head and digging your heels in (fig. 16-24).

In the event that a slip on low-angle or gentle snow or ice becomes a slide, try to prevent the slide from becoming an uncontrolled fall by using the ice axe self-belay described later in this section.

Self-Arrest from Four Falling Positions

If your slip becomes a slide and the techniques you use to stop a slide fail, the last resort to stop what has now become an out-of-control fall is to perform a self-arrest as quickly as possible. It is usually only possible to self-arrest on low-angle and gentle snow. If a slope is too steep or the snow too hard, a falling climber will build up speed too quickly to control the fall. Self-arrest technique is shown in Figures 16-25, 16-26, 16-27, and 16-28.

push pick into snow

foot slips

Fig. 16-24. *Catching a slip before it becomes a slide while descending.*

Self-arrest technique depends on the position the climber is in after a fall. A falling climber will be sliding in one of four positions: head uphill or head downhill and, in either case, facedown or on their back.

Head uphill, facedown. This is the easiest position to perform a self-arrest (as shown in Figure 16-25c). First, you must grasp the axe with both hands, one hand on the head in the self-arrest grasp and the other hand at the base of the shaft near the spike. If the fall occurred while climbing in the cane position, rotate the shaft with the hand down by the spike so that the hand on the head is now in the self-arrest grasp. Getting into this position and performing this technique is the final step to stop a fall from the other three positions, as referenced below. Here is how to do it:

1. **Hold the axe in a solid grip.** Place one hand in the self-arrest grasp, with your thumb under the adze and fingers over the pick (see Figure 16-10b), and your other hand wrapped around the shaft just above the spike. Place the shaft across your chest diagonally and hold the spike end close to the hip that is opposite the axe head.

2. **Press the pick into the snow above your shoulder.** Place the adze near the angle formed by your neck and shoulder with the pick facing forward. Sufficient force cannot be exerted on the pick into the snow if it is not in the proper position.

3. **Gently pull up on the spike end.** Prevent the spike from penetrating the snow and getting wedged. If the spike gets wedged in the snow instead of the pick, this could wrench the ice axe from your hands or flip you over backward into an uncontrolled fall.

4. **Press your chest and shoulder down on the ice-axe shaft.** Pulling up on the spike levers the shaft across your chest, which acts as a fulcrum, driving the pick into the snow and forcing you to a stop.

Keep your head facedown, bend your knees slightly, and spread your legs apart to help stabilize your body position. On softer snow, your slightly bent knees can dig in to help with a stop, but on harder surfaces, the stopping power will come almost entirely from the ice-axe pick penetrating the snow. In most conditions, and when you are in doubt, keep your toes up off the snow to avoid getting flipped over backward. In some conditions and depending on skill and whether or not you are wearing crampons, it may be possible to try to slow a fall by applying different amounts of pressure with your toes. Knowing if and when to dig in your toes requires experience and intermediate or advanced skills.

Head uphill, on your back. When falling with your head uphill, on your back (fig. 16-25a), get into the self-arrest

16

Fig. 16-25. *Correct self-arrest technique when falling head uphill, on your back:* **a,** *falling;* **b,** *rolling toward the ice-axe head;* **c,** *rolling facedown onto your stomach to complete the self-arrest.*

Fig. 16-26. *Incorrect self-arrest technique when falling head uphill, on your back:* **a,** *falling;* **b,** *rolling toward the spike;* **c,** *ice axe wrenched out of your hand(s).*

position as in step 1 above, without digging in your heels (which would flip you forward). Do this by rolling toward the head of the axe and aggressively planting the pick into the snow at your side as in step 2 above (fig. 16-25b). Roll over onto the shaft with your chest as in step 4 above (fig. 16-25c).

When you fall with your head uphill, on your back (fig. 16-26a), beware of rolling toward the spike (fig. 16-26b), which can jam the spike in the snow before the pick, as described in step 3 above, and wrench the axe from one or both of your hands (fig. 16-26c).

Head downhill, facedown. Self-arrest from a headfirst fall is more difficult because you must first swing your feet downhill. In this facedown predicament, with the ice axe in the self-arrest position as in step 1 above, reach downhill and off to the axe-head side (fig. 16-27a) and get the pick into the snow (fig. 16-27b) to serve as a pivot to swing your body around (fig. 16-27c). Work to swing your legs around (fig. 16-27d) so they are pointing downhill (fig. 16-27e). Then self-arrest as described in steps 2, 3, and 4 above.

Head downhill, on your back. Again, self-arrest from a headfirst fall is more difficult because you must first swing your feet downhill. In this face-up predicament, hold the ice axe across your torso similar to the self-arrest position in step 1 above except the pick is jabbed into the snow near your hip to serve as a pivot point (fig. 16-28a), then swing your legs downhill (fig. 16-28b). Twist and roll your chest onto the shaft with the ice-axe head near the angle formed by your neck and shoulder while swinging your legs around to point downhill to complete the self-arrest (fig. 16-28d).

Challenges in Self-Arresting

Practice self-arrest in all four positions on increasingly steeper slopes and hard snow above a safe runout. Practice while carrying a full pack. The key to success is to quickly get into the four-step arrest position described above and then dig in. When you practice, remove your ice-axe leash from your wrist so there is less chance of the axe striking you. Cover or pad the adze and spike to minimize chances of injury. Although crampons are often worn on snow slopes where self-arrest may be necessary, do not wear crampons when practicing self-arrest.

The effectiveness of self-arrest depends on your reaction time, the slope's steepness and length, and the snow

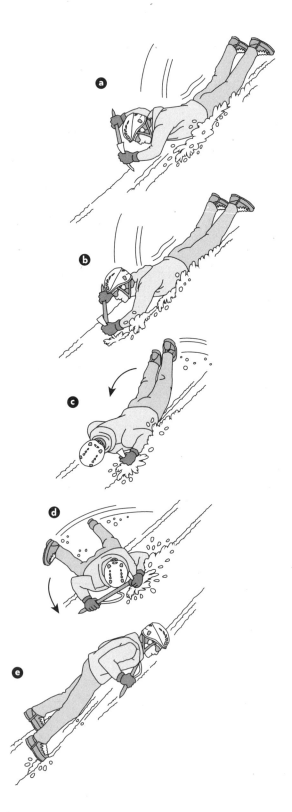

Fig. 16-27. *Self-arrest technique when falling head downhill, facedown:* **a,** *reach downhill and to same side as ice axe's head;* **b,** *plant pick into snow;* **c,** *pivot body around pick;* **d,** *swing legs downhill;* **e,** *press chest and shoulder onto ice-axe shaft, while slightly lifting the spike end, to complete the self-arrest.*

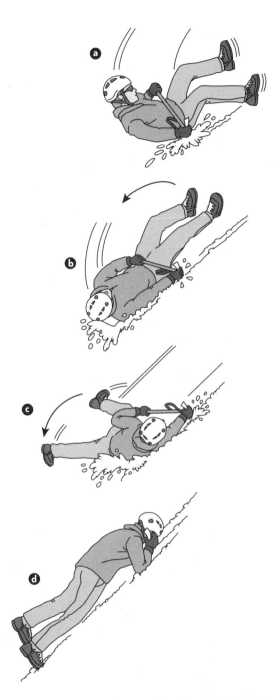

Fig. 16-28. *Self-arrest technique when falling head downhill, on your back:* **a,** *plant the pick near your hip;* **b,** *swing your legs downhill;* **c,** *twist and roll your chest onto the shaft;* **d,** *swing your legs downhill and press your chest and shoulder onto ice-axe shaft while slightly lifting the spike end.*

conditions. Do not trust the possibility of self-arrest if a slope seems too icy or steep, if the runout seems too dangerous, or if members of the climbing party doubt their strength or skill. If any of these possibilities is the case, the general recommendation is to use some type of belay, back off and look for another route, or rope up and put in protection (see Roped Techniques, below).

On steep or icy slopes. When the slope is too steep or icy, even the best self-arrest technique will not stop a slide. Acceleration on ice, on even a low-angle slope, can be so rapid that the climber cannot get the ice-axe pick to penetrate the surface before completely losing control of the fall.

On hard or very soft or loose snow. Arresting on hard snow is very difficult and takes considerable skill, but it's not impossible. Practicing self-arrest will increase your skill and ability to stop a fall in difficult conditions. In certain types of very soft or loose snow, the pick will not provide enough resistance to slow and stop a falling climber. The best brakes in this case are the self-arrest plus feet, knees, and elbows, widely spaced and deeply pressed into the snow. If the initial efforts at self-arrest are unsuccessful, do not give up. Keep fighting. The attempt itself may slow the fall and help prevent you from rolling, tumbling, and bouncing. It may also help keep you sliding feet first, the best position if you end up hitting rocks or trees.

Without an axe. If you lose your ice axe in a fall, use hands, elbows, knees, and boots to dig into the snow slope, using positioning similar to what you would use if you still had the axe. Try to claw at the snow or clasp your hands together against the slope so that snow accumulates in your clasped hands and creates more friction.

Trekking or ski poles may be an aid for balance on lower-angle slopes, but they provide minimal means to arrest and should be used only on low-angle terrain when the consequences of an out-of-control fall are not a concern. Some ski poles are equipped with a whippet head that has a pick like an ice axe. It is possible to attempt a self-arrest with a whippet ski pole, but it would not be as effective as using an ice axe. A whippet should not be used at steeper angles or on dangerous runouts.

Ice Axe Self-Belay

In the event that a slip on low-angle or gentle snow or ice becomes a slide, try to prevent a slide from becoming an uncontrolled fall by using the ice axe self-belay. As your legs slide out from underneath you, drive the spike of the axe down hard into the ice with your grip hand (fig. 16-29a), then use your free hand to grab the axe shaft and slide that hand down to the surface of the ice (fig. 16-29b). Press downward firmly with your grip hand on the axe head, and

367

keep your bottom hand locked onto the shaft to keep from sliding down the slope.

Roped Techniques

On a glacier, teams rope up for protection from crevasses, especially ones that may be hidden (see Chapter 19, Glacier Travel and Crevasse Rescue). On low-angle or gentle snow and ice slopes, whether to rope up or belay each other is less clear-cut and depends on several factors (see the "Decision-Making for Roped Snow and Ice Travel" sidebar). The party may ascend unroped, relying on each climber to

Fig. 16-29. *Ice axe self-belay: **a,** as your legs slide out from underneath you, drive the spike down hard into the ice with your grip hand; **b,** use your free hand to grab the shaft of the axe and slide that hand down to the surface of the ice.*

stop their own fall. Another option is to rope up for travel but not belay each other, which may enable team members to self-arrest and stop a falling team member. But recent tests show that such team arrests usually fail and often result in the falling climber pulling the entire roped team down the slope. Well-trained trip or rope leaders can offer better security for their less-skilled team members by short roping them to prevent a fall from gaining enough momentum to make it difficult or impossible to stop. But short roping requires a

DECISION-MAKING FOR ROPED SNOW AND ICE TRAVEL

When deciding whether to rope up for low-angle and gentle snow and ice travel, consider these questions:

- Do all team members have the skills and ability to self-arrest, given the slope and conditions?

- Does the rope team have one or more experienced members with the ability and skill to short rope less experienced team members given the slope and conditions? If not, the choice to rely instead on a team arrest to hold a less skilled partner who might fall and not be able to self-arrest poses a high risk that the other team members will also be unable to self-arrest and that a falling climber will pull everyone off.

- Given the slope and conditions, is it possible for anyone in the party to self-arrest?

- If there are not enough members with the skill to short rope the team, plus the slope and conditions make it improbable for unroped team members to perform a successful self-arrest, and fixed belays are too time-consuming, should a running belay with snow or ice anchors be used to protect a roped team? If so, does the party have enough experience and equipment to execute and manage running belays?

- Do the climbing conditions and the situation require using fixed snow and ice belays?

The risks of roping up are not trivial: one climber can fall and pull an entire rope team off the mountain. A climbing party can always consider turning around, especially if the conditions and/or route surpass the skills and ability of the team. If the party decides it is more secure overall to rope up, they can choose from several methods to match the type of rope protection to the conditions and the climbers' abilities.

high level of skill for the rope leader(s). Although it is slower, a party may also decide to rope up for travel and use fixed or running belays because route conditions or the climbers' skill levels make it prudent to use this level of protection.

SHORT ROPING AND TEAM ARREST

If conditions on low-angle or gentle snow and/or ice slopes make it unlikely that a trained individual can perform a self-arrest, then roping up to protect everyone with a team arrest often creates a false sense of security. In these conditions, a falling climber will more likely pull off their team members attempting a team arrest so that everyone is now falling down the slope. In this situation, deciding whether to rope up and climb without belaying each other depends on whether there are enough skilled climbers in the party to protect the team by short roping.

Short Roping

Short roping is when a trained leader uses a small portion of the rope to prevent a slip or fall by reducing the likelihood of a slip and by stopping a slip before it becomes a fall (fig. 16-30). To short rope, a rope leader with advanced skills must perfect the following procedures:

- **The rope leader (leader) and less experienced team member being led (follower) move together,** usually less than 6 feet (2 meters) apart so that the leader has a high degree of control over the group.
- **The leader moves and holds the rope in such a way to be prepared to stop a slip,** with the rope held firmly in one hand and while in a secure stance with the feet.
- **If the follower slips, the leader pulls up on the rope aggressively,** pulling the follower back into balance, and preventing a minor slip from becoming a fall.
- **The leader must be very close to the follower to watch and sense the follower's movement** and balance, and to keep an absolute minimum of slack in the rope.
- **The leader must watch, feel, and listen to the follower and be alert to potential slips,** and then if necessary, move and hold the rope in such a manner that a slip can be stopped.
- **The climbers get set up by shortening the rope with coils** (see Figure 19-9) so that there is about 20 feet (7 meters) between the leader and follower.
- **The leader carries most of these 20 feet (7 meters) in small coils** so that there is only about 5 or 6 feet (approximately 2 meters) remaining between the leader and follower.
- **The leader should hold the end of the short rope to the follower in their downhill hand,** keeping it below

chest level and not using it for anything else! When short roping on snow and ice, it can be helpful for the leader to tie a small loop in the rope with an overhand knot to hold onto.

- **Body position is critical to short roping** because the leader's feet are the follower's belay anchors. Move using diagonal ascent or descent, with the downhill and uphill legs braced to catch a slip. The leader must place their feet securely in steps kicked into the snow.
- **The leader should move and then stop** to maximize the amount of time spent standing with legs braced.
- **The leader should keep a small amount of tension in the rope** to feel the follower's movement. Ask the follower how much tension they prefer for security without being pulled off-balance. Keep the tension constant except when catching a slip.
- **The leader must know at what level of difficulty and on what type of climbing the follower** has a significant chance of falling.

Fig. 16-30. *Short roping.*

In difficult terrain where the follower has a significant chance of falling and the limits of short roping are being pushed, the leader must determine if there is greater security in traveling slower by belaying. How difficult any given terrain is for a climbing party is determined mostly by the leader's and follower's skills and experience. One of the greatest advantages of short roping is the follower climbs extremely close to the leader and can therefore watch them to learn the best foot sequence and pace.

It is much more difficult for the leader to short rope with two followers, and the leader must have extensive practice with this arrangement. Two followers will not be as careful as the leader in keeping the slack out of the rope between them, risking a fall that is harder to catch. Leaders using this technique must know that with followers of different abilities, the less skilled climber should be kept close to the leader and the more skilled not far behind (or ahead on descent). The leader can effectively short rope the less skilled follower and at the same time provide a somewhat lesser degree of security for the more skilled follower. With multiple followers, the leader will probably want to use a roped belay system on some terrain where it would feel reasonable to short rope with only one follower. Because it requires an incredible degree of concentration and extremely demanding, complex decision-making, short roping is mentally exhausting. Amateur leaders should get instruction from a professional guide on how to perform this technique to achieve a high level of competency before taking on this responsibility.

Team Arrest

Under all of the following circumstances, a team arrest can be a reasonable choice to protect a falling climber:

- Team members have solid self-arrest skills.
- The slope is low angle or gentle and conditions are soft enough for climbers arresting a fall to also dig their knees and boots into the slope.
- The sliding climber doesn't generate a lot of force with the given slope and conditions.
- There isn't excessive slack between team members.
- The other rope team members react quickly to a fall.

Under these circumstances, members of the rope team can self-arrest and likely stop a rope mate who has fallen but is not able to self-arrest. To perform a team arrest on a snow or ice slope, use the following procedures:

Carry a few feet of slack rope coiled in your hand if any climbers are below you. If a climber falls, drop the loose rope, which delays the moment that the rope is loaded. Use this moment to drop onto the slope in a self-arrest position and

hold onto the ice axe firmly with the pick embedded, before the falling climber's weight loads the rope. Avoid carrying too much slack, which increases the distance that your rope mates will slide before the rope is weighted, which increases the load on the arresting climber(s) due to momentum.

Put the least-skilled climber on the downhill end of the rope. As a rule, position the least-skilled climber last on the rope while ascending and first on the rope while descending. With this approach, the climber most likely to fall is below the other climbers, where the impact along the rope will be lower.

Climb on a shortened rope. Using only a portion of the rope when climbing together can reduce the sliding distance and the pull on the rope if one partner falls. It is also easier to walk together on varied terrain without dragging the full length of a longer rope that may be needed for another section of the climb. To shorten the rope, see Figure 19-9 featuring "Climbing in Coils" in Chapter 19.

Handle the rope properly. When traversing a slope, keep the rope on the downhill side so there is less chance of stepping on it. Hold the rope in a short loop in your downhill hand. You can then take in or pay out rope, adjusting to the pace and position of the person ahead of you or behind you, rather than getting into a tug-of-war.

Yell "Falling!" whenever any climber falls. This heads-up alerts all rope partners to self-arrest and avoid getting pulled off their feet (see Figure 19-15 in Chapter 19).

RUNNING BELAYS

Roped climbers can move together on snow and ice with the help of running belays (also called simul-climbing), which offer an intermediate level of protection, somewhere between short roping or team arrest and fixed belays. Running belays are an advanced technique, and teams need to be skilled at placing anchors and at how to travel together without excessive slack. With a skilled team, running belays save time over regular belayed climbing but still provide protection. On low-angle and gentle slopes where a team determines that protection is needed and team members do not have the skill to short rope, a successful team arrest is improbable, and fixed belays are too time-consuming, use a running belay with snow or ice anchors. Ice screws are used in hard ice; pickets can be driven into very hard snow; T-slot anchors can be used in soft or hard snow for protection (see Snow and Ice Anchors, below). Running belays are also useful for rock and technical snow and ice climbing (see Chapters 14 and 17).

The leader places ice screws, pickets, or T-slot anchors when necessary and uses carabiners and a runner to clip the rope in to each one. All rope team members continue to

Fig. 16-31. *A running belay setup with a cabled picket in snow and an ice screw in ice.*

climb at the same time, just as in unbelayed travel, except that now there is protection in place designed to stop a fall (fig. 16-31). To pass each running belay point with more than a two-person team, the middle climber(s) uses the Cascade clip. Before unclipping the rope in front of them, they reach down and clip the rope behind them into the carabiner, underneath the existing clipped rope. Then, they can unclip the rope between them and the person ahead. That precaution ensures that the team remains attached to each piece of protection as the middle climber passes it. The last climber on the rope removes each piece of protection.

SNOW AND ICE BELAYS

Climbers typically use fixed belays on steeper, more difficult snow or ice (see Chapter 17, Technical Snow and Ice Climbing). But in some conditions or situations when this level of security is needed, fixed belays are also used for ascending or descending low-angle or gentle snow and ice. On low-angle or gentle snow, climbers can give quick and less formal belays using an ice axe or a sitting hip belay, or they can set up belays using snow or ice anchors and a belay device. No matter the belaying technique used, make every snow and ice belay as secure and dynamic as possible to help limit the force on the anchor.

Set up a belay close to the climbing difficulties. To belay the lead climber, set up the belay stance to one side of the fall line

to get out of the path of falling snow and ice. If the leader is heading up on a diagonal, get away from any point where that climber's route would cross directly above you. On a ridge crest, it is not always possible to predict a fall line and plan a belay in advance. If a rope mate slips off one side of the ridge, the best tactic may be to jump off the opposite side, with the rope running over the ridge and thus saving both climbers.

Carabiner–ice axe belay. To set up the carabiner–ice axe belay, plant the axe as deeply as possible, the pick perpendicular to the fall line. Girth-hitch a short sling to the axe shaft at the surface of the snow and clip a carabiner to the sling (fig. 16-32a). Stand at a right angle to the fall line, facing the same side as the climber's route, with a control carabiner on your harness. Brace the axe with your downhill boot, standing atop the sling but leaving the carabiner exposed (fig. 16-32b). Keep crampon points off the sling. The rope runs from the potential direction of pull up through the carabiner at snow level, through the control carabiner on your harness, and then around the back of your waist and into your uphill (brake) hand. With the carabiner–ice axe belay, the force of a fall pulls the belayer more firmly into the stance. The carabiner–ice axe belay provides better security than a boot-axe belay (see below), with easier rope handling.

Boot-axe belay. A fast and easy way to provide protection is the boot-axe belay, but it is weaker than other techniques for belaying on snow. The boot-axe belay cannot

16

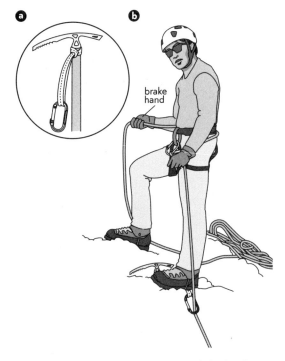

Fig. 16-32. *Carabiner–ice axe belay:* **a,** *girth-hitch a short runner to axe shaft and clip carabiner to runner;* **b,** *plant axe, stand on runner, and run rope up through carabiner at snow level, through control carabiner on harness, and around waist.*

hold the force of a fall from high above the belay, and the belayer's hunched-over stance makes it difficult to manage the rope. The boot-axe belay is better for letting rope out when doing something like protecting a rope mate who is probing a cornice or crevasse edge. It is not efficient to use a boot-axe belay to take in rope when providing a top belay. With practice, this belay can be set up in a few seconds by pushing the ice axe into the snow and quickly sweeping the rope around the axe shaft near its head, then in front of your ankle (fig. 16-33a and b).

Sitting hip belay. Used with or without a snow anchor, the sitting hip belay is a dynamic and often secure way to provide a top belay. The seated belayer may face the prospect of a cold, wet assignment, but sitting on a pack, foam pad, or other insulation can position the belayer too high, and they could be easily pulled off their seat. Build the seat deep enough so that holding weight on the rope pulls the belayer farther down into the seat and not out of it. To set up the belay, stamp or chop the seat in the snow, as well as a platform to brace each boot against, then settle into a standard hip belay (see Hip Belay in Chapter 10), with legs outstretched and stiffened (fig. 16-34). The hip belay can pull the belayer down into the seat and provide a more gradual, dynamic belay than a belay using a belay device, but it takes practice to execute correctly.

Snow and ice anchors and belay device. A belay device used with a snow or ice anchor offers a very secure belay. If a belay device is not available, a munter hitch also works

Fig. 16-33. *Boot-axe belay:* **a,** *position of axe, hands, and feet;* **b,** *overhead view of rope configuration.*

Fig. 16-34. *Sitting hip belay in snow, while attached to a T-slot anchor clipped to harness belay loop.*

(see Figure 8-26 in Chapter 8). Standing or sitting while attached to the snow or ice anchor and belaying from the harness provides a more dynamic system than belaying directly off the anchor, but be aware of surrounding ice or rock formations that you could get pulled or dragged into when holding a leader fall (see Position and Stance in Chapter 10). When belaying directly off the anchor, it is important to have multiple anchor points that have been weight tested (see Figure 16-38)—except multiple ice screws in reliable ice, which probably do not need to be weight tested.

SNOW AND ICE ANCHORS

In snow and ice, a medium of variable density that is not solid like rock, specialized anchors provide protection and the means to secure rappels and belays. The strength of snow anchors depends on the type of anchor, the area of snow the anchor pulls against, the snow's density, and ultimately, proper placement and snow conditions. Before relying on a snow anchor for a belay or rappel, weight test it by clipping your harness to the anchor and pulling on it abruptly with all your body weight. Be careful not to perform a weight test with too much force to avoid injuring your back. If the anchor moves, the test failed, so start over and place it deeper in the snowpack or use a different type of snow anchor. The strength of ice anchors depends on the quality of the ice (see Chapter 17, Technical Snow and Ice Climbing). Common snow and ice anchors are pickets, T-slot anchors, bollards, ice screws, and V-threads.

Picket

A picket is a specialized large stake driven or buried into the snow as an anchor. Aluminum pickets come in lengths ranging from 18 to 36 inches (46 to 90 centimeters) and in different styles, including V- or T-profile pickets (Figure 16-34 shows a T-profile picket), with carabiner attachment holes at the end (and, in many models, along the picket's length). Some pickets also come with a cable affixed to a carabiner hole in the middle of the picket (as in Figure 16-35b). Tests comparing a traditional top-clip picket with a mid-clip cable picket show that the mid-clip cable picket is stronger because it spreads the load across the entire length of the picket, whereas only the top third of a top-clip picket is loaded. Tests have also shown that loading the mid-clip cable picket produces stronger results in softer snow than for a top-clip picket, which works only in very firm, hard snow (in soft snow, a top-clip picket will lever out when loaded). A mid-clip cable picket can work in both hard and softer snow.

Place a top-clip picket at about 25 degrees offset from an imaginary projection perpendicular (90 degrees) to the snow slope, away from the direction of pull. Drive the picket as far into the snow as possible with the side of an ice axe (or an ice-tool hammer—see Ice Tools in Chapter 17). Attach a carabiner and/or runner to the picket at the

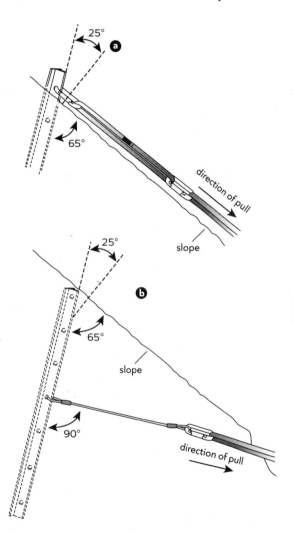

Fig. 16-35. *Picket placements: a, only in very firm snow, place a top-clip picket at 25 degrees offset from an imaginary projection perpendicular to snow slope, then clip carabiner and runner at snow's surface; b, place a mid-clip cable picket at same angle as top-clip picket, but drive it below snow's surface so cable (not to scale) pulls on picket at 90-degree angle.*

snow's surface (fig. 16-35a)—not higher on the picket, or a pull may lever it out of the snow. Place a mid-clip cable picket also at about 25 degrees offset from an imaginary projection perpendicular to the snow slope, away from the direction of pull. But drive the mid-clip picket below the snow's surface and use an ice-axe pick to cut a slender trench for the cable; make it deep enough so that the cable extends from the picket at an angle of 90 degrees (fig. 16-35b) and the picket is being pulled down into the snow. It's common to attach the rope to pickets using a locking carabiner.

If a vertical picket placement fails the weight test, the snow is probably too soft for this type of anchor; a stronger option in these conditions is to use the picket as a T-slot anchor (see Figure 16-36a).

T-Slot Anchor

A T-slot anchor properly constructed in reasonably dense snow takes more time to build but is considerably stronger than a top-clip picket and somewhat stronger than a mid-clip cable picket. Although pickets are often used as T-slot anchors (fig. 16-36a), many other objects buried in the snow can be equally strong. Ice axes (fig. 16-36b), ice tools, and even stuff sacks filled with snow (fig. 16-36c) can be used as T-slot anchors. Here are the steps to build a T-slot anchor:

1. With the ice-axe pick and adze, dig a trench as long and narrow as the item being used and perpendicular to the load. The softer the snow, the deeper the item must be placed. Make sure there are no visible cracks in the snow in the area against which the item exerts force, and consider boot packing and hardening the area against which the item exerts force.

2. Girth-hitch a runner or tie a cord to the item at its midpoint and place the item in the trench. Use a clove hitch if the item is likely to rotate. It's common to attach the rope to a T-slot anchor using a locking carabiner.

3. Cut a slot in the snow to allow the runner or cord to lie in the direction of pull. Make sure this slot is as deep as the trench, so there will be a downward pull on the anchor.

4. Backfill the trench and cover the item being used with snow. Compact the trench-backfill, and consider hardening the snow in the area where the item exerts force by boot packing.

5. Perform a weight test. If it fails, start over, placing the item deeper until it passes the weight test.

In soft snow, increase the anchor placement's strength by burying it deeper (the softer the snow, the deeper it should be placed) or by increasing the area of snow it pulls against. Do this by using a larger object such as a pack, a pair of skis, or a large stuff sack tightly filled with snow. Ski or trekking poles are not strong enough; do not use them. Using items like an ice axe, pack, or skis for a T-slot anchor is OK for belays and protection, but not for rappel anchors: these are items you would not want to leave behind except in an emergency. T-slot rappel anchors are normally constructed with a picket or a stuff sack filled with snow.

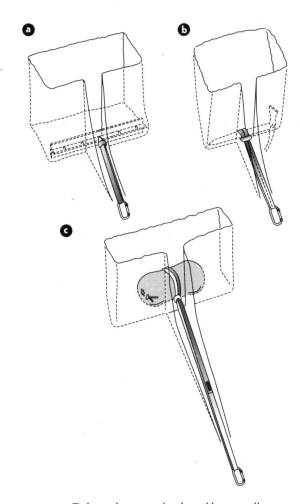

Fig. 16-36. T-slot anchors: **a,** picket, buried horizontally; **b,** ice axe, buried horizontally; **c,** stuff sack packed tightly with snow, buried horizontally.

Bollard

A bollard is a short, thick vertical pillar chipped or carved out of very firm snow or ice. When rigged with rope or webbing, bollards can be strong, reliable anchors. Building one, however, can be time-consuming. Practical use of bollards is limited because the different types of T-slot anchors described above are quicker to build and can provide safe snow anchors in a wider range of snow conditions. In hard ice, it would be much faster, easier, and more secure to build an anchor using ice screws or a V-thread.

Build a traditional bollard by making a horseshoe-shaped trench in snow or ice, with the open end of the horseshoe pointing downhill (fig. 16-37a). In hard, firm snow, chop out the trench using the ice-axe adze; soft snow is generally too weak for constructing a bollard because the rope or webbing around it can cut through, resulting in a catastrophic failure. However, snow or ice bollards can be constructed from an existing dense snow or ice formation that can be easily modified so a rope or piece of webbing can be looped around it. Good examples of this situation include moats or the lower lip of a bergschrund or crevasse. Two trenches can be cut a few feet apart from each other and well down into the lip of one of these sturdy, finlike snow formations (fig. 16-37b). A shallow groove can be cut into the back of the snow fin between the two trenches so that the rope or webbing will not slip off when placed around the newly constructed bollard. Similarly, slings can be wrapped around pillars of hard ice

for a strong and easy-to-build anchor (see Figure 17-26 in Chapter 17).

To spread the load and make the rope easier to pull if the bollard is used as a rappel anchor, line the rear and sides of the bollard with natural solid items like flat rocks or branches. If you are concerned about pulling the rope when rappelling, use a long piece of at least 7-millimeter or larger-diameter accessory cord around the bollard.

Ice Screws or V-Thread

When it is necessary to build an anchor on low-angle and gentle slopes in hard ice, use ice screws or a V-thread. See Chapter 17 for ice-screw placement and V-thread construction.

Equalized Snow and Ice Anchors

At least two equalized anchors are standard practice for belaying and rappelling. Equalized snow and ice anchors are independent anchors that are connected to share the load (fig. 16-38). Keep snow anchors several feet apart so they do not share any localized weaknesses in the snow. (For more details on joining multiple anchors, see Equalizing the Belay Anchor in Chapter 10, Belaying, and Equalizing Protection in Chapter 13, Rock Protection.) As with all snow anchors, weight test it, but take care not to injure your back. If the anchor moves, start over and place it deeper or use a different type of snow anchor. Equalize the two snow anchors only after each one has passed the weight

16

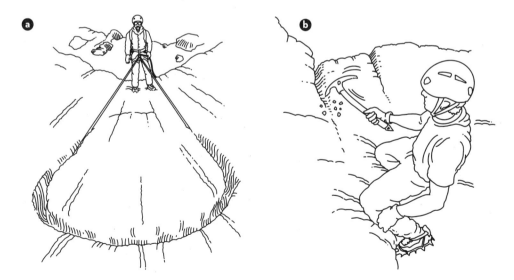

Fig. 16-37. *Bollards:* ***a,*** *traditional bollard cut into firm snow;* ***b,*** *bollard constructed at edge of moat.*

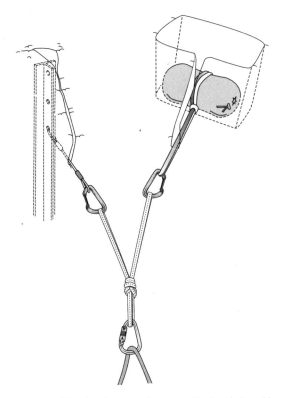

Fig. 16-38. *Equalized snow anchors: equalized mid-clip cable picket and stuff-sack T-slot anchors.*

test. Equalize ice anchors by placing either two ice screws or one ice screw and one V-thread. (Building a V-thread anchor is discussed in Chapter 17.)

Routefinding on Snow

Snow can provide a smooth, uniform surface that is easy to travel on. It can also be too soft to support your weight or hard and perilously slick. It can obscure trails, cairns, rocky ridge crests, and other guideposts to the route, especially above tree line. Dangers often lie beneath the surface: moats, creeks, or glacier crevasses hidden by a thin layer of snow. Unstable snow slopes may avalanche.

Studying the medium will minimize the frustrations and pitfalls of snow travel. For information on snow formation, types of snow, and the creation of glaciers, see Chapter 27, The Cycle of Snow. Learn how seasonal weather patterns affect snow accumulation and avalanche conditions (see Chapter 20, Avalanche Safety). Be aware that with the effects of climate change, weather patterns are more extreme and snow may be icier or nonexistent compared with previous years.

Hone your navigation skills. A skilled routefinder uses a variety of tools, including map, compass, altimeter, GPS device (see Chapter 5, Navigation and Communication), wands, the sun, and visual landmarks. Make the snow work for you: read the snow surface and terrain features to determine a safe, efficient route.

SURFACE CONSIDERATIONS

The best snow to travel on will support climbers' weight, as well as be stable enough not to avalanche (see Chapter 20). The location of the best snow varies from day to day, even from hour to hour. If the snow in one spot is too slushy, hard, or crusty, look around: there may be better snow a few feet away. Here are some tips for making the best use of the snow surface:

- **A slushy slope.** Walk in shade or find patches of firmer snow.
- **A slope that is too firm to kick useful steps into.** Try to find patches of softer snow or use crampons.
- **Postholing.** Detour toward any surface nearby that looks firmer, or possibly use flotation equipment like skis or snowshoes.
- **Depressions that may indicate a stream under the snow.** Stay on thicker snow and use caution.
- **South- and west-facing slopes in the northern hemisphere.** These areas catch the heat of afternoon sun and consolidate earlier in the season and more quickly after storms. When not unstable from wind loading or solar effect, they offer hard surfaces when north- and sometimes east-facing slopes are still soft and unstable.
- **Firm crusts on open slopes.** Take advantage of these crusts before they melt. Get an early start after a clear, cold night that follows a hot day.
- **Hidden holes next to logs, trees, and rocks.** Beware of places where snow has melted away from these warmer surfaces.
- **Unfavorable conditions on one side of a terrain feature.** Try the other side of a ridge, gully, clump of trees, or large boulder—the difference may be considerable.
- **Questionable firmness.** When in doubt, use the ice-axe spike to check the snow's firmness.
- **Much softer conditions than on the ascent.** When descending, look for the best snow; use a different route if necessary.

VISIBILITY CONSIDERATIONS

Using several routefinding methods creatively becomes especially important when visibility is poor. In a whiteout, it is possible to become disoriented. You may be unable to distinguish between uphill and downhill and between solid snow and dense clouds. A whiteout can be caused by cloud cover or blowing snow that limits visibility and makes navigation challenging or hazardous.

A GPS device can keep a party on track even when visibility is poor. Without GPS in a whiteout, get out a map, compass, and altimeter to navigate. Other options include placing wands, waiting for the weather to clear somewhat before proceeding, or turning back.

TERRAIN FEATURES

Major terrain features present obstacles as well as opportunities. Know which landmarks to use and which to avoid. In addition to crevasses (fig. 16-39j), which are covered in Chapter 19, some of these features are described below.

Snow Ridges

A snow ridge (fig. 16-39bb) may be the route of choice if it is not too steep, corniced, or composed of very soft snow. Snow ridges are generally free of rockfall and avalanche hazard. However, snow ridges take the full brunt of wind and bad weather.

Cornices

Cornices form when windblown snow accumulates horizontally on ridge crests, hanging suspended out past the supporting rock (fig. 16-39d). The shape of a ridge and the amount and direction of wind and snowfall determine the size of the cornice that can develop. A ridge that slopes on the windward side and breaks into an abrupt cliff on the leeward side is a good candidate for a gigantic cornice. A knife-edge ridge (where snow usually doesn't accumulate) or a ridge that is gentle on both sides (where snow can disperse) typically has only a small cornice, if any at all—although exceptions do exist.

When the physical features are right for building cornices, wind direction decides the exact location of the cornice. Because storm winds have definite patterns in each mountain range, most cornices in the same area face the same way. In the Pacific Northwest region of the United States, for example, most snowstorms come from the west or southwest, so most cornices form on the north and east sides. These same northern and eastern exposures were made steep by past glaciation, creating ridges ideally shaped for cornice formation.

Cornices are a hazard. They can collapse spontaneously, triggering large avalanches on the slopes below. If climbers are traveling on a corniced ridge, it is easy to wander onto an unsupported cornice that could collapse under the added weight, or the climbers could fall through it. Cornices can separate slightly from their host ridge, forming a crack or cornice crevasse. (See Figure 20-3 in Chapter 20, Avalanche Safety.)

The safest course along a corniced crest is well behind the unsupported cornice and probable fracture line. Do not be misled by appearances. On a mature cornice, the probable line of fracture could be dozens of feet or more back from the lip—farther back than might be expected on examination. Usually the fracture line is not visible. Look for any crack or indentation in the snow, which might indicate a cornice that has partially collapsed along the edge of the supporting ridge below.

Warm weather can cause cornices to collapse. If possible, avoid traveling under them.

Approaching from windward. The back side of a cornice appears to be a smooth snow slope that runs out to meet the sky. Look at nearby ridges for an idea of the frequency, size, and location of cornices in the area. Try to view the lee side of the ridge from a safe vantage point, such as a rock or tree jutting through the crest.

Although rocks and trees projecting from the snow can be safe, they do not indicate a stable route between them across the entire ridge. These protrusions can easily be on the tops of buttresses that randomly jut out perpendicular to the ridge (fig. 16-39w). The area directly in front of and between these outcroppings may be all cornice. Many climbers have had the enlightening experience of looking back along a ridge only to discover that their tracks go along the top of an unsupported cornice.

When approaching from windward, stay well back from the crest if a cornice is suspected. If the crest must be approached, consider belaying the lead climber, who should probe carefully with an ice axe or ski pole while advancing.

Approaching from leeward. A cornice cannot be missed from the leeward side, where it resembles a wave frozen as it is breaking. If a cornice's stability is doubtful, do not travel below it.

Occasionally it may be necessary to climb directly through a cornice to attain a ridge crest or pass. The lead climber should cut straight uphill at the point of least overhang, carefully tunneling and upsetting as little of the mass as possible.

16

Fig. 16-39. *Alpine terrain features.*

ALPINE FEATURES

a. Horn or aiguille
b. Rock ridge
c. Rock arête
d. Cornice
e. Glacier basin
f. Seracs
g. Fallen seracs
h. Icefall
i. Glacier
j. Crevasses
k. Lateral moraine
l. Snout
m. Moraine lake
n. Terminal moraine
o. Glacial runoff
p. Erratic blocks
q. Rock band
r. Shoulder
s. Col
t. Couloir or gully
u. Hanging glacier
v. Bergschrund
w. Buttress
x. Cirque or bowl
y. Headwall
z. Flutings
aa. Ice wall
bb. Summit of snow ridge
cc. Ice arête
dd. Towers or gendarmes
ee. Avalanche chute
ff. Avalanche debris
gg. Snowfield

16

Couloirs

Couloirs—steeply angled gullies (fig. 16-39t)—can provide a main avenue to the summit. Their overall angle is often less than that of the cliffs they breach, offering technically easier climbing. Couloirs are also the deadly debris chutes of mountains (fig. 16-39ee): snow, rocks, and ice blocks that become loose fall down couloirs naturally (fig. 16-39ff). Here are some tips for using couloirs:

- **Try to be out of couloirs before the sun hits them.** Couloirs are often safer in early morning when the snow is solid and rocks and ice are frozen in place.
- **Stay on the sides of the chute.** Spend as little time as possible in the center, where most of the debris comes down.
- **Listen for suspicious sounds from above.** Listen for slides and falling rock.
- **Examine a gully carefully before ascending it.** Couloirs can become steeper and have moats (see below), rubble strewn loosely over smooth rock slabs, thin layers of ice over rock, and cornices at the top. Determine if slopes connected to the couloir higher up may be in the sun sooner than the couloir itself. Many avalanche incidents in couloirs arise from a failure to consider or assess the snow stability higher up.
- **Bring crampons.** Deeply shaded couloirs may retain a layer of ice year-round. Early in the season, they are covered by hard snow and ice, caused by freezing or avalanche scouring. Later in the season, climbers encounter the remaining hard snow and ice, sometimes with steep moats lining the edges.
- **Observe snow and avalanche conditions above steep gullies and on their floors.** Avalanches scour deep ruts in the floors of many steep couloirs. Cornices can hang above. The floors of the ruts may offer the soundest snow available, and in cold, stable weather, the risk from falling debris may be low. But if favorable conditions do not exist, cross the ruts rapidly or avoid them altogether.
- **On the way up, look for alternative descent routes.** If snow conditions change, descending the couloir may be too risky on the return.
- **Research the area beforehand.** It can be challenging to find the correct couloir on a particular route. They often look alike, and there may be several in the area.

Rely on route information and your knowledge of the terrain to choose the one that gives access to the summit rather than leading to a dead end.
- **Beware of meltwater streams running above or underneath the snow.** Listen for water. Look for sagging snow or holes in the snow where there may be a stream and a risk of falling through the snow. Walk on the gully's sides and avoid any water; it may be slick with ice.
- **Carry avalanche rescue gear** when in avalanche terrain.

Bergschrunds

The giant crevasse found at the upper limit of glacier movement, formed where the moving glacier breaks away from the permanent snow or ice cap above, is called a bergschrund (fig. 16-39v). A bergschrund's downhill lip can be considerably lower than its uphill edge, which may be overhanging. (For more information, see Chapter 19, Glacier Travel and Crevasse Rescue.)

Moats

Where snow partially melts and settles away from warmer rocks or trees, a moat forms. Moats are encountered on snowfields (fig. 16-39gg), around rock outcroppings (fig. 16-39q) and trees, on ridges and along slopes, and in couloirs. Crossing a moat at the top of a snowfield where it separates from the rock can be difficult.

Moats can form around trees and rocks, and there may be an unstable layer of snow covering a hole. Stay away from treetops poking through the snow, and probe uncertain areas with an ice axe before stepping onto them. If a wide moat borders both sides of a slope in a steep couloir, it may indicate an equally wide moat at the head of the gully. Climbers may have to cross it or retreat and find an alternate ascent.

Rockfall

Snowfields, glaciers, and couloirs are subject to rockfall generated from bordering walls and ridges. Wear helmets in hazardous areas. Try to schedule climbs for less-dangerous periods. Early-season outings can face less rockfall than summer climbs because seasonal snow still cements loose rock in place. In the northern hemisphere, southern and eastern slopes get the sun first, so climb these slopes early. Sometimes shaded northern exposures can offer less rockfall danger.

TRAVEL CAREFULLY ON SNOW AND ICE

Snow and ice change constantly. Traveling across them without mishap requires alertness, preparation, and constant vigilance. Remember these points to minimize your risk:

- **Climb in balance and do not fall.** If a slip occurs, go into a position that doesn't allow a fall to begin (see Figures 16-23 and 16-24). It is important to prevent falls because if a fall occurs and becomes out of control it may be difficult to self-arrest.
- **Continually assess the runout and snow and ice conditions.** If a runout looks hazardous, consider roping up or choosing another route.
- **Do not climb unroped if the runout is dangerous or unknown.** If climbers are uncomfortable with the terrain, use a running belay or an anchored belay, or turn back and find another route.
- **Do not get caught in an avalanche.** Understand snow conditions and avalanche potential, and carry avalanche rescue gear if avalanche conditions exist (see Chapter 20, Avalanche Safety).
- **Do not climb under overhead hazards like unstable cornices or seracs.** Overhead hazards can release without warning and injure or wipe out any climbers beneath.
- **Monitor weather forecasts and climb when conditions look favorable.** (See Chapter 28, Mountain Weather.)

Forecasts are often inaccurate. Be prepared for a storm and be able to navigate in a whiteout.

- **Bring crampons on snow and ice climbs, even in warm weather.** Even if the snow surface is soft, you may encounter a shady couloir or slope with unexpected ice or hard snow.
- **Wear gloves on snow or ice where it may be necessary to perform a self-arrest or team arrest.** Wear gloves even when the weather is warm and it would be more comfortable to take them off.
- **Continually observe the party's overall condition and climbing ability.** Exhaustion can diminish reaction time and cause mistakes.

Practicing for the Freedom of the Hills

Ascending low-angle and gentle snow and ice to reach a climbing objective is one of the most rewarding experiences in the backcountry. In summer, encountering snow can be delightful, while winter snow creates a wonderland-like experience. The basic techniques discussed in this chapter can help you be more efficient, confident, and secure while traveling over low-angle and gentle snow and ice, enabling you to revel in the freedom of the hills.

16

CHAPTER 17

TECHNICAL SNOW AND ICE CLIMBING

The steep gullies, mixed climbing, and summits of many alpine peaks harbor challenging and thrilling terrain, including moderate, steep, very steep, vertical, and overhanging slopes. Climbers exploring this realm need specialized techniques and equipment to minimize their risk while climbing technical snow and ice.

Technical snow and ice climbing is complex and involves considerable risk, primarily because the strength and stability of snow and ice vary greatly. It's critical to learn how conditions affect the techniques used for ascending and descending and how to avoid getting swept away by an avalanche. (See Chapters 20, Avalanche Safety, and 27, The Cycle of Snow, for descriptions of different types of snow and ice and avalanche risks.) This chapter explores the equipment, techniques, and roped systems used to climb technical snow and ice steeper than 30 degrees.

The techniques used to climb different types of technical snow and ice at different angles, along with the necessary skill level, are shown in Table 17-1. As the table indicates, there are several options for which movement technique to use. Choosing the best technique for the situation depends on a climber's experience, skill, conditioning, and degree of fatigue, as well as the consequences of a fall. On the same descent, a skilled climber might face out and scurry down while a climber with a different skill level faces in and descends methodically. Less experienced climbers can reasonably decide to use a slower technique if it provides them greater security and comfort. Meanwhile, watching more experienced climbers as they move over the same terrain using alternate techniques with efficiency and confidence can be motivating and educational. Note that expert techniques are beyond the scope of this book.

Descriptions and illustrations of techniques for climbing technical snow and ice are found later in this chapter. Basic techniques for climbing low-angle and gentle snow and ice are discussed in Chapter 16, Basic Snow and Ice Climbing (see Table 16-1); climbers should master these basic skills before learning how to climb technical snow and ice. Managing the risk from dangers like rockfall or snow or ice avalanches, poor protection, stormy weather, the potential for a leader fall, getting stranded, or insecure rappel anchors

are discussed in Chapter 23, Risk Management. Knowing how to manage these kinds of complex situations comes from years of experience, usually beginning under the mentorship of a guide or skilled teacher.

Equipment

Refinements in equipment have helped technical snow and ice climbers expand their capabilities and take on greater challenges. Manufacturers have been producing a steady stream of specialized and innovative clothing, boots, crampons, snow and ice tools, and protection tailored to technical snow and ice. (See Chapter 16, Basic Snow and Ice Climbing, for a general description of ice axes and crampons.)

CLOTHING

Clothes for snow and ice climbing should provide both comfort and function. Employ a layered system appropriate to the conditions, and ensure that the layers work together. Clothing manufacturers regularly develop new fabrics and designs that dissipate excess body heat while offering warmth, water repellency, and wind protection. Choose clothing designed to move as you move. See Chapter 2, Clothing and Equipment, to learn more about technical climbing clothes for various conditions. Two items deserve additional information related to technical snow and ice climbing: handwear and gaiters.

> **KEY TOPICS**
>
> **EQUIPMENT**
> **TECHNICAL SNOW AND ICE TECHNIQUES**
> **ROPED SYSTEMS**
> **CLIMBING STEEP SNOW AND ICE**

Handwear

When you are climbing technical snow and ice, proper handwear is as important as ice tools and crampons. Handwear must provide a balance between dexterity and warmth. Your hands need protection from dampness, cold, and abrasion, but the type of handwear you choose depends on the difficulty, steepness, and conditions of the ice or snow.

Ill-fitting handwear is dangerous on steep terrain. Too loose a fit (the wrong size or too much insulation) prohibits a proper grip on ice tools; too tight a fit (the wrong size or underinsulation) leads to cold or numb hands. Climbing steep, deep snow on a cold day and repeatedly plunging snow and ice tools and hands under the surface calls for a well-insulated pair of gloves or mitts with waterproof taped seams or an internal waterproof, breathable liner. When ascending steep to overhanging snow and ice, the best choice is gloves with a comfortably snug fit, just enough insulation to keep hands reasonably warm, and material on the palms and fingers with enough friction to allow a slip-free grip on ice tools. These snug, minimally insulated gloves provide dexterity to grip tools, place screws, or manipulate gear. It takes experience to pick the right handwear for the situation.

Some climbs may demand several different pairs of gloves or mitts. For example, on long, cold technical routes, climbers often choose a lightweight pair of gloves or liners for the nontechnical approach, a pair of snug, thin gloves for climbing—plus a spare in case those get wet or lost—and a thick, warm pair of gloves or mittens to keep hands warm at belays or rests.

Gaiters

Few technical snow and ice climbers use full-length gaiters. This is because many modern pairs of climbing pants feature either an integrated gaiter, hooks or straps that go under the boot so the pant leg itself acts as a gaiter, or pant cuffs that fit close enough to the boots so that gaiters are not needed. Some climbing boots also have a built-in gaiter. Reinforced material on the lower part of the pants or hardshell pant legs minimizes abrasions and snags from crampon points.

Full-length gaiters may, however, be useful in deep snow or very cold temperatures. Make sure they fit your boots securely, can accommodate the layers of insulation you wear on your legs, and mesh well with your crampon attachment method.

BOOTS

When selecting boots, get a precise fit. Toes should have a little wiggle room, but the instep and heel should be snug.

There should be no heel lift inside the boots to prevent blisters and reduce calf stress when front-pointing or walking. The instep should be snug and secure but not so tight over the top of the foot that it impedes circulation to the toes. Freedom to rotate the ankle is critical; boots must permit sufficient lateral range of motion but still be supportive. Be sure to fit boots to accommodate your preferred sock system. Spend time breaking in your new boots—and your feet—gradually building up miles before taking them out for a longer excursion.

Modern mountaineering boots intended for technical snow and ice climbing have molded toe and heel grooves or lips, called welts, to accommodate clip-on crampons. Boots used for extensive front-pointing must have very stiff soles to provide a platform to stand on when front-pointing, to prevent overstressing the crampon frame, and to keep the foot from twisting out of a clip-on crampon binding. Boot toe and heel welts should be wide enough so that the crampon toe bail and rear heel clip stay firmly clamped. Note that repeated abrasion from alpine rock climbing can wear the toe welt on the boot down so that it becomes too small to safely accommodate clip-on crampons.

For alpine ice climbing in moderate to cold conditions, modern leather or high-performance synthetic mountaineering boots are the best choice. Leather boots are typically heavier but are more durable and will last longer if properly cared for, while synthetic leather and fabric boots are generally lighter but less durable than leather boots. For extreme cold or at high altitude, double boots with a removable insulated liner provide extra warmth. The outer and inner boot materials on modern double boots are an ever-changing combination of innovative fabrics, foams, and insulation materials; some even feature carbon fiber midsoles. As mountain-boot technology advances, there are ever-lighter and better options each year.

TECHNICAL SNOW AND ICE CLIMBING CRAMPONS

Crampons intended for technical snow and ice climbing are generally heavier and can withstand more wear than those described in Chapter 16, Basic Snow and Ice Climbing. Crampon manufacturers specify the intended use for different models in their marketing materials. Technical snow and ice crampons usually have either hybrid vertical-horizontal or vertical front points that are often removable. Removable front points allow you to replace them if they wear out from climbing on rock, which is more economical than having to replace the entire front half of each crampon if they have fixed front points. Removable

17

TABLE 17-1. TECHNIQUES FOR TECHNICAL SLOPE ANGLES IN DIFFERENT CONDITIONS

SLOPE ANGLE	CONDITIONS	ASCENDING: BOOTS	ASCENDING: ICE AXE OR ICE TOOL	DESCENDING: BOOTS	DESCENDING: ICE AXE OR ICE TOOL	EXPERIENCE LEVEL AND COMMENTS
Moderate: 30° to 45°	Soft snow	Step-kick, with or without diagonal ascent; with crampons	Cane, self-arrest, stake, or cross-body position (see Ch. 16)	**Facing in and backing down:** step-kick, front-point, or hybrid technique with crampons. **Facing out:** plunge-step or diagonal descent with crampons.	**Facing in and backing down:** stake, low-dagger, or middle-dagger position. **Facing out:** self-arrest or cross-body position (see Ch. 16).	Intermediate skills required. Avalanche potential (see Ch. 20).
Moderate: 30° to 45°	Hard snow	French technique, front-pointing, or hybrid technique; with crampons	Cane, self-arrest, or cross-body position (see Ch. 16); low-dagger, middle-dagger, or traction position	**Facing in and backing down:** front-point or hybrid technique with crampons. **Facing out:** French technique with crampons. Consider rappelling.	**Facing in and backing down:** low-dagger, middle-dagger, or traction position. **Facing out:** self-arrest or cross-body position (see Ch. 16). Consider rappelling.	Facing in on descent is an intermediate skill that provides added security compared with facing out, which is a more difficult advanced skill. Self-arrest may be difficult or impossible.
Moderate: 30° to 45°	Hard ice	French technique, front-pointing, or hybrid technique; with sharp crampons	Cane, self-arrest, or cross-body position (see Ch. 16); traction position	**Facing in and backing down:** front-point or hybrid technique with sharp crampons. **Facing out:** French technique with sharp crampons. Consider rappelling.	**Facing in and backing down:** traction position. **Facing out:** self-arrest or cross-body position (see Ch. 16). Consider rappelling.	Facing in on descent and backing down for more than a short distance is an advanced skill. French technique while ascending is an advanced skill, and while descending is an expert skill. Impossible to stop a fall with self-arrest.
Steep: 45° to 60°	Soft snow	Step-kick, with or without diagonal ascent; with crampons	Stake position	Back down using step-kick, front-point, or hybrid technique with crampons. Recommend rappelling.	Back down using stake, low-dagger, or middle-dagger position. Recommend rappelling.	Do not face out. Facing in and backing down is an advanced skill. Recommend rappelling. Avalanche potential (see Ch. 20).
Steep: 45° to 60°	Hard snow	Front-point or hybrid technique; with crampons	Low-dagger, middle-dagger, or traction position	Back down using front-point or hybrid technique with crampons. Recommend rappelling.	Back down using low-dagger, middle-dagger, or traction position. Recommend rappelling.	Do not face out. Facing in and backing down is an advanced skill. Recommend rappelling.

TABLE 17-1. TECHNIQUES FOR TECHNICAL SLOPE ANGLES IN DIFFERENT CONDITIONS						
SLOPE ANGLE	**CONDITIONS**	**ASCENDING: BOOTS**	**ASCENDING: ICE AXE OR ICE TOOL**	**DESCENDING: BOOTS**	**DESCENDING: ICE AXE OR ICE TOOL**	**EXPERIENCE LEVEL AND COMMENTS**
Steep: 45° to 60°	Hard ice	Front-point or hybrid technique; with sharp crampons	Traction position	Back down using front-point or hybrid technique with sharp crampons. Rappel; see comments.	Back down using traction position. Rappel; see comments.	Do not face out. Facing in and backing down is an expert skill. Rappel on hard ice where it's easier to get good anchors.
Very steep: 60° to 80°	Soft snow	Step-kick or front-point; with crampons	Stake or traction position	Rappel	Rappel	Climbing and descending very steep, soft snow requires expert skill and techniques, some of which are beyond scope of book. Avalanche potential (see Ch. 20).
Very steep: 60° to 80°	Hard snow	Front-point or hybrid technique; with crampons	Middle-dagger or traction position	Rappel	Rappel	Advanced skill
Very steep: 60° to 80°	Hard ice	Front-point or hybrid technique; with sharp crampons	Traction position	Rappel	Rappel	Advanced skill; anchors easier to build than in soft or hard snow.
Vertical	Soft snow	Step-kick or front-point; with crampons	Stake or traction position	Rappel	Rappel	Expert skill: See comments for very steep, soft snow. Avalanche potential (see Ch. 20).
Vertical	Hard snow	Front-point or hybrid technique; with crampons	Traction position	Rappel	Rappel	Advanced skill; see comments for very steep, soft snow.
Vertical	Hard ice	Front-point with sharp crampons	Traction position	Rappel	Rappel	Advanced skill; anchors easier to build than in soft or hard snow.
Over-hanging	Snow or ice	Front-point with sharp crampons	Stake or traction position	Rappel	Rappel	Expert skill. See comments for very steep, soft snow.

17

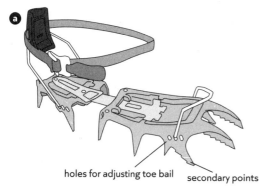

holes for adjusting toe bail   secondary points

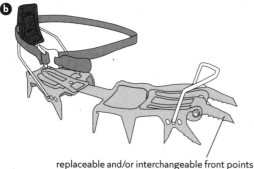

replaceable and/or interchangeable front points

Fig. 17-1. *Technical snow and ice crampons: **a,** with fixed hybrid horizontal-vertical front points; **b,** with replaceable vertical front points.*

front points can usually be adjusted for how far they stick out and enable the crampon to be configured with either dual or mono front points.

Systems for attaching and fitting crampons to boots are discussed in Chapter 16. Most crampons have a set of holes for attaching the toe bail or toe strap that can be used to adjust how far forward the front part of the crampon is positioned on the boot (see Figure 17-1). This adjustment is important for technical snow and ice climbing because when front-pointing, the front points and the secondary points (the first forward-slanting points on each side of the crampon) must both contact the ice when placed with the foot level. If the toe bail or toe strap is adjusted too far forward, then only the front points will contact the ice. The bail or strap should be adjusted so that the secondary points are even with or protrude slightly past the front of the boot. That way, the forefoot, not just the front points, takes the load. If the toe bail or toe strap is adjusted too far back on the crampon, then the front points and secondary points will protrude too far forward, reducing stability. Having

your weight too far back from the ice when front-pointing can cause severe calf muscle strain.

The front points on all crampons, no matter their intended use, are angled downward, and the secondary points are angled forward. Compared with approach, touring, or general mountaineering crampons—which have front points usually oriented horizontally to give them more purchase in softer snow—technical snow and ice crampons have either hybrid horizontal-vertical (fig. 17-1a) or vertical (fig. 17-1b) front points that are well suited for penetration into hard snow or ice. Vertically oriented front points, with height greater than width, provide less support in soft snow, but when climbers front-point in these conditions the boot toe usually penetrates as well and can provide adequate purchase.

Check to see that all the fastening bolts and nuts on replaceable front points are tight after each use—they often come loose. Check and sharpen the points as necessary before each climb; the harder the ice, the sharper the points need to be. Also check and consider replacing the crampon toe bail on a regular basis, as these have been known to break. See Equipment in Chapter 16 for details on crampon maintenance and sharpening.

ICE TOOLS

As mentioned in Chapter 16, Basic Snow and Ice Climbing, ice axes or ice tools are categorized into three main types: general mountaineering ice axes (intended for low-angle and gentle snow and ice climbing, described in Chapter 16); technical mountaineering ice tools (fig. 17-2a), for use on moderate, steep, very steep, vertical, and overhanging snow and ice; and waterfall ice tools (fig. 17-2b), for use on very steep, vertical, and overhanging snow and ice (see Chapter 18, Waterfall Ice and Mixed Climbing).

QUESTIONS TO CONSIDER WHEN SELECTING ICE TOOLS

Ask the following questions when selecting ice tools:

- Is the tool designed for the kind of climbing I intend to do?
- Does the tool swing and penetrate the ice well?
- If I am going to use the tools for both mixed climbing and dry tooling, do they work well on both ice and rock?
- Can I comfortably grip the tools with gloves appropriate for the conditions and difficulty?

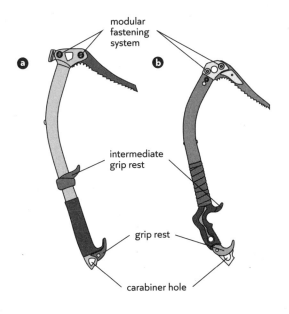

modular
fastening
system

intermediate
grip rest

grip rest

carabiner hole

Fig. 17-2. *Typical ice tools:* **a,** *technical mountaineering ice tool with hammer;* **b,** *waterfall ice tool.*

Technical mountaineering ice tools and waterfall ice tools have bent shafts with a grip rest and usually a spike at the base of the shaft (some waterfall ice tools do not have a spike). While the styles of ice tools vary greatly, the principal parts are the shaft, pick, adze or hammer, and handle or grip rest.

Technical mountaineering ice tools have modular and semimodular heads. On semimodular tools, only the pick is interchangeable. Modular tools have interchangeable picks plus interchangeable hammers or adzes opposite the pick. Being able to replace picks, hammers, and adzes offers flexibility. The tool can be assembled to accommodate different types of climbing, or a broken pick can be replaced in the field. When water-ice climbing, using an adze is not recommended because it's easy to hit yourself in the face, as described below.

There is no standard fastening system on modular ice tools. Components of one manufacturer's system are not compatible with those from another company. The trend has been toward designing fastening systems that require minimal tools, all of which are easy to carry in the field.

The best ice tool is whatever works best for you in terms of weight, technical features, how it swings and feels, and the type of climbing it will be used for most of the time. Try a variety of tools to determine which you prefer. See the "Questions to Consider When Selecting Ice Tools" sidebar.

Shafts

Technical mountaineering ice tools are around 20 inches (50 centimeters) in length and are not designed to perform as well for self-arrest as a general mountaineering ice axe. But on moderate (30- to 45-degree) soft snow slopes, a skilled climber should be able to perform self-arrest with a technical mountaineering ice tool. On moderate hard snow or ice and on slopes steeper than 45 degrees, even a highly skilled climber would find it difficult or impossible to perform self-arrest. Depending on the runout, falling on steeper slopes while unroped can be deadly. If climbers believe there is a chance they could fall, they should use fixed or running belays (see Chapter 16).

Ice-tool shafts are mostly manufactured from aluminum alloy or carbon fiber composites. Bent-shaft ice tools intended for terrain steeper than 45 degrees can reach around bulges and usually keep the climber's fingers from hitting the snow or ice face when swinging the tool. The angles of bent shafts vary. Check to see that the shaft's curve and the swing weight allow good penetration in snow and ice and complement your natural swing. The bent shaft makes hammering pitons awkward; when climbers anticipate a lot of piton work, they often carry a light piton hammer to make that job easier.

To facilitate grip and provide insulation, shafts on technical mountaineering and waterfall ice tools are usually partially covered in rubber, and most technical mountaineering ice tools also have an intermediate grip rest partway up the shaft.

Picks

Nearly all technical mountaineering or waterfall ice tools have a pick with a reverse curve. The ice tool's pick must penetrate ice, hold against a downward pull, and be easy to pull out. The holding and removing characteristics of a pick are determined by its reverse-curve angle, tooth configuration, and thickness. The teeth are shaped to bite into the ice when a climber pulls down on the ice tool's shaft.

Many ice-tool manufacturers produce several types of picks intended for different types of climbing. A thinner pick is intended primarily for pure ice climbing. A thicker pick is more apt to shatter the ice but is also stronger and intended for mixed climbing and dry tooling. Torquing the pick in cracks and other rock-climbing techniques might break a thinner pick. Some picks can be equipped with pick weights that make it easier to penetrate the ice when swinging the tool. Pick weights are used primarily with some tools on waterfall ice (see Chapter 18, Waterfall Ice and Mixed Climbing), and not when it's important to have light gear for alpine ice climbing.

17

When tools are swung into thin ice and the pick inadvertently hits rock underneath, the sharp edge is usually damaged and dulled. They also get worn from climbing on rock in mixed climbing and dry tooling. A dull pick can be sharpened with a file, but once a pick gets filed back to the first tooth, it is time to replace it. A pick lasts longer if it is sharpened only enough to reestablish its original shape and edge. Unless you are an expert, do not use a grinder—it may remove more metal than necessary and could weaken the pick by overheating it.

Hammers and Adzes

At least one ice tool should be equipped with a hammer when you are climbing alpine routes. Hammers are primarily used for driving or testing pitons and pickets. Some manufacturers produce different-sized hammers, providing additional weight for driving pitons but also for easier pick penetration when swinging into ice. Hammers can also be used for clearing loose ice or rock or testing suspect holds.

Ice-tool adzes, used primarily for alpine climbing and not for waterfall ice climbing, come in an array of shapes and sizes. The most common adze is straight, extending perpendicular to the shaft or drooping slightly downward. Some technical alpine routes might require excavating snow to make steps or digging a tent platform in snow, dirt, or gravel, so some climbers prefer to equip one ice tool with an adze. However, use caution when climbing on steep snow or ice with an adze. When you pull on a tool, it can unexpectedly pop out of the snow or ice, or off of a hold, and fly back into your face. If it's equipped with an adze, this sudden movement can cause a nasty gash. Climbing vertical ice with an adze is not recommended.

Handle or Grip Rest

The ergonomic handle at the bottom of the shaft on waterfall ice tools and the grip rest on technical mountaineering ice tools make it easier to climb steep snow and ice and mixed terrain, but they may impede plunging the shaft into snow. Some technical mountaineering ice tools come without a grip rest or have a folding grip rest, which might be a better choice when there is a lot of steep snow. The size and shape of the handle affect your grip and might be too large or too small for your hand, though the grip rest on many models is adjustable. Your choice of handwear also affects your grip (see Handwear, above). Nearly all technical mountaineering ice tools are equipped with either a spike or teeth on the bottom of the grip rest. Waterfall ice tools may or may not have a spike or teeth on the bottom of the

handle (see Chapter 18, Waterfall Ice and Mixed Climbing). Most spikes have a hole (see Figure 17-2) to which a climber can clip a tether (see Figure 17-3).

Tethers

For the most part, climbers no longer use wrist leashes for climbing technical snow and ice, waterfall ice, and mixed terrain. Instead, to prevent the loss of a dropped tool, climbers use a tether (also called an umbilical). A single tether is usually made of an elastic cord with a clip on one end, for attaching to the ice tool, and a loop with a swivel on the other, for clipping to the harness belay loop with a carabiner. Tethers are usually made for two tools and feature two cords and clips that are attached to a single loop and swivel (fig. 17-3). Using a carabiner to attach tethers to the harness makes it easier to move them out of the way while belaying or rappelling, or to remove and clip to the

Fig. 17-3. *A tether, or umbilical, for two tools, attached to harness belay loop with a locking carabiner.*

Fig. 17-4. *Ice screws of different lengths, with a folding knob attached to the hanger.*

rope when seconding belayed pitches. When seconding or top roping with tethers, they should be clipped to the rope and not the harness. If the tethers are attached to the harness and the climber falls with the tools still in the ice, the tools usually get ripped out and can hit the climber and cause an injury. If the second clips the tethers to the rope, a fall won't rip them out and the rope slides through the attachment carabiner (as discussed later in this chapter).

Maintenance

Inspect ice tools before each outing, checking for rust, cracks, and other signs of wear or damage. Be sure that picks are sharp. If the tools are a modular design, check to see that all fastening bolts and screws are tight.

ICE SCREWS

Modern ice screws are made of steel or aluminum with steel teeth, and they come in a variety of lengths ranging from 10 to 22 centimeters (ice screws are commonly measured in metric units). Except for a 10-centimeter screw, ice screws have the same length of thread and are similar in holding strength in reliable ice. Using a longer screw may offer more strength if the threads are able to extend farther into good ice. Modern screws include hangers with folding knobs (fig. 17-4), which you unfold and use like a crank to turn the screw when placing or removing it.

OTHER GEAR

Snow and ice climbers use other gear adapted specifically for this type of climbing, including gear carabiners, head

Fig. 17-5. *Gear carabiner on a harness waist belt with an ice screw racked on it.*

and eye protection, V-thread tools for making ice anchors, and ropes.

Gear Carabiners

Climbers use nonrated specialized plastic or aluminum gear carabiners for racking ice screws or carrying ice tools. Gear carabiners attach directly to the harness waist belt (fig. 17-5) and provide easy, one-handed unclipping when gear is needed. Although plastic gear carabiners are more common, they can break if overloaded or pressed against a hard surface—for example, in a rock chimney on a mixed climb. Metal gear carabiners are less available and more expensive, but they provide a stronger racking system for costly and important items. A full-sized, lightweight oval climbing carabiner can also be used as a gear carabiner by clipping it through a harness gear loop and securing it with heavy rubber bands or zip ties.

Head and Eye Protection

When swinging ice tools or crampons into the ice, climbers dislodge large pieces of ice. To reduce the chance of a serious head injury from falling ice or rock, be sure to wear a helmet. Some climbers wear safety glasses or sunglasses to keep their eyes safe from flying debris; however, in this high-moisture environment, glasses can easily fog up. Some manufacturers make a clear plastic visor that attaches to

17

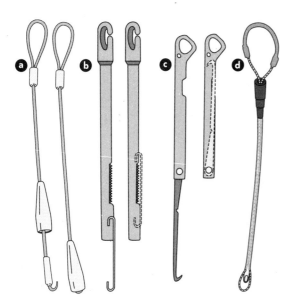

Fig. 17-6. *V-thread tools: **a**, cable hook with rubber sliding hook guard; **b** and **c**, folding hooks that are equipped with a knife for cutting cord and can also be used to clear ice from tubular ice screws; **d**, snare type tool.*

their helmets, allowing airflow and protection for the eyes and face.

V-Thread Tools

On multipitch snow and ice climbs, a V-thread tool is a critical piece of equipment for hooking a rope end, length of cord, or webbing and pulling it through the drilled tunnel of a V-thread anchor (see V-Threads later in this chapter). Each climber should carry one. Several styles of V-thread tools are available commercially (fig. 17-6), and on several models the hook folds up so it does not catch on clothing (fig. 17-6b and c). Some climbers prefer a snare tool, which requires some practice to use but has less potential for damaging the rope ends when making a no-thread anchor (fig. 17-6d). Some budget-conscious climbers make crude V-thread tools from a bent piece of coat hanger wire. Remember to keep a V-thread tool's hook sharp and protect it from catching on clothing or gear.

ROPES

Standard 60- or 70-meter half ropes (see Half- and Twin-Rope Techniques in Chapter 14, Traditional Rock Climbing) are commonly used for technical snow and ice climbing, though the rope length chosen by climbers depends on

the type of climb and their preferences (see also Table 8-1 in Chapter 8, Essential Climbing Equipment). Half ropes are each individually lighter than a single rope, and they allow for full-length rappels on the descent. Half ropes are often used on ice climbs, whereas on rock a larger-diameter rope is usually used because it provides greater resistance to abrasion and cuts from sharp edges. Manufacturers of all ropes, both single and half, continue to develop ropes of increasingly smaller diameters that satisfy international testing standards. These smaller-diameter ropes are much lighter, but the trade-off is that they may be less durable than larger-diameter ropes.

Snow and ice climbing is wet; use water-repellent ("dry") ropes. Compared with untreated ropes, dry ropes retain more strength and are less likely to freeze—though a dry rope can still become coated in ice. It can also be more difficult to stop a fall when belaying or control the rope while rappelling while using untreated ropes that have become wet or frozen. Rope manufacturers use different types of dry treatments. Sheath treatments cover the surface and can wear off, especially if the rope is also used for rock climbing. Sheath treatment plus core treatment, which coats the fibers inside the rope, provides a longer-lasting dry treatment, but these ropes are more expensive. Climbers get more use from snow and ice climbing ropes that have a more durable dry treatment.

Technical Snow and Ice Techniques

Steep snow and ice is complex and varies in strength and consistency, and conditions can change quickly. Many techniques for climbing technical snow and ice are based on those used for lower-angle terrain (see Chapter 16, Basic Snow and Ice Climbing) and are also used for waterfall ice (see Chapter 18, Waterfall Ice and Mixed Climbing).

ASCENDING WITH BOOTS AND CRAMPONS

Different boot techniques and equipment can be used for ascending technical snow and ice, depending on slope angle, snow conditions, and climbers' strength and skill (see Table 17-1). With the possible exception of duck walk (*pied en canard*), the basic techniques described in Chapter 16 for low-angle and gentle snow and ice are also used on technical terrain, including flat-footed (*pied à plat*), step-kick, diagonal ascent, and hybrid technique (*pied troisième*). This chapter describes how these basic techniques can be adapted for steeper slopes, covering French technique (a combination of flat-footed

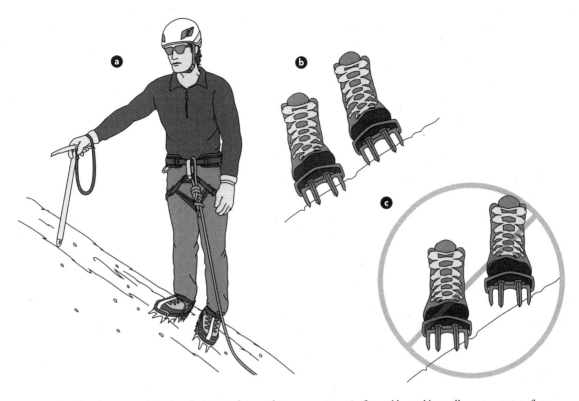

Fig. 17-7. *French technique:* **a,** *French technique with ice tool in cane position;* **b,** *flex ankles and keep all crampon points flat against snow or ice;* **c,** *do not edge with only the inside crampon points.*

17

and diagonal ascent), front-pointing (German technique), and a hybrid technique that uses flat-footed and front-pointing.

Flat-Footed with Diagonal Ascent (French Technique)

The basics of flat-footed and diagonal ascent are discussed in Chapter 16, but as the slope steepens to a moderate angle, the combination of these techniques is commonly referred to as French technique. French technique is an efficient method of ascent for most climbers on 30-degree snow slopes, but as the angle increases to 45-degree hard snow, this becomes a technique for advanced climbers. Only expert climbers should be using French technique on 45-degree hard ice, and in this case it would probably be more efficient to front-point (see Table 17-1). French technique is not appropriate for steep slopes greater than 45 degrees.

Zigzagging up the slope using French technique effectively lessens the slope angle. Well-executed French technique demands balance, rhythm, joint flexibility, and confident use of crampons and ice axe. As a slope steepens, it is important to keep all crampon points weighted into the snow or ice (fig. 17-7a and b). When using French technique, do not edge with the inside points of the crampons (fig. 17-7c). It is even more dangerous to lean into the slope, which can cause the points to skate off hard snow or ice, resulting in a fall. Keep your weight centered over your crampons, and keep the points flat against the snow or ice at all times.

As the slope steepens, rotate the toes of both feet downward, keep the boot soles flat against the slope, and keep your body centered over your crampons (fig. 17-8a). Move diagonally upward in a two-step sequence, bringing the downhill foot up and in front of the uphill foot (fig. 17-8b), then moving the new downhill foot up from behind to place it in front of and above the uphill foot (fig. 17-8c), without snagging the front points on a pant leg. Step on lower-angle spots and natural irregularities in the ice to ease ankle strain and conserve energy.

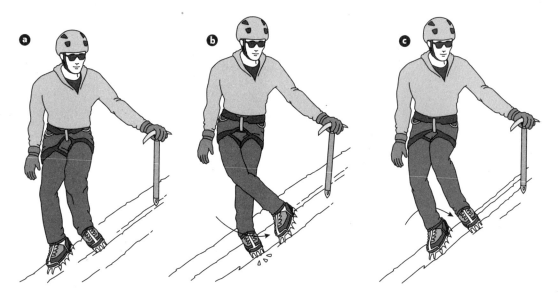

Fig. 17-8. *French technique on a diagonal ascent using a two-step sequence:* **a,** *start from a position of balance;* **b,** *bring downhill foot in front of and above uphill foot;* **c,** *bring downhill foot up from behind and in front of and above uphill foot.*

When using French technique to change direction (switchback) on a moderate slope of snow or ice, use the same technique as described in Chapter 16 for a diagonal ascent on a gentle snow slope (see Figure 16-16).

Practice using French technique on gentle to moderate snow slopes, and when the angle becomes steep enough that climbing flat-footed feels insecure, face into the slope and start front-pointing. However, front-pointing puts more strain on the smaller calf muscles, which burn out much faster, whereas French technique puts most of the strain on the large, powerful thigh muscles. Work to improve your French technique to give your calf muscles a rest. Climbing safely and in control is the highest priority. When the going gets steep enough that you want the security of facing into the slope and front-pointing, never be concerned if others around you are still using French technique. Your primary responsibility to the team is not to fall.

Front-Pointing

Front-pointing (German technique) is very similar to kicking steps straight up a steep snow slope. But instead of kicking a boot into soft snow, a climber kicks the front crampon points into hard snow or ice firmly enough to step up onto them and be supported by them. Front-pointing is the most secure method for ascending steeper hard snow or ice. Well-executed front-pointing is an efficient, rhythmic motion with the body's weight balanced over the crampons'

front points. Front-pointing is easier to learn than French technique: kicking front points straight into snow or ice is easier than balancing flat-footed on crampons while moving diagonally upslope.

Front-pointing uses the crampon's primary front points and the secondary points behind them to penetrate the snow or ice. The front four crampon points, when attached to a rigid pair of boots and placed properly in the ice, provide a stable platform that a climber can stand up on with their center of gravity balanced over the toes (fig. 17-9).

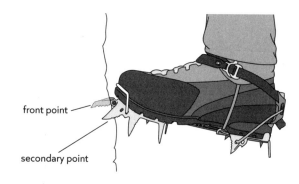

Fig. 17-9. *Front-pointing (German technique): keep toes and front points horizontal, with heels slightly down to engage secondary points.*

When front-pointing, bend your knees, lift your toes, and kick into the snow or ice; at the moment your points hit, your foot should be very close to level. Once the boot placement is made, it's fine to drop your heel a bit to further engage the secondary points and create a stable platform that will reduce the strain on your calf muscles. After making a boot placement, do not raise your heels when front-pointing. This rotates the secondary points out of the snow or ice and pushes the boot toe against the slope, which pulls the front points out and weakens or causes the boot placement to fail. To become comfortable with the essential skills of crampon placement and foot positioning, practice on a top rope with an experienced ice climber who can make suggestions about how you can improve your technique.

Based on snow and ice conditions, determine the amount of force and number of kicks required to secure a firm placement with your front points. Look for any flat places in the slope to kick into that will create a more stable platform to stand on. In good conditions, a single confident leg swing may be all you need. In fractured and hollow snow and ice, it might take several kicks to get a secure foot placement. Kicking too hard and too often in one place is fatiguing and usually isn't necessary for a secure foot placement. After making a crampon placement, avoid foot movement, which can make the points rotate out of the ice.

Hybrid Technique

The hybrid technique discussed in Chapter 16 combines step-kick and duck walk. Adapting this technique for technical snow and ice climbing on steeper slopes with crampons is often called combination technique because it combines flat-footed and front-pointing. As one foot is front-pointing, the other is flat-footed and points to the side (fig. 17-10): to three o'clock if it is the right foot—also called the three o'clock position (*pied troisième*)—or to nine o'clock if it is the left.

The hybrid technique is a less tiring way to make a direct ascent than front-pointing with both legs. The leg that is flat-footed experiences much less calf strain than the leg that is front-pointing. Climbers will reduce overall leg fatigue by alternating which leg is flat-footed. When climbing, seek out flatter areas in the snow or ice surface, or kick a small platform with your crampon points for the flat-footed leg to stand on, allowing those calf muscles to rest.

ASCENDING WITH ICE TOOLS

Different ice-axe or ice-tool techniques can be used to climb technical snow and ice, depending on slope angle,

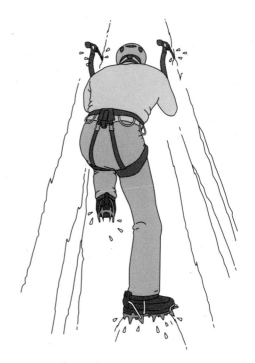

Fig. 17-10. *Hybrid technique: flat-footed (here with the right foot) and front-pointing (here with the left foot).*

snow conditions, and climbers' strength and skill (see Table 17-1). The basic ice-axe and ice-tool techniques described in Chapter 16 for low-angle and gentle snow and ice are also used on technical snow and ice, including the cane position, the self-arrest position, and the cross-body position. In this chapter, these techniques are described again, but only for how they are applied on steeper slopes. This section focuses on techniques used to climb moderate, steep, very steep, vertical, and overhanging snow and ice, which include the stake position, low-dagger position, middle-dagger position, and traction position.

Stake Position

On moderate to vertical slopes with soft deep snow, the primary technique to use with your ice axe or ice tools—for balance or to pull up—is the stake position (fig. 17-11). Face into the slope and reach up with one hand on the head of the ice axe or ice tool in the self-arrest position and plunge the shaft as far as it will go into the snow. Move up by kicking a couple of steps, standing up, and lifting the ice axe or ice tool out of the snow and reaching up and plunging it again into the snow in the stake position. When feeling insecure or in need of a rest or additional security, face into

the slope and place the ice axe in the stake position, shoving it into the snow with both hands, then kick a platform in the snow (this is also known as the self-belay position).

When soft snow is very steep or vertical, climbers should be using two ice tools and the stake position with each arm. Climbing very steep or vertical soft snow requires expert skill and techniques that are beyond the scope of this guide, such as digging, trenching, bridging, and boot packing.

Low-Dagger Position

While front-pointing on moderate to steep slopes with soft or hard snow, hold the axe by the adze or hammer in the cane position, and push the pick into the snow near waist level, to aid balance (fig. 17-12). The low-dagger position (*piolet panne*) tends to hold you away from the slope and out over your feet, the correct stance for front-pointing. This technique is also very useful for down-climbing while facing in on moderate to steep slopes. Low or medium dagger positions are ineffective on hard ice, where good placements can only be made by swinging the ice axe or tool.

Fig. 17-11. *Using ice axe in stake position.*

Fig. 17-12. *Front-pointing with two tools, both in low-dagger position.*

Fig. 17-13. *Front-pointing with ice axe in middle-dagger position.*

Middle-Dagger Position

While front-pointing on moderate to steep slopes with soft or hard snow, wrap your hand around the ice-axe or ice-tool shaft below the head and push the pick into the snow near shoulder or chest level, to aid balance (fig. 17-13). The middle-dagger position (*piolet appui*) also holds you away from the slope and out over your feet, the correct stance for front-pointing. This technique is very useful for moving quickly upward while saving energy by not swinging the axe or tool into the slope. This technique is also very useful for down-climbing while facing in on moderate to steep slopes. Like the low-dagger position, the middle-dagger position is ineffective on hard ice, where good placements can be made only by swinging the ice axe or tool.

Traction Position

The most important ice-axe or ice-tool technique to learn for climbing technical hard snow and ice is the traction position (*piolet traction*). When using the traction position, hold the ice tool's handle or grip rest at the bottom of the shaft and start the swing with the ice tool's head behind and slightly below your shoulder. Swing the tool forward, using your shoulder and wrist to plant the pick in the snow or ice. Climb up by pulling straight down on the tool or axe while front-pointing (fig. 17-14). More information on swinging ice tools can be found in Chapter 18, Waterfall Ice and Mixed Climbing.

On moderate to steep slopes, climbers usually feel confident using *piolet traction* with a single tool. But on steep to overhanging slopes, it is nearly impossible to balance on front points and not fall while removing and then replanting a single tool. On slopes of this angle, it is necessary to use a second ice tool. Using two tools provides three points of support—for example, two crampons and one ice tool while you plant the second tool, or two ice tools while you move one foot up. The placements must be secure so that

Fig. 17-14. *Front-pointing with ice axe in traction position* (piolet traction): *pull straight down on the tool.*

Fig. 17-15. *Front-pointing using two tools in the traction position* (piolet traction): *both feet and the left ice tool provide three points of support while the right hand makes a new ice-tool placement.*

17

if one of the three points of support fails, the other two will hold you until you replace the third point. Your legs carry most of the weight, but your arms help with both weight-bearing and balance (fig. 17-15). More information on ascending steep to overhanging snow and ice can be found in the next section.

When using *piolet traction*, minimize fatigue by establishing a solid placement with a minimum number of swings. Learning tool placement takes practice, especially when swinging with your nondominant arm. Learning proper swing technique and using tools designed for climbing steep snow or ice enables swift and precise tool placements that are both secure and easy to remove. (For more on swing technique, and on tool placements and how they are affected by different snow and ice conditions, see Chapter 18.)

Removing the Tool

In addition to learning how to place a tool, climbers must learn the best way to remove it. Normally the tool is easily removed by pulling the handle or grip rest away from the ice and pushing it back in to disengage the teeth, and then sliding the pick up and out. If the tool penetrates the snow or ice too deeply, removing it can be more tiring than placing it. Try to loosen a stuck placement by rocking the handle or grip rest away from and back toward the ice, and then slide the pick up and out. In most cases, that will be enough to free the tool.

Another method for removing ice tools with a handle or grip rest is to hit up against the bottom of the handle with your palm. Use a tether because the tool may suddenly break free from the ice and go flying. If all else fails and you are climbing with two tools, get into a secure position, place a reliable screw, and clip a sling from it into your belay loop. Use one tool to chip away at the surface ice surrounding the stuck pick on the other tool. Then replace the non-stuck tool back into the snow or ice, and retry freeing the stuck tool using the methods described above. Only use this technique as a last resort and carefully chip ice from around the stuck pick. If too much ice is chipped away, the stuck tool placement that you are now using for support (while chipping with the other tool) could fail and cause a fall.

ASCENDING VERY STEEP OR VERTICAL SNOW AND ICE

The most efficient and secure method of climbing extremely steep or vertical hard snow or ice is front-pointing while using two ice tools in piolet traction. The basic position is to keep your hips close to the ice and your back slightly arched, your feet slightly apart and in the front-point position (heels low), and one arm as straight as possible (fig. 17-16).

Fig. 17-16. *Basic position for climbing steep, very steep, or vertical hard snow or ice.*

The basic progression is used for ascending steep, and sometimes very steep, hard snow or ice. Start with your feet slightly apart and level with each other and the tools level with each other, shoulder-width apart, with the handles or grip rests even with your shoulders (fig. 17-17a). Place one tool above your head about 4 inches (10 centimeters) below your maximum reach (fig. 17-17b), then place the other tool at the same height, and maintain the shoulder-width separation from the first tool (fig. 17-17c). With your arms straight, move your butt out and look down while lifting one foot to about the level of the opposite knee and place it

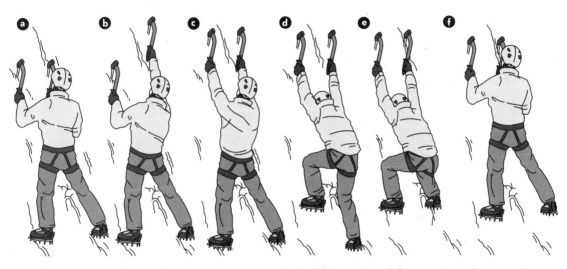

Fig. 17-17. *Basic progression for ascending steep, very steep, or vertical hard snow or ice, with front-pointing and two ice tools in piolet traction: **a,** stand on both crampons with feet slightly apart and both tool handles or grip rests even with the shoulders; **b,** place one tool above your head; **c,** place other tool at same height as first tool, shoulder-width apart; **d,** move butt out, look down, lift one foot, and front-point; **e,** lift other foot and front-point; **f,** pull down on ice tools and stand up to straighten legs and pull hips in.*

using front-pointing (fig. 17-17d), then lift the other foot and place it at the same level as the first foot, heel low with your feet slightly apart (fig. 17-17e).

To move up, pull down on the ice-tool handles or grip rests and stand up on both crampons, straightening your legs and returning to the original starting position with your hips in (fig. 17-17f). Let your legs do most of the work when you stand up; do not burn out your arms by doing pull-ups. Take steps that are small enough so that you stay below your tools—the handles or grip rests should be about even with your shoulders so that you are pulling down on the tools, not out.

Now repeat the sequence. Establish a rhythm that produces an efficient, balanced, methodical placement of crampon points and ice tools. The outline of tool and crampon placements when using the basic progression is shaped like a rectangle. This is an efficient way to climb snow and ice that is less than vertical when most of the weight is carried by the legs. But often when climbing very steep snow and ice—and almost always when climbing vertical or overhanging snow and ice—the advanced progression should be used. On steeper ice, the body weight needs to be centered under the upper tool that together with the feet forms the outline of a triangle. Being in the triangle is accomplished by using the advanced progression described in Chapter 18, Waterfall Ice and Mixed Climbing.

DESCENDING TECHNICAL SNOW AND ICE

Climbers can use different techniques to descend technical snow and ice, depending on the slope angle, the snow conditions, and their strength and skill (see Table 17-1). The basic techniques described in Chapter 16 for descending low-angle and gentle snow and ice are also used, including the plunge step, diagonal descent, and facing in. This chapter focuses on how these techniques are used on steeper slopes, particularly diagonal descent and facing in, which can be adapted to backing down using front-pointing.

Diagonal Descent

Also known as descending using French technique, diagonal descent is usually the easiest and most efficient method of descending gentle to moderate snow (see Chapter 16), but on moderate slopes, it requires intermediate to advanced skills. Descend diagonally flat-footed with the ice axe or tool in the self-arrest position (fig. 17-18). As the descent angle steepens, bend your knees more, with your body weight over your feet so that all crampon points bite securely.

A diagonal descent of hard ice on a moderate slope is precarious, requires expert skills, is impossible to self-arrest, and is not recommended. Diagonal descent on anything steeper than moderate snow and ice is not recommended.

Fig. 17-18. *Diagonal descent of a moderate slope using French technique: flat-footed with ice axe in self-arrest position.*

Backing Down and Front-Pointing

On technical snow and ice slopes, backing down and front-pointing (German technique) generally uses the same techniques as for ascending, described earlier in this chapter. Take smaller downward steps; stepping down too far keeps your heels too high and risks your front points failing. When backing down moderate or steep snow slopes, you can use the ice axe or tool in either the low-dagger (fig. 17-19), middle-dagger, or traction position, but it's often better to rappel (see Table 17-1), even though snow anchors may be time-consuming and difficult to place.

On moderate or steep ice slopes, backing down is possible using the *piolet traction* ice-tool position. But doing this for long distances is slow, tedious, exacting, and dangerous and requires advanced to expert skills. In these icy or steep conditions, it is easier and less risky to rappel unless you are backing down for only a short distance. On very steep, vertical, and overhanging snow and ice, all climbers should rappel (see Rappelling on Technical Snow and Ice later in this chapter).

direction of travel

Fig. 17-19. *Backing down and front-pointing (German technique) on a moderate snow slope with ice axe in low-dagger position.*

Roped Systems

Most climbers usually rope up on technical snow and ice. Depending on the conditions, slope angle, and team expertise, climbers decide whether to belay individual pitches or to climb roped together using running belays, known as simul-climbing (see Running Belays, below). For speed and efficiency, an experienced team may choose to simul-climb on moderate to steep slopes, but on very steep, vertical, or overhanging terrain, the team would most likely belay individual pitches. When a roped team faces a section of technical snow and ice that is impossible to protect, where a fall by one climber would pull the whole team off the slope, they must decide whether to turn around (if that is possible) or to keep climbing but do so unroped. When climbing unroped (soloing), all climbers must be completely confident they can manage the terrain without falling.

PLACING PROTECTION

Snow and ice anchors to protect roped teams on low-angle and gentle snow, such as pickets, T-slot anchors, bollards, and ice screws (see Chapter 16, Basic Snow and Ice Climbing), are also used on technical snow and ice. This chapter describes how to place ice screws, V-threads, and rock gear for protection and or belay and rappel anchors on technical snow and ice.

Ice Screws

In hard ice, strong ice-screw placements for protection or an anchor depend on the quality and depth of the ice. Look for areas where the ice is the thickest and most homogeneous, without cracks, visible air bubbles, air pockets, or voids. Look for flat or concave surfaces where the screw can be placed in solid ice and not in a bulge or formation that might fracture off. An ice screw is only as strong as the ice in which it is placed.

Find a natural resting spot or the most relaxing position from which to place a screw. On continuous low-angle, gentle, and moderate ice slopes, there are usually plenty of places to choose from. On steep, very steep, vertical, or even overhanging ice, find a lower-angle spot or bulge to stand on, to help relieve the calf strain of standing on front points. If high-quality, solid ice is readily available, try to place a screw between waist and chest level to conserve energy. *Note:* When climbing popular ice routes, climbers may encounter old ice-screw holes from previous ascents. If the ice-screw hole is in solid ice, tests have shown that placing a screw in this old bore hole is a secure placement, and it takes less effort, but only if the new ice screw is equal to or larger in diameter than the existing hole, such as an aluminum screw placed in a steel screw hole.

The procedure for placing a screw can vary with ice conditions but is basically as follows:

1. Avoid or chop away any ice that is soft, aerated, cracked, or hollow-looking or that will interfere with placement. On ice topped with a layer of snow or rotten ice, use the pick (or possibly the adze) to chop down to a hard, solid surface (fig. 17-20a). In deep rotten ice, keep chopping or digging down to solid ice that will take a secure screw placement (fig. 17-20b). It helps to create a small starting hole—with the pick on steep ice or the spike on low-angle hard ice—to give the screw's teeth and starting threads a solid grip. Pick a screw length that looks like it will be able to penetrate all the way to the hanger without hitting any underlying rock.

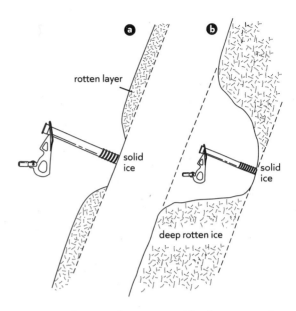

Fig. 17-20. *Ice-screw placements:* **a,** *with soft or rotten surface layer;* **b,** *in deep rotten ice.*

2. Start the screw at a right angle to the ice surface and press the screw in firmly with one hand (fig. 17-21a).
3. Twist the screw a quarter turn clockwise and counterclockwise several times to start a hole with the screw's teeth (fig. 17-21b).
4. Twist the screw a few more turns by hand until the threads are fully engaged in the ice (fig. 17-21c).
5. Use the crank incorporated into the hanger on most modern ice screws to turn the screw in (fig. 17-21d) until the hanger is flush with the ice surface and pointed in the direction of load (see Figure 17-22a). As you turn the screw crank, there should be slight resistance as the teeth cut their way into the ice. If the crank suddenly turns without resistance, the screw has penetrated a void. One or two turns with the teeth inside the void is OK if the screw then offers slight resistance in good ice. If the void is larger than that, it will weaken the placement, so remove it and find a new location with thicker solid ice. If the screw hits rock before it is inserted all the way, remove that screw: select a shorter screw or look for thicker ice. After placing the screw, be sure to rotate the crank back in so it is not a hazard for the rope in the event of a fall.

17

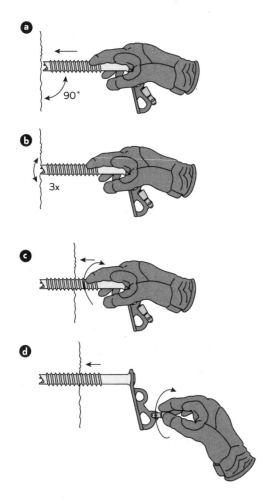

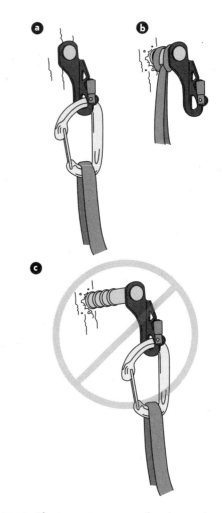

Fig. 17-21. *Placing an ice screw:* ***a,*** *press screw in perpendicular to ice surface;* ***b,*** *twist in and out a few times to start a hole,* ***c,*** *twist a few turns by hand until threads are well engaged;* ***d,*** *screw in with the crank until hanger is flush with ice and facing down.*

Fig. 17-22. *Clipping an ice screw:* ***a,*** *clip a hanger that is flush with the ice;* ***b,*** *girth-hitch a sling to a slightly protruding screw and clip rope to sling;* ***c,*** *do not clip to a screw that protrudes too far (more than ½ inch, or about 1 centimeter) from the ice.*

With practice, climbers should be able to place an ice screw with either hand. It may help to chop or kick a step to stand in while placing the screw. Maintain your body weight on your feet and always hang on to one tool while placing a screw in case the ice underfoot breaks or shifts, which would cause you to lose balance and fall. But do not wear yourself out by overgripping the tool while placing screws.

To use the ice-screw placement, clip a quickdraw or runner in to the screw hanger's eye (fig. 17-22a), then clip the rope(s) to the quickdraw or runner. If a 13-

centimeter-long (or longer) screw protrudes no more than ½ inch (about 1 centimeter) from good-quality ice after hitting underlying rock, girth-hitch a sling around the protruding tube (fig. 17-22b), then clip the sling to the rope—this method should still provide sufficient holding power. If the screw protrudes farther from the ice than ½ inch, do not use this placement (fig. 17-22c)—find another that allows the screw to be fully engaged in the ice.

To remove an ice screw, unscrew it (fig. 17-23a) and then immediately clean the ice from inside its core. The

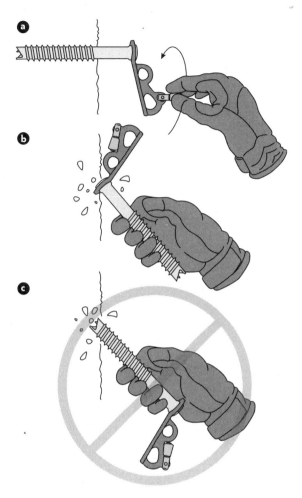

Fig. 17-23. *Removing an ice screw:* ***a,*** *unscrew it;* ***b,*** *clear ice out of its core by banging hanger end against the ice;* ***c,*** *do not bang the teeth or threads.*

screw is not reusable until all the core ice is removed. To remove the core ice, tap or hit the hanger end of the screw against the ice (fig. 17-23b). Do not hit the screw's teeth or threads against anything hard (fig. 17-23c), which can damage them and dull the screw. If the ice inside the screw is difficult to remove, try to melt it out by breathing or blowing into the screw's center (take care not to freeze your lips to the metal) or placing it inside a jacket pocket. Some V-thread tools function as a plunger to help clean ice from inside screws. Some ice climbers use a silicone gun cloth ahead of time to clean and lubricate the inside of their ice screws to make it easier to remove core ice.

V-Threads

Strong and easy to construct, a V-thread anchor requires climbers to leave behind only a short piece of cord (or nothing at all), making it a popular rappel anchor in hard ice. V-threads are generally not used for running belays, leader protection, or belay stations because ice screws are easier and quicker to use in these situations. Also known as the Abalakov, after its originator, a V-thread is built by boring a V-shaped tunnel into ice, pulling accessory cord through the tunnel with a V-thread tool, and then tying the cord to form a sling. The V-thread anchor is only as strong as the ice in which it is constructed. Here are the steps to construct a V-thread anchor:

1. Clear away cracked, rotten, or uneven ice from the surface and screw a 21- or 22-centimeter-long ice screw into the slope, angling the screw about 60 degrees from the surface of the ice (fig. 17-24a).
2. Back this screw out and clear the ice from it, possibly inserting another screw into this hole as a guide to get the angle of the second hole correct.
3. Insert the 21- or 22-centimeter-long screw into the ice 8 inches (about 20 centimeters) from the first hole, angling the screw about 60 degrees from the surface of the ice, to form a triangle or V (fig. 17-24b). Remove the guide screw from the first hole and look inside to make sure the bottom of the hole intersects with the end of the second screw placement.
4. Remove the second screw placement and clear the ice from it. Hold the end of this screw in the opening of one of the holes and blow into it to clear loose ice from the V-shaped tunnel, checking whether ice particles fly out the other hole, which indicates the two holes intersect. Getting the angles correct so that the two holes intersect at the bottom is the most difficult skill to learn in building a V-thread anchor, and it comes with practice.
5. Thread a length of 6- to 8-millimeter accessory cord into one side of the V-shaped tunnel. Use a V-thread tool to fish the end of the cord out through the other side of the tunnel (fig. 17-24c). Try to grab the end of the cord (especially with larger-diameter cord or if pulling a climbing rope), rather than farther back along the cord, which could cause it to double over on itself and be harder or impossible to pull through the other side of the tunnel.
6. Tie the cord to form a sling (fig. 17-24d).

17

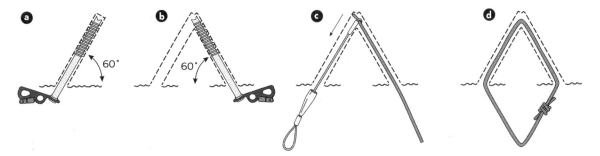

Fig. 17-24. *V-thread anchor:* **a,** *bore first hole with ice screw tilted out to one side at a 60-degree angle;* **b,** *bore an intersecting hole with an ice screw tilted out to the other side at a 60-degree angle;* **c,** *pull a piece of accessory cord through the V-shaped tunnel, using a V-thread tool;* **d,** *tie the cord to form a sling, completing the anchor.*

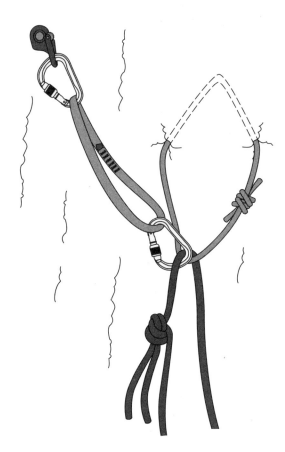

Fig. 17-25. *Backup for V-thread rappel anchor: back up the V-thread with an ice screw that the last rappeller removes before descending.*

To use a V-thread with a sling as a rappel anchor, thread the rappel rope directly through the sling; when the rappel is completed, the rope can be pulled free of the sling. As discussed in Chapters 10, 11, and 13, it is important to have redundant rappel anchors, especially for the first rappeler who applies weight to it. Multiple V-thread placements can be constructed and rigged together to create an equalized anchor point. It's also common practice to place an ice screw above a V-thread anchor as a backup. Clip this screw to a runner clipped to the rappel rope with a small amount of slack so that the ice screw doesn't take any weight from the rappel rope (fig. 17-25). Then the first rappeler(s) can jump-test the V-thread anchor. The last rappeller removes the backup screw and rappels on the single V-thread anchor.

If you do not have any accessory cord to spare or you want to leave no trace, thread the rappel rope itself through the V-thread tunnel (sometimes referred to as a "0-thread" or "naked thread")—but be aware that if the ice or the ropes are wet, the rope can freeze in the V-thread tunnel and get stuck.

Many climbers place the V-shaped tunnel in a vertical rather than horizontal orientation and refer to it as an A-thread. Tests have shown the A-thread to be slightly stronger, but in good ice, either orientation should have adequate strength as a climbing anchor.

Many rappel and/or belay stations on popular ice climbs have abandoned V-thread anchors. As with any other fixed anchor, check it carefully before trusting your life to it. Inspect the sling material for burn marks, wear, or other damage, and check that the knot is secure. Sometimes the knot's free tails may be frozen in place, resembling a secure portion of the sling. Take care! Be sure to rig the rope through the sling instead of these frozen tails. Inspect the integrity of the V-shaped tunnel to be certain it has not melted out, becoming shallow or insecure, or is otherwise damaged. If you have any doubts about the anchor, back it up with an ice screw and jump-test it, add another V-thread and equalize them, or replace it.

Rock Gear and Natural Protection

If rock borders on or protrudes through the route's snow or ice, it may be possible to place pitons, nuts, or camming devices, or perhaps to fix slings around rock horns or other features (see Chapter 13, Rock Protection). Other natural protection, such as sturdy ice columns or other ice formations, may be used by placing a runner around them (fig. 17-26). Sturdy trees may provide similar opportunities for protection. In ice curtains about the thickness of a long ice screw, climbers can drill two holes and thread them with webbing or accessory cord as for a V-thread anchor.

BELAYING ON TECHNICAL SNOW AND ICE

As in other types of roped climbing, technical snow and ice climbers can use either fixed or running belays.

Fixed Belays

Fixed belays for multipitch climbing on technical snow and ice are performed the same way as on rock, and climbers can swap leads on snow and ice the same way they do on rock (see Chapters 10, Belaying, and 14, Traditional Rock Climbing). A standard anchor setup for a snow or ice belay must be as SERENE (Solid, Efficient, Redundant, Equalized, and with No Extension) as a rock anchor (see Chapter 10). Equalized snow or ice anchors can be used for belay anchors (building equalized snow anchors is shown in Chapter 16). In hard ice, at least two ice screws are used for belay anchors and should be placed at least 12 inches (30 centimeters) apart to reduce the danger of fracture lines from one placement reaching the other and weakening both.

Running Belays

Ice screws and V-threads can be used for running belays when climbing technical ice; performing a running belay with snow anchors is described in Chapter 16. Because using running belays sacrifices much of the security of belaying individual pitches, it is not commonly used on technical snow and ice. A running belay is an advanced technique that requires sound judgment based on extensive experience. Newer climbers, looking for time savings, should not use running belays before they have the experience to use them effectively. Running belays require good communication, adequate protection in the system, the skill to manage slack, and the ability to plan ahead for anchor locations and

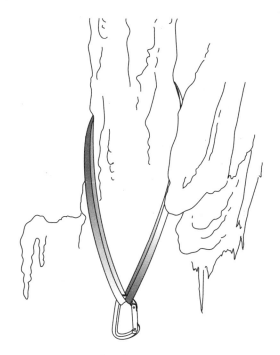

Fig. 17-26. *Runner threaded around a sturdy ice pillar.*

gear requirements, plus the climbers need to possess the skill to not fall. Running belays on technical snow and ice should be considered free soloing, with a rope strictly to protect against catastrophe. As the difficulty of the route changes, the team can easily shift between running belays and pitched climbing with fixed belays.

Anchor Setup

Near the end of a technical snow or ice pitch, the leader needs to keep an eye out for a suitable belay location: a slight depression or a place with less steep snow or ice, where it would be easier to stand or possibly chop out a platform. It's important to choose a belay location off to the side to avoid having the belayer get hit by any falling snow or ice generated by the leader on the next pitch. On steep ice, it may be possible to chop only a simple ledge the width of your foot. Belay the follower directly off the anchor, preferably using an auto-locking belay device (fig. 17-27) or, if a belay device is not available, a munter hitch (see Belaying a Follower in Chapter 10).

When climbing multipitch snow and ice routes with ice-screw anchors, it may be preferable to belay the leader off the anchor using a fixed-point belay. Consider doing this instead of belaying the leader off the harness if the belayer could be slammed into features like a wall or up into the roof of an ice cave in the event of a leader fall. This could seriously injure the belayer and/or cause them to lose control of the belay.

To belay the leader with a fixed-point belay with ice-screw anchors, use a munter hitch on a locking carabiner attached directly to a small 2- to 3-inch (5- to 7.5-centimeter) loop on a 60-centimeter sling created with a bowline. This small loop is also clipped directly in to one ice screw with another locking carabiner so this system is not pulled upward in the event of a leader fall. Back up this primary ice screw with the other end of the 60-centimeter sling clove-hitched to a second screw (fig. 17-28). There is an advanced option to use a belay device

rather than a munter hitch on a locking carabiner—but with this option, the brake end of the rope(s) from the belay device must be clipped through another locking carabiner clipped to the locking carabiner attached to the ice screw until the leader clips the rope(s) through the first piece of protection. This preserves the braking action of the belay device prior to an upward pull. When using a fixed point belay, this first piece of leader protection needs to be as strong as an anchor used in a belay, or

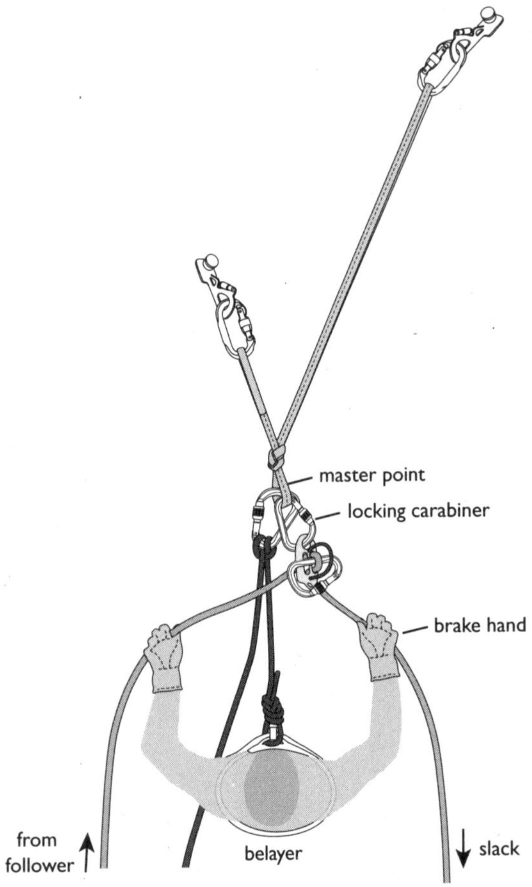

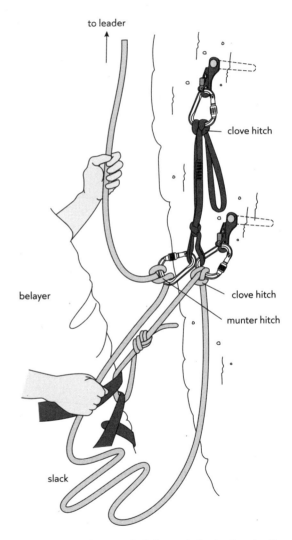

Fig. 17-27. *Anchor setup for belaying a follower directly off the anchor using two ice screws and an auto-locking belay and/or rappel device in auto-lock position.*

Fig. 17-28. *Anchor setup for belaying the leader directly off the ice anchor, using two ice screws and a munter hitch on a locking carabiner.*

the belayer needs to keep the brake end clipped through this locking carabiner until the leader has placed reliable protection that would hold a fall.

RAPPELLING ON TECHNICAL SNOW AND ICE
Deciding when it is preferable or necessary to rappel when descending technical snow and ice depends on conditions, slope angle, and skill (see Table 17-1). The principal considerations for rappelling on snow and ice are the same as for rappelling on rock (see Chapter 11, Rappelling)—to avoid long distances of difficult backing down and to protect against dangerous exposure. It is also essential to build secure anchor placements. The most popular rappel anchor for snow is some type of T-slot (see Chapter 16), and on hard ice it is the V-thread (see earlier in this chapter). The types of equalized anchor setups used for belay stations when climbing technical snow and ice are the same as those used to anchor climbers at rappel stations when descending. When making multiple rappels, the climber leading each rappel must build these anchor setups and use their personal anchor system to secure themselves to it before the next rappeller can come down.

Climbing Steep Snow and Ice

With experience, you will learn to assess conditions and develop the skills and confidence to climb technical snow and ice. Link up with a steady climbing partner and practice together often. Work on ice-tool and crampon techniques. Climbers make risk-management decisions together, such as when to rope up for protection—and when it is more secure not to. If the climbing team disagrees on the appropriate method to minimize risk, they should either default to the least risky option or turn around. Experienced snow and ice climbers learn these skills, continue to hone them, and apply them with confidence and adept judgment so that they can meet the rigors of their chosen routes on technical snow and ice.

17

CHAPTER 18

WATERFALL ICE AND MIXED CLIMBING

As the temperature falls below freezing, liquid water transforms into its solid state, and one result can be the formation of water ice. If the temperature stays below freezing long-term in a place with falling water, ice can accumulate from above and build up from below. Soon these growing ice formations meet and form a sheet or column of chandelier-like ice crystals. The flowing water fills in voids and freezes into a growing monolith.

Water ice can take many forms: smooth and broad sheets, runnels, cauliflower-textured walls, chandeliered curtains, massive ice pillars, and free-hanging icicles. The life span of waterfall ice formations is very brief compared with that of glacial ice. During a single winter's freeze-thaw cycles, waterfall ice can form, collapse, and re-form, only to collapse again when the spring thaw arrives.

Many climbers who enjoy climbing waterfall ice also practice dry tooling: climbing on technical rock with ice tools and crampons. The combination of pure ice climbing and dry tooling, called mixed climbing, has long been part of ascending Scottish gullies in winter and climbing technical routes in the Alps.

When establishing dry-tooling or mixed routes, consider the local ethics. Avoid climbing in culturally sensitive areas and popular rock climbing zones. Since waterfall ice climbing occurs primarily during the winter months and requires travel up steep slopes, in gullies, or below basins, snow conditions are also a big concern. Assess avalanche risk and exercise prudence any time you venture into the backcountry (see Chapter 20, Avalanche Safety).

Waterfall ice climbing and mixed climbing require advanced to expert climbing skills, as well as a reserve of strength. Protection systems are intended to keep a lead climber from falling to the ground, but in most cases these systems would not prevent a serious injury. Falling and catching a crampon on the ice usually results in a fractured ankle or worse. With the exception of steep bolted dry tooling and steep bolted mixed climbing, waterfall ice climbing and mixed climbing are like alpine climbing—the leader should not fall. Leading on waterfall ice and mixed terrain is bold and committing. Be honest about your ability and climb responsibly.

Waterfall Ice Climbing

It is important to lead water-ice climbs within your ability because, as mentioned above, there should be no leader falls. In the following ratings, WI stands for "water ice" and the degrees indicate the angle of the slope, followed by generally accepted descriptions of seasonal waterfall ice climbing conditions.

- **WI1:** Low-angle ice.
- **WI2:** Less than 60-degree ice with one or two body lengths of 60-degree ice.
- **WI3:** Consistent 60-degree ice with possible bulges of 70-degree ice.
- **WI4:** Sustained 70-degree ice with one or two body lengths of 80 to 90 degrees; reasonable rests and good stances for placing screws.
- **WI5:** Continuous 80-degree ice with long sections of 90-degree ice broken up by occasional rests.
- **WI6:** A full rope length of 90- or nearly 90-degree ice offering few good rests; or a shorter pitch of thin or bad ice. Highly technical.
- **WI7:** Overhanging or same as WI6 but on thin, poor-quality, or poorly bonded, or poorly adhered ice.

EQUIPMENT

This section includes a few considerations specific to climbing waterfall ice. For discussions of snow and alpine ice

---

KEY TOPICS

WATERFALL ICE CLIMBING
ICE CONDITIONS AND FORMATIONS
MIXED CLIMBING
CLIMBING ICE

climbing equipment, see Chapters 16, Basic Snow and Ice Climbing, and 17, Technical Snow and Ice Climbing.

Crampons

Manufacturers specify in their marketing materials the intended use for different crampon models. Most technical snow and ice crampons described in Chapter 17 are also adequate for waterfall ice. Systems for attaching and fitting crampons to boots, plus crampon maintenance and safety, are discussed in Chapter 16. Crampons designed specifically for waterfall ice climbing often come in a monopoint configuration (fig. 18-1a) that is adjustable and replaceable and usually can be converted to dual front points (fig. 18-1b).

Ice Tools

Many of the alpine ice tools for technical snow and ice climbing described in Chapter 17 can also be used for waterfall ice climbing. There is considerable overlap between tools designed for technical snow and ice climbing, waterfall ice climbing, and mixed climbing. All these types of tools have modular heads, and each manufacturer makes picks designed for specific purposes that are usually interchangeable within their different models. But for waterfall ice climbing tools, the bent shaft angle can vary: the sharper the bend, the steeper the terrain the ice tool is intended for.

Most waterfall ice climbing tools also come with an ergonomic handle at the bottom, some of which are adjustable

(fig. 18-2a, b, and c), with another grip rest just above the lower one. There are a variety of waterfall ice and mixed climbing tools on the market, each with slightly different characteristics, including grip, degree of shaft bend, weight, and balance. Some have a hammer; some have a spike (fig. 18-2a and d). Try out several models and choose the one that best fits your needs.

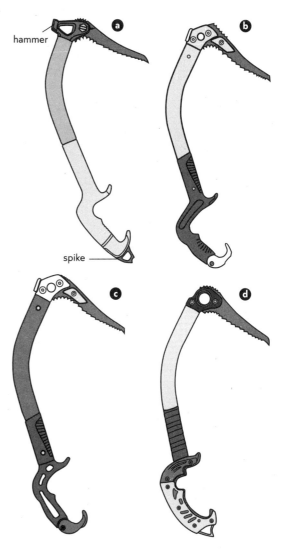

Fig. 18-2. *Modern technical ice tools:* **a,** *ice tool with adjustable handle and removable spike;* **b,** *steep ice climbing and dry-tooling axe with adjustable handle;* **c,** *ice climbing axe with adjustable handle;* **d,** *hammerless ice tool.*

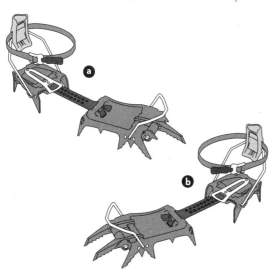

Fig. 18-1. *Crampons with replaceable front points:* **a,** *mono;* **b,** *dual.*

TYPICAL RACK FOR WATERFALL ICE

A typical ice climbing rack for a multipitch pure ice climb might contain some or all of the following gear:

- Two long (19- or 22-centimeter) screws for anchors and/or constructing V-thread anchors

- Eight to 12 ice screws of 17-centimeter or 13-centimeter lengths, depending on the ice's thickness; bring a few 10-centimeter screws if you anticipate encountering thin ice.

- Eight to 14 quickdraws and alpine draws (see Figure 14-4 in Chapter 14, Traditional Rock Climbing)

- Two long runners or cordelettes for equalizing belay anchors

- V-thread tool (see Figure 17-6 in Chapter 17, Technical Snow and Ice Climbing)

- A few pieces of 6- to 8-millimeter accessory cord for constructing V-thread anchors

- Knife (see Figure 8-38) for cutting webbing and cord

- Belay device, locking carabiners, and rappel prusik

Leashes are almost never used on water-ice tools. Without leashes, you can match both hands on a single tool and readily let go of a tool to rest and shake out your arms or to place an ice screw. Climbers, however, may wish to use tethers to prevent the loss of a tool (see Chapter 17).

Protection

Ice screws remain the most common type of protection used on waterfall ice (see Figure 17-4), but in unusual circumstances, pound-in ice pitons, such as the Spectre Ice Piton, are sometimes used. Placing ice screws is described in Chapter 17. Protection placed in nearby rock or slung around natural ice features can also be used, if available, as described in Placing Protection in Chapter 17.

Ice climbers usually rack quickdraws, alpine draws, accessory cord, and rock gear directly on their harness gear loops. Ice screws are usually racked on specialized gear carabiners (see Figure 17-5). When carrying a full rack of ice screws (see the "Typical Rack for Waterfall Ice" sidebar), as well as two ice tools when rappelling, it is helpful to have four gear carabiners—two on each side of the harness.

Clothing and Gloves

Waterfall ice climbing is different from other types of climbing because of the extremes: you are either standing around in very cold temperatures or moving and working hard. Layered clothing systems designed for continuous movement allow climbers to adjust insulation relative to the air temperature and their work-generated heat. But for waterfall ice climbing, you need two climbing outfits: one stripped down and the other well insulated. On the approach, it is easy for a climber to overheat and sweat. Manage your clothing layers, including handwear, to minimize perspiration (see Chapter 2, Clothing and Equipment).

The discussion about handwear in Chapter 17 also applies to waterfall ice climbing. Choosing and managing gloves is hugely important for the waterfall ice climber. Have extra pairs of climbing gloves so that if one pair gets wet, you can readily change into dry ones.

Once you arrive at the route, consider replacing sweaty layers with dry clothing to stay warm as your body cools. After you have stopped sweating from the approach, warm up a thinner pair of ice climbing gloves inside your jacket to wear at the start of the climb (but do not let any sweat remaining inside the jacket get the gloves wet). Experiment with different glove thicknesses to find the thinnest pair that keeps your hands warm for the air temperature. If you stay warm as well as dry, it will be easier to keep your hands warm when climbing. If your body and hands are warm and dry when you start the pitch, yet your hands still grow cold—and even after shaking them out periodically—the gloves are probably too tight and/or the insulation too thin for the conditions.

However, if gloves are thicker than needed, climbers tend to grip harder, which compresses the extra insulation, constricts blood flow, and makes for even colder hands. Thick gloves also cause hands to sweat when climbers are moving—even small amounts of moisture inside gloves will make hands cold. Thick insulated gloves are for keeping hands warm while belaying and standing around.

On multipitch climbs, switch into thick gloves at the belay and put on an insulated jacket (and maybe even insulated pants) to keep your body and hands warm before climbing again. It is common for hands to become very cold after belaying because the body is largely at a standstill. Place ice climbing gloves inside your jacket to warm them before donning them for the next pitch.

WATER-ICE TECHNIQUES

The following sections describe different techniques for using crampons and ice tools and for progressing vertically. Practice at grades you are comfortable with, and gradually move into harder grades when you have gained the necessary confidence and skill. This chapter builds on the steeper techniques for hard ice listed in Table 17-1 in Chapter 17.

Cramponing

Chapter 17 describes the crampon techniques for ascending technical snow and ice of increasing steepness—including front-pointing (German technique)—and details the basic movements. Front-pointing is the primary crampon technique used for climbing waterfall ice and is discussed in this chapter only to the extent that the technique is applied differently on waterfall ice.

Using Ice Tools

The mainstay of footwork on waterfall ice is front-pointing, and the most frequent ice-tool placement is the traction position (*piolet traction*, described in Chapter 17). This chapter builds on the basics of *piolet traction* by providing more information about how to swing the ice tool to make solid water-ice placements.

Experience gained by climbing a wide variety of ice conditions is the best way to develop an understanding of the stability and strength of waterfall ice. At the base of a route, try a few tool placements to get a feel for the ice's density. Is the ice brittle or fractured so that it shatters, requiring several swings to excavate down to solid uniform ice? Or is the ice soft and easy to penetrate for a solid placement with one swing? Ice is less likely to shatter in small depressions than in bulges. Bulges shatter or break off under the impact of an ice tool.

Because swinging tools is tiring, it is important to develop an efficient swing that achieves a secure placement with the minimum number of swings. While gripping the tool handle, have your shoulder, elbow, and hand all in a single two-dimensional plane with the tool head and pick. Keeping your swing's arc contained in this flat plane focuses all the power transmitted by your arm and the moving weight of the tool's head into the tip of the pick as it penetrates the ice. If all these components do not swing in a single plane, the tool will wobble sideways when the pick hits the ice, and the force will go into twisting the tool's shaft instead of driving the pick into the ice. Make solid, planar swings with precision and firmness. At the end of the swing, flip the wrist downward just before the pick hits the ice to give it more force.

Without this powerful motion with every swing, upward progress can quickly fall apart. Poor swings result in excessive swings, causing added fatigue, which leads to more poor swings: a downward spiral that is difficult to recover from and especially frightening and dangerous when a climber is leading. Take your time, do not overgrip, and stay in control. Shake out each arm while climbing to manage strength. When leading, always maintain a margin of strength and never allow your muscles to get pumped to the point of losing grip strength.

Avoid swinging and placing your tools too close to each other, which can fracture the ice, and seek out solid-looking concave surfaces for a place to strike. The surface of some ice formations consists of suspect fragile ice that the climber must clear away before making any potentially trustworthy tool placements in the ice underneath. A solid *thunk*-like sound and a small vibration in the shaft indicate a well-founded placement. Avoid swinging the tool too hard and penetrating the ice so deep that it is difficult and tiring to remove.

After placing the tool and before relying on it, examine it carefully. First, note the pick's penetration depth and whether it entered or created any fractured or weak ice. If so, remove the tool and chop away any suspect ice, then swing into the intact ice beneath. Before pulling hard on a tool placement, test it from a stable stance by loading it with some of your body weight.

PROTECTING THE ICE CLIMB

If you decide that you can climb and protect a pitch safely, keep these tips in mind:

- **Examine the crux(es) carefully.** Figure out the moves before you get up there. Devise both a plan and a backup plan for protecting and climbing through the crux.

- **Once on route, place gear at rests.** Place gear before the hard parts instead of halfway through a crux sequence.

- **Relax, stay in control, and breathe deeply.** These techniques will calm stressed nerves.

- **Shake out.** Never let your arms get so fatigued that you are about to fall. Take your time and manage your arm strength. Holding on to big tool handles or grip rests makes it possible to alternately shake out each arm and regain enough strength to make the next set of moves or to place a screw. If you cannot recover adequate strength to continue safely, it is best to descend.

- **Be prepared to leave some gear behind.** If for any reason continuing to lead poses a serious risk of taking a leader fall, do not hesitate to place a V-thread or leave ice screws or other gear behind to lower or rappel from. Sacrificing gear is a small price to pay to avoid serious injury or worse.

18

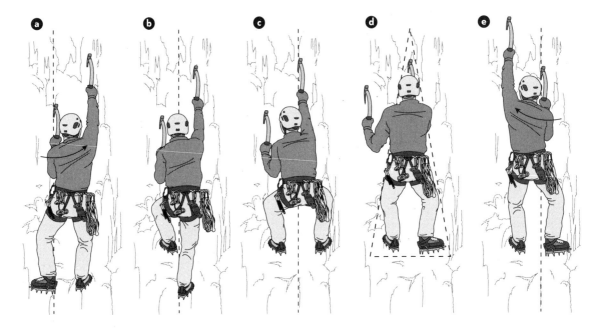

Fig. 18-3. *Advanced progression technique:* **a,** *swing one tool into the ice overhead;* **b,** *move one foot up;* **c,** *move other foot up so you are centered under the higher tool;* **d,** *stand up "in the triangle";* **e,** *remove the other tool and place it overhead with the other hand to begin the sequence again. Dashed lines indicate center of gravity. Arrows indicate direction that center of gravity shifts to be in line with the upper tool.*

Using Advanced Progression

The basic progression for climbing moderate to steep ice is described in Chapter 17 and shown in Figure 17-17. This section discusses advanced progression technique that can be used on moderate to steep ice but should be used on very steep to vertical ice. Unlike the basic progression, the body is centered beneath each ice tool that is placed at different heights in the advanced progression to maintain balance. Also, staggering the tools reduces the number of tool placements, decreasing the workload on the arms and hands.

Swing one tool into the ice overhead, keeping your center of gravity under the tool that remains placed (fig. 18-3a). Move one foot up (fig. 18-3b), then the other, to position your center of gravity beneath the higher tool (fig. 18-3c). Stand up so that you are "in the triangle," with your feet and the higher tool forming an isosceles triangle of three points of contact (fig. 18-3d). Remove the lower tool and place that tool overhead to begin the sequence again (fig. 18-3e).

This general pattern is described for progress on flat, smooth ice. In actual practice, climbers perform variations of this advanced progression based on the ice features they are climbing.

Climbing from Vertical Ice onto Lower-Angle Ice

"Pulling over the bulge" from vertical to lower-angle ice requires a specific technique that is important to learn. It is tempting to pull over onto a potential resting spot before taking the time and energy to chop away unreliable ice and move your feet into the proper position. Climbing from vertical ice onto lower-angle ice requires placing one or both feet high before moving your upper body forward and losing sight of your feet. Swinging tools over a bulge is awkward, albeit easier with bent-shaft tools, and it is often difficult to get solid placements in convex ice that fractures off in layers (dinner-plating; see Dinner-Plate Ice later in this chapter).

The proper technique for pulling over a bulge is to first chop away any dinner-plate or fractured ice in the lower-angle ice above, then place both tools into solid ice, but only as far forward as you can while still being able to look down and see your feet (fig. 18-4a). Lean back, holding on to your tools with straight arms, and move one or both feet up high near the lip where you can still see them (fig. 18-4b). While keeping your heels low, pull your head and torso over the lip while still pulling down and not upward on the tools. Move one tool (or both tools,

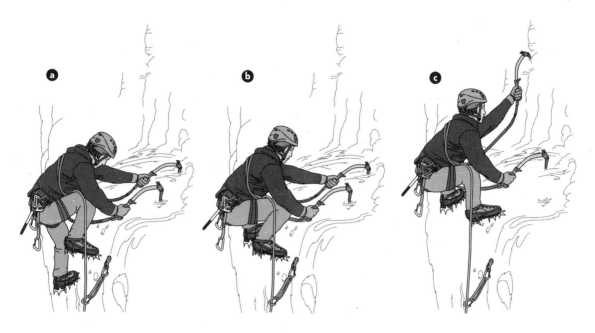

Fig. 18-4. *Pulling over a bulge:* **a,** *plant tools as far forward on a low-angle area as possible while still being able to see your feet;* **b,** *lean back and move feet, still visible, high on the vertical ice near bulge lip;* **c,** *move tool(s) farther forward, and then step over lip onto low-angle area.*

one at a time) farther forward, then move your feet up one at a time onto the lower-angle ice (fig. 18-4c). In some situations, the ice farther forward is nonexistent or too poor to take tools. Then it is necessary to keep your tools in the original position over the lip of the bulge and to mantel (see Chapter 12, Sport Climbing and Technique) onto the lower-angle ice by pushing down on the tops of the ergonomic handles.

Placing an ice screw in the vertical ice near the lip for protection before pulling a bulge, as shown in Figure 18-4, is a sound practice. Being fatigued while executing this maneuver, which requires strength and skill, poses one of the greatest risks of falling when climbing waterfall ice.

Traversing Steep or Vertical Ice

The principles for traversing are much the same as for front-pointing up steep ice. However, because the climber moves to the side instead of straight up, it is more difficult to keep feet perpendicular to the ice. If your heel rotates to either side, the front points will also rotate and come out of the ice. There are two methods for traversing on vertical ice: shuffling the tools and matching on them.

With the tool shuffling method, start from a secure position with both feet at the same level. Lean in the direction of travel and plant the leading tool in the ice (fig. 18-5a), but not so far to the side that it causes your body to rotate out from the wall (barn-door) when you remove the trailing tool. Now shuffle sideways on your front points, first with the leading foot (fig. 18-5b), then with the following foot (fig. 18-5c). Remove the trailing tool and place it closer to the leading tool (fig. 18-5d). Then lean in the direction of travel and replant the leading tool to repeat the process.

The tool matching method is shown in a dry-tooling context (on rock rather than on ice) in Figure 18-8. Traverse as described in the tool shuffling method except after removing the trailing tool, hang it over your leading shoulder and match hands on the leading tool by grabbing the leading tool's upper grip with your trailing hand. Now grasp the tool hanging over your trailing shoulder with your leading hand and place it farther along in the direction of the traverse. Tool matching while traversing vertical ice is more efficient than tool shuffling and saves strength because it uses half as many tool placements.

18

Fig. 18-5. *Traversing on vertical ice with tool shuffling method:* **a,** *plant leading tool to the side in the direction of traverse;* **b,** *shift leading foot to under leading tool;* **c,** *shift trailing foot closer to leading foot;* **d,** *plant trailing tool closer to leading tool.*

Belaying

Setting up belay anchors and belaying on waterfall ice uses the same procedures as those discussed in Belaying on Technical Snow and Ice in Chapter 17. Take extra care in locating belays away from the fall line to avoid being hit with falling ice generated by the leader. In gullies, site the belay to one side of the route, seeking protection from one of the sidewalls. When climbing large features like pillars, daggers, or curtains, it's very important to place the belay behind or to the side of these massive formations to avoid any risk of being hit if they collapse.

Leading

Waterfall ice climbs are led and followed in pitches. On some long climbs there are lower-angle sections where experienced ice climbers might feel comfortable using running belays that also require the leader to take care to avoid knocking ice on the follower. Ice pitches may be climbed with a single rope or with two ropes using either half-rope or twin-rope technique (see Half- and Twin-Rope Techniques in Chapter 14, Traditional Rock Climbing). Placing ice screws is discussed in Chapter 17.

DESCENDING

Some waterfall ice climbs allow walk-off descents to one side or the other. Most, however, are descended by rappelling. Some short, low-angle portions of waterfall ice climbs can be descended by down-climbing, and those techniques are discussed in Chapter 17.

Rappelling

The principal techniques for rappelling on ice are the same as for rappelling on rock (see Chapter 11, Rappelling). Many rappels on popular waterfall ice climbs are done from fixed anchors, usually a combination of bolts and chains, slings on trees, fixed pitons, or abandoned V-thread anchors. As with any fixed anchor, inspect these thoroughly before trusting them. Make sure bolts are secure, and test fixed pitons with the hammer on your ice tool. Check slings or accessory cord on a tree, pitons, and any V-threads for damage, wear, or burn marks, and check all knots. When in doubt, remove and replace the material. Check old V-threads to ensure they are still solid and not melted out. If an existing anchor is suspect in any way, place your own.

If there are no fixed anchors, the most common anchor to use in hard ice is a V-thread. The technique for building and testing a V-thread anchor is described in Chapter 17. Back up V-threads, whether old or new, with an ice screw, then have the first rappeler jump-test it with caution to avoid injuring your back. Before the last climber rappels, ensure that the rappel lines are running over smooth surfaces and are not frozen in place, buried in snow, set in a crack, or jammed in any way. Have the first rappeler test the pull from the next anchor (or from the bottom) to ensure the ropes can be pulled free from below. The last rappeler then removes the backup screw and rappels. How to build intermediate stations for making multiple rappels is described in Chapter 17.

Ice Conditions and Formations

Waterfall ice comes in an amazing and beautiful (and, many times, terrifying) array of formations, shapes, and features. Waterfall ice conditions and formations vary according to how well it is attached to the underlying rock and supported at the base, as well as how the ice formed. Learning to climb on all these varied types of ice takes years of experience, but it is also one of the most intriguing aspects of waterfall ice.

The textures and quality of water ice change with conditions and the location, quantity, and type of ice can change from year to year, making the same ice climb a different experience each season.

SOLID, SUPPORTED ICE

The easiest and most secure type of waterfall ice is thick, solid, and fully supported by underlying rock from behind and along the bottom. This type of ice is free of voids and takes ice screws easily. But even solid, well-supported ice can be difficult to climb in extreme cold when it is hard and brittle, causing tool placements to shatter the ice. In moderate temperatures, with soft or "plastic" ice, it is possible to get secure tool placements with a single swing. Solid, supported ice climbs are found at any water-ice grade.

BRITTLE ICE

The result of very cold temperatures, brittle ice is usually found on the surface layers of ice formations that are affected by the cold. Brittle ice can be found on ice climbs of any angle or difficulty. When you strike brittle ice, it shatters around your pick, leaving a very weak placement. Remove the pick from a shattered ice placement and use the tool to chop away the shattered, brittle ice to get to the softer, more plastic ice below. When placing ice screws, do the same thing by chopping away the surface brittle ice and putting the screw in the better ice found beneath.

ROTTEN OR SUN-AFFECTED ICE

Waterfall ice baked by the sun has a weak surface layer that must be chopped away so climbers can access the solid ice that is usually underneath. Often when the sun has baked the surface of a waterfall ice climb, it has also heated up the supporting rock behind it. The ice melts away from the warm rock and is much more fragile than ice that is frozen to the rock wall behind it. If the sun has weakened the ice to the point that the entire formation is detached and might fall, it is best to walk away.

THIN ICE

Depending on the steepness, ice that is thick enough over the rock to hold one or two teeth in the tip of the tool pick is usually climbable, as long as there is good cohesion between the ice and the underlying rock. Make both tool and crampon placements with the gentlest of taps to avoid shattering what little ice there is to climb on. Sometimes climbers must use a combination of scratching, small chipping, and hooking to create tool placements.

Thin ice is impossible to protect unless you can obtain traditional gear placements or use bolts placed in the surrounding rock. If there is no available rock protection, carefully assess from below whether ice that is too thin to take even the shortest ice screws might lead to thicker ice that may offer the security of deeper tool placements and solid protection. It is very difficult and dangerous to down-climb thin ice after starting up. If you are uncertain about protection, it is best for all but the most experienced and confident climbers to walk away. Be careful not to drill ice screws into the underlying rock. When a screw stops turning—stopped by rock—do not force it, to avoid damaging the teeth.

FREESTANDING PILLARS OR COLUMNS

Freestanding pillars (fig. 18-6a) form when water flows off an overhang during long-term freezing temperatures, creating ice stalactites above and stalagmites on the ground below. Soon these growing formations meet, forming a freestanding column of new chandelier-like ice crystals. The flowing water fills in the voids, and the ice freezes into a solid column.

It is critically important to assess the stability of a freestanding pillar before deciding to climb it. Is the column large enough in diameter and strong enough so that it will not collapse under the added weight and blows from a climber? Is the column attached at the top? Has it fractured and settled, which could make it more stable because the tension was released and the base is supporting all the weight? Does the foundation of the column at the bottom look substantial? Having the ability to make a well-informed assessment of a freestanding column requires years of experience that begins with the guidance of accomplished mentors and guides. Monitor the air

18

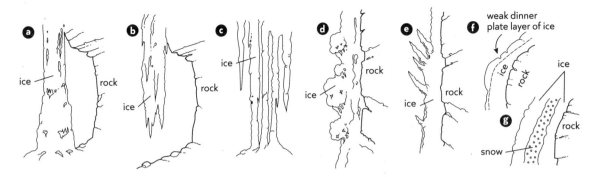

Fig. 18-6. *Water-ice conditions and formations: **a,** freestanding pillar; **b,** ice daggers; **c,** chandelier ice; **d,** cauliflower ice; **e,** ice leaves; **f,** dinner-plate ice; **g,** onion-skin ice.*

temperature in the days before and during an attempt to climb a freestanding column. Abnormally warm or cold temperatures can weaken them, and a sudden large drop to very cold temperatures can cause a freestanding pillar to fall spontaneously. Freestanding pillars are generally WI5 and harder.

Climbing freestanding pillars requires some amount of deft and delicate treatment. Do not kick or swing the ice tools too hard on a smaller column, or the impact might cause it to collapse. It is also dangerous to place ice screws in small columns, because if the pillar collapses while being climbed, protection screws would pull the roped climber down amid tons of falling ice. To minimize this risk, the leader may decide that it is less risky to solo the freestanding pillar, placing ice screws only after arriving where the free-standing portion ends and the ice column is now attached to and supported by the underlying rock. Climbing free-standing ice pillars or columns is a serious undertaking for even the strongest and most experienced waterfall ice climbers.

ICE DAGGERS

Free-hanging ice daggers (fig. 18-6b) form when water flows off an overhang during long-term freezing temperatures, creating ice stalactites that do not touch down. Or they can be the upper remnants of columns or pillars that have bro-ken off. A free-hanging ice dagger is generally WI5 or harder and usually requires hard dry tooling to get up to where it is possible to step over onto it. Like freestanding columns, they require careful assessment and delicate tool and cram-pon placements to keep from breaking the dagger off.

To climb an ice dagger, place rock protection in the wall behind it while dry tooling up and then step out onto it. If the dagger breaks while you are moving onto it, a fall would cause you to swing back under the rock overhang and away from the falling ice. Do not put ice screws for protection into the dagger, because if it breaks, the screw will pull a climber down and into a massive piece of falling ice. Step-ping out onto a dagger is an airy and exhilarating move. But before committing to it, assess again whether it is strong enough to hold your weight. Do not kick the dagger with your front points to get started. Reach over with an ice tool and gently chop a small foothold that you can step over onto. It might be possible to make several stemming moves between the dagger and the rock to keep weight off your arms and obtain more rock protection higher up before committing to the ice.

After stepping onto the ice with one foot, make your first tool placement in the ice in the back of the dagger. Then grab it using the hand opposite the foot you stepped over with, to prevent barn-dooring when stepping across with the other foot. Once you are completely on the dagger, lean around toward the dagger's front, pulling on the tool in the back of the dagger, until your arm is partly wrapped around it. Reach up with your other tool to get a placement up above you on the outside of the dagger, then move your feet around into a stable position under the outside tool so you do not barn-door when you release the tool behind the dagger. Once you are established on the outside of the dagger, climb straight up and put in a screw as soon as you reach where the dagger is attached to the rock. Phew!

BULGES AND LEDGES

These formations in waterfall ice can be a short horizontal step or a deeper ledge. Snow, rotten ice, and dinner-plate ice (see below) often accumulate on ledges and bulges and must be cleared away before proceeding. See Climbing from Ver-tical Ice onto Lower-Angle Ice earlier in this chapter.

CHANDELIER ICE

Waterfall ice forms when formations growing from above and sometimes below eventually meet to form a dense latticework of chandelier glass–like ice. Usually, water keeps flowing through this delicate formation and freezes into dense solid ice. But sometimes after the chandelier glass–like ice forms, the water stops dripping or it gets diverted elsewhere, and this chandelier ice remains (fig. 18-6c). Chandelier ice is beautiful to see, insecure to climb, and difficult to protect.

Since chandelier ice is formed by dripping water, it is usually found on steeper ice. But ice filled with similar types of air pockets can be found at just about any water-ice grade. A WI3 climb with solid supported ice is much easier to climb and protect than a WI3 climb that formed with chandelier-type ice. Climbing waterfall ice in these conditions requires strength, years of experience, and a cool head.

Aggressive tool swinging can be a useful technique on solid, supported ice, but it would destroy any structure in chandelier ice that might support body weight. Instead, swing tools lightly, and gently hook between icicles and test them with a firm pull. Use light kicks and strategic crampon placements to prevent the ice feature from falling apart. In chandelier ice, you may find places to get a solid screw in for protection, such as in small bulges or ledges where water has filled in the voids to form solid ice. Sometimes, by moving from one side to the other, you can follow a line with the most solid ice. It's also possible in these conditions to ascend most of a rope length before good protection and solid ice appears. Break up the pitches so that the belays are located where there is solid ice for the anchor and where you will be protected from or out of the way of ice dislodged by the leader on the next pitch.

CAULIFLOWER ICE AND ICE LEAVES

Water can drip and splash its way down the outer face of vertical or near-vertical ice climbs to form unusual shapes resembling everything from cauliflowers to oversized artichoke petals. These formations can range in size from several inches to several feet wide and deep. These types of formations, called cauliflower ice (fig. 18-6d) or ice leaves (fig. 18-6e), are sometimes too fragile to climb and must be cleared away with ice tools to access solid ice underneath. Terrain must be sufficiently steep for dripping water to form cauliflower ice and ice leaves, and these formations are generally found on WI4 climbs and harder.

Cauliflower ice or ice leaves can offer more comfortable places to stand when compared to smooth sheets of ice. But good tool placements can be harder to find on these formations than on thick solid ice. The ice above and behind a cauliflower, in between cauliflowers, or behind a chopped-off cauliflower can offer good tool placements. A swift strike with your pick behind a cauliflower blob will usually chop it off and reveal solid ice for placing a screw. Secure ice-screw placements can also be found in solid ice deep between these formations.

When climbing ice leaves, kick off the tops of the "petals" down to where they are thick and strong enough to stand on. Hooking over ice leaves often works, but secure tool placements and strong ice-screw placements can usually be found by chopping off the leaves down to solid ice that is part of the mass of underlying ice.

DINNER-PLATE ICE

A 1- to 3-inch-thick (2- to 7-centimeter-thick) thick layer of ice that fractures away when hit with the pick of an ice tool is called dinner-plate ice (fig. 18-6f). Dinner plates can form on the ice surface from cold temperatures, or they can form on convex surfaces where the ice is in tension. Dinner-plate ice can be found on ice climbs of any angle or difficulty.

As with brittle ice, chop away any dinner plates so that you can make tool placements in the solid ice beneath. Stagger tool placements far enough apart so that the fracturing created by one tool does not reach the other, causing it to fail. Always place ice screws in the better ice found beneath the dinner-plate layer. Also, beware of dislodging large pieces of ice that can hit you in the arm, chest, thigh, or front points and throw you off balance.

ONION-SKIN ICE

When running water within a frozen waterfall sprays out onto a layer of fresh snow sitting on top of lower-angle waterfall ice, it can freeze to form a crust of ice over the snow, sometimes several inches thick. This crust is called onion-skin ice (fig. 18-6g). These formations are notoriously unstable because the ice is not attached to an underlying solid surface. Before climbing onto an area that looks like onion-skin ice, place an ice screw for protection; and never place a screw in an onion skin, which can easily slide off. Ice climbers should never be connected to insecure formations like this.

Generally, you must clear away the onion skin, dig away any loose snow, and climb up on the firmer snow or ice beneath. To clear away the onion skin, whack the surface of it with the side of the ice-tool head. This should fracture a relatively thin skin into pieces that will slide away. If the onion skin is too thick to break up and slide away, and

18

if instead it seems strong enough to support your weight, punch holes in it with a boot and take care in this very delicate situation not to break it while standing up on the onion-skin layer.

Mixed Climbing

The combination of climbing on rock, snow, and ice—and sometimes on frozen mud and moss as well—is called mixed climbing. This type of climbing might mean ascending snowed-up rock with ice-filled cracks in the winter. Or it may involve ascending an icy face broken by a rock band. Mixed climbing can involve placing the front points of one crampon on rock holds and front-pointing with the other in ice, one tool hooked on rock and one ice tool placed in a frozen smear.

Modern "sport" mixed climbing involves climbing sections of rock with crampons and ice tools—called dry tooling—sometimes with preplaced bolted rock protection combined with ice climbing. Walking or scrambling on low-angle rock between sections of low-angle or gentle snow and ice with crampons on does not require any special techniques other than learning how to stay in balance (see Climbing Low-Angle Rock with Crampons in Chapter 16, Basic Snow and Ice Climbing). Mixed climbing on steeper technical terrain does require special equipment and techniques.

EQUIPMENT

The equipment chosen for steep mixed climbing depends on the type of mixed climbing that will be encountered. On a steep alpine climb, "mixed climbing" most likely means climbing on rock using gloved hands, dry tooling, or ice climbing with technical mountaineering ice tools and technical mountaineering crampons. When the route entails a combination of waterfall ice climbing, dry tooling, and mixed climbing, it is likely to involve waterfall ice tools and monopoint crampons.

When mixed climbing (like on waterfall ice), the thinnest gloves that keep your hands warm enough will make it easier to hold on to the tools than thicker gloves will (see "Equipment" under Waterfall Ice Climbing earlier in this chapter). Most mixed climbers wear a pair of low-profile, close-fitting gloves, prewarmed inside a jacket, and carry a thick insulated pair clipped to the harness or inside a small pack for belays. Have on hand a second pair of dry, close-fitting gloves in case the first pair gets wet.

The equipment you bring for protection depends on the type of climbing. On a bolt-protected mixed sport route, quickdraws and some ice screws may be all you need (see Chapter 17, Technical Snow and Ice Climbing, for how to place ice screws). On a traditionally protected mixed climb, you will need a rack of nuts, spring-loaded camming devices, and possibly pitons (see Chapter 13, Rock Protection), in addition to ice screws.

When carrying a full rack of ice screws, as well as two ice tools, it is helpful to have four gear carabiners (see Other Gear in Chapter 17)—two on each side of the harness. See "The Mixed Climbing Rack" sidebar, as well as "Protection" under Waterfall Ice Climbing earlier in this chapter.

Crampons

When faced with climbing a steep technical mixed route, it may be impractical to remove crampons only to put them back on when the route returns to the ice. Technical mountaineering or waterfall ice crampons are used for steep mixed climbing (see "Crampons" under Waterfall Ice Climbing earlier).

Nearly all technical snow and ice and waterfall ice crampons have vertical front points (see Figure 18-1a and b). Monopoint crampons (see Figure 18-1a) are particularly handy for precise placement on minuscule ledges, vertical seams, and other subtle rock features.

THE MIXED CLIMBING RACK

A rack for mixed climbing contains gear appropriate for each individual climb. Some modern sport mixed climbs are fully bolted, requiring only a set of quickdraws for protection. Longer traditional mixed climbs require a full rock rack combined with a full ice rack. A typical mixed climbing rack might contain some or all of the following gear:

- Six to 12 ice screws of varying lengths appropriate for the thickness of the ice
- Assortment of nuts that can be slotted into cracks
- Spring-loaded camming devices (SLCDs)
- Assortment of pitons
- A dozen or more runners, alpine draws, or quickdraws
- A double runner and a cordelette
- V-thread tool
- A few pieces of 6- to 8-millimeter accessory cord for constructing rappel anchors
- Knife for cutting webbing and accessory cord
- Belay device, locking carabiners, and rappel prusik

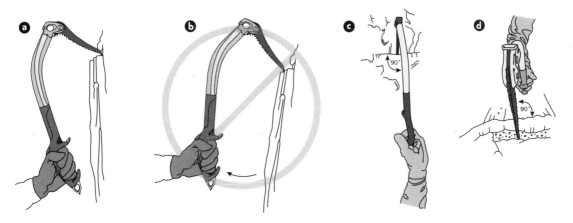

Fig. 18-7. *Dry-tooling technique:* **a,** *pull straight down on the shaft, keeping it close to the rock;* **b,** *do not pull out on the shaft—the pick will skate off hold;* **c,** *hold shaft firmly perpendicular to hold so it does not swing from side to side;* **d,** *keep wrist tight and hold the pick at 90 degrees to the surface of the rock.*

Some climbers prefer crampons with horizontal front points for mixed climbs that are snowy (see Figure 16-5 in Chapter 16, Basic Snow and Ice Climbing) because they are less prone to shearing through snow, owing to their greater surface area. Some manufacturers make crampons with hybrid horizontal-vertical front points. On sport mixed climbs that involve mostly dry tooling, some climbers use special "competition boots," which have crampon points bolted on to the sole.

Ice Tools
Ice tools for mixed climbing are the same as those used for waterfall ice climbing (see Figure 18-2). One exception is that, for pure dry tooling, some climbers prefer a tool with a spikeless ergonomic handle that is tilted farther back than on other models (see Figure 18-2b). A thicker, stronger pick is used for dry tooling.

MIXED CLIMBING TECHNIQUES
To ascend mixed terrain, climbers must combine precision crampon and ice-tool placements with calculated body positioning. It is often necessary to lean to one side or another, use a drop knee, hang off a tool placement, and then move the feet up and make a big reach to the next hold. This type of body positioning is similar to rock climbing techniques (see Chapter 9, Basics of Climbing). Climb mixed routes on a top rope initially to get a feel for using crampons and ice tools on rock. With practice on mixed terrain, climbers gain confidence in their technique.

Cramponing
When climbing on rock with crampons, an experienced mixed climber selects a foothold and delicately places crampon point(s) on that spot. Smooth weight transfer is critical while gradually testing the foothold until it is completely weighted. Once that foot is weighted, it is important to keep the front points still, to prevent them from rotating off the hold. Careful footwork is the key to mixed climbing. Use your feet and position your body as you would when making rock climbing moves (see Chapters 9 and 14, Traditional Rock Climbing). But the choice of footholds is different. Crampons do not have as much friction on rock as rubber-soled boots, but the front points can stay on small edges that boots cannot.

Using Hands on Rock
Usually on mixed climbs the rock is cold, so it's necessary to climb with gloves on to keep your hands from going numb. Rock climbing with gloves takes some practice but uses all the same techniques as rock climbing gloveless (see Chapter 14). It takes experience on different types of rock to judge whether the route's moves will be easier to climb with tools or with your hands.

When using your hands on rock, especially when switching back and forth between using hands and using tools, it is good to have two empty gear carabiners, one attached to either side of the harness, for securing and retrieving your ice tools. Some mixed climbers prefer to hang their tools over a shoulder when using their hands to rock climb. On multipitch mixed routes, it's easy to

18

Fig. 18-8. *Matching: **a,** place leading tool; **b,** hang following tool over leading shoulder; **c,** grab upper grip on leading tool with following hand; **d,** move tool from leading shoulder to following shoulder, then with both hands on leading tool, move feet up; **e,** stand up while pulling down with both hands, then remove tool from following shoulder with leading hand; **f,** place it as the new leading tool.*

drop a tool when switching back and forth between hands on rock and tools, and so using tethers can keep you from dropping a tool (see Ice Tools in Chapter 17). Dropping a tool on a one-pitch sport-style mixed route may be annoying and embarrassing—but dropping one on a multipitch mixed route could have more serious consequences.

Dry Tooling

Normally on steep mixed terrain, the rock is too cold to climb barehanded, or the holds are too small to climb with gloves on, or the cracks are filled with ice. In these conditions, it is necessary to climb rock using tools, employing a set of techniques referred to as dry tooling. The most difficult thing to learn when dry tooling is how to find and use holds that the pick can rest on, especially if you are more accustomed to doing this using your fingers while rock climbing. The tip of the pick on most ice tools is about 9 inches (23 centimeters) above your arm's reach, so it is harder to see the pick placement and you lack the sensory ability that you have in your fingers to find potential holds. It takes practice and experience with different types of rock, searching around with your pick, to find an edge or a crack that will hold your weight and where the pick won't slip off.

Once you have made what you believe is a secure placement, pull down on it, with the tool's shaft against the rock (fig. 18-7a). Lock off with your arm, and do not pull out with the grip rest or handle as you reach up for the next hold, or the pick will skate outward off the hold (fig. 18-7b). To prevent the pick from skating sideways off the hold, keep the shaft steady and perpendicular to the hold by using body tension, making sure this pull angle remains constant throughout the move (fig. 18-7c). Keep your wrist tight and the pick perpendicular to the rock so it doesn't move side to side (fig. 18-7d), and roll off the hold. Also, it is easier to hang on if you don't overgrip and relax your thumb, letting your pinky finger wedge into the bottom of the ergonomic handle.

Matching. Tool placement while dry tooling is a progression from one pick hold to another hold higher up. Rather than having to do a series of one-arm pull-ups, or to enable a move right or left, it is possible to match both hands on one tool, then pull up on it with both arms to reach the next hold or to reach a new hold off to one side.

After placing the leading tool's pick on a hold (fig. 18-8a), hang the following tool's pick over the leading shoulder (fig. 18-8b) or on your leading hand's thumb, and grab the leading tool's upper grip with the following hand (fig. 18-8c). Move the tool from the leading shoulder to the following shoulder (or hook it on the thumb of the following hand). Then with both hands on the leading tool, move your feet up (fig. 18-8d). Stand up while pulling down, lock off with the following hand still on the leading tool's upper grip, and grab the tool off the following shoulder (or thumb) (fig. 18-8e). Reach up to place the pick on the next hold (fig. 18-8f).

Torquing. Basic tool placement and matching techniques are the most important skills when you are first learning to

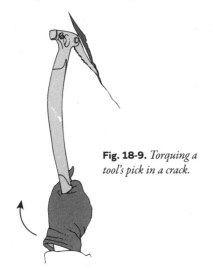

Fig. 18-9. *Torquing a tool's pick in a crack.*

dry tool, but several other techniques are useful. When climbing cracks, the tool may come out when pulled straight down. But it is possible to twist the pick inside the crack by pushing or pulling the shaft perpendicular to the crack to wedge it (fig. 18-9). Keep pushing or pulling and using body tension to maintain torque on the twisted pick. With wider cracks, you can push the entire tool head up inside the crack and torque the tool's shaft by pulling on it perpendicular to the crack.

Stein-pulling. To reach high for a hold, sometimes it is possible to do what is called a stein-pull: insert the pick upside down into a downward-facing seam or crack or under a flake (fig. 18-10a). Then, just as a bartender would pull down on a tap handle, pull down on the tool's shaft, engaging the pick into the hold and forcing the tool's head against the rock, creating opposing force (fig. 18-10b). The closer to the handle you grab the shaft and the harder you pull down, the stronger the tool placement becomes. Maintain your grasp on this tool, then move your feet up and stand up and reach with the other tool for a new placement (fig. 18-10c).

Stacking. Another technique used frequently in dry tooling is stacking. If there is one good tool placement and you do not want to match hands on it, you can hook the free tool's pick over the tip of the well-placed tool and pull up using both tools (fig. 18-11). Lock off with the arm

a   **b**   **c**

Fig. 18-10. *Stein-pull:* **a,** *invert tool and hook under lip;* **b,** *pull down on shaft;* **c,** *step up and reach for another hold with second tool.*

18

holding the well-placed tool and reach up to the next hold with the free tool.

Climbing Ice

Waterfall ice and mixed climbing require specialized equipment, a high level of skill, and an excellent understanding of conditions and ability. Equipped for the winter environment, the waterfall ice and mixed climber combines the disciplines of rock climbing and ice climbing with snow travel and backcountry risk management. Waterfall ice and mixed climbing builds on the skills of basic and technical snow and ice climbing, as well as rock climbing, and the combination of all these skills defines what it means to be an alpinist.

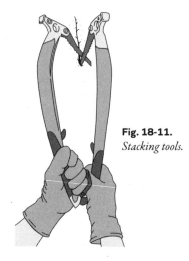

Fig. 18-11.
Stacking tools.

CHAPTER 19

GLACIER TRAVEL AND CREVASSE RESCUE

Glaciers can offer a convenient route to alpine summits, but they hold many hazards. As a glacier's mass of consolidated snow flows slowly downhill, it splits in places known as crevasses. Glacier travel is a specialized and important skill for mountaineering. Climbers must learn how to travel while mitigating hazards in this terrain.

To minimize risk while traveling on a glacier, climbers first need all of the fundamental snow-travel skills outlined in Chapter 16, Basic Snow and Ice Climbing. In addition to those fundamental skills, climbers must develop the skill and experience to detect and avoid crevasses and other glacier hazards. With good routefinding and some luck, climbers may never fall into a crevasse. But if they should, it is imperative that climbers know how to extricate themselves or their partners. Before stepping onto a glacier, climbers must have a clear appreciation of the dangers as well as confidence in their ability to deal with those dangers.

Glaciers and Crevasses

Glaciers constantly change as snow supply and temperature changes influence their advance and retreat. Climate change is dramatically altering glaciers, with many shrinking and retreating and, in some cases, disappearing altogether. Glaciers are like a river of ice slowly moving down a mountain (as shown in Figure 19-1). Some glaciers are relatively small, stagnant pockets of snow that have metamorphosed into ice. Most climbers experience medium-sized glaciers; but there are also icefields of immense proportions, with huge crevasses and full of teetering ice formations that can collapse (see Chapter 27, The Cycle of Snow, for information on the formation of glaciers).

Glacial flow patterns can be very complex. But research since the early 1960s indicates that, with few exceptions, glaciers around the world have retreated at unprecedented rates over the last hundred years. Most glaciers move faster in the warmth of summer than in winter because they are lubricated by increased meltwater. The flow of ice over underlying substrate, around bends, or in other circumstances that exceed the ice's plasticity leads to fracturing and the formation of crevasses.

Crevasses often form where the slope angle increases significantly, putting tension on the ice, which then splits open (fig. 19-1f). At the place where a glacier moves by a permanent snow or ice face on the mountain above, a large crevasse called a bergschrund forms (fig. 19-1b). Crevasses also commonly form where a glacier turns (fig. 19-1g); where the distance between valley walls either narrows or expands; or where two glaciers meet. Crevasses may also develop around a bedrock feature that obstructs the glacial flow, such as a rock formation protruding through the ice—a nunatak (fig. 19-1e).

Crevasses are most dangerous in the accumulation zone (fig. 19-1c), the portion of a glacier that receives more snow every year than it loses to melting. Here, crevasses are difficult to detect because they are frequently covered with a layer of snow (fig. 19-2a and b) that may be too weak to support a climber. Below the accumulation zone is the ablation zone, where the glacier's annual melting matches or exceeds the yearly snowfall. But in fall, winter, and spring, the ablation areas can also be covered in snow, obscuring crevasses in this area of the glacier as well. The boundary separating these two zones is the firn line (fig. 19-1d), from a German word for "old snow."

19

ICE FEATURES

a. Moat
b. Bergschrund
c. Accumulation zone
d. Firn line
e. Nunatak
f. Crevasses
g. Marginal crevasses
h. Terminus (snout)

MORAINE FEATURES

i. Medial moraine
j. Lateral moraine
k. Terminal moraine
l. Moraine lake

m. Braided outwash stream
n. Old terminal moraine
o. Old lateral moraine
p. Outwash plain and ground moraine
q. Erratic (boulder)

Fig. 19-1. *Aerial view of a glacier showing principal features of ice and moraine.*

The deeper layers of glacial ice are denser and more plastic than the upper section and can move and deform without cracking (fig. 19-2c). If this deeper, older ice becomes exposed, the glacier is usually fairly flat, with narrow, shallow crevasses that are easy to cross. Below it all is bedrock (fig. 19-2d).

OTHER GLACIER HAZARDS

Besides crevasses, other common hazards on glaciers include ice avalanches, moats, glacial moraines, meltwater, whiteouts, and rockfall.

Ice avalanches. When the steep, jumbled glacial sections known as icefalls (see Figure 16-39h in Chapter 16, Basic Snow and Ice Climbing) avalanche, seracs (towers of ice) can come crashing down (see Figure 16-39f and g). A glacier's inexorable movement means that ice avalanches can occur anytime; their activity is only partly related to season, temperature, or snowfall. Travel through icefalls and under seracs is dangerous and best avoided. On some routes, climbers may decide to assume the risk of traveling through short sections of these dangerous areas, moving quickly to minimize their exposure to this hazard.

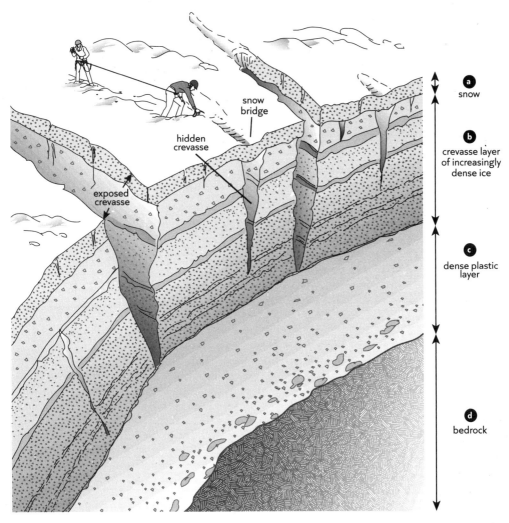

Fig. 19-2. *Cross-section of a glacier:* **a,** *upper snow layer on a glacier;* **b,** *crevasses open up in snow and ice layers as glacier angle increases;* **c,** *denser lower area moves without splitting;* **d,** *bedrock.*

Moats. Big gaps that appear when snow or ice melts back from a rock face are called moats (fig. 19-1a). Moats can present major barriers to climbers who need to gain the rock as part of their route. Belayed mountaineers may be able to cross a snow bridge over a moat or climb into the moat and back up onto the rock on the other side.

Glacial moraines and dry glaciers. Mounds of rocky debris previously carried and then deposited by a glacier—typically composed of compacted, unsorted boulders, rocks, gravel, and soil—are called glacial moraines (fig. 19-1i, j, k, n, and o). Lateral moraines often appear as steep-sided ridges with exposed faces that contain partly buried boulders ready to dislodge at the slightest touch. Traveling anywhere on a dry glacier in the summer below the firn line often involves insecure footing on loose rocks that slide around like ball bearings on top of the hard ice, as well as the need to avoid large boulders that could roll over onto a climber.

Meltwater. The runoff flowing from a glacier (fig. 19-1m) or surface meltwater on top of a glacier can be a chilling obstacle if the climbing route requires a crossing. During warm weather, consider waiting to cross until the cooler hours of the next morning, when flow is often at its lowest. Beware of being swept away by surface meltwater that usually cascades into moulins, the holes that channel this flow into subglacial channels. (For more advice on crossing rivers, see Rivers and Streams in Chapter 6, Wilderness Travel.)

Whiteouts. In a whiteout on a snowy glacier, sky and snow merge into a seamless blend of white, sometimes described as feeling like being inside a ping-pong ball. Without navigation tools, these conditions make routefinding difficult or sometimes impossible. Climbers can navigate in a whiteout by noting compass bearings and altimeter readings, or GPS readings. During the ascent, climbers can place route-marking wands or record GPS waypoints—even when it looks as though clear weather will prevail. If snow or clouds close in and leave the climbing party in a whiteout, these simple precautions will pay off on the descent.

Rockfall. Parts of glaciers can be subject to rockfall from bordering walls and ridges, and these zones are usually best avoided. If the route passes through an area subject to rockfall, cross the area when it is cold and move quickly. Nighttime cold freezes rock in place and reduces rockfall hazard, whereas warmer temperatures melt these bonds and release the loose rock.

Equipment

When traveling on glaciers, use specialized equipment to minimize risk and to protect and extract a climber who falls into a crevasse. This includes ropes, harnesses, ice axes, crampons, ascenders, belay devices, rescue pulleys, prusiks and runners, and more.

ROPES

Ropes with "dry" treatment (see Ropes in Chapters 8, Essential Climbing Equipment, and 17, Technical Snow and Ice Climbing) absorb much less water from wet snow and pick up less grit from a glacier, which makes them lighter, stronger, and easier to work with, especially in freezing conditions. The type of rope needed depends on the glacier and the route.

Depending on the size of the team, 30- to 60-meter (100- to 200-foot) half and twin ropes are used and generally adequate for most glacier travel. The lighter, thinner ropes are sufficient for general glacier use because there are generally no sharp edges that might cut the rope. An added advantage is their lighter weight.

If the route consists of glacier travel and steep technical climbing, it requires a variety of types of ropes used in different ways (see Chapters 14, Traditional Rock Climbing, and 17, Technical Snow and Ice Climbing).

HARNESS

For glacier travel, be sure the seat harness's waist belt and leg loops can adjust to fit over several layers of cold-weather clothing. When carrying large packs, glacier travelers sometimes wear a chest harness, which can help a climber who falls into a crevasse maintain an upright position (see Chest Harness later in this chapter, as well as Harnesses in Chapter 8).

ICE AXE AND CRAMPONS

An ice axe and crampons are as important for glacier travel as they are for travel on any firm, sloped surface of snow or ice. The ice axe aids balance and provides a means for self-arrest. If a rope mate drops into a crevasse, other climbers on the rope use their ice axes to go into self-arrest, controlling and stopping the fall. For basic glacier travel, choose a general mountaineering ice axe (see Chapter 16, Basic Snow and Ice Climbing).

When walking roped on a glacier, climbers may consider using a wrist leash or tethering their ice axe to the harness. The benefit is that if climbers drop their ice axe, it will not get lost. The downside is that climbers may get injured by the ice axe in the event of a fall (see Wrist Leash or Umbilical in Chapter 16).

For glacier travel, use general mountaineering crampons. These crampons are described in Chapter 16, along with their use on a range of slope angles and in different snow conditions.

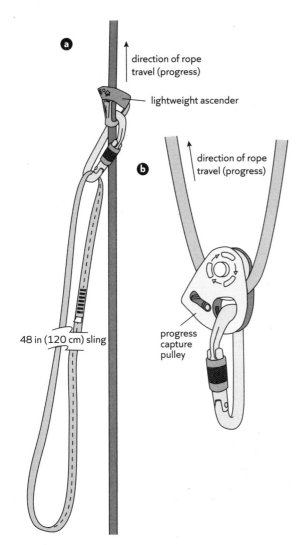

Fig. 19-3. *Preferred devices for ascending a rope after a crevasse fall:* **a,** *lightweight ascender with locking carabiner;* **b,** *progress capture pulley (PCP) with locking carabiner.*

ASCENDERS

Climbers traveling on glaciers also carry lightweight ascenders and progress capture pulleys (see below). Prusik slings can be used instead of these mechanical devices, but prusiks do not perform as well.

Lightweight Ascender and Progress Capture Pulley System

The preferred system for ascending the rope after a crevasse fall incorporates a lightweight ascender and a progress capture pulley (PCP). A lightweight ascender (fig. 19-3a) is a very compact device for rope ascents or hauling that is slipped over and secured to the rope with a locking carabiner so that the teeth inside are pressed against the rope to enable the braking action. A PCP (fig. 19-3b) is a pulley combined with a toothed camming device that allows the rope to advance through it in one direction but acts as a brake in the other direction. This system also requires two 48-inch (120-centimeter) runners and three locking carabiners.

Prusik System

Although using a mechanical lightweight ascender and PCP system is preferable, climbers should have the materials and know-how to tie and use a prusik system if the mechanical system is unavailable. Prusik slings consist of two pieces of 5- to 7-millimeter accessory cord, one for the feet with one or two loops (fig. 19-4a) and one for the waist loop (fig. 19-4b), attached to the climbing rope with friction hitches. When a climber puts weight on a prusik sling, the hitch grips the rope firmly; when the climber removes the weight, the hitch can be loosened and moved up or down the rope. A cordelette (see Static Equalization in Chapter 10, Belaying) tied in a loop can serve well as a single-foot alternative to the double-foot sling shown in Figure 19-4a.

19

TABLE 19-1. SIZING PRUSIK SLINGS		
CLIMBER'S HEIGHT	FOOT SLING LENGTH (2 LOOPS)	WAIST SLING LENGTH
5 ft. (1.5 m)	11 ft. (3.4 m)	5 ft. (1.5 m)
5 ft. 6 in (1.7 m)	11 ft. 6 in (3.5 m)	5 ft. 6 in (1.7 m)
6 ft. (1.8 m)	12 ft. (3.7 m)	6 ft. (1.8 m)
6 ft. 6 in (2 m)	13 ft. (4 m)	6 ft. 6 in (2 m)

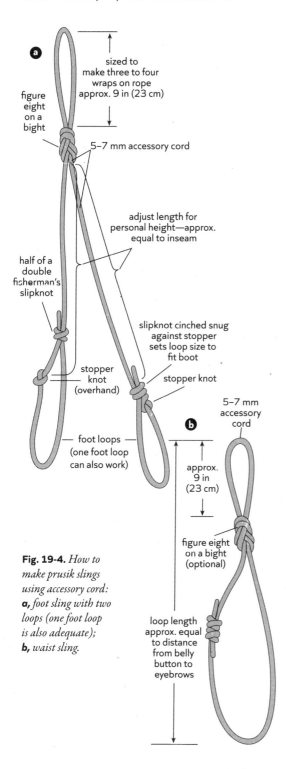

As with all prusik systems, it is important to size the slings correctly for each climber's height. Table 19-1 shows the correct length of cord needed for each untied sling for four sample climber heights. Note that the waist sling's length is the same as the climber's height.

Size the top of the foot sling at about waist level when a climber is standing in the sling (fig. 19-5a), and the top of the waist sling at about eye level when the sling is clipped to the belay loop on the harness (fig. 19-5b). Before taking the slings out onto a glacier, check their sizing at home. Practice ascending a rope thrown over a garage rafter or a tree limb to find out how you need to adjust it.

a sized to make three to four wraps on rope approx. 9 in (23 cm)

figure eight on a bight

5–7 mm accessory cord

adjust length for personal height—approx. equal to inseam

half of a double fisherman's slipknot

slipknot cinched snug against stopper sets loop size to fit boot

stopper knot (overhand)

stopper knot

foot loops (one foot loop can also work)

5–7 mm accessory cord

b approx. 9 in (23 cm)

figure eight on a bight (optional)

Fig. 19-4. *How to make prusik slings using accessory cord:* **a,** *foot sling with two loops (one foot loop is also adequate);* **b,** *waist sling.*

loop length approx. equal to distance from belly button to eyebrows

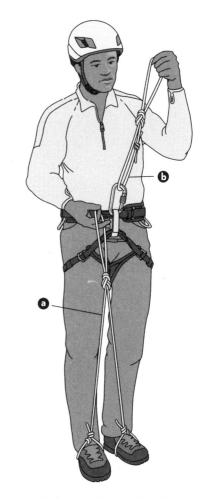

Fig. 19-5. *Prusik sling lengths:* **a,** *tied foot sling extends from both boots to belly button;* **b,** *tied waist sling extends from belly button to eyebrows.*

Climbers commonly attach the slings to the rope with prusik hitches. But experiment also with the klemheist and bachmann hitches to find the system most comfortable for you to use (see Knots, Bends, and Hitches in Chapter 8, Essential Climbing Equipment).

OTHER STANDARD GLACIER GEAR

A climbing party may want to carry a shovel to flatten campsites and minimize rope entrenchment in rescue situations. Each party member also carries the following gear.

Rescue pulley. If you are using a lightweight ascender and PCP system for self-rescue, you do not need a separate rescue pulley. If you are using prusiks for self-rescue, each climber carries a pulley designed for use in rescue hauling systems.

Anchor. Depending on conditions, carry either a snow or ice anchor or both, such as a snow picket and a couple ice screws for each climber (see Snow and Ice Anchors in Chapter 16, Basic Snow and Ice Climbing, and Ice Screws in Chapter 17, Technical Snow and Ice Climbing).

Runners. Bring at least two double-length (48-inch, 120-centimeter) runners (part of the lightweight ascender and PCP system described above) and two single-length (24-inch, 60-centimeter) runners for self-rescue systems and for attaching to anchors. Also consider a cordelette or quad-length runner for constructing an equalized anchor for crevasse rescue.

Belay device. See Belay Devices in Chapter 10, Belaying.

Carabiners. Carry at least three locking carabiners (part of the lightweight ascender and PCP system described above) and three regular carabiners.

CLOTHING

Climbers need to be prepared for cold weather but also minimize overheating. If a climber should fall into a crevasse, the glacier's interior will be frigid even when the day is hot. For the base layer, wear a light-colored, long-sleeved top that reflects the sun's heat but provides some warmth in case you end up inside a crevasse. Long sleeves also protect elbows from abrasive snow during self-arrest.

Similarly, wear lightweight gloves to protect the hands. A lightweight wind jacket that takes the edge off breezy conditions is a valuable layer that weighs little and takes up little space in your pack. A thin neck gaiter can be pulled up over your face or converted to a head covering for sun and wind protection. Keep a large insulated jacket accessible at the top of your pack for quick access in an emergency or during breaks. Stash a warm hat and gloves in the jacket pockets.

SKIS AND SNOWSHOES

Skis or snowshoes are essential for winter and some types of expedition mountaineering: they provide necessary flotation to keep climbers from sinking too deeply into snow, which allows for more efficient travel and reduces fatigue. Skis or snowshoes also reduce the chance of a climber breaking through snow bridges over hidden crevasses. Snowshoes are usually more practical than skis for roped glacier travel unless all members of the rope team are highly skilled skiers (for further information on ski mountaineering, see Resources).

WANDS

Wands can be used as a navigational aid to mark the climbing party's ascent route and identify known hazards, such as weak snow bridges or crevasses. Even if visibility is satisfactory while ascending, route-marking wands can be an alternative to GPS waypoints if a whiteout occurs on the return.

Climbers usually make wands using 30- to 48-inch-long (76- to 120-centimeter-long) green-stained bamboo garden stakes topped with a colored duct-tape flag. Label the flags with the party's initials for easy identification.

Wands placed during the ascent indicate the direction of travel. Space the wands at a distance equal to the total length of the climbing party when roped and moving single file. Wands are typically placed on the uphill side of the route and inserted deeply enough to prevent them from falling over in melting snow or high winds. If firm snow makes placing the wand difficult, use the ice axe's pick or spike to create a suitably deep hole.

Two wands inserted at opposing 45-degree angles to cross one another, forming an X, indicate a known danger such as a weak snow bridge over a crevasse. Climbers also use wands when setting up camp on a glacier to mark the boundaries of the safe areas for unroped walking and the location of buried supplies (caches).

On the descent, remove all wands placed by your party. Do not remove any wands placed by other parties.

GPS DEVICE

A GPS device can be used as a navigational aid on glaciers instead of or together with wands (see GPS in Chapter 5, Navigation and Communication).

Fundamentals of Glacier Travel

Strong, capable snow and ice climbing skills (see Chapters 16 and 17), proper timing, and routefinding experience are important to have when traveling on glaciers. Climbers should plan their ascent and descent to avoid being out on the glacier during the time of day when the sun and heat can be debilitating, weaken snow bridges, and create soft and wet snow conditions. If possible, observe and take photographs of the glacier from far enough away to determine a general line of ascent that avoids traveling through icefalls, under seracs, and among dense networks of large crevasses. Looking at these photos can be very helpful later when making routefinding decisions on the glacier. But even skilled climbers using all these precautions can encounter and sometimes fall into hidden crevasses.

ROPE MANAGEMENT

Assessing conditions to decide when to rope up for glacier travel requires considerable experience. However, the general rule is to rope up whenever the team is in glaciated terrain. This general guideline applies even if climbers are familiar with the glacier and believe they can see and avoid crevasses. Roping up is especially important in areas where snow cover conceals crevasses.

It is tempting to walk unroped on a glacier that looks like a benign snowfield, especially if climbers have recently traveled the same way without punching through the surface into a hole beneath. But taking the time to rope up, like wearing a seat belt in a car, greatly increases a climber's chances of surviving the most likely accident on a glacier: falling into a crevasse.

When walking on a gentle or low-angle glacier where there is more danger of someone falling into a crevasse than of simply falling downslope, climbers may want to hold their ice axes in the self-arrest position. However, for climbers traveling on a bare-ice glacier, crevasse falls are almost impossible to arrest, so it might be prudent to use running belays or fully belayed pitches with ice-screw anchors (see Running Belays in Chapter 16).

Rope Team Size

The number of climbers in each rope team is usually determined by the type of climb and the number of climbers in the overall party (subject in part to the land manager's limits on group size). Generally, smaller parties are faster and better suited to steeper climbs with belayed pitches; they also have less of an environmental impact. When traveling on a glacier, larger rope teams are better able to arrest a fall and larger parties have more people and resources available for crevasse rescue.

Rope teams of three or four climbers are ideal for glacier travel to allow for efficient movement while still having multiple people available to stop a fall or aid a climber who has fallen into a crevasse. A party size of two rope teams provides a rescue backup if a climber on one of the teams falls into a crevasse. While the person who is on the same rope as the fallen climber remains in an arrest position, the second team can set up a snow anchor and initiate the rescue (see Reacting and Responding to a Crevasse Fall later in this chapter).

The distance between adjacent climbers on a rope is an important consideration with its own trade-offs. Shorter distances between climbers allow for better team communication, a quicker response to falls, and easier rope management. Longer distances, however, may reduce team risk when crossing crevasses. When roping up, choose a spacing that is larger than the widest crevasse you expect to encounter, ensuring that only one person at a time is at risk when crossing a snow bridge. Parties traveling on extensive glaciers with giant crevasses will arrange rope teams to have greater spacing between climbers than parties traveling on smaller glaciers.

Glacier travelers usually put three or four people on a 30- to 60-meter (100- to 200-foot) half or twin ropes. These configurations ensure there is enough rope to create appropriate spacing between climbers and extra coils for crevasse rescue for most routes.

How to Tie In

Climbers on either end of the rope tie in directly through the tie-in points on the harness with a rewoven figure eight (fig. 19-6). Climbers in the middle of the rope clip a butterfly knot or an overhand on a bight to the harness belay loop with a locking carabiner (fig. 19-7). After being weighted, the butterfly knot is much easier to untie than the overhand, and some climbers prefer it. (See Basic Knots in Chapter 8 for more information on these tie-in options.)

Climbers should tie in at equal intervals along the rope unless this spacing is longer than needed for efficient glacier travel. The spacing between climbers can be shortened by tying and carrying shoulder coils (see Shorten the Rope with Coils, below).

Considerations for teams of two. When climbing with a rope team of two, there is only one other climber to try to arrest a fall. In this situation, having a larger distance between climbers of between 50 and 75 feet (15 and 23 meters) allows more time for a climber to react and arrest in the event of a crevasse fall. It also provides more room between the arresting climber and a potential crevasse edge (fig. 19-8). The two climbers each tie in at one end of the rope, then adjust their spacing with shoulder coils to provide some free rope for a hauling system or other rescue use. Spacing within this range will depend on the size of the crevasses.

Another technique that is important to use with two-person teams and can also be used with larger rope teams is to tie butterfly knots in the rope between the climbers. Provide an initial 15- to 18-foot (5- to 6-meter) space between the climber and the first knot, and space subsequent knots 6 to 10 feet (2 to 3 meters) apart beyond the first knots (as shown in Figure 19-8). In the event of a fall into a crevasse, the knots in the rope will

Fig. 19-6. *Rigged and ready climber on end of rope: note lightweight ascender, progress capture pulley (PCP), and 48-inch (120-centimeter) sling with two locking carabiners clipped to gear loops.*

Fig. 19-7. *Rigged and ready climber in middle of rope: tied in to rope with butterfly knot and locking carabiner; note lightweight ascender, progress capture pulley (PCP), and 48-inch (120-centimeter) sling with two locking carabiners clipped to gear loop.*

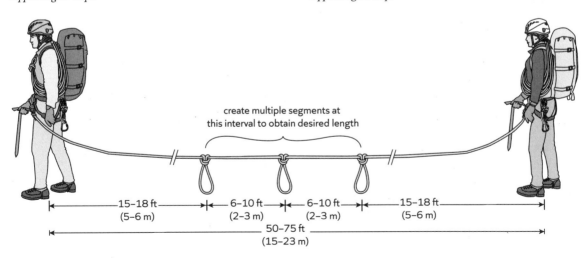

Fig. 19-8. *Two-person glacier-travel rope team with shoulder coils: adjust spacing to 50–75 feet (15–23 meters), with butterfly knots in rope to help arrest a fall by catching in crevasse lip. Butterfly knots can also be used with larger rope teams.*

become entrenched and catch in the crevasse lip. This takes most of the weight off the arresting climber, which makes it easier to set up the initial rescue anchor. See Special Rescue Situations later in this chapter for more information regarding these knots.

Shorten the Rope with Coils

"Climbing in coils"—shortening the rope by coiling it over one shoulder (fig. 19-9)—is a fast and convenient way to adjust the length of rope between each climber. This technique allows flexibility based on the terrain. On an alpine

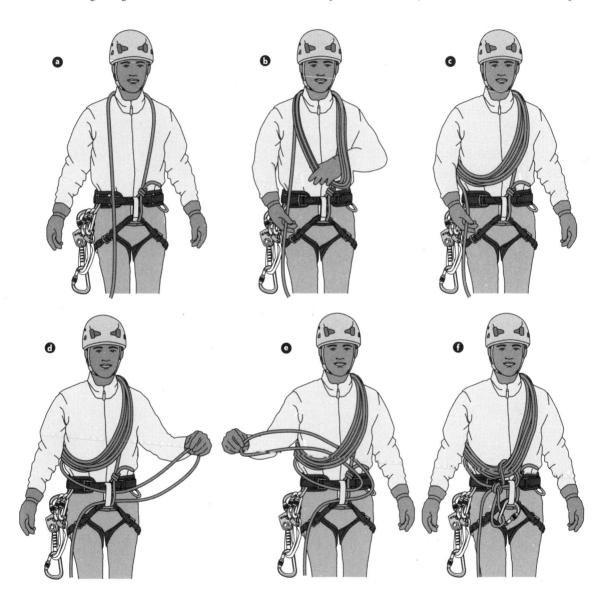

Fig. 19-9. *Shortening the rope with a coil:* **a,** *tie into harness and drape rope over neck;* **b,** *coil desired amount of rope around neck and hand;* **c,** *put arm through coil;* **d,** *take loop of rope and pass it through belay loop;* **e,** *bring loop up, behind, and over the coil;* **f,** *tie loop around ropes fed through belay loop with overhand knot and clip loop to belay loop.*

climb, for example, climbing in coils allows the team to quickly transition between medium spacing when traveling on a glacier, shortened spacing while short roping, and full-rope-length belayed climbing for pitches of rock or ice. To create the coil, follow these steps:

1. Tie the rope end to your harness, and drape rope around neck (fig. 19-9a).
2. Coil the rope around the neck and hand with the elbow at a right angle until there is enough remaining for the desired spacing between climbers (fig. 19-9b).
3. Put arm through coil (fig. 19-9c).
4. Take a loop of rope and pass it through the belay loop on the harness (fig. 19-9d).
5. Bring the loop up, behind, and over the coil (fig. 19-9e).
6. Tie the loop around the ropes fed through the belay loop with an overhand knot (fig. 19-9f), and clip loop to belay loop with a locking carabiner.

Maintain Proper Slack

When traveling roped up on a glacier, mountaineers need to maintain proper slack in the rope. Keep the rope extended, but not taut, and with only as much slack as the climbing team finds useful—often a small loop of about 3 feet (1 meter) as a buffer between each person as they travel (to keep climbers from dragging or pulling on each other or being stopped by the person behind them). Keeping the rope fully extended between climbers helps prevent a long plunge into a hidden crevasse and a longer climb out. Increased slack in the rope puts more force on the arresting climber in the event of a crevasse fall, making it harder to stop the fall and increasing the risk that the arresting climber will be dragged along into the hole. Falling deeper into a crevasse also increases the chance that the fallen climber will hit something and get injured or become wedged in as it narrows.

To make it easier for others to maintain proper rope slack, the rope leader should set a steady pace the others can follow for a long time. Rope leaders pay particular attention to maintaining their pace as the route transitions from an uphill section to a flat or downhill stretch. The impulse to immediately increase the pace in easier terrain strains the trailing climbers who must move quickly through the uphill section to keep up. Likewise, followers should be alert going downhill, when it becomes easy to walk too fast and increase the slack in the rope.

Keep the Rope Downhill

As you perform a diagonal ascent while roped up on a glacier, keep the rope on the downhill side of the track. This

helps prevent the rope from getting entangled with your feet. To make sure rope management at switchbacks is smooth, follow these steps:

1. **About 10 feet (3 meters) from the apex of the turn:** The leader and subsequent climbers step over the rope that goes to the climber behind. Perform the step-over in stride, maintaining a steady pace. Until you reach the apex, the rope will temporarily be on the uphill side.
2. **At the apex of the turn:** Switch the ice axe to the uphill hand and walk in the new direction (see Diagonal Ascent in Chapter 16, Basic Snow and Ice Climbing). The rope should now be on the downhill side once again.
3. **As the following climbers make the turn:** Give the rope ahead a flick to help keep it from becoming entangled with their crampons.

Try to move steadily through the turn, without any unnecessary stopping or starting. As each climber approaches the turn, they match the pace of the climber in front of them. Moving too quickly introduces slack in the rope after the turn is complete; moving too slowly makes it difficult to reach the apex of the turn before the rope tautens. In either case, climbers can make small adjustments to their pace as needed so that they arrive at the corner with the proper amount of slack in the rope.

Belay In and Out of Breaks

When the party reaches a rest stop or campsite surrounded by crevasses, consider belaying climbers into and out of that location. Keep the rope to the leader extended and free of slack until the leader has thoroughly checked and/or probed the location for crevasses.

Having secured the area for the team, the leader belays the next climber(s) into the secured area using one of the

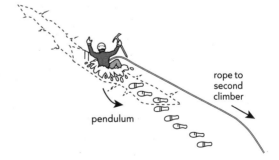

rope to second climber

pendulum

Fig. 19-10. *Where the direction of travel runs parallel to a crevasse, a lengthy pendulum could make a fall worse.*

snow and ice belays described in Chapter 16, Basic Snow and Ice Climbing. When leaving the secured area to resume climbing, climbers heading out should again be belayed using a suitable snow and ice belay.

Travel Perpendicular to Crevasses

When possible, the rope team should travel at right angles (perpendicular) to crevasses. A rope team that travels parallel to a crevasse risks a lengthy pendulum fall for a climber who drops in (fig. 19-10). Traveling at right angles to crevasses, and with proper rope slack, positions the rope to minimize the length of a fall.

CARRYING AND PRERIGGING SELF-RESCUE GEAR

Self-rescue gear such as slings, carabiners, a lightweight ascender, and a progress capture pulley (PCP) can be racked on the harness gear loops. Some self-rescue gear can be prerigged so it is easier to use when needed.

Extraction Loop

Hidden crevasses may be wide enough at the top for a climber to fall into but then taper to body width a short way down, making it easy for a climber to get wedged in the ice. The fallen climber cannot self-rescue in this situation and must be pulled out. It's very difficult to extricate a wedged

extraction loop

Fig. 19-11. *Climber equipped with an extraction loop attached between the harness and the pack's haul loop.*

climber who fell in while traveling unroped because their harness is now inaccessible. For roped up climbers, pulling at the harness's waist belt can rotate the wedged climber in the crevasse, which might make it more difficult to pull them out or require using so much force that it could cause serious injuries.

It's helpful (and in some places like the Alps, it's required) when traveling on glaciers to rig an extraction loop so that rescuers can haul a fallen climber straight up and out of a tight crevasse. An extraction loop is a 48-inch (120-centimeter) sling girth-hitched to the harness, extended up over the climber's shoulder, and clove-hitched to the pack's haul loop so that the portion of the sling between the harness and haul loop is taut (fig. 19-11). Rescuers can reach down to a wedged climber and clip a rope to the top of this loop, which can be used to pull straight up.

Lightweight Ascender and PCP System

One of the benefits of using the preferred lightweight ascender and PCP system for self-rescue is that climbers do not need to prerig these devices on the rope as they would for prusik slings. It is relatively easy to deploy this system, so the lightweight ascender, PCP, and two 48-inch (120-centimeter) slings with three locking carabiners can all be racked on the harness gear loops for ready access as needed.

Prusik Slings

If the equipment for the preferred lightweight ascender and PCP system is *not* being used, prerig prusik slings as an acceptable substitute (see Equipment earlier in this chapter). Immediately after roping up to begin glacier travel, attach the waist prusik sling to the climbing rope, ideally on the side of the rope going to the climber behind you. Clip the waist prusik to the harness belay loop with an extra locking carabiner to be used during self-rescue.

Optionally, attach the leg prusik to the rope as well, taking care to secure the one or two free foot-loop ends—either stuffing them in pockets or clipping them to the harness—so they do not become a tripping hazard during the climb. If you opt to not attach the leg prusik at the start of the climb, clip it to a gear loop on the harness so it is out of the way, does not present a tripping hazard, and remains accessible in case you need it for self-rescue after falling into a crevasse. Prerigging the prusiks reduces the work required in the event of a crevasse fall.

Climbers attached to the middle of the rope will not know which end they might have to climb after a fall. If they attach a leg prusik, they should put it on the section of rope opposite that of the waist prusik. That way, if they fall, they only need to move one of the prusik slings to the side of the rope that they will need to climb.

Chest Harness

A chest harness is mainly used in glacier travel if you are carrying a heavy pack (see Chest Harness in Chapter 8, Essential Climbing Equipment). The chest harness, clipped to the rope after a crevasse fall, helps keep the climber upright when hanging from the rope and encumbered by a pack.

DETECTING CREVASSES

Figuring out where the crevasses are and picking a route through them is fundamental to risk management in glacier travel. Climbers can try to plan the route before a trip by studying recent photographs of the glacier. But because of climate change and seasonal variations, it's challenging to find accurate comparative photographs, unless they are from parties who have recently climbed the route or visited the area.

On the approach hike, try to get a look at the glacier before you reach it, from the valley below or perhaps alongside the glacier. Climbers may see an obvious route from a distance that would be impossible to discover once they are on the glacier. Take photos and make notes to help you remember major crevasses, landmarks, and route options.

Photographs and distant views of a glacier are useful, but the situation can be much different once you get there. What appeared to be small cracks may be gaping chasms. Crevasses can be hidden when covered by a thin layer of snow, or they may not be visible from your perspective. Sagging trenches, for example, are a prime characteristic of a hidden crevasse, marking where gravity has pulled the thin snow cover down over the fissure's opening. See the "Tips for Detecting Crevasses" sidebar. Stay alert and be prepared to backtrack and take an alternate route.

Snow Probing

One technique of searching a suspicious-looking area for crevasses is called snow probing. If a climbing party discovers a crevasse via probing, continue probing in all directions around this area to find the crevasse's true lip. Probe by thrusting an ice-axe shaft or a ski pole into the snow a couple of feet ahead, keeping the axe or pole perpendicular to the slope. Thrust with enough force to measure resistance that would most likely hold body weight.

If the axe or pole breaks through the surface layer into a void, you have found a crevasse. If the route must continue in the direction of this hole, use further axe or pole thrusts

TIPS FOR DETECTING CREVASSES

- **Keep an eye out for sagging trenches in the snow.** These sags are visible as a linear dip in elevation compared to the surrounding snow and may have a slight difference in sheen, texture, or color, especially when the low-angle light of early morning and late afternoon tends to accentuate them. (These depressions may be difficult to detect in the flat light of fog or in the glare of midafternoon sun.)

- **Be wary after storms.** New snow can fill a sagging trench and make it blend into the surrounding surface. (At other times, however, new snow can make a sagging trench more apparent by creating a hollow of new snow that contrasts with surrounding areas of old snow.)

- **Remember that where there is one crevasse, there are often many.**

- **Be especially alert in areas where crevasses are known to form.** Where a glacier makes a turn or where slope angle increases are examples of such places.

- **Regularly sweep your eyes to the sides of the route to check for open cracks to the left or right.** Cracks could hint at crevasses that extend beneath your path.

to establish the extent and direction of the crevasse. The leader can chop away thin surface layers to expose the crevasse for followers to see.

The effectiveness of probing to discover hidden crevasses depends on climbers' skill and experience at interpreting the changes they feel in the snow layers. An ice axe is a limited probe because it is relatively short, but it is also the handiest and, therefore, the most commonly used. Ski poles are longer and allow climbers to probe deeper, but if the basket limits probing depth, consider turning the pole around and probing with the handle.

CROSSING A CREVASSE FIELD

Climbers employ various methods to avoid falling into a crevasse when traveling on a glacier. The techniques described below are typical, but they are usually adapted to conditions in the field. Routefinding on a glacier involves finding a path around or over crevasses, many of them hidden, and other obstacles. The crossing is seldom without detours as climbers carefully pick their way across.

19

Make an End Run

The most common way to negotiate a crevasse is to make an end-run detour from the line of ascent and go around it. In late summer, when winter snow has melted down to old snow or ice, it may be possible to see the true end of the crevasse. But if snow blankets the glacier, the end of the crack may not be visible. Make a wide swing around what appears to be the end, probing carefully (fig. 19-12). Look closely at adjacent crevasses to judge whether one of them could be an extension of the crevasse you are trying to end run—you might actually be crossing a snow bridge.

Use a Snow Bridge

If an end run is not possible or requires a lengthy detour from the climbing route, crossing on a snow bridge may be a better option. Deep winter snow hardened by wind, or the area between parallel crevasses, can form a bridge over the void beneath. A snow bridge's longevity and strength vary tremendously depending on time of year and temperature. A bridge that exists in late spring might be melted out by late summer. A bridge that supported substantial weight in early morning may collapse under its own weight during a summertime afternoon thaw. Use caution every time you cross a snow bridge. Do not assume that a bridge that held in the morning during the ascent will remain sturdy on the way down that afternoon. Setting up a belay for questionable snow bridges may better protect the party from a lengthy, dangerous fall with a difficult and time-consuming rescue.

Snow bridges that form where two crevasses are parallel but not quite connected are often sturdy, with foundations that extend deep into the body of the glacier. Treat the ends of these crevasses carefully and swing wide around them, as these ends may be covered with snow (fig. 19-13).

Study a snow bridge carefully. Before venturing out onto a bridge, look for a side view to see beneath it and gauge how thick and strong it might be. If in doubt, the leader can approach it to probe and get a close-up look while the second climber stays braced against the taut rope, prepared

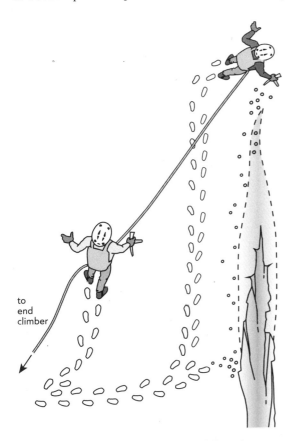

Fig. 19-12. *End run around a crevasse: the follower keeps rope fully extended, and at more of an angle and less parallel to the crevasse, by not following the leader's footsteps.*

Fig. 19-13. *Crossing a snow bridge between parallel crevasses: swing wide around potentially covered ends.*

Fig. 19-14. *Probing a snow bridge with caution before crossing it.*

to drop into self-arrest in case the leader possibly breaks through (fig. 19-14). After the leader gets across, the rest of the party follows exactly in the leader's steps, also receiving protection from a taut rope.

Take a Long Step Across

Before attempting a long step across a crevasse, probe to find the true edge of the crevasse to establish a stable starting place. From there, determine if the crevasse is narrow enough to cross with a long step or a very short hop. Do so by visually inspecting the opposite side of the crevasse, or if possible, probe with a long ice axe or a ski pole to determine if it seems sturdy enough to hold a climber's weight. Protect the climber stepping across with a taut rope or a belay. Be wary of making a desperate long jump across a crevasse while wearing crampons. While leaping across looks dramatic and fun in videos, it often results in a sprained or broken ankle. Attempt a long leap across a crevasse only in an emergency when the consequences of such an injury are less than the risk from other dangers.

Go Into the Crevasse

On rare occasions, it may be practical to get to the other side of a shallow crevasse by climbing down into the crevasse, crossing it at the bottom or at a narrow point, and climbing up on the other side. Only a strong, highly trained, well-equipped party that is ready to provide a secure belay should attempt this tactic. Inspect the crevasse carefully and probe while moving ahead. Often, what appears to be a solid bottom could collapse.

Reacting and Responding to a Crevasse Fall

If a member of a rope team (usually the first person on the rope) breaks through the surface snow layer or a snow bridge over a crevasse, reacting quickly can often prevent their entire body from falling into the hole. If the crevasse is narrow enough or the snow layer on the edges strong enough, perhaps only your legs will penetrate and you can stop the fall with support from your outstretched

19

end climber

middle climber

lead climber

Fig. 19-15. *Leader reacts by extending their arms to keep from plunging deeper into a crevasse; the middle and end climbers drop into self-arrest with a taut rope, ready to hold the lead climber to prevent a deeper fall. (Length of rope is not to scale.)*

arms bridged across the crevasse on either side (see Figure 19-15). Immediately after feeling the snow collapse underfoot, you can also try to prevent a deep plunge by twisting around 180 degrees and lunging backward with your upper body to perform a self-arrest into the crevasse lip.

By reacting quickly, the middle and end climbers on a three-person rope team also play an important role in preventing the leader from taking a deep plunge. Keeping the rope taut when traveling across a suspicious area, the middle and end climbers can lunge backward if they see the leader start to fall in, and immediately drop into a self-arrest position (facing away from the direction of pull, fig. 19-15). Pulling the leader backward with the rope this way makes it easier for the fallen leader to twist around and self-arrest onto the crevasse lip. The middle climber can then perform a sitting belay as the leader climbs out (see Chapter 16).

Most of the time, these kinds of quick reactions can keep a climber from falling completely into a crevasse. But sometimes the route must negotiate crevassed areas with thin snow coverings or weak snow bridges that, should they collapse underfoot, would result in a climber falling all the way in. To stop a fall, the middle and end climbers drop immediately into self-arrest as described above (see Figure 19-15). Once the fall has been stopped, the climbers still on the surface perform a crevasse rescue. It is uncommon for climbers to fall all the way into a crevasse, but learning and practicing crevasse rescue procedures gives climbers the necessary skills to perform a rescue when it does happen. Developing these important skills requires training in the field, augmented with periodic practice. See the "Crevasse Rescue Precautions" sidebar.

The principal steps to perform a rescue are listed briefly here and discussed in detail in the sections that follow. (The more involved Seven Steps in Accident Response are discussed in Chapters 24, First Aid, and 25, Self-Rescue.)

Step 1. Communicate with the fallen climber and devise a rescue plan. Determine if it is possible for the fallen climber to self-rescue by using a technique such as the traction position and front-pointing (see Chapter 17, Technical Snow and Ice Climbing) to climb out, protected with a sitting hip belay. If not, proceed to step 2; the team will need to build an anchor system so that the fallen climber can either perform a self-rescue by ascending the rope or the team can use a hauling system to pull the climber out. If it's not possible to communicate with the fallen climber, immediately proceed to step 2.

CREVASSE RESCUE PRECAUTIONS

When rescuing a fallen climber inside a crevasse, ensure that these precautions are in place.

- **All anchor systems are strong enough to hold the applied forces.** Use equalized or backup anchors to prevent an anchor failure.

- **All rescuers are connected to anchors at all times.**

- **The rescue needs to proceed as quickly as possible.** Minimize how much time the fallen climber spends in a cold crevasse.

Step 2. Set up a secure anchor system appropriate for the rescue plan. If it was possible to communicate with the fallen climber in step 1, and it was determined that it was not possible to climb out protected with a sitting hip belay, set up an anchor system that will accommodate the agreed-upon rescue plan. If it was not possible to communicate with the fallen climber, set up an anchor system that will accommodate a rescue plan deemed most appropriate for the situation.

Step 3. Continue to communicate with the fallen climber and carry out the plan. Once the rope has been anchored, it should be easier to communicate with and assist the fallen climber. Implement a self-rescue for the fallen climber to ascend the rope if that is the plan. For a team rescue, set up the chosen hauling system, then haul the climber out.

STEP 1. COMMUNICATE AND DEVISE A RESCUE PLAN

If possible, rescuers while they are still in self-arrest should communicate with the fallen climber to determine the quickest and easiest way to get the person out of the crevasse. Ask questions to evaluate the situation:

- Is the climber wedged in?
- Is the climber injured?
- Is it possible for the person to simply climb out with a belay?

After falling into a crevasse, it's usually possible to climb out using front-pointing and a few *piolet traction* moves. Sometimes, the inside of the crevasse has tunnels or ice features that can be followed as a way to get out. If the fallen climber tries to climb out, team members above who have stopped the fall and are still in self-arrest can set up a sitting hip belay in the snow once the climber has gotten their weight off the rope (see Figure 16-34 in Chapter 16).

If the party determines the fallen climber cannot climb out protected with a sitting hip belay, then proceed to step 2 after establishing whether the fallen climber will ascend the rope or be extricated using a team rescue.

STEP 2. SET UP THE ANCHOR SYSTEM

If it isn't possible to self-rescue by simply climbing out, the fallen climber works to be as comfortable as possible, zipping up and adding additional warm layers. If there is a nearby ledge inside the crevasse, the fallen climber can ask to be lowered to it. If it's not possible to be lowered onto a ledge, the fallen climber should clip the ice axe to a harness gear loop with a carabiner and gain an upright position. If the weight of the pack makes it impossible to pull upright, remove it, girth hitch a sling through its haul loop, and clip the sling with a carabiner to the harness belay loop to let

the pack hang (see Figure 19-16). It's also possible for the rescuers to lower a rope and pull up the stranded climber's pack and ice axe.

Build the Initial Anchor

Building the initial anchor will be much easier if the weight can be taken off the rope by lowering the fallen climber to a nearby ledge if one is available inside the crevasse. If the fallen climber is carrying an ice screw, it might be possible to place it in the wall of the crevasse and take the weight off the rope by hanging from it. If the weight cannot be taken off the rope, and another trained rope team is available to help, the second team begins setting up a rescue anchor—a distinct advantage of traveling with more than one rope team. Otherwise, the end climber on the three-person rope team generally is responsible for setting up the initial anchor. To free the end climber, the middle climber stays in self-arrest to support the fallen climber's weight, which hopefully is not too difficult if rope friction across the snow holds much of the weight.

The end climber slowly gets out of self-arrest, after first making sure the middle climber can hold the weight alone. The end climber then approaches the middle climber's position, using a progress capture pulley (PCP) or a prusik

Fig. 19-16. *End climber sets up initial anchor while middle climber remains in self-arrest to hold fallen lead climber, who is upright and has removed pack and attached it and ice axe to harness.*

sling to self-belay and remaining ready to drop back into self-arrest if the middle climber begins to slip. Once the two top-side rescuers are together, the end climber can establish an initial anchor (fig. 19-16).

In snow, a picket with a midpoint cable attachment (a mid-clip cable picket) is often a good choice for the initial anchor because it can be placed quickly in a vertical position and is stronger than a top-clip picket. An ice axe may also be used as a T-slot anchor (see Snow and Ice Anchors in Chapter 16). If there is ice not far beneath the snow surface, dig down and use an ice-screw anchor (see Ice Screws in Chapter 17). Place the anchor 5 to 10 feet (1.5 to 3 meters) down-rope from the middle climber, if there is enough room away from the lip of the crevasse.

Attach the Rope to the Anchor

The person who has set up the anchor now attaches a PCP to the climbing rope and clips the pulley with a locking carabiner to another locking carabiner attached to the end loop of the mid-clip cable picket (fig. 19-17). The next move is to slide the PCP down the rope toward the crevasse, until the anchor's cable is tight and ready to take the load. The middle climber—or anyone still in self-arrest—can now ease the load onto the anchor, but still remain in the arrest position to back up the initial anchor. Confirm that the anchor is solid and that the PCP grips the climbing rope.

If a PCP is not available, attach a short sling to the climbing rope with a prusik hitch (or a bachmann or klemheist friction hitch), and clip it to the anchor with a locking carabiner. Back up the friction hitch by tying a figure eight on a bight in the climbing rope and clip the knot to the anchor.

Build the Second Anchor

Never trust a single anchor. Always back it up with a second anchor to make the system as secure as possible. While the end climber builds the second anchor, the middle climber remains in the self-arrest position as a temporary backup to the initial anchor. For the second anchor, use a T-slot anchor for snow (fig. 19-18) or an ice screw if there is ice just beneath the snow.

Clip the second anchor to a sling that is then clipped to the locking carabiner clipped to the PCP, which is attached

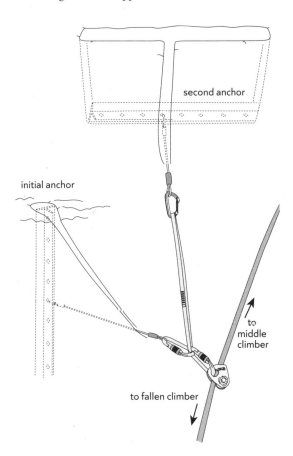

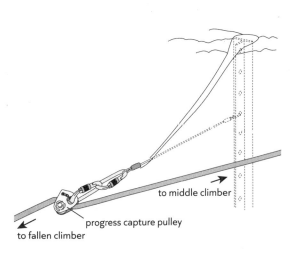

Fig. 19-17. *Climbing rope fed through progress capture pulley (PCP) that is attached with a locking carabiner to another locking carabiner clipped to the mid-clip cable picket.*

Fig. 19-18. *Install a second anchor: here, a T-slot using a picket.*

to the climbing rope. Try to make a taut connection from anchor to sling and remember the principles of equalization: keep the angle between the two anchors small (see Equalizing the Belay Anchor in Chapter 10, Belaying).

Once a secure anchor system is in place, the team members can proceed to the next steps in the crevasse rescue plan.

STEP 3. CONTINUE TO COMMUNICATE AND CARRY OUT THE PLAN

Now that the rope is anchored, one of the rescuers approaches the lip of the crevasse (fig. 19-19) while self-belayed from the main anchor using a PCP or prusik sling clipped to their harness belay loop with a locking carabiner attached to the rescuer's tie-in rope. From there, the rescuer can better communicate with the fallen climber and confirm or revise the rescue plan developed in step 1. The rescuing climber at the crevasse lip should be skilled in rescue techniques and first aid. The other team members similarly anchored can move around to adjust or tend to the snow anchors and begin implementing the rescue plan.

Investigate and Choose the Rescue Plan

When the rescuer approaches the lip of the crevasse, aim to go to either side of where the climber fell, to prevent knocking snow and ice down onto the climber in the crevasse. Also, probe with an ice axe while approaching to discover where the snow surface may be undercut or unsupportive. The rescuer is now positioned to prepare the lip to keep the rope holding the fallen climber from becoming more entrenched. A better option is to lower a separate length of rope that is not entrenched, from either side and not directly above the fallen climber. Use the opposite end of the accident rope or another rope entirely, lower it with a locking carabiner to the fallen climber for them to clip to their harness, and then anchor the new rope to the main anchor with a PCP. An entrenched rope adds a lot of friction to the raising system and exerts tremendous force on the anchors during team rescues. If the entrenched rope is equipped with brake knots, it will be almost impossible to use it for a raising system or for the fallen climber to ascend the rope over the lip. Lowering a separate rope to the fallen climber to be used for the rescue, one that is not entrenched or knotted, will make it much easier to carry out the rescue plan.

To prevent either the entrenched rope holding the fallen climber from digging in farther—or the nonentrenched rope that was lowered down to the fallen climber from digging in at all—slide an ice-axe shaft, a ski with padded edges, a foam pad, or even a pack under the rescue rope as

Fig. 19-19. *Anchor system complete: self-belayed rescuer able to communicate with fallen climber; anchored ice axe protects rope from entrenchment at lip of crevasse.*

close to the edge of the crevasse as you can reach safely. Be careful when working with sharp objects (ice-axe picks, ski edges, et cetera) to keep from damaging the rope. Anchor the rope support items so that they cannot fall into the crevasse (see Figure 19-19). It is also helpful to use a shovel or ice axe to round out the crevasse lip to a low-angled ramp, but only when it is off to the side and not directly above the fallen climber. Rounding off the edge of the crevasse can make the transition from inside the crevasse to the glacier surface much easier for everyone.

If it wasn't possible to communicate effectively with the fallen climber in step 1, try to talk now at the lip to determine if they have any injuries. If there is still no answer, the fallen climber may simply be out of earshot, or noisy wind on the glacier may mask the response. If further attempts still elicit no response, the rescuer must rappel or be lowered into the crevasse, to further assess the situation and perform urgent first aid if needed. Some crevasse rescue systems are better for dealing with a seriously injured or unconscious climber than others; see Special Rescue Situations later in this chapter.

If rescuers initially had voice contact with the fallen climber in step 1, they know whether the fallen climber can climb up and out. Now that a rescuer is at the edge of the crevasse, ask many of the same questions as before plus more questions to evaluate the full situation:

- Is the climber wedged in?
- Is the climber injured?
- Is the climber cold and in need of more clothing?

Most important, assure the climber that the team is making progress on the rescue.

If the fallen climber was unable to communicate with the rescuers in step 1, the fallen climber and the rescuers can confirm now whether self-rescue—by climbing up the side of the crevasse or up the rope—is a possibility or whether the climber needs to be hoisted from above. If there is a nearby ledge and the fallen climber was unable to communicate that in step 1, the rescuers can discuss the possibility of lowering the fallen climber to a ledge from where it may be easier for the climber to self-rescue or be hauled up.

After deciding between self-rescue and team rescue, the party must still choose among the various methods of either option. Deciding factors include the fallen climber's condition, the number of rescuers, available equipment (ice-climbing tools, additional ropes, PCPs, ascenders, and so forth), weather conditions, the topography of the crevasse area, and any other variables that affect the risk to the fallen climber and rescuers. The two sections below provide a brief overview of the various options, which are described and illustrated in more detail under Rescue Methods, below.

Option 1. Self-Rescue

If the fallen climber is uninjured and is familiar with self-rescue techniques, it is usually easier to perform a self-rescue. For small parties pinned down holding the rope, self-rescue may be the only practical option. This is especially true for a two-person rope team traveling without other parties around to help.

Climb out. If the fallen climber is uninjured and able to maneuver, climbing up the wall of the crevasse—assisted by pulling from above—is often the easiest and fastest form of rescue, regardless of party size. An uninjured climber may spot other ways to climb out, perhaps not exactly where they fell in. Always check the possibility of lowering the fallen climber or having them swing to an inside ledge, where they may find a different, easier way to ascend with a belay from above.

Ascend the rope. The other self-rescue method is for the fallen climber to ascend the rope with the lightweight ascender and PCP system, which is much easier to perform than using prusik slings (see Rescue Methods, below).

Option 2. Team Rescue

Several choices for team-rescue methods are summarized here. For complete descriptions and illustrations, see Rescue Methods, below. When performing a team rescue, clear communication between team members is especially important as the fallen climber approaches the lip to ensure that the rope, if entrenched, does not pull the climber into the crevasse wall (another reason to set up a nonentrenched rope to perform the rescue).

Direct haul. For a large party with an unentrenched rope, it's possible to try a direct pull using brute force, but this approach takes a tremendous force and usually doesn't work unless the fallen climber is only a short distance down inside the crevasse. It takes a large group of strong rescuers hauling on the rope, and it helps if the hauling climbers are on flat ground or downhill from the fallen climber.

2:1 (single) pulley system. When there isn't enough horsepower to perform a direct haul, try a 2:1 (single pulley) method. The fallen climber must be able to contribute to the rescue, with at least one hand available for clipping in to the rescue PCP and for maintaining balance. An entrenched fall rope does not matter because this method requires a separate length of rope—either the unused end of the accident rope or another rope entirely. The length of rope available must be at least twice as long as the distance from the anchor to the fallen climber. The mechanical advantage of the pulley makes hoisting this way a lot easier than a direct haul.

3:1 (Z) pulley system. When a fallen climber is unable to help in the rescue or when the haulers cannot pull up the fallen climber with a single pulley, the 3:1 (Z) pulley may be the best method. The pull force is either on the accident rope, which may be partially entrenched, or a separate length of unentrenched rope that was lowered down as described above. This system's high mechanical advantage gives haulers the power to overcome some entrenchment, but the additional load this system puts on the snow anchors and the problems associated with pulling the fallen climber over the lip make using a separate length of unentrenched rope for the rescue a better option.

Other rescue methods. Though the crevasse rescue systems mentioned above are among the most common, other team-rescue methods are worth considering. Piggybacking two systems together, such as a 2:1 pulley setup hauling on a 3:1 pulley system, creates a higher mechanical advantage and, thus, even more hauling power. But for hauling the weight of a fallen climber, it's usually not necessary to build a system with a mechanical advantage greater than 3:1 (see Piggyback Systems later in this chapter).

Carry Out the Plan

Now the party must get the fallen climber out of the crevasse. If self-rescue is the chosen plan, the rescuers assist as needed. If the rescue is a team effort, the rescuers set up the selected hauling system and pull the fallen climber out. See Rescue Methods, next section.

Rescue Methods

If you are unable to climb out, you can perform a self-rescue by ascending the rope a couple different ways. When performing a team rescue, you can choose from various hauling methods.

OPTION 1. SELF-RESCUE BY ASCENDING THE ROPE

The preferred method for self-rescue by ascending the rope is the lightweight ascender and progress capture pulley (PCP) system. If this equipment is unavailable, it's possible to ascend the rope with the prusik system.

Lightweight Ascender and PCP System

The lightweight ascender and PCP system permits plenty of upward progress per cycle as well as comfortable rests. This system is easy to learn and execute, and it keeps the climber upright without having to be connected to a chest harness. Here are the steps for setting up the system to climb up the rope, which should now be attached to the anchor (fig. 19-20).

1. **Attach the PCP to the climbing rope.** Make sure the capture end is toward the anchor (arrows on the pulley indicate the direction of rope travel). Clip a locking carabiner through the PCP and, for now, leave it attached to the rope only.
2. **Attach the lightweight ascender to the rope above the PCP.** Use a locking carabiner and clip a 48-inch (120-centimeter) foot sling to this locking carabiner.
3. **Slip one foot into the 48-inch sling clipped to the lightweight ascender.** Slide the lightweight ascender up the rope to where it is snug on the foot sling,

and pull up on the locking carabiner attached to the ascender while standing up in the foot sling to take your weight off the rope tied to your harness.
4. **Clip the locking carabiner on the PCP to the belay loop on your harness.** Pull all the slack rope through the pulley.
5. **Sit down in your harness so the PCP takes the weight.**
6. **Girth-hitch another 48-inch sling to your harness's belay loop.** Clip this backup sling to the locking carabiner on the lightweight ascender.
7. **Lift leg and slide the lightweight ascender up, stand up in the foot sling, and pull more rope through the pulley.** Alternate steps 5 and 7 several times until there is about 3 feet (1 meter) of rope between the pulley and the rope tie-in knot on your harness.

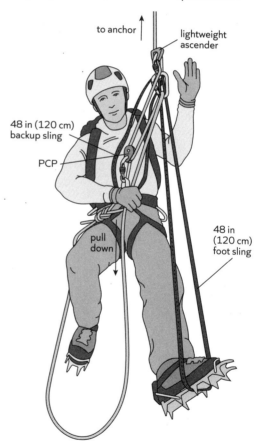

Fig. 19-20. *Self-rescue using the lightweight ascender and progress capture pulley (PCP) system to ascend the rope.*

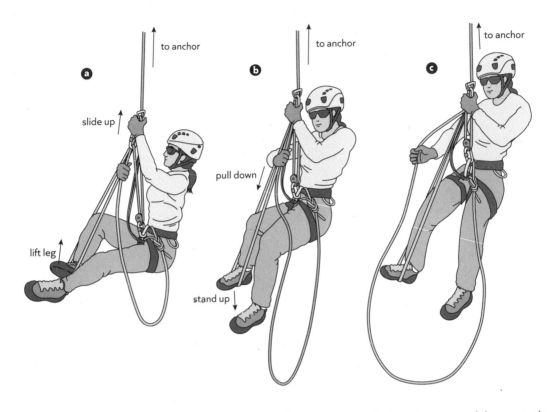

Fig. 19-21. *Ascending a rope using the lightweight ascender and progress capture pulley (PCP) system: **a,** while sitting in the harness, lift leg and slide up ascender clipped to foot sling; **b,** stand up in foot sling while pulling down on ascender's locking carabiner, and with your other arm pull down on rope from PCP running through carabiner attached to ascender's carabiner (removing slack); **c,** sit in harness again.*

8. **Clip another locking carabiner in to the locking carabiner already attached to the lightweight ascender.** Clip the rope slack from step 7 in to this second carabiner.

Now that the self-rescue system is set up, repeat the following three steps to ascend the rope:

1. While sitting in your harness, **lift leg and slide the lightweight ascender attached to the foot sling up the rope** (fig. 19-21a).
2. **Stand up in the foot sling** while pulling up with one arm on the locking carabiner attached to the ascender. At the same time, to remove the slack, pull down with the other arm on the rope running from the PCP through the carabiner attached to the lightweight ascender's carabiner (fig. 19-21b).
3. **Sit down in your harness again** (fig. 19-21c).

Prusik System

It is much easier to climb a rope using the lightweight ascender and PCP system than using prusiks. But if that equipment is not available, another option is to use a traditional prusik system, which is very similar to the one described above except that prusik knots (or another type of friction hitch) are used to grip the rope instead of the two mechanical devices. In this system, a foot sling (with one or two foot loops; see Figures 19-4a and 19-5a) is already attached to the climbing rope with a prusik knot, and a waist sling (see Figures 19-4b and 19-5b) is clipped with a locking carabiner to the harness belay loop and is also attached to the rope with a prusik knot (see Carrying and Prerigging Self-Rescue Gear earlier in this chapter).

To deploy and use the prusik system (fig. 19-22) to perform a self-rescue by ascending the rope, follow these steps:

Fig. 19-22. *Prusik system setup: slide waist loop prusik knot up the rope until tight and remove foot loop prusik sling from pocket ; place a foot in one or both loops, then stand up and slide the waist loop prusik up again.*

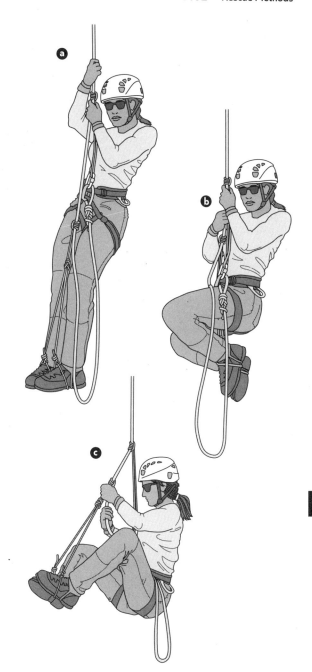

1. **Slide the waist sling prusik knot up the rope** until it is tight.
2. **Remove the foot loops end of the foot sling** from your pocket (the prusik end is already attached to the climbing rope) and place your feet in one or both foot loops (see Figure 19-22).
3. **Stand up in the foot loops.** Loosen the waist sling's prusik knot or friction hitch attached to the rope and slide it up the rope until the sling is taut (fig. 19-23a).
4. **Sit down in your harness.** Put all your weight on the waist sling, which releases your weight from the foot sling (fig. 19-23b).
5. **Loosen the foot sling's prusik knot** (or other friction hitch) attached to the rope and **slide the hitch up the rope.** This raises the foot sling and your feet with it (fig. 19-23c).
6. **Repeat steps 3 to 5 to ascend the rope.** While ascending the rope, it's a good idea to periodically clip backup knots to your belay loop.

Fig. 19-23. *Ascending a rope using the prusik system (pack and ice axe omitted for clarity):* **a,** *stand in foot loops and move waist sling's friction hitch up until it is taut;* **b,** *sit in harness to unweight foot sling;* **c,** *move foot sling's prusik hitch up.*

19

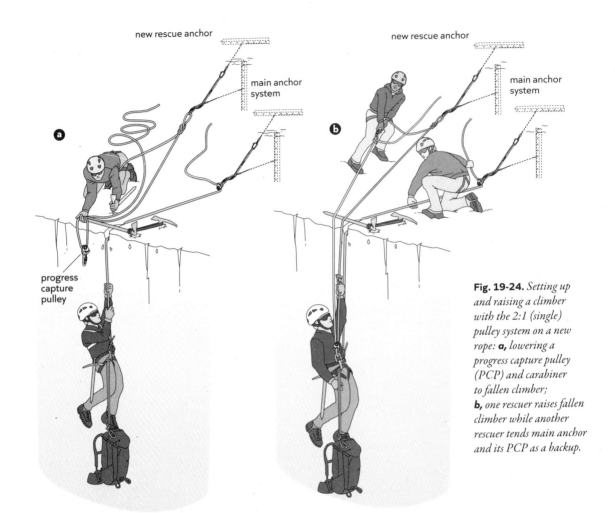

Fig. 19-24. *Setting up and raising a climber with the 2:1 (single) pulley system on a new rope:* ***a,*** *lowering a progress capture pulley (PCP) and carabiner to fallen climber;* ***b,*** *one rescuer raises fallen climber while another rescuer tends main anchor and its PCP as a backup.*

OPTION 2. TEAM RESCUE

A team rescue involves hauling the fallen climber to safety. The principal hauling methods—direct haul, 2:1 (single) pulley, 3:1 (Z) pulley, and piggyback systems—are described in the sections below. In any rescue system calling for pulleys, carabiners can be substituted if necessary. However, carabiners create far more friction and make the rope harder to pull, and the load on the anchor system is correspondingly increased.

Direct Haul

It takes a lot of horsepower to pull a fallen climber out of a crevasse using a direct haul. It requires a large group of strong haulers to line up along the accident rope and grasp it, either with gloved hands or via a PCP or friction hitch attached to their harness with a locking carabiner. They position themselves up-rope beyond where the anchor is attached to the climbing rope with a PCP (or a friction hitch, if a PCP is not available). The PCP (or friction hitch) will hold the rope if the haulers slip or need a rest.

The haulers pull on the rope hand over hand, or move step by step away from the crevasse, while one rescuer tends the PCP (or friction hitch, if a PCP is not available) on the anchor, making sure the rope moves smoothly through it and also keeping an eye on the anchor system. If there are enough people, another person stationed at the lip of the crevasse continues to communicate with the fallen climber.

The haulers pull the rope at a slow, steady pace, especially as the fallen climber reaches the crevasse edge. If the rope is entrenched in the lip, the fallen climber could be injured by being pulled into the crevasse wall. At this point, rescuers may ask the fallen climber to scramble over the lip (with the help of an ice axe) while they pull.

2:1 (Single) Pulley System

To reduce the pulling force in half for the rescuers relative to a direct haul, use the 2:1 (single) pulley system—though friction lowers this ratio somewhat. This method requires that the fallen climber clip a carabiner to their harness, but if the victim is unable to, a rescuer can rappel into the crevasse to clip the carabiner to the victim's harness and provide additional assistance and first aid.

Use a rescue rope at least twice as long as the distance from the anchor down to the fallen climber, either the unused end of the accident rope or a separate rope altogether. Attach this rope to either the main anchor system or a new rescue anchor off to the side to keep the systems separate. Prepare the lip of the crevasse to prevent the rescue rope from entrenching itself in the snow and perform any additional edge prep work as necessary.

With lightweight ascender and PCP. To carry out a rescue with the 2:1 pulley system using a PCP and lightweight ascender, follow these steps:

1. **Double the rescue rope into a big loop.** Affix a PCP to the loop, making sure the rope going through the capture end of the pulley comes from the main anchor. Attach a locking carabiner to the pulley and leave the carabiner unlocked.
2. **Lower the PCP and carabiner attached to the loop of rope to the fallen climber (fig. 19-24a).** Have the fallen climber clip the carabiner and lock it to the harness belay loop. Confirm that this has been done and check that all the fallen climber's equipment is secure and ready for hauling to begin.
3. **Assign a rescuer to attend to the slack that will develop in the original accident rope as the fallen climber is raised.** The PCP will transfer the climber's weight to the rescue anchor and hold it. But as a backup, a rescuer can also pull slack through the PCP attached to the original fall rope clipped to the main anchor.
4. **Start pulling on unanchored end of rescue rope with a lightweight ascender when everything is ready (fig. 19-24b).** To ease the haulers' task somewhat, the fallen climber can use a lightweight ascender to pull

up on the anchored side of the rescue rope while the hauling proceeds.

With simple pulley and carabiner. Note that this 2:1 pulley system can also be performed with a simple pulley and carabiner lowered to the fallen climber—steps 1 and 2 above—and a prusik (or other friction) hitch used to anchor the original fall rope to the main anchor. If using this system, it is critically important that a rescuer actively attend the main anchor (step 3 above), pulling slack through this friction hitch so that the rope is always ready to accept the fallen climber's weight.

3:1 (Z) Pulley System

To reduce the pulling force for the rescuers, relative to a direct haul or 2:1 system, use the 3:1 (Z) pulley system that offers a three-to-one mechanical advantage using two pulleys (note that friction lowers this ratio somewhat). It can be set up and operated with no help from the fallen climber. The 3:1 pulley system can use either the unused end of the accident rope or a separate length of rope if the accident rope is too entrenched. The 3:1 system requires more equipment and is more complicated than the other hauling methods described above.

Start by confirming the solidity of the main anchor system. The 3:1 pulley system puts more stress on it than the 2:1 pulley system. Take the loose end of the climbing rope attached to the fallen climber, or if that is too entrenched, take the loose end of a separate length of rope that was lowered and clipped to the fallen climber, and then clipped to the main anchor with a PCP and pulled taut. Extend this unweighted rope beyond the main anchor, and form it into a giant flat S or Z in the snow.

With PCPs and lightweight ascender. The first bend in the Z is the stationary PCP (or ratchet PCP) that is already in place as part of the main anchor (see Figure 19-17). At the second bend in the Z (the slack bend, closer to the crevasse lip), install a second PCP (the traveling PCP) on the rope, making sure the rope going through the capture end of the PCP comes from the anchor. Attach a lightweight ascender with a locking carabiner to the taut section of rope going to the fallen climber, and clip it to the traveling PCP (fig. 19-25). The 3:1 pulley system is now ready to be used. Here is how to haul using this system:

1. **Start pulling at a steady rate.** Either pull hand over hand or hold tight and walk backward. (Both methods are easier when pulling on the rope using a lightweight ascender.) If you walk backward, be sure the area you are walking toward is free of hazards.

2. **The hauling soon brings the second (traveling) PCP close to the stationary (ratchet) PCP at the main anchor.** Stop hauling when the PCPs are about 2 feet (0.6 meter) apart. If they are pulled too close, the figure Z collapses and the mechanical advantage is lost.

3. **Once hauling has stopped, relax the pull on the rope.** Relax the rope enough to transfer the fallen climber's weight back onto the stationary or ratchet PCP.

4. **Reset the traveling PCP.** Slide the lightweight ascender back down the taut fall rope toward the crevasse lip once again.

Repeat these four steps until the fallen climber is raised. The rescuers pull the rope at a slow, steady pace, especially when the fallen climber reaches the crevasse lip. If the rope you are using has cut into the lip, the fallen climber could be injured by being pulled into the crevasse wall. At this point, rescuers may ask the fallen climber to scramble over the lip (with the help of an ice axe) while they hoist.

With simple pulleys and friction hitches. It is easier to operate this pulley system using PCPs and a lightweight ascender, but if this equipment is not available, a 3:1 pulley system can be built using standard pulleys and

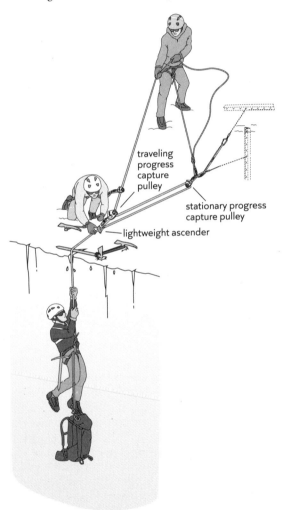

Fig. 19-25. *Raising a climber with the 3:1 (Z) pulley system using two progress capture pulleys (PCPs) and a lightweight ascender: the stationary (ratchet) PCP is on the main anchor and a traveling PCP is attached to the lightweight ascender.*

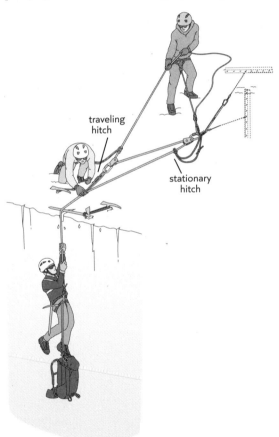

Fig. 19-26. *Raising a climber with the 3:1 (Z) pulley system using two standard pulleys and friction hitches: one set is the stationary prusik (here, a bachmann hitch) and pulley, the other is the traveling prusik and pulley.*

friction hitches. To set up this system, equip the main anchor to hold the fallen climber's weight with a friction hitch (the stationary hitch) and a standard pulley (the stationary pulley) attached to the Z rope, instead of the PCP described above. Attach a traveling hitch to the rope leading to the fallen climber, instead of the lightweight ascender described above, and clip it to the second (traveling) pulley with a locking carabiner (fig. 19-26). Follow these steps to lift the fallen climber with standard pulleys and friction hitches:

1. **Unclip the backup figure-eight loop (used with prusiks) from the main anchor system.** Untie the knot as soon as the haulers and fallen climber are ready for pulling.

2. **Assign a rescuer to tend the stationary hitch attaching the accident rope to the main anchor system.** If the stationary hitch is a prusik friction hitch, tend it so the rope slips freely through it as the rope is pulled in. If the stationary hitch is a bachmann hitch, the attachment should tend itself, and the hauler closest to the anchor can simply keep an eye on this hitch to see that all is well.

3. **Start pulling at a steady rate.** Either pull hand over hand or hold tight and walk backward. If walking backward, be sure the area you are walking toward is free of hazards.

4. **The hauling will soon bring the second (traveling) pulley close to the first (stationary) pulley at the main anchor.** Stop hauling when the pulleys are about 2 feet (0.6 meter) apart. If they are pulled too close, the figure Z collapses and the mechanical advantage is lost.

5. **Once hauling has stopped, relax the pull on the rope.** Relax the rope enough to transfer the fallen climber's weight back onto the stationary hitch at the main anchor.

6. **Reset the traveling pulley.** Loosen the traveling hitch clipped to the traveling pulley and slide the traveling hitch back down the taut accident rope toward the crevasse lip once again.

Keep repeating steps 3 through 5 until the fallen climber is raised. The rescuers pull the rope at a slow, steady pace, especially when the fallen climber reaches the crevasse lip. If the rope you are using has cut into the lip, the fallen climber could be injured by being pulled into the crevasse wall. At this point, rescuers may ask the fallen climber to scramble over the lip (with the help of an ice axe) while they hoist.

Piggyback Systems

To get even more mechanical advantage out of a rescue hauling setup, it is possible to combine or "piggyback" two of the systems discussed above. Systems with a greater mechanical advantage put higher loads on the snow anchors; if they are not operated carefully, they can also generate forces capable of seriously injuring a climber being hauled. It's usually unnecessary to build a system with a mechanical advantage greater than 3:1 to haul a fallen climber. If more force is needed, there may be other problems in the system to solve first, like having an entrenched rope. High-force hauling systems should only be operated by trained rescue teams, so they are beyond the scope of this guide.

Special Rescue Situations

Rescuing a climber from a crevasse can be complicated by special situations. Climbers must find a way to adapt and deal with them. Every crevasse rescue situation is different, so finding creative solutions while managing the team's risk is often necessary. (See Chapter 25, Self-Rescue, for more details on accident response and additional rescue techniques.)

WHEN THE MIDDLE PERSON FALLS IN

When the middle person on a three-person rope team falls completely into a crevasse, the other members of the rope team are separated by a crevasse, each in self-arrest. To get out of this fix, the climbers need to begin by deciding which side of the crevasse will be the rescue side—that is, which side they will try to help the fallen climber out on. Usually, one of the two rescuers in self-arrest is holding more weight than the other. The one holding the least weight usually has the best chance of getting up and establishing an anchor, while the rescuer on the other side stays in self-arrest to hold the fallen climber. The shape and steepness of the crevasse lip is also a major determining factor; choose the side where it will be easier for the fallen climber to self-rescue or be hauled out. If the climber above holding the most weight is on the easier side to perform a rescue, the fallen climber's weight may need to be eased onto the climber in self-arrest on the other side temporarily until the anchor can be built on the easier side.

After the climber on the rescue side sets up the rescue anchor (see Step 2: Set Up the Anchor System earlier in this chapter), the climber in self-arrest on the other side of the crevasse can slowly release tension on the climbing rope and ease the fallen climber's weight onto the anchor, which will also cause the victim to swing to the other side of the crevasse. Sometimes the shape of a crevasse or the predicament of the fallen climber makes it unwise to transfer weight and swing the victim back and forth to opposite sides of the crevasse. Try to communicate with the fallen climber to see if they are able to help themselves by climbing out with a belay or be lowered to a ledge.

If the climber on the non-rescue side is needed to help in the rescue operation, the climber on the rescue side now tries to belay the climber on the non-rescue side over to the rescue side. The rope on the rescue side can be used for belaying, if it is long enough. If no belay or secure route across the crevasse is available, however, the climber on the non-rescue side could be stuck there. This climber on the non-rescue side would then set up an anchor and stay put.

The most advantageous rescue plan now is for the fallen climber to self-rescue by climbing out or ascending the rope, coming out on the rescue side, where the anchor has been placed. If a self-rescue is not possible, then a 3:1 (Z) pulley system could be tried. This all takes plenty of time, competence, equipment, and resourcefulness. If progress capture pulleys (PCPs) are not available, learn to use the bachmann hitch (see Friction Hitches in Chapter 8, Essential Climbing Equipment) for times when you might have to haul alone, because the hitch requires less tending than a standard prusik hitch in a hauling system.

In the case of a four-person rope team, the situation is a little simpler if one of the two middle members falls into a crevasse. Conduct the rescue in a routine manner from the side that has two climbers top-side, if the crevasse lip on that side is also the easier side to perform the rescue.

WHEN A TWO-PERSON TEAM IS ALONE

For a party of two climbers without another rope team nearby, travel on a heavily crevassed glacier is riskier than for a larger party, and the prospect of crevasse rescue is very challenging and complex and requires significant training. Both climbers need to know their rescue techniques. If one of the climbers falls entirely into a crevasse, and the climber top-side stops the fall with a self-arrest, it is difficult, maybe even impossible, for the top-side climber to set up an anchor alone while still holding the weight of the fallen climber. In this situation, the team will need to rely much more on the fallen climber, to either climb out or get the weight off the rope so the climber top-side can set up an anchor.

To relieve weight from the rope, the fallen climber could locate a ledge or stance and down-climb or be lowered there. They could also place an ice screw in the wall of the crevasse and hang from it. If the fallen climber can reliably take the weight off the rope, the climber top-side is able to build an anchor, attach the fall rope, or throw down an anchored, nonentrenched rope. The topside climber can then work with the fallen climber to develop a rescue plan and carry it out as described earlier in this chapter under Reacting and Responding to a Crevasse Fall.

If the fallen climber is unable to get the weight off the rope, then the top-side climber may need to remain in self-arrest and act as the anchor while the fallen climber ascends the rope.

If the fallen climber is injured, the top-side climber will need to get creative and assume the risk involved in finding a way to dig their feet into the snow and use their body weight to keep from being dragged into the crevasse while building an anchor.

Each climber in a two-person team should carry equipment that is readily available to build an anchor, as well as extra PCPs, lightweight ascenders, carabiners, and slings to set up a hauling system. Rope teams of two often shorten their rope by taking in coils (see Shorten the Rope with Coils earlier in this chapter), which automatically makes an extra length of rope available for rescue use.

If you are using brake knots (see Figure 19-8), there is a greater chance that the rope will get stuck when it becomes entrenched going over the lip of a crevasse during a fall (see How to Tie In earlier in this chapter). The entrenched brake knots may hold the weight of the fallen climber, which would allow the top-side climber to set up an anchor. Once the rope is anchored, these knots may complicate a rescue process that needs to use that portion of the fall rope. But shortening the rope with coils would make an extra length of rope available for rescue use.

Traveling on a glacier alone as a party of two requires a high degree of competency with crevasse rescue systems. Study and practice before attempting it.

WHEN THE FALLEN CLIMBER IS UNCONSCIOUS

If a climber is injured falling into a crevasse, a rescuer must descend as quickly as possible by rappelling from the anchor or being lowered. This rescuer must descend with enough clothing and equipment to warm or insulate the victim, provide appropriate first aid, and ascend independently if needed. The rescuer can administer urgent first aid and get the fallen climber right side up if necessary. If possible, try to lower the injured climber to a ledge inside the crevasse where first aid can be administered more easily.

If the fallen climber is injured badly or unconscious, any additional movement could cause further injury (see First Aid in Chapter 24). The injured climber may need to remain in the crevasse in a location where they can be stabilized as much as possible until a trained rescue team can be called to the site. If the team is in a remote location with no possibility of calling for a rescue, the rescuers must then consider how to immobilize the injured climber, possibly build a litter, and evaluate which of the hauling methods they will use, keeping in mind that the fallen climber is unable to participate. Helping an unconscious or injured climber over the lip of the crevasse requires a rescuer to work right at the edge of or from inside the crevasse. Monitor the condition of the unconscious person, taking care to avoid causing further injury. See Chapter 25, Self-Rescue, for next steps in evacuation and accident response.

WHEN THE SELF-ARREST IS CLOSE TO THE EDGE

The climber who drops into self-arrest to stop a rope mate's fall could be lying so close to the lip of the crevasse that there is very little room to place an anchor or pulley system. If the party has more than two climbers, the climber who is not in self-arrest can set up the main anchor where there is enough room beyond the climber in self-arrest. The anchor can be placed there instead of the usual place between the rescuer and the crevasse. Extend a long sling, a cordelette, or the free end of a rope from the main anchor to where a PCP (or prusik sling) can be attached to the rope between the rescuer in self-arrest and the crevasse. Tensioning this sling or cordelette allows it to take the weight of the fallen climber and permits the rescuer to get up from their self-arrest position. The anchor point on the rope to the fallen climber can then be moved closer to the main anchor using another PCP or prusik knot so that there is space to work.

WHEN THE WORKING SPACE IS NARROW

When working in a narrow space, such as between two crevasses, it's possible for rescuers to change the direction of pull on a 3:1 pulley system. Clip a third pulley via a sling and carabiner to the main anchor, and run the hauling end of the rope through it (fig. 19-27). Now the rescuers can pull in a direction that accommodates the site.

WHEN THE ROPE IS ENTRENCHED

As mentioned previously, it is usually advantageous to switch to a new rescue rope if the upward progress of a person climbing out or being pulled out of a crevasse is hampered by a fall rope that has become deeply entrenched into the crevasse lip. If the entrenched rope seems manageable, it can be used for a rescue with some improvisation.

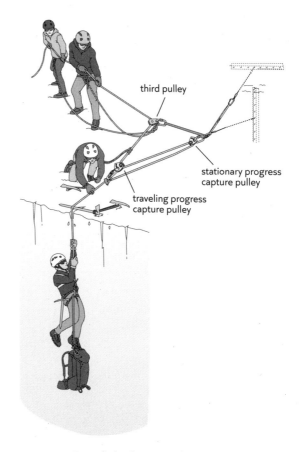

Fig. 19-27. *Setup for hauling in a tight space, such as between two crevasses: to change the direction of hauling in a 3:1 (Z) pulley system, attach third pulley with sling and locking carabiner to main anchor and run hauling rope through it.*

Remove weight from the entrenched rope. If the fallen climber can be lowered to a ledge or find some other means to unweight from the rope, the rescuers can free the entrenched rope and pad it at the lip.

Bypassing the entrenchment. A rescuer can attach prusik slings above the entrenched portion of the rope and then drop them down for the climber to step into or pull on to get around the entrenchment.

Switching to a new rescue rope. As mentioned earlier, a rescuer can lower a new rope to the fallen climber for a 2:1 hauling system (as shown in Figure 19-24). Or as also mentioned earlier, a new rescue rope, supported at the lip of the crevasse to keep it from becoming entrenched, can be lowered to the fallen climber to open up several other rescue possibilities, such as the fallen climber can switch from

19

ascending the original climbing rope to ascending the new free rope. Or the rescuers can haul the fallen climber up and out on the new rope. Or the fallen climber can merely transfer all of their weight to the new rope, to give rescuers a much better chance of freeing the entrenched line.

Paths to the Summit

Although glaciers appear to be rather convenient, obvious routes to alpine summits, they are massive, dynamic systems that hold many hazards—especially with climate change reshaping the glacial landscape. Climbers who seek the freedom of the glaciated peaks must learn how to negotiate crevasses and other dangers while minimizing their risk of falling into a crevasse. Even when climbers take precautions, they sometimes fall or experience other accidents. Anyone planning to travel on a glacier must master the techniques for dealing with the hazards and performing a successful rescue if necessary. With these skills, climbers can securely take advantage of these glacial paths to alpine summits.

CHAPTER 20

AVALANCHE SAFETY

Mountaineers seek the freedom of the hills, and no freedom is harder to earn than that of the snowy hills. In North America, according to the Colorado Avalanche Information Center (CAIC), avalanches kill more winter recreationists than any other natural hazard. Nearly all avalanches involving people are triggered either by the victims or a member of their party. To lower their risk, climbers must learn to recognize and evaluate the hazards presented by avalanche terrain.

According to avalanche expert Bruce Tremper, about 90 percent of avalanche victims trigger their own slide. According to the Colorado Avalanche Information Center, over the past seven decades in the US, the majority of avalanche fatalities in May and June have involved climbers. When mountaineers plan to enter avalanche terrain, it is important that they focus first on avoiding an avalanche, and then on surviving one and searching for and rescuing companions.

Climbers, backcountry skiers, snowmobilers, and snowshoers are the primary victims of avalanches. Advances in mountaineering and skiing gear and changing trends in backcountry recreation are leading more and more people to have fun where there are avalanche-prone slopes. Two factors explain the high level of risk to climbers and backcountry skiers:

1. With a combination of unstable snow, terrain capable of producing an avalanche, and a trigger—often someone in your party—mountains big and small possess the potential to bury or injure you.
2. The longer and bigger the objective, the more climbers and backcountry skiers increase their exposure to the risk of involvement in an avalanche.

Reaching a climbing objective often involves traveling up cliffs and narrow couloirs, across exposed crevasses or boulder fields, on steep and exposed avalanche start zones, and other terrain traps. These kinds of hazards increase the likelihood of serious injury or deep burial, making an encounter with a small avalanche potentially fatal. When choosing routes, climbers must contend with the challenges of evaluating avalanche hazard. Early start times, traveling fast, and brute ambition can help lower avalanche risk, but such measures will not help climbers evade all avalanches. Unlike high-mountain exposure and severe weather, avalanche hazard is not always obvious. At the same time, the consequences of an avalanche for mountaineers in spring and summer are at least as great as they are in winter. It is not only important for climbers to recognize these hazards but also to have the discipline to respect the problem and choose another route or wait until the risk decreases.

Avalanche Training

Avalanches are not a mysterious phenomenon. Learning about avalanches and how to manage your risk of being caught in one is a lifelong process that requires frequent practice, continued education, and regular informal and formal assessment. In North America, avalanche education for recreationalists consists of a one-hour awareness class, a three-day level 1 course for beginners, a one-day rescue course to improve companion rescue skills learned in the level 1 course, and a three-day level 2 course for people who want to lead a group of friends on a hut trip

20

or an overnight climbing trip. Avalanche education provides helpful information to assist backcountry travelers in making informed decisions while traveling in a snowy environment.

This chapter describes types of avalanches, reviews some ways that snow travelers can evaluate hazards and minimize their risk, and explains basic methods of companion rescue techniques. This material is not meant to be comprehensive. For a thorough understanding of how to navigate avalanche terrain while minimizing your risk, consult specialized publications (see Resources). Before you venture into avalanche terrain, learn how to recognize such terrain and the hazards it may entail by taking a level 1 course from a reputable organization, such as AIARE (the American Institute for Avalanche Research and Education), the Alaska Avalanche School, or the American Avalanche Institute (see Resources). Refresh your knowledge and skills at regular intervals. It is only through mentorship, continuing education, and assessment that you can be sure that you are prepared to evaluate terrain and hazards out in the field.

Follow up that level 1 course with an avalanche rescue course to learn how to locate and rescue climbers buried in a slide, which requires a methodical and efficient approach to be effective. Level 1 courses do not cover how to make decisions without an avalanche forecast. After the forecast centers close and climbing season begins, you will need to be able to identify potential problems and gauge their extent. On a climb, mountaineers must be prepared for the possibility of multiple burials, since avalanches in glaciated terrain and on popular routes have a higher probability of involving more than one climber. For an explanation of how avalanches form and an assessment of dangers associated with various forms of snow, see Chapter 27, The Cycle of Snow.

Most backcountry skiers and winter mountaineers in avalanche-prone areas have some knowledge of the hazards and carry basic avalanche safety equipment, such as transceivers, probes, and shovels. Many seek out formal training in avalanche avoidance and rescue. But preparation for avalanche hazards in the spring and summer mountaineering season is less systematic. Most professional avalanche training is skewed toward using information from the local avalanche center to help navigate winter avalanche problems. However, many avalanches that affect mountaineers occur in terrain not covered by avalanche forecasts or after avalanche centers have stopped forecasting for the season. The difference in conditions in late spring and summer in the mountains

challenges climbers to recognize the same red flags and prepare with the same gear as they do in winter.

Types of Avalanches and Related Snow Features

When storm loads deposit new snow on the previous layers of snowpack, that snow adds more stress and can trigger a natural avalanche. A skier or climber may add sufficient stress to trigger a slide—as can falling chunks of snow, ice, or rock. The two principal types of avalanches that climbers encounter in a typical spring and summer climbing season are slab avalanches and loose-snow avalanches. (See How Avalanches Form in Chapter 27, The Cycle of Snow.) If you expect to be in avalanche terrain often, and as an alpine climber, you most likely will, you will probably want to dive into this topic in far more depth. As part of AIARE training, you will learn about the Snow and Weather Avalanche Guidelines (SWAG), a set of guidelines published by the American Avalanche Association for observing and recording snow, weather, and avalanche phenomena; those guidelines more formally classify avalanches into nine types and explore this topic in much more depth than this context allows. This brief introduction to avalanche types and response presents the hazards climbers are most likely to encounter without getting too far into the science of snow and the terminology used by avalanche professionals, which you could spend a lifetime studying.

SLAB AVALANCHES

Dangerous and destructive to skiers and snowshoers, as well as to winter climbers and scramblers, a slab avalanche occurs when a cohesive layer of snow, referred to as a slab, breaks free and slides downhill along a weak layer of snow underneath it (fig. 20-1). A slab composed of densely packed snow deposited by wind and the accumulation of snowfall.

The slope fails first in compression, with a *whumph* that climbers sometimes hear, and then in tension, as the slab breaks off and begins to move. As the large area of snow begins to move, the slab often breaks up into large plates and blocks of snow (fig. 20-2). Slab avalanches can strip away the snow all the way to the ground or can involve only the top layer(s) of poorly bonded snow. Wet springtime slab avalanches occur when the intense warming and higher sun angles of long spring days soften layers in the existing snowpack that formed during the winter. Wet slab avalanche conditions are very sensitive to the slope aspect, time of day, and temperature.

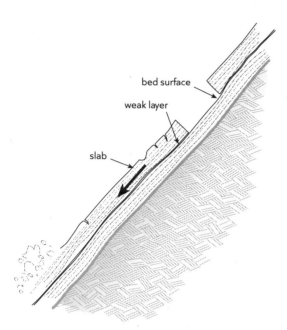

Fig. 20-1. *Layers of a slab avalanche in cross-section.*

Storm Slabs

A storm slab occurs when a soft, cohesive layer (a slab) of new snow breaks within the storm snow or on the old snow surface and is released. Storm-slab problems typically last between a few hours and a few days. Because storm-slab avalanches are the most common avalanche climbers encounter, recognizing the red flags in recent weather conditions and the forecast is critical. Mountaineers also need to be careful to avoid exposure to avalanches when choosing camp locations. Climbers should ideally wait up to 48 hours before attempting a route that has had more than a foot of new snow, is on a leeward aspect, and/or has exposure to terrain traps, such as cliffs or crevasses.

Wind Slabs

Wind-slab avalanches happen when strong winds (at least 15 miles per hour) move loose snow into dense layers and a cohesive layer of snow (a slab) is released. Wind typically transports snow from the upwind sides of terrain features and deposits snow on the downwind side. Strong winds during storms can turn 6 to 8 inches of new snow into slabs that are up to 2 feet deep on leeward slopes, such as the Roman Wall on Mount Baker in the Cascades and Tuckerman and Huntington Ravines in New Hampshire, to name a few. Often smooth and rounded, wind slabs range from soft to hard and they sometimes sound hollow. Wind slabs form in specific areas and are confined to lee and cross-loaded terrain features. By sticking to sheltered or wind-scoured areas, you can usually avoid wind-slab avalanches.

Persistent Slabs

A persistent slab occurs when a cohesive layer of soft to hard snow (a slab) in the middle to upper snowpack releases. Typically, this layer's bond to an underlying persistent weak layer breaks. Persistent layers include surface hoar, depth hoar, near-surface facets, or faceted snow. Persistent weak layers can continue to produce avalanches for days, weeks, even months, making them especially dangerous and tricky. As additional snow and wind events build a thicker slab on top of the persistent weak layer, this avalanche problem may develop into a deep persistent slab.

The best way to manage the risk of persistent slabs is to be conservative when choosing terrain. Light loads can trigger persistent-slab avalanches up to weeks after the last storm, making them tricky. The slabs often propagate in surprising and unpredictable ways, making them difficult to predict and manage. Increasing your safety buffer when persistent slabs are a possibility will help you avoid them.

LOOSE SNOW AVALANCHES

Loose snow avalanches, consisting of wet or dry snow, originate from a single point of release. They often resemble a teardrop shape that starts from one point and fans out as the avalanche runs downslope. Dry loose snow avalanches occur when unconsolidated dry snow detaches and cascades downhill in a powdery, dispersed manner. These avalanches are most dangerous in steep, confined, and isolated terrain.

Common in spring, wet loose snow avalanches, on the other hand, are often triggered by rising temperatures, direct sunlight, or rain. Melting within the snow causes bonds of the snow to break down, which in turn causes an underlying weak layer to fail, resulting in an avalanche.

CORNICE FALLS

Cornices form when wind drifts snow onto the downwind side of a ridgeline or summit (fig. 20-3). Cornices present risks for climbers along snow-covered ridges or when climbers fail to notice one on a snow-covered summit. When cornices fail, they often break quite far back on the slope the snow has been blown across, and can take a climber down with them. When a collapsing cornice falls onto the slope below, it can also trigger deep slab avalanches. Avoid climbing below cornices or approaching them too close, especially during the heat of the day.

20

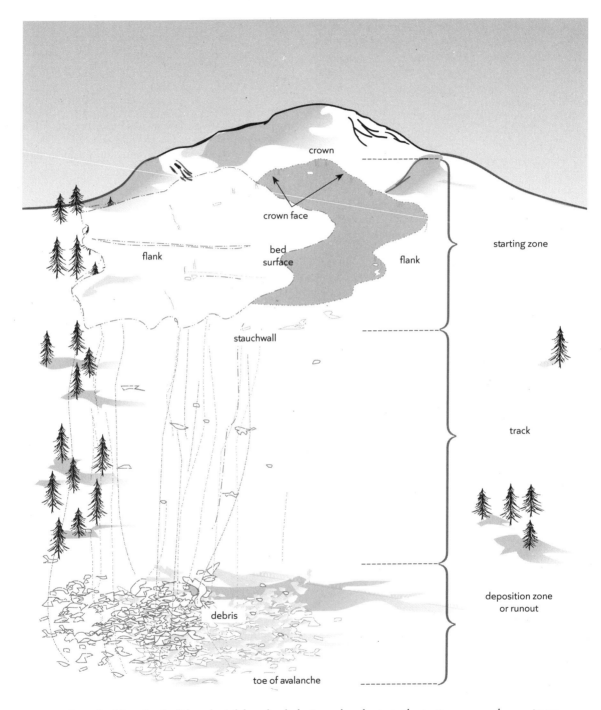

crown

crown face

bed
surface

flank

flank

starting zone

stauchwall

track

debris

deposition zone
or runout

toe of avalanche

Fig. 20-2. *Parts of a slab avalanche slide path: A slab avalanche begins and accelerates in the starting zone, reaches maximum velocity and mass in the track, and then decelerates and deposits snow in the deposition zone or runout.*

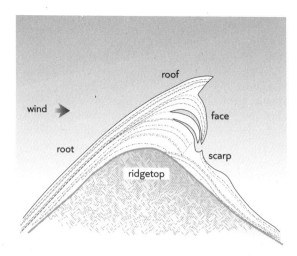

Fig. 20-3. *As the face of a cornice grows, it becomes heavier and eventually breaks—sometimes due to a trigger such as a person stepping out onto it.*

ICEFALL

When a portion of a serac or ice cliff fails in a steep, unstable glacier, ice can fall and present a hazard, possibly triggering an avalanche on the slopes below. Picture, for instance, the massive and dangerous Khumbu Icefall on Mount Everest. As with cornices, falling ice may trigger deep slab avalanches that can run far down a mountainside, threatening camps placed close to large faces. The random nature of icefalls makes predicting these events very difficult. The only way to reduce your risk is to minimize how much time you spend moving through or under icefalls, especially during the day, and to avoid placing camps in areas that are exposed to collapsing ice.

GLIDE AVALANCHES

After a long period of warming, in which running water has lubricated the slope underneath the seasonal snowpack, the snowpack may move downhill. This movement in turn creates glide cracks, which run through the entire snowpack from the surface to the ground. When these cracks break apart completely, large and destructive glide avalanches may result. These dangerous avalanches are incredibly difficult to predict. In alpine areas, these avalanches occur most often on glacier-polished slabs and glacial slabs. Selecting routes that limit your exposure to such features, or that avoid them altogether, will help you minimize your risk of experiencing this kind of avalanches.

Recognizing and Evaluating Avalanche Terrain

Mountaineering avalanches typically happen in terrain steeper than 30 degrees, above tree line, often on glaciers, and in areas subject to snowstorms. In other words, the types of terrain that climbers love. Most avalanche victims are involved in small- to medium-sized slides. Picture a snowfield the size of a couple of tennis courts poised on a slope, with weak layers hidden beneath the surface. A climber or rider enters the start zone, and the additional load causes a failure. *Crack*—the slab is off and away.

The snow breaks and shears along the bed surface (the ground, ice, or hard snow layer that forms the sliding surface) between the weak layers. Across the top of the snowfield, a fracture line marks the point where the tension holding the snow failed. Below the avalanche start zone (typically a 30- to 45-degree slope), the slab breaks up, and the churning snow accelerates down the avalanche track and into the runout zone. The snow stops moving due to the change in terrain, and the dense deposit accumulates and buries victims. The suddenness, speed, and power of an avalanche typically sweep victims off their feet, sometimes hurtling them into dangerous terrain and/or burying them in a cement-like medium.

In the spring and summer, when mountaineering activity peaks in North America, climbers may face exposure to significant storms leaving more than a foot of new snow on a route; strong winds (more than 15 miles per hour), transporting snow and building slabs on leeward slopes; and strong UV (solar) radiation, increasing the risk of triggering wet loose and slab avalanches. Understanding the basic mountaineering avalanche types helps you recognize the hazards you face and what solutions may help you mitigate or avoid them.

Choosing terrain is the key to minimizing your risk in snow-covered mountains. You cannot control the weather, and while an unstable snowpack can persist over large areas for long periods, climbers can choose to travel in terrain that will not generate an avalanche. Choosing terrain based on an understanding of the local conditions is the central concept of minimizing your risk when moving through avalanche country.

Learning to recognize avalanche terrain is the first step in the process of evaluating avalanche hazard. The steepness of a slope, its aspect (which direction it faces), and the slope's shape and natural features (its configuration) are all important factors in determining whether a slide could occur on a particular slope.

20

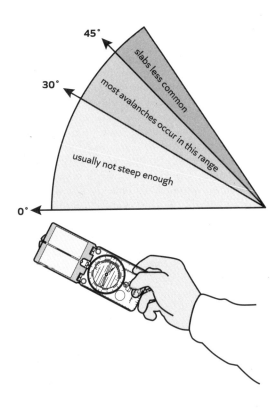

Fig. 20-4. *Slope angle, defined as steepness of the slope, is the most important terrain factor affecting avalanches. Most avalanches occur on slopes ranging from 30 to 45 degrees.*

SLOPE ANGLE

The steepness, or slope angle, is the most important terrain factor. Slab avalanches commonly occur on slopes with starting-zone angles of about 30 to 45 degrees, but they also occasionally occur on slopes of less than 30 and greater than 45 degrees (fig. 20-4). Slopes steeper than about 50 to 60 degrees tend to sluff snow regularly, and slopes of about 25 degrees or less are generally not steep enough or require highly unstable snow before they can slide.

It is difficult to estimate the angle of a slope simply by looking at it. Use a clinometer to measure slope angles in the field. Simple plastic models are available, and many compasses have built-in clinometers (see Chapter 5, Navigation and Communication, for a discussion of clinometers and how to measure slope angle). Learn to measure slope angle accurately on topographical maps; special scales make it easy to measure slope angle directly from the map based on the spacing of contour lines (fig. 20-5).

Slope angle is not the only factor to consider—an avalanche could start from an adjacent slope. All of the snow is connected. A party does not have to be climbing or skiing on a slope for it to avalanche. If the snowpack is unstable enough, climbers traveling on a gentle slope or even a snow-covered road can trigger a slide on a steeper slope above them. It is critical to know what is above you as you travel. Because adjacent terrain is often out of view or obscured by the weather, study a topographical map to identify possible sources of hazard above or below your route.

SLOPE ASPECT

The direction a slope faces—its slope aspect—determines how much sun and wind it gets, which may indicate its avalanche potential. Understanding the aspect of slopes is crucial for assessing avalanche hazard. Various aspects respond differently to weather conditions like precipitation, solar radiation, wind, and temperature. Here is how it works in the northern hemisphere (it is the opposite on mountains south of the equator).

South-facing slopes. South aspects receive more direct sunlight and tend to be warmer, which can lead to wet loose avalanches, especially in spring. The increased solar radiation can lead to melting and refreezing of the snow, forming crusts on the surface.

North-facing slopes. North aspects tend to receive less direct sunlight, resulting in colder and shadier conditions.

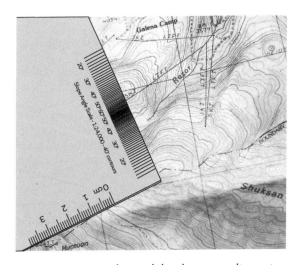

Fig. 20-5. *Measuring slope angle based on contour lines, using the 1:24,000 scale on the American Institute for Avalanche Research and Education (AIARE) Field Book.*

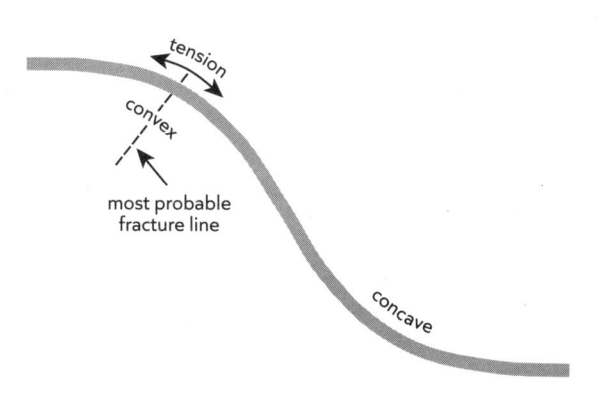

Fig. 20-6. *Most likely fracture line on a convex and concave slope.*

These slopes may retain colder, drier snow and are more likely to develop a weaker, faceted snow layer, which can contribute to unstable snow and increase the risk of avalanches.

Windward slopes. Slopes that face directly into the prevailing wind direction, windward slopes may be blown clear of snow. Snow that stays on the slope may be compacted by the force of the wind and create specific snow and avalanche conditions.

Leeward slopes. Slopes that face away from the wind are particularly dangerous because of wind-loading, which happens when the wind transports snow rapidly from an exposed area to a less exposed area. A slope can become top-loaded by wind blowing snow over the top of a ridge crest and depositing it on the lee side, or it can become cross-loaded by the wind blowing across the slope and depositing the snow in gullies between ridges. Leeward slopes can collect snow rapidly even in moderate winds. Such wind-loading can cause cornices to form on the lee side of ridges, can result in deeper, less consolidated snow, and can cause avalanche-prone wind slabs to form. In some storms, the wind frequently shifts directions, rapidly loading a slope or ridge.

SLOPE CONFIGURATION

As you plan a climb in a specific route, look for certain route features that either make avalanches more likely or increase the hazard of a slide:

- **Cliffs** with steep (>30-degree) slopes above and below can expose climbers to small avalanches.
- **Slopes with rock features poking through the surface** can increase the risk of triggering a storm slab.

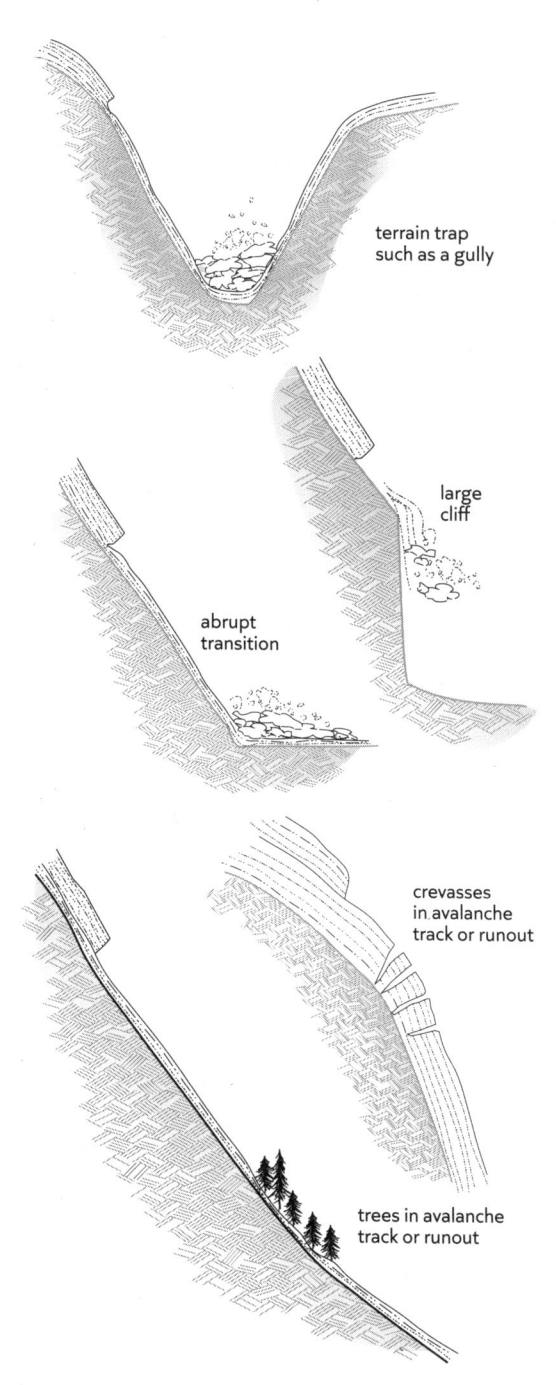

Fig. 20-7. *Convex and concave slope configurations: All these types of terrain increase your risk of encountering an avalanche.*

20

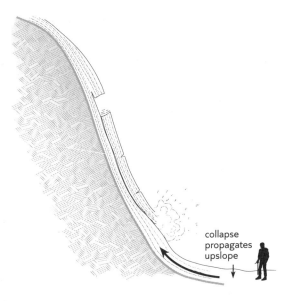

collapse
propagates
upslope

Fig. 20-8. *You can trigger an avalanche nearly as easily from below a slope as on the slope itself, especially in very unstable conditions.*

- **Seracs or cornices** above a slope are large, unstable features that can injure you or trigger large avalanches.
- **Crevasses** below a slope increase the chance of a deep burial and fatal outcome.
- **Convex areas**, where the slope angle suddenly increases, are places where the tension is highest, increasing the chances of triggering an avalanche (fig. 20-6).
- **Concave areas**, where the slope angle suddenly decreases, are also zones of stress (fig. 20-7). The entire

slope above might be supported by an area where the slope transitions rapidly from steep to flat.

Be alert, too, when traveling below snow-covered slopes. Avalanches can be triggered from the bottom of a slope, especially in unstable conditions (fig. 20-8).

TERRAIN TRAPS

Terrain traps are hazardous terrain in which climbers risk a higher chance of being buried or injured if they become caught in an avalanche. These traps occur in a wide variety of terrain, including cliffs or a grove of trees below the route. It is particularly important to be aware of terrain configurations that will concentrate or funnel an avalanche into a smaller runout zone. In that situation, a person caught in the slide will likely be buried very deeply.

Even a relatively small and shallow avalanche that might be harmless on an open slope can bury and kill a climber if it flows into a narrow gully. Many ice climbing routes follow gullies that, though too steep to be a source of avalanches, are routinely swept by powerful avalanches that start above the gully. Other examples of terrain traps include buried streams, glacier crevasses, lakes, valleys, and flat roadways cutting across a slope—essentially any place where the terrain changes abruptly from steep to flat.

AVALANCHE TERRAIN EXPOSURE SCALE

Developed in Canada and used around the world, the Avalanche Terrain Exposure Scale (ATES) is a system to rate terrain based on how much exposure to avalanches an individual will experience while moving through an area (see Table 20-1). ATES is used by Parks Canada, the Canadian Avalanche Center, New Zealand National Parks, and in the US guidebooks and maps published by Beacon

TABLE 20-1. AVALANCHE TERRAIN EXPOSURE SCALE		
DESCRIPTION	**CLASS**	**TERRAIN**
Simple	1	Exposure to low-angle or primarily forested terrain. Some forest openings may involve the runout zones of infrequent avalanches. Many options to reduce or eliminate exposure. No glacier travel.
Challenging	2	Exposure to well-defined avalanche paths, starting zones, or terrain traps. Options exist to reduce or eliminate exposure with careful routefinding. Glacier travel is straightforward, but crevasse hazards may exist.
Complex	3	Exposure to multiple overlapping avalanche paths or large expanses of steep, open terrain. Multiple avalanche starting zones and terrain traps below. Minimal options to reduce exposure. Complicated glacier travel with extensive crevasse bands or icefalls.

Guidebooks, among others. There is even an online tool, https://atesmaps.org, used to plan winter tours in the Pyrenees.

Most popular mountaineering routes across North America, from Mount Rainier to Mount Washington's Huntington Ravine, from climbing routes in Colorado and the Tetons to the classics of the Canadian Rockies, are rated complex on this scale due to factors like their steepness, exposure to multiple avalanche paths, and sometimes glaciation. A complex rating means that it is impossible to avoid avalanche hazards entirely. Acknowledging that a given route travels through complex terrain allows you to focus on identifying the areas of greatest exposure, which in turn helps you identify decision-making points along the route—places you will need to stop and evaluate the likelihood of avalanche activity. In the ATES, small avalanches in complex terrain carry a high risk of being swept off or buried in a feature like a moat or crevasse. Awareness of exposure helps climbers develop points along the route—places you can reassess the avalanche risk they face.

Such routes generally share three characteristics that make avalanche accidents more common:

- Ascents in features, such as gullies, couloirs, or large faces, where climbers cannot avoid exposure to avalanches.
- Approaches that travel through terrain traps with unavoidable exposure to avalanche terrain above, such as creeks, cliffs, or moraines.
- Descents via a different route where conditions are substantially different from the ascent route.

North American Public Avalanche Danger Scale

Avalanche danger is determined by the likelihood, size, and distribution of avalanches. Safe backcountry travel requires training and experience. You control your risk by choosing when, where, and how you travel.

Danger Level		Travel Advice	Likelihood	Size and Distribution
5 - Extreme		**Extraordinarily dangerous avalanche conditions.** Avoid all avalanche terrain.	Natural and human-triggered avalanches certain.	Very large avalanches in many areas.
4 - High		**Very dangerous avalanche conditions.** Travel in avalanche terrain not recommended.	Natural avalanches likely; human-triggered avalanches very likely.	Large avalanches in many areas; or very large avalanches in specific areas.
3 - Considerable		**Dangerous avalanche conditions.** Careful snowpack evaluation, cautious routefinding, and conservative decision-making essential.	Natural avalanches possible; human-triggered avalanches likely.	Small avalanches in many areas; or large avalanches in specific areas; or very large avalanches in isolated areas.
2 - Moderate		**Heightened avalanche conditions on specific terrain features.** Evaluate snow and terrain carefully; identify features of concern.	Natural avalanches unlikely; human-triggered avalanches possible.	Small avalanches in specific areas; or large avalanches in isolated areas.
1 - Low		**Generally safe avalanche conditions.** Watch for unstable snow on isolated terrain features.	Natural and human-triggered avalanches unlikely.	Small avalanches in isolated areas or extreme terrain.

Fig. 20-9. *North American Public Avalanche Danger Scale.*

20

The North American Public Avalanche Danger Scale (NAPADS) is a system that rates avalanche danger and provides general travel advice based on the likelihood, size, and distribution of expected avalanches (fig. 20-9). It consists of five levels, from least to highest amount of danger: 1 for low, 2 for moderate, 3 for considerable, 4 for high, and 5 for extreme. Danger ratings are typically provided for three distinct elevation bands. Although the danger ratings are assigned numerical levels, from one level to the next the danger increases exponentially. In other words, the hazard rises quite significantly with each step up the scale. When using the ATES and NAPADS, as the danger increases, you need to decrease your exposure to the avalanche problem.

Assessing Avalanche Risk

Avalanche risk refers to the level of potential danger or probability of avalanches occurring in a specific area or region. Backcountry travelers need to assess avalanche risk so that they can make informed decisions about how they travel mountainous terrain. Avalanche risk is determined by many components, including consequences, likelihood, exposure, and vulnerability (fig. 20-10).

Avalanche hazard. Avalanche hazard is the potential that avalanches will occur in a given area and possibly cause harm to people and/or their property. Avalanche hazard consists of consequences and probability. Consequences means what will happen if an avalanche occurs. Probability means the likelihood that it will occur. The size and destructive potential of avalanches vary. The consequences depend on factors like the volume of snow, slope length, and the presence of terrain traps or areas where avalanches can have severe impacts, such as damaging buildings or roads and/or burying or injuring people.

Likelihood. Likelihood assesses the probability that people will unintentionally trigger an avalanche. Certain conditions, such as a persistent weak layer of snow or day when the hazard level is high, can significantly increase the likelihood of triggering an avalanche.

Exposure. This component of avalanche risk is defined as the people or property affected by the hazard. The climbers must take into account the route chosen, the overall plan, and the amount of time they plan to spend in avalanche-prone areas. Traveling through avalanche terrain, such as underneath steep slopes or another objective hazard, increases the climbers' exposure time and their risk.

Vulnerability. This component considers the likelihood that people will be injured or killed or that property will be damaged if an avalanche were to occur.

To assess avalanche risk, backcountry travelers need to consider the combination of all these components when forming their understanding of the potential dangers in a given region. Avalanche centers and professionals use various tools, collective public observations, data, and their expertise to communicate avalanche risk to the public. This information is presented in public advisories, bulletins, and state or local warning systems to help the public make informed decisions and take appropriate precautions when traveling in or around avalanche terrain. It is critical for anyone who is venturing into the backcountry or in avalanche-prone areas to be familiar with avalanche risk and to practice measures to reduce their risk, thereby minimizing the potential for avalanche-related accidents.

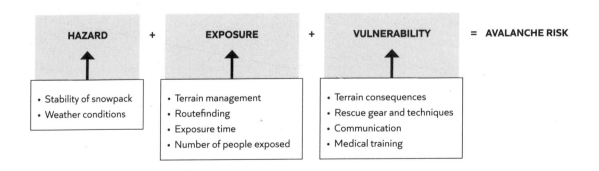

Fig. 20-10. *Several factors affect each component of avalanche risk. The greater the hazard, exposure, and vulnerability, the higher probability you will face higher avalanche risk with more severe consequences.*

PLANNING A TRIP

To plan a trip, you need to identify areas of exposure to avalanches and examine the prevailing conditions and forecast to determine whether they increase or decrease the possibility of an avalanche on your chosen route.

Assemble the group, making sure everyone has the appropriate winter travel skills and avalanche training to carry out the group goal. All members should be familiar with and capable of using their avalanche safety equipment (shovel, probe, and transceiver) and comfortable communicating about terrain choices.

The next step in the planning process is to review the weather and avalanche forecast (if such tools are available). Consider the wind, precipitation, and freezing levels, as well as recent events from local weather stations. Then evaluate what, if any, terrain is too exposed given the current conditions, and identify possible routes or peaks that allow you to avoid unnecessary exposure. With all this information in mind, draw up time plans for as many options as you can think of to get outside and climb while minimizing your avalanche risk.

Consult Avalanche Forecasts

An avalanche forecast or bulletin provides information regarding the avalanche hazard rating; avalanche problems; recent events, such as observed avalanches on a specific slope; snowpack synopsis; and anticipated weather conditions that may affect the possibility of triggering an avalanche. The main difference between a forecast and a bulletin is the frequency with which they are issued—forecasts are issued daily, while bulletins are issued up to several times a week. A forecast and/ or bulletin describes the avalanche problems of the day and indicates their location (distribution); size (how destructive they may be); and likelihood of a person triggering one.

Most avalanche forecasts are issued between late November and April. Most mountaineering avalanche accidents, however, occur outside this period. The local avalanche center may issue seasonal recommendations, with general advice outside the time frame of regular forecasts. Rangers, climbing guides, and the general climbing community in the area of your objective may have more relevant and recent information. Before your trip, visit local blogs (such as a ranger blog, available for some popular destinations such as Denali and Mount Rainier), guides' reports (such as the Mountain Conditions Report featured on the Association of Canadian Mountain Guides, or ACMG, website), or community outlets (such as regional forums and Facebook groups) to get a general sense of conditions and perhaps even specific reports about your planned objective.

Consider Weather Conditions

When seasonal avalanche centers are not issuing forecasts, it's up to climbers to use the nearest mountain weather forecast to help determine what avalanche problems they may encounter. Learn to use the detailed forecasts from NOAA (within the US), Windy.com, and Mountain-Forecast. com. Forecast accuracy drops off dramatically after 24 to 48 hours—it is a good idea to check the weather forecast daily at least a week before your trip to get a sense of the overall trend and any possible periods of stormy or challenging weather. Start by learning what data you need and becoming proficient at reading short- and long-range weather models.

Here are some key data points to look for when checking the forecast:

- **Freezing level:** This piece of data tells you where the snow will start to accumulate and where the avalanche problems will develop, such as wet loose below the freezing level when the sun comes out or looking out for storm and wind slabs above the freezing level during or just after a big storm.
- **Precipitation totals:** This data is often provided in inches of water (millimeters outside the US) for a 6-, 12-, or 24-hour period. (A good rule of thumb is that 1 inch of water equals 1 foot of snow.) Precipitation intensity tells you how fast slopes will get loaded. A rate of 1 inch (2.5 centimeters) per hour of snow is considered high intensity and indicates how fast slabs are forming.
- **Wind direction:** The predominant wind direction affects which slopes will get loaded. For example, southwest winds will load northeastern slopes. Wind speed forecasts include hourly average and maximum gust. Pay attention to sustained wind speeds stronger than 15 miles per hour and that last longer than two hours—winds in that category contribute to the formation of wind slabs.

If your trip is in North America, you can gather data from remote SNOTEL (snow telemetry) sites. These sites provide a lot of information about past and current weather. You can find their locations through Natural Resources Conservation Service and on local avalanche forecast center websites. All the weather information is tabular or in graphs, helpful if you need to look at only a few weeks' worth of weather.

Be Aware of the Snowpack Conditions

In the spring and summer, the snowpack typically undergoes multiple melt-freeze cycles, which can lead to avalanche problems. Early spring (March to mid-April in North America), when the snowpack is first beginning to warm up due to increased exposure of daylight and UV radiation, is a very dangerous period. These conditions can reactivate weak, old layers, leading to large, destructive avalanche cycles in high-alpine zones.

Key red flags for an alpine snowpack include:

- Persistent weak layers present within the top 3 feet of the snowpack.
- Early spring warm-ups, when the winter snowpack has not adjusted to the extra heat it is exposed to on longer days through UV radiation.
- Large rain- or snowstorms that release more than 1 inch of water or more than 12 inches of snow in 24 hours.
- Strong winds (more than 15 miles per hour) on the upper mountain that persist for more than 6 hours.

Your party should develop a time plan to decide what time you need to leave camp to avoid specific hazards on your route that may increase in likelihood as the day warms. Web-based planning tools such as CalTopo and onX Backcountry offer the ability to measure distance and vertical gain on your planned route. With this information, you can estimate how much time you will need to go up and back down.

There are two ways to estimate how long your trip will take and then use that information to craft a time plan. A general rule of thumb is that is takes about one hour to ascend about 1,000 feet (300 meters), and that 3 miles (5 kilometers) without any elevation gain will also take about an hour. The Munter formula, developed by Swiss guide Werner Munter, uses the metric system to estimate one hour for every 400 meters of elevation gain and about an hour for every 4 kilometers without any elevation gain. There are entire courses dedicated to this skill, as well as apps that will help you make a plan and navigate using it. A time plan helps you evaluate your timing around definitive spots on a route.

WATCH FOR RED FLAGS ON THE ROUTE

Even when the forecast and conditions reports are positive, red flags warning of potential avalanche hazard may appear. Recent avalanche activity indicates that an avalanche problem is present.

If a route has had observed, recent avalanches, find out some key information:

- How recent is any avalanche debris (from the last 24 to 72 hours)?

- What aspect and elevation did the avalanches occur on? Is the terrain that recently experienced an avalanche similar to the terrain on your route?
- How deep was the layer that avalanched (more than 1 inch)? Which specific layer failed? What type of avalanche was it? What triggered it, a human or natural cause?

As the weather changes, new avalanche problems can develop, when snow or rain falls on the snowpack and/or the sun heats up the upper snowpack.

Key weather-related red flags include:

- **Rapid warming** (more than 3 to 5 degrees in a couple of hours) from rain or sun. Signs include roller balls coming from above or below steep rock features.
- **Rain on new snow or heavy rain on steep slopes** (over 30 degrees) that softens the surface quickly.
- **Isothermal snow**, indicated by deep wet snow, without cohesion.
- **More than 12 inches (30 centimeters) of snow falling in 24 hours** and/or precipitation intensity of greater than 1 inch per hour. The layer created in such conditions will feel denser than the layer below and above it. Shooting cracks or whumpfing (rapidly collapsing snow underfoot) are signs of unstable storm snow.
- **Wind speed over 15 miles per hour** during a storm that creates wind slabs. Slabs created in these conditions will feel denser than the surrounding snow on leeward features, such as large boulders, cliffs, and slopes.

RESPECT THE RED FLAGS

If you observe red flags on a climb or expedition, it's time to consider contingency plans: maybe an alternative route or a nearby peak with less avalanche exposure. Perhaps your schedule allows you time to descend and move to another part of the range, where the mountains may be drier and offer a route with little to no risk of avalanches.

On expeditions, respecting red flags may involve waiting while other teams summit or even abandoning your climb. Trusting the process means trusting what you have learned and observed—not believing that other groups know something you don't. Do not be persuaded by the fact that other groups of climbers choose to continue—they are just as easily influenced by the human factors that contribute to many accidents. Human factors stem from cognitive biases, and nearly two hundred known bias affect our perception and processing of information. With that in mind, it's easy to see how skewed our view of reality can be.

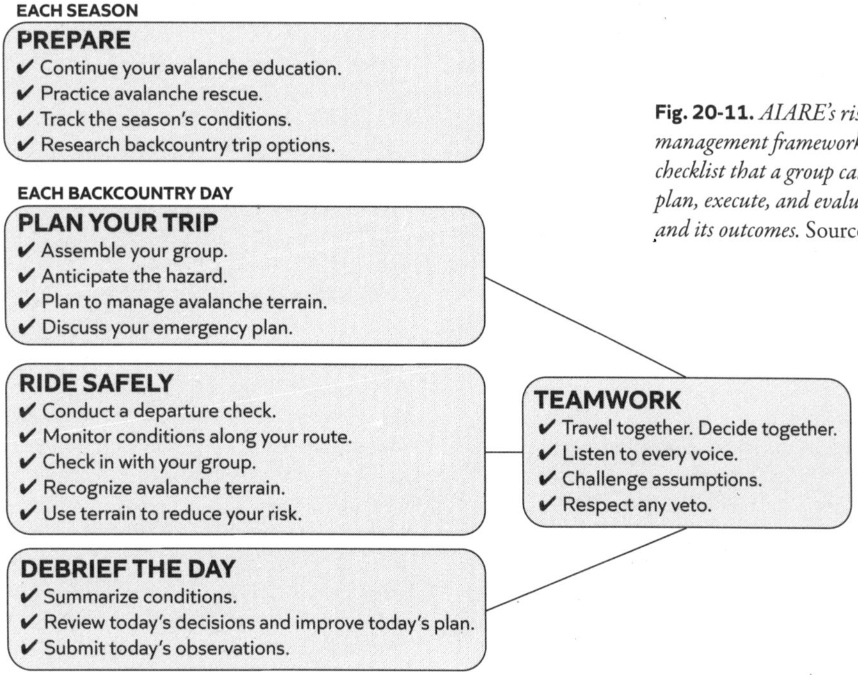

EACH SEASON

PREPARE
- ✔ Continue your avalanche education.
- ✔ Practice avalanche rescue.
- ✔ Track the season's conditions.
- ✔ Research backcountry trip options.

EACH BACKCOUNTRY DAY

PLAN YOUR TRIP
- ✔ Assemble your group.
- ✔ Anticipate the hazard.
- ✔ Plan to manage avalanche terrain.
- ✔ Discuss your emergency plan.

RIDE SAFELY
- ✔ Conduct a departure check.
- ✔ Monitor conditions along your route.
- ✔ Check in with your group.
- ✔ Recognize avalanche terrain.
- ✔ Use terrain to reduce your risk.

TEAMWORK
- ✔ Travel together. Decide together.
- ✔ Listen to every voice.
- ✔ Challenge assumptions.
- ✔ Respect any veto.

DEBRIEF THE DAY
- ✔ Summarize conditions.
- ✔ Review today's decisions and improve today's plan.
- ✔ Submit today's observations.

Fig. 20-11. AIARE's risk management framework is a checklist that a group can employ to plan, execute, and evaluate a trip and its outcomes. Source: *AIARE.*

ACCOUNT FOR HUMAN FACTORS

Human factors contribute to poor decision-making. The Dunning-Kruger effect is an example of a cognitive bias that affects our perception of risk in a dynamic, ambiguous natural environment like the alpine zone. This particular effect leads people to believe that they are smarter and more capable than they really are. Essentially, people with limited competence are unable to recognize their own incompetence, making it hard to identify complex problems that exceed their skill and knowledge.

Heuristics related to cognitive bias can be grouped into four categories:

- **Information bias.** We notice things that we are familiar with, and develop a blind spot for anything we don't understand.
- **Lack of understanding.** To avoid our doubts, we are likely to confer expert status to groups or individuals who are doing something we are unsure about. In avalanche terrain, this may mean watching a group successfully traverse a cornice and therefore believing you will also be able to pass through the area.
- **Feeling pressure to act fast.** This category involves the idea of sunk cost. The thought process is you are here, so go ahead and do it. You may also feel overconfident due to time constraints.
- **Attention bias.** We don't notice everything but instead apply meanings to things or events without knowing the whole story.

Cognitive biases can impair your ability to differentiate the risks and consequences of travel through hazards. Despite being confronted with multiple red flags, even with only a small amount of bias, your mind will create rational reasons why you should continue. You need to be aware of your own biases and be able to recognize them before you make a decision.

The most important avalanche safety tool is your judgment and willingness to recognize and accept that the red flags you observe point to an avalanche problem. Developing these skills will help you understand that you need to leave that route alone for the time being, despite all the time and effort you have invested in planning and getting there. Be humble in the face of natural hazards, and you will find that as one door closes another opens—whether it is another route, peak, activity, or epiphany. Being open to change will help you continue to climb for a long time—which after all is the point!

20

USE THE RISK MANAGEMENT FRAMEWORK

Used to make decisions effectively and efficiently in the field, the risk management framework (RMF) developed by the American Institute for Avalanche Research and Education (AIARE) is a checklist tool that fosters open, clear group communication (fig. 20-11). The RMF helps keep the team's emotions from overriding its logic and addresses the level of uncertainty that the team may have when making decisions as a group. Teams can use the framework repeatedly as they continually reassess the conditions related to the forecast and determine whether avalanche danger is increasing or decreasing.

In an attempt to decide simply "go" or "no go," it is often best to think in terms of the party's levels of certainty, instead of agonizing over the particulars. Examine the available information and then determine whether you know enough to make a decision that minimizes the party's risk and is within their skill and experience. If you cannot decide whether the terrain will expose the group to unacceptable amounts of risk, then there is simply too much uncertainty to proceed. In this situation, it is best to choose to travel on alternative terrain that you are confident will minimize your party's risk in the current conditions. Include a low-risk, alternate destination in every trip plan.

When a party encounters potential avalanche hazard along the way, ask these questions:

- How does the group feel? Is anyone uncomfortable with the plan and current conditions?
- Are the conditions we are observing different from the avalanche forecast?
- Are there red flags present?
- Are any changes in weather increasing your exposure to the avalanche problem?

To respond effectively, think holistically and apply concrete observations. If anyone in the party answers yes to the first question, respect that person's veto, and move on to discuss the alternate destination.

Carry Avalanche Gear

If you will be exposed to avalanche risk while climbing, you should carry and know how to use avalanche rescue gear. If someone gets buried in an avalanche, rescuers have roughly 10 minutes to find them, dig them out, and clear their airway before they asphyxiate. Each party member needs to carry an avalanche transceiver, probe, and shovel. Even if you're climbing a route on which you believe no one would survive an avalanche, friends or family will still want your

body to be retrieved, which means SAR teams will end up searching for you.

Wearing a transceiver and using clothing equipped with the RECCO system does everyone a favor. RECCO is a rescue technology used by organized rescue teams as an additional tool to locate people buried by an avalanche or lost in the outdoors. The system is based on a harmonic radar system and composed of a detector and a passive reflector integrated into some outdoor clothing and gear.

AVALANCHE RESCUE TRANSCEIVERS

A digital avalanche rescue transceiver, often called an *avalanche beacon*, is a crucial tool for finding buried victims. Rescue depends on each member of the party carrying a transceiver. A rescue transceiver can be switched to either transmit or receive signals. Digital transceivers convert the analog signal to a digital readout, and they typically provide both audible and visible signals in receive (search) mode. The international standard frequency for avalanche transceivers is 457 kilohertz. Steady progress in the avalanche safety field has produced transceivers with increasingly sophisticated digital processor capabilities. The transceivers recommended for backcountry travelers and climbers operate exclusively at 457 kilohertz and use three or more antennas to generate the most accurate readings and make searching efficient.

A valuable feature of newer digital transceivers is the ability to quickly separate and isolate signals in a scenario in which two or more victims have been buried. While some people argue that multiple-burial scenarios are rare, they do occur, and if a searcher inadvertently reverts to transmit in a single-victim burial, it is very useful for searchers to be able to know whether multiple transceivers are in transmit mode.

All members of a party must know how to use their transceivers correctly—a skill that requires regular practice before and during every season. Local ski areas have beacon parks with multiple targets buried in close proximity to assist people who are learning how to operate their transceivers.

PREPARING TO TRAVEL

At the trailhead and at the beginning of an outing, the group needs to verify that all transceivers in the group can send and receive signals properly. Fresh batteries usually last for about 300 hours (a lot less time when used in search mode), but carry extras in case the signal from any transceiver weakens due to a drop in battery power. Test the battery life of your transceiver while practicing search methods. Become familiar with your device so that you know at what battery-level indicator you need to change the batteries, and before each trip, check the charge level.

Strap the transceiver around your neck and torso. Carry it under your clothing, just outside your innermost garment, to keep it from being lost in an avalanche. Do not carry it in your pack. A zipped front pants pocket has also been determined to be a reliable place to carry a transceiver. Use a leash to secure the device to you as well. During the climb, leave your transceivers on and set to the transmit mode. When you are staying overnight in a snow cave or in an avalanche-prone area, consider leaving the transceiver on and set to transmit even at night.

Electromagnetic interference from phones, radios, watches, heated gloves, GPS devices, and other devices with a battery can disturb the function of avalanche transceivers. Consider turning such devices off if you do not need them for travel or communication. If they are turned on, keep them at least 12 inches (30 centimeters) from your transceiver. When searching for a signal, keep the transceiver 22 inches (50 centimeters) from your body and any such devices.

Traveling in Avalanche Terrain

Snow is a medium that changes constantly. When you travel in avalanche terrain, you must be prepared, stay alert, and regularly reassess terrain and conditions (fig. 20-12). Here are some ways to protect yourself:

- **Continually assess the group's exposure** relative to the avalanche problem. Evaluate the relative level of avalanche danger. Start by researching the area and conditions before your trip, and reassess throughout the climb.
- **Practice secure travel techniques** in avalanche-prone areas. Always choose the safest path of travel, and consider crossing avalanche-prone slopes one person at a time to limit the group's exposure.
- **Carry rescue gear** in avalanche terrain. Climbers should bring and know how to use avalanche transceivers, probes, and shovels. The group should also bring a well-stocked first-aid kit and a repair kit for any crucial gear.

Unfortunately, many climbers consider avalanche safety an abstruse specialty, more of a concern for skiers and winter mountaineers than the average climber, so they may not bother to become familiar with how to assess avalanche

Fig. 20-12. *Open, clear communication keeps the group focused on relevant observations and evaluations of avalanche hazards, terrain, snowpack, and weather.*

20

hazard and minimize their risk. Yet avalanches can and do occur year-round in many mountain ranges. Everyone who travels on steep snow will benefit greatly from avalanche safety training. The study of snow and avalanches is both fascinating and useful; the more you learn, the more interesting the topic becomes. The knowledge you will gain overlaps with many other topics in mountaineering. In particular, modern avalanche training emphasizes planning and decision-making—valuable skills that are directly applicable to all backcountry travel. The cycle of snow is both an art and a science that you can study for a lifetime. Avoiding avalanches is only one of many benefits of such study. Understanding snow and mountain weather is vital—even outside avalanche terrain—to truly gaining the freedom of the hills (see Chapters 27 and 28 to learn more).

When traveling in and around avalanche terrain an important component to manage is the human factor.

It is particularly important to manage the human factor of a group. The acronym FACETS represents the six heuristic traps: familiarity, acceptance, commitment, expert halo, tracks (aka social proof), and scarcity.

- **Familiarity:** A trend among backcountry travelers to make riskier decisions in familiar terrain than when traveling in unfamiliar terrain.
- **Acceptance:** The action or process of being received as adequate or suitable, typically to be admitted into a group.
- **Commitment:** The state or quality of being dedicated to a cause, activity, et cetera.
- **Expert halo:** Deferring to the perceived expert in the group and not making decisions or contributing to the decision-making process.
- **Tracks or social proof:** Where people follow and copy the actions of others in order to display accepted or correct behavior. Iinformed decision-making by the group is a must; don't follow unknown tracks in the backcountry.
- **Scarcity:** A mindset that leads to the belief that there are limited opportunities, options, and favorable conditions.

Each group member must understand the possible consequences of decisions and any alternatives. Everyone should understand any assumptions underlying the decision to enter avalanche terrain, including assessments of the party's risk tolerance and its ability to deal with an avalanche and or avalanche conditions.

A group should base its decision-making process on an open, forthright discussion that covers these topics:

1. Identify potential hazards.
2. Collect, evaluate, and integrate information continuously during a trip.
3. Consciously challenge assumptions, evaluate the consequences of a particular decision, and consider alternatives.
4. Make a decision, but be willing to reevaluate based on new information, especially if avalanche danger is increasing.

Formalize this decision-making process by identifying places along a route where a group will need to make decisions. Include these decision-making points in the trip plan or on the map to ensure that the group takes time to reevaluate conditions and discusses options as a team.

OBSERVING SNOW CONDITIONS

Climbers should understand the terrain they are heading into and incorporate where and when they could observe the conditions and terrain into their trip plan. Consider conditions on terrain similar to that of the climb, and reevaluate your assessment as often as possible. Observe the big picture first: on the road, up the trail, at camp, out on the terrain. Then evaluate how the party's plans and situation fit into that picture. Use this perspective to decide where the party may be able to test the snow, identify weaker layers of snow, and decide which snowpack tests the group will apply. All this information will assist the party in avoiding avalanche hazard.

Climbers should use snowpack tests to gain a general understanding of local conditions and look for any unexpected signs of danger—but snowpack tests do *not* predict the stability of adjacent slopes. If overall conditions lead a party to conclude that a slope may be dangerous, the party should not change their minds based on field tests that happen to show a stable result. On the other hand, if the party's forecast was for good stability and a local snowpack test uncovers unstable conditions, climbers should assume that other unstable areas exist on similar slopes.

To minimize risk while traveling in the backcountry, climbers must be able to recognize increased exposure to avalanche terrain. Generally, when unstable snow conditions exist, the majority of results from observations and tests will confirm that conditions are unstable on certain slope aspects, at certain elevations, and within a certain range of slope angles. When the weather is changing, climbers should operate within an extra margin safety and look for red flags (see Watch for Red Flags on the Route earlier in this chapter).

Testing the Snowpack

Interpretation of snowpack tests is beyond the scope of this guide. If you want to learn that skill, take an avalanche course in the snow in your local range. It is often more practical for a climbing party to make many quick tests and observations of the snowpack as it progresses steadily upward than to stop and carry out scientific snowpack tests or dig a full snow profile (figs. 20-13 and 20-14) to gather detailed observations from a single location. Nevertheless, it is a very good idea for anyone who travels in avalanche terrain to become familiar with the range of snowpack tests and observation techniques that snow professionals use to evaluate the snowpack.

Carrying out these tests provides backcountry travelers with information comparable to what the professional avalanche forecasters take into account when preparing their bulletins. Knowing how to perform these tests will also help climbers identify the basis for avalanche forecasting. Practicing these snowpack tests and digging baseline profiles, when time allows, will help you become knowledgeable about current snow conditions. Comparing what you discover in the snow and the snowpack discussion with daily avalanche forecast reports will help you develop a much deeper understanding of avalanche hazard. Snowpack tests can also be useful for discovering unexpected danger in the snowpack, but they have limited value in decision-making. Do not rely on tests that indicate a stable snowpack to enter avalanche terrain in questionable conditions.

A well-equipped climbing party should carry tools to evaluate the snowpack. A snow study kit with a snow crystal card, clinometer, and snow saw is useful in analysis of slopes and the snowpack. Climbers well educated in avalanche safety should understand the procedures and terminology used in the extended column test (ECT), compression test (CT; see fig. 20-15), propagation saw test (PST), and any other tests commonly performed by professional forecasters in the part of the world they are climbing in. It also pays to learn the correct methods used in making snowpack observations, as well as the standardized ways of noting the data from these tests and observations. Full profiles dug in the snow allow a close inspection of the layers in the upper 3 feet (1 meter) of the snow. They allow observers a detailed look at the snowpack, but they are time-consuming to create and represent only a single sample in a vast landscape. Professional avalanche courses—in the US; throughout Europe; in Argentina and Chile; and in Nepal, Kyrgyzstan, and other places in Asia and cover this material and introduce people to the basics of snow science and avalanche forecasting.

Fig. 20-13. *Evaluating layers in a correctly constructed snow pit.*

Fig. 20-14. *Isolating the snowpack with a snow saw for a compression test.*

20

Test profiles, performed quickly by isolating the snow using a shovel or saw and targeting the weak layer, can give you an idea of what is going on in the upper layers. It is a good idea to push your trekking pole or ice-axe spike into the snow regularly as you travel, to look for weaker and stronger layers near the surface. However, these informal tests will not offer any information about the bonding of snow layers.

TRAVEL TECHNIQUES

Even after a party has made every effort to choose safe terrain in existing conditions, the group must also use travel techniques designed to reduce their risk when crossing a potential avalanche slope. The goal is to disturb the slope as little as possible and therefore minimize the consequences of a possible avalanche.

Choose a Safer Line of Travel

When a route meanders, seek out lower-angle terrain and avoid trigger points (like convex rollovers) and exposure to terrain traps. Look ahead and make use of topographical maps, GPS, and route plans to avoid more complex areas in the terrain. The route should follow as high of a line on a slope as is practical. For instance, it may be possible to hug cliff bands at the top of a slope. Choosing the most efficient and least risky line up a mountainside while setting a skin track is an advanced route-finding skill that requires training and practice.

Stay Together

On steep tricky traverses, everyone else monitors from less risky locations, ready to respond if a slide starts, while one person at a time moves across. (Alternatively, the group may spread out and travel far apart simultaneously, but within view of each other.) Cross with long, smooth strides, with folks spaced out on the slope. If your group is crossing one at a time, each climber follows in turn, stepping in the leader's footprints or skiing in the same track. In conditions with very low visibility, it is often safer to stay close together and even to rope up to keep the team together and assist with routefinding.

In whiteout conditions, keep all group members in sight of others. Pairing people up to look after each other can prevent an individual from getting separated from the group, or even buried, without anyone noticing. Move from one position you trust to another, minimizing how long you are exposed to the hazard. Do not fall. Falling suddenly loads the snowpack and could trigger an avalanche. The impact of a falling body on an avalanche-ready slope can trigger a slide. Be aware of other parties; try not to travel or ski above others who are moving up the slope.

Surviving an Avalanche

After an avalanche starts, there is limited time to arrest or escape the start zone. Think ahead about what would you do if an avalanche were to occur. While traveling, keep an eye out for escape paths.

If you are caught in an avalanche, fight to survive. When an avalanche starts, try to prevent yourself from being swept away. Grab a rock or tree, or dig your ice axe or a ski pole into the snow to arrest, and hold on. Try log rolling to the side of the moving snow where there is less turbulence. If that does not work, use swimming motions, flail your arms and legs, and/or roll to stay as close to the surface as you can. If possible, discard any gear like skis and ski poles that may pull you down into the avalanche. Keep your backpack on to protect your spine and help protect you from trauma. Larger objects tend to be pushed to the surface of avalanche debris; having a pack on may help keep you near the surface. Plus, if you survive the traumatic forces of the avalanche, you will need the clothing and emergency gear in your pack.

If your head goes below the surface, do your best to keep your airway from being suffocated by snow. As the avalanche slows, thrust an arm upward so that your hand may end up above the surface, and if you are buried, try to put an elbow or hand in front of your face to create a breathing space. Inhale deeply and expand your ribs before the snow stops; as the snow comes to a stop around you, relax and try to conserve oxygen and your energy. If you are buried in snow, you most likely won't be able to move. Your climbing partners should know what to do, and they will begin rescue efforts immediately.

Rescuing a Companion

Mountaineers should focus on following travel techniques and evaluating avalanche terrain to avoid avalanches altogether. Rescue skills are very important, but keep in mind that self-rescue is the last resort—used only after an avalanche has occurred. Every party needs a baseline of avalanche rescue skills and safety equipment, but skills and gear are no substitute for making sound judgments that reduce your risk while traveling in avalanche terrain. This section briefly describes one approach for handling the situation if you or a member of your party experiences an avalanche. For a list of several widely available books about avalanche rescue, as well as useful website, see Resources near the end of the book.

People buried in a large avalanche very seldom live long enough to be rescued by people who are not close by when the accident occurs. It can often take hours, or even days, to bring outside rescuers to the scene of an avalanche. If you survive the physical trauma of an avalanche, you will almost certainly be depending on your companions and possibly nearby climbing parties to rescue you quickly, before you suffocate or die of hypothermia.

FIRST STEPS IN A RESCUE

Following a step-by-step approach to rescue will improve your chances of finding someone buried in an avalanche. If they survive the trauma of the avalanche itself, buried victims have limited oxygen and warmth. It is important to be methodical and efficient.

Identify the Area Where the Person Was Last Seen

Rescue efforts start even before the avalanche has stopped. In the shock of the moment, the first step in a successful rescue is a tough one: pay attention to the point where the victim was last seen. Identify the search area based on this last-seen area. Perform a head count to make sure you know how many people are missing.

Select a Leader

Choose a leader to direct a thorough and methodical rescue effort. The leader should evaluate the potential for other slides in the area and choose the least risky approach to the search area; it is usually easier to move downhill while searching. The leader should also designate an escape path in case another avalanche were to occur. To be as effective as possible, the leader should assign tasks and recruit everybody in the group to search. If the search party is large enough, the leader should avoid participating in the hands-on process, which can narrow their focus and distract them from evaluating the big picture. The initial transceiver search requires only enough people to cover the search area.

If someone is available, it is often a good idea to have that person make an initial call to alert outside rescuers to the situation, even to simply report the ongoing search and the party's location and arrange to call back. (The specifics of your communications process and response will be determined in part by whatever devices your group brought, such as a satellite phone, inReach or other messaging device, or smartphone, a decision you should make when planning your trip.) Mobilizing outside search and rescue

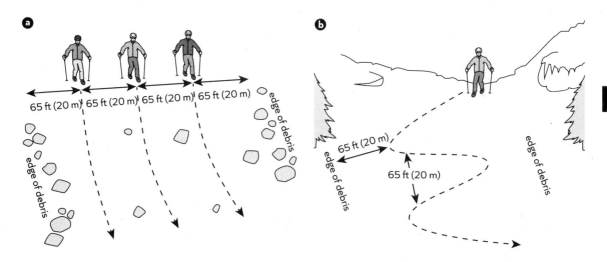

Fig. 20-15. *Paths taken during a signal search phase:* **a,** *multiple searchers;* **b,** *single searcher. Space the search paths closely enough to stay in range of the victim's transceiver.* ·

organizations to mount a search can take a long time. In the event that a trauma victim may need to be evacuated, the leader should get this process started as soon as possible. Sometimes, with a long downhill search zone, rescuers may not have a signal at the bottom of the slope, which in turn might severely delay that first call to outside rescuers. On the other hand, if carrying out an effective companion rescue requires the entire party, it may be best to postpone any calls for help until after the victim is recovered. When placing a call for outside help, be careful to share all the pertinent details rescuers will need: who, where, what equipment and supplies you have, and how many people are missing; confirm that you will call back when you have further information.

A critical principle of avalanche rescue: Do not send anyone for help. Stay and search. The victim's survival depends on finding them quickly. If a person survives an avalanche without hitting rocks or trees or suffering trauma, they have a roughly 90 percent chance of survival if rescuers are able to locate them, uncover them, and clear their airway—all within 10 minutes. Their probability of survival drops off steeply after 10 minutes. After 90 minutes, the victim's probability of survival is around 25 percent. Wait to send someone for help until after the victim has been dug out or after search efforts turn out to be futile.

Prepare to Search

Once you begin to search, all the active searchers should unstrap their transceivers and switch them to search mode to locate the transmission from the victim's transceiver. This step is critically important. Otherwise, searchers will waste valuable time receiving a signal from one of their own transceivers rather than the victim's device.

Once a signal has been acquired, a rescuer needs to be proficient enough to locate a buried victim as quickly as possible. The 10-minute survival statistic mentioned above includes finding a victim, digging them out, *and* clearing their airway. Practice using rescue transceivers regularly to ensure that you and your fellow climbers have the best chances of locating a victim before they suffocate.

THREE PHASES OF A SEARCH

Work rapidly and efficiently. Don't forget to search with your eyes. Try to determine if anyone can point out the last place the victim was seen, then move quickly into the transceiver search. Look for items of clothing or other clues, and consider the location of terrain traps where a person may be lodged. Anyone not needed for the transceiver search should follow the transceiver searchers while getting their

probes ready. All searchers should carry their packs and keep all emergency gear with them. The digital transceiver search for an avalanche victim or victims occurs in three phases: signal, coarse, and fine.

Phase 1: Signal Search

In the signal search phase, a signal has not yet been detected. Starting from the last point where the victim was seen, searchers fan out no more than 65 feet (20 meters) apart—about the effective range of a modern digital transceiver with some overlap—across the slope. Searchers should move straight down the fall line with their transceivers in receive mode until they pick up a signal (fig. 20-15a). If there is no agreed-upon last-seen point, the searchers much check the entire slope. If only one person is searching, they must switchback down the slope with no more than 65 feet (20 meters) between switchbacks (fig. 20-15b).

Once searchers have detected a signal, they can move to the coarse search while other rescuers prepare to dig out the victim. If there is more than one victim, the rest of the rescuers should continue the coarse search until all the victims have been found. Modern transceivers have a flagging or signal suppression function that allows them to continue searching without interference from the recovered victim's transceiver. To decrease confusion for the search party, it

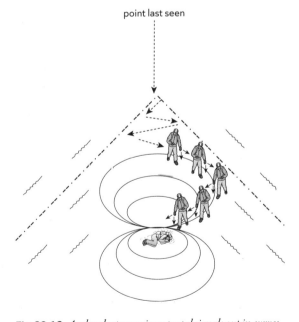

Fig. 20-16. *Avalanche transceivers propel signals out in curves.*

is possible change the victim's transceiver settings to search to eliminate overlapping signals from other buried people's transceivers.

Phase 2: Coarse Search

The coarse search phase begins when the searchers detect a consistent signal. Use the directional lights and distance meter on the transceiver to follow the signal to roughly where the victim is buried. Because the signal transmissions from the victim's transceiver are propelled outward in a curve, the transceiver will likely be following a curved path, the flux line (fig. 20-16).

Move as quickly as is practical during this phase. The digital distance readout on a transceiver is not precise, but it will give you a good idea of the distance to the traveler's transceiver beneath the snow. After practicing with your transceiver, you will begin to get a good idea of what the distance readings mean, and you will become familiar with the range of curves that search lines may follow. This experience will greatly improve your search times, and practicing can teach you how to pace yourself to be efficient but not

move so fast that you outpace the transceiver's processor or make mistakes that waste time.

Phase 3: Fine Search

Once a searcher is within roughly 10 feet (3 meters) of the victim, the searcher should slow down and begin the fine search. At this point, it is usually best to remove skis (if you are wearing them) to make it easier to get as close as possible to the snow surface with the transceiver and move with precision. You may need to take off your skis or snowshoes in order to dig.

Search along a straight line to try to pinpoint the victim more closely (fig. 20-17a). When the rescuer is within 2 meters, ignore the transceiver's directional arrows and audible signals from this point on (some beacons switch them off automatically at this stage), and instead use the distance indicator numbers to find the point along this straight line that is closest to the victim. As you move along the line, maintain a steady speed, not too fast, and keep the transceiver oriented exactly the same way as when you came into the field—avoid moving the transceiver like a flashlight.

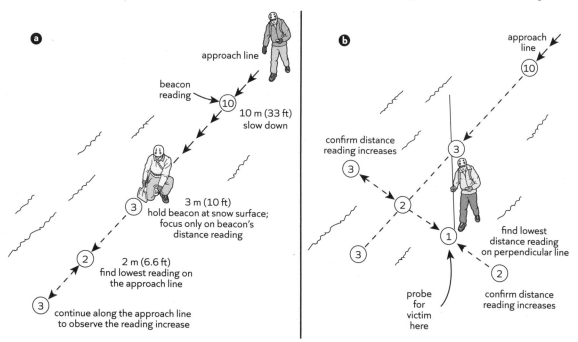

Fig. 20-17. *Steps of a fine search:* **a,** *When the beacon reads 10 meters, slow down. Continue until the beacon distance reading starts to increase. Mark this point. Then return along the line past the lowest reading until the reading starts to increase again, and mark this point;* **b,** *Now strike a new line perpendicular to the approach line at the midpoint between these marks. Repeat the process to find the closest point to the victim along this second line, and probe for the victim where the beacon indicates the lowest number.*

20

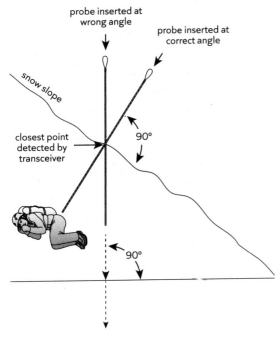

Fig. 20-18. *After locating the person with the beacon, insert the probe perpendicular to the slope. If you insert a probe on a plumb line, you will most likely end up missing the victim.*

At some point along the line, the distance numbers will dip to a low point and then start to climb again. Make a mark in the snow where the distance number first began to go up again. Then without changing the transceiver orientation, move back along the line at the same steady pace until the number dips low and rises to the same higher number again, and mark that point. Now mark the midpoint of the span between the two marks you made along your straight line. This is the point along your first line where you are closest to the victim, but you may not yet be directly above them.

Now strike a line perpendicular to your original line that crosses it at this close-to-the-victim point (fig. 20-17b). Follow along this second line in either direction (again, with the transceiver in the same orientation it has been in all along) until you again find the lowest distance reading by marking the two points where the reading first rises above the low and then marking the midpoint. The victim should be below this mark.

At this point, probe *perpendicular to the snow surface*— not straight up and down (fig. 20-18). The shortest distance from the closest point detected by a transceiver to the buried beacon (and victim) is along a line perpendicular to

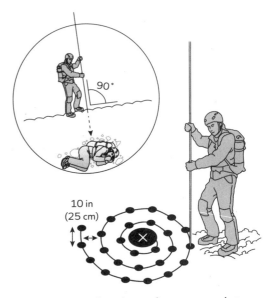

Fig. 20-19. *Starting where the signal is strongest, probe in a spiral pattern in increments of about 10 inches (25 centimeters). Be sure to probe perpendicular to the surface of the snow.*

the snow surface; probing on a plumb line can easily miss a buried person.

If you missed the person the first time probing, continue probing in a spiral pattern outward from this point, moving in 10-in (25-centimeter) increments out from the closest point found in the transceiver search (fig. 20-19). Take care to keep the probe perpendicular to the snow surface, and push it down as far as you can. People buried deeply are less likely to survive long enough to be dug out, but you would not want to miss them because you were probing too shallowly. As soon as the person is located, leave the probe in place and begin digging.

To find a buried person, use a real avalanche probe and sturdy metal shovel. Ski-pole probes and plastic shovels have a reputation for failing.

HOW TO SHOVEL EFFICIENTLY

After locating the person using the fine search and then pinpointing with the probe, take care while digging to avoid injuring the person you are rescuing. Some victims have reported that the most terrifying part of their avalanche experience was having their air space trampled on as they were being rescued. Nevertheless, dig as fast as you can while following a systematic and efficient process, rotating positions every 30 to 60 seconds, and working as a team.

probe

lead digger

1.5 x burial depth

Fig. 20-20. *When digging out a buried avalanche victim, shovel at an angle downhill from the victim's estimated location.*

Practicing efficient shoveling methods with your climbing team is a very valuable exercise that has certainly saved lives.

Expect to work very hard: snow in an avalanche undergoes a transition as it slides. When it finally stops and settles, it sets up like concrete. Digging a person out is the hardest and most time-consuming phase. The most important goal in this phase is to uncover the victim's airway and remove any snow from it so that they can breathe.

Start shoveling on the downhill side, away from the victim at a distance of approximately one and a half times the estimated depth of the probed target. Move snow downhill. Excavate either in steps or at an angle to the victim, rather than straight down (fig. 20-20). Organize the shovelers so that one person at a time spearheads the shoveling. Other rescuers can hang back and extend the digging area while also sweeping the lead digger's snow piles and chunks out of the way. Take turns in the lead digging position, rotating as often as you need to avoid slowing down.

Keep a wide area open behind the lead digger where other rescuers can clear snow away rapidly. Even though it moves more snow, this method is much faster than tunneling straight down. An open and relatively level area may be very important if the rescuers need to provide emergency care when they extract the person.

EVALUATE AND TREAT THE VICTIM

As you uncover the victim, check to see that the person's mouth is not filled with snow and that there are no other obvious obstructions to their breathing. Clear snow away from their chest to allow room for their lungs to expand and take in air. Be prepared to start cardiopulmonary resuscitation (CPR), before the person is completely extracted from the snow if necessary. Be aware that suddenly moving a burial victim may cause cardiac failure as cold blood from the extremities moves to the heart (read more about "afterdrop" in Cold Stress and Hypothermia

20

in Chapter 24, First Aid). Make sure the person is as warm and comfortable as possible, and be prepared to treat for hypothermia and injuries (see Chapter 24, First Aid). Once your party has determined that the rescued individual does not need urgent care, continue to search for other buried victims.

Applying These Skills in the Field

Once you have learned and practiced the fundamentals of avalanche safety, keep practicing these skills in the backcountry until you are confident that you are proficient. Identifying avalanche terrain or suspect weather patterns is not enough to minimize your risk; you must know how to put it all together. As with other aspects of avalanche safety, practice these techniques before you venture into hazardous terrain, become involved in an avalanche, or have to search for and and rescue a companion. Climbing in mountainous environments means being exposed to certain risks. Proper training and regular practice with avalanche safety equipment is a lifelong learning process, and continued avalanche education is essential to fully understand the risks associated with climbing. Mountaineers should train with local avalanche educators to develop their skills evaluating and managing avalanche hazard and minimizing their risk.

CHAPTER 21

EXPEDITION CLIMBING

Climbers who want to explore the world's highest and remotest peaks will need
to learn about the planning and preparation required to fulfill their dreams.
Executing an expedition teaches climbers a great deal about their destination, their
climbing partners, and themselves.

What makes a climb an expedition? Expeditions require significant time, commitment, planning, and preparation. Just getting to base camp may involve two or three days of air travel, followed by a day or two of land travel, then a 10-day trek. On an expedition, climbers may take a few days or several weeks to acclimate to high elevation. Plus, climbers must navigate local languages and customs, etiquette, and the red tape that larger objectives often entail.

Mastering the mountaineering skills needed for the chosen objective is a prerequisite for expedition climbing. The techniques covered in other chapters in this book are used in expedition climbing, but often at extreme altitude on objectives that are orders of magnitude larger than any mountains team members may have climbed previously. It is beyond the scope of this overview of expedition climbing to cover techniques specific to some types of expeditions (to learn more, see Resources).

Planning

Expedition planning involves researching and choosing an objective, selecting a style and type of climb, choosing the team, and developing an itinerary. Proper planning is key to setting up an expedition for success. There is a wealth of information for climbing destinations worldwide. Sort through it to choose an objective and learn more about it. Getting firsthand information from people you know and trust is invaluable.

CHOOSE AN OBJECTIVE

In deciding what peak to try and which route to climb, choose a destination that excites you. Ask yourself whether you are committed to the substantial effort involved in researching, planning, financing, and preparing for an expedition.

Location

Choosing your destination is the first important step. Africa, Antarctica, Central and South Asia, Europe, New Zealand, and North and South America all boast difficult, remote peaks. After choosing a peak, research the mountain and its routes, as well as objective hazards. Talk to climbers who have been there; look for descriptions in the journals of the United Kingdom's Alpine Club, the American Alpine Club, the Alpine Club of Canada, and other climbing organizations. Seek out guidebooks, videos, and articles in climbing magazines, and research online sources. Select and research another objective on a nearby peak in case the original objective is abandoned because of avalanche hazard, bad weather, inability of party members to continue, or any other reason.

Route

When considering an objective, think of the trip as an opportunity to apply well-practiced climbing skills in a new environment rather than to push the limits of any individual's technical ability. The chosen route should be well within the party's climbing ability because the added challenges of remoteness, altitude, changeable weather, and routefinding will compound the route's difficulties. Identify a backup route in case the preferred route choice on the chosen peak is not feasible.

21

> ### KEY TOPICS
> **PLANNING**
> **PREPARATION**
> **IN THE FIELD**
> **EMBRACING EXPEDITION VALUES**

Time of Year

Seek out information from knowledgeable climbers and literature on seasonal temperatures, winds, storms, precipitation, snow conditions, and amount of daylight for the prospective expedition's area. These factors will affect the decision for the best time for the expedition, as well as its duration and needed supplies and gear.

Climb Duration

Do not underestimate the time that acclimatization requires in the world's higher-elevation regions. Allowing enough time to wait for the right conditions and a sufficient window of good weather to make the ascent increases the chance of success. However, spending a long period on an expedition must be reconciled with the difficulties of an extended absence from other commitments back home.

CHOOSE THE EXPEDITION TYPE AND STYLE

An expedition can be either guided or run by the team members—or a hybrid of these two options—and the climb can employ either alpine- or expedition-style tactics. The choices of type of expedition and climbing style greatly influence planning; thus, make these important decisions early in the planning process. These choices affect the required climbing skill, the trip's commitment and risk, the equipment and supplies needed, and the party who is responsible for logistics.

Type of Expedition

If this is the climbers' first expedition, if they lack capable partners, or if the prospect of organizing such a major adventure is overwhelming, they can consider a fully guided expedition or a commercial expedition rather than doing it all themselves. Each of the three expedition types described below offers a very different experience, and each has advantages and disadvantages. All expeditions, no matter the type, generally use local adventure-travel services, but the range of services needed varies depending on the type of expedition.

Guided expeditions. Using a guide service is the easiest and most reliable way to reach a major summit because all of the client oversight, logistics, decision-making, and (in some cases) load carrying is provided by experienced personnel. Climbers can focus entirely on their mental and physical exertions. Guide services offer climbing expeditions to many of the world's major peaks. But guided expeditions bring together climbers who often do not know

> ### WHAT TO CONSIDER WHEN SELECTING A GUIDE SERVICE
>
> - Is the guide service permitted, licensed, and insured as required by the governing authority of the destination?
> - What is the safety record of the guide service?
> - Does the guide service employ certified guides? What are the qualifications of the guide(s)?
> - What experience and qualifications do other party members have?
> - What reputation does the guide service have among climbers? Personal references are very helpful.
> - Does the guide service engage in socially responsible environmental, economic, and employment practices?

each other, and the process of understanding the mountain, evaluating conditions, developing strategy, making decisions, and doing much of the work is delegated to guides (see the "What to Consider When Selecting a Guide Service" sidebar).

DIY expeditions. A do-it-yourself expedition is just that: the climbing team is responsible for organizing all the expedition logistics, developing strategy, making decisions, and managing all aspects of the trip. The advantages and disadvantages of DIY expeditions are the opposite of guided expeditions. DIY expeditions usually consist of a team of friends who must work together to learn about the mountain and conditions, do all the work, and make their own decisions. An expedition that assumes these responsibilities rather than delegating them to professionals may offer a smaller chance of success, but this kind of self-reliance can provide a more complete and authentic experience.

Commercial expeditions. A hybrid of guided and DIY expeditions, commercial expeditions delegate the pre-climb logistics to a professional organizer, and the participants are responsible for the climbing. Companies offering commercial expeditions charge a fee to organize all the logistics of getting to and living at base camp. These companies do not provide guides to escort climbers up the mountain, so individual climbers or predetermined climbing teams are responsible for their actions above base camp.

Climbing Style

Any expedition can employ one of two styles of climbing—expedition or alpine—although guided expeditions rarely are alpine style.

Expedition style. Climbers work their way up a mountain in "expedition style" by installing infrastructure such as fixed ropes or other climbing aids to facilitate travel between a set of fixed camps. In some cases, the infrastructure and camps are set up and stocked using skilled labor from local high-altitude workers. Expedition-style climbing provides a systematic way to acclimatize. Climbers slowly ascend the fixed ropes between camps and descend the same fixed ropes going down. Nearly all guided and some DIY and commercial expeditions employ expedition style.

Alpine style. When a party climbs "alpine style," they carry all of their food, shelter, and equipment as they climb in a single push, eschewing expedition-style infrastructure such as fixed lines and a series of camps. There is greater risk in climbing alpine style, because only the bare minimum of equipment and supplies can be carried, and descending is more involved. However, alpine-style climbing is considered to be a purer expression of the sport, and because it involves small teams, there is less environmental impact.

As mentioned previously, fast and light alpine-style climbing generally involves more risk than infrastructure-laden, expedition-style ascents. But in some instances, having greater speed lessens some risks, such as exposure to objective hazards or time at high altitude (see Chapters 7, Protecting the Outdoors, and 23, Risk Management). Many DIY expeditions climb alpine style, and some commercial expeditions break up into smaller teams that climb alpine style.

CHOOSING THE TEAM

The greatest factor that determines whether an expedition will be prudent and enjoyable is the choice of the climbing team. This task includes evaluating the optimal number of team members and their compatibility and climbing skills. Climbers on a guided expedition can assess the guide service's choice of team size and skill, and they will learn team member compatibility once the expedition is under way. A DIY expedition will choose its team members. Commercial expeditions can attract both individual climbers and prearranged teams and therefore have attributes of both guided and DIY expeditions.

Team Size

The size of the climbing team depends primarily on the chosen objective and climbing style. For lightweight alpine-style expeditions, a party of two to four climbers is best because of the speed and efficiency of smaller rope teams and limited space at bivouac sites. However, a small team faces a big impact if one person becomes ill or cannot continue. This loss may weaken the team to the extent that the other member(s) may have to abandon the climb. It is also more difficult for smaller parties to carry out self-rescue than larger teams.

For expedition-style climbs, parties of six or more have the advantage of strength and reserve capacity for doing work like breaking trail in deep snow or carrying loads. Larger teams have more flexibility if a climber is unable to continue, because there will still be enough team members to carry out the expedition. But the team may reject this style of climbing out of principle, and as the number of climbers increases, the feasibility of doing a technical climb decreases and issues of transportation, lodging, food, equipment, and environmental impact can also become more complicated (see Logistics below).

Compatibility

Expedition team members must be able to live harmoniously with others in close quarters under stressful conditions. Climbers on an expedition will spend considerable time together and must be flexible and prepared to deal with unknowns.

On guided expeditions, group compatibility is difficult to determine ahead of time, but knowing your climbing partners is less of an issue on this type of expedition because the guides facilitate and lead much of the group interaction and decision-making, and they perform much of the work.

For DIY expeditions, making decisions, assessing risk, performing group tasks, and developing strategy can be challenging, and good partners do these things effectively, even under hardship. Ideally, team members would agree ahead of time on the expedition's philosophy in terms of climbing goals and style, degree of acceptable risk (see below), environmental impact (see Chapter 7, Protecting the Outdoors), and communication style (see Chapter 22, Leadership). Personalities need to be compatible. Make it a goal to head out as friends and return as even better friends.

Determining compatibility on commercial expeditions is a hybrid of how this is done on guided expeditions and on DIY expeditions.

21

Behavior. Team partnerships are driven by how members behave with each other. Ask yourself these questions about the prospective team, especially if it is a DIY expedition, before embarking with them on a weeks- or months-long expedition:

- Are team members supportive of each other and the climbing goal?
- Is everyone encouraged to have an equal voice?
- Do the climbers have enough experience and discipline to take care of themselves?
- Are people psychologically prepared to deal with uncertainty and separation from friends and family?
- Do members pitch in and help each other? Are they self-reliant with the things they need to do for themselves?
- Can members stay calm under duress?
- Do they have a sense of humor?

Risk tolerance. The team should discuss the party's willingness to accept or not accept different mountain hazards before leaving on the expedition. Disagreement over risk management strategies is a common source of conflict between expedition team members (see Chapter 23, Risk Management). Disagreements might still arise on the mountain related to risk. But transparency and communication over this issue when choosing the team is important and will establish productive ways for the team to have ongoing communication about it.

Skill

The team members' level of skill must be equal to the demands of the climb. On guided expeditions, team members need to have a minimum skill level, but they also depend heavily on the guides' skill, decision-making, and assessment of the team's capabilities. The skill of a DIY team or of any individual team included in a commercial expedition is usually equal to that of its least experienced member. Team members' skill levels can be different and their levels of ambition can change. Some climbers may discover that they do not possess the skill nor the desire to continue when faced with the realities of a big, committing objective. Less confident and skilled climbers being pressured to continue or assume risks by other team members who are more skilled and comfortable with the situation usually creates conflict and increases risk. Skilled climb leaders recognize these dynamics and address them. For more on these topics, see Chapters 22, Leadership, and 23, Risk Management.

Preparation

The detailed planning and preparation begins once a team has chosen an objective, time of year, trip duration, type and style of expedition, and the team. On a guided expedition, the guide service carries out most of the detailed planning and logistics, and climbers focus on physical training and obtaining personal equipment, visas, and medications. On a DIY or commercial expedition, team members must also plan the itinerary, research and obtain climbing permits, prepare a budget and secure financing, obtain equipment and supplies, arrange travel and local transport, secure lodging, and purchase rescue and/or medical insurance.

LOGISTICS

Find out what travel visas are necessary and determine how long in advance any permit applications must be made. Research potential health problems for the specific travel location, including availability of safe drinking water. Obtain details on what to budget for and the types of food, fuel, and equipment that are available locally. Determine what type of communication devices work and are allowed in the area (see Chapter 5, Navigation and Communication). Consider whether anyone in the party speaks the local language.

Itinerary

An itinerary includes an estimate of the number of days needed for the entire roundtrip journey from home and back again. It reflects the answers to questions such as these:

- What is the best day to fly to the destination area to avoid arriving on weekends or holidays when tasks like changing money, shopping, or meeting with government agencies cannot be accomplished?
- Will extra time be necessary if local air travel is unreliable or weather-dependent?
- Will extra time be needed at towns along the way to base camp for provisioning and arranging for vehicles and porters?
- How much time is needed for the trek or flight to base camp?
- How much time is needed to do the ascent based on the chosen climbing style and potential delay waiting for good weather and conditions?
- How much time is needed for the journey home after the expedition?

It is not easy to estimate how much time is needed above base camp for acclimatizing, carrying loads up the mountain (if climbing expedition style), waiting for favorable weather, making the actual climb, and resting between failed attempts. Allowing time to wait for satisfactory weather is the most unpredictable factor when determining the itinerary. The more time allowed, the greater the chance of success. Try to plan a flexible schedule for the climb above base camp, to account for unknowns like weather, conditions, and climbers' health. Trying to force a rigid climbing itinerary when faced with these uncertainties is a poor strategy that can also create added risk.

Permits

Climbing expedition permits are required by many parks and countries around the world. Research what permits might be required for the climbing destination. There is usually a fee associated with a permit. Guided and commercial trips usually obtain the necessary permits and pass on any of these costs to their clients. DIY team members are responsible for obtaining permits, which can be easy to get in many places but difficult in others—especially where access is restricted for security or political reasons. If permits are difficult to obtain, the team may need to develop a permitting strategy in consultation with other climbers who have been there before or with a local adventure-tour company.

There can be a specified length of time before the start of the expedition in which the party must register or apply for a permit. Climbing permits may also limit, for environmental reasons, the number of people in an area or on a particular peak. There is usually a set of regulations associated with the permit. Understand and comply with all permit requirements; violating them can result in fines, a ban from climbing in that country for many years, and possibly a loss of access for future expeditions.

Budget and Financing

Expeditions can be costly because of the large amounts of time, equipment, supplies, and travel expenses required. A guided expedition usually includes all costs in its per-climber fee, except for personal equipment and airfare to a specified departure point. A commercial company should specify exactly what its services include and what the costs are for the team or for each climber. A DIY team must figure out all expedition expenses.

Major costs include equipment for the climb, transportation to the peak, accommodation en route to the climb (if necessary), meals during the entire expedition, permits and fees, and support staff, hired porters, and/or pack animals, if needed. It is best not to scrimp on gear, guide or adventure-travel-company services, local support services, or weather forecasting. In the broader perspective, a slightly higher fee or slightly more expensive sleeping bag could make or break a climber's chance to reach the summit on a trip of a lifetime.

Prepare a budget spreadsheet that itemizes all the elements of the chosen type of expedition. Develop unit costs for each element based on quotes from such companies as airlines, tour operators, guide services, bush pilots, and hotels, as well as on information from other climbers who have been there. Use government agencies or other sources to budget both fair wages for porters and other support staff and the costs to provide them with the equipment and supplies they need to stay safe and be comfortable.

Expeditions are often financed by the climbers themselves. But for expeditions that meet certain criteria, there may be grants available from national alpine clubs or private foundations. If expedition members plan on applying for support, research the criteria and consult with previous grant recipients on how to apply, and make sure to note the application deadline.

Insurance

Research whether buying travel insurance is a worthwhile investment. Local regulations may require an expedition to provide its local workers some amount of life and medical insurance. Having rescue insurance can cover the cost of what would otherwise be an expensive evacuation (see below). Individual team members should make sure their medical insurance will provide coverage in the event they are injured or sick and require medical care in another country.

Rescue Services

Climbers can get sick or injured on expeditions in remote areas, so the team must be prepared to handle medical emergencies (see Chapter 24, First Aid). In the event of a serious illness or injury that cannot be managed with first aid in the field, a medical evacuation may be required. In some parts of the world, suitable helicopter equipment that can fly to the necessary altitude to perform an evacuation may not be available. Do not wait until the team is in the middle of an emergency to figure out how to arrange a helicopter rescue. Research this ahead of time and develop an emergency response plan. Ask other climbers who have been to the area what kinds of rescue services are available and how to mobilize them if necessary. See Chapters 23, Risk Management, and 25, Self-Rescue.

21

In most countries, climbers are responsible for the cost of a helicopter evacuation, which from remote areas can be substantial. Obtain rescue insurance or subscribe to a rescue service that can cover these costs. In some countries, climbers must have proof of rescue insurance coverage, a subscription to a rescue service, or ability to pay, or they must pay a deposit ahead of time before rescue services will be deployed. Research the rescue services available and rescue protocols for the region or country the team will visit. Choosing not to comply with these protocols could result in a refusal to send a helicopter if a life-threatening medical emergency occurs or a search is needed for missing climbers.

If the team does obtain a medical helicopter evacuation to a local hospital, they may end up needing a medevac flight back to their home country. Make sure the team's medical or rescue insurance or service covers this. Insurance coverage for climber rescue and evacuation services is often available through national alpine clubs.

In addition to arrangements for a helicopter rescue, the expedition's emergency response plan should include a list of emergency contacts for each team member, each team member's medical and insurance plan information, and relevant phone numbers for local contacts and embassies. In the event of an emergency overseas where the team must coordinate with officials of a foreign government, call the team member's state department or foreign ministry; they will assign someone in their local embassy or consulate to help.

To initiate a medical evacuation, the expedition will need a satellite communication (satcom) device or the type of personal locator beacon (PLB) that can send text messages, or a satellite phone (see Chapter 5, Navigation and Communication). Leave a copy of the team's emergency response plan with a trusted individual at home. Make sure this person understands the nature of the climb and has a clear directive from the team on when and how to engage in organizing rescue efforts.

Weather Forecasting

It can be difficult to pick a sufficient weather window to make a summit attempt, and having dependable weather forecasts reduces the team's risk and improves their chances of success. If a team has access to satellite communications, weather forecasts are available anywhere on the globe. Research the types of forecasts available for the area you will be visiting. In some places, dependable weather forecasts are available online with internet access. In other places, a team may not have internet access, or weather forecasts for the altitude where the team will be climbing may be difficult or impossible to obtain.

In the latter situation, the team may decide to pay for custom weather forecasts from an experienced mountain-weather professional and obtain this information using a satcom device or PLB with texting capability. When putting together the trip budget, be willing to pay for access to accurate weather forecasts. Having the best possible information about weather enables decision-making that minimizes the risk of a committing attempt to reach the summit. After picking appropriate team members, having accurate weather forecasts is arguably the next most important element that contributes to making the summit or not.

Even with dependable weather forecast information, expedition climbers should know something about mountain weather. When the expedition reaches base camp for its objective, talk to other climbers (if there are any around) and to people who live there about local weather patterns. Find out the direction of the prevailing winds. Most sports watches have a barometer and altimeter, so make a record of weather patterns at different readings that might signal weather changes (see Chapter 5, Navigation and Communication). Take clues from the clouds: cirrus clouds warn of a front bringing precipitation, and lenticular clouds mean moisture aloft and high winds. For more information, see Chapter 28, Mountain Weather.

EQUIPMENT

The combination of the route, the chosen climbing style, and the type of expedition determines what equipment is needed. Having the necessary gear—and having it in working order—is critical. An expedition needs a complete equipment list, agreed on by all team members, that includes both group and personal gear. On guided expeditions, the guide service provides the group equipment and a list of personal equipment that each climber is required to bring. Gear lists can be found in books or other resources specifically about expedition climbing.

Personal Equipment

No matter whether it is a guided, commercial, or DIY expedition, or whether it is an alpine- or expedition-style climb, personal equipment is mostly the same: crampons, ice axe(s), personal climbing hardware, harness, headlamp, pack(s), sunglasses, clothing, shoes and boots, sleeping bag(s) and pads, and other personal items. Having a journal to record daily events and thoughts is a helpful way to keep track of the trip. Expedition climbers need clothing that can stand up to prolonged use under severe conditions. The suggestions on clothing and equipment in Chapters 2, Clothing and Equipment; 16, Basic Snow and Ice

Climbing; and 17, Technical Snow and Ice Climbing, are generally applicable to expeditions. But make sure the comfort rating of your clothing and sleep systems is based on the area's anticipated temperatures, climate, and altitude. For some expeditions going to extreme altitude, specialized sleeping bags, clothing, and double boots are necessary.

Hygiene kit. On expeditions, each climber must bring a personal hygiene kit that includes an adequate supply of prescription and over-the-counter medications, as well as a toothbrush, toothpaste, floss, lotion, soap and wipes, shampoo, comb, razors, toilet paper and blue bag (see Packing Out Poop in Chapter 7), and other items tailored to the location and individual needs. For those that need them, bring extra contact lenses and solution, or prescription sunglasses (along with an extra pair). Make sure to have an appropriately labeled pee bottle and female urination device (Chapter 7) to eliminate unpleasant trips outside the tent in storms and on cold nights.

Electronics. There can be a lot of downtime resting or waiting for weather, so it is a good idea to bring an e-reader for entertainment, which is much lighter than carrying multiple books. Depending on the expedition, it may be necessary to have a portable solar charging device to power a headlamp, a camera, a phone and other communication devices, an e-reader, a watch, and possibly a computer. Charging systems can be complicated, so ensure yours serves the power-supply needs of all personal electrical and electronic items (see Chapter 5, Navigation and Communication).

Group Equipment

Items of group gear include technical hardware for the climb, stoves and pots, tents, the group repair kit, communication devices, water storage and filtration systems, solar chargers for group power needs, wands, a group first-aid kit (see Medical Supplies, below), and other similar items. On guided expeditions, all base-camp items are normally provided, such as a kitchen tent, base-camp cooking pots and pans, dishes and utensils, table(s) and chairs, and a mess tent, plus climbing hardware, tents, ropes, stoves, and other group equipment listed above. On commercial expeditions, all base-camp group equipment is usually provided similar to on a guided expedition, but typically not repair kits for personal items or personal electronic items. With DIY expeditions, the party arranges for all these things themselves, and they also must be sure to bring or locally purchase sufficient equipment for any porters or other local individuals who will be part of the expedition.

Group climbing gear. As with any climbing trip, the type of technical rock, snow, and ice climbing hardware needed on an expedition is determined by the type of climbing anticipated (see Chapters 13, Rock Protection; 16, Basic Snow and Ice Climbing; and 17, Technical Snow and Ice Climbing). Beyond what would be brought along on an alpine-style expedition, expedition-style climbs also need ample gear for fixing lines—thousands of feet of rope and dozens of additional rock or ice anchors, as well as multiple tents, stoves and pots, sleeping bags, and insulating pads for the fixed camps on the mountain.

Stoves and pots. The type of stove used on an expedition must be determined by whatever fuel is available locally, since stove fuel cannot be transported on commercial airlines. Lightweight mountaineering stoves use small compressed-gas cartridges or liquid fuel dispensed from a small hand-pressurized tank. Expedition base camps with kitchen staff have large stoves, usually run off large, refillable compressed-gas tanks or liquid fuel. Base-camp stoves that burn compressed propane provide a healthier work environment for kitchen staff than those that burn kerosene, because propane does not give off fumes like kerosene. Liquid fuel used in mountaineering stoves is usually either white gas or kerosene; if kerosene is the locally available fuel, make sure the stove has the appropriate jet for kerosene.

Many climbers prefer mountaineering stoves that use compressed-gas cartridges in parts of the world where the liquid fuel available is kerosene. Stoves burning kerosene emit noxious fumes, don't function well at high altitude, and can clog. But in places like Alaska, where base camp is often on a glacier above the firn line and all drinking water must be melted from snow, many climbers prefer white-gas stoves because of their high heat output and compatibility with large pots. In high-altitude regions, choose a stove that will work efficiently in that environment. Learn to take apart, clean, and troubleshoot stove repairs *before* the trip. See Stoves in Chapter 3, Camping, Food, and Water. If using liquid fuel, bring a fuel filter and filter all local fuel before using it, and carry empty fuel containers compatible with the stove and fuel type.

Group repair kit. Bring a group repair kit with tools like a multi-bit screwdriver, an adjustable wrench, pliers, a multitool, a sewing awl and heavy thread, and an Allen wrench and other small wrenches for adjusting and tightening ice tools and crampons. Other repair-kit items include duct tape and fiberglass tape; different types of glue; sewing supplies; spare parts for stoves, crampons, and ice tools; and repair tape or kits for patching clothing, tents, and inflatable sleeping pads.

Other group gear. Team members could consider some or all of the following as group gear rather than have individual

21

climbers each carrying one: water treatment system, map, compass, GPS device, satcom device(s), solar charging devices and associated power banks or battery packs, wands, and latrine equipment.

SUPPLIES

Expedition supplies consist primarily of fuel and food, as well as a group first-aid kit and other medical supplies.

Fuel

Most climbing destinations have compressed-gas cartridges available in local shops or through a local tour operator; but if the expedition will need compressed-gas cartridges, verify that they are locally available before leaving on the trip. White gas is available in North America and some places in Europe (where it is called naphtha or Coleman fuel), and it is usually consistent in quality. But in Asia and many other parts of the world, kerosene is the available liquid fuel, and it often has impurities that can clog non-local stoves that are used for climbing. As discussed under Group Equipment, above, the type of stove must be compatible with whatever fuel is available locally.

On guided expeditions, the stoves and fuel supply are generally taken care of by the guide service. On commercial expeditions, the stoves and fuel supply at base camp are usually taken care of by the tour company, but the stove(s) and fuel supply used above base camp are usually the responsibility of individual climbers (although arrangements for fuel can often be made through the tour operator). On DIY expeditions, team members are responsible for bringing stoves and obtaining all fuel supplies.

The amount of fuel needed greatly depends on whether the stove is used to melt snow for water. Calculate fuel needs before leaving on the trip. For formulas and factors, see How Much Fuel? in Chapter 3, Camping, Food, and Water. Bring sufficient stoves and fuel for any porters or other local individuals who will be part of the expedition or will be carrying loads to base camp. To help reduce the entire team's impact on the environment, do not allow porters or kitchen staff to burn locally obtained wood (see Leave No Trace in Chapter 7, Protecting the Outdoors).

Food

Like fuel, food provisioning depends on what is available locally and whether the expedition is guided, commercial, or DIY. On guided expeditions, the guide service generally provides all the food, though they need information about climbers' food allergies and preferences. Commercial trips generally take care of the base-camp food, with food above base camp usually the responsibility of individual climbers. For DIY trips, team members are responsible for base-camp as well as on-mountain food supplies.

If expedition team members are responsible for some or all of the food supply, determine ahead of time which food items must be brought from home and which can be purchased from local markets. Many items, such as freeze-dried food; energy bars and drink mixes; high-quality cheese, dried meat, and nuts; instant soups and potatoes; and foods that are not eaten or available locally (such as peanut butter) often must be brought from home. Base-camp food items, which are heavier and can take longer to prepare than on-mountain food items—like sugar, powdered milk, rice, beans, flour, fresh fruit and vegetables, condiments, spices, common candy bars, crackers, cookies, and tea bags—can often be purchased locally. Local tour operators or other climbers familiar with the area can provide this information.

If the expedition will work with a guide, cook, or other staff, these workers often make the local food purchases. When working with a guide or cook, be sure to communicate dietary restrictions. If expedition members will prepare their own food, they also usually do the local food purchasing.

On-mountain food above base camp should be lightweight and tasty and require minimum preparation. As much as possible, sample foods ahead of time that will be brought from home. When calculating food weight, plan on roughly 40 ounces—2.5 pounds (about 1.1 kilograms)—of food per person per day. For specific menus, see Food in Chapter 3, Camping, Food, and Water. For nutrition for climbers, whether in training or on the mountain, see Fundamental Training Concepts in Chapter 4, Conditioning.

Medical Supplies

Every expedition must have a comprehensive first-aid kit. A guided expedition will have a group first-aid kit, but individual climbers should carry personal first-aid items and medications they may need. A commercial expedition usually will have a group first-aid kit at base camp, but the climbers will need a first-aid kit beyond base camp. A DIY expedition must assemble a group first-aid kit for base camp and one for higher on the mountain.

Consider how isolated the peak is and the specifics of medical issues and diseases in that region or country.

Consult with a doctor who is a travel specialist or is familiar with mountaineering to discuss the vaccinations and preventive care needed in the destination country, and ask specifically for prescriptions for medications needed for the first-aid kit. The first-aid kit may include such specialized or prescription items as altitude medications, strong painkillers, antibiotics, a dental repair kit, and a suture kit (see Chapter 24, First Aid, and The Mountaineers' Ten Essentials in Chapter 2, Clothing and Equipment).

Find out whether different climates or altitudes adversely affect the efficacy or side effects of medications that will be taken on the expedition. Know the specific medical conditions of team members and their medical knowledge. Team members should prepare by obtaining wilderness first-aid training and understanding how the contents of a first-aid kit can be used. Check online with the Centers for Disease Control and Prevention and other travel medicine resources as part of your planning.

TRAVEL AND LODGING

Traveling for an expedition includes commercial flights to climbing destinations around the world. Expeditions also usually involve some local transportation, and climbers may need to secure local lodging en route.

Commercial Flights

Expeditions can take climbers to the most remote, far-flung parts of the world, and making travel arrangements with commercial airlines can be complicated. Seek help from a professional travel consultant rather than trying to tackle these arrangements on your own. These itineraries demand attention, so leave that to an expert and do not burden yourself with the details about how to get there and how to get home.

Expedition climbers usually have a lot of baggage, which can get lost or delayed. Split important items between the bags, rather than packing all the important items and equipment in a single bag. That way, if one bag is lost or delayed, only part of the equipment, clothing, food, et cetera is lost or delayed. Try to wear or carry on the most important items rather than checking them as baggage.

The amount of time it takes to complete an expedition is hard to predict and more often than not climbers need to change their return flight. Work with a travel consultant to buy your ticket, and that person will make the changes for you. When trying to get home after an exhausting and lengthy expedition, you will not want to have to struggle

with airlines and third-party websites. Do internet research, but use experience-based judgment when accessing that information, and take it with a grain of salt.

Local Transportation

After the expedition members arrive at the area's major air hub, they may need to take some sort of local transportation. Depending on the location, that may include a bush flight, ground transportation, and/or an approach hike to base camp.

Bush flight. It is possible to reach some remote climbing destinations that lack a prepared landing strip or runway with either a helicopter or a bush plane. Bush planes can be equipped with large tires, floats, or skis. Some locations may have only one bush-flight service that will take the team where it wants to go; for some popular destinations, there may be several services available. On guided expeditions, it is common for bush flights to be included in the packages the guide service offers. For DIY and some commercial expeditions, the team may need to talk to other climbers who have been there to find out what their experience was with the bush-flight service they used. Talk to the flying service ahead of time to learn more about their operations. To reserve a flight, you may need to pay a deposit.

Ground transportation. Often, part of the journey to reach a remote climbing objective includes local road transportation. The type of vehicle(s) used depends on the road quality and could be anything from a bus, truck, van, and/or passenger automobile to a four-wheel-drive vehicle. On guided or commercial expeditions, the guide service or tour operator arranges the ground transportation. On DIY expeditions, it is a good idea to hire a local tour operator whose services include road travel arrangements with safe drivers and reliable vehicles.

Foot travel. The final stage of getting to a remote objective is usually by foot, which often includes using porters or pack animals to carry equipment and supplies. On guided expeditions, these arrangements are made by the guide service, and on commercial and well-organized DIY expeditions, a tour operator is usually responsible for this. Although the arrangements for porters are usually made by others, it is the responsibility of all expedition members to ensure that workers are paid a fair wage and have proper equipment; their health and well-being should be everyone's highest priority. It is also the expedition's ultimate responsibility to see that any pack animals are treated humanely.

21

Local Lodging

Accommodations en route from the commercial airport to the trailhead or bush-flight service are arranged by the guide service or tour operator for guided and commercial expeditions. DIY trips may use a local tour operator to make these arrangements, but in some parts of the world it might be easy enough for team members to make the arrangements as they go.

CONDITIONING

Because expeditions require significant commitment, it is important for each climber to start physical, mental, and technical conditioning many months before the trip. Traveling to the peak and then being unable to reach the top because of inadequate conditioning can be frustrating and discouraging.

Expedition climbers ideally aim to achieve a level of physical fitness commensurate with the size of the objective and technical difficulty of the climb. Emphasize both cardiovascular and strength training (see Components of Fitness in Chapter 4, Conditioning). Climbers can find plans online, and many guide companies provide written programs to follow for physical conditioning. Working with an individualized training plan or personal trainer will complement each climber's preparation for the trip. Conditioning for a major climb can be time-consuming, requiring months of daily or twice-daily training sessions.

Train for what the planned climb will require. Will climbers be hauling a sled? Will they be carrying heavy loads? Will they need excellent endurance as they move to high altitude? Will there be steep technical climbing that requires strength and skill? Team members must make sure their conditioning plan prepares them for the type and style of climbing they will do.

Soft skills such as the ability to handle decision-making under stress, being comfortable with uncertainty, and communicating risk to climbing partners are also essential. Climbers should practice and master these important skills. Consider whether the team members have met with and worked with one another. Evaluate whether they have learned to communicate effectively and work together as a team. Dealing with extreme cold, possible sickness, cramped quarters, sometimes poor food, conflict with teammates, the stress of technical climbing, and the lethargy brought on by high altitude demands much more than physical strength. Remember to use your sense of humor, and be flexible. Do not underestimate the mental component of conditioning (see Mental Conditioning in Chapter 4).

Additionally, dialing in technical skills is essential to a successful climb. Will the expedition require techniques such as steep snow and ice climbing? (See Chapters 17, Technical Snow and Ice Climbing, and 18, Waterfall Ice and Mixed Climbing.) Will it require any particular rock climbing techniques? (See Chapters 13, Rock Protection, and 14, Traditional Rock Climbing.) Will the team be traveling on heavily crevassed glaciers? (See Chapter 19, Glacier Travel and Crevasse Rescue.)

Work on physical, mental, and technical conditioning by seeking out experiences that come as close as possible to what can be expected on the expedition. Prepare for the expedition by going on longer trips. If possible, do these as a team so everyone can learn to work together before they are subjected to physically and mentally stressful situations.

In the Field

Once the expedition gets under way, the team will face demands such as maintaining their physical health, adapting to weather changes, communicating with one another, respecting the local culture, heeding security issues, and minimizing their environmental impact.

MAINTAINING PHYSICAL HEALTH

Gastrointestinal problems, high-altitude-related ailments, and extreme-cold injuries are all potential health hazards that can occur on expeditions. Such trips can be in remote, hard-to-access places far from health-care facilities. The team needs to recognize, prevent, and treat any health problems as they arise. The first step in staying healthy is for each team member to take care of their personal health issues. Everyone must check with their doctor and make sure they have an adequate supply of any personal prescription medications. Any team members susceptible to allergies, sinus or respiratory problems, or similar conditions should bring over-the-counter or prescription medications to treat these conditions.

Gastrointestinal Disorders

Suffering from vomiting and diarrhea caused by drinking or eating contaminated water or food is the most common expedition ailment when climbers travel outside their home country. Contaminated water and food plagues many parts of the world, and getting sick from it can ruin a trip. Research the destination to ascertain the quality of the local water, and when in doubt, filter all water. In many countries, water may need to be filtered in cities and towns as well as in the backcountry. Do not eat any raw food, and do not consume soft drinks from a glass or with ice. Drinking bottled water in cities and towns will prevent waterborne sickness, but it also contributes to plastic waste; some expeditions filter and disinfect water from the local distribution system instead.

Beyond the trailhead in areas where drinking-water quality is in doubt, expedition members must filter all their drinking water. If there is any doubt about the water's quality after it has been filtered, add a chemical disinfectant. Always filter water before using a chemical disinfectant or UV wand, because those chemicals or devices are ineffective in water with a high concentration of suspended solids. Do not make the mistake of thinking that water from a mountain stream, even one flowing from a glacier, will be safe for human consumption. Plenty of pollutants from animals and other dispersed sources can make climbers sick. When camping on a glacier, it is important to ensure that the snow supply for drinking water and cooking is kept separate from and free of human waste and other pollutants.

Do not rely on drinking water that was supposedly boiled. At high altitude, water boils at a lower temperature that may not be hot enough to disinfect it properly. If water is boiled by kitchen staff, there are too many opportunities for it to get contaminated before it reaches climbers. Expedition members must control their water filtering operation to ensure it meets their standards for cleanliness. For more information, see Water Treatment in Chapter 3, Camping, Food, and Water.

If the expedition hires a local cook and kitchen staff, that operation will have more to do with the team's gastrointestinal health than almost anything else. Be sure the kitchen staff know how to prepare food and clean dishes so that the team stays healthy. Guide services and commercial operations have considerable experience working with locals and usually hire kitchen staff who understand how to keep the team healthy. If the expedition is DIY, ask climbers who have been there if they can refer a cook and kitchen staff who know how to run a clean kitchen.

High-Altitude-Related Ailments

Expedition climbing often takes place at extreme altitude, which can cause different ailments that climbers need to be able to recognize. Every climber is affected to varying degrees by reduced oxygen at higher elevations, which can cause acute mountain sickness (AMS). Also called altitude sickness, AMS can lead to the life-threatening conditions of high-altitude pulmonary edema (HAPE) and high-altitude cerebral edema (HACE).

Climbers are much less likely to suffer from these illnesses if they take the time and effort to acclimatize properly. This process can only take place by spending time at different altitudes before progressing upward (see High-Altitude Conditions in Chapter 24, First Aid). Climbers often lose their appetite at high altitudes, and the degree to which this happens is an indication of acclimatization level. Hydration is also critical in avoiding altitude illness (for detailed information, see Dehydration in Chapter 24; also see Resources for that chapter). If climbers are not able to eat and drink enough to maintain strength, they should descend to become better acclimatized at a lower elevation.

Besides ailments caused by low oxygen, expedition members must also be aware of cold-weather dangers like frostbite, as well as windburn and sunburn (see Chapter 24).

ADAPTING TO CHANGING WEATHER

Big mountains typically have big storms, strong winds, and rapidly changing weather. On an expedition, it is safer to descend from high on a mountain before the weather gets too severe. The team can then wait out storms in a comfortable, secure place with adequate supplies. Trying to stick it out during storms high on the mountain while waiting for better weather is almost always a poor strategy. Lying around in a flapping tent at altitude for days, with limited food supplies and poor sleep, will leave team members too exhausted or sick to make a summit bid when the weather improves.

Warm temperatures also pose problems. If it is hot and sunny, glaciers intensify solar radiation that can sap a climber's strength. Warm weather can also lead to deteriorating conditions, such as softened snow and deep trail breaking, collapsing snow bridges, and triggered avalanches. In such conditions, it is best to wait until temperatures drop or to climb at night, when temperatures are lower and snow and ice are the most stable. As the effects of climate change accelerate, climbers must increasingly adapt to warmer temperatures.

COMMUNICATING AMONG TEAM MEMBERS

Expedition members are partners—people who are committed to each other's success and well-being. Open and clear communication among team members supports this partnership and is usually a prerequisite for expeditions to be both successful and gratifying. Volumes have been written on communication, but it is worth discussing a few things about how it applies to expeditions. In other situations, poor communication might result in a business or relationship failure, but on a climbing expedition, it can have tragic consequences.

Expedition members need to understand the different types of leadership that are appropriate for different types

21

of expeditions and how leadership affects the way the team cooperates and makes decisions (see Chapter 22, Leadership). Guided expeditions have a designated trip leader who is responsible for managing all the logistics and making all the important decisions. Clients on guided expeditions are expected to cooperate with the leader, to communicate honestly about their health and their ability to do what is required, and to express any other concerns. On commercial expeditions, the tour company or trip organizer is responsible for managing all the logistics and making all the decisions while getting everyone and everything to base camp. Above base camp, the team members interact with each other as they would on a DIY expedition.

DIY expeditions usually designate a leader for permitting purposes or for taking charge in an emergency. Small DIY teams share the actual logistical management, work tasks, and decision-making. On DIY expeditions, it is important for the team to agree on how decisions will be made before the trip gets under way, to ensure everyone has a voice. Assignments can be delegated to various team members to distribute the workload and to keep everyone involved. Designated team members can take the lead on areas such as finances, food, medicine, and equipment.

RESPECTING LOCAL CULTURE AND HEEDING SECURITY ISSUES

With some climbing destinations, expeditions become immersed in the local culture that they also rely on for delivering many needed services. A large part of this overall experience is the opportunity to interact with people and customs that are very different from your own. Guided and commercial expeditions have relationships with local tour companies and service providers and can share information on cultural norms that need to be respected. For DIY trips, the team must research this subject, including consulting climbers who have been there.

Circumventing any local rules and regulations is unethical. It is the host country's prerogative to establish rules for foreigners that govern their visiting and climbing activities. Violating these rules can also jeopardize access for future expeditions.

Some climbing destinations are located where land ownership is disputed between adjacent countries. Permits to climb in these high-security areas can be hard to obtain, and when they are issued, they usually include strict rules on where the team can go and what they are allowed to see and do. In these situations, the expedition is typically assigned a liaison officer, usually a military officer responsible for ensuring that the climbers adhere to the rules. Work to maintain a positive relationship with this person, who has the power to either help the expedition run smoothly or make it a nightmare.

Other climbing destinations pose potential security risks from crime and religious or political violence. Consult with your country's state department or foreign ministry for any travel advisories. Talk to other climbers who have been there to get the latest information on security issues. The best way to minimize security risks is to obtain current information from a reliable source on the geographic location and demographics of these risks, and whether it's possible to avoid them. Be aware that some local adventure-tour companies downplay security risks as a way to encourage tourism.

MINIMIZING ENVIRONMENTAL IMPACTS

The two main sources of pollution that humans generate in the backcountry are human waste and solid waste (garbage). Expeditions last for long periods of time and generate large amounts of both kinds of waste. It can be difficult to manage these waste streams, with the goal of leaving the area as pristine as possible. For details, see Chapter 7, Protecting the Outdoors. Many expeditions go to places in the world where other expeditions are taking place, and the larger number of people compounds these waste problems. It is important to learn how waste is managed in the location you will be visiting.

Solid waste. The adage of "pack it in, pack it out" applies to expeditions. In some places, all trash is collected and transported out of the mountains and then disposed of properly. In other places, it is acceptable to separate solid waste; burn combustible items completely; pack out bottles, cans, and other items that cannot be burned or composted; and compost items that can decompose. Every expedition is ultimately responsible for following local rules, regulations, and standard practices for managing the expedition's solid waste. When this work is done by a cook or kitchen staff, expedition members must provide oversight to make sure solid waste is properly managed.

Human waste. The disposal of expedition human waste can be managed in many ways, depending on the location. In some places where climbers camp on snow or ice, feces and sometimes even urine is collected and flown or carried out. If the infrastructure for disposal of human waste doesn't exist, then waste is usually disposed of in a hole dug in the snow or in a crevasse, far away and downstream from where water or snow is collected for drinking and cooking. When an expedition camps on soil, an outhouse may be available or can be constructed. Some of these methods are better than others at minimizing pollution. See Leave No Trace in Chapter 7.

Embracing Expedition Values

Roger Baxter-Jones, an elite British alpinist, is known for his golden rule: "Come back alive, come back as friends, get to the top—and in that order." Sayings like his reflect the values that an expedition and its members need to talk about and agree on before leaving home.

An expedition has a greater chance of survival if the team is not obsessed with its goal. Goals are important—they inspire us to accomplish great things—but they should not be the sole priority. By themselves, summits are simply a set of GPS coordinates on the planet. What is meaningful about the experience of trying to reach them is the opportunity to learn things about ourselves in challenging situations. Spending time in these beautiful places is a tremendous gift and an arena where personal values regarding partnership, fortitude, stewardship, creativity, and independence can develop. Embracing these values will help climbers return home alive and well, hopefully after having reached the top. Ultimately, this kind of personal growth is much more enduring than standing on a summit.

21

PART V
LEADERSHIP, RISK MANAGEMENT, AND RESCUE

CHAPTER 22

LEADERSHIP

Just as all climbing parties need navigation tools, they also need competent leadership—but the optimal style and form of that guidance varies, depending on the venture. Heading out with longtime companions for a sunny weekend of peak bagging is vastly different from undertaking an extended technical climb on an unfamiliar peak with people you met only recently.

Climbers who know each other well often achieve good leadership informally, probably without even realizing it, while climbers who are getting to know one another may require a more formal structure and organization. Effective leadership brings everyone together to create an enjoyable experience and work toward common goals. Fostering a supportive atmosphere so that team members know their companions are there to help them is another important aspect of leadership. A leader who sets this kind of tone expands opportunities for a wider variety of people to feel comfortable and welcome on a climbing team.

The Climb Leader

A climb leader has the important responsibility of organizing the climb and making decisions en route. Depending on the nature of the party, formal organization may vary from highly structured to virtually nonexistent.

Informal small parties of friends often do not select a leader. Everyone feels responsible for organizing, sharing work, and team building. Communication is open enough that each member knows what their fellow climbers are doing, which makes it easy for them to coordinate. The climb organizer or most experienced party member may be tacitly recognized as the leader.

Large groups function better with a designated leader. All the members of such a large group cannot be aware of what every person is doing, so the lead organizer takes responsibility for making sure that no critical details get overlooked. Large groups may also need to focus more intentionally on team building, especially if the members do not all know one another.

TYPES OF LEADERS

How leaders are chosen may influence the scope of their authority and legitimacy. The leader for most climbing parties tends to result from the relationships between the party members. Climb leaders often fit into one or more of the following categories.

Peer. Acquaintances who decide to climb together are peers, often without a designated leader. Instead, members informally allocate key functions and make most decisions by consensus. Even in this least formal type of organization, one member usually emerges as "first among equals." The person who displays the most initiative, solid judgment, and concern for the group and who inspires the most confidence is often regarded as the leader.

Climb organizer. The person who has the initial idea for the venture and recruits others is a climb organizer. The organizer is often recognized as a de facto leader, even if that position is never formalized.

Subject-matter expert. A group may bestow leadership on and defer to the judgment of the climber who is clearly the most experienced. That experience may consist of specific climbing skills, number of completed climbs, or familiarity with the peak or climbing area.

Accredited instructor. Leadership may be formally conferred by a sponsoring group when a climb is part of an organized program such as a climbing club or school. There is no doubt who is the leader, and the participants do not select one. Often, these leaders must go through an accreditation process to ensure a specified level of experience and competence. There may even be a leadership hierarchy, with a primary leader and assistant instructors. The leader organizes the climb and coordinates equipment, transportation,

THE CLIMB LEADER
ORGANIZING AND LEADING A CLIMB
BECOMING A LEADER

and other logistics. Such climbs are often teaching situations: students are expected to follow the leader's guidance but are also learning and gaining self-sufficiency.

Guide. Climbers can pay guide services to provide competent leadership. Professional guides, often outstanding climbers, are in charge of their group. Guides make decisions for their clients and assume responsibility for their well-being.

LEADERSHIP STYLES

Each climb leader develops a personal style through learning the craft of mountaineering and discovering effective ways of relating to climbing companions to help them become a happy, effective team. All kinds of people can be successful leaders. While some people are jolly and talkative, others are more reserved. It is more important to be genuine than to try copying some idealized style.

That said, two general categories characterize the extremes of style in which leaders perform their roles. While many leaders lean toward one or the other, most operate somewhere between the two.

Goal-oriented. A goal-oriented leadership style has to do with process and structure—what to do, who will do it, how they will do it. Leaders with this style concentrate on making decisions and directing others.

Relationship-oriented. A relationship-oriented leadership style has to do with helping a group of people become a supportive, cooperative team. Leaders with this style show consideration by taking an interest in people and their perspectives, consulting with them to make decisions, and building group cohesion and morale.

Emotional Intelligence and Cultural Sensitivity

Effective leaders use emotional intelligence and cultural sensitivity to balance the two leadership styles described above, based on the specific group, its needs, and how those needs may change throughout the climb. Developing emotional intelligence (see the "Emotional Intelligence" sidebar) and cultural competency (see the "Cultural Competency" sidebar below) is an ongoing process of increasing your self- and social awareness, as well as developing skills in understanding and interacting effectively with people of various backgrounds.

An effective leader respects and values the diversity of perspectives that people with backgrounds different than their own may bring. These skills help a leader create a team environment built on trust and rapport—an approach that helps foster the interconnected emotional and physical well-being of team members.

EMOTIONAL INTELLIGENCE

Daniel Goleman is credited with popularizing the term **emotional intelligence** through his book of the same name and many subsequent publications (see Resources). Goleman characterizes it as comprising these broad components:

- **Self-awareness:** the ability to understand your strengths and weaknesses, moods, emotions, and motivations and their effect on others.
- **Self-management:** the ability to control and sometimes suppress your impulses and moods and to think before acting on them.
- **Social awareness:** the ability to identify and understand the emotions of others and to tailor your treatment of others to their emotional reactions; also, the ability to be aware of interpersonal dynamics between others.
- **Relationship management:** the ability to influence, mentor, manage conflict, promote teamwork, and inspire.

LEADERSHIP ROLES

The climb leader's task is to help the party achieve its objectives securely and enjoyably, with minimal environmental impact. A leader must be experienced and have technical skills appropriate for the climb but is not necessarily the best climber in the group. A leader need not be the fittest in the party but does need to exercise an abundance of solid judgment and feel a palpable sense of responsibility for the entire party's welfare. Along the way, a leader simultaneously adopts many roles.

Risk manager. Keeping all of its members physically and emotionally secure is the paramount concern of any climbing party. In the planning stage, a leader checks to ensure that everyone has appropriate equipment, experience, and physical fitness. They assess whether the chosen route is reasonable for the party and in suitable condition. During the climb, a leader monitors climbers and notices when they become tired, impatient, or excited—conditions that warn when climbers may be more error-prone—and becomes more alert. When tough decisions have to be made, such as turning back due to weather changes or time constraints, it is often up to the leader to initiate the unpleasant discussion before the situation becomes critical (see Chapter 23, Risk Management). Beyond physical well-being, a leader's cultural competency, or their ability to understand and interact with people who are different from them, will

22

help ensure the emotional well-being of the party members as well.

Guardian of the environment. Climbers must do their best to avoid disturbing the environment so that future generations may sample the same pleasures. Leaders set the example by practicing minimum-impact techniques (see Chapters 3, Camping, Food, and Water, and 7, Protecting the Outdoors). If other climbers fail to follow this example, it is up to the leader to remind them of Leave No Trace principles and practices, gently and perhaps in private at first, then insistently if necessary.

Planner. Getting people to the right place at the right time with the right equipment to climb a summit requires a lot of coordination. A leader does not plan every aspect of a trip but is responsible for ensuring that someone in the group attends to all necessary preparations.

Delegator. A leader is responsible for seeing that things get done but not necessarily for doing them. Delegating tasks allows the leader to maintain an overview of the trip and builds team spirit by getting people involved and having them feel useful. Delegation also fosters individual responsibility by clearly demonstrating that everyone can participate and help decide. If someone is having difficulty and needs special help, an experienced climber may be delegated the role of personal coach. In a larger group, especially in a teaching situation, the leader can appoint an assistant to help keep things moving and to take over if the leader becomes incapacitated.

Expert. Giving advice is an important leadership role that requires prerequisites such as training, experience, and solid judgment. A person does not have to be the party's best climber to be an effective leader, but they need to have enough experience to have developed "mountain sense." In addition to technical knowledge, leaders must possess a range of skills: a robust understanding of equipment, navigation, first aid, rescue techniques, weather—all addressed in various chapters in this book.

Teacher. If some party members are less experienced, teaching becomes part of the leadership role. Usually teaching of this nature involves occasional advice and demonstrations. However, if some members lack techniques required for secure progress, it may be wise to halt for a teaching moment and conduct hands-on learning. Many seasoned mountaineers find passing along their hard-won knowledge to be a fulfilling experience, but they need to be careful to do so thoughtfully. Novices may be embarrassed by their relative lack of skill or intimidated by the physical danger. The best teaching in these situations may come in the form of a "let me show you what works for me" approach. If a student starts doing something dangerous, a more direct approach may be necessary.

Coach. Different from the role of teacher, a coach helps people overcome difficulties by encouraging and supporting them. The leader-as-coach also considers whether everyone is respectful of cultural, gender, and other differences, such as communication styles. Lack of self-confidence is often a real obstacle. Assisting a companion through some difficulty helps that person and also keeps the entire party cohesive and moving forward. Coaching effectively, helping people do their best and emerge smiling, can be one of the delights of leadership.

Facilitator. A climb progresses through a series of decisions the party makes: Where would we like to make camp? Which route should we take? What time will we get up? When should we rope up? Often, the decisions themselves are not challenging, but they must be made in a timely fashion. The function of leadership is not necessarily to dictate answers but to get the right issues on the table at the appropriate time.

Arbiter. Once a discussion is under way, differences of opinion can arise. It is good to collect opinions and get all viewpoints out into the open, but this approach can result in indecision ("Which course do we select?") or argument

---

CULTURAL COMPETENCY

Cultural competency is the ability to understand and interact with people who are different from us. As outlined by Suzanna Windon and Tanya Lamo in a 2020 article (see Resources), to hone your cultural competence, you should strive to do the following:

- **Practice openness** by demonstrating acceptance of difference.
- **Be flexible** by demonstrating acceptance of ambiguity.
- **Demonstrate humility** through suspension of judgment and the ability to learn.
- **Be sensitive to others** by appreciating cultural differences.
- **Show a spirit of adventure** by showing curiosity and seeing opportunities in different situations.
- **Use a sense of humor** through the ability to laugh at ourselves.

("You are wrong!"). Anyone in a position of leadership, whether formally conferred or not, has some leverage in these instances. If the party seems to be making a technically incorrect or dangerous decision, if tempers are rising, or if the discussion is aimlessly wandering, the weight of the leader's opinion often settles matters and gets the climb moving again.

Anticipator. Leaders avoid trouble by anticipating it. In camp, they think about the climb; on the ascent, the descent; on the descent, the trip out. They watch companions for early signs of fatigue, take note of bivouac sites and water sources, keep track of the time and progress, and note any changes in weather. By thinking ahead, they avoid problems or catch them as they begin to develop, before they become crises.

LEADING IN A CRISIS

Everyone hopes it will never happen, but sometimes things go wrong. Perhaps conditions turn dangerous or someone is injured. Then the group's focus shifts from recreation to recovery and survival. If the group has a designated leader, that person often switches to a more authoritative style. An informal small group may find that a leader emerges. When a clear need for coordination arises, people tend to look to the most experienced person or the one who, for whatever reason, inspires the most confidence.

When an accident occurs, a party must act promptly and effectively, and the leader's role changes. The leader stays hands-off as much as possible, instead directing others, focusing on the big picture, and thinking ahead to the next steps. The rescuers' security comes first—even before that of the victim(s). An accident's outcome is usually determined by factors beyond the climbers' control, but the climb leader draws on training and experience to devise an appropriate plan and carry it out as prudently and effectively as conditions permit. The leader guides the group to act promptly but deliberately and calmly, using procedures that they have learned and practiced.

Accidents are unexpected, but climbers can prepare by taking courses in mountain-oriented rescue, reading about the subject, and rehearsing accident scenarios (see Chapters 23, Risk Management, and 25, Self-Rescue). First-aid training is crucial. Chapter 24, First Aid, describes how to prevent and treat medical conditions commonly experienced by mountaineers—but reading about first-aid techniques is not a substitute for hands-on training. Public and private agencies offer wilderness-oriented first-aid courses, and some climbing clubs offer rescue training.

Organizing and Leading a Climb

Even a simple climb can be a complex undertaking. Once an objective is chosen, the leader has many tasks to complete before the group begins to climb. On the way to the trailhead and at the trailhead, last-minute checks and updates keep the outing organized. The leader continues to coordinate the outing until it is over, usually when the party has returned to the trailhead. This section introduces two systems approaches for leaders—Nine Planning and Preparing Steps and Eight Trip Checks. Considered alongside the Ten Essentials described in Chapter 2, Clothing and Equipment, these checklists help climb leaders think through the entire process of planning and executing a trip.

BEFORE THE CLIMB: NINE PLANNING AND PREPARING STEPS

Once a destination has been chosen, the leader gathers information on the approach, climbing route, and descent. The leader chooses team members and decides what equipment the group needs and who will bring it. They draft a schedule that includes enough time to complete the climb, with a prudent margin for contingencies, and coordinate transportation to the trailhead. In the days leading up to the climb, the leader monitors weather trends (and snow conditions, if applicable). Nine steps (see the "Nine Planning and Preparing Steps" sidebar below) help guide a leader through this process. (For a useful breakdown, see the checklist in Table 22-2 at the end of this section.)

1. Establish Leadership

A climb leader must be capable and qualified, but they may also want to designate a competent assistant (or two) who can take on some tasks and serve as a consultant for key decisions. For example, on larger trips with multiple rope teams, the climb leader needs to make sure that each rope team with inexperienced climbers has an experienced rope leader.

2. Research the Trip

Typically, climbers research their planned trips so that they know what to expect and can prepare accordingly. Guidebooks covering most popular climbing areas provide written descriptions of approaches and routes, maps, drawings, and sometimes photos. Topographic maps are indispensable. The internet is also an invaluable resource for route information. Some climbing clubs keep files of trip reports from their outings or post these trip reports online. Useful not only in themselves, they also often list the people who went on the climb. Firsthand recent accounts can

22

NINE PLANNING AND PREPARING STEPS

Follow these nine key steps before the climb:

1. Establish leadership.
2. Research the trip.
3. Choose a party.
4. Make the plan.
5. Check on equipment.
6. Assess communications.
7. Build in a contingency margin.
8. Monitor weather and route conditions.
9. Evaluate preparedness.

---

add significantly to data from other sources, particularly regarding current conditions. For peaks on public land, government agencies such as the National Park Service and US Forest Service can be useful sources of information. Check road and trail conditions—the approach can sometimes present as many challenges as the technical climb. (For details on researching a route, see Gather Route Information in Chapter 6, Wilderness Travel.)

Permit, registration, and recreational fee requirements vary greatly from region to region. Many publicly owned parks, forests, and wilderness areas have some form of governmental regulation. Some agencies may limit where parties can camp, which can affect the climb logistics. Typically, regulations are designed to preserve the ecology of an area or to increase the value of the wilderness experience. Some are created to protect the well-being of visitors; others are in place to gather fees to maintain an area's infrastructure and support recreation. Groundwork for the climb includes determining regulations, securing any necessary permits, and paying any applicable fees. Consider researching the land's original inhabitants and acknowledging them and their cultural norms as part of your trip plan.

3. Choose a Party

Researching the route helps determine what party attributes are needed for a particular climb. Is the route or the approach physically arduous? What level of technical challenge, routefinding, or decision-making does the climb pose? Is the place so remote that the party will rely completely on its own resources, or are there likely to be other people in the vicinity?

Who should go? Every member of a climbing party must be up to the challenge, both physically and technically.

Expedition leaders sometimes request written résumés, but for a weekend climb, a brief, probing conversation is often enough to ascertain a person's physical fitness. When attempting a route near the limit of their abilities, some climbers will go only with companions who have done similar routes in the past. Leaders should ask some key questions of a climber they do not know before including them on a climb.

Experience is the surest indicator of ability; someone who has climbed several times at a given rating level is likely capable of doing so again. A climber's skills should match the chosen route's requirements. For instance, climbing-gym experience can be adequate for crag climbs but does not immediately translate to an alpine environment.

Leaders need to be aware that inexperienced climbers may not realize they are unprepared for a given climb. A party that includes novices, or even experienced people who have never climbed at the route's required level of skill, will need to include veteran climbers who are willing and able to lead rope teams and coach less experienced climbers. The climb will almost certainly take longer, and the chance of success will decrease. Be sure everyone in the party understands this situation and accepts it.

Leaders consider compatibility when forming a climbing party, especially for a long or arduous trip. Fortunately, most people are respectful and eager to cooperate while the group is on a climb. Relying on each other fosters a supportive environment. The fact that climbing companions often end up holding one another's lives in their hands does much to promote cooperation. Nevertheless, expedition literature is filled with engaging tales of squabbling parties. Interpersonal conflict may reduce a party's chance of success and diminish enjoyment—it can even compromise risk management.

How many should go? The size of the party must be appropriate for the objective. Leaders need to consider both efficiency and speed.

Minimum recommended party size is three climbers for glacier travel. That way, if one climber is hurt, the second can go for help while the third stays with the injured person. It is also a good idea for groups to travel in at least two rope teams on a glacier. That way, if one team is pinned down holding a rope mate who has fallen into a crevasse, the second team will be there to aid the rescue. Leaders of a rock climbing outing need to make similar considerations as to their party size and ability to extricate themselves and/or care for injured party members.

The specifics of the proposed trip may introduce other considerations. A prolonged wilderness venture may require a larger group to carry equipment and supplies, as well as to provide backup in case of emergency. Some rock climbs require double-rope rappels on the descent, which lends itself to a second team unless a single team is willing to carry two ropes. Technical rock and ice climbs are often best done with just two climbers on each rope. For these climbs, whatever the size of the party, an even number of climbers may be advantageous.

Maximum party size is also determined by considerations of speed and efficiency, as well as by land-use regulations and concerns about environmental impact. A large group can carry more gear and offers more people to help in an emergency. But a bigger party is not necessarily safer. A larger party tends to get spread out and may kick down more loose rock, snow, or ice. Sometimes being able to travel quickly is more prudent, and experienced alpinists know that a larger group always moves more slowly. On certain routes, for example, climbers must move fast to ensure they finish before dark.

As a general rule, the more difficult the route, the smaller the group should be. Two fast, experienced people can do some long technical climbs, but a party of two must carry an emergency communication device (see Chapter 5, Navigation and Communication) or make other arrangements in case of an emergency.

Large groups are more likely to damage a fragile environment. They also diminish the wilderness experience. National parks and wilderness areas typically enforce party size limits (often 12 people maximum) to protect the land and preserve aesthetic values. Responsible mountaineers may choose to impose even tighter restrictions on their party in especially fragile places.

4. Make the Plan

Prepare the overall trip plan—the route, participants, equipment, assignments, meeting times, and other pertinent information—and share it with party members to ensure that all participants have the same knowledge and expectations. Ask all participants to avoid scheduling important meetings, airplane flights, or social events for several hours after the scheduled end of a trip, since climbs frequently take longer than expected. When developing the trip plan, include each party member's name, contact information, and emergency contact.

Develop a trip itinerary: establish a schedule for the climb, and use it to manage time spent en route. Time must be carefully rationed on a climb. It is more important that a party use the time it has wisely than move as fast as it possibly can. As you estimate the length of each

segment—driving to the trailhead, hiking the approach, making the ascent, making the descent, and returning to the trailhead—allow extra time for the unexpected. Be realistic when estimating how long the climb will take.

Most guidebooks estimate times for popular climbs and sometimes for the approaches as well. Keep in mind, though, that times vary greatly from party to party and may not include breaks. Experience with a particular guidebook will indicate whether its estimates tend to be faster or slower than your personal times; adjust your plans accordingly. Another good source for time estimates is someone who has done the climb.

If no information is available, use rules of thumb based on individual experience. For example, many climbers have found that, with light packs, they can average 2 miles (3-plus kilometers) per hour on a well-established, maintained trail and 1,000 vertical feet (300 vertical meters) per hour on a nontechnical approach.

A typical time estimate could resemble the one in Table 22-1. In that scenario, if the climbers want to be back at the trailhead by dark, which occurs at 9:00 PM, they must start their drive to the trailhead by 6:30 AM.

Setting a turnaround time is a good practice. In the example below, the party estimates four and a half hours from summit to trailhead for the descent, without any margin for contingencies. Allowing an extra hour for unexpected delays, they must start descending by 3:30 PM or risk walking out in the dark. If the leader observes that the party is moving slower than the estimated times, the party should candidly assess its progress well before the turnaround time.

TABLE 22-1. SAMPLE TRIP ITINERARY

TRIP SEGMENT	ESTIMATED TIME HOURS)
Drive to trailhead	2
Hike the trail	2
Continue approach (off trail)	1
Climb the route	4
Descend	2
Return to the trail	1
Hike out to trailhead	1.5
Total time estimate	13.5
Allow for contingencies	1
Total time allowance	14.5

22

The leader selects or creates maps and route plans—and prints out backup copies of both. The leader also registers the party with park or forest agencies, if required, but all members must confirm that they have current valid passes for whatever area they are visiting. All team members are also responsible for setting their individual compass declination for the climbing area and making sure their GPS device is set to the correct datum. Everyone on the team downloads waypoints and route information to their GPS device, tablet, or phone, as applicable.

Once the trip plan is complete, the leader will leave a copy at home with a responsible person, specifying when the party expects to return, how long the person should wait if the party is overdue before notifying authorities, and which authorities to notify. For example, in the United States, the National Park Service has responsibility for mountain rescue in national parks; in most other areas of the western United States, it is the county sheriff.

5. Check on Equipment

The party needs to make decisions about equipment, both personal and shared. Personal equipment is what each climber may need to bring, such as clothing, an ice axe, a helmet, crampons, an avalanche transceiver, or a harness, in addition to the Ten Essentials (see Chapter 2, Clothing and Equipment). These personal items are often useful only if everybody brings them, so it is essential to coordinate.

Group equipment is shared: for instance, tents, stoves and cook pots, food, ropes, rock and snow protection, snow shovels, GPS devices, and satellite communication (satcom) devices. The leader—or a designated party member—determines what the group needs, surveys the climbers to see who owns what, and then decides who will bring which items. (See Chapter 21, Expedition Climbing, for more on personal and group gear.)

6. Assess Communications

Bringing communication devices, such as phones, satcom devices, or radios, on an outing can dramatically shorten the time it takes to summon rescuers in case of emergency. The devices are also useful for telling people back home that the party will be late but is not in trouble, avoiding the launch of unnecessary rescue efforts. A NOAA weather radio or similar device may also be able to give a current weather forecast or updates about avalanche hazard. Inexpensive handheld walkie-talkie two-way radios may be useful for communication between rope teams or the front and rear of the party on a trail. They are also helpful when sorting out navigation options, for checking in with an ill climber

who stayed back at camp rather than heading for the summit, or for coordinating during emergencies. Such devices may also allow climbers to communicate with responding search and rescue authorities.

Understanding device limits is as important as understanding their usefulness. Phone batteries run down, and in many mountain locations, phones with GPS apps are unable to transmit or receive. View them as an adjunct to, not a substitute for, self-reliance. (For detailed information, see Communication Devices in Chapter 5, Navigation and Communication.)

7. Build In a Contingency Margin

Plan for self-reliance and develop contingency options. For example, the party may want to arrive at the trailhead with extra equipment in case conditions become more severe than earlier forecast, or in case someone forgets an item or fails to show up. If the party does not need the surplus gear, they can stash it out of view in vehicles.

Climbs often exceed their prescribed schedule. A prepared climbing party can take care of itself in case of travel delays, navigation errors, unexpected route conditions, a mishap, or a downturn in the weather. Bringing a little extra offers a contingency margin: extra clothing, extra food, extra flashlight batteries or a power bank, extra climbing hardware, and the like. Balancing the benefit of extra supplies against their weight is an art every mountaineer must develop.

Having a little extra can also mean allowing extra time and, above all, reserving stamina. Generally, leaders plan for the party to be self-sufficient for several hours beyond the estimated trip time.

8. Monitor Weather and Route Conditions

Understanding current and anticipated weather and route conditions remains as much an art as a science. Although mountaineers have ever-increasing access to current weather and route conditions, primarily via the internet, the amount of information available for a given area, mountain, or specific route varies greatly. For many ranges and mountains, there may be little or no current information.

Useful internet resources include local and regional governments, national or regional parks, and private recreation areas, as well as sites that detail weather and road conditions. Some resources include real-time weather cams and webcams for an up-to-the-minute view of conditions. Local climbing sites are useful for researching current route conditions or posting a question to solicit information.

TABLE 22-2. NINE PLANNING AND PREPARING STEPS

STEP	TASKS
1. Establish Leadership	• Choose a leader.
2. Research the Trip	• Check whether roads, particularly dirt access roads, are open. • Check hiking trail conditions. • Review the climbing route in guidebooks, on maps, and in trip reports. • Determine the route's technical level and any special problems. • Determine what regulations, permits, fees, and/or reservations are required.
3. Choose a Party	• Ascertain party members' levels of climbing skill, physical conditioning, and compatibility. • Determine appropriate party size for the area and route.
4. Make the Plan	• Include name, contact information, and emergency contact for each party member. • Estimate time: miles and/or hours of driving; miles and/or hours of trail hiking and/or off-trail approach to high camp or start of climb; hours to summit; hours to descend and hike back to trailhead. • Select or create maps and route plans. • Set GPS datum to match maps and download waypoints and route information to GPS devices, tablets, or phones, as applicable. • Set compass declination for climbing area. • Register with park or forest agencies, if required. • Leave trip itinerary with a responsible person.
5. Check on Equipment	• Determine equipment needs and which party members have what equipment. • Coordinate to make sure each party member brings necessary personal equipment: clothing, Ten Essentials, climbing gear. • Arrange who will bring what group equipment: tents, stoves, cookware, food, water filter or other water treatment equipment, ropes, climbing protection, GPS devices.
6. Assess Communications	• Bring an emergency communication device. • Consider bringing walkie-talkie two-way radios.
7. Build In a Contingency Margin	• Develop contingency options. • Bring extra gear and supplies for the unexpected.
8. Monitor Weather and Route Conditions	• Look up current route conditions, the weather forecast, and expected shifts in the weather window. • Understand how a change in weather will affect the route and the party's objectives. • Look into alternative trips in case of poor weather. • Consider bringing a NOAA weather radio or other device for accessing updated forecasts.
9. Evaluate Preparedness	• Critique the plan holistically: Does it add up favorably? Does it feature any unprepared or underprepared areas? Could it be improved? If so, identify how and adjust those details of the plan. • Double-check the status of required registration and/or permits a day or two before the trip starts.

22

The best source for route conditions is often a reliable individual who has recently been on the mountain and route the party is considering. Searching the internet for information or calling a park office, climbing shop, bush pilot, or friend in the area is a great idea, especially if the climb involves a long drive or approach.

The "art" aspect of understanding conditions and weather forecasting involves knowing how a change in weather will affect the route and the party's objectives. Forecasting is based on inexact models that may vary widely from conditions in specific locations on a trip, especially with significant elevation gain and loss (see Chapter 28, Mountain

Weather). Relying too heavily on the timing of a forecast is risky. Note how the end of a favorable weather window may come into play if a trip ends up taking longer than expected. Consider how specific changes in temperature, wind, humidity, and precipitation will affect the climb. Have alternate trips in mind, perhaps even in another area altogether, to avoid forcing a group to tackle a specific climb—nearly always a flawed decision.

9. Evaluate Preparedness

How can climb organizers gauge their group's preparation? One reliable approach is to ask whether the party has the people, proficiency, and equipment it needs to be self-reliant under the circumstances. Being prepared means the group has the ability to accomplish the climb and cope with situations that arise. The members' mountaineering proficiency, their physical condition, the number of climbers, and their equipment all determine the party's preparedness. Intangibles such as morale, degree of commitment to the climb, and quality of leadership also affect party preparedness.

A prepared party may consist of several experienced, proficient climbers who are in strong physical condition and are well equipped; a team with diverse skills; or even a relatively inexperienced group with high commitment, morale, and readiness. A party is prepared or not only in relation to its goals. On a very challenging climb, where retreat options are limited and the group is at or near the limit of its technical abilities, a single unprepared member may affect the entire party. On easier trips, where retreat options are abundant or the technical demands are less substantial, two experienced, proficient climbers may balance several less experienced ones, a common dynamic on guided climbs. A party consisting entirely of inexperienced members should consider gaining experience on easier objectives, to avoid finding themselves overmatched in a more demanding situation.

Seasoned climb leaders know that taking the time and effort to plan and prepare positions the party for success. This step looks at the entirety of that effort. Does the plan set the party up for success? Are there prudent contingency margins? Are there areas of unpreparedness? Can the plan be improved? Double-check the status of required registration or permits a day or two before the start date. Setting out ill-prepared or inadequately equipped, or attempting a route beyond a group member's ability, imperils both the climbing party and possible rescuers.

UNDER WAY: EIGHT TRIP CHECKS

How does a climb leader know whether a trip is on course for a successful summit or headed for a disaster? Careful planning and preparation go a long way in making sure the trip goes favorably. Once the trip begins, monitoring ongoing progress can either provide further assurance or illuminate issues that may threaten well-being or success. Even with the best-prepared plan and thorough preparation, the unexpected can occur. Formal trip checks (see the "Eight Trip Checks Overview" sidebar) help the party stay on track and spot potential pitfalls (see also the checklist in Table 22-3 at the end of this section).

1. Trailhead: Check Gear and Plans

At the trailhead, set the tone for the trip by discussing expectations and goals and inviting open communication around questions and concerns. If group members are not already acquainted, have them introduce themselves. An effective leader builds camaraderie and facilitates the party's emotional well-being and inclusivity. They also consider acknowledging the original inhabitants of the area.

Take a few minutes to check that all necessary equipment and supplies are in the climbers' packs. Experienced climbers know that a single missing critical item can ruin a trip. Pay particular attention to the packs of less experienced climbers. Coordinate distribution of group equipment. Are pack weights appropriate? Is group gear distributed fairly?

Before the party leaves the trailhead, go over the itinerary one last time to make sure everyone understands the same timetable. Is there any new information or reason to modify the plan? Are there any cautionary warning flags? Discuss the planned pace, breaks, hazards, and water sources with the party.

2. Navigation: Check Map and GPS

Most experienced leaders can share several stories of navigation misadventures that may only be amusing in hindsight. Orient your surroundings to the map early on rather than waiting until someone has a concern. Set altimeters in a location where you are certain of the elevation, often at the trailhead but perhaps at a trail junction. Check now and then to ensure the party is on the correct route. Involve the party in these tasks. The more people who are actively navigating, the better the chances of avoiding serious mistakes.

When you are unsure about navigation, take time and effort to regain your confidence. Sometimes it may prove easier to eliminate options than to confirm which one is correct. Photograph, make notes about, or create GPS waypoints of key junctions. Record a GPS track if the party is concerned about routefinding on the return journey—for example, if they may travel at night or in a storm or whiteout.

3. People: Check Nutrition and Hydration, Monitor Pace, and Stick Together

Team member skills and fitness may vary considerably. Leaders monitor party members for concerns that may arise. On the approach and on the climb, set a steady pace. In the long run, the party cannot move faster than its slowest member; progress may be even slower if that person becomes exhausted. The important thing is to keep moving steadily. Watch newer climbers who may have less stamina or may be carrying too much gear, making for an overly heavy pack. Deal with blisters before they begin.

Take rest stops for the whole party, at specific intervals, rather than halting randomly whenever someone decides to stop, which is inefficient. When timing rest stops, wait for the slowest member to catch up, then allow the entire party to rest before continuing. Make sure that everyone is eating and drinking at rest stops.

Is anyone lagging? A climber will likely fall farther and farther behind unless the group's pace, nutrition, and hydration are adequate. If someone is lagging, offer them support. For instance, ask one of the faster climbers to carry some of the slower person's pack weight, allow for longer recovery time at rest stops, or slow the pace a bit. Try to catch potential problems early, when the party has more options for preventing the problem or dealing with it.

Generally, success reflects the degree to which the party members share common values and work cooperatively to reach their goal. A climbing party that stays together—not necessarily in a tight knot, but at least close enough to be in communication with one another—is more secure than a party that splits up. A party that develops an interest in splitting up may have underlying issues with fitness, travel speed, or trip objectives.

More experienced members tend to want to forge ahead, leaving the climbers who are the most likely to need help isolated from the people who are best able to give it. Parties are more likely to become separated on the technical portions of a climb, where the more skilled

---

EIGHT TRIP CHECKS OVERVIEW

Keep track of these elements on the approach, during the climb, and on the descent:

1. **Trailhead:** check gear and plans.
2. **Navigation:** check map and GPS.
3. **People:** check nutrition and hydration, monitor pace, and stick together.
4. **Time:** check progress and adjust schedule.
5. **Hazards and risk management:** check preparedness, techniques, and alternatives.
6. **Weather and route conditions:** check changes.
7. **Perspective and decisions:** check the big picture and evaluate judgment.
8. **Leadership:** check effectiveness and responsiveness.

---

climbers can move much faster, or on the descent, where some people want to sprint while others lag. If a party becomes spread out, make sure the last two people pair up. Keep rope teams close enough to communicate with each other.

A small party of friends will naturally tend to stick together; problems are more likely to arise with larger groups. A large party benefits from having a designated leader who coordinates its movement and keeps the party together or in communication. The leader can give party members some flexibility to hike up the trail at their own pace, but they should regroup with the rest of the party at designated rendezvous points. Regrouping is especially important at trail junctions, to make sure everyone goes the right way; at riskier spots, such as hazardous stream crossings, in case anyone needs help; and at the bottom of glissades, where parties naturally tend to split up.

4. Time: Check Progress and Adjust Schedule

Manage time and progress. Daylight can be priceless if the unexpected occurs—start early. Optimize breaks, taking into account location, timing, and duration, as well as the party's fatigue, water supplies, et cetera. Consider adjusting the campsite location to fit the party's progress and schedule. Failure to reach an intended camp at the expected time may suggest the party will be slow the following day too. Choose a turnaround time that will accommodate unexpected delays.

22

5. Hazards and Risk Management: Check Preparedness, Techniques, and Alternatives

Stay alert for hazards (see Recognizing Hazards in Chapter 23, Risk Management). Some, such as falling, may be anticipated; you can then bring ropes and equipment to mitigate falls. Others, such as a swollen stream, may be unexpected, requiring impromptu measures. Outcomes from exposure to hazards are unpredictable. In a questionable situation, consider whether the party would be able to retreat later if conditions were to worsen. Avoid hazards, possibly by finding less risky alternatives, or mitigate the consequences of exposure to such hazards. Sometimes the only prudent solution is to retreat so that the group can come back another day when the hazards are easier to control or are less threatening.

Practice well-reputed climbing techniques. Never climb beyond the party's ability and knowledge. Rope up on exposed places and glaciers. On technical climbs, two ropes will often be advantageous in terms of security. Anchor all belays. (See A Climbing Code in Chapter 1, First Steps.) Redundancy greatly increases the security of belay and rappel anchors, as well as of many other systems (see Equalizing the Anchor in Chapter 10, Belaying).

Be mindful of how small errors may compound and increase the amount of risk the group is exposed to. With extra time and a good contingency margin, the party may proceed with caution despite small errors, all while continuing to monitor their progress.

6. Weather and Route Conditions: Check Changes

Watch for, and adjust to, adverse changes in weather and route conditions. Obtain updated weather forecasts if possible. (See more about weather in Chapter 28, Mountain Weather.)

7. Perspective and Decisions: Check the Big Picture and Evaluate Judgment

Stay alert to the big picture; avoid fixation on a particular aspect of the trip to the detriment of others. Think ahead; anticipate. Is the situation stressful? The more stressed you are, the harder it is to escape tunnel vision and maintain a broader perspective.

Climbers sometimes have to make decisions based on incomplete information and when saddled with fatigue, hunger, dehydration, discomfort, or injury. Guard against biases in risk assessment and decision-making. What are the facts? What are the options? What do others think? Can the party minimize its risk exposure? Make clear-headed decisions that maintain prudent margins.

One technique to help guard against bias in decision-making is to come up with three responses to a problem, then choose the best alternative. Thinking up multiple options counters the tendency to go with an impulsive first solution, which may not be the best resolution. Or ask yourself what could go wrong and write a mental "incident report." Should the worst occur, will you be able to justify your anticipated decisions? Working through these types of exercises promotes objectivity and rational thought.

Never let desire overrule judgment—for example, don't let the desire to summit overrule sound judgment when it comes to choosing a route or deciding whether to turn back (see A Climbing Code in Chapter 1). The outcome of exposing the party to a potentially lethal hazard is unpredictable. If the consequences cannot be mitigated, help the party find a more secure alternative, which may mean turning around.

8. Leadership: Check Effectiveness and Responsiveness

A leader's primary goal for any outing is to have the whole party return home in good condition. Practice sound leadership techniques. During the trip, check whether your leadership is effective at pulling together the many elements to help the party stay physically and emotionally secure and remain on schedule. Start from a place of humility; give your leadership skills time to develop and improve through experience.

Give new climbers the benefit of your experience. Look for teaching moments: opportunities to impart knowledge, involve the party, and continue climbers' development.

The leader need not be at the front of the party. In fact, many prefer to lead from the middle or rear, to monitor the entire group. However, the leader must be ready to step up when a difficulty arises, such as a routefinding puzzle or a patch of demanding technical terrain. It may be wise to appoint a strong member as trail sweep, especially on the descent, to avoid losing track of any stragglers. Be sure that no one leaves the trailhead until everyone is back and all the climbers have started their cars.

Consider enjoying a group meal on the trip home or planning for some other opportunity to debrief the trip. Ask what went well and what could have gone better. Did anyone ever feel insecure, either emotionally or physically? Did anyone feel left behind? Creating a supportive space for participants to share open feedback after the trip, together as a group or privately, and demonstrating your receptiveness to their feedback may further facilitate your learning process as a leader.

TABLE 22-3. EIGHT TRIP CHECKS CHECKLIST

CHECKPOINT	TASKS
1. Trailhead: Check Gear and Plans	• Set the tone for the trip. Discuss expectations and goals, invite open communication for questions and concerns, have group members introduce themselves if not acquainted, and consider saying a land acknowledgment aloud. • Make sure everyone has enough personal equipment and food. • Inventory group equipment and distribute group equipment to equalize loads. • Share an overview of the plan.
2. Navigation: Check Map and GPS	• Orient early to the map. • Set altimeters at a place where you are certain of the elevation. • Check occasionally to ensure the party is on route. • Note important route decision points such as trail junctions. • Create GPS waypoints and tracks for returning in the dark or declining visibility.
3. People: Check Nutrition and Hydration, Monitor Pace, and Stick Together	• On the approach and the climb, set a steady pace that all party members can maintain. • Monitor party members for problems such as fatigue or too much pack weight. • Take rest stops for the whole party; make sure everyone eats and drinks at rest stops. • Keep the party reasonably together. Avoid letting anyone lag. Regroup at specified times or places—especially trail junctions. Keep rope teams close enough to communicate with each other. • Assign a responsible person to sweep the trail to watch for and help any stragglers. Be sure that no one leaves the trailhead until everyone is back and all cars have been started.
4. Time: Check Progress and Adjust Schedule	• Start early to maximize travel in daylight. • Optimize the location, timing, and duration of breaks. • Monitor progress and adjust the schedule if necessary. • Choose a turnaround time.
5. Hazards and Risk Management: Check Preparedness, Techniques, and Alternatives	• Watch for hazards—both anticipated and unexpected. • Where hazards are unavoidable, find a less risky alternative, mitigate their outcome, or turn around. • Practice well-reputed climbing techniques. Do not climb beyond the party's ability and knowledge. • Rope up on technical, exposed terrain. • Anchor all belays. Redundancy increases the security of belay and rappel anchors.
6. Weather and Route Conditions: Check Changes	• Watch for, and adjust to, adverse changes in weather and route conditions.
7. Perspective and Decisions: Check the Big Picture and Evaluate Judgment	• Stay alert to the big picture. Avoid fixating on a particular aspect of the trip to the detriment of others. • Think ahead, and anticipate challenges. • Try to catch problems early, when options for dealing with them are most numerous. • Make clearheaded decisions. Guard against risk-assessment and decision-making biases. • Make decisions that maintain prudent margins. Never let desire overrule judgment when deciding whether to turn back. • Consider several solutions to a problem, and then choose the best alternative.
8. Leadership: Check Effectiveness and Responsiveness	• A leader's primary goal for any outing is to have the whole party return home in good condition. • Practice sound leadership techniques. • Start from a place of humility. Give leadership skills time to develop and improve. • Look for teaching moments. • Consider creating an opportunity to debrief the trip, and solicit feedback.

22

Becoming a Leader

The responsibility of leadership is a burden, but it gives an experienced alpinist the opportunity to pass along their knowledge. Mountaineers climb because they love the mountains. It can be deeply satisfying to help others enjoy and become proficient at the sport.

Some climbers may never want to take on a leadership role, but as they gain experience, they may find that they inevitably possess a certain degree of leadership. A party naturally tends to look to its more seasoned members for guidance, especially in a crisis. Therefore, all climbers should give some forethought to what they would do if they were suddenly called upon to take charge.

Climbers who aspire to leadership can climb with people they regard as capable leaders to study them and observe how they organize the trip, make decisions, and work with people. Offer to help in order to participate in some of these activities. To develop your people skills and cultural sensitivity, consider taking a class or participating in a workshop (see Resources).

While studying respected leaders is worthwhile, it may be a mistake to model yourself too closely after anyone in particular. A group must believe that its leader is genuine. Focus on exercising leadership in a way that feels natural. For example, a reserved person should not strain to act outgoing. Anyone who has technical skill, confidence, and a sincere interest in the party's welfare can succeed as a leader.

On your first time out as a leader, choose a climb comfortably within your abilities. Perhaps invite a proficient friend, someone to rely on. Spend some extra time organizing, seek input from the party's more experienced members, and delegate in order to put those members' skills to good use. Veteran leaders report that they think ahead, anticipating problems that may arise and considering possible solutions. This type of experience sometimes takes time to develop. Start your leadership path with smaller, achievable objectives to build confidence and experience.

The Climbing Code in Chapter 1, First Steps, is a time-tested, deliberately conservative set of guidelines for making leadership decisions. Following that Climbing Code may cost you a summit, but it is unlikely to cost a life. Seasoned leaders may draw on experience to modify some of the rules with confidence, but they are not likely to radically depart from it—the code embodies using sound, experience-based judgment for secure mountaineering.

Every participant on a climb should be engaged in the endeavor. Each individual must be invested in the climb and share responsibility. Be aware of the group and its progress: Is someone lagging behind? Ask whether there is a problem, offer encouragement, and look for ways to help. A group becomes vulnerable when climbers become separated. Work at being aware of where companions are, and help to keep the party together. When you are out front and moving fast, look behind from time to time. Stop and let the group catch up if you are far ahead—then let someone else set the pace for a while.

Participate in routefinding. Study guidebooks and maps to become familiar with the approach and the climbing route. A climbing party is much less likely to get lost if everyone is actively involved in navigation. Use the map and compass, and refer often to the route description so you are always oriented (see Chapter 5, Navigation and Communication). Everyone should participate in the group's decision-making. Each person's experience is a resource for the party, but if people fail to speak up, that resource goes untapped.

Establishing a supportive atmosphere is part of successful leadership. People need to know that their companions care about and will help them. Be part of this effort: help set up a tent, fetch water, carry the rope, share a cookie or other treat you brought. While intangible, morale can be the deciding factor in party success and often makes the climb enjoyable. It is everyone's responsibility to contribute to morale.

Assume responsibility for your knowledge, skill, and preparedness. Research the climb and make sure it is within your abilities before committing to it. Make sure you have the proper supplies and equipment. If you have questions about whether the climb is appropriate for you or about what gear to take, ask your companions ahead of time. If you ever think that you are getting in over your head, speak up. It is better to get some help over a rough spot, or even quit a particular climb, than to end up hurting yourself or contributing to an emergency on a climb. Thinking about the party's welfare, and how you can contribute to it, is part—perhaps the most important part—of being prepared to lead.

CHAPTER 23

RISK MANAGEMENT

Although climbers anticipate and consider risks when planning a trip, novice and experienced climbers alike are sometimes injured or killed in the mountains. Increasing awareness of risks associated with mountaineering activities and learning the skills to avoid or minimize exposure to such risks can help mitigate them.

A s climbers explore terrain that is more technical, venture farther from assistance, and extend the season to include shoulder periods that may involve extreme shifts in weather and conditions, their exposure to risk increases. Mountaineers balance that exposure by broadening and deepening their knowledge and honing and expanding their capabilities. Balancing risk, knowledge, and capability increases the likelihood of avoiding serious incidents, injuries, and fatalities. Everyone's number one priority should be that each member of the group return home alive and well, both emotionally and physically.

For people who spend a significant amount of time in the mountains, serious injury or death is not a hypothetical probability. A misplaced foot or hand, a moment of distraction, or a minor gap in communication at a critical juncture may bring climbers within a hair's breadth of calamity. Rarely would a climber view the objective of an outing as more important than avoiding injury or damaging a close friendship. Yet they may inadvertently expose themselves and their adventure partners to unacceptable levels of risk by not possessing or engaging sufficient capabilities. Mastery of competencies—knowledge, skill, experience, conditioning, and paying attention to intuition—prepares climbers to manage risk in increasingly challenging mountaineering situations. As Mark Twight writes in *Extreme Alpinism*, "As an alpinist who carries a long list of dead friends and partners, I approach the mountains differently than most. I go to them intending to survive, which I define as success. A new route or the summit is a bonus."

Keeping risk management in mind runs counter at times to a natural inclination to discount risk ("the weather does not look that that bad") or take shortcuts to speed up progress and reduce effort ("we do not need to belay each other in this area this time"). Most of the time, when climbers follow these inclinations, they pass through unscathed. Occasionally, their next level of risk preparation kicks in (for instance, surviving an unexpected bivy because you brought suitable gear) or a common safety backup skill saves the day (knots at the end of the rope prevent you from rappelling off the ends). Near misses and minor injuries are wake-up calls that alert climbers to reexamine their decision-making around risk. Over time, unnecessary exposure to risk increases the odds of serious accidents. In rare instances, people win the wrong kind of lottery. The risk they have exposed themselves to is not addressed by any preparation or inherent capability, and the worst imaginable incident occurs.

While mountaineering adventures are riskier than staying home, they are not as dangerous as they are often portrayed. Deploying sufficient capabilities can address risk when climbing—even difficult, challenging climbing—and focusing on risk management in a straightforward manner can help climbers avoid most incidents. Following sound practices leads to greater chances of having successful adventures. In some instances, using sufficient capabilities to manage risk may take more time, gear, knowledge, experience, or conditioning. Appropriately managing risk may mean deciding to turn around in the hopes of attempting an objective another day. People who consistently manage their risk can expect to live longer and enjoy more years of climbing adventures and successful summit attempts.

Ed Viesturs, the first American to climb the world's 14 highest peaks above 8,000 meters (26,247 feet), all without

23

KEY TOPICS

UNDERSTANDING WHAT CAUSES ACCIDENTS
DEFINING TERMINOLOGY
RECOGNIZING HAZARDS
MITIGATING HAZARDS
MANAGING RISK TO MEET OBJECTIVES

supplemental oxygen, has spoken extensively about turning back on many climbs because he insisted on secure conditions. Several of his contemporaries with similar aspirations but who exercised less prudence have perished.

The strategy for managing risk in the mountains is straightforward to describe but harder to put into practice consistently. First, climbers need to recognize the hazards associated with the adventure. Then they must address those hazards when planning and preparing for the trip. During the adventure, it is crucial to be present and mindful of immediate as well as upcoming hazards, avoid them when possible, and mitigate the risk of negative consequences. For example, if the objective is at the other end of a knife-edge ridge with extensive exposure, a climbing party can use technical gear to avoid the immediate negative consequences while enjoying the thrill of the positive experience.

Understanding What Causes Accidents

Climbing adventures are often perceived as unsafe because of mountain hazards largely beyond the control of the climbers. People may conclude that accidents, injuries, and fatalities are inevitable, making comments such as "stuff happens" while shrugging their shoulders. Yet most mountaineering incidents are instead the result of "user error" due to insufficient planning, preparation, knowledge, skills, practice, conditioning, or communication.

Although there is no official organization responsible for soliciting, collecting, or analyzing data on mountaineering accidents, *Accidents in North American Climbing* (*ANAC*), published annually by the American Alpine Club and the Alpine Club of Canada (see Resources), is a reliable source of information on injurious and fatal climbing incidents in North America. Since most of this data comes from voluntary contributions, the number of incidents is underreported, but *ANAC*'s cumulative data represents decades of accident reporting, providing historical statistics and trends.

ANAC data shows that mountaineering incidents are generally spread across age groups and experience levels. Many reports are gripping accounts by the victim or party members. In these accounts, it becomes apparent that most incidents could have been avoided by following sound mountaineering practices and employing sufficient capabilities in balance with the risk exposure.

Table 23-1 shows the most common causes of North American mountaineering accidents in descending order of relative frequency. An immediate cause, such as a fall, is generally a surprise. A contributing cause is something that increases exposure to risk, in effect enabling the incident or increasing the significance of the resulting injury or harm.

Contributing causes often precede an incident. Frequently the climbing party either failed to identify such causes or dismissed them as inconsequential. According to *ANAC*, falls and slips dominate immediate causes, while a variety of other contributing causes, from climbing unroped to poor weather, are roughly equal in frequency. A typical incident results from one immediate cause and several contributing causes.

In one specific example, a climber was on steep snow when she slipped—the immediate cause—then lost her ice axe, was unable to self-arrest, and broke her leg after sliding 150 feet (45 meters). The contributing causes were climbing unroped, not using an ice-axe leash, and exceeding her abilities. An alert climber identifies and does not discount contributing causes, viewing them as early-warning signals; this climber will employ sufficient capabilities to address each contributing cause and thus prevent an incident.

Although ineffective decision-making is not included in *ANAC*'s list of accident causes, analyses of individual reports in *ANAC* discuss flawed decisions participants made, illustrating that poor decision-making is the reason behind an overwhelming number of injuries, much more so than inherent hazards such as loose handholds, rockfall, or thin snow bridges. Mountaineering is not inherently dangerous—rather, climbers' insufficient decisions, preparation, and capabilities are factors that most frequently lead to climbing incidents (fig. 23-1).

Defining Terminology

Learning some terms will help climbers understand how and why incidents occur and how to reduce the probability of their occurrence.

Accident. A popular and general catchall term, *accident* suggests either chance or an unavoidable outcome, which is almost never true. This book uses terms such as *outcome* and *incident* instead.

Hazards. Hazards include sources of serious illness, injuries, or death, such as people, the route, the time of year, the time of day, or weather conditions (see Recognizing Hazards later in this chapter). Climbers who open themselves to hazards, either through making flawed decisions or being insufficiently aware of, or prepared for, the hazards, become subject to exposure to the hazard, which leads to outcomes that can include serious climbing injuries.

This chapter excludes very low probability hazards that are not likely to—but theoretically could—result in serious injury or death. Examples include tripping on a root while crossing a trail, slipping on exposed Class 2 terrain, using equipment with a manufacturing defect, ineffectively treating water, losing your footing on a modest snow slope, experiencing a car accident driving to the trailhead, or poking an eye with a hiking pole or tree branch.

As an individual's capabilities increase, including knowledge, skill, experience, conditioning, and paying attention to intuition, their exposure to a given hazard decreases. For example, highly capable individuals often have better balance and technique and more-solid foot placements when ascending or descending steep faces and slopes, reducing the hazard presented by such terrain to these climbers compared with people with fewer capabilities.

Exposure. This refers to being subject to the influence of a hazard. If you are not exposed to a hazard, you cannot experience a negative outcome, such as injury or death. *Exposure* is also used by climbers to denote a place where there is a danger of falling, termed *fall exposure*. Extent of exposure is often ranked from high to low, based on the consequence or outcome resulting from experiencing the hazard.

Exposure time. This refers to the amount of time an individual is exposed to a hazard. A longer exposure time increases the risk (see below) that an incident will occur. For example, on a route known to have rockfall, an exposure time of several hours is riskier than an exposure time of a few minutes. Similarly, crossing a snow slope with suspect stability or below a large overhanging cornice quickly is less risky than spending more time on that slope.

Outcome. The unpredictable consequences of exposure to hazards, outcomes range from favorable to lethal. For instance, a climber may choose to save time by not donning crampons for a couple of steps across an exposed icy runnel. If the climber slips during the crossing, however, the outcome could be lethal. Most exposure to hazards will not result in injury—in this example, the individual may pass through the exposure unscathed. However, every exposure can result in the full range of outcomes. Repeated exposure to hazards without experiencing the possible extreme consequences may lead a climber to downplay risk, develop an unrealistic perception of a prudent margin (see below), and have a tendency or willingness to be exposed to similar hazards in the future.

Incident. Any undesirable outcome, incidents are usually grouped as near-miss, non-injurious, injurious (minor, significant, and major), or critical (fatal). In everyday life, injurious incidents are commonly called accidents.

Risk. This refers to the probability that exposure to a hazard will lead to an undesirable outcome. An individual's risk for a particular hazard depends on their capabilities, exposure time, and the nature of the hazard. Each hazard's risk is unique for each climber because the risk is a function of the individual's capabilities and decision-making. Regardless of how many times a climber takes a risk, the outcome of the next risk they are exposed to is unforeseeable—it does not depend on the accumulation of past outcomes.

Prudent margin. How far an individual is from—rather than how close they are to—a negative outcome, a prudent margin is an inverse way of describing risk. By employing capabilities sufficient to protect themselves, climbers can improve their prudent margin and lower their risk. Each individual's capabilities influence their prudent margin, just as the amount of risk climbers experience is unique to each of them.

Here are some illustrations of prudent margins. A climber who walks around the end of a crevasse rather than crossing a snow bridge that spans it has a wider prudent margin. They have opted for the greater prudence of circumnavigating the crevasse over the greater risk of crossing it, even if

TABLE 23-1. REPORTED CAUSES OF MOUNTAINEERING ACCIDENTS

MOST FREQUENT *IMMEDIATE* CAUSES

- Falling on rock
- Falling on ice
- Falling rock, ice, or objects
- Stranded or lost
- Illness
- Rappel failure and/or error

MOST FREQUENT *CONTRIBUTING* CAUSES

- Climbing unroped
- Inexperience
- Placing no or inadequate protection
- Using inadequate equipment or wearing inadequate clothing
- Weather
- Climbing alone
- Not wearing a helmet
- Inadequate belay

Source: ANAC 2023 (see Resources).

23

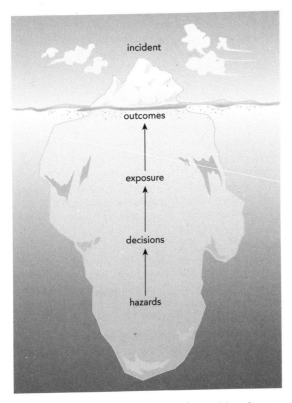

Fig. 23-1. *An incident is like the proverbial tip of the iceberg: several underlying hazards and decisions contribute to increased exposure to risk and the outcomes that cause an incident.*

the latter could save time. A climbing move with high fall exposure (free-falling a significant distance with a clearly calamitous outcome) has a slimmer margin than the same move with little to no fall exposure. Crossing a tumultuous stream by walking across a wet log is less prudent than scooting astride the log on your haunches. An anchored belay is more prudent than an unanchored one.

Risk perception. This refers to how each person evaluates risk for serious injury or death from an exposure to a hazard. Unfortunately, most people have biased risk perception in that they tend to overestimate their prudent margin and underestimate the risk of serious injury or death. Also, people new to mountaineering tend to overestimate risk, while experienced alpinists tend to underestimate it.

Risk tolerance. Each climber's personal perception of risk, risk tolerance varies and can change over time. Factors that may change risk tolerance include age; influence of family, friends, and loved ones; having children; experiencing a personal close call or the close call of a friend;

experiencing a significant personal incident; or the loss of a friend or peer in a critical incident.

Mitigation. This refers to an action that can help avoid, but does not necessarily prevent, injuries; an intervention that does not prevent an incident but may prevent or lessen an adverse (injurious) outcome. Belays are a good example. If a climber slips while rock climbing where there is considerable hazard of a catastrophic fall exposure, without a belay, the outcome could be fatal, but with a belay and arrest, the climber may keep climbing—an example of successful risk mitigation. However, the arrest may fail or the falling climber may pull out the protection and strike a ledge (or hit the ground) before the belay stops the fall, resulting in injury—unsuccessful mitigation. In another example, if an avalanche buries a climber, their beacon (mitigation) may allow other party members to find and save them—successful mitigation. If, however, other party members find the buried victim, only to discover that they died from trauma or suffocation, that's an example of unsuccessful mitigation.

Secure climbing: avoiding or adequately mitigating hazards by employing sufficient capabilities. Examples of secure climbing include wearing a helmet, building SERENE anchors (see the "SERENE Anchor Systems" sidebar in Chapter 10), ensuring that gear (ropes, protection, shoes, et cetera) is in serviceable condition, having experience with and knowledge about using protection, placing protection with sufficient frequency, building safe rappelling systems, and using critical judgment in determining whether the climbing party has sufficient skills, tools, experience, capabilities, and conditioning to mitigate the present risk.

Recognizing Hazards

Some hazards are obvious, but many are not. Climbing hazards have historically been classified as either objective (mountain-based) or subjective (human-based). In the analogy of driving a car, road and driving conditions such as road surface, curves, shoulders, potholes, lane width, lighting, and the choices and actions of other drivers are objective hazards. Speeding, tailgating, weaving, diminished alertness, mechanical deficiencies of the vehicle, and distractions such as the radio, a phone, or conversation are subjective hazards.

Mountain hazards. Examples of mountain hazards include steepness, dangerous route conditions, falling distance, extent of exposure, river crossings, bad weather, loose rock, rockfall, avalanches, icefall, crevasses, moats, cornices, unstable snow and ice, thin snow bridges, and many more.

Human hazards. "To err is human"—people make mistakes. Human hazards are often the result of heuristics:

mental shortcuts people take to help them through a process, draw conclusions, or make decisions. Usually, these brain habits help people move along adroitly, but sometimes the oversimplification of heuristics leads to deficiencies in how people think—in other words, biases. Cognitive biases adversely affect memory, interactions, and decision-making. Psychologists have verified dozens of biases that distort thinking and lead people to draw inaccurate conclusions. Unless people are trained to spot these biases, they are unaware of how such mental shortcuts influence their perception and understanding.

For example, a bias leads people to confidently believe they are objective when assessing situations and making decisions, even when they are not. Another bias leads people to believe they are better at these same thought processes than others in their group, even when they are not. Many biases adversely affect decision-making. Here are other examples of how biases manifest: feeling overconfident, dismissing the probability of negative outcomes, underestimating how much time it will take to do something, having inaccurate memories, favoring statistical outliers, relying on inaccurate information and flawed presumptions, making a faulty analysis, and drawing flawed conclusions.

In many instances, people are biased toward downplaying risk. The human brain convincingly justifies exposures to hazards. But it is important to remember that the outcome of exposure to a hazard is unpredictable, no matter what you think, how experienced or skilled you are, or how steadfastly you believe otherwise. Most people are unaware of the extent to which cognitive biases distort observations, analyses, and decisions regarding risk.

Besides bias, climbers must also recognize other human-related hazards, such as stress, fatigue, dehydration, injury, emotional distraction, adrenaline, and incomplete or poor information, which further corrupt the ability to assess risk accurately. While in the mountains, climbers may tend to attribute incidents to mountain hazards instead of acknowledging that they could have employed more capabilities to manage the hazard's risk, and that they could have mitigated the outcome of the hazards they exposed themselves to.

Mitigating Hazards

People new to the mountains often embrace climbing adventures while focused narrowly on specific climbing objectives. As a result, they may end up in situations beyond their capabilities and get hurt. While images of leading or soloing sheer rock walls and ice couloirs are inspiring, people beginning their climbing journeys cannot fully appreciate the years of training and experience that prepare climbers to attempt such routes. Nor do sensational pictures reveal the detailed planning and preparations undertaken prior to the photo shoot.

Education, training, practice, and experience all help climbers to become better at recognizing hazards, to become mindful of their natural biases, and to compensate for such biases when making decisions to avoid or mitigate hazards. Until mountaineers gain this wisdom, they are not fully aware of their personal limits, nor will they anticipate all the ways things can go wrong. As the common saying goes, "You don't know what you don't know." Spending time in the mountains, practicing techniques, making mistakes, and learning from experiences will help you become a more objective decision-maker capable of consistently mitigating risk.

MANAGE RISK BY AVOIDING HUMAN HAZARDS

Studying the *ANAC* reports helps climbers learn from the experience of others. These reports are poignant reminders that very few incidents arise from extraordinary situations. Instead, most result from climbers not adhering to well-accepted practices and techniques, and many incidents would have been shockingly simple to prevent. Reading *ANAC* every year is a sobering and useful practice for keeping human hazards in the forefront when making decisions.

An uninhibited desire to achieve a climbing objective is the most common bias leading to poor decisions: as the Climbing Code (see Chapter 1, First Steps) recommends, "Do not let desire overrule your judgment when choosing a route or deciding whether to turn back." Individuals have unfortunately suffered serious and even fatal injuries while attempting to realize an objective—such as reaching a summit or completing a well-recognized list of peaks—by letting their focus on the objective override their rational evaluation of risk. A group motivated by the overall experience of the trip—relations between party members, everyone's comfort with the level of risk, open communication about mitigating hazards—is less likely to press on through hazards beyond the combined party's capabilities than is a group motivated by a "must achieve the objective" mentality.

Sometimes many small things—none of which are significant enough by themselves to begin eroding the prudent margin for a particular move, route, or even the trip itself—accumulate and result in a catastrophic outcome. These unanticipated human hazards may be anything from a routefinding mistake, the party moving more slowly than planned, a climber's lack of sleep, or a mildly ill party member (blisters, lack of fitness, leg cramps), to a trailhead

23

argument that leads to distracting emotions. At some point, even little things add up and have an impact.

MANAGE RISK BY MAKING SOUND DECISIONS

One technique to help make decisions less biased is to think up multiple solutions to a hazard, which increases objectiveness and broadens analysis. Some proponents suggest coming up with three alternatives, evaluating their merits, and then picking the best one (fig. 23-2).

When climbers are unsure whether a hazard presents risk significant enough to be dangerous, they can consider what would happen if dozens of climbers—with their individual levels of capability and decision-making—were to pass through the hazard. Would it be reasonable to expect some to suffer a mishap resulting in serious injury or death? In other words, is the group confident they could pass through the hazard several dozen times without incident? If not, is it worth risking serious injury or death to go ahead with this level of exposure? How can the party mitigate the risk to such a degree that they can move forward?

When a positive outcome follows a poor decision, bias can lead to future incidents. If you pass through a hazard unscathed this time, you may end up finding a dangerous practice more tolerable. What about next time? Will you act differently, or will one slightly different parameter lead to a devastating outcome? Be sure your biases and decision-making habits are not setting you up for an incident.

PLAN AND PREPARE FOR A CLIMB

Identifying and avoiding specific trip-related hazards starts as you plan and prepare for the trip (fig. 23-3), long before the party takes the first step on the trail. Climbers can avoid many hazards through planning: assessing leadership, researching the area and route, assessing party members, crafting an itinerary, and setting a prudent margin. Following checklists for anticipating, evaluating, and preparing for hazards helps guard against forgetfulness and memory errors (see Organizing and Leading a Climb in Chapter 22, Leadership).

An oft-quoted climbing adage is "The number one rule is don't fall." It is wise to choose a route below the party's technical best so that the climbers can focus on orchestrating all the components necessary for a successful trip. The technical portion may be the highlight, but it is only one of many aspects of a mountaineering trip. There is a tendency to focus too intently on the technical aspects, only to be tripped up by something "simple."

Risk mitigation also involves selecting party members who have sufficient capabilities for the intended objective.

Careful and thoughtful conversations with potential participants can help avoid the human hazard of including people with less than sufficient capabilities in a climbing party. Rather than placing the entire party at increased risk, discuss whether this is the right trip for them.

Craft an itinerary and evaluate objective route hazards, setting a prudent margin such as a turnaround point should the party move more slowly than planned. When heading into an environment subject to adverse weather, be prepared with a backup plan for another objective elsewhere to improve the odds for a successful outing on a given date. Similarly, when a particular objective is the foremost goal, schedule the climb on several possible dates to improve the odds for acceptable (even stellar) weather.

Once a group has outlined a plan, participants need to prepare for it. Learning and practicing technical skills in a less risky environment such as at a crag, climbing area, or indoor climbing gym, rather than trying to do so in a more remote environment, allows the party to focus on developing and enhancing their skills. Most trips require a certain level of fitness, so all participants must work up to at least that level. If specific gear is essential, participants need to acquire it and become skilled at using it. Making lists to confirm who is bringing what avoids embarrassing moments at the trailhead or potentially hazardous moments on the climb.

In general, careful planning and preparation help reduce the number of surprises on the trip. Ineffective and insufficient planning and preparation increase the probability of unanticipated hazards, decrease the likelihood of avoiding or mitigating exposure to these hazards, and increase the overall risk of negative outcomes.

MITIGATE HAZARDS DURING THE CLIMB

On the climb itself, participants who are alert for both expected and unexpected hazards help to reduce exposure to risk. As climbers identify hazards, the key to managing risk is to reduce exposure to them or mitigate the possibility of an injurious outcome. If neither is an option, the prudent course is to retreat and return when the risk can be managed by employing sufficient capabilities.

To use the driving analogy again, maintaining the car, driving slower, selecting a prudent driving route, avoiding traffic congestion, leaving sufficient space between your vehicle and others, taking a rest break, being patient, and allowing extra time are all examples of avoiding hazards. Using shoulder restraints and driving a car with airbags and modern vehicle construction are examples of mitigation. While these choices will not prevent an incident, they will

Fig. 23-2. *Decision-making framework for managing risk.*

likely mitigate the outcome of an incident and lessen injury in the event that an incident occurs.

On a climb, recognize that best practices for one type of activity may not be sufficient for another type. Following risk management practices contrary to the local norm may be socially intimidating, which may in turn lead climbers to develop unsafe habits. For example, at sport climbing areas with bolted anchors and established landings, it may be standard practice to forgo stopper knots in the ends of the rappel rope. A climber habituated to this practice is unlikely to tie stopper knots in the backcountry, where a secure landing is not necessarily ensured.

Redundancy substantially improves risk management. The probability of multiple independent backups failing is the product of the failure rate of each independent backup—comparatively, a very low number. For example, lead climbers normally place two or three pieces of protection when building an anchor, which results in strong redundancy. In contrast, many climbers rappel from a single anchor point without a second thought. While single rappel anchors are frequently used and "proof tested" by each person, lack of redundancy exposes climbers to a falling risk if the anchor fails and there is no backup. Temporary backup of new or infrequently used rappel anchors introduces a substantial prudent margin compared with the risks associated with a single anchor. Leaving behind extra cord brought specifically for that purpose or being willing to leave behind expensive climbing gear may make the difference between an uneventful rappel and a fatality.

Decision-making requires you to be objective, which human hazards may affect. For instance, perhaps you are hoping to use the last day of your vacation to achieve a long-desired objective. But if it began raining in base camp last night and the weather looks unsettled, will the climbing party attempt the objective even though the route could be hazardous? Does the party have secure alternative destinations? How long can the group wait for a meaningful change in weather? Or, by waiting, will the group inadvertently lose opportunities to retreat if hazards persist? Will the party be able to retreat in time to return home without incident and try again another day?

Managing Risk to Meet Objectives

Few activities engage people both physically and mentally as mountain adventures do. Perhaps mountaineering challenges climbers in ways for which our minds and bodies evolved eons ago. Most contemporary climbers do not grow up with the challenges of traversing in the mountains as a daily activity, so they must learn and practice multiple capabilities to manage risk while enjoying the freedom of the hills. Climbers with ample experience seek to identify, prepare for, minimize exposure to, and mitigate the risks associated with hazards prior to their trips. During a climb, they remain vigilant in recognizing unanticipated hazards and make decisions to avoid or mitigate their exposure so that the party returns home without incident and remains friends.

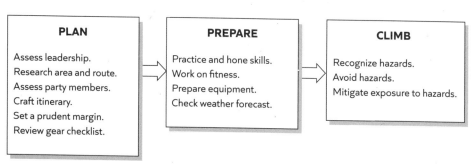

Fig. 23-3. *Three-part focus for managing risks on a climbing trip: plan, prepare, climb.*

CHAPTER 24

FIRST AID

Most skilled mountaineers learn to avoid and mitigate hazards in the mountains, because preventing injuries is vastly preferable to having to treat them. Yet accidents and illnesses can strike mountaineers, just as they can anyone at any time. First-aid knowledge and training are crucial, supportive skills of a competent, self-reliant climber.

The physical demands of climbing and wilderness travel involve unique injuries and illnesses. Because mountaineers are often far from emergency medical services, climbing parties must be able to provide first aid. Additionally, mountaineers have a proud history of aiding injured and ill people in other parties.

The two components to accident response when mountaineering are (1) the framework for responding to an accident and (2) the techniques for treating specific conditions. This chapter begins with planning and preparation, then presents the response framework appropriate to most backcountry accidents. Following that are medical conditions associated with the backcountry, from mountain-specific maladies to injuries to illnesses. This book is not a comprehensive first-aid text. The best way to learn these skills is by taking classes and then periodically practicing and refreshing your knowledge.

Planning and Preparation

While planning a climb, a mountaineering party determines its members' general first-aid skills and any relevant personal medical information, such as asthma or a prior history of altitude illness (also called acute mountain sickness, or AMS). Some climb leaders collect each climber's personal medical information before a trip. Another approach is to ask participants to provide this information to the group at the trailhead before the climb. Other elements of planning for emergency response are identifying rescue and emergency medical resources that serve the area and making sure that everyone in the mountaineering party carries a basic first-aid kit.

FIRST-AID KIT

The "Basic First-Aid Kit" sidebar highlights contents of a personal mountaineering first-aid kit, which climbers can add to. Some first-aid items may be found elsewhere in a climber's personal supplies, such as a multitool in a repair kit. Clearly label personal emergency medications, such as epinephrine for allergies or an inhaler for asthma, and let other party members know where these are located. It may be useful to talk with your doctor about prescription antibiotics and opioid pain medication for emergencies.

Put the first-aid kit in a resealable plastic bag to keep it dry and label it clearly. On longer trips or in remote areas, adjust the items and quantities; a group first-aid kit may make sense. Avoid the temptation to strip it below the bare minimum to reduce weight.

The party must choose an appropriate emergency communication device, such as a phone, satellite communication (satcom) device, or personal locator beacon (PLB), to expedite medical assistance or rescue if necessary. Remember that cellular service is often limited over great distances (see Requesting Outside Assistance in Chapter 25, Self-Rescue).

Responding to Accidents

A shared framework for responding to an emergency is key to a climbing party translating their knowledge and skill into effective, not chaotic, action. An effective response can be simplified into seven steps, covered below in detail (see also "The Seven Steps in Accident Response" sidebar).

> **KEY TOPICS**
>
> **PLANNING AND PREPARATION**
> **RESPONDING TO ACCIDENTS**
> **MOUNTAIN MALADIES**
> **INJURIES**
> **ILLNESSES**
> **PREPARING FOR THE UNEXPECTED**

STEP 1. TAKE CHARGE OF THE SITUATION

The climb leader is responsible for managing the overall accident response. The security of survivors is the top priority. Identify and then avoid or mitigate threatening hazards. Designate a first-aid provider—usually the person with the best medical skills—and assistants. Choose a readily accessible spot for team members to gather resources such as first-aid kits, ropes, and racks.

The climb leader maintains the big picture, thinks ahead, delegates tasks, communicates with rescue resources, and stays focused on managing the entire response. If the situation appears to require outside rescue assistance, the leader requests assistance immediately, since mounting a rescue response takes time. If there are several patients, use triage to direct the party's limited resources toward priority actions and away from those that can wait.

STEP 2. APPROACH THE PATIENT PRUDENTLY

Gather first-aid supplies, rescue equipment, and other needed supplies. Pause to assess the situation. Do not endanger party members in the effort to reach an injured person. Remain cognizant of objective hazards such as falling rock or ice or dangerous avalanche conditions. The climb leader selects the best approach strategy, which in technical terrain could require ropes and rescue techniques (see Chapter 25, Self-Rescue).

STEP 3. PERFORM URGENT FIRST AID

Move a patient only if there is imminent danger to the patient or rescuers, taking steps to minimize further injury. Patients do not have to be lying on their back to be examined and treated. Try to determine whether a spine injury may have occurred. If a patient needs to be extricated, support and immobilize any obviously injured area, as well as the neck and spine.

Take precautions to protect rescuers from body fluids that could transmit communicable infectious diseases. Protective measures include disposable gloves, eyewear, or perhaps a bandanna. If a patient is bleeding or vomiting, wear raingear for additional protection.

If the patient is unresponsive, check their P-MARCH vital indicators (see below) and begin emergency first aid if necessary.

Pulse: Is a pulse present?

Massive hemorrhage: Is there heavy bleeding that needs immediate control?

Airway: Is the airway clear?

Respiration: Is patient breathing adequately?

Circulation: Is the patient in shock?

Head injury and/or Hypothermia: Does the patient have a head injury? Is the patient at risk for hypothermia?

If a pulse is absent and someone in the party has sufficient training, begin cardiopulmonary resuscitation (CPR). Performing CPR in the wilderness rather than a hospital requires special consideration; see the "Special

---

THE SEVEN STEPS IN ACCIDENT RESPONSE

1. Take charge of the situation.
2. Approach the patient prudently.
3. Perform urgent first aid.
4. Protect the patient.
5. Check for other injuries.
6. Make a plan.
7. Carry out the plan.

BASIC FIRST-AID KIT

- Commercial tourniquet
- Adhesive bandages
- Skin closures or cyanoacrylate skin glue
- Hemostatic gauze pad
- Nonadherent dressings
- Self-adhering roller bandage or wrap
- Medical tape
- Antiseptic wipes and hand sanitizer
- Blister prevention and treatment supplies
- Nitrile gloves, eye protection, surgical or N95 mask
- Tweezers
- Needle
- Nonprescription painkiller (acetaminophen)
- Nonsteroidal anti-inflammatory (naproxen, ibuprofen)
- Antidiarrheal and antiemetic medications
- Antihistamine
- Topical antibiotic and ophthalmic antibiotic ointment
- Accident report form (see Figure 24-1) and pencil
- Personal prescriptions: asthma inhaler, epinephrine, et cetera

24

Circumstances for Withholding or Terminating CPR" sidebar. These guidelines are based on recommendations from the International Commission for Alpine Rescue on the termination of CPR in mountain rescue (see Resources).

Manage Serious Bleeding

In remote locations, any blood loss beyond that from superficial wounds is harmful. If a victim is bleeding seriously from an extremity, apply a tourniquet to control bleeding until an effective pressure dressing can be applied. A tourniquet must be at least 1.5 inches (4 centimeters) wide to obstruct blood flow. If a tourniquet fails to control bleeding, place a second tourniquet next to the first. Apply a tourniquet to bare skin on an upper arm or upper leg. The tourniquet must have a windlass device to provide sufficient force to overcome arterial pressure, which can be confirmed by the absence of a pulse at the farther end of the arm or leg. A standard belt cannot be pulled tight enough to impede arterial flow and may instead increase bleeding.

After a tourniquet has been applied, move the injured individual or further treat them until you can apply a proper dressing. Then reassess the need for the tourniquet and release it if it is no longer required. The released tourniquet may be left loosely in place for rapid reapplication in case bleeding recurs. Leave the tourniquet in place until the patient undergoes a definitive medical evaluation.

For less severe bleeding, use direct pressure over a hemostatic dressing or clean clothing. If bleeding persists, apply a pressure dressing. Elevating a limb is not effective for controlling bleeding. Applying pressure to a pressure point is effective for about a minute, which can give rescuers time to apply a tourniquet. For bleeding in areas not amenable to a tourniquet, apply direct pressure and pressure dressings or a hemostatic dressing packed into the wound to "fill the bowl."

Traumatic bleeding causes metabolic abnormalities, causes hypothermia, and interferes with the blood's ability to clot. Hypothermia results in worsening metabolism, both of which contribute to bleeding severity. Controlling hypothermia in an injured person is critical. Hypothermia can occur in an injured patient even on a warm, sunny day, and even mild hypothermia in a trauma patient can result in devastating physiologic consequences. Stopping bleeding and preventing hypothermia (see Cold Stress and Hypothermia later in this chapter) are the most effective treatments for serious bleeding (see the "Tips to Manage Bleeding" sidebar).

STEP 4: PROTECT THE PATIENT

The first-aid provider must focus on protecting the patient from the environment—heat, cold, precipitation, et cetera—usually without moving the patient, to prevent shock. Make every effort to maintain the patient's body temperature. Worsening shock is characterized by symptoms such as lessening responsiveness, deteriorating mental status, and a collapsing circulatory system: falling blood pressure, wrist pulse becoming weak or absent, and other indicators (see Table 24-1). Shock is difficult, if not impossible, to treat in the backcountry; evacuation is a priority for patients who develop this condition.

STEP 5: CHECK FOR OTHER INJURIES

Once the patient has been stabilized and treated initially for life-threatening conditions, the first-aid provider

TABLE 24-1. SYMPTOMS AND SIGNS OF SHOCK	
SYMPTOMS A PATIENT MAY EXPERIENCE	**SIGNS AN OBSERVER MAY NOTE**
Nausea	Face pale
Thirst	Eyes dull
Weakness	Pupils dilated
Fear and/or restlessness	Pulse rapid but weak
Sweating	Restlessness
Shortness of breath	Skin cool and clammy
	Lips and nail beds blue
	Breathing rapid and shallow
	Unresponsiveness (a late sign)

TIPS TO MANAGE BLEEDING

- First, take precautions (gloves, sunglasses, raingear) to shield rescuers.
- Apply a tourniquet to control heavy bleeding.
- Apply a hemostatic dressing.
- Apply direct pressure to control bleeding.
- Use pressure dressings on top of existing ones.
- Prevent and treat for hypothermia.
- Treat for shock: elevate the feet 6 to 12 inches (15 to 30 centimeters).

checks for other injuries. Conduct a systematic head-to-toe secondary survey, looking for the clues listed in the "Signs of Injury" sidebar. The exam needs to be visual and hands-on. For best results, examine bare skin while making thorough observations for injuries. Expose the area of interest, and then cover the area to protect against hypothermia.

The person conducting the examination should use a first-aid or accident report form (fig. 24-1) to guide the exam. The report provides information in the event that the patient's condition changes or the injured person is turned over to outside assistance. To detect changes, reassess at regular intervals, such as every five or ten minutes, depending on the injury severity.

STEP 6: MAKE A PLAN

Up until this point, the accident response steps primarily include urgent first aid and thorough assessment. A patient may also require other first aid, such as wound care, splintng an injured limb, hydration, medicating for pain, and preventing shock and hypothermia. If the patient needs to be evacuated, the party may require resources from outside organizations. Finally, consider the remaining party members' needs. Taking all of this into account, the leader then makes a plan.

A patient who cannot walk nearly always needs assistance for evacuation. Carrying a patient by litter requires proper equipment and many people, which is beyond the capabilities of most climbing parties. The party should not attempt to evacuate a patient who may have serious head, neck, or back injuries (see Injuries later in this chapter). In deciding whether to attempt an evacuation, consider the terrain, the weather, the time of day, how long an evacuation will take, and strength and skills of other party members. If the party

SPECIAL CIRCUMSTANCES FOR WITHHOLDING OR TERMINATING CPR

The first-aid provider may withhold or terminate CPR if any of these conditions occur:

- There is unacceptable risk to the rescuer.
- The rescuer is exhausted.
- The environment is one in which CPR is impossible.
- The injuries are incompatible with life.
- The patient's body is frozen solid.
- The avalanche victim does not have a pulse, has an obstructed airway, and was buried for more than 35 minutes.
- The victim's heartbeat does not return after 30 minutes of CPR (excluding hypothermic patients).

chooses to evacuate with outside help, the members must plan and organize the effort.

If the climb leader decides to seek outside help, the party needs a plan for obtaining assistance and taking care of all members remaining in the wilderness. If the party has an emergency communication device, it is better to request rescue assistance early, rather than finding themselves with a deteriorating patient in the middle of the night or a rainstorm. If the plan is to dispatch people to request help, send at least two of the party's more fit and experienced members, along with a completed accident report form and rescue request form (fig. 24-2) with the condition of both the patient and the rest of the party, the adequacy of survival supplies, and the party's specific location. See Chapter 25, Self-Rescue, for details on rescue and evacuation methods.

STEP 7: CARRY OUT THE PLAN

While executing the plan, the party monitors progress and looks for opportunities to improve it. Monitor the patient and offer reassurance and support. Give fluids and carbohydrates if the patient can swallow and tolerate them. If in doubt, start with occasional sips of water. Remain vigilant because a patient may develop symptoms of shock after an injury as their condition deteriorates.

At this stage, psychological support becomes important for the patient and anyone involved in helping the seriously injured. Keep an eye out for anyone whose behavior seems irrational, agitated, or dazed. Often, assigning people a simple task will refocus them. Party members may need to set up a shelter, ration food, or prepare to spend a night in the wilderness.

SIGNS OF INJURY

- Discoloration or bruising
- Deformity
- Bleeding or loss of other fluids
- Swelling
- Pain or tenderness
- Limited range of motion
- Guarding of a body part
- Numbness

24

FIRST-AID AND/OR ACCIDENT REPORT FORM

Date	Time	Completed by		
Name				Age
Allergies		Medical Problems		
Initial Rapid Check	Massive bleeding?	Airway?	Breathing?	Shock?
What happened?				
Assessment of Problems				
Where does it hurt?				

Consciousness:	Alert?	Verbal?	Painful?	Unconscious?
Skin:	Color	Warm? Cool?	Moist? Dry?	
Pupils:	Equal?	Regular size?		
Head:	Scalp—Wounds?	Ears, Nose—Fluids?	Jaw—Stable?	Mouth—Wounds?
Neck:	Tenderness?	Deformity?	Wounds?	
Chest:	Movement?	Symmetry?		
Abdomen:	Rigid?	Wounds?	Tender?	
Pelvis:	Stable?	Deformities?	Sensations/movement?	Pulse below injury?
Extremities:	Stable?	Deformities?	Sensations/movement?	Pulse below injury?
Back:	Wounds?	Tenderness?	Deformity?	
Pain: (Location)				

VITAL SIGNS RECORD

TIME	Pulse (rate and location)	Breaths (rate and character)	Pupils (equal and reactive?)	Skin (color, temp., and moisture level?)	Other (pain, anxiety, thirst)

INJURIES—MARK WITH AN X

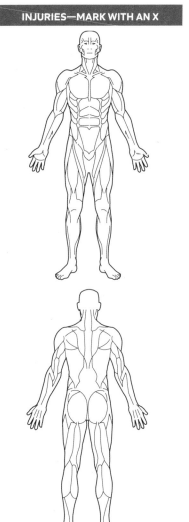

Fig. 24-1. *First-aid and/or accident report form.*

RESCUE REQUEST FORM

My name is _____. I am calling to request a rescue.

Location: _____ (include lat./long., UTM, and/or prominent terrain feature)

Method(s) of contacting me: _____ (phone number, inReach, SPOT, radio frequency)

Number of patients: _____

MOVING

Mechanism of Injury and/or Nature of Illness (What happened?)

    Excessive ☐ Heat ☐ Cold

    Fall on ☐ Rock ☐ Snow ☐ Crevasse ☐ Ice

    Struck by ☐ Avalanche ☐ Rockfall

    Medical emergency: _____

    (Chest pain, respiratory difficulty, abdominal pain, diabetes, fatigue, intoxication?)

Obvious Injury and/or Medical Symptoms: _____

(Bleeding, fracture, shortness of breath, vomiting, confusion, weakness, etc.?)

Vital Signs

    Heart rate: _____

    Breathing rate/quality: _____

    Skin temperature/color: _____

    State of consciousness: _____

    Pain/location: _____

Interventions (first aid given): _____

Needs: What do I need? Special equipment to evacuate, food, water, warmth?

Go Now or Can Wait? Helicopter rescue, technical rescue, carry out, or walk out?

    Method of marking up pickup site: _____

    Terrain description (altitude, tall trees, steep terrain): _____

    Local conditions, weather, wind, hazards: _____

Fig. 24-2. *Rescue request form.*

24

Mountain Maladies

The mountain environment exposes climbers to extremes of heat, cold, sun exposure, and altitude Treating some conditions in the field may be challenging since an ill climber can rarely be removed from the causes. If one person is suffering, others in the party could be close behind. This section describes maladies ranging from milder (and more common) to more serious (and less common).

DEHYDRATION

Maintaining sufficient hydration reduces the risk of heat-, cold-, and altitude-related illnesses by maintaining adequate blood flow in the body. Hydration also improves overall physical performance. Climbers may be unaware of how much water their body is losing. If they do not urinate periodically or if their urine becomes darker, they are not drinking enough fluids. Other indications of dehydration are a flushed feeling, headache, or a decrease in or lack of sweating.

Individuals vary in the rate at which their bodies lose water. Climbers at higher altitudes experience increased water loss through urination and respiration. Various medications can influence the body's ability to maintain water balance, by changing how much a person sweats or feels thirst or by affecting urine output. Conditioning also affects the body's water balance.

Begin mountaineering outings well hydrated. Drink a cup (or more) of water 15 minutes before starting out. Once under way, continue drinking fluids at a rate of 1 to 1.5 cups (0.2 to 0.3 liter) for every 20 to 30 minutes of intense aerobic activity. This rate of drinking helps maintain hydration without distending the stomach. Most people can tolerate drinking a pint (0.5 liter) of water without stomach distension. If you want a second pint, consume it more slowly, over a span of 15 minutes, to avoid bloating.

Commercial sports and electrolyte drinks help replace electrolytes (body salts) lost via sweat. The electrolytes sodium and glucose are necessary for adequate water uptake in the gastrointestinal (GI) tract. Prior to the creation of electrolyte solutions and oral rehydration salts, doctors treated fluid loss with intravenous fluids. In the 1960s, physiologists found that consuming glucose helped to increase the absorption of water and sodium. When a mixture of sodium, glucose, water, and other electrolytes reaches the small intestine, the body rapidly rehydrates. Eating snacks with some salt content can also help replace electrolytes.

EXERCISE-ASSOCIATED HYPONATREMIA

The belief that individuals should "drink as much fluid as possible" is an alarming misconception. Climbers should instead drink according to the dictates of thirst. A relatively uncommon although very dangerous fluid-electrolyte disorder called exercise-associated hyponatremia (EAH), or overhydration, is generally caused by drinking too much water, which decreases blood sodium levels for up to 24 hours after prolonged activity. The body can excrete and sweat about 1 to 1.5 quarts (1 to 1.5 liters) of water per hour. Consuming water in excess of this amount may eventually result in EAH and decreased sodium levels.

To differentiate between dehydration and overhydration, track the patient's water intake (How big is the water bottle? How often was it filled?) and urination. Indicators like increased thirst, rapid heart rate, diminished urination (darker-colored urine), and dizziness, faintness, or lightheadedness only on standing are less likely with EAH and more likely with heat-related conditions. In EAH, the urine and blood are very dilute; signs include weakness, malaise and fatigue, irritability, headache, a bloated feeling and weight gain, nausea and vomiting, dizziness, and variable urine output. EAH can lead to seizures, coma, and death.

To prevent EAH, keep salt and salty snacks readily available and maintain appropriate fluid intake, particularly during long, hot outings. This strategy depends on not overhydrating. To treat mild EAH, restrict fluids until urine is dark, offer salty snacks, and provide concentrated oral electrolyte solutions. For severe EAH, evacuate immediately.

HEAT-RELATED CONDITIONS

If a person builds up more heat with exertion or exposure than their body can lose, heat-related illness can result. Humans lose heat largely through their skin. High humidity impairs heat dissipation because it slows evaporation of perspiration. High air body temperature ≥ combined with high humidity and strenuous exertion *are dangerous conditions* that can lead to overheating and a range of problems, from the crippling pain of heat cramps to heat exhaustion or heatstroke (fig. 24-3). Treating a patient in the field can be challenging, especially when it is hot and sunny and there is little water, shade, or snow. It is vastly preferable to prevent someone from overheating in the first place.

Heat Index

In Figure 24-4, the heat index provides a measure of apparent temperature increase due to the effect of increasing humidity. For example, if the ambient air temperature is 90 degrees Fahrenheit (32 degrees Celsius) at a relative humidity of 45 percent, the perceived temperature will be 93 degrees Fahrenheit (34 degrees Celsius), indicating extreme caution is necessary. At a relative humidity of 90

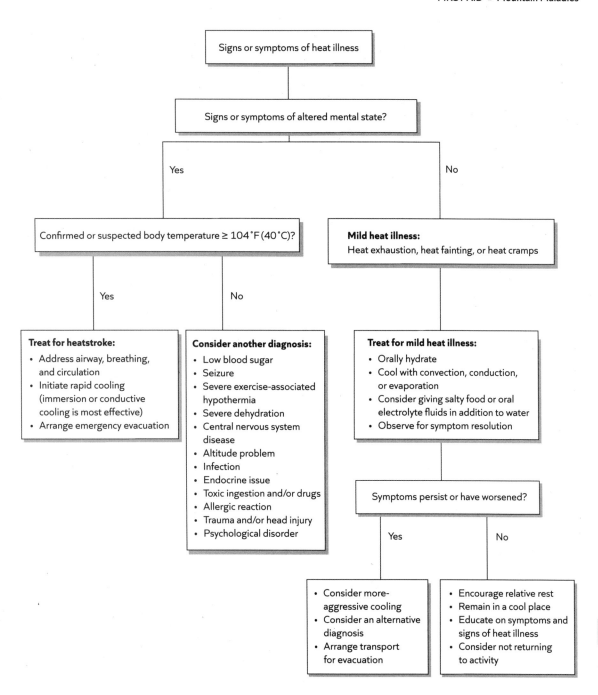

Fig. 24-3. *Flowchart for determining whether someone has a heat-related condition.*

24

percent, however, the perceived temperature will be 122 degrees Fahrenheit (50 degrees Celsius), indicating dangerous conditions.

When the heat index range is 91–103 degrees Fahrenheit (33–39 degrees Celsius), prolonged exposure and physical activity can result in heatstroke, heat cramps, and heat exhaustion. When the heat index range is 103–124 degrees Fahrenheit (39–51 degrees Celsius), heatstroke, heat cramps, and heat exhaustion are likely. When the heat index is 126 degrees Fahrenheit (52 degrees Celsius) and above, heatstroke is imminent.

Heat Cramps

If a climber becomes dehydrated or electrolyte-imbalanced during sustained exertion, muscle cramps—especially in the legs—can develop. Less conditioned climbers are more likely to develop heat cramps. Replenish water and electrolytes throughout the climb to avoid this painful condition and to treat it. Treatment also consists of rest, massage, and gentle, slow stretching of the affected muscles. Severe leg cramps on an approach or strenuous climb may be a warning sign of impending heat exhaustion.

Heat Exhaustion

Heat exhaustion is a milder affliction compared with heatstroke (see below). In the body's effort to reduce core temperature, blood vessels in the skin become so dilated—and sweating-related moisture loss so pronounced—that circulation to the brain and other vital organs becomes inadequate. The result is an effect similar to fainting (see the "Signs and Symptoms of Heat Exhaustion" sidebar). An individual's susceptibility includes a history of heat exhaustion or being dehydrated or salt-depleted.

Treatment of heat exhaustion consists of resting—reclining with feet up—preferably in the shade, removing excess clothing, and drinking plenty of fluids and electrolytes. Applying water over the head, skin, and clothing promotes evaporative cooling. On average, it takes one hour to get a quart (liter) of fluid into the circulatory system.

Heatstroke

Also called sunstroke, heatstroke is a life-threatening emergency that must be treated immediately. The body's heat gain is so substantial that body core temperature rises to dangerous levels: 104 degrees Fahrenheit (40 degrees Celsius) or more. The most reliable symptom is an altered mental state, which may manifest as irritability, combativeness, delusions, or incoherent speech (see the "Signs and Symptoms of Heatstroke" sidebar).

Heatstroke victims must be treated immediately. Move the patient to the shade. Cool the head and body by packing them in snow, splashing water on them, or fanning them vigorously. Remove clothing that retains heat. Add ice packs or snow to the neck, groin, and armpits. Once body temperature has dropped to 102 degrees Fahrenheit (39 degrees Celsius), the cooling efforts can be stopped. Continue to monitor the patient's temperature, mental status, and general condition. Temperature instability may continue for some time, and body temperature could climb again, necessitating more cooling. If the patient is able to swallow, provide cold drinks—rehydration is critical. The ill person may not be able to begin moving again for several hours. A heatstroke patient should not resume activity until competent medical personnel have evaluated their condition.

SIGNS AND SYMPTOMS OF HEAT EXHAUSTION

- Headache
- Cool, clammy skin
- Dizziness
- Fatigue
- Nausea
- Thirst
- Rapid pulse and respiratory rate

SIGNS AND SYMPTOMS OF HEATSTROKE

- Altered mental state: confusion or uncooperativeness, advancing toward unconsciousness
- Rapid pulse and respiratory rate
- Headache
- Weakness
- Flushed, hot skin (wet with sweat or sometimes dry)
- Seizures
- Loss of coordination

Air temperature (°F)

Relative humidity (%)	80	82	84	86	88	90	92	94	96	98	100	102	104	106	108	110
40	80	81	83	85	88	91	94	97	101	105	109	114	119	124	130	136
45	80	82	84	87	89	93	96	100	104	109	114	119	124	130	137	
50	81	83	85	88	91	95	99	103	108	113	118	124	131	137		
55	81	84	86	89	93	97	101	106	112	117	124	130	137			
60	82	84	88	91	95	100	105	110	116	123	129	137				
65	82	85	89	93	98	103	108	114	121	128	136					
70	83	86	90	95	100	105	112	119	126	134						
75	84	88	92	97	103	109	116	124	132							
80	84	89	94	100	106	113	121	129								
85	85	90	96	102	110	117	126	135								
90	86	91	98	105	113	122	131									
95	86	93	100	108	117	127										
100	87	95	103	112	121	132										

Heat index 91°F–103°F (33°C–39°C) **Extreme caution**	Heat index 103°F–124°F (39°C–51°C) **Danger**	Heat index 125°F (52°C) and higher **Extreme danger**

Fig. 24-4. *Heat index, showing likelihood of heat disorders with prolonged exposure or strenuous activity: white boxes, use caution; light gray boxes, use extreme caution; gray boxes, dangerous conditions; dark gray boxes, extremely dangerous conditions.* Source: *National Weather Service, NOAA.*

Air temperature (°F)

Wind speed (mph)	40	35	30	25	20	15	10	5	0	-5	-10	-15	-20	-25	-30	-35	-40	-45
5	36	31	25	19	13	7	1	-5	-11	-16	-22	-28	-34	-40	-46	-52	-57	-63
10	34	27	21	15	9	3	-4	-10	-16	-22	-28	-35	-41	-47	-53	-59	-66	-72
15	32	25	19	13	6	0	-7	-13	-19	-26	-32	-39	-45	-51	-58	-64	-71	-77
20	30	24	17	11	4	-2	-9	-15	-22	-29	-35	-42	-48	-55	-61	-68	-74	-81
25	29	23	16	9	3	-4	-11	-17	-24	-31	-37	-44	-51	-58	-64	-71	-78	-84
30	28	22	15	8	1	-5	-12	-19	-26	-33	-39	-46	-53	-60	-67	-73	-80	-87
35	28	21	14	7	0	-7	-14	-21	-27	-34	-41	-48	-55	-62	-69	-76	-82	-89
40	27	20	13	6	-1	-8	-15	-22	-29	-36	-43	-50	-57	-64	-71	-78	-84	-91
45	26	19	12	5	-2	-9	-16	-23	-30	-37	-44	-51	-58	-65	-72	-79	-86	-93
50	26	19	12	4	-3	-10	-17	-24	-31	-38	-45	-52	-60	-67	-74	-81	-88	-95
55	25	18	11	4	-3	-11	-18	-25	-32	-39	-46	-54	-61	-68	-75	-82	-89	-97
60	25	17	10	3	-4	-11	-19	-26	-33	-40	-48	-55	-62	-69	-76	-84	-91	-98

Frostbite times

30 minutes   10 minutes   5 minutes

Fig. 24-5. *Windchill index.* Source: *National Weather Service, NOAA.*

24

TABLE 24-2. STAGES OF COOLING BODY CORE TEMPERATURE

STAGE	TEMPERATURE (°F)	TEMPERATURE (°C)	SELF-CARE	SHIVERING	MENTAL STATUS
Cold stress	95–98.6	35–37	Yes	Yes	Alert
Mild hypothermia	90–95	32–35	No	May cease	Diminished, uncooperative
Moderate hypothermia	82–90	28–32	No	Will cease	Confused, irrational
Severe to profound hypothermia	<82	<28	No	No	Loss of consciousness; coma

COLD-RELATED CONDITIONS

When body heat is lost to the environment through evaporation (sweating and breathing), radiation (from uncovered skin), convection (from windy conditions), and conduction (from touching, sitting, or lying on something cold), cold-related illnesses and injuries occur. Cold stress and hypothermia involve systemic heat loss; Raynaud's disease, frostnip, frostbite, and immersion foot involve localized heat loss. Localized cold-related illnesses are less urgent concerns than hypothermia.

Windchill

As wind speed increases, it draws more heat from exposed skin by convection. The windchill index (fig. 24-5) provides a mathematical measure of how wind can accelerate the rate of cooling from exposed skin in relation to the ambient temperature. Windchill is calculated based on heat-transfer theory. For example, if the air temperature is minus 552degrees Fahrenheit (minus 23 degrees Celsius) and the wind is blowing at 25 miles (40 kilometers) per hour, then the windchill Air temperature is minus 37 degrees Fahrenheit (minus 38 degrees Celsius), At this temperature and at this wind speed, exposed skin can freeze in 10 minutes.

By definition, the windchill index temperature is lower than the air temperature. But it is a measure of cooling and not a measure of ambient temperature. Windchill is of greater significance when the air temperature is relatively cool—that is, when there is risk of frostbite or hypothermia. Windchill cools all warm surfaces, while the windchill index depicts cooling only on exposed skin; dressing properly in windproof materials can reduce or eliminate the windchill effect (see Layering in Chapter 2, Clothing and Equipment).

Cold Stress and Hypothermia

Systemic cold-related conditions occur when the body tries to maintain normal core temperature in cold temperatures but blood is diverted away from the skin surface and extremities. Wet clothing and exposure to wind chill the body. Direct contact with snow or cold rock also robs the body of heat. Dehydration, inadequate food intake, and fatigue are risk factors. Cold stress is mild; hypothermia is more severe.

Cold stress occurs when heat loss outstrips heat generation, resulting in a lower core temperature, between normal and 95 degrees Fahrenheit (35 degrees Celsius). A classic example occurs when active backcountry skiers stop for lunch and wait until they start to feel cool before donning more clothing. The added clothing, at ambient temperature, initially draws more heat from the skiers' bodies, and they progressively feel colder and start shivering, an initial indication of core cooling. To avoid cold stress, use passive rewarming: add more clothing as soon as you stop, or exchange sweaty base layers for dry ones. If you are cold-stressed, get moving again to warm back up.

Unlike cold stress, hypothermia is an emergency condition that will lead to death unless treated. Usually hypothermia occurs after prolonged exposure to a chilly environment

TIPS FOR PREVENTING HYPOTHERMIA

- Avoid wet skin or clothes from sweat or precipitation.
- Wear adequate insulation and shells.
- Avoid windchill by covering exposed skin.
- Maintain hydration.
- Stay well fed.
- Pace yourself to avoid sweating and becoming fatigued.
- Prior to prolonged stops, don chilled clothing to warm it up.
- If you start to feel cool, put on more warm clothing.

rather than exposure to extreme cold. A drizzly day where the temperature is around 25 degrees Fahrenheit (minus 4 degrees Celsius) with a strong breeze is a more typical hypothermia setting than minus 10 degrees Fahrenheit (minus 23 degrees Celsius) at the ice cliffs. An active climber immobilized suddenly by injury in a cool, cold, or windy environment is particularly susceptible.

The party must know when to call off a summit quest. Watch out for each other. When a party member becomes exhausted, that person is often "too tired" to bother adding clothing, eating, or drinking, which makes hypothermia more likely to occur. Because hypothermia interferes with judgment and perception, climbing partners must be annoyingly persistent in telling a shivering climber to don warmer gear, eat calories, and drink fluids (see the "Tips for Preventing Hypothermia" sidebar).

Hypothermia symptoms vary depending on the individual and both the extent to which and the amount of time that body core temperature has been reduced (see Table 24-2). Initially, signs and symptoms of cooling lag behind the drop in body core temperature. Typically, the patient does not notice the early signs. Shivering is the body's attempt to rewarm itself through muscular work. As the body cools further, cognitive and physical processes progressively decline. The symptoms and severity fall into three stages: mild, moderate, and severe to profound.

In mild to moderate hypothermia, body core temperature ranges from 95 to 82 degrees Fahrenheit (35 to 28 degrees Celsius), but the distinction between the two is blurry since there is no practical way to measure core temperature in the mountains. Symptoms of mild hypothermia include intense shivering, fumbling hand movements, stumbling, dulling of mental functions, and uncooperative or isolative behavior.

The climbing party can evaluate coordination by having the person walk an imaginary tightrope for 15 feet (about 5 meters), heel to toe. As core temperature decreases into moderate hypothermia, shivering becomes increasingly violent but may cease if heat loss is unchecked. The patient may not be able to walk but may still be able to sit or stand. As muscle and nervous-system function continue declining, muscles become stiff and movements uncoordinated. Behavior is confused or irrational.

In severe hypothermia, the body's core temperature drops below 82 degrees Fahrenheit (28 degrees Celsius) and shivering stops; consciousness is gradually lost to the point of coma. As profound hypothermia progresses, it may be extremely difficult to observe a pulse or tell whether the patient is breathing. The patient's pupils may dilate.

Hypothermia must be treated aggressively to prevent the patient's decline and death. Treat preventively rather than waiting for signs and symptoms to appear. Focus on stopping heat loss and rewarming the patient (see the "Tips for Preventing Hypothermia" sidebar). Help a patient who can walk put on clothing, consume food and water, and keep traveling—muscle activity is the quickest way to warm up.

To treat a hypothermic patient who is unable to walk (for example, an excavated avalanche victim), protect the person from the elements. In mild cases, insulate the patient from the ground, shelter them from wind and precipitation, and remove wet clothing and put on dry. If the patient has a working gag reflex and can swallow, offer liquids. Treat dehydration until urine output is restored. Also offer energy gels and carbohydrates to enable shivering.

Most mildly to moderately hypothermic patients with altered consciousness require active rewarming. In the wilderness, do what you can. Wrap bottles of hot water in mittens or socks and place them on the patient's chest, neck, armpits, and groin. Wrap the patient in clothing, sleeping bags, and sleeping pads to insulate against heat loss. Using direct body contact with a (warm) party member is less effective than using heat packs or hot water bottles. It may be possible to use a tarp or rain fly set up around the seated patient to capture heat, sauna-like, from a portable stove—being careful to prevent carbon monoxide poisoning as well as burns.

A severely hypothermic patient must be handled gently to avoid sending cold blood that circulates near the skin and in the extremities back to the heart. This "afterdrop" could cause heart rhythm abnormalities such as cardiac arrest. Rewarm the patient slowly. Do not offer liquids to a semiconscious patient. Limit limb movement and keep the patient horizontal. Allow the recovering patient to shiver for at least 30 minutes to thermally stabilize their body before exercise. Once a patient has adequate energy reserves, the most effective means of heating may be for the patient to walk.

A profoundly hypothermic person may appear dead. Before starting CPR, feel for a carotid pulse for one minute. If a pulse is not detectable, start chest compressions, including rescue breathing. It is essential not to give up on resuscitation efforts until the patient is warm, has received adequately performed CPR, and still shows no signs of life. Remember the saying that "no one is dead until warm and dead." Severely hypothermic patients have tolerated delayed and interrupted CPR and made a full neurologic recovery. Once the severely hypothermic patient has a normal core temperature, monitor them because their temperature-regulating mechanisms may be unstable for a considerable period.

24

Raynaud's Disease

A chronic condition often triggered by cold, Raynaud's disease involves intense temporary constriction of blood vessels, usually of the hands. Initially, involved fingers turn white and stiff and feel numb due to diminished blood supply. Later they may turn bluish due to lack of oxygen. These changes may be harder or easier to see, depending on your skin color. After the blood vessels reopen, flushing may be painful and turn the area red.

A climber suffering an episode may appear to have frostbite, but those with a history of Raynaud's will be familiar with the course of an episode. Climbers with Raynaud's are more susceptible to frostbite or cold injuries and must use preventive measures, avoiding triggers like exposure to cold weather without adequate clothing, and using gloves or mittens and chemical heat packs to keep their hands warm (or to treat an episode). Treat as for frostnip.

Frostnip

Commonly mistaken for frostbite, frostnip is a superficial, nonfreezing cold injury associated with intense constriction of blood vessels in exposed skin—usually fingers, cheeks, ears, or nose. It is a common occurrence. Waiting too long to don handwear is a frequent cause.

Treat by putting on insulated clothing, warming the skin with direct contact with something warm (warm skin, such as putting your hands in your armpits, or bottles full of hot water), breathing with cupped hands over the nose, and using chemical heat packs. Exercise increases dilation of blood vessels in limbs, which should help. Rewarming may be painful, but frostnip does not result in long-term damage. The occurrence of frostnip may signal conditions favorable for frostbite.

Frostbite

When tissue truly freezes, frostbite occurs; ice crystals form in the body's internal fluids, leading to tissue dehydration and eventual tissue death. Frostbitten tissue is cold, hard, numb, and pale or darkly discolored. Frostbite can be classified as superficial (little permanent tissue loss expected) or deep (tissue loss expected). The distinction is usually difficult to make in the wilderness. The affected body part can be severely and permanently damaged, and effects can persist for years. Skin injury is common. Frostbitten tissue is fragile; do not massage it. Preventing frostbite from occurring is vastly preferable to having to treat it.

Avoid frostbite by wearing non-constrictive clothing in layers that is appropriate for the expected conditions, and

cover exposed areas. Mittens can be warmer than gloves. Keeping feet dry is important; also avoid overly tight boots. Chemical hand and toe warmers are helpful. Prompt party members to check by wiggling toes and fingers and to notify the trip leader early if they are having problems keeping warm. Avoid skin contact with cold metal or stove fuel, which can cause frostbite on contact. Stop and warm fingers and toes before they go numb. Exercise is a specific method to maintain peripheral blood flow.

Treatment for frostbite starts with treating for any accompanying hypothermia (see above). Superficial frostbite can be warmed against another warm body—for example, placing a cold finger or foot against a warm belly. In the wilderness, it is undesirable to rewarm a deeply frozen body part, because if the thawed body part then refreezes, tissue death will be more extensive. Instead, evacuate the patient to a medical facility for rewarming.

If at all possible, do not use a frozen extremity for walking, climbing, or other maneuvers until definitive care is reached. If you are considering using a frozen extremity to move, conduct a risk-benefit analysis weighing the potential for further trauma and a possibly poorer outcome. Although it is reasonable to walk on a foot with frostbitten toes for evacuation purposes, it is inadvisable to walk on an entirely frostbitten foot, because of the potential for resulting tissue death. If a frozen extremity must be used for locomotion or evacuation, pad and splint it, and keep it as immobile as possible to minimize additional trauma. However, do not attempt to retard spontaneous rewarming by deliberately packing the area in snow, keeping it in cold water, or traveling in a chilled vehicle.

In the rare instance in which you wish to rewarm the frozen extremity in the wilderness, warm the frostbitten part in a water bath of 98.6 to 102.2 degrees Fahrenheit (37 to 39 degrees Celsius), about the temperature of a hot tub. In the wilderness, it will be challenging to maintain water in this temperature range. Do not use hotter water, as a frostbitten body part is extremely susceptible to thermal injury. Rewarming of an extremity takes 30 to 45 minutes and is painful; pain medication may be necessary. Have the frostbitten patient lie down and elevate the injured part.

Blisters often emerge during rewarming; do not rupture them. Gently wash any open wounds or already ruptured blisters with a skin antiseptic, and cover them with sterile dressings loose enough to accommodate some swelling. Patients require additional treatment in a hospital setting to minimize secondary effects.

Immersion Foot

Also called trench foot, immersion foot occurs when a person's feet are wet and cold for a prolonged period, from several hours to days. The injury is believed to be caused by constriction of blood vessels to prevent heat loss, resulting in skin damage that, if untreated, can lead to tissue death. Infection and gangrene may occur in severe cases. Immersion foot can occur after a climber wades across a stream and hikes for several hours with wet boots and soggy feet, or on a long trip when the feet stay damp for days. Immersion foot results in pale, pulseless, tingling feet; typically, the unhappy mountaineer discovers these symptoms in the tent at night. Prevention consists of keeping the feet dry for at least eight hours a day.

Treat immersion foot by drying, gently rewarming, and slightly elevating the feet. Following rewarming, the affected feet shift through a painful phase that may last for several days in which they fill with congested blood and other body fluids; they become reddened and swollen, with a bounding pulse. It may be necessary to cool the feet to tone down the intensity of this phase. After the feet have been rewarmed, the climber may not be able to walk for 24 to 48 hours due to pain. The patient is also at a higher risk for recurrence of immersion foot.

CONDITIONS RELATED TO ULTRAVIOLET RADIATION

Intense ultraviolet (UV) radiation from the sun, particularly reflected off snow and ice, can burn human skin at high altitudes. For every 1,000 feet (about 300 meters) above sea level, UV radiation increases about 5 to 6 percent. Burn injuries from overexposure to UV radiation are potentially serious but preventable.

Sunburn

Cloud cover does not effectively filter out UV radiation. Certain medications such as tetracycline, sulfa drugs, and diuretics can increase the skin's sensitivity to sun. Burned skin can range from bright red to blistered. Treat sunburn like any other burn: cool the burned area, cover it, and treat for pain. In particular, cover blistered areas with sterile dressings to minimize risk of infection.

The most effective prevention methods are to cover exposed skin with clothing and to use adequate sunscreen. Special clothing with an ultraviolet protection factor (UPF) rating is unnecessary; tightly woven clothing effectively screens UV radiation. Wear a hat with a wide brim or a sunshirt with a hood to protect the back of the neck as well as the face and ears. A handkerchief, neck gaiter, or thin balaclava can help cover the face. (See 3. Sun Protection in Chapter 2, Clothing and Equipment.)

Snow Blindness

Ultraviolet keratitis, commonly called snow blindness, is a potentially serious problem that results when UV radiation burns the outer layers of the eyes. The cornea (the clear layer at the front of the eye) is burned most easily. With further radiation, the eye's lens can become burned as well. Snow blindness sets in 6 to 12 hours after the UV radiation exposure. Dry, sandy-feeling eyes become light sensitive, then reddened and teary, then extremely painful. Recovery takes at least a full day.

Preventing snow blindness is straightforward. In high-UV environs, wear either goggles or glacier sunglasses with side shields. Choose sunglasses that block 99 to 100 percent of both UVA and UVB rays. A darkly tinted or polarized lens can filter out glare but not the burning UV light. If climbers lose their eye protection, they can fashion crude emergency goggles out of duct tape or cardboard by cutting narrow horizontal slits for each eye (see 3. Sun Protection in Chapter 2).

Treatment of snow blindness includes providing pain relief and preventing further injury. Cool compresses may reduce pain, and sunglasses help with photosensitivity. Remove contact lenses unless the patient can tolerate them and/or they are needed for evacuation. Advise the patient to avoid rubbing their eyes and to rest. There is no evidence to support therapeutic bandaging of the eyes. Topical antibiotic ointments, anti-inflammatories, and systemic pain medications may be used. Recheck for light sensitivity at half-day intervals.

HIGH-ALTITUDE CONDITIONS

At increasing elevations, atmospheric pressure, air temperature, and humidity decrease while UV radiation increases. It becomes difficult to climb as efficiently or powerfully as at lower elevations. As elevation increases, the body's organs and tissues struggle to get adequate oxygen. Eventually, climbers enter a state of reduced oxygen called hypoxia, which is greatest during sleep.

One physiological adaptation to high-altitude hypoxia is an increase in the rate and depth of breathing. After ascending to high altitude, a climber's respiratory rate continues to increase for several days. This increase also results in greater expiration of carbon dioxide, which lowers dissolved carbon dioxide in the blood. Another normal adaptation to high-altitude hypoxia is that the kidneys send more water to the bladder as urine, ridding the body of more fluid. This diuresis makes the blood slightly thicker; the change begins promptly on ascent and continues for several weeks. Eventually the body produces a greater number of red blood cells to increase oxygen-carrying capacity.

Although the body adapts to high altitude, complete acclimatization takes time—and the single most critical reason people get sick at high altitude is that they ascend too high too fast. Effects can include insomnia and altered vision as well as acute mountain sickness, high-altitude cerebral edema, and high-altitude pulmonary edema. The most important way to prevent altitude illness is to undertake a slow ascent to high elevation. On lengthy trips above 10,000 feet (about 3,000 meters), limit increases in sleeping elevation to about 1,000 to 1,500 feet (about 300 to 460 meters) per night. Two or three times a week, allow an additional night at the same elevation as the night before. Be sure to maintain adequate fluid intake.

Insomnia

The ability to sleep soundly deteriorates at high altitude. Most mountaineers have insomnia at altitude, waking up more often and getting less deep sleep. Commonly, mountaineers may experience an irregular breathing rhythm—periods of apnea (no breathing) interspersed with periods of hyperventilation, an alternating rhythm known as Cheyne-Stokes respiration—while sleeping and sometimes while awake too. The blood's low carbon dioxide content appears to drive this odd change in breathing. A small dose of acetazolamide (see Acute Mountain Sickness, below) at bedtime decreases Cheyne-Stokes respiration and may aid sleep. New evidence suggests that prescription sleeping pills help with insomnia at altitude; despite concerns that they depress respiration, they have been used at altitude without adverse consequences.

Altered Vision

Hypoxia at altitude causes temporary edema and thickening of the corneas, which may cause increased farsightedness and decreased visual acuity in climbers who have had the radial keratotomy (RK) procedure. One approach is to take along glasses or goggles of different corrective prescriptions. Research is unclear as to altitude effects on laser-assisted in situ keratomileusis (LASIK) or photorefractive keratectomy (PRK).

At high altitude, an increase in retinal blood flow and subsequent retinal vein dilation can lead to retinal hemorrhages in many climbers. If climbers develop altered vision, they should descend. The presence of high-altitude retinal hemorrhage has been associated with altitude illness.

Acute Mountain Sickness

At least half the people who live at sea level and travel rapidly to moderate altitude—8,000 to 14,000 feet (2,400 to 4,300 meters)—experience some degree of acute mountain sickness (AMS). These nonspecific symptoms can resemble a case of flu, a hangover, or carbon monoxide poisoning. Headache is the cardinal symptom, often accompanied by fatigue, loss of appetite, nausea, and, occasionally, vomiting (see the "Signs of Acute Mountain Sickness" sidebar). Often localized in the occipital or temporal areas, a headache will start usually after 2 to 12 hours at a higher altitude, and often the first night or the next morning.

AMS can vary widely in severity but generally resolves with 24 to 72 hours of acclimatization. Controlling the rate of ascent, in terms of the elevation gained per day, is highly effective at preventing acute altitude illness. The altitude at which someone sleeps is considered more important than the altitude reached during waking hours.

AMS can progress in severity. When symptoms such as headache and nausea progress, a descent of 2,000 to 3,000 feet (about 600 to 900 meters) in elevation is the best treatment. If the condition improves on descent, the diagnosis of AMS is confirmed. It is important to differentiate AMS from the more ominous high-altitude cerebral edema (HACE) and high-altitude pulmonary edema (HAPE); see below.

Some medicines can be used to deal with altitude-related health problems; climbers can ask their physician about the appropriateness of such drugs for their situation. Acetazolamide (Diamox) has an established role in preventing

SIGNS OF ACUTE MOUNTAIN SICKNESS

People with AMS usually have a headache, plus one of the following:

- Insomnia
- Listlessness and/or lassitude
- Loss of appetite
- Nausea
- Vomiting
- Lightheadedness or dizziness that worsens when upright

AMS. It is ideal to start acetazolamide the day before ascent, though it still has beneficial effects if started on the day of ascent. Some mountaineers use it through the first 48 hours at high altitude to prevent AMS or block its recurrence. Potential adverse effects are tingling of the extremities, ringing in the ears, nausea, frequent urination, and a change in the sense of taste. It is better to test this possibility at home. Acetazolamide does appear to be effective in preventing and treating AMS as well as mitigating the respiratory changes brought on by high altitude.

The steroid dexamethasone is used in preventing and treating AMS as well as HACE and HAPE. It is usually reserved for treatment of these conditions or when rapid elevation gain prevents normal acclimatization, such as in very high-risk situations—for example, when military or search and rescue personnel are airlifted to altitudes above 11,500 feet (3,500 meters) and must immediately be physically active. Dexamethasone should be used only in these limited circumstances. It does not facilitate acclimatization like acetazolamide, but it can help prevent AMS. Start dexamethasone the day before ascent, though it still has beneficial effects if started on the day of ascent.

High-Altitude Cerebral Edema

High-altitude cerebral edema (HACE) may be a severe manifestation of AMS: HACE rarely arises out of the blue, occurring more often as a progression of AMS. Generally, it takes from one to three days at high altitude for HACE to develop. Vessels in the brain respond to the stress of high altitude by becoming leaky, resulting in the brain swelling with increased fluid. Ultimately, the brain swells inside its rigid container of cranial bones. HACE usually develops in climbers above 10,000 feet (about 3,000 meters) who are not acclimatized, although it can occur as low as 8,500 feet (2,600 meters).

Early signs of this deadly condition include deteriorating coordination, headache, loss of energy, and altered mental status, ranging from confusion or signs of not thinking clearly to hallucinations. Use the coordination test: ask the person to walk an imaginary tightrope for 15 feet (about 5 meters), heel to toe, to check for impaired coordination. Nausea and forceful vomiting may be present. Once HACE develops, it may advance rapidly. The patient may become somnolent and lapse into a coma.

HACE is deadly. Descent is critical to survival. Descending to a lower elevation remains the single best treatment for AMS and HACE. Individuals should then stay at a lower elevation until symptoms resolve, unless terrain, weather conditions, or injuries make descent more dangerous than the condition. Symptoms typically resolve following descent of 980 to 3,300 feet (300 to 1,000 meters), but the required altitude decrease varies among individuals. Climbers suffering from HACE should not descend alone.

Some expeditions use a portable hyperbaric chamber (such as the Gamow bag) to create an artificial lower elevation in the effort to stabilize a patient for a few hours. Supplemental oxygen can also be helpful. Drugs such as dexamethasone are beneficial; acetazolamide may be part of the treatment.

High-Altitude Pulmonary Edema

In high-altitude pulmonary edema (HAPE), body fluids leak into the lungs to a degree that interferes with respiration. A different disease from AMS or HACE, HAPE can occur quite suddenly in climbers who are otherwise performing well. Occasionally, HAPE and HACE do occur together.

Early signs of HAPE may overlap with more-benign problems, such as a persistent cough caused by simple bronchial irritation from dry high-mountain air. Decreasing ability to exercise, needing to take more frequent rest breaks, or falling behind companions may be subtler signs of HAPE. Breathlessness and a hacking cough appear as HAPE develops. Breathing rate and pulse increase.

If HAPE is allowed to advance, breathing requires effort and includes bubbling noises. Lips and nail beds may appear dusky or tinged with blue, reflecting the body's inability to transfer oxygen into arterial blood. Some affected people also develop a low-grade fever, making it difficult to distinguish HAPE from pneumonia; one indicator of HAPE is how rapidly it worsens with continued ascent. HAPE is a potentially fatal condition, and survival depends on a rapid response.

The key to treating HAPE is to descend. A descent of 3,000 feet (900 meters) will resolve nearly all HAPE cases that are caught early. If descent is impossible, supplemental oxygen and portable hyperbaric therapy (a Gamow bag) are useful. Ultimately, however, real descent must occur.

In the field, where resources are limited, nifedipine, a drug that enlarges blood vessels (a vasodilator), can be used in addition to descent, oxygen, or a Gamow bag. Nifedipine should be used as primary therapy only if none of these other measures are available. Studies suggest that other vasodilators, including tadalafil and sildenafil, also can be used for treatment of HAPE in both men and women,

24

particularly when descent is not feasible. Using multiple pulmonary vasodilators at the same time is not recommended due to concerns of provoking abnormally low blood pressure. A climber who develops HAPE should not consider ascending to a higher altitude until symptoms have resolved completely and the person maintains stable oxygenation while off supplemental oxygen and vasodilators, both at rest and during mild exercise.

Injuries

This section describes injuries ranging from milder (more common) to more serious (less common). One study of the National Outdoor Leadership School's courses over five years showed that 80 percent of injuries suffered by course participants were sprains, strains, and soft-tissue injuries. To minimize injuries, apply first aid as described below. Specific treatments for serious injuries are beyond the scope of this book, so hands-on instruction in mountaineering first aid is essential (see Resources).

BLISTERS

Nearly everyone dreads blisters. These bubbles under the skin, filled with clear or blood-tinged fluid, are the most common health-related reason for ending or truncating wilderness outings. Small blisters are a source of minor irritation and discomfort, but larger blisters can cause significant pain and can lead to serious infection and ulceration if they rupture. Blisters result from friction where the skin rubs against a sock and/or the inside of a boot. Blisters often happen when boots are too large or too loosely laced or when socks are lumpy or wrinkled. Moisture tends to soften the skin, so wearing wet boots or socks promotes blister formation.

To prevent blisters, fit boots properly, and break them in slowly and thoroughly. The areas most prone to blistering are over the heel or Achilles tendon at the back of the ankle and on the toes. If you blister easily, pad the blister-prone areas with blister tape (for example, Leukotape), a blister cushion (such as Compeed), or adhesive foam, but do not pad them so much that you create a new pressure point. Keep feet dry, and wear adequate, well-fitting socks. Threadbare socks can cause blisters.

A blister usually becomes noticeable first as a hot spot (fig. 24-6a), a localized sensation of heat or pain that increases in size and intensity over time. When you feel a hot spot, take measures immediately to prevent it from growing more severe. Place a generous strip of waterproof adhesive tape or a moist wound-healing dressing, such as Compeed (fig. 24-6b) or Spenco 2nd Skin, over the spot; these active-gel (hydrocolloidal) dressings can last for days. Other products include Moleskin and Dr. Scholl's Molefoam; some sufferers are successful with duct tape or waterproof first-aid tape. Avoid using adhesive bandage strips (such as Band-Aids) for covering hot spots—their nonadhesive dressing pads can ball up and rub against already sensitive skin.

Once a blister has formed, avoid opening it unless absolutely necessary, to avoid infection. The body will reabsorb the fluid after several days, and the blister will heal. Pad a blister and protect it from rupturing by layering a "doughnut" of padding thick enough to keep pressure off it (fig. 24-6c). The padding doughnut must be deeper and wider than the blister. Tape the padding to prevent it from becoming displaced.

If a blister breaks open, wash and dress it with sterile dressings when not wearing footwear, as you would treat any open wound. If you must continue to hike, treat the blister as you would a hot spot. If infection is a concern, clean the wound twice daily and apply a topical antibiotic ointment. If the wound does not improve, seek medical attention.

CHAFING

Poor-fitting clothing, cotton fabrics, dirty clothing, sweat, and sand or dirt—combined with the repetitive motion of hiking or climbing—can chafe or, in severe cases, even painfully rub away the skin. Quickly identify and eliminate the irritant and change into clean, well-fitting clothing. Using a lubricating product may help. Take immediate action—chafing will only get worse without intervention.

BURNS

Burns happen in the wilderness when climbers handle hot cookware and stoves (see also Sunburn earlier in

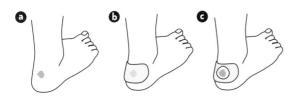

Fig. 24-6. *Blisters: a, starting out as a hot spot; b, apply tape or a dressing over the hot spot, to prevent blister from forming or to protect an emerging blister; c, doughnut-cushion a blister once it forms.*

this chapter). Burned skin can range from bright red to blistered to charred. Cool a burn within 30 minutes to reduce pain and the depth of the injury; use cold water—filtered or treated, preferably—or snow if available. Do not drain any blisters; if the skin has broken, avoid contaminating it. Cover superficial burns or those with a few blisters with a topical antimicrobial agent and a nonadherent dressing. More-extensive blistering or deeper skin damage, especially to the face and hands, requires urgent medical care and evacuation to a medical treatment facility.

Burns can also occur from friction against skin. Wearing gloves when performing activities like rappelling minimizes this risk. Treat these as you would other burns. For other kinds of burns, see Lightning Strikes later in this chapter.

EYE INJURIES
Protect your eyes in the backcountry. Sunglasses, glacier glasses, and goggles all guard against direct trauma and provide reliable protection from UV radiation. Corneal abrasions, one of the most common eye injuries in the backcountry, are usually caused by a foreign body entering the eye, a blow to the eye, or extended use of contact lenses. Symptoms include feeling as though there is something caught in the eye.

Check the affected eye and use clean hands to remove any small foreign bodies from it. Treat corneal abrasions with topical antibiotics and frequent use of artificial tears. Sunglasses may help reduce sensitivity to light, but there is no evidence supporting eye patching for corneal abrasions.

If the injury is still bothersome after 24 hours, seek further treatment. If deep scratches are apparent in the cornea or if the eyeball is ruptured, evacuate the affected individual immediately.

WOUNDS
Scrapes, cuts, and puncture wounds are common in the wilderness. The goals of wound care are to prevent infection, avoid further trauma, preserve function, and optimize healing. When providing first aid to someone else, put on protective gloves to prevent exposure to any possible blood-borne pathogens.

Thoroughly irrigate all grossly contaminated wounds with filtered, chemically treated, or boiled water as soon as possible, to reduce the bacterial load and remove foreign debris. Pressure irrigation using a syringe or a hydration bladder is more painful but also more effective. Gently scrub the wound with gauze or a clean cloth as needed.

Apply topical antimicrobial agents to reduce the risk of infection before covering the wound with a nonstick dressing and bandage. Cleaned lacerations can be closed with skin-closure bandages (Steri-Strips) or cyanoacrylate glue. Do not close puncture wounds and animal bites. Use a hemostatic gauze pad if bleeding persists.

STRAINS, SPRAINS, AND FRACTURES
Strains are injuries to muscles, while sprains are injuries to ligaments. Strains can be quite painful and debilitating; to help prevent them, be well conditioned, hydrated, and properly warmed up. Take care not to push yourself or your party too quickly. The most common type of injury that keeps a party from self-rescue and requires outside assistance is injury to the ankle or foot. While this chapter cannot adequately cover the details of fractures, emergency splinting in the backcountry can be used for severe sprains or fractures until the patient can be evacuated or rescued.

Taping an Ankle Strain or Sprain
The most common ankle sprain results in an injury to the ankle's outer ligaments. Taping a severe ankle sprain or strain, as well as some fractures, may allow a party to self-rescue; and practicing ankle taping keeps it in your climbing first-aid repertoire. The standard prescription for ankle taping is the "closed basket weave" using 1.5-inch-wide (4-centimeter-wide) adhesive tape, as shown in Figure

MANAGING FRACTURES
- Protect first-aid provider from contamination from injured person's blood.
- Assess limb and joint for circulation, sensation, and function.
- Expose injury site and control any bleeding.
- Apply dressings to wounds as needed.
- Prepare a splint.
- Stabilize injured extremity and apply splint without excessive movement of extremity.
- Use padding to fill any large gaps between limb and splint.
- Immobilize fracture site and joints above and below it.
- Reassess circulation, bleeding, and sensation periodically.

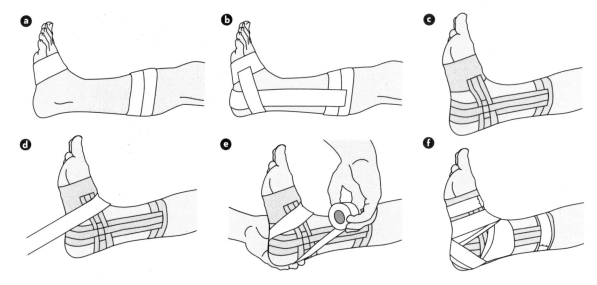

Fig. 24-7. *Taping an ankle:* **a,** *attach anchor strips;* **b,** *add U-shaped stirrup and horseshoe strips;* **c,** *create basket weave with layered U-shaped strips;* **d** *and* **e,** *apply figure-eight heel locks;* **f,** *add cover strips.*

24-7. Ideally, the skin should be dry, clean, shaven, and free of lotions or oils. To tape an ankle, follow these steps:

1. **Attach anchor strips.** First place two adjacent anchor strips all the way around the leg just below the calf (fig. 24-7a). Place a third anchor strip all the way around the foot at the arch.

2. **Add U-shaped strips.** With the foot flexed (toes pointing up), run a U-shaped arch strip (stirrup strip) from the inner calf anchor strip to beneath the foot and, under tension, up to the outer calf anchor strip. Place a U-shaped heel strip (horseshoe strip) from the arch anchor strip back around and above the heel and forward to the other side of the arch anchor, perpendicular to the stirrup strip (fig. 24-7b).

3. **Create basket weave.** Alternate three stirrup strips with three horseshoe strips, overlapping each strip by a half strip lengthwise, working from back to front of the leg and from bottom to top of the heel for a basket-weave appearance (fig. 24-7c).

4. **Apply heel locks.** Apply two figure-eight heel locks, overlapping each strip by a half strip lengthwise, as shown in Figure 24-7f: starting from the high outer ankle, descend across the inner ankle (fig. 24-7d), under the foot, around the heel, and then up the inside of the foot (fig. 24-7e) to return to the start.

5. **Add cover strips.** Add strips to cover the ends of the stirrup and horseshoe strips (fig. 24-7f).

After taping the ankle, ask about the patient's comfort and check circulation. Gently squeeze the toes; the nail beds should turn paler or white. When you release the squeeze, the toes should return to a more normal color within a second or two. If the climber develops pain or the skin turns bluish or cold or numb, loosen or remove the tape.

Splinting a Sprain or Fracture

Several principles apply in backcountry splinting (see the "Managing Fractures" sidebar above). A structural aluminum malleable (SAM) splint is highly versatile, lightweight, and reusable. Because a SAM splint can be rolled, flattened, curved, cut, or folded, it can be adapted for many types of injuries. Pad the splint well, to avoid damaging superficial tissues, by wrapping elastic bandages around it or by covering the injured limb with a soft material.

Immobilizing a limb or joint to its natural anatomic alignment, splinting offers tremendous pain relief and can make even a severe fracture tolerable. A SAM splint can be doubled to brace a neck injury (fig. 24-8a). When splinting an extremity, immobilize the joints above and below the injury (fig. 24-8b); splint the injury in a comfortable and natural position. In an upper-extremity injury, the patient

SAM splint

Fig. 24-8. *Stabilizing an injured area with SAM splint:*
a, *doubled to brace neck;* ***b,*** *doubled over to appropriate length to splint forearm or wrist;* ***c,*** *splinted arm or hand immobilized with triangular bandage;* ***d,*** *wrapped around foot and secured with bandannas to splint ankle. Stabilizing an injured area with improvised available materials:*
e, *injured finger taped to adjacent finger;* ***f,*** *injured leg splinted with ice axe, trekking pole, and sleeping pad and secured with cloth strips.*

will generally cradle their injured arm in toward their chest using their uninjured arm. Splint the injured arm in this position and immobilize it with a triangular bandage (fig. 24-8c). For a lower-extremity injury, contour the splint around the foot and up each side of the leg to make it as comfortable as possible and in line with the patient's body (fig. 24-8d).

In mountain environments, you will often have to improvise to create a splint. For example, a lower-leg injury can often be protected by taping the injured leg to the uninjured leg. Similarly, an injured finger can be temporarily secured to the adjacent finger (fig. 24-8e). Splints can be fashioned from a wide variety of materials, including sticks and mountaineering equipment such as a backpack's internal stays, a rolled-up backpack, sleeping pads, trekking poles, or an ice axe (fig. 24-8f). Spare webbing, twisted duct tape, bandannas, clothing, or athletic tape can secure an improvised splint.

Following a severe sprain or fracture, it is normal for the area to swell for hours. Avoid applying a splint too tightly, which can impair circulation to the affected area. After applying a splint, periodically reassess it by checking below the injury for pulse, skin temperature, and sensation. To minimize swelling, wrap a bag of snow or ice in the elastic bandage that secures the splint, but do not apply snow or ice for more than 20 minutes at a time, to avoid cold injury to soft tissue. Elevating an injured extremity helps minimize swelling.

HARNESS SUSPENSION TRAUMA
A motionless climber hanging from a harness faces a life-threatening emergency. Harness leg straps restrict blood flow, which leads to blood pooling in the legs and lowered core blood pressure. The loss of blood pressure may lead to death within minutes. The priority is to end suspension.

If possible, lower the climber to a ledge. If the climber is conscious, ask them to move their legs, transfer weight to any available feature, or stand in aiders improvised from slings or a prusik. If a climber is unconscious, have a rescuer immediately raise and keep the legs horizontal until the climber can be relocated. Have the rescued climber lie flat to help restore normal blood circulation and body chemistry. Monitor and treat any secondary effects.

HEAD, NECK, AND BACK INJURIES
Head and spine injuries are common causes of death in wilderness accidents. Blunt force injuries are often caused by falling objects, such as rock or ice, or in a fall onto the head or back. For all head injuries, assume that there is a neck

24

INDICATORS OF POSSIBLE HEAD INJURIES

- Blunt force trauma to head or neck
- Unconsciousness
- Drainage of blood or clear fluid from ears, nose, or eyes
- Unequal eye pupil size or unequal constricting response of pupils to light
- Black eyes ("raccoon eyes")—bruising around the eye where blood collects
- Very slow pulse
- Fluctuations in respiratory rate
- Headache
- Disorientation and confusion
- Seizure
- Vomiting

(cervical spine) injury until an examination indicates this is less likely. For all cervical spine injuries, monitor the patient for potential head and brain injury (see the "Indicators of Possible Head Injuries" sidebar below).

Indicators of possible neck and spine injuries include significant pain or tenderness over the bones (midline) of the spine and numbness, tingling, or paralysis of extremities; the patient also may be holding their head and neck stiffly and very still. Some factors that may make it hard to determine if there is a cervical spine injury include head injury, severe or distracting injuries elsewhere, and intoxication (which causes a person to feel less pain and tend not to sense an injury).

Less serious injuries may be treatable by the party. A cervical collar is unnecessary with an uninjured spine or stable spine injury, including neck strains, sprains, and even mild fractures—for example, a mild compression fracture. The challenge is to determine whether the injury is serious or not. Patients who have had a minor accident, do not have tenderness in their midline cervical spine, do not have any numbness or tingling in the extremities, do not have any disability, and are able to actively rotate the neck and spine 45 degrees in each plane should not require a cervical collar. If a trauma patient is unconscious or intoxicated, it is nearly impossible to rule out a cervical spine injury.

Serious injuries to the head, neck, and/or spine can permanently disable the victim. With severe injuries, the best treatment is to immobilize the head and spine until outside rescuers arrive. Restore and maintain neutral alignment, unless such a maneuver causes the patient to resist, experience increased pain, or exhibit a new or worsening numbness, tingling, or paralysis. Do not use traction when returning a cervical spine to the neutral position. To keep the spine immobile in a neutral position, use an improvised cervical collar (see Figure 24-8a).

A patient significantly at risk of further injury or death may need to be moved. When transferring someone with possible neck injuries, grab their trapezius muscles (tops of the shoulders between the neck and point of the shoulder), place your forearms approximately at the level of their ears, and firmly squeeze their head between your forearms. Move their entire body all at once, minimizing movement of the climber's legs, head, neck, and back.

LIGHTNING STRIKES

High-mountain environments endure many more thunderstorms each year than coastal areas do, as the weather systems mass against the mountains before rising over them. Summer afternoons are the most likely time for thunderstorms and lightning to endanger mountaineers. Most lightning ground strikes occur directly below a cloud and hit the nearest high point. But lightning strikes can emanate from several miles away, shooting toward high points ahead of (or, less frequently, behind) the main thunderhead formation—"out of a clear blue sky." Therefore, mountaineers can be in danger of a lightning strike even when the storm is not directly overhead (see the "Various Ways Lightning Can Cause Injuries" sidebar). For information on how to avoid being struck by lightning, see Thunder and Lightning in Chapter 28, Mountain Weather.

VARIOUS WAYS LIGHTNING CAN CAUSE INJURIES

- **Direct strike:** lightning hits someone in the open who could not find shelter
- **Splash strike:** lightning current jumps from an object onto someone sheltering nearby
- **Contact injury:** someone holds an object that lightning hits
- **Step voltage:** a strike is transmitted along the ground or through an object (even a wet rope) near someone
- **Shock wave:** a nearby strike creates blunt trauma or a blast effect

Lightning-caused injuries include cardiac arrest, burns, and internal injuries; a victim may be knocked unconscious or temporarily paralyzed, which can lead to respiratory arrest. The most immediate danger from being struck by lightning is cardiac arrest. Lightning burns often take several hours to develop after the strike; such burns are usually superficial (similar to first-degree burns), although serious internal injuries can also occur. The eyes, a vulnerable point of entry for electrical current, can be damaged in a lightning strike. Ear damage also may occur; a patient may not respond to your questions because of a loss of hearing caused by the strike.

After a lightning strike, a victim does not present an electrical hazard to rescuers. Triage victims in reverse: direct the most care first to those who appear dead. If victims appear lifeless and are not breathing, they may have respiratory arrest from being temporarily paralyzed; perform CPR immediately. Proceed promptly with first aid, assessing P-MARCH: Pulse, Massive hemorrhage, Airway, Respiration, Circulation (shock status), Head injury and/or Hypothermia (see Responding to Accidents earlier in this chapter). Get lightning-strike patients to a medical facility, because vital body functions may remain unstable for a considerable time after resuscitation. Lightning burns do not usually require treatment (see Burns earlier in this section).

Illnesses

This section describes illnesses ranging from more common to less common. One study of the National Outdoor Leadership School's courses over five years showed that 60 percent of the illnesses experienced by course participants were nonspecific viral illnesses or diarrhea. Hygiene has a significant impact on these illnesses.

GASTROINTESTINAL DISORDERS

Gastrointestinal (GI) disorders can cause a wide range of symptoms, from a mildly upset stomach to weeks of diarrhea. The onset of any GI disorder will ruin a trip. Understanding, preventing, and treating these disorders is of utmost importance to climbers. If the party plans to head into regions with questionable hygiene and water disinfection practices, seek medical advice before the trip about adding antibiotics (to ward off infection) and antimotility (antidiarrheal) drugs to the first-aid kit. Taking such drugs is not, however, a substitute for dietary discretion or prudent water treatment practices (see Chapter 3, Camping, Food, and Water).

Fecal-Oral Contamination

In mountaineering environments, the most common cause of GI infections that entail diarrhea and abdominal cramping is fecal-oral contamination. Most often, the source of the feces is mountaineers themselves. Some rock climbing routes may be contaminated with feces. On glacier routes, handling ropes that have been dragged through soiled snow and ice can lead to contamination. Water bottles as well as food can become contaminated. Animal waste also presents a risk.

To clean your hands, simply wash them with biodegradable soap and water or treat them with alcohol-based hand sanitizer before eating and especially after defecation. This simple step helps a climber avoid many intestinal disorders. Climbers are often gregarious at rest stops, but think twice before offering your snack bag for each person to plunge a hand into; pouring food into each person's hands is less risky. Secure food and water at night from rodents and other animals (see Protecting Food from Animals in Chapter 3).

Food Poisoning

The symptoms of food poisoning—generally vomiting and diarrhea, or perhaps simply an upset stomach—arise rapidly following the ingestion of food contaminated by pathogenic bacteria, viruses, or parasites, as well as chemical or natural toxins. Symptoms tend to subside within 12 hours. Dehydration is a dangerous side effect of vomiting and diarrhea, so drink treated water and electrolytes as tolerated. You may need a few hours to regain strength.

To prevent food poisoning, use dietary discretion when traveling; avoid consuming raw fruit or vegetables, raw meat, raw seafood, and tap water (as well as ice made from tap water). Instead, stick to boiled or treated water, properly cooked meat and vegetables, bottled beverages, and reputable eating establishments.

Contaminated Water

While the water flowing in streams and rivers in the backcountry may look pure, it can still be contaminated with bacteria, viruses, parasites, and other contaminants that can cause infection in the GI tract (gastroenteritis). Pathogens can also get into a water source via infected animal feces. The incubation period of the pathogens can be a clue to the source: Bacterial and viral pathogens have an incubation period of 6 to 72 hours. Protozoal pathogens such as *Cryptosporidium*, *Giardia intestinalis*, and *Giardia lamblia* generally have an incubation period of one to three weeks and rarely present symptoms in the first few weeks.

24

Bacterial and viral infections begin with the sudden onset of bothersome symptoms that can range from mild cramps and urgent loose stools to severe abdominal pain, flatulence, fever, vomiting, and bloody diarrhea. Untreated bacterial diarrhea lasts three to seven days. Viral diarrhea generally lasts two to three days. Parasitic diarrhea, such as giardiasis and cryptosporidiosis, generally has a more gradual onset of low-grade symptoms, with two to five loose stools per day, that can persist for weeks to months if not treated. An acute bout of gastroenteritis can lead to persistent GI symptoms, even in the absence of continued infection.

For most intestinal infections associated with diarrhea, treatment during a climbing trip consists of replacing fluids and electrolytes. Mix replacement electrolytes into treated drinking water; one packet is generally equal to 1 teaspoon (5 milliliters) of salt and 8 teaspoons (40 milliliters) of sugar. If electrolyte replacements are not available, simply replace fluids. Provide palatable foods and broths with a substantial salt content. If the climber is also nauseated, antiemetic medication such as ondansetron (Zofran) can relieve nausea and vomiting and allow them to consume fluids and rehydrate.

TICK-BORNE DISEASES

Ticks are arachnids that can carry Lyme disease, Rocky Mountain spotted fever, and other infections. Tick bites may appear anywhere on the body. Anywhere from 3 to 30 days after a tick bite (7 days on average), disease signs and symptoms can appear, including fever, chills, headache, fatigue, muscle and joint aches, and swollen lymph nodes. A rash at the site of the bite occurs in 70 to 80 percent of infected persons, expanding in area up to 12 inches (30 centimeters) across and sometimes resembling a target or "bull's-eye" in appearance. Skin may feel warm but is rarely itchy or painful. A tick attached for less than 24 hours is extremely unlikely to transmit Lyme disease, although other diseases transmit more quickly. Check for ticks frequently when traveling in infested areas and during prime seasons.

Conduct a full-body check using a mirror to view all parts of your body. Examine gear for hitchhiking ticks. If you find a tick attached to your body, avoid trying folklore remedies such as coating the tick with nail polish or petroleum jelly or using heat to make it detach. Do not wait for it to detach. Follow these steps to remove it:

1. **Use fine-tipped tweezers:** Grasp the tick at its mouthparts as close to your skin's surface as possible. Do not grab a tick around its body, as squeezing the tick could express infection into the wound.
2. **Pull outward with steady, even pressure:** Do not twist or jerk the tick, which can cause its mouthparts to break off in your skin. If you are unable to easily remove a fragment of a mouthpart, leave it alone.
3. **Thoroughly clean the bite area:** Use soap and water to clean the area and wash your hands.

Reducing exposure to ticks is the best defense against tickborne infections. Avoid wooded and brushy areas with high grass and leaf litter. Repel ticks by applying 20 to 30 percent DEET or 20 percent picaridin to exposed skin and clothing; 0.5 percent permethrin applied to clothing and gear such as boots, pants, socks, and tents remains protective through several washings (see Insect Repellent in Chapter 2, Clothing and Equipment). Light-colored clothing helps you spot ticks, which are usually dark brown. After spending time in tick habitat, shower as soon as possible to wash ticks off before they attach and to find and remove them. Back at home, tumble clothes in a dryer on high heat for an hour to kill any remaining ticks.

POISONOUS INSECTS, PLANTS, AND ANIMALS

From centipedes, scorpions, and rattlesnakes to poison oak, ivy, and sumac, some insects, plants, and animals are poisonous and can cause painful or debilitating conditions. Check with sources knowledgeable about local risks and prevention for the area you are visiting.

ANXIETY AND PANIC

Mountaineering outings are usually refreshing and rejuvenating experiences. In extreme situations, such as a serious accident, most climbers must deal with their own as well as other climbers' stress, anxiety, or even panic. Some people also have a tendency toward intense anxiety in response to certain physical situations, such as exposure to heights or enclosed spaces. This tendency can erupt in a panic response during a step-across move on a cliff face or while squeezing up a rock chimney. An affected climber may freeze up. The climber may breathe rapidly (hyperventilate) and temporarily be unable to fully assess the situation; their physical movements may become clumsy, raising the potential for a mishap.

To treat hyperventilation, have the climber try breathing into a bag, which can increase the concentration of inhaled carbon dioxide and slow the breathing rate. Redirecting the climber's focus onto a useful physical task can interrupt the snowballing effect of panic. Fellow climbers can help by maintaining an atmosphere of confident acceptance and support, by pointing out retreat options, and by calmly prompting a panicked climber to use these self-calming techniques:

- Recognize panic as an adrenaline reaction to perceived risk.
- Focus on slow, steady, deep breathing.
- Run through options for prudent movement.
- Follow these options one at a time.

For more strategies to anticipate and counteract anxiety and panic, see Mental Conditioning in Chapter 4, Conditioning.

Preparing for the Unexpected

It is tempting to assume that carefully reading first-aid texts is sufficient training, but first aid is much like any other skill. People can read, even memorize, all the greatest texts on skiing, yet if they do not practice, they will not become a proficient skier. The same is true with first aid: to be competent in first aid, climbers must periodically practice and refresh their skills. The best strategy is to take advantage of the courses offered by many respected organizations.

Practicing first aid helps a climber prepare for dealing logically with the uncertainty that accompanies many mountaineering accidents and injuries—uncertainty about what happened, the nature and extent of injuries, what should be done, and the outcome. Practicing will also help you prepare for the alarm and emotion that accompany accidents. Serious accidents tend to flood people's minds with a spectrum of emotions, which can interfere with a thoughtful, rational response. Practicing scenarios in outdoor first-aid classes can help climbers learn how to respond methodically, even to overwhelmingly stressful situations. Learning tactics for keeping a cool head and having the skills to provide first aid will instill confidence that you can face whatever a climbing expedition—and the freedom of the hills—may present.

24

CHAPTER 25

SELF-RESCUE

Climbing instruction emphasizes strategies for preventing and mitigating accidents. But even the most prepared mountaineers may encounter a situation requiring first aid and rescue skills. With outside assistance often hours or even days away, a climbing party must be able to perform first aid, initiate small-party search and rescue (SAR) efforts, and work effectively with SAR authorities.

This chapter introduces techniques for small-party rescue from high-angle alpine terrain, search strategies, and guidelines for interacting with SAR agencies. If a nearby party incurs an accident, climbers should forgo their planned climb and offer them assistance.

Learning Rescue Techniques

First aid and self-rescue are key components of responding to an accident or serious illness. The skills taught in most urban and workplace first-aid classes are designed to help a severely injured patient survive for the short time it takes for emergency medical services to arrive. Wilderness-oriented first aid, in contrast, helps treat and take care of a patient for hours, possibly days, in an outdoor environment (for first-aid references throughout this chapter, see Chapter 24, First Aid). Alpine rescue involves actions a party can take to locate a missing climber, rescue an injured climber from steep terrain, and evacuate an ill or injured climber from the backcountry.

As climbers build and broaden their technical skills, they must also add to their knowledge of first aid and rescue techniques. Consider taking a course from an organization that offers classes in self-rescue (see Resources), and practice setting up and running the systems to keep your skills fresh.

The Seven Steps in Accident Response

Accidents are not inevitable. Planning and preparing, practicing sound climbing strategies and techniques, and recognizing and mitigating hazards all help prevent accidents (see Chapter 23, Risk Management). The challenges of rescuing and evacuating can be just as difficult for an ill climber as for one who is injured. Identifying a serious illness early is the best strategy. Share unusual signs and behaviors with

other party members. Discussing these clues may facilitate a prompt diagnosis and faster response. The party has more options if an ill climber can still walk. While this chapter focuses on accident rescue, many of the techniques are also appropriate for rescuing an ill climber.

Serious accidents happen unexpectedly, often stimulating an intense adrenaline response. This evolutionary response of "freeze, fight, or flight" compromises our ability to think clearly, while at the same time producing a powerful motivation to act immediately, which may make things worse and either exacerbate injuries, cause other climbers to become injured, or delay rescue efforts.

Devastating accidents can overwhelm and emotionally paralyze people. To interrupt the snowballing effect of these emotions, redirect an anxious, panicky, or traumatized climber's focus onto a useful task. Maintain an atmosphere of confidence and support while also matter-of-factly prompting the climber to focus on slow and steady deep breathing. To treat hyperventilation, have the climber breathe into a stuff sack or resealable plastic bag; increasing the concentration of carbon dioxide in the air they inhale will slow their breathing rate. Providing psychological first aid is important for helping all party members regain mental health in the months and even years afterward.

If you feel overwhelmed, acknowledge what occurred, tell yourself to address that aspect later, then focus on what needs to be done. Start with something small that you have control over. Focus on personal and team security until the party can take calm, deliberate action.

The seven steps in accident response outlined in Chapter 24, First Aid, serve as guidance for rescue response too. These steps help the party focus on the tasks they need to accomplish (see "The Seven Steps in Accident Response" sidebar below). This section provides an overview of these steps as they relate to rescue. To implement these steps in an accident scenario, see Putting It All Together later in this chapter.

STEP 1. TAKE CHARGE OF THE SITUATION

The climb leader has overall responsibility for accident response. The immediate priority is to ensure the security of the whole group. Throughout the situation, the climb leader keeps the big picture, plans ahead, delegates specific tasks, and avoids being drawn into time- and attention-robbing details. If the climb leader is incapacitated, an experienced party member will need to step forward and fill that role.

STEP 2. APPROACH THE PATIENT PRUDENTLY

The rescuer and first-aid provider need prudent access to the injured climber. In steep or dangerous terrain, they may need to climb, rappel, or be lowered to the patient. The climbers are likely to be desperate to reach their injured team member, but acting hastily increases the chance of additional injuries and delays. The party must work deliberately rather than reactively, remembering that survivors' security always comes first. Considering several solutions for reaching the patient fosters objectivity and improves the likelihood of finding the best approach. The time it takes to ensure the party's well-being contributes to a positive outcome for the entire situation. The adage "half as fast, twice as efficient" is applicable in rescue response.

STEP 3. PERFORM EMERGENCY RESCUE AND URGENT FIRST AID

Check the patient's vital P-MARCH indicators: Pulse, Massive hemorrhage, Airway, Respiration, Circulation, Head injury and/or Hypothermia. Provide life-saving CPR, manage serious bleeding, and perform other critical first aid. Do not move the patient unless they are in danger, such as from an avalanche, rockfall, icefall, or immersion in water, or need urgent first aid that cannot be administered at the current location, such as midpitch on a rock route.

STEP 4. PROTECT THE PATIENT

Communicate with the injured or ill climber to reassure them. Protect the patient from precipitation, wind, heat, cold, and other environmental factors. Move the injured party immediately if hazards such as rockfall present imminent danger. Anticipate and provide care to prevent dehydration, shock, and hypothermia, since these conditions are much harder to treat once symptoms begin.

STEP 5. CHECK FOR OTHER INJURIES

Make a thorough examination of the patient to determine what injuries, illnesses, or medical conditions exist and their extent. This may be difficult in steep terrain, so repeat this process as soon as the injured or ill climber can be moved to a more suitable location and after the initial shock of the incident has worn off.

STEP 6. MAKE A PLAN

Input from other party members helps the climb leader take all crucial factors into account in preparing the rescue plan. To recall these steps, remember the acronym **WE-RAPPED.**

Weather. Take into account anticipated temperature, wind, and precipitation, which may impact both the patient and the rescue team.

Evacuation. In assessing how to evacuate the party, consider these questions: How far is it to the trailhead? Can the patient walk? If not, can the patient tolerate the rigors of party evacuation? If not, outside assistance is needed—where is the best place to wait? Where is there helicopter access?

Rope. Is roped climbing required to reach the patient, move rescue personnel, or send a messenger for help? Will a rope system be required to raise or lower the patient?

Assistance. Are there climbing parties nearby who can help? Unless it is obvious that the injured climber can self-evacuate, seek additional assistance. It is better to have outside assistance on the way—even if it turns out later that it might not have been needed—than to delay the request until need is certain, because it typically takes hours for rescuers to mobilize and reach the site. Phones are unreliable in the backcountry, so also carry emergency communication devices, such as a satellite communication (satcom) device, or personal locator beacon (PLB), or satellite phone to initiate outside rescue assistance.

Patient. Is the patient improving, stable, or deteriorating? Is the patient at a good location? Can the patient be moved without significantly aggravating their injuries?

Party. Are other members of the group injured or traumatized? To ensure traumatized survivors do not inadvertently endanger themselves or wander off, they may

25

need to be secured to an anchor or relocated to a prudent location. What are the party's capabilities? Does the team need food, water, or rest? Can they remain on-site for several hours or overnight?

Equipment. What equipment is available? What can be done with the available equipment? Was any important equipment lost or damaged in the accident?

Daylight. How much daylight is left? Everything will be much harder after dark. What are the nighttime impacts?

Once the **WE-RAPPED** assessment is complete, the team puts together a plan of action, which initially may be more conceptual than detailed. The party can expect to modify their plan as they gather new information and the situation changes.

STEP 7. CARRY OUT THE PLAN

As the party carries out the plan prepared in step 6, they must continually assess the team and situation so that they can adjust the plan. With the leader focused on the overall situation, climbers focused on specific tasks may suggest improvements to the plan.

Rescue

When an injured climber or stranded hiker is on steep terrain, a team may need to use ropes to lower or raise the patient. Figure 25-1 gives an overall picture of what this may look like: a lowering system that may be a main rescue line (fig. 25-1a) and belay line (fig. 25-1b), with anchors that are SERENE (Solid, Efficient, Redundant, Equalized, and with No Extension) (fig. 25-1c), and a climber anchored near the edge (fig. 25-1d) to communicate with the rescuer as she stabilizes the patient (fig. 25-1e). For knots and anchors, see Chapters 8, Essential Climbing Equipment, and 10, Belaying. The climber controlling the lowering at the anchor may choose to add a carabiner redirect, as shown in Figure 25-1a, or use a standard belay device, but only if she finds the load to be controllable using the latter method.

THE SEVEN STEPS IN ACCIDENT RESPONSE

1. Take charge of the situation. .
2. Approach the patient prudently.
3. Perform emergency rescue and urgent first aid.
4. Protect the patient.
5. Check for other injuries.
6. Make a plan.
7. Carry out the plan.

THREE WAYS TO TEST A ROPE SYSTEM

Evaluate a rescue rope system using these three field tests:

- **Whiteboard analysis.** Look at all the components of the rescue system to ensure they will do what is intended, such as catch a fall or provide the desired mechanical advantage.

- **Critical-points examination.** Take a second look at every component in the rescue system to ensure all necessary points are backed up so that if a single piece of gear fails or a person slips or loses their grip, it will not cause a serious or fatal accident.

- **Whistle test.** If, at the sound of a whistle, every person takes their hands off the system, would the system prevent a fall?

Instead of one main rescue rope and one belay rope, a twin-tension rope system can be used, where both ropes share the load as equally as possible and are tensioned equally by rescuers during all phases of operation. The rope setups are usually identical: that is, two systems, each using a belay device that may be redirected to provide additional friction if needed.

RISK MANAGEMENT

In a stressful rescue situation, ensuring security is paramount. Humans tend to underestimate hazards during an emergency and take dangerous shortcuts. A climbing party must guard against this tunnel-vision urgency, which can make the situation worse.

To contribute to party security, everyone continually observes and analyzes the plan, rope systems, activity, and environment for hazards. Before a party uses a raising or lowering system, a party member who was not involved in constructing the system needs to inspect every component. This redundant check is an important safeguard for catching stress-induced errors (see the "Three Ways to Test a Rope System" sidebar).

Redundant components significantly improve the risk management of a raising or lowering system. The probability of both components failing is the product of the failure rates of each independent component, comparatively a much smaller number. Independent backups are one way to provide system redundancy. For example, a separate belay rope system provides redundancy to the primary rescue rope system. Twin-tension rope systems offer redundancy, as each system is capable of supporting the rescue load by itself.

EQUIPMENT CONSIDERATIONS

Modern climbing protection and belay systems are designed to absorb or transfer the forces generated by a one-person, not a two-person, fall—yet rescue situations may require that two people be supported by the rope and gear. Because typical climbing gear and protection placements may not be strong enough to withstand the fall of two people, to securely use recreational climbing gear in a rescue, lowering

Fig. 25-1. *Small-party rescue:* **a,** *lowering system on rescue rope using a belay device and prusik, with a climber tending the prusik;* **b,** *belay rope with climber tending to tandem prusik belay with tension-release hitch (could use a second redirected control device and prusik instead);* **c,** *SERENE anchor;* **d,** *climber anchored near edge, communicating;* **e,** *rescuer stabilizing patient in front of her.*

25

and raising systems must be designed to minimize the potential fall factor and be built to withstand higher fall forces. For example, strive to raise and lower from solid anchors that are best aligned for the rescue situation.

Anchors

Strong anchors are the foundation of rescue systems. Due to the probability of two people relying on the anchor, it must be very strong. Follow the principles of building SERENE anchors, just as the party would when climbing, until everyone is confident the anchor system will not fail (see Belay Anchors in Chapter 10, Belaying). A basket hitch around a tree is a strong anchor that is easy to set up and remove (fig. 25-2). If it is the only option, a single tree that appears healthy and well rooted and that provides appropriate alignment for the rescue system should be adequate to anchor both rope systems in nearly all rescue scenarios.

Snow and ice anchors are weaker than rock anchors, so create them using several linked pieces of protection (see

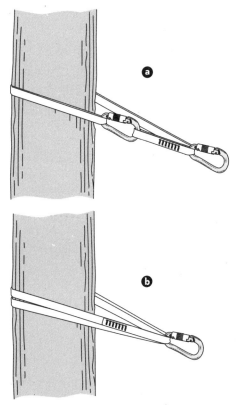

Fig. 25-2. *Basket-hitch variations around a tree:* **a,** *using two carabiners;* **b,** *using a single carabiner.*

Snow and Ice Anchors in Chapter 16, Basic Snow and Ice Climbing, and Placing Protection in Chapter 17, Technical Snow and Ice Climbing).

A prusik hitch may be useful to connect pieces of protection to the rope and fine-tune load distribution within the anchor system (see Friction Hitches in Chapter 8, Essential Climbing Equipment). In the event of a fall, an anchor with legs of similar length will better distribute forces among the pieces of protection.

Ropes

Designed for a single climber, dynamic climbing ropes typically stretch 6 to 10 percent under the weight of one suspended person; when 30 meters (100 feet) of a dynamic rope is extended, it will stretch 2.5 meters (nearly 8 feet). The amount of stretch increases with a two-person load. On a steep face, this stretch translates into a rubber-band-like effect: each time the patient and rescuer hang freely, the rope stretches; each time they transfer weight to a feature or ledge, the rope contracts. For example, during a two-person lower, after stepping from a small ledge onto a face, the pair could drop several feet during the rope extension, potentially striking something. The sheath on climbing ropes is subject to more abrasion with a two-person load than with a one-person load, and the rubber-band-like stretching accentuates this abrasion. Pad places where the rope runs over sharp edges as you are able.

The original climbing rope may have been damaged in the fall. Prudence calls for transferring the patient to a different rope, if possible. A low-stretch or static rope is better suited for a rescue (see Ropes in Chapter 8). Such ropes are, however, unsuitable for catching a fall, and the anchor system must be built to handle large forces since less energy is dissipated through rope stretch.

When a party performs a rescue, distinguish ropes by labeling them according to their function. The rope used to raise or lower a patient and/or a rescuer becomes the "rescue rope." A backup rope used whenever two people are raised or lowered becomes the "belay rope." Or for a twin-tension rope system, the party could refer to the rope color or the name of the person operating it.

Descent Control Method

Most belay and rappel devices are designed to belay either one or two individual climbers. Incorporate additional friction, such as by using a redirect, when controlling a rescue load if the normal belay method proves difficult. The double munter hitch (see Figure 25-4b) also provides sufficient friction for two-person rescue loads.

Pulleys

In a raising system, even the best pulleys suffer friction losses. Due to these frictional losses, a theoretical 3:1 pulley system may have a real ratio of 2.7:1 or less; a 9:1 (3:1 on a 3:1) pulley system will have an actual ratio of between 6:1 and 7:1 (see Figure 25-6). If you do not have enough pulleys, carabiners can be used without pulleys, but they will introduce more friction into the system. Since pulleys will almost always be in short supply, use the best pulleys nearest the hauling end of the rope for best overall efficiency.

Prusiks

Prusiks are useful as rope grabs. Prusiks in combination with a pulley simplify the resetting of raising systems by enabling rescuers to hold the load during resets. They act as an automatic, hands-free belay if the belayer must temporarily let go of the belay rope to help pull when raising, or if the belayer is forced to let go by rockfall, bees, or other problems. Prusiks can be used to piggyback supplemental anchor protection and mechanical-advantage systems to the rescue rope.

The development of sewn eye-to-eye prusik material, such as the Valdotain Tresse (V-T) prusik, enables tying of asymmetric prusik hitches that are releasable under load. These eliminate the need for including a tension-release hitch to transfer load from a loaded standard prusik.

Tension-Release Hitch

The tension-release hitch, or TRH, is used to release tension on a weighted rope system. It consists of a prusik(s), a locking carabiner, a figure eight on a bight, and a munter hitch around a pear-shaped locking carabiner with a mule knot finish (see Figure 25-3b).

Belays

The belay rope is an independent backup for the rescue rope. The belay system consists of a SERENE anchor (fig. 25-3a) and a TRH (fig. 25-3b) that includes two (tandem) prusiks spaced at least 4 inches (10 centimeters) apart around the belay rope to keep the prusiks from interfering with each other (fig. 25-3c). The belayer pulls rope through the prusiks, maintaining a few inches of slack to back up the rescue rope during the raise or lower. The slack keeps the prusiks from inadvertently tightening or grabbing during routine raising or lowering on the rescue rope. If the rescue system fails, the resulting force on the belay rope will cause it to be pulled from the belayer's hands, and the prusiks will grab the rope to catch the load. Although one prusik should be sufficient, the second prusik offers redundancy. Rescuers can then use the TRH to transfer the load from the belay rope back to the rescue rope, if necessary.

RAISING AND LOWERING SYSTEMS

An injured climber may need to be extricated from steep terrain. The party may use a mechanical advantage to help raise the climber or a friction device to lower them, if they are unable to climb under their own power. For injuries

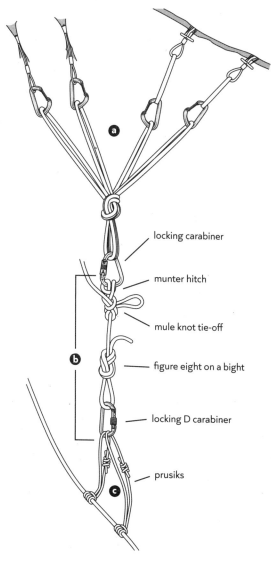

locking carabiner

munter hitch

mule knot tie-off

figure eight on a bight

locking D carabiner

prusiks

Fig. 25-3. *Tandem prusik belay with tension-release hitch (TRH):* **a,** *SERENE anchor;* **b,** *TRH—locking D carabiner clipped to prusiks, with figure eight on a bight and munter-mule-overhand knot made from tail of rope and clipped to locking carabiner;* **c,** *tandem prusiks spaced 4 inches (10 centimeters) apart.*

25

that are more severe, a rescuer can help support the patient while the team raises or lowers them both. Lowering is preferable, when feasible, due to the problems of raising with limited person-power to haul, the stretch of climbing ropes to overcome, and the potential for significant friction to develop when hauling over unprotected rock surfaces.

Commands

In addition to the typical commands outlined in Table 10-1 of Chapter 10, Belaying, a few specific to rescues are helpful. Anyone who notices anything unsafe or amiss should shout "Stop!" The rescue should not resume until the issue has been resolved. A climber may need to shout "Stop" several times before fellow rescuers understand. The rescue leader uses "Up" or "Down" to direct those operating the raising or lowering system and "Reset" when the haulers need to reset the traveling pulleys in a raising system. Those rescuers receiving the commands should repeat the commands to help ensure that everyone has heard them.

Unassisted Rescue

A single person puts less stress on the rope and anchor system than two people (see Ropes in the preceding section), so if the fallen climber is uninjured or has only upper-body injuries, the rescuers may decide to raise or lower the patient without an accompanying rescuer. The patient ties in to the rescue rope and is then raised or lowered off the steep terrain by others.

Assisted Rescue

If the fallen climber has more severe injuries, an accompanying rescuer ties in at the end of the rescue rope and, upon reaching the patient, clips a sling between the rescuer's harness and the patient's harness using locking carabiners. The patient and rescuer are now linked redundantly to each other and to both ropes.

For assisted raising or lowering, the rescuer attaches the patient to the rescue rope using a prusik hitch girth-hitched to a sling, which is then attached with a locking carabiner to the patient's harness belay loop. This setup replaces the double sling used initially to safeguard the patient. Slide the friction hitch up or down the rescue rope to place the patient alongside the rescuer, in the rescuer's lap (as shown in Figure 25-1e), below the rescuer, or on the rescuer's back with the patient's chest even with the rescuer's upper back. With an optimal adjustment of the prusik extension, the patient's weight hangs from the rescue rope and not from the rescuer; the rescuer maneuvers and stabilizes the patient as they are being moved. A second rope is used as the belay rope.

As the angle decreases, less weight hangs from the rescue rope and more on the rescuer. If the rescuer cannot manage the patient's weight on low-angle terrain, such as a wide bench, it may be helpful to have another rescuer rappel from a separate anchor and rope to assist.

Lowering Systems

It is much easier and faster to lower a patient than to raise one. To lower two people, use either a munter hitch or double munter hitch. For instance, a rescuer can be lowered to the patient using a munter hitch (fig. 25-4a), which can easily be converted to a double munter hitch (fig. 25-4b) to lower both patient and rescuer if additional friction is needed to control the load. On the rescue rope, a prusik and TRH serve as a backup. The TRH is essential to ensure the prusik can be released after being engaged. If a rescuer will be stationary for a while, secure the double munter hitch using a mule knot tie-off (see Figure 25-3b). If the party has the necessary equipment, a redirected belay device and prusik backup is another useful method to control a two-person rescue load (fig. 25-4c). Asymmetric prusiks, such as the Valdotain Tresse (V-T) prusik, are releasable under load and therefore eliminate the need for a TRH. These prusiks are versatile and worth carrying on the harness for many climbers for this reason (fig. 25-4d). Do not lower two people from a harness; instead, lower directly off the anchor.

It is preferable to lower a patient and rescuer than to use an assisted rappel. Tandem rappelling requires the rescuer to do all the work, whereas lowering allows other climbers to control the descent, stops, and raising if needed; the rescuer can focus on controlling the patient. Furthermore, if the patient becomes unable to continue during a tandem rappel, the rescuer will end up in a tough predicament. Also, there may be insufficient friction to securely control the rappel, due to some combination of rope diameter, weight, rappel device, and terrain steepness. If a tandem rappel must be used, two climbers attach themselves to the same rappel device with a rappel extension made from a double runner, and the rescuer backs up the rappel with an autoblock (fig. 25-5).

Raising Systems

A raising system multiplies the force the puller(s) can exert. The 3:1 (Z) pulley system (fig. 25-6a) is usually the most useful of the simple raising systems; for details, see 3:1 (Z) Pulley System in Chapter 19, Glacier Travel and Crevasse Rescue. When there is a two-person load or only a few haulers, a second 3:1 system can be added to the pulling end of the first 3:1 system to create a compound 9:1 raising

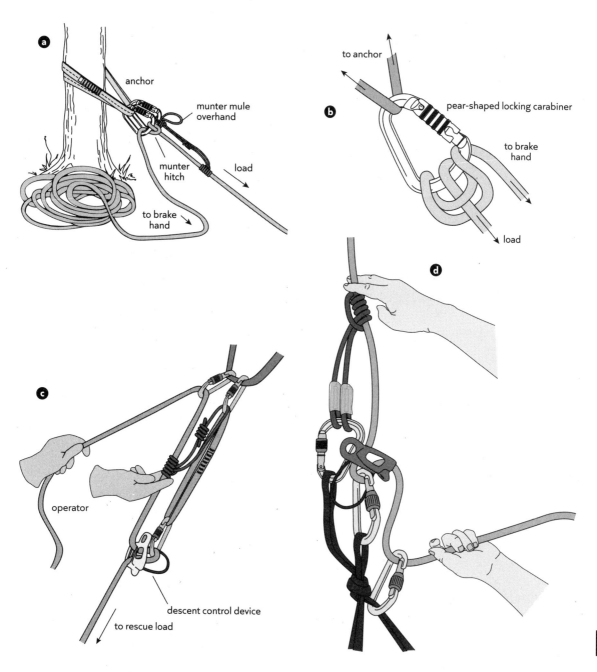

Fig. 25-4. *Lowering systems:* **a,** *using a munter hitch;* **b,** *using a double munter hitch;* **c,** *using a belay device with a carabiner redirect and prusik backup;* **d,** *Valdotain Tresse (V-T) prusik.*

25

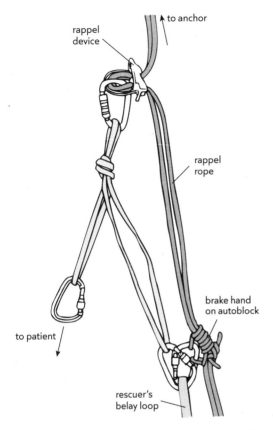

Fig. 25-5. *Tandem rappel setup with rappel extension to the patient and autoblock backup tended by the rescuer.*

system (fig. 25-6b). If a 9:1 system provides too much mechanical advantage, it can be easily converted to a 5:1 system by removing the last prusik and connecting that prusik's pulley or carabiner directly to the same carabiner as the second pulley (fig. 25-6c). The V-T prusik used in lowering will function as an excellent progress capture device for raising systems.

A fast, jerky raise makes it difficult for the rescuer and patient to negotiate broken terrain and maintain a stable position. If the rope jams and the haulers keep pulling, the system then applies its mechanical advantage to the anchors instead of raising the climbers, which may pull out the anchors. During raising, the belayer takes accumulating slack out of the belay system to keep the belay tight by pulling the rope through the tandem prusiks. When practicing rescue techniques, always use a belay rope (see Figure 25-1b).

Putting It All Together

No definitive step-by-step procedure will work for all rescues. Rescue techniques can be used to solve numerous problems that arise in a variety of accident scenarios. Following the seven steps in accident response and using the party's technical climbing, rescue, and first-aid skills will guide climbers through what needs to be done to respond to an accident in steep terrain.

This section presents possible raising and lowering solutions to a scenario in which a lead climber has fallen on high-angle terrain, to illustrate how to use the seven steps, interwoven with many climbing, rescue, and first-aid skills. In this scenario, the climbing party is made up of two rope teams of two climbers each. Each team has a rope, rack, and two-way radio. The lead climber has fallen on a steep face more than halfway through a pitch on a multipitch climb and is unconscious and out of sight of the belayer. The climbing rope has been damaged. The other rope team has already completed the climb.

Step 1. Take charge of the situation. The fallen climber's belayer arrests the fall, and after the climber fails to respond or move, the belayer radios to the two other climbers already on the summit. The belayer takes charge. The other team rappels to the belay ledge at the top of the pitch, observing the unmoving, hanging climber below. The party contacts emergency first responders by using a satcom device, or a phone if a signal is available.

Step 2. Approach the patient prudently. The top team builds a SERENE anchor system beefed up for a two-person load. One of these two climbers lowers the other, who is now the rescuer, with a munter hitch. The rescuer takes down first-aid supplies, a warm jacket, and the rack. As the rescuer is lowered past the patient's highest remaining protection, from which the patient is hanging, the rescuer notices that the sheath of the patient's rope has been stripped from the core.

Continuing down, the rescuer stops above the patient and builds an anchor in a crack while secured by the rescue rope. Using a TRH, the rescuer attaches the hitch's prusik to the patient's rope below the damaged core. The fallen climber's belayer lowers the patient onto this new anchor. The top belayer lowers the rescuer farther down to the patient, and the rescuer attaches a sling between the belay loops of both the patient's and the rescuer's harnesses.

Step 3. Perform emergency rescue and urgent first aid. The rescuer determines that the fallen climber is breathing and is not bleeding profusely but is unconscious. Concerned the patient has sustained spinal injuries, the rescuer strives to

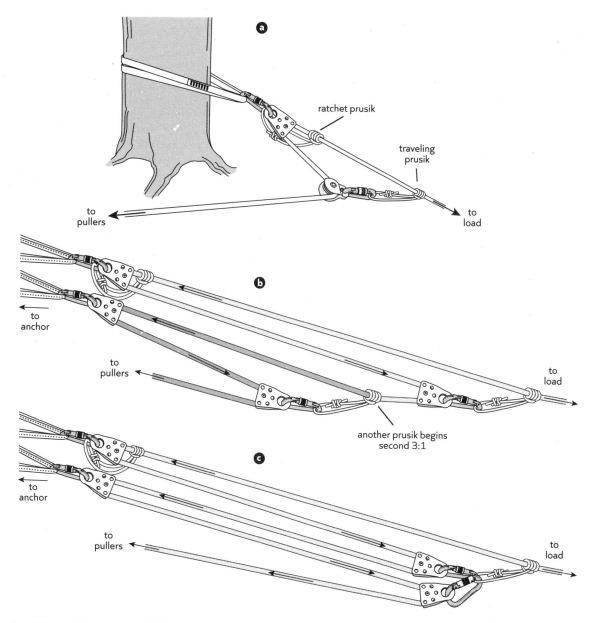

ratchet prusik

traveling prusik

to pullers

to load

to anchor

to pullers

to load

another prusik begins second 3:1

to anchor

to pullers

to load

Fig. 25-6. *Raising systems: **a**, 3:1 (Z) pulley system; **b**, 9:1 system; **c**, 5:1 system.*

minimize movement of the patient's head, neck, and spine. The rescuer places a sling around the patient's knees and attaches it to the anchor, adjusting it to raise the patient's legs toward a more level orientation to treat possible harness suspension trauma (see Chapter 24, First Aid).

Step 4. Protect the patient. The rescuer zips a warm jacket around the patient's torso and arms to help prevent hypothermia.

Step 5. Check for other injuries. The rescuer examines the patient but can find no obvious injuries.

25

FIRST SOLUTION: RESCUE BY RAISING

The uninjured climbers now continue with the remaining two steps in their accident response.

Step 6. Make a plan. The three climbers decide that the best course of action is to raise the patient to the top of the pitch and await rescue.

Step 7. Carry out the plan. The patient's belayer unties from the rope; the rescuer pulls the climbing rope through the pieces of protection, isolates the damaged core with a butterfly knot (see Basic Knots in Chapter 8), and tosses the end back down to the patient's belayer.

The rescuer now belays the patient's partner, who climbs and cleans protection up to the rescuer. The patient's partner then takes both racks, attaches a prusik backup from his or her harness to the rescue rope, and then climbs, sliding the prusik up the rescue rope (self-belaying) while also being belayed by the rescuer, until able to tie in to the unused end of the rescue rope that has been dropped down. The patient's partner removes the self-belay prusik and continues ascending, now top belayed, to the ledge.

The two climbers at the top of the pitch use the damaged climbing rope to set up a tandem prusik belay with a TRH on a new anchor, and they use the rescue rope to set up a 9:1 raising system (see Figure 25-6b). The top climbers maneuver the rescuer with the 9:1 system so that the patient can be secured to the rescuer's back with a nylon webbing carry (see Figure 25-9f). As these two are hoisted and belayed past the mid-face anchor the patient had been suspended from, the rescuer removes the TRH holding the patient. (The tension-release hitch is no longer needed.)

Once they are all at the top of the pitch, the party reassesses the patient's injuries, provides more spinal immobilization, and adds clothing and insulation to help prevent hypothermia and shock. They consider their own survival needs and resources, then prepare to wait for outside help from a local search and rescue agency.

Later the three climbers decide it makes little sense for all four to remain at the belay ledge, so two of them leave their extra clothing, food, and water and descend.

SECOND SOLUTION: RESCUE BY LOWERING

The uninjured climbers may come up with a different solution, now continuing with the remaining two steps in their accident response.

Step 6. Make a plan. In this case, the party's plan is to lower the patient.

Step 7. Carry out the plan. The patient's belayer unties; the rescuer pulls the climbing rope through the pieces of protection, clips to it with a butterfly knot beyond the damaged core, threads the rope through the new mid-face anchor, and tosses the free end back down to the patient's belayer, who builds a tandem prusik belay with a TRH (see Figure 25-3).

The rescuer connects a sling from the patient's harness belay loop to a prusik on the rescue rope, then releases the mid-face anchor TRH to transfer the patient onto the rescue rope. The climber at the top lowers the rescuer and patient on a double munter hitch while the patient's partner operates a bottom belay until the rope runs out.

The rescuer takes the belay rope from the bottom belayer and sets up a self-belay with tandem prusiks from the harness belay loop. The rope now runs from the tandem prusiks up through the mid-face anchor and back down to the butterfly tie-in on the rescuer's harness.

The top climber continues to lower the patient and rescuer to the belay ledge while the rescuer self-belays with the tandem prusiks. The top climber rappels the route, cleaning it.

Evacuation

When an injury occurs, the party may be miles from a trailhead or even a trail. The patient's condition, distance to be traveled, and party's strength determine the feasibility of evacuating the patient to the trailhead. The party may decide to evacuate the patient to a better location where they can wait for outside assistance or an area suitable for helicopter pickup.

For some time after an injury, endorphins in the bloodstream may help control a patient's pain. As time goes on, endorphin levels drop and swelling tissues may add to pain or limit range of motion. Moving a patient soon after an injury is generally less painful than waiting until later.

SNOW EVACUATIONS

The party may be able to improvise a sled with typical gear carried by the group (fig. 25-7). Spread out a tarp, bivy sack, tent, or rain fly. (Figure 25-7 shows this as an 8-by-10-foot [2.5-by-3.5-meter] tarp.) Place two skis flat on top, far enough apart (two to three ski widths) to support the patient's head, torso, and pelvis (Figure 25-7 shows this distance as 9 inches [23 centimeters]).

Then tie the skis together near the tips, midpoints, and tails with a 60-foot (18-meter) piece of 7-millimeter cord (or the climbing rope), extending the cord (or rope) beyond both ends of the skis to form the hauling end and the trailing end. Next, wrap a piece of 1-inch tubular webbing around each ski near the tips, another around

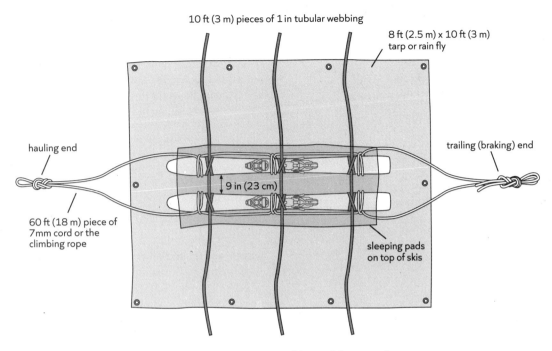

10 ft (3 m) pieces of 1 in tubular webbing

8 ft (2.5 m) x 10 ft (3 m) tarp or rain fly

hauling end

trailing (braking) end

9 in (23 cm)

60 ft (18 m) piece of 7mm cord or the climbing rope

sleeping pads on top of skis

Fig. 25-7. *Improvised sled for snow evacuation using a tarp, a pair of skis, and sleeping pads.*

the midpoints, and a third around the tails, extending the webbing out past both sides of the tarp (Figure 25-7 shows these as 10 feet/3 meters long)—the webbing helps prevent shifting, maintaining the spacing between the skis. Now place layers of sleeping pads, packs, clothing, and/or sleeping bags on the skis to protect the patient from heat loss and bumps from the ground.

The improvised sled is now ready for the patient to be placed on top of the padding. Wrap the tarp around the patient and secure the tarp with the three pieces of webbing. At the top of the patient's head, gather the tarp material together and tie a cord or sling around this point; also do this at the ends of the patient's feet. An overhand knot in the tarp material is one way of keeping the cord or sling from slipping off.

To ready the sled for hauling, make a figure eight on a bight in the hauling end of the cord (or rope) to connect to the haulers' harnesses. Also make a figure eight on a bight in the trailing end emerging from the rear of the sled, and use it as a brake on steeper downhill slopes to keep the sled from overrunning the haulers. Following the fall line is the easiest path; traversing on a firm slope is difficult. On steep slopes, lower the patient with a lowering system rather than pulling the sled.

CROSS-COUNTRY OR TRAIL EVACUATIONS

It is almost impossible to move a nonambulatory patient even a short distance off trail. Even on a trail, it takes considerable effort.

Assisted Walk

If the patient can walk, one or more rescuers can walk alongside to provide physical support. A rescuer close behind can help in difficult terrain. Have party members ahead select the easiest route and remove loose branches and other obstacles. Having the patient use trekking poles may help. Along some stretches, such as crossing boulder fields or logs, the patient may choose to scoot across on their own.

Back Carries

A strong climber may be able to carry a patient on their back for a short distance if the weight is distributed properly. The techniques described below are difficult to use off trail. Have rescuers take turns as carriers, and choose a pace that will not exhaust the party.

Coil carry. Coil the climbing rope, sizing the loops to fit from the patient's armpits to their crotch, then separate the coil in half to form a pair of loops, and secure them

25

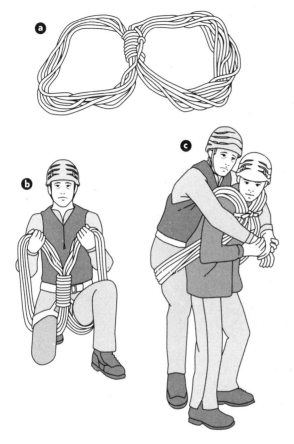

Fig. 25-8. *Coil carry:* **a,** *coil the rope, sizing it for two loops to fit from patient's armpits to crotch, then separate the coil in half to form a pair of loops;* **b,** *place patient's legs through loops;* **c,** *lift patient up so upper part of loops can be slipped over carrier's shoulders, then tie these loops together at carrier's chest with a short piece of webbing.*

by wrapping the rope several times around where the coils join, tying it off with a square knot (fig. 25-8a). Place the patient's legs through the loops (fig. 25-8b) and have someone lift the patient up so that the upper part of the loops can be slipped over the carrier's shoulders (fig. 25-8c). Then tie these loops together at the carrier's chest with a short piece of webbing.

Nylon-webbing carry. Use a 15- to 20-foot (4.5- to 6-meter) piece of 1-inch webbing and place it around the patient's back and under their shoulders, crossing in front of their chest (fig. 25-9a), then place the ends over the carrier's shoulders from back to front (fig. 25-9b). Bring these ends alongside the carrier's ribs, between the patient's legs

near their crotch, and around the outsides of the patient's thighs (fig. 25-9c), then tie the ends of the webbing together around the carrier's waist, which raises the patient off the ground (fig. 25-9d). Have the patient put their arms around the carrier's neck, if they're able (fig. 25-9e); for a lower, raise, or rappel, the patient hangs primarily by a prusik from the harness to the rescue rope, with the webbing securing and stabilizing the patient to the rescuer, and the belay rope prusiked to the webbing for redundancy (fig. 25-9f). Pad pressure points for greater comfort.

Rucksack carry. For this simple option, make slits in the sides of a large backpack near the bottom. Have the patient step into the pack as though it were a pair of shorts. Then the carrier wears the backpack as usual, with the patient as the load.

Stream and Obstacle Crossings

A rescue party may need to cross slippery streams or jumbled boulders on an evacuation. Loss of footing could prove disastrous to both the patient and rescuer. Form two lines of rescuers across the obstacle from one side to the other to provide handholds and supports for the rescuer carrying the patient.

It is easy to underestimate the hydraulic forces of swift water. It is dangerous to tie in to a rope; if someone were to slip when tied in, the rope may entrap them underwater or midstream. Instead, place a rope across the stream as a hand line, not perpendicular to the banks but at an angle downstream, so the current helps you move across. A Tyrolean traverse may be possible if it can be rigged high enough to ensure that the patient will not sag into the water (see Leading Tyrolean Traverses in Chapter 15, Aid and Big Wall Climbing).

RESCUES INVOLVING OUTSIDE RESOURCES

When the climbing party lacks the resources to deal with a search, injuries, rescue, or evacuation, it needs outside rescue assistance. Organized search and rescue (SAR) groups bring to the scene the benefits of training and experience, combined with specialized equipment and techniques. When planning a climbing trip, find out what outside agency to contact if assistance is required in that location, and include their contact information in the itinerary.

Worldwide, there are a variety of approaches to SAR. Many countries have nationalized SAR services. In urban North America, the local fire department is responsible for rescue. In the backcountry, SAR responsibility most frequently rests with the county sheriff's department for locations in US national forests and on state land; in national parks, the National Park Service is responsible. In the United States, the responsible SAR agency frequently requests assistance from volunteer SAR teams due to the SAR agencies' limited capabilities and staffing. Mountain rescue teams in the United States consist of volunteer climbers who receive training in wilderness-oriented first aid, search, rescue, specialized rigging, and helicopter operations.

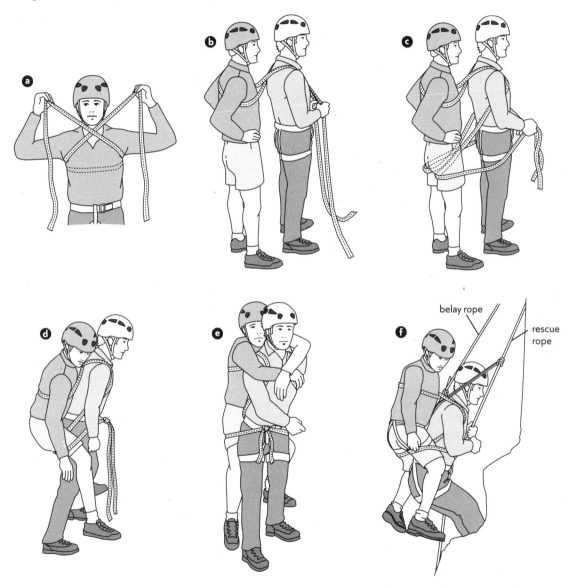

Fig. 25-9. *Nylon-webbing carry:* **a,** *place webbing around patient's back and under shoulders, crossing in front of the chest;* **b,** *place ends over carrier's shoulders (from back to front);* **c,** *bring ends alongside carrier's ribs, between patient's legs near crotch, and around outsides of patient's thighs;* **d,** *carrier ties ends of webbing together around waist, raising patient off the ground;* **e,** *patient puts arms around carrier's neck, if able;* **f,** *for a lower, raise, or rappel, patient hangs primarily by prusik from harness to rescue rope, with webbing securing and stabilizing patient to rescuer, and belay rope prusiked to webbing for redundancy.*

25

Patients in North America are rarely charged for SAR costs. In Europe and many other parts of the world, climbers are usually charged. Insurance policies for climbing may cover these costs. An expedition fee with a guide service often includes insurance, but climbers are responsible for understanding when they may need additional travel insurance.

REQUESTING OUTSIDE ASSISTANCE

It is essential to communicate clearly with the SAR agency. From a SAR perspective, the patient's location and whether the patient is ambulatory are the most important pieces of information. The next priority is information on the injury, condition of the patient, and best access to the accident site. The rescue request form in Figure 24-2 in Chapter 24, First Aid, provides a sample format for documenting this information.

A hallmark of competent climbers is being prepared for the unexpected and having the ability to summon help in an emergency. Outside rescuers can be contacted using various emergency communication devices such as satellite phones, personal locator beacons (PLBs), and other satellite communication devices (collectively called satcom devices); amateur radios and smartphones (both usually unreliable in the backcountry); or human messengers. With all devices, service may improve if the caller moves, reorients the antenna, or transmits from a higher elevation. For details, see Communication Devices in Chapter 5, Navigation and Communication.

Personal Locator Beacons

The most reliable means of summoning help, PLBs use technology similar to that used on aircraft and ships for non-land-based emergencies. The signal's GPS location is routed via satellite to the local government SAR authority. These robust, lightweight devices send signals for at least 24 hours in extreme environments.

Satcom Devices and Satellite Phones

Satellite communication (satcom) devices have richer features than PLBs (sometimes including two-way calling) but are significantly more expensive and require a paid subscription. All of these kinds of devices determine the party's position using GPS, then send a message using commercial satellite networks.

Depending on the device, climbers can enable ongoing location tracking, send notifications, summon help, and send—or send and receive—text messages. When a party is behind schedule, being able to keep friends and family informed provides peace of mind and may head off an unnecessary SAR call. Location tracking may be activated solely by the receiving agency when an SOS is initiated on the device.

Amateur Radios and Smartphones

Climbing parties save hours in obtaining help if they can get through with a radio or phone, but in the mountains and wilderness, radios and phones are limited by the available repeater or cellular signal network. Amateur radios, together with amateur repeaters, are generally the most reliable radio for remote locations; these radios are regulated by the federal government and their operation requires a license.

Where phones have network coverage, they are invaluable for communicating with outside rescuers. However, phone batteries can deplete rapidly, especially in cold temperatures, and are vulnerable to extreme temperatures (see Limitations in the Backcountry in Chapter 5, Navigation and Communication). When battery life becomes an issue, inform the SAR authorities; it may be best to shut the phone off for an agreed-upon period of time. Texting helps preserve instructions without having to write them down and saves battery life, and a phone's texting function may be able to access the cellular network when voice calls cannot. It is increasingly possible to text 911 to reach emergency call centers.

Human Messengers

In some situations, sending someone from the climbing party may be the only means of communicating with outside help. If this is the case, try to send two messengers for contingency margins. Resist rushing to send the messengers on their way. Instead, take a few minutes to make sure the messengers have everything they will need, such as car keys, the party's plans, emergency contacts, and the like; again, the rescue request form in Figure 24-2 in Chapter 24 is a useful tool for providing comprehensive information. Have the messengers carry a map (electronic and print backup) showing the patient's precise location.

Messengers must pace themselves and travel prudently, avoiding the natural tendency to rush. It is more important to be certain that they will be able to get help than to worry about the time it will take them to do so.

INTERACTING WITH SAR

For the initial call for outside assistance, use the normal procedure for local fire, police, or medical emergencies, such as dialing 911 in the United States. The dispatcher will connect the party to the appropriate SAR authority. When there is no cellular phone signal, make an SOS call via a PLB or satcom device. When no other option is available, send a human messenger to get into cellular phone range and call in a report.

Communicate the Location

The accident location must be communicated unmistakably. Use more than one way (redundancy) to describe it. Start with simple information such as the state or province, county, closest city or town, and road names. This approach may seem too basic, but heartrending stories abound of rescuers searching the wrong side of a mountain or of a desperate climbing party watching a helicopter hover over an adjacent peak. Give information such as map coordinates and datum; the type of map and its name, along with a description of the location; and the route name, including the guidebook that describes it.

The party's elevation can be an invaluable piece of information for establishing location. If you are using a GPS coordinate system, specify the datum and format, especially when using latitude and longitude, since there are several formats (see Coordinate Systems in Chapter 5). Specify whether any compass bearings are true or magnetic. When you communicate via PLB, satellite phone, satcom device, or phone, most dispatchers will be able to obtain location coordinates for the transmitting device, so it is almost always advantageous to stay put once you have made an assistance call.

Assist the Rescuers

Make an effort to speak with the rescue team that will enter the field. Mountain rescuers will have specific questions about access and route conditions that dispatchers or SAR mission leaders are unlikely to ask. This information will assist them in formulating the best strategy and selecting the most useful equipment. The party's human messengers may be asked to escort rescuers back to the accident scene.

At the scene, do everything possible to help the arriving SAR team, from having drinking water available to setting up fixed lines to help rescuers reach the accident scene. When a mountain rescue team arrives, they will assume responsibility for providing first aid and completing the rescue and evacuation. The SAR leader will look to members of the arriving teams to perform most of the vital tasks.

The climbing party can help by cooperating closely with the mountain rescuers. The climb leader remains in charge of the remaining climbing party and is responsible for its security. The climbing party may be escorted out. However, the climbing party should be prepared to lend a hand in the rescue if requested.

HELICOPTER RESCUE

Helicopters have revolutionized mountain rescue. They can deliver rescue teams to remote areas and pluck injured climbers from cliffs and glaciers, and many are capable of a significant level of life support. Helicopters can transport an injured climber to the hospital in minutes or hours, whereas ground evacuation can take days. However, do not base rescue plans on an immediate helicopter rescue just because helicopters are used in the area. Bad weather, darkness, hot temperatures, or high altitude may limit helicopter operation. A helicopter also may not be available due to another assignment or maintenance. If a helicopter can rescue an injured climber(s), the remaining party members may or may not be evacuated by helicopter.

Prepare for the Helicopter

While awaiting a helicopter rescue, the climbing party can prepare by making their location easier to see, clearing debris from a landing site, and taking precautions when the helicopter arrives.

Make the party visible. In many types of terrain, it is surprisingly difficult to see people on the ground from a helicopter. Help the crew by waving brightly colored items; flashing any lights; using mirrors, watch or electronic device display faces, stove windscreens, or shiny pots; making tracks in snow; or moving around on a contrasting background such as snow, a forest clearing, a ridge, or a riverbed. If a helicopter approaches at night, presume the pilot is using night-vision goggles. If so, too much light can be disruptive to such vision. A single small light directed at the ground is sufficient once you believe the helicopter is headed toward you. Once the helicopter has positively identified the party, it may fly off to prepare for the rescue or to land rescuers a short distance away.

Prepare the area. For an anticipated landing, clear a level area for the helicopter. Move all loose objects, such as branches and saplings, well away from a landing site. Fly a brightly colored wind indicator from a nearby location as high as possible. Secure anything that could be blown away when the helicopter lands.

Take prudent precautions. When dealing with helicopters, safety concerns are of utmost importance. Many things pose a danger, including static electricity buildup on the helicopter, as well as rotor effects such as blowing dust and debris, intense windchill, and loss of visibility from blowing rock, dirt, debris, and snow. The helicopter's downwash and noise are overwhelming; wear eye protection and climbing helmets and protect the patient from the downwash.

25

Assist the Crew

A rescue helicopter loads an injured person in one of three ways: it lands (or hovers just above the ground) and takes the patient aboard, it hovers overhead while hoisting the patient aboard, or it hovers overhead to connect the patient to a fixed-length cable. If a radio is lowered to the party, you may need to press a button to talk to the pilot. Remove any loose or sharp items from the patient and place the items inside their pack; send the written accident report (see Figure 24-1 in Chapter 24) with the patient.

If the helicopter lands: Stay out of the proximate landing area and behind protection from windblown debris. Expect a crew member, on landing, to come to you; approach the helicopter only when signaled to do so. If you must approach, do so from the front or sides of the helicopter, as long as you can stay well below the main rotor. *Do not approach from behind,* to avoid the nearly invisible low tail rotor.

If the helicopter hovers and lowers a crew member to the ground: Prepare to assist this crew member in loading the injured climber. This person will not necessarily be a climber and may be unfamiliar with glaciers, steep terrain, and prudent climbing practices. Do not touch any cables and baskets from the helicopter until after they touch the ground, which discharges the static electricity.

If the helicopter hovers and lowers a bare hook: Allow the helicopter cable's hook to touch the ground to discharge static electricity before touching it! Do not anchor the hook to the ground, and ensure that the hook and cable do not snag on anything. Expect the hook and cable to move as the helicopter adjusts to hold a stationary hover.

For the patient to remain upright when hoisted, make sure that both a seat harness and a chest harness are on the patient. Girth-hitch a single-length sling to the seat harness belay loop and pass it through the chest harness to create the attachment point. Press the helicopter hook's safety latch to open it, and place the attaching sling in the hook. If a pack is also being hoisted by hook, girth-hitch a double-length sling through both the pack's shoulder straps (the haul loop may not be strong enough) and insert the sling into the same hook with the climber; the pack will hang below the climber.

Once the attaching sling is secured in the hook and the patient is no longer attached to any anchor, make eye contact with the hoist operator and raise your hand overhead, pointing to the sky.

Searches

The Climbing Code described in Chapter 1, First Steps, instructs climbers to stay together. Separating the group sets up less experienced members for a mishap. The smaller the party, the higher the risk of becoming lost. Solo travelers are at greatest risk. If possible, do not allow a single person to descend on their own. Also, do not allow a group to become spread out in unfamiliar terrain and/or on poorly marked trails.

SEARCHES BY THE CLIMBING PARTY

If a climbing party realizes that a member is missing, it is time to initiate a search; start by devising a search plan. If bad weather, difficult terrain, or medical considerations suggest that the missing climber may need help, implement the plan without delay.

Prepare a search plan. In preparing to search, examine the topographical map for possible alternate paths the climber may have taken. Try to visualize errors the person could have made. Consider the lost person's skill level, resources, and remaining stamina. Lost people tend to head downhill and take the path of least resistance. Look at the map for inviting pathways, choke points that focus travel, and barriers that block travel altogether. Forming a careful strategy saves time and energy.

Before sending out party members, the climb leader needs to set a meeting or return time and place, based on a reasonable amount of search time. If radios or phones are available, have the search teams agree on a scheduled call-in time.

Start the search. The most effective search strategy is to return to the location where the missing person was last seen and retrace the route, looking for places where the climber could have left the path. Use whistles, shouting, or any other noisemaking to extend your reach. Look for clues, especially footprints. Inform any travelers you encounter of the search and inquire as to whether they have encountered the missing person. Prominently identify and mark all physical points (with flagging, clothing, or whatever you have available) you want outside searchers to be able to locate.

Request outside help. If, after the designated period of searching, the party members check in or meet up only to find that they have found no sign of the missing climber, it is time to request outside help. The longer a lost person is on the move, the farther they can travel and the harder it is to find them.

SEARCHES INVOLVING OUTSIDE RESOURCES

The science of searching has advanced over the years. Leaders from government agencies responsible for searches have models to help predict the behavior of lost people and determine search segment probabilities. A number of specialized SAR teams may search. Search dogs can follow scents and disturbances, while human trackers can spot signs of passage. Teams on foot and/or horseback can search less difficult terrain, and mountain rescue teams can cover steep terrain. Helicopters cover large areas quickly, while drones can sweep smaller parcels. Four-wheel-drive and all-terrain vehicles can travel rough roads and be parked and waiting at trailheads.

Each search has different needs. Once the climb leader has notified authorities, the best action for the original climbing team is to meet with the SAR leader, who will want specific information that only the climbing team can provide. The party will be directed where to meet the SAR leader, which usually means waiting at the trailhead. After an initial debriefing, the SAR leader may ask the climbing team to remain at the SAR base to answer questions that arise.

The climb leader calls the emergency contact person for the missing climber. When the climbing party leaves the SAR base, they must always leave their contact information. Friends of the missing person and other untrained volunteers are often prohibited from participating in a SAR-organized search because of liability concerns.

Going Forward

Planning and preparation help a party identify many hazards before a climb begins. During the climb, identifying and avoiding hazards goes a long way toward ensuring the party's security. Still, unforeseen circumstances do arise, so being prepared to organize and perform a rescue operation is important. Learn leadership, first aid, and rescue skills, and make sure to practice (see Chapter 23, Risk Management) the rescue techniques outlined in this chapter. Consider contributing to the community by joining your local mountain rescue group.

With the knowledge to rescue and evacuate an injured person in treacherous terrain, you will become confident in your leadership, accident prevention, first aid, and rescue skills. With such knowledge and skills, you will be more fully prepared to pursue the freedom of the hills.

25

CHAPTER 26

MOUNTAIN GEOLOGY

Some kinds of rocks are very durable, whereas others crumble under pressure. Mountaineers learn from experience that different types of rock make for vastly different climbing experiences. Having a baseline knowledge of what mountains are made of and how they are formed can help climbers more easily evaluate a destination when planning and help them assess conditions out on a climb.

Climbers can gain a better understanding of mountains by examining them on three scales: a close-up of individual rocks, a midrange view of outcrops, and a wide-angle view of an entire mountain or even a mountain range. Each perspective contributes to a broad comprehension of the mountain environment.

At arm's length, climbers can identify rock types and recognize textures that may either be difficult to climb or harbor solid holds. By focusing on specific outcrops from 10 to 100 feet (3 to 30 meters) away, climbers can identify features that could help—or hinder—an ascent: for example, a pattern of cracks is probably a good bet for nut and cam placements. Using satellite images, interactive mapping programs, and/or binoculars to examine the mountain as a whole, climbers can look for areas with strong, supportive rock and areas where rock may be weak and unreliable; for instance, sudden differences in slope angle may indicate an abrupt change in rock type. Recent rockfall is also an indicator of potentially less stable rock, which can be difficult to climb and protect.

How Mountains Form

When we step back and look at the mountain ranges on a global scale, we can see clear patterns explained by plate tectonics. Plate tectonics describes the movement of the continents on Earth's surface. The energy for this movement is the heat in the planet's core. As molten rock heats and expands, it becomes less dense and is pushed up by the hot material below it. As it moves away from the core, the magma starts to cool but continues to be forced up by heated material below it. Then closer to the surface, the cooler, heavier flow divides into two currents moving in opposite directions. The rising and sinking of molten rock creates convection currents, and these complete circles are the engines that provide energy to move continents (see Figure 26-1).

Earth's surface is composed of two kinds of plates. The continental plates are less dense (lighter) and the oceanic plates are more dense (heavier); both are floating on the molten rock below. The mountain ranges are formed when two plates run into each other (a convergent boundary). If the colliding plates are both continental plates, the contact zones will fold and form a series of folded mountains and valleys, like eastern North America's Appalachian Mountains. If the collision is between a dense oceanic plate and a continental plate, the heavier oceanic plate will be forced under the lighter continental plate. This is a subduction collision zone (heavier moves under the lighter). This collision represents the mountains of the western coast of North America.

Unique to this boundary is that heat builds up from friction as the denser oceanic plate sinks and rubs against the continental plate. Anywhere from 50 to 100 miles (60 to 80 kilometers) from the subduction boundary, there will be enough heat to melt rock and give off gases. These gases and melted rocks rise to the surface and form a string of mountains 50 to 100 miles inland from the subduction boundary. These lines of mountains can easily be seen from a plane or by mountaineers from a perch high in the mountains.

The patterns that form mountain ranges are generated by immense forces that squeeze rock masses together or pull them apart. Edges (or margins) where tectonic plates move toward each other are convergent. Margins where tectonic plates pull away from each other are divergent.

> ## KEY TOPICS
>
> **HOW MOUNTAINS FORM**
> **GEOLOGIC BUILDING BLOCKS**
> **MOUNTAIN FORMATIONS**
> **FINDING GEOLOGIC INFORMATION**

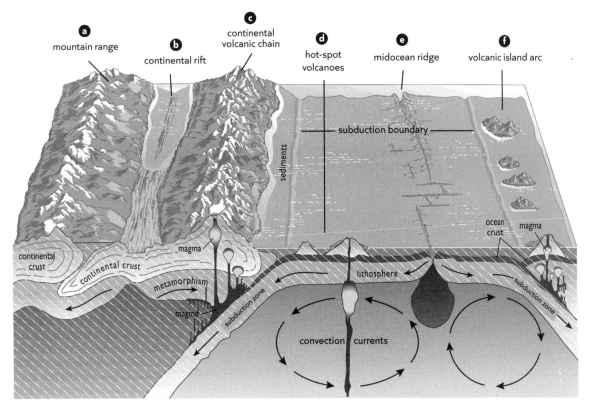

Fig. 26-1. *Features of various formations in tectonic plates:* **a,** *continent–continent convergent boundary producing a suture-zone mountain range;* **b,** *continent–continent divergent boundary producing a continental rift;* **c,** *ocean–continent convergent margin producing a continental volcanic chain;* **d,** *mantle plume inside an oceanic plate producing a chain of seafloor hot-spot volcanoes;* **e,** *ocean–ocean divergent margin producing a midocean ridge;* **f,** *ocean–ocean convergent boundary producing a volcanic island arc.*

WHERE PLATES CONVERGE

Three varieties of convergent boundaries each produce a somewhat different type of mountain: ocean–ocean margins, ocean–continent margins, and suture zones. Many of Earth's major mountain ranges are found in suture zones, where continental plates or island arcs have collided and combined as they have converged (fig. 26-1a). For example, the Himalayan range has been uplifted by the collision of two continental plates, the Indian and Asian Plates; Europe's Alps were created by the African Plate's northward push into Europe; and North America's Rocky Mountains were uplifted by the collision of numerous microplates that have extended the edge of North America hundreds of miles westward over the past 170 million years. In these mountain ranges, faulting may thrust one part of the range over another. These huge thrust-faulted structures are well

exposed in the Alps, the Canadian Rockies, and the North Cascades (see Figure 26-4).

Where oceanic crust is pushed under the edge of a continent (an ocean–continent convergent boundary), it forms a subduction zone that produces a chain of volcanic mountains on land (fig. 26-1c). This process can form three types of volcanoes. Most of the climbing destinations along these margins are stratovolcanoes (also known as composite volcanoes), composed mainly of andesite and having steep slopes, such as Washington State's Mount Rainier or Japan's Mount Fuji. Shield volcanoes, great conical stacks of basalt flows with gentle slopes, such as Belknap Crater in the Cascade Range of central Oregon, are uncommon. Cinder cones, composed of pyroclastic fragments, are generally only a few hundred feet high and tend to be of little interest to mountaineers.

26

Margins where two plates of oceanic crust converge are ocean–ocean margins. The colder, older slab forms a subduction zone by sinking beneath the warmer, younger slab. Deep within the subduction zone, 55 to 60 miles (about 90 to 100 kilometers) below Earth's surface, abundant molten rock (or magma) is formed and rises buoyantly. Over time, much of the magma makes its way to the surface, where a chain of oceanic island volcanoes grows (fig. 26-2f). The island mountains of the Aleutians, Hawaii, and Indonesia are a few examples.

As tectonic plates move, they cause various stresses—faulting, folding, and uplift—that create mountain structures (see Mountain Formations later in this chapter). These movements, as well as erosion, expose deeper layers of Earth's crust. For example, the schist and gneiss exposed in Washington's North Cascades originated as clay and silt on the seafloor 250 million years ago. During plate convergence, this material was buried as much as 100,000 feet (30,000 meters) beneath the surface, where it was metamorphosed by heat and pressure into schist and gneiss. Continued plate convergence has now moved these rocks back to the surface in the northern part of the North Cascades. To the south, volcanism has buried the metamorphic basement yet again and has built a chain of large stratovolcanoes that extends from British Columbia to Northern California. Mountain ranges of similar origin include the Andes of South America and the Japanese Alps.

WHERE PLATES SPLIT

Where plates diverge, Earth's crust is stretched and ultimately breaks apart. Divergent margins develop within continents, producing terrain of great interest to mountaineers. As the crust's plates move apart along continental rifts (fig. 26-1b), vertical faults break the crust into huge block-shaped mountains with nearly vertical faces on one side and gentler slopes on the other. These form large escarpments, such as eastern Africa's Great Rift Valley. Some mountains of the western United States, including Utah's Wasatch Range and California's Sierra Nevada, are fault-block ranges associated with stretching (extension) within the North American Plate rather than along its margin (see Figure 26-3). Mountains created by stretching like this generally have less relief (or contrasting elevations) than those created by convergent boundaries.

Volcanism also affects the topography of rifted margins. Magma from the upwelling mantle beneath the rift can rise through faults to the surface, where over time it builds up both shield volcanoes and composite volcanoes, such as Africa's Mount Kilimanjaro. The most extensive divergent margins are the submarine mountain ranges of the mid-ocean ridges (fig. 26-1e), but obviously these ranges are inaccessible to climbers.

WHERE HOT SPOTS FORM

The tallest mountain on Earth is not Mount Everest but, rather, a volcano on the island of Hawaii. Mauna Kea extends 30,000 feet (9,000 meters) above the seafloor, part of a chain of volcanic islands and underwater mountains that extend from the mid-Pacific nearly to Japan. These gigantic basalt islands form when hot spots within one tectonic plate rise up underground and burn through the crust on the seafloor (fig. 26-1d). Because hot spots produce mainly shield volcanoes with gentle slopes, summiting them rarely requires technical skills.

Hot spots can also form within a continental plate. One well-known example is the chain of volcanoes and lava flows that extends across the Snake River Plain from near Boise, Idaho, northeast to Yellowstone National Park.

Geologic Building Blocks

Rocks form the foundation of the climbing experience. Each type of rock has a different fracture pattern, surface texture, and durability, and the minerals rocks are made of affect their strength and resistance to erosion and weathering. Minerals are solid inorganic crystals, and they have unique properties such as color, hardness, cleavage (the tendency to split along definite crystalline planes), luster, and crystal shape. Most rocks in Earth's crust are made up of only seven minerals: calcite and six silicates—feldspar, quartz, olivine, pyroxene, amphibole, and biotite. These silicates, except for mica or sheet silicates, are generally hard, durable materials; only calcite is soft and soluble.

Rocks are classified into three categories: igneous, sedimentary, and metamorphic. Weathering, lichens, and biofilms (groups of microorganisms that grow together and stick to a surface) obscure the exterior of many rock outcrops. To identify a rock, look for a fresh surface that has recently broken open. Beneath a brown exterior, you may discover black basalt, white rhyolite, or even glassy obsidian. A climber does not need to be an expert in classifying rocks. However, since different types of rock require different climbing and protection strategies, it is useful to be able to identify them and plan a trip accordingly.

IGNEOUS ROCKS

Rocks that solidify from magma or liquid rock are called igneous. If the rocks form from magma that reaches the surface, they are extrusive, called lava. Because lava cools so quickly on the surface, the crystals have little time to grow large, making lava a fine-grained rock—though liquid magma that erupted as lava or ash can contain small holes from air bubbles. When igneous rocks form from magma that never reaches the surface, they are called plutonic (named after Pluto, the god of the underworld). Because they cool slowly underground, their crystals have more time to grow; plutonic rocks are classified as large- or coarse-grained rock. They can have a wide range of crystal sizes.

The two types of volcanic rock are lava flows and pyroclastics. Most lavas crystallize rapidly under conditions of supercooling, and while they consist mainly of tiny mineral grains invisible to the naked eye, they often include large crystals that formed in underground magma chambers before eruption. Most lava flows feature rock well suited to climbing. Lavas that are full of small cavities formed by gas bubbles and flows that have been chemically altered by corrosive volcanic gases (which are found on most volcanoes) are, however, crumbly and hazardous to climb.

Pyroclastics are deposits of volcanic rock fragments produced by explosive eruptions, including outcrops of ash and pumice that tend to fail unpredictably; avoid such features if possible. Many pyroclastics also show some degree of chemical alteration and thus are less stable than other rocks for anchors. Anyone climbing stratovolcanoes around the

world, from the Aleutians to the Andes to Africa's Kilimanjaro, must be aware of this potential hazard.

The most common plutonic rocks are the coarse-grained granitoids—granite, granodiorite, and diorite. Granitoids tend to be very durable, with fracture planes from weathering resulting in crack systems and chimneys, often attractive to climbers. In addition, granite tends to provide robust anchor points for climbing protection. A good way to check the reliability of protection in granitoid rock is to hit it with a hammer; if it rings, it is likely solid rock. A dull thud could indicate damage or voids under the surface, such as a flake that may break off.

SEDIMENTARY ROCKS

Most sedimentary rocks are made of one of three types of material: fragments of preexisting rocks, precipitates from dissolved rocks, or accumulated organic material (for example, coal). Rocks made up of fragments of preexisting rocks are classified according to the size of fragments. Large, coarse-grained fragments, including sand and pebbles, are transported and deposited in higher-energy areas of stream channels and beaches (fig. 26-2a). The sand grains cemented into the layered rock form sandstone; pebbles cemented into the rock form conglomerate. Small, fine particles, such as mud, clay, and silt, are deposited in low-energy environments (fig. 26-2b), such as the seafloor, where they sink and accumulate to form the layered

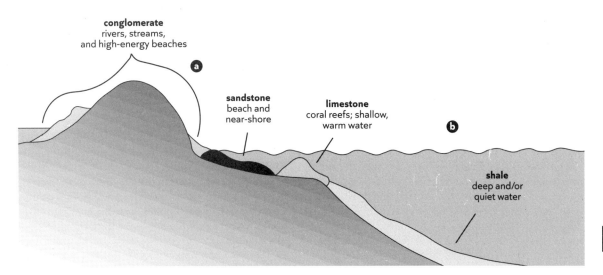

26

Fig. 26-2. *Environments of deposition of various kinds of sedimentary rocks:* **a,** *high-energy areas include rivers, streams, and beaches;* **b,** *low-energy areas include shallow to deep quiet water.*

sedimentary rock shale. Once-living matter accumulates here too, drifting down to be entombed in the rock.

Many climbers find sandstone with silica cement, or gritstone, desirable for climbing. It has continuous fracture systems, similar to granitoids, coupled with high friction from its sandpapery surface formed of quartz and feldspar grains. Sandstone outcrops commonly have reliable hand- and footholds. Unless it is highly weathered or poorly cemented, sandstone generally offers spots for climbers to place protection, but sandstone can be weak when wet. In contrast, because it is composed chiefly of soft clay, shale crumbles easily. Avoid shale if possible, but be aware that it is commonly found in layers between sandstones.

Limestones are rocks deposited at the bottom of warm equatorial seas (see Figure 26-2b). The seawater contains dissolved limestone and other minerals. The limestone rocks are formed as water evaporates. The evaporation of water causes the concentration of limestone to increase high enough that, with additional evaporation, the lime- stone begins to precipitate out of solution and form lime- stone on the bottom of the sea. Of concern to climbers, crack systems are far less continuous on limestone than on granitoid rocks. Also, limestone is composed of calcite, a soft mineral, so if protection points are stressed during an ascent, as in a leader fall, they can degrade and fail. Lime- stone that has formed below the water table before being uplifted can have many solution cavities, caves, pockets, and overhangs both large and small that make for interesting climbing.

METAMORPHIC ROCKS

Igneous or sedimentary rocks that have been stressed by heat and pressure become crystallized, with similar min- erals moving together in repetitive layering, or foliation. Each layer is a different mineral. If the minerals heat up more, they might melt. But if they cool in this crystallized state, they form a metamorphic rock. The most distinctive change—foliation, where the mineral layers are aligned like the grain in wood—is found in slates, phyllites, schists, and gneisses. From a climber's perspective, foliation indi- cates a plane of weakness in the rock—planes particularly prevalent in slate. If you try to drive a piton parallel to the foliation, a slab of rock resembling a piece of a chalkboard may easily split off. Schist, which has mineral grains coarse enough to be visible, resists splitting more than slate, but protection placed parallel to the foliation will still be poor. Most gneisses are similar to granitoids in strength, but climbers must still be alert to the foliation planes they contain.

If a sedimentary rock is made of only one kind of min- eral, then as it metamorphoses, no layers form. The mineral grains are all the same and simply fuse together. Several nonfoliated types of metamorphic rock include quartzite (made from pure quartz crystals), marble (made from pure limestone), and hornfels. A climber's favorite, quartzite is slabby, has continuous long fractures, and forms very solid outcrops. But it lacks the friction of sandstone, especially when wet, and in the alpine zone, where freezing and thawing can be extensive, quartzite can sluff off in slabs. Marble, similar to limestone, is composed of soft calcite that degrades easily and is soluble in humid climates, but it tends to have more continuous fractures than limestone. Very hard and brittle, hornfels is formed by heat along the margin of granitoid plutons. Nuts and cams work well in it, but driving pitons and drilling bolts into hornfels can splinter it.

Metamorphic changes along fault zones affect climbers. In the shallow part of faults, movement shatters or grinds rock into mineral rock fragments called gouge. Decom- position can also occur if hot fluids circulate through the fractured rock. Both the gouge and decomposed rock are dubious and feeble as holds. Deeper in the fault zone, rocks tend to flow rather than break, producing mylonites, which have intense foliation and are generally unreliable.

Mountain Formations

The movement of even the fastest-moving tectonic plates cannot be detected by the human eye, but their effect on Earth's surface is profound. This movement stresses rocks, forming mountains and moving them up, down, or from side to side and breaking them apart. Most sedimentary rocks are originally deposited in horizontal layers (or beds), but the brittle layers near the surface move along faults or fracture into joints. Where the temperature and pressure are higher deeper underground, the beds tend to bend into folds rather than breaking.

FAULTS

The fractures that the layers of Earth's crust move along are called faults. Such movement can vary widely, from shifting a fraction of an inch to uplifting an entire mountain range, such as Wyoming's Teton Range. Faults can bring layers of very different types of rock together, and fault zones can also consist of very weak, ground-up rock that may present a hazard to climbers.

Faults are classified according to their relative move- ment. Normal faults involve vertical movement that occurs

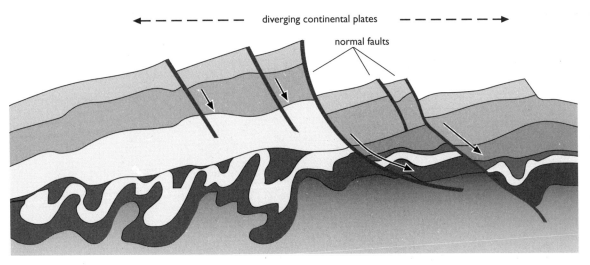

Fig. 26-3. *Typical structures that form where continental plates diverge: normal faulting forms steep escarpments where Earth's crust downslips.*

when the crust is stretched to the point of breaking, causing a chunk of crust to downslip (fig. 26-3), as in the Basin and Range region of Nevada, Utah, and California.

Vertical movement also occurs where the collision of continental plates causes compression, creating reverse faults (where a chunk of crust is uplifted) and thrust faults, which are reverse faults with an angle of less than 20 degrees (fig. 26-4). Examples include Europe's Alps and the Himalaya. Strike-slip faults move the crust in a horizontal plane, rather than up and down—for example, California's San Andreas Fault.

FOLDS

In mountains such as Colorado's Front Range, rock beds have been compressed into folds, which commonly dip steeply or are even vertical, producing a series of archlike anticlines and trough-like synclines (see Figure 26-4). These folds can range in size from microscopic to a mile or more high, in patterns creating ramps, overhangs, and resistant ridges that can be crucial factors in planning a route to a summit.

JOINTS AND VEINS

Rock masses that expand or contract can crack. When hot rock cools and shrinks, for example, contraction joints can form. Lava flows, for instance, can solidify into an array of roughly hexagonal columns typically 10 feet (3 meters) tall. The columns are examples of columnar jointing. Exceptionally tall columns such as Devils Tower in Wyoming provide spectacular climbing opportunities.

Joints also develop when erosion exposes rocks from deep within our planet. As the overlying rocks are stripped away, the once-buried rocks expand upward and fracture. If the expansion joints develop parallel to the exposed surface, rocks peel off in layers called exfoliation joints (see Figure 26-4). Half Dome in California's Yosemite National Park is a prominent example. Sets of joints commonly occur at angles of 30, 60, or 90 degrees to each other—and these angles tend to be persistent as long as the rock type is the same. Being able to recognize such joint patterns is essential for routefinding, especially on vertical faces in granitic rocks.

Veins (or fractures filled by minerals, most commonly quartz or calcite) can affect the texture of weathered rock surfaces. Quartz veins tend to project out as resistant ridges, whereas softer calcite veins are often recessed. On some sheer faces, these veins can feature the only holds suitable for climbing, so the pattern of fractures determines where climbers should look for the next hand- or foothold.

Finding Geologic Information

The primary provider of geologic maps and information in the United States is the US Geological Survey (USGS). Its website is the gateway to an abundance of geologic data for the entire world (for all websites mentioned in this section, see Resources). The USGS map locator is an interactive feature that allows users to figure out the name and location of 7.5-minute topographic maps (also see Chapter 5,

26

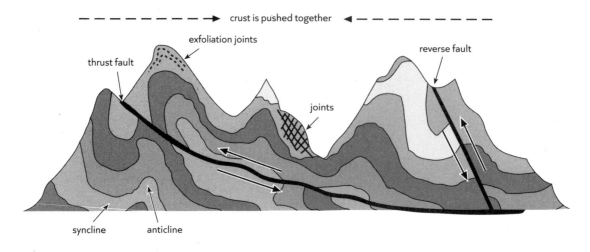

Fig. 26-4. *Typical structures that form where continental plates converge: thrust and reverse faults, folds (synclines and anticlines), and joints that sometimes exfoliate.*

Navigation and Communication). Another useful service of the USGS is the National Geologic Map Database.

Other federal agencies in the United States that dispense geologic data are the US Forest Service and the US Bureau of Land Management. Nearly all of the state geological surveys also maintain websites with abundant geologic information; links to state geological surveys are found online.

Another useful tool for planning climbing trips is Google Earth, a virtual mapping program that displays satellite images. Users can download the free program or access it online. Climbers can easily see the terrain and specific features for almost any mountain on Earth, which helps immensely with route planning. Many apps offer accessible and useful information via phones and other mobile devices, but since backcountry areas are often out of cellular data range, climbers must download what they need ahead of time for offline access in the field.

For climbers seeking a site-specific geologic map or details on the geology of a chosen climbing route, there is no better place than the nearest college or university geology department. Many have websites with a lot of local geologic information, and faculty and students are often avid climbers who know exactly what rocks and structures they have seen on different routes.

Better still, start looking carefully and making detailed notes on the geologic features of the routes that you climb. Mountaineers are in effect practicing geologists, interpreting rock types and structures as they ascend. Personal observations are the best way to learn how to read the rocks and mountains for future climbs.

CHAPTER 27

THE CYCLE OF SNOW

Understanding how snow forms, ages, and changes—the cycle of snow—helps climbers anticipate how conditions can differ from valley to chute to mountaintop. Snow changes most dramatically during storms, but it also changes during the course of a single day or over days and weeks. Subtle changes caused by exposure to sun, by wind, or by other aging processes can significantly affect the snowpack and climbers' circumstances as well.

When water vapor condenses at below-freezing temperatures, snow crystals form around foreign matter, such as microscopic dust particles, in the atmosphere. These snow crystals grow as more atmospheric water vapor condenses onto them. Tiny water droplets also may contribute to these crystals' growth. While generally hexagonal, snow crystals can vary widely in size and shape, including plates (fig. 27-1a), dendrites (fig. 27-1b and e), columns (fig. 27-1c and f), and needles (fig. 27-1d). The shape that forms depends on the air temperature and amount of water vapor available.

When they fall through air masses that have different temperatures and water vapor contents, snow crystals may combine or become more complex. In air temperatures close to freezing, snow crystals stick together to become snowflakes (aggregates of individual crystals). When snow crystals fall through air that contains water droplets,

the droplets freeze to the crystals, forming rounded snow particles called graupel (fig. 27-1g), or soft hail. When snow crystals ascend and descend into alternating layers of above- and below-freezing clouds, layers of glaze and rime build up to form hailstones (fig. 27-1h). Sleet (fig. 27-1i) is made up of either raindrops that have frozen or snowflakes that have melted and refrozen.

The density of freshly fallen snow depends on weather conditions. Generally, the higher the temperature, the denser (heavier and wetter) the snow, but density varies widely in the range of 20 to 32 degrees Fahrenheit (minus 7 to 0 degrees Celsius). High winds break falling crystals into fragments that pack together into dense, fine-grained snow; the stronger the wind, the denser the snow. The lightest and driest snow falls in moderately cold and very calm conditions. At extremely low temperatures, new snow is fine and granular, with somewhat higher densities. The highest densities are associated with graupel or needle crystals falling at temperatures near freezing.

The amount of water (solid or liquid) in layers of snow can indicate its density. Higher water content means that ice or water occupies more space and the snow contains less air, making it denser. The water content of freshly fallen snow ranges from 1 to 30 percent, sometimes even higher, and the average for mountain snowfall is 7 to 10 percent.

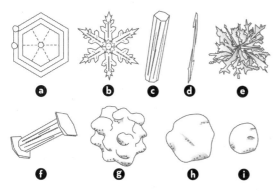

Fig. 27-1. *Snow crystal forms:* **a,** *plate;* **b,** *dendrite (stellar crystal);* **c,** *column;* **d,** *needle;* **e,** *spatial dendrite (combination of feathery crystals);* **f,** *capped column;* **g,** *graupel (soft hail);* **h,** *hail (solid ice);* **i,** *sleet (icy shell, inside wet).*

KEY TOPICS

SURFACE FORMS OF SNOW
HOW AVALANCHES FORM
HOW SNOW AGES
HOW GLACIERS FORM
UNDERSTANDING THE CYCLE OF SNOW

27

Surface Forms of Snow

Snow and ice undergo endless surface changes as wind, air temperature, solar radiation, freeze-thaw cycles, and rain affect them. This section describes most permutations that mountaineers typically encounter. Table 27-1 summarizes the travel considerations and dangers associated with these various forms of snow.

Rime

When water droplets freeze on trees, rocks, and other objects exposed to moisture in the air (think freezing fog), the ice that forms is called rime. Rime deposits build into the wind and may form large, feathery flakes or a solid incrustation, but rime lacks regular crystalline patterns. Typically it forms a weak crust on snow and makes for an unreliable anchor on rock or ice faces. Of note, it can form heavily on camping and climbing tools used in the mountain environment.

Hoarfrost

A type of snow that forms at ground level, hoarfrost is created when objects cool quickly and moisture is deposited on them. Unlike rime, hoarfrost displays distinct crystalline shapes such as blades, cups, and scrolls that appear fragile and feathery, sparkling brilliantly in sunlight. When deposited on snow, generally on a cold, clear night, hoarfrost is known as surface hoar. A heavy deposit of surface hoar makes for fast, excellent skiing. (For depth hoar, see How Snow Ages later in this chapter.)

TABLE 27-1. SNOW CONDITIONS AND THEIR DANGERS AND EFFECTS ON MOUNTAIN TRAVEL AND PROTECTION

SNOW CONDITION	EFFECTS ON TRAVEL	EFFECTS ON PROTECTION	DANGERS
Rime	Breakable; can trap feet or skis	Unreliable for anchors on rock or ice faces	
Hoarfrost	Fun skiing		Buried hoarfrost may pose avalanche danger.
Powder snow	Difficult walking; good skiing	Ropes cut through it; ice axes do not hold in it; it clogs crampons; T-slot anchors need reinforcing with buried packs.	Possible avalanche danger
Corn snow	Walking and skiing on it best in morning before it thaws	Bollards must be large to hold in corn snow.	In frozen corn snow, avalanche possibility is low. When it melts, stability depends on water content and strength of underlying layer.
Rotten snow	Difficult traveling	Ropes cut through it; ice axes do not hold in it; T-slot anchors need reinforcing with buried packs.	Potential avalanche danger
Meltwater crust, sun crust, rain crust	Breakable; can trap feet if crust thin; good walking if crust thick; skis require edges	These types of crust may require crampons. Climbers need to get down to a solid snowpack to set anchors.	Slippery
Wind slab	Good walking		Potential avalanche danger, especially on leeward slopes
Firnspiegel	Breakable		
Verglas	Breakable; impedes rock travel		Slippery
Suncups	Uneven, tedious, but solid walking and skiing		Avalanche danger is low because suncups usually form in stable, old snow. Ski edges may catch on them.

TABLE 27-1. SNOW CONDITIONS AND THEIR DANGERS AND EFFECTS ON MOUNTAIN TRAVEL AND PROTECTION			
SNOW CONDITION	EFFECTS ON TRAVEL	EFFECTS ON PROTECTION	DANGERS
Nieves penitentes	Difficult to negotiate	Ropes can catch on them and be damaged depending on how sharp the frozen edges are.	Avalanche danger is low because they usually form in stable, old snow.
Drain channels (runnels)	Uneven but solid walking and skiing; turning while glissading or skiing a bit difficult on downhill slopes		Avalanche danger is low if channels are frozen. If newly formed channels are soft, meltwater may have weakened a buried layer.
Sastrugi, barchans	Difficult traveling	Ropes can catch on them.	Sastrugi are a sign of wind transport and possible slabs. Ski edges may catch on them.
Cornices	Difficult to negotiate; best to avoid	Ropes can easily cut through them.	Can break away underneath or above traveler
Crevasses	Difficult to negotiate; may be hidden by snow; best to avoid	These hazardous features require rope protection (see Chapter 19).	Easy to fall into, especially if hidden
Seracs, ice avalanches	Difficult to negotiate; best to avoid	Ropes can catch on them.	Very unstable; can break catastrophically
Avalanche paths	Hard surface; good walking		Slippery; relatively free of avalanche danger unless portion of slab remains or is recharged by new snow
Avalanche debris	Difficult to negotiate		Relatively free of avalanche danger unless portion of slab remains or is recharged by new snow

Powder Snow

A popular term for light, fluffy fresh snow, powder snow is more specifically defined as new snow that has lost some cohesion. This change happens because large temperature differences between its feathery branching (dendrite) crystals cause recrystallization (see Figure 27-1b and e). Loose and uncohesive, powder snow commonly affords fun downhill skiing, but may form dry loose-snow avalanches. It is difficult to climb or walk through powder, as most objects that are not feather-light will readily sink.

Corn Snow

Once snow begins to melt in early spring, fair weather may lead to coarse, rounded crystals forming on the surface. These crystals, often called corn snow, form when the same surface layer of snow melts and refreezes for several days. Before corn snow thaws each morning, it is great for skiing and step-kicking. As it thaws throughout the day, corn snow can become too thick and mushy for uphill travel.

This is why early-morning starts are often necessary to reach a climbing destination, before this change happens. By the afternoon, the associated meltwater may lubricate the underlying snow and promote wet loose-snow avalanches, especially if the snow is stressed by people glissading on it or by the sliding and turning actions of skis, snowboards, and snowmobiles.

Rotten Snow

A spring condition, rotten snow is characterized by soft, wet lower layers that offer little support to the firmer layers above. Rotten snow forms when lower layers of depth hoar (see How Snow Ages later in this chapter) become wet and lose what little strength they have. It is a condition that often leads to wet loose-snow or slab avalanches running all the way to bare ground.

Continental climates, such as that of the North American Rockies, often produce rotten snow. Maritime climates, such as that of the Pacific coastal ranges, which usually have

27

deep, dense snow covers, are less likely to produce conditions that lead to rotten snow. In its worst forms, rotten snow will not support the weight of even a single skier. Snow that promises good skiing on a spring morning may deteriorate to rotten snow later in the day.

Meltwater Crust

When water melts on the surface of snow, refreezes, then bonds with the snow crystals, the resulting cohesive layer is a meltwater crust, which often exists below the surface. Meltwater crusts are caused by various sources of heat such as warm air, condensation on the surface of the snow, direct sunlight, and rain.

Sun crust. The name of this common variety of meltwater crust is derived from the main source of heat that melts snow: the sun's radiation. Sun crusts form only on sunny slopes. In winter and early spring, a sun crust's thickness over dry snow is usually determined by how far into the snowpack the sun's radiation extends. In late spring through summer, when liquid water is found throughout the snow cover, the sun crust's thickness—usually less than about 2 inches (5 centimeters)—depends on how cold nighttime temperatures are: colder temperatures overcome the melt and protect the snow beneath. Often a sun crust is thin enough that skiers and hikers break through it.

Rain Crust

Another type of crust forms after rainwater percolates into the snow's surface layers. As it percolates through the snow, rainwater often creates fingerlike features that pin the crust to the underlying snow after it refreezes. This pinning action helps stabilize snow against avalanching and makes for strong walking surfaces, especially in coastal ranges where heavy seasonal rainfall is common, even at high elevations. Glazed rain crusts can be extremely slippery and dangerous. On top of glacier ice, rain nearly always freezes, even during summer, making glaciers particularly hazardous immediately after a rainstorm.

Wind Slab

After wind disturbs the snow's surface layers, they can harden and form a wind slab. When wind breaks snow crystals into fragments that then come to rest, they are compacted together. Wind can heat and melt these snow crystals. Even when there is too little solar heating to melt the crystals, the disturbed surface layer warms, then cools when the wind dies down, providing additional metamorphic hardening. Travel across hard wind slabs is usually fast and easy, but slabs can break in long-running fractures, and

if the slabs overlie a weak layer or form a cornice, added stress can trigger an avalanche.

Firnspiegel

The thin layer of clear ice that sometimes develops on the snow's surface in spring or summer is *firnspiegel* (FEARN-spee-gull, German for "snow mirror"). Under the right conditions of sun and slope angle, sunlight reflecting on *firnspiegel* produces a brilliant sheen called glacier fire. *Firnspiegel* forms when solar radiation penetrates the snow and causes the layer just below the surface to melt, while freezing conditions prevail at the surface. Once *firnspiegel* forms, it acts like a greenhouse, allowing snow beneath it to melt while the transparent layer on the surface remains frozen. *Firnspiegel* is usually paper-thin and quite breakable. However, breaking through *firnspiegel*, unlike breaking through sun crusts, causes little negative effect on travel or comfort.

Verglas

A layer of thin, clear ice formed by water—either rainfall or snowmelt—freezing on rock, verglas is most commonly encountered at higher elevations in the spring or summer when a freeze follows a thaw. Verglas (vair-GLAH, French for "glazed frost" or "glass ice") also may form by supercooled raindrops freezing directly as they fall onto exposed objects—a phenomenon known as freezing rain, also sometimes inaccurately called silver thaw. Verglas forms a very slippery surface, and like black ice on a roadway, it can be difficult to anticipate.

Suncups

Where sunshine is intense and air is relatively dry, cups can form in the snow, deepening with increasing elevation and decreasing latitude. On each cup's ridges, sun-heated water molecules evaporate from the surface. In each cup's hollow, sun-heated water molecules are trapped near the surface, forming a liquid layer that promotes further melt. Because melting requires only one-seventh of the heat needed for evaporation, the hollows melt and deepen faster than the ridges evaporate (fig. 27-2a). When dirt in the hollows absorbs solar radiation, the hollows grow even deeper. Suncups can vary in depth from 1 inch to 3 feet (2.5 centimeters to 1 meter) or more. In the northern hemisphere, suncups melt faster on southern (sunny) aspects, and the pattern gradually extends northward across a snowfield.

Warm, moist winds tend to destroy suncups by causing faster melt at the cups' high points and edges. A prolonged summer storm accompanied by fog, wind, and rain often

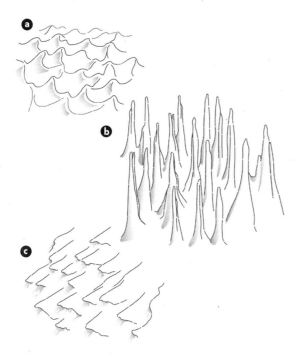

Fig. 27-2. *Surface features on snow:* **a,** *suncups;* **b,** *nieves penitentes;* **c,** *sastrugi.*

erases a suncup pattern completely, but the suncups start to form again as soon as dry, fair weather returns. While skiing over suncups, it is easy to catch an edge, especially if the suncups are frozen hard from nighttime cooling. The unevenness of suncupped surfaces makes walking uphill tedious, but traveling downhill is a little easier if travelers "skate" into each hollow.

Nieves Penitentes

When suncup hollows become very deep, accentuating their ridges into columns or knifelike rises resembling stalagmites in caves, they are called *nieves penitentes* (nee-EH-vays pen-ih-TEN-tays, fig. 27-2b). Spanish for "snow penitents," the term is derived from the forms' similarity to the shape of a monk's cowl. These pillars are peculiar to snowfields at high altitudes and low latitudes, places with intense solar radiation and atmospheric conditions conducive to suncups. The columns often slant toward the midday sun, ranging in size from an inch to several yards (a few centimeters to several meters) high. *Nieves penitentes* reach their most striking development among the higher peaks of South America's Andes and Asia's Himalaya, where these forms may make mountain travel very difficult.

Drain Channels

After snow begins to melt in spring, water runoff forms drainage patterns (also called runnels) on and within snowfields. As snow melts at the surface, the water percolates down until it encounters either impervious layers that deflect its course or highly permeable layers that it can follow. Much of the water also reaches the ground. Water flowing within the snow often creates branching drain channels; the flowing water accelerates the snow's settling around these channels, which are then outlined by surface depressions. Material collects in these depressions and absorbs solar radiation, causing differential melting that deepens the drain channels.

On a sloping surface, drain channels flow downhill and form a parallel ridge pattern that can make it a little difficult to turn while glissading or skiing. On flat surfaces, drain fields create a dimpled surface, similar to suncups but more rounded. The appearance of dimples or drain channels suggests that a significant amount of water has percolated into the snow cover. If these dimples or channels are frozen, it can be a good sign of stability against avalanches. However, if the channels are newly formed and still soft, the snow's stability may be compromised by meltwater that has weakened a susceptible buried layer.

Sastrugi and Barchans

When wind scours the surface of dry snow, the snow erodes into various forms, such as small ripples and irregularities. On flat, treeless territory and high ridges, both of which are fully exposed to the wind, these forms can grow to substantial sizes. These features potentially form slab avalanches, and ski edges or crampon points may catch on them.

Sastrugi. This characteristic hard form features a wavelike pattern, with sharp prows directed into the prevailing wind (fig. 27-2c). A field of unyielding sastrugi (sass-TRUE-gee, Russian for "grooves") up to several feet high can make for difficult alpine travel.

Barchans. High winds over featureless snow plains can produce dunes similar to those found in desert sand, with the crescent-shaped dune (or barchan) being most common. These stiff, uneven features also can make travel challenging, especially when ice or rocky ground is exposed between them.

Cornices

Snow deposited on the lee edge of a ridgetop, pinnacle, or cliff can form a cornice. Cornices can also form from or be enlarged by snow blown from snowfields to the windward side of a ridge or feature (see Figure 20-3). As a general rule,

27

cornices formed during snowstorms are softer than those produced by wind drift alone.

Cornices present a particular hazard because they overhang, forming an unsupported, unstable mass—which may not be solid clear through—that can break off due to natural causes or human disturbance. Walking on a cornice is dangerous; falling cornices are dangerous to people below and can also set off avalanches.

How Avalanches Form

Each snowstorm deposits a fresh layer of snow. Even during the same storm, a different type of layer may be deposited each time the wind shifts or the temperature changes. After snow layers are deposited, wind, temperature, sun, and gravity continually alter the character of the layers. Each layer is composed of snow crystals similar in shape and bonded together in similar ways. Because each layer is different, each reacts differently to various forces. Understanding these differences can help climbers recognize the conditions that contribute to avalanches and avoid them.

Snow avalanches are categorized by the mechanism that releases them. Loose-snow avalanches start at a point, while slab avalanches begin in blocks. Slab avalanches are usually much larger and involve deeper layers of snow. However, loose-snow avalanches can be equally dangerous, especially if they are wet and heavy, if they catch victims above cliffs or crevasses, or if they trigger slab avalanches or serac falls (see Ice Avalanches later in this chapter). To learn more about avalanches, see Chapter 20, Avalanche Safety.

LOOSE-SNOW AVALANCHES

When new snow builds up on steep slopes and is not stable enough to remain on the slope, it rolls downhill, collecting more snow as it descends. Sun and rain also can weaken the bonds between snow crystals, especially if they are newly deposited, causing individual grains to roll and slide into loose-snow avalanches. Skiing, glissading, and other human activities can disturb the snow and set off loose-snow avalanches, which can easily sweep climbers or skiers into crevasses and over cliffs, destroy tents, and bury or carry away vital equipment.

SLAB AVALANCHES

Because slab avalanches involve buried layers that often cannot be detected from the surface, they are more difficult to anticipate than loose-snow avalanches. Usually a buried weak layer or weak interface is sandwiched between a slab layer and a bed layer or the ground (fig. 27-3). When the

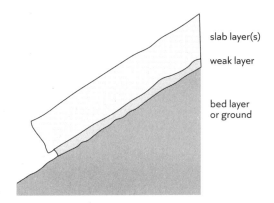

Fig. 27-3. *Typical layers of snow in a slab avalanche: a weak layer between slab and bed layers.*

buried weakness is disturbed in a way that reduces its frictional hold on the overlying slab, the slab avalanches.

These unpredictable avalanches can be even more destructive than loose-snow avalanches, including for climbers and skiers. Not only can slab avalanches fling people and equipment off slopes or bury them, but the tremendous speed of a slab avalanche and the force of impact have been known to move buildings and transport objects and people hundreds of yards downslope. It is difficult to survive an avalanche that is hurtling downslope, and once a person is buried, the snow hardens, making it difficult to breathe and hampering rescue.

The Buried Weak Layer

Depth hoar and buried surface hoar (hoarfrost) are the most notorious weak layers. They can withstand a significant amount of vertical load but slide easily along their horizontal interface. Their structure of faceted crystals loses all strength when crushed and becomes very soft and weak when wet. Depth hoar and buried surface hoar can survive weeks to months with little change in their fragile structure.

Surface hoar (or frost) can form all across the snow cover, persisting most in shaded places protected from wind. Buried by subsequent snowfall, it becomes a weak layer that can promote avalanching. If the first storm following hoarfrost formation begins with cool, calm conditions, the buried surface hoar can quickly form a thin, dangerous layer, even in a matter of hours. While hard to detect, this layer can support subsequent layers of snow.

Depth hoar matures fastest in the shallow snow of early winter, when the ground is still warm and the air is cold (common in continental regions), but it can develop wherever and whenever the snow temperature varies greatly at different depths (see How Snow Ages later in this chapter). It is a loose, sugar-like collection of ice grains; immature depth hoar (solid faceted shapes) may be just as weak as mature depth hoar (open, cup, and scroll shapes).

Another classic weakness is buried graupel (soft hail; see Figure 27-1g), which can act like ball bearings if disrupted. Other weaknesses that can make it easier for slabs to avalanche include plate-shaped crystals (see Figure 27-1a).

Buried weak layers may persist longer on glacier ice than on bare ground. The ice reduces the amount of geothermal heating reaching the snow from the ground, keeping temperatures cooler and slowing metamorphism. Buried weaknesses in seasonal snow underlain by glaciers can persist following storms and well into summer, long after adjacent snowy slopes have stabilized.

The Slab Layer

Once the underpinning of a snowpack is sufficiently weakened, the overlying snow (either a single layer or group of layers) begins to slide. If the overlying snow is cohesive enough to develop tension as it begins to slide—that is, if it forms a slab—it may break in long fractures across the slope. Lengthy fractures can result in large, heavy blocks that easily pull away from the rest of the slope, such as along the sides and bottom of a slope where more-stable snow may exist.

Slabs commonly are formed by brittle, wind-deposited snow layers. Wind often deposits snow in pillow-like patterns on the leeward side of ridges, thickest in the middle of the slope (where most of the weight of the slab, and thus the greatest avalanche danger, exists) and thinner on the edges. Wind slabs can maintain their blocky integrity throughout a slide, thrusting powerful masses downslope.

Slabs also are commonly formed by layers of needle-shaped crystals (see Figure 27-1d), deposited like a pile of pickup sticks, and by layers of branching crystals with many interlocking arms (see Figure 27-1b and e). These fragile crystals often pulverize immediately after a slide is triggered, forming fast-moving powder avalanches.

Thick rain crusts, which often bridge over weakened surfaces, are rarely involved in avalanches until they begin to melt in spring. Sun crusts, on the other hand, are usually thinner and weaker than rain crusts and can be incorporated in a group of slab layers.

If the overlying snow is too warm or wet relative to the underlying weakness, it may instead deform slightly and stay on the slope. However, if the underlying weak layer fails quickly and initial movement is significant, even this pliable wet slab can avalanche. This scenario occurs commonly in spring, when meltwater percolates into and weakens thick layers of old depth hoar. The depth hoar can then collapse, which overstresses the slab and leads it to fracture and slide. This effect can also occur in dry snow.

If the overlying snow is fragile and noncohesive (technically not a slab), the failure of a weak layer may result in snow grains in the overlying snow collapsing but remaining in place. However, if the weak layer consists of buried surface hoar or slightly rounded branching or plate crystals, it can fail rapidly enough that even the most fragile snow layers above can turn into slab avalanches.

The Bed Layer

The initial sliding surface of an avalanche is a bed layer, often the smooth surfaces of old snow, meltwater crust, glaciers, bedrock, or grass. Temperature changes can cause depth hoar to form, or meltwater or percolating rainwater can lubricate the interface of these smooth surfaces and the snow above it, further weakening it. The bed layer can also be the collapsed fragments of old depth hoar.

AVALANCHE TRIGGERS

Humans are efficient mechanisms for triggering avalanches. Climbers glissading down a slope, snowshoers walking across snow, and skiers skinning upslope—especially when they execute kick turns—can all disturb layers of depth hoar or buried surface hoar. The sweeping turns or sharper turns of downhill skiers and snowboarders can release loose-snow avalanches and fragile but fast-moving soft-slab avalanches. Making snowplow turns or "hockey stops," sideslipping downhill, or falling may release wet loose-snow and wet slab avalanches. Even traveling below a slope can trigger an avalanche, especially if the buried weak layer is surface or depth hoar. As the delicate crystal structure collapses, the failure can propagate uphill. The weight and vibration of snowmobiles can set off avalanches in places where traveling on foot would not.

Storms can also trigger avalanches. Many types of buried layers (such as thin layers of slightly rounded branching and platelike crystals) fail when a force is applied evenly over a broad surface, as when storms deposit layers of new snow. Earthquakes, cornice and serac falls, and other effects both within and outside the snowpack can cause avalanches at unpredictable times and places. Loud sounds alone cannot trigger avalanches; it is the concussive impact (not the percussive noise) of bombs set off by ski professionals that triggers a controlled slide.

27

How Snow Ages

Snow on the ground changes over time. The crystals undergo metamorphism, a process that usually results in smaller, simpler forms and a snowpack that shrinks and settles. Metamorphism begins the moment snow falls and lasts until it melts completely. Because the snowpack changes over time, mountaineers must check an area's recent weather history and snow conditions to determine what the snow cover will be like.

DEPTH HOAR

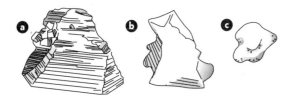

Fig. 27-4. *How depth hoar changes when temperatures affect water vapor in the snowpack:* **a,** *depth hoar begins as scroll- or cup-shaped snow crystals that appear layered and may be relatively large;* **b,** *it loses strength when crushed;* **c,** *it becomes soft and weak when wet.*

A type of metamorphism happens when water vapor moves from one part of the snowpack to another, depositing ice crystals that are different from those of the original snow. This process produces faceted crystals that often end up with a scroll or cup shape, appear to be layered, and may grow to considerable size—up to 1 inch (2.5 centimeters) or so (fig. 27-4a). These crystals form depth hoar, a fragile structure that loses all strength when crushed (fig. 27-4b) and becomes very soft and weak when wet (fig. 27-4c). This weak, unstable snow form is popularly referred to as sugar snow when dry and rotten snow when wet. Depth hoar forms when temperatures differ widely at different snow depths and air space allows water vapor to diffuse freely. These conditions are most common early in winter, when the snowpack tends to be shallow and unconsolidated.

AGE HARDENING

Snow can also age by mechanical means, such as wind. Snow particles disturbed in this way undergo a process known as age hardening for several hours. Snow's variations in strength are among the widest found in nature: New snow is about 90 percent air, and the unconnected individual grains make it a fluffy, weak material that is easy to break apart. In contrast, wind-packed old snow may be less than 30 percent air, with the small broken particles forming interconnected strong bonds that can create layers 50,000 times harder than fluffy new snow. This is why it is easier to follow others' tracks through hardened snow. The variations between the extremes of new and old snow, and the continual changes in strength caused by changes in temperature, pressure, and wind, make for highly variable conditions from place to place and hour to hour.

FIRN OR NÉVÉ

Another type of metamorphism gradually converts the varied snow crystal forms into homogeneous, rounded grains of ice, with both temperature and pressure affecting the rate of change (fig. 27-5). When temperature within the snow is near freezing—32 degrees Fahrenheit (0 degrees Celsius)—change is rapid; the colder it gets, the slower the change: it virtually stops below minus 40 degrees Fahrenheit (minus 40 degrees Celsius). Pressure from the weight of new snowfall speeds changes within older layers. Snow that has reached old age—surviving at least one year, with all original snow crystals converted into grains of ice—is called firn or névé. Any further changes to firn snow lead to the formation of glacier ice (see below).

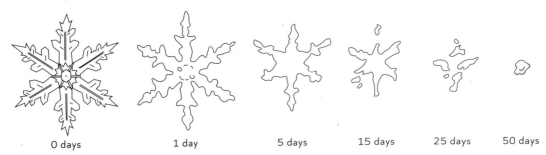

| 0 days | 1 day | 5 days | 15 days | 25 days | 50 days |

Fig. 27-5. *How a dendrite snow crystal changes with temperature and pressure: days indicate time required for shapes to change under average temperature and pressure in a typical seasonal snow cover.*

How Glaciers Form

Snow that does not melt or evaporate during the course of a year persists to the next winter. Each spring when the lower snow layers are still below freezing temperatures, percolating meltwater refreezes when it reaches them. This refrozen meltwater forms layers of ice within the old snow—the firn or névé—where the snow crystals have also compacted and changed into grains of ice. Thus, by the time compaction and metamorphism have prepared an entire area, the firn may already contain irregular bodies of ice. As the air between the grains seals off, the mass becomes airtight and these grains of ice become glacier ice (fig. 27-6).

Once glacier ice forms, some grains continue to grow at the expense of their neighbors, and the average crystal size increases with age (fig. 27-7). Large glaciers, in which the ice takes centuries to reach the foot of the formation, may produce crystals with a diameter wider than 12 inches (30 centimeters)—gigantic specimens that grew from minute snow particles.

To understand how a simple valley-type alpine glacier is born, picture a mountain in the northern hemisphere without glaciers. Now suppose snow begins to persist from year to year high on the mountain in a sheltered spot with northern exposure. From the beginning, snow starts to creep (or flow) toward the valley in very slow motion. As new layers are added each year, the patch of firn snow grows deeper and bigger, and the amount of snow in motion increases. While melting and refreezing, the creeping snow dislodges soil and rock, and the flow of water around and under the snow patch influences the surroundings. This small-scale process of erosion eventually forms a hollow where the winter snow is deposited in deeper drifts. After the snow depth exceeds about 100 feet (30 meters), the many upper layers of firn exert increasing pressure on the lower layers, and they begin to turn into glacier ice. If snow continues to accumulate year after year, eventually consolidating and beginning to move slowly downhill, a glacier is born.

With continued nourishment from heavy winter snows, the glacier flows toward the valley as a stream of ice. At

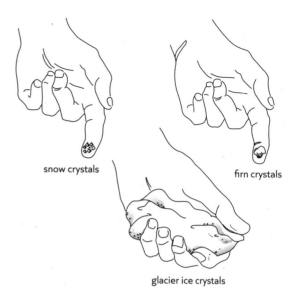

Fig. 27-7. *Ice crystals increase greatly in size as they transform from snow and firn into glacier ice.*

snow crystals

firn crystals

glacier ice crystals

some point, the glacier reaches an elevation low and warm enough where new snow no longer accumulates, and the glacier ice begins to melt. When the glacier reaches an even lower and warmer point, where all glacier ice melts each year, this becomes the glacier's lower limit.

Glaciers vary from stagnant expanses with little motion to vigorously flowing rivers of ice that transport large masses from higher to lower elevations each year. Glaciers in relatively temperate climates flow both by internal deformation (deeply buried ice that under pressure flows like honey) and by sliding on their beds. Differences in speed within the glacier are somewhat like those in a river: fastest at the center and surface and slower at the sides and bottom where bedrock creates drag. Small polar glaciers appear strikingly different from their temperate cousins, for they are frozen to their beds and can flow only by internal deformation. The polar glaciers look much like flowing molasses, whereas temperate glaciers are rivers of broken ice.

CREVASSES

Important features of glaciers, crevasses are fractures that occur when ice encounters a force greater than it can bear. Near a glacier's surface, where ice begins to form, it is full of tiny flaws and weakly bonded crystals. When the glacier stretches or bends too fast, it can break apart like glass, resulting in a crevasse.

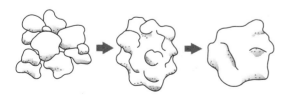

Fig. 27-6. *Rounded grains of ice are pressed and squeezed together to form a large crystal of glacier ice.*

27

Crevasses typically are 80 to 100 feet (25 to 30 meters) deep. At greater depths, ice layers become stronger, with increasingly large and well-bonded crystals. When stresses try to pull this deeply buried ice apart, overlying pressure squeezes it further, causing it to flow and deform like thick goo. In colder glaciers—at high elevations or in polar climates—crevasses can penetrate somewhat deeper because colder ice is more brittle and tends to break more easily.

Temperate glaciers normally have more, and shallower, crevasses than polar glaciers because temperate glaciers usually move faster. When glaciers move very fast, such as over a precipitous drop, they fracture extensively, forming an icefall. The icefall's numerous crevasses intersect, isolating chunks of ice in columns called seracs, which can be huge.

ICE AVALANCHES

Hanging glaciers, icefalls, and any serac-covered portion of a glacier can release ice avalanches. They are caused by a combination of glacier movement, temperature, and serac configuration. On warm, low-elevation glaciers, ice avalanches are most common during late summer and early fall, when enough meltwater flows underneath the glacier to increase its movement. On high-elevation glaciers and cold glaciers that are frozen to the bedrock, there is no such seasonal cycle of ice avalanches.

Ice avalanches can occur at any time of year and any time of day or night, although field observations suggest that they are most common in the afternoon. This may occur in a snow-covered serac field if daytime heating loosens snow enough for it to avalanche into seracs and cause them to fall in an ice avalanche. However, scientists have discovered that ice avalanches are likeliest in the deep cold of early morning, when the ice is most brittle.

Understanding the Cycle of Snow

Researching the terrain and both typical and recent weather patterns before a trip can help climbers anticipate snow conditions (see Chapter 28, Mountain Weather). During a trip, understanding how wind, sun, and precipitation affect snow at different elevations and on different slope aspects will help climbers and skiers choose a route and what equipment to use.

Dense snow can make for a great walking surface and sound bollards for rope belays, but snow that has transformed into ice can be slippery and difficult to carve. Fluffy new snow is fun for skiing downhill but makes uphill travel arduous and provides little support for belaying. The variety, combination, and timing of how snow layers form can promote avalanching. From the first falling flake to glacier ice to meltwater, the cycle of snow creates a dramatic, dynamic environment that challenges and delights climbers.

CHAPTER 28

MOUNTAIN WEATHER

My climbing partners and I could not see the avalanche, but we could hear it and feel the shock wave set off by the explosive collapse of snow and ice somewhere up mountain. We were at the foot of the Coleman Glacier on Mount Baker, roping up for a summit climb. Months of mountain weather had led to this moment, and knowledge of it shaped our climbing decisions.

Whiteout conditions made it difficult to see climbers more than a few dozen yards away, much less the avalanche. But experienced mountaineers know that ignoring what they cannot see—or choose not to see—is not conducive to survival. Smart climbers recognize changing and/or poor weather and adjust their route and their plans.

Failing to pay attention or engaging in wishful thinking can be lethal in the mountains, as can believing the weather will hold or improve when evidence suggests otherwise. It is difficult to abandon a planned summit attempt in the face of deteriorating weather, particularly when climbers have invested considerable vacation time and money in an expedition. Yet climbers benefit from understanding the ways weather systems develop and move, and particularly how mountains influence weather patterns, so that they can consult and interpret forecasts as they plan their climbs.

Forces That Create Weather

Understanding weather forecasts and reports requires a basic grasp of the forces that create weather. Not only does such knowledge help mountaineers better digest such information before leaving home, it also helps them detect important changes on the trail or climbing route as the weather changes over time.

THE SUN

The sun does far more than simply illuminate planet Earth. It is the engine that drives the earth's atmosphere, providing the heat that, along with other factors, creates the temperature variations that are ultimately responsible for wind, rain, snow, thunder, and lightning—everything known as weather.

The key to the sun's impact is that the intensity of its radiation varies across the earth's surface. Closer to the equator, the sun's heat is more intense. The extremes in temperature between the equator and the poles come as little surprise.

However, those differences in air temperature also lead to air movement, which moderates those temperature extremes.

AIR MOVEMENT AND PRESSURE

Wind, the horizontal movement of air, is all too familiar to anyone who has pitched a tent in the mountains. Air also rises and descends. When air cools, it becomes denser and sinks; the air pressure increases. But when air warms, it becomes less dense and rises; the air pressure decreases. These pressure differences, the result of temperature differences, produce moving air. Air generally moves from an area of high pressure, a high, to one of low pressure, a low (fig. 28-1). Remember, wind direction is defined as the direction the wind is coming from, not the direction it is moving toward.

Air moving from high to low pressure carries moisture with it. As that air moves into the zone of lower pressure, then rises and cools, the moisture may condense into clouds or fog. As the air cools, it is not able to hold as much water vapor. That is why you can "see" your breath when in cold air temperatures: the water vapor in your mouth condenses into liquid water droplets as you breathe out. The process of cooling and condensation operates on a large scale in the earth's atmosphere as air moves from high-pressure systems into low-pressure systems, where it rises.

Because Arctic and Antarctic polar air is colder and denser than air closer to the equator, it sinks. The zone where

> **KEY TOPICS**
>
> FORCES THAT CREATE WEATHER
> THUNDER AND LIGHTNING
> LOCALIZED WINDS
> FIELD FORECASTING IN THE MOUNTAINS
> APPLYING WHAT YOU LEARN

28

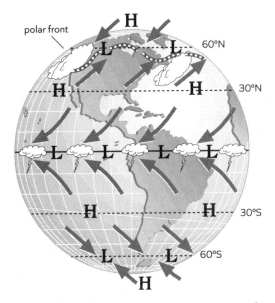

Fig. 28-1. *The earth's air circulation patterns: movement from areas of high pressure (H) at the poles toward areas of low pressure (L) at the equator, deflected in the middle latitudes by the earth's rotation.*

it sinks and piles up is a region of high pressure. As the air sinks and its pressure increases, it warms a bit. The effect is similar to what happens to football or rugby players caught at the bottom of a pile: they get squeezed the most, and their temperature (and possibly temperament) heats up. In the atmosphere, this warming within a high-pressure area tends to cause some of the moisture to evaporate. That is why the Arctic receives very little precipitation. Although this sinking motion heats the air enough to cause much of

the moisture in it to evaporate, the air does not heat up enough to transform the poles into the tropics!

Changes in Air Pressure

A barometer or barometric altimeter can give excellent indication of changes in air pressure. A barometer measures air pressure directly; a barometric altimeter measures air pressure and reports elevation. A decrease in air pressure shows on an altimeter as an increase in elevation even when the party has not changed its elevation; an increase in air pressure shows on an altimeter as a decrease in elevation—again, even when the party has not changed its elevation. (See Altimeter in Chapter 5, Navigation and Communication.) Table 28-1 evaluates a developing low-pressure system, but rapidly building high pressure can also have its troublesome effects—principally, strong winds.

THE EARTH'S ROTATION

If the earth did not rotate, cold polar air would slide toward the equator. However, the air sinking and moving from the poles toward the equator and the air rising from the equator do not form a simple loop moving from north to south (or from south to north) and back again. The earth's rotation around its axis deflects this air. Some of the air rising from the equator descends over the subtropics, creating a region of high pressure. In turn, part of the air moving from these subtropical highs moves north into the air moving south from the North Pole (or, south of the equator, moves south into the air moving north from the South Pole). The boundary layer between these two very different air masses is the polar front (see Figure 28-1). When the boundary does not move, it is called a stationary front. It often serves as a nursery for the development of storms.

TABLE 28-1. AIR PRESSURE AND ALTIMETER CHANGE CLUES		
IF PRESSURE CHANGES OVER THREE HOURS	**IF ALTIMETER CHANGES OVER THREE HOURS**	**THEN CHECK FOR**
Decrease of 0.04–0.06 inch (1.2–1.8 millibars)	Increase of 40–60 feet (12–18 meters)	Clouds lowering hourly or thickening; begin checking pressure changes hourly
Decrease of 0.06–0.08 inch (1.8–2.4 millibars)	Increase of 60–80 feet (18–24 meters)	Winds ranging from 18–33 knots (21–38 miles or 34–61 km per hour); continue monitoring conditions
Decrease of more than 0.08 inch (more than 2.4 millibars)	Increase of more than 80 feet (more than 24 meters)	Winds of 34 knots (39 miles or 63 kilometers per hour) or greater
Increase of air pressure	Decrease of altimeter reading	Strong winds

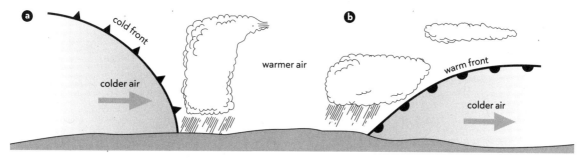

Fig. 28-2. *Fronts:* ***a,*** *cold front displaces warmer air;* ***b,*** *warm front displaces colder air.*

COLD FRONTS AND WARM FRONTS

Because of the great contrast in temperatures across the polar front, together with imbalances caused by the earth's rotation and differing influences of land, sea, ice, and mountains, some of the cold, dry air from the north slides south (or, in the southern hemisphere, air from the south slides north). The zone where cold air replaces warm air is referred to as a cold front (fig. 28-2a), and the zone where warm air gradually replaces cooler air is referred to as a warm front (fig. 28-2b). Both types of fronts appear as a wave or bend on the stationary front. An occluded front, which combines characteristics of warm and cold fronts, is typically found near the center of a mature low-pressure system.

The wave or bend that develops along what started out as a stationary front may build into a low-pressure system, with air circulating counterclockwise around the low (the opposite direction of air moving around a high)—again, a consequence of the earth's rotation and friction.

Clouds Signal Moving Fronts

Both cold and warm fronts are marked by unique clouds, which help the mountaineer distinguish one type of front from the other. Clouds seen ahead of, along, or just behind a cold front include puffy clouds resembling cotton candy: the name *cumulus* refers to their "pile" or "heap" shape. Cumulus clouds (fig. 28-3a) have upward growth that suggests showers later in the day. High-based altocumulus clouds (fig. 28-3b) often indicate potential for thunder and rain showers. Cumulonimbus (fig. 28-3c), dense, towering vertical clouds, produce rain, snow, or thunder and lightning. Stratocumulus clouds (fig. 28-3d) are lumpy, sheetlike layers of cumulus that often follow a cold front, suggesting showers. The name *stratus* refers to the "sheetlike" or "layered" characteristics of these clouds.

Clouds seen ahead of or along a warm front include a halo (fig. 28-3e), commonly seen 24–48 hours ahead of precipitation; lenticular (lenslike) clouds (fig. 28-3f)

TABLE 28-2. CLOUD COVER CLUES		
IF	**THEN**	**CHECK FOR**
High cirrocumulus or cirrostratus clouds; halo around sun or moon	Precipitation possible within 24–48 hours	Lowering, thickening clouds
High cirrocumulus or cirrostratus clouds forming tight ring or corona around sun or moon	Precipitation possible within 24 hours	Lowering, thickening clouds
"Cap" or lenticular clouds forming over peaks	Precipitation possible within 24 to more than 48 hours; strong winds possible near summits or leeward slopes	Lowering, thickening clouds
Thickening, lowering, layered, and flat stratus, altostratus, or nimbostratus clouds	Warm or occluded front likely within 12–24 hours	Shifting wind; dropping pressure
Breaks in cloud cover closing up	Cold front likely within 12 hours	Shifting wind; dropping pressure

28

Fig. 28-3. *Cloud types:* **a–d,** *seen ahead of, along, or just behind a cold front;* **e–l,** *seen ahead of or along a warm front.*

g stratus

h cirrocumulus

i cirrostratus

j altostratus

k nimbostratus

l fog

28

TABLE 28-3. WIND DIRECTION AND SPEED CLUES (NORTHERN HEMISPHERE)

IF	AND IF	THEN
Winds shift to east or southeast	Air pressure drops; low-pressure system approaching	Clouds lower, thicken; precipitation possible
Winds shift from southwest to northwest	Air pressure rises	Drying and clearing likely; showers possible on windward slopes, especially along western US or Canadian coast
Increasing winds from east to southeast	Continued air pressure drop; low-pressure system approaching	Winds likely to increase
Winds shift from southwest to west	Air pressure rises; high-pressure system approaching	Showers possible along windward slopes, especially along western US or Canadian coast

over mountains, often suggesting precipitation within 48 hours; stratus (layerlike) clouds (fig. 28-3g) associated with widespread precipitation or ocean air; cirrocumulus (fig. 28-3h), very high clouds typically made of ice crystals, a warning of approaching storms; cirrostratus (fig. 28-3i), high, very thin clouds composed of ice crystals; altostratus (fig. 28-3j), made up of large, thin sheets that, when part of an approaching warm front, follow cirrostratus; nimbostratus (fig. 28-3k), amorphous, usually dark gray stratus clouds producing widespread precipitation and low stability; and fog (fig. 28-3l), visible fine particles of water or ice crystals suspended in the air. Overall, lowering and thickening clouds signal the approach of precipitation and lowered visibility. See Table 28-2 for a summary of clues provided by the cloud cover.

Thunder and Lightning

Thunderstorms can be set off by the collision of different air masses when fronts move through or by air heating rapidly when it comes in contact with sun-warmed mountain slopes. This warm air becomes buoyant and tends to rise. If the atmosphere above is cold enough, the air tends to keep rising, producing air-mass thunderstorms. A single lightning bolt can heat the surrounding air up to 50,000 degrees Fahrenheit (approximately 25,000 degrees Celsius). That heating causes the air to expand explosively, generating ear-splitting thunder.

Thunderstorms in the mountains can and do kill (fig. 28-4). Lightning is the biggest killer, claiming an average of two hundred lives in the United States alone each year. It can also spark dangerous wildfires, and even a moderate thunderstorm may release up to 125 million gallons (473

million liters) of rainwater. The resulting flash floods can inundate streambeds and small valleys, sweeping away entire campgrounds. The growing popularity of canyoneering, particularly rappelling in deep slot canyons, increases climbers' exposure to flash floods and drowning. Thunderstorms can also produce lethal winds, capable of leveling entire stretches of forest.

By taking a few precautions, climbers can avoid most accidents caused by mountain thunderstorms (see the "Tips If Thunderstorms Are Forecast" sidebar). Before you hit the trail, consult up-to-date weather reports and forecasts.

GAUGING A THUNDERSTORM'S MOVEMENT

How is it possible to gauge the movement of a thunderstorm? It is easy with a watch or simply by counting. Use

TIPS IF THUNDERSTORMS ARE FORECAST

- **Do not camp or climb in a narrow valley or gully.** Anticipate and avoid flash floods.
- **Do not climb or hike in high, exposed areas.** Take precautions to avoid lightning strikes.
- **Climb high early and descend by the afternoon.** Thunderstorms tend to develop with afternoon heating.
- **Watch small cumulus clouds for strong upward growth.** This change may signal a developing thunderstorm.
- **Watch for cumulus clouds changing from white to dark gray or black.** This change may also signal a developing thunderstorm.

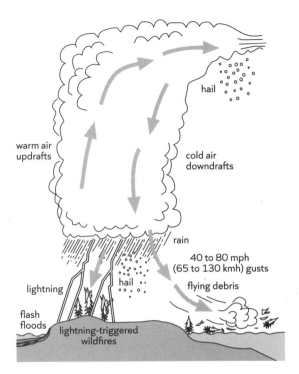

Fig. 28-4. *Thunderstorm hazards include lightning, lightning-triggered wildfires, flash floods, and high winds.*

the "flash to bang" principle: The moment lightning flashes, start counting the seconds. Stop counting once you hear the bang of thunder. Divide the number of seconds by five; the result is the thunderstorm's distance away in miles. (For climbers using the metric system, divide the number of seconds by three to obtain the thunderstorm's distance in kilometers.) Continue to time the interval between lightning and thunder discharges to judge whether the thunderstorm is approaching, remaining in place, or receding: if the time interval between the lightning and thunder is decreasing, the thunderstorm is approaching; if the interval is increasing, it is moving away.

This technique works because the light from lightning moves much faster than the sound from thunder. Although thunder occurs at virtually the same instant as lightning, its sound travels only 1 mile (1.6 kilometers) every five seconds, whereas the lightning flash, traveling at 186,000 miles (300,000 kilometers) per second, arrives essentially instantaneously. That is why the lightning is seen before the thunder is heard, unless the thunderstorm is very close—too close.

TABLE 28-4. ESTIMATING THE SNOW LEVEL

IF	AND IF	THEN
Stratus clouds or fog present	Steady, widespread precipitation	Expect the snow level to be 1,000 feet (305 meters) below the freezing level.
Cumulus clouds present or a cold front approaching	Locally heavy precipitation	Expect the snow level to be as much as 2,000 feet (610 meters) below the freezing level; snow will stick at 1,000 feet (305 meters) below the freezing level.

REACTING TO AN APPROACHING THUNDERSTORM

If you are caught out in the open during a thunderstorm, try to seek shelter. Tents are poor protection: metal tent poles may function as lightning rods; stay away from poles and wet items inside the tent. Take the following precautions to avoid being struck by lightning.

- **Get away from water:** it readily conducts electricity.
- **Seek low ground** if the party is in an open valley or meadow.
- **Move immediately** if your hair stands on end.
- **Avoid standing on high ground**—ridgetops, at lookout structures, or near or under lone tall trees, especially isolated trees, which are more likely to fall in strong winds.
- **Look for a stand of even-sized trees** if the party is in a wooded area.
- **Do not remain near or on rocky pinnacles or peaks.**
- **Do not remain near, touch, or wear metal or graphite equipment,** such as ice axes, crampons, climbing devices, and frame packs.
- **Insulate yourself from the ground** if possible. Place a soft pack or foam pad beneath you to protect against step-voltage transfer of a lightning strike through the ground—though ground currents may move through such insulation.
- **Crouch to minimize your profile.** Also cover your head and ears and close your eyes.
- **Do not lie down:** this puts more of your body in contact with the ground, which can conduct more electrical current.

28

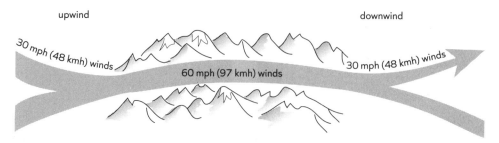

Fig. 28-5. *Wind accelerates—as much as doubling—through gaps and passes.*

Localized Winds

Understanding large-scale wind patterns, both at the earth's surface and in the upper atmosphere, is important to gauging the weather. However, mountains alter wind considerably, so understanding localized patterns can mean the difference between successfully reaching the summit and being tent-bound—or getting blown off the mountain. See Table 28-3 for a summary of clues in changes in wind direction and speed.

GAP WINDS

Winds are often channeled from open areas through gaps in the terrain, such as major passes or even between peaks. Wind speeds can easily double as they move through such gaps (fig. 28-5).

Climbers can use this knowledge to their advantage. If possible, gauge the surface wind speeds upwind of a gap or pass before traveling into the vicinity of these terrain features. Knowing the upwind velocities can prepare a climber for gap winds that may be twice as strong. Avoid camping near the downwind portion of the gap, and consider selecting climbing routes not exposed to such winds. A major peak can block or slow winds for a few miles or kilometers downwind.

VALLEY AND GRAVITY WINDS

Sparsely vegetated ground is typically found close to ridges. Because it heats more rapidly than forest-covered land near valley floors, and because heated air rises, wind is generated that moves up either side of a valley, spilling over adjoining ridgetops. Such uphill breezes, called valley winds, can reach 10 to 15 miles (16 to 24 kilometers) per hour, attaining maximum speed during the early afternoon and dying out shortly before sunset.

At night the land cools, and the cool air flows downslope in what is called a gravity wind. Such downslope breezes reach their maximum after midnight, dying out just before sunrise. Camping at the base of a cliff may result in an uncomfortably breezy evening. The more open the slopes between a campsite and the ridge above, as opposed to forested slopes, the faster the winds will be.

FOEHN WINDS

When winds descend a slope, air temperatures may increase dramatically in what is called a foehn wind or, in the western United States, a chinook. The air heats as it sinks and compresses on the leeward side of the crest (fig. 28-6), sometimes warming 30 degrees Fahrenheit (17 degrees Celsius) in minutes, melting as much as a foot of snow in a few hours. These winds are significant because of their potential speed, the rapid rise in air temperature associated with them, and the potential they create for both rapid snowmelt and flooding. Such winds can increase the risk of avalanches, weaken snow bridges, and lead to sudden rises in stream levels.

Warning signs make it possible to anticipate a potentially dangerous foehn wind. Expect such a wind, with temperatures warming as much as 6 degrees Fahrenheit per 1,000 feet (3 degrees Celsius per 305 meters) of descent, if these three conditions are met:

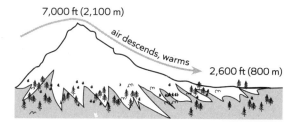

Fig. 28-6. *As foehn winds descend, they warm quickly: here, a descent of 4,400 feet (1,300 meters) causes air to warm from 22 degrees Fahrenheit (minus 5 degrees Celsius) to 48 degrees Fahrenheit (9 degrees Celsius).*

1. You are downwind of a major ridge or crest, primarily to the east of mountains.
2. Wind speeds across the crest or ridge exceed 30 miles (48 kilometers) per hour.
3. You observe precipitation above the crest.

BORA WINDS

The opposite of a foehn wind is a bora or, as it is called in Greenland, a *piteraq*. A bora is simply wind consisting of air so cold that its sinking, compressing motion as it flows downslope fails to warm it significantly. Such cold winds are most common downslope of large glaciers. Their speeds can easily exceed 50 miles (80 kilometers) per hour. A bora can blow away tents, throw climbers off balance, lower the wind-chill to dangerous levels (see Figure 24-5 in Chapter 24, First Aid), and obscure visibility by blowing snow around.

Field Forecasting in the Mountains

Gathering and evaluating weather data does not end at the trailhead. The weather in the mountains, which can cause accidents, rarely changes without warning. At times, the clues can be subtle, but sometimes they are as broad as daylight.

MAJOR INDICATORS OF AN APPROACHING STORM

The following four factors can alert climbers to an approaching storm:

- **Changes in air pressure.** See Table 28-1.
- **Changes in cloud cover.** See Table 28-2.
- **Changes in wind direction.** See Table 28-3.
- **Changes in wind speed.** See Table 28-3.

No single factor tells you all you need to know; you must examine each element carefully. This section adds some guidelines for estimating freezing and snow levels and for creating custom weather briefings, which can enhance the weather reports and forecasts that climbers obtain before leaving home.

Occasionally, weather reports and forecasts can also be updated en route via smartphone, although that information is subject to having both an adequate signal and reliable phone apps and sources. There are many weather apps available, including from a number of commercial sources, but shiny marketing claims do not guarantee sparkling performance. National forecast sources, including the National Weather Service in the United States, Environment Canada, the Met Office in the United Kingdom, and Meteo France, all offer apps that provide a good foundation. Talk to fellow mountaineers to benefit from their experience and suggestions.

FREEZING LEVEL AND SNOW LEVEL

It can be useful to estimate both the freezing and snow levels. Such estimates are subject to error because they are based on the average decrease in temperature as altitude increases: 3.5 degrees Fahrenheit per 1,000 feet (2 degrees Celsius per 305 meters) of elevation gain; see the formulas and examples below. Still, such estimates are usually better than no estimate.

Estimating Freezing Level in Feet and Degrees Fahrenheit

To estimate the elevation at which the temperature drops to 32 degrees Fahrenheit, climbers simply need to know their elevation in feet and the temperature in degrees Fahrenheit at that elevation:

1. Subtract 32 from the temperature in degrees Fahrenheit.
2. Multiply this number by 1,000.
3. Divide this number by 3.5.
4. Add this number to the elevation in feet to estimate the freezing level.

In the following example, the climber's elevation is 1,000 feet and the temperature at that elevation is 39 degrees Fahrenheit:

1. 39 minus 32 equals 7.
2. 7 times 1,000 equals 7,000.
3. 7,000 divided by 3.5 equals 2,000.
4. 2,000 plus 1,000 feet equals 3,000 feet—the estimated freezing level.

Estimating Freezing Level in Meters and Degrees Celsius

To estimate the elevation at which the temperature drops to 0 degrees Celsius, climbers simply need to know their elevation in meters and the temperature in degrees Celsius at that elevation:

1. Multiply the temperature in degrees Celsius by 304.
2. Divide this number by 2.
3. Add this number to the elevation in meters to estimate the freezing level.

In this next example, the climber's elevation is 1,000 meters and the temperature is 3 degrees Celsius at that elevation:

1. 3 times 304 equals 912.
2. 912 divided by 2 equals 456.
3. 456 plus 1,000 meters equals 1,456 meters, or approximately 1,500 meters—the estimated freezing level.

28

Estimating the Snow Level

Once the freezing level has been estimated, climbers can use the guidelines in Table 28-4 to estimate the snow level.

CREATING CUSTOM WEATHER BRIEFINGS

Obtaining updated weather forecasts is basic to maximizing the success and safety of any climbing trip, be it a local weekend outing or a major expedition. It is true that forecasts are not perfect, but it is equally true that the accuracy of weather forecasts has improved significantly over the last few decades. Specifically, four-day forecasts are as accurate today as one-day forecasts were in 1980. The 24-hour forecast temperatures are within two degrees of those actually observed more than 90 percent of the time. Precipitation and wind forecasts have also improved considerably.

The more complex the terrain, however, the greater the chance of forecast errors. And mountainous terrain is quite complex. Climate change is also increasing the variability of weather—for example, by producing more frequent extreme events. Forecast accuracy fades at about one week and beyond, approaching 50/50—the flip of a coin. If a forecast service suggests otherwise, go elsewhere for weather information. Using a week-old forecast to guide decision-making is at best unwise and at worst unsafe.

Consider gathering weather information at least one day, and preferably two to three days, before a planned departure. That gives the party a chance to verify the forecasts by observing conditions. If the forecasts are pretty close to what the party actually sees, climbers can proceed on the trip with more confidence than if the forecast and observed weather conditions are 180 degrees apart.

TWO TO THREE DAYS BEFORE TRIP

Check these elements two to three days before the planned departure:

- **Overall weather pattern:** positions of highs, lows, and fronts.
- **Projected weather forecast:** for the next two or three days.

ONE DAY BEFORE TRIP

Check these elements the day before the planned departure:

- **Current weather:** evaluate the accuracy of the previous day's forecasts.
- **Overall weather pattern:** recheck positions of highs, lows, and fronts.
- **Projected weather** for the next two days.
- **Updates every six to eight hours:** *if* weather projections mention the possibility of strong winds, thunderstorms, or significant snow or rain—the lead time on such forecasts is short because of the rapid changes that sometimes occur.

DAY OF TRIP

Take these steps on the day of departure:

- **Check the current weather:** evaluate the accuracy of the previous day's forecasts.
- **Check the projected weather** for the trip's duration.
- **Make decisions:** evaluate current forecasts, the track record of earlier forecasts, personal experience, and demands of the trip; base decision-making on this information.

Applying What You Learn

Mountaineers can consult a rich supply of weather forecast sources, information of great value. Begin with the vital step of gathering forecasts for the locale of the climb, followed by careful observation during the outing. Analyze changes in cloud cover, air pressure, and wind speed and direction. Estimate the freezing and snow levels if applicable. Consider all such weather information thoroughly when selecting approach and climbing routes, camp locations, and start and turnaround times. Being aware of the environment and its impact on the party's plans will widen your margin of safety during your pursuit of the freedom of the hills.

APPENDIX: RATING SYSTEMS

A rating system helps a climber choose a climb that is both challenging and doable. Rating systems for climbing were first developed in the late 19th and early 20th centuries in Britain and Germany. In the 1920s, Willo Welzenbach used roman numerals and British adjectives to compare and describe routes in the Alps. This system became the basis of the Union Internationale des Associations d'Alpinisme (UIAA; International Climbing and Mountaineering Federation) system of rating. Rating systems have since proliferated. Internationally in the 21st century, no fewer than seven systems are used for rock, while there are four for alpine climbing, four for ice, and two for aid climbing.

Rating climbs is a subjective task, which makes consistency between climbing areas elusive. Climb ratings assume fair weather and availability of the best possible equipment. Variables that affect the rating include a climber's size, strength, and flexibility, as well as the type of climb (for instance, face, crack, or friction climbing) and the types of holds or features. Ideally, a route is rated by consensus to reduce personal bias, though the first-ascent party often rates a climb. A guidebook author typically does not climb every route in the guidebook and therefore has to rely on other climbers' opinions.

Ratings described as "stiff" indicate that the climb is harder than its rating, whereas a "soft" rating indicates the climb is easier than its rating. When you climb in an area for the first time, it's a good idea to start out on recommended or "starred" routes below your usual ability until you have evaluated the local ratings and nature of the rock.

Alpine Climbing

The National Climbing Classification System (NCCS), developed in the United States, assigns grades (also called commitment grades) to describe the overall difficulty of a multipitch alpine climb or long rock climb in terms of time and technical rock difficulty. The NCCS takes the following factors into account: length of climb, number of difficult pitches, difficulty of hardest pitch, average pitch difficulty, commitment, routefinding problems, and ascent time. A climb's approach and remoteness may affect the grade given, depending on the guidebook and area. Higher grades require more psychological preparation and commitment.

Grade I. Normally requires several hours; can be of any technical difficulty.

Grade II. Requires half a day; any technical difficulty.

Grade III. Requires a day to do the technical portion; any technical difficulty.

Grade IV. Requires a full day for the technical portion; the hardest pitch is usually no less than 5.7 (in the Yosemite Decimal System for rating rock climbs; see Free Climbing below).

Grade V. Requires a day and a half; the hardest pitch is at least 5.8.

Grade VI. A multiday excursion with difficult free climbing and/or aid climbing.

Grade VII. Requires at least 10 days on a huge wall, in poor weather, in a remote area. The climbing grades are at least as difficult as those on a Grade VI climb, with all other factors increasing in intensity.

Like other rating systems, the grade is subjective. For example, the *Nose* on El Capitan in California's Yosemite National Park is rated Grade VI. Warren Harding and companions took 45 days for the first ascent, in 1958. John Long, Billy Westbay, and Jim Bridwell made the first one-day ascent in 1975. Hans Florine and Peter Croft cut the time to less than four and a half hours in 1992, and Lynn Hill (accompanied by a belayer) led the first free ascent in 1993 and the first one-day free ascent in 1994. In 2018, Alex Honnold and Tommy Caldwell pushed the speed record to under two hours.

The time needed for a climb is as relative as the abilities and technologies of the climbers. The type of climb affects what factors of the given grade are emphasized. Proper planning, including studying a route description, is more valuable in determining a party's climbing time than the given grade.

Rock Climbing

Rating systems for free climbing, aid climbing, and bouldering help climbers in each discipline compare routes and evaluate difficulty.

FREE CLIMBING

In 1937, a modified Welzenbach rating system was introduced in the United States as the Sierra Club System. In the 1950s, this system was modified to more accurately describe the rock climbing being done at Tahquitz Rock in California by adding a decimal to the Class 5 rating. This is now known as the Yosemite Decimal System (YDS). This system categorizes terrain according to the techniques and physical difficulties encountered when rock climbing.

Figure A-1 compares the YDS with other international rating systems.

Class 1. Hiking.

Class 2. Simple scrambling, with possible occasional use of the hands.

Class 3. Scrambling; hands are used for balance; a rope might be carried.

Class 4. Simple climbing, often with exposure. A rope is often used. A fall could be fatal. Typically, natural protection can be easily found.

Class 5. Where rock climbing begins in earnest. Climbing involves the use of a rope, belaying, and protection (natural or artificial) to protect the leader from a long fall.

The decimal extension of Class 5 climbing originally was meant to be a closed-end scale—that is, ranging from 5.0 to 5.9. Up until 1960 or so, a climb that was the hardest of that era would be rated 5.9. The rising climbing standards in the 1960s, however, led to a need for an open-ended scale. Strict decimal protocol was abandoned, and 5.10 (pronounced "five-ten") was adopted as the next highest level. As this open-ended system developed, not all climbs were rerated, leaving a disparity between the "old-school ratings" and the new ratings.

The YDS numbers reached 5.15 in the first few years of the 21st century. The ratings from 5.10 to 5.15 are subdivided into a, b, c, and d levels to state the difficulty more precisely. The most difficult 5.12 climb, for instance, is rated 5.12d. A plus or minus sign is used to refine a classification. Sometimes a plus sign indicates that the pitch is sustained at its particular rating, while a minus sign might indicate that the pitch has only a single move at that level.

The extended numbers of the fifth-class rating system can't be defined precisely, but the following descriptions offer general guidelines:

5.0–5.7. Easy for experienced climbers; where most novices begin.

5.8–5.9. Where most weekend climbers become comfortable; employs the specific skills of rock climbing, such as jamming, liebacks, and mantels.

5.10–5.11. A committed recreational climber can reach this level.

5.12–5.15. The realm of true experts; demands much training and natural ability, as well as often, repeated working of a route.

The YDS rates only the hardest move on a pitch and, for multipitch climbs, the hardest pitch on a climb. The YDS gives no indication of overall difficulty, protection, exposure, runouts, or strenuousness. Some guidebooks, however, will rate a pitch higher than the hardest move if the pitch is very sustained at a lower level. A guidebook's introduction should explain any variations on the YDS that may be used.

Because the YDS does not calculate the potential of a fall, but only the difficulty of a move or pitch, a seriousness rating has been developed. This seriousness rating (introduced by Jim Erickson in 1980) appears in guidebooks in a variety of forms; read the introduction to any guidebook for an explanation of its particular version.

PG/PG-13. Protection is adequate, and if it is properly placed, a fall would not be long.

R. Protection is considered inadequate; there is potential for a long fall, and a falling leader would take a real "whipper," suffering serious injuries.

X. Inadequate or no protection; a fall would be very long with serious, perhaps fatal, consequences.

Ratings of the quality of routes are common in guidebooks. If anything, they are even more subjective than the basic climb ratings because they attempt to indicate aesthetics. The number of stars given for a route indicates the quality of the route in the eyes of the guidebook writer. A standard number of stars for the very best climbs has not been established. A climb with no stars does not mean the climb isn't worth doing, nor does a star-spangled listing mean that everyone will like the route.

AID CLIMBING

Rating aid moves or aid climbs is different from rating free climbs in that the rating system is not open-ended like the YDS. An aid climbing rating primarily indicates the severity of a possible fall, based on the quality of protection available. To some extent, an aid rating indicates the difficulty of the climbing, but only in that there is a loose correlation between easy-to-place protection and its ability to arrest a fall. However, following a series of "easy" hook moves for a distance of 40 feet (12 meters) with no protection left to arrest a fall might garner a rating of A3, while conversely some A1 pitches might accommodate high-quality protection at regular intervals but could be extremely difficult to climb if the crack is a deep, awkward flare with protection available only at its very back.

The scale is from A0 to A5 or from C0 to C5. The "A" refers to aid climbs in general, which may utilize pitons, bolts, or nuts. The "C" refers to clean aid climbing, meaning that a hammer is not used to make placements. A rating such as C2F, with the "F" indicating "fixed," indicates that the pitch can be climbed clean only if critical gear normally placed with a hammer has been left in place by other parties. It is sometimes possible to climb a pitch clean that is

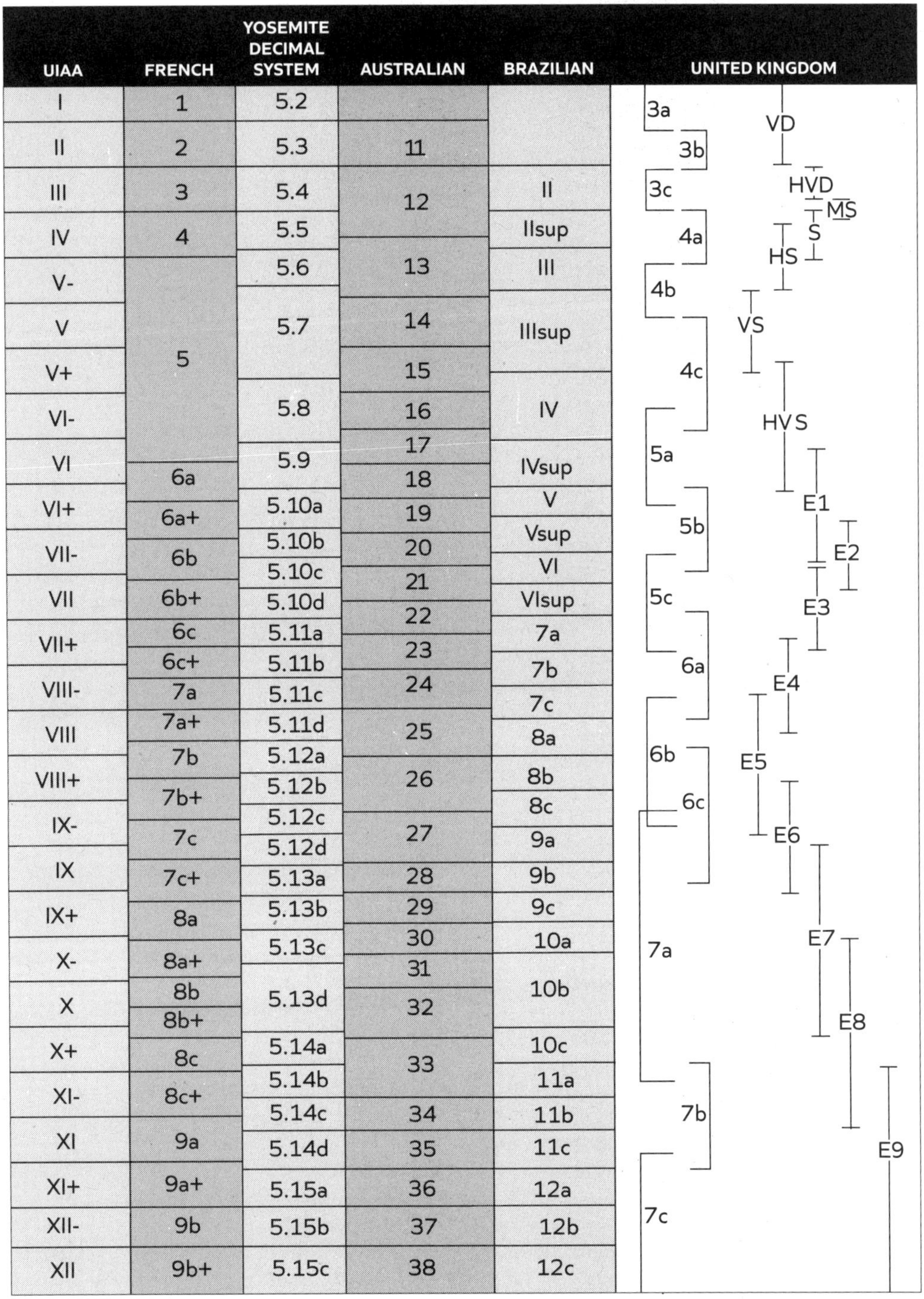

UIAA	FRENCH	YOSEMITE DECIMAL SYSTEM	AUSTRALIAN	BRAZILIAN
I	1	5.2		
II	2	5.3	11	
III	3	5.4	12	II
IV	4	5.5		IIsup
V-		5.6	13	III
V	5	5.7	14	IIIsup
V+			15	
VI-		5.8	16	IV
VI	6a	5.9	17	
			18	IVsup
VI+	6a+	5.10a	19	V
VII-	6b	5.10b	20	Vsup
		5.10c	21	VI
VII	6b+	5.10d	22	VIsup
VII+	6c	5.11a	23	7a
	6c+	5.11b		7b
VIII-	7a	5.11c	24	7c
VIII	7a+	5.11d	25	8a
VIII+	7b	5.12a	26	8b
	7b+	5.12b		8c
IX-	7c	5.12c	27	
		5.12d		9a
IX	7c+	5.13a	28	9b
IX+	8a	5.13b	29	9c
X-	8a+	5.13c	30	10a
			31	
X	8b	5.13d	32	10b
	8b+			
X+	8c	5.14a	33	10c
XI-	8c+	5.14b		11a
		5.14c	34	11b
XI	9a	5.14d	35	11c
XI+	9a+	5.15a	36	12a
XII-	9b	5.15b	37	12b
XII	9b+	5.15c	38	12c

UNITED KINGDOM (bracketed grades): 3a, 3b, 3c, 4a, 4b, 4c, 5a, 5b, 5c, 6a, 6b, 6c, 7a, 7b, 7c; VD, HVD, MS, S, HS, VS, HVS, E1, E2, E3, E4, E5, E6, E7, E8, E9

Fig. A-1. *Six of the world's seventeen climbing rating systems.*

rated with the A0–A5 system, and some pitches have two ratings, one A rating and one C rating, which indicates the grade with or without a hammer.

The following rating system is used worldwide except in Australia (which uses M0 to M8; the "M" stands for "mechanical"):

A0 or C0. No aiders are required. Fixed gear such as bolts may be in place, or the climber may be able to simply pull on a piece of gear to get through the section, a technique sometimes called "French free."

A1 or C1. Good aid placements; virtually every placement is capable of holding a fall. Aiders are generally required.

A2 or C2. Placements are fairly good but may be tricky to place. There may be a couple of bad placements between good placements.

A2+ or C2+. Same as A2, though with increased fall potential—perhaps 20 to 30 feet (6 to 9 meters).

A3 or C3. Hard aid. Several hours to lead a pitch, with the potential of 60- to 80-foot (18- to 24-meter) falls, but without danger of grounding (hitting the ground) or serious injury.

A3+ or C3+. Same as A3, but with the potential of serious injury in a fall. Tenuous placements.

A4 or C4. Serious aid. Fall potential of 80 to 100 feet (24 to 30 meters), with very bad landings. Placements hold only body weight.

A4+ or C4+. More serious than A4. More time on the route, with increased danger.

A5 or C5. Placements hold only body weight for an entire pitch, with no solid protection such as bolts. A leader fall at the top of a 150-foot (45-meter) A5 pitch means a 300-foot (90-meter) fall or a fall that would cause a serious impact on a rock feature, the latter of which may be equivalent to hitting the ground.

A5+. A theoretical grade; A5, but with bad belay anchors. A fall means falling to the ground (anchor failure).

Aid ratings are always subject to change. What was once a difficult A4 seam may have been beaten out with pitons to the point that it will accept large nuts, rendering it C1. Camming devices and other examples of newer technology can sometimes turn difficult climbs into easy ones. Some climbs once considered A5 might now be rated A2 or A3 after repeated traffic and with the use of modern equipment.

Big wall climbs are rated like this: The *Nose*, El Capitan: VI 5.8 C2. This notation means that the *Nose* route on Yosemite's El Capitan is a Grade VI (a "multiday excursion");

YOSEMITE DECIMAL SYSTEM	SHERMAN V-SCALE (BOULDERING)
5.8	V0-
5.9	V0
5.10a-b	V0+
5.10c-d	V1
5.11a-b	V2
5.11c-d	V3
5.12-	V4
5.12	V5
5.12+	V6
5.13-	V7
5.13	V8
5.13+	V9
5.14a	V10
5.14b	V11
5.14c	V12
5.14d	V13
5.15a	V14
5.15b	V15
5.15c	V16

Fig. A-2. *The Sherman V-scale for rating boulder problems, compared to the Yosemite Decimal System for rating rock climbs.*

the most difficult moves that you must free climb (with no option to aid) are YDS 5.8; and the most difficult aid is C2.

BOULDERING

Bouldering—climbing on large rocks, fairly close to the ground—is a popular discipline. Though once a game played by alpinists in mountain boots on days too rainy for climbing, bouldering has become an all-out pursuit of its own. John Gill created his B-scale to rate boulder problems:

B1. Requires moves at a high level of skill—moves that would be rated 5.12 or 5.13.

B2. Moves as hard as the hardest climbs being done in standard rock climbing (5.15 currently).

B3. A successful B2 climb that has yet to be repeated. Once it is repeated, the boulder rating automatically drops to B2.

John Sherman created the open-ended V-scale, which gives permanent ratings to boulder problems (unlike Gill's scale, with its floating ratings). As shown in Figure A-2, Sherman's scale starts at V0- (comparable to 5.8 YDS); it moves up through V0, V0+, V1, V2, and so on, with V16 being comparable to 5.15c YDS. Neither the B- nor V-scale takes into account the consequences of a rough landing on uneven terrain.

Ice Climbing

The variable conditions of snow, ice, and ice formations make rating climbs on those surfaces difficult. The only factors that usually do not vary throughout the season and from year to year are length and steepness. Snow depth, ice thickness, and temperature affect the conditions of the route; these factors plus the nature of the ice and its protection possibilities determine a route's difficulty. These rating systems apply mainly to waterfall ice and other ice formed by meltwater (rather than from consolidating snow, as on glaciers).

COMMITMENT RATING

The important factors in this ice climbing rating system are the length of the approach and descent, the length of the climb itself, objective hazards, and the nature of the climbing. (The roman numeral ratings used in this system have no correlation to the numerals used in the grading system for overall difficulty of alpine climbs; see Alpine Climbing above.)

I. A short, easy climb near the road, with no avalanche hazard and a straightforward descent.

II. A route of one or two pitches within a short distance of rescue assistance, with very little objective hazard.

III. A multipitch route at low elevation, or a one-pitch climb with an approach that takes an hour or so. The route requires from a few hours to a long day to complete. Descent may require building rappel anchors, and the route might be prone to avalanche.

IV. A multipitch route at higher elevations; may require several hours of approach on skis or foot. Subject to objective hazards; possibly involves a hazardous descent.

V. A long climb in a remote setting, requiring all day to complete the climb itself. Requires many rappels off anchors for the descent. Sustained exposure to avalanche or other objective hazards.

VI. A long ice climb in an alpine setting, with sustained technical climbing. Only elite climbers will complete it in a day. A difficult and involved approach and descent, with objective hazards ever present, all in a remote area far from the road.

VII. Everything a grade VI has, and more of it. Possibly requires days to approach the climb, and objective hazards render survival as certain as a coin toss. Needless to say, difficult physically and mentally.

TECHNICAL RATING

The technical grade rates the single most difficult pitch, taking into account the sustained nature of the climbing, ice thickness, and natural ice features such as chandeliers, mushrooms, or overhanging bulges. These ratings have been further subdivided, with a plus or minus added to grades of 4 and above if the route is usually more or less difficult than its stated numerical grade.

1. A frozen lake or streambed (the equivalent of an ice rink).

2. A pitch with short sections of ice up to 80 degrees; a lot of opportunity for protection and good anchors.

3. Sustained ice up to 80 degrees; the ice is usually good, with places to rest, but it requires skill at placing protection and setting anchors.

4. A sustained pitch that is vertical or slightly less than vertical; may have special features such as chandeliers and runouts between protection.

5. A long, strenuous pitch—possibly 165 feet (50 meters) of 85- to 90-degree ice with few if any rests between anchors. Or the pitch may be shorter but on featureless ice. Good skills at placing protection are required.

6. A full 165-foot pitch of dead-vertical ice, possibly of poor quality; requires efficiency of movement and ability to place protection from awkward stances.

7. A full pitch of thin, vertical or overhanging ice of dubious adhesion. An extremely tough pitch, physically and mentally, requiring agility and creativity.

8. Thin, gymnastic, overhanging, and bold. Pure ice climbs at this level are extremely rare.

These ratings typically describe a route in its first-ascent condition. Therefore a route that was rated a 5 on its first ascent might be a 6- in a lean year for ice, but only a 4+ in a year with thick ice. The numerical ice ratings are often prefaced with WI (water ice, or frozen waterfalls), AI (alpine ice), or M (mixed rock and ice; historically, mixed climbs were described with the YDS).

NEW ENGLAND ICE RATING SYSTEM

A system developed for the water ice found in New England applies to a normal winter ascent of a route in moderate weather conditions:

NEI 1. Low-angle water ice of 40 to 50 degrees, or a long, moderate snow climb requiring a basic level of technical expertise for safety.

NEI 2. Low-angle water ice with short bulges up to 60 degrees.

NEI 3. Steeper water ice of 50 to 60 degrees, with bulges of 70 to 90 degrees.

NEI 4. Short vertical columns, interspersed with rests, on 50- to 60-degree ice; fairly sustained climbing.

NEI 5. Generally multipitch ice climbing with sustained difficulties and/or strenuous vertical columns, with little rest possible.

NEI 5+. Multipitch routes with a heightened degree of seriousness, long vertical sections, and extremely sustained difficulties; the hardest ice climbing in New England to date.

MIXED CLIMBING

Jeff Lowe introduced the Modern Mixed Climbing Grade to simplify crux ratings on mixed ice and rock routes. It is an open-ended scale with routes rated M1 to M13. A plus sign or a minus sign is added to broaden the range and to prevent grade compression. It is the consensus of top climbers that the M ratings in Europe are inflated by one grade. See Figure A-3 for a comparison of the M grades to YDS ratings.

Other Major Rating Systems

A variety of rating systems are used throughout the world. Figure A-1 compares the principal systems. These systems are unique to their own treatment of seriousness and local weather and conditional phenomena. The Alaska Grade, for example, is a grading system unique to Alaska that takes into account severe storms, cold, altitude, and cornicing; it extends from Grade 1 to 6 (instead of overall commitment ratings I to VII).

MODERN MIXED GRADE	YOSEMITE DECIMAL SYSTEM
M4	5.8
M5	5.9
M6	5.10
M7	5.11
M8	5.11+/5.12-
M9	5.12+/5.13-
M10	5.13+/5.14-
M11	5.14+/5.15-
M12	5.15
M13	5.15+

Fig. A-3. *The Modern Mixed Climbing Grade for mixed rock and ice climbs, compared to the Yosemite Decimal System for rating rock climbs.*

When climbing in a new area, be sure to check with local authorities and/or guidebooks and become knowledgeable about any possible local grading systems and their peculiarities.

ROCK CLIMBING

Here are some of the most well-known systems for rating rock climbs around the world.

Australian. The Australian system uses an open-ended number series. The Australian number 38, for example, is equivalent to 5.15c in the YDS.

Brazilian. The rating of climbs in Brazil is composed of two parts. The first part gives the general level of difficulty of the route as a whole, ranging from first to eighth grade (or degree). The second part gives the difficulty of the hardest free move (or sequence of moves without a natural rest). Figure A-1 shows only the second part of the Brazilian system, the part that is most comparable to the other systems shown. The lower range is expressed in roman numerals; the designation "sup" (for "superior") is added to refine the accuracy of the rating. The upper range is expressed in arabic numerals with letter modifiers.

United Kingdom. The UK system is composed of two elements: an adjectival grade and a technical grade.

The adjectival grade—such as Very Difficult (VD) or Hard Severe (HS)—describes the overall difficulty of a route, including such factors as exposure, seriousness, strenuousness, protection, and runouts. The list of adjectives to describe increasingly difficult routes became so cumbersome that the British finally ended it at Extremely Severe (ES) and now simply advance the listing with numbers: E1 for Extremely Severe 1, E2 for Extremely Severe 2, and so forth:

E. Easy.

M. Moderate.

D. Difficult.

VD. Very Difficult.

HVD. Hard Very Difficult.

MS. Mild Severe.

S. Severe.

HS. Hard Severe.

VS. Very Severe.

HVS. Hard Very Severe.

E1. Extremely Severe 1.

E2. Extremely Severe 2.

E3. Extremely Severe 3.

The technical grade is defined as the hardest move on a particular route. This numeric component of the British system is also open-ended and is subdivided into a, b, and c.

The two grades are linked to each other. For example, the standard adjectival grade for a well-protected 6a, which is not particularly sustained, is E3 (and the combined rating would be expressed as E3 6a). If the route is a bit run-out, it would be E4; if it is really run-out, it would be E5. See Figure A-1.

French. In the French open-ended system, ratings of 6 and above are subdivided into a, a+, b, b+, c, and c+. The French rating of 9b+ is comparable to 5.15c in the YDS.

UIAA. The UIAA open-ended rating system uses roman numerals. Beginning with the fifth level (V), the ratings also include pluses and minuses. The UIAA rating of XII is comparable to 5.15c in the YDS. German climbers use the UIAA system.

ALPINE CLIMBING AND ICE CLIMBING

The International French Adjectival System (IFAS) is an overall rating of alpine and ice climbs used primarily in the Alps. The system is used by several countries, including France, the United Kingdom, Germany, Italy, and Spain. It expresses the seriousness of the route, including factors such as length, objective danger, commitment, altitude, runouts, descent, and technical difficulty in terms of terrain.

The system has six categories that are symbolized by the initials of the French adjectives used. It is further refined with the use of plus or minus signs, or the terms "sup" (superior) or "inf" (inferior). The ratings end with an adjective readily understood in English:

F. *Facile* ("easy"). Steep walking routes, rock scrambling, and easy snow slopes. Crevasses possible on glaciers. Rope not always necessary.

PD. *Peu difficile* ("a little difficult"). Rock climbing with some technical difficulty, snow and ice slopes, serious glaciers, and narrow ridges.

AD. *Assez difficile* ("fairly difficult"). Fairly hard climbs, steep rock climbing, and long snow and/or ice slopes steeper than 50 degrees.

D. *Difficile* ("difficult"). Sustained hard rock and snow and/or ice climbing.

TD. *Très difficile* ("very difficult"). Serious technical climbing on all kinds of terrain.

ED. *Extrêmement difficile* ("extremely difficult"). Extremely serious climbs with long, sustained difficulties of the highest order.

ABO. *Abominable*. Translation—and difficulty—obvious.

GLOSSARY

A

accessory cord Core-and-sheath-constructed cord of diameters ranging from 2 to 8 millimeters, fabricated from aramid (Kevlar), nylon, Perlon, polyester, and polyethylene (Dyneema or Spectra) fibers. Often shortened to cord. *See also* Dyneema, Kevlar.

accumulation zone The portion of a glacier that receives more snow each year than it loses each year to melting.

acute mountain sickness (AMS) An altitude-related illness.

aid climbing Using gear to support a climber's weight while climbing.

aiders Webbing ladders that allow an aid climber to step up. Also called *etriers*.

alpine rock climbing Rock climbing that requires mountaineering skills.

alpine start Starting before daybreak.

altimeter Instrument for determining altitude.

AMS *See* acute mountain sickness. Also called altitude sickness.

anchor The point on the mountain to which the climbing system is securely attached; there are belay anchors, rappel anchors, and protection in rock, snow, and ice.

approach shoes Lightweight, sticky-soled shoes designed for both trails and moderate rock climbing.

ascender Mechanical device used to ascend a rope. Also called *jug, jumar.*

autoblock A hitch that provides modest friction to simulate the grip of a hand. Commonly used while rappelling.

B

back-cleaning A procedure in which the leader cleans some protection while ascending the route.

bearing The direction from one place to another measured in degrees from true north.

belay anchor *See* anchor.

belay device A piece of equipment that applies friction to the rope to arrest a fall.

belaying Fundamental technique of generating friction to stop a rope's movement and the climber attached to that rope.

bergschrund Giant crevasse found at the upper limit of glacier movement, formed where the moving glacier breaks away from the ice cap or snowfield above.

bight A 180-degree bend in a rope.

big wall climbing Climbing on a large, sheer wall, which usually requires bivouacs and extensive aid climbing.

bivy From the French *bivouac*, meaning "temporary encampment."

bivy sack Large fabric envelope that serves as a lightweight alternative to a tent.

body belay *See* hip belay.

bollard A mound carved out of snow or ice and rigged with rope, webbing, or accessory cord to provide an anchor.

bolt Permanent piece of artificial protection consisting of a threaded bolt that is placed into a hole drilled into rock.

brake hand The belayer's hand that secures the belay; must be kept in contact with the rope at all times.

C

cairn A pile of rocks used as a route marker.

cam *See* spring-loaded camming device, Tricam.

camming Application of torquing or counterpressure with climbing gear.

carabiner Metal snap-link that comes in various shapes and sizes; indispensable and versatile climbing tool used for belaying, rappelling, clipping in to safety anchors, securing the rope to points of protection, and numerous other tasks.

CEN European Committee for Standardization, Comité Européen de Normalisation. The European nonprofit organization responsible for creating and maintaining climbing equipment standards. The "CE" mark signifies that a product meets all applicable European legislation. *See also* UIAA.

chimney A crack wide enough to fit a climber's body and narrow enough to allow a climber to apply opposing force to both walls.

chlorine dioxide Chemical water treatment method (not to be confused with chlorine) for purifying water.

chock Removeable protection for climbing; mostly outdated term. Also called stopper. *See also* hex, nut, spring-loaded nut, Tricam, tube chock, wired nut.

chockstone A rock firmly lodged in a crack or between gully walls.

circlehead *See* copperhead.

clean climbing Climbing without permanently marring the rock.

cleaning Removing protection.

cleaning tool *See* nut tool.

climbing in coils The preferred tie-in method for two-person glacier-travel teams—for closer spacing between rope partners and more efficient travel.

combination technique *See* hybrid technique.

contour lines Lines on topographic maps that represent constant elevations.

coordinate system A system, such as UTM or latitude and longitude, to describe a location on the earth.

copperhead Malleable hardware used in aid climbing. Also called *head, circlehead.*

cord *See* accessory cord.

cordelette A long runner usually made of 7- to 8-millimeter nylon or small-diameter, high-strength accessory cord.

crag climbing Technical rock climbing in an area close to roads and civilization that does not require alpine skills.

crampons A set of metal spikes that attach to boots in order to penetrate hard snow and ice.

crevasse A crack or chasm in a glacier.

crux The most significant, committing, or difficult section of a pitch or climb.

D

daisy chain Sewn sling with stitched loops.

datum The anchoring points for a coordinate system. Critical when using a map with a GPS device.

deadman *See* T-slot.

declination Compass adjustment needed to correct for local difference between magnetic north and true north.

dihedral Where two walls meet in approximately a right-angled inside corner. Also called *open book.*

dry rope Rope treated to make it more water-repellent.

dry tooling Climbing on rock with ice tools and crampons.

dulfersitz Configuration for rappelling in the event that a harness or carabiners are not available.

DWR Durable water-repellent. A chemical coating applied to fabrics to make them hydrophobic and able to shed water. Currently essential to the functioning of virtually all waterproof, breathable fabrics.

dynamic rope A rope that stretches under loads.

Dyneema Brand name for ultra-high-molecular-weight, ultra-strong polyethylene fibers. Material is highly abrasion-resistant and very lightweight but has a low melting point and is very slippery, making knots difficult. Commonly used in climbing runners; also called *Spectra.*

E

edging Climbing technique using either the inside or outside edge of the foot so that the edge of the sole is weighted over the hold.

emergency communication device A device that can be used to summon help in an emergency. Includes radios, smartphones, personal locator beacons (PLBs), satellite phones, and satellite communicators (Garmin inReach, SPOT). *See also* personal locator beacon, satellite communicator.

equalette A cordelette with pretied knots used to rig anchors. *See* cordelette.

equalization Equalizing forces on a multipoint anchor.

Esbit fuel Waxy fuel tablets made of hexamine and used in ultralight stoves.

etriers *See* aiders.

F

fall factor The length of a fall divided by the length of the rope between belay device and fallen climber.

fall line The line of travel of a freely falling object.

fixed line Rope anchored in place.

fixed pin Permanent piton.

flagging Climbing technique that involves extending a limb for counterbalance, to prevent pivoting or the "barn-door" effect.

flaking Uncoiling the rope, one loop at a time, into a neat pile.

flat-footed *See* French technique.

follower *See* second.

free climbing Using ropes and other means of climbing protection to protect against injury, not assist progress. Originally meant "free from aid."

free solo climbing Climbing without any rope or other means of protection where a fall would result in serious injury or death.

French technique Cramponing technique used on moderately steep snow and ice in which the feet are placed flat against the surface of the snow or ice. Also called *flat-footed.*

friction climbing *See* smearing.

front-pointing Kicking front crampon points into hard snow or ice. Also known as *German technique.*

G

gaiters Article of clothing used to seal boundary between pant legs and boots from water, snow, and debris.

German technique *See* front-pointing.

glissade A controlled slide on snow.

Global Positioning System (GPS) Collective term for satellite-based navigation system run by US Department of Defense and similar agencies in other countries. Often referred to as GPS.

grade A ranking from I to VII describing the overall difficulty of a multipitch alpine climb or long rock climb in terms of time and technical rock difficulty. Also used as a general term for a climb's rating.

guide hand The belayer's hand that pays the rope in and out.

guylines Cords attached to a tent or tarp and staked out to brace it.

H

HACE *See* high-altitude cerebral edema.

halbmastwurf sicherung (HMS) German for "half clove-hitch belay"; another term for the munter hitch. Carabiners stamped "HMS" accommodate the munter hitch.

HAPE *See* high-altitude pulmonary edema.

hardshell Typically uninsulated rain parka or pants made from waterproof, breathable fabric. *See also* softshell.

heads *See* copperhead.

hero loop *See* tie-off loop.

hex Hexagonally shaped, passive removable protection. A type of chock.

high-altitude cerebral edema (HACE) An altitude-related illness affecting the brain.

high-altitude pulmonary edema (HAPE) An altitude-related illness affecting the lungs.

hip belay A method of applying friction to the rope with the belayer's body that does not require a mechanical device. Also known as a *body belay*.

HMS *See* halbmastwurf sicherung.

hybrid technique Cramponing technique that combines flat-footed (French technique) and front-pointing (German technique) on steep snow or ice. Also called *combination technique*. *See also* French technique, German technique.

I

ice axe Specialized tool used by climbers, generally for snow and ice travel.

ice screw A tubular, hollow screw used as protection in ice.

ice tool Short ice axe or hammer used for technical ice climbing.

icefall Steep, jumbled section of a glacier. Also a term for falling ice.

J

jamming A basic technique of crack climbing in which a hand or foot is jammed into a crack, then turned or flexed so that it is snugly in contact with both sides of the crack and it will not come out when weighted.

jugging Ascending the climbing rope with mechanical ascenders in aid climbing. Also called *jumaring*.

jumaring *See* jugging.

K

kernmantle rope Rope composed of a core of braided or parallel nylon filaments encased in a smooth, woven sheath of nylon; designed specifically for climbing.

Kevlar Aramid synthetic fiber trademarked by DuPont; used in accessory cord, among other things. *See also* accessory cord.

L

leader The climber who takes the lead on a roped pitch.

leashless tool Ice tools specifically designed to be used without leashes.

Leave No Trace Principles of minimum impact developed by the organization of the same name.

lieback To use hands in opposition to feet to create a counterforce.

load-limiting runner A presewn runner with a series of weaker bar tacks that fail at lower impact forces and absorb high loads.

M

mantel To use hand down-pressure to permit the raising of the feet.

matching Placing both hands or both feet on the same hold, often to transition from one hold to the other.

microfilter Drinking water filter designed to filter parasites, protozoa, and bacteria, but not viruses. *See also* purifier-filter.

moat Gap between snow and rock.

moraine Mounds of rock and debris deposited by a glacier.

mountaineering boot Crampon-compatible, stiff-soled footwear.

multipitch A route with two or more pitches.

munter hitch A friction knot used for belaying and rappelling. *See also* halbmastwurf sicherung.

N

nieves penitentes Snow pillars produced when suncup hollows become very deep, accentuating the ridges into columns of snow that look like a person wearing a penitent's cowl.

nut Passive removable protection that is a wedging-type chock. Also called *stopper, wired nut*. *See also* spring-loaded nut.

nut tool Tool used for removing protection. Also known as a *cleaning tool*.

nylon cord *See* accessory cord.

O

objective hazard Physical hazard associated with a climbing route, such as rockfall, exposure, or high altitude.

off-width A crack that is too wide for a hand jam but too narrow for chimney technique.

open book *See* dihedral.

P

pearabiner A carabiner large enough at its wider end to accommodate a munter hitch or multiple anchor tie-ins.

PCP *See* progress capture pulley.

Perlon A brand name for nylon 6. *See* accessory cord.

personal anchor A runner, sling, or other material (such as the rope itself) a climber uses to attach themselves to belay and rappel anchors.

personal locator beacon (PLB) Electronic device that broadcasts a user's GPS location to emergency first responders via government-based satellites. Also called PLB. Similar to *satellite communicators*.

picket An aluminum stake used for an anchor in snow.

piolet French word for ice axe; used to describe various ice-axe positions used to negotiate technical snow slopes.

pitch The distance between belays on a climb.

piton A metal spike used as protection.

plunge-stepping A technique for walking down a snow slope that involves assertively stepping away from the slope and landing solidly on the heel with the leg vertical (but not with the knee locked), transferring weight to the new position.

posthole To sink deeply with each step in snow.

progress capture pulley (PCP) Pulley device with integrated cam that allows a user to capture progress immediately without the need of prusiks. Used in crevasse rescue rope systems.

protection Point of attachment that links climbing rope to the terrain. Also known as pro.

prusik A friction hitch. Also a technique for ascending a climbing rope using friction hitches.

purifier-filter Drinking water filter designed to filter parasites, protozoa, bacteria, and viruses. *See also* microfilter.

Q

quad A cordelette tied into an equalette and then doubled over and tied with limiter knots. Popular as anchors on sport climbs.

quickdraw A presewn runner, typically 4 to 8 inches (10 to 20 centimeters) long, with a carabiner loop sewn into each end through which a carabiner is attached.

R

rappel anchor *See* anchor.

rappelling Fundamental climbing technique of safely descending a rope using friction to control speed.

rest step Ascent technique that ends every step with a momentary stop relying on skeletal structure to give muscles a rest.

rock shoe Specialized rock climbing footwear with a sticky rubber sole.

rope drag Friction that impedes the rope's travel.

runner Length of webbing or accessory cord used to connect components of the climbing safety system. Also called a *sling*.

running belay Climbing technique in which all members of the rope team climb at the same time, relying on immediate protection rather than a fixed belay. Also called *simul-climbing*.

S

satellite communicator Electronic device that broadcasts a user's GPS location to emergency first responders via commercial satellites. Also called satellite messengers. May include texting, location tracking, and other nonemergency communication.

scrambling Unroped, off-trail travel that requires some use of hands.

scree Loose slope of rock fragments smaller than talus.

second The climber who follows the leader on a roped pitch. Also known as a *follower*.

self-arrest Ice-axe technique used to stop a fall on snow.

self-belay Ice-axe technique in which the ice axe is jammed straight down into the snow and held by the head or head and shaft.

serac Tower of ice on a glacier.

simul-climbing *See* running belay.

single-pulley system *See* 2:1 pulley system.

ski mountaineering Involves climbing mountains, either on skis or while carrying skis, and skiing down using randonée (also known as alpine touring) or telemark gear and style.

skins Strips of textured material that attach to the bottoms of skis for traction, designed to let the ski slide forward on snow but not backward.

SLCD *See* spring-loaded camming device.

slider nut *See* spring-loaded nut.

sling *See* runner.

smearing Rock climbing technique in which the foot points uphill and the climber maximizes contact between the rock and the sole of the shoe for friction. Also called *friction climbing*.

snow pit Pit dug into snow in order to observe snow conditions.

softshell Article of clothing made from dense, stretchy, woven synthetic fabric. *See also* hardshell.

Spectra *See* Dyneema.

SPF Sun protection factor, the rating system that quantifies the degree of sun protection provided by a sunscreen product.

sport climbing Technical rock climbing that relies on fixed protection (bolts) and does not usually require mountaineering skills; compare *trad climbing*.

spring-loaded camming device (SLCD) Active removable protection that uses spring-loaded cams to create opposing force in a crack. Also called a *cam*.

spring-loaded nut A chock that uses a small sliding piece to expand the profile of the chock after it is placed in a crack. Also called a *slider nut*. *See also* chock.

static rope A rope that does not stretch; used for fixed lines and hauling.

stemming Climbing technique using counterforce in which one foot presses against one feature while the other foot or an opposing hand pushes against another feature; commonly used to climb chimneys or dihedrals.

step kicking Climbing technique that creates ascending steps in snow.

stopper *See* chock, nut, wired nut.

suncup Small hollow in snow or ice that is created by melting and evaporation.

T

talus Rock fragments large enough to step on individually. *See also* scree.

team arrest Arrest attempted by several members of a rope team on a snow slope.

technical climbing Climbing in which belays or protection should be used for safety.

Ten Essentials Essential gear that should be carried on all wilderness trips. Developed by The Mountaineers.

3:1 pulley system Raising system that theoretically triples the amount of weight a rescue team could haul without a pulley. Also called *Z-pulley system*.

tie-off loop Short runner commonly used for tying off belays, for self-belay during a rappel, in aid climbing, and in rescue. Also called *hero loop*.

topos Topographic maps or climbers' sketch maps.

top roping A crag or sport climbing technique in which the climber is belayed using a rope that runs up from the belayer, through a preplaced top anchor, and back down to the climber.

trad climbing Technical rock climbing in which climbers place and remove protection; compare *sport climbing*.

Tricam Removable protection with a lobe-shaped camming wedge; can be set actively or passively. A type of chock.

T-slot Any object buried in the snow to serve as an anchor. Also any piece of hardware such as an ice screw or ice tool placed in ice to protect climbers.

tube chock Telescoping protection used for off-width cracks. *See also* chock.

2:1 pulley system Raising system that theoretically doubles the amount of weight that a rescue team could haul without a pulley. Also called *single-pulley system*.

U

UIAA International Climbing and Mountaineering Federation, Union Internationale des Associations d'Alpinisme. The internationally recognized authority in setting standards for climbing equipment. *See also* CEN.

UPF Ultraviolet protection factor, the rating system that quantifies the degree of sun protection provided by a garment.

UTM The Universal Transverse Mercator is one of the principal coordinate systems used to define a location on the earth. *See also* coordinate system, datum.

V

verglas The thin, clear coating of ice that forms when rainfall or melting snow freezes on a rock surface.

V-thread anchor A V-shaped tunnel bored into the ice, with accessory cord or webbing threaded through the tunnel and tied to form a sling.

V-thread tool A hooking device used to pull accessory cord or webbing through the drilled tunnel of a V-thread ice anchor.

W

webbing *See* runner.

whippet Ski pole with an attachment resembling an ice-axe pick for self-arrest on snow slopes.

wired nut Passive removable protection. Also known as *chock, nut, stopper*.

Z

Z-pulley system *See* 3:1 pulley system.

RESOURCES

CHAPTER 1: FIRST STEPS

Barcott, Bruce. *The Measure of a Mountain: Beauty and Terror on Mount Rainier*. Seattle: Sasquatch Books, 2007.

Blum, Arlene. *Annapurna: A Woman's Place*. Reprint ed. Berkeley, CA: Counterpoint Press, 2015.

Bonatti, Walter. *The Mountains of My Life*. Translated and edited by Robert Marshall. London: Penguin Classic, 2010.

Caldwell, Tommy. *The Push: A Climber's Journey of Endurance, Risk, and Going Beyond Limits*. New York: Penguin Books, 2018.

Chin, Jimmy. *There and Back: Photographs from the Edge*. New York: Ten Speed Press, 2021.

DesLauriers, Kit. *Higher Love: Climbing and Skiing the Seven Summits*. Seattle: Mountaineers Books, 2021.

Garton, Johanna. *Edge of the Map: The Mountain Life of Christine Boskoff*. Seattle: Mountaineers Books, 2020.

Gillman, Peter, and Leni Gillman. *The Wildest Dream: The Biography of George Mallory*. Seattle: Mountaineers Books, 2001.

Herzog, Maurice. *Annapurna: The First Conquest of an 8,000-Meter Peak*. Translated by Nea Morin and Janet Adam Smith. Lanham, MD: Lyons Press, 2022. First published 1952 by Dutton (New York).

Honnold, Alex, with David Roberts. *Alone on the Wall*. Expanded ed. New York: W. W. Norton, 2018.

Ives, Katie. *Imaginary Peaks: The Riesenstein Hoax and Other Mountain Dreams*. Seattle: Mountaineers Books, 2021.

Krakauer, Jon. *Eiger Dreams: Ventures Among Men and Mountains*. Reprint ed. Lanham, MD: Lyons Press, 2019.

Messner, Reinhold. *My Life at the Limit*. Seattle: Mountaineers Books, 2014.

Miller, Lauren DeLaunay. *Valley of Giants: Stories from Women at the Heart of Yosemite Climbing*. Seattle: Mountaineers Books, 2022.

Molenaar, Dee. *The Challenge of Rainier: A Record of the Explorations and Ascents, Triumphs and Tragedies on the Northwest's Greatest Mountain*. 40th anniversary/updated 4th ed. Seattle: Mountaineers Books, 2011.

Moro, Simone. *The Call of the Ice: Climbing 8000-Meter Peaks in Winter*. Translated by Monica Meneghetti. Seattle: Mountaineers Books, 2014.

Muir, John. *John Muir: The Eight Wilderness Discovery Books*. Seattle: Mountaineers Books, 1992.

Muir, John. *Nature Writings: The Story of My Boyhood and Youth; My First Summer in the Sierra; The Mountains of California; Stickeen; Essays*. Edited by William Cronon. New York: Library of America, 1997.

Nash, Roderick Frazier. *Wilderness and the American Mind*. 5th ed. New Haven, CT: Yale University Press, 2014.

Roberts, David. *Limits of the Known*. New York: W. W. Norton, 2018.

———. *The Mountain of My Fear and Deborah: Two Mountaineering Classics*. Seattle: Mountaineers Books, 2012.

Simpson, Joe. *Touching the Void: The True Story of One Man's Miraculous Survival*. New York: Perennial, 2004.

Steck, Ueli, with Karin Steinbach. *My Life in Climbing*. Translated by Billi Bierling. Seattle: Mountaineers Books, 2017.

Synnott, Mark. *The Impossible Climb: Alex Honnold, El Capitan, and the Climbing Life*. New York: Dutton, 2019.

Tharkay, Ang, with Basil P. Norton. *Sherpa: The Memoir of Ang Tharkay*. Translated by Corinne McKay. Seattle: Mountaineers Books, 2016.

Turner, Jack. *Teewinot: Climbing and Contemplating the Teton Range*. New York: St. Martin's Press, 2001.

Washburn, Bradford, and David Roberts. *Mount McKinley: The Conquest of Denali*. New York: Abrams, 2000.

Wood, Sharon. *Rising: Becoming the First North American Woman on Everest*. Seattle: Mountaineers Books, 2019.

CHAPTER 2: CLOTHING AND EQUIPMENT

Beck, Jessie, and Fred Perrotta. "The Best Merino Wool Clothing for Travel: Buyer's Guide." Tortuga. https://blog.tortugabackpacks.com/merino-wool-clothing/.

Dixon, Alan. "Ultralight Backpacking and Hiking." Adventure Alan. Accessed in 2022. www.adventurealan.com.

Evenson, Laura. "Layering Basics." REI Expert Advice. Accessed 2021. www.rei.com/learn/expert-advice/layering-basics.html.

Federal Trade Commission (FTC). "Guides for the Use of Environmental Marketing Claims." *Federal Register* 77, no. 197 (October 11, 2012): 62122–23. www.ftc.gov/sites/default/files/documents/federal_register_notices/guides-use-environmental-marketing-claims-green-guides/greenguidesfrn.pdf.

Kirkpatrick, Andy. "A Short History of Man Made Fabrics." November 8, 2008. www.andy-kirkpatrick.com/articles /view/a_short_history_of_man_made_fabrics.

Mutebi, John-Paul, and John E. Gimnig. "Mosquitoes, Ticks, and Other Arthropods." In *CDC Yellow Book 2024: Health Information for International Travel*, by the Centers for Disease Control and Prevention, 211–16. New York: Oxford University Press, 2023. www.nc.cdc.gov /travel/yellowbook/2024/environmental-hazards-risks /mosquitoes-ticks-and-other-arthropods. An updated *CDC Yellow Book* is released every two years.

National Academies of Sciences, Engineering, and Medicine. *Review of Fate, Exposure, and Effects of Sunscreen in Aquatic Environments and Implications for Sunscreen Usage and Human Health*. Washington, DC: National Academies Press, 2022. https://doi.org/10.17226/26381.

Nichols, Maggie. "The 4 Best Budget Windbreakers for Women of 2023." Outdoor Gear Lab, March 9, 2023. www.outdoorgearlab.com/topics/clothing-womens /best-budget-wind-breaker-jacket-womens. Article updated annually.

NOAA (National Oceanic and Atmospheric Administration) Marine Debris Program. "Plastics." Office of Response and Restoration, National Ocean Service, NOAA. Accessed 2022. https://marinedebris.noaa.gov/info/plastic.html.

Patagonia, Inc. "Product Care." Accessed 2021. www.patagonia.com/product-care.html.

Peeken, I., M. Bergmann, G. Gerdts, C. Katlein, T. Krumpen, S. Primpke, and M. Tekman. "Microplastics in the Marine Realms of the Arctic with Special Emphasis on Sea Ice." In *Arctic Report Card 2018*, by the NOAA (National Oceanic and Atmospheric Administration) Arctic Program. November 19, 2018. https://arctic.noaa.gov/Report-Card /Report-Card-2018/ArtMID/7878/ArticleID/787 /Microplastics-in-the-Marine-Realms-of-the-Arctic-with -Special-Emphasis-on-Sea-Ice.

Rosenberg, Ronald, Nicole P. Lindsey, Marc Fischer, et al. "*Vital Signs*: Trends in Reported Vectorborne Disease Cases—United States and Territories, 2004–2016." *Morbidity and Mortality Weekly Report* 67, no. 17 (May 4, 2018): 496–501. www.cdc.gov/mmwr/volumes/67/wr /mm6717e1.htm.

Schimelpfenig, Tod. *NOLS Wilderness Medicine*. 7th ed. Guilford, CT: Stackpole Books, 2021.

US Environmental Protection Agency (EPA). "Find the Repellent That Is Right for You." Accessed 2021. www.epa .gov/insect-repellents/find-insect-repellent-right-you.

———. "Fluorinated DWRs Contain the Chemical Contaminants Perfluorooctane Sulfonate (PFOS) and Perfluorooctanoic Acid (PFOA)." December 2017. www.epa.gov.

———. "Repellents: Protection against Mosquitoes, Ticks, and Other Arthropods." Accessed 2021. www.epa.gov /insect-repellents.

Wilkerson, James A. *Medicine for Mountaineering and Other Wilderness Activities*. 6th ed. Seattle: Mountaineers Books, 2010.

CHAPTER 3: CAMPING, FOOD, AND WATER

Anderson, Kristi, ed. *Wilderness Basics*. 4th ed. Seattle: Mountaineers Books, 2013.

Backpacker Geek. "Closed Cell Foam Pads—Part 2." May 22, 2017. https://backpackergeek.wordpress.com /2017/05/22/backpackergeek/closed-cell-foam-pads -part-2.

Burbidge, John, ed. *Backpacker Magazine's The Complete Guide to Backpacking: Field-Tested Gear, Advice, and Know-How for the Trail*. Guilford, CT: Globe Pequot/Falcon, 2016.

Centers for Disease Control and Prevention (CDC). "A Guide to Drinking Water Treatment and Sanitation for Backcountry and Travel Use." Accessed 2021. www.cdc .gov/healthywater/drinking/travel/backcountry_water _treatment.html.

Fisher, James, and *Backpacker* editors. "Backpacking Nutrition: What Hikers Need to Know About Eating on the Trail." *Backpacker*, March 2, 2022. www.backpacker .com/skills/the-essential-rules-of-performance-nutrition.

Gerber, Katie, and Heather Anderson. *Adventure Ready: A Hiker's Guide to Planning, Training, and Resiliency*. Seattle: Mountaineers Books, 2022.

Hassapidou, Maria. "Carbohydrate Requirements of Elite Athletes." *British Journal of Sports Medicine* 45, no. 2 (2011): e2. https://doi.org/10.1136/bjsm.2010.081570.23.

Helmuth, Diana. *How to Suffer Outside: A Beginner's Guide to Hiking and Backpacking*. Seattle: Mountaineers Books, 2021.

Hostetter, Kristin. *Backpacker Magazine's The 10 Essentials of Outdoor Gear: What You Need to Stay Alive*. Guilford, CT: Globe Pequot/Falcon, 2014.

Kirkpatrick, Andy. "Stoves." March 20, 2019. www.andy-kirkpatrick.com/blog/view/stoves.

Lichter, Justin, and Shawn Forry. *Ultralight Winter Travel: The Ultimate Guide to Lightweight Winter Camping, Hiking, and Backpacking*. Guilford, CT: Globe Pequot/Falcon, 2017.

Martin, Brian. "The 5 Best Bivy Sacks of 2023." Outdoor Gear Lab, October 21, 2023. www.outdoorgearlab.com/topics /camping-and-hiking/best-bivy-sack. Article updated annually.

Paul, Susan Joy. *Woman in the Wild: The Everywoman's Guide to Hiking, Camping, and Backcountry Travel*. Guilford, CT: Globe Pequot/Falcon, 2021.

Pugh, Griffith. "The Importance of Nutrition in Mountaineering." International Climbing and Mountaineering Federation (UIAA), April 21, 2017. www.theuiaa.org/mountaineering/the-importance-of -nutrition-in-mountaineering.

REI. "How to Choose Energy Food and Drinks." REI Expert Advice. Accessed 2021. www.rei.com/learn/expert-advice /energy-foods.html.

REI. "Hydration Basics: How to Choose a Water Filter or Purifier." REI Expert Advice. Accessed September 2022. www.rei.com/learn/expert-advice/water-treatment -backcountry.html.

Timmermann, Lisa F., Klaus Ritter, David Hillebrandt, and Thomas Küpper. "Drinking Water Treatment with Ultraviolet Light for Travelers: Evaluation of a Mobile Lightweight System." *Travel Medicine and Infectious Disease* 13, no. 6 (2015): 466–74. https://doi.org/10.1016 /j.tmaid.2015.10.005.

Wallace, Maggie. "The Complete Guide to Female Urination Devices." *Backpacker*, September 10, 2015. www .backpacker.com/gear-reviews/the-complete-guide-to -female-urination-devices.

Woolf, Marcus. "A Beginner's Guide to Camping Gear." Sea to Summit. October 17, 2016. https://seatosummit.com /blogs/adventure-tips/beginners-guide-camping-gear.

CHAPTER 4: CONDITIONING

Abramson, Ashley. "Read This Before You Buy a Massage Gun." *Consumer Reports*, August 17, 2021. www.consumerreports.org/massage-guns/massage -gun-buying-guide-a1197181514.

Absolon, Molly. *Backpacker Magazine's Fitness and Nutrition for Hiking*. Guilford, CT: Globe Pequot/Falcon, 2016.

American College of Sports Medicine. *ACSM's Fitness Assessment Manual*. 6th ed. Edited by Yuri Feito and Meir Magal. Philadelphia: Lippincott Wilkins & Williams, 2021.

Berardi, John. "Top Five 'Best Practices' for Elite Fitness Pros." Precision Nutrition. Accessed 2021. www.precisionnutrition.com/5-best-practices-for-pros.

Bergland, Christopher. "Longer Exhalations Are an Easy Way to Hack Your Vagus Nerve." *Psychology Today*, May 9, 2019. www.psychologytoday.com/intl/blog/the-athletes -way/201905/longer-exhalations-are-easy-way-hack-your -vagus-nerve.

Burbach, Matt. *Gym Climbing: Improve Technique, Movement, and Performance*. 2nd ed. Seattle: Mountaineers Books, 2018.

Colver, John, with M. Nicole Nazzaro. *Fit by Nature: The AdventX Twelve-Week Outdoor Fitness Program*. Seattle: Mountaineers Books, 2011.

Donahue, Topher, and Craig Luebben. *Rock Climbing: Mastering Basic Skills*. 2nd ed. Seattle: Mountaineers Books, 2014.

Ellison, Julie. *Climb to Fitness: The Ultimate Guide to Customizing a Powerful Workout on the Wall*. Guilford, CT: Globe Pequot/Falcon, 2018.

Harvard Medical School. "Understanding the Stress Response." Harvard Health Publishing, July 6, 2020. www.health.harvard.edu/staying-healthy/understanding -the-stress-response.

Hörst, Eric J. *How to Climb 5.12*. 3rd ed. Guilford, CT: Globe Pequot/Falcon, 2012.

———. *Maximum Climbing: Mental Training for Peak Performance and Optimal Experience*. Guilford, CT: Globe Pequot/Falcon, 2010.

———. *The Rock Climber's Exercise Guide: Training for Strength, Power, Endurance, Flexibility, and Stability*. Guilford, CT: Globe Pequot/Falcon, 2017.

———. *Training for Climbing: The Definitive Guide to Improving Your Performance*. 3rd ed. Guilford, CT: Globe Pequot/Falcon, 2016.

House, Steve, and Scott Johnston. "8 Week Mountaineering Training Plan." Uphill Athlete. Accessed September 3, 2021. uphillathlete.com.

———. *The New Alpinism Training Log*. Ventura, CA: Patagonia, 2015.

———. *Training for the New Alpinism: A Manual for the Climber as Athlete*. Ventura, CA: Patagonia, 2014.

House, Steve, Scott Johnston, and Kilian Jornet. *Training for the Uphill Athlete: A Manual for Mountain Runners and Ski Mountaineers*. Ventura, CA: Patagonia, 2019.

Imtiyaz, S., Z. Vegar, and M. Y. Sharzeef. "To Compare the Effect of Vibration Therapy and Massage in Prevention of Delayed Onset Muscle Soreness (DOMS)." *Journal of Clinical and Diagnostic Research* 8, no. 1 (January 2014): 133–36. https://doi.org/10.7860/JCDR/2014/7294.3971.

Iodice, P., P. Ripari, and G. Pezzulo. "Local High-Frequency Vibration Therapy Following Eccentric Exercises Reduces Muscle Soreness Perception and Posture Alterations in Elite Athletes." *European Journal of Applied Physiology* 119, no. 2 (February 2019): 539–49. https://doi.org/10.1007 /s00421-018-4026-5.

Layton, Julia. "How Fear Works." HowStuffWorks.com. Accessed March 19, 2022. https://science.howstuffworks .com/life/inside-the-mind/emotions/fear.htm.

Mayo Clinic Staff. "Male Menopause: Myth or Reality?" Mayo Clinic. Accessed June 2020. www.mayoclinic.org /healthy-lifestyle/mens-health/in-depth/male-menopause /art-20048056.

Naney, Alison, in conversation with Scott Johnston. "Training, Stress, and Success for Female Athletes with Uphill Athlete Coach Alison Naney." Uphill Athlete. Live Zoom event on May 28, 2020. YouTube video, 1:01:14. www.youtu.be/81_lRcZjK4U.

Pollmeier, Mercedes, and Maria Hines. *Peak Nutrition: Smart Fuel for Outdoor Adventure*. Seattle: Mountaineers Books, 2020.

Schurman, Courtenay W., and Doug G. Schurman. *The Outdoor Athlete*. Champaign, IL: Human Kinetics, 2009.

St. Pierre, Brian. "Best Workout Nutrition Strategies." Precision Nutrition. Accessed 2021. www.precision nutrition.com/best-workout-nutrition-strategies.

Tsong, Nicole. *Yoga for Climbers*. Seattle: Mountaineers Books, 2016.

Twight, Mark, and James Martin. *Extreme Alpinism: Climbing Light, Fast, and High*. Seattle: Mountaineers Books, 1999.

Uphill Athlete. "Uphill Athlete Training Zones Heart Rate Calculator." Accessed September 3, 2021. https://uphillathlete.com.

Wharton, Josh, and Uphill Athlete. "Josh Wharton's 4 Week Beginner to Intermediate Rock Climbing Training Plan." TrainingPeaks. Accessed September 3, 2021. www .trainingpeaks.com/training-plans/other/tp-107095/josh -whartons-4-week-beginner-to-intermediate-rock -climbing-training-plan.

World Health Organization (WHO). "Physical Activity." Accessed 2021. www.who.int/news-room/fact-sheets /detail/physical-activity.

CHAPTER 5: NAVIGATION AND COMMUNICATION

AllTrails. Good source for GPS tracks. www.alltrails.com.

Burns, Bob, and Mike Burns. *Wilderness Navigation: Finding Your Way Using Map, Compass, Altimeter, and GPS*. 4th ed. Seattle: Mountaineers Books, forthcoming 2025.

CalTopo. Backcountry mapping and trip-planning software for personal computers and phones. www.caltopo.com.

CanMaps. Canadian topographic maps. www.canmaps.com.

Caudill, Craig, and Tracy Trimble. *Essential Wilderness Navigation: A Real-World Guide to Finding Your Way Safely in the Woods with or without a Map, Compass, or GPS*. Salem, MA: Page Street Publishing, 2019.

Gaia GPS. Backcountry mapping and trip-planning software for personal computers and phones. www.gaiagps.com.

Godino, John. Alpine Savvy. Website dedicated to modern navigation and climbing techniques. alpinesavvy.com.

Google Earth. Satellite imagery. www.google.com/earth.

GPS.gov. Information about GPS provided by the US government for students and teachers. www.gps.gov/students.

GPS World. Lists international sources of GPS service and knowledge. www.gpsworld.com/resources/gps-resources.

Green Trails. Digital or printed trail maps for much of the western United States plus British Columbia, Canada. https://greentrailsmaps.com.

Magnetic-Declination.com. Magnetic declination information. www.magnetic-declination.com.

Mexico Maps. Printed and GPS maps, including INEGI (National Institute of Statistics and Geography) products, from US vendor. https://mexicomaps.com.

National Association for Search and Rescue. *Basic Navigation for Search and Rescue and Survival*. Tampa, FL: Waterford Press, 2016.

———. *Fundamentals of Search and Rescue*. 2nd ed. Burlington, MA: Jones and Bartlett Learning, 2019.

National Geographic Maps. www.natgeomaps.com.

OpenStreetMap (OSM). A collaborative project to create a free editable map of the world; makes maps available through apps such as CalTopo and Gaia GPS. www.openstreetmap.org.

Peakbagger.com. An online resource where climbers and hikers create lists of peaks, share trip reports, post photos, and more. https://peakbagger.com.

Prescott, Travis. Alpine Geek. Website dedicated to alpine travel. www.alpinegeek.com.

Randall, Glenn. *Outward Bound Map and Compass Handbook*. 4th ed. Guilford, CT: Globe Pequot/Falcon, 2019.

Trantham, Gene, and Darran Wells. *NOLS Wilderness Navigation*. 3rd ed. Guilford, CT: Stackpole Books, 2019.

US Forest Service (USFS). Standard maps and other map products. www.fs.usda.gov/visit/maps.

US Geological Survey (USGS). US Topo maps and other mapping products. https://store.usgs.gov.

US National Park Service (NPS). Maps and map finder. www.nps.gov/planyourvisit/maps.htm.

CHAPTER 6: WILDERNESS TRAVEL

Anderson, Dave, and Molly Absolon. *NOLS Expedition Planning*. Mechanicsburg, PA: Stackpole Books, 2011.

Anderson, Kristi, ed. *Wilderness Basics*. 4th ed. Seattle: Mountaineers Books, 2013.

Bisson, Christian, and Jamie Hannon. *AMC's Mountain Skills Manual: The Essential Hiking and Backpacking Guide*. Boston: Appalachian Mountain Club Books, 2017.

Bombieri, G., J. Naves, V. Penteriani, et al. "Brown Bear Attacks on Humans: A Worldwide Perspective." *Scientific Reports* 9 (2019): 8573. https://doi.org/10.1038/s41598-019-44341-w.

British Columbia Parks. "Wildlife Safety: Wolves." https://bcparks.ca/plan-your-trip/visit-responsibly /wildlife-safety.

Fletcher, Colin, and Chip Rawlins. *The Complete Walker IV*. New York: Alfred A. Knopf, 2002.

Google Earth. Satellite imagery for route planning. www.google.com/earth.

Gookin, John, and Tom Reed. *NOLS Bear Essentials*. Mechanicsburg, PA: Stackpole Books, 2009.

Kosseff, Alex. *AMC Guide to Outdoor Leadership*. 2nd ed. Boston: Appalachian Mountain Club Books, 2010.

Mountain Project. Website featuring trip reports and photos of climbing routes, as well as information on conditions, climbers trails, access trails, and more. www.mountainproject.com.

Paul, Susan Joy. *Woman in the Wild: The Everywoman's Guide to Hiking, Camping, and Backcountry Travel*. Guilford, CT: Globe Pequot/Falcon, 2021.

Smith, Dave. *Backcountry Bear Basics*. 2nd ed. Seattle: Mountaineers Books, 2006.

US National Park Service. "Bear Attacks." Updated July 22, 2022. www.nps.gov/articles/bearattacks.htm.

———. "Mountain Lion Safety Tips." Updated July 20, 2018. www.nps.gov/nava/planyourvisit/upload/MountainLionSafetyAndFactsNAVA.pdf.

Western Wildlife Outreach. "Tips for Coexistence with Wolves." Accessed September 25, 2021. www.westernwildlife.org/tips-for-coexistence-with-wolves.

Zawaski, Mike. *Snow Travel: Skills for Climbing, Hiking, and Moving across Snow*. Seattle: Mountaineers Books, 2012.

CHAPTER 7: PROTECTING THE OUTDOORS

Access Fund. *Climbing Management: A Guide to Climbing Issues and the Production of a Climbing Management Plan*. Boulder, CO: Access Fund, 2008.

Ahmad, Taimur. "Climbing and Respect for Indigenous Lands." Access Fund, April 23, 2019. www.accessfund.org/latest-news/open-gate-blog/climbing-and-respect-for-indigenous-lands.

Attarian, Aram, and Kath Pyke, comps. *Climbing and Natural Resources Management: An Annotated Bibliography*. Raleigh: North Carolina State University; Boulder, CO: Access Fund, 2001.

Brame, Rich, and David Cole, with original text by Bruce Hampton. *NOLS Soft Paths: Enjoying the Wilderness Without Harming It*. 4th ed. Mechanicsburg, PA: Stackpole Books, 2011.

Gosalvez, Emma. "Nature Gap: Why Outdoor Spaces Lack Diversity and Inclusion." College of Natural Resources News, North Carolina State University, December 14, 2020. https://cnr.ncsu.edu/news/2020/12/nature-gap-why-outdoor-spaces-lack-diversity-and-inclusion.

Hautamaki, Andria. "As Crowds Swell on Public Lands, Visitors Learn How to Minimize Their Impact." *National Geographic*, November 11, 2020. www.nationalgeographic.com/travel/article/how-to-care-for-national-lands-despite-coronavirus-wildfire-pressures.

Humphrey, Naomi. "Breaking Down the Lack of Diversity in Outdoor Spaces." National Health Foundation, July 20, 2020. https://nationalhealthfoundation.org/breaking-down-lack-diversity-outdoor-spaces.

Khadka, Navin Singh. "Climate Change 'Making Mountaineering Riskier.'" BBC World Service, November 1, 2019. www.bbc.com/news/science-environment-50237551.

Leave No Trace Center for Outdoor Ethics. *Ethics Reference Cards*. Set of 18 waterproof cards, 5 by 3 inches (13 by 7.5 centimeters), that provide a framework for making decisions related to the outdoors, to fit specific areas, activities, or age groups. www.lnt.org.

———. *Leave No Trace for Mountaineering*. Quick-reference brochure annotating the seven principles of Leave No Trace with general mountaineering techniques and information. www.lnt.org.

———. *Skills and Ethics*. Booklet series covering regions of the United States and various outdoor activities. www.lnt.org.

———. *Skills and Ethics: Rock Climbing*. Boulder, CO: Leave No Trace Center for Outdoor Ethics, 2001. www.lnt.org.

Leopold, Aldo. *For the Health of the Land*. Washington, DC: Island Press, 2001.

———. *Think Like a Mountain*. New York: Penguin Books, 2021.

Marion, Jeffrey. *Leave No Trace in the Outdoors*. Mechanicsburg, PA: Stackpole Books, 2014. (Includes an excellent bibliography.)

Meyer, Kathleen. *How to Shit in the Woods*. 4th ed. New York: Ten Speed Press, 2020.

Mills, James Edward. *The Adventure Gap: Changing the Face of the Outdoors*. Seattle: Mountaineers Books, 2014.

Mourey, Jacques, Mélanie Marcuzzi, Ludovic Ravanel, and François Pallandre. "Effects of Climate Change on High Alpine Mountain Environments: Evolution of Mountaineering Routes in the Mont Blanc Massif (Western Alps) over Half a Century." *Arctic, Antarctic, and Alpine Research* 51, no. 1 (2019): 176–89. https://doi.org/10.1080/15230430.2019.1612216.

Noble, Chris. *Women Who Dare: North America's Most Inspiring Women Climbers*. Guilford, CT: Globe Pequot/Falcon, 2013.

Walls, Margaret A. "The Outdoor Recreation Economy and Public Lands." Resources for the Future, October 18, 2018. www.resources.org/archives/the-outdoor-recreation-economy-and-public-lands.

Waterman, Laura, and Guy Waterman. *Wilderness Ethics: Preserving the Spirit of Wildness*. 2nd ed. Woodstock, VT: Countryman Press, 2014.

Williams, David. *Homewaters: A Human and Natural History of Puget Sound*. Seattle: University of Washington Press, 2021.

Wilson, Edward O. *The Social Conquest of Earth*. New York: W. W. Norton, 2012.

CHAPTER 8: ESSENTIAL CLIMBING EQUIPMENT

American Mountain Guides Association. How-to videos for rock climbing. https://amga.com/rock-videos.

Donahue, Topher, and Craig Luebben. *Rock Climbing Anchors: A Comprehensive Guide*. 2nd ed. Seattle: Mountaineers Books, 2019.

———. *Rock Climbing: Mastering Basic Skills*. 2nd ed. Seattle: Mountaineers Books, 2014.

Ellison, Julie. "How to Make a Backpack Coil." *Climbing Magazine*, June 20, 2013. YouTube video, 5:06. www.youtu.be/ppYanQ5DDPM.

Fitch, Nate, and Ron Funderburke. *Climbing: Knots*. Guilford, CT: Globe Pequot/Falcon, 2015.

Godino, John. Alpine Savvy. Website dedicated to modern navigation and climbing techniques. alpinesavvy.com.

Grogono, Alan "Grog," David Grogono, and Martin Grogono. "Climbing Knots." Animated Knots. Accessed 2018. www.animatedknots.com/climbing-knots.

InnerBark Outdoors. "The Eight Climbing Knots You Need to Know." February 21, 2020. YouTube video, 10:06. www.youtu.be/FIHCwmMuXY8.

Long, John, and Bob Gaines. *Rock Climbing: The Art of Safe Ascent*. Guilford, CT: Globe Pequot/Falcon, 2021.

Luebben, Craig. *Knots for Climbers*. 3rd ed., revised and updated by Clyde Soles. Guilford, CT: Globe Pequot/Falcon, 2011.

Olliffe, Neville, and Madeleine Rowles-Olliffe. *Knots: The Step-by-Step Guide to Tying the Perfect Knot for Every Situation*. Seattle: Skipstone, 2010.

Owen, Peter. *The Ultimate Book of Knots*. Guilford, CT: Globe Pequot/Lyons Press, 2003.

ReferenceReady. *Crag Cards: Essential Climbing Knots*. Salt Lake City, UT: ReferenceReady, 2016.

REI. "Best Knots for Climbing: The Five Knots Every Climber Should Know." REI Expert Advice, July 9, 2019. YouTube video, 5:13. www.youtu.be/V1yq9XoAbCQ.

REI. "How to Coil a Climbing Rope." REI Expert Advice, June 15, 2019. YouTube video, 4:53. www.youtu.be/Aqt1ntSVjJA.

REI. "How to Tie into a Climbing Harness (with a Figure-Eight Knot)." REI Expert Advice, July 16, 2019. YouTube video, 3:59. www.youtu.be/XQ1r7iddc1w.

Soles, Clyde. *The Outdoor Knots Book*. Seattle: Mountaineers Books, 2004.

CHAPTER 9: BASICS OF CLIMBING

American Mountain Guides Association. How-to videos for rock climbing. https://amga.com/rock-videos.

Bridgeman, Gavin. "Gym to Crag: Learning to Climb Outdoors." REI Expert Advice. Accessed 2021. www.rei.com/learn/expert-advice/learning-climb-outdoors.html.

Donahue, Topher, and Craig Luebben. *Rock Climbing: Mastering Basic Skills*. 2nd ed. Seattle: Mountaineers Books, 2014.

Kirkpatrick, Andy. *1001 Climbing Tips*. Seattle: Mountaineers Books, 2017.

Layton, Michael A. *Climbing Stronger, Faster, Healthier: Beyond the Basics*. 2nd ed. Self-published, 2014.

Long, John, and Bob Gaines. *Rock Climbing: The Art of Safe Ascent*. Guilford, CT: Globe Pequot/Falcon, 2021.

Mountain Project. Website featuring trip reports and photos of climbing routes, as well as information on conditions, climbers trails, access trails, and more. www.mountainproject.com.

REI. "Lead Climbing: How to Clip Quickdraws." REI Expert Advice. Accessed 2021. www.rei.com/learn/expert-advice/clip-quickdraws.html.

———. "Leave No Trace Climbing Ethics." REI Expert Advice. Accessed 2021. www.rei.com/learn/expert-advice/climbing-ethics.html.

Samet, Matt. *Crag Survival Handbook: The Unspoken Rules of Climbing*. Seattle: Mountaineers Books, 2013.

CHAPTER 10: BELAYING

Ahmed, Naz, Rick Dotson, and Matt Vodjansky. "How to Belay." REI Expert Advice. Accessed 2021. www.rei.com/learn/expert-advice/belay.html.

American Mountain Guides Association. How-to videos for rock climbing. https://amga.com/rock-videos.

Donahue, Topher, and Craig Luebben. *Rock Climbing Anchors: A Comprehensive Guide*. 2nd ed. Seattle: Mountaineers Books, 2019.

———. *Rock Climbing: Mastering Basic Skills*. 2nd ed. Seattle: Mountaineers Books, 2014.

Fitch, Nate, and Ron Funderburke. *Climbing: From Gym to Rock*. Guilford, CT: Globe Pequot/Falcon, 2015.

Gaines, Bob. *Advanced Rock Climbing: Mastering Sport and Trad Climbing*. Guilford, CT: Globe Pequot/Falcon, 2018.

———. *Toproping: Rock Climbing for the Outdoor Beginner*. 2nd ed. Guilford, CT: Globe Pequot/Falcon, 2020.

Long, John, and Bob Gaines. *Climbing Anchors*. 3rd ed. Guilford, CT: Globe Pequot/Falcon, 2013.

———. *Climbing Anchors Field Guide*. 2nd ed. Guilford, CT: Globe Pequot/Falcon, 2014.

———. *Rock Climbing: The Art of Safe Ascent*. Guilford, CT: Globe Pequot/Falcon, 2021.

REI. "How to Build Anchors for Climbing." REI Expert Advice. Accessed 2021. www.rei.com/learn/expert-advice/climbing-anchors.html.

Samet, Matt. *The Climbing Dictionary: Mountaineering Slang, Terms, Neologisms, and Lingo.* Seattle: Mountaineers Books, 2011.

CHAPTER 11: RAPPELLING

American Alpine Club. "AAC Know the Ropes: Rappelling." February 13, 2018. YouTube video, 8:49. www.youtu.be/ZCZjMG7UJqQ.

———. "Rappelling." March 14, 2018. https://americanalpineclub.org/news/2018/2/14/rappelling.

American Mountain Guides Association. How-to videos for rock climbing. https://amga.com/rock-videos.

Donahue, Topher, and Craig Luebben. *Rock Climbing Anchors: A Comprehensive Guide.* 2nd ed. Seattle: Mountaineers Books, 2019.

———. *Rock Climbing: Mastering Basic Skills.* 2nd ed. Seattle: Mountaineers Books, 2014.

Gaines, Bob. *Advanced Rock Climbing: Mastering Sport and Trad Climbing.* Guilford, CT: Globe Pequot/Falcon, 2018.

Hays, Brian, with additional contributors. *Technical Rescue Handbook.* 12th ed. Washington, DC: US Department of the Interior, National Park Service, Emergency Services, 2023.

Janicula, Jesse. "How to Rappel." REI Expert Advice. Accessed 2021. www.rei.com/learn/expert-advice/how-to-rappel.html.

Kirkpatrick, Andy. *Down: The Complete Descent Manual for Climbers, Alpinists and Mountaineers.* Ireland: Andrew Kirkpatrick Ltd., 2020.

Long, John, and Bob Gaines. *Rock Climbing: The Art of Safe Ascent.* Guilford, CT: Globe Pequot/Falcon, 2021.

Viesturs, Ed, with David Roberts. *No Shortcuts to the Top: Climbing the World's 14 Highest Peaks.* New York: Broadway Books, 2006.

CHAPTER 12: SPORT CLIMBING AND TECHNIQUE

American Mountain Guides Association. How-to videos for rock climbing. https://amga.com/rock-videos.

Fitch, Nate, and Ron Funderburke. *Climbing: From Gym to Rock.* Guilford, CT: Globe Pequot/Falcon, 2015.

———. *Climbing: From Toproping to Sport.* Guilford, CT: Globe Pequot/Falcon, 2016.

Gaines, Bob. *Advanced Rock Climbing: Mastering Sport and Trad Climbing.* Guilford, CT: Globe Pequot/Falcon, 2018.

———. *Toproping: Rock Climbing for the Outdoor Beginner.* 2nd ed. Guilford, CT: Globe Pequot/Falcon, 2020.

Gaines, Bob, and Jason D. Martin. *Rock Climbing: The AMGA Single Pitch Manual.* Guilford, CT: Globe Pequot/Falcon, 2014.

Green, Stewart M., and Ian Spencer-Green. *Knack Rock Climbing: A Beginner's Guide; From the Gym to the Rocks.* Guilford, CT: Globe Pequot/Knack, 2010.

Hörst, Eric J. *How to Climb 5.12.* 3rd ed. Guilford, CT: Globe Pequot/Falcon, 2012.

Ilgner, Arno. *The Rock Warrior's Way: Mental Training for Climbers.* 2nd ed. La Vergne, TN: Desiderata Institute, 2006.

Janicula, Jesse. "How to Set and Clean a Top-Rope Anchor." REI Expert Advice. Accessed 2021. www.rei.com/learn/expert-advice/set-and-clean-anchors.html.

Long, John, and Bob Gaines. *How to Rock Climb.* 6th ed. Guilford, CT: Globe Pequot/Falcon, 2022.

Pease, Kent. *The Crack Climber's Manual: Jamming with Finesse.* Boulder, CO: Fixed Pin Publishing, 2014.

Petzl. *Access Book #5: Sport Climbing: Climbing and Belaying.* Accessed 2021. www.petzl.com/US/en/Sport/Downloads-eBooks/AccessBook-RockClimbing.

REI. "Lead Climbing: How to Clip Quickdraws." REI Expert Advice. Accessed 2021. www.rei.com/learn/expert-advice/clip-quickdraws.html.

Whittaker, Pete. *Crack Climbing: The Definitive Guide.* Seattle: Mountaineers Books, 2019.

CHAPTER 13: ROCK PROTECTION

American Mountain Guides Association. How-to videos for rock climbing. https://amga.com/rock-videos.

British Mountaineering Council. *Passive Protection: A Guide for Climbers and Mountaineers.* n.d. www.thebmc.co.uk.

Donahue, Topher, and Craig Luebben. *Rock Climbing Anchors: A Comprehensive Guide.* 2nd ed. Seattle: Mountaineers Books, 2019.

———. *Rock Climbing: Mastering Basic Skills.* 2nd ed. Seattle: Mountaineers Books, 2014.

Fitch, Nate, and Ron Funderburke. *Climbing: From Sport to Traditional Climbing.* Guilford, CT: Globe Pequot/Falcon, 2016.

———. *Climbing: Protection.* Guilford, CT: Globe Pequot/Falcon, 2015.

Gaines, Bob. *Advanced Rock Climbing: Mastering Sport and Trad Climbing.* Guilford, CT: Globe Pequot/Falcon, 2018.

Hörst, Eric J. *How to Climb 5.12.* 3rd ed. Guilford, CT: Globe Pequot/Falcon, 2012.

Long, John, and Bob Gaines. *Climbing Anchors.* 3rd ed. Guilford, CT: Globe Pequot/Falcon, 2013.

———. *Climbing Anchors Field Guide.* 2nd ed. Guilford, CT: Globe Pequot/Falcon, 2014.

———. *Rock Climbing: The Art of Safe Ascent.* Guilford, CT: Globe Pequot/Falcon, 2021.

———. *How to Rock Climb.* 6th ed. Guilford, CT: Globe Pequot/Falcon, 2022.

Long, John, and Peter Croft. *Trad Climber's Bible*. Guilford, CT: Globe Pequot/Falcon, 2014.

REI. "Lead Climbing: How to Place Trad Gear." REI Expert Advice. Accessed 2021. www.rei.com/learn/expert-advice /place-trad-gear.html.

Whittaker, Peter. *Crack Climbing: The Definitive Guide*. Seattle: Mountaineers Books, 2019.

CHAPTER 14: TRADITIONAL ROCK CLIMBING

American Mountain Guides Association. How-to videos for rock climbing. https://amga.com/rock-videos.

Chauvin, Marc, and Rob Coppolillo. *The Mountain Guide Manual: The Comprehensive Reference—From Belaying to Rope Systems and Self-Rescue*. Guilford, CT: Globe Pequot /Falcon, 2017.

Donahue, Topher. *Advanced Rock Climbing: Expert Skills and Techniques*. Seattle: Mountaineers Books, 2016.

Donahue, Topher, and Craig Luebben. *Rock Climbing Anchors: A Comprehensive Guide*. 2nd ed. Seattle: Mountaineers Books, 2019.

———. *Rock Climbing: Mastering Basic Skills*. 2nd ed. Seattle: Mountaineers Books, 2014.

Fitch, Nate, and Ron Funderburke. *Climbing: From Sport to Traditional Climbing*. Guilford, CT: Globe Pequot/Falcon, 2016.

———. *Climbing: Protection*. Guilford, CT: Globe Pequot/ Falcon, 2015.

Funderburke, Ron. *Climbing: From Single Pitch to Multipitch*. Guilford, CT: Globe Pequot/Falcon, 2019.

Gaines, Bob. *Advanced Rock Climbing: Mastering Sport and Trad Climbing*. Guilford, CT: Globe Pequot/Falcon, 2018.

Hays, Brian, with additional contributors. *Technical Rescue Handbook*. 12th ed. Washington, DC: US Department of the Interior, National Park Service, Emergency Services, 2023.

Hörst, Eric J. *How to Climb 5.12*. 3rd ed. Guilford, CT: Globe Pequot/Falcon, 2012.

———. *Training for Climbing: The Definitive Guide to Improving Your Performance*. 3rd ed. Guilford, CT: Globe Pequot/Falcon, 2016.

Ilgner, Arno. *The Rock Warrior's Way: Mental Training for Climbers*. 2nd ed. La Vergne, TN: Desiderata Institute, 2006.

Long, John, and Bob Gaines. *Climbing Anchors*. 3rd ed. Guilford, CT: Globe Pequot/Falcon, 2013.

———. *Climbing Anchors Field Guide*. 2nd ed. Guilford, CT: Globe Pequot/Falcon, 2014.

———. *Rock Climbing: The Art of Safe Ascent*. Guilford, CT: Globe Pequot/Falcon, 2021.

———. *How to Rock Climb*. 6th ed. Guilford, CT: Globe Pequot/Falcon, 2022.

Long, John, and Peter Croft. *The Trad Climber's Bible*. Guilford, CT: Globe Pequot/Falcon, 2014.

Nicholson, Ian. *Climbing Self-Rescue: Essential Skills, Technical Tips, and Improvised Solutions*. Seattle: Mountaineers Books, 2024.

Samet, Matt. *Crag Survival Handbook: The Unspoken Rules of Climbing*. Seattle: Mountaineers Books, 2013.

CHAPTER 15: AID AND BIG WALL CLIMBING

Abdullah, Kia. "20 Most Stunning Big Wall Climbs from Around the World." Atlas and Boots, October 4, 2023. www.atlasandboots.com/travel-blog/big-wall-climbs.

Donahue, Topher. *Advanced Rock Climbing: Expert Skills and Techniques*. Seattle: Mountaineers Books, 2016.

Elli, Fabio, and Peter Zabrok. *Hooking Up: The Ultimate Big Wall and Aid Climbing Manual*. English ed. Milan, Italy: Versante Sud, 2019.

Green Gear. *The Video Guide to Aid Climbing*. Joshua Tree, CA: Green Gear Productions, 2005.

Kirkpatrick, Andy. *Higher Education: A Big Wall Manual*. Self-published, 2018.

Long, John, and John Middendorf. *Big Walls*. Guilford, CT: Globe Pequot/Falcon, 1994.

McNamara, Chris. *How to Big Wall Climb*. Mill Valley, CA: SuperTopo, 2012.

———. "How to Big Wall Climb: Basic Aid Climbing Techniques." SuperTopo, February 10, 2010. YouTube video, 2:59. www.youtu.be/QyVtbmuQ7bI.

McNamara, Chris, and Chris Van Leuven. *Yosemite Big Walls*. 3rd ed. Mill Valley, CA: SuperTopo, 2011.

Miller, Lauren DeLaunay. *Valley of Giants: Stories of Women from the Heart of Yosemite Climbing*. Seattle: Mountaineers Books, 2022.

Ogden, Jared. *Big Wall Climbing: Elite Technique*. Seattle: Mountaineers Books, 2005.

Robbins, Royal. *Advanced Rockcraft*. Glendale, CA: La Siesta Press, 1990.

CHAPTER 16: BASIC SNOW AND ICE CLIMBING

Alford, Monty. *Winter Wise: Travel and Survival in Ice and Snow*. 2nd ed. Victoria, BC: Heritage House, 2013.

Bloemsma, Katrina. "How to Use Crampons." REI Expert Advice. Accessed 2021. www.rei.com/learn/expert-advice /how-to-use-crampons.html.

———. "How to Use an Ice Axe for Mountaineering." REI Expert Advice. Accessed 2021. www.rei.com/learn/expert -advice/how-to-use-an-ice-axe-for-mountaineering.html.

———. "Snow Travel Techniques for Mountaineering." REI Expert Advice. Accessed 2021. www.rei.com/learn/expert -advice/snow-travel-techniques-for-mountaineering.html.

Coppolillo, Ron. *The Ski Guide Manual: Advanced Techniques for the Backcountry*. Lanham, MD: Globe Pequot/Falcon, 2020.

George, Caroline. "IFMGA Alpine Guide Answers Top FAQs about Ice Climbing." Outdoor Curious. Eddie Bauer, March 16, 2022. Video, 16:16. www.eddiebauer.com /stories/ifmga-alpine-guide-answers-top-faqs-about-ice -climbing.

Gooding, Dunham, and Jason D. Martin. "Know the Ropes: Snow Climbing; Fundamentals to Save Your Life." In *Accidents in North American Mountaineering 2014*, by the American Alpine Club and the Alpine Club of Canada, 10–25. Golden, CO: AAC, 2014. https://publications .americanalpineclub.org/articles/13201212891/Know -The-Ropes-Snow-Climbing.

MSR Team. "Winter Climbing: 9 Tips for Getting Started." MSR, March 6, 2018. www.msrgear.com/blog/winter -climbing-tips.

Nies, Sam. "Snow Anchors for Mountaineering." REI Expert Advice. Accessed 2021. www.rei.com/learn/expert-advice /snow-anchors-for-mountaineering.html.

Volken, Martin, Scott Schell, and Margaret Wheeler. *Backcountry Skiing: Skills for Ski Touring and Ski Mountaineering*. 2nd ed. Seattle: Mountaineers Books, forthcoming 2025.

Zawaski, Mike. *Snow Travel: Skills for Climbing, Hiking, and Moving across Snow*. Seattle: Mountaineers Books, 2012.

CHAPTER 17: TECHNICAL SNOW AND ICE CLIMBING

American Mountain Guides Association and Outdoor Research. How-to videos for ice climbing. https://amga .com/ice-videos. Video library available on Outdoor Research's YouTube channel: www.youtube.com /playlist?list=PLajYFniMZtJh9QEEI3zCS2r_n29ehppa5.

Banfield, Tim, and Sean Isaac. *How to Ice Climb!* 2nd ed. Guilford, CT: Globe Pequot/Falcon, 2021.

Blanc-Gras, Jérôme, and Manu Ibarra. *The Art of Ice Climbing*. Chamonix: Arvesa/Blue Ice, 2012

Climbing Tech Tips. "Alpine and Mountaineering: 1. Ice Axe Positions." February 2, 2018. YouTube video, 2:32. www.youtu.be/6TtDf1DD_ig.

Funderburke, Ron. *Climbing: From Rock to Ice*. Guilford, CT: Globe Pequot/Falcon, 2019.

Gadd, Will. *Ice and Mixed Climbing: Improve Technique, Safety, and Performance*. 2nd ed. Seattle: Mountaineers Books, forthcoming 2025.

Garrison, Hal. *Ice Climbing*. New York: Gareth Stevens Publishing, 2018.

Gresham, Neil, and Ian Parnell. *Winter Climbing+*. Hinckley, UK: Cordee/Rockfax, 2008.

Isaac, Sean. *Mixed Climbing*. Guilford, CT: Globe Pequot/Falcon, 2004.

Messenger, Alex. "Winter Skills Films Series Four: Climbing Grade III." British Mountaineering Council, November 29, 2017. www.thebmc.co.uk/winter-climbing-videos -technical-grade-skills.

Ormond, Patrick. "How to Place Ice Screws." Outdoor Research, December 1, 2016. YouTube video, 6:17. www.youtu.be/DJ5RXYB6MWw.

Petzl. "Ice Climbing Basics: Ice Screw Placement, Anchors and V-Threads." November 27, 2013. Video, 6:56. https://vimeo.com/80485814.

Twight, Mark, and James Martin. *Extreme Alpinism: Climbing Light, Fast, and High*. Seattle: Mountaineers Books, 1999.

CHAPTER 18: WATERFALL ICE AND MIXED CLIMBING

Banfield, Tim, and Sean Isaac. *How to Ice Climb!* 2nd ed. Guilford, CT: Globe Pequot/Falcon, 2021.

British Mountaineering Council. Winter skills video series. www.youtube.com/playlist?list=PLTodUXkQjZwxa 2g6yfV21wLRXffbAdFxT.

Buhay, Corey. "Why (and How) You Should Learn to Mixed Climb." REI Uncommon Path, February 8, 2017. www.rei.com/blog/climb/learn-mixed-climb.

Chouinard, Yvon. *Climbing Ice*. San Francisco: Sierra Club Books, 1978.

Funderburke, Ron. *Climbing: From Rock to Ice*. Guilford, CT: Globe Pequot/Falcon, 2019.

Gadd, Will. *Ice and Mixed Climbing: Improve Technique, Safety, and Performance*. 2nd ed. Seattle: Mountaineers Books, forthcoming 2025.

———. "Three Drytooling Tips, One Ice Tip." WillGadd.com, January 4, 2014. willgadd.com/three-drytooling-tips -one-ice-tip.

Isaac, Sean. *Mixed Climbing*. Guilford, CT: Globe Pequot/Falcon, 2004.

Lowe, Jeff. "Jeff Lowe's Waterfall Ice Climbing Technique (Part 1)" and "Jeff Lowe's Waterfall Ice Climbing Technique (Part 2)." Posted August 29, 2015, by Ivan Gonchar. YouTube videos, 1:04:06 and 46:13. www.youtu.be /nDujpX7hQKY and youtu.be/VKF-PWE9CUI.

Petzl. "Ice Climbing Technique: The Basics." Video, 3:56. www.petzl.com/US/en/Sport/Ice-climbing-technique— -the-basics.

Petzl, with François Damilano. "Waterfall Ice Study." www.petzl.com/US/en/Sport/Waterfall-ice-study.

Twight, Mark, and James Martin. *Extreme Alpinism: Climbing Light, Fast, and High*. Seattle: Mountaineers Books, 1999.

CHAPTER 19: GLACIER TRAVEL AND CREVASSE RESCUE

Bloemsma, Katrina. "Crevasse Rescue Skills." REI Expert Advice. Accessed January 21, 2022. www.rei.com/learn /expert-advice/crevasse-rescue-skills.html.

———. "Glacier and Roped Travel for Mountaineering." REI Expert Advice. Accessed January 21, 2022. www.rei.com/learn/expert-advice/glacier-and-roped -travel-for-mountaineering.html.

Chauvin, Marc, and Rob Coppolillo. *The Mountain Guide Manual: The Comprehensive Reference—From Belaying to Rope Systems and Self-Rescue.* Guilford, CT: Globe Pequot/Falcon, 2017.

Fasulo, David. *Self-Rescue.* 2nd ed. Guilford, CT: Globe Pequot/Falcon, 2011.

Nicholson, Ian. *Climbing Self-Rescue: Essential Skills, Technical Tips, and Improvised Solutions.* Seattle: Mountaineers Books, 2024.

Nicholson, Ian. *Glacier Climbing and Crevasse Rescue: Essential Skills for Snow Travel.* Seattle: Mountaineers Books, forthcoming 2025.

Tyson, Andy, and Mike Clelland. *Glacier Mountaineering: An Illustrated Guide to Glacier Travel and Crevasse Rescue.* Rev. ed. Guilford, CT: Globe Pequot/Falcon, 2009.

Volken, Martin, Scott Schell, and Margaret Wheeler. *Backcountry Skiing: Skills for Ski Touring and Ski Mountaineering.* 2nd ed. Seattle: Mountaineers Books, forthcoming 2025.

Ward, Jeff. "How to Rope Up for Glacier Travel." Outdoor Research, June 15, 2018. YouTube video, 4:09. www.youtu.be/QwBOLjin67U.

CHAPTER 20: AVALANCHE SAFETY

Achelis, Steve. Beacon Review. beaconreviews.com.

Alaska Avalanche School. www.alaskaavalanche.org.

American Avalanche Institute. www.americanavalanche institute.com

American Avalanche Association. www.americanavalanche association.org.

American Institute for Avalanche Research and Education (AIARE), https://avtraining.org.

Atesmaps.org. An online planning tool for winter tours in the Pyrenees.

Avalanche.org. Comprehensive website run by several avalanche research organizations that provides international statistics, links to avalanche courses, and links to avalanche information centers.

Avalanche Canada, www.avalanche.ca.

Colorado Avalanche Information Center, US avalanche accident reports. avalanche.state.co.us/accidents /statistics-and-reporting.

LaChapelle, Edward R. *Secrets of the Snow: Visual Clues to Avalanche and Ski Conditions.* Seattle: University of Washington Press, 2001.

McClung, David, and Peter Schaerer. *The Avalanche Handbook.* 4th ed. Seattle: Mountaineers Books, 2022.

Mountain-forecast.org. A website that provides both animated and static weather maps for more than 1200 regions around the world.

Natural Resources Conservation Service. Great for remote SNOTEL (snow telemetry) sites in North America. www.nrcs.usda.gov/wps/portal/wcc/home.

Northwest Avalanche Center. www.nwac.us.

O'Bannon, Allen, with illustrations by Mike Clelland. *Allen & Mike's Avalanche Book: A Guide to Staying Safe in Avalanche Terrain.* Guilford, CT: Falcon, 2012.

Schonwald, Matt. "Know the Ropes: Avalanches--Spring and Summer Hazards for Mountaineers." *Accidents in North American Mountaineering* 12: 73 (2020): 8.

Tremper, Bruce. *Avalanche Essentials: A Step-by-Step System for Safety and Survival.* Seattle: Mountaineers Books, 2013.

———. *Avalanche Pocket Guide: A Field Reference.* Seattle: Mountaineers Books, 2014.

———. *Staying Alive in Avalanche Terrain.* 3rd ed. Seattle: Mountaineers Books, 2018.

Windy.com. A website that provides interactive weather forecasting worldwide.

CHAPTER 21: EXPEDITION CLIMBING

Anderson, Dave, and Molly Absolon. *NOLS Expedition Planning.* Mechanicsburg, PA: Stackpole Books, 2011.

Centers for Disease Control and Prevention (CDC). "Traveler Advice." Accessed 2022. wwwnc.cdc.gov/travel/page /resources-for-travelers.

Central Intelligence Agency. *The CIA World Factbook 2022–2023.* New York: Skyhorse Publishing, 2022. www.cia.gov/the-world-factbook. (*The CIA World Factbook* is updated annually.)

Farris, Mike. *The Altitude Experience: Successful Trekking and Climbing above 8,000 Feet.* Guilford, CT: Globe Pequot/Falcon, 2008.

Hörst, Eric J. *Maximum Climbing: Mental Training for Peak Performance and Optimal Experience.* Guilford, CT: Globe Pequot/Falcon, 2010.

House, Steve. "High-Altitude Climbing: 14 Tips for a Successful Expedition." Uphill Athlete, March 25, 2019. https://uphillathlete.com.

House, Steve, and Scott Johnston. *Training for the New Alpinism: A Manual for the Climber as Athlete.* Ventura, CA: Patagonia Books, 2014.

Howe, Steve, and Pete Rognili. "Go Deep: How to Plan Your First Big Expedition." *Backpacker*, October 25, 2021. www.backpacker.com/skills/beginner-skills/pre-trip -planning/the-manual-plan-an-expedition.

Lewis, Paul. "Expedition Planning." Peak Mountaineering. www.peakmountaineering.com/expedition-planning.

REI. "How to Plan a Mountaineering Trip." REI Expert Advice. Accessed February 18, 2022. www.rei.com/learn /expert-advice/how-to-plan-a-mountaineering-trip.html.

Stuck, Hudson. *The Ascent of Denali (Mount McKinley): A Narrative of the First Complete Ascent of the Highest Peak in North America.* New York: Charles Scribner's Sons, 1914.

Winser, Shane, ed. *Royal Geographic Society Expedition Handbook.* London: Profile Books/RGS, 2004. www.rgs.org.

CHAPTER 22: LEADERSHIP

American Alpine Club and Alpine Club of Canada. *Accidents in North American Climbing* (formerly *Accidents in North American Mountaineering*). Annual publication distributed by Mountaineers Books, Seattle. https://publications.americanalpineclub.org/about_accidents.

Anderson, Dave, and Molly Absolon. *NOLS Expedition Planning.* Mechanicsburg, PA: Stackpole Books, 2011.

Atlantic Re:think. "Five Ways to Make the Outdoors More Inclusive." Created by *The Atlantic*'s marketing team for REI, 2018. www.theatlantic.com/sponsored/rei-2018/five-ways-to-make-the-outdoors-more-inclusive/3019.

Bass, Bernard M., with Ruth Bass. *The Bass Handbook of Leadership.* 4th ed. New York: Free Press, 2008.

Brown Girls Climb. Facilitates mentorship, provides access, uplifts leadership, and celebrates representation in the outdoors and climbing. www.browngirlsclimb.com.

Chatfield, Rob, and Lewis Glenn, eds. *Leadership the Outward Bound Way: Becoming a Better Leader in the Workplace, in the Wilderness, and in Your Community.* Seattle: Mountaineers Books, 2007.

Cloos, Kassandra. "We Need More Women of Color Working in the Outdoors." *Outside Magazine*, April 3, 2018. www.outsideonline.com/culture/opinion/where-are-all-women.

De Jesus, Marinel. "The Outdoor Industry's Inclusion Problem." *Adventure Journal*, February 1, 2018. www.adventure-journal.com.

Enoksen, Elisabeth, and Pip Lynch. "Learning Leadership: Becoming an Outdoor Leader." *Journal of Adventure Education and Outdoor Learning* 18, no. 2 (2017): 176–88. https://doi.org/10.1080/14729679.2017.1391105.

Finney, Carolyn. *Black Faces, White Spaces: Reimagining the Relationship of African Americans to the Great Outdoors.* Chapel Hill: University of North Carolina Press, 2014.

Goleman, Daniel. *Emotional Intelligence: Why It Can Matter More Than IQ.* 25th anniversary edition. London: Bloomsbury, 2020.

———. *What Makes a Leader? Harvard Business Review Classics.* Boston: Harvard Business Review Press, 2017. (Article first published in the November–December 1998 issue of *Harvard Business Review*; reprinted in the January 2004 issue.)

Goleman, Daniel, and Richard E. Boyatzis. "Emotional Intelligence Has 12 Elements. Which Do You Need to Work On?" *Harvard Business Review*, February 6, 2017. https://hbr.org/2017/02/emotional-intelligence-has-12-elements-which-do-you-need-to-work-on.

Harvey, Mark. *The National Outdoor Leadership School's Wilderness Guide.* Rev. ed. New York: Touchstone, 1999.

Kosseff, Alex. *AMC Guide to Outdoor Leadership.* 2nd ed. Boston: Appalachian Mountain Club Books, 2010.

Martin, Bruce. *Outdoor Leadership: Theory and Practice.* Champaign, IL: Human Kinetics, 2006.

Melanin Base Camp. Inspires diversity in outdoor adventure sports with blog posts, trip reports, and gear reviews. www.melaninbasecamp.com.

Mills, James Edward. *The Adventure Gap: Changing the Face of the Outdoors.* Seattle: Mountaineers Books, 2014.

Powers, Phil. *NOLS Wilderness Mountaineering.* 3rd ed. Mechanicsburg, PA: Stackpole Books, 2009.

Rajagopal-Durbin, Aparna, and Marina Fleming. "Cultural Competency for the Outdoor Professional." National Outdoor Leadership School (NOLS). Prezi slide presentation, January 19, 2017. https://prezi.com/rpqtecp_zou1/cultural-competency-for-the-outdoor-professional.

Shooter, Wynn, Karen Paisley, and Jim Sibthorp. "Trust Development in Outdoor Leadership." *Journal of Experiential Education* 33, no. 3 (2011): 189–207. https://doi.org/10.1177/105382590113300301.

Stawski, Jeannette. *The Outdoor Leader: Resilience, Integrity, and Adventure.* Seattle: Mountaineers Books, 2024.

Wilderness Education Association. "DEI [Diversity, Equity, and Inclusion] Resources." https://wea.wildapricot.org/DEI-Resources.

———. Outdoor Leadership Training Course (and other credentialing outdoor leadership courses); annual International Conference on Outdoor Leadership. www.weainfo.org.

Windon, Suzanna, and Tanya E. Lamo. "What is Cultural Competence and How to Develop It?" PennState Extension. Accessed 2022. https://extension.psu.edu/what-is-cultural-competence-and-how-to-develop-it.

CHAPTER 23: RISK MANAGEMENT

American Alpine Club and Alpine Club of Canada. *Accidents in North American Climbing* (formerly *Accidents in North American Mountaineering*). Annual publication distributed by Mountaineers Books, Seattle. https://publications.americanalpineclub.org/about_accidents.

Barton, Bob. *Safety, Risk, and Adventure in Outdoor Activities.* London: Paul Chapman, 2007.

DJ Smith. "Feeling Like I Had a Near-Death Experience." Mountain Project, Injuries and Accidents Forum post, February 1, 2022. www.mountainproject.com/forum /topic/121931630/feeling-like-i-had-a-near-death -experience.

Guthrie, Stephen P. "Actual Risk and Perceived Risk: Implications for Teaching Judgement and Decision-Making to Leaders." Paper presented at the 11th International Conference on Outdoor Recreation and Education, Merida, Mexico, November 1997. https://files.eric.ed.gov /fulltext/ED419652.pdf.

National Outdoor Leadership School. *Risk Management at NOLS*. NOLS report. September 15, 2023. www.nols.edu/en/filer/public/1479753396/699.

Raue, Martina, Ronnie Kolodziej, Eva Lermer, and Bernard Streicher. "Risks Seem Low While Climbing High: Shift in Risk Perception and Error Rates in the Course of Indoor Climbing Activities." *Frontiers in Psychology* 9 (2018): 2383. https://doi.org/10.3389/fpsyg.2018.02383.

Saupe, Ashley, producer and host. *The Sharp End Podcast*. Sponsored by the American Alpine Club. www.thesharpendpodcast.com.

Twight, Mark, and James Martin. *Extreme Alpinism: Climbing Light, Fast, and High*. Seattle: Mountaineers Books, 1999.

Viesturs, Ed, with Dave Roberts. *No Shortcuts to the Top: Climbing the World's 14 Highest Peaks*. New York: Broadway Books, 2006.

CHAPTER 24: FIRST AID

Alton, Joseph, and Amy Alton. *The Survival Medicine Handbook: The Essential Guide for When Help Is Not on the Way*. 4th ed. Gatlinburg, TN: Doom and Bloom, 2021.

Auerbach, Paul S., Benjamin B. Constance, and Luanne Freer. *Field Guide to Wilderness Medicine*. 5th ed. Philadelphia: Elsevier, 2019.

Bennett, Brad L., Tamara Hew-Butler, Mitchell H. Rosner, Thomas Myers, and Grant S. Lipman. "Wilderness Medical Society Clinical Practice Guidelines for the Management of Exercise-Associated Hyponatremia: 2019 Update." *Wilderness and Environmental Medicine* 31, no. 1 (March 2020): 50–62. https://doi.org/10.1016 /j.wem.2019.11.003.

Carline, Jan D., Martha J. Lentz, and Steven C. Macdonald. *Mountaineering First Aid: A Guide to Accident Response and First Aid Care*. 5th ed. Seattle: Mountaineers Books, 2004.

Mountaineers Books. *Emergency Essentials Pocket Guide: A Field Reference for Survival*. Seattle: Mountaineers Books, 2016.

National Association of Emergency Medical Technicians (NAEMT). "First on the Scene." Accessed 2021. www.naemt.org/education/fots.

National Weather Service. "Heat Forecast Tools." National Oceanic and Atmospheric Administration (NOAA). Accessed 2022. www.weather.gov/safety/heat-index.
———. "Wind Chill Chart." National Oceanic and Atmospheric Administration (NOAA). Accessed 2021. www.weather.gov/safety/cold-wind-chill-chart.

Otten, Edward J., and Warren C. Dorlac. "Managing Traumatic Brain Injury: Translating Military Guidelines to the Wilderness." *Wilderness and Environmental Medicine* 28, no. 2 (June 2017): S117–S123. https://doi .org/10.1016/j.wem.2017.02.008.

Paal, Peter, Mario Milani, Douglas Brown, Jeff Boyd, and John Ellerton. "Termination of Cardiopulmonary Resuscitation in Mountain Rescue." *High Altitude Medicine and Biology* 13, no. 3 (September 2012): 200–8. https://doi.org/10.1089 /ham.2011.1096.

Schimelpfenig, Tod. *NOLS Wilderness Medicine*. 7th ed. Guilford, CT: Stackpole Books, 2021.

Wilderness Medical Society. "Wilderness Medical Society Clinical Practice Guidelines and Summaries." *Wilderness Medicine Magazine*. https://wms.org/magazine/magazine /1191/WMS_Clinical_Practice_Guidelines/Default.aspx.

Wilkerson, James A., ed. *Medicine for Mountaineering and Other Wilderness Activities*. 6th ed. Seattle: Mountaineers Books, 2010.

CHAPTER 25: SELF-RESCUE

Absolon, Molly. *Backpacker Magazine's Outdoor Survival Stories and the Lessons Learned*. Guilford, CT: Globe Pequot/Falcon, 2014.

Chauvin, Marc, and Rob Coppolillo. *The Mountain Guide Manual: The Comprehensive Reference—From Belaying to Rope Systems and Self-Rescue*. Guilford, CT: Globe Pequot/Falcon, 2017.

Donahue, Topher, and Craig Luebben. *Rock Climbing Anchors: A Comprehensive Guide*. 2nd ed. Seattle: Mountaineers Books, 2019.

Fasulo, David. *Self-Rescue*. 2nd ed. Guilford, CT: Globe Pequot/Falcon, 2011.

Hays, Brian, with additional contributors. *Technical Rescue Handbook*. 12th ed. Washington, DC: Department of the Interior, National Park Service, Emergency Services, 2023.

Kirkpatrick, Andy. *Down: The Complete Descent Manual for Climbers, Alpinists and Mountaineers*. Ireland: Andrew Kirkpatrick Ltd., 2020.

Lipke, Rick. *Technical Rescue Riggers Guide*. 4th ed. Bellingham, WA: Conterra.

Long, John, and Bob Gaines. *Climbing Anchors*. 3rd ed. Guilford, CT: Globe Pequot/Falcon, 2013.

National Ski Patrol. *Mountain Travel and Rescue: National Ski Patrol's Manual for Mountain Rescue*. 2nd ed. Seattle: Mountaineers Books, 2012.

Nicholson, Ian. *Climbing Self-Rescue: Essential Skills, Technical Tips, and Improvised Solutions*. Seattle: Mountaineers Books, 2024.

Prattley, Grant. *Rope Rescue and Rigging: Field Guide*. 3rd ed. Christchurch, NZ: Over the Edge Rescue, 2020.

Saupe, Ashley, producer and host, with Aaron and Ian Davis. "Getting Rescued in Zion National Park." *The Sharp End Podcast*. Sponsored by the American Alpine Club. Episode 71, December 1, 2021. www.thesharpendpodcast.com /episode-71.

Saupe, Ashley, producer and host, with Dave Weber. "Covid, Climbing and Rescue: Advice from Ranger Dave Weber." *The Sharp End Podcast*. Sponsored by the American Alpine Club. Episode 52, May 1, 2020. www.thesharpendpodcast .com/episode-52.

Walker, Emma. *Dead Reckoning: Learning from Accidents in the Outdoors*. Guilford, CT: Globe Pequot/Falcon, 2021.

CHAPTER 26: MOUNTAIN GEOLOGY

Association of American State Geologists (AASG). www.stategeologists.org.

Ball, Jessica. "Geology and Rock Climbing." American Geophysical Union, February 27, 2011. https://blogs .agu.org/magmacumlaude/2011/02/27/geology-and -rock-climbing.

Ellis, Gene, and Jack Reed. *Rocks Above the Clouds: A Hiker's and Climber's Guide to Colorado Mountain Geology*. Golden, CO: Colorado Mountain Club, 2009.

Fleming, Anna. *Time on Rock: A Climber's Route into the Mountains*. Edinburgh: Canongate Books, 2022.

Garlick, Sarah. *Flakes, Jugs, and Splitters: A Rock Climber's Guide to Geology*. Guilford, CT: Globe Pequot/Falcon, 2009.

Geological Survey of Canada. https://nrcan.gc.ca/science -and-data/research-centres-and-labs/geological-survey -canada/17100.

Google Earth. www.google.com/earth.

Hiking the Geology series (various states). Seattle: Mountaineers Books, various dates.

Kaligi, Azad, and Lydia Yang. "Geology for Climbers." Geo Forward. Accessed 2022. www.geoforward.com/geology -rock-climbers.

McPhee, John. *Assembling California*. New York: Farrar, Straus and Giroux, 1993.

———. *Basin and Range*. New York: Farrar, Straus and Giroux, 1981.

Roadside Geology/Geology Underfoot series (various states). Missoula, MT: Mountain Press, various dates. https://geology.com/store/roadside-geology.shtml.

Rost, Harald, and Ulfi. "Rock Types and Geology for Climbers." theCrag ("the largest collaborative rock climbing and bouldering platform"). www.thecrag.com/en /article/rocktypes.

Tabor, Rowland, and Ralph Haugerud. *Geology of the North Cascades: A Mountain Mosaic*. Seattle: Mountaineers Books, 1999.

University of Washington Department of Earth and Space Sciences. www.ess.washington.edu.

US Bureau of Land Management (BLM). www.blm.gov.

US Forest Service (USFS). www.fs.usda.gov.

US Geological Survey (USGS). www.usgs.gov.

———. Map locator tool. https://store.usgs.gov/map-locator.

———. The National Geologic Map Database. https://ngmdb .usgs.gov.

CHAPTER 27: THE CYCLE OF SNOW

Hock, Regine, Golam Rasul, et al. "High Mountain Areas." Ch. 2 in *The Ocean and Cryosphere in a Changing Climate: Special Report of the Intergovernmental Panel on Climate Change*, by the IPCC, 131–202. Cambridge, UK, and New York: Cambridge University Press, 2019. https://doi.org/10.1017/9781009157964.004. Also see www.ipcc.ch/srocc/chapter/chapter-2/executive-summary.

Benn, Douglas I., and David J. A. Evans. *Glaciers and Glaciation*. 2nd ed. Abingdon, UK: Routledge, 2010.

Carry, Joe. *Handbook of Snow, Ice, and Glaciers*. New York: Syrawood, 2016.

Cuffey, K. M., and W. S. B. Paterson. *The Physics of Glaciers*. 4th ed. Cambridge, MA: Academic Press, 2010.

Ferguson, Sue A. *Glaciers of North America: A Field Guide*. Golden, CO: Fulcrum Publishing, 1992.

Gray, D. M., and D. H. Male, eds. *Handbook of Snow: Principles, Processes, Management and Use*. New York: Pergamon Press, 1981.

Hobbs, Peter V. *Ice Physics*. Oxford Classic Texts in the Physical Sciences. Oxford: Oxford University Press, 2010.

Intergovernmental Panel on Climate Change (IPCC). Body of the United Nations responsible for assessing the science related to climate change; resources about glaciers worldwide and climate change. www.ipcc.ch.

International Association of Cryospheric Sciences. *The International Classification for Seasonal Snow on the Ground*. IHP-VII Technical Documents in Hydrology no. 83, IACS Contribution no. 1. Paris: UNESCO/IHP, 2009. https://unesdoc.unesco.org/ark:/48223/pf0000186462.

LaChapelle, Edward R. *Field Guide to Snow Crystals*. Cambridge, UK: International Glaciological Society, 1992.

———. *Secrets of the Snow: Visual Clues to Avalanche and Ski Conditions*. Seattle: University of Washington Press; Cambridge, UK: International Glaciological Society, 2001.

Lindsey, Rebecca. "Climate Change: Mountain Glaciers." NOAA (National Oceanic and Atmospheric Administration) Climate.gov, February 14, 2020. www.climate.gov/news-features/understanding-climate /climate-change-mountain-glaciers.

Martin, James. *Planet Ice: A Climate for Change*. Seattle: Mountaineers Books, 2009.

McClung, David, and Peter Schaerer. *The Avalanche Handbook*. 4th ed. Seattle: Mountaineers Books, 2023.

National Oceanic and Atmospheric Administration (NOAA). "How Do Snowflakes Form? Get the Science Behind Snow." December 19, 2016. www.noaa.gov/stories /how-do-snowflakes-form-science-behind-snow.

National Snow and Ice Data Center (NSIDC). "Snow." https://nsidc.org/learn/parts-cryosphere/snow.

Nelson, Steven A. "Glaciers and Glaciation." Tulane University. November 19, 2015. www2.tulane .edu/~sanelson/eens1110/glaciers.htm.

Post, Austin, and Edward R. LaChapelle. *Glacier Ice*. Rev. ed. Seattle: University of Washington Press; Cambridge, UK: International Glaciological Society, 2000.

Sturm, Matthew. *A Field Guide to Snow*. Fairbanks: University of Alaska Press, 2020.

Tremper, Bruce. *Staying Alive in Avalanche Terrain*. 3rd ed. Seattle: Mountaineers Books, 2018.

US Environmental Protection Agency (EPA). "Climate Change Indicators: Glaciers." Updated August 24, 2022. www.epa.gov/climate-indicators/climate-change -indicators-glaciers.

Wood, Anthony R. *Snow: A History of the World's Most Fascinating Flake*. Guilford, CT: Globe Pequot/ Prometheus, 2020.

CHAPTER 28: MOUNTAIN WEATHER

Anderson, Jay, John A. Day, and Jay M. Pasachoff. *Peterson Field Guide to Weather*. Boston: Mariner Books, 2021.

Avalanche.org. Partnership between American Avalanche Association and US Forest Service National Avalanche Center. List of US avalanche centers: https://avalanche.org /us-avalanche-centers.

Avalanche Canada. "Mountain Weather Forecast." www.avalanche.ca/weather/forecast.

Ballard, Lisa. *Backpacker Magazine's Predicting Weather: Forecasting, Planning, and Preparing*. Guilford, CT: Globe Pequot/Falcon, 2010.

Barry, Roger G. *Mountain Weather and Climate*. 3rd ed. New York: Cambridge University Press, 2008.

Henning, Ryan. *Field Guide to the Weather: Learn to Identify Clouds and Storms, Forecast the Weather, and Stay Safe*. Cambridge, MN: Adventure Publications, 2019.

Mass, Cliff. *The Weather of the Pacific Northwest*. 2nd ed. Seattle: University of Washington Press, 2021.

Mersereau, Dennis. *The Skies Above: Storm Clouds, Blood Moons, and Other Everyday Phenomena*. Seattle: Mountaineers Books, 2022.

Met Office (the Meteorological Office, the UK's national weather service). "Mountain Weather Forecast." www.metoffice.gov.uk/weather/specialist-forecasts /mountain.

Mountain Forecast. "Mountain Weather Forecasts for Mountains around the World." www.mountain-forecast.com.

Northwest Avalanche Center (NWAC, a US-based forecaster for the Pacific Northwest). "Mountain Weather Forecast." https://nwac.us/mountain-weather-forecast.

Perkins, Oliver. *Reading the Clouds: How You Can Forecast the Weather*. New York: Adlard Coles, 2023.

Renner, Jeff. *Lightning Strikes: Staying Safe Under Stormy Skies*. Seattle: Mountaineers Books, 2002.

———. *Mountain Weather: Backcountry Forecasting and Weather for Hikers, Campers, Climbers, Skiers, and Snowboarders*. Seattle: Mountaineers Books, 2005.

———. *Mountain Weather Pocket Guide: A Field Reference*. Seattle: Mountaineers Books, 2017.

Whiteman, C. David. *Mountain Meteorology: Fundamentals and Applications*. New York: Oxford University Press, 2000.

Williams, Jack. *National Geographic Pocket Guide to the Weather of North America*. Washington, DC: National Geographic, 2017.

Woodmencey, Jim. *Reading Weather: The Field Guide to Forecasting the Weather*. 3rd ed. Essex, CT: Globe Pequot/ Falcon, 2022.

WITH GRATITUDE

Thank you to the members, volunteers, and donors whose financial contributions help keep nonprofit publishing thriving. With your support, our publications can reach more people and help them enjoy the natural world respectfully and sustainably. To learn more about how you can elevate the work and impact of Mountaineers Books, please visit mountaineersbooks.org/donate.

$5,000 Donation
Madeline T. N.

$2,500 Donation
Doug & Rachel McCall
In memory of Tab Wilkins

$1,000 Donation
In memory of A. L. "Loo" Crittenden, former Climbing Committee chairman and contributor to first edition, 1960
David Einert, in memory of Louie A. Einert
Don & Marci Heck
Ed Lucas
Leigh Noble
Bruce & Jill Sanchez
Anne Smart & Frank McCord
Cody Smith & Virginia Brown
Tom Vogl & Katie Koepke

$500 Donation
Anita Arbini Wilkins
James T. Burke
Kathryn Celia Roddy Capps
Bill Chaput
The Crichton Family
David & Brita Enfield
Lee Fromson & Twala Coggins
Tiffany Gilbert & Kendrick Efta
Jeffrey Hancock & Virginia Felton
In loving memory of Ian Harford
Edward Henderson, Board of Trustees President 2000–2002
Dan Irwin
Craig Kartes
TJ, Tanya & Eli King
Lauren Kisser
Hazel & Madelyn Koethe
Yu-Hang Kuo
In honor of Sumiko and Yuichi Kuraishi

Robert & Marion McIntosh
Ericka Mitterndorfer & Justin Bland
David Paul Orsmond
Joyce Reynolds
Chris & Kathy Robertson
The Climbing Smiths: George, Flint, Quade, Cody & Tyle
Lowell Skoog & Nancy Mattheiss
Tim Tan
In loving memory of Don C. Taylor
Brianne Vanderlinden, in honor of Jack Vanderlinden
Jon & Vera Wellner
Robert & Ashley White
Alexander Whitlow
LaVerne Woods

$250 Donation
Nicole & Sam Bulow
John M. Cary
Helen Cherullo, in memory of Tom Hornbein, *Everest: The West Ridge*
climbitjason
Tim Coulter
Billy and Courtney Cundiff
Dallas Damianick
Kai Davey
Donna DeShazo
Douglas Diekema
Ted Doughty
Carolyn Driedger-Mastin
Debbie Due
Dave Foong & Laura Handley
The Freeburgs
Christian P. Fuchs
Mark Gnadt
Don & Natala Goodman
Danielle Graham & Andrew Pedersen
Calvin Hall

Hannah Ann Hergert
Dan Hicks
Deborah K. Hiney
Art Hogling
Homestretch Foundation
Raymond Huey
Garth Jacobson
Jean Johnson
Michael T. Kovacs
Ken Lans
Geoff Lawrence
Ryan Mansfield
Michael McCracken
Roger Mellem & Gisela Stehr
Brittney Moraski
Harry Morgan
Lloyd Murray
Joanne Najdzin
The Nelson Family, in honor of Jack Stansfield
Peter F. O'Connor
John Ohlson
Steven Payne, in memory of Karen Sykes
Dena (Dee Dee) Peel
Amanda PiroDaniel Poor
Hany & Adam Ramadan
Stephen A. Reynes
David Roche
Henry F. Romer
Curt W. Rosler, Olympia Branch
Ben D. Schafer
Samuel Shadwell
Scott Shafer
The Shand Family
Terence Stanuch
Alan Stewart
Will Tooker
Elizabeth Watson
James Pierce Whinston
Dean Wingfield

INDEX

A

access and inclusion in wilderness, 150
accidents. *See also* falls
    accident report form (fig.), 514
    causes of, 504, 505
    injuries, 526–31
    response, 510–13, 534–56
Accidents in North American Climbing,
        233, 504, 507
acute mountain sickness (AMS),
        524–25
adzes and hammers, 388
aerobic exercise, 81–82
aid climbing
    aid placements, 319–21
    basic aid techniques, sequence,
        322–23
    changing leads, 338–39
    clean, 306
    equipment, 306–19
    generally, 305
    leading aid pitches, 325
    overhangs and roofs, 328–29
    racking, 322
    rating system, 582–584
    spirit of, 343
    switching with free climbing, 326–27
    tension traverses and pendulum
        swings, 327, 336–38
    top-stepping, 323–26
    traverses and overhangs, 334–36
    Tyrolean traverses, 330–32
    uses of, 306
aiders (etriers), 310
air movement, 571–72
air pressure and altimeter changes
        (table), 572
alpine ice climbing
    boot(s), 383
    rating systems, 581, 587
alpine rescue, 534
alpine terrain features, 376–80
altimeters, 39, 106–08, 572
American Institute for Avalanche
        Research & Education (AIARE),
        464
anaerobic exercise, 82
anchoring tents, 56–57
anchor(s)

belay, 206–14
belaying off, 216
equalized, 375
fixed, 149
for glacier travel, 427
how to equalize, 208–14
personal, 172–73
rappel, 226–28
for rescues, 437–39
in rescue systems, 538
SERENE systems, 214, 227, 536,
        538
setup on snow, ice, 403–05
snow and ice, 373–75
trees as, 269–70
T-slot, 56, 374
angles, 316
animals. *See also specific type*
    protecting food from, 59–60
anticlines, 559, 560
anxiety and panic, 532–33
aperture belay devices, 200–01, 308
archaeological artifacts, 147
area position, 118–19
arm rappel, 236
ascenders, 312, 332–34
ascending, 425–27
    with boots, crampons, 390–93
    boots, ice axes, 347, 354
    cleaning a pitch, 298
    with ice tools, 393–96
    lead belay, 194
    and pace, 133
    steep or vertical snow, ice, 396–97
    steep terrain, 333
    technical terrain, 177
assisted-braking belay devices,
        202–03, 308
Australian rock climbing rating system,
        586
autoblock hitch, 166–67, 238–39,
        240–41
auto-locking belay devices, 201–02
avalanche beacons, 464. *See also*
        transceivers
avalanches
    avalanche training, 451–52
    ice, 423, 570
    North American Public Avalanche
        Danger Scale (fig.), 459

red warning flags, 462–63
rescue gear, carrying, 464–65
rescuing a companion, 468–74
risk, assessing, 460–64
slope angle, aspect, configuration,
        456–58
surviving, 468
terrain and, 455–60
traveling in avalanche terrain,
        465–68
triggers, 567
types of, 452–55
Avalanche Terrain Exposure Scale
        (ATES), 458–60
avalanche transceivers, 47, 452, 460,
        464–65
axes. *See ice axes*

B

Bachmann hitch, 166
back carries, 545–46
backing down and front-pointing,
        397–98
back injuries, 529–30
backpacks, 34–37
bacteria, 72
barchans (snow), 565
barometric altimeters, 106–07, 572
barrel knot, 231
batteries, 39, 47–48, 103–04, 106
Baxter-Jones, Roger, 487
bearings, 39, 103, 109, 110–19, 424,
        529
bear-resistant containers, 60
bears, 58–60, 135
belay devices, 165, 199–200
belay jacket, 25, 27–28
belays and belaying
    anchors for, 206–14
    belay devices, using, 199–204
    braking force, 199
    choosing spot, 196
    climbing use, 194–95
    escaping the belay, 221–22
    establishing belays, 330
    firefighter's belay, 241
    hip belay, 204–06
    lead belay, 197

BRAND NAMES AND TRADEMARKS

The following trademarks and brand names are referenced in this tenth edition, including some items used as the basis for specific illustrations that are not necessarily identified by name:

ActiveIce Sun Gloves (Outdoor Research), Alien and Hybrid Alien (Fixe Hardware), Allen wrench, Apple Watch (Apple), ATC and ATC-Guide (Black Diamond), Attache (Petzl), Avenza Maps (Avenza Systems), Ball Nut (C.A.M.P. USA), Band-Aid (Johnson & Johnson), BaseCamp (Garmin), Biffy Bag (Ledo Environmental, LLC), Big Bro (Trango), Buff, Bug (DMM), CalTopo, Camalot (Black Diamond), Camalot C3 (Black Diamond), Camalot C4 (Black Diamond), Candela (Grivel), Clean Mountain Can (Paul Becker GTS, Inc.), Clepsydra S K10GS (Grivel), Coleman, Compeed (Laboratoire HRA Pharma SAS), Connect Adjust (Petzl), Croakies (The Hilsinger Company), Darn Tough Vermont (Cabot Hoisery Mills), Dart crampons (Petzl), Deuce of Spades (The Tent Lab), Diamox (Lederle Laboratories), Double Doodie (Reliance Outdoors), Dyneema (DSM), Eddy (Edelrid), 8003 full-body harness (Petzl), Ergonomic ice tool (Petzl), Esbit (Esbit Compagnie GmbH), EpiPen (Viatris), eTrex 32x (Garmin), European Committee for Standardization (CEN or CE), eVent (eVent Fabrics), Fat Cam (Metolius), FATMAP (Strava), Forerunner 935 (Garmin), Friend (Wild Country), Fuel Hammer ice tool (Black Diamond), G7 Pod (Grade VII Climbing Equipment), Gaia GPS (Outside Interactive and Trailbehind, Inc.), Gamow bag (Chinook Medical Gear), Garmin, GigaPower (Snow Peak), Glacier ice axe (Petzl), GO Anywhere Toilet Kit (Cleanwaste), Google Earth, Gore-Tex (W. L. Gore and Associations GmbH), Green Trails Maps, Grigri+ (Petzl), Half Dome helmet (Black Diamond), Hexentric (Black Diamond), Hiker Filter (Katadyn), HMS Bulletproof Screw FG (Edelrid), Ibex, Icebreaker, inReach Explorer+ and inReach Mini (both Garmin), Intervals.icu, The Israeli Bandage (OM Performance, Inc.), Kevlar (DuPont), Leave No Trace, Leukotape (BSN Medical GmbH), LifeStraw (Vestergaard), Link Cam (Omega Pacific), Lost Arrow (Black Diamond), Lycra (Invista), Lynx crampons (Petzl), Mega Jul (Edelrid), microSD (3D-3C, LLC), Micro Traxion (Petzl), Molefoam (Dr. Scholl's), Moleskin (Dr. Scholl's), Mountain House, Mountain Project (onX Maps), MSR (Cascade Designs, Inc.; PocketRocket, Reactor, Whisperlite Universal, and XGK EX stoves and Groundhog tent stakes), Mylar (DuPont), Nano-Air (Patagonia), National Geographic Maps (National Geographic), Nature Valley (General Mills), Nepal Cube GTX (La Sportiva), Neve Strap crampons (Black Diamond), New-Skin (Advantice Health), Nomic ice tool (Petzl), Ocún Crack Gloves, OpenStreetMap (OpenStreetMap Foundation), OS Locate (Ordnance Survey), Outdoor Research, Pacific Link Cam (Omega), PAS 22 (Metolius), PeakFinder, Pecker (Black Diamond), Perlon (Perlon Monofil GmbH), Polar (Polar Electro Oy), Polartec Alpha (Polartec), Poo Powder (Cleanwaste), PrimaLoft, Pro Traxion (Petzl), Pyramid (Trango), Rapid Tourniquet (Rapid Medical), Recreational Equipment, Inc., ResQLink (ACR Electronics), RESTOP2 (American Innotek, Inc.), Reverso 4 (Petzl), Rite in the Rain (JL Darling, LLC), RURP (Black Diamond), Sarken crampons (Petzl), 2nd Skin (Spenco), Serac crampons (Black Diamond), Shewee (TSBN Ltd.), Smartwool (TBL Licensing, LLC), SnowClaw Backcountry Snow Shovel, Spectra (Honeywell), Spectre Ice Piton (Black Diamond), SportTracks (Zone Five Software), SPOT (SPOT, LLC), Squeeze (Sawyer), Starlink (SpaceX), Steripen (Katadyn), Steri-Strip (3M), Stopper (Black Diamond), Strava, Suunto 7 (Suunto), Swift ice axe (Black Diamond), Talon (Black Diamond), TCU (Metolius), Technical Friend (Wild Country), Technora (Teijin Aramid), Teflon (DuPont), Therm-a-Rest (Cascade Designs, Inc.), Tibloc (Petzl), Totem Cams (Totem Cams), TrainingPeaks, Tricam (C.A.M.P. USA), Trivex (PPG), Tyvek (DuPont), UIAA (International Climbing and Mountaineering Federation), Ursack, Vapor helmet (Black Diamond), Vasak crampon (Petzl), Vaseline (Unilever), Velcro, Vergo (Trango), V-LINK (Petzl), Wallnut (DMM), Waste Case (Metolius), WD-40, Whippet ski pole (Black Diamond), Zofran (Novartis), ZOLEO, and Z piton (Leeper).

recreation · lifestyle · conservation

MOUNTAINEERS BOOKS is a leading publisher of mountaineering literature and guides—including our flagship title, *Mountaineering: The Freedom of the Hills*—as well as adventure narratives, natural history, and general outdoor recreation. Through our two imprints, Skipstone and Braided River, we also publish titles on sustainability and conservation. We are committed to supporting the environmental and educational goals of our organization by provid ing expert information on human-powered adventure, sustainable practices at home and on the trail, and preservation of wilderness.

The Mountaineers, founded in 1906, is a 501(c)(3) nonprofit outdoor recreation and conservation organization whose mission is to enrich lives and communities by helping people "explore, conserve, learn about, and enjoy the lands and waters of the Pacific Northwest and beyond." One of the largest such organizations in the United States, it sponsors classes and year-round outdoor activities throughout the Pacific Northwest, including climbing, hiking, backcountry skiing, snowshoeing, camping, kayaking, sailing, and more. The Mountaineers also supports its mission through its publishing division, Mountaineers Books, and promotes environmental education and citizen engagement. For more information, visit The Mountaineers Program Center, 7700 Sand Point Way NE, Seattle, WA 98115-3996; phone 206-521-6001; www.mountaineers.org; or email info@mountaineers.org.

Our publications are made possible through the generosity of donors and through sales of 700 titles on outdoor recreation, sustainable lifestyle, and conservation. To donate, purchase books, or learn more, visit us online:

MOUNTAINEERS BOOKS

1001 SW Klickitat Way, Suite 201 · Seattle, WA 98134

800-553-4453 · mbooks@mountaineersbooks.org · mountaineersbooks.org

An independent nonprofit publisher since 1960

Mountaineers Books is proud to support the Leave No Trace Center for Outdoor Ethics, whose mission is to use the power of science, education, and stewardship to ensure a sustainable future for the outdoors and the planet. The Leave No Trace program is focused specifically on human-powered (nonmotorized) recreation. For more information, visit www.lnt.org.

OTHER TITLES YOU MIGHT ENJOY

MOUNTAINEERS OUTDOOR EXPERT SERIES

WILDERNESS SKILLS & CONDITIONING

AVALANCHE SAFETY

PERSONALITIES & STORIES

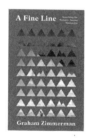

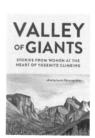